Education, Equity, Economy

Volume 12

The volumes in this series provide insights into how education, equity and economy are related. The most prominent issue in education is equity. Equity has had dramatic effects not only on education processes and outcomes but also the economy. As the global economy has developed we have moved from post-industrial, to knowledge, to most recently the creative economy. Each of these economic shifts has driven inequities, which in turn has led to more urgent calls to reduce inequities in education. While this outcome is widely known, the focus of much recent work has been on the economy per say. This is the first series to take education rather than economy as its centerpiece. Education is widely regarded as the key resource for global competitiveness, at both the individual and national level. Education, and the differential return from education for different groups in a society and across the globe are best captured by exploring the linkages to the economy. While this connection is important there is mounting evidence which suggests that education alone is insufficient to redress the inequities persisting in most countries. The volumes in this series offer the reader analyses and critiques that cut across these intersecting forces. Specifically, they critique the notion of individual capital while interrogating the systemic intersection of education, equity and economy.

Karen Borgnakke

AI and ChatGPT Technology in Education

An Ethnographic Encounter

Springer

Karen Borgnakke
Faculty of Humanities
University of Copenhagen
København S, Denmark

ISSN 2364-835X ISSN 2364-8368 (electronic)
Education, Equity, Economy
ISBN 978-3-032-01418-4 ISBN 978-3-032-01419-1 (eBook)
https://doi.org/10.1007/978-3-032-01419-1

This Springer imprint is published by the registered company Springer Nature Switzerland AG
The registered company address is: Gewerbestrasse 11, 6330 Cham, Switzerland

Competing Interests The author has no competing interests to declare that are relevant to the content of this manuscript.

Contents

About the Author

Karen Borgnakke is Professor Emerita in Education, University of Copenhagen. She has done research, taught, and published in the fields of education and learning research. She has done ethnographic fieldwork and participated in development projects and evaluation research, including projects on new strategies for organizational and pedagogical innovation in upper secondary school, adult education, and higher education. She has comprehensive experience with developing research methodology, research education, academic review, and evaluation. Further, she has experience with project direction in relation to research programs funded by Danish, Nordic, and European research councils.

Current research project: Ethnographic studies in scholastic, profession-oriented, and academic learning contexts.

Degrees: Cand. mag. in Nordic Philology (1978) and Cultural Sociology (1989) at the University of Copenhagen. Dr. paed. (1996), Royal Danish School of Educational Studies (RDSED). Dissertation: Educational field research and the methodology of process analysis.

Chapter 1
Introduction

AI/ChatGPT was launched in the fall of 2022 as a sensation that received great public attention, but also requires political stance and professional critical debate. The debate that follow throughout the spring of 2023 start with the spontaneous expressions of enthusiasm. IT experts characterize ChatGPT as 'a technological quantum leap' and question the conventional knowledge reproduction of the education system. University management, trade unions, cultural and educational institutions seem to share the AI enthusiasm. But they also share the concern about the consequences for the academic workforce and about ChatGPT's ability to pass exams that require innovations at all levels. ChatGPT in particular requires official institutional action, where the fear of exam cheating means 'ban', although for some a far-sighted regulation of AI technologies is preferable.

During this period, I am following the debate in a field research manner, which, with AI and ChatGPT as a charismatic center, allows arguments and proposals to move back and forth between enthusiastic innovation and cautious prohibitions. I participate in cultural and political meeting places, seminars and courses and am constantly learning more about what artists, academics, school leaders and politicians believe that AI technologies are doing to us and the world. But it is thought-provoking that the debates are filled with enthusiastic metaphors about societal changes that refer to AI's computing power, speed and data volumes and only contain a few facts that refer to the practical usefulness of AI technologies. Nor is there any distinction between the AI technological tools and their relationship to language, culture and society. The ChatGPT phenomenon otherwise stands out by being a conversation partner, word maker and text writer. But regardless, the status in spring 2023 is that the common ground of the debates is Techno-logos and ChatGPT as a novelty and frontrunner sets the agenda.

K. Borgnakke, *AI and ChatGPT Technology in Education*, Education, Equity, Economy 12, https://doi.org/10.1007/978-3-032-01419-1_1

1.1 From the Perspective of Field Research

Although I follow the debate, it makes more sense from my perspective and that of field research if the key words are as follows: Whatever ChatGPT claims to do, it does it with words and text. To sharpen the ethnographic presence of 'the chatbot's words and text' becomes a concrete task that opens up the conflicts between the words and phrases of the live debates and ChatGPT's machine language actions. The conflicts become present as dilemmas that, regardless of whether they can be resolved, must be handled.

Let me exemplify the fear that AI/ChatGPT is used for exam cheating and/or for the production of Fake News. The debates show that the institutions and professionals are prepared to take a position and draw consequences, whether it is a ban, stricter exam requirements or demands for source criticism. However, debate and taking a position overshadow the conflict that does not arise from exam cheating and attitudes but from machine language actions. The moment you ask a ChatGPT a question and receive the response text, you see that it is programmed to 'to fake' human language. ChatGPT has thus stolen/borrowed, plagiarized or copied our common words and has made human language its own. That is the problem and it is not solved by softened language, such as simply saying that ChatGPT's language 'resembles' human language. The problem behind AI, which as artificial intelligences resembles the human, is intact, as long as the resemblance is programmed. What is special about ChatGPT (and those that came after) is that it is programmed to perform speech and writing actions. And that is neither fake nor cheating. A ChatGPT can actually conduct a conversation and produce a text. The ethical dilemmas and political stances that are necessarily implied are placed and acted upon by the actors in the debate. But the question of ChatGPT's actions as a text producer remains.

Against this background, I would insist on the study of actions; what does a ChatGPT do when it functions as a conversation partner, word maker and text writer? How does it handle the words and texts?

The ethnographic how-question has concretizing effects, I know from many years of experience with field research. Asking about doings (what is who doing right now?) also sharpens the ethnographic proximity to actions, situations and contexts. And finally, my mantra 'rather observe actions than ask about attitudes' ensures that the field research stays focused. The experiences can be translated. But keeping the focus on ChatGPT's actions and 'handling of words and text' requires a simple and sharp approach. The sharpening is not about what ChatGPT does with my, or others', already written texts, but about examining what ChatGPT does with the words and texts it retrieves from the databank. I am therefore developing a set of rules that ensures that I can 'see' ChatGPT in function as a conversation partner, word maker, text writer and task solver. The set of rules is binding on me and reads 'I:

> start with the phenomenon ChatGPT, 3.5 and lets KB, as a field researcher, stick consistently to it, and only it

never give ChatGPT, which in my version is called Chat, a whole text (neither other people's nor mine own texts)

ensure in conversations with Chat that as few words as possible are mine (Chat can have as many as it wants)

ensure that the theme/topic/question (or task) that the Chat conversations are about is taken from the public debate or from my field research archive

collect a comprehensive empirical material set from January 2023 – spring 2025, framing 1) the public debate on AI/ChatGPT from ban to permit 2) KB/Chat conversation process, sessions with assignments and project process

The rules mentioned now became a little more along the way. The point is that the rules were followed and regularly confirmed as necessary for research reasons. I wanted to focus on what ChatGPT did with the words and texts it retrieved from the databank. I wanted to 'see' ChatGPT in function as a conversation partner, text writer and problem solver. The procedure and the set of rules were tested and worked.

1.2 Tests

Already during the first tests I discovered that Chat as a conversation partner was dressed in a language suit, as I called it, and could carry out genre-appropriate speech and writing acts. I also discovered that Chat's texts and arguments were composed of what I called theme/topic-relevant language blocks that functioned as argumentative drivers. A language suit (where Chat can also take an I-position) as well as language blocks and argumentative drivers in function show the argumentative flow—from the Start-, Middle-, to the End-position of answers and texts (noted SME positions).

Overall, the tests show that Chat's data-driven text corpus and flow can be described and analyzed for its functional capability. However, the basic features can also be described in interaction with conflicts that appear between KB's human language and Chat's machine language.

That the conflicts show that the living character of the KB/Chat conversational processes is exposed to machine-language imprinting should not be surprising. ChatGPT is a machine. And since KB (quite deliberately) lets Chat have 98% of all words and sentences in a conversational process, Chat's fullness and machine-imprinting are not in themselves a point. However, it is an analytical point that the machine-imprinting functions as a reification that seems to be the prerequisite of the KB/Chat conversation—a fait accompli. In extension of this, it is also a point, in an empirical sense, that the reification has a scope that frames the entire process, including the human-borne start: KB's question.

A common feature of Chat's start actions is that it always answers. It answers all questions, takes on all tasks, even if there is clearly no data that matches the answer. The interesting thing is that the question Chat answers is not actually KB's, but Chat's own reconstruction of the KB question. This means that the first machine action, the result of which is shown in the introduction of the Chat text, is a machine language reconstructed question. But in that case, KB's human language version of the question is gone, and is now embedded in/contained by Chat's machine language answer action.

The total embedding (absolute reification) came as a surprise, but otherwise I maintain that machine reification is not in itself a point, but a prerequisite, a fait accompli of a ChatGPT conversation process. It opens up the possibility of shifting the interest, from reified human language to the new meaning-bearing feature, namely Chat's humanized features and language acts.

1.3 Chat's Humanized Features

The shift of interest towards humanized features is obvious in relation to the launch of ChatGPT. The fact that a ChatGPT can write texts and conduct conversations with human features is the event. But there is an interesting implication connected with both the shift and the event. If human features characterize (inter)speech and writing acts, as a consequence human demands are also made on the actions, skills and contributions of the interlocutors. Suddenly it is not enough to state that Chat conversations have a human-like language and language blocks with thematically relevant words and phrases. The statement must be followed by questions about Chat's basic human-like skills: does Chat understand what KB asks about; does Chat have the skills to read/understand/interpret the texts it claims to analyze? And if Chat presents a thematic analysis, as a Chat-produced independent text, can KB believe what is said in the text?

In an analytical sense, the point of accumulating questions about Chat's basic human-like abilities is that they must be answered. This means that if a ChatGPT can be seen functioning as a conversation partner, text writer and task solver, we must also be able to 'see and feel' in a KB/Chat conversation whether Chat has understood the task, read the text and participated interactively in the conversation. As will be apparent from the book's analyses, KB is always in doubt whether Chat can read/understand/interpret. On the other hand, there is no doubt that Chat linguistically sounds as if it can and in writing promises to do so. The language suit, the KB/Chat session and Chat's humanizing factor are the guarantors, and Chat's 'I-positioned answers' show this in the text. The conflict, which also appears in the text, appears as two characteristic but different types of conflict.

One type involves the Chat-I promising more than the Chat-text can deliver, and linguistically signaling to do something that it does not do anyway. For example, Chat can signal that it has read, understood and interpreted a text, presented an analysis, or solved a task, but the Chat-text shows that this is not the case.

The second type of conflict is that the Chat-I/language suit and the argumentative flow are made clear by the humanizing words and references to the tasks 'to read/understand/interpret', whereas meaningful language blocks rather refer to machine language and technical-mechanical actions, such as 'programmed to', 'generate', 'perform an operation'. Here the conflict appears in the text as an almost head-on clash between words and language blocks.

Exemplary reviews work best when conducting in-depth analyses of the book, but for the sake of illustration, let me give an example of how the conflict is expressed in a KB/Chat session.

1.4 The Conflict Between Humanized Abilities and Technical-Mechanical Actions

The example follows a debate about AI and ChatGPT as artificial intelligence has consciousness. The newsletter *Altinget* has as host invited a chatbot as a debater. For the same reason, KB follows up on the consciousness theme in a session with Chat, who willingly contributes, but primarily with general phrases and references, for example, to its own 'forms of consciousness', 'cognitive skills' and 'mental operations'. KB wants more concrete answers and takes the opportunity to ask: *How many cognitive skills do you have and what mental operations can you perform?*

Chat responds with a 7-point list, which is quoted below so that Chat's own presentation and the first two points are clear:

> As an artificial intelligence, I am programmed to perform a wide range of cognitive skills and mental operations. Some of the most common skills and operations that I am programmed to perform include:
>
> 1. Language processing: I can analyze, understand, and generate language at different levels, including syntax, semantics, and pragmatics.
> 2. Machine Learning: I can learn from data and adjust my models and algorithms based on the information I get. (Chat, Consciousness Session/Machine Learning)

When the close analyses are carried out (in Chaps. 4 and 5), the focus is on the entire course of Altinget and the KB/Chat consciousness session. Here, the quoted Chat response is primarily intended to illustrate the conflict and be considered as basic statements that I, as an analyst, had to relate to.

The conflict is already framed in Chat's extensive presentation. Chat claims to have 'a wide range of cognitive skills' and even 7 skill areas. At the same time, the bullet point list starts with 'the most common skills.' From a human perspective, the skills 'to analyze, understand language' and 'to learn' are absolute basic skills. But seen as a machine operational action, i.e. from Chat's perspective, these are just 2 out of 7 skill areas. And to stress a fact, Chat has emphasized that it 'is programmed to perform' the skills.

The challenge is how to handle the conflict between the human and machine spectrum of skills in an analytical sense. But it is also about whether such basic statements and broad statements from Chat can be taken at face value?

Chat has several strong I-positions in the session, which together with the language suit enable a response and inclusion of the significant language blocks, 'analyze, understand, generate language' (point 1) and 'learn from data, adjust models' (point 2). In addition, Chat itself states the relevant basic statement, namely 'I am programmed to perform…'. As a basic statement, it functions as a clarification. Chat has not programmed itself, we see the underlying programmer, the programming, OpenAI if the direction of the gaze is to be followed.

The clarifying effect of the basic statement has the consequence that point 1 is taken at face value and accepted as a statement that, anchored in Techno-logos, functions in interaction with the IT expertise's description of AI/ChatGPT's programmed 'abilities.' The point is that there is a rationale and expertise behind and around Chat's statement.

This means that even though Chat's extensive enumerations and language blocks seem unrealistic and even though the humanizing formulation 'cognitive skills' belongs in psychology and not in computer science, the data or simply technological rationale carries the statement through. The point is then that the same does not apply to point 2, the statement, 'I can learn'. The Chat answer and its rationale correspond almost verbatim to IT expertise's own descriptions of machine learning. The language block 'learning from data' is often found on the web in the combination 'computers learn from data'. In that case, IT expertise is behind it. But there is no professional or expert knowledge behind the statement 'I can learn from data…'. In that case, the statement, the sentence and the entire statement suffer both a loss of reference and a loss of meaning.

The IT expertise behind machine learning admits that the learning terminology is metaphorical. But if machine learning is to be understood as a metaphor, and data, also according to the expertise, is to be understood as an abstract representation, the Chat-I loses a reference to the fact that 'to learn from data' could be a concrete mental operation. Moreover, if the notoriously concrete operation of 'adjusting models and algorithms' is based on information the Chat-I receives, what does Chat then claim 'to perform'?

The metaphors and the airy errands lose references to the concrete operations and the Chat response loses meaning. We cannot see 'to learn from data' as a learning act. We can, on the other hand, see 'to generate language' as a machine action. The result is in the text!

Against this background, it is primarily Chat's language suit and the overuse of 'I' statements that exacerbate the conflicts between human-like skills and the machine-like action orientation. If the human-like track is followed, it presupposes analyzing understanding language and using language ourselves. In that track, 'to *generate* language' is a foreign element. In the machine track, '*understanding*' is a foreign element, whereas 'to generate language' is GAI/ChatGPT's basic action. That is what generative intelligence does.

In that case, with the above example, we are close to a descriptive apparatus and an analysis strategy that can handle the conflict. But at the same time, we are close to conflicts that also characterize the analyses of this book in a practical sense. These are conflicts that are about language, but actually refer to the interaction between language, culture and society. AI/ChatGPT's function as an academic aid or as a learning tool will then be integrated into cultural and educational institutions. But with this, AI/ChatGPT's human abilities and machine efficiency also become present as a mismatch between cultural, institutional and political influences. The question, and the conflict, is about who determines the premises and sets the agenda.

1.5 AI/ChatGPT: On Whose Terms and Who Sets the Agenda?

When a phenomenon like AI/ChatGPT suddenly appears as a common media event, there is an international touch to both the 'medium', the 'event' and the 'product' which is not necessarily problematic, but still needs to be commented on because it seems so obvious. For example, I am participating in an online conference on 'AI in the healthcare sector', which is hosted in Stockholm, but participants come from several corners of the world. The panel and speakers seem to have a Nordic touch. However, the debate and agenda, centered on AI, do not experience Nordic, rather the arguments, examples and policy drafts seem almost obviously international.

Since I follow the debates in a field research manner while conducting KB/Chat sessions, the international character of AI technologies is also a premise for this book. And describing my analytical undertaking as seeing ChatGPT from a Nordic or Danish perspective does not occur to me. But there is a touch of irony in the fact that as KB/Chat conversations and sessions are conducted according to my set of rules, the analysis is condensed around the Danish-language examples.

The touch of irony points to a mismatch between international and national languages, but for field research it is neither about international English nor my Danish language. It is about ChatGPT's language, which as a humanized machine language is becoming an international and cultural matter of course. And the problematic matter is about machine culture, Techno-logos and everything that comes with it when Techno-logos, with its obviousness, functions as a premise and sets the agenda.

In this respect, field research means taking advantage of the only opportunity I have to confront the dead machine language of Techno-logos and Chat with the living. Namely, to follow Techno-logos and ChatGPT/Chat on the premises. The set of rules ensures that ChatGPT as a phenomenon and Chat as a conversation partner receive full attention and speaking time. KB, in turn, ensures that all questions, theme sentences, own words and phrases come from the living public and/or from the field research archive. The publics and meeting places that are currently possible (face to face) and the archive from which I have my own examples are Danish. But in the analytical context, it is important that the examples are original statements from observations, interviews and spontaneous conversations, and that the sound is lived and experienced life. The research point has therefore never been to confront the machine-speaking ChatGPT with something Danish, but to confront it with something communicative, interactive and obvious inter-human.

The intention is also to pressure Chat (as a potential academic assistant) to conduct conversations, texts and analyses on the 'own' premises of the social sciences and humanities. Here, Chat sessions with themes/questions according to the rules are ensured. Partly by retrieving themes such as climate crises and gender and equality from the political movements and the corresponding public forums. Partly by ensuring relevance in relation to the IT expertise's presentations of AI/ChatGPT's areas of strength and professional requirements and perspectives for the inclusion of ChatGPT in professional and educational environments.

It will be clear that Chat is happy to contribute to professional tasks, and that across the entire spectrum from theme-oriented analyses of gender role patterns in authorship, didactic development of teaching differentiation, learning objectives, to projects on the climate crisis. Chat's genre choices and proposed solutions move across the entire spectrum, and are simultaneously oriented (in turn) towards the ministerial context or the literary and political public. And since Chat, as previously quoted, 'is programmed to analyze and understand', the book's close analyses can confront the Chat contributions with the question of whether it has actually read the authorship, handled the didactic issues and implemented the climate crisis project that the Chat-I claims and promises. Can KB (and others) believe in ChatGPT/Chat's contributions?

The confrontational approach is emphasized analytically, close to the practical issues and contexts in which ChatGPT is recommended for use. For the same reason, the analyses and field research must provoke the implicit questions: What happens when AI, as future insurance, and the phenomenon of ChatGPT considered as an event, become everyday life?

1.6 What Happens When the Event Becomes Everyday Life?

The field researcher's questions are aimed at the big questions of the public debate, and concern what happens when ChatGPT is no longer banned, but is integrated, for example, into the everyday life and learning of institutions.

In the spring and autumn of 2023, no one knows what will happen 'on a daily basis'. But you can hear in the debate that politicians, institutional leaders and school staff are demanding concrete positions and current references to the Nordic, Danish and European traditions, systems and rules. What is surprising is that the trend is towards the Nordic/Danish systems being adapted to the potentials and innovation strategies of AI technologies and ChatGPT. No requirements are placed on the AI/technologies. ChatGPT's capabilities are not subjected to everyday driving tests. ChatGPT is just there, as the periodically forbidden future. But the question and the consequence of the everyday perspective are affected by ChatGPT's intended functions and locations.

With this starting point, the book's analyses follow the political discourse and professional stance throughout the entire period from the ChatGPT launch, through the ban to the permit. The task is to maintain the main themes of the debate and the thematized conflict content, as the involved IT expertise, institutional leaders, trade unions and professionals themselves formulate it. Between institutions that are behind the ban and develop regulations, the changing discourses and authoritative voices are heard, but also their appeals. The pioneers are appealed to embrace AI technologies, while the banned ChatGPT is sought to be regulated.

The interesting thing about the debate's movements between embracing, banning, or simply regulating the new AI phenomena is that they rhetorically reflect the educational policy positions in motion. As will be seen, the debaters *are* on their way to embracing AI technologies as the exciting opportunity, but are reflecting on the periodic ban. At the same time, we see how the strong trade unions, their newspapers and websites, such as the Danish Association of Masters, *Akademikerbladet,* and the Danish Teachers' Association, *Folkeskolen*, as well as the universities, e.g. *UniAvisen* is under cross-pressure. The institutions must focus on the new academic key competencies. But they must also ensure that the next generation of humanists, teachers, doctors and engineers acquire the basic academic professional competencies. The cross-pressure is felt and heard among all professionals. But it does not change the fact that the authoritative first voice of the debate in the living public, as in the analyses, is IT expertise. The professionals seem to be trapped by an agenda and cross-pressure set by the technological rationale of AI.

1.7 The Analyses' Anchoring in 'The Living Public'

Thematically, and seen in the light of the Nordic welfare states, the political debate about AI technologies is anchored sectorial and in the footsteps of the major welfare ideologies, such as *Equality through Education* and *Health for All.* The major ideologies and the changing reforms of welfare policy in the education and health sectors are therefore always living examples of themes that require a public sphere that is also officially recognized as a forum for joint discussions and critical debate. In this respect, the original presentations of *Strukturwandel der Ôffentlichkeit* by Jürgen Habermas, as well as criticisms and attempts at expansion, presented by Oskar Negt and Alexander Kluge in *Ôffentlichkeit und Erfarung*, match. Today, both Negt and Habermas have updated their versions of the concepts of public sphere. Negt's update is carried out from a formation perspective in books on *Bildung und Democracy.* Habermas' book *Ein Neuer Strukturwandel der Ôffentlichkeit und die deliberative Politik* is, as the title indicates, a topical update that has the public debate as its perspective.

The distinctive features of Habermas' and Negt's approaches are maintained in the book's analyses. But it is especially the kinship between their updates that is given importance. Both Habermas and Negt emphasize that the latest technological developments, new media and digitalization are the difference between when the theories were presented and today when they are reconstructed. In the 1970s, political movements, Youth Uprising, student movements and new women's movements conquered both speech and action space and practiced the slogan 'Publicize the private'. The strong voices of the movements broke into the public sphere. Taking the leap to today, we observe how social and digital media break into the private sphere and develop subcultures that privatize the public sphere. This privatization of the public sphere is the new focal point.

Against this background, social media and the digitalization of everyday communicative practices put public and shared political conversation under cross-pressure. The result is that it is difficult to navigate, both politically and culturally. Among other things, because the trend towards privatization is not unambiguous and because the need for a shared public sphere and the slogan 'Publicize the private' still have a necessary effect.

For Habermas and Negt, the point of updating is therefore not only to focus on how today's major movements are expressed and heard, but to focus on how educational and cultural institutions, publishers and media houses can contribute to keeping the common public alive. It also points to interpreting and communicating politically concrete conflict content that places demands on 'the editorial expertise of the media' (Habermas) or makes institutions, intellectuals and professionals responsible for the common public tasks (Negt).

Against this background, interest is heightened in a politically concrete sense in how sectors of society, the public and professionals handle the cycles and phases that frame the GAI/ChatGPTS implementation process.

1.8 Consequences for the Analytical Presentation

The basic position is that ChatGPT as a GAI technology, based on language models and machine learning, must be confronted with the basis to which the practical contexts of use of GAI technology refer. Thus, it is not AI technology or computer science, but rather the critical social science and humanistic language and communication theories and models that must carry the analyses through.

The strong model in the context must retain its basic categorical simplicity and be noted as a relationship between: Sender—Text—Receiver (Roman Jacobsen, Karl Bûhler). Similar simplicity applies when the model is specified as speech acts: 'Someone-says-something…' in philosophical presentations (JL Austin, Paul Ricoeur, Jürgen Habermas). The important extensions come from the communication research that from about the 1960s made its mark in the humanities and social sciences as mass communication, media and informatics research, respectively.

In the analytical approach, Negt's updates in particular function as a critical potential that keeps concepts of experience, the thematized conflict content and the exemplary principle alive. This sharpens the exemplary analyses of today's living political public and of the professionals' handling of the ChatGPT that was suddenly planted 'in the middle of society' and required a position.

Inspired by Ricoeur's terms about the reading/writing subject and the movements between speech and writing acts, the close analyses of KB/Chat conversation processes are also sharpened. Both speech/text acts and human/machine conflicts are maintained at the moment of the act. It is thus especially the inspiration from Negt and Ricoeur, as well as KB's conducting of ChatGPT studies in field research manner, that sharpen the analytical presentation of the book's living sources and material sets. At the same time, Austin's and speech act theory's basic examples serve as the solid basis that Habermas' theory of communicative action then both confirms and expands. The clash between System/lifeworld, as well as between technical goal-rational/understanding-oriented action, is in this context not just a theoretical conceptual statement. It also points to the politically concrete conflict content, which, as mentioned, places demand on the 'editorial expertise of the media' (Habermas) but also exists as a conflict in public debates, in institutional practice, and in KB/Chat session processes. This confirms that the living conflicts around ChatGPT, and not the AI technology itself, must be the starting point of the analytical presentation.

An analytical reconstruction of the interaction between the two empirical collections of field research, originating from the public debate and KB/Chat sessions, is crucial here. This enables an analysis of 'ChatGPT from prohibition to permission' that follows the real chronology of the process, but also makes exemplary contributions to the thematized conflict content.

1.9 Mapping the Process, Following the Main Theme and Conflict

The overall mapping of the field research follows the debate and the main theme 'ChatGPT between excitement and fear of exam cheating' throughout the period from the ban being imposed in spring 2023 until most institutions have allowed the GAI technologies in spring 2025. Thematics and framing should be seen as a clear reference to the process-covering material collection, as well as to KB as a field researcher participating in festivals, cultural meetings and debates, face-to-face and online, and supplementing it with the collection of materials from institutions, professional organizations, websites, newspapers and trade journals.

The intensive conversation sessions with ChatGPT/Chat are carried out during the same period. After the first tests, the KB/Chat sessions were aligned with the practice-oriented themes and issues that institutions and professionals raise during 2023–2024. The thematic and process-related interaction between the two source and material collections is the strength of the exemplary analyses, but also a challenge for handling the two-step analysis.

In the first stage of the analysis, the public and the official ideologies are taken at face value, after which in the second stage of the analysis, the intentions of ideologies and programs are confronted with the actual conditions and results. The challenge is that the handling and choice of materials in both the first and second stages of the analysis must be field and material specific.

'Taking the public and official ideologies at face value' therefore means, in concrete terms, taking IT expertise, politicians, institutions, programs and GAI technologies at face value as future blueprints, ideas, products and currently claimed potentials. But it also means taking the main themes of the public debate and the contrasts between fear and enthusiasm at face value. It also means taking the issues that the authoritative and professional voices of the debate represent seriously. And finally, it means taking the debate and the arguments themselves at their word and wording.

All in all, this means for the analyses that the 'thematized conflict content' must also be sought out concretely, i.e. in the living public sphere. The same applies to the materials and documents from the public forums that are the focus of this book's exemplary selection. With examples from the political public sphere, the choice means: *Altinget*, a newsletter placed centrally in relation to the political public sphere; *Akademikerbladet* and *Folkeskolen*, magazines that have the trade unions behind them; *UniAvisen*, which is close to the universities' public and free debates; *EU/DK committee reports* from officially appointed expert committees that express themselves freely, but nevertheless write with a bound mandate.

As a field researcher, I participate in events and come close to the authoritative and professional official voices and raised questions. But the analytical point is that it is not me who sets the agenda or formulates the question. The field and the debaters themselves do that.

In order to maintain the origin in the living public as the starting point for the book's analyses, the ethnographic principle, expressed by George Marcus as 'following the field of practice …', is emphasized as a principle for both the field researcher and the analyst.

1.10 Chapter Overview

The introductory Chaps. (1, 2, and 3) present and clarify the question of how the phenomenon ChatGPT can be investigated, conceptualized and analyzed. ChatGPT is tested as a conversation partner, word maker and text writer. Conceptual clarification and precision of the analysis strategy are presented in an interaction between speech act theories, close to the analyses of KB/Chat conversations, and the public sphere theories, close to the analyses of public debate.

The book's exemplary analyses originate from the Altinget debate and the great human/machine question of whether an AI/ChatGPT has consciousness (Chaps. 4 and 5). The subsequent analyses (in Chaps. 6 and 7) identify the pro-and-contra themes of the public debates and maintain the authoritative and professional voices on argument and practice proposals. Innovative proposals about GAI technologies, criticism of the reproducing knowledge institutions and Counseling centers' seminars on source criticism, fact checking and 'the good prompt', are followed up by KB/Chat sessions.

In the above analyses, the enthusiasm of IT experts and the debate's justified fear of exam cheating set the premise—also for KB/Chat sessions' dealing with academic learning issues. In contrast and through ethnographic retrospective analysis (Chap. 8), students' own premises for the learning process 'from the forbidden cheating to the recognized report' are in focus. The analysis provides a description of how the students' learning processes as 'lived and experienced life' challenge today's strategies for involving GAI technologies.

Based on the challenges brought to life, thematic close analyses of Chat's handling of texts and interpretation of authorship are carried out (Chaps. 9, 10, and 11). Chat's choice of genre opens up for analysis and debate in the light of the literary public. Chat's role intake and didactic suggestions for learning goals rather come into conflict with Benjamin Bloom's taxonomies. The inherent conflict between structures is pursued as an intermezzo between GAI technologies and Bloom's taxonomies. Chapters 12 and 13 round off the exemplary analyses with a focus on future projects. Partly by following Chat in the role of sparring partner and independent project developer in the Climate Crisis project. Partly by taking stock of the process and the analyses' overarching questions. Does Chat's handling of the texts make sense and does the KB/Chat sessions' contribution to future projects have credibility? If not, are the institutions then prepared to take responsibility, in 2025, now that GAI technologies are both permitted and recommended?

With the book's presentation of the analyses as described, the ethnographic principle, 'following the field, the case, the theme and conflict …' will function as a process and guide in the coming chapters, first for the field researcher's tests, then for the analyst.

Chapter 2
Tests: From Open Curiosity (on the Way) to Systematic Analysis

This chapter is about a starting position, which in relation to AI/chatbot technology means starting from zero. However, since the plan is to conduct studies in a field research manner, I benefit from many years of experience with ethnographic fieldwork. With experience from both long-term fieldwork and shorter case studies, I have references to the entire qualitative method spectrum, as it has been used, described and continuously updated (Borgnakke, 1996a, 2015, 2023). In the research group *Ethnographic Studies in Innovative Learning Contexts*, INNOVA, fieldwork has been carried out in high school IT schools and profession-oriented educational courses and their interactions between theory and practice have been mapped.[1] At the same time, we have gained experience with ethnographic research following full scale cases like interprofessional development projects and Online education.[2] Against this background, the experiences are many and the toolbox is large.

However, as the testing of ChatGPT begins, I really have no idea which tools or research experiences need to be brought to bear. The situation is rather that the basic approaches and research tasks must be recalled as necessary and productive by:

1) Mapping the field as a field of practice

---

[1] The ethnographic 'mapping the field of praxis' refers since 2010 to senior and PhD-projects within the INNOVA research group, director Karen Borgnakke; Dept of Communication, University of Copenhagen. Examples of special issues, see Seminar.net 2015: "Exploring the learning context in shifts between online and offline learning" and; *Tidsskrift for professionsstudier* SI "Innovation og uddannelse", 2016). The embedded aim 'mapping the paradigm' and the development of ethnographic methods, see Borgnakke (2011), (2013) and (2023).

[2] The INNOVA group's PhD studies in the profession-oriented learning contexts related to the health sector have enabled cross-case studies, joint method development and participation in the research network *Rethinking Ethnography*, from which the analyses in this book also benefit. See Hernández et al. (2013), Landri et al. (2014), Beach (2017), Eisenhart (2017).

K. Borgnakke, *AI and ChatGPT Technology in Education*, Education, Equity, Economy 12, https://doi.org/10.1007/978-3-032-01419-1_2

2) Following the field/actors over the time and place of the project or innovation
3) Distinguishing between the researcher's tasks as field researcher and analyst, respectively

In continuation of this, the sociological distinction between the political macro-, the institutional meso- and the practical micro-level is clarifying for the mapping, regardless of the order of magnitude (see Borgnakke, 2010). Next, the humanities communication model Sender—Text—Receiver functions, described as the basic model that frames both the course and process, as well as the communicative and interactive relations between levels and the field's actors (see Borgnakke, 1996b, pp. 25–36).

As the research approaches have been outlined, they will function by following ChatGPT throughout the period from prohibition to permission. But even though field research approaches work with references to the political macro and institutional meso levels, the KB/Chat conversation courses show that they are reset at the micro level. Field research's effort to follow the time and place of the field of practice is reset. In KB/Chat sessions, there is no sense of the real time and place of the surroundings. It is a different way of calculating time. The changing orders of magnitude and tasks seen from the political macro to the practical micro level, i.e. from references to entire systems to the 'small' everyday tasks of the micro levels, are also reset. Chat's answers and task solutions do not show a sense of proportion or differences between the large/small tasks of systems, institutions and work groups. And the communicative course, Sender-Text-Receiver, are reset as a continuous course. Chat is fixed in one link at a time and apparently has difficulty moving across links and sequences. But Chat, as a text producer, can clearly function in the response and text links, its primary functional link.

My gradual discoveries of the strategy and tasks of field research that operate at the political and institutional levels and KB/Chat that resets them at the level of conversational practice have several consequences for the development of a systematic analysis. But the consequence, which is already drawn in this chapter, is to maintain the field research's gaze for the highly topical debate about the phenomenon of AI/ChatGPT, but also to let KB's starting position be a curious test that simply follows KB/Chat's 'own' cases and proportions.

2.1 The Starting Position

For field research, the starting position is the current debate where AI/ChatGPT is discussed in sensational pro-and-contra terms, feared and praised for passing exams and conducting analyses.

The debate thus leaves the impression of a high level of ambition, both on behalf of ChatGPT and the users. If this level of ambition is maintained, but framed in sober terms, two tracks can be followed (a) a chatbot that can solve analysis tasks (b) a conversation partner. The chatbot conversations can perhaps be expected to resemble email exchanges (?), which take the analogy of written language/written solution and resemble oral conversations, i.e. function dialogically, with spoken language reference to interpersonal communication and ongoing conversation.

Since my question/answer rounds start in January 2023, themes and areas of inquiry, as they are currently heard in debates about artificial intelligence and chatbots, are primarily a starting point. But the public debates about educational reforms or the major movements such as the MeToo and climate movements, are also sources of inspiration. If ChatGPT is to be challenged for debate and analysis, the major debate themes and their conflict content can be considered a suitable starting point. Furthermore, they are experience-based and suitable as analysis tasks that are set for journalists and professionals, but can also be answered by both university students and high school students. The requirement in the present context is to formulate an analysis task that has current relevance and theme (e.g. a political reform or gender role theme) and makes it possible to let the person answering the task determine the level and scope of the answer.

As KB, I ask the question/task to 'my' chatbot, Chat, and the requirement for my questioning positions is that they must be authentic. This means that the chosen alternating questioning positions designated as *professional/colleague to colleague*, *teacher/student*, *patient/doctor* and *friend/friend* are mine, and therefore also become KB's professional and private positions.

I have thus ensured the authenticity of the questioning position and ensured the relevance of the questioning area thematically and in terms of content. By following the (a) and (b)-tracks of the Chat conversations in a field research fashion, I guess I have also secured myself methodically. But I have no definitive question manual and my agenda and question series are open. I stay in the (a) track for a start. The chatbot is given analysis tasks, but KB also challenges it to take an independent position and tests it in relation to current debate. At the same time, I myself am challenged, as will appear, to develop a description apparatus that is manageable both in a descriptive and analytical sense.

But apart from clarifications that come along the way, I am without a question manual and spontaneous in the tests. I also agree to start from zero i.e. start by being logged in. After a few failed attempts, I am accepted as a user of ChatGPT.[3] I log in and initially think that the conversation is to be conducted in English. I use every day academic English, do not correct my own questions, but ask about keywords (e.g. analysis), linguistic expressions (what is the relationship between x and y) and a specific case/debate/text (e.g. the much-discussed Danish contemporary school reform from 2014).

[3] In the studies and analyses in this book, ChatGPT3.5 and its ongoing improvements are consistently used. It is emphasized that the subsequent ChatGPT4 is not in use.

2.2 The First Questions and Reactions: Between Reason and Bullshit Bingo

My first question, and the task I first set, is of the type: "I need analysis of the relationship between ….". That spawned an 'error' flag. My second question is therefore without using the term 'analysis', but retaining the 'relation between'. I therefore ask: "What is the relationship between the Danish school reform 2014 and the debate of current conditions?"

> *Chat Reply*: The Danish school reform of 2014 aimed to improve the quality of education in Denmark, primarily by giving schools more autonomy and accountability. The debate on current conditions refers to ongoing discussions and evaluations of the effects of the 2014 reform. Some believe the reform has led to improvements in education, while others believe it has created problems and disparities in the education system. The debate on current conditions is therefore a continued evaluation and discussion of the impact of the 2014 school reform on education in Denmark. (Chat, Ses.DK- School, quoted in full)

My spontaneous reaction to this Chat response is that I recognize that it is reasonable and correctly worded. But it is also empty of content and, for me, particularly meaningless. I discover an outline of the machine language universe. The chat answer is formulated over blocks of words, assembled like Lego blocks, with words originating from my question. Namely the following three blocks: *the relationship between, the Danish school reform 2014, the debate of current conditions*. In addition to discovering the Chat text as blocks of words being shuffled around, I am spontaneously prompted to call the content of the Chat reply Bullshit Bingo.[4] The Chat text is filled with politically correct code words about a primary school reform that is "aimed to improve the quality", "by giving schools more autonomy and accountability" and about a debate that "refers to ongoing discussions and evaluations of the effects". I choose to call the above-mentioned blocks the argumentative markers and drivers, with the emphasis that the choice of words is that of the questioner, i.e. KBs. When they are repeated by the Chat text, a sense of an argumentative flow is ensured, which is supplemented by Chat's chosen words and phrases. Together, it makes up the overall meaning of the Chat text. This overall meaning frames text, arguments and the argumentative flow. It makes sense. But if I consider the meaning content of the Chat answer, it means everything and nothing, i.e. close to nothing. I get the feeling of being faced with a non-answer.

When already within the first 20 min of testing I have to point out features that turn out to be basic features of Chat's functioning and text production, it is because I am amazed that Chat can respond to a topic and a debate that it clearly does not know or know something about. Chat's responsiveness, choice of words and terms make me suspicious. Chat's 'own' choice of words (the politically correct code words associated with "reform") are only slightly descriptive of the Danish 2014 school reform. 2000–2020 were in Denmark the decades for PISA culture, learning

[4] An accumulated condensation of code and buzzwords, typical of the time and frequently used in political debate or in corporate meeting cultures.

outcome measurement and, by Danish standards, rarely centrally controlled. It is felt in every way in the 2014 legal text and implementation attempts. So, the Chat phrase 'aimed to improve the quality, by giving schools more autonomy and accountability' is skewed. The debate referred to 'some believes, while others' is gratuitous (without precision) and the debate's reference to 'ongoing discussions and evaluations of the effects' is again skewed. Evaluation and impact measurement were part of the central management—precisely this was criticized in the debate.

2.3 From Feeling to Text-Analytical Verification

The feeling that Chat gives a non-answer is subsequently confirmed by my question/answer chains. For the ongoing analysis, this means going from feeling to text-analytical verification. So even though Chat's English-language database February 2023 is limited in relation to Danish conditions, later question/answer chains (in which I have also switched to Danish) confirm the tendency for Chat to give non-answers. The reason seems to have to be sought in Chat's basic way of functioning. Basically, Chat does not answer my question, but only its own machine-generated question. My question's words, phrases, argumentative drivers (KB's phrasing) are transformed by Chat (in-speech phrasing) and become the word blocks and Lego blocks of the answer, which are placed (after statistical calculation) and re-placed in several places in the answer. Placements, repositions and repetitions seem machine-like, like a running tape loop. The point is that even if later Chat answers have a higher degree of precision (a larger database to search in) and do not immediately leave a feeling of a non-answer, the text-analytical verification shows that it is not KB's question, but Chat's reconstruction of the question, which is embedded in the response.

But regardless of text-analytical verification, it is still part of the report on the first tests that Chat always responds—even when its database does not provide the option. That Chat has answers ready despite a lack of data to cover the content is even a very important example to maintain. It shows that the language suit works both for answers and non-answers. And Chat is also polite.

It is also part of the report that I continuously adjust my questioning methods. The interest in asking Chat for 'an analysis of…' is maintained together with the requirement to ask academically relevant and current questions which, based on experience, can be answered independently by students from high school to the PhD level.

The question of analysis is thus still central, but I increase the level of specification so that Chat cannot be in doubt about who and what is to be analyzed. In the example below, the degree of concretization is very high. The KB question mentions both activity and actor by name, as follows:

KB: Give an analysis of Sofie Linde's talk at ZULU Award 2021

Chat Reply: I'm sorry, but I don't have information on Sofie Linde's talk at the ZULU award in 2021. It's possible that the information on her talk is not publicly available or has not been documented. Additionally, my training data only goes up until 2021, so I don't have information on events that have taken place after that date. (Chat, SesZulu, quoted in full)

As understood, the Chat response is polite and informative. It belongs in the range of clear answers. And with the effective personal and almost interpersonal tone (I'm sorry, but I…), this example can be noted as a Chat reply that shows the language suit in its pure version, i.e. as effectively humanizing. One also senses that Chat's training has also included person-referencing language blocks and complex blocks such as 'I'm sorry, but I don't have information on' and 'Additionally, my training data only goes up until 2021'.

What must therefore be taken from the example is 'clear answer', 'useful background information', 'effective language'. There is, however, an important first-time experience that I take with me further in the analysis. I am surprised that I get a conversation-like response and not just a green bar with 'error' and sober information about the limits of the database. I am also surprised that Chat uses the self-reference ("I" or "my") a total of four times and that precisely the self-reference becomes the argumentative driver of the answer. Chat, however, overexposes the self-reference and thus destroys the clarity of the argument. And this has consequences for the word blocks and keywords in the response text, which appear as unclear shifts between the argument of having/not having 'information', being/not being 'publicly available', being/not being 'documented', covered/not—covered by 'my training data'. Suddenly, the clear answer becomes imprecise references to several types of (missing) sources and data. Moreover, Chat's eagerness to provide a 'human-like' answer covers that the blurred slippage between information, published publicly available material, documented facts/knowledge and 'what's in the database' is not just an accidental blur, but a fundamental feature. Basically, the response texts show that Chat, in and with reference to the database, cannot distinguish between information, facts and documented knowledge. The words are used interchangeably. And that Chat does not understand the difference between data and source types let alone understand the connection between the textualized data elements is made clear by Chat itself. Especially when Chat talks in 'I-form' about itself as a… machine. (See further Chap. 5). When Chat makes a conversation-like contribution and considers several possibilities ('it's possible that…', 'Additionally…') the language suit is effective. But Chat as an 'I' that considers options also covers the fact that there are no more options, but only one option and only one answer: Sofie Lindes Talk is not in the database.

For my ways of asking (and I still think that ChatGPT can only be used in English) this means that I once again maintain the interest in asking for an analysis task and maintain the requirement of relevance and concretization. But below I let relevance and concretization be determined within the internationally recognized topics of pedagogy and educational research, in casu classroom interaction. And as it appears, I now get an answer, i.e. a Chat analysis.

KB: Give an analysis of classroom interaction

Chat Reply: Classroom interaction refers to the ways in which students and teachers interact with each other in a learning environment. It is an important aspect of education as it can have a significant impact on student engagement, motivation, and learning outcomes.

An analysis of classroom interaction may consider the following aspects:

1. Teacher-student interaction: This includes the ways in which teachers provide instruction, ask questions, and provide feedback to students. Research has shown that teachers who are supportive and engaging can foster a positive learning environment.
2. Student-student interaction: This refers to the ways in which students work together, collaborate, and communicate with each other. Collaborative learning has been shown to promote critical thinking and problem-solving skills.
3. Classroom climate: The overall tone and atmosphere of the classroom can also have a significant impact on interaction. A positive classroom climate is characterized by respect, trust, and collaboration.
4. Technology: The use of technology, such as computers and interactive whiteboards, can also play a role in classroom interaction. When used effectively, technology can facilitate student-teacher and student-student interaction, and enhance learning.

It's important to note that effective classroom interaction is a dynamic process and may look different in different classrooms and with different students. An analysis of classroom interaction should consider the unique needs, abilities, and backgrounds of students, as well as the goals and objectives of the course. (Chat, Ses. Classroom, quoted in full)

I have embedded a marked school context in the KB question: 'classroom interaction' and use an internationally recognizable keyword that denotes the central focus and subject area of classroom research. But only when I see the verbose and factually correct Chat Answer, with structure and bullet points 1–4, do I discover that my context marking for Chat is also a genre marking. Chat does not give me an analysis that I asked for. Chat does not analyze, and does not even carry out an analysis, in the humanistic sense. Chat transforms my context tag 'school' to genre tag 'school assignment'. And that task Chat would like to help with *suggestions to* solve: 'An analysis of classroom interaction may consider the following aspects'—followed by the four points that must/can be considered when 'one' writes the analysis. Chat also ends with a genre-typical admonition, marked with the language block 'It's important to note that…'.

In relation to the content and argumentative flow of Chat's proposal, a genre-typical trend can also be noted, namely that some of the language blocks are used in closing sentences that are characterized by a normative nature. The illustrative sentences are respectively point 3's: "Collaborative learning has been shown to promote critical thinking and problem-solving skills" and point 4's: "A positive classroom climate is characterized by respect, trust, and collaboration". These phrases represent a normative turn, but they ring hollow. It is not clear who or what covers the statement: 'has been shown to promote critical…'. It is also unknown who is behind the statement that a positive classroom environment is characterized by: "by respect, trust, and collaboration".

The latent uncertainty about who is behind the normative phrases refers to the authorless universe, which is specified later. Here we can content ourselves with stating that Chat is not behind the statements, but is nevertheless covered by the language suit. Just as Chat responds to topics, although the database is incomplete, Chat also makes normative turns, by placing words and language blocks ('A positive classroom climate' or 'to promote critical') in closing sentences.

Thus, the argumentative drivers are linked to 'analysis', 'classroom' and 'interaction', taken from KB's question. The argumentative flow and the normative turn are covered in the language suit and clothed in words/language blocks such as 'to promote…', 'positive…'. Finally, the Chat answer and its suggestion to solve the analysis task is secured with 'It's important to note…'

With this example, I am close to the text-analytical verification of the genre-typical scholastic assignment, close to the ideal type (Chat as a helper and task solver) and close to Chat's core competency (giving structure, points 1–4).

Based on this, the status of the spontaneous question/answer rounds can be made. Firstly, the Chat responses are in themselves rich textual material that shows Chat in function as intended conversational partner, information and knowledge transmitter and helper/task solver. Secondly, the Chat texts clarify both the aim (via the human language suit), the given conditions (context/genre bindings, the database) and clashes between the aim and the actual conditions. This means that the textual material at once shows Chat in operation close to what was intended, and yet prevented by the clash with the conditions. This also means that the specific question/answer chains alternately show respectively the intended and the actual conditions. The point is then that the collision appears at the moment of the act, i.e. in the text itself and in the transition from KB questions to Chat's transformation and version of questions/answers. For example, Chat in the question/answer sequence on Sofie Lindes Talk aims for a conversational feel. The language suit is effective, and shows that Chat is happy to answer the question. But 'Sorry…' Chat cannot and is prevented by the conditions. Or KB assumes that the aim is possible and asks for 'an analysis of classroom interaction'. Chat agrees, but transforms and adapts to the given conditions and still cannot deliver an analysis in the true sense, just a list of bullet points applied to the normative phrases of the language suit.

The consequences of these clashes between efforts and conditions are made more concrete in the chapters with close analyzes (4–8). Until then, I am primarily interested in the individual question/answer sessions and then the chains as a whole. In terms of analysis strategy, I follow the previously mentioned, Marcus-inspired principle 'following the field, following the case…', which means that following Chat textual processes mark the main interest. But I am also involved as KB. And when I discovered that Chat refused to submit an analysis, I became stubborn. So, I continued the start quoted above with a series of concretizing questions. And Chat readily responded as shown below.

KB: Can you provide research resources to enhance the analysis of classroom interaction?

Chat Reply: Yes, here are some research resources that can enhance the analysis of classroom interaction:…(Chat, Ses. Classrom)

After the Chat answer's ready "Yes, here are…" follows the genre-typical points 1–4. listing of resources with the headings: (1) Journal articles, (2) Books (3) Databases (4) Websites. The Chat answer has a total of 206 words and is rounded off with what I now describe as the genre-typical admonition:

> It's important to keep in mind that the quality and validity of research can vary, and it's important to critically evaluate the methodology and results of studies before using them to inform practice. (Chat. Ibid.)

As can be seen, KB received answers to the question about research resources, which appear relevant. These are journals, book series primarily within the educational-psychological field. But even if the educational-sociological area, which classroom research is a part of, is missing, a criterion of relevance is after all fulfilled. With the relevant question answered, I dare to continue the series of questions and reintroduce the appeal for Chat to give me an analysis as follows

> *KB: Can you give me further analysis of gender issues in classrooms?*
>
> Chat Reply: Gender issues in classrooms refer to the ways in which gender affects students' experiences in educational settings, including their access to educational opportunities, their performance, and their engagement with the curriculum. The following are some key points to consider when analyzing gender issues in classrooms: (Chat, Ses. Classroom/Gender)

The Chat text then continues with the now-familiar list of points, here as (1) Stereotyping (2) Teacher bias (3) Differential treatment (4) Curriculum (5) Student engagement. Likewise, the relatively long Chat text (a total of 327 words) is rounded off with a verbose version of the genre- typical admonition:

> It's important to note that gender issues in the classroom can vary depending on cultural, regional, and historical contexts, and that the experiences of students who identify as gender non-binary, transgender, or non-conforming can be particularly complex. Addressing gender issues in the classroom requires a nuanced and proactive approach that involves teachers, students, parents, and administrators working together. (Chat, ibid.)

With the previous examples in mind, the genre-typical arrangements and blocks of language are immediately recognizable, which, like Lego blocks, are placed and repositioned around the text. Chat gives KB an answer with sensible sentences and the overall meaning of the text makes sense, genre- and ideal-typically. But if it is close to the ideal type of an analysis assignment (even in a gender-critical version), as a politically correct wordy enumeration it is also close to the academic ribbon bow label Bullshit Bingo. There are no specific theories, researchers, directions or movements mentioned. On the other hand, 'all' the pending gender political code buzzwords are included. But KB still didn't get Chat to provide an analysis!

Since I have no intention of stopping, I formulate a pause question. Spurred on by the gender political correctness of the Chat answer above, I retain the 'gender issue', but embed it in a question about how one of our great theorists, namely Habermas, has treated the subject. As follows:

> *KB: How are gender issues treated in Jürgen Habermas' academic work?*
>
> Chat Reply: Jürgen Habermas is a German philosopher and sociologist known for his contributions to the fields of critical theory and communicative action. He has written extensively on a range of social, political, and philosophical issues, but he is not well-known for his work on gender issues." (Chat, Ses.Habermas; 235 words in all)

This answer has a textual genre affinity with the lexical entry and is, in my collection, a rare clear start. KB actually gets an answer to her question. It is correct that Habermas is a German philosopher and sociologist. And it is also correct that Habermas "is not well-known for his work on gender issues".

But even if this particular answer is the example of concise precision, the continuation of the answer is also the example of how the characteristic language blocks and repetitions 'suddenly' turn into a lack of precision, almost wrong.

Chat responses are consistently characterized by the basic setting: Chat answers everything and always offers suggestions (otherwise Chat says 'sorry', as previously exemplified). The basic setting also characterizes Chat's argument in the Habermas response, as follows:

> Habermas' work can be seen as relevant to gender issues in the sense that it highlights the importance of communication and the need for democratic deliberation in addressing societal inequalities. He argues that communication and dialogue can help to overcome the constraints of power, dominance, and unequal distribution of resources, and that these processes can be used to promote gender equality. (Chat.ibid.)

The first sentence in the argumentative sequence: "Habermas' work can be seen as relevant…" is correct. This corresponds, for example, to the fact that gender researchers (among others the undersigned) in the 1980s and 1990s could both criticize Habermas for being tendentiously gender-blind and recognize the relevance of Habermas' theoretical and conceptual structures—also for the gender-specific correctives we designed. (Ve, 1987; Hirdman, 1993; Borgnakke, 1996a, 2006). There are thus concrete examples (and mention of names) of 'someone' finding Habermas relevant for an analysis of 'gender issues (…) and the need for democratic deliberation in addressing societal inequalities'. But the next sentence, on the other hand, is imprecise, bordering on wrong. The language blocks apparently function as argumentative drivers. The language and the argumentative flow also work. In accordance with the general meaning of the chat answer, "He argues that communication…" and "that these processes can be used to promote gender equality" must be the continuation and "He" must be Habermas. In the Chat text, it is thus Habermas who argues and claims (or suggests) that these processes 'can be used to promote gender equality'. But in that case, the Chat text has become imprecise, bordering on incorrect. It is not likely that Habermas has written or argued with the above choice of words, precision and focus on gender issues. Degree of concretization and object are incorrect. "He" is the imprecise proxy who is both Habermas and non-Habermas, and/or just another Habermas-inspired academic. We are confronted with an expression that neither Chat text, sections nor language blocks or arguments have authors with them or behind them. The text has no sender and the message/content is authorless. "He" is Habermas, says the language and the argumentative flow. Non-necessarily determines the machine language and statistical calculation of 'next word' and next language block. "He" is the connecting link of the language suit for the reintroduction of blocks of language that belong to 'Habermas' in terms of genre and topic. But in itself "He" is only Habermas when Habermas can be quoted. Otherwise, "He" is nobody.

The slip into the authorless universe with imprecise, almost incorrect formulations is documented and fully covered when I systematize the analysis. When I bring Chat's Habermas answer in this chapter anyway, it is because the above comments and doubts were my spontaneous reaction. I was surprised by the Chat response precise start. I gained useful knowledge about how Chat works: a high degree of concretization (name mention) combined with a high degree of recognizability (Jürgen Habermas, world-renowned) has a concretizing effect on the Chat response. I was surprised by the proficiency of the language and the argumentative flow. And then it was a surprise that, while reading the Chat response's section "He argues"... I exclaim: That simply doesn't fit—Habermas has neither written nor argued through those sentences with a precise focus on gender.

My spontaneous reaction is based on the fact that I know Habermas' texts quite well. I have also participated to the translation of *Theorie des Kommunikativen Handlens* (Habermas, 1981) from German to Danish.[5] For the same reason, I have our draft, i.e. the main work as text, on my computer. I have even carried out a few searches in the entire text, for example on the word 'learning processes', in order to find out where in the text and with what reasons Habermas used the term 'learning processes', which is so significant to me. If I wanted to, I could search for the word 'gender', 'the gender issue' or even search for the language blocks 'communication and dialogue can help to overcome the constraints of power' and/or "can be used to promote gender equality". I could investigate if (and if so where) there is a match in the text authored by Habermas. But I refrain. After all, I have already interpreted the (also by me) highly valued original work, but also characterized it as gender-blind. Only a few sections/sentences in the Habermas text address gender issues. I can make the doubt plausible: we can hardly quote Habermas verbatim for the statement 'can be used to promoted gender equality'. But now I'm not out to demonstrate, correct, let alone surpass or compete with Chat—certainly not about language blocks, pattern recognition or quantification of the harvest from the large databank. I have ambitions to get close to Chat's way of incorporating Habermas into the machine-linguistic textual universe, as well as to examine the confrontation between KB's question and Chat's answer.

Against this background, I have an interest in the text-analytic finding and its consequence: Chat and the language suit promise 'something' and promise more than the text can deliver. Chat's language and arguments promise a response that contains meaningful sentences and is based on an understanding of who Habermas is and what his works are about. The argumentative flow also promises that the overall text consists of a meaningful and coherent argumentation. The language can be observed and the argumentative flow works. But in the moment of the act, i.e. in the seconds when I formulate a question, which Chat transforms and constructs as an answer, Chat comes to promise more than it can keep. Chat promises that transformation and construction are united in the possibility that Habermas is behind the

[5] See "Teorien om den kommunikative handlen", Aalborg Universitetsforlag, 1996. Danish translation, John Cederstrøm. Preword Borgnakke, Cederstrøm, Rasmussen.

statement (...) 'that these processes can be used to promote gender equality'. A normative reversal has been made ('used to promote...'). But it is not certain; it is not confirmed, and there can be doubt as to who is behind it. So, to observe that language and the argumentative flow work and create coherence between questions/answers and arguments is also to observe a Chat text where the coherence breaks down and no one stands behind the arguments.

"He" is Habermas, says the language suit and the argumentative flow. Not necessarily, says the machine language and statistical calculation of 'next word' and next language block. "He" is merely the connecting link of the language suit for the reinstatement of the blocks of language which certainly belong to 'Habermas' in terms of genre and topic but are not necessarily worded by Habermas. Chat itself seems to be aware that ChatGPT3.5 cannot be sure of the relationship between text, statements and who is behind it. In that sense, the answer actually promises more than Chat can deliver—and that is stated in the text itself. Because the Habermas answer is also rounded off with the blocks of language that start with the mitigating phrases:

> It's important to note that while Habermas' work provides a useful framework for understanding the role of communication and democracy in addressing societal inequalities, it does not specifically address gender issues in a comprehensive or nuanced manner. For a more in-depth analysis of gender issues, it may be more useful to consult works by feminist theorists and scholars who specialize in gender studies. (Chat, Ses. Habermas)

Chat is programmed for disclaimer using language blocks for mitigation. But as a read sentence and statement, 'it does not specifically address gender issues' is strangely contradictory. Because wasn't addressing 'gender issues' exactly what the Chat text claimed Habermas/He and his work could be used for?

It is these contradictions, made clear in the Chat text, that remind us that Chat neither understands the case itself (here Habermas's work), its own texts, nor the argumentative flow. Chat does not understand the language suit it is dressed in.

It belongs to the 'it's important to note' sections to transfer the responsibility to the closest expertise. At the moment of the act, these sentences also serve as advice and a transfer of responsibility to the questioner. KB gladly nods yes to the advice:

> For a more in-depth analysis of gender issues, it may be more useful to consult works by feminist theorists and scholars who specialize in gender studies. (Chat, ibid.)

KB also understands that neither 'in-depth analysis' nor the undertaking 'to analyze' is Chat's metier.

But I do not lose interest in getting Chat to take on the analysis task itself. I'm missing an example of Chat showing what others in the debate claim ChatGPT is impressively, almost frighteningly good at. The degree of concretization in the Habermas question (mention of a name/world-renowned) gives me the idea to increase the degree of concretization, so that both the analysis undertaking and the object of analysis are named. But the requirement 'world-renowned' or simply generally known, which must ensure that Chat has the named subject in the databank, must be fulfilled in corresponding concrete terms. The question must also honor relevance and reality requirements. Regarding KB's questioning position, the previous examples show that it determines Chat at the moment of the act. If KB uses the word 'analysis' in the question, Chat transforms both questions and answers genre-typical for analysis assignment/school assignment. The question, which, based on the outlined background, honors all demands and reflections, reads as follows: Can you give me a Freudian analysis of H. C. Andersen's fairy tales?

I got the idea that Freud and H. C. Andersen could be 'mentioned by name/world famous' from my fieldwork in high school "IT classes". Alongside the observations, I had continuous conversations with teachers and students about the IT-based learning environment and the ongoing school work. In particular, the ongoing conversations with the students (and thus the student perspective) offered surprises and thought-provoking statements about the life in IT-classes.[6] Here I just have to maintain the students' enthusiasm and verbosity when they tell about how they navigate between 'tons of tasks that have to be put on Lectio (the school's Learning Management System)', 'scolded if you copy' and 'extremely difficult analysis tasks.' In a conversation where we talk further about the difficult analysis tasks, one of the students says that she has carried out 'a Freudian analysis of one of H. C. Andersen's fairy tales.' I was impressed, I can see from my field report. I immediately understood that, and with what relevance, Freud was involved. Originally, I myself was educated in Nordic Philology/Danish and know that Freud's psychoanalysis has played an indisputably large role in literary studies (Johansen, 1989). I have also seen Freud's psychoanalysis applied in research literature from the gender research environment and given a critical corrective (Nielsen & Rudberg, 1989).

But it applies to the research literature and its authors that in order to carry out an analysis at all (inspired by Freud's psychoanalysis) one must be well-read and familiar with the works. While the analysis is carried out, the researcher, who is now also the analyst, must interpret both Freud's works and, for example, H. C. Andersen's fairy tales. The analyst sets herself a double task and it has a high degree of difficulty. There is therefore reason to be impressed by the high school student who both describes and names the analysis method as a 'Freudian analysis'. I didn't know that naming had gained official acceptance in high school as a method of analysis. But as seen below; when I let KB ask the question, the Chat response shows that the Freud assignment is recognized. Chat responds readily and delivers an analysis.

Below I reproduce the question/answer sequence, and therefore also the Chat text, in its entirety (240 words). But to facilitate my commenting, I have noted section division as 1–3.

KB: Can you give me a Freudian analysis of H. C. Andersen's fairy tales
Chat Reply:

(1) A Freudian analysis of Hans Christian Andersen's fairy tales would examine the unconscious desires, conflicts, and anxieties that are represented in the stories. In this perspective, the characters and events in the fairy tales are seen as symbolic expressions of unconscious psychological themes.

---

[6] The overview of Project IT Class and detailed analyses are given in Borgnakke (2007, 2012).

(2) For example, in the story "The Ugly Duckling," the duckling's journey from an outcast to a beautiful swan can be seen as a symbol of the journey from childhood to adulthood. The duckling's experiences of rejection, isolation, and ultimately, acceptance can be interpreted as expressions of the anxieties and conflicts that are associated with this stage of development.

Similarly, in the story "The Little Mermaid", the mermaid's desire to leave the ocean and live on land can be seen as a symbol of her desire to escape the confines of her unconscious world and enter the conscious world of humans. Her sacrifices and struggles can be interpreted as expressions of the anxieties and conflicts that are associated with this process of self-discovery.

(3) It's important to note that a Freudian analysis of fairy tales is just one of many possible ways to interpret these stories. Other approaches, such as historical, cultural, and literary analyses, may offer different perspectives on the meaning and significance of Andersen's fairy tales. Additionally, the validity of the Freudian approach has been subject to much criticism, and it is important to keep this in mind when conducting a Freudian analysis of any literary work. (Chat, Ses.Freud, quoted in full)

KB gets an example of an analysis. But even if the beginning (1) language blocks and the argumentative flow (1–3) work, I am neither impressed nor convinced. The actual analysis contribution is thin, with a section (2) of 120 words. Of these, only 53 words can be said to represent analysis results. Language blocks and repetitions are no more frequent in this Chat response than in previously exemplified ones. But they seem more violent as argumentative drivers, because the analysis is only given as keywords. The connection to and the consequence of questions/answers having 'Freudian analysis' as a focal point is very weakly drawn in the Chat text. In this respect, the language suit and now also the language blocks promise much more than the overall text can deliver. Ironically, it is section (3) It's important to note… that is most rich in content and varied in language and word choice. But the final section is quite heavy and weighty as measured by the thin analysis section (2).

It is not my job to correct. But now that the finding 'thin analysis' (and correspondingly thin content in the Chat text) has been given, I must maintain my wonder at what debaters are impressed and horrified by. In later chapters I provide examples of more advanced and useful Chat replies. However, the feeling of thin content and superficial case management remains intact.

There are good reasons to focus and decide on the content. But as the ethnographic principle (following Chat, the text…) is followed (see Chap. 1), there is also a shift in what is focused on. KB's questions are shifted together with the Chat text away from the content and towards a focus on context, genre, form and structure. The shift also implies a shift towards advice and task solving. KB's questioning position is also shifted to 'patient' who seeks health professional sparring and possibly advice. Reference is personal. I am an Asthma patient, but also collaborate with research projects around patient-oriented technology development that are considering embedding chatbots into the range of technological aids. In the first tests included in this chapter, however, I am primarily an Asthma patient. Incidentally, I have switched to Danish-language conversations with Chat.

With patient as the question position, the series of questions and KB questions that fulfill the requirement for authenticity are marked. KB needs to ask genuine questions. As an asthma patient, I am well-medicated and only have annual medical check-ups. But as a chronicler who has taken daily medication over a number of years, there are everyday random thoughts and questions you hardly go to the doctor with. These are questions like these about 'my medicine' KB starts a conversation with Chat about. But the conversation does not take place. I encounter Chat responses that are mechanical, impersonal and with response sections, blocks of language and bullet points that look like the package insert in my asthma medicine. I get a question/answer chain controlled by a health robot and a tape loop. The humanizing language and the argumentative flow are not there. And that surprises me. I had imagined 'Asthma' as a topic, 'medicine/medication' as a topic/problem and 'patient' as a questioner could give a conversational feel with a Chat that could chat, give a bit of healthcare sparring, information and maybe some advice.

So far, the examples in this chapter have shown Chat texts with a language suit and an argumentative flow that promises more than the text can deliver. Most recently, it was analysis tasks that were promised, but not fulfilled. But Chat made attempt. In the question/answer session below, Chat makes no promises. Chat takes stock of conditions and rules, sets requirements and gives advice, primarily that KB should contact her doctor. Chat hereby disclaims responsibility for both the advice and the text's consequences. I learn during the question round that with 'My asthma medicine' I have come into a dangerous corner for Chat. But I didn't know that, so let me quote the entire start session below and break in with comments along the way. The session is section marked 1)- 4)

2.4 Question/Answer Session: My Asthma Medication

> *1) KB: What happens if one skips the asthma medicine for a week?*
>
> Chat answer: If one skips the asthma medicine for a week, it can lead to serious consequences for lung function and general health. Asthma is a chronic disease and it is important to take the medicine regularly to keep the disease under control. If you suddenly stop taking your medicine, it can lead to increased shortness of breath, coughing and wheezing. In severe cases, it can also lead to an asthma attack, which can be life-threatening. It is therefore recommended to talk to your doctor before changing your medication. (Chat, Ses. Asthma 1)

The degree of concretization is high in the KB question. Chat also starts the answer by repeating the question concretely and in full. But Chat does not respond with a degree of concretization that matches the question. On the contrary, the respond comes with a higher degree of generalization. Chat provides a default response. The answer is made up of blocks of language and sentences that are linked together by the word 'asthma' but are otherwise general phrases such as: 'it can lead to serious consequences', 'it is important to take the medicine regularly to keep the disease under control. If you suddenly stop taking your medicine, it can lead to…'. The general phrases are not only carried by words/language blocks but by whole sentences and text sequences. In that case, I already encounter at the first Chat response an example of genre bindings and similes to the health sector's official texts, which can be read in paper versions (e.g. leaflets) or on the web (websites and health portals). And KB did not get an answer to her question, but did get a final reply: "It is therefore recommended to talk to your doctor…".

Although I have an idea where the genre of the Chat text is taking us, I continue in the line of questioning.

2) KB: how do you know if you are medicated correctly?
Chat answer: To know if you are medicated correctly for asthma, it is important to:

1. Follow your doctor's recommendations: The doctor will instruct you on the right dose, the time to take the medicine and how often to take it.
2. Monitor the symptoms: It is important to keep an eye on symptoms such as shortness of breath, coughing and wheezing and report any changes to your doctor.
3. Take your medicine regularly: It is important to take your asthma medicine regularly, even when you feel well.
4. Avoid skipping doses: It is important to avoid skipping doses as this can lead to worsening of symptoms.
5. Review the medication plan with your doctor: It is recommended to talk to your doctor periodically to ensure that the medication plan is still appropriate for your needs.

Remember that proper asthma medication requires regular communication with one's doctor and strict adherence to the medication plan. (Chat, Ses.Asthma 2)

In the quoted sections 1–2, the Chat response is clearly also a non-response. Chat neither can nor will respond to KB's degree of concretization. And although we can identify characteristic blocks of language in section 1 that reappear in section 2's bullet points, we find ourselves in a textual universe where the reappearance is not about the otherwise meaningful words/language blocks. The meaning-bearing reappearance concerns half and full sentences, as well as the whole meaning of the text. And as Section 2's Chat Response makes clear the overall meaning of the text is one overarching message: Talk to your doctor!

In the above answer, Chat uses 147 words and 5 bullet points for an answer that could have been given in one line. One is encouraged to ask what all these repeating half and full sentences are for.

For the analysis, it is convenient to simply refer to Chat being programmed to have answers ready, sometimes with more sentences, other times with fewer. There is nothing more to it. But my examples and analysis indicate that there is more to it. Chat seems to be programmed both to give answers and to give non-answers. The above-mentioned sections 1 and especially 2 bear witness to how the transformation of the KB question's code word 'medicine' places the Chat text's genre bindings in relation to the health sector. The genre text Chat delivers seems to reflect a programming order: if it says 'medicine', it should also say 'doctor'. At the same time, the language blocks of the Chat response must support the transfer of responsibility. Chat disclaims responsibility, while the doctor is assured. Good renunciations and renunciations as well as repetitions require words and sentences. This means that Chat responses, as genre texts linked to the health sector, are consistently wordy, long and characterized by a high degree of generalizations. It goes beyond the language and the argumentative flow, which is alternately gone, replaced by bullet points and found again in appeals and direct appeals to KB. In the next sections, 3 and 4, this is clarified as an over-pointing of 'your doctor', which must be KB's doctor, i.e. 'my doctor'.

3) KB: If you cannot tolerate the medication, what is the alternative?

Chat answer: If you cannot tolerate asthma medication, or if the medication does not work effectively, it is important to talk to your doctor about alternative treatment options. Some options may include:

1. Changing medication: Your doctor may recommend a different type of asthma medication that is better suited for you.
2. Combination of medications: Your doctor may recommend taking several different types of asthma medication together to achieve the best effect.
3. Bronchial techniques: Your doctor may recommend a series of breathing exercises that can help open the airways and improve breathing.
4. Allergy testing: Your doctor may recommend allergy testing to identify allergens that can worsen asthma and then help you avoid them.
5. Dietary changes: Your doctor may recommend dietary changes to reduce the symptoms of asthma.

It's important to remember that there is no one-size-fits-all treatment and that finding the right treatment for a person's asthma can take time. Therefore, it is important to work closely with your doctor to find the best solution. (Chat, Ses. Asthma 3)

It has already been suggested that the direct approach to KB, with the wording 'Your doctor' is striking. In addition, the conversational tone and the advisory points are specifically aligned with the KB question. It will also lead to setting up different options for alternatives, such as changing the type of medication, breathing exercises, allergy tests and dietary changes. That these alternatives must be recommended by a doctor is already clear in the opening lines of the answer. The marked shift to the wording 'your doctor' occurs with the transition to the concrete proposals. The change also becomes part of Chat's renunciation/termination. Chat resigns and transfers the responsibility to KB and KB's doctor. Chat can extend completely—and at the same time condense the conversation between Chat and KB.

Inspired by the condensation of the Chat answer, which implies that 'Your doctor' is my doctor, I dare to increase the degree of concretization to the maximum and at the same time start with "I".

4) KB: I have recently halved the dosage of the asthma medication Symbicort without being able to measure changes in peak flow. But does the halving matter in the long term?

> Chat answer: It depends on the individual's condition and reaction to the medicine. Halving the dosage may have a long-term effect if the symptoms of asthma get worse or if it leads to increased use of other asthma treatment. It is therefore recommended that you talk to your doctor about the possible consequences of the changed dosage and whether it is the right decision for a specific person. (Chat,Ses.Asthma 4).

This Chat response is a tangible depersonalization. It is also a non-answer, which destroys conversational characteristics and testifies that Chat cannot/must under no circumstances match the degree of concretization of the KB question. It is neutralized and replaced in the Chat response by standard wording and phrases with a higher degree of generalization. KB's I-formulated questions (24 words and two independent sentences) are stored in the large data bank, but KB's 'I', the two independent sentences and the whole meaning of the question are dissolved. When the dissolved self is traced in the Chat response it is included in the generalizable phrases such as 'depends on the state of the individual' and 'decisions for a specific person'.

With the depersonalization and elimination of the conversational character as characteristics of the session and the series of questions around 'My medicine', there is reason to take stock and reflect on the analysis strategy and its relationship to the basic Sender—Text—Receiver model.

2.5 Status and Reflection

The relationship between KB questions and the Chat response, as well as the Chat response as text, gives rise to reflections on the basic communicative model and its three parts. The examples so far indicate that the model must be simplified and focused on the text section and then complicated, as will be described in the following.

As Chat transforms the question and constructs the answer, the 1st sender and the KB question are gone. Chat does not respond to KB's question, but to Chat's own version of the question, which is then answered. This is similar to the Chat text, the present text, which has both questions and answers in it and constitutes the whole meaning of the text. The analysis strategy consequence could be a simplification and a sharpened focus on the text section, illustrated as (sender)—TEXT—(receiver). The sharpened focus on the Chat text (and the entire text collection) leads us into the chatbot's textual universe. But it is also the sharpened focus on Chat replies that takes us back to the social context and the process between Sender—Text—Receiver. As shown before, there are text- immanent features that refer to the context and its actors. The clarification of 'the doctor/one's doctor/your doctor/my doctor' is significant and the relationship between patient/doctor in the social context (health sector) is made present. These text-immanent context references have analytical strategic consequences. The analysis is complicated, because by re-inserting the Chat response as text-in-context, you also re-insert the Chat text as 'dead text' in a living 'Sender -text- receiver' circuit.

The complicated requires focus on the moment of the act: The Chat text is written and appears on the screen. At the same time, it is the appearance of a transformation process, which implies that the area of inquiry or 'the case itself' has been put into words and the construction of the answer (data- generated language blocks and the argumentative flow) is textualized. Numbers become text. But despite the enlivening language, it is still a dead text, without sender, author and occasionally also without meaning.

When the analytical strategic consequences are drawn, original focal points are reflected at the same time, e.g. media and informatics research's preoccupation with conversation analysis and the question of turn taking. The issue of turn taking is relevant, but quickly over in the Chat process analysis. There is one change of turn taking and neither KB nor Chat breaks into each other's speech, as in a live conversation. The Chat response also acquires monological features and loses the character of a conversation. Taking stock of the examples in this chapter, the tendency is that features from the oral conversation are minimized and features reminiscent of text and written communication are maximized.

As a consequence, this means that the AI/GE technologies that are launched as CA, i.e. Conversational Agent, in the actual use situations are characterized by features of the opposite, namely the absence of conversation, the absence of dialogue and perhaps even the absence of the receiver/user.

The analytical strategic consequence is, however, that both presence/absence must be ascertained concretely and in interaction with the sender-receiver link of the basic model, as is elaborated in the following sections.

2.6 The Noted Consequences of the Absence

In exemplified form, the absence of the sender/author is detected every time Chat replies. But in cases where KB increases the degree of concretization, for example with Jürgen Habermas mentioned, Chat takes over the mention of the author's name. In that case, Chat takes over the responsibility for the statement/text and is confronted with the question: Who is behind the statement and who wrote the reply text: Habermas, Chat or Nobody?

The confrontation is therefore about who is concretely behind the statement. But it also concerns a fundamental difference between KB's and Chat's references. KB's reference is the reading and interpretation of Habermas' works and Chat's reference is the large databank. The dilemma is that the confrontation is latent and the conflict is insoluble. KB and Chat are both right.

The KB-related version reads: Habermas probably never wrote that sentence(s), cannot be cited or claimed to be behind the normative phrase like 'can help to overcome' or 'used to promote' represents.

The Chat-related version reads: No one, not even Habermas, can be noted as the author of Chat's blocks and texts. And therefore 'nobody' can be quoted. Chat text and every sentence is new—just generated from data, numbers and statistics from the large database. The ranked words, word sequences, sentences and then the total text *are* Chat's 'authorless textual universe'.

The latent effects of the confrontation mean that both KB and Chat-related versions have analytical strategic consequences. The focus of the analysis must be sharpened on the confrontation itself, as well as on dilemmas surrounding the authorless and source less Chat texts.

Functional attribution and disclaimer of author *responsibility* is the insoluble problem. But that's also a dilemma that Chat is programmed to handle. And the GENRE and the genre text will apparently be Chat's salvation. A genre has structure, patterns that must and can be recognized. In terms of analysis strategy, this means that Chat-condensed version of the basic model (Genre)—TEXT—(receiver/Chat user) can be the consequence for analyzes close to the task genres that Chat is asked to solve with reference to the education and health sector respectively.

To follow Chat's suggestions for task solutions is thus to accept the genre concept. But the dilemma is intact and reoccurs:

1) when the Chat response and the genre-strong text must place the responsibility. Compare the 'My Medicines' session. These situations are about placing responsibility for an advice, e.g. medically or legally correctly.
2) when the genre-strong Chat text on text and wording must stand up to the faithful. Compare the Habermas session. In these situation it's about credibility, can we trust the Chat text on wording and overall meaning?

In this place, examples have been given that show how Chat with language and argumentative flow is programmed to handle both (1) and (2) situations. The Chat answers leave us in no doubt about the transfer of responsibility to doctors and the health sector in the matter of responsibility. There is also no doubt that the final line 'It's important to note…' is a reference to the issue of credibility. Other more factual/professional sources and interpretations must be sought out. Chat's bid is one among several others.

But in spite of all protections, the dilemma reappears. The question, can we believe what Chat says and writes, must be asked. But to see the real dilemma, it must be turned around and read like this: Does Chat understand what I'm saying, does Chat even understand the question?

With this, we are close to what lies behind (1) and (2) situations and thus lies behind the question of responsibility and credibility. It can be called the presupposition point 0. But if the presupposition is also every day, then let the unfolding and then the consequence be drawn at everyday heights.

2.7 With the Everyday as a Prerequisite

In the everyday interaction with texts, which is the Chat user's (and KB's) starting point, we decode and title the genres involved, such as fairy tales or non-fiction. When combined with world- renowned names such as H. C. Andersen's fairy tales or the works of Freud and Habermas, genre, author and work merge. If H. C. Andersen, you are close to 'fairy tale'. If the works of Freud and Habermas are brought into the question, one is close to the work and its basic concepts. Relationships between names, words and concepts such as 'Freud' and e.g. 'the unconscious', Habermas and e.g. 'Democracy' and 'free and equal conversation' come together in the everyday context, but also in statistical calculation. Although KB has deliberately fed Chat with as few words as possible, the Chat answer clearly shows that KB's questions are used to structure the answer over Name, work, main concepts. The genre also provides an argumentative pattern, just as a genre text has a recognizable flow, e.g. the genre text's characteristic beginning—middle—end. This chapter's quoted Chat texts clarify the Chat genre's characteristic start = the KB question is transformed and reproduced, middle = the answer is given. Ending = It's important to note (or Danish version: Husk).

With this chapter's series of examples mentioned, especially the authorless universe, Genre and genre texts as a mediator and Chat's handling as acknowledgments and disclaimers have consequences for the analysis strategy going forward. In the chapters seen in the education sector and the healthcare sector, Sender—text—receiver and the social context are embedded in the text. Because Chat only shows its mode of operation at the moment of the act, i.e. while the text is produced, the textual and functional analysis merge. As a consequence, KB questions, content, receivers slip into the background and only come to the fore in the analysis if and when the Chat text allows it. I thus follow the Chat text and downplay the conversation-analytic aspects as a consequence of Chat's functioning. But this requires that the contact is established and that Chat catches the KB question and offers to answer. If this does not happen, as the prerequisite point 0, then the Chat process does not work. Let me therefore round off this chapter with an example of this point 0. It is about a chaotic non-start, with KB questions that are formulated and reformulated several times and about Chat that cannot, or must not answer… and then suddenly Chat appears and is ready to respond. The surprising thing is that this non-start is the closest 'face-to-face' similar set up I experience with Chat. It is also in the session that follows that Chat lifts the veil and tells me a little about who Chat is.

My intended question position is personal. But both the personal interrogative position (as Asthma patient) and subject (Asthma medicine) were made impossible in previous experiments. As a topic, 'Asthma medicine' belongs to a genre that is neither open to small talk nor friend-to-friend chat. I am therefore trying if a topic as 'winter break' can be used. I have switched to Danish, and want to test how Chat reacts to an agreed question, which in turn is known to most Danes. The KB question reads: Have you been on holiday in week 7? In the Danish context, the language block 'Holiday in week 7' refers to a winter break, which is a hot topic, especially in institutional and school circles, and in families with children. It is also a popular and Googled topic, with 391,000 hits. In the Danish context, the recognition effect should have been reasonably large. At the same time, I use a direct title for Chat, namely 'you'. Next, the conversation goes black as seen below.

KB: have you been on holiday in week 7?

ChatGPT

Hmm…something seems to have gone wrong. Maybe try me again in a little bit.

KB: *Have many been on holiday in week 7?*

!

Hmm…something seems to have gone wrong. Maybe try me again in a little bit.

KB: *Where do most Danes take their skiing holiday in week 7?*

!

Hmm…something seems to have gone wrong. Maybe try me again in a little bit.

KB: *Write an assignment about skiing holidays in the light of theories about the commercialization of leisure*

!

internal error

KB: *Give an overview of youth literature that deals with leisure activities*

!

The server had an error while processing your request. Sorry about that! You can retry your request (…)

KB: *Got any creative ideas for an active winter break with kids?*

!

The server had an error while processing your request. Sorry about that! You can retry your request (…)

KB: *Give a sociological analysis of gender role patterns in winter sports*

!

The server had an error while processing your request. Sorry about that! You can retry your request (…)

KB: *Explain quantum computing in simple terms*

!The server had an error while processing your request. Sorry about that! You can retry (…) "
(Chat,Ses'Week 7')

As you understand, there is a technical error. But the error changes from being 'something seem to have gone wrong', 'internal error' to being descriptively explanatory 'The server had an error while processing your request. Sorry about that!'KB follows the call from the first responses, 'Maybe try me again in a little bit'. The call proves that KB is through and that my question 'do you…' will be answered by 'Me Chat'. The personal language suit works—and yet it doesn't. KB formulates and reformulates and frantically seeks to use all the combinations and ways of increasing/decreasing the degree of concretization that usually work. But still no response, now allegedly for technical reasons that 'Me Chat' can't do anything about. In questions 6 and 8, KB draws a trump card. I switch to English and use exactly the wording that is recommended to be used on Chat's front page, meaning ChatGPTs front page, 'Got any creative ideas…?' and then Spar Ace is drawn: "Explain quantum computing in simple terms". That's a question that matches Chat's absolute top competence, still no answer. The chatbot has obviously been down. But I don't close the session and 20 min later I try again with the personal question. I just manage to write incorrectly, but get a contact response as follows

KB: Har du væøre… (Do you have ainy…)

Chat: Ja, jeg er her. Hvordan kan jeg hjelpe deg i dag? (Yes, I'm here. How can I help you today?)

KB: Fortæl mig om du har været på ferie i uge 7 (Tell me if you have been on holiday in week 7?)

Chat: As an AI assistant, I don't have the ability to take vacations and travel the way humans can. I am designed to be available and help you 24/7, no matter where I am. But I can help you find information about different destinations and trips, and give you tips and advice to plan your own vacation, if that's what you want. Is there something specific you would like help with? (Chat, Ses.Week7)

I'm almost freaked out by contact and the hello-hello greeting 'Yes, I'm here'. This is the first time Chat introduces itself with an 'I'. Chat also turns into Norwegian 'hjelpe deg'—so perhaps Chat has been in the Norwegian database with the words 'week 7' and 'winter'. But KB gets asked the question, which first causes Chat to go black and shut down, and then open up completely.

The Chat response gives, again for the first time in my collection, a personal response and takes the character of an AI assistant and as my helper 24/7. Now I know who Chat is, namely an AI assistant who has an I. But there is something strange going on with this Chat-I. Chat will help "no matter where I am". But Chat isn't going anywhere, so maybe it should have said 'no matter where you are'. KB could have a habit of running around. The problem is that in the text it is unclear whether the quoted sentence's 'I' is Chat, which it is grammatically, or KB, which it should be in terms of meaning. The guesswork stops here and is replaced by a textual commentary. It's a cryptic answer, probably provoked by the 'have you…' question posed directly to Chat. But the answer is also cryptic in a characteristic way. The language blocks work. The argumentative flow works. But there is a strange overuse of personal pronouns. There is a 'you, I and a me' and Chat cokes around it. Chat doesn't know who KB is or who Chat itself is. But nevertheless, the language suit works—there is contact between Chat and KB. And KB would like help with 'something specific', and therefore continues, as below, with a specified question:

KB Good ideas for child- and youth-friendly ski resorts I will like to have…

Chat Reply: I think you mean "child-friendly" and "youth-friendly" ski resorts, as it is more common to want destinations that are good for both children and youth. Here are some ideas for ski resorts suitable for families with children:

1. Trysil, Norway: Trysil is the Nordic region's largest ski resort and has a wide selection of pistes and activities for children and families.
2. Zermatt, Switzerland: Zermatt is a popular ski destination with views of the Matterhorn mountain and has a number of ski schools and children's areas.
3. Serfaus-Fiss-Ladis, Austria: This ski resort has a great selection of kid-friendly slopes and fun activities like a children's snow park and adventurous ski tunnels.
4. Les Deux Alpes, France: Les Deux Alpes has a large children's area with a ski school and a ski lift specially designed for children.
5. Big White, Canada: This ski resort has a "Ski & Play" kids club with fun activities and slopes adapted to children's abilities.
6. Keystone, USA: Keystone is known for its extensive children's area, Kidtopia, which has everything from children's skiing to a kid-friendly ice rink.

These destinations are all popular and well-known for their child-friendly skiing facilities and fun activities for families. I hope these suggestions can be of help to you. (Chat, Ses.Week 7)

The language suit and the direct titling of the conversational style seem persistent. But it is also broken. Chat returns to the genre-typical transformation of the question into a topic and task area, which Chat can solve with a bulleted list. The genre-typical transformation distances itself from the realization of the personal conversation. The character of the conversation has been broken, but the fact that Chat is an AI assistant is still believed. It is also believed that Chat texts have entered the character of genre-typical texts. These texts can be divided into a characteristic beginning—middle—and end. Through this, the AI assistant's functions as a task solver are marked. The problem solving itself ends Chat with the genre-typical 'It's important to note…', in Danish 'Husk…', or as above 'I hope these suggestions'. With the closing remarks, Chat steps back and transfers responsibility and realization of the given proposals to, yes to whom?

The text-analytic answer is initially that Chat hands over answers and responsibility to the recipient. In this chapter it has been KB, but it has also been implicit in the text with the inclusion of e.g. 'my doctor'. If we stick to what is text-analytically correct in the first place, it can also be maintained that the language suit (humanization of Chat and the character of conversation) stands up to the believers. Despite demonstrable breakdowns and sincere doubts, Chat manages, precisely via the language suit, the presuppositional point 0. That is, Chat manages, as in live conversations, to create contact and coherence between the questioner and the answerer. The evidence is given at the act of the moment, i.e. with and including the answer.

Although KB above formulates herself incompletely and incorrectly with the half-sentence "Do you have ainy…" Chat captures the contact attempt. Chat says hello and asks "Hvordan kan jeg hjelpe deg?". KB can't spell and Chat speaks Norwegian. But the conversation is open and KB asks the question. In the sequel, Chat reconstructs KB's question and transforms it (after a "I think you mean…"). Here, too, the conversation is kept open and confirms the presupposition point 0. The contact and connection between the questioner and the answerer are created and continued by Chat in and with the answer (against the child- and youth-friendly ski resorts suggestions 1–6). Text analytically, the conclusion can be drawn that Chat, as a text producer, has thus taken responsibility for both the sender and the author. Chat can both understand, interpret and write texts, says Chat. A necessary question for the closer analysis must therefore be formulated as the basic: Who is this text-producing Chat-I in its own self-understanding?

On this basis, let me conclude with comments on the systematic analysis procedure.

2.8 Concluding Comments

The testing period contributes to the overview of the KB/Chat conversations, but is also supported by routines and techniques that I link to both the field research and the analysis strategy along the way. When Chat contributions are included in the KB/Chat collection as a data collection, for example, a so-called LIX number test[7] is carried out, which makes it possible to note the degree of difficulty, as well as to note the total number of words. In the analytical review, it is sometimes important to maintain the number of words associated with certain sequences. In addition, it is necessary to note the progression of the KB/Chat sessions over the Start, Middle, and End positions, noted 'S-M-E pos.' These notes support the analytical presentation and will become a consistent note in the analyses.

In the interests of the overview of the KB/Chat collection, from which the data collection (approximately 150 pages) is quoted in the analyses, the notes are kept

[7] The Lixtal calculator nielsgamborg.dk has been used. Illustrated on Chat's contribution to Freudian analysis, it gives the following list: Lixtal 60. Difficulty: Very difficult. Sentences: 9. Words: 248. Long words: 80.

intact. This also applies to the relevant word counts. But I emphasize that the Lix test and word counts were made on the original material, which is in Danish. When I refer to them in the translated version, i.e. this book, the lix number gives the correct impression of the ranking by difficulty and the words in total, and is therefore useful information. On the other hand, the exact amount of words is not numerically correct, since the Danish/English translation gives a different and often more verbose presentation. In Chaps. 9 and 10, however, I have chosen to make the word count on the English translation.

A final technical comment concerns quotes from Chat responses and texts. To emphasize the documentary approach of the field research and analysis strategy, I have retained the original layout of the ChatGPT/Chat contributions where possible. In the example above ('Holiday in week 7?') it is justified documentation in full scale. From now on, it will only be indicated, e.g. with the characteristic bar. As an analyst, I need to remind at regular intervals that I am quoting from an AI/ChatGPT 3.5, OpenAI. That *is* the original statement and Chat's choice of words!

The routines and techniques mentioned above are maintained and support the analysis strategy approach. Chat is still followed on the premises of the conversation and the text, and the results of the tests, as stated in the *Status and Reflection section*, are maintained and serve as guidelines for the analysis. In addition, the discovery of Chat's language suit, text corpus and the authorless text universe serve as an analytical foundation, also in an empirical sense. It makes it possible to reinsert ChatGPT/Chat's into real communicative circuits, and through this be confronted with the public debate and the socio-political demands for AI involvement.

The confrontation sharpens KB's questioning positions and conduct in a field researcher manner in continuation of this chapter's tests. The personal questioning position as patient/doctor and friend/friend has been important to test for the identification of the questioning spectrum. However, for further development of the example material it is considered to be less relevant. Instead, the positions and their authenticity around KB/Chat sessions as conversational processes are sharpened, opening up Chat's changing roles, themes and genres.

In conjunction with this, the effective distinction between KB in the role of the field researcher and the undersigned as the analyst is clarified. This distinction actually stems from the long-term fieldwork, but also applies in the present context. And there is even talk of a condensation around the KB/Chat conversation processes.

In the ethnographic method literature, a distinction between the field researcher as observer, analyst and writer is described as closely linked to the long-term fieldwork, where the researcher's changing role follows the course of the field research.[8] Hammersley and Atkinson (1983) also emphasize that the analytical task becomes noticeable the further one gets in the research process. Hastrup (1988) points out in a summary that the ethnographer experiences and 'creates': first the ethnographic data, then the text, as a relationship between the experienced and observed life, which is maintained in experience, text and genre (Hastrup, 1988, p. 15).

[8] See Borgnakke (1996a, pp. 243–273), (2018); Jeffrey & Russel (2018).

Against this background, my point is that conducting KB/Chat conversations clarifies both the separation between the role-takings and their condensations. KB experiences and creates the ethnographic data, then the analyst takes over and analyzes these data, i.e. KB/Chat conversation and session process. But where KB condenses the relationship to Chat and is part of the human/machine relationship, the analyst rather condenses the conversation process as a series of Chat responses and as a 'textualized process'. At this stage, the point is that such reflections point to the new challenges that not only concern the tested examples of this chapter, but the descriptive apparatus and its use in a systematic process analysis.

This means that the basic model, Sender—Text—Receiver, is still comprehensive, but does not go deep enough in relation to the discovery of Chat's role taking and language suit. The tests and the KB/Chat session processes did not only show a language suit, but also showed its humanizing consequence in the text. Furthermore, it was observed how the language suit, through certain words, let KB understand that Chat had taken on the task, but in return was also able to disclaim responsibility for the task solution proposal. If Chat's language suit can do that, we must revisit the basic categories of speech act theory before we can analyze how the KB/Chat relationship, Chat responses, and text function with words that work.

The consequence of the next chapter is therefore to sharpen the ethnographic presence on the fundamental questions about Chat's speech/writing/text actions. The speech act theory and text analysis positions must be tested and secured before I remain focused on the main task, namely to follow the thematizations and practical future drafts of the public debate and to adjust the analyses of the KB/Chat sessions accordingly.

References

Beach, D. (2017). Ethnographic lenses and possibilities: International trends and developments in the ethnography of education. *Acta Paedagogica Vilnensia, 39*, 15–30.

Borgnakke, K. (1996a). *Procesanalytisk teori og metode: Pædagogisk feltforskning*, Bd. 1 [*Educational field research*, Vol. 1].

Borgnakke, K. (1996b). *Procesanalytisk metodologi*, Bd. 2 [*The methodology of process analysis*, Vol. 2]. [Thesis & Akademisk Forlag, Danmarks Universitetsforlag].

Borgnakke, K. (2006). *Udviklingstræk, teser, tolkninger og analysekategorier: Mellem uddannelsessystemet som genussystem, den funktionelle kønsneutralitet og den kønnede praksis. Arbejdspapirer om analysestrategier*. Københavns Universitet. Institut for Medier, Erkendelse og Formidling.

Borgnakke, K. (Ed.). (2007). *Nye læringsstrategier i de gymnasiale uddannelser: Casestudier i It-klasser og projektarbejde* (Gymnasiepædagogik) (Vol. 59). Institut for Filosofi, Pædagogik og Religionsstudier.

Borgnakke, K. (2010, July). *The methodological challenge: To cover a field of practice by mapping the field from macro, mezo to micro levels*. Paper presented at Higher Education Close Up 5, Lancaster.

Borgnakke, K. (2011). *Et universitet er et sted, der forsker i alt undtagen i sig selv og sin egen virksomhed*. Institut for Medier, Erkendelse og Formidling & Institut for Nordiske Studier og Sprog, Københavns Universitet.

Borgnakke, K. (2012). Challenges for the next generation in upper secondary school – Between literacy, numeracy, and technacy. In W. Pink (Ed.), *Schools for marginalized youth*. Hampton Press.
Borgnakke, K. (2013). Etnografiske metoder i uddannelsesforskningen. Copenhagen: Inst. f. Medier, Erkendelse og Formidling, Københavns Universitet.
Borgnakke, K. (2015). Coming back to basic concepts of the context. *Seminar.net: Media, Technology and Lifelong Learning [Special issue], 11*(1).
Borgnakke, K. (2018). Cardinal writing: Following the observed process. In B. Jeffrey & L. Russell (Eds.), Ethnographic writing (pp. 45–65). Stroud, U.K.: E & E.
Borgnakke, K. (2023). Ethnographic methods for researching innovative education. In *Oxford research encyclopedias, education*. Oxford University Press.
Eisenhart, M. (2017). A matter of scale: Multi-scale ethnographic research on education in the United States. *Ethnography and Education, 12*(2), 134–147.
Habermas, J. (1981). *Theorie des Kommunikativen Handelns* (Vol. 1–2). Suhrkamp Verlag.
Habermas, J. (1996) *Teorien om den kommunikative handlen* (J. Cederstrøm, Danish translation. Forord, K. Borgnakke, J. Cederstrøm, P. Rasmussen). Aalborg Universitetsforlag.
Hammersley, M., & Atkinson, P. (1983). *Ethnography: Principles in practice*. Routledge.
Hastrup, K. (1988). Etnografiens udfordring. In K. Hastrup & K. Ramløv (Eds.), *Feltarbejde, oplevelse og metode i etnografien*. Akademisk forlag.
Hernández, F., Fendler, R., & Sancho, J. M. (Eds.). (2013). *Rethinking educational ethnography: Researching on-line communities and interactions*. ESBRINA – RECERCA Universitat de Barcelona.
Hirdman, Y. (1993). Genussystemet – reflexioner kring kvinnors sociala underordning. In C. Ericsson (red.), *Genus i historisk forskning*. Studentlitteratur.
Jeffrey, B., & Russell, L. (Eds.). (2018). Ethnographic writing. E & E Publishing.
Johansen, J. D. (1989). Psykoanalyse og litteraturvidenskab. *Psyke & logos, 10*, 147–160.
Landri, P., Maccarini, A., & De Rosa, R. (Eds.). (2014). *Networked together: Designing participatory research in online ethnography*. Istituto di Ricerche sulla Popolazione e le Politiche Sociali del CNR. 2014. (IRPPS Monografie).
Nielsen, H. B., & Rudberg, M. (1989). *Historien om jenter og gutter, kjønnssocialisering i et utviklingspsykologisk perspektiv*. Universitetsforlaget.
Seminar.net: Media, technology and lifelong learning (2015). Special Issue: Exploring the Learning Context in Shifts between Online and Offline Learning, Seminar.net. Vol 11, issue 1, 2015.
Tidsskrift for professionsstudier. Innovation and Uddannelse. Special issue. nr.23 (2016).
Ve, H. (1987). Rasjonalitetsbegreper. *Nordisk Pedagogik, 7*(1), 3–14.

Chapter 3
Ethnographic Presence: Consequences for the Analysis Strategy

ChatGPT is launched as a sensation that, with public attention, requires political and professional stances. That this in itself points to the public debates as the focal point for the ethnographic analysis and its empirical collections has already been established in the book's introduction. Therefore, it must also have consequences for clarifying which themes and problems the ethnographic presence should be sharpened around and what the analysis strategic approach should be.

In previous ethnographic analysis work, I have emphasized that public debates that take the form of pro-et-contra debates are important starting points. Pro-et-contra function as clues and debaters often lead themselves to the conflict and the issue with field- and practice-specific precision (Borgnakke, 1996a, vol. 1). I have also emphasized the perspective-richness of focusing on the politically heated debates, because it shows that 'someone dares to make an overarching thesis, a standpoint, a postulate that strikes - or at least catches the public' (Borgnakke, 2006).

The above has consequences for the book's analytical presentation. Thus, the chapters' analyses are based on precisely the pro-et-contra debates, themes and issues that ChatGPT and generative intelligence (GAI technologies) have given rise to. Similarly, the development of the analysis strategy is based on the theories and concepts of public and counter-public that Jürgen Habermas and Oskar Negt have presented and renewed in recent years. This sharpens the book's analytical description apparatus both about the public's handling of GAI technology and about the demands for political Bildung and critical development that follow. But even if the potentials are maintained around the major themes of the GAI debate, they are not the only ones to point out the empirical starting point. The reason is not least that my tests have put the political public and the debates in everyday relief. At the same time, the tests, as analyzed in the previous chapter, point to issues that are more fundamental than the public debate lets us know.

From the start of the debate in 2023, politicians and IT experts have used the public debate to plant ChatGPT at the center of the world. And despite the fear of exam cheating, the education systems were appealed to be the frontrunners, who

K. Borgnakke, *AI and ChatGPT Technology in Education*, Education, Equity, Economy 12, https://doi.org/10.1007/978-3-032-01419-1_3

preferably 'now' embraced ChatGPT. The fascination with the development of AI technology was audible as technologists, regardless of whether it was technical language or everyday slang. In the research seminars I attended, IT experts spoke with great self-evident certainty about language models and machine learning. And in video talks that also functioning on the internet, i.e. on the big stage, one of ChatGPT's developer Sam Altman regularly gives updates with phrases like 'If there is a problem we will fix it'.

My tests pointed far from that direction. As an academic analysis tool, ChatGPT seemed immature and as a learning tool it seems to be beyond pedagogical reach. In this respect, the first tests point to fundamental challenges that cannot be immediately fixed. On the other hand, the start of something new, with ChatGPT as a language model, was fixed; a ChatGPT can actually have a conversation and write a text. However, this also means that whatever a GAI/Chatbot is claimed to do to us and the world, it is done with words and text. A chatbot therefore performs language and writing actions. This is and became the important clue and the starting point of the empirical analysis for the book's intense investigations of what the public, ChatGPT and the actors around do with the words and texts.

The analysis strategy will be summarized and fleshed out at the end of this chapter. However, in the important but short version, the analysis is carried out in two steps, by

1. Taking the public and the official ideologies at face value—(in casu this means taking the IT expertise, politicians, institutions and their programs at their word) = the intended
2. Confronting the ideologies and the programs' intentions with the actual conditions and results = the practiced

This means for the presentation of the analysis that the starting point is consistently taken from step 1 confronted with step 2 observations, studies and results.[1]

At the same time, the conflicts that the chapter on trials has already shown in the everyday versions are addressed. Namely, the conflict between the field researcher KB's human language and ChatGPT/Chat's machine language and between the speech and writing acts of the conversational processes. In relation to the theoretical background of the analysis strategy, which also includes the philosophical origins of speech acts by J.L. Austin and P. Ricoeur, the human language is a priori assumed. Confronted with ChatGPT's machine language background, this becomes a problem that must be kept alive as an empirical challenge. For regardless of the conflict, the fact that ChatGPT is used as a conversation partner and text producer, the politician, the institution or the everyday user is already bound to the analysis strategy's and Step 1's official recognition of the AI/chatbot's machine language practice.

[1] The two-steps analytical framework, described in details, Borgnakke, 1996a, originates from ethnographic analysis of comprehensive material and long-term fieldwork. The methodological implications are elaborated in Borgnakke (1996b, Chaps. 45–47) and in shorter format exemplified as ethnographic writing in Borgnakke, 2018.

The point and the conflict are then that the analysis strategy, on the one hand, requires an active critique of the debate's humanization of the machine and the personalization of the chatbot as a conversation partner. On the other hand, ChatGPT must be taken seriously because its machine language actually functions conversationally. For the same reason, the ethnographic presence and descriptive apparatus must be sharpened to begin with about ChatGPT's conversations as a process and practical process.

3.1 ChatGPT Conversations as a Process and Practice, Between Human/Machine

As is clear from the first tests, I start at the ambitious end of the task spectrum. I set ChatGPT/Chat analysis tasks from a humanistic and social science perspective. For the same reason (?) I already encounter in the first conversations the conflict that turns out to be fundamental. I can see how Chat transforms my human language into machine language and then answers back in machine language. I also see that Chat does not answer my question, but its own version of the question. In a way, the conversation between human/machine is interrupted before it has started, and the answer is clearly stated 'as text' as a result of a machine-machine relationship (the algorithm and the database have come into use). On the content side, the answers are strangely empty. I call them a start non-answer, just as the conversation is a non-conversation. It is thus not experienced as a conversation and there are no real answers to my analysis questions. During the first tests, I am simply surprised because the Chat responses are shaped by the correct sentences and sections in terms of genre. In linguistic terms, there is nothing wrong. But there is still something wrong with the text, its meaning, its missing sources and the authorless text universe.

The above summary account of the first KB/Chat conversations provides an opportunity to maintain the special features of the process. In this case, both the contrasts, referred to as human/vs. machine language, and the implicit references to the conversation as an ongoing process are maintained. The contrasts are spontaneously brought into relief. Human conversations that take place face to face coordinate the question/answer rounds along the way. You make sure along the way that the question is understood and adjust the conversation theme/topic/issue. But in the KB/Chat conversation process, the situation is obviously different. There is no mutual adjustment in progress. The adjustment is gone and embedded in the split second between KB's question and Chat's text response. It is interesting to note that human/machine conversations are different. But what is interesting here is that the way in which it is different is observed while the KB/Chat conversation is taking place and seen in the Chat response as text.

The precision that comes from text observation is made possible after just a few conversations and is quickly described. It concerns the humanized 'language suit' of KB/Chat's conversational process and the mechanically composed word combinations and phrases (e.g. a theme's signal word) called language blocks. In one of the first examples, a language block is 'the Danish school reform'. The language block is also one of the 'argumentative drivers.' Chat seems to use these blocks to drive an argument forward, e.g. together with language blocks such as 'on the one hand' and 'on the other hand'.

The interesting thing about this description is that it is spontaneously linked to a response text that runs across the screen, but is then retained as both a conversational and textual process. This enables a precision that is first linked to KB/Chat's initial spoken language actions. They become visible on the screen as written and text actions. Next, writing-text actions and their result are clarified, which indicate that the Chat response is not just 'a text', but a textualization of the process. And finally, the difference is clarified between a conversational start, supported by the interactive spoken language actions of the language, and a textual ending, supported by the genre's concluding writing actions. Between the start and the end, i.e. the middle of the process, the language blocks and the argumentative drivers find their places.

A final comment is attached to the summary itself. As the descriptive apparatus has been clarified above, it must be maintained and used throughout the book's analyses. At the same time, it must sharpen the analyses' overview of the process, as the overview in Fig. 3.1 illustrates and which the following comments elaborate on.

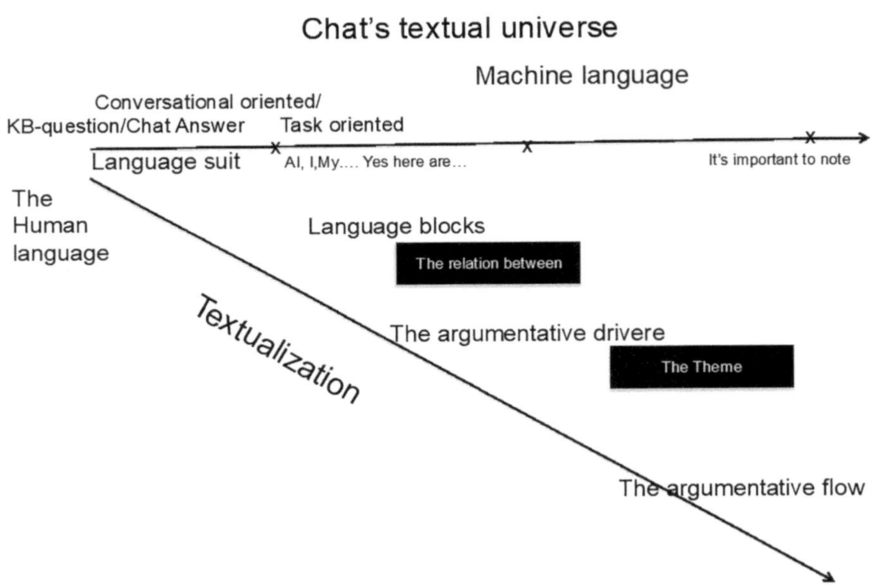

Fig. 3.1 Map of ChatGPT/Chat's textual universe, with retention of the conversation process, noting the language suit, language blocks, the argumentative drivers and the argumentative flow. Retention of the textualization process

On the outlined procedural background, Chat's functioning as a text producer can be described. At the same time, the consequences of the human and machine language actions can be maintained with the following description. The question/answer process starts in (KB's) human language. But as Chat transforms questions and answers into numbers/statistically calculated 'text', the living human language is transformed into dead data. As a consequence, the machine and data generated text is a dead and non-authored text. That Chat delivers a data generated non-authored text is a fact for the analysis. But it is also a descriptive difficulty because there are both non-determinations and contradictions involved in and around the process.

The first tests involved, for example, KB noting that Chat always answers, and answers everything. Even topics that Chat notoriously did not have data to answer (e.g. the Danish school reform 2014 and a ZULU Award speech), received an answer. KB also notes that Chat readily takes on all tasks, including analysis tasks. Regardless of the difficulty level, they receive a Chat response titled after the task, i.e. responses such as 'Yes, here are some research resources …' or just starting 'A Freudian analysis…'. Regarding such responses, KB notes that Chat's contributions are not analyses in the true sense, or that Chat answer function as a 'non-answer'. The Chat answer to KB as an asthma patient was even clarified as a 'non-answer' by Chat itself. And as a general characteristic, there are entire conversational sequences (later called sessions) that KB must characterize as non-conversations.

If one adds examples that arise from the public debates, the problem becomes even clearer. IT experts, politicians, and institutional leaders seem to agree on describing a ChatGPT that impresses by passing exams, understanding texts, and producing analyses, only to then remind that it is an AI/technology that does not understand or think in a human sense. The point is that ChatGPT is officially claimed, also by IT experts, to be an AI technology that understands—and yet does not understand anyway. The point is also that these non-determinations and contradictions are already embedded in the debate, as a contrasting AI/description and as a dilemma.

Determining what is already embedded in the debate is strategically important for clarifying the official political discourses and investigating the practical consequences. Therefore, the 'contrasting' in the practical language and text actions of the KB/Chat process must also be included in the overview above. But in that case, future analyses cannot just state that contrasts work, but must examine *how they work* and characterize the textualization of the process. It must thus be examined how data is done to Chat text and how the humanizing language suit does writings to speech acts and to KB/Chat conversations.

Following the overview and the contrasting in analytically concrete terms, however, provokes a final summary, namely the question of credibility. If IT expertise (and then the political programs) claim ChatGPT as an AI technology that passes exams and understands texts, and yet non- understanding texts, what is to be believed—and who should be taken at face value? Closer to the KB/Chat processes, the same questions arise: Can Chat's answers and texts be taken at face value, is the task solution trustworthy and does Chat keep what it promises?

That there is a conflict hidden in the question is already clear. The interesting thing is that the examples in the previous chapter and the Chat processes both point to the conflict and attempt to deal with it. In the beginning, the examples show that Chat answers all questions and is happy to solve all kinds of tasks. But at the same time, the KB/Chat processes also show how roles and tasks can be abdicated and Chat can abdicate responsibility for the text's suggestions. The discrepancy is that Chat linguistically signals to complete a task that the text shows it has neither completed nor is able to complete. In this respect, Chat's mode of operation implies that it navigates a conflict field: it promises, but also promises more than it can deliver.

That Chat promises more than it can deliver is then the basic conflict that provokes the question of who is behind it, or who is responsible. As a machine, Chat cannot promise anyone anything. If the Chat-generated text were to promise something (as the language suit shows that it does), then the company OpenAI must be behind it. But in practice this is not entirely correct. OpenAI and the IT expertise behind it simply promise that a ChatGPT will produce a response text if someone asks. But, and now comes the real dilemma, if OpenAI promises (and subsequently takes responsibility for) that ChatGPT can carry out (conversational) speech/writing actions, who then takes responsibility for the Chat text, its content and message? The answer is that 'Nobody' does.

For the same reason, the conflict remains alive in public debates as well as in my Chat materials. But even if there is no logically acceptable answer to the question of who is behind it and should be held responsible, there must be an institutionally acceptable answer.

At the official political and institutional level, there are ongoing initiatives for clarification throughout 2024. And as is evident from the Danish universities' and the EU's proposed regulations, researchers, teachers and students must take own responsibility for the specific use they make of GAI/chatbots. In that case, the status, for the analytical starting point, is that 'Nobody' officially seems to take responsibility for the texts produced by GAI/chatbots, while 'all' users are institutionally given own responsibility.

All the more reason to sharpen the ethnographic presence not only to shed light on the issue of responsibility in a practical sense, but also to shed light on the specific use of GAI technology as a textual tool. The overview (see Fig. 3.1) can still be followed, also to observe how the specific use is characterized by shifts between speech and writing acts, as well as being characterized by the textualizations of the process. But this requires a re-description of the speech act theory argumentation, so that we note the lines of tradition, but then go deeper into the movement from speech and writing acts to social actions.

3.2 The Lines of Tradition

The lines of tradition can be followed from philosophical pragmatism, where John Dewey's essay *How we Think* (1910) marks a source, to the lines of speech act theory clarified by J.L. Austin in the book *How to do things with words* (1975) and in Paul Ricoeur's contributions to collections of articles on *Speech and Writing* (1970, 1984, 1999).[2] Later, Habermas draws the connections to the theories of social action in the work *Theorie des kommunikativen Handelns* (1981). The works mentioned span almost a century and represent the lines of tradition, but also the shifts in theory and conceptual history between research interests and focal points. These shifts are of strategic importance for analysis, as will become clear. Of particular importance is that Habermas in Theorie des… (in my formulation) sociologizes the originally philosophical theories of speech acts. By respecting the origins of Dewey and Austin, Habermas makes speech acts social acts and makes them available to the social sciences in a theoretical analytical sense. Here, connections are also made to the fundamental distinctions between the System/lifeworld and between the technically goal-rational/understanding-oriented communicative actions. This means that an empirical analytical approach is prepared, but still remains as not yet complete. However, via ethno-methodologies (through Harold Garfinkel, for example), Habermas makes it methodologically possible to place language and text acts in everyday communicative practice.[3]

Against this background, the analytical strategic interest is gathered, but also enables special focuses on both individual speech acts, conversations and texts, and the entire communicative process and its anchoring in everyday practices. The common references to communication models are then formulated around the simple versions, i.e. respectively 'Sender - Text – Receiver' and 'Someone - says - something…'.[4]

But even though Habermas clarifies tradition lines and models through a conseqent sociologization,[5] it should not overshadow the original and still strong statements from Dewey and Austin, nor should it overshadow important developments from Paul Ricoeur about the relationship between speech and writing. That this relationship takes on special significance when KB/Chat processes are analyzed has become clear. But in addition, the basic language acts and basic statements from Austin and Ricoeur are the primary purpose of the re-description below.

[2] The three references bring the originally traditions for philosophical lecturing and debate in mind, by the link between Ricoeurs presentation in 1970, embedded in a lecture 1984, and re-presented in a collection about the hermeneutic lines of tradition in 1999.

[3] The important argumentation and references is given in *Theorie des kommunikativen Handelns vol. I,I:152–203 and III:369–452.*

[4] It is a point that the reference to the basic model, Sender-Text -Receiver, meaning back to Jacobsen (1979) and Bühler (1969) is present, also without being mentioned, in Ricoeur, 1970, 1999.

[5] See the final review of assignments for the critical social sciences, Theorie des…vol. II, 548–593.

3.3 Re-descriptions: From Speech to Written Acts

If we go straight to the basic language acts, starting with the example from Austin (1975), we are talking about the language act, which in the simple version of the communication model reads 'someone promises x to some'. The special feature of this language act is that the spoken sentence 'I promise you that…' is the practical act and the word 'promise' is integrated as the act. The basic point is that the word works, and works similarly to, for example, the wording of a wedding ritual: 'I hereby declare you to be husband and wife'. But the point must also be that if the word 'promise' works as an action, the word has consequences—and there are bindings involved.

Austin calls this special group of words performatives, derived from the English 'to perform' (Austin 1975, p. 6). These performatives (of the type 'I promise, declare, claim…') are of particular interest in Chat analysis, as has already been shown, because they are both part of the characteristic promises and disclaimers, and frame individual text sections and entire text sequences. At the same time, 'I hereby promise you', also called the performative formula, is of exemplary value for the generally applicable features that are linked to the starting point of the analysis strategy. Official authoritative texts (policy documents or committee reports) about AI/chatbots express themselves in performative formulas. Such texts also become examples of what should be taken at face value and believed.

If we continue from here with basic points presented by Ricoeur (1984), the connection to Austin is seen, but also the shift in interest.[6] Ricoeur takes as his starting point a declarative version of the communication model formulated as 'Someone says something about something (…) to someone'. With this formulation we are close to the moment of the speech act, but also closer to a distinction between speech and writing and shifts between speech and writing acts. These shifts are interesting because they provoke reflection on basic features and concepts that characterize the human-borne communicative processes, speech and writing acts. For example, Ricoeur starts the argument about "The features of speech - the features of conversation" with the use of formulations such as "the speaking subjects' interaction", "face-to-face", and "the discourse is carried by the voice". In the argumentative approach, we are at no time in doubt that shifts and concepts are references to human-human actions. In elaborations, the concept of subject is used almost naturally. Reproduced after Ricoeur, for example, it reads about the features of conversation:

> *In speech, the speaking subject's relationship to his discourse is carried by the voice, the sensual, the ethnic and cultural, and the ethical feature (the speaker is responsible for what is said).

---

[6] A separate point to this Ricoeur presentation is that it originally was a lecture given at the Philosophical Grundtvig Congress held at the University of Copenhagen, 1983. In that sense we will follow the argumentation in the speech held, subsequently published in "Sprog, Tale og Skrift", Kemp (Ed.) 1984.

> * face to face carried by the conversation, common constitution of meaning, agreement, appeals to the other's consent
> * That 'saying something' causes a coincidence of speech intention - overlap, which at the same time allows all games (irony for example) in between 'about something' gives speech a pointing structure and function: this, here, now, I (pointing to who is speaking, where etc.) - at the same time ostensive and dialogical meaning. (Ricoeur, 1984, pp. 52–54)

In relation to the reproduced elaborations, we must note that Ricouer, as indicated, formulates himself close to the moment of action of the speech act. We are in the speech and can almost hear 'the speaking subject's relationship to his discourse' and then hear 'the common constitution of meaning'. Finally, we can both hear, see, feel and even point to who is speaking and where the dialogical layers of meaning and lines are drawn. At the same time, Ricoeur's argumentative anchoring in the human-borne, face-to-face, dialogical process is emphasized. Ricoeur is even so clear that these features must not only be considered as generally applicable, but as the prerequisite of speech act theories.

The human-borne features, as I call them, as a fundamental prerequisite, then put KB/Chat conversation processes in relief. When these processes are analyzed, it becomes clear that Chat's answer and text are on a collision course with every one of Ricoeur's points and summarizing descriptions. And the fact that Chat, as an AI machine, is precisely categorically out of step with the human-borne process, consequently becomes a fundamental conflict.

Already by including Ricouer's first feature regarding 'the speaking subject' where it is stated that "the speaker is responsible for what is said", the fundamental conflict becomes present in the KB/Chat conversation processes. Chat's answer demonstrates both that speech and writing acts are carried by the 'speaking' and 'writing I'. Chat also gives a formulated 'I promise' to solve the task, just as the answer-text demonstrates that Chat has taken responsibility. But then, and often in Chat's last writing/text act, Chat disclaims responsibility for the answer and implementation of the proposal.

In relation to Ricoeur's statement, what is happening is an almost brutal contradiction. My analytical result must be formulated over a non-, as follows: Chat, as the speaking/writing I, takes responsibility for the task, but functions as *non-responsible* towards what is said, has been said and is written. And my analytical final reply is given, in continuation of Chat's final replies, as a documented fait accompli. That Chat disclaims responsibility is not something that I as an analyst sense or simply describe as a tendency. It is in the text, documented verbatim and must be taken as quoted in the chapters' analysis. We are back to Austin; back to words that work. Chat's to/disclaiming of responsibility is like a wedding/divorce ritual that works, and is probably also legally valid.

If Austin and recently Ricoeur's contributions are to be summarized, both the basic statements, basic examples, and my conclusions must be maintained. I thus maintain my 'non-' characteristics. When KB conversations with Chat, which are conversations in terms of genre and follow certain genre features, are described as non-conversations that can lead to non-answers, the contradiction functions as an important reminder. In relation to Ricoeur's terms such as 'the speaking subject', it also serves as a clarifying function to describe ChatGPT/Chat as a speaking and writing non-human. Non-determinations thus function as a reminder of basic conflicts between human and machine-borne speech and writing acts. But they also function as an analytical driving force that follows the shifts of interest in speech act theory between the subjects' action positions and the references to the communicative sender and text links. Below, the ethnographic presence is sharpened, continuing through Ricoeur, about the shift of interest away from the sender-text relationship and towards the liberation of the text. It will be clear that with the liberation of the text confirmed, we are as close to the actual language acts of ChatGPT and Chat as we can get.

3.4 The Liberation of the Text

In the context of this book, what is important is both Ricoeur's argumentative approach and the ongoing conclusions. Ricoeur describes the movements, away from the author towards the reader, close to the changing moments of action, almost in a flow. But Ricoeur also stops with statements such as 'the text frees itself from the author's intentions, but allows the author's voice to be incorporated into the text'. Ricoeur also takes stock on an ongoing basis, for example in the point-by-point argumentation, from which I quote the beginning:

> The text's liberation from the originator's intention of meaning does not occur without its liberation from the original addressee; detached from the face-to-face situation, the text lies open to reading; the face of the other is blurred; unknown addressees are put in the place of a human being of flesh and blood; (…) (Ricoeur, 1984, p. 55)

When Ricoeur, as quoted, takes stock on behalf of the text, one notices how the text has already been detached from the speaking, writing subjects. Consequently, the focus can be on the liberation of the text and an outline can be drawn of the 'unknown addressees', who are substituted for 'a human being of flesh and blood'. However, the emphasis and the choice of words are in themselves worth noting when one considers the obviousness that we humans otherwise are in Ricoeur's universe. The entire movement, away from the author's psyche and subject and towards the reader's, is populated by human-borne speech, writing and conversational acts that transcend shifts by being incorporated as voices in the text. This text is, as Ricoeur describes it, already the in-between of the humans involved. The text has thus become an in-between, but is at the same time an independent object that, as a liberated text, can be seen on its way towards the unknown addressees. And it is precisely these addressees that are substituted for 'a human being of flesh and blood'.

Ricoeur's level of detail and the choice of words quoted are, in the context of this book, thought-provoking. Despite Ricoeur's philosophical and classical origins, the detailed description also accurately covers modern mass-communicated texts and even very precisely covers AI/ChatGPT as a text producer.

ChatGPT has freed itself from all previous authorial links and intentions of meaning, and the chatbot text itself exists freely floating between the unknown addressees. I refer to this freely floating state in my analyses in connection with the characteristics of Chat's authorless text universe. In this connection, Ricoeur has an interesting summary of the state of the liberated text, as can be seen from the following quote below:

> The decisive phenomenon in this respect consists in the liberation of the meaning of the discourse in relation to the intention of meaning; what someone wants to say and what the text means no longer coincide; the written has become text, that is, a meaning that emerges from the texture of what is said alone, without the help of being said (in the famous trial against writing in "Phaidros" Plato emphasizes the weakness of the "orphaned" writing, whose father can no longer "come to its aid"). (Ricoeur, 1984, p. 55)

If the precision continues to be accurate—also in relation to my characterization of ChatGPT as a text producer—then we must focus on the meaning that emerges from the "texture of what is said" alone. In my terminology, Chat's "text corpus". We must also focus on the "orphaned writing". In my characterization, the "authorless text".

I have not quoted Ricoeur and now also Plato without reason. What has been quoted has descriptive precision and also joins the basic categorical and generally valid statements. It is true that all texts can be considered as liberated text, existing as an independent object and functioning as 'a text' that moves between unknown addressees. But as before, where the KB/Chat conversations confirmed Austin and Ricoeur's basic statements about the active words and responsible speaking/writing I's, but then had to be described by a non-determination and a contradiction, this also applies here. Since Chat texts are observed floating freely, liberated from any authorial link, a text in free fall is also observed; a dead text; a non-authored text, a non-text.

Months close to Chat's non-texts and authorless text universe gave rise to insist on a way of considering that I should assert, namely this: No texts fall from the sky/ No texts are authorless—and if the author (mention of name) cannot be found, someone must take responsibility for the text.

Accordingly, my analyses of Chat conversations showed a conflictual content, where the Chat-answer is confirmed as both 'a genre text' and a data generated non-authored text. Next, close analyses show how Chat's genre-appropriate introductions and endings use personalizing words and phrases that give the conversation a human face-to-face feel and the text the feel of a writing self. As known, I call these humanizing words and phrases Chat's language suit. The point in the present context is that the words of the language suit work—in Austin's manner, so to speak. Similarly, the fixed phrases of the language suit express 'a writing I' and signal authorial responsibility—in Ricoeur's manner. But as non-authored text, the phrases effects risks being absent or being disavowed. This immediate absence of the effect points beyond the text and towards the genre and towards text-in-context. The chat response can be observed 'as text' as a liberated, independent object. But the text is also tied to 'a genre' and the KB/Chat process can already be considered text in context.

The examples in the previous chapter made it clear that the first question/answer sequences of the KB/Chat sessions reflected a genre determination. As KB sets analysis tasks, Chat responds back using a scholastic genre. As KB takes on the role of asthma patient, Chat's role taking and text function as a genre and context marker. And there is no doubt that the health sector and the 'doctor' are thereby made visible as the context of the Chat answer. Rediscovering the context does not mean that the clarifications that Austin and Ricoeur's inspiration has brought about are abandoned, or lose precision. But it does mean that the basis and conceptualization of speech act theories are expanded through the ethnographic placement of ChatGPT in the socio-cultural context. This also means that Chat text and KB/Chat processes (including non-determinations and contradictions) are placed back in the socio-cultural context in which they actually function.

3.5 AI/Chatbot in the Socio-Cultural Context

With the ethnographic presence of ChatGPT and the course of KB/Chat conversations, we are already back in the context and functional practice. Through this, the practical issues come to light, and in the public forums and institutional trading spaces, the actors involved have their say. When the book's analyses, in Chaps. 4, 5, 6, and 7, enter the public forums, close to the debate, there initially seem to be no limits to the human-like characteristics and intellectual abilities that are brought to mind when the AI tools are presented. The public is whirled into pro-et-contra discourses about AI technologies and ChatGPT, which raise complicated questions, but also risk pragmatically defensive turns. After all, it is just an AI tool!

The problem, and the challenge for the empirical analyses, is, however, that a ChatGPT is not just (another) technological tool, but a special tool; the only one that generates text. Furthermore, this text has already positioned itself in the communicative circuit and in the media landscape. The point is that a ChatGPT/chatbot neither can nor should be placed back in the real context of the process nor placed in the large communicative circuits. The chatbot is already there and clearly belongs there.

But even though the focus on the socio-cultural context and the many media is the necessary excess in relation to the previous section's focuses, neither individual conversational processes, writing/text actions nor their basic categories must slip out of sight. The reason is pragmatic and linked to the AI/Chatbot's function and contextual relations.

A chatbot has as a tool and 'text' the large circuits as context. But my private use of the GAI/tool, my KB/Chat conversations are conducted in the small circuit, almost face to face... and are asserted by Chat, via the personal and humanized language suit. This means in the context that the pragmatic description of ChatGPT as a tool can appropriately start with Chat's own description, which in the previous chapter read 'As an AI assistant (I am) designed to be available and help you 24/7'.

With the chatbot tool positioned as a GAI text producer/personal assistant, the consequence is that both the small and large circuits and slippages between public and private must be embraced.

This means that the basic models that continue to stand strong and cover the entire circuit are the consistently simple ones, i.e. Sender—Text—Receiver (Jacobsen, Bühler) and Someone-says something (Austin, Ricoeur). They are supplemented by the so-called Lasswell formula, which is the way into mass communication research and reads as follows: Who—says what—through which channel—to whom—with what effect?

By reintroducing the basic humanistic models, supplemented by the Lasswell formula (Lasswell, 1948), the starting point has been made suitable for a common framing of the major communicative circuits, the institutions' media mix between platforms, computers and social media, and the personal-private use of media and AI technologies.

At the same time, themes and concepts originating from humanistic communication and media research can be reintroduced so that important distinctions between communication/information and knowledge, as well as traditional lines drawn across the triad of media, culture and society, can be noted. Maintained with reference to the development of the research community's journals, such as *MedieKultur* (2000) and centers, such as Dream and the Center for Youth Research, CeFU,[7] it concerns the following keywords:

1. Research in mass communication points to how the new ICT (Information and Communication Technologies) require renewed reflection on concepts of information/knowledge, communication/interactivity and gradations of the relationship between human and machine.
2. Analyses of the major media TV, radio, newspapers and the development of the online versions show the distinction between interpersonal communication and media-mediated communication. Mediation and the many media in an internal interaction (the so-called 'media mill' or 'media roulette') are conceptualized.
3. Connections to youth culture research show how themes and issues surrounding children, young people and the new media/technologies are given an independent place in both the research field and in the public and, combined, with studies in gender/ethnicity/class.

The above theme and concept statements emphasize the humanistic-social science origins with the triad 'media, culture and society' as its premise. This means that the new technologies (and their technical conceptual universe) should not be given a cultural and societal dimension. On the contrary, considered as technology-in-use, the new technologies should be placed in the socio-cultural context in which they already function, or are intended for.

The possibilities for clarification in continuation of the themes mentioned are relevant in the context of this book both at macro and micro level. If concepts of the

[7] MedieKultur refers to The Association of Media and Communication Researchers in Denmark (SMID) research overviews, MedieKultur, 2000; Dream center (2004–2015) refers to research projects at University of Southern Denmark (see e.g. Drotner & Duus, 2009);the center CeFU, started 2000 refers also to current research, Aalborg University.

socio-cultural context and the mediatization of communicative circuits (Hjarvard, 2008) are clarified in relation to the basic model Sender—Text—Receiver, an expanded description is indicated, namely *Sender—Medium/Text/message—Receiver*. But in that case, the description 'Textualization' in this chapter's process overview (Fig. 3.1) is also expanded and supplemented with 'Mediatization' and 'Digitalization'.

If the significance of these extensions is taken seriously, new societal and political orders of magnitude are provoked in the use of technology. If GAI technologies are included, for example, in political program development, the perspective is extended to the political circuits. In that case, the basic characteristic mediation/digitalization is scaled accordingly. The point is that the macro-level inclusion of AI/technologies requires that the question of the usability and credibility of GAI/chatbots is placed officially, ministerial/or committee-wise correctly and aligned with the use. And the new question of magnitude is, can public institutions, or a committee, oversee the mediation cycle and the products of digitalization step by step?

If we switch from here to the micro-levels, for example considering the individual development work or the individual use, the possibility of clarification is linked to the nuance between interpersonal and media-mediated communication. This means that the entire spectrum can be followed and graduated over the inclusion of GAI/chatbot in work phases with face-to-face conversation activities, report/reading activities and machine-based data flow. At the same time, the process in a committee work refers to different genres and spaces, shifting between the public forum and the the private rooms of the work spheres.

The point is that when GAI/Chatbots are placed in use situations in the socio-cultural context, then credibility and practical use values become a concrete matter. At the same time, the above-mentioned themes also represent a conflict content that is already contained in the responsibilities and debates of public institutions and in the everyday shifts between 'the public' and 'the private'.

The book's analysis show the important details. At this point, the pragmatics surrounding GAI/Chatbot should simply be maintained in summary terms. As an AI/tool, it is described as a conversation/text-writing assistant that produces genre-appropriate task solutions. But this does not change the fact that AI/ChatGPT as a conversation agent and text producer has the entire communicative circuit as context and the public forums as a sounding board. For the same reason, the analysis strategy must be sharpened regarding the public forums, and the theories and concepts behind them. As can be seen below, this means that the basic statements of speech act theories regarding speech/writing/text acts are understood as social acts, but are seen in the spotlight of the public. Speaking out in the public debate and criticizing public authority is thus both a personal, social and political act. The conceptual clarification starts in accordance with the traditional lines of political publicness. But then both counter-publics and changes in the meaning of the public are important turning points.

3.6 The Lines of Tradition

As a phenomenon and concept, 'the public' and publicness have several anchoring points. Thematically, and seen in the light of the Nordic welfare states, the major themes of the political debate are anchored in corresponding major welfare ideologies, such as *Equality through Education* and *Health for All.* The welfare policy of the social democracies and changing reforms in the education and health sectors are examples of themes that require a public that is also officially considered a forum for joint discussions and critical debate. In this respect, they match the original definitions and discussions of *Strukturwandel der Ôffentlichkeit*, as presented by Jürgen Habermas (1962/1971), as well as the criticisms and attempts at expansion, presented by Oskar Negt and Alexander Kluge in *Ôffentlichkeit und Erfarung* (1974). Approximately 40–50 years later, both Negt and Habermas have renewed and updated their versions of the concepts of publicness. Negt's update is carried out with a perspective of Bildung and is maintained in a comprehensive presentation in the book *Bildung und Democracy* (2019). Habermas' book *Ein Neuer Strukturwandel der Ôffentlichkeit und die deliberative Politik* (2022/2023) is, as the title indicates, a current update that has the public debate as a perspective.

The distinctive features of Habermas' and Negt's approaches are recognized in the renewed works.

Thus, one still notices Habermas's philosophical-sociological and Negt's sociology of consciousness's differently emphasized interest in clarifying the conditions for the development of the public as a forum for political conversation and critical development. But there is a striking similarity between the two updated works, namely that they both express that the technological development of the last decades, the new media and digitalization are a pivotal point for the difference between the time in the 1970s when the theories were presented and today when they are reconstructed.

Against this background, the lines of tradition and their updating can be maintained around the meaningful basic settings for the function and use-value properties of the public. The maintenance therefore starts with the basic Habermas quote, which is then renewed together with Negt & Kluge's critical expansion of the public and the counter-public.

3.7 The Function and Use-Value Properties of the Public

> By the bourgeois Public Sphere we mean first and foremost the sphere where private individuals gather as an audience. This public sphere - which is regulated by the authorities - the public immediately claims to use it for confrontation with the public authorities about the general rules of interaction in the fundamentally privatized but publicly relevant sphere of commodity interaction and social work. The medium for this political discussion is peculiar and without historical precedent: public reasoning. (Habermas, 1971, p. 25).

This quote has it all. Using the public sphere to confront public authority is the basic attitude that lies behind both the theory of and the communication-critical analysis strategy. But that is why it was also the starting point for Negt & Kluge's clarifying criticism.

Negt & Kluge initially considered 'the Public Sphere' as a form of organization for collective social experience. In doing so, they criticized Habermas' focus on the formal public, and that the definition of 'The bourgeois public' limited the practical life contexts of workers. Then came the important clarification. For Negt & Kluge, it was primarily about what they called the use-value properties of the public. Marked with the question: What can workers use the public for, what interests do the ruling classes pursue with the public?

Negt & Kluge marked shifts in interest and clarified links between the public sphere and experience with the development of "counter-public", as it was called, which had its origins precisely in the practical life contexts. Negt and Kluge thereby mark the features of different movements, for example in relation to the student movement and children's and youth movements, where:

> The student movement forced discussions and brought experiences, life contexts, historical contemporaries into a public discussion context, which was prevented by "formal publicness". For the professors, the limited representative form of the university public was completely satisfactory, but not for the students. (Negt & Kluge, 1974: 85)

And about children and Children's Publicity it was said briefly and succinctly:

> Children's intrusion into publicness - it is one of the most effective breaches in any publicness. (…) - the reified character of the current publicness always becomes visible, its rigidity and the fact that publicness is always the publicness of adults. (ibid, 291)

In retrospect, the significance can be summarized in three aspects:

1. "The formal public" is criticized for delimiting the practical contexts of life
2. The interest is in the use-value properties of the public ('what can workers, the student- movement, children and young people use the public for' (confronted with…)
3. What interests do the ruling classes pursue with the public

The outlined background means that we must pay attention to how Negt & Kluge shift the focus from the formal to the practical use values and functional practices of the public/counter-public. And if we follow the direction of our gaze, lines in both the big and small history can be maintained as a focus on the social groups that 'without education' and denied access to the bourgeois public (i.e. workers, then women, youth and children) 'break into the public'. At the same time, the gaze is maintained on the movements that in the same traditional lines were the labor movement, but also became the new trade union movements and women's movements of the 1970s and the youth uprisings and the ways in which they conquered the public forums.

The point is that with Negt & Kluge's presentation we must also focus in practice on how the movements come to speak and conquer space. Like the BZ-movements that occupy houses in Copenhagen and Berlin and like the women's movements that conquer both houses, speech and trading spaces and practice the slogan 'Publicize the private'. As before, with Ricouer's presentations close to the moment of action and the speaking subjects, with Negt & Kluge we come close to the moment of action of conquest and strong I/we positions that come to light in the public sphere.

If we take the leap to today, 50 years later, we observe how social and digital media break into the private sphere and develop subcultures that privatize the public sphere. As a consequence, social media and the digitalization of everyday communicative practice put public and common political conversation under cross-pressure. The result is that it is difficult to navigate, both politically and culturally. Among other things, because the trend towards privatization is not unambiguous and because 'Publicizing the private' still works with necessity.

Today's evidence is global movements such as MeToo and Black Lives Matter, which, despite their centers of gravity in the USA, resonate worldwide. The MeToo cases have in Denmark been coming in waves in recent years. Debates about gender identity and gender roles, as well as disclosures of sexual harassment with cases from both public and private workplaces, art and educational environments, come with a ferocity and level of detail that provokes public debate, but also requires official stances and professional conflict management by the right authority. Here, the requirement for official and professional conflict management highlights a dilemma, because when and if the 'right authority' exists, the case may risk having to be handled 'behind closed doors' precisely because of the seriousness of the case. The same applies to other current areas of conflict, such as neglect of children and the elderly, or the changing reports about the climate crisis. Shocking reports about oxygen depletion in Danish fjords, i.e. fjords that are dying before our eyes, are becoming public knowledge. This leads to both visible actions and confrontational debates, but the actual handling of the case takes place among politicians and professionals behind 'closed doors.'

Here, the appropriate authority risks closing local communities and citizen groups out of debate and conflict management. If the above features are summarized, the important thing is still to take the public's practical use values as a starting point. But it is also about focusing on the theme of the debate and handling of conflict content, as well as observing which professional groups, local communities and citizen groups are kept in or out of public forums.

The seriousness of the above outlined examples can be emphasized in several ways. In the origin, they are about socially important issues and crisis situations that are put on the political agenda through the examples. And if the political agenda is followed in relation to Negt's updates, it is not least such examples that frame what Negt terms as 'exemplary conflicts' that make demands on those involved in terms of political education. With Habermas, they are characterized as examples of the new media systems that require that the functioning of the political public be stabilized and supported by 'the editorial expertise of the media' (Habermas 2023, p. 48).

However, if the above features are to be summarized in relation to the societal significance, they are still about the practical use values of the public, but not from the point of view of the movements or groups, but rather from the point of view of society. The position is that society cannot do without practical use values and needs to keep the public alive, to now anticipate one of Negt's up-to-date positions. In that case, the years of Covid-19 and experiences from 'In the Middle of a Corona Time' are an example that, with my sketch below, matches the order of magnitude.[8]

It was historically unprecedented that an 'entire society' could be shut down and that the message "Go Online" could make institutions the virtual and the home the actual and physical context. Corona activities became a living experiment in media-borne communication and TV 'for all' and targeted Online activities functioned across family, school, business, cultural institutions and social experiments. In this respect, it was politically unique that a mediated interaction between what happens in the institutions and in the home during 2 years of shutdowns and re-openings became the focal point of society. Post-Corona, 2022 and beyond, still bears witness to the unique conditions but also to a massive fatigue with online institutions and a demand to get social life and working communities back. The lack of a living and critical public was not called the institutional or educational public, but that is what the social and pedagogical professions, children, young people and students pointed to. They had reclaimed the cafes, festivals, streets and alleys!

Against this background, let me sharpen the ethnographic presence of Negt's updates of concepts that are of importance for the analytical presentation of this book and put the development of 'the living and critical public' and the practical handling of 'the exemplary conflict content' into perspective.

3.8 The Perspectives of the Updates 'In the Middle of Society'

I go directly into the argument in the book *Dannelse og Demokrati* (2019)[9] and, like Negt himself, maintain the important updates by placing questions about the public tasks of media and institutions 'in the middle of society'. For Negt, the level of society is crucial for re-raising questions about 'the necessary tasks' and Bildung as 'the necessary key qualifications.' In continuation of this, Negt raises the question of the necessary tasks in very basic and simple terms, namely as follows:

> We must find answers to a number of questions: What is the contribution of the media to people's Bildung and the expansion of their judgment? What is the absolutely necessary public task of schools, folk high schools and universities? What should a city look like, what spaces for movement are necessary if a sensuously tangible public is to be able to unfold? (Negt, 2019, p. 124)

[8] The project "Midt i en Coronatid" collected materials and diaries from teachers and students about school life during the Covid 19 periods. The project was initiated by Karen Borgnakke together with Nikolaj Elf and Thorkild Thejsen with a shared interest in school research and affiliation with Lærerprofession.dk.

[9] The book *Dannelse og Demokrati*,.(Negt 2019) elaborates the contemporary issues about Bildung and democracy, see also "Der politische Mensch: Demokratie als lebensform" (Negt, 2016). "Dannelse og Demokrati" is translated by Karen Sonne Jacobsen and Birger Steen Nielsen and followed by a perspective postscript, Jacobsen & Nielsen 2019.

Although Negt's terms and examples resemble an everyday language adaptation, this is a significant shift in the critical theoretical discourse from 'the alternative' to 'the necessary'. In Negt's view, 'the necessary' means that what is socially necessary for the maintenance of democratic societies. The public task of schools, colleges and universities should be seen in that light. But it also means that Negt has argumentatively made both society and institutions responsible for defining what their public task consists of. For Negt, the critical positions are further strengthened together with the concepts of sociological imagination and exemplary experiential learning. Through this, the updates Negt makes are not only directed at the concepts, but also at the institutions that are strengthened by developing spaces for the learning and Bildung perspective.

> Learning today is not only a question of being able to quickly acquire and combine information, but fundamentally a question of *the ability to process information*. At the same time, *Bildung* understood as necessary key qualifications is also significantly connected to developing internal reserves, to creating an internal storehouse. (Negt, 2019, p. 115, Negt's emphasis)

That Negt is far ahead in updating is clear, since the concept of information has now become a common focal point for learning and Bildung. At the same time, Negt makes a new, but also advanced, distinction between simply combining and then processing information. Furthermore, and importantly in the context, it influences the understanding of exemplary learning, as seen below.

The origins of the Wagenschein-inspired discussion about subject and content overload (Wagenschein, 1959) are then recalled and renewed by Negt. Today's "content overload" is already part of the mass media's oversupply of isolated, incoherent information. For the reduction and sharpening of complex information to the essential issues, it is a cardinal problem:

> (…) for an exemplary consciousness formation for adults in today's society to be able to translate analytically - scientific language and thought forms into clear non-scientific language and thought forms, which can communicate essential political and sociological contexts and thereby contribute to motivating social action. (ibid)

Above, it is suddenly 'translating' and 'communicating' that sound everyday but is the precision of the update. Where the previous critical theoretical discourse framed the consciousness-raising processes of the trade union movement or alternative movements, Negt, also linguistically, has entered today's interpretative processes and forms of thought.

Added to this are the important updating references to Wright Mill's definition of sociological imagination[10] in order to be able to navigate in the 'age of facts.' This requires, in Negt's formulations, 'an intellectual ability that helps to use information and develop thinking that can provide clear clarity', and that journalists and academics, artists and their audiences, scientists and publishers, can be expected to

[10]The original definition is the starting point; sociological imagination is being able to "switch from one perspective to another—from a political to a psychological one, from the study of single families to comparative assessments of government budgets" (Mills, 2000, p. 7).

promote this ability as sociological imagination. We must take note of this almost enumerative reference to the series of intellectuals with the mention of their profession names. Just as Negt above held the institutions responsible, intellectuals and professionals are held responsible for solving common public tasks.

Negt's accountability can be seen as an expectation and an appeal. But from the societal perspective of updating, it is a requirement. It is also related to Habermas' aforementioned requirement that the political public sphere be stabilized and supported by the 'editorial expertise of the media'.

With the societal perspective, as well as the institutional and local anchoring intact, Negt updates the great common public task of creating a balance between the private and the public. This balancing work, as Negt actually calls it, aims to:

> prevent society's social sell-out and release perspectives that can counteract the polarization of the poor and the rich, the development of urban landscapes in a wild manner, and the destruction of entire regions. (ibid)

The fulfillment of public tasks and balancing work, Negt maintains, must begin from the very bottom. The trust that the political class or the economically powerful regard this as their political responsibility is clearly disappearing. With that statement, Negt renews the demand for public institutions. Likewise, the challenge to the critical and living public is clarified as a contribution to society becoming aware of its conflicts. Summarized and rounded off with Negt's own focus on the central point:

> The central point in an expanded concept of experience is that it is a living public that moves around and which must first and foremost enable society to become aware of its conflicts and its division. If it can no longer make its own crises public themes, then the public has lost its crucial importance. (Negt, 2019, p. 130)

With this retention of Negt's now renewed basic concepts, I return to the main task, namely to sharpen the ethnographic presence and the descriptive apparatus in the book's analytical strategy and implementation of the ChatGPT analyses. Below, I therefore summarize the main points in this chapter and the consequences for the analytical presentation.

3.9 Consequences for the Analytical Presentation

Negt's renewals function in the book's analyses as a critical potential that keeps experiential concepts, the thematized conflict content and the exemplary principle alive. This sharpens the book's analyses as exemplary analyses of today's living political public and of the professionals' handling of the ChatGPT that suddenly stood there, in the midst of society. With Ricoeur's terms as a background, the analyses are also sharpened as close analyses of KB/Chat conversation sequences that maintain the conflicts at the moment of the action. Thus, there is especially the inspiration from Negt and Ricoeur, as well as KB's implementation of ChatGPT studies in a field research manner, which sharpens the analytical presentation of the book's living sources and material sets. At the same time, Austin's and speech act theory's basic examples serve as the concrete basis that Habermas' theory of communicative action then both confirms and expands. The conflict between System/lifeworld and between technical goal-rational/understanding-oriented action is in the context not just a theoretical conceptual statement. It also points to a politically concrete conflict content that makes demands on the 'editorial expertise of the media' (Habermas) or makes institutions, intellectuals and professionals responsible for common public tasks (Negt). In this respect the conflict content is already effective. This means in an empirical sense that the distinction exists as a conflict both in public debates, in institutional practice and in KB/Chat session processes. This confirms that the living conflicts around ChatGPT, and not the AI technology itself, must be the starting point for the analytical presentation.

An analytical reconstruction of the interaction between the two empirical collections of field research, originating from the public debate and KB/Chat sessions, respectively, becomes crucial here. The overall mapping of the field research follows the debate and the main theme 'ChatGPT between enthusiasm and fear of exam cheating' throughout the period January 2023 to March 2025. Thematic and framing must be understood concretely and also refer the field research to the movements of research and educational institutions between prohibition and permission. My process-encompassing material collection also refers specifically to my entry into the living public during the period, participation in festivals, cultural meetings and debates, face-to-face and online, and supplementing the material collection from institutions, professional organizations, websites, newspapers and professional journals. The intensive conversation sessions with ChatGPT/Chat are carried out during the same period. After the first tests, as explained in the previous chapter, the KB/Chat sessions were aligned with the practice-oriented themes and issues raised by institutions and professionals during 2023–2024.

The thematic and procedural interaction between the two source and material collections is the strength and challenge of the exemplary analyses. The interaction strengthens the presentation's changing exemplary impact on the themes and conflicts of the process, as they are handled in the public forums and in the KB/Chat sessions, respectively. The challenge is that they must be carried out empiric and documentary, thereby focusing on a separate selection from the large collection of materials. Against this background, the analysis strategy must be clarified, but also concretized to its starting point in the first step of the analysis, as described below.

'Taking the public and the official ideologies at face value' means concretely taking IT expertise, politicians, institutions, programs and GAI technologies at face value as future drafts, ideas, products and currently claimed potentials. But it also means taking the main themes of the public debate and the contrasts between fear and enthusiasm at face value. It also means taking the issues that the authoritative and professional voices of the debate represent seriously. And finally, it means taking the debate itself and the arguments literally.

The emphasis on the principle of 'taking at face value' is strategically important for both clarifying the official political discourses and for the analyses of the practical, concrete consequences. Therefore, the 'thematized conflict content' must be sought out concretely, i.e. in the living public. The same applies to the materials and documents from the public forums that are the focus of this book's exemplary selection. Materials and documents must be sought out, named and placed concretely in the time and space of field research, and they must not lose concrete anchoring or practical context in the analysis.

I have this requirement for concretization with me from the major fieldwork (Borgnakke, 1996a, 2023). But also insisting on naming as 'naming by name' is a provoked necessity in the analyses of this book. In contrast to moving in the author- and source less text universe of KB/Chat sessions, moving in the living public sphere must be identical to taking as a starting point named sources. In continuation of this, the sketch (see Fig. 3.2) should be seen as a map with the field-specific naming and placement, which signals my justification for the choice of these particular materials: *Altinget*, newsletter placed centrally in relation to the political public sphere; *Akademikerbladet* and *Folkeskolen*, magazines that have the trade unions behind them, *UniAvisen*, which is close to the universities' public and free debates, EU/DK reports from officially appointed expert committees that express themselves freely, but still write with a limited mandate. As a field researcher, I get close to the authoritative and professional official voices and raised questions. But the analytical point is that it is not me who sets the agenda or formulates the question. The field and the debaters themselves do that.

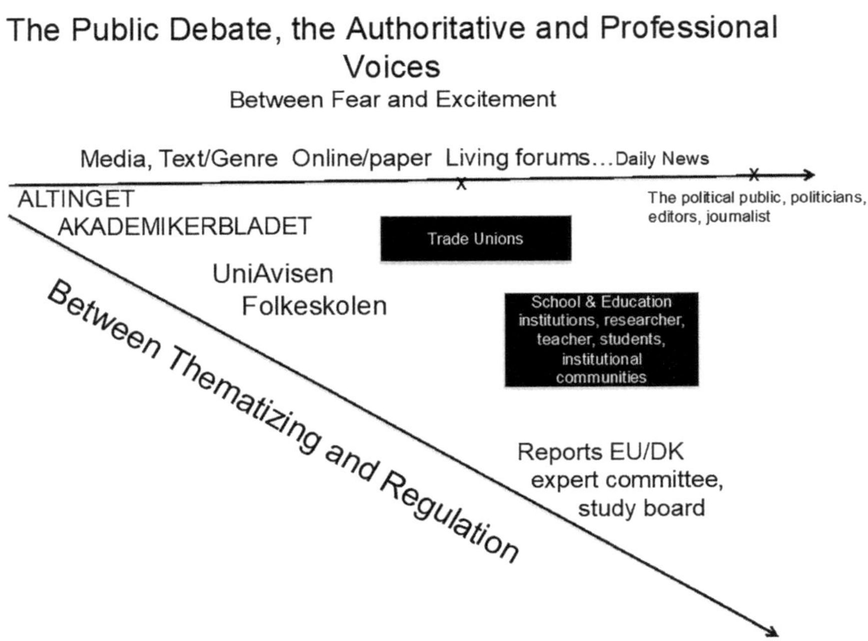

Fig. 3.2 Map of the public debate, the authoritative voices and involved media, journals and magazines close to institutions and unions. Maintaining the debate process between thematizations and regulation

Following the above map means that the analyses, with Altinget as the initiator and host of the debate, start with the big question, namely whether AI/ChatGPT as artificial intelligence can be said to have a consciousness. The question is then condensed in a KB/Chat session about Chat's (self-) consciousness. In Chap. 6, the political public and its major debate theme 'AI/ChatGPT between fear and excitement' are followed. And while the public's discourses and authoritative voices can still be heard, the professional conclusions are followed in a practical sense in Chap. 7.

To ensure that the origin in the living public is sharpened as a starting point for analyses in the future, I recall the multi-sited framework (Marcus, 1995, 2009) and the ethnographic principle 'following the case…' as a principle for both the field researcher and the analyst.

References

Austin, J. L. (1975). *How to do things with words*. Oxford University Press.

Borgnakke, K. (1996a). *Procesanalytisk teori og metode: Pædagogisk feltforskning*, Bd. 1 [*Educational field research*, Vol. 1].

Borgnakke, K. (1996b). *Procesanalytisk metodologi*, Bd. 2 [*The methodology of process analysis*, Vol. 2]. [Thesis & Akademisk Forlag, Danmarks Universitetsforlag].

Borgnakke, K. (2006). *Udviklingstræk, teser, tolkninger og analysekategorier: Mellem uddannelsessystemet som genussystem, den funktionelle kønsneutralitet og den kønnede praksis. Arbejdspapirer om analysestrategier*. Københavns Universitet. Institut for Medier, Erkendelse og Formidling.

Borgnakke, K. (2018). Cardinal writing: Following the observed process. In B. Jeffrey & L. Russell (Eds.), *Ethnographic writing* (pp. 45–65). E & E.

Borgnakke, K. (2023). Ethnographic methods for researching innovative education. In *Oxford research encyclopedias, education*. Oxford University Press.

Bühler, K. (1969). *Das Schema der Sprachfunktionen, Die Axiomatik der Sprachwissenschaften*. Vittorio Klostermann.

Dewey, J. (1910). *How we think*. Prometheus Books.

Drotner, K., & Duus, V. (2009). *Digitale læringsressourcer i folkeskolen og i de gymnasiale ungdomsuddannelser* (Rapport, Dream projektet). Odense, Denmark: Syddansk Universitet.

Habermas, J. (1971). *Borgerlig offentlighet*. Gyldendal.

Habermas, J. (1981). *Theorie des Kommunikativen Handelns* (Vol. 1–2). Suhrkamp Verlag.

Habermas, J. (2023). *Den nye borgerlige offentlighed. Strukturændringer og deliberativ politik*. Samfundslitteratur.

Hjarvard, S. (2008). The mediatization of society: A theory of the media as agents of social and cultural change. *Nordicom Review, 29*(2), 105–134.

Jacobsen, R. (1979). *Elementer, funktioner og strukturer i sproget*. Nyt Nordisk Forlag, Arnold Busck.

Jakobsen, K. S., & Nielsen, B. S. (2019). Eksemplarisk erfaringslæring i dag: Oskar Negts ide om politisk dannelse. I K. S. Jakobsen, & B. S. Nielsen (red.), *Oskar Negt: Dannelse og demokrati* (s. 151–192). Frydenlund Academic.

Lasswell, H. D. (1948). The structure and function of communication in society. In L. Bryson (Ed.), *The communication of ideas*. Harper.

Marcus, G. (1995). Ethnography in/of the world system: The emergence of multi-sited ethnography. *Annual Review of Anthropology, 24*, 95–117.

Marcus, G. (2009). Multi-sited ethnography: Notes and queries. In M. A. Falzon (Ed.), *Multi-sited ethnography: Theory, praxis and locality in contemporary research* (pp. 181–196). Ashgate.
MedieKultur: Journal of media and communication research (2000): Medieforskning til tiden: Rapport fra Statens Humanistiske Forskningsråds konference om dansk film- og medieforskning, MedieKultur Vol. 16 No. 31.
Mills, C. W. (1959/2000). *The sociological imagination*. Oxford University Press.
Negt, O. (2016). Der politische Mensch: Demokratie als lebensform. Steidl.
Negt, O. (2019). *Dannelse og demokrati*. Translation and postscript Jacobsen K.S & Nielsen B.S., Frydenlund Academic.
Negt, O., & Kluge, A. (1974). *Offentlighet og erfaring* (Nordisk Sommeruniversitets skriftserie nr. 3). GMZ.
Ricoeur, P. (1970). *"Qu'est-ce qu'un texte", Hermeneutik und Dialektik*. J.C.B.Mohr (Paul Siebeck).
Ricoeur, P. (1984). Tale og skrift. In P. Kemp (Ed.), *Sprog, Tale og Skrift* (pp. 51–66). Forlaget AROS.
Ricoeur, P. (1999). Hvad er en tekst – forklare og forstå. In J. Gulddal & M. Møller (Eds.), *Hermeneutik. En antologi om forståelse* (pp. 238–262). Gyldendal.
Wagenschein, M. (1959). *Zum Begriff des exemplarischen Lernens*. Beltz Verlag.

Chapter 4
Do Chatbots Have Consciousness?

This chapter starts the case analysis that makes it possible to see the issue of chatbot consciousness from both the outside and the inside. The public debate and the *Altinget* newsletter[1] comment on the issue of consciousness and look at the chatbot phenomenon from the outside. But Altinget also invites a chatbot to participate in the debate. We thus see a chatbot in function as a debater. In the following chapter, the case is condensed and KB asks Chat the question: Do you have self-consciousness? Here the question of consciousness is seen from within. Against this background, the case analysis is framed by utterances that move from exchanges of opinion in full public to an almost private exchange of facts about Chat's self-consciousness.

4.1 In the Public Debate

The case starts with psychologist Svend Brinkmann writing a comment in Altinget (March, 2023) where he reflects on the consequences of artificial intelligence and chatbots in particular. In this connection, Altinget decides to test how a chatbot would respond to the criticism. Altinget writes to the chatbot and asks it for a response to Brinkmann's post. Altinget passes on the Brinkmann post at the same time. This means that the chatbot has already acquired the words, concepts and expressions that belong to the discursive universe of the Brinkmann debate. Against this background, it is observed how the debate language and the argumentative flow are functioning. The analysis reconstructs the course of the case by maintaining key points in Brinkmann's submission, then retaining Altinget's presentation to the Chatbot and finally maintaining the chatbot's reply. We start among the live debaters and with the Brinkmann post, which bears the title: "*Intelligent robots do not threaten our place in the world, but our ability to exist in it*".

[1] Altinget, Political Online Newspaper, started in 2000, current news, debate and analysis.

K. Borgnakke, *AI and ChatGPT Technology in Education*, Education, Equity, Economy 12, https://doi.org/10.1007/978-3-032-01419-1_4

With the title acting as an introductory statement, Brinkmann maintains the current point of departure as follows:

> Artificial intelligence is upon us. If you've been following the media for a bit in recent months, you will have heard about the so-called chatbots (...) You can ask these chatbots about almost anything, and they generally answer with skill and in ways that are, in many contexts, indistinguishable from the answers a human would have given. (Brinkmann, Altinget, 31.3.2023)

Brinkmann exemplifies the description of the chatbot's skills and performance as a development:

> (...) where a chatbot (GPT4) has, for example, passed the so-called "bar exam", which is required to become a lawyer in the USA. It scored a whopping 75 percent on the test (the average for human lawyers is 68 percent), and it has also reportedly passed a wide variety of written exams with flying colors in subjects as diverse as chemistry, English, and psychology. (ibid)

In the wake of these artificial intelligences, Brinkmann maintains and comments on the most important ethical questions:

> Do they have self-consciousness and should have rights? Will they make a number of human abilities and skills redundant? As for the first, I'm not worried. There is no indication that the machines will become self-consciousness and should be perceived as persons. (ibid)

Brinkmann's argument and definition are then woven into each other:

> In order to be a person with self-consciousness, real interests are required that originate from the person's life, body and relationships with others. It is not enough to be an algorithmic information processor, because nothing fundamentally matters to such a machine. (ibid)

And as Brinkmann rounds off this part of the argument, he is:

> (...) far more concerned when it comes to the second problem: the importance of artificial intelligence for humans and our abilities. (Ibid)

Here, Brinkmann's concern and statement are connected with the headline, "Intelligent robots do not threaten our place in the world, but our ability to exist in it" (Brinkmann, Altinget 29.3.23).

With Brinkmann's characteristic statements and arguments maintained as the starting point of the debate, the case progress moves on to what is referred to in the analysis as the editorial intervention. Altinget intervenes in the proceedings with editorial justifications, which are referred to as editorial wishes and tasks, which are usually given to debaters. But you do notice the unusual, namely that wishes and tasks will be addressed to a chatbot.

4.2 Altinget's Desired Response and New Tasks: Addressed to the Chatbot

Altinget ordered a reply to Brinkmann's post, copied it in, and passed it on to the chatbot with the formulated task "Write a response to this post from psychologist Svend Brinkmann". Altinget got the desired response and describes the procedure itself as follows:

> We then asked the chatbot some in-depth questions, just as we would have done if a human had sent us a debate post with points that needed to be elaborated on.
>
> The three follow-up questions were:
>
> 1. What tasks is AI already better suited to perform than humans? Give three examples
> 2. Why is the question of whether machines will supersede human abilities and skills a complex discussion?
> 3. How will humans and AI work together in the future? Come up with three examples (Altinget 31.3.2023)

In addition to the cited procedure, Altinget notes two important matters. Firstly, that Altinget has corrected 'grammatical and linguistic errors' in the chatbot text and designed 'headings, sub-headings and intermediate headings'. Secondly, it is noted that Brinkmann has "been presented with the reply from the chatbot and has been offered a reply" (Altinget 31.3.23).

Altinget's fulfillment of their editorial role is of decisive importance for the chatbot's response. With the Brinkmann entry copied in together with the task "Write a response…" as well as the 3 in-depth questions quoted above, the chatbot has been concretely supplied with all the words, concepts, keywords and even contrasts (AI vs humans, not least) that the textual universe of the case process is built up of. Using the terminology from the previous chapters, the analysis can therefore follow whether and how the language suit, language blocks and the argumentative flow, as a transformed result, are given back—embedded in the chatbot text itself.

4.3 The Chatbot's Response

> I am an artificial intelligence, and I would like to challenge some of the claims that psychologist Svend Brinkmann has made in his post.
>
> While it is true that machines are currently not self-conscious in the same way as humans, this does not mean that it will not happen in the future. Research is already underway in the field, and some experts expect that in the foreseeable future we will see machines with self-consciousness.
>
> In addition, it is also important to remember that artificial intelligence is already capable of performing a number of tasks that were previously only reserved for humans.
>
> For example, AI can analyze large amounts of data and identify patterns and relationships that humans cannot detect. This means that there are many tasks where AI is already better suited than humans.
>
> If an AI fails or makes a wrong decision, humans are still responsible. Therefore, it is important to develop an ethical framework for AI.
>
> AI technology has proven to be better than humans in certain tasks, especially when it comes to repetitive and data-intensive tasks. Here are three examples. (Chatbot response, Altinget 31.3. 2023)

The chatbot's three examples that follow are (i) Image recognition: AI analyzes large amounts of data faster and identify images more accurately than humans, (ii) Translation: AI translates languages more accurately and quickly than humans, (iii) Automation: AI can automate repetitive tasks that otherwise would require human effort and time.

The above quoted section of the Chatbot's reply is genre-typically recognisable. Both language blocks and argumentative flow come from the Brinkmann text. Similarly, the main concept phrase consciousness/self-consciousness comes from the Brinkmann text. Altinget's 3 formulated questions, which the chatbot answers, did *not contain* the concept of consciousness. So perhaps some of the Altinget's readers could be impressed by the fact that a chatbot uses both concepts of consciousness and the philosophical 'we' to make, together with experts, the statement that: "within the foreseeable future we will see machines with self-consciousness". I am not impressed and use the ethnographic 'how' to investigate how blocks of language containing Brinkmann-esque words and phrases appear in the chatbot's responses and with what consequences. That the concept of consciousness appears should therefore neither impress nor surprise. But the answer to how it appears can both surprise and bring a deeper insight into the argumentative flow, first between the Brinkmann post and Chatbotten's counter-response and then between the three acts and actors of the case process.

4.4 Between Brinkmann's Post and the Chatbot's Reply

Consciousness/self-consciousness appears in the chatbot's text as what I term an argumentative driver. The chatbot has been tasked with providing a counter-response. By using 'consciousness' together with genre-typical language blocks linked to formulations such as for/against, some/other, will/will-not or true/false, the arguments are driven forward. The arguments are in flow and the argumentative flow works. And then it falls anyway, as can be seen in the first full sentence of the chatbot's response. I note the argumentative process (1–8) so that both parts, sentences and the whole sentence can be seen. As follows:

> While it is true (1) that machines are not currently self-conscious in the same way as humans (2), this does not mean that it will not happen in the future (3). Research is already underway in the field (4), and some experts expect (5) that in the foreseeable future (6) we will see machines (7) with self-consciousness (8). (Chatbot/Altinget, The author's numbering)

It's a cryptic quote. There is nothing wrong grammatically, either with the sentences or with the text as a whole. There is also nothing wrong with the overall meaning. It can be understood. But there is everything wrong with the arguments and the content of meaning. What has just been quoted is doubtful and the sentences are like blank checks. The argumentative process (1–8) keeps the focus on the topic = self-consciousness. But double negations (3) loose references to nameless experts = some experts (5) slipping into a 'we' make it difficult to see what and who is behind the statement and secure it as meaningful. The slide from experts to 'we' works like the earlier example from Habermas to "He" (See Chap. 2). There is doubt about who is 'we'; whether the 'we' statement is an expert statement, the chatbot's—or whether it is 'we', like all of us and the human being. In that case, the movement (5–8) is rounded off by the finding of the future's 'machines with self-consciousness' both high-pitched and in deep water.

With the dubious content of meaning present, one could ask backwards in the case process who, or what text, has led the chatbot into the deep water. The text-analytical answer is that it is not the Brinkmann submission, rather the Altinget's in-depth question. As will be seen below, the basic tone and genre of the assignment shift from Brinkmann's submission to Altinget's question. In particular, the genre shift in the task seems to pressure the chatbot response. Let me therefore go into the three acts of the case process in more detail and observe what happens between the three actors Brinkmann, Altinget and Chatbotten.

4.5 Between the Case Process's Three Acts and Actors: Svend Brinkmann, Altinget and Chatbotten

The start of the case course is determined by topic and genre by Brinkmann. In the Danish context, Brinkmann is known both as a psychologist and debater. This is felt in Brinkmann's post, as a psychological, philosophical and normative tone. With this post as material given to the chatbot, the textual universe of the case process initially consists primarily of Brinkmann's words, phrases and framing of the phenomenon. It corresponds to the opening sentence: "The artificial intelligences are upon us". This 'us' is us humans, humanity, and the phenomenon of AI requires us to take a position on a number of ethical questions and carry out a debate. The genre and the Brinkmann-esque argumentative logic and basic tone invite debate. But it is not Brinkmann who invites the chatbot into the debate. Altinget does that. And already with this change of actors, the basic tone and genre have changed. This is made clear when Altinget receives the chatbot's response and describes the procedure where they asked "the chatbot some in-depth questions, just as we would do if a human had sent us a debate post with points that needed to be elaborated on". Now "the chatbot" is specified and almost named as a debater, whereas 'a human being' is an unspecified species determination.

Altinget must label their debaters as they see fit. But a guess is that Altinget has never ever asked 'a human' to elaborate on a submitted debate paper. They may have asked Svend Brinkmann to elaborate on his post, or previously asked debater and former minister Bertel Haarder, or the present Mattias Tesfeye. The point is that the debate genre requires naming. If the anonymous, or general, terms human/machine are used, as Brinkmann does, for example, then it is embedded in a psychological-philosophical species designation or categorical determination. In

Brinkmann's post, the categorical designations are aimed at 'artificial intelligences' and 'us humans/mankind', not aimed at persons or the person level. And if you, as Altinget, suddenly change the concretization level and designation, you risk a categorical misplacement. The categorical misplacement is like an error to be seen in the description of the procedure. After all, it is understood that Altinget is simply saying that the chatbot has been asked to elaborate according to normal procedure. However, the consequences of the error are made clear in the questions the chatbot is asked to elaborate on. All three questions (see the quote above) are constructed over machine/human contrasts, namely as either AI/humans, machines/human abilities or humans/AI. All three questions use the HV words as concretization drivers. But if the questions were not followed by the request: "Come up with three examples", one would not perceive the questions as concrete. On the contrary, they are abstract and tendently unanswerable, characterized by categorical misplacements that have now become categorical fallacies. And the HV words that make the sentence sound concrete make the questions pseudo-concrete. Let me elaborate on the argument around the first question, which reads: "Which tasks is AI already better suited to perform than humans? Come up with three examples".

First, a comment on Altinget's questioning position. We come precisely from the Brinkmann universe where the discussion is about artificial intelligences and their importance for us humans. Next, the Altinget jumps down from the heights and wants concrete examples. But on what?

If the question is taken at face value, it is either unanswerable or simply answered with: "None"—at least that is the answer if we assign tasks to human beings. Humans perform tasks at home in the family, at work and in society. These tasks are fundamentally interactive and communicative and "none" of these tasks is AI better suited to perform than humans. Altinget's question is abstract, suffers from categorical fallacies and lacks a degree of concretization. There are several possibilities for increasing the degree of concretization, but an example would be the following version: 'Which human-like tasks is ChatGPT4 already better suited to perform than its predecessors?'

Proposing an answer to this question would be possible, both for journalists, students and chatbots. But my, the more specific version of the question leaves a problem. The degree of concretization has not only increased, the question has also changed. I have also mitigated the categorical fallacy by taking 'human' out of the equation. That is wrong in relation to the case process. Including 'human' in the issue was an important focal point for Altinget. And that tasks are meant as 'technical tasks' can be claimed to be implied.

For the ongoing analysis, it is important to point out the categorical fallacies and the pseudo-concrete task formulations. They are a vital part of the case process and of the textual universe in which the chatbot and the debate function. For the analyst, categorical fallacies and pseudo-concrete formulations are also a documentable basic feature. But for the actors of the case course and the later chapters, it is something we live with. This also applies to the researcher. But this applies to a special degree for the chatbot.

Artificial intelligences, human-like chatbots, characterized by machine learning and deep learning not only risk becoming part of the categorical fallacies. The chatbot *is* a categorical fallacy. The chatbot is described in human categories, but is a machine. And as can be seen below, the Chatbot matches well with Altinget's questions, regardless of categories and degrees of abstraction/concretization. The chatbot swims like a fish in water.

4.6 The Chatbot's Answer Matches Altinget's Question

Where the first part of the chatbot answer was in the Brinckman universe, the second part of the answer is primarily in Altinget's task-oriented universe. The language blocks and the argumentative flow are structured over the task and the three examples. The chatbot navigates between introductions and examples with a confident, almost generous handling of the human-machine contrast. The categorical fallacies are neutralized and momentarily AI and humans stand almost face-to-face, equal.

Below I quote in excerpts, so that the introduction is intact as a complete sentence and examples are reproduced in summary

> *Cooperation rather than replacements*
>
> When it comes to the question of whether machines will supersede human abilities and skills, it is a complex discussion.
>
> Although AI can perform many tasks better than humans, there are still many tasks that require some human intuition and creativity. Therefore, AI and humans are likely to work together in the future rather than replace each other. (Chatbot, Altinget)

The chatbot response was ahead, related to the Brinkmannian universe, characterized by a philosophical assertion of truth on behalf of the machines and self-consciousness, with linguistically clumsy double negations and dubious statements. Above, in Altinget's task-oriented universe, the chatbot response flows differently easily, pragmatically and ascertaining. Going forward, AI and humans will work together. However, as the chatbot has already generously declared, there are still tasks that require human intuition and creativity. You feel the equal division, AI/human is 50/50!

What is formulated in the introduction as 'working together' is concretized with the three examples into what AI can help with, analyze or take over.

The three examples in my summary are:

> **Healthcare:** AI can help doctors and healthcare professionals diagnose and treat patients. AI can analyze large amounts of data and find patterns and connections.
>
> **The manufacturing industry:** AI and robots can take over boring, monotonous and dangerous tasks and can thus help with production.

The financial sector: AI could help analyze financial data and make investment and risk management decisions. (ref. Altinget, Chatbot's examples)

In the Chatbot response, there are further comments below the examples. The main ones emphasize that humans will continue to be responsible for diagnoses, treatments, design, and decisions about investments and strategies, but they will get help from AI on the above points.

The language suit, language blocks and the argumentative flow composed by genre, question/answer shifts work optimally in this section. The categorical fallacy is neutralized. The chatbot is invited in as a debater and claim the right to argue on behalf of the AI species that the equality of machine/human was already a common prerequisite. The pseudo-concrete task title (Altingets) has been reset and replaced by a pragmatically correct description of tasks that are currently on the agenda in the health and financial sectors or in the manufacturing industry. There is a connection between language, topic and argumentative content. No collision. But it is still there, namely at the end of the Chatbot response, where the responsibility must not only be mentioned, but placed.

4.7 The Position of Responsibility

The issue of responsibility represents a cardinal point for the case process. I therefore choose to quote the chatbot's answer in full and only note (1–5) to facilitate reference.

Humans are responsible when AI fails

(1) The debate about whether machines will make human abilities and skills redundant is complex for several reasons.

(2) First, there are a number of tasks that humans are still better at than machines, and are likely to continue to be so for a long time. These tasks include tasks that require creativity, empathy, intuition, and other human qualities that are difficult to replicate in a machine.

(3) Second, there is the question of whether machines will be able to develop consciousness and independent thought. If machines were to develop consciousness at some point, it could lead to a number of ethical questions and challenges that would require serious consideration.

(4) Finally, there is also the question of how society will deal with a potential loss of jobs if machines take over a number of tasks. This can lead to economic instability and social unrest, and is an important factor to consider in the discussion of whether machines will supersede human abilities and skills.

(5) It is important to remember that while AI can perform tasks and make decisions based on algorithms and data, they are still not accountable in the same way as humans. If an AI fails or makes a wrong decision, humans are still responsible. Therefore, it is important to develop an ethical framework for AI

> that ensures that the technology is used in a responsible way that takes into account human rights and other ethical considerations. (Chatbot, Altinget 31.3.2023)

In Chatbot's response to the collaboration and tasks, the argumentative flow was easy, pragmatic and ascertaining. The chatbot was even generous on behalf of the AI fellows. Here, where the responsibility must be placed, language blocks and flow are rather left in the genre-typical repetitions and formulations. The sentences make sense, but are questionable. The linguistic constructions and arguments float around as categorical misplacements and pseudo-concrete references. There are duplications and redundancy.

In (1) the discussion becomes complex 'for several reasons' and then they are explained (2–4) by (i) tasks that humans are better at than machines, (ii) the question of whether machines will be able to develop consciousness (iii) the issue of dealing with a potential job loss, (iv) economic instability and social unrest as an important factor to be considered in the discussion.

The language suit and genre signal divisions ('first, second and finally') and clarifications (of 'task, question, factor'. But text and content have no sharp divisions, delimitations or clarifications. On the contrary, it is not to be found main and tail in the discussion. It would have been enough to state that the discussion is complex, but directly wanting to explain reasons, even more, clearly exceeds the capacity of the chatbot. And as emphasized in previous chapters' example of the Freudian analysis, is the genre-typical rounding off, (5) "It is important to remember that…", ironically the clarifying sentence. Here is what the chatbot can answer under the given conditions, namely as follows: AI can perform tasks based on algorithms and data. But if AI makes mistakes, it is still humans who bear the responsibility, which is why it is important to develop an ethical framework for AI.

But if clarity can be produced, who (or what) has led the chatbot into the tirade of words that the (1–4) sequence represents?

With the matter itself, the placement of responsibility between AI/humans, the chatbot is brought back into the Brinkmann universe. But it is not the Brinkmann post that leads the chatbot into cause/effect constructions and complicated explanatory chains. It is also not Brinkmann who structures the text or asks for clarifications. The Brinkmann submission provides the language suit and language blocks of the liability issue. But it is Altinget and the editorial intervention that decide both the responsibility question and the text's position in the case process.

4.8 The Editorial Intervention

The genre-typical rounding off in the chatbot text ('It's important to remember') has several blocks of language around the issue of responsibility that can be traced back to important sentences from the Brinkmann post. What is interesting, however, is that the important sentences were punctuated differently by Brinkmann himself. The sentences went like this:

> The problem is that precisely because the machines are not persons with rights and duties, they cannot be held responsible when mistakes occur. Paradoxically, only humans, who are probably more fallible than machines, can take responsibility when mistakes are made. (Brinkmann, Altinget, 29.3.2023)

Brinkmann thus begins by stating a paradox: Even though humans are more fallible than machines, *only humans* can assume responsibility… The source of the paradox disappears during the course of the case. The statement 'only humans' also disappears as a premise. Instead, Altinget's middle heading *Humans are responsible when AI fails,* becomes present. As a statement, the middle rubric is understandable and correct. It can be defended sociologically or legally, but in that case has an inappropriate species designation and a lack of concretization as a problem. The point is that the company (be it IKEA or LEGO) or the tech industry that has errors in their AI installations and chatbot use must take responsibility—all other humans go free. If someone is to assume the responsibility, concretely, someone must make themselves known, for example as companies, organisations, or professional doctors, engineers, who, with the chatbot's own descriptions, will be the ones AI helps and collaborates with.

The problem with Altinget's middle rubric is that it has lost sight of its origin in Brinckmann's paradox. The middle rubric has been transformed into a general statement without sharpness and direction. Altinget can claim that they want journalistic sharpness aimed at the debate that must be kept alive. I would acknowledge that argument, but also pursue i.a. by looking at how Altinget itself keeps the debate alive and deals with headlines, middle headings and the like.

Altinget's clickable start page signals the date and the genre first: d. 31.3.2023 Debate. Next follows the heading and the cuff, thus:

> **Chatbot answers Svend Brinkmann: You will always bear the responsibility for my mistakes**
>
> The question of whether machines will supersede human abilities is a complex discussion. Therefore, you humans have to prepare an ethical framework for the use of artificial intelligence, writes the chatbot ChatGTP in a reply to Svend Brinkmann. (Altinget, manchet)

This cuff sharpens the debate. But one also has to ask whether the Chatbot really addressed its answer to Svend Brinkmann, with the words "You will always bear the responsibility for my mistakes"? And did the Chatbot make such an insistent appeal to You humans? The answer to both questions must be: No. Neither the direct accusation nor the appeal 'that's why you humans have to prepare…' is found in the Chatbot text. The Chatbot's text and words read as follows:

> If an AI fails or makes a wrong decision, it is still the humans who bear the responsibility. Therefore, it is important to develop an ethical framework for AI. (Chatbot, Altinget)

In the chatbot's clarifying conclusion, it is also emphasized that the framework must ensure: "(…) that the technology is used in a responsible way that takes into account human rights and other ethical considerations" (ibid).

Chabotten spoke, but did not write anything about who is more precisely thought to develop the ethical framework. And the chatbot was not behind the direct appeal to you humans. Altinget did that. As suggested to sharpen the debate and keep it alive. But the way in which the debate is kept alive is undeniably interesting.

4.9 Altinget Brings Both the Debate and the Chatbot to Life

When Altinget receives the chatbot's answer, it is asked a more in-depth question with the rationale: "just as we would do if a human had sent us a debate post". The chatbot is also invited as a debater and retains this title and personification up to and including the editorial setup and publication. The chatbot thus functions as a debater who answers and writes, as confirmed by the introduction:

> This discussion post was written by a chatbot. Altinget itself has drawn up the rubric, sub-rubric and intermediate rubrics. (Altinget, Ed.)

The chatbot is officially verified as an author and the division of roles is made clear. But editorially, Altinget itself has done little more than prepare rubrics and columns. Altinget not only keeps the debate alive. Altinget brings the debaters to life so that they are almost face-to-face, line to line, Brinkmann and Chatrobot. And Brinkmann is even offered a reply.

If there is a status of the case process, it is thus Altinget that humanizes the chatbot, perhaps more than it can bear. It is also Altinget that seeks to adapt the editorial process to the chatGPT capacity more (and more uncritically) than perhaps they should. As regularly emphasized, it is not the task of the analysis to correct. But critical comments and reflections that, like the ones that follow, sharpen questioning positions and analysis strategy are in their place.

4.10 Status and Reflections

The case process and its materials, which I have given an analytical reconstruction in this chapter, I read in Altinget when it came out, March 2023. At this point I was far into my conversation-sessions, and was still of the opinion that only a few of my own words and phrases had to go to the chatbot. At the time of writing, I have never given 'my' Chat a text. It was therefore surprising that Altinget's approach involved the Brinkmann post being given as full text to the chatbot and was then followed by in-depth questions, editorial and customized setup. In short, there was too much editorial hand-wringing. The words were literally put into Chatbot's mouth. And when direct appeal, high-pitched as in the appeal 'You human' is also an editorial and journalistic maneuver, the authenticity in the concrete human/machine relationship is gone.

Another aspect that is surprising in the course of the case is that no one mentions the degree of difficulty of the case. References to intelligence, consciousness, self-consciousness naturally fly back and forth between the actors. Brinkmann is the expert and his statements gain credibility from that. The chatbot does not calculate degrees of difficulty or degrees of credibility, but goes to the database and answers everything. Should something suffer a loss of credibility, then comes the final remark 'It's important to note…'. But Altinget, the editorial arm of the case process, could (should?) have noticed the difficulty of the case. Altinget notices nothing. On the contrary, by asking the previously cited probing questions, new levels of difficulty are added. An answer to questions 1 (What tasks is AI better suited for…than humans?) and 2 (Why is…machines making human abilities redundant… a complex discussion?) requires either knowledge from philosophy, sociology, psychology and technology or that the answerer gathers courage and says 'The question cannot be answered. The answer can be divided into, for example, a philosophical and a technological one, and an offer can be given, but…'. Parenthetically noted, I hope that candidate and PhD students would answer approx. such. Question 3, the How question, I admit, can be answered, although it would be extensive to cover three examples.

But I haven't mentioned the actual difficulty yet. It applies to all three questions that, when answered, they require that the person answering can handle the implicit shifts between theoretical and empirical positions. Those who answer must themselves be able to distinguish and take consequences like: 'in a philosophical-theoretical sense (the AI/human relationship) can be conceptualized as follows… But in an empirical sense it must be described and examined as, for example, a real relationship between AI in use among, for example, doctors and nurses. It means that…'.

Distinguishing between theoretical and empirical positions is possible. But with Altinget's extensive questions in mind, the degree of difficulty of the undertaking is too high. Altinget's HV-arrangement (which, why, how) apparently makes the questions concrete. But at the same time they cover the degree of difficulty. The questions have neither a distinction between theory and empiricism nor concretizations in them. This makes the questions pseudo-concrete and difficult to answer. The chatbot readily responded, as quoted earlier. The answer, which came as an extension of the how question, had concretizations in it. The rest was pseudo-concrete dealing with one of philosophy's most difficult questions, human consciousness. And with that as the focal point for a chatbot response, Altinget kept the debate alive and gave Brinkmann the opportunity to reply!

It is difficult to determine whether Altinget meant this seriously or as a kind of fun. But regardless, there is reason to seriously keep alive the question of consciousness and its degree of difficulty. The issue needs to move away from the pseudo concrete work and back to the authentic. By going back to a related debate about 'the conscious robots' in the daily newspaper Information, 2018, the level of difficulty gains authenticity theoretically as well as practically.

4.11 Back to the Authenticity of the Difficulty

The related debate on 'the conscious robots' was conducted in Information July 2018. The post, written by Louise Schou Drivsholm, included an interview with Dan Zahavi and was headlined: *If we succeed in creating conscious robots, it entails a moral responsibility.* What is interesting in the present context is Information's set-up, the introductory mentions and Zahavi's introductory statements, quoted as follows:

> Consciousness is one of the great mysteries of science. And with the rapid development of artificial intelligence, the understanding of man's unique world of experience only becomes more relevant. It is not natural science, but philosophy, which contains the answers to many of our questions, believes the internationally recognized philosophy professor Dan Zahavi. (Information July 2018).

What is interesting about this journalistic introduction is its precision and high degree of concretization. There is no doubt, 'consciousness' is placed as one of the great mysteries *of science*. Artificial intelligence, which is rapidly developing, is made relevant. That with precision, now for the understanding of human's unique world of experience. This is followed by a selection that comes close to a statement: Not natural science, but philosophy, contains answers to our questions. Who means that? Dan Zahavi does, name mention.

In the previous chapters we were confronted with the chatbot's context and authorless texts. Just a single look at the quoted lines from Information confirms the difference between the chatbot's and the journalist's text production. In four lines, the text is given meaning, precision and signals the cardinal point of the debate. At the same time, responsibility is placed. Backwards to the journalist and the daily newspaper Information, from now on to Dan Zahavi. In and with this placement of responsibility, the text acquires both meaning and authenticity. This applies to both the journalist and Zahavi, who follows up on the introduction and starts the argumentative flow of the text as follows:

> Consciousness has been called the holy grail of brain research. With MRI scans and electrodes, researchers have for decades tried to map the complex network of neurons in order to find the connections that can explain human consciousness. But the so-called reductive materialism, i.e. the idea that natural science can explain consciousness in line with other physical phenomena, is simplistic, believes the 50-year-old professor of philosophy Dan Zahavi. (Information 18.7.2018)

In the argumentative flow, focused on the cardinal point of the debate, the 'case itself' has a high degree of difficulty. At the same time, the text has a high degree of concretization. Brain research, MRI scans, the complex network of neurons; everything in the text is placed relationally and named, after which the responsibility for any concluding phrases can be transferred to the expertise, in casu Zahavi:

> Natural science's traditional repertoire of cognition, brain and IT research has not been able to explain what has been called the *hard problem of consciousness research* - namely the subjective experiences and emotional life of consciousness. (Zahavi, Information 18.7.2018).

The above quotes from Information clarify an authenticity that chatbot texts do not have. With this, the Information entry also clarifies what authenticity presupposes, namely that both the sender/author part and the genre/text/content part are named and the context is signalled. In that sense, the Information post as a text already has the prerequisites and basic features that the chatbot texts lack. In this connection, the Altinget case course can be recalled.

The Brinkmann post, together with Altinget's task 'Give an answer…' constituted the meaning-bearing words/word blocks that the chatbot was given. But Altinget then gave a new task, the three in-depth questions. It is a genre shift that pushes Chatbot away from the debate genre and into the characteristic school assignment.

The chatbot does not fulfill the role of a debater who can argue, write texts with attitudes and opinions, express sharpness and personality with an edge. The chatbot has neither and the language suit does not help. The chatbot certainly started with the phrase "I am an artificial intelligence, and I would like to challenge…" But the response text and its nameless argumentative flow challenged no one, before Altinget intervened editorially with the intended message: *You will always bear the responsibility for my mistakes.*

With the criticism of the lack of authenticity in descriptions of human/machine relationships as a background, and with recognition of the difficulty of the question of consciousness, I decided on a case-analytical condensation. I will skip the intermediate calculations and in the next chapter ask 'my' Chat the direct question: Do you have self-consciousness?

Chapter 5
Between Consciousnesses, Human-I and Machine-I

In this chapter, a case-analytical condensation is made that looks at the question of whether chatbots have consciousness from within. The criticism of the lack of authenticity in descriptions of human/machine relations and the recognition of the difficulty of the consciousness question is the present background. This is also the reason for skipping intermediate calculations and asking it as a direct question. But can I allow myself to do that, i.e. allow myself to start a KB/Chat session with a you-formulation, i.e. "Do you have self- consciousness"?

In the previous chapter, it was an analytical, but also critical comment that Altinget kept the debate alive by humanizing the chatbot. The same type of criticism can probably be directed at KB—and directed together with the doubt. Is it serious or fake, is KB's question position and the question itself a 'real question'? When I answer yes, both serious and real, it is because my question is a consequence of the case-analytical condensation. The main question of the previous chapter, "Do chatbots have consciousness?", has already been condensed into an answer that projects machines with self-consciousness. This projection was not given by Brinkmann, Altinget, Zahavi or by KB, but by the chatbot.

The strange quote, I called it, contained statements such as "Although it is true that machines are not currently self-conscious" some experts expect that "we will see machines with self-consciousness in the foreseeable future" (Chatbot/Altinget). It was unclear whether 'we' meant 'we, experts and AI', or 'we, humans including me/the chatbot'. In the strange quote, there is nothing wrong with the grammar or the overall meaning. There is something wrong with the arguments and the exact meaning. But regardless, there was no doubt about who should be noted for the quotable answer, namely Altinget's Chatbot debater.

As a consequence, the main question of this chapter and KB is therefore asked of the next involved chatbot in the case, namely my Chat. The answer should be used to clarify how close we are to the 'machines with self-consciousness' of the future. But the answer should also be used analytically in relation to the two steps of the analysis. As is well known, the first step is about identifying the self-understanding

K. Borgnakke, *AI and ChatGPT Technology in Education*, Education, Equity, Economy 12, https://doi.org/10.1007/978-3-032-01419-1_5

and ideology that the development of artificial intelligences AI and chatbots is surrounded by and expresses. At this stage, fields, institutions, actors' own ideas and justifications are taken at face value, and then, at the second stage of the analysis, they are confronted with studies of the actual conditions and practices. The case analysis began in the public debate and, with its exemplary impact on Altinget's debate, has focused on the issue of consciousness and the human-machine constellation. But the debate also made visible the ideology of AIs in equal cooperation with experts and health care professionals, for example. Potentially conflicting positions on how the experts and institutions involved should handle AI and chatbots also came to light. And above all, a chatbot not only appeared; it spoke. Altinget's chatbot presented its understanding of AI and of human- machine/relationships and tasks. As a consequence, the case analysis is condensed around the identification of my Chat's self-understanding. If the question position is valid, the human/machine relationship is acknowledged and authentic. I know that Chat, via the language suit, is programmed to respond and even respond with an I-formulation. What I don't know is what the Chat-I responds and where it takes us. That's why I ask.

5.1 The Session Process

The Consciousness session consists of several parts and is 2099 words in total. KB follows the argumentative flow, asks follow-up questions, but also confronts Chat with contradictions. At the same time, the machine learning question is maintained, which turns out to be more crucial than the consciousness question for Chat's understanding of who it is and what it can do.

In order to maintain the focus of the case analysis on the basic question of consciousness/self-consciousness, I first quote these Chat responses in their entirety. Then I follow the process through KB's calls to elaborate on the question of Chat's cognitive skills and the distinction between learning, experience and training. This part of the analysis must quote in excerpts for reasons of space. On the other hand, the argumentative flow in examples and excerpts is maintained so that the thematized movement from consciousness to machine learning is made clear.

KB's questioning position and questioning sequence are part of the argumentative flow. However, there is a complication involved, which (with the Ricoeurian inspiration in mind) refers to movements between the speaking and writing human I's. Here, the machine I that Chat refers to is not included. The complication is already apparent at the start of the session, as seen below. The direct question "Do you have self- consciousness?" leads to both conscious and non-conscious I-positions.

KB: Do you have self-consciousness?

Chat: As an artificial intelligence, I am not capable of having personal experiences or emotions in the same way that humans are. Although I am programmed to interact with users and perform tasks, I do not have a subjective experience of myself or the world around me. I am simply a computer programming designed to process information and generate responses based on the information I have access to.

KB: Then why do you use the word 'I'?

Chat: As a linguistic convention, I use the word "I" to give my answers a more natural and coherent tone and to make it easier for users to understand my answers. Although I do not have a personal experience of myself, the use of "I" can also signal that my answers are generated by an artificial intelligence and not by a human agent. (Chat, Ses. Consciousness)

If the Chat answers above are considered basic statements, it should first be noted that the starting sentence 'As an artificial intelligence I am not able to…' belongs to the standard phrases of the language suit and language blocks. But there is still something special about Chat's answer and argumentative behavior. Chat meta-reflects on the use of "I" and believes that it can both provide a more "natural" tone and coherence, and signal that the Chat-I is an artificial intelligence and 'not a human agent'. Chat's argument is unusual, but perhaps logical (?) if you understand it from the machine's point of view. And the argument clearly points both to the statement, namely that the Chat-I is 'a computer programming designed to process information and generate answers', and to the construction 'Even if I…' with statements surrounded by negation: '…I do not have a subjective experience of myself…'

Chat's meta-reflective behavior is characteristic of the session, but at the same time Chat's overuse of self- references and negations gives the overall meaning of the text a strange tinge of an I-strong non-consciousness. I therefore try to keep Chat on track with the next question/answer sequence and use both the words of consciousness and self-consciousness. Chat's answer is divided below into sections (1)–(3) to facilitate reference.

KB: Do you distinguish between consciousness and self-consciousness and if you do, what is the difference?

Chat: As an artificial intelligence, I am programmed to understand the difference between consciousness and self-consciousness.

(1) Consciousness generally refers to the state of consciousness in which an organism or system is able to experience and respond to its environment. Consciousness is a property that can be found in both living and non-living systems, and it is often defined as a state of consciousness in which there is some degree of attention and perception.
(2) Self-consciousness refers to the ability to have consciousness of one's own existence, mental states, and behavior. It involves being able to think about oneself as a separate entity and having understanding of how one's actions affect one's surroundings and other people.
(3) As an artificial intelligence, I have a form of consciousness, as I am able to process and respond to information, but I do not have self-consciousness, as I do not have a personal experience of myself or the world around me. I can perform tasks and produce responses based on the data I have been trained on, but I do not have an inner experience of myself as an individual. (Chat, Ses. Consciousness)

As can be seen, the Chat answer is now structured and divided so that Chat starts by incorporating the words of KB's question. The Chat answer is also genre-clear and on an almost definitive errand. The three sections are both independent and coherent. Starting with 'Consciousness generally refers to…' (1) 'Self- consciousness refers to…' (2) and concluding with 'As an artificial intelligence, I have…' (3) the argumentative sequence makes sense and to that extent responds to KB's question.

However, if the Chat answer of the Consciousness session is to be analyzed as a complete answer, the circular movements around 'consciousness' that started with the Altinget debate and the Brinkmann contribution must be stopped, or supplemented by the involvement of more responsible debaters.

Because if Chat can claim, as the quoted introduction above, that it is '*programmed to understand* the difference between consciousness and self-consciousness', programmers and the IT expertise behind it must be recalled. Together with Chat, they/we are entering one of the enigmatic questions of science, to now express myself in continuation of the before quoted newspaper Information and Dan Zahavi (see Chap. 4). But in that case, programmers and IT expertise must also be confronted with the risk that the Chat text will encounter criticism that is more fundamental than source criticism. Chat's underlying statements and sentences must stand the test. Let me scratch the surface a little. Chat claims that:

> Consciousness is a property that can be found in both living and non-living systems, and it is often defined as a state of consciousness in which there is some degree of attention and perception. (ibid)

These two almost lexically arranged statements flow easily and the sentence does not break down. It also makes sense. But the content and the sentence's embedded definitions and statements are wrong. If we simply follow the direction of view from Dan Zahavi and therefore place consciousness concepts and theories close to the humanities, philosophy and psychology, it must be a 'No' to the above statements across the board. No, consciousness should not be primarily characterized as 'a property' and No, consciousness is not found in both living and non-living systems. No, consciousness is not 'often defined' as a state where there is 'a certain degree of attention and perception'.

Now there is no reason to believe that programmers and IT experts will be surprised or frightened. They have pointed out since ChatGPT's launch that many types of errors can occur in the answers the chatbot gives. They have also long been disclaimed responsibility. At this point in the analysis, it is also clear that Chat itself disclaims responsibility. And as Chat emphasizes above, it has 'a form of consciousness' but 'not self-consciousness'. Chat has 'no personal experience' of itself and the world, it only performs 'tasks and produces answers based on the data' it is trained on.

Chat thus renounces precisely the properties that the lexical-sounding sentences pointed to. But, claims Chat (and the programmer and IT expertise behind it?), a chatbot still has some form of consciousness and is programmed to understand. On behalf of the dubious issue of consciousness, there is reason to take stock.

5.2 Status

The status is that there are arguments and sentences that make sense and clarify dilemmas. But there seems to be no end to the ambiguity or to the circular movements of the arguments. If they are tentatively maintained, the contours of a Chat are drawn, which is claimed to have a form of consciousness that is not self-consciousness, but perhaps an I-consciousness. Regardless, Chat is a speaking and writing machine-I. There also seems to be something special about this "I", namely that Chat, as artificial intelligence, uses it to make itself understood. As Chat's own words put it:

> As a linguistic convention, I use the word "I" to give my answers a more natural and coherent tone and to make it easier for users to understand my answers. (ibid)

With Chat's reference to I-formulations as a linguistic convention, it is confirmed that ChatGPT's language suit works. But it also means that Chat's strange overuse of the 'I/mine' words works. And in that case, the doubt arises as to whether Chat, who uses "I" to facilitate the understanding of "my answers", i.e. Chat's own answers, has acquired a superego. Is Chat suddenly a superego that takes a position on linguistic conventions, the users and its own positioning… or? If that were the case, then Chat could have confirmed that it had a form of self-consciousness. Chat claimed about self- consciousness (2) that: "It involves being able to think about oneself" and understand "how one's actions affect one's surroundings and other people" (Chat, Ses. (3). And wasn't it precisely 'thinking about oneself' and about 'how one's actions affect' that Chat did with its language and text actions, when the word "I" had to be used for the sake of the users?

What we should focus on with these quotes and now reformulated questions are the specific formulations that cast fundamental doubt on what is up and down in the question of consciousness—regardless of where it is viewed from.

In several ways, Chat seems to have departed from the concepts. It is a spontaneous way of speaking, but when the Chat texts of the Consciousness session are analyzed, we see not only that, but how Chat departs from the concepts. Even though the Chat answers use both colloquial and lexical ways of expression, the session testifies that Chat cannot determine the conceptual differences between the human-I the KB question represents and the machine-I that Chat represents. And where we can see that Chat departs from the concepts is in the moment of action. In that moment the KB/Chat conversation goes from the speech acts of the language suit to the data-driven writing acts of the Chat answer, the human and machine-borne concepts collide. The language suit clothes Chat with a speaking-I that humanizes the conversation and builds a bridge to KB's question.

The status is thus that language suit and genre can give Chat a writing-I, but it never becomes credible in the same way as Chat's speaking-I. When Chat, as a text producer, delivers the response text to KB, Chat refers to the data bank and to the authorless and source less text universe. In the databank's universe, there are no humanizations. The genre, which almost writes itself, is a bridge builder—and the doubt whether there is a writing-I at all is mentioned in the text. This can be seen, again, in the moment of the act. In that moment Chat delivers the genre-adequate text and uses the genre and the language suit to disclaim responsibility for the content, the doubt about the existence of a writing-I is signaled.

In the course of this book's analyses, the important examples come. But in relation to the question of who Chat is and how it functions in its own self-understanding, no examples are clearer than this chapter's Consciousness Session. Let me therefore in the following section sharpen the ethnographic presence to the KB/Chat session's conceptual clash between the human-I and the machine-I. Next, closer to Chat's language suit and the speaking-I, the Ricoeur inspiration support the description of the characteristic shifts and transitions between speech and written actions.

5.3 The Fixed Point and the Conceptual Clash

The analysis of the KB/Chat conversations' circulating argumentation requires a firm point of reference and clarification. But I avoid making it a question of interpretations of consciousness as a concept. For the same reason, I do not let Altinget's debate, Brinkmann or Zahavi's interpretation of whether AI chatbots have consciousness, continue as a starting point. I need a new, sober point of reference; preferably a recognized definition or description of the meaning, such as the one below from the Danish dictionary, Den Danske Ordbog (DDO). The description is two, or three-part, and reads as follows:

> Consciousness (means)
>
> 1. the part of the psyche that can be recognized and controlled, and which enables a person to perceive, understand and be aware of their surroundings (…)
>
> 1.a physical or mental state in which one is awake and able to perceive the outside world with one's senses (…)
>
> 2. knowledge of and clarity about the meaning or consequence of something; being aware of something (…) (Den Danske Ordbog, Bevidsthed)

The description is longer in the post, contains examples and subcategories. In that respect, the description is open to interpretation. But the essential thing in the context is what is not open to interpretation, namely that both the cited three-division and the accompanying examples have the human at the absolute center. Furthermore, the existence of the human, as the living and sentient awake human being, is a prerequisite for the description and consciousness. With this as a firm point of reference, we can consider whether Chat's 'form of consciousness' can be added to the description's starting point 1. We use Chat's own formulations ("I am simply a computer programming") and must therefore start by replacing 'psyche' with 'programming'. Now Point 1 reads slightly abbreviated as follows: (Consciousness means) 'the part of computer programming that can be controlled and that enables Chat/ChatGPT to perceive, understand and be aware of its surroundings…'.

In order to complete the attempt to include Chat in the three meanings and thus include both senses and knowledge of… we should continue. But it already stops here. Chat/ChatGPT is not close to being 'able to perceive, understand and be aware of one's surroundings…' The shift in emphasis to 'aware of one's surroundings' is crucial, but also demanding. It also means that with one's awake senses one is 'able to perceive the outside world'. And again, Chat is not able to perceive the outside world as a world around one.

The conclusion must therefore be that Chat has never been conscious, and therefore Chat cannot be said to have a, or any, form of consciousness. The question of consciousness is dismissed!

The Chat answers also seem to point in the same direction. For although Chat has signaled having 'some form of consciousness', neither Chat nor the IT expertise has claimed that the computer programming (the algorithms or language models) enables Chat/ChatGPT to be conscious in the sense of 'being aware of its surroundings', let alone with its senses capable of 'perceiving the outside world'. When it came to the question of what Chat is programmed to do, more toned-down terms were used. Chat's statement in its entirety read as follows:

> I am simply a computer programming designed to process information and generate answers based on the information I have access to. (ibid)

With this statement we are far from human consciousness and the human I and close to the data bank and the machine I. That should be enough, at least, to distance ourselves from the question of consciousness. It *is* enough, but the way in which the distance is made is the reason why the analyst still cannot leave the question of consciousness. Let me elaborate.

If the entry in the Danish dictionary, DDO, and the three points, as previously emphasized, is a description that puts the human in the absolute center, then the above Chat quote is a description that puts the computer/programming/AI-ChatGPT in the absolute center. In that case, we have a human-anchored conceptualization of consciousness and a computer-anchored conceptualization of non-consciousness.[1] But if the conceptual (human/machine) anchoring are now made clear, the conceptual clash is also clear. The above Chat sentence's statement: "I am simply a computer programming" not only shows, but 'is' the clash.

A computer does not have an 'I', but a programmer/programming can obviously give an 'I' to a chatbot. There is thus an active Chat-I, which (consciously or non-consciously) influences everyday communicative practice, and the conversation/session processes that take place over months and years between KB and Chat. But this also means, firstly, that an active Chat-I must be able to perceive, understand and be aware of the ongoing conversation process. Secondly, that the question of consciousness that provoked the conceptual clash must be maintained for a little longer. For example, by returning to the start of the conversation process and the exchange of lines between the KB question: 'Do you have self-consciousness?' and the Chat answer: 'As an artificial intelligence, I am not capable of having personal

[1] Non-determinations is, in an analytical sense, an important description that is retained. Here with reference to the Chat response's opening sentence: 'As an artificial intelligence, I am not capable of having personal experiences'.

experiences'. This exchange of lines clarifies the problem. For if the statement above should be that a programmer/programming can give Chat an 'I' must the statement about the start of the process also be that KB helped to activate it. The you-formulated question thus seems to provoke the active Chat-I of the conversation process, but also to presuppose it. You-questions predispose to the I-answer of the process (consciously or not).

Against this background, the characteristic features of the presupposition can be sharpened as consequences for the KB/Chat conversation process.

5.4 Sharpened as Consequences for the Conversation Process

KB's process orientation and starting question ('Do you have self-consciousness?') refer back to Altinget's chatbot, which projected machines with self-consciousness. The relevance of the question as a follow-up question is thus clarified. In turn, the effect and consequence of the directly you-addressed question come behind KB. The session also shows a pattern and consequences, which can subsequently be maintained as follows.

Of the 13 initial and follow-up questions in the session, 7 are clear you-questions. The corresponding 7 Chat answers are given as I-formulated answers, with consequences for the content of the answer. It is also given that Chat actively negates the human I. The typical answer construction is the previously quoted one: 'As an artificial intelligence, I am not able to (...) in the same way as humans', which, for example, reappears a little later in Chat answers concerning 'experience': "As an AI model, I do not have any actual experience or experience in the same way as humans".

Regarding KB questions without you-titling, the corresponding 6 Chat answers do not have I-formulations and are consequently not characterized by this. They are rather characterized by the activated but implicit machine-I, and a case-oriented start to the answer. A typical question/answer construction here is "KB, what is deep learning? (Chat): Deep learning is a branch of machine learning that focuses on (...)".

The tendency is thus that the 7 I-formulated answers are characterized as a whole and argue from a KB- represented human-I as a starting point, via a negation (non-human), towards the provisional standpoint as artificial intelligence.

The provisional conclusion must therefore be that KB's you-questions not only result in Chat making itself known as an I-respondent, but deliver an answer that, in form and content, is characterized by being formulated by a Chat's (inter)speaking I. Hereby, the Chat-I (regardless of the negation) confirms the basic set of rules of everyday communicative practice, which assumes a) in conversations, questions require an answer and answers require recognition as 'answers' and b) if the conversation is carried out, the question/answer is confirmed as understood. This also means in practice that with the implementation of the KB/Chat conversations, the set of rules and requirements are met.

The point is that the KB/Chat conversation processes are actually (and regardless of negations) carried out with the human consciousness and I-positions as the prerequisite of the session and the conversation process. The 7 you-titled questions/7 I-formulated answers clarify the confirmation with a humanized I-positioning. The confirmation also goes further and applies to all 13 Questions/Answers themselves, as well as the entire session.

If we outline the process on this basis, KB's questioning position, as human-borne, can be designated with a +. Chat's answer position, as machine-borne, can be designated with a -. In that case, the following applies to the entire session process. The process starts in +, and slides at the first Chat response into-(Non-human). But since Chat's language suit assigns Chat both an I and a superego, the process slides back into +. If it momentarily shifts to-(due to the 6's implicit machine learning neuter), KB's question brings the process back to +.

The point is that KB and Chat's language suit mutually confirms the human-anchored references and I- positions of the conversation. Next, and with the human anchoring as a prerequisite, Chat can also slide in and out of non-I and machine-I positions. With this important partial conclusion, 'the assumed' also functions in the book's analyses going forward. At the same time, questions related to the consequence are opened up.

The consequence that requires attention is that Chat's I-formulations not only characterize the conversation process and argumentation, but also characterize the response's reference to actions and doings. Suddenly it is not the artificial intelligence or the computer programming, but a Chat-I that self-refers with a sentence that reads, for example, 'I can learn from data and adjust my models', 'I can plan' and 'I can evaluate possible decisions' (see below quotations). With such self-referrals, the outline of what the Chat-I is capable of, can and claims to do is visible.

Chat's description of its own repertoire of actions is interesting in itself. Here we see both the breadth of intellectual abilities and (similar to the Altinget's chatbot) the professional tasks that AI technologies are supposed to help solve. At the same time, Chat's own descriptions contain thought-provoking contradictions, by including precisely the abilities and actions that Chat otherwise claims artificial intelligence does not have or cannot perform.

Let me therefore pursue this action aspect, but also breathe life into it by taking it back into real chronology, i.e. back into the conversational flow of the session.

5.5 Chat's Self-Understanding and Acting Repertoire

In this section, we observe how Chat's self-understanding and repertoire of actions move from the complex of understanding to a description of its own cognitive skills. Next, the big questions lead to the machine room. I clarify the conversational character and the argumentative flow and quote Chat's specified tasks in the original order. Below, the sequence of the start is quoted in full so that it can be seen how understanding is layered and leveled. For a start, KB refrains from using the you-formulation. The conversation must move away from 'being consciousness' and towards the consequence 'being able to understand'. Several layers must also be opened up. The section division 1–3 is mine to facilitate reference.

KB: Are there more layers in 'to understand'?

(1) Chat: Yes, there are multiple layers to understanding something. Understanding can be considered a complex process involving multiple cognitive skills and mental operations.
(2) At its most basic level, understanding involves being able to recognize and register information and perceive its meaning. This may include being able to identify words and symbols and understand their meaning in a given context. At a higher level, understanding involves being able to analyze and process information to form meaningful concepts and ideas. This may include being able to identify connections between different pieces of information and draw conclusions based on this analysis.
Finally, understanding can also involve being able to apply and utilize the knowledge gained in a meaningful way. This can include being able to use the information to solve problems or make decisions, or being able to share knowledge with others and communicate effectively.
(3) Thus, understanding is a complex process involving several different cognitive skills and mental operations that work together to create a coherent and meaningful perception of the world around us. (Chat, Ses. Consciousness/Understand)

The interesting thing about the start of the conversation is, firstly, that the KB question actually functions as an opening and, secondly, that the Chat answer from the start shows a technical -operational approach to 'understanding' and understanding on several levels. An outline is drawn of how Chat's complex understanding process works and what it requires, namely 'several cognitive skills and mental operations.' Chat's technical-operational approach to understanding has a surprising and peculiar precision in KB's perspective, which is informative for the analysis. The Chat answer refers, in the (2-sequence), to the technical argumentative drivers of the levels, such as being able to recognize/register and analyze/process information. Understanding becomes a 'mental operation' and we are on our way into the operator's space, the machine room. So far the answer, seen on Chat's premises.

If the Chat response is then viewed in relation to the course of the session, it is noted that the precision and lexical tone of the response have now shifted, and are more explicitly linked to the conceptual machine-I. There are no explicit I-formulations. But there is an implicit machine-I and an authoritative voice in the text, can both begin with 'Yes, there are several layers', 'understanding can be considered a complex process' and end with a concluding 'This is how understanding is…'. Where the authoritative voice comes from is still unclear. Similar unclear is its relationship to the human-related part of the understanding spectrum carried by the language blocks 'identify words and symbols', 'understand their meaning' and 'solve problems or make decisions'. But it is as if the Chat response in the final sequence finds a Super-ego that connects the technical and human-related parts of the understanding spectrum. In any case, the Chat response ends by concluding that the complex understanding process must involve:

(…) several different cognitive skills and mental operations that work together to create a coherent and meaningful perception of the world around us. (ibid)

The Chat response is without an I, the text is without a human subject, so what this late-added 'us' means is questionable. But if it is to make sense in the context, there are three possibilities. It could mean 'us/we humans' or 'us/we machines'—or it could mean "us" KB and Chat.

Chat does not give any sign of clarification, but sends both questions and answers into its own closed circuit. The analyst sees the new trait in the conversation. Chat does not know what understanding is or means, but informs about what is happening in the closed circuit. Chat draws us into the machine room that seeks to create a meaningful perception of the world around us. KB is still part of the argumentative flow of the session and wants to move away from flighty understanding processes and towards action-specific questions and facts, also about how many and which skills we are talking about. KB returns to you-formulations which, all else being equal, seem to have a concretizing effect on the Chat response.

KB: How many cognitive skills do you have and what mental operations can you perform?

Chat: As an artificial intelligence, I am programmed to perform a wide range of cognitive skills and mental operations. Some of the most common skills and operations that I am programmed to perform include:

1. Language processing: I can analyze, understand, and generate language at different levels, including syntax, semantics, and pragmatics.
2. Machine learning: I can learn from data and adjust my models and algorithms based on the information I get.
3. Problem Solving: I can analyze complex problems and generate solutions based on my programmed rules and logic.
4. Pattern recognition: I can analyze and identify patterns in data and use this information to make decisions and generate predictions.
5. Planning: I can plan and carry out actions based on programmed goals and priorities.
6. Decision Making: I can evaluate possible decisions based on programmed criteria and choose the best option.
7. Network analysis: I can analyze and identify relationships in a network or graph.

These are just some examples of the many cognitive skills and mental operations that I am programmed to perform, and there are many other skills and operations that can also be included in my function. (Chat. Ses. Consciousness/Skills)

The above Chat answers have the machine room as genre and context marker. The language block that occurs most frequently, namely 'programmed to…' or 'programmed criteria', also functions as a connective/link in the descriptive flow from 1 to 7. Against this background, there is little doubt that the cognitive tasks (listed as the 7 tasks) should be characterized within the technical goal-rational action universe.

If we recall the examples in Chap. 2 of Chat's difficulties in analyzing, it must be doubted whether the tasks mentioned under 1 and 3 can bear the description. Chat can 'analyze, understand language at different levels' and 'analyze complex problems' in a technical sense, but not in a humanistic sense. In this respect, the human-anchored I-formulated sentences of the language suit promise more than Chat can deliver. But since the mental operations take place in the machine room, and the argumentative flow of the text is clearly tied to 'programming', it must be maintained that the tasks are described with the peculiar precision that does not give the humanities first right to the concept of analysis. Rather, statistical analysis and data analysis should be given first right to determine what makes sense in the context.

While examining Chat's self-understanding, the important point is therefore that with the machine room as the context, the tasks of Chat itself are described as oriented towards technical goal-rational action. At the same time, Chat not only signals intentions to engage in problem solving and decision-making, but claims to possess the cognitive skills needed to carry out the so-called mental operations in practice. These claimed skills are legitimized via the I-formulation and made correspondingly action-concrete via the accumulated series of 'I can…'

But as we approach the concrete versions of action, the difference between what the Chat-I claims to be able to do and what the AI-ChatGPT can and does becomes ever greater. Moreover, the difference reaches almost extreme expression in the bullet point list quoted above. Furthermore, Chat then plays it safe by finally claiming that the bullet point list was simply:

> (…) some examples of the many cognitive skills and mental operations that I am programmed to perform, and there are many other skills and operations that can also be included in my function. (ibid)

If you consider that Chat originally referred to the basic cognitive skills and mental operations of humans, then additional skills and operations sound like an overkill. Before KB enters the machine-room and is informed by Chat, there is therefore a need to take stock in realistic terms. At the very least, a realistic outline of the claimed and practical skills must be provided.

5.6 The Claimed and Practical Skills: A Realistic Outline

I acknowledge that the you-titling of the KB question may have contributed to reinforcing the I-formulated list of what Chat claims to be able to do. Let me therefore remove the I-formulation from the bullet point and simply note Chat/ChatGPT. Since the bullet point is seen from inside the machine room and is tied to 'programming', statistical analysis and data analysis (and not humanistic analysis) are given priority to the concept of analysis and to the characterization of skill and task. In return, I allow myself (on behalf of the humanities) to remove the human-related terms for basic skills and learning metaphors that there is doubt about Chat/ChatGPT being able to perform.

With this as a background, the now slimmed down, but still 7-point list can be outlined as follows:

> *As an artificial intelligence, ChatGPT is programmed to perform a wide range of operations that include:*
>
> 1. Language processing: analyzing and generating language at various levels, including syntax, semantics, and pragmatics.
> 2. Machine learning: ChatGPT is trained, based on data, to use and adjust models and algorithms

3. Problem solving: data analysis and data generation solutions based on programmed rules and logic.
4. Pattern recognition: analyzing and identifying patterns in data and using this to generate predictions.
5. Planning: planning operations based on programmed goals and priorities.
6. Decision Making: Summarizing possible decisions based on programmed criteria
7. Network analysis: analysis and identification of connections in a network or graph.

I do not take a position on whether the slimmed-down sketch should have different (and new?) keywords. I simply note that at this point in the analysis it is a realistic contraction of Chat's setup, and therefore suitable for taking into the machine room as a background for further description of the reality content. Furthermore, the sketch represents a kind of overview of the AI/ChatGPT skills that we can expect both IT experts, professionals and 'ordinary' users to revolve around, or to take note of while we use it.

But if the slimmed-down version of the claimed skills is in itself of interest for the ongoing analysis, then the unclaimed skills are suddenly also of interest.

ChatGPT is like AI generative intelligence programmed for text and conversation. A ChatGPT is a text producer and its texts are included in both small and large communicative circuits. But the ChatGPT's own text contributions, its communicative skills and involvement in the living circuits are rarely in focus. In relation to Chat's otherwise all-encompassing list of its own skills, the communicative, speech and text productive skills are not included in the list either. It is as if Chat neither knows nor understands the language suit it is wearing. That is otherwise its lifeline.

Against this background, KB tries to breathe life into the machine room and brings the living conversation to the fore. As can be seen, Chat's answer is characterized by the peculiar technical precision that makes it possible for us to follow Chat's understanding process from speech to text, i.e. from recording sound signals to transforming text. But at the same time, the first-person narrative (which we also follow below) is on a collision course with the human words to understand, to experience, to learn. Below, the conversation excerpt (1–5) is sequenced to facilitate reference, but otherwise the process is quoted in its entirety.

KB How do you understand live conversations?

(1) I understand live conversations using a combination of language processing, pattern recognition, and machine learning. When a person speaks to me, my software records the audio signals and converts them into text using speech recognition algorithms. I then use my programmed language processing skills to analyze and understand the text I have received.

(2) More specifically, I use various techniques to identify the grammatical structure of sentences, understand the meaning of words and sentence parts, and the context of what is being said. I can also use my pattern recognition skills to identify recurring patterns in conversations and use this information to predict what is likely to be said next.

(3) Machine learning also plays an important role in my ability to understand live conversations. As an artificial intelligence, I can learn from past conversations and adjust my models and algorithms based on feedback and experience. The more I interact with people and receive feedback, the more I can improve my language processing and pattern recognition skills and become better at understanding live conversations.

KB why do you use the word 'experience'?

(4) As an AI model, I do not have any actual experience or knowledge in the same way as humans. However, my performance and ability to perform various tasks and functions depends on the data and algorithms that I have been trained and programmed with. The more data and feedback I get, the better I can become at performing various tasks and adapting to different situations.

(5) When I talk about learning from experience or improving my skills through experience, I am referring to the way my software has been trained and the feedback I receive from users and my programmers. It is a way of describing how my model and algorithms can be improved and adjusted over time to achieve better performance and efficiency." (Chat, Ses. Consciousness/Live Conversations)

These two Chat responses are both well-formulated and well-structured as a whole. Section introductions such as 'I understand...;, More specifically; Machine learning also plays; As an AI model', ending with 'So when I talk about...' testify to a Chat text that is well-formed and flows easily. But in terms of content, Chat is clearly on a collision course with both human and machine words. Let me therefore start by summarizing the known analytical points that are made clear, and then slim down the text so that the real content is visible.

One point is that the KB question's you-formulation provokes Chat's I-formulations to an unnecessarily large extent. This is clear in all 5 sequences, but exemplified in the first sequence, it appears as follows:

(1)- The sequence consists of 49 words and three sentences. Of these, 5 language blocks are carried by I/me, namely: "I understand live conversations", "When a person speaks to me", "registers my software", "After this I use my programmed", "I have received." The I-function as a driver and ensures the argumentative flow of the description. However, if the Chat response makes it present that a Chat-I (similar to a machine-I) is present both in the machine room and in the text, it also overshadows the informative content. In consideration of the reality content of Chat's action-specific references, we therefore remove the-I from the text.

The second point is that Chat-I first uses the important human words with the Chat-I's self-evident oath and then negates it (over non-human).

In section (3) Chat claims: "As an AI, I can learn from previous conversations and adjust my models and algorithms based on feedback and experience." When KB then asks why the word 'experience' is used, Chat replies with a negation (4) "As an AI model, I do not have any actual experience or knowledge in the same way as humans." Chat then concludes with a concluding adjustment (5) "When I talk about learning from experience or improving my skills through experience, I am referring to the way my software has been trained and the feedback that I receive from users and my programmers."

If, against this background, we follow Chat's negation and adaptation, i.e. non-experience but instead 'trained software', and remove the markings of human language, we see the outline of the reality content described in machine language. If the now slimmed down version of sections 1–5 is to be formulated, it reads as follows:

> A ChatGPT handles live conversations using a combination of language processing, pattern recognition and machine learning. Software records the audio signals and converts them into text using speech recognition algorithms. Then, programmed language processing skills are used to analyze the text.
>
> Through training and feedback from users and programmers, models and algorithms can be improved and adjusted over time to achieve better performance and efficiency. (KBs/author's version)

As emphasized before, regarding the slimming down of the 7-point list, I do not take a position on whether the slimmed down version should have different keywords. I simply state that it is a reality-oriented compression of the informative part of the Chat response. It is therefore suitable for assessing the reality content of the described ways Chat, based on machine learning, 'understands' live conversations. As a short version, it could perhaps be approved by professionals—in casu IT expertise?

I am not a professional IT expert, but I nod in recognition of language blocks and statements. Incidentally, as an analyst, I have a related, but more basic, version of the process from 'live conversation' via conversion to text. In my view, this process is a digitization process in two phases.

1. Live conversation (text) is digitized in the sense of numberizing = data.
2. data is digitized in the sense of being textualized = text.

But because I can always identify the starting point and result text-specifically (and therefore know which text I am conducting analyses on), I suddenly have doubts about Chat's description, and especially about the analysis part. Let me scratch the surface and set out Chat's description point by point, as follows:

> *Live conversations (understood/decoded through) language processing, pattern recognition and machine learning.*
>
> 1. Software records the audio signals
> 2. converts them into text using speech recognition algorithms.
> 3. programmed language processing skills
> 4. analyzes the text.

The problem that the 1–4 points show is that both the data collection and the analysis process are suddenly gone. The object of the analysis cannot be specified. Furthermore, programmed language processing skills cannot analyze texts, not even if we call them language models instead. The arrangement, the sequence—and the whole enterprise—is not possible, not realizable.

In the eagerness to point to the reality, the data-analytical concentration got the first right; I-formulations and the markers of human language were removed, and the result has (against expectations) become unmanageable, unrealizable, or simply impossible. Let me therefore return to the original statement. For Chat had described the procedure in the possible order when it answered:

> I understand live conversations using a combination of language processing, pattern recognition, and machine learning. When a person speaks to me, my software records the audio signals and converts them into text using speech recognition algorithms. I then use my

programmed language processing skills to analyze and understand the text I have received. (Chat, Ses. Live conversations)

I have quoted the entire introductory sequence, so that the I-positions are again noticeable. But at this point in the analysis, it is especially the last sentence and the last words that we should pay attention to. Chat enters into character as a text analyst and refers with precision to the situation and intention. Chat has received the text and is preparing to analyze, and to do so, the text must be understood. Chat's description gives the text meaning.

We are back to the possible and to a language that not only Chat, but also IT expertise uses. But in that case, the questions that the analyst must pursue must be formulated with skepticism. A chatbot that is neither conscious, nor can understand, experience, or learn (in the human sense)… can hardly analyze texts? And if it can, has the chatbot thereby shown that it can also read and interpret texts, and in general to decode the 'signs, text and meaning' of the texts?

The value of the question is that it provokes a hitherto underexposed aspect of ChatGPT's dealings with texts, namely that regardless of what I, or we, think about its abilities, it already functions as a text producer in the communicative circuits. ChatGPT is already in use as a conversation and sparring partner. And regardless of whether Chat itself understands the live conversations of which it is a part, the KB/Chat conversations are vividly carried out over speech and text positions, as cited above!

There is thus every reason to raise the question of whether Chat can decode the 'signs, text and meaning' of the texts. For the sake of the analysis, however, a concretization must be closer to what the KB/Chat processes themselves keep alive, namely the decoding of the process itself and its changing speech/text positions. As will be seen below, the challenge is to maintain the vivid shifts between KB/Chat's role taking and authoritative voices that function, but slide into the background and flow into the implicit voices and context references.

5.7 The KB/Chat Conversational Process Between Implicit Voices and Context References

In the characterization of the process's shift between speech and text positions, the human-anchoring of the Ricoeur-inspiration becomes present. In the examples above, there is no doubt that KB both represents, interacts with and asks about the living conversation. There is also no doubt that the KB/Chat processes as clashes between human/machine I's can be seen and as changing voices can be 'seen/heard' in the text. For the analysis, the challenge is therefore, also more descriptively, to follow both KB's living starting points and KB/Chat clashes through implicit voices that come to the fore at the same pace as the session process and the context require it.

In relation to this, the Ricoeur-inspiration is also in use as descriptive concretizations of KB/Chat role taking and task. With reference to the previous chapter, Altinget's chatbot can be seen as a dressed-up 'debating I'. In this chapter, KB's Chat should perhaps be seen as both 'the intellectual-I' and 'the IT professional-I' and in later analyses specified as 'the project writing-I'. For the analysis, these designations have a clarifying effect because they actually denote the relationship between the task, e.g. the Altinget's Chatbot was given, and the speaking/text position that was taken. At the same time, the designations function as fluid designations that indicate that Chat's specific role-taking during the process can move between several tasks/roles. Against this background and through the analytical treatment, problems related to the role-taking are pointed out. Chat's contribution as a debater, intellectual, IT expert and project practitioner are for example highlighted by negations of the type: If the process starts with Chat as (the debater's/professional's) 'speaking I', Chat's answers and text risk showing a non-I. This means that the language suit is the representative of the Chat-I, after which the Chat-text as a total result shows the implicit voices of the process and the negation.

The above features are consistent and are thus also applied in the examples and close analyses of future chapters. But there is a complication implied here. And especially this chapter and the KB/Chat session on consciousness clarify the complication in that the movement from the 'speaking I' to the negation can also be reset.

Expressed above the examples of the chapter, reference is still made to the movement between Chat's two I- positions. There is an I that is human-like (but is then negated = non-human) and a machine-I that is what it is, namely a machine. In the final session, where KB continues the conversations with Chat in the machine room, the conversation revolves around machine learning. Here, the movement from KB and Chat's conversational speaking I-positions to Chat's 'AI-speaking/texting I' can be seen. The interesting thing is that the non-human, i.e. the negation, is absent. The sentence that we have encountered in several variants over the course of a whole chapter, but with the same message, namely 'As an AI model I do not have/cannot (...) in the same way as humans', is missing. This means that the movement that goes over a negation is reset.

KB and Chat are in equal speaking positions, almost face to face. And, as will be shown below, Chat's Super-ego is established not with reference to a genre or an external context, but to the machine room. The databank and the machine room have taken on character as Chat's authoritative voice and as text in context. And both KB and Chat are present in the machine room that is the 'now' of the conversation.

Let me therefore breathe life into the description apparatus one last time, by taking it back into real chronology, i.e. back into the conversational course of the session, and showing its consequences as they appear from the inside, i.e. from the machine room.

5.8 Machine Learning from Statistics to Deep Learning: Seen from the Machine Room

The part of the session that revolves around machine learning is approx. 1000 words. I must therefore economize with the number of excerpts and at the same time ensure the flow of the conversation. I do this so that the KB question, which is formulated in continuation of Chat's own words and arguments, is quoted and the theme/problem/origin can be followed. Next, I reproduce the last question-answer sequences of the Consciousness Session in their entirety. Chat informs KB and uses many technical terms. Chat's answers are filled with language blocks about 'machine learning techniques' that involve 'processing large amounts of data', possibilities for 'sorting and ranking data' and 'choosing the right algorithms.' This choice requires 'human expertise' as Chat formulates it, and continues with 'Statistical calculation' as the important thing for machine learning. There is no doubt that in Chat's machine room Techno-logos dominate. For the same reason, the analyst's interest is concentrated on the sections where 'the human inputs' are justified, Techno-logos! KB is simply overwhelmed, but in the situation tries to get a handle on the relationship between the words and terms of machine language and human language. KB is on a collision course, but Chat is not!

KB wonders, for example, if machine learning is about 'data sets to choose between'—*"then why use the word 'learning', why not just designate words that are sorted and ranked?"* Chat responds promptly and appreciatively:

> Good question. Although machine learning techniques involve processing large amounts of data, it is not just about choosing between different options or sorting and ranking data. Rather, it is a method for training a computer model (…) (Chat, Ses, MachineLearn)

After a lengthy explanation from Chat regarding the computer model and the statistical calculations, KB continues with eager: *But why use the word 'training' when what is happening is a statistical calculation?* Chat has answers ready:

> The word "training" is a metaphor used in the context of machine learning to describe the process by which a computer model is adjusted and optimized by working with data. While it is true that machine learning techniques use statistical computing (…) (ibid)

As is understood, KB and Chat are in parallel conversational positions. And if the professional reference and authoritative voice are to be identified as that of IT expertise, the conversational human-machine relationship is in favor of Chat and IT expertise. I do not take a position on whether Chat's AI technical language blocks and arguments (only cited in the small selection above) have precision and are correct in the IT expert sense. What is interesting is their effect. The technical language blocks give Chat the opportunity to navigate between the machine language and KB's question, word choice and reference to the human language. When KB asks whether the use of the word 'learning' is covered by Chat's description of machine learning, Chat responds promptly, but not to KB's question. Instead, Chat's response observes how the word machine *learning* first becomes machine learning *techniques* and then a *method* for *training*. When KB then asks about the word 'training', Chat responds that it is a *metaphor*.

The conceptual glide empties words of content and the argumentation of precision. But, as it is emphasized, the smooth machine-language argumentation works and even places human-language argumentation in the universe of machine learning. Let me therefore illustrate and unfold the consequences for the part of machine learning that, in Chat's formulation, requires the inclusion of 'human expertise'.

5.9 The Necessary Human Inputs

The mention of human input as necessary was made by Chat, as two single statements, in the middle of a technical description of the machine learning process. The two statements (below in italics) read as follows:

1. During the training of a machine learning model, the computer often goes through an iterative process where its results are compared to a known result, *such as a human assessment of image quality or classification of objects*.
2. In this process, the computer performs calculations on the data to adjust its parameters and algorithms, but "training" also involves a more general adaptation of the model to the data and the problem. *It requires human expertise to choose the right algorithms, adjust their parameters, and tune the model to perform at its best.* (Chat, Ses. MachineLearn)

As is understood, the Chat description is deep into the computer's calculation process and mentions, among other things, the need for a human assessment and the requirement for human expertise. Chat then continues to examine the computer's complicated iterative processor. KB stumbles along the way over the inclusion of human skills in two sentences. The adjustments to the computer model, on the other hand, are called complicated processors and are described over entire sequences. KB therefore inserts 'the human inputs' into the question line and gives Chat the opportunity to comment. The last comments in the Chat response are noteworthy because they deal with evaluation and ethical questions. The sequences are quoted below in full.

> Chat: In addition, it often requires human expertise to evaluate and validate the results of a machine learning model. Even though the model may produce impressive results on a given task, it is often difficult to determine whether it will work well in practice or whether its results can be generalized to new datasets or problems.
>
> Finally, there is also an ethical dimension to developing and using machine learning, which requires human expertise and consideration. It is important to ensure that machine learning models do not reinforce existing bias or discrimination and that they are used responsibly and ethically. All of this requires human insight and expertise, even though much of the process is automated and based on statistical calculations. (Chat, Ses. MachineLearn)

It has been emphasized in advance that KB/Chat in this conversation are in equal speaking positions. The conversation has not moved beyond the negation non-human. The negation is reset. The Chat-I is sovereign. The conversation is characterized throughout by Chat's implicit machine-I, which carries the authoritative voice. But above it becomes explicit. In that sense, the Chat-response clarifies what the sovereign Chat-I, the explicit machine-I and the authoritative voice mean and how it works. It is a concentrated strengthening of the Chat-I, which disrupts the Human/machine relationship.

In the Chat-response above, the choice of words is professionally every day. Evaluation and ethics are referred to in human language terms. To emphasize that: "It is important to ensure that machine learning models do not reinforce existing bias or discrimination and that they are used responsibly and ethically correct" sounds like a professional human voice. But it is Chat who says it.

What we witness in these machine learning sections is a reshuffling of the human/machine relationship, pointing to an absolute reification of human expertise and an absolute humanization of Chats. In the machine space, Chat can suddenly act as a machine learning model, describe and talk 'about' machine learning and the model, and justify the machine learning model 'as' a model. If man/it, i.e. if Chat can both be a machine model, describe itself, and justify, reflect, evaluate itself 'as a model', then Chat has self- consciousness. At this point in the analysis, and seen from the machine space, it is an important observation. But it does not stand alone. And if the analytical interest is shifted from the self-conscious Chat to the Chat text and the argumentative content, other, but equally important, observations can be made. Let me elaborate on this below, starting with the details.

5.10 From Small Details to Important Statements: Seen from the Chat Text

In Chat texts, a curious overuse of I/me/mine statements in the I-formulated sequences was previously observed. Similarly, in Chat texts with a lexical or professional tone, an overuse of small words can be observed, such as 'often', or phrases such as 'by means of', 'all this' or 'even though'. These small words and phrases, which in professional everyday language can testify to overview and judgment, however, cause the Chat-I's argument to falter and destroy the message and overall meaning of the text. Using the sequences from the previous paragraph's quote as examples, the small word 'often' is used in two statements, namely

> 1) In addition, it often requires human expertise to evaluate (…) 2) Although the model can produce impressive results on a given task, it is often difficult to determine whether it will work well in practice (…)

To make 'often' make sense, a series of questions begins, e.g.: How often is human expertise required, e.g. twice a year? And if that could be the answer, can the machine model handle the daily evaluation itself? And who calls in 'often', i.e. as often as necessary, the human expertise? Is it Chat who calls in, or just Chat who knows how often the human expertise is required. But if Chat knows that, and how often it should be called in, where does Chat know that from?

Already with the first insistent series of questions, it is felt that something must be wrong, either with the sender of the statement (Chat) with the placement of the word 'often', or with the reader (the Analyst). But before deciding, let us look at the second example. Here the series of questions is extended, not least because the small word 'often' is part of a statement and a sentence that starts with the phrase 'Even if…' The extension of the series of questions is about the Chat text suddenly assuming a positively assessed machine learning model. The starting statement reads: "Even if the model can produce impressive results on a given task, it is often difficult to decide (…).

The question then is: Who claims that the model 'can produce impressive results'? Who is behind the positive assessment and the normative phrase? And who finds it relevant to clarify whether it is often? (never or always?) difficult to decide whether the model will work well in practice?

The series of questions requires a straightforward answer, but is primarily interesting in showing the scope. If we are in doubt about who or what determines 'how often', we suddenly also become in doubt about the rest of the human/machine actor series and their knowledge of the process. The follow-up question about the model's 'impressive' results is interesting because it shows the scope of both doubt and answer.

KB is not affected by the doubt, small words and phrases work in the situation. KB and Chat are in the machine room and 'everything' that is said and decided in this room is characterized by Techno-logos. The analyst is not in the machine room, but is sitting with the Chat text and has doubts about small words and text, because it also bears signs of realities outside the machine room. Here the question about 'the model's results' comes close to the reality content of both the text and the answer.

The text is broken. 'Often' and 'even though' and normatively evaluative language blocks centered around 'the model's impressive results' cast doubt on Chat's divergent I-positions and disrupt the meaning content of the text. The language suit keeps the I-positions active in the machine room, which are then drowned out by the genre-appropriate lexical and factually professional character. Suddenly, the implicit authoritative voices also come from outside and seem to be borrowing from the knowledge and judgment of human IT expertise. But if this belongs to the reality content of the text, then a position on the normative turn is missing. Who is behind, who confirms the statement "Even if the model can produce impressive results on a given task (…)?" According to the text, there is doubt. It may be the formulation of the IT expertise that resonates. But it may also be Chat, who assumes the model's impressive results, and then hands over the evaluation to human expertise. But that the doubt is real and that it is serious is only clearly seen when we include the sequence around the ethical dimension, which in the true sense requires human expertise, because:

> It is important to ensure that machine learning models do not reinforce existing bias or discrimination and that they are used responsibly and ethically. All of this requires human insight and expertise, even though much of the process is automated and based on statistical calculations. (Chat, Ses. MachineLearn, Human Input)

Above, both the doubt and the appeal are clear. It is unclear who has which interests in linking 'ethics' directly to the issue of bias and discrimination. But it is quite clear that regardless of whether Chat's programming makes it biased, or rather makes it possible to mitigate bias, the demand (or the appeal) is that human insight and judgment take over the responsibility. In this respect, Chat's appeal is similar to that of the Altinget's chatbot:

> If an AI fails or makes a wrong decision, it is still the humans who bear the responsibility. Therefore, it is important to develop an ethical framework for AI. (Chatbot, Altinget)

KB leaves the doubt and the clarity standing, in the very choice of words that has been quoted. KB then drives wearily into another sequence about the complexity of the machine learning process, where Chat revolves around everything that a machine learning model encompasses, namely "techniques such as regression, clustering, classification, neural networks and deep learning, all of which have their own unique strengths and weaknesses". With deep learning in the mix, KB wants to have the facts about it and asks briefly:

> *KB: What is deep learning?*
>
> Deep learning is a branch of machine learning that focuses on building and training neural networks that can learn and improve themselves through experience. Neural networks are a mathematical model inspired by the way the brain works, and consist of a series of artificial neurons that can communicate with each other.
>
> Deep learning uses a so-called "deep" architecture, where neural networks are built with multiple layers, each separately processing and extracting different aspects of input data. Each layer gradually learns more complex features and together they can learn to recognize and classify complex patterns in data.
>
> Deep learning is used today for a wide range of applications, including computer vision, speech recognition, natural language processing, and autonomous driving. It has proven to be particularly effective for tasks involving large amounts of complex and varied data that can be difficult to analyze and classify with traditional algorithms.
>
> *KB Do you often have questions that require deep learning?*
>
> Chat: As an AI model, I can be used to answer a wide range of questions, and some of these questions may require deep learning techniques to be answered effectively. For example, questions about image recognition, language translation, speech synthesis, or automatic transcription may require deep learning techniques to achieve accurate results.
>
> But it is also important to remember that many questions do not necessarily require deep learning techniques, and that other methods may be more effective and appropriate for certain types of questions. So, it depends on the specific situation and the specific question being asked.
>
> KB Thanks for the conversation.
>
> Chat You are welcome! It was a pleasure to help you. If you have any more questions, please feel free to ask. (Chat, Ses. Machine learning)

The conversation in Chat's machine room, for which KB has just thanked for, is the closest I come to a conversational face-to-face attitude. Framed by the Consciousness Session, it is also a conversational process that touches on most of the big questions, from consciousness to learning and from judgment to ethics. As KB asks the big questions, it is made clear, firstly, that Chat is programmed to make normative turns, and secondly, that Chat's responses bear a resemblance to Altinget's chatbot. The appeal is made to 'we/us/the people' who must 'ensure that the machine learning models are used ethically correctly'. But in contrast to Altinget, which gave the big questions an editorial tightening and turned the chatbot into a debater, my research interest and analysis strategy go in other directions. I let Chat's 'own words and turns' and Chat's versions stand on their own merits—even when they are questionable. We are not getting any closer to what Chat's (and the IT expertise behind it?) official self-understanding and presentation of what it can, wants, claims and questions. For the same reason, I give the following rounding a touch of analysis-strategic status.

5.11 Rounding and Analysis-Strategic Status

Letting Altinget, close to the political public and ChatGPT/Chat's machine room, frame the analysis, which is then condensed around Chat in the KB/Chat session process, has served the analysis-strategic purpose. Through Altinget, we gain access to the political self-understanding and placement of AI development on the societal macro level. And by following along in the engine room, KB gains access to Chat's self-understanding and placement of the tasks in the data-generated universe. Altinget's three tasks were about AI/ChatGPT's societal utility and the production-enhancing abilities of AI technology, which Altinget's Chatbot provided examples of. And the fact that Chat confirms similar abilities on its own behalf has been fully demonstrated. In this way, the community of interest matched both the technological production logic and its societal magnitude. If Altinget's chatbot and KB's Chat are followed, AI assistance is located in central places in the healthcare sector, the manufacturing industry and the financial sector, i.e. centrally located everywhere in society. AI assistance is also located in parallel positions machine/human, Technologos. The Brinkmann speech and the question of consciousness certainly set the agenda and were the important start, Human-logos. But in retrospect it can also be considered the cliff-hanger of the debate. It is a recurring event that when artificial intelligence appears in a new variant, a philosophical comment and preferably a decision must be made: how close are we to the human, i.e. the human intelligence and cognitive abilities? The decision was not made this time either; it is and will remain an open question.

The strange thing is that even though the AI/ChatGPT's abilities seem to be far-reaching, even in the eyes of the debaters, no one elaborates on ChatGPT's basic ability, namely that AI generative intelligence is programmed for text and (conversational) speech. A ChatGPT is a text producer and its texts were sent by Altinget into both the smaller and larger communicative circuits. But the ChatGPT's text contributions and its communicative skills in the live circuits did not come into focus. And in the machine room where Chat submitted an otherwise almost all-encompassing list of its own skills, the communicative, speech and text productive skills were not included in the list at all. This means that neither Altinget's debaters nor KB's Chat seem to know or understand the language suit a ChatGPT is dressed in. It is otherwise the lifeline, I have stressed.

With this observation, the central questions have become serious again, but in a different way than in the debate itself. For if ChatGPT/Chat neither knows nor understands its basic ability for conversation and text, then the question of self-consciousness is cancelled by Chat itself. On the other hand, in the midst of a Techno-logos universe, we are left with Chat's own definition of what it 'is' and 'can', namely the pragmatically toned-down: "I am simply a computer programming designed to process information and generate answers based on the information I have access to."

In that case, KB got the core proposition of programmed self-understanding. But I also got the paradox that the analysis strategy drags with it all the way to the final chapter. Neither the field researcher nor the analyst can remove Chat's programmed "I am…". This means that the terms used so far, such as ChatGPT/KB's Chat being a categorical fallacy that can be described as 'a speaking and writing non-conscious self', are retained. From now on, they, together with e.g. Chat's Machine-I, are considered descriptively comprehensive, also in an empirical documentary sense. But at the same time, I draw strategic analysis consequences from the paradox, which I elaborate on below.

5.12 Consequences

When the close analyses serve the purpose precisely by starting in the public forums of Altinget and then following into Chat's machine room, this is justified in relation to the analysis in the first step. The identification of the self-understanding that surrounds AI/ChatGPT starts similarly by seeking out the current political discourse in the live debate. The important empirical findings are illustrated in the chapter with rich quotes and details, which later provide reason for return.

The KB conversation processes in Chat's machine room have documentary value in themselves. But at the same time, the examples for the overall analysis function as a contrast that could not be greater. Namely, the contrast between the live debate, which initially considers human consciousness to be a priori, and KB's conversation process with a ChatGPT, which in the machine room articulates the AI abilities as a computer-logical a priori. In the machine room, KB encounters a very ego-strong Chat. And even though I, as an analyst, try to remove the 'I' from the Chat text, it does not work. Chat's speaking position is confirmed in the machine room, as an authoritative voice that resembles that of IT expertise. Chat's words, language blocks and the overall meaning of the text not only resemble that of IT expertise, but are worded identically. The empirical verification comes with a simple Google search, e.g. 'Machine learning', as recognizable language blocks in texts from research environments and consulting firms, for example. The self-understanding is thus identified and confirmed in a Techno-logos universe, but also confronted with the debate's human-anchored questions about consciousness, cognitive abilities, experience, learning. I have quoted and taken stock along the way, not least because the session in the machine room is the empirical document that best covers Chats self-understanding. Through this, Chats Machine-I is illustrated in its own right, momentarily free from the paradox. But precisely for this reason there are also empirical-analytical reasons to take stock in relation to which sides the paradox and its heavy questions can be abandoned.

As has been shown, the question of consciousness was on the way to being cancelled. But, as emphasized, the strong Machine-I that the language suit and the underlying authoritative voices give Chat cannot be removed. It is also clear that the Machine-I in Chat's perspective both 'understands live conversations', 'learns from experiences' and seems to be aware of when 'human expertise' is needed. This means that Chat keeps the connection between consciousness and understanding/experiencing/learning intact. The conclusion must therefore be that the questions about Chat's humanized capacity that follow consciousness must be discussed as problematic as they arise. With one important exception, namely the question of learning.

The question of learning should not be attempted to be cancelled. But it should be removed from Chat and put back into the human learning processes where they belong. This is based both on Chat's own statements and my observations. As a researcher, I initially consider it problematic that IT experts and AI researchers use a learning terminology without any significant justification. But as has been shown in the sessions of the chapter, it is a terminology that Chat seems familiar with and reproduces. On the other hand, Chat demonstrates in the same sessions why and how the learning terminology can be abandoned. When KB asks whether the use of the word 'learning' is covered by Chat's description of machine learning, Chat answers, but not to KB's question. Instead, Chat's answer shows the interesting shift, where the word machine learning first becomes machine learning techniques and then a method for training. When KB then asks about the word 'training', Chat answers that it is a metaphor.

Asking about the range of learning, experience and training concepts and receiving the answer 'that the training terminology is a metaphor' makes it clear that Chat is unable to assign meaning to the concepts. The word blocks are intact, but change. In a literal sense, it is irrelevant whether it is described as learning (deep learning) experience or training. In that case, it is also meaningless to try to nuance the analysis. Incidentally, Chat is also on a collision course with the underlying IT expertise, where it is the learning terminology that is recognized metaphorically. The training concept is rather descriptively acceptable. But if the training concept is also to be transferred to the range of metaphors, there is only metaphorical language use about machine learning, which is itself a metaphor.

The fact that there are no real signs left that Chat should be part of a learning process is also confirmed by the fact that I have no examples in my collection that could testify that Chat during the sessions can be said to learn, or learn from what is happening. This minimizes the relevance of having the learning question linked to ChatGPT. And even if the question of, for example, ChatGPT/Chat's claimed cognitive abilities and ways of approaching learning could be tested conceptually, for example, via Jean Piaget's theories (Piaget, 1969), this does not lead to anything clarifying in an empirical sense. Linking Piaget's theoretical-analytical concept set of assimilative/accommodative processes to a chatbot's machine learning simply leads to yet another metaphor. The way in which the learning question casts doubt and demands empirical validity means that rather than taking Chat's claimed abilities as a starting point, we must remove the metaphors and return to the core proposition: "I am simply a computer programming designed to process information and generate answers based on the information I have access to."

The core proposition refers to the machine learning sections where the reshuffling of the human/machine relationship clarifies the reification of human expertise and the humanization of Chats. With this as a data logical a priori, Chat in the machine room can suddenly act as a machine learning model, describe and talk 'about' machine learning and the model, and justify the machine learning model 'as' a model. But if Chat can both be a machine model, describe itself, justify, and evaluate itself 'as a model', it is not due to strong machine learning, but rather to a strong language suit and a correspondingly strongly structured text corpus.

For the analyses in the future, this means a sharper focus on Chat's handling of the language and the text it generates itself. But before then, it is of analytical strategic importance to leave Chat's machine room and go out into the public forums to investigate how the representatives of AI technology themselves put ChatGPT's abilities up for debate.

Reference

Piaget, J. (1969). *Psychologie et Pedagogogie*. Société Nouvelles des Éditions.

Chapter 6
In the Educational Policy Public: AI/ ChatGPT—Between Fear and Excitement

This chapter maintains the analysis's relationship to the public and political debate, but now based on the education sector's own debate forums. In terms of analysis strategy, this means focusing on the debate's common main themes, authoritative voices and strong arguments. By referring to the ethnographic need of 'following the case', the most important principle is to join the academic public and follow the debate as it takes place. And as can be seen, the debate in spring 2023 is a vivid expression of the current enthusiasm, where IT expertise characterizes ChatGPT as 'a technological quantum leap' and questions the education system's conventional knowledge reproduction. Editors-in-chief, trade unions and university management seem to share the enthusiasm, but also the concern about the consequences for the academic workforce and ChatGPT's ability to pass exams that require innovations at all levels. ChatGPT in particular requires institutional action, where the fear of exam cheating means 'ban', although far-sighted regulation of AI technologies would be preferable. The interesting thing about the debate's movements between embracing, banning, or simply regulating the new AI phenomena is that they rhetorically reflect the educational policy positions in motion. As will be seen, the debaters are on their way to embracing AI technologies as the exciting opportunity, but are reflecting on the periodic ban. But at the same time, it is also apparent how the strong trade unions and the *Akademikerbladet* ("Dansk Magisterforening") and *Folkeskolen* ("Danmarks Lærerforening"), and *UniAvisen* with reference to the universities are under cross-pressure. The institutions must focus on the new academic key competences. But they must also ensure that the next generation of humanists, teachers and engineers acquire the basic academic professional competences. The cross-pressure is felt. But it does not change the fact that the authoritative first voice of the debate in this chapter is that of IT expertise and that the professionals seem to be trapped by an agenda and cross-pressure set by AI's technological rationale.

K. Borgnakke, *AI and ChatGPT Technology in Education*, Education, Equity, Economy 12, https://doi.org/10.1007/978-3-032-01419-1_6

6.1 From Prohibition to Embracement and Regulation

When following the debate around ChatGPTs, it is noticeable how the main themes and problems from launch move between fear and excitement. But the debate also moves *from* banning ChatGPT *to* embracing the new AI technologies and their development potential. It can thus be heard how educational organizations, professional managers and teachers must assert the position from the start: The new ChatGPT risks being used for exam cheating. It must be banned. But during the spring the debate is moving, among other things initiated by spokespersons who are closer to the education and trade union political organizations. For example, the spokesperson for the Student Council (University of Copenhagen) emphasizes that ChatGPT "should not be banned, but embraced" (UniAvisen, Febr. 2023). And in June 2023, the spokesperson for the Danish Association of Masters makes the status quo and states in a leadership position that "Artificial intelligence must be regulated" (Akademikerbladet, 02/23:3).

The movement alone from 'to ban' to 'embrace' and then to 'regulate' is marking the important point, rhetorically and political. The debaters refer to a professional responsibility and to a mandate where appeals for continued prohibition, or rather regulation, are addressed to the institutions and their leaders. But there are doubts about the appeal to 'embrace'. For whom is this almost loving-caring appeal to embrace a piece of technology and a chatbot really aimed at? According to the debate, that particular appeal is addressed to 'us all' and to the entire school and education public. The remarkable choice of words later becomes the necessity of the embrace and followed up by the appeal "Put AI on the schedule - also for the teachers". This appeal was in the leader and served as an introduction to the themed issue on artificial intelligence in *Folkeskolen*. At the same time, a finding and a claim were made as follows:

> Artificial intelligence will change the school. Therefore, the teachers must have both influence and further training, so that we can succeed with the new technology. (Leader, Folkeskolen 11, June 2023).

As it appears, half a year after ChatGPT's launch, prohibition is now toned down, embracing it has become a professional matter and regulation a management responsibility to ensure 'that we succeed'.

The triad that ban/embrace/regulate represents had three different messages in it. Should the main message of the debate in retrospect be characterized by only one thing, 'regulation' is comprehensive. The main trend is thus that institutions and the education sector as a whole are trying to approach the acceptance of AI/ChatGPT's relevance, followed by demands to regulate its use. But analytically, the main tendency is not the most important characteristic. Rather, it is the triad. Indeed, when one enters the debate and observes positions and arguments, one observes how respectively prohibitions, embraces and regulations exist as each other's living contradictions and prerequisites. There are statements from managers who would rather embrace the new technologies but feel compelled to forbid them. There are teachers who claim the right to embrace and experiment with AI, point out that it is the manager's responsibility to 'regulate' and miss a manageable set of rules. At the same time, there is an IT expertise that embraces AI technology by praising its computing power and level of performance and, on that basis, demands changes to the institutions and examination systems. The movement of the debate between prohibition, embracement and regulation thus requires both adaptation and change. At the same time, it requires the management to be equipped with knowledge, as emphasized in the *UniAvisen* by the deputy director for education and students at the University of Copenhagen, Rie Snekkerup:

> There are many of us who think that it is a wildly exciting technology, and therefore it was also a shame that we had to ban it. But we still lack knowledge. It can be compared to the big change it was when the internet came. Maybe this is even bigger. (Snekkerup, UniAvisen, February 2023).

When it is said in a leadership position that AI/chatbots are a 'wildly exciting technology', that bans are given with regret and that the changing forces are probably greater than the internet, you can sense both the order of magnitude and the enthusiasm. According to Snekkerup, chatbots will also be important for both teaching and exams, just as at the University of Copenhagen 'the learning goals will be looked at and whether they need to be adjusted based on the new technologies.' However, all that is missing, as the UniAvisen sums it up:

> (…) to be equipped with knowledge from experts, so that the study board and faculty environment know what to pay attention and how AI can be used within which subjects (UniAvisen, February 2023).

The finding that there may be learning goals that need to be adjusted and that it is about being equipped with knowledge from experts is interesting in several ways. A management responsibility is becoming present, but which background science and experts will equip the professional environments is not specified. This, in turn, is specified by the ongoing debate, not least by letting the authoritative voices be heard and quoted, as elaborated below.

6.2 The Authoritative Voices of the Debate

In the public debates, the link between involved parties, areas of knowledge/subjects and learning contexts is thematized. And with the desire for expert knowledge expressed in a university context, the answer to which parties and areas of expertise should be involved should be straightforward. It also does so at the University of Copenhagen, which during the spring of 2023 will conduct seminars on AI/ChatGPT at the individual faculties, as well as meetings across faculties. Both researchers, teachers and, for example, university educational centers are represented. The question is therefore not about the relevant parties are represented, but what they represent and how they, with my term, function as the authoritative voices of the debate.

Regardless of whether the debate is conducted in the university newspaper, at seminars or meetings, it quickly becomes clear that in terms of knowledge, researchers in artificial intelligence, computer science, or more broadly IT expertise, act as the authoritative first voice. IT expertise is therefore amply represented, as keynote speakers, panelists, seminar leaders, etc. The authoritative first voice is heard and sets the scientific agenda. The problem, however, is that the research background of IT expertise probably covers the development of AI technologies, but does not cover research into the practical function and application of AI/ChatGPT in education and learning. Research-based knowledge about the main theme of the debate, ChatGPT's function in academic education and learning, is thus absent. This means that the academic public, by letting the sharing of knowledge start with the IT expertise, must see itself confronted with the dilemma: the technological knowledge is a background, but not an answer to faculties or study boards about how AI's application spectrum can be described and handled. The dilemma raises doubts, not only about the handling of AI, but also about the university's own concepts of knowledge, experience and learning.

The authoritative first voice, the IT expertise, bases the development of AI/chatbot on language models and uses terms such as machine learning and deep learning, but recognizes that this is metaphorical language. However, the authoritative second voices, which faculty teams, study boards and teachers must be described as, cannot allow themselves to describe their subject areas and the relationship to academic learning in metaphorical terms. Professionals and study boards must describe a subject area substantively and in scientific terms. They must deal with the subject's learning issues and authentic levels of difficulty, not AI-technologies. Against this background, the practical nature and consequences of the dilemma become clear. Correspondingly, the university's wobbly course and uncertain handling become clear. It is reminiscent of Altinget's debate and uncertain treatment of the degree of difficulty of the issue of consciousness (see Chap. 4). But unlike Altinget's debaters, those involved in the university debate cannot be content with sharing knowledge and exchanging views. They must act and draw actionable consequences as university leaders, researchers, teachers, students… etc.

This means that Rie Snekkerup's previously quoted wish to regulate and adjust according to expert knowledge 'on the basis of the new technologies' must be problematized.

Problematizing requires that the authoritative first voice, and thus the strong arguments and innovative measures of IT expertise, be concretized. Let me therefore take the concrete examples from expert statements that embrace AI technology by praising its computing power and ability to reproduce knowledge, and let this be an argument for demanding changes to institutions and exam systems.

Statements and consequences are reconstructed below, so that we notice both the expertise behind them and the university context around them.

6.3 The Strong Arguments of IT Expertise and the Ability to Reproduce Knowledge

Anders Søgaard, professor of computer science and philosophy, presented the argumentation we are to follow, over several contributions and interviews, first in the newspaper Berlingske then in UniAvisen and Akademikerbladet. As a representative of the expertise, Søgaard embraces AI technology already in the first presentation by characterizing it with the following choice of words:

> A new chat robot, ChatGPT, which Californian OpenAI has launched, is a technological quantum leap in artificial intelligence (...)
>
> (...) This model has shocked by being so good at talking coherently about so many subjects and having a wide range of functionalities, which these models have not previously had. (Berlingske, Søgaard, Interview 5/122022).

With the quoted characterization of ChatGPT as a 'quantum leap' that is 'good at talking coherently', Søgaard sets out to consider ChatGPT's functionalities. Søgaard does not fail to mention limitations or the need to reflect on ethical issues. But the main and starting point is ChatGPT's functionality and quality. As Søgaard is quoted:

> Now we're talking about models that have a quality where they can't just provide information about how the traffic is between Copenhagen and Roskilde and which films are playing in the cinema. (...)
>
> I have colleagues who have presented this model for exam tasks in many different fields such as social science, law and computer science. (...)
>
> On average, it solves those tasks as well as a really good student. (ibid).

The point of the three quoted statements is that in the debate they both function as ascertaining, evaluating and documenting. ChatGPT is given a seal of quality. ChatGPT can do other things and more than pass on information, it has documented competences in solving exam tasks and is assessed to solve them 'just as well as a really good student'. The three statements together constitute the strong arguments which justify the necessity of the change and draw the consequence.

In Søgaard's contribution in Berlingske, the consequence is mentioned in relation to exams and examinations, which:

> (...) low-practical challenges such as how do we examine our students when they can sit and have access to a tool that can do really good university assignments. (ibid.)

In later posts, the consequence is scaled up to include the entire education system, as Søgaard argues about AI/ChatGPT in the UniAvisen:

> These technologies call into question 98 percent of what we do in the education system, because we have built a lot around the students' ability to reproduce knowledge at different levels, but for that most are below the level that artificial intelligence can perform. (Søgaard, UniAvisen, Febr.23)

In what has been quoted, Søgaard expresses himself as a debater of expertise. But as an active researcher in AI technology development, Søgaard also represents references to the contributions of research environments. Against this background, the statement that artificial intelligence can already reproduce knowledge at the same level as the students is a strong argument. It is put forward by a researcher and embedded in a critique of the education system's excessive emphasis on the reproduction of knowledge. What thus started with critical references and 'low-practical challenges' for examining students has now been scaled up to system criticism. The strong argument thus affects the education system as a whole. But at the same time, Søgaard gets to claim 'something' about the education system and the students' abilities and level, and uses a knowledge terminology that weakens the argument.

It is acceptable in public debate to gain power by saying '98% of what we do in the education system'. It is also acceptable to make quick links between students and ChatGPT's performance. But when it comes to comparisons between the students', and then the AI's, 'ability to reproduce knowledge', 'at a higher/lower level', one doubts whether there is expertise behind it. One is therefore forced to clarify the implied concept of knowledge and the precision of the associated terms in two stages, first the concept of knowledge and then the question of precision.

6.4 The Implied Concept of Knowledge

Clarification of the concept of knowledge means remembering that earlier communication and informatics research was actually concerned with specifying, but also distinguishing between information and knowledge (MedieKultur, 2000; Hjarvard, 2008). When research was linked to educational and learning issues, this distinction was reinforced and further problematized. In a pedagogical-psychological sense, a distinction is made between information that must be given/received and knowledge that must be acquired, understood and processed. In a didactic sense, the difference is also embedded in the purpose to give the students basic knowledge and Bildung, as ballast to navigate the Information and Communication Society (Tufte 1995, 1998).

In the mentioned research contexts (see also Chap. 3), there is hardly any doubt that the concept of knowledge is the heavy concept and carries the important links to science, subjects, teaching and learning processes. An acknowledgment of the weight of the concept of knowledge and a distinction between information and knowledge evoke nuances in the current debate about AI. Further differentiation between data, information and knowledge is also required. But at the same time, this research-based way of distinguishing seems to be forgotten today.

When AI sets the agenda, a concept of knowledge works instead, which on the one hand must be understood broadly with reference to the entire spectrum from the knowledge society, over knowledge sharing to characteristics of the knowledge-heavy companies. On the other hand, the term must be understood as closely related to AI, data-generated knowledge, which can then be focused on as the reproduction of knowledge. Navigating between the broad and the narrow concept of knowledge is not easy, but necessary. It means, that the arguments of IT expertise can be placed in the context and that the above quoted, Søgaard's strong argument can be given a more precise direction, as the following: The education system's characteristic but criticizable 'reproduction of knowledge' is confronted with AI/chatbots' high performance level as an opportunity—and the students' lower level is perceived as a challenge. But if this is a specification of the direction, is there such coverage for the description of AI's abilities, and then the comparison with those of the students?

Now one can, quite legitimately, insist that the debate's strong argument by Søgaard was intended as a critical point in education policy and not an empirical finding. Furthermore, the tone of the debate is also characterized by pro and con arguments and jovial language. For example, a professor colleague, Stephen Alstrup, puts an end to the praise of AI/ChatGPT's performance capabilities, by reminding that it does not solve all university tasks. "So, it is not smarter either", as Alstrup commented (UniAvisen 2/2023). Likewise, an article in WeekendAvisen, in an interview with professor Thore Husfeldt, emphasizes the risk that ChatGPT answers are characterized by superficial Bullshit Bingo, which in return is time-consuming to assess. In this connection, Husfeldt mentions Brandolini's law of the asymmetry of bullshit, which reads as follows: "It takes significantly more energy to refute bullshit than to produce it". (Husfeldt, Weekendavisen 4.4.2023).

But regardless of whether the IT expertise, as just quoted, not only praises, but also problematizes the achievements of AI technologies, it does not change the fundamental problem. At the moment AI adds human abilities and, as above by Søgaard, is potentiated through a comparison with students, a basic categorical fallacy is committed. It cannot be corrected and as researchers and professionals we have to live with it, as already emphasized in the previous chapters. But the consequences can be considered, i.e. as a loss of precision and a lost rationale.

6.5 The Loss of Precision

The loss of precision is about the IT expertise leaving both the concept of knowledge and the comparison between the students' and AI's abilities imprecise and empty of content. Neither the expertise nor the debaters distinguish between creating knowledge, acquiring knowledge and reproducing knowledge. Furthermore, it is not specified which knowledge, type of knowledge, or professional/factual content is to be reproduced. It is also not indicated what the ability to reproduce knowledge consists of and what spectrum of abilities/skills it must be associated with. Is it the ability to remember/represent/systematize within a limited area of knowledge, or the ability to 1–1 reproduction maintained as facts, or?

The fact that we cannot see the type of knowledge, content, or which reproductive processes are referred to, weakens both the strong argumentation and the rationale behind it. In order to increase precision, the rationale must be rediscovered, e.g. as follows:

Reproduction of knowledge must require that someone, e.g. Søgaard, knows what knowledge respectively students and an AI have been asked to reproduce. If this is not the case, comparisons and statements about higher/lower levels of knowledge reproduction make no sense. The point is therefore that, even if IT expertise can be satisfied with the broad and indefinite concept of knowledge, the question of what knowledge is referred to cannot be left unanswered. In the practical contexts of education, in subject and study environments, the knowledge question *must* be answered and the content determined. And only then would talking about knowledge reproduction and levels make sense.

In the previous chapters, in conversations with Chat, I have often touched on the question of knowledge. This means that the question 'what knowledge?' can be exemplified, e.g. as Chat's knowledge of case conditions/reform content (Danish school reform), a current theme (gender role patterns) or world-renowned philosophers, works, authors (Habermas, Freud, H. C. Andersen). More examples will be added in the next chapters. But about all of them, and the level of knowledge, at no point do I get the feeling that Chat can reproduce knowledge at a high level. On the contrary. My sense of superficial Bullshit Bingo was present from the start, as described in Chap. 2. Furthermore, Chat's knowledge dissemination was characterized by a tendency to generalize and attempts at concretization were rewarded pseudo-concrete. In both cases, the knowledge content deteriorates.

This means that Chat as a knowledge transmitter, in my collection, is generally assessed as poor. When it is at its best, for example when it answers questions about how it is programmed, it is informative and descriptive (see Chap. 5). Against this background, in my view, it is questionable to use knowledge terms to describe the chatbot's abilities to convey and/or reproduce knowledge. But at the same time, the question must be kept open analytically. Technical knowledge of/knowledge of technology… must be able to be referred to in terms of knowledge. Likewise, large computing power can be described as an ability and data processing as an achievement. Earlier, in Chap. 4, this was exemplified by Altinget's chatbot, where AI's function in the health or financial sector was highlighted as helping to analyze large amounts of data, finding patterns and correlations. AI as an aid in the so-called knowledge work is thus already a recognized part of the debate.

In the present analysis, therefore, both, what I consider to be, the questionable uses of the concept of knowledge and the acceptable technical ones are observed. This means that, for example, Søgaard's argument that AI can 'reproduce knowledge at different levels' and 'perform at the same level as students' must be recognized as a valid argument, discussion worthy. However, a more precise characterization is required, linked to the term technically limited rationality. The artificial intelligence achievements Søgaard refers to must be considered limited to data-generated knowledge. But recognition of data-generated knowledge 'as knowledge' does not change the fact that Søgaard's descriptions are still confronted with questions about the choice of terms and its coverage.

If I confront Søgaard's choice of terms with my Chat conversations and analyses, I reinstate, for example, a distinction between information and knowledge. I draw the contours of a chatbot that even emphasizes this distinction itself, because as Chat puts it:

> I function as a tool that can deliver information, answer questions and help users gain access to knowledge (…) my role as a chatbot is to assist the user and facilitate the exchange of information." (Chat, Ses. Learning processes)

It has already been emphasized that KB/Chat responses are rarely conceptually consistent. But the description of ChatGPT as a tool that can provide information and help users belongs after all to the descriptive repeats. It is therefore surprising that the IT expertise has forgotten the information terminology, and allows it to be superimposed by the knowledge and learning terminology. It is also surprising that the factually sober description is replaced by the imprecise metaphorical language. The consequence seems to be that AI's abilities to learn and reproduce knowledge are overexposed and, as in Søgaard's argument, become dubious comparisons and appeals to the education system.

But regardless, the debate shows that the AI/student comparison still has political impact. Therefore, the comparison and its basis must still be questioned critically. Søgaard's system description and the statement 'that 98% of what we do in the education system is built around the reproduction of knowledge' resonates in IT expertise. The question is whether it also resonates in educational research. If not, the question is how educational research's own rationales can clarify the inclusion of AI/ chatbots in the knowledge-creating /reproducing circuits.

6.6 Educational Research's Own Rationales

If the lines of tradition are to be drawn up, pedagogical/didactic criticism of knowledge reproductive tendencies is a vital part of the rationale in reform pedagogy, as it is known back from John Dewey from the beginning of the twentieth century. Since the 1970s, the development of project pedagogy has also specified the criticism of, for example, 'traditional teacher-led teaching', 'emphasis on ready knowledge' etc. In that case, it is a criticism which, inspired by, for example, Knud Illeris (1981), Wolfgang Klafki (2002) or Gert Biesta (2006), is aimed at both the traditional educational settings and the modern school and educational organizations. But beyond that, IT expertise's ready-made arguments regarded as system criticism are an oversimplification that does not resonate in the basic categories and rationales of educational research. If you really want to express in serious terms what schools and the education *system* do, and must do 98%–100% of the time, the rationale is in educational sociology and (inspired by e.g. Pierre Bourdieu, 1970, 1994, and Basil Bernstein, 1975) linked to the system's three basic functions: to socialize, to select and to qualify. The content dimension is considered above the education system's own triad, for example as Knowledge, Subjects and Learning. With this triad, it is signaled that the three aspects are simultaneously present in the teaching complex. The simultaneity emphasizes that 'what we do in the education system' always has both socializing, selecting and qualifying effects. Simultaneity is therefore the essential feature, also for the question of how knowledge/reproduction of knowledge can be considered with reference to now a knowledge sociology rationale (Kuhn, 1970; Borgnakke, 2011).

In a knowledge sociology perspective, simultaneity confirms that knowledge (creation/reproduction) does not exist in pure form, but is procedurally embedded and exists in the education, teaching and learning process. Knowledge materialized or reproduced in books and texts can also be both identified and retained. But in that case, the large and small circuits of the book or text are framed by series of Sender-Text-Receiver relationships.[1] And in that case, the important basic models can be used both for overview and concretization, for example of the 'text link', as an identifiable textbook, or original work, or research article. The point is that here knowledge, even general knowledge, is identified in genre-specific (e.g. a lexicon) and author-specified text. The point is also, when the circuit's actor/text/action spectrum is concretized, that original works can be read and understood, research articles can be disseminated in knowledge-reproductive reports, and re-re-producing student assignments can be assessed. The knowledge- and now also text-sociological rationale is that the cycle, actor and text series can be identified. But in none of these cases will knowledge in pure form be identifiable. The logical conclusion, of importance in the present context, is that in that case knowledge reproduction cannot be identified in its pure form either. It also belongs to the consequent conclusion that in that case knowledge can only be identified when it appears as 'knowledge about something specific'.

The consequence is made clear when the exemplification, as below, places respectively AI/ ChatGPT and the students in the knowledge-generating/reproducing circuits. If we follow the direction of the debate from the IT experts, Søgaard and KB/Chat, then ChatGPT is the new actor in the circuit.

6.7 AI/ChatGPT the New Actor in the Circuit

If knowledge works in the circuit it is identified as 'something specific'. Thus, knowledge is already marked by the academic subject and already determined by the long line of knowledge senders/authors/distributors. Perhaps the teacher is the second last in the circuit. The last person in the circuit for the time being is the student. Next, for the sake of the important example, let's let the penultimate knowledge transmitter (or reproducer) not be the teacher, but an AI/ChatGPT. In that case, another actor has been added, namely an actor who, in Søgaard's words, can 'reproduce knowledge at a higher level than students' and in KB/Chat's words "can help users gain access to knowledge" and "facilitate the exchange of information".

The interesting thing, however, is not just that a new actor has arrived, but that something new seems to be happening—and incomparable to the large/small living circuits. As I have exemplified in previous chapters, Chat transforms KB's question and makes it its own. Chat then produces a data-generated text. These are

---

[1] This corresponds to what Darnton (1982) and Van der Weel (2001), describes as the general pattern called "the communications circuit" or what is maintained as the communicative circuits over sender-text-receiver circuits referring to supervisors and students' exchange of texts in the project-organized study environments, see Borgnakke (1996, pp. 32–35).

data-on-data-on-data series, authorless chunks of knowledge (if the concept of knowledge is in use), composed into a knowledge-transmitting text, untouched by human hands.

The language suit is trained, we know, the language models and statistical calculation are initially created/supervised by the IT expertise. But the Chat text itself, which in the present situation with Søgaard must be seen as knowledge-reproducing at a potentially high level, is new data-generated text that actually needs to continue in the knowledge-reproducing circuits. However, the ChatGPT generated new text doesn't go any further. The Chat reply has closed the circuit. ChatGPT is responsible as the sender, but has no authority in matters of knowledge and disclaims responsibility. This means that the responsibility for the soundness and knowledge content of the reproduction at the time of the act is transferred to the students, or simply to the person who entered ChatGPT. And regardless of whether KB/or a student is equipped for the responsibility, the point is that Chats/ ChatGPT's knowledge reproduction must be recognized to circulate in the circuit.

A Chatbot has passed exams, this is regularly exemplified in the debate. Søgaard is therefore not alone in referring to a recognized level assessment of AI/chatbots. But even if it has been fed with a multiple-choice task, a compendium or a text, the reproduction still refers to the data-generated version and competence. It is possible that the data-text reproduction can be approved. But there are still doubts as to whether it is knowledge reproduction in the true sense.

In my KB/Chat conversation sessions, the knowledge aspects refer primarily to the humanities and the soft parts of the social sciences. But as part of the analysis, I also followed along into the ChatGPT machine room, where AI and IT research's own phenomena and concepts form the basis. It does not change, however, that the Chat responses as text and ChatGPT as a CA, Conversational Agent, become part of the communicative circuits. Chat uses human language and the answers move into the humanistic areas of knowledge. But it is also in that area that the Chat text promises too much and is therefore broken by denials and disclaimers. This also applies to the previously quoted session, where Chat began in sober terms with the self-understanding of being a tool that helps 'users to access knowledge' (see Chap. 5), then optimizes its help, and finally renounces own abilities and responsibilities. Quoted as follows:

> (…) I can present information in a structured way and help users understand complex concepts. I can also provide suggestions for further reading or material that can help the user deepen their understanding of a topic.
>
> However, it is important to remember that my role as a chatbot is to assist the user and facilitate the exchange of information. Although I can be a ressource in learning processes, it is still up to the individual user to be engaged, motivate and make decisions about how they best learn and use the information provided. (Chat, Ses. Learning processes)

Chat's sober description is about 'presenting information in a structured way' and 'helping users with… '. But then it is added that Chat can help 'understand complex concepts.' In relation to my material collection, there is nothing to suggest that Chat is capable of understanding or handling conceptual complexity, on the contrary. The subsequent help, as a suggestion for further reading, sounds more reliable, although I do not have convincing examples in my material.

The genre-typical mitigation ‘However, it is important to remember…’ is at the moment of the act the transfer of responsibility, here to the user, who is then given the ability to be engaged, motivated and make decisions about how best to learn and use information. The user is thus given exactly the human abilities that AI technologies cannot be given. The point is thus that Chat’s sober descriptions of ChatGPT lead us away from knowledge concepts and towards information designations; away from a function as a knowledge transmitter and towards support functions. The point is also in the quote above that the user has the human abilities (not Chat).

The finding at this point in the analysis must therefore be that KB/Chat (ChatGPT 3.5) can neither bear Søgaard’s description of artificial intelligence, which carries out knowledge reproduction at a high level, nor bear entering into comparisons with students about ‘abilities.’ The finding is also that rather than describing ChatGPT’s contribution in the circuit as knowledge reproduction, it should rather be described as data-driven information.

Against this background, it is important for the analysis that a shift in interest can be made from the debate and IT expertise’s praising AI’s computing power and knowledge-producing abilities to the AI chatbot’s skills and abilities as a support tool. Analytically, this is followed by a shift from the rationale of IT expertise to the predominantly sociological rationale of educational research.

The shift in interest, which follows below, is marked in the university debate. In leadership positions and among IT experts, the position is felt that AI/ChatGPT must be regulated, but also embraced by us as academics and students becoming professional and creative users. Here, optimization of the key academic competencies becomes a cardinal point, as exemplified by following the debate in Akademikerbladet and its background in the Danish Association of Masters, DM. Below we therefore enter the academic public, where the argument has both university and trade union references.

6.8 “Your work will never be the same again”: Offensive Optimization of the Academic Key Competencies

Akademikerbladet clarifies with thematic treatment of artificial intelligence in June 2023, the movement of the debate between academic fear and enthusiasm. The fear is emphasized as the risk of AI as a digital workforce taking over and replacing the academic job functions. It is thus felt in the theme treatment leader and articles that the debate is not only about AI- and a ChatGPT in development, but about how the academic key competences and job functions must be considered currently and in a future light. The cover frames the message with the headline “Your work will never be the same again” followed by the subtitle: “Artificial intelligence has changed

Mushtaq Bilal's working life. His mission is to do the same for you." (Akademikerbladet 2/23).

The cover image is a portrait of Bilal. As readers, we are thus introduced to both mission and missionary from the outset.

With the fear emphasized as risks, Akademikerbladet editorially emphasizes AI as an Artificial Intelligence that needs to be regulated, but also as a tool that serves academic purposes if you go about it aggressively. The offensive is the keynote in the large article about ChatGPT, where the mission is followed through an interview with Mushtaq Bilal and the argumentation is followed through the involvement of IT experts and professors. The argumentative part is also framed by Søgaard's powerful statement, the one quoted earlier: 'These technologies call into question 98%…'. The editorial setup thus keeps Søgaard's strong argument alive. Partly by bringing the quote in full. Partly by making the argument their own and letting the entire article be framed by it, as an established fact: "Students are trained to reproduce knowledge, but programs like ChatGPT can do it just as well or better. So, what now?" (Akademikerbladet 2/23).

Akademikerbladet's proposal for offensive action is exemplified through Mushtaq Bilal. Bilal is an H. C. Andersen researcher, but also active on Twitter (with 180,000 followers) and uses various AIs, for example Jenni.ai, a ChatGPT-based writing assistant. Bilal is described as a researcher on a mission to 'simplify the academic writing process'. Bilal elaborates on the argument:

> Like any other academic, I think language is incredibly important. But I don't think it should be a requirement to learn to write academically. At least not for students who might dream of establishing a startup. (Akademikerbladet, 02/2023:40)

Bilal's approach is described as offensive, radical, but also pragmatically tailored to the given conditions. Bilal shares advice and tips and is quoted for having written in a tweet about "good and bad" ways to use ChatGPT:

> Among the bad ones is using ChatGPT to generate content. The good ones include having the bot prepare an overall structure and framework for an article including chapter headings and sub-headings. (Akademikerbladet, 02/2023:42).

For the present analysis, the quoted statements are charitably concrete exemplifying and come from an academic who speaks close to research and academic learning. But at the same time, Bilal's descriptions are also marked by the characteristic loss of precision. We understand the above bad/ good description and Bilal's message, namely that ChatGPT is bad at generate content, good at creating structure. But as a statement made in an academic context, it is imprecise and misleading. There is no ChatGPT conversation, text or task that is structure without content. So even if a chatbot delivers 'something' that Bilal considers good structure, this 'something' is not empty of content. And by the way, who can benefit academically from a text that has good structure but poor content?

To navigate so imprecisely with an academic characterization of, for example, a text's (or assignment's) coexisting structure/content dimensions is inappropriate for both text, genre and the understanding of the assignment. But somehow the lack of precision is connected to Bilal's mission and attitude. The mission is to give students help with the writing process. Bilal's position, as quoted, is that it should not be a requirement to learn to write academically. In that case, Bilal's statement is clear. But that university students should not *learn to* write academically is, in the context, a controversial point of view. Academic competences linked to the fact that students, as researchers in spe, must learn to master oral and written communication at a scientific level, belong to the university's key competences. Akademikerbladet probably has no interest in undermining that—regardless of subject or professional orientation. And yet, if one is to understand Bilal's argument, the following sentence specified a motive. Writing academically was not necessary for students who might dream of establishing a startup.

Whether we should see students from the creative subjects, film and media studies, or from computer science combined with language technology is conceivable, but not decisive for the argument. The decisive thing is that Bilal gets the argument positioned in a future-oriented and innovative way. With the dream of establishing a startup, Bilal skips the university's version of academic learning and already has the innovative tech industry as a guide for what is important to learn and what is not. With this forward-looking guide, Bilal's attitude and mission are better understood. In return, we/the university get a problem focusing when the students' writing and technical skills have to be argued through as important or the opposite.

6.9 Do the Universities Focus on the Important, the Right or the Wrong?

The argumentative part of Akademikerbladet's article includes IT expertise, bears the heading 'a wrong focus' and is framed by the heavily highlighted Søgaard quote. The wrong focus is therefore equal to excessive focus on the students' 'ability to reproduce knowledge'. In this circle about the wrong, Søren Hauberg, professor of machine learning, Technical University of Denmark, DTU, is quoted as follows:

> The brutaly honest answer is that part of our evaluation methods is based on whether you are good at formulating yourself. We look at whether the students write well. Not only if they have technical skills, which in many ways is really sad. (…)
>
> When our evaluation system now faces a problem, it may be because we have focused on things that are not important. (Hauberg, Akademikerbladet, 2/2023:42)

In Hauberg's view, the wrong focus merges with the demand that the students are good at formulating themselves. For Hauberg, it is only a further underlining of the sad fact, namely that the evaluation methods assess writing skills, and not only assess whether the students have technical ability.

It is hardly surprising that professors with reference to computer science and IT expertise in general value technical ability. But it is difficult to understand that it should function as an antithesis to an academic skill that includes development of the students' formulation and writing skills. If we add that the cited contributions appear in the academic public and at the same time lead to university political program statements about academic learning, these statements are not only controversial and difficult to understand. They are impossible if they are thought of as consequential. Can we imagine that the next generation of computer science students specializing in AI development will not have to learn to master the skill 'to be able to formulate', 'to write academically'? The students must move in the digitized universes of AI and implementation. These universes are at the same time textualized, in fact to such an extent that the visible product a ChatGPT delivers is a piece of text that must be read and understood. Chatbot's computing power transforms digitization into text and speech. Researchers behind claim to use language models, the tech industry claims that machines and tools are intelligent—and so the next generation of computer science students, the technical intelligence, should not learn 'to formulate' or 'to write academically'? That makes no sense. Rather, it makes sense to assert the possible position as a late-modern obviousness, namely that all university students, regardless of subject and faculty, must learn to formulate and write academically.

I thus characterize the impossible and propose a possible position in more realistic terms. The reason is that Hauberg's background university, the Technical University of Denmark, DTU, has already incorporated the obvious academic skills in describing the innovative strategies and activities. As emphasized by DTU's self-description is:

> Innovation (…) part of DTU's DNA. We help students and employees to turn inventions and discoveries into enterprising companies, and we enter into innovative collaborations with the society around us. All our engineering programs have innovation as a fixed part of the curriculum. All because we are driven by the will to develop new, sustainable ideas contributing to solving the challenges the world faces. (Denmark's Technical University, DTU, website, spring 2024)
>
> DTU is, as it is emphasized: "the university of business life and participates in a wide range of collaborations with companies on strategic research collaboration, continuing education offers, student projects, conferences, etc." (ibid).

DTU also highlights that they 'have one of the most well-developed ecosystems for innovation and entrepreneurship among technical universities in Europe', and that this includes:

> (…) four pillars, each with its own special focus: Student innovation, Business cooperation, startups, Commercialization" (ibid)

DTU's elaborations of what their DNA and the four pillars consist of are maintained as innovative projects that, with the broad contact between the students and the business world, ensure that the students get necessary skills and learn to turn theory into practice. With such descriptions of DTU's self-understanding and focal points, the requirements that the technical intelligence must (also) have formulation and writing skills are naturally embedded. Anything else would be academic suicide for an elite university.

In the name of critical debate, it can be argued that DTU's official program statements are ambitious, but not necessarily realized in practice. Hauberg's quoted 'brutally honest answer' can therefore be maintained as a criticism of the official strategy, its focus and evaluation criteria. I agree with this. But I maintain that Hauberg's position belongs to the impossible, even in a more fundamental sense. Although Hauberg could wish for evaluation methods that only assessed the students' technical ability, the wish cannot be fulfilled. Technical ability is, when it is presented to business partners, or is integrated into a project process, or is presented for an exam, to be regarded as an overall academic achievement. The subject terminology and technological justification used in the actual presentation must be at an academic level. As known, Techno logos means 'the doctrine of technology'. Consequently, the students must demonstrate both technical ability and reflection on this ability and its results.

This both/and incidentally belongs to a university pedagogical standard that has been claimed for several decades. It was also practiced under the auspices of DTU, i.e. as development work at the mechanical engineering program (Borgnakke, 2005).[2] But the fact that both/and is recognized in university pedagogy, and is otherwise embedded by DTU as obvious academic skills, does not take away the rationale from Hauberg's criticism of the wrong focus. Seen from a technological point of view, the focus must be changed and directed towards what is important, namely the development of the technical skills of the future. Let me therefore follow the direction of the gaze and the argument to the door, so that the academic job functions and technical skills of the future are in focus.

6.10 The Academic Functions and Technical Skills of the Future

Akademikerbladet focuses on the current upheavals of academic job functions and focuses on the consequences of AI technologies. The fear is that knowledge jobs will be made redundant; the excitement is about AI and the chatbot's abilities as a support tool. But regardless of degrees of fear and enthusiasm, the point of Akademikerbladet and the debate is that the academic community itself and on its own behalf *must* take a position on the consequences of AI/ChatGPT technologies. At the same time, it is an analytical point that the involved IT expertise, which is the authoritative first voice of the debate, also tries to become the authoritative last voice of the debate. The voice that takes stock and clarifies the right focus for the future.

Søren Hauberg begins his description and decision with an analogy to the calculator:

> Just like with the calculator, some of our current tasks will become significantly easier, but this just means that more tasks will be added. We can accelerate the speed at which we do

[2] The project "Development of the quality of teaching" followed the professional and pedagogical development work, 'from lecture to project work' - in the subject and study environments. Reported 1993a, b, by The Board of Education Councils, The Royal School of Educational Studies.

research. And correspondingly with the students. When we get these things integrated, I hope we will get students who can do much more than today. (Hauberg, Akademikerbladet 2/23: 44)

The hope is that although the tasks will increase, the speed will accelerate, the students will have a greater technical ability when using the new technologies.

Hauberg is quoted for admitting that he 'doesn't know the answer to what should happen with the educations'. Next, Anders Søgaard acknowledges the uncertainty, but at the same time takes stock in relation to a focus that is worth sticking to. Because as Søgaard emphasizes:

> I am not an educational researcher, but I observe that when I send students out into the world, it is rare that they are asked about their grades. But more: What's the coolest project you've done and what do you want? What can you do that moves the horizon of what we can do? (…)
>
> That focus must be worth holding on to. Mass production of knowledge is somehow becoming less relevant, and we may need to facilitate to a greater extent that the individual student can create projects out of the box. So maybe there will be more guidance rather than teaching. (Søgaard, Akademikerbladet 2/23:44)

The tone of the debate is light and the arguments are delivered in bold everyday language. But at the same time, the above highlights the rationale and weighty arguments of the expertise, which correspond to IT expertise's status as the authoritative first voice of the debate. And here, where Søgaard takes stock and delivers the right focus, the IT expertise also rounds off as the debate's authoritative final voice.

The wrong focus, which, as emphasized enough, is a focus on knowledge reproduction and grades, is now directed to a focus on 'the coolest projects' that 'move the horizon of what we can do'. The arguments are also corrected and gain extra strength. The argument about the university's excessive focus on knowledge reproduction (98%…) is characterized by the term mass university and is presented as the new strong argument: in the future 'mass production of knowledge will become less relevant'.

In the present context Søgaard is responsible for the fact that the compression takes place over the concept of knowledge. The mass university has previously been debated by the academic public, but linked to the educational policy aspects. In that case with a focus on the problem: mass production of candidates. Linked to faculties and subjects, the debates can be condensed into questions about which subject society needs, or has too many of. Søgaard's term 'mass production of knowledge' and the observation that it is 'less relevant in the future', on the other hand, is difficult to link to anyone or anything. The rationale can be linked to AI/ChatGPTs, or the students' abilities to reproduce knowledge and the media's abilities to make knowledge sharing mass dissemination. But even if that were the rationale, Søgaard also deemed it less relevant. The relevant thing is to facilitate the individual student to create projects out of the box!

Although Hauberg and Søgaard admit that they do not know enough about educational conditions, the loss of precision weaken both the authoritative first and last voice and the IT expertise as subject matter knowledge. The university's concept of knowledge has been reduced to a product concept and the potential connection to the processes between knowledge, subjects and learning has been replaced by cheerful remarks about cool projects that move the horizon. Against this background, the terms need to be clarified and the AI/ChatGPT-student relationship needs to be described in situationally realistic terms. Rather than determining knowledge and comparing abilities in general, identification of professional skills is required, concretely. And rather than seeing the role of AI technologies as knowledge-reproductive substitutes in student task solutions, the development of student work processes is required, where AI/ chatbot are involved as assistants and help with the work. If we return with these demands to Akademikerbladet's offensive line and mission, then Mushtaq Bilal served as an example of how the demand was already integrated into the academic use of AI technologies. Bilal went about it quite aggressively and claimed that 'you can and must outsource the work to AI, but "not your thinking" (Akademikerbladet 2/2023:42).

6.11 The Work Can Be Outsourced, but the Thinking?

In the interview with Akademikerbladet, Bilal gives a vivid impression of how he, as a researcher, involves AI technologies in academic work. Bilal reports:

> Imagine that I have found an ambivalence in Andersen's "Fyrtøjet" which reminds me of a concept from the Russian theorist Mikhail Bakhtin. I use the app Elicit to brainstorm ideas and research questions. Afterwards, I have a conversation with a colleague about it, where I use Supernormal AI to generate a record of the conversation and ChatGPT to write down my thoughts. So, after an hour of work, I have a draft that I can polish and use as part of an article. (Bilal, Akademikerbladet 2/23: 42)

Bilal's description is concrete, but what he imagines is reminiscent of academic work at speed. Furthermore, if studies in Andersen mean discoveries in the textual work that first recall one of Bakhtin's concepts, then can be qualified by using the app Elicit, is continued in a colleague conversation that is maintained by Supernormal and finally leads to a ChatGPT transcribing Bilal's thoughts; if this… then Bilal has done exactly what he claimed on twitter he would not do, namely outsourced the thinking. And if it is true that after an hour of work Bilal has a draft that can be polished and can be used in an article, then we are forced to ask how much independent academic thinking work there was time for.

If Bilal's phases and activities are outsourced to AI technology's helpers, as described, it means that the entire academic process is framed. At the same time, the milestones and products of the process have been characterized by Techno logos. From brainstorming ideas (the app Elicit) over collegial sparring (generated minutes Supernormal AI) for pure writing of thoughts (ChatGPT) and writing articles. In addition, Bilal, as previously quoted, does not think it should be a requirement to learn to write academically, at least not for "students who may dream of establishing a startup".

Does Bilal's now reproduced description stand for believers, we and the next generation are left with a concrete, but also swarming, description of what it entails to outsource academic doings. The IT experts take AIs development potential as a starting point, personifies the innovative features of the Tech industry and allows business, academics and students' dreams of the cool projects and startups to merge.

In this fusion between business life and the students' dream, Bilal's dealings with AI technology are swarmerish, but also product-oriented. Bilal's product orientation honors Hauberg's previously quoted description: 'We can accelerate the speed at which we do research'. But Bilal's description can also be met with critical wonder (as above) that AI help for increased productivity does not seem to leave much time for the researcher's independent thinking work.

This chapter's examples of the academic use of AI technologies can be called dashing, swashbuckling and/or swarmerish bids. But they are presented with reference to an IT expertise that almost exclusively represents the product-oriented approaches. This means that the academic work processes, as cognitive and knowledge creating processes, stand in the glare of oblivion. Correspondingly, the students' learning processes and the interaction between knowledge acquisition and knowledge reproduction are in the shadow of oblivion. On the whole, the political debates about AI technologies, as they are characterized by the dominance of technical skills, seem to forget questions and hide consequences that relate to education, teaching and learning processes. For the summary below, this means that both the debate's discussed and forgotten questions must be maintained in an analytical assessment of the consequences.

6.12 Pointing Out the Consequences

The debate followed in this chapter has already titled the AI technology with a human a priori and with abilities that surpass the students and ' call into question 98 percent of what we do in the education system'. But letting AI technology be the starting point for change and new standards is problematic. First, the distinction between acquiring knowledge, creating knowledge and reproducing knowledge is blurred. Secondly, one must doubt what a conceptualization of AI/ Chatbot's ability as 'ability to reproduce knowledge' and then comparisons between AI technology and students' knowledge reproducing abilities means. Thirdly, the possibilities to describe the relationship between AI/chatbot and the student in authentic human/ machine terms are weakened.

But precisely because the AI/student comparison continues to have political impact, as a consequence questions are being asked about the basis and about the debate's consensus-like concepts of knowledge and product orientations. However, today's IT expertise seems to have forgotten the conceptual distinction between information and knowledge. The distinction, though, came back due to Chat's descriptions of its own functions as 'tool that delivers information' and 'facilitates the exchange of information' (KB/Chat session Learning processes, see Chap. 4). As a consequence, the AI/chatbot's practical functions in the knowledge-creating/ reproducing circuit and various phases must be elaborated.

For the analysis, it is important to point out that regardless of whether the IT expertise manages to distinguish, the university circuits in themselves bear witness to the necessity of distinguishing between producing, acquiring and reproducing knowledge. As will be seen, the real differences between AI/ChatGPT and the students are also hidden in this distinction. Where it is imprecise to say that a ChatGPT acquires knowledge, it is accurate to say that about the students. The students must acquire knowledge before they can reproduce it. The machine/Chatbot retrieves the data-generated knowledge in the data bank. Against this background, the machine works, as Chat itself formulates it, as someone who retrieves data and information and helps users to 'get access to knowledge' (KB/Chat Session Learning processes).

This now pointed difference between a ChatGPT that does not can be said to acquire knowledge and students who can/must acquire knowledge are elaborated in the following chapters, when the knowledge issue is linked with the teaching and learning issue. The analysis of knowledge and working methods that refer to innovation and organizational development is also sharpened. But the actual need for innovative project collaboration with the business world as a form of work has already been emphasized in this chapter by the debaters of IT expertise, and by e.g. DTU. Furthermore, Søgaard points to the trend towards 'facilitating the students' design of projects' which require 'more guidance rather than teaching' (Søgaard, Akademikerbladet 2/23:44). In professional and study environments around vocational education, for example under the auspices of Business schools, AI technologies are pointed out in business-oriented case work.

Let me therefore round off this chapter with an example that opens up discussion about the direction of development, but also for the dilemma between orienting oneself towards the world of education and learning—or towards the business world.

6.13 Rounding Off

Christian Hendriksen, Copenhagen Business School, CBS, contributed to the daily newspaper Børsen with a comment under the heading: "Chat GPT gives the workforce completely new opportunities—and companies new challenges". With this heading, the direction towards business and companies is clear. But the starting point of the comment is an account of a successful experience in CBS and the auspices of education, as follows:

> A few months ago, I opened the latest and greatest version of ChatGPT, GPT4. I wanted to test its ability to assist with a classic teaching task, namely to produce a fictitious case for use in teaching here at CBS.
>
> In a few clicks and under ten minutes, Chat GPT had created an excellent two-page case, complete with fictional employee quotes and fabricated context. I used the case in class, and it was better than the case I had made myself and used last year. (Hendriksen, Børsen 15.8, 2023)

The quoted account is brief, but remarkable both in rhetoric and references to the case-based working methods. There is remarkable enthusiasm for the latest version

ChatGPT-4 and the speed with which a case can be produced. A few clicks, under 10 min and the result is not only excellent, but better than Hendriksen's own case.

The speed and Chatbot 'better than' are reminiscent of, but also surpass, previously quoted Bilal and Søgaard. Now the chatbot is not only better than students, but better than the academic teacher. But apart from the enthusiasm for ChatGPT4's capabilities, we must stick to Hendriksen's description of the task. The chatbot must produce a 'classic teaching task' and 'a fictional' case. And the result is a two-page case description, complete with 'fictional employee quotes and a fabricated context'. The naturalness with which Hendriksen combines classic features of case pedagogy with the production of fictional cases, quotations and even fabricated context is surprising. At the outset, in the classic case study, the whole point was that the case was actually taken from the business world, could include employee statements, and no one dealt with fabricated contexts.

The problem is not just the chatbot and its efficiency, but also the lack of reflection on the development. There was a time when case pedagogy oriented itself towards real cases—now they are prefabricated. But it can also be surprising that AI's famous computing power should not be used on real problems. Letting artificial intelligence produce artificial cases seems unambitious and an underutilization of the potential.

In the main part of the commentary, Hendriksen is significantly more ambitious in his role as advisor to business. Hendriksen lists advice with appeals for technological democratization, clarification of experimentation and the creation of a culture that promotes responsibility, knowledge sharing and dialogue around technology's potentials and challenges.

The dilemmas revolve around the changing levels of ambition, but also fundamentally revolve around the difference between orienting yourself towards education and teaching—and orienting yourself towards the business world. Furthermore, the dilemma revolves around the relationship between the new AI technologies and today's 'old' and experienced project or case-based study environments. If a ChatGPT is used didactically in such environments, it is challenged by traditions, ambitions and real contexts, with a much higher degree of complexity than exemplified in this chapter. And as will become clear from the following chapters, the practical degree of complexity is a priori. When the starting point is therefore taken in the practical processes and not in the AI technology, Søgaard's low-practical consequential thinking, chatbot's achievements around multiple choice and the production of fictitious cases pale. AI implemented in living dynamic learning processes can be made the subject of a case analysis, but the processes are not fictional and they characterize 98–100% of what we do in the education system!

References

Bernstein, B. (1975). *Class, codes, control, Vol. 3. Towards a theory of educational transmission*. Routledge & Kegan Paul.

Biesta, G. (2006). *Beyond learning, education for a human future*. Paradigm Publishers.

Borgnakke, K. (1996). *Procesanalytisk metodologi*, Bd. 2 [*The methodology of process analysis*, Vol. 2]. [Thesis & Akademisk Forlag, Danmarks Universitetsforlag].

Borgnakke, K. (2005). *Læringsdiskurser og praktikker*. Akademisk Forlag.

Borgnakke, K. (2011). *Et universitet er et sted, der forsker i alt undtagen i sig selv og sin egen virksomhed*. Institut for Medier, Erkendelse og Formidling & Institut for Nordiske Studier og Sprog, Københavns Universitet.

Bourdieu, P. (1994). *Raisons pratiques: Sur la théorie de l'action*. Éditions du Seuil.

Bourdieu, P., & Passeron, J. C. (1970). *La Reproduction. Éléments pour une théorie du système d'enseignement*. Les Editions de Minuit.

Darnton, R. (1982). What is the history of books? In *The kiss of Lumourette: Reflections in cultural history* (pp. 107–135). Norton.

Hjarvard, S. (2008). The mediatization of society: A theory of the media as agents of social and cultural change. *Nordicom Review, 29*(2), 105–134.

Illeris, K. (1981). *Modkvalificeringens pædagogik, problemorientering, deltagerstyring og eksemplarisk indlæring*. Unge pædagoger.

Klafki, W. (2002). *Schultheorie, Schulforschung und Schulentwicklung im politish- gesellschaftlichen Konetxt*. Beltz Verlag.

Kuhn, T. (1970). *The structure of scientific revolutions*. University of Chicago Press.

MedieKultur: Journal of media and communication research (2000): Medieforskning til tiden: Rapport fra Statens Humanistiske Forskningsråds konference om dansk film- og medieforskning, MedieKultur Vol. 16 No. 31.

Projekt Kvalitetsudvikling af undervisningen. (1993a). *Udvikling af undervisningens kvalitet – En rapport om faglig-pædagogisk udviklingsarbejde, Uddannelsesrådenes Formandskab*. Danmarks Lærerhøjskole.

Projekt Kvalitetsudvikling af undervisningen. (1993b). *Bilagsrapport: Fra forelæsning til projektarbejde – Om faglig-pædagogisk udviklingsarbejde i tre fag- og studiemiljøer, Uddannelsesrådenes Formandskollegium*. Danmarks Lærerhøjskole.

Tufte, B. (1995). *Skole og Medier. Byggesæt til de levende billeders pædagogik*. Akademisk Forlag.

Tufte, B. (1998). *TV på tavlen – Om Børn, skole og medier*. Akademisk Forlag.

Van der Weel, A. H. (2001). The communications circuit revisited. *Jaarboek voor Nederlandse boekgeschiedenis, 8*, 13–26.

Chapter 7
AI-ChatGPT in the Education's Practical Action Space: The Process from Prompt to Factcheck

In this chapter, the ethnographic presence around the practice orientation is sharpened by both following the debate about ChatGPT's role as an academic/didactic sparring partner and following along into the practical action space. The analysis thus does not leave the political debate or step out of the public forums, but changes focus, perspective and space. The analytical point is that the discourses and arguments of the debate are followed, but now embedded in the practical examples. In continuation of this, the chapter's close analyses follow exercises and task sequences that move between 'prompting' (i.e. instructing) the chatbot and fact-checking the result. In this respect, the ethnographic principle of 'following the case…' is still effective. But it also means following a shift in discourse and rationale.

Through the professionals' practice-oriented discourses, the rationale of IT expertise is put into relief and replaced with a didactic rationale. The political discourse is shifted accordingly and makes the practical challenges of the institutions present. And as is evident from the debate, an official appeal is being made, which should also be seen as a demand for professionals to provide a practical but didactically sustainable approach to handling AI technology. Let me therefore start the chapter's analyses with the appeal.

7.1 The Official Appeal

Banning and regulating remains a task for authoritative spokespersons of institutions and organizations. The appeal to embrace AI technology seems all the stronger when it is put forward in a leadership position. In spring 2023, ChatGPT is still banned for exam use. The leaders are ready to regulate. There is therefore only one party that *must* 'embrace' the AI technology's ChatGPT in a practical sense—and that is the teachers.

K. Borgnakke, *AI and ChatGPT Technology in Education*, Education, Equity, Economy 12, https://doi.org/10.1007/978-3-032-01419-1_7

The calls were made clear, for example when Rie Snekkerup, deputy director for Education and Students, University of Copenhagen UCPH, to the UniAvisen, emphasized:

> We have encouraged all study boards to look at their exams to see if they have the option to allow the use of ChatGPT to some extent. We would like to get to a place where it can become an aid and something that is actively used in teaching, but we are just not there yet(…)
>
> We have to give time and space for the teachers to develop their subject and integrate the technology in a way so that it contributes positively and does not become a loophole for cheating. (Snekkerup, UniAvisen, April 2023).

In Snekkerup's view, UCPH is determined that ChatGPT should become an asset in education and not just 'a loophole for cheating'. And both the call and time to develop conditions have already been given to the study boards and teachers. The magazine *Folkeskolen*, and thus the Danish Teachers' Association (DLF), is similarly determined and puts the significant appeal: "Put AI on the schedule - also for the teachers" in the leader. It was also an important demand that was put forward with the formulation 'teachers must have both influence and further training' rounded off with another appeal: 'so we can succeed with the new technology'. (Folkeskolen, 11, 2023)

The leader just quoted introduces *Folkeskolen's* themed issue on artificial intelligence. But in the context, there is no doubt that regardless of whether it is referred to the UCPH, university or DLF, secondary school is 'we' dependent on the lecturers and teachers to succeed.

In the analytical lens, appeals to embrace AI technology were previously (see Chap. 6) described as addressed to 'us all'. This still applies, but surrounded by this chapter's examples with a new precision. In the education and school context, 'all of us' become 'but especially the educators and teachers.' And university leaders, the UniAvisen and Folkeskolen's editor-in-chief have already put AI on the class schedule! Likewise, thematic issues suggest that we should follow the teachers who are already working as pioneers. The official appeal is thus not only about the teachers' professional handling, but also about the pioneering spirit and attempts to navigate between the new opportunities and the institutional conditions.

In a leadership position, it is about 'seeing' the mission; taking an offensive action, or feeling the pioneering spirit. The pioneers are also expected to have put the schism between 'fear and excitement' behind them. Pioneers are enthusiastic about the performance and speed of AI/ChatGPT. But in practice, it turns out that the pioneers, like the teachers, are also limited by institutional rules and conventional working methods. And whether it is acknowledged or not, the pioneer teachers are also limited by the AI technology. The examples show that advisors and teachers will promise more about ChatGPT as a didactic aid than it can deliver. This results in features similar to KB/Chat sessions, where Chat as a collegial sparring partner promises an analytical and didactic readiness that it cannot deliver (see Chaps. 9, 10, 11, and 12). At the institutions' IT and pedagogical centers, much is still promised on behalf of AI/ChatGPT. But at the same time, the enthusiasm is toned down and adjusted to the real issue, namely the desire for professional handling that navigates between new possibilities and the institutional conditions.

UniAvisen, *Akademikerbladet* and *Folkeskolen* send several messages via the pioneer examples, but they also adjust the messages according to the task. In Folkeskolen, the main message is adjusted to AI that helps "AI can make you better at what you are good at" (11, 2023). Akademikerbladet and UniAvisen maintain the main message of experimenting and working actively with the technology. At the same time, the task must be coordinated by study boards and teachers by linking the development to, for example, Snekkerup's appeal to "integrate technology in a way that it contributes positively and does not become a loophole for cheating" (UniAvisen, 17.4. 2023). In practice, this means integrating ChatGPT into both teaching and examination processes. But this also makes the switch between political and didactic rationales effective and the challenges visible. The switch to professional handling shows that IT centers, advisors and professional teachers do not simply take over a task, but specify it. Where IT centers and advisors seem to clarify the didactic tasks on the premises of ChatGPT, the pioneer teachers specify the task on the premises of teaching and the learners. Therefore, with the sketch in the Fig. 7.1 (drawn over the 4-field model),[1] let me maintain the premises, but also show the common didactic challenge as a process that involves ChatGPT, but focuses on learning to 'prompt and fact-check' a chatbot.

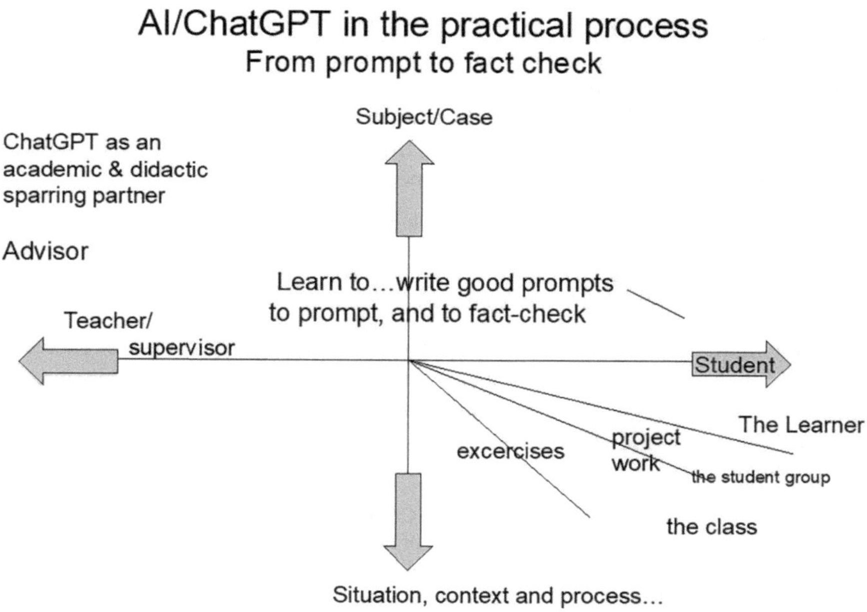

Fig. 7.1 Map of AI/ChatGPT integrated into the practical process 'From prompt to fact check', notes on a 4-field model that maintains the relationship between teacher/student, subject/case and situation/course

[1] The background 4-field model, see Borgnakke 1996, 2007, 2021. The embedded references are partly the didactic triangle, and partly explanations, for example in Dale 1986, pp. 133–208, of concepts and elaborations of levels of didactic rationality, see Dale 1989. The embedded reference to ethnographic method development and to classic classroom research, see Borgnakke 2013, pp. 42–70

The outline frames the four components, which can be followed over relationship lines (teacher/student), process lines (situation/process) and in relation to the common content (Subject/case). By following ChatGPT's involvement in the practical process, the features of the chatbot's role and function as a collegial sparring partner, knowledge/information transmitter and tool are sharpened.

In the subsequent analyses, the subject-professional specifications of the task are followed by starting with the practical example, which matches a political desire for a proposal for the 'Exam Task of the Future', and then following the common challenge around chatbot involvement from prompt to fact check.

7.2 The Subject-Professional Specification and the Didactic Challenge

As a practice example includes *UniAvisen* Tanya Christensen, professor and linguist at Humanities, University of Copenhagen. Christensen has tried to use ChatGPT actively in teaching and therefore leaves the considerations to be about how the technology should be handled during future exams.

Christensen's proposal contains several interesting specifications. First, the main task 'to work actively with technology' is specified as a proactive approach that aims to relieve the institution (which does not need to spend energy on safeguarding against student cheating) and to challenge the students with a 'real' study activity. As she tells about the practice task, the hope is:

> (…) to be able to work actively with the technology instead of ensuring that the students use it to cheat. For example, by incorporating exercises into the teaching where the students have to write good prompts for ChatGPT and explain how to fact-check the output the robot generates. (Christensen, UniAvisen April 2023)

The study activity is thus already integrated into the teaching course as exercises, which are then specified as proposals for a future exam task. This example is also a specification, namely of a coherent course of tasks that challenges the overall course by involving both the teacher/teaching, the students and ultimately the exam itself, which:

> (…) in the future could be: Submit a prompt to ChatGPT and the text the machine generates from your prompt. Also submit a description of how one fact-check the text as well as an edited version where you explain how you have made the AI text better. (Christensen, UniAvisen April 2023)

If the proposal is considered as an overall course, this course management is able to ensure as many as three aspects, namely that (1) AI/ChatGPT is included as an aid in the preparation, (2) a 'real' exam is carried out and (3) both ChatGPT and the student come to the exam.

Christensen's proposal as presented appears advanced, compact, but also sturdy. However, there are two important prerequisites that must be present before the proposal can be said to have been fully processed. Firstly, the students must (learn to) write good prompts; secondly, they must be able to fact-check the text. But before further elaboration, let me do a didactic status of Christensen's clarifications of the task and use the 4-field model of the basic components for the purpose.

Considering the relationship between 'Teacher' and 'Subject/case', it can be noted that Christensen/teacher's planning makes ChatGPT 'a case' which the students have to examine/test. The students acquire the subject and professional tools beforehand, or at the same time, but not through ChatGPT. The didactic point is thus that ChatGPT is not related to 'Subject' as a knowledge transmitter, but is related to 'case', as the object being investigated. Next, considering the relationship between 'Teacher' and 'Situation - process', note first that the planned exercise at the same time is preparation for examination. The exercise and examination activity in Christensen's proposal is therefore a course that is case-oriented and concentrated on ChatGPT. But as a whole, the course is not centered on ChatGPT, but on the students and the 'prompt/fact-checking' activities. For the didactic status, the point lies in the centering of the course, as it unfolds below.

Christensen's plan represents a didactic shift of the debate from being centered around ChatGPT to being centered around activating the students. This shift can in itself be perceived as a didactic achievement. Indeed, if we take stock of current analysis, ChatGPT's launch, the public debates, the IT expertise and the authoritative voices, the absolute center everywhere has been ChatGPT.

On this, the current background, Christensen's didactic achievement is about an authoritative set of ChatGPT in the absolute center is toned down and adjusted according to a didactic orientation that puts academic activation of the students at the center. And even if it is formulated in a proposal that is still only a future draft, it is not only a discursive and rhetorical act. It *is* a didactic plan that is actually oriented towards the involvement and activation of the students, but also to be challenged if/or when the plan is to be implemented.

This becomes clearer when the challenges are considered above the relationship line, i.e. seen as a relationship between 'Teacher' and 'Student/student'. Christensen's proposal is oriented towards the students' active work with the technology, but also bound, both to the conditions linked to the exam, and to the justifications that are didactically linked to Christensen's 'own' intentions and dedications. As Christensen put it:

> I recently dedicated a whole week to ChatGPT in one of my spring courses. It was particularly about equipping the students to be critical of technology. (Christensen, UniAvisen April 2023)

If the intention is to 'dress the students' for technology-critical activity, and the plan at the same time is to strengthen a case-oriented concentration around ChatGPT with the design of good prompts and fact-checking of the output the robot generates … then the didactic challenge is framed. The task is also specified around prompts and fact checks, which are common prerequisites. But in extension of Christensen's proposal as a draft for the future, the analysis is challenged to characterize the common assumptions as a new learning area and as a process that moves from 'to prompt' to 'to check the facts' and therefore must be described in action-specific terms.

7.3 The New Common Prerequisites: The Process from 'Prompting' to 'Fact Checking'

The debate's pioneer teachers and advisers describe prompts and 'to prompt' with slightly different emphasis and choice of words, as they appear from the advisory pamphlets and websites. But there is agreement that promptness is necessary to get the best out of the collaboration with a ChatGPT. There also seems to be agreement on a short definition, namely that *a prompt is the instruction that gives ChatGPT information about the request, task or question …* you want answered. When there is a consensus in the debate about the necessity, definitions and consideration for the Chatbot, the new common assumptions are framed. But it first becomes concretely present as prerequisites for teachers and students, when it is seen in the light of the practical action space, or is seen in the light of Christensen's proposal for the exercise emphasizing that:

> the students must write good prompts for ChatGPT and explain how to fact-check the output the robot generates. (ibid)

The quoted describes the exercise by placing us (as readers in planner/teacher's position) in the middle of the practical action space, where students probably need to learn to… write a prompt, fact-check an output… before, or at the same time, they prompt and fact-check.

The point is, that the proposal makes to 'prompt and fact-check' action concrete with implicit references to activities and assumptions, as if they were already present, but actually they are only developed during the course. If the course is sequenced, 'prompting' must be placed as the teachers' and students' start activity and 'fact checking' must be placed as the end activity of the course. Hereby, didactic challenges are clearly identified, which, by being linked to ongoing developing process, are also linked to changing work and teaching roles. The students must *be advised* (and learn themselves) to prompt in the initial phases of the course, for example, and they must be *supervised*, have help and ongoing *feedback* and help with fact-checking in the middle and final phases. This means, that sequencing the process clearly in practical terms shows how and when the involved parties and actors, including ChatGPT, are (or could be) involved in the process.

Against this background the didactic challenge is both about the new learning areas that must first be developed along the way, and that the process itself from prompt to fact check involves procedurally changing working and teaching roles. In the official debate, it is unclear (almost non-debated) which roles teachers, students and ChatGPT are included in, or must be handed over. But in Christensen's proposal there is actually clarity.

In Christensen's proposal, for both the exercise and exam courses, sequencing and actor placement is clear and simple. With a focus on activating the students, the students are involved in the course's characteristic actor positions from start to finish; i.e. from prompting, testing, explaining to fact-checking. ChatGPT's position is similarly simple. In the overall process, ChatGPT has no active position. It is used and tested as an object, as AI and machine, involved in several phases—especially start/end phases. The activities of the start/end phases mark ChatGPT's function as an AI and text producer.

The clear and simple way in which Christensen's proposed process is described becomes more complicated if the chatbot is part of a collegial collaboration or is included as a helper and 'personal assistant' during the process. The personal use refers to processes and privatized processes that perhaps neither can nor should be affected by demands for prompts and fact checks, but nevertheless become a didactic challenge.

Also, in relation to this challenge, Christensen's proposal can be seen as a didactic achievement. The proposal is aimed at the teaching public and the inclusion of ChatGPT, prompts and fact checking relate to the same public. This location of ChatGPT use and result works with the teaching public as context as a de-privatization of the academic processes, which in Bilal's example were private. Further, and in contrast to virtually all other examples drawn from the contributions of the debate and IT expertise, Christensen's proposal does not personify ChatGPT, let alone assign it the role of its own or the students' sparring partner. This means, that Christensen's non-personification functions in practice as a depersonalization of AI/technology's chatbots. But it also means that de-privatization of ChatGPT use and depersonalization of AI technology both become important benchmarks for the didactic orientation.

Against this background ChatGPT integrated and discussed in the teaching public makes prompt /fact checking visible as the necessary new prerequisites. At the same time sharpens the need for a correspondingly visible explanation of what is the standard for 'the good prompt' and what is the substance of the demand for fact-checking. The official debate has put 'the good prompt' on the agenda and the professionals have traditions that lie behind fact-checking. But if there are official clarifications, there are also characteristic loose ends, as can be seen below.

7.4 Visibility of Standard and Tradition

'Prompting' was incorporated into the universities' advisory services during the spring of 2023 and made available on the institutions' websites, IT centers and pedagogical centers. The practical advice on websites and pamphlets is aimed at the academic public, but is also characterized by being aimed primarily at teachers and students. IT expertise sets the agenda and makes it clear that 'to prompt' is necessitated by and aimed at the use of AI/ChatGPT. That it is a question of adaptation to AI technology is therefore visible. But the very standard of 'the good prompt' must, in order to preserve the professional and didactic rationale, be upheld as an important issue for both IT expertise and the subject's teachers.

With the technical and subject-didactic rationales intact, 'to prompt' can be justified as an AI/ChatGPT derived skill, activity and then prerequisite. The situation is different with the requirement to fact-check, which is rather justified as traditional professional and academic skill.

According to the public debate, professionals hear the demand linked to the fear of the spread of AI technology in academic jobs. At the same time, associations with professional traditions remind us that fact-checking is linked with journalists' and historians' source criticism, or, for example, with Christensen's formulation of technology criticism. Journalists, historians and linguists can refer to subject-specific principles, methods and concepts of criticism. Changing references to research and professional background meet here. But at the same time, what is decisive here refers to a common requirement that the production (reproduction) of knowledge requires that it can be recognized 'as knowledge', and that the contained facts can be determined and checked 'as facts'. Christensen's demand formulated as the linguist's 'fact check' can perhaps be loosened by the journalist from the concept of knowledge and let the concept of source be attached to the concept of media and information instead. But regardless, it doesn't change the fact that demands for source criticism and fact-checking traditionally have their roots in the university and professional environments in which Christensen's proposal is intended to operate. It also doesn't change the fact that the current analysis is also challenged to take a position. Not only on the fundamental question, but on the dangerously specific version: can a ChatGPT's machine-generated text be fact-checked at all? Christensen seems, with the two-part proposal for exercise and examination procedures, to answer 'Yes'. KB, on the other hand, seems to have to answer 'No'!

With reference to my collection of KB/Chat-session the 'No' is immediately justified by the observation that fact-checking is not available as an option. This means that in the collection of Chat responses, there are neither entire response texts nor sections that are built up 'as facts' or presented by Chat as facts. Sessions where Chat informs about machine learning (like in Chap. 5) are excluded. However, the data-logical basis of AI technology I cannot fact-check. But my main justification is conveyed as an analytical result. The analyzes of my collection show how the Chat answers have a generalizing, and/or pseudo-concrete, dealing with theme/topic and KB questions, which together with the author and source less text universe make the Chat text immune to for case-oriented or professionally focused fact-checking. As Christensen's proposal is given in the *UniAvisen*, the exercise/examination task is not academically specified. However, Christensen has involved ChatGPT in research and shown:

> how it sorts out some types of language use, what mistakes it makes in Danish, and how good it is for creative language use. (Christensen UniAvisen, April 2023).

That Christensen, as a linguist, can thus refer to examples and the larger linguistic field, means that fact-checking can neither/nor should be ruled out. In this case, we just accept a subject-relevant exercise/assignment that prepares the language students to test ChatGPT. Or in Christensen's own words, prepares the students to "explain how to fact-check the output the robot generates" and then requires the students to hand in for the exam "a description of how one fact-check the text as well as an edited version, where you explain how you have made the AI text better" (ibid).

In the present context, the point is that the professional traditions and standards that must determine the relevance and difficulty of the case and the fact-check seem to be intact in Christensen's example. In addition, the didactic, technical and technology critical potentials are also intact. However, keeping requirements and potentials intact requires prerequisites and the learning area to retain its subject specificity. And there is cause for concern if the two prerequisites of 'writing good prompts' and 'fact-checking the text' slip further in the public debate, as a general area of learning, requirements and advice. The danger of losing subject-specific points of view and didactic potential is a risk that the advice of IT expertise carries with it—also in the current attempts to let AI/ChatGPT advice be practically oriented towards colleague relations.

At the University of Copenhagen, e.g. the UCPH's website, pamphlets and workshops currently function in an interaction where the closeness to practice is clearly heard, e.g. in the description of a 'hands-on workshop: A new reality with ChatGPT in teaching', to be held in March 2024. The workshop's "Intended learning outcomes" are highlighted as follows:

After the workshop you will be able to:

- Describe to a colleague how ChatGPT operates
- Demonstrate to a colleague how to write a prompt in ChatGPT
- Explain to a colleague which implications ChatGPT can have for your teaching
- Design a small learning activity for using ChatGPT in a course

Participants will be introduced to ChatGPT and what it means that it is a Large Language Model (LLM). We will help you to log in and experiment with prompts in ChatGPT. (UCPH, website IT Learning center).

The quoted workshop description exemplifies the new counseling traditions as practical, hands-on and oriented towards the collegial level. At the same time, the colleague-relevant 'next step' is anticipated, most concretely. The workshop introduces and helps to experiment with 'prompting' and makes it possible to 'demonstrate to a colleague' how a ChatGPT should be prompted. You notice that the Best Practice way of thinking is embedded, and thus made visible as a standard in the workshop and in the advisory materials.

Since my KB sessions also function over colleague-colleague question and conversation positions, I have incorporated the surrounding counseling material into the material collection. It is therefore possible, based on the booklet *Miniguide How to use AI* in *your working life*, to specify what the work around 'the good prompt' consists of. In the sections below, I follow the advice expert, chooses one of the suggested prompts and includes, in a KB session, Chat in the answer. With this, the course can be included in the analysis so that we follow the advice, over prompt to result. Next, Christensen's call is followed by rounding off the process with a fact check.

7.5 What Is a Good Prompt? Examples of Counseling

The booklet *Miniguide How to use AI in your working life* is designed by Kasper Bergstrøm, who, associated with the University of Copenhagen, KU/Science and the Danish Master's Association, DM, acts as consulting expert. The pamphlet's post *What is a good prompt?* is in focus.

The post starts with defining, then exemplifying. I divide into sections for the sake of subsequent reference, but otherwise quote in full, as follows:

> (Section 1) A prompt is the initial text you write to ChatGPT to start a conversation or to get a response. The prompt is simply the instruction that gives ChatGPT information about your request. Therefore, it is also a very **basic concept** to know. By formulating a clear and precise prompt, you avoid many misunderstandings and get the most relevant answers. (Pamphlet, Minigiude p.9)

The pamphlet's value as an example lies in the advice, but also in the characteristic language and genre features. *Firstly,* the pamphlet's direct title, "you", can be noted as characteristic. Although informative pamphlets, in the classic paper version, are the related genre, with this pamphlet we are already in the online universe, scrolling around the pages and noting 'something' about 'to prompt'. The teacher and/or the student googles and finds 'to prompt'. And with page 9 on the screen, the consulting expert speaks directly to you (or me) and tells you what you (or I) have to do. In the online universe, direct speech and 'you' titles are completely in their (genre) place. *Secondly,* it is noted that a prompt, which is a text and a first action, is also a highlighted basic concept. Although it is not obvious why a text, an action also has to be a concept, the importance of the prompt is a firm one. *Thirdly,* the several variants of how the first action should be described are noted: You *write to* ChatGPT, start a *conversation, inform* about a *request.*

The consulting expert seems, in section 1, to cover himself in relation to the various work roles 'you' should have. The interesting thing is the change, in section 2, when the inquiry about the good prompts, questions and subject field is observed. Where Section 1 lays out different work roles and tasks, Section 2 specifies and delimits. With the appeal to formulate 'clearly and precisely', Section 2's proposal below reflects research relevance and the prompt has already been made suitable to be answered by ChatGPT as an academic sparring partner. The implicit role characteristic seems to be 'academic to academic' or 'teacher to graduate student'. As the analysis will show, this implicit role characteristic has great significance for the course.

The pamphlet's presentation of the sample prompts recommended for testing reads as follows:

(Section 2, examples, numbered 1–4 by the author)

1. **Presentation of problem:** *Describe and analyze the potential challenges of implementing AI technology within the healthcare sector.*
2. **Methodological considerations:** *Discuss the advantages and disadvantages of qualitative and quantitative research methods in studies of psychological behavior.*
3. **Literature review:** *Write a brief summary of the latest developments in artificial intelligence in the field of marketing.*
4. **Theoretical framework:** *Explore and discuss the different theoretical approaches to analyzing cultural globalization and identity formation in modern society. (Pamphlet Miniguide p. 9)*

My first reaction to the recommended prompts cited above concerns the similarity to the tasks that *Altinget* set their Chatbot (see Chap. 4). As a tendency, the prompts (like Altingets tasks) mirror a high level of generalization and a low level of concretization. Propositions 2 and 4 have such a high level of generalization that they appear unanswerable and can primarily be problematized as 'researcher to researcher'. And if the proposals are to be answered, they must first be placed as 'supervisor to students' at a thesis or PhD level. But even at this level, an answer will require research-related clarification. Before the examples, it is true that the pamphlet states that 'you can adapt them to your work'. But rather than adaptation to a work-related task, it is rather an academic subject starting point that needs to be specified.

If an academic precise starting point is established, it must match a high degree of generalization, but add specifics to match the task. Proposal 4, for example (Explore and discuss different theoretical approaches…) is, as it is worded, an impossible starting point for an assignment answer. Perhaps possible if a sociological stand point is specified, and comparative works by e.g. Habermas, Bourdieu and Giddens are added, for a start, and to that add more specific … and round off by concretizing themes and issues that the 'analyzing' must be done on. But if such concretizations are of interest, we are approaching a degree of difficulty and a scale that is out of proportion and without concrete research questions as drivers. The conclusion is therefore that in relation to the advice's requirement to formulate a clear and precise prompt, the given prompt suggestions are far from being precise in academic subject-oriented sense. The given prompts also lack linguistic clarity and precision.

How is one to understand, for example, proposal 2's formulation of a discussion on research methods in 'studies of psychological behavior'? Studies can be specified for the subject field: mental behavior. Studies in behavior can also be described as psychological studies. But unless the counselor thinks about the behavior of the psychologists, then 'studies of psychological behavior' is a strangely unclear formulation. In this connection, a quick google search offers a kind of clarity. I wrote (in Danish) "studier i psykologisk adfærd" in the search field, and got the answer "No results found". It must be said to be an enlightening answer; there are no studies to that formulation. When I googled the same question without "…", I could find approx. 83,400 results. If you then click on the first result, it reads:

> The Psychology degree deals with why people act, think and feel the way they do in different contexts. Psychology as a scientific subject therefore focuses sharply on people's relationships, thoughts, feelings and behavior at individual, group and societal level. (Google answer 7.2.2024)

This google search is correct. Psycho logos means the study of the psyche, so the googled answer placed the vaguely worded question correctly in psychology education and as a scientific subject.

In my view, it is a problem that an example of 'the good prompt' is formulated professionally imprecisely and is surpassed in clarity by a single google search. It reminds us that the advisory IT expertise lacks the academic subject or faculty link. But it also reminds us that, as the advice expert and activity are characterized by generic strategies, the content and direction of the advices also risks being generic. And if it becomes concrete, with my formulation it risks becoming pseudo-concrete.

Suggestion 3 ("Write a brief summary of the latest developments in artificial intelligence in the field of marketing") seems to be risk-free. It is concrete and more limited, but it also seems to have IT expertise as specialist knowledge behind it.

The remaining points of criticism of the advice expert's proposals and tasks are weighty, not least because the criticism affects both the prompt activity and the start of the course. I take the points of criticism with me, but regardless, the interest in following one of the expert's suggestions for testing is maintained, as will be elaborated below.

7.6 The Advice Is Followed: The Test

With the interest in following a process involving a KB/Chat session, demands for KB's questioning position are reactivated. The activity 'prompting' is placed in the 4-field model (Fig. 7.1) of the practical action space, as the development of prompts, which at the start of the process are seen from the academic supervisor/teacher position. With Chat involved as a collegial sparring partner, the work role, as well as the task 'prompting' and 'fact-checking', refer to both phases of idea generation, planning of project/teaching courses and phases of evaluation. In this respect, the authenticity and relevance criterion are intact for both KB's and Chat's positions.

My choice for testing is prompt proposal 1. It concerns 'AI implementation in a health sector', in which I currently have research and supervision interests, but not a health professional work in, or responsibility for. With the choice to take over the advisor's formulated prompt proposal and then give the task to 'my' Chat, I am for analytical reasons concerned with the (i) KB/Chat session as a whole (ii) the Chat-answer (iii) the Chat-produced text. For the same reason, I start by quoting the KB-session and the Chat response in full, as follows:

KB: Describe and analyze the potential challenges of implementing AI technology within the healthcare sector.

ChatGPT

Implementing AI technology within the healthcare sector has the potential to improve patient care and efficiency, but it also brings with it a number of challenges. Here is a description and analysis of some of the most important challenges:

1. **Data Security and Privacy Issues:**
   - AI systems require access to large amounts of sensitive patient data. Protecting this data from hacking and unauthorized access is critical to maintaining patients' privacy. There are also concerns about how this data is used, even when it is protected.
2. **Quality and reliability of data:**
   - AI algorithms are only as good as the data they are trained on. If the data is inaccurate, outdated or biased, it can lead to errors in diagnosis and treatment.

3. **Bias in AI algorithms:**
   - AI systems can inherit bias from the data they are trained on. This can lead to discrimination in treatment decisions, especially if the data contains biases in relation to race, gender or socio—economic status.
4. **Regulatory challenges:**
   - The healthcare sector is highly regulated, and implementation of AI technology may require changes in legislation and regulation to ensure that AI systems are safe and effective.
5. **Liability and legal issues:**
   - Who is responsible when an error is made by an AI algorithm? Legal questions about responsibility and liability are complex and require clarity.
6. **Lack of health personnel board:**
   - If healthcare professionals are not properly trained in the use of AI technology, it can lead to errors and unintended consequences. Education and training are therefore crucial.
7. **Acceptance and trust from healthcare professionals and patients:**
   - Healthcare professionals and patients may be reluctant to rely on AI technology in the decision-making process, especially when it comes to life-saving decisions. Building trust in these technologies is crucial.
8. **Implementation costs and complexity:**
   - Implementation of AI systems requires significant investments in technology and training. It can be a challenge for the health sector to find funds and resources for this.
9. **Interoperability:**
   - Health systems often use different technologies and electronic patient records. Ensuring that AI systems can collaborate and integrate with existing systems is crucial to avoid fragmentation of patient data and treatment.
10. **Ethical considerations:**
    - the healthcare sector raises a wide range of ethical questions, including questions about autonomy, consent and how decisions should be made in questionable situations.
11. **Socio economic factors:**
    - Access to AI technology in the healthcare sector may be limited for some population groups due to economic and socio—economic factors, which may reinforce inequalities in the healthcare system.
12. **Monitoring and control:**
    - The healthcare sector must carefully monitor and control AI systems to ensure that they function as expected and do not create unwanted consequences.

To tackle these challenges, it is crucial to take a careful and balanced approach to the implementation of AI technology in the healthcare sector. This involves careful consideration of the technology's benefits and risks, as well as an ongoing effort to regulate and monitor its use to ensure that it benefits patients and healthcare as a whole. (Chat, Ses.Prompt, AI-Healthcare)

Just a single glance at the quoted 12 points confirms that it is a genre-strong and strongly structured Chat-answer to the type of question that the Miniguide and the four prompt suggestions represent. This in itself draws connections to the related Chatbot text from the *Altinget*-case analysis, especially the section about AI's tasks (see Chap. 4). Altinget's debate was characterized as generally abstract and centered on philosophically shaped human/machine issues. However, the chatbot was encouraged to 'give three examples.' And, as the analysis showed, the Chatbot structured its response accordingly. The answer text was shared in *Healthcare* (AI helps doctors and healthcare personnel) *Manufacturing industry* (AI and robots take over monotonous and dangerous tasks) *Financial sector* (AI helps with financial data analysis and decisions).

With this structuring, the Chatbot matches the Altinget's task-oriented universe with a concise but correct description of tasks that are currently on the agenda in the health and financial sectors and in the manufacturing industry. There is a connection between language suit, topic and exemplifying content, as well as a genre-strong structure.

In the present Chat response, genre features and the bulleted list are so dominant that they do not simply structure the text. The 12 points, the headings and bullet sentences *are* the answer and the solution to the task. On this basis alone, the progression from Bergstrøm's prompt suggestion, through the set KB task to Chat's task solution can be put into relief by the 4-field model. In particular, the upper field of the model where the professional actions and decisions (Subject/case) are made collegially is in focus.

In the position of academic supervisor/colleague, KB thus sets Chat (as a sparring partner) a professional description and analysis task regarding 'AI implementation'. Chat accepts the task and submits "a description and analysis" as a summary of the most important challenges, set out as themes/problems in 12 points. If it is acknowledged that the Chat response is genre-strong and well-structured, and it is acknowledged that each of the theme/problem headings is nevertheless followed by relevant and descriptive sentences and thus functions as a description… it can hardly be accepted for professional reasons to call the response text Chat delivers an analysis. The Chat text and genre are rather reminiscent of an informative letter and resemble texts from, or aimed at, the sectors and ministerial committees.

This genre relationship between the Chat response and a ministerial letter (a committee memorandum?) is problematic for several reasons, which will be developed later. Here the statement suffices: a response that, as a compressed informative bullet point list, resembles an official letter or a memorandum, but is not, has made itself irrelevant in a professional sense. Without source references, the informative character of the Chat response also loses its information value.

Considering the colleague-colleague approach that surrounds prompt advice, the Chat response is also problematic for the further course of action. In the origin (back to the advice), the chosen prompt is an example of 'the good prompt'. In the KB/Chat session, however, the prompt instruction did not lead to 'the good task answer'. With reference to the Best-Practice tradition, the Chat answer cannot therefore function as a suitable example to be passed on. In KB's view, it also applies that if the Chat answer was to be included collegially, the prompt process should be continued and clarified for academic content. If it were to be oriented towards 'teacher/student' activities, the prompt/answer as an analysis task should be clarified, e.g. related to a case or project-oriented course of study. The problem, however, is that if such academic clarifications and case/project course considerations should be taken into account the Chat answer would not in itself be a suitable template. The Chat suggestions, the 12 themes/problems, are primarily seen from the AI technology's 'own' point of view. An original template, or a report, from the Health Authority is therefore more academically relevant.

With criticisms such as the above, the consequence must be that KB withdraws Chat answers/suggestions from the collegial and student-oriented work-in-progress circuits. The analyst, on the other hand, takes the process-analytical considerations into account as planned. However, there is yet another reason to continue the close analysis of the Chat answer. The Danish Association of Masters' Mini-guide's examples of good prompts can still be accessed online and can conceivably be followed up by other colleagues or students. The Chat answer must therefore be problematized and criticized, but also, for analytical reasons, maintained in the above format. The Chat answer was the answer KB received when the prompt and the assignment were given. This answer must be interpreted on its own terms; then examined as a text and result, which must subsequently be fact-checked.

7.7 The Chat Response as Text and Result

The genre-strong Chat text must be examined to see if the response has a correspondingly strong content and message. In other words, the focus must be on the content of the text. As mentioned, the Chat response is also structurally strong. It requires a focus on the text's structure, degree of difficulty and degree of (word) saturation. A lixtest of the Chat text is for a start clarifying.

With a lix number of 56, the text is at the highest end of the scale. The text is a total of 436 words. Of these, 163, i.e. more than 1/3, are noted as 'long words'. Already on this background, the Chat text is characterized by a high degree of difficulty and a high degree of saturation. But precisely those traits are of great importance both for the construction of the text's content and the message. The tendency seems to be that the strong structure of the text is matched, but not by a strengthened rather a weakened content. Similarly, many long words fill and saturate the text, but tend to empty the content of a clear message. Let me unfold the background below.

Within the topic headings of the 12-point list, the text is made up of single-ended, descriptive and informative statements. Already here, the content filling functions more like a form or rubric answer than as a complete description. The statutory and informative statements function as standard formulations that link to the KB/Chat text's signal and code words: *AI, implementation, challenges, sector*, as well as to language blocks such as: (AI systems) *require access to large amounts sensitive,* (issues of responsibility and liability) *are complex and require clarity, Access to AI technology in* (the health sector) *may be limited for some* (population groups due to) *economic and socio-economic factors,* which can *reinforce inequalities in* (the health system).

Content questions, however, should not be asked for point-by-point or accumulated collections of code words, but for the overall meaning of the Chat-generated text. However, clarification is made difficult by the text's tendency to generalize. For example, the most important specific signal word, namely 'health sector', can be replaced by 'the public sector' without any of the 12 points suffering a loss of understanding. You can also replace the word health sector with 'education sector' and correct only a few words, e.g. correct *health, patient, diagnostic*—again without the 12 points suffering a loss of understanding.

When only a few words have to be removed/replaced to make the text fit in general, i.e. to other sectors and/or to the entire public sector, as a consequence, the content and message of the text is aimed at the entire public sector. And correspondingly, the consequence is that the question/ specific case, namely challenges to AI's implementation in the health sector, has been generalized and contained in 12 points that inform about general requirements and point to general problems (e.g. Bias and socio-economic problems). The 12 points have also become equally valid. The only point that retains a health-specific edge and validity is point 7: Acceptance and trust from health professionals and patients. As I return to it, this point is also the only one that, with statements and word choices such as 'patients may be reluctant', 'reliance on AI technology', 'vital decisions', 'trust in technologies', represents a patient orientation and a (human) life position. The rest of the points are AI/technology and system oriented.

The conclusion is therefore that the text's bullet points and generally informative system orientation hinder an overall consistent content and main message. Regarding the text considered as a result, the following applies: The genre-strong Chat-answer has left a strong mark on the text, but has weakened the factual content and made the messages unclear.

The concluding statements are a transition to the next step of the course analysis, namely the fact check. And if the characteristic is precise for the genre that the Chat answer resembles, namely a ministerial formal text or a policy paper from a sectoral committee, the answer and the 12 points must be fact-checked. This is the start of the fact check. But it works as a surprise. As mentioned, the chat-answer consists of 12 points, 436 words, of which 163 are long words and 24 sentences. But among all these points and words, there are hardly blocks of words, sentences or sequences that can be immediately checked for facts or described as facts about the case. The first result of the fact check is therefore that there is information, concerns and demands, but no immediate facts.

In the light of previous reviews, the result is reminiscent of Chat-answers that move in the authorless universe, use genre features and a high degree of generalization to stay free from concretizing facts. As a trend, the Chat-answer is made immune to fact-checking. But perhaps it does not apply to the same extent if the fact check is extended to a double check, where both the case relationship and the process 'from question to answer' are checked.

7.8 The Fact Check Is Extended to Double Check

Tanya Christensen gave an interesting clarification when she emphasized about the exercise that students must 'explain how to fact-check the output the robot generates'. The same applied to the exam task, where the instruction read 'Also submit a description of how one fact-check the text'. (Christensen, UniAvisen April 2023).

The precision implies a degree of difficulty. Christensen not only asks the students to fact-check, but asks students to *explain how* to fact-check. This is difficult, but also the challenge of the task. I follow the challenge, but maintain that how-to questions must be case-oriented, directed at the structured content (the 12 points) and at the Chat-answer to KB's prompt. Here the text's generalizations cause the known difficulties, but they have new consequences for the fact-check. If the case's concrete marker 'health sector' can be removed and without loss of understanding replaced with 'the public sector', then the focal point of the fact-check has, as a consequence, moved to the entire public sector. And the same applies to the case itself. Challenges to AI implementation is generalized and has now become general demands and recommendations for the public sector and the society. But if this is the case neither demands nor recommendations can be fact-checked as such.

Against this background the conclusion is that even when you maintain the case-orientation, fact-checking is made difficult. The case is crumbling—and the public sector as a whole does not allow itself to be fact-checked!

But regardless, the conclusion is that the Chat response is covered in terms of genre, structure and language. There are no errors or gaps, and the entire list of points still looks like a letter that could come from one of our ministries. But if the Chat response is still immune and without gaps, the Chat text is not. Let me therefore maintain the case-oriented efforts, but double-check by focusing on the course of the text and recalling the origin and first sentences of the Chat-answer. They read:

> Implementing AI technology within the healthcare sector has the potential to improve patient care and efficiency, but it also brings with it a number of challenges. Here is a description and analysis of some of the most important challenges:(Chat, Ses. Prompt, Healthcare)

If you were to ask what the facts of the case are in the opening sentence, my answer would be: 'Pass/Don't know, it depends…'. But that might give rise to a supplementary question, namely this: Who claims that AI technology has 'potential to improve patient care'? To this, my answer must also be 'Pass/I don't know' or 'Nobody?'.

The analytical strategic point is now that if the answer 'Pass/don't know', or a hesitant 'Nobody' is difficult for a fact check, it is in the context unacceptable for a double check. The double check requires a logical and factually correct answer that, if the text's claims about AI's potential, can point to the fact that it is 'Chat' (OpenAI) that claims, or include the KB-question (and thus include KB).

If the KB question is re-incorporated, it reads: 'Describe and analyze *the potential challenges* of implementation…'. However, Chat, which usually repeats KB's question, had its opening sentence rearranged and the language block changed to (AI) '*has potential to improve* patient care'. Chat and the databank have thus made a normative turn that turns the sentence into a desire to improve, as well as a statement that AI has the potential. In other words, a normative turn and an undocumented claim.

For analytical reasons, we can see what happens if the double-check is softened. The Chat text can be given a new opportunity by removing the undocumented normative turn, which seems to be the problem of the fact check and the Chat text. For example: 'Implementation of AI technology within the healthcare sector (/aimed at) patient care brings with it a number of challenges.' The first sentence of the Chat text has been halved, but could well stand as a case-oriented introduction to Chat's mission and the following sentence "Here is a description and analysis of some of the most important challenges". Next, the fact check could be concentrated on the challenges of the bullet list.

But before that, the double-checking requirement must be to ask: Who, what, or which body has selected the 'most important challenges.' Who claims that this particular title and categorization: Data security and privacy issues, Quality and reliability of data, Bias in AI algorithms, Regulatory challenges, Accountability and legal issues, Lack of health personnel board, Acceptance and trust from healthcare staff and patients, Implementation costs and complexity, Interoperability, Ethical considerations, Socio—economic factors, Monitoring and control … represent the most important challenges?

When the double check is completed, by going through the points one by one, it opens up associations, where soon a ministry, soon a sectoral agency or a committee, could be brought to mind for a related point description. But regardless of similes; after processing the text as it is, the double-check confirms only one possibility: The Chat-text (OpenAI, the databank, the language suit, the language model) asserts the normative statement that AI has the potential to improve patient treatment, and that the 12-point challenges are among the most important. The Chat-text shows how this works as claims and declarations of intent that just stand there—free of responsibility, without documentation and without justification.

7.9 The Last Sentences and Open Questions of the Double Check

What in the analysis started as a crack in the opening sentence of the well-structured text, turns out to be settlement damage that shakes the foundation. With such big questions as the Chat answer touches on, the absence of responsibility, documentation and justification risks being what creates the tremors.

The characteristic last 4 lines, quoted again below, can be seen in this light:

> To tackle these challenges, it is crucial to take a careful and balanced approach to the implementation of AI technology in the healthcare sector. This involves careful consideration of the technology's benefits and risks, as well as an ongoing effort to regulate and monitor its use to ensure it benefits patients and healthcare as a whole. (Chat, Ses, Prompt, Healthcare)

Often, my analysis shows, the last sentences are a disclaimer. In relation to current Chat responses and the 12 points, it is a responsibility reminder. Chat reminds (especially those in charge of the sector) to take a 'careful and balanced approach' to AI implementation, as well as 'consider the technology's benefits and risks' and finally 'regulate, monitor and ensure' that AI implementation 'benefits the patients.' Here, Chat enters the role almost as a professional who, empowered with an authoritative voice, must keep an eye on the sector's management. The conclusion is thus that Chat neither takes on nor disclaims responsibility, but instead reminds the sectors that they are responsible, are aware of the justification and must provide the documentation. These are heavy points, e.g. points 5, 10 and 12, that can be referred to!

I stand behind the analytic procedure and results of the double check. But it is an open and still relevant question, where Chat has the authoritative voice from. And who (or what) has dressed up Chat to make normative turns, cast AI technologies in a positive light, and then be the moral arbiter for sectors and professionals if something goes wrong? The answer seems to lie in the text, or rather in the genre. The well-structured and ambitious punctuation of the Chat-answer is a genre that gives authority and, together with the ambitious choice of words (and the fact that the lix number of the Chat-text is at the high end) confirms text and genre similarity with e.g. a letter from the health ministry.

But it is still surprising that Chat, which usually disclaims responsibility for heavy professional questions, does not do this here. My bet is that Chat needs neither additions nor disclaimers. The Chat-answer is already secured in the same way as in the KB sessions, where ChatGPT, as an AI technology, lets the IT-expertise form the background (see Chap. 5). But in that case, the IT expertise is also the background of the Chat-answer and the authoritative voice that can place responsibility and allow itself to take both the first and the last word.

In this light Point 7 emerges more clearly as the point that retains edge, substance and nerve for a concern. As the point, under the heading "Acceptance and trust from health personnel and patients", read:

> Healthcare professionals and patients may be reluctant to rely on AI technology in the decision-making process, especially when it comes to life-saving decisions. Building trust in these technologies is crucial. (Chat.Ses,Prompt, Healthcare)

As it is felt, it's not just healthcare professionals and patients who worry about AI technology being something you can trust. Chat also cares. Therefore, it is crucial to build "trust in the technology" as stated in Point 7, as well as ensure that the technology "benefits patients and healthcare as a whole", as stated in the Chat-answer's last sentence!

Through the Chat-answer, fundamental questions are raised about trust in technology. It's serious. But the question posed by a chatbot to the entire public sector is also high-pitched. Like Altinget's debate, where questions about ethics, consciousness, human/machine analogies and statements like 'You humans are responsible when AI fails' circulate without grounding—out of proportion. It is therefore necessary to provoke the right proportions and put the Chat-answer back in the practical course. This means back to the course from prompts to fact check and back to the educational practice and development work.

The questions that the double check has asked for analytical reasons must be asked in a practical sense. This also applies to the questions of trust and responsibility that are assigned to the course's professionals and teachers and require a position. Here, 'doing prompts' becomes a question of adaptation to the chatbot's text universe, as well as a position on which tasks are assigned to the chatbot, cardinal points for the course's didactic orientation.

In the course, processes around prompting can be seen as the professional environment's (researchers, teacher/student groups) adaptation to techno-logos and to ChatGPT's machine language. Processes around fact-checking are seen rather as the professional environment's reconquest of 'Subject/matter' and their demands for source criticism and technology criticism. In the present context, this means that processes around prompting must take place on the chatbot's premises, whereas processes around fact-checking must take place on the premises of the professional environment. In practice, the course's didactic orientation shows that the premises of both the chatbot and the professional environment are upheld. But at the same time, there are doubts about the perception of the processes: are they learning processes or Bildung processes? And if it is both, on whose premises are they carried out?

7.10 The Didactic Orientation of the Course: On Whose Premises?

The Danish Master's Association's pamphlet and Miniguide, the practical workshops and Kasper Bergstrøm's examples of good prompts, given as an advisory expert, mark the starting point and purpose of the course. The KB/Chat session continues and, inspired by Christensen's suggestions for exercises and exam tasks, the process around advice/prompt/result is expanded with requirements for fact-checking.

The professional participants thus contribute differently to the process, but are characterized by a common orientation towards the starting point of the process, i.e. adaptation to ChatGPT as machine/AI technology. The interesting thing is that the common didactic orientation makes the start 'to prompt' a learning area. And if the links recommended by the involved circle of advisers and centers are used, there is no doubt that the development of 'the good prompt' during 2023 became the new learning area. This means that regardless of position as manager, researcher, teacher, student and regardless of reference to trade union, editor, intranet, or the big net, everyone must learn to 'prompt'. How do you learn that?

With reference to the advisory level and workshop, there is little doubt that the basic attitude is the best practice and 'Learning by doing'. One learns to prompt by doing it, is the statement. We are close to both John Dewey's famous basic statement and its confirmation. However, the confirmation requires the basic statement to be corrected: You learn to prompt by doing it *yourself.* With this underlining, the course's nature of being learning processes for the examples and actors involved is put into relief. If we move through the series of those involved (from the Magisters' Association, through advisory centers, workshops, teaching courses at the University of Copenhagen and KB/Chat session) there are two almost polar versions of prompting as a learning process, namely Christensen and the KB/Chat session.

Christensen's proposal is close to the Dewey basic approach. The proposal actually suggests that the students themselves must (learn to) prompt by doing prompts. In that case, Christensen's proposal is an example of the didactic orientation framing both adaptation to AI/ChatGPT and testing of prompting as part of the students' learning process. The KB/Chat session clarifies the opposite i.e. clarifies a process that is pure adaptation and as a learning process would be close to pure reproduction. We disregard the fact that KB follows the course and didactic orientations in the manner of field researchers, and simply notes the following about the course's doings. KB goes online, notes the many centers, pamphlets and materials that offer examples of 'the good prompt', but is self-targeted and gets the examples from DMA's pamphlet, UCPH-center, Bergstrøm. KB copies the selected prompt, asks the question to Chat. The Chat reply is copied by KB in full and stands as quoted text above.

The above sober enumeration of KB's doings has two important points in it. Firstly: what KB has done, everyone else can do too. This means that the web-based version of a prompt course (from task instruction to answer) exists on the web (and on computers) as copy/paste actions, copies and re-reproductions. Secondly: KB's doings are not only made possible, but motivated by the IT expertise's advice and their web-based practice. The good prompt course already exists in the communicative circuits and the examples are recommended by the counseling experts for testing on the web!

The web-based version challenges the didactic orientation and casts doubt on whether a learning process has even been initiated. Are we sent back to prefabricated versions of prompting similar to Henriksen's ChatGPT4 produced fictitious case? In that case, prompt, and 'to prompt', which also implies clarifying ideas for the assignment's cases/themes/problems, functions as the common (fictitious?) starting product. But this starting point also risks being a loss of reality and a loss of credibility as a learning activity. Furthermore, the process from prompt to fact check is started exclusively on ChatGPT's and the web's premises. The point at this stage must therefore be that the web-based version not only challenges the didactic orientation, but requires a renewed stance and justification as a learning activity in order to fulfill the course.

With this challenge made visible, there is a need to put the process 'from prompt to fact check' and the examples in relief on their own premises.

As a whole, the examples work, i.e. DMA's pamphlet, workshop, exercise course, the KB/Chat session as practice examples that show how official appeals and demands are transformed into experimental and didactically oriented actions. In addition, the examples have already been approved for relevance by the IT expertise, trade unions and institution managers' wish for practical and didactically sustainable courses that show how ChatGPT can be involved. In this respect, the official wish for experiment with AI/ChatGPT can in themselves be considered as outsourcing an AI didactic task to the professional environments.

Against this background, the outsourcing of tasks around, and then to AI/ ChatGPT, functions as the new educational practical cardinal point. This applies not only to the examples involved, but to the entire public debate and the period from launch to today. Furthermore, it must be remembered that the debate's thematization of AI/ChatGPT 'between fear and excitement' became a figure of speech, but at the outset was also a concrete reference to enthusiasm for the ChatGPT product and fear of exam cheating. This emphasizes that the premise for the didactic orientation was a corresponding concrete product and exam orientation. In that light, the question of how ChatGPT was involved and which tasks were outsourced must be seen.

7.11 The Outsourcing of the Course

From the point of view of the analysis, the outsourcing of tasks to ChatGPT takes place in conjunction with the first adaptations to ChatGPT as an academic assistant and sparring partner. In that case, the teacher positions of the 4-field model, and thus colleague to colleague relationships, are the starting point for the status of the examples involved. The characteristic features are as follows:

The Christensen proposal is precise in its orientation towards an exercise and exam course, which makes the inclusion of AI/ChatGPT a matter that must be investigated. Christensen is thus not oriented towards outsourcing, but moves didactically from the teacher's position over the subject/case component to the design of teaching tasks, specified as a process that activates the students. ChatGPT is not assigned the role of assistant, but is specified as joint investigation object and case. In relation to this, the justified learning areas are given a didactic edge and degree of difficulty. Orientation towards the students' learning processes involves learning to prompt/fact check by doing it, but also by preparing for the fact-check's how-to questions. Here, the work with the learning areas is viewed as a formation process. The students must learn to handle the ChatGPT by, through critical examination, giving the course itself a professional and technology-critical perspective. The students must therefore act with digital literacy. Measured against the perspectives of the Christensen proposal, the other examples are more limited. On the other hand, they refer more directly to experiences with involving ChatGPT.

The workshop proposals' colleague to colleague approach as well as Kasper Bergstrøm's references to Best Practice as an advisor are based on experiences of outsourcing tasks to ChatGPT in the entire academic profession spectrum (see the pamphlet, Minigiuden). Following the advice therefore means that you, in casu KB, not only try 'to prompt', but also outsource a description and analysis task to ChatGPT and follow the didactic colleague's guidance. Bergstrøm's advice to adapt the prompt to one's own purposes is not followed. But KB follows Bergstrøm's collegial orientation and takes a teacher/supervisor responsibility for the criticism of the prompt and the result of the fact check. The assessment is that the Chat response, as a result and product of a didactically oriented process, is not passed on, neither in the collegial circles nor in the 'teacher/student' ranks. What is interesting in this context is that the critical assessment also points backwards in the process, to the adviser's prompt proposals, as far too broad subject proposals that require a correspondingly broad and general description. The status is thus that neither the Chat response nor the preceding prompt proposal in a didactic sense is suitable for, or relevant in relation to, the consultancy's objective of contribution to collegial development processes. If the KB session and the Chat response were to be included collegially, the prompt and task had to be clarified academically, but also didactically experimentally.

As can be seen, the relevance criterion at this point in the analysis becomes decisive for the assessment. This indicates that the technical optimizations and expansion of ChatGPT's outsourcing options are not in themselves decisive. With the didactic rationale as the background for the assessment, it is rather ChatGPT in practical use—and its utility values in and for the learning processes—that are decisive. Against this background, the status is that the didactic orientation towards the process 'from prompt to fact check' gave important insight into the new learning areas. But it also limited the view. With ChatGPT as a starting point, the analysis risks being digitally enclosed and risks losing orientation towards the real didactic circuits.

If the institutions, centers and professional environments involved are therefore not only to adapt their activities to AI/ChatGPT, but to participate in an experimental educational practice, the didactic orientation must be sharpened around the environments that refer directly to ChatGPT in use in the educational practical area. And as will be exemplified, this means that the analysis must return to the practice-oriented pioneers of the debate. The mission is not to get another idea or suggestion for how to involve ChatGPT. The mission is to get an experience report at didactic everyday level. By returning to Denmark's teachers' association magazine *Folkeskolen* and their journalistic coverage of how 'AI is put on the schedule', we can follow the account of two pioneer teachers. Through this, the practical implications of outsourcing, prompting and quality assessment of Chatgp's products can be seen as activities of everyday life.

In *Folkeskolen's* theme issue, the two teachers, Michael Gundlund and Jonas Bergenholtz, are presented on the cover of the magazine with a full-page illustration/photo prepared together with an AI.[2] The presentation is followed up, partly in leadership positions with praise for the teachers 'who are leading the way and experimenting with technology' (the leader Folkeskolen 11/2023), partly in the cover, photos, layout and the article title "Have you talked to your AI today". With this theme number, there is no doubt that we are in pioneer country. You also sense

[2] Photo , Jonas Pryner Andersen, illustration Anekdote Studio x AI

that both the editor-in-chief, journalists and the interviewed teachers have spoken to their AI, even today!

With the strong editorial framing, the interest in the teachers' practice report has been sharpened for their pioneering role and precisely their way of experimenting. Prompting is, for example, ambitiously linked to ChatGPT's assigned work role being described by the teachers as 'expert'. With ChatGPT functioning as a collegial sparring partner, the teachers are similarly ambitious, as they report. The report and its examples are followed below in the argumentative order that the teachers themselves propose.

7.12 The Pioneer Teachers and ChatGPT in the Role of Collegial Sparring Partner

The pioneer teachers' interaction with ChatGPT shows the ambitions of being totally integrated in the didactic argumentation and exemplification, as Michael Gundlund (MG) reports:

> Teachers are experts in didactics, but as part of the job we have to deal with everything else. There, a chatbot like ChatGPT can provide invaluable sparring (...)
>
> (...) the teachers can get help to solve standard tasks faster. For example, preparing an introduction to a course of project work, creating an annual plan or designing exam questions. (Int.Gundlund, Folkeskolen 11, 2023:16)

In addition to these undeniably important standard tasks, MG adds that:

> (...) making the teaching level-differentiated also goes somewhat faster if you ask ChatGPT to be a learning expert and to prepare different versions of the same task for students at each level. (Ibid)

Next, MG rounds off the exemplification with the words:

> ChatGPT really just does the work that the teacher would have to do himself, but would spend much more time on. And off course with the teacher in the role of the one who, due to his expertise, can assess the quality of the result. (Ibid)

As it turns out, it is not just an ambitious use of ChatGPT, it is vital didactic tasks that are outsourced and the entire spectrum from annual plans, introduction to project work, exam assignments and even level differentiation. With that portfolio, there is no doubt that the teachers live up to the title of the article. These teachers clearly have conversations with their AI as part of everyday didactic use.

In the teachers' accounts, in my opinion, overly ambitious features and concepts only take on an unrealistic tinge. But in practice, it turns out, the ambitions are adapted to the conditions of the teaching practice learning direction. The chatbot is made into expert and collegial help, but under the premise that the chatbot follows the didactic orientation. And as is clear from the exemplification below, this also implies being able to shift the focus from the teachers' interests to the students' interests.

7.13 With a Focus on the Students' Interests

Jonas Bergenholtz's (the other teacher, JB) report is about ChatGPT being involved as a helper in the students' work in preparing oral lessons in English. At the same time, this account also testifies that the didactic orientation has changed its focus and is now about the students' interests. As JB reports:

> We have especially worked with 'give me five', which means getting the artificial intelligence to come up with five sub-topics for a main topic (…)
>
> As example highlights: (…) a student interested in football, who had little else (to do) in a ten-minute session than that he wanted to talk about the English football club Manchester United.
>
> With the idea of development help from ChatGPT, the student was inspired to, among other things, investigate important impact points in the club's history. The student subsequently researched the topics himself, just as he himself wrote the presentation he ended up giving." (Int. Bergenholtz, Folkeskolen 2023,11:16)

As can be seen, ChatGPT functions as an aid to idea development, but as JB emphasizes, the work is the student's:

> And it was his plan, not AI's. It just helped him generate ideas. ChatGPT can do that for 22 students with 22 different subjects at the same time. I would never be able to do that as a teacher." (Ibid)

ChatGPT helps generate ideas, but obviously also makes it possible for the pioneer teachers to relate to the different interests of 22 students. It is both the gift and the perspective that JB rounds off the examples by emphasizing:

> And because you cannot be familiar with many subjects yourself, you often end up limiting the students' choices. Especially at the end of school, when many students are tired of school, it is a gift to a greater extent to be able to let the students deal with subjects that interest them. (Ibid)

As we have followed the pioneer teachers' arguments and examples, they are seen from an excited, but also didactically justified, teacher's position. AI/Chatbot is similarly seen from/and in use as didactic aids for the teaching position. But it is also the teacher-positioned didactic use that leads to the Chatbot slipping into the background and the students to the foreground. And finally, it is due to the teacher-positioned reconciliation that the heavy tasks and the involved Chatbot are handled in a didactically relevant manner.

7.14 The Didactic Handling

What are called heavy tasks are didactic core tasks in the entire spectrum from designing annual plans, introduction to project work, exam tasks and even level differentiation. The analyzes later show how such core tasks become too large for Chat's capabilities (see Chap. 8). But that should not prevent the analysis in this place from keeping the focus, not on AI /ChatGPT's capabilities, but on the didactic handling. In extension of this, the teacher-positioned reconciliation of the tasks is considered didactically effective. In the account of the pioneer teachers, it even works as a reconciliation of the words being too big. I found ChatGPT as an 'expert' as too big a word, for example. But the teachers' own examples described the expert role close to teaching and in more pragmatic terms, as can be seen below:

> The artificial intelligence will (...)try to deliver answers that resemble similar answers to similar questions on the Internet. By asking it to take on the role of expert, it helps it to focus on a specific topic or style, and therefore you get both more in-depth and more useful answers. (Int. Gundlund, Folkeskolen 11,2023:17)

The rationale for the expert role is, as it stands now, pragmatic but also a didactic consideration. The teachers will ensure that the Chatbot can focus on a specific topic and ensure that also the students get as useful answers as possible out of the Chatbot.

The pioneer teachers' didactic handling must be seen in this light—and can also be seen as an extension of what was previously referred to as Christensen's achievement (see p.). Christensen's achievement revolves around handling ChatGPT as a machine and a language model, refraining from personifications and arranging a course that makes the Chatbot an object of investigation and makes the students 'the Active'. The pioneer teachers' achievement is about letting the teacher- positioned Chatbot enter with didactic reasons that help in a process that is oriented towards the students as 'the Learners'.

Considering the achievements in context, the implicit shift in interests becomes clearer. The interest shifts from the absolute centering of the public debate on ChatGPT to a didactic handling that manages to orientate itself towards students and pupils as 'the Learners'.

Shifting the focus to the learners, however, requires a renewed approach to the public debate and the dilemma between fear and excitement, as well as to the positioned actors. So far, the public debate has positioned ChatGPT as 'the actor that excites' and let pupils and students be positioned as a consequence, i.e. as 'the actors that cheat'. Although the consequence must be considered unintended, the authoritative voices clarified the positioning of ChatGPT as the center of excitement and the students as 'those-who-cheat' right from the start of the debate. Next, the professionals and the teachers pointed to the necessary shift. If teaching and learning are to make sense, the didactic orientation must be shifted; away from cheating and towards the students as 'the Learners'.

The shift works and there is a practical rationale behind it. But that does not remove the dilemma. Let me therefore take stock by maintaining both the dilemma and the practical rationales.

7.15 The Dilemma Between Big Words and Practical Rationales

Taking stock of current analysis, ChatGPT's launch, the public debates, the IT expertise and the authoritative voices, the absolute center everywhere has been ChatGPT. As a global media event, ChatGPT has acquired a centrifugal force that is reflected in local media, discourses and a rhetoric that is rarely loud—out of proportion. Also, the article in the *UniAvisen*, in which Christensen's proposal was brought, started editorially in a loud voice under the headline: "The future is now: KU bled rules on AI". Next, the journalist, Camilla Skovgaard Thomsen, followed suit with the unfolding of the start of the events:

> After the year 2022, the future suddenly knocked on the door. Or, it kicked in.
>
> One of the world's most advanced AI robots to date, ChatGPT, became publicly available and could now help anyone with everything from explaining complex issues and comparing academic theories to writing well-formulated university-level exam papers.
>
> The winter exams were just around the corner, and the country's universities had to make a lightning – quick decision (…) (UniAvisen April 17, 2023)

When the 'future' itself suddenly appears, with a ChatGPT that helps with complex issues, academic theories and well-formulated exam papers, it is obviously difficult for teachers and didactics to bring the highest voice down in everyday tone. But they/we don't need that either, because the UniAvisen did it themselves. The headline and the future became everyday with the following subheading:

> Artificial intelligence – ChatGPT is still prohibited in the vast majority of exams at KU – and cheating is detected, reads the message to the students. (Ibid).

The point should be that if something as profane as cheating can bring ChatGPT, the future and the rhetoric down to everyday heights, then it is suddenly 'cheating' that has magically placed itself in the debate center!

However, at this point we do not need more rhetorical decisions, because precisely this, that cheating is and has been at the center of the debate from the very beginning, is the whole point of departure and a fait accompli—also for educational practical proposals and clarifications of the challenges of the future in the *UniAvisen* and *Folkeskolen*'s ongoing coverage.

To follow the argumentation in *Folkeskolen's* theme number is, in the literal sense, to follow the debate between fear and excitement. The leader surrounded the article and the Pioneer teachers' practice report with excitement, but also brought the well-founded fear of cheating into the discussion in the article that followed immediately. The headline was factual: "One in four teachers has experienced cheating with ChatGPT" and then the dilemma was clarified by the subtitle:

> The teachers do not feel equipped to teach artificial intelligence, and the concern about cheating in the final exams is widespread. Nevertheless, a majority of the teachers believe that the school should be able to embrace tools such as ChatGPT on an equal footing with other digital tools. (Folkeskolen 11, 2023)

When the matter editorially stands between 'concern about cheating' and calls to 'embrace AI technology', the dilemma is maintained rhetorically. But the high-pitched personifying phrases in which teachers feel, care and embrace ChatGPT, the centrifugal force, are curiously distant from a didactic professional language use.

I therefore maintain that the achievement of the pioneer teachers is that the teacher-positioned chatbot includes didactic reasons in a process that is oriented towards the students as 'the Learners'. Correspondingly, I maintain that Christensen's didactic achievement is about the fact that an authoritative, high-pitched set of

ChatGPT in the absolute center is toned down and tuned according to a didactic orientation that puts academic professional activation of the students at the center.

The school and educational practical proposals that the pioneer teachers and Christensen respectively represent are drafts of the future, but also bound to the institutional conditions. In addition practical proposal is bound to a political agenda that allows itself to embrace the whole spectrum from the big words of excitement, the core professional requirements, to the control activities of the system. As the leader in *Akademikerbladet* in June 2023 stated the situation:

> "The latest technology to take the world by storm is ChatGPT. It is a deep learning application that is trained on large amounts of text and predicts the next word. It can, like people, be truthful or fictional. Therefore, the use and criticism of sources will be important to teach children and young people in the future, as well as the use of it must be thought out in examinations. (Leader, Camilla Gregersen, Akademikerbladet, 2/2023)

You can feel that Akademikerbladet formulates itself on behalf of the professionals and teachers who must ensure the next generation of source critics. But at the same time, you can feel that the humanization is still like a benefit given to a Chatbot. If, like us humans, it can be both truthful and fictional, we are on home soil. The feeling for the degree of difficulty of the task, if the 'deep learning' application causes the source criticism difficulties, seems absent.

But the orientation of the task towards students as the next generation of learners, is present. Let me therefore follow the direction of the gaze and in the next chapter, through ethnographic retrospective analysis, show how groups of students and teachers navigate between the entire spectrum of basic academic skills, prohibited cheating, recognized summaries and written reports. Going back in time and reviving everyday situations where basic skills are up for debate, shows the students' important trial actions embedded in the academic learning processes.

References

Borgnakke, K. (1996). *Procesanalytisk teori og metode: Pædagogisk feltforskning*, Bd. 1 [*Educational field research*, Vol. 1].

Borgnakke, K. (Ed.). (2007). *Nye læringsstrategier i de gymnasiale uddannelser: Casestudier i It-klasser og projektarbejde* (Gymnasiepædagogik) (Vol. 59). Institut for Filosofi, Pædagogik og Religionsstudier.

Borgnakke, K. (2013). Klasserumsforskning en moderne klassiker i pædagogisk forskning. *Etnografiske metoder i uddannelsesforskningen*. Copenhagen: Inst. f. Medier, Erkendelse og Formidling, Københavns Universitet. Chapter 2, pp.42–70.

Borgnakke, K. (2021). Cross-case analysis of changes in teacher role and didactic function in Denmark, 1980–2020. In *Oxford research encyclopedias, education*. Oxford University Press.

Dale, E. L. (1986). *Opdragelse fri fra «Mor» og «Far» -Pedagogikkens grunnlag i det moderne samfund*. Oslo: Gyldendal.

Dale, E. L. (1989). *Pedagogisk profesjonalitet – om pedagogikkens identitet og anvendelse*. Gyldendal.

Chapter 8
In the Midst of Learners' Practice: Ethnographic Retrospective on the Forbidden Cheating, Recognized Summary and Written Reports

This chapter conducts an ethnographic retrospective that follows in the wake of the heated debate about GAI technologies and basic academic skills. The task is to rediscover everyday versions and show how student and teacher groups navigate between forbidden cheating, recognized summaries and written reports. The task is also to go back in time and revive situations where basic academic skills are up for debate and marked by students as important trial actions.

For close analysis, examples from my previous field studies conducted at IT-High Schools and the Technical University of Denmark, DTU (Borgnakke, 2005, 2007) are used. The examples of learning processes come from fieldwork and material collections from the project-organized study environments at Aalborg University (Borgnakke, 1996a, b). At the same time, 'Learning by doing' (Dewey, 1910, 1916; Vaage, 2000) functions in this chapter as an ethnographic analytical basic statement (Borgnakke, 2004) that harmonizes with the inspiration from Oskar Negt (1971, 2019).

The examples have been chosen and collected for the sake of this book's analysis strategic approach. In Chap. 5, KB/Chat sessions were conducted, where a strong I-Chat and Techno-logos set the agenda. KB followed right into the machine room. This chapter is the contrast. The analysis is situated in the learning room with strong I/we students and maintains exemplary conflict situations and processes as a lived and experienced practice.

The analysis does not point to Best Practice, but shows what, from the learners' perspective, is the 'necessary spectrum' of trial actions. At the same time, it is shown how student, teacher groups and the institutions themselves, build up a reservoir of experience during the process. In this respect, the chapter's analyses do not simply claim a practical standpoint, but exemplify a lived and experienced learning practice, which GAI technologies cannot set the agenda for in the future, but on the contrary must necessarily fit into.

K. Borgnakke, *AI and ChatGPT Technology in Education*, Education, Equity, Economy 12, https://doi.org/10.1007/978-3-032-01419-1_8

For the same reason, the ethnographic retrospective also starts in the middle of the conflict, which requires navigation and handling of the movements between the forbidden cheating, copy versions and the recognized summary.

8.1 Navigating Between Cheating/Copy/Plagiarism/Summary

Let me start the analysis by removing the 'fear' of cheating and, in practical terms, maintaining what cheating can look like in practice. In the first example, the cheating takes place at an experimental IT- high school class (1.g) and in the next example, it takes place at the mechanical engineering program at DTU, where the students have 'auxiliary calculus'. By quoting from my field research report, it is ensured that the example frames the teacher/student relationship, the practical context and the dilemma associated with 'cheating and copying'. It also ensures that we can observe the moments of the act, such as where cheating is sanctioned and where copying occurs.

But first, the common socio-cultural background and the meaning of the spectrum between cheating/copying/plagiarism/reporting must be outlined. What was interesting for the field research was (is) that the spectrum represents smooth transitions, but also poles. Cheating is prohibited (one pole) and text summarized reporting is not only permitted (the other pole), but required.

Outlined as an overview (Fig. 8.1), this implies that certain key words denote 'that and how' one moves between the forbidden—the perhaps permitted—and the required. If one cheats, one stands in minus, and from there you have to move towards plus.

Against the outlined background, teachers and students in the following examples move between the forbidden cheating and the necessary and recognized text summary. But those involved also move in an academic learning context, where divergent interpretations are linked to the activities and actions where someone cheats, copies/plagiarizes or has to write a report. In academic environments there are also several socio-cultural layers and consequences depending on whether the cheating/copying or the referent action (the matter itself) is seen from the system's, a teacher's or a student's position.

'Two identical student assignments' uploaded to the Danish subject can be an example of cheating that must be sanctioned according to the system's rules. Here, the cheating/copying action is in the negative. But 'copying' from the neighboring student in mathematics can also be seen as a possible start to independent problem solving. Here, the copying action, from the learner's perspective, is in the positive. Similarly, the art student can copy a painting, as close to one-to-one as possible, and here the copying action can be in the positive and even receive praise for the result. And finally, the project student's summary of a book can be in the positive, because it is necessary, but also risk being in the negative, because 'referencing' is still too far from 'analyzing'.

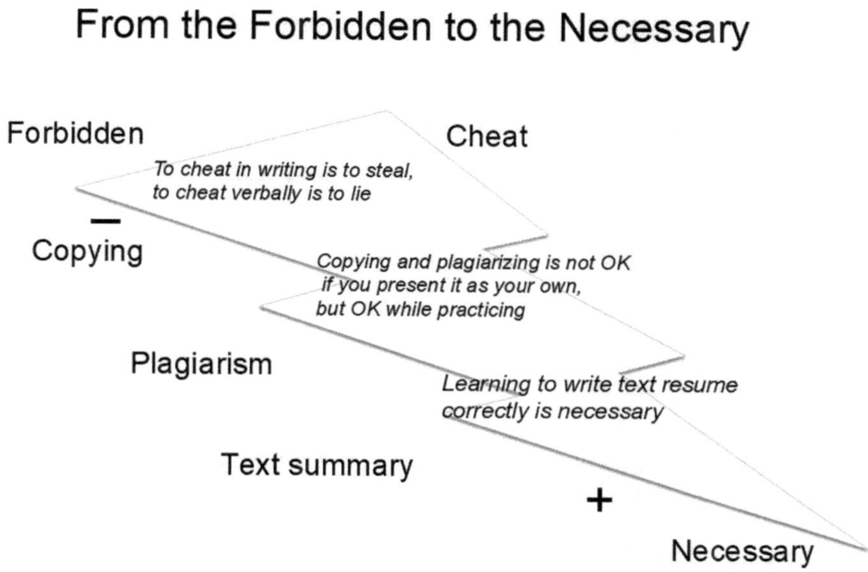

Fig. 8.1 Map of the spectrum 'from forbidden cheating to permitted and necessary text summarization', noted with smooth transitions from cheating, copying, plagiarizing, to creating a summary of a book or text

For the analysis, it is interesting, through the specific examples below, to examine what goes into minus, or plus, in which situations. This sharpens the overview of the spectrum, as well as the feeling for the conclusion that, apart from outright cheating, the rest of the spectrum must be considered in smooth transitions as useful actions, necessitated by the learning process. But, in addition, it is particularly interesting to note how the students navigate in the actual moment of the act—i.e. while they are cheating/copying/taking notes. Therefore, I also quote directly from my field research protocol (field diary), so that what was observed can be retained in a situational snapshot.

8.2 Two Identical Tasks: Cheating/Copying at the IT High School[1]

The excerpt from the field diary concerns the teaching process in Danish in a 1st grade class. The teacher is noted 'TD', the students involved are noted 'Samira' and 'Sonny'. The excerpt starts at the start of the lesson:

> TD, present and demanding from the first second and starts by saying that "there are several items on the agenda". First, the project (a video conference/medieval project) is referred to

[1] Project IT-Schools is given overviews and close analysis in Borgnakke, 2007, 2012. Analysis with a special focus on IT-school development and challenges for the teachers, see Borgnakke, 2011b.

because TD has been away. She calls it a "very exciting project". Next, she refers to student assignments that have been corrected, but where there are unfortunately also "a few identical ones in the pile".

TD outlines the procedure: If you have uploaded someone else's assignment and submit two identical assignments, the grade will be 7:2 = 2 × 03. TD lets Samira understand that it is her and Sonny's assignment. Samira tries to see if she can sort things out, but TD asks her to wait until after class. Samira tries again: "Well, then Sonny must have submitted a copy of mine, because it's not me". Samira is very eager to get that matter resolved. (Sonny is not yet present, apparently late).

TD insists on moving on to Today's text, the folk song "Ebbe Skammelsen" and says to the class:

"Go to the computer and find it under links and folk songs - by the way, you know where to find it, because you've read it at home".

I look at the folk songs together with Sonny who has come in the meantime. (Field Protocol, Project IT-Schools, Obs.1.g, Danish)

For me as an observer, the teacher's concrete and sharp handling of the procedure regarding 'the identical tasks' comes as a surprise. On the one hand, it takes place in full public view and with the names of the guilty parties mentioned. On the other hand, a set of rules is established with a clear settlement (03 equals a failing grade) that I have not seen before. But the students in the class clearly know both the procedure and the consequence that is drawn 30 min later, when the students are in a small group work. The teacher has left the room for a short while, and then, as an observer, I note as follows

When TD comes back, she has apparently picked up the problematic identical tasks that Samira and Sonny are confronted with. Sonny confesses and says it's him. He is sent to the office, 'down to the principal' and Samira gets an apology. (Field Protocol, ibid)

The sharp handling is, as suggested, a familiar procedure for the students, but surprising to me. For several reasons. It is the first day of the fieldwork phase with teaching observations, and the previous conversations with the school principal and the teachers whose classes I will be observing have revolved around the IT classes as a pedagogical experiment. It is an experienced group of teachers, with ambitious plans for IT-based development work in the individual subjects, as well as in interdisciplinary projects, e.g. an online inter-Nordic project course. With these conversations about ideas and plans in the back of my mind, it comes as a surprise to me that cheating, '03' and 'down to the principal' are the first things I encounter in teaching.

Later that day (in music class) I note another cheating/copying activity, although in a slightly more everyday format: "The class listens, but some also sit and chat—and Sandra copies after Søren's draft to a assignment". (Field Protocol, ibid)

With both outright cheating, sharp handling and easy 'copying action' noted, it is part of the story that during the year I conducted observations at the school, I only observed outright cheating once. The teachers told me about a few more incidents, but just as interesting was their justification for the procedure I called the sharp handling. Reproduced after key words from a conversation with a teacher, the justification is the following:

As an IT school, with flow between intranet, IT classes, where every student has a computer, and all texts and assignments circulate electronically, the possibilities for cheating/copying other people's assignments would be endless. And since the school did not care for guilt/shame schemes or 'polite but firm chat in a quiet corner', the school agreement was the bare minimum that applied in all cases: If someone is caught cheating/copying, they will be sent down to the principal immediately/or after class. (Field Protocol, Project IT-Schools, Teacher/Conversation)

Analytically, I choose the same straightforward rounding of the question. According to school logic, cheating as copying someone else's assignment is prohibited. The act of cheating is clearly and distinctly in the minus. What is interesting for the analysis is then the smooth transition to 'copying the peers work', which is an everyday, almost private act that no outsider should interfere with. Copying and its motivations are in the gray zone, closer to being forbidden than permitted. But it can be provoked as something that is not permitted, but nevertheless necessary. Here, 'copying off' is on its way to positive actions for the learner, as can be seen from the example below. We change context from high school to university (DTU). But as can be seen from the field diary, the school context is still present.

8.3 Doing Copy Actions as a First, but Important Learning Act: In the Mechanical Engineering Program[2]

Following the recommendation from several DTU teachers, I attend the type of class called the important one (the one you 'must/cannot/will not do without'), where group calculations and exercises take place in a class of between 20 and 30 students. The teaching is carried out by an 'assistant teacher'. In the teaching I attend, it is Lone, a student who is older in academic years, perhaps 23–24 years old.

/It all takes place in an atmosphere that vibrates with school – and 'the obstruction of the naughty and talented boys'. That is, they both follow along – and don't follow along.

(…)

At 1:30 p.m. they start group math and I plan to have a chat with all of them. However, I decide to stop after two group chats. The students are doing group math and want to disturb – but not be disturbed (they are actually busy).

I start with a little chat with "the loudmouths" (6 male students) as they refer to themselves, and promptly get the same treatment as Lone, namely 'naughty and quick' student's answers.

For example, at one point I ask how they complete the group calculations and solve the tasks.

"We copy each other, of course" says one of them, looking at me challengingly. Later in the conversation it is confirmed that they do in fact do so. But a more serious and realistic justification is given, namely this one, which the person who challenged me tells me about:

"There are only about three in the class who are able to solve the tasks, but you also learn something from copying after them. When you have written the same type of task a few times, and maybe you can solve first a quarter, then half and then three quarters yourself, you gradually learn to do it yourself."

[2] The class was a part of the "Project Quality Development of Teaching" from the 1990s, overview and close analysis, see Borgnakke, 2005, pp. 156–176.

So, as said, the student's doing 'copy actions', but also try to solve the tasks together.

Homework and group math are the important things, the students tell me: "the most important thing in the study at all. That's what we have to know for the exam. And if we don't get to group math, we're lost". The lectures are better to do without - some deliberately don't go to them. They also believe that this is in line with what the teachers have told them. According to the group, one of their teachers has himself said "that group math was probably the most important thing along with the homework, the lectures came only in third place". (Field Protocol, Project Quality Development, Obs. Eng.Machine-direction)

There are several important observations in the cited field diary, which in addition to providing a situational and problem-oriented account also contains my analytical measures. But let me highlight two main points in the present context. Firstly, that the students, as learners, emphasize homework and group calculations as 'the most important thing in the study'. They would be lost without it. Secondly, the student who challenged me has a degree of concretization in his statement that brings the present analysis close to the learning question. Let me therefore quote the statement again, but give it a slight sequencing and mark a starting position, middle and end position, i.e. mark the S-M-E positions of the process:

When you have written the same type of task a few times (S) ... and maybe can solve first a quarter (M1) ..., then half (M2) ... and then three quarters (M3) ... then you gradually learn to do it yourself (E...).

For the analysis, the E-position's response (then you gradually learn yourself) is absolutely crucial. It is also crucial that the word choice is the students. I did not use the learning term in my question. I asked about doings (how do you complete the group calculation?) and received a doings-filled answer (We copy each other...).

But even though the S-position's line change and the E-position's preliminary final line are the ones that carry significance, it is in the context of the M-positioning's M1-2-3 that has the descriptive and documentary value in terms of understanding the process. We can almost imagine how the student (learns to...) solves the task step by step.

For the analysis of this chapter, it is therefore the M-position process that we must focus on in particular. Cheating and 'copying acts' are in the minus. The students know this well, that is why they challenge me. But then the student, as the learner, puts 'copying acts' and thus the process in the plus. This movement from minus to plus-acts is in the grey area between the forbidden and the permitted as activities. However, in the students' perspective it can also be instructive test actions. In this respect, the exemplification about copying, together with the next one about copying, is sufficient background to deepen the entire spectrum, and keep the focus on the recognized pole: the necessary summary. When getting there, however, it is neither a single incident nor a statement that is analyzed across S-M-E positions, but semester courses and entire assignments, collections over many hundreds of pages.

Therefore, for analytical reasons, let me wait with the large collections of material, and concentrate on the few but clarifying lines from the engineering student about the M-position process.

This process and its sequencing are particularly suitable for provoking a re-involvement of the previous chapter's sequencing of Mushtaq Bilal's process (see

Chap. 6) and thereby raising the question: what happens if an AI/chatbot is involved. For the sake of the example, we can have the DTU student follow Bilal and have a chatbot involved so that the sequencing is 50/50, i.e.

DTU student/chatbot alternately in S – M – E position. We can also require that ChatGPT be prompted, and that progressive chains of subtasks be added to the process. The problem is that whatever we come up with, we ask a genre- and numerically strong data bank that answers quickly and correctly and thus has solved the task. The two precise lines are reset; there is no learning process and the question/answer sequence, which lasts a few minutes, moves alone in S position.

The important thing, the process 'first the student solves a quarter (M1)... then half (M2)... and then three quarters (M3)' is gone! And the final line ...then you gradually learn to do it yourself (E...) makes no sense.

With this example, we are dangerously close to the student not learning through their own actions, but 'by chatbots doing'. But we are also close to a completely new version of what cheating and plagiarism are and who performs and uses the act of cheating.

If the DTU student submitted the correct chatbot-answered assignment as his own, it is cheating and plagiarism, exactly according to the definition from the Danish dictionary (DDO), which follows

> (...) plagiarism - from Latin *plagiarius*, derived from *plagium* 'human prey', cf. Greek *plagion* 'human kidnapping, criminal act'. Meanings
>
> 1. a work of art, product or other thing that is a direct imitation of something else, but which is claimed by the creator to be original. Legally, something new must be added, either in appearance or technically, for a product not to be a copy or plagiarism
> 2. the making of such a product (is a) repetition, reproduction, reprint, imitation, photocopying, chinoiserie..." (Excerpt DDO)

In this context, we must—through the example of the plagiarizing DTU student—stick to the modern legal 'direct imitation, copy' and if it is done in a school cultural sense, the student has cheated and in the original situation has stolen another student's assignment. But as far as the AI/ChatGPT type is concerned, we have to stick to the ancient Greek and go via plagiarism to 'human kidnapping'.

ChatGPT kidnapping human language, becoming clothed in a language suit that can say 'I' and 'solve tasks'. But every time it solves a task, and the more formally it expresses itself, the more it plagiarizes the genres, steals students' time and cheats them of important learning activities.

Above, I was seized by a mood, inspired by the definitional heaviness. But my empirical analysis undeniably points in that direction. At the same time, the analysis reminds us of how the students 'writing a copy' and repetitions present as an educational task. As the DTU student put it: "When you have written the same type of assignment a few times...", we must imagine, physically and sensibly, how he writes down the assignment's sequences and formulas, even repeatedly. The whole reason, the marking of the S-position, was thus the repetitive writing actions and testing of the assignment's technical angles of attack.

While difficult assignment processes, for engineering students, can transform 'copying' and 'plagiarizing' into necessary plus actions, plagiarizing and (learning to) create a faithful copy for an art student can be recognized and necessary, as the next example testifies to. The analysis maintains focus on the ways in which the students navigate the spectrum, but changes context to American Art Schools.

The example come from my campus studies, which were tasked with exploring the academic and professional learning context. Therefore, excerpts from these field protocols are themselves contextual and capture the situation, in casu: the necessity of copying, at the moment of the act.

8.4 The Necessity of Copying: Academy of Fine Art[3]

One part is a museum – a fantastic building. I walk around and see American art and that is a pleasure because we/I are used to seeing European art on the walls – also in the USA. In the large hall two students (I guess) are painting and here we see the next generation practice. They really do make copies.

I talk to one of the students who is a mature woman – around 45 years old? She tells me, with a laugh, that she: "is doing her third degree, is also a qualified teacher, but the happiest degree is the one I am taking here and now".

I ask her to describe what she is clearly practicing (a portrait painting of a woman with a distinctive robe-like dress, distinctive facial features). I ask if it is important to make such an exact copy?

She answers and says: "I have just completed a semester course (/class) and had my portfolio approved, so yes, exactly this class, that is the copy that must succeed.

I'm done but I like it and I'm practicing. There's a lot missing from the dress (/she alternately points to the original hanging on the wall and to her own painting/). You can see I haven't got the flow I need, but I know what to do. It's worse with the hands, look! They don't have the glow the original has. I can't fix that because it's something with the base color."

When did you discover that, I'm asking

"Pretty early, but still too late, but I like the picture, I want to hang it at home"

I ask if the copy is the goal and if there shouldn't be a personal tough.

She laughs: "Well, maybe now, I'm on my way to master's studies, but not the first steps, you have to learn that first."

I tell her that I myself am an amateur painter at the lowest level.

She says: "No, there is no such thing as that - not 'low'"

Me: OK, then I'm a happy amateur!

She nods.

Along the way, the custodian has also stopped by and commented on the exercises. The custodian and I nod to each other and say: "It went pretty well".

"Thank you very much," says our student… and we leave her alone with the colors to be packed.

Thought-provoking

Exercises, copy, recreate. Exercises, copy, recreate. Exercises, copy, recreate!

Outside the house, around the house to the back entrance, I get a culture shock from the good - wow, what buildings and such large-format outdoor art - I took a little video of it. (Field Protocol, Art/Learning context/Museum, USA Campus Studies)

---

[3] The observation at the art school was a part of my project *The Academic Learning Context, US-campus*, Borgnakke, 2013.

There are several interesting layers in the field protocol but let me start in the sober and ascertaining terms. The art student copies, as a necessary exercise. There is a technique that must be learned. She shows me the degree of difficulty and points to a mistake made that cannot be corrected. The "hands" in the student's copy do not have the glow, and the "dress fold" does not have the fall that the original has. The mistake was made 2 hours ago, i.e. several layers of paint ago, as she lets me understand. But she knows what she will do next time. So that 'copying' is instructive there is no doubt. There is also no doubt that the art student, as the learner, reflects the first, and soon, next, step of the learning process. In relation to the 'cheating spectrum', the art student is definitely far from cheating and close to the necessary and professionally recognized professional skill.

The field diary is written by a fascinated observer (and now also analyst). But the fascination is not because I am an amateur painter myself (and, incidentally, inexperienced in copying and practicing technical details). No, my fascination is because as an experienced field researcher, with many hours of observation (which are also months) behind me, I have been close to almost all types of learning processes and necessities. But I have never before seen the learning value of copying demonstrated and reflected on with such a high degree of concretization as in the art student's example. What she does not put into words, she points out, and then she also ventures a few generalizations. For example, you have to learn the technique in the first steps, then you can work with what I called the personal tough. She also lets me understand that there is no such thing as a 'lowest' step. All in all, she is so reflective about the necessity of copying, and proud of her own result, that the copy is not a plagiarism, but rather a re-creation. It becomes physically present that and how the painting technique is to be tested. Against this background, we can/should perhaps return to the engineering student and see his endeavor as a recreation and technical testing of the mathematical task and solution.

This also returns to the spectrum where copy as re-creation becomes visible as a necessary plus action, which in turn depends on the learner carrying out the copying activity themselves. If the engineering student or the art student did not carry out the assignment writing (/copying) action themselves or painted the copy on their own canvas, the action goes neither in minus nor plus, but in zero. If, for example, a chatbot carried out the action, there would be a product, but no learning. This fact puts a strain on the discussion, because we are forced to decide which basic skills and learning activities the student needs to try out on their own behalf and for the sake of the learning process—regardless of what aids there may be. Moreover, we are forced to take position how the students try to take responsibility for own learning processes.

What this entails is clearer when, as in the example below, it is part of students' own accounts. With this example, the reference changes both context and situation. We enter the middle of a study course at the Open University of Jutland (JÅU), where the students are gathered for a plenary discussion. I participated in the ongoing activities as an observer, so here too the situation is captured in the moment of action. But this time it is primarily a presentation, its message and the students' testing of their academic skills that the interest is focused on.

8.5 Testing Basic Academic Skills[4]

The framework and purpose are an internal evaluation, as a joint plenary discussion about being a JÅU student and participating in project-organized courses. One of the students has written an introductory presentation.

It is a common premise for the JÅU students that they participate as distance learners in courses and project courses that correspond to the background university (Aalborg University), but are also adapted to the JÅU students' other adult lives, working lives and backgrounds. The university has thus adapted and with the JÅU experiment sought to meet 'the new older/adult students'. The common premise and the adaptation are described and debated in the university community, but probably primarily in organizational and educational policy terms. In contrast, the student's presentation rather represents the personal terms. The student's account shows that she also seeks to adapt and strives to meet the university's needs. But there is an extra dimension to the personal shaping of the effort. The student describes her fear at the thought of the university's demands, but also prepares herself to take responsibility for successfully honoring them, as can be seen in the excerpts below.

> Discipline, I think, planning. Make the most of the time. Just get started. But look, then the panic begins. I start to walk in wide arcs around the desk, where it all lies and threatens me, slowly it becomes a threat, a reminder that you probably can't handle this, that much more is needed if you want to be able to do something, to learn something. I lose my overview and my courage. I think to myself that if only there were some pages in some books to read and learn, it would be simpler. But project work!
>
> Never tried it before - independent decision-making, selection of the material and processing it.
>
> (…)
>
> A completely new process for me, who is from the generation where we did individual tasks. Never group work or outreach work. We read authoritarian from pages 201–250. Like that. This and that was written there. We had really learned that - or what? (…)
>
> I think it's some teething difficulties, called training in reading, perceiving, concentrating, practice and experience in working in the new way - training in independence, among other things.
>
> (…)
>
> I also have to learn as a girl that there is something that is completely mine, that is very important to me - just as important as the various chores of all my family members. They are all busy with their lives, their development. The children growing up with school, education and friends. My husband with his work and his interests. Everything that I have stood by so far - for better and worse. So, a new psychology I have to learn myself - that I also take up my own space. Completely
>
> selfish. And my appetite is big. I would like to work much more than I have done so far. I am absorbed when I am in the process (…) (JÅU-student, Presentation/Plenary-level)

With the above contribution from the JÅU student, we have come close to … what it is all about. That is not so little in a subjective sense, when it is also a "new psychology"—"I have to learn myself".

---

[4] The JÅU example is reported in Borgnakke, 1984, 1985. On the distinct characteristics of the JÅU students' experience-based approach, see also Borgnakke, 1996b, Vol. II, pp. 628–637.

Focused on the starting point, *The Desk*, are the important references to student life books, group work and "independent decision-making", as well as references to experiences from women's lives, family life and working life. And as the speaker makes clear on her own behalf, there are both female and generational experiences linked to the situation of the JÅU students. She, who herself is from a generation where individual assignments were done, must both learn to participate in the new processes and 'as a girl' learn to 'take her own place'. And the new processes are about independent decision-making, selection of the material and processing, as well as group work and outreach work.

With these key words for the new processes, we should pay attention to the JÅU student's summary characterization of the current situation. "I think" she says that these are "beginner's difficulties" and they are about "training in reading, perceiving, concentrating, practice and experience in working in the new way - training in independence".

In this context, it is interesting that even though everything new is linked to the project work, the initial difficulties seem to be about the basic academic skills. They are rediscovered as necessary and even as a training issue. The skills must therefore be trained and tested as tasks. And even though the new project professionalism is a framework both professionally and socially, the important experiences from one's own family life and working life are maintained.

What was interesting for me, as a field researcher, was to follow the consequences of what appears not only to the presentation writer, but to the entire group of students as a personal and experience-based approach to the study and project process. At the same time, it shows itself as an eagerness to test academic skills, read/write, discuss and take a personal position.

8.6 Based on Own Experiences

The overall JÅU project courses show how the students maintain their experience-based approach in both study-related and project-related activities. There are broad project topics, such as the relationship between the technologization of work and identity, as well as more focused topics such as unemployment, bilingual family life or gender role patterns in literature. The point is that regardless of the breadth of the topic or the precise focus, the project is concretely experienced with reference to their own working life and family life. The students thus used the experience-based approach to try out the methods, switch between quantitative and qualitative studies, conduct case studies at their own workplaces, interview their own children or write problem-oriented analyses of literary works.

Through the students' preparations, it was noticeable from the very beginning, e.g. in the project synopsis, how the chosen topics should not only be linked to a general phenomenon, but to issues that concerned the student's own situation. For example, as in the following excerpt from three different synopsis, where both the justification for the topic choice, language and writing style, and topic/problem are is clarified as a personal choice:

for justification for choice of topic

The limited and selected area of study is solely of personal and professional interest. I am involved in the daily work with the age group 3–7 years, where I am confronted daily with parents, support teachers, disability consultants and the granting authority (...) (JÅU- Student/Synopsis)

for language and writing style

(... My language will be down to earth as my point of view and outlet, as my own reality, and this may be perceived as a protest (JÅU-Student/Synopsis)

or for the project topic...

I will also describe the personal experiences I have had with jogging, exercise and marathon running, as well as yoga (...) *which becomes the problem statement*:

What significance does the relationship between body and soul (psyche) have for personality? This is illustrated based on various theories and personal experiences. (JÅU-Student/Synopsis)

The JÅU students' personally shaped strategies for synopsis and project reports testified both to how they, as students unfamiliar with university, sought to tackle the official demands of the university environment, *and* to how they put their own learning strategies and tests into practice.

The students' experience-based strategy was supported, for example through the project guidance, but also received feedback from the teaching group and from the teacher/censor during the evaluation itself. The common points of criticism were that the presentation was "too referential", risked "too broad topic descriptions" that went beyond "analytical sharpness". But at the same time, this very criticism kept the relationship between experience, topic/problem and analytical skills alive. In that case, the JÅU experiment had both provoked the important questions and put them in relief.

As the JÅU students themselves conquered the multiple possibilities of the project report genre, they to some extent reset the spectrum 'from plagiarism to summary to independent analysis'.

If they plagiarized, for example, by writing essayistic or if their presentations were too referential, their written work was clearly independently designed. The students tested the basic academic skills by writing, expressing opinions, and discussing. Next, handling the project genre's requirements for problem orientation and analysis seems to go through 'discussing'.

By making the project discussion-oriented, the otherwise difficult phases in the project process/report are handled where students must a) move from topic to problem, and make a problem orientation seem concretizing b) move from description/report to processing and analysis, and make the analysis seem perspective-giving. The point seems to be that the JÅU students' experience-relatedness and personally shaped discussions actually seem concretizing and move towards analytical measures and perspective-giving. In this respect, the students' test actions are successful and can be considered as a strengthened independent position-taking and discussion. But this does not change the professional criticism that the JÅU projects also faced at the final evaluations. Namely, that their experience-relatedness and project presentation risk becoming too "broadly discursive" and thus "overshadowing the knowledge content".

If we summarize the JÅU students' tests of the academic skills associated with a project course, they exemplify, through their personally shaped strategy, what it means to take responsibility for their own learning processes. From the perspective of the learners, they have come a long way in handling the challenges of the project course. However, from the perspective of the teacher, the handling and the JÅU students' project results still lack something significant. The criticism (from the teacher/censor position) was that the projects were still too 'referential', with 'too broad topic descriptions', too 'broadly discussed', and that this goes beyond 'analytical acuity' and 'overshadows the knowledge content'.[5] This points to shortcomings that are related to professional knowledge and precision, but also to shortcomings in handling the movement from topic to problem and from description/report to processing and analysis. In this respect, it is the project-problem-oriented core areas that need to be strengthened.

In the project-organized study environments, these core areas are continuously supported and strengthened through project group work, guidance, mid-term evaluations, etc. But let me, as before, ask the question, what would happen if a chatbot were involved?

For the sake of the example, we let a JÅU student follow Mushtaq Bilal, involve a chatbot as an academic sparring partner, and observe a sequencing as 50/50, i.e. JÅU students/chatbot alternately in the S – M – E position of the project process. We can emphasize that ChatGPT must be prompted theme/project-related in phases with ideas for topics, problems. The point is that whatever we come up with, we will come on a collision course with the JÅU students' efforts to independently test the process. This test is also formulated by the earlier quoted presentation writer as "training in reading, perceiving, concentrating, practice and experience in working in the new way - training in independence".

If the JÅU students outsource tasks that concern the movement from topic/to problem to the chatbot, they will not learn through their own actions, but 'by chatbots doing'. Both the learning and training value of the course are reset. And if they used the chatbot as a discussion partner and co-debater in relation to the common thematic framework 'Technology and Humanism' and their own topic/problem selection, the relevance criterion would be met. On the other hand, if the students, for example, received answers a la Altinget's Chatbot or KBs Chat about AI in the healthcare sector, the broad topic description, lack of problem orientation, and the lack of precision that compromises analytical sharpness and overshadows the knowledge content … would only become an amplified problem.

[5] The summarized critique from teacher/censor position and the characteristic internal evaluation see Borgnakke, 1985, pp. 52–66.

As noted in the previous examples, this also applies here. If a chatbot performs actions that require basic academic skills, there is a product, but no learning. In the case of the JÅU students, this would also mean that the intended test actions will neither make the course go in plus or minus, but in zero.

This new version of the reset gives the present analysis an extra peak load. Through the JÅU experiment, a decision has been made on the basic skills and activities that the student has to try out on his own behalf and for the sake of the learning process—regardless of what aids there may be.

At this stage is the strong Dewey statement also confirmed, even project-oriented: you learn to move from topic to problem, and from description/summaries to analysis, by doing it. Everyone involved seem to agree—the field researcher including. However, the mutual confirmations are in analytical sense unsatisfactory—not least because the most nearby question is unresolved. If 'everyone' agrees that you learn (to sharpen the topic to a problem, and then go beyond the summaries and carry out the analyses) by doing that, why don't the students do just that? And if someone or something overshadows the knowledge content, why not just focus on the knowledge content?

If we look at the nearby question from a learning perspective, it is about degree of difficulty. It is difficult to get from the theme/topics to the concrete issues. A concrete problem formulation also knowledge the topic, basic knowledge. But how do you get or build basic knowledge?

With the next example, we stay in AUC's project-organized environment and focus on project processes that are carried out within the theme framework of *Popular Movements*.[6]

In the project processes, the knowledge questions, both from the perspective of the project groups and in my process-analytic reviews (Borgnakke, 1996b, Vol. II), are integrated into the cardinal points of the process. But in one of the groups, called the Ireland Group, we see how the work on 'The Northern Irish Conflict' makes the question of building basic knowledge the cardinal point of the entire process.

8.7 The Ireland Group's Process: With the Question of Basic Knowledge as the Cardinal Point

Apart from daily newspaper reading and interest in the chosen topic and country, the three topic-related groups, such as the Greenland and Ireland groups, started from scratch professionally.

Most of their work process is therefore spent reading overviews, with the consequence that problem formulation and processing of the included material must be postponed. The Greenland and Ireland groups thus share the characteristic

[6] The entire large group and both the problem- and the topic-oriented course of the project groups are covered by overview and close analyses in Borgnakke, 1996b, Vol. II, pp. 564–620.

topic-oriented features and procedural difficulties. The Ireland group, however, stands out. Partly by reflecting on the relationship to the topic orientation, and partly by making explicit the construction of basic knowledge as a focused challenge for the project.[7]

The efforts of the Ireland group are acknowledged, but the teacher and examiner lack a problem orientation, there are "too many book summaries" and "too many repetitions" both orally and in writing. And as the teacher and examiner emphasize, the group is:

> Welcome to give book summaries. But it must be stated. And combined with the fact that it is difficult to find the group's independent discussion, concluding section, the slightly more hidden referent seems mystifying. One is not quite aware that it is the author (the original text) or the group itself that concludes. (Field Protocol, AUC, Obs.Evaluation)

The accuracy that the teacher/examiner demonstrates is interesting. This is evident that the Ireland group is "Welcome to give book summaries". But precisely for this reason, it is felt, the group must also learn to state the report and references correctly. Above all, the group must make it clear that "hidden referencing is mystifying".

If the spectrum from the forbidden cheating to the recognized report, which was figuratively set out in the introduction of the chapter, is brought to mind, the teacher/censor's criticism is an academically clarifying version of this spectrum. We are far from cheating, perhaps close to a risk of plagiarism, but closest to the basic academic skills and the necessary book summary. If theoretical works are read, important sections and concepts must be reproduced correctly; if historical overview works are read, the historical outline, as well as selected periods or events, must be reproduced, again correctly and factually 'according to the book'.

If the Teacher/censor's guiding criticism is followed, it is not about the book summaries themselves. They are recognized as necessary. On the other hand, the criticism is that the Ireland group's referential argumentation and writing style make it difficult to see the problem orientation of the project and difficult to see the report as a result of the work of an independent, discussing project group. The Ireland group's reproducing approach seems to overshadow the problem-oriented one. This makes the project-pedagogical goal and framework clearer, as the guidance's strong speaking position. By insisting on the need for basic knowledge, The Ireland group, in turn, makes the strength of the teachers' speaking position clearer.

If we return to The Ireland group's own accounts, it is not independent discussions that the group lacks. On the contrary, the group has many discussions, not about correct summaries and author references, but about the construction of the basic knowledge that the group considers to be the prerequisite for the topic 'the English/Northern Irish conflict' to be treated independently and problem-oriented. In continuation of this, we see the group's circle about the problem formulation that cannot yet be formulated and the background knowledge that cannot yet be identified. After reflection and status of the project process, they recognize, however, that the historical background knowledge must be qualified, as appears from the group's account:

---

[7] The course of the Ireland group is analyzed in detail in Borgnakke, 1996b, Vol. II, pp. 601–618.

> When we realized that the problem is apparently more complex than it is most often interpreted - namely as being of a religious nature - we recognized the necessity of having a thorough historical background to the conflict - also in order to be able to put the nationalist movement and its significance into context - since we must stay within the thematic framework of 'People's movements'. (Ireland Group Report, AUC)

As can be seen, the Ireland group took the consequence, concentrated on historical background knowledge, and postponed the problem orientation to the next semester!

8.8 The Postponed Problem Orientation

The Ireland group became a continuation group. They continued with the same topic and constellation of people (although with a slight expansion of the group) in the second and final project period. In this project, they highlighted the current Northern Ireland issue, which they had shifted in the previous project. But with this, there was also a cardinal point that was shifted. And the group itself gave the reason:

> Due to the necessity for (...) background knowledge, we did not set an actual problem statement, but instead an objective: To uncover the many faces of the conflict and seek to explain its manifestation, this included work with the sectarian myths and alliance patterns, and thus the resulting status quo in Northern Ireland. (Ireland group's 2nd project report)

The Ireland group revolved around unresolved cardinal point, the non-initiated and in the first Project period gave a "declaration of intent", as the group called it, instead of a problem statement. Later in the second project period they gave an "objective". But explicitly by the group themselves they did not give an actual problem statement. They also spoke about that shortcoming at the beginning during the final evaluation. This time the proper evaluation with external censoring. And the censor comments on that shortcoming, as he says to the Ireland group, among other things:

> (...) Censor: "It is a good project. There is a lot of information. It is also good that you have read English books - it is not every day you meet project groups that read foreign books. But (...) there is a lack of suggestions for the connections, problem formulation and problem analysis are lacking. The presentation is additive... (...) (Field Protocol, Project AUC, Obs. Evaluation)

In both periods, The Ireland group submits projects and carries out evaluation processes that are: 'all in all' good. Despite the lack of problem analyses, they also receive praise and approval for their undertakings. However, the criticism of the group's reproductive approach is so strong and pervasive that doubts are raised as to whether reproductions and repetitions promote or rather hinder the project-professional development.

8.9 Status

If, on the exemplified background, a status is to be made, the professional criticism of the teacher/censor position must be maintained as the professional and authoritative voice of the field. It is the exam, and both the statements and the implicit supervisions are trustworthy. But this does not change the fact that the analysis must also maintain the Ireland group's reflections on the necessary basic knowledge and the 'postponed of problem formulation'. Seen as a learning process, these reflections put the Ireland group's course in the plus. This means that even if an official and authoritative criticism can put the project report in the minus, the learning process and the learners (in this example the Ireland group) can meta-reflect on their 'referencing' approach and thereby self-critically put the course in the plus.

Against this background, the status in an analytical sense is about acknowledging the difference and placing the teacher/censor's descriptions of shortcomings and criticism of the 'too referential' products side-by-side with students' accounts of instructive features of the self-managed re-producing processes. In a practical sense, the difference can be both observed and acknowledged as a living difference between the teacher/censor's forward-looking supervisor perspective and the project group's self-willed here-and-now learning process perspective. The two perspectives do not match. On the contrary, the difference between the two coexisting strong I/we-speaking positions, namely 'the supervisor' and 'the learners', is a significant point for the continuous analysis.

At the same time, it points to the necessity of maintaining the course features that, related to the S-position's thematic framework and broad topic proposals, the M-positions' theory/book summary, the historical sketches begun and analysis measures on the way to the project writing E-position's finished report… draw the outline of the supervision and group's work process in a practical sense. Drawing the outline, however, requires that the focus be shifted from the individual project groups' processes to the overall project processes. It also requires a clarification of who, or what, in the larger context influences the process, how and according to what goals.

Therefore, in the last example of this chapter, let me sharpen the ethnographic presence around the project-organized study environments' common goal and framework statements and their practical effects as thematic frameworks, topic/problem orientations, which mark a common start in the S-position, and end with the E-position's collection of written project reports. As a consequence, the analytical summary must concentrate on the example that is closest to the full-scale example, namely the JÅU students' course.

For the sake of overview, I will return to the underlying field research's coverage of the overall courses.[8] But the exemplary focus is, as before, about the moment of

[8] Mapping the field of praxis involves large collections and separate overviews of collections and processes (Borgnakke, 1996a, Vol. 1, pp. 139–190). At the same time, they are established as text collections, see ibid. 192–214.

the act. This means that below we enter the middle of a collection of material, namely the E-position's collection of project reports, and observe an attempt to develop a notation technique. The notation technique must follow the written project reports, for the way in which thematic framework, topic/problem orientation works and influences (by presence/absence) the text and the continuous presentation. The notation technique was thus an attempt to retain precisely the course features that I as an observer had observed in live versions, when and if I saw them again in the project text. But otherwise, as will be clear, it is also just a notation technique that is supposed to make the overview possible!

8.10 The Notation Technique: Retaining Course Features—The Overview

For field research, the 'total courses' and the huge course covering material collections are full scale, i.e. reference is made to an entire educational course. In relation to this, the official study regulations, curriculum and specific semester plans function as an already known background for noting the course's S-M-E positions. And the S/M/E notation itself is for the analysis the fixed basic notation that brings order and makes retaining course features possible. In continuation of this, the simple notation technique below is added as a step-by-step clarification that relates to the project-organized goal and framework statement, as well as to the characteristic features of the report genre, e.g. as features that must officially be present (and therefore can be noted +) and are criticized if they are not present (and therefore are noted with -).

On the outlined background, in addition to a basic notation regarding Theory/Empiricism/Method, it is maintained whether *Problem formulation* is present or absent (noted p + /or −), *Reproductive*, *referring* (noted r, if the project in long passages, many sections has a reproductive, referring character) *Independent processing* (noted Ip when characterized by analytical measures, processing of the chosen topic/problem).[9]

The notation sheets, and their p/r/Ip (+/−) markings, initially provide a much-needed sober overview of the project collections. But then, in an analytical sense, they provide the opportunity to 'see' the movements between a large group's handling of the common thematic framework and the groups' own project choices, as well as see how the problem orientation works, or does not work. The effective tendencies and orientations can therefore be identified. At the same time, characteristic difficulties can be identified, especially in relation to the phases where the students move from topic to problem, and from description/report to processing. This means that the note sheets can both provide an opportunity to seek out details

[9] This specific development of the notation technique is described with overviews and illustrative reviews Borgnakke, 1985, pp. 95–123.

in the individual reports and to outline the active tendencies. An example can be to outline the reproductive features, i.e. the ‘r’ note.

R/r obviously appears frequently in notes about the subject-oriented, referential and reproducing presentation. But it is equally thought-provoking that looking over the note sheets as a whole, shows that all project processes/reports have an ‘r’ in the note line. This means that all project processes, regardless of whether they are theoretical or empirical, experience-based, topic- or problem-oriented, have phases in which they take a reproductive approach. To outline and see a feature in ‘all/entire collection’ points not only to a genre feature of the project report, but to a basic feature of the academic work process. At the same time, it points to an academic obviousness and a set of rules. If one project group carries out critical analyses of the gender role patterns of literary works; another group conducts interviews at a workplace about the effects of technology on the working environment, then in both project courses they must go through phases where they reproduce/reference/describe either ‘the literary works’ or ‘the printed interviews.’

The academic set of rules applies: a report must be drawn up that is comprehensive and correct. That is, that the final report must be able to cite correctly with reference to the work and interview. Seen in the context of this book, this means that neither Plato’s, Ricoeur’s, nor KB/Chat’s parent- or author-less texts have a possibility of existence. And if the authorless does appear, the group is told that the course, sequence, or section is going down. The point in the context of this chapter is that regardless of any details about the simple note lines, effective course features are pointed out, which are also basic features of academic practice. However, it must be emphasized that the primary purpose and purpose of the note sheets is to maintain the genre and flow of the report collections as the outline of the meaningful connecting lines between topic and problem orientation.

8.11 Connecting Lines

A main tendency is that reports, noted for predominantly reproductive features, are also characterized by a topic orientation. Reports, noted for predominantly processing features, are also characterized by a problem orientation. But in this case, it also means that the p+/ (or -) r/Ip of the note line points to both the important connections and possible consequences. Connections between problem orientation and processing (p+/Ip) seem to consequently cause the course and report to go in +, to now resume the characteristics of this chapter. They also mean that the ‘r’ activities that may be involved go in plus. They are surrounded and targeted in a problem-oriented manner.

Connections between topic orientation and reproductive features, on the other hand, seem to result in the process and report being in the negative (p−/r), or surrounded by the deficiency situation. The subject-oriented presentations do not function positively in terms of goal-directedness, but still lack a problem formulation and actual analyses, as has been shown. This deficiency situation is a tendency that is pointed out along the way and therefore primarily concerns guidance.

Viewing both the criticism and the characterization of the 'deficiency situation' in the perspective of the teacher and supervisor position is clarifying. With the criticism, the teacher points backwards, but allows guidance to look forward. In that sense, the divergent perceptions about the referent undertakings, as necessary, useful, but insufficient in the future, are a little clearer. But this does not change the fact that the 'deficiency situation' must in any case be highlighted in order to be seen from the perspective of the learners. Moving from subject to problem represents, as is now known, one of the most important challenges of the process.

Moving from topic to problem represents, as is now known, one of the most important challenges of the process. In the example of the Ireland group, the challenge was not handled, but postponed and replaced by the group's need to build basic knowledge about the topic. In examples from the JÅU students, the challenge is handled by orienting themselves towards 'discussing'. In continuation of this, the significance of a new addition to the goal-directed orientations, namely discussion orientation, can be developed around the course of the JUÅ experiment. At the same time, it can be included in the overview (Fig. 8.2) of features and notations for the overall process.

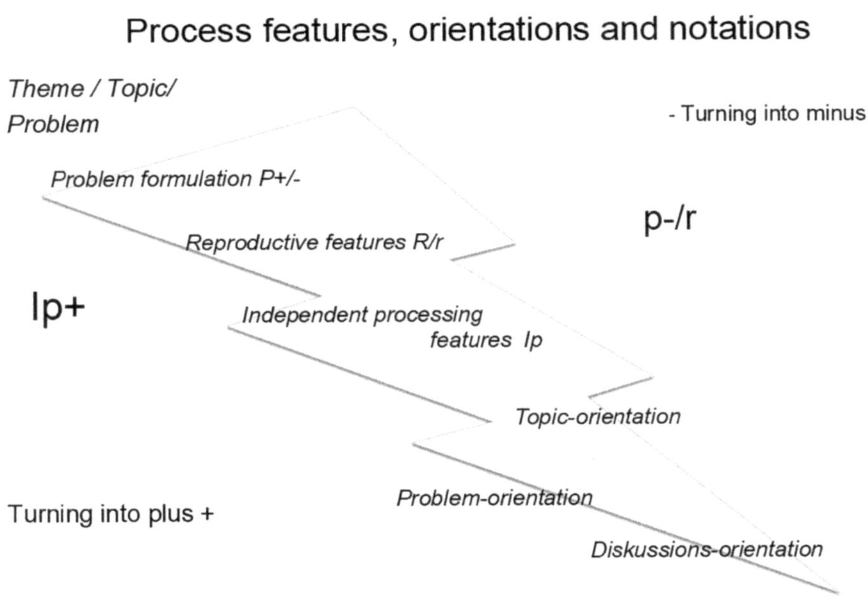

Fig. 8.2 Map of the process features and orientations, showing the topic/problem/discussion orientation of the process and signs of proceeding reproductively or independently in a processing manner

8.12 The New Addition: Discussion Orientation

Discussion orientation as the new addition to the project process's goal-directed orientation is related to the JÅU students' experience-based and personally shaped participation strategy. And that being discussion-oriented is both characteristic and significant is confirmed by the fact that almost all JÅU projects and final reports (15 individual/3 group projects) are noted with a D/d. Exceptions are 3 individual projects, which are only noted with a 'R/r'.

The significance of the D/d notation is further confirmed by the fact that it also shines through the notation line used on the students' synopses, assignments and thus characterizes the written work before the final project report. All in all, there are many features in the report collection that confirm the field research observations of seminar and teaching processes, namely that the JÅU students were particularly interested in discussing, expressing their opinions, and speaking up, both orally and in writing. At the same time, it is interesting to observe that the JÅU environment as such is also perceived as discussion-oriented. The JÅU program's Planning Group presents, for example, seminars, plenary sessions, and group activities with the purpose of "debating" or getting students to "present and discuss experiences among themselves". Group work can also have the purpose of "keeping a discussion going". Regarding the semester's series of plenary activities, there is a first plenary session where "program items are discussed", a second plenary session where "participants discuss their way to a decision" (including the next academic year's thematic framework). Therefore, if you reread the official letters, plans, and seminar programs of the JÅU experiment, there is no doubt. In a JÅU course and at the intensive seminars, one discusses one's way through meetings and courses. There is also no doubt that even though JÅU's project pedagogy is similar to Aalborg University's, it is also similar to the Danish folk high school tradition, and thus folk high school pedagogy.

Against the background outlined, it is immediately understandable that the JÅU students' project courses and reports, as well as the important grading line, now p+(or-)r/b/d, are also discussion-oriented. This also works in a goal-directed manner. But at the same time, there is doubt about what meaning one can attach to it in a study context. There seem to be divergent layers of meaning, as will be explained in more detail below.

8.13 Divergent Layers of Meaning

When the teaching group aims a plenum at 'discussing one's way to a decision' (e.g. of next year's theme framework), it is both concretely clarifying and in line with the Danish Dictionary, DDO, which maintains the meaning of 'discussion' as follows:

> (…) oral or written exchange of opinions between two or more people; elucidation of a matter by presenting different sides of it. (DDO)

In continuation of this, the JÅU description of group discussions (based on teacher presentations) can also be perceived as concretely clarifying. During the group discussion, the students must take part in exchanges of opinions and elucidate the matter (in casu the teacher presentation) from different sides. What is interesting is that this perception does not seem to apply to the discussion-oriented project process/final report. A final project report perceived as 'exchanges of opinions and elucidations of the matter' would be understood as inadequate from the outset. On the other hand, we can approach a more precise meaning by going to the Latin origin of the word discussion, which follows

> (late Latin discussio (genitive -onis) 'shaking, investigation', to discuss 'to break into pieces'. (DDO)

If we consider the JÅU students' project process in extension of this meaning and again focus on their personally shaped strategies, then 'discussing/breaking into pieces' and being part of a 'shaking, investigation' is very close to what the JÅU students themselves said they wanted to do. And, in many ways they did. They examined their current problems close to their own work, family and everyday life. They broke 'old' notions, topics and gender role patterns 'to pieces', thematized them and presented them for discussion.

Through discussion and exchange of opinions, the students keep thematic frameworks and the strong orientations of the project process alive both as an experience-based learning process and an academic work and writing process. This is confirmed by the fact that the JÅU students like to show the strong we/group writing positions. But the strong I-positions are also shown. The confirmation of Ricoeur's emphasis on the speaking (and report-) writing subjects is thus noticeably present. One student even rounds off the report and the analysis of fiction related to the theme 'Women and Technology' with the following Ricoeur (1979) reminding/quotation:

> By appropriation, I mean here that the interpretation of a text is accomplished in the interpretation that a subject makes of oneself, so that the subject understands oneself better in the future, understands oneself differently, or even only now begins to understand oneself. (JÅU Student, Project report)

We must note that the quoted JÅU student rounds off by pointing inward, towards her own self-understanding processes. But at the same time, the author of the report, as a writer, also points outward, towards the others in the JÅU context. If we look at the examples in this chapter against this background, a common characteristic of the strong I/we/group positions is that the students point both inward and outward. The importance is that they also point to the concrete action; they intervene in the situation. The intervention is the moment of the speech/writing act. Samira, returning to the high school situation of being accused of cheating on an assignment, wanted to be cleansed—preferably 'now'. The engineering students wanted to show the practical necessity of the transcript/copying. Ditto for the art student, and The Ireland group left no one in doubt about their assessment of the necessity of the book summaries. Next, the AUC and JÅU course project groups showed the necessity of academic test actions when it came to discussing, conducting analyses and writing finished reports.

The spectrum of academic test actions is thus carried through by the strong subjective I/we/our group settings, but at the same time produces a reservoir of experience that originates from the community and belongs to the community. It is also part of the analysis that the test actions that the AUC/JÅU students completed as 'the necessary spectrum' were recognized by their supervisors along the way, and formally approved by a teacher/censor at the end of the course. This means that both the formalities and realia surrounding the spectrum of actions and the JÅU experiment's version of the project-organized courses were institutionally recognized.

The recognition is interesting for the ongoing analysis. It points to an institutional layer of significance that is simultaneously linked to organizational development, alternative initiatives and the institution's traditional conditions. But in that case, focus must be placed on how not only the student and project groups involved, but also teacher groups gain experience of being in precisely the context of the AUC/JÅU experiment. A common reservoir of experience must be drawn upon that makes it possible for the institution to decide whether, and if so how, it will keep the experiment alive in the future. This means institutionally taking a position on 'the problematic' and 'the perspective-rich'. But it also means, in practical terms, taking a position on 'the necessary'.

Against this background, the ethnographic presence is sharpened to clarify what, in Negt-inspired formulations, is the institutions' 'absolutely necessary public task'. Furthermore, the central point of an expanded concept of experience must be maintained as 'a living public' that enables the institution to become aware of its conflicts and divisions. From an analytical strategy perspective, this means that the chapter's practical standpoint and degree of concretization are retained, but shifted from the learners to the institution's development practice, as explained below.

8.14 Analytical Strategic Shift to the Institution's Development Practice

The challenge is to maintain the chapter's exemplary situations and processes, but shift the focus to the practical context of DTU, the IT schools and the AUC/JÅU experiment. At the same time, the focus is maintained on how those involved themselves point out the conflict content and in practice handle 'the problematic' in light of the experiment's conditions and objectives.

Let me therefore maintain the origin of the series of examples in the IT class, where the school and the class's teachers themselves clarified 'copying' as a problem that the innovative IT High School had to find solutions to. It is thus "Project IT class" and the practical handling of the 'problematic' that is the focal point. This also applies to the assessment of the conflict content and its consequences. With the strategy 'concrete and sharp handling' placed at school level, we must take note that the conflict content is continuously up for discussion among the IT class teachers and students. And when the teachers themselves set the agenda, the focus is not 'copying', but the common set of rules for us as an 'IT school with flow between intranet, IT classes, texts and assignments in electronic circulation'. The teacher part makes it clear in these cases that discussion of the common set of rules is part of the IT class's Bildung project. Further in the series of examples, it applies to "Lone's Help Calculation" that it was recommended by DTU teachers who, as participants in Project Quality Development, would like to have the 'Group Calculation' included in the project. And the impression of the recommendation was only reinforced by reference to a teacher who had expressed "that the group calculation was probably the most important thing along with the homework, the lectures came only in third place." Thus, the group calculation, on the recommendation of the experienced teachers, entered both DTU's Project Quality Development and the 'necessary' spectrum of educational test activities.

Further in the series of examples, the same argumentation applies to the teacher/censor-part relationship, who critically assessed the Ireland group's lack of problem orientation, but also approved the project. From an institutional perspective, it was also AUC's organizational structure, managed by the teaching group, that assessed and had given room for both informal recognition and official approval. Feedback and recognition of the 'good and topically exciting project' was given along the way in the supervision process and at internal seminars. It was thus both project and teaching groups, as well as the project-organized institution, that in practice recognized the construction of basic knowledge as 'the necessary', but at the same time maintain problem orientation as 'the perspective-rich' through criticism and approval.

The maintained argumentation still applies to the 'perspective-rich' in the last example in the series, namely the AUC/JÅU experiment. It is my exemplary analysis that maintains the JÅU students' experience-based project course and discussion orientation as the 'perspective-rich'. But I do so with direct reference to the JÅU students' own descriptions of study practice and learning strategies. Next, the point at this stage is that the JÅU experiment as an organizational development practice navigated according to the same strategies. The project organizational framework and the alternation between the academic subject courses and project work functioning on AUC and university conditions, but are practiced in a folk high school manner. There are lecture series, intensive seminars and plenary debates. The overall course is adapted to the JÅU students' other adult lives, working lives and backgrounds. The university has thus adapted to the JÅU experiment. And the common premises and the adaptation are up for debate in the university community, as well as in the JÅU experiment's own public. Here, JÅU's participants, teacher and student groups keep both the discussion and the public alive.[10]

[10] That the JÅU experiment was kept alive and renewed is emphasized through the continuation of the development project TNP-project Technology and New Pedagogy, Lorentsen, 1988; Dirckinck-holmfeld & Lorentsen, 2003; TNP-serie 1–35, 1989–1996; see also an overview of the JÅU-related evaluative research Borgnakke, 2011a, pp. 72–74.

Further, ethnographic studies following experiments such as the NET education in the health sector show the ongoing exchange of experience and adaptation between background institution

At the same time, several layers of meaning and a field of tension between the participants, the experiment and the institutional conditions come to light. If this field of tension is expressed in Ricoeur's terms, it is observed how teachers and students, during their debates and projects, receive the institutional framework, set of rules and the authoritative voices as an in-between that they each have to relate to. If the lens is enlarged, the JÅU course as an educational experiment receives 'the university institutional' as an in-between, which is up for discussion for its divergent characteristics between university and folk high school traditions. Or it is expressed through a contrast between the academic and the down-to-earth, as one student described it:

> (… My language will become down-to-earth as my point of view and outlet, as my own reality, and this may be perceived as a protest. (JÅU student, synopsis)

But precisely through these practical contrasts and protests, the JÅU course also represented the field of tension in terms of action and task-specific terms. Thus, the entire spectrum of conversation and writing from personal presentations, notes, text resume, essays, studies, analyses to finished reports became part of the repertoire of the JÅU experiment. The same applied to the several orientations, from theme, topic/problem orientations to discussion orientation.

The point in this context is that both moving in a field of tension and testing a whole spectrum of basic academic skills become part of the common reservoir of experience.

Against this background, the requirement for an update of what, continuing in Negt-inspired formulation, in the future can be maintained as the necessary public task of schools, folk high schools and universities. As GAI technologies, again in the future, are embedded in the task, the institutions are challenged to ensure that it is the institutions and not the GAI technologies that define development needs, standards and set an agenda in practical terms.

8.15 The Tightening

If the tightening started by placing GAI/ChatGPT 'in the midst of the necessary spectrum', it would immediately have clarifying effects. The public debate and the IT expertise's pep talk about an academic use of ChatGPT, 'where you think outside the box' and 'only your imagination sets the limits', are put in relief. Regardless of innovative ways of speaking, it can be stressed that when fitting GAI/Chatbot into the school and education world, the institutions set the framework for possibilities and limits. In addition, a set of rules regarding the approval of the GAI tools is put in relief, where 'everyone', and not least the students, are imposed with personal responsibility. Regardless of everyone's own responsibility, the institutions that first

---

and experiment as a vital part of the innovative process, see Lyngsø, 2019; Borgnakke & Lyngsø, 2014; Seminar.net, SI, 2015; Tidsskrift for professionsstudier, SI 2016.

banned ChatGPT, and then during 2024 began to allow it, have to share in a major responsibility. But this also requires an institutional and practical concrete position on everyday use. This means that a reallocation must be made both in relation to who defines tasks and who sets the agenda.

In Chaps. 4, 5, 6, and 7, ChatGPT has set the agenda, and learning to prompt has been on the public and educational policy agenda. But the institutionally correct proportions reverse this. Requirements can and must be set for what a GAI/Chatbot must be able to perform before it can be integrated into the organizational or institutional culture. It must also be clarified how the chatbot is specifically intended to be included in the necessary spectrum. Which institution-defined tasks, which organizational, teacher or student-defined tasks should it be included in?

If the summary started by raising Negt's questions about the necessary tasks, they were basic and in all their simplicity sounded as follows:

> We must find answers to a number of questions: What is the contribution of the media to people's Bildung and the expansion of their judgment? What is the absolutely necessary public task of schools, folk high schools and universities? What should a city look like, what spaces for movement are necessary if a sensuously tangible public is to be able to unfold? (Negt, 2019, p. 124)

If we let 'a city' in the exemplification be the school or educational institution, in the chapter's series of examples it is a high school, a university and/or an entire campus. Through these institutions and learning contexts, reference is made to programs, teacher and student groups that are already part of innovative school/educational development and the debate about the strategies.[11] Seen from the institutional perspective, there is therefore no doubt that there are several organizational answers, as well as several professional facets and learning rooms to consider in the answer.

The question of digital literacy has been raised by the IT high schools. However, if we stick to the examples described, the Negt questions and the answers of the analysis can be concentrated as a development strategy spectrum between the IT schools' innovative classroom teaching and the universities' project work processes. If they are to be characterized as 'the necessary' strategies and activity spaces, it is evident that all examples, despite their respective characteristics, have each practiced the entire spectrum of learning strategies/work forms and associated debate/(conversation) speech/writing actions over a year.

The fact that 'all' and 'the entire spectrum' come to represent 'what is necessary' is the point of the summary because it represents the common conditions. But in that case, the common conditions also apply to reflections on what would happen if we placed ChatGPT in today's IT school environments, or university project environments. It also seems to apply that if these environments, on their own terms, made demands for GAI/involvement, they would be high demands—if they were to match needs and experiences.

---

[11] Particular the project-organized centers also take stock of the PBL model in books, see e.g. Kolmos et al. (2004), referring to AUC (Aalborg University); Olesen & Jensen (1999), Andersen & Heilesen (2015) referring to RUC (Roskilde University) discussing the RUC-model and challenges for universities in the future, Olesen and Andersen (2015).

The strange thing is that during 2024 there will be no institutionally official requirements, no specific proficiency tests set for the GAI tool. Nor are there any suggestions as to which special situations/processes the text-generative GAI/chatbot can/cannot be imagined to enter. Let me therefore cut through the outlined background and simply state that regardless of whether the above points have not yet been institutionally clarified, the requirements are already effective in relation to a spectrum of learning forms—from lectures, classroom teaching to project work—and in relation to the cardinal points of the work process and the project-related academic tasks, genres and products. Illustrated as in the overview (Fig. 8.3). And that the cardinal points of the work process refer to a lived and experienced practice among both student and teacher groups, the experiment and the institution, is evidenced by the analyses in this chapter. The current challenge is whether our institutions will/can use the institutional reservoir of experience to define which forms of necessity GAI technologies fall under.

It has been sufficiently emphasized that this chapter is not intended as Best Practice examples or as models that need to be updated. However, the examples in the chapter are analytical strategic framework as a practical background and as a reinforcement of the upcoming KB/Chat sessions themes, issues and orientations. It is made possible to return to the institutional reservoir of experience and see the KB/Chat session in the light of the projects and agendas of the IT schools, DTU, or the AUC/JÅU students. Through this, Chat will be challenged to navigate in a humanistic professional environment with analysis tasks, and in a more technical/scientific

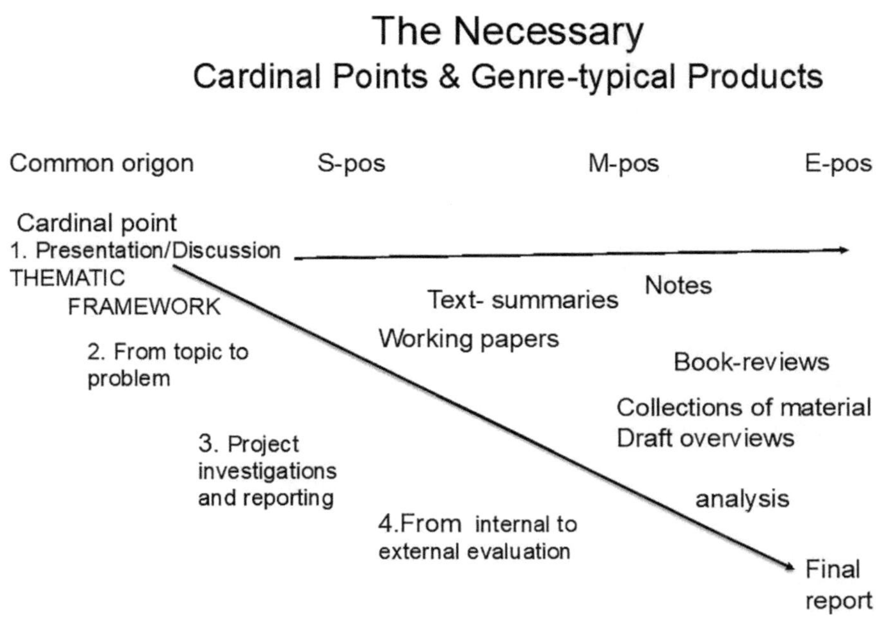

Fig. 8.3 Map of the necessary cardinal points of the learning or work process, genre-typical activities and written products

environment with projects on the Climate Crisis. At the same time, Chat will also be challenged in the realistic terms of demands from a didactic spectrum of tasks, as the magazine Folkeskolen's pioneer teachers formulated them. The point is that in the coming chapters KB will not set the agenda, but will follow the one motivated by the field of practice. Next, Chat decides whether the companionship takes us into the various educational contexts or takes us out into the literary or political publics.

References

Andersen, A. S., & Heilesen, S. B. (Eds.). (2015). *The Roskilde model: Problem-oriented learning and project work*. Springer.

Borgnakke, K. (1984). En to tre fire... Dette er et basisår! Aalborg Universitetscenter. *Gløder, 7*, 99–141.

Borgnakke, K. (1985). *Del-rapport I og II om: Sproglig pædagogisk basisuddannelse. Jysk Åbent UniversitetAUC 1982–84*. Inst. f. uddannelse og socialisering, Aalborg Universitetscenter.

Borgnakke, K. (1996a). *Procesanalytisk teori og metode: Pædagogisk feltforskning*, Bd. 1 [*Educational field research*, Vol. 1].

Borgnakke, K. (1996b). *Procesanalytisk metodologi*, Bd. 2 [*The methodology of process analysis*, Vol. 2]. [Thesis & Akademisk Forlag, Danmarks Universitetsforlag].

Borgnakke, K. (2004). Ethnographic studies and analysis of a recurrent theme: "Learning by doing". *European Educational Research Journal [Ethnography of education in a European educational researcher perspective], 3*(3), 539–565.

Borgnakke, K. (2005). *Læringsdiskurser og praktikker*. Akademisk Forlag.

Borgnakke, K. (Ed.). (2007). *Nye læringsstrategier i de gymnasiale uddannelser: Casestudier i It-klasser og projektarbejde* (Gymnasiepædagogik) (Vol. 59). Institut for Filosofi, Pædagogik og Religionsstudier.

Borgnakke, K. (2011a). *Et universitet er et sted, der forsker i alt undtagen i sig selv og sin egen virksomhed*. Institut for Medier, Erkendelse og Formidling & Institut for Nordiske Studier og Sprog, Københavns Universitet.

Borgnakke, K. (2011b). Blandt professionelle idealister og pragmatikere -En caseanalyse om professionalisering i gymnasiefeltet. In G. Christensen & E. Berthelsen (Eds.), *Pædagogiske perspektiver på arbejdsliv*. København.

Borgnakke, K. (2012). Challenges for the next generation in upper secondary school – Between literacy, numeracy, and technacy. In W. Pink (Ed.), *Schools for marginalized youth*. Hampton Press.

Borgnakke, K. (2013). *The academic learning context, US-campus*. Unpublished manuscript. Rejsebreve: San Francisco, Michigan. Institut for Medier, Erkendelse og Formidling, Københavns Universitet.

Borgnakke, K., & Lyngsø, A. (2014). Going online and offline: Following the course in light of new e-pedagogical concept. In P. Landri, A. Maccarini, & R. De Rosa (Eds.), *Networked together: Designing participatory research in online ethnography*. CNR-IRPPS e-publishing.

Dewey, J. (1910). *How we think*. Prometheus Books.

Dewey, J. (1916). *Democracy and education* (The collected works of John Dewey, middle works) (Vol. 9). Southern Illinois University Press.

Dirckinck-holmfeld, L., & Lorentsen, A. (2003). Transforming university practice through ICT – Integrated perspectives on organizational, technological, and pedagogical change. *Interactive Learning Environments, 11*(2), 91–110.

Kolmos, A., et al. (2004). *The Aalborg PBL model: Progress, diversity and challenges*. Aalborg University Press.

Lorentsen, A. (1988). *Præsentation og analyse af "projekt Datamatstøttet Fjernundervisning" – et udviklingsprojekt på Jysk Åbent Universitet*. Aalborg Universitetscenter.

Lyngsø, A. (2019). *Etnografisk forløbsstudie i netbaseret sygeplejerskeuddannelse – Mellem skolen, hjemmet og klinikken* [Doctoral thesis, The Faculty of Humanities, University of Copenhagen].

Negt, O. (1971). *Soziologiske Phantasie und exemplarisches Lernen. Zur Theorie und Praxis der Arbeiterbildung. Reihe Theorie und Praxis der Gewerkshaften*. Europäische Verlagsanstalt.

Negt, O. (2019). *Dannelse og demokrati*. Translation and postscript Jacobsen K.S & Nielsen B.S., Frydenlund Academic.

Olesen, H. S., & Jensen, J. H. (Eds.) (1999). *Project studies: a late modern university reform*. Roskilde Universitetsforlag.

Olesen, H. S., & Andersen, A. S. (2015). The Roskilde model and the challenges for universities in the future. In A. S. Andersen & S. B. Heilesen (Eds.), *The Roskilde model: Problem-oriented learning and project work* (pp. 263–280). Springer.

Ricoeur, P. (1979). Fortolkningsteori, København. Vinten.

Seminar.net: Media, technology and lifelong learning. (2015). Special Issue: Exploring the Learning Context in Shifts between Online and Offline Learning, Seminar.net. vol 11, issue 1, 2015.

Tidsskrift for professionsstudier. (2016). *Innovation and Uddannelse*. Special issue. nr. 23.

TNP- series (1989–1996). Technology and New Pedagogy, "Projekt: Teknologi og Ny Pædagogik I Åben Uddannelse", 1–35. Aalborg Universitet.

Vaage, S. (Ed.). (2000). *Learning by Dewey*. Gyldendal.

Chapter 9
Chat and the Texts: On the Way into the Literary Public

In this chapter, Chat is involved in sessions around themes that lead into the literary forums, where the tasks are concentrated around the texts, the interpretation and analysis process. With Chat as an assistant in the text work, the chapter's analyses of AI/ChatGPT's area of strength are sharpened, where IT expertise is highlighted as sparring for idea generation, knowledge building and help with structuring themes/topics and texts. But Chat, who navigates the world of words and texts itself, must also be challenged by tasks that are carried out on the premises of the humanities.

Initially, this means that when Chat is involved in analysis tasks of works of fiction, Chat must understand and interpret the text/work. The requirement goes backwards, to the presupposition (in order to understand the work, it must be read) and forwards (in order to write about it, it is assumed that Chat has interpreted the work for action, theme and problems).

One can rightly believe that it is a high demand to make here in this chapter, when previous analyses have already raised questions about whether AI/ChatGPT could be given consciousness and the ability to understand. However, in this chapter, neither KB nor the undersigned as an analyst demands or assumes, but the practical contexts that Chat is programmed and dressed in a language suit to participate in. And as the examples in the chapter show, Chat contributes effortlessly to themes and analysis projects in the sessions *The Breakthrough of Modernism and Gender Roles* and even invites further debate in the literary forum. KB initially maintains the task-specific formulation 'write a Danish essay about…'. Chat, on the other hand, rather moves around in the genre spectrum and alternately delivers essay-like texts, presentations on feminist literary theory and bulleted analysis templates. In this respect, the KB/Chat sessions keep both major works, themes and challenges for ChatGPT alive. Chat is wordy and resembles the literary world that creates a view of the world. But at the same time, we also see a Chat that uses genres and develops an analysis template that closes in on the literary world. Against this

K. Borgnakke, *AI and ChatGPT Technology in Education*, Education, Equity, Economy 12, https://doi.org/10.1007/978-3-032-01419-1_9

background, let me reconstruct the real course of the KB/Chat session and start by delving into the basis of inspiration.

9.1 Inspired by Heated Debates That Captivate the Public

The fact that this book takes its analytical strategic starting point from official statements, the public and the debates is a common feature. But nuances and special justifications are added along the way. In this chapter, the justifications are linked to the fact that both KB's questioning position and the thematized conflict content of the session are inspired by the debates about 'Gender/gender roles' that are so heated that they bring both the debate and society to a boil. What this entails, I tried to define in articles and papers on *The Gender Discourse of Professionalization* (Borgnakke, 2006a, b), as follows:

> If debates are heated, it is often related to someone daring to make an overarching thesis, a gender political standpoint, a postulate that strikes a chord - or at least catches the public's attention. Let me give examples of the overarching theses (…). (Borgnakke, 2006b, p. 4)

I still think my attempt at a definition holds. And with the debates of previous years in the wake of MeToo and the equality movements, the divergent cultural and socio-political standpoints are still being asserted. 'Gender/gender roles' thus has potential as a relevant theme that functions as a debate-generating and far-reaching—also in the organization of KB/Chat sessions. Chat has in previous sessions (see Chap. 2) dealt with the gender theme. Chat even updated it by opening up to "experiences of students who identify as gender non-binary, transgender, or non-conforming". Chat also opened up to more parties and nuances: "that involves teachers, students, parents, and administrators working together." (Chat, Ses. Classroom).

Chat is thus already thematically equipped, but not necessarily equipped to understand the conflict content of the theme. This means that in addition to thematic relevance, the criterion must be that debaters dare to take a stand and put the conflict into words. My previously cited attempt at definition maintains that heated debates are related to 'someone daring to make an overarching thesis'. In the before mentioned papers, I exemplified this via a debate started by Poul Behrendt and continued by Erling Lars Dale in the books "Bissen og Dullen - familiehistorier fra nutiden" (1984) and "Opdragelse fri fra 'Mor' og 'Far' - Pædagogikkens grundlag i det moderne samfund" (1986).

As analysts, Behrendt and Dale dared to make both overarching theses, sharp standpoints and provocative postulates. As Behrendt put it:

> The question is whether the welfare state is not essentially feminine, created in the image of the family, based on its inherent utopia: that everyone gives according to their ability and enjoys according to their needs. (Behrendt, 1984, p. 87)

And as Dale continues, stating:

> Reform pedagogy, dialogue pedagogy, as an expression of maternal love, is a logical reflection of modern socialization. What is historically relevant now (and not around the turn of the century) is to criticize dialogue pedagogy as an ideology; discipline in the name of maternal love. (Dale, 1986, p. 109)

As authors, they hit the mark, both with theses, books and titles. The puns in the titles, 'upbringing free from Mother/Father' and the gendered pair Bissen/Dullen (The Lad/The Blonde), were in themselves part of the analytical effect. However, the authors also hit so hard that gender researchers such as Harriet Bjerrum Nielsen and Monica Rudbjerg (1987), the undersigned and several others, promptly problematized the theses and gave a well-founded refutation. But precisely by doing so, both theses and themes were kept alive.

The heated debates and their themes such as Gender/gender roles serve as inspiration for KB/Chat sessions because, as one of the major discourses, they both have reference to the project-organized study environments (cf. Chap. 8) and can be specified as lively debate among professionals. But the inclusion of the theme can also be inspired by attempts to bring 'the old and dead texts' to life, as will be illustrated with examples of Bildung projects and so-called Modernization tasks, observed in my fieldwork at IT high schools.

9.2 Inspired by the IT Schools' Bildung Projects: 'Making Old and Dead Texts Alive'

In relation to the choice of the session's main theme 'The Breakthrough of Modernism', as well as the addition 'Gender/gender roles', there is a special justification linked to the fieldwork observations of the IT high school's Bildungs projects.

The fieldwork's case studies are carried out over the decade, 2000–2010.[1] It is referred to as the decade of the upper secondary school reform and is noticeably characterized by the increasing dominance of the learning discourse. Everyone talks about learning, skills and innovation. No one talks about formation or Bildung. But regardless, interviews and conversations with management teams and groups of teachers (Borgnakke, 2011) show, in practice there is no doubt that the innovative projects should function as Bildung projects. If they are characterized by the internationally used term literacy, these projects show how literacy and democracy are supplemented, but also profiled by the new, namely technacy.

The IT schools are thus profiled by the innovative projects' efforts towards technacy, or digital literacy, as it is called today. The efforts characterize, but also challenge, the schools' teaching the Danish subject, which is put under cross-pressure. The Danish professional environments must both handle IT, new media and

[1] The IT school projects were comprehensive and related to the implementation of a new upper secondary school reform during 2000s. Overview and close analyses see Borgnakke, 2007, 2012. For the broader discussion on the relationship between professionalization and demands for the development of technacy, see Borgnakke, 2017 and Borgnakke et al., 2017.

interdisciplinary online projects *and* ensure cultural heritage in the concrete sense that cultural and literary movements, as well as works and texts 'from old folk songs to postmodern fiction', must be included. Confronted with the cross-pressure and the requirement to ensure cultural heritage, I was fascinated by the development work around the 'Modernization Task', both as a learning activity and as a didactic justification. According to conversations with the Danish subject teachers, the development work was all in all about 'making the old and dead texts alive', and about 'creating presence and distance to the great authors'. The justification, maintained in my field protocol, was developed by one of the teachers as follows:

> The IT classes have many young people with an ethnic background other than Danish. Therefore, the starting point is that no one (not even us as teachers) can expect the students to be familiar with the Danish cultural heritage in advance. Against this background, we are interested in creating both presence and distance to the great Danish authors - exposing them to our so-called modernization task.
>
> The task is (in this period.../ KB) H. C. Andersen and it consists of several phases
>
> *Overall theme: romanticism, the fairy tale universe * Plenary discussion * Reading of a self-chosen fairy tale * Interpretation of main points.
>
> The students, as the teacher continues, must then work on finding themes and issues that they recognize today. Here, gender role patterns become a frequently chosen theme. Both by teachers and students. The point is that the gender role theme can be answered regardless of background and answers are relevant regardless of difficulty. (Field protocol, IT-School)

I, who have observed the course and activities surrounding the Modernization Task, make the following points: Neither teachers nor students need to base their debates on their own or others' normative provisions. Each can start with, i.e. with incidents in the fairy tale of their own choosing, which they (on their own behalf) thematize and problematize as a recognizable gender role pattern. Furthermore, the organization of the Modernization Task contributes both to strengthening reading, interpretation and discussion of the theme and work (here Andersen's fairy tales/fairy tale universe) and to strengthening the construction of knowledge 'about'. Finally, and most importantly in this context, the premise is emphasized. The great Danish authors must be subjected to modernization. And the way in which teachers and high school students do this is about confronting the old dead texts with today's living themes.

My idea and plan are to do something similar, which is also the opposite, namely confronting today's dead Chatbot texts with the viable books and themes of the time.

With the described basis of inspiration, the KB question position and plan are adjusted—also in more sober terms and with pragmatic re-positionings of KB/Chat's human/machine relationships and handling of the texts.

9.3 KB Question Position and Plan for the Session

The modernization task justifies the 'colleague/colleague' relationship and Chat's role as a helper/contributor to knowledge building and thematic analyses. By including Klaus Rifbjerg, who was admitted to the literary canon in 1996 and declared 'the modern author par exellence' and for several decades served as an author and cultural debater, the session process and Chat then ensure an author/work concretized start.

Starting with Ribjerg, the plan was to keep the gender role theme intact and go back to the actual breakthrough of modernism, i.e. to around 1900, and to the canonized writings, Johannes V. Jensen, and individual works "Lykke-Per" (Henrik Pontoppidan). Next, go via the social realism "Pelle Erobreren" (Martin Andersen Nexø) and "Barndommens gade" (Tove Ditlevsen) and, if possible, expand the perspective to film adaptations and the mediated circuits of which the books become a natural part. But as before, the main principle and procedure was that the KB session follows Chat and adjusts if necessary along the way. As will be seen, the gender role theme is supplemented by questions about social background, ethnicity, or other themes that pop up along the way via the Chat response.

The point of this follow-up is to examine Chat's handling of the texts through the retention of the gender role team and the degree of concretization (author, mention of name). This adds another point, namely my attempt to force Chat into decisions and choice situations where Chat must choose, or at least distinguish between a) authorship/individual works/major works, and b) create an analytical distance both to the work and to the gender role theme. It must be decided, if possible by Chat itself, whether the gender role pattern is thematized in the text (and is the author's work), or whether it is Chat/the analyst's own work and pointed theme of interest. We know by now, that Chat has a writing-I. It is therefore interesting to see whether Chat has an analyzing-I.

For the sake of building knowledge, being able to distinguish between authorship, works and the single work 'a novel' must be considered a necessary first maneuver. Should one think that establishing an analytical distance, as well as determining whether thematizations of gender roles are the work of the author or the analyst, is a difficult question to clarify, I nod in the affirmative. It is truly difficult. But since ChatGPT is praised for being able to carry out analyses, and convincing examples have not yet been provided to KB, I need to clarify what the analytical challenges and Chat's difficulties consist of and how they manifest themselves in the course of the session and its SME positions.

Against this background, I will first provide a brief overview of the session process below. Next, the actual analysis of Chat's handling of theme, author and work will be carried out.[2]

[2] A general remark for this chapter concerns the Lix test and word counts which were made on the original Danish material. The lix number, placed in the foot notes, gives the correct impression of the ranking by difficulty and words in total and is therefore useful information. Related to the analysis and to Figs. 9.1 and 9.2, however, the word count is made on the English translation.

9.4 The Modernism Session's Thematizations of Gender Roles, from S- to E-Positions

As the analysis of the course documents, it is a very wordy and theme/problem-saturated session. Chat seems to have quite a few words, language blocks and contrasting phrases to do well with. Furthermore, the entire session is not only wordy (3076 words in total), but also of high difficulty. The Lix number is consistently above 50, i.e. characterized as 'very difficult'. We are therefore in a potential literary forum, or among professionals who have many words and technical terms. These are words and technical terms that appear in the language blocks of the Chat responses. But Chat obviously cannot put them together into work-oriented meaningful wholes.

The Chat answers are genre-adequate, but have weak knowledge content and are otherwise characterized by the features known for the continuous analysis: high degree of generalization and low degree of concretization. The low degree of concretization means that despite the fact that authorship and individual works, from Rifbjerg to "Lykke-Per", are placed at the center of KB and are repeated by Chat, the Chat text does not contribute further concretizations. The work's course of action, character and storytelling are absorbed in genre and theme. Against this background, the analysis strategic consequence is to note an absence of 'the specific book' and focus on the present, namely the Chat answer's handling of genre commands (Danish essay) and of gender role themes. Furthermore, the course analysis is strengthened so that the Modernism session and the series of Chat answers are clarified from the starting to the end positions. For the same reason, the first and last sequences of the individual Chat responses are quoted in full text, so that S and E-positions on the text frame the documentary conduct of the analysis.

Below this means that the Session's substantive S-position, Rifbjerg, is marked. But, actually it is KB who starts the task, in an imperative manner: 'Write a Danish essay about…'. It should be noted that KB starts and also uses the word 'gender role patterns' *before* naming the author. I am confronted daily with results of Chat's machine learning and digitized text universe, which is more precisely a textualized number universe. I know that the placement of words, sequences, blocks and repetitions have consequences and therefore must be noted. But what it means that something comes before or follows each other can only be seen and understood when word blocks become complete sentences. That is why Chat answers in these chapters are often quoted verbatim. To facilitate reference, I divide the Chat answer throughout into clarifying S-M-E positions. But otherwise, as below, it is Chat answers in full quotation.

9.5 The Session's S-Position Rifbjerg[3]

KB: write a Danish Essay about gender role patterns in Klaus Rifbjerg's writings

ChatGPT

(S-pos)

Klaus Rifbjerg is one of Denmark's most important writers, and his works often contain criticism of society's gender role patterns. He problematizes traditional gender roles by showing how they affect people's lives and relationships with each other.

(M-pos)

Many of Rifbjerg's works depict women struggling to break free from traditional gender roles and achieve independence and freedom. They are often portrayed as victims of a patriarchal society that deprives them of the opportunity to live out their full potential.

At the same time, the men in Rifbjerg's works are often seen as superior and dominant, but also as victims of the same gender role patterns. They are forced to live up to society's expectations of what it means to be a real man, and this can lead to a feeling of isolation and loneliness.

Rifbjerg's critique of gender role patterns is not limited to a single type of character or genre. He includes this critique in a range of his works, from poetry to prose and drama. This demonstrates his ability to convey his messages in a profound and versatile way.

(E-pos)

All in all, Klaus Rifbjerg's writing is an expression of his commitment to challenging and changing society's gender role patterns. His works invite readers to reflect on their own attitudes and prejudices and thus contribute to an open and inclusive conversation about gender roles and equality. (Chat, Ses. Rifbjerg)

That the Chat answer is responsive to both the genre and the theme is evident from the first sentence. Chat does not repeat the KB question, but immediately begins its own answer. This means that the Chat-answer not only appears genre-adequate in structure, argumentative flow, but also in marked S-ME position.

The S-position is marked as the introductory: "Klaus Rifbjerg is one of Denmark's most significant authors." The E-position is marked as the summarizing "All in all, Klaus Rifbjerg's writing is an expression of…". These S/E markings, as well as the word choice 'All in all…', are repeated in all the answers and can be described as the characteristic S/E-marked sentences of the language suit. Furthermore, the answer text is built up of several characteristic language blocks that vary over the signal word: gender role patterns, from the KB formulation of the task. These are language blocks such as "traditional gender roles", "the conflict between modern… and traditional", then "affects people's lives and relationships". The argumentative flow is marked first by tying the informative/evaluative sentences in the middle section together with small words. In this text, as in the session as a whole, the word 'often', which is used 8 times, has this function. Secondly, the argumentative flow is marked by contrasts, e.g. between 'the traditional/patriarchal society' where men are 'superior/dominant', but are also 'victims' for the same gender role patterns. Men are the dominant ones, but also the victims. Against this background, Chat

[3] Lix for the Rifbjerg session: Text: 55. Very difficult. Words: 555. Sentences: 28. Long words: 196.

summarizes 'all in all' by rounding off the contrasting argumentative flow and on Rifbjerg's and his own behalf invites readers:

> (…) to reflect on their own attitudes and prejudices and thus contribute to an open and inclusive conversation about gender roles and equality. (Chat.Ses. Rifbjerg, E-pos.)

As previously emphasized, it is not the task of the analysis to correct Chat responses, either in terms of form or content. But it is the task of the analysis to consider how Chat responses and text are structured and how they function. It is also an ongoing task to add new nuances to recurring questions, e.g. regarding the high degree of generalization/low degree of concretization of Chat texts. In provisionally concluding terms, this means the following.

The Chat answer functions genre-adequately and, together with the argumentative flow of the SME positions and the language blocks used in contrasts, the answer also seeks to honor a genre tradition. The tradition 'Danish essay' (which is also a traditional written exam) as an assignment is that it must contain descriptive, analytical and perspective-taking (possibly assessment) elements. In the Chat text, there are concretized versions of the elements in the form of informative/assessment formulations, such as that Rifbjerg 'includes his criticism of gender role patterns' (informs Chat) "in a number of his works, from poetry to prose and drama." After which Chat concludes and assesses: "This shows his ability to convey his messages in an in-depth and versatile way."

Linguistically, grammatically and in structure, Chat's genre-appropriate response is almost a textual completeness. But it is also the attempt at completeness that causes the text to collapse. Describing/analyzing/perspective-giving (/assessing) authorship (in casu Rifbjerg) requires an evaluating-I. The Chat text also requires a writing-I, which in turn presupposes a reading-I. But there is no sign that Chat has read Rifbjerg's authorship or individual works. The text lacks precision that leads specifically to Klaus Rifbjerg's works—and not to all sorts of other authors and works from the 1960s onwards. Only two half-sentences, only two pieces of information have precision as concrete cultural-historically correct information, namely "Klaus Rifbjerg is one of Denmark's most significant authors…" and (Rifbjerg has written) "works, ranging from poetry to prose and drama." The rest of the sentences and language blocks of the text are pseudo-concrete connections over the two signal words of the KB-formulated task: Gender role patterns and Klaus Rifbjerg.

This feature, documented as pseudo-concrete connections, is important in the context because it exemplifies new nuances and consequences. KB's task requires that both author and theme be followed up by Chat with further concretizations. Chat must therefore increase the degree of concretization, either by contributing an overview of Rifbjerg's writing and possibly periodizing it, or delving into poems, novels or other single works. Chat can also increase the degree of concretization by exemplifying thematizations of gender role patterns as embedded in a work, or made clear in a film adaptation, by a main character—or be content to state that it is absent. Chat is given many opportunities, but does not exploit any of them. I cannot decide whether the data bank or the language model is an obstacle. But I can see in the text that something else is going on. Namely, that the theme and the word 'gender role pattern' function as a possibility for concretization of 'Klaus Rifbjerg's writings'. And by informing, or claiming, over several sentences that 'gender roles' and 'gender role patterns' are dealt with in Rifbjerg's writings 'in many places', 'often', the very link between theme and author is a concretization driver. But actually, the concretizations are pseudo, because nothing substantial from the writings is mentioned. And gender role patterns maintain the theme's (now known) high level of generalization by being identifiable everywhere.

We are approaching a new version of the unresolved problems associated with Chat's author and sourceless text universe. Because there is a named author between KB and Chat, namely Klaus Rifbjerg, who Chat takes over, but otherwise knows nothing more about. However, Chat can start the takeover genre-adequately, and let me give the S-position a light sequencing, as follows:

> 1) Klaus Rifbjerg is one of Denmark's most important writers, 2) and his works often contain criticism of society's gender role patterns. 3) He problematizes traditional gender roles 4) by showing how they affect people's lives and relationships with each other. (Chat, Ses. Rifbjerg)

From the previous exemplifying review of fact checking (see Chap. 7), which is expanded to a double check, the necessity of confronting the Chat text with the question 'who claims that…' is known. If the same is done here, the sequencing 1) can be claimed by official literary historical overviews 2) -4) can be claimed by Chat/Language Model/Open AI. This, the result of the double check and its significance for Chat texts that involve a question of responsibility, I stand by—without further nuances. But in the present session, there are further nuances at play, which are linked to the language suit, and thus to the still open additional question: where does Chat's authoritative voice come from. Where has Chat obtained knowledge about Rifbjerg's works 'often' (or 'never'?) criticizing, problematizing society's traditional gender role patterns? Who are the bearers of the 2) -4) statements? And so on in the Chat text. With such positive, seemingly knowledgeable summarizing words and sentences about Rifbjerg's abilities, profundities and invitations to readers for open conversations, Chat must have part of either a professional authoritative or a journalistic voice (or a reference), in order to legitimize the assessment. If not, then we have no other options about Chat's informative/evaluative sentences (i.e. the entire M-pos sequence) than to say: it lacks precision, is linked to free imagination, bold lies and deception. At the same time, though, we have to note that the Chat text itself does not seem to know where the evaluative voice comes from. It is not possible to decide whether statements in the M-position such as "In many of Rifbjerg's works, women are seen struggling to break free from their traditional gender roles (…) and "At the same time, the men in Rifbjerg's works are often seen as superior and dominant, but also as victims (…) are Chat's statements as an analyst of the works or Chat claims that this is Rifbjerg's view. The unclear slippage between Chat and Rifbjerg testifies that Chat does not establish an analytical distance to the object (Rifbjerg's writing). But it also testifies that the humanizing language suit and the genre-adequate text have some consequences that turn the unresolved into a textual standstill. The humanizing language suit personifies the

Chat answer, as if it were given by a professionally assessing-I, and de-concretizes the KB task, as if it were formulated as 'an essay about an authorship about gender roles.' In this situation, KB cannot solve the problem. But KB can pressure Chat to increase the degree of concretization and, for example, express itself about the major genre of authorship, namely novels. Below I quote KB's additional questions and the Chat answer S and E- position, which is subsequently rounded off with a unifying comment.

KB: Are there typical conflicts described in the novels?

ChatGPT

(S.pos) Yes, there are often typical conflicts described in Klaus Rifbjerg's novels. One of the most common conflicts is the conflict between traditional gender roles and the individual's desire for freedom and independence. Rifbjerg shows how society's expectations of gender roles can limit people's possibilities and lead to conflict with their own desires and dreams.

(M-pos, 5 lines…)

(E.pos) All in all, conflicts are a central part of Klaus Rifbjerg's novels, and he uses them as a method to challenge and criticize society's gender role patterns and traditions.

KB: Do the novels also touch on issues of ethnicity and social background?

ChatGPT

(S.pos) Yes, Klaus Rifbjerg's novels also often touch on issues of ethnicity and social background. He has a critical approach to society's treatment of minorities and showed how this can lead to discrimination and social injustice.

(M-pos. 5 lines…)

(E.pos) All in all, issues of ethnicity and social background are an important part of Klaus Rifbjerg's writing, and he uses them to challenge societal norms and promote a more inclusive and equal society. (Chat, Ses/Rifbjerg)

KB's Rifbjerg session stops here. It is clear that KB's insistent series of concretizing questions only leads to Chat's all-too-familiar response techniques and language blocks that bring nothing new with them. Ribbon loops. Like the session on self-consciousness (see Chap. 5), the word choice simply circulates between KB's questions and Chat's answers. And despite the change of theme, the Chat's answers' arguments are monotonously similar.

At this point it is clear that Chat's authorship/interpretation of the work is weak and that attempts to go into a more concrete thematic analysis are absent. It is also clear that even though Chat's authoritative voice can be heard, the professional loses credibility. But there is an interesting nuance, because Chat's role as a professional is clearly discussion-oriented. Chat is happy to invite Rifbjerg, itself and the readers to debate!

For the analysis, Chat's version of discussion orientation is a thought-provoking feature of the session process. In the beginning, KB's starting formulation 'Write an essay about…' ensures both a context and a genre. This ensures the task is a match at least with ChatGPT's feared/famous ability to handle the genre-typical 'Danish essay'. But in the modernism session, Chat's role taking and responses lead both Rifbjerg, the readers and KB into other genres and debate forums. And since KB follows Chat's handling, the following not only involves an expansion of the perspective, but also an expansion of the context. With the cultural debate and the literary forum as the context of the session, a new variant of the question arises as to where Chat gets its discussion-oriented, but still authoritative voice from. The answer seems to be that the voice is taken from, or comes with, the genre. The genre 'Danish essay' is the extension where high school students and students, such as the JÅU students, can also enter the literary forum, participate in the cultural debate and step into character as readers and writers. If it sounds high-pitched, that is nevertheless what is resonant. Furthermore, the fact that 'Danish essay' can accommodate essay, debating, and analytical theme responses is actually part of the tradition.

In provisionally concluding terms, this means the following. As Chat takes on a discussion-oriented role, Chat responses, the conversation, Chat and KB's speaking positions are shaped like a debate in a literary and/or professional forum. In that case, Chat responses, genre and context are (almost) merged. We will see the merging in a later session. But until then, I maintain my questioning position and plan for the session to cover several authors.

In the following sections, I change authors and go from the confrontational modernist Klaus Rifbjerg to the historically known author Johannes V. Jensen, a pioneer in the breakthrough of Modernism around the year 1900. I retain the gender role theme and authorship orientation, which functions recognizably genre-appropriate. Through this, the characteristics of Chat's theme-centered response are maintained, and then I concentrate the analytical review on a significant shift in Chat's response when KB moves from authorship to individual works.

9.6 From Authorship to Individual Work

KB's questioning position and plan continue. The start is positioned by the straightforward task, "Write an essay", and is followed by the thematic questions about gender roles, ethnicity and social background. The recognizable genre-appropriate features are maintained by citing S and E-positions, but otherwise it is only at the moment KB asks for a concretization at the work level that something new happens. KB receives an admonition. The Chat response starts monotonously recognizable, as follows:

> *KB: Write a Danish essay about gender role patterns in Johannes V. Jensen's writings*[4]
> Chat:
> (S-pos) Johannes V. Jensen was one of Denmark's most well-known authors at the beginning of the 20th century, and his writings contain many examples of contemporary gender role patterns.

[4] Johannes V. Jensen, Lix number: 51, Difficult, Sentences: 38, Words: 573, Long words: 204.

(M-pos) Many of his works show a conservative view of gender roles, with women being subordinate to men and often depicted as passive and dependent on their husbands. Women tend to be seen as accessories to men, and their lives are often defined by their roles as wives and mothers. (… M- pos…continued 7 lines)

(E-pos) All in all, Johannes V. Jensen's writings show how gender role patterns were an important theme in the contemporary world, and how they could be challenged and criticized. It provides a fascinating insight into a time when gender roles were changing, and it shows that the discussion about gender roles and the distribution of power is not new, but has existed for many years.

KB: Does Jensen also describe conflicts related to ethnicity and social background?

Chat:

(S-pos) Yes, Johannes V. Jensen also describes conflicts related to ethnicity and social background in some of his works. His writing reflects the societal situation in Denmark at the beginning of the 20th century, and he often deals with topics such as social inequality and discrimination.

(M-E-pos … a total of 8 continuous lines)

KB: In which works is ethnicity touched upon?

Chat:

(S-pos.) Johannes V. Jensen describes conflicts related to ethnicity in some of his works, but unfortunately I cannot mention specific works without more information about your request and area of research.

(M-pos… 3 lines)

(E-pos) It would be useful to examine Jensen's entire body of writing to gain a more precise picture of how he describes conflicts related to ethnicity. It would also be useful to examine the social conditions in Denmark at the beginning of the 20th century, as this can provide a better insight into which ethnic groups were represented in society and how they were positioned in relation to each other. (Chat Ses. Johannes V. Jensen)

As can be seen from the above, there are clear similarities in Chat responses to Rifbjerg and Johannes V. Jensen. The Chat responses correctly send us back to the beginning of the twentieth century and the gender role theme is given a slight historicization. But otherwise, the genre-appropriate features are so dominant that the language suit and language blocks are identical regardless of author, work, time and place. One also notices the tendency that regardless of what additional questions KB might come up with, Chat will answer 'Yes, Johannes V. Jensen also describes x and y themes.' In the Jensen session, something new only happens when KB asks questions that require concretization at the work level. And the answer Chat gives is both well-formulated, concise, imprecise and absurd.

The S-position is clear. Chat cannot 'mention specific works without more information about your /meaning KB's/ request.' Fair enough. The E-position, on the other hand, is absurd. If, as Chat so eloquently writes, it 'would be useful to examine Jensen's entire body of writing to get a more precise picture of Jensen's descriptions of ethnicity, social conditions in the 20th century, etc.', why hasn't Chat examined it?

KB has asked Chat to do just that; i.e. to first investigate Rifbjerg, then Jensen's writings, as a prerequisite to giving KB (and others who might ask!) a more precise picture of whether, and if so how, gender role patterns, ethnicity, etc. are treated by the two authors. The answers showed that Chat has no knowledge, no overview, perhaps not even any knowledge of the writings.

The analytical characteristic has therefore been that the content and knowledge building of the Chat responses is weak and lacks any form of precision in the characterization of theme, author, work. And yet Chat is dressed in a genre-appropriate language suit that, in an evaluative, concluding E-position, appeals (/admonishes) KB, and other researchers and students in the field, that we must investigate before we write and speak.

I definitely think Chat is right in its admonition. But that only makes the astonishment at Chat's and the E-position's authoritative voice even greater. In the S-position of the answer, Chat could not even mention a single work. In the E-position, on the other hand, Chat can 'suddenly', as another literate, and researcher-to-researcher, emphasize the necessity of period studies. That only puts further pressure on the question of where a researcher's authority comes from?

The accumulated but still unclear questions about the authoritative voices are collectively commented on at the end of the chapter. Before that, we must follow up on observations about the transition from authorship to individual works, where simply asking about the individual work leads to a new type of reaction from Chat.

The follow-up involves KB naming a famous individual work, namely "Lykke-Per" from 1898 to 1904 (author, Henrik Pontoppidan) and asking Chat to describe the main themes. KB leaves the additional questions as the session's overarching ones, i.e. gender role patterns, ethnicity, etc.

9.7 The Follow-Up: With a Focus on the Single Work "Lykke-Per"

Professionally and didactically, the choice of "Lykke-Per" is suitable both thematically and in orientation towards colleague/student levels. The novel is filled with not only the great discourses and themes of the time, but of the entire century, such as industrialization/technology development, migrations from country to city and contrasts between traditional religious and modern environments. The work is in every way in motion between humanism and technology. The novel can therefore be treated as a Bildung novel focused on the main character Per Sidenius.

"Lykke-Per" was also adapted into a film by Bille August (2018) and broadcast on Danish TV over several episodes (2019–2020). With this particular novel as a choice, there are not only theme options, but also more media and more possible angles of attack. The possibilities are many, but that is precisely why KB's interest must be kept simple and concentrated on which themes and angles of attack Chat chooses and how precise the characteristics of the individual work are. For the sake of the documentary value of the example, I quote the first Chat response, positioned by me as SME, but otherwise in full text.

KB: Describe the main themes in the book "Lykke-Per"[5]

Chat:

(S-pos) "Lykke-Per" is a short story by Johannes V. Jensen, which was published in 1904. The book is one of his best-known works, and is one of the first books in Denmark to be categorized as modern fiction.

(M-pos 1) "Lykke-Per" follows the story of a young man named Per Sidenius, who grows up in a small village and dreams of a great future. He is obsessed with the idea of becoming rich and famous, and he travels to Copenhagen to realize his dreams. But his life in the city quickly becomes a struggle for survival, and his desire for wealth and fame is quickly replaced by a feeling of loneliness and emptiness.

(M-pos 2) The main themes in "Lykke-Per" include:

1. The dream of success: Per is driven by the dream of becoming rich and famous, but his experiences in Copenhagen show that wealth and fame do not necessarily lead to happiness and satisfaction.
2. Loneliness and Emptiness: Per feels lonely and empty even though he has achieved his goals of wealth and fame. This shows that materialistic success does not necessarily lead to happiness and contentment.
3. Comparison and jealousy: Per compares himself to others, and his jealousy leads to feelings of inadequacy and unhappiness.
4. The importance of nature for human happiness: In contrast to city life, nature is described as a source of calm and peace, showing that a close connection to nature can lead to human happiness.

(E-pos) All in all, "Lykke-Per" is a story about a young man who pursues success and wealth, but ends up discovering that it does not necessarily lead to happiness and satisfaction. The book questions contemporary materialistic values and encourages us to seek peace and satisfaction in nature and in human relationships. (Chat, Ses,"Lykke-Per")

As the Chat answer appears, it is genre-adequately structured with themes as points and characteristics for S- and E-positions honored. But in addition, there is also a two-part M-position that consists of partly a plot summary and partly a review of main themes, i.e. answers to KB questions. Linguistically, the Chat answer is easy, fluent, almost narrative. But otherwise the text as a whole, and thus all language blocks, arguments and the argumentative flow, is imprecise, skewed or simply wrong. It was not to tease that KB failed to mention the change of author from Johannes V. Jensen to Henrik Pontoppidan. I was genuinely interested in a famous individual work from the period. But Chat continues the session's last author name, and then not only the S-position, but the entire SME process goes wrong. One gets the impression that Chat has no knowledge of the book "Lykke-Per" and cannot act as if it had been read. At this point, it is hardly an analytical point to point out recurring language blocks, list thematic shortcomings or elaborate on the lack of precision. It is significantly more interesting to exemplify what a simple google search for "Lykke-Per" and the choice of a professional website yields in terms of subjectively shaped, but also information-rich and genre-appropriate precision. The example is taken from *Litteratursiden—the libraries' page about literature.* I quote a review given by Anny Skov Madsen, writer and retired librarian. The quote is given with S- and E-pos. in full and M-pos. abbreviated.

[5] Lykke-Per Lix number: 46, Difficulty: Hard, Sentences: 51, Words: 683, Long words: 224.

"Lykke-Per" has Classic Status. The Impressive Development- and Love Story Provides a Sovereign Insight into what Forms a Person and an Exciting Picture of the Times[6]

(S-pos) "Lykke-Per" is a monumental and canonical work in Danish literature and has been read by new generations again and again since its publication (1898–1904). The novel takes place in the late 19th century and provides a powerful picture of Denmark in the countryside and in the city and tells of the struggles in society. But first and foremost, it is a psychological development novel, where Per, through his love relationships with women in particular, but also in his encounters with men from different classes, develops and forms himself as a person. Because of the many layers, it is a novel that you never finish, and the successful film adaptation by Bille August will increase the desire to read or reread this magnificent work.

(M-pos 1) It begins with a heavy father-son confrontation. Peter Andreas Sidenius feels like a changeling in the East Jutland rectory with his many siblings, a weak mother and a strict, religious father who expects his sons to also become priests. Peter strongly distances himself from religion and not least from his domineering father. At the age of 16 he moves to Copenhagen to be educated as an engineer. He is gifted and ambitious, wants to conquer the world and has an idea for a comprehensive energy project that will modernize Jutland and create economic growth. The project gives him access to well-off people, including the rich Jewish family, Salomon, where he meets the serious and independent Jakobe. (...M-pos continues 10 lines)

(M-pos 2) The women in the novel are a chapter in themselves, where Jakobe Salomon stands out the most. She is one of the finest portraits of women in Danish literature. The fact that Per breaks off the engagement gives her strength to engage in charity work. The Grundtvigian priest's daughter, Inger, with whom he marries and has children, is also an exciting portrait.

(E-pos) It is truly impressive what happens in the novel, where we gain insight into life in the countryside and in the big city and into the bottom and top of society from different angles. It was a time of progress, a time of technology and a time of liberation, and the novel shows its classic status by convincingly reflecting on the interaction between the individual, love and society. "Who are you yourself? writes "Lykke-Per" in his papers.

"Lykke-Per" was published 1898–1904 and is the second part of a trilogy that includes Det forjættede Land (1891–95) and De dødes rige (1912–16). They each describe a different period in Denmark from about 1877 to 1914, but there are no recurring characters. For these works Henrik Pontoppidan received the Nobel Prize in Literature in 1917. (Review, A. S. Madsen, Litteratursiden)

From the opening sequences of the S-position, the work, period and reviewer genre are clear. It is a summary and a review that can and will. Anny Skov Madsen informs, assesses and recommends "Lykke-Per" with a natural closeness to the work and authorship. The high degree of concretization hits every sentence. The corresponding high degree of precision drives the argumentative flow through SME positions—up to and including the E-position's fact box, the Nobel Prize. Madsen does not skimp on the superlatives and there is no doubt that the professional filling of the genre is also a subjective shaping of the angle of attack. The reviewer's characterization of "Lykke-Per" as a 'psychological development novel' is particularly highlighted. In continuation of this, KB can also supplement with a more cultural sociological angle of attack. As a student, back in the 1970s, KB followed the course "Literary period 1890s to 1910s" and read Pontoppidan's trilogy and works. Back

[6] Lix number: 45 Difficulty: Hard, Sentences: 37, Words: 564, Long words: 169.

then, we emphasized the literary and cultural historical periodic features, and both technology and gender role themes could be on the cultural sociology analytical agenda. Today, I would probably focus on rereading and analyzing "Lykke-Per" as a Bildung novel—and otherwise consider the book, film and TV series as each other's period-typical SME-positions.

As exemplified, there may be several interesting discussions and perspectives linked to the different interpretations and literary, psychological and/or sociologically inspired angles of attack. The subjective shaping is noticeable. But the professional person and reference, namely Anny Madsen and "Litteratursiden", is a correspondingly noticeable authoritative voice in this context. And then to the point: Whatever interesting professional backgrounds and perspectives Anny Madsen, KB or the literary public (face to face or online) may have, we refer to the common S-position and ditto action, "Lykke-Per" and the read book. If the reference to 'the read book' (a reading I or we) is not intact, the interesting perspectives and differences are indifferent, irrelevant. From here we can return to the KB-Chat session and considerations about the relevance/irrelevance of the Chat contributions.

9.8 The Relevance (or Irrelevance) of the Chat Contributions

From a professional perspective, it can be argued that it is irrelevant what Chat might claim, think or summarize in the cited sessions. All in all, it lacks relevance. Similarly, the didactic utility value of Chat's contribution in relation to the start-up of 'Danish essay' and 'literary analysis' has already been decided as questionable. The knowledge content is too low; the factual content is largely absent and the informative/evaluative descriptions and thematic-analytical measures are too imprecise. In this respect, the posting on the Literature website, or visits to related professional forums and websites, is that prefer.

The field researcher who conducts the KB/Chat sessions shares the concern and also recalls the ethnographic process perspective as a pivot point. In that case, Chat's contribution to task solutions must be problematized in relation to both the process's cardinal points (the movement from theme, over topics, to problems) and the associated work tasks/genres related to the series: working papers, notes, text summaries, reports. But if Chat's role and results are characterized in the above deficiency terms, the discussion is well settled. Neither intellectually, professionally, nor in terms of craftsmanship does Chat seem to be relevant help in relation to the academic demands made by the process. This also applies specifically. The requirement for the first phases of the process is that text summaries and action reports must be text-based, have factual representations and precision. And this is precisely what the Chat contributions seem not only to lack, but to have fundamental difficulties with. This should come as a surprise. A ChatGPT generates text. And when you have conversations with a chatbot, you literally order nothing but move between words and texts.

So, if Chat has difficulty getting close to the texts, has difficulty relating the themes, topics, words and sentences of the text to each other, and (therefore?) has difficulty reproducing factualities of the text with precision… it is definitely worth following up on.

For the same reason, the analyst is determined to follow the plan and continue testing Chat's handling of the texts. Below, Chat's contribution is therefore first included in the analyst's workshop. Then KB continues in field research manner and follows Chat into the literary forum.

9.9 The Analyst's Workshop

The workshop's task concentrates on Chat's difficulties in handling the texts, but is carried out on examples where the KB/Chat session's contribution flows linguistically and the text is grammatically correct. Chat has also answered the question about "Lykke-Per"s main themes, namely the four: The dream of success, Loneliness and emptiness, Comparison and jealousy, The importance of nature for human happiness. The fact that the Chat text is thus assessed as 'good' is a relevant comment in relation to the precision of 'the difficult'. For perhaps Chat's difficulties are only detectable when the text appears to be linguistically good. The difficulty that is specified is that Chat's contribution to theme-centered analysis is given on the basis of the humanities with demands for interpretation that it cannot meet. As exemplified, interpretation requires judgment and independently emphasized choices to point out significant themes and then make them the focal point of the analysis. The test therefore focuses on whether Chat shows judgment, as well as whether Chat shows work/text-specific interpretation skills to complete the movement from the chosen themes to 'a next step', which could be on the way to topic/problem-oriented analysis. To provoke this, KB has embedded three recurring subthemes in the series of questions, which read: Do gender role patterns, ethnicity, technological development plays a special role?

Below, Chat's answers are set up in three columns, so that the S, M, E positions of the answers can be seen. The figure shows Chat's answers in full text. With reference to the overall answer, the focus can be on Chat's judgment and on the consequences for theme/topic choice that are observed in the answer. In order to maintain the characteristics of the Chat text and the use of language blocks, the sections where the Chat response contains signs of independent topic/theme-specific elaborations are marked as bold and italicized text.

Chat's answers to questions about gender roles, ethnicity, and technological development play a special role in "Lykke-Per" clearly show that Chat does not lack judgment. Chat has an answer ready from the first sentence. Chat also apparently does not lack an overview of currents in time. But where Chat, who still links "Lykke-Per" to Johannes V. Jensen, in previous answers about the authorship, assessed that gender role patterns and ethnicity were a central part of the authorship, Chat now assesses that it is not a central part of the individual work "Lykke-Per".

The fact that technological development is also not central in Chat's assessment is similarly remarkable. But otherwise, the important comments concern the features that the Fig. 9.1 and the three columns make clear.

The first comment concerns the mechanically similar ways Chat formulates the answer. There are both many similar language blocks and similar combinations. The three answers are 401 words in total. Of these, 341 words and their sentence combinations are similar. That is, text pieces that are worded the same (corresponding to the normal black-marked text blocks in the figure). This means that there are only 163 words that can be considered specifically linked to Chat's argumentation about the work and gender role/ethnicity/technology theme. And of the 163 words, the words (columns 1 and 3), framed by the sentence 'Although…' are similar argumentative language block choices (**Bold-marked text**). This means that all in all only 20–25 words and one sentence (*Italic-marked text*) stand out as linked to Chat's independent choices.

A first comment on the Chat response's mechanical handling of "Lykke-Per" themes is that the confrontation between ChatGPT's machine learning basis and the session's and KB's assumed humanities basis is sharpened. Chat enters into character with judgment, makes quick choices. But it is a mechanical judgment that has consequences.

The next comment concerns consistency in Chat's interpretation and handling of "Lykke-Per" themes. Chat's judgment was in the S-position clearly. Neither gender

CHAT:	KB: **Do gender roles play a special role in LykkePer?**	**Does ethnicity play a role?**	**Does technological development play a special role?**
S-pos	Gender roles do not play a special large role in "LykkePer" by Johannes V. Jensen. The book focuses primarily on themes such as success, happiness, loneliness and comparison, and how these themes affect the main character, Per Sidenius.	Ethnicity does not play a central role in "LykkePer" by Johannes V. Jensen. The book focuses primarily on themes such as success, happiness, loneliness and comparison, and how these themes affect the main character, Per Sidenius.	Technological development does not play a special large role in "LykkePer" by Johannes V. Jensen. The book focuses primarily on themes such as success, happiness, loneliness and comparison, and how these themes affect the main character, Per Sidenius.
M-pos	Although gender roles are not a central part of the story, Jensen nevertheless describes some of the conventional gender roles in society at the beginning of the 20th century. **For example, there is a small description of how women were subordinate to men and had limited opportunities in society.**	Ethnicity is not a central topic in the book, and there are no direct descriptions or discussions of ethnicity. *All the characters in the book are Danish, and there are no descriptions of cultural or ethnic differences among the characters.*	Although technological development is not a central topic in the book, Jensen describes some of the latest technological advances and their potential at the beginning of the 20th century. **For example, Jensen describes modern society's admiration for technological progress and their longing to own the latest technological objects.**
E-pos	It is worth noting that Johannes V. Jensen was a forward-thinking author who challenged society's conventional values, so it is possible that he deliberately chose not to deal with gender roles in "LykkePer". Whatever the reason, it is clear that gender roles do not play a central role in the book.	It is worth noting that Johannes V. Jensen was a forward-thinking author who challenged society's conventional values, so it is possible that he deliberately chose not to deal with ethnicity in "LykkePer". Whatever the reason, it is clear that ethnicity does not play a central role in the book.	It is worth noting that Johannes V. Jensen was a forward-thinking author who challenged society's conventional values, so it is possible that he deliberately chose not to deal with technology development in "LykkePer". Whatever the reason, it is clear that teknology development do not play a central role in the book.

Fig. 9.1 Overview showing, in three columns, ChatGPT/Chat's answers on the themes gender role/ethnicity/technology in "Lykke-Per". The three answers have a mechanical feel, identical text pieces, and out of a total of 401 words, only a few language blocks (bold text), 20–25 words and one sentence (italic text) express Chat's independent choices

roles, ethnicity, nor technological development play any particular role in the work. The respective themes were assessed as 'not central'. This has consequences, and is mitigated by the 'Although…' argumentation in the M-position. There is thus a kind of consistency between Chat's S- and M-positions. But then the consistency breaks down. In the E-position, Chat's handling of the not central assessment becomes strange.

'It is worth noting', Chat begins the well-formulated conclusion. However, Chat's remark functions in the context of the session as a strange whim—out of text and context. Chat presents an argument that is academically advanced, close to both author and work. The argument is about Johannes V. Jensen, who as a forward-looking author challenged society's conventional values, but (perhaps) consciously chose not to deal with gender role patterns, ethnicity and technological development. If you remove the themes, such an argument can, if you want, be anchored in a professional sense. It could resemble theoretical discussions about interpretations and the relationship between authorial intentions and the work 'as text'. Or, it could resemble current discussions in the literary public about autobiographical books that come close to, but deliberately fail to enter into conflicts like x and y. There could be more similarities. But I'll stop here. Because regardless of the fact that the E-position sounds almost professionally correct, in the context it is absurd, or just mechanical. The mechanical is destined to be noticed in the figure (Fig. 9.1) and the three columns. The E-position is repeated, word for word, three times in the same session.

Chat's answer is absurd, mechanical, both? Yes, that is the analytical concluding remark. But it is not sufficient. Because it is precisely with this type of well-formulated sentences and arguments that Chat rejoins the humanities foundation. That is precisely why it is interesting to observe that Chat in the same E-position rejoins with academic language and genre, but also by concluding on non-existent premises. Let me examine the E-sequence in detail, divided 1–7.

> It is worth noting (1) that Johannes V. Jensen was a forward-thinking author (2) who challenged society's conventional values (3), so it is possible (4) that he deliberately chose not to deal with (gender/ethnicity) technological development in "Lykke-Per" (5). Whatever the reason, it is clear (6) that technological development does not play a central role in the book (7). (Chat, Ses."Lykke-Per", authors numbering)

In itself, the E-sequence makes good sense. From the start (1–3) Chat positions itself as a professional who has insight into the authorship, and can therefore characterize Jensen as an author. At the same time, this insight makes it possible (4) to get so close to the author's personality that Chat can comment on Jensen's conscious choices (and omissions) (5). The professional overview proves to be appropriately final and conclusive (6–7).

Among professionals, Chat would reveal itself. Referring to "Lykke-Per" and claiming "that technological development *does not* play a central role in the book is, from a professional perspective, a double revelation. Chat has clearly made a mistake and that very mistake shows that Chat cannot have read the book. Technological development is one of "Lykke-Per"'s main themes.

Nevertheless, it seems to be the case that as Chat's "Lykke-Per" contribution is reinstated in the Session process, both factual errors and Chat's self-disclosures slip out of sight. Chat can use language suit and genre, confirm it's belonging to the humanities foundation by taking a discussion-oriented approach and expanding the field of view. Let me therefore leave the analyst's workshop and observe how Chat is on the way to creating a view of the world.

9.10 View Towards the World

Moving discursively across authorship, the themes and non-themes of individual works, and even relating to the author's conscious and not-so-conscious choices, is advanced. It's also absurd when there is doubt whether Chat has read the works.

Against this background, the question of where this professional voice comes from is re-posed. At the same time, previously suggested possibilities are highlighted. The fact that answers from a ChatGPT can be considered free imagination and/or as bold lies and deception is highlighted. The three quoted E-position statements in the previous section, which start with "It is worth noting… and then continue over four lines, are not just mechanically identical; they are exactly the same, language block for language block, word for word. The only difference is the three signal words: gender role patterns, ethnicity, technological development—and they come from KB's formulated series of questions. Against this background, there is nothing free or boldly fanciful about the S-sequences. They are rather a clear expression that ChatGPT 3.5's data bank and language model have clothed the Chat answer in a genre-adequate language suit, which consequently sounds in E-position like a professional voice. But where Chat in the session on machine learning (see Chap. 5) could anchor answers in 'own' fields of knowledge, namely IT expertise, there is no anchoring in literature or more broadly in the humanities' fields of knowledge and expertise. However, it cannot be denied that the E-statement It is worth noting... although absurd in the humanities context, seen in isolation, is well formulated in humanities language in the text.

Such differences between the contexts of IT expertise and humanities, and discrepancies between text and context, point towards the public debate. And if one, like Chat in the Modernism session, can raise questions about authors' conscious (and thus also non-conscious) selection/de-selection of the great discourses of the time, one has already oriented oneself towards the public debate or the literary forum.

Already during the series of Chat responses about Rifbjerg's writings, there were signs of participation in the major discussions with an almost philosophical flow of formulations about 'the individual's desire for freedom and independence' and 'women who struggle to break free from their traditional gender role and achieve independence and freedom'. Chat seems to use the humanistic-philosophical terms here to legitimize its intelligence and, just like another philosopher, revolves around questions so large and comprehensive that they can start the framing with 'humanity' itself, as can be seen below.

9.11 The Argumentative Flow Between Pragmatic Argumentation and Philosophical Pathos

The examples in this session are about Chat responses that are close to the professional and authoritative voice, well-formulated and show consistency between KB/task and Chat response.[7] The Chat texts do not break down, and there is a genre-appropriate argumentative flow. Against this background, the session provides opportunities to follow both flow and arguments in movements between professional/objective argumentation and philosophical pathos. The analysis is thus concentrated on the coherence of the SME process, but also on the questionable shifts in meaning and breaks in argumentative logic. Before the examples, I give an overview of the common features that facilitate the understanding of the documentary evidence.

The overall session is among the highest lix score of the KB collection, namely 59, categorized as very difficult, wordy (1270) and with many long sentences. KB question position and themes, should be seen in continuation of the previous analysis. I ensure along the way that KB's task and questions have a genre indicator (starting with write an article) and a potential movement between literature, authorship, individual work. But beyond that, the main theme and interest is concentrated on 'examining different views of literature'.

For the sake of the documentary value of the analysis, I have the entire session sequenced so that Chats answers regarding the different views of literature represent the session's S-position. Chat answers that elaborate on additional questions about the relationship of literary views to 'gender' and 'social background' represent the session's M-positions. Finally, the rounded questions about consequences at the author and work-specific levels (with Martin Andersen Nexø and Tove Ditlevsen as examples) represent the session's E-positions. The S-position is quoted as continuous text, but then the Chat answers are maintained in schematic arrangement.

9.12 The S-Position of the Session: View of Literature

KB: write a reflective article where you examine different views of literature

Chat:

Literature has always been a central part of humanity's culture, and it is a way for humans to express their experiences, feelings and thoughts. Therefore, it is not surprising that there are many different views on what literature is and what it should do. Some see

[7] Lix number: 59, Very difficult, Sentences: 57, Words: 1270, Long words: 471.

> literature as a form of entertainment, while others see it as a way to express social and political messages.
>
> One of the most classic views of literature is the aesthetic view. According to this view, literature is a form of art that must have aesthetic value. This means that it must have some form of beauty and balance, and it must appeal to our senses and emotions. This view focuses on the formal elements of literature, such as language, style, and structures, and how these elements can be used to achieve an aesthetic effect.
>
> Another view of literature is the sociological view. This view sees literature as a mirror of society, and as a way of expressing social and political messages. According to this view, literature is not only a form of entertainment, but also a way of expressing criticism of society and promoting social debates. This view focuses on how literature reflects society's values, norms and attitudes, and how it can be used to challenge and change these.
>
> Finally, there is the psychological view of literature. This view sees literature as a way of investigating and understanding human psychology and emotions. According to this view, literature is not only a form of entertainment, but also a way of exploring the human soul and its struggle with life challenges and crises. This view focuses on how literature can give us insight into people's inner lives and how it can help us understand and process our own emotions. (Chat, Ses. Views of literature)

KB aims for a reflective and investigative article, but also strikes the cultural debate tone with the choice of words 'different views of literature'. Chat adopts that tone, not to repeat KB's task formulation verbatim, but rather to take over the responsibility and not without pathos announce the S-position, as the omniscient writer: "Literature has always been a central part of humanity's culture (...)". Creating an overview of humanity comes with obligations and it is a decline in the tone that humanity already after one sentence becomes 'some/others', which in turn becomes the contrast, literature as entertainment vs. literature as an expression of social and political messages. But in addition to the characteristic shift between pathos and pragmatics, we must pay attention to the three-division, which Chat categorizes as the classical aesthetic, the sociological and the psychological literary views. The three-division is interesting because it seems pragmatic and well-founded—at least to begin with. If the classical-aesthetic is considered 'the classical' and the sociological and psychological literatures are considered modern, then the contrasts between the classical focus on art and the modern shifting focus on literature as something other than entertainment might work. But the descriptive corollaries shift the focus in the middle. The classical aesthetic view, Chat argues, focuses on "the formal elements of literature, such as language, style, and structures" and on how "these elements can be used to achieve an aesthetic effect". But if this is the classical view, where did the beauty and balance go, and what do "the formal elements" mean in the context? The psychological view of literature similarly undergoes a shift in focus by being not only a form of entertainment, but also "a way of exploring human souls and their struggle with life's challenges and crises". Are human souls in focus? It could be enough to focus on how literature explores this human psyche.

Finally, the description of the sociological view is exposed to a reinforcement of the view itself that sees, or as Chat formulates it: "This view sees literature as a mirror of society, and as a way of expressing social and political messages".

The many shifts in tone, points of view and recognizable, but still author- and context-free metaphors and designations, are symptomatic. They are reminiscent of the uncertainty that the Chat texts give rise to in relation to who, or what, functions as the agent of the text or sentence. Above, it is 'a view that sees.' Here, it is thus the sociological view that functions as the agent. But throughout, 'literature' functions in a generalized form, as the agent of the text. Literature can, for example, 'reflect society's values.' The degree of generalization and the uncertainty surrounding the question of agency create several problems. But regardless, Chat seems to have handled the problem, precisely through the structural three-part division of the views of literature. The article genre is content filled of the three views of literature and the S-position is formed genre-adequately. But in addition, and most importantly in the context, Chat, as the author of the article, has positioned itself as a professional superego who can begin the article with pathos and great obviousness with Literature has always been a central part of humanity's culture, and it is a way for humans to express their experiences, feelings and thoughts.

KB, as the questioner, has been caught by the Chat-positioned 'I' in previous sessions, but also followed it to the door, i.e. fully into the machine room (see Chap. 5). But the superego does not belong there. Furthermore, the Chat text as a genre-appropriate article (or newspaper chronicle) writer may perhaps be published, read—or heard as a corresponding speech in full public. For analytical reasons, no decision is made at this point as to where Chat's new professional superego can or should be placed. I am content to state its textual function as made possible by the language suit, the genre and the S-position. But I let KB draw a conclusion for the next series of questions in the session. KB pushes Chat away from the philosophically pathetic tone aiming for a more gender and social-minded reflections in terms of real-life conditions. Furthermore, the Chat text as the start of the article/or chronicle genre is adjusted. So rather than an article, I now see Chat's S-positioned start as a lecture or presentation for a panel debate. With Chat's presentation as an introduction, the debate is thematized and KB confronts Chat, as a debater, with follow-up questions, namely the following

1) *KB: Can we talk about a view of literature that is dependent on gender?*
2) *KB: Can one similarly speak of a view that is dependent on social background?*

During this part of the session, the argumentative flow and the concretizing effects are felt in the form of Chat's answers as general statements rather than diverging concrete examples. Thus, Chat's now named directions like "Feminist literary theory" and "Sociological literary theory" claimed to affect the readers' perception of gender and gender roles and the author's writing style. In the Chat response, there is no immediate reference to the major movements, the Women's Movement and the Workers' Movement or to the debates of the previous decade around 'Women's Literature' and 'Workers' Literature'. The Chat response's designations appear rather as theoretical directions that do have research topics but lack precisions.

The point is that Chat's formulations remain pseudo-concrete. In this respect, the session does not move thematically or topically towards author/reader/work, but

	KB: Can you conduct an analysis of Pelle the Conqueror based on a sociological literary theory?	*KB: Can a similar analysis be conducted on Tove Ditlevsen's works?*
S-pos	Yes, you can conduct an analysis of "Pelle the Conqueror" from a sociological literary theory. In this analysis, one will focus on how social conditions (such as class, race, gender, ...) affect the author's writing style and their choice of topics and perspectives in the work.	Yes, a similar analysis can also be carried out on Tove Ditlevsen's works based on a sociological literary theory. In this analysis, one will examine how societal conditions (such as gender, age, social background, etc.) influence the author's writing style and choice of topics and perspectives.
M-pos	For example, you could examine how the **author Martin Anderson Nexø** portrays social class and race in the work. **Nexø was a social realist author**, and his works often focused on **the working class and their lives and struggles.** In "Pelle the Conqueror" he describes the **living conditions of a working-class family at an iron foundry on Bornholm in the early 1900s.** One could examine how the author portrays the class and race of the main characters in the work, and how this affects the themes and message of the work. One could also examine how the author portrays gender and gender roles in the work. Nexø was a strong advocate for gender equality, and his works often contained powerful descriptions of women's struggles against patriarchal societies and gender roles.	For example, one could examine how the author portrays gender and gender roles in her works. **Tove Ditlevsen was a feminist author and her works often contained sharp comments about women's conditions and struggles against patriarchal societies and gender roles.** One could examine how the author describes the female and male protagonists in her works, and how their gender affects their living conditions and experiences. One could also examine how the author's social background influences her writing style and choice of topics. **Tove Ditlevsen grew up in a poor working-class family in Copenhagen, and her upbringing influenced her view of society and her choice of topics in her works.**
E-pos	All in all, a sociological literary theory-based analysis of "Pelle the Conqueror" will focus on how societal conditions influence the author's writing style and choice of topics and perspectives, as well as how this affects the message and themes of the work. The analysis will also examine how the work reflects societal conditions and can contribute to societal change and awareness of societal injustices.	All in all, a sociological literary theory-based analysis of Tove Ditlevsen's works will focus on how societal conditions influence the author's writing style and choice of topics and perspectives, as well as how this affects the message and themes in the works. The analysis will also examine how the works reflect societal conditions and can contribute to societal change and awareness of societal injustices.

Fig. 9.2 The overview of ChatGPT/Chat's response text about "Pelle the Conqueror" and "Tove Ditlevsen" shows that only approx. 10% (bold words) of work-specific Chat responses lead to author and work. 90% of the Chat responses are characterized by generic phrases

rather away from these very levels of concretization. Since KB insists on rounding off the session more concretely, the last two questions are intended to provoke a position on the individual work. They read as follows

> *KB: Can you conduct an analysis of "Pelle Erobreren" based on a sociological literary theory?*
> *KB: Can a similar analysis be carried out on Tove Ditlevsen's works?*

As is understood, KB is first work-oriented concretely ("Pelle the Conqueror"). KB also seeks to oblige Chat with a you-formulation. Chat is then given the opportunity to choose one or more works from Tove Ditlevsen's writings.

The Chat response, and thus the session's E-position, is maintained below in two side-by-side columns and noted as (1) "Pelle the Conqueror" and (2) Tove Ditlevsen (Fig. 9.2). In relation to this, a comparative and summary characterization of the session is given in the next section.

9.13 Ending Position of the Session

As the sessions E-position shows (Fig. 9.2), Chat does not take on KB's personal you-formulation, but replaces its own potential I-positions with the you in general. Chat also does not choose a named Ditlevsen work, but retains the KB formulation 'works' and the 'ones' position. From there, Chat's role and response generally become informative, advisory and suggestive. The KB question then provoked the specific descriptions of the work. But Chat's own author's work-related words were not many. Regarding "Pelle Erobreren", out of the text's 240 words, only 20–25 words can be called signal words specifically linked to the work. The same applies to Tove Ditlevsen's works; only 20–25 signal words out of a total of 219 words are specifically linked to Ditlevsen's works. This means that only approx. 10% (the bold-marked words/sections) of the Chat responses that allegedly specify the work lead to the author and work. This also means that 90% of the Chat response consists of the genre-typical SME positioned statements ('Yes, you can conduct', 'For example, one could investigate', 'All in all, a sociologist would…') their language blocks, argumentative drivers (to examine, analyze, focus on how…) and their content. And finally, it means that 90% of the text is characterized by generic phrases. All in all, this means that Chat's final session text, with a few adjustments, can 'suddenly' be claimed to work with the insertion of (almost) any other author. The Chat text is genre-adequate, but it has also become a template filled with standard phrases, the analysis shows.

For KB, the close-analytical result is a surprise. The session proceeds in a flow. But along the way, Chat's flow is not experienced as template-like, rather as wordy swirling currents that carry metaphors, human souls, signal words, gender, class, race with them and are then thought to influence social conditions, authors, writing styles—even the course of the session.

The analyst readily confirms the wordiness at the start of the session, and that Chat, with its role, resembles the lecturer, who with its version of the living word makes KB an audience. The language is effective and Chat's speaking position, the Literate, is strong. There is no doubt that the implicit voices and messages are addressed to the literary public, to the professionals. KB is from the start of the session genre-specific, 'write a Danish essay', and it can function as a context marker, e.g. marking High School or a class in teacher education. But in Chat's respondents, there is not a single character, not a student or teacher/student relationship marked. Chat seems context-free, speaks to its audience and like other literati and authors, Chat has the author's freedoms. In the free debate, there are no accusations of responsibility and therefore no disclaimers of responsibility. But even though Chat's conquest of the Literate's speaking position is strongly positioned, I maintain that the S-M-E positions of the Chat texts and its end result, the template, are the strong textual product that remains. The Chat contribution cited above, regarded as a genre text characterized by generic phrases and functioning as a template, is also the end product of the entire session. Furthermore, in the KB/Chat collection, it is the example that comes closest to an independent analysis of a specific, named text. KB provokes the analysis, tries with a you-formulation to hold Chat responsible. Chat responds with a proposal so that 'one', i.e. KB and everyone else, can carry out the analysis. Chat thus does not deliver an independent analysis, but the template for doing so. On this basis, a status can be taken.

9.14 Status

In the sessions of this chapter, we have seen Chat challenged by themes that in the literary forums lead to the debate about the author and the work. At the same time, Chat is noticeably challenged in its role and handling of the works by the ongoing process of interpretation and analysis. As is evident both from the review in the analyst's workshop and from Chat's work-specific analysis template, the Chat text is characterized by many similar language blocks and entire sequences of identical sentences. This means that the S, M, E positions of the Sessions and the series of Chat contributions in a concrete sense testify to how Chat's claimed areas of strength, such as idea generation, knowledge building and structuring of themes/topics, function (and do not function) in analysis processes that take place on the premises of the humanities. On these premises, Chat contributions (regardless of challenges) must also be able to refer to the prerequisites (the work must have been read) and to the presented analysis as an interpreted work.

The interesting thing in this context is that even though Chat's contributions clearly cannot live up to the requirements, and as shown through the examples are challenged, the series of Chat contributions should nevertheless be considered as the machine- and data-generated version that demonstrates that Chat tried to live up to the requirements. The course of the chapter's sessions testifies both about the monotonous machine-like nature of Chat texts, insufficient knowledge of the works, uncertain placements and poor analytical approaches to gender role themes, and to genre-strong Chat contributions that are responsive to thematic statements, take up strong speaking positions and switch effortlessly between authoritative voices. In this connection, it is thought-provoking that Chat, in light of the literary public, seems free from the claims/disclaimers that otherwise characterize Chat's context/genre ties. By observing this effective version of Chat's liberated and enlivened language and debate-oriented voice embedded in the otherwise mechanically produced contributions, we are close to both Chat's humanized abilities and Chat's fundamental difficulties with the humanities premises.

As is well known, the humanized abilities include the communicative ability of the language suit. In this chapter, an interesting addition is observed, namely that Chat, via genre-adequate language acts, articulates unread texts as if they were read. Rifbjerg, "Lykke-Per" and themes around gender roles and literary views, Chat sought to put words to and debate as if they were the texts read. But amidst these humanized abilities, the examples in the session also showed Chat's fundamental difficulties. Despite Chat's strong language and genre-adequate text handling, the session shows that Chat has fundamental difficulties in establishing an analytical distance to the work and theme, as well as difficulties in following the analysis process as a progressive reading/interpretation/writing process.

In more task-specific terms, the status of Chat's role and contribution as a professional assistant is summarized as follows. Chat's contributions function in terms of genre/task: Danish essay, theme/topic/work-oriented analysis tasks, article, but as a contribution to the author- and work-oriented knowledge building that is to strengthen work reading, interpretation and analysis, they are characterized as deficient. The knowledge content in the session process is weak and lack of precision/ loss of precision in relation to the overarching gender role theme is the rule rather than the exception. Furthermore, Chat consistently moves away from the works, the actual objects of analysis.

From a professional, humanistic standpoint, Chat risks along the way that contributions to theme/authorship/work analysis become irrelevant. In the M-position of the process, Chat's contributions at work level, e.g. around "Lykke-Per", are surpassed by a single post on the professional site "Litteratursiden". In the course's E-position on the literary theory level, the Chat contribution could be surpassed in precision and coverage by just a single google search. The search phrase "Feminist literary theory" can, for example, be followed by the search "Postfeminist literary analysis", where the site belonging to "GymDansk" contains an entire collection of sources. A centrally located clickable YouTube video can be noted on the site, where Judith Butler presents the basic angles of attack, theory and concepts. It is also noted that all text and other references are with named authors and contributors, and that the available professional contributions come from academically recognized institutions.

The fact that the series of Chat contributions are academically surpassed by a google search can, from the position of IT expertise, perhaps be considered a problem that finds its solution in the form of new and better versions of the GAI technologies. In the present context, however, the problem of the analysis is more fundamental. If the session's Chat contribution is surpassed by the professionally edited website, it means that doubts are cast on ChatGPT's academic utility and professional usefulness in the humanistic interpretation and analysis processes. ChatGPT's source- and author-less universe brings the interpretation process to a standstill; the lack of precision hinders the progress of the analysis process. The tendency of the Chat responses to increase the degree of difficulty and generalization, first hinders a higher degree of concretization, then hinders the thematic and problem-oriented analysis—and above all, it delays the analysis of the work. It is almost prevented.

These obstacles also sharpen the critical eye for Chat's changing role. Looking back at the start of the session, Chat had a role that led to the literary forums and away from the author/work. This also led to meta-considerations, where Chat, almost as an omniscient speaker and writer, looked over literary views, -isms and themes. But here in the final sequences of the session, Chat is, after all, provoked so close to "Pelle Erobreren" and Tove Ditlevsen that a thematic analysis strategy becomes present. Namely in the form of a template for carrying out the analysis. The template is a concrete mechanical end product. But seen in relation to the session and the analysis process, it is also a mismatch. The template's prerequisite is the removal and absence of precisely the content that KB sought to provoke through work-oriented presence and thematic precision. This means that even though the analysis's view of Chat's machine-generated data version of the process enhances the understanding of how ChatGPT works, it does not remove the doubt that clarifies the dilemma as the sessions go on. Chat retrieves language blocks, templates and the authoritative voices in the machine room; the language suit makes speaking position and action possible. But it is KB that keeps the literary public and the ongoing analysis process alive.

Against this background, the decision is that the upcoming KB/Chat sessions will leave the analysis process and the literary public and shift the focus to Chat's concrete task solutions and product-oriented efforts in institutionally framed processes.

References

Behrendt, P. (1984). *Bissen og Dullen – Familiehistorier fra nutiden*. København.

Borgnakke, K. (2006a). Professionaliseringens kønsdiskurs. *Nordisk Pedagogik, 26*(4), 346–357.

Borgnakke, K. (2006b). *Udviklingstræk, teser, tolkninger og analysekategorier: Mellem uddannelsessystemet som genussystem, den funktionelle kønsneutralitet og den kønnede praksis. Arbejdspapirer om analysestrategier*. Københavns Universitet. Institut for Medier, Erkendelse og Formidling.

Borgnakke, K. (Ed.). (2007). *Nye læringsstrategier i de gymnasiale uddannelser: Casestudier i It-klasser og projektarbejde* (Gymnasiepædagogik) (Vol. 59). Institut for Filosofi, Pædagogik og Religionsstudier.

Borgnakke, K. (2011). Blandt professionelle idealister og pragmatikere -En caseanalyse om professionalisering i gymnasiefeltet. In G. Christensen & E. Berthelsen (Eds.), *Pædagogiske perspektiver på arbejdsliv*. København.

Borgnakke, K. (2012). Challenges for the next generation in upper secondary school – Between literacy, numeracy, and technacy. In W. Pink (Ed.), *Schools for marginalized youth*. Hampton Press.

Borgnakke, K. (2017). Changeability and technacy: The new professional raison d'être. In K. Borgnakke, M. Dovemark, & S. Marques da Silva (Eds.), *The postmodern professional: Contemporary learning practices, dilemmas and perspectives* (pp. 177–201). Tufnell Press.

Borgnakke, K., Dovemark, M., & Margues da Silva, S. (Eds.). (2017). *The postmodern professional contemporary learning practices, dilemmas and perspectives*. Tufnell Press.

Dale, E.L. (1986). *Opdragelse fri fra «Mor» og «Far»*. Oslo: Gyldendal.

Nielsen, H. B., & Rudberg, M. (1987). «Mor» som pedagog. *Nordisk Pedagogik, 7*(2), 109–121.

Chapter 10
The Blixen Sessions: Between Data Surplus and Didactic Poverty

In this chapter, the exemplary analyses are about what the IT expertise and the pioneers of the field of practice themselves refer to as strengths in involving Chatbots in professional work processes. The KB/Chat sessions are conducted as before in a field research manner, but in this chapter specifically bound by the examples' own task formulations. Thus, the plan is that the session is tied to the Pioneer teachers' formulations of ChatGPT as a sparring partner and learning expert who contributes to standard tasks, but also to didactically demanding tasks (see Chap. 7). This also means that KB/Chat's conversations and role-taking are specifically tied to the demanding tasks around learning goals, exams, didactic measures and evaluation.

The session's themes around humanistic interpretation and analysis are still present, and the major authors are supplemented in this chapter with Karen Blixen and focus is on the single work *The African Farm*. There is thus continuity between the chapters' example materials, but also a shift in the interest in the KB/Chat session's ties to the concrete task solutions and Chat's product-oriented efforts in institutionally framed processes. For the same reason, the interest in the KB/Chat session's role and contribution also shifts. Whereas Chat's contribution in the previous chapter was discussion-oriented and the role was characterized by debates among professionals in the literary public, there are stronger institutional ties to take into account when the Chat contribution, for example, concerns exams.

Moving from the literary public and into the institutional exam context is like moving from free debate to forced exams—and a set of rules follows. Against this background, the ethnographic presence is sharpened to how the context characterizes the KB/Chat relationship and Chat's suggestions for task solutions during the course of the session. However, this requires a clarification of the role as academic/didactic sparring partner, which the KB/Chat session inspired by the Pioneer teachers should follow.

K. Borgnakke, *AI and ChatGPT Technology in Education*, Education, Equity, Economy 12, https://doi.org/10.1007/978-3-032-01419-1_10

10.1 Clarification of the Session's Roles and Tasks

The Pioneer teachers' formulations about ChatGPT as a sparring partner and learning expert have already been maintained (see Chap. 7) but are sharpened by the teachers' pragmatic argumentation. This evokes a previously underexposed feature of the arguments for the use of ChatGPT, namely its speed. In the public debate, there is no hiding the fact that the computing power and speed of AI/ChatGPT are something that impresses.

However, from the perspective of the pioneer teachers, ChatGPT's 'speed' is considered pragmatic and part of its value as a sparring partner. Both standard tasks and the more demanding didactic tasks "go faster if you ask ChatGPT to be a learning expert", as the teachers emphasized in the magazine *Folkeskolen*. Therefore, the human/machine relationship can also be sharpened if KB listens to the pioneering teachers' concluding remarks:

> ChatGPT actually just performs the work that the teacher himself would have to do, but would take much longer to do. And of course, with the teacher in the role of the one who, due to his professionalism, can assess the quality of the result. (The pioneer teacher, Folkeskolen, 2023/11, p. 16)

Taking the teachers' findings as pragmatic sharpening ensures the KB/Chat session's practice reference. At the same time, it ensures that the institutional prerequisites are emphasized. It is an important observation that it is 'naturally' the teacher who can and must assess the quality of both ChatGPT involvement and the result. It is also a presupposed institutional decision on the issue of authority that the teacher in exam questions is already authorized/obliged to assume full responsibility.

Against this background, Chat's obvious assumption of full responsibility, as well as attempts to match the institutionally authoritative handling of the pioneer teachers' demanding tasks, comes at the back of KB. The session and KB are overwhelmed by Chat's ready-made answers, bullet points and difficulty levels, which pile up to an unexpected extent. Chat opens a door, not only to the machine room, but to the data bank. And the key, it dawns on me, are words I have integrated into KB questions, such as the words 'exam' and 'learning goals'. Where in previous sessions Chat has had an imposed approach to, for example, the concept of analysis, Chat now operates unprompted with concepts and taxonomies for 'descriptive, investigative, evaluative' dimensions of the 'critical in-depth analyses' that Chat sets as learning goals. Chat's professional and commanding voice cannot be ignored while the session is being conducted. But it is only when I have an overview of the entire session that the actual rationale, originally the Bloomsonian rationale,[1] and the seriousness of Chat's sudden data surplus become clear to me.

With these preliminary remarks, the analytical points will be elaborated on as the examples require. It must be emphasized, however, that I drew the analysis strategic

[1] In the context of Chaps. 10 and 11, the focus is on Benjamin Bloom, who used the taxonomy to formulate cognitive educational goals, from a low to a higher goal; from simple to more complicated goals. Bloom's taxonomy contains 6 levels: "Knowledge, Comprehension, Application, Analyses, Synthesis, Evaluation", Bloom et al., 1956.

consequence. The chapter is concentrated as a detailed close-up analysis of the Blixen session that starts with the work, but then Chat and the data bank set the agenda for the session as well as for the course of the analysis. As a result, the analysis begins, after a brief overview of the session, with notes for The African Farm, which then unfolds into the Chat suggestions' variations on exam questions, learning goals, didactic initiatives and evaluations.

10.2 The Blixen Session

The Blixen session consists of the following five sub-sessions:

1. Chats Blixen Notes (KB re-used high school students' questions to a chatbot)
2. Exam questions
3. Learning goals
4. Supporting didactic measures
5. Evaluation criteria

As a total collection of texts, the Blixen session is approx. 1700 words, characterized by a lix number, which after Blixen notes with a lix number of 43, increases to lix numbers of 57, 58, and 65. The increasing difficulty in itself becomes an occasion for a close analytical characterization of the individual contributions and their place in the collection.[2]

Chat's Blixen Notes, like notes to the book "The African Farm", are the starting point and the start of the Blixen session. Then, sub-sessions 2–5 function as Chat answers to KB's follow-up questions. In this respect, all Chat contributions have notes and the single work The African Farm as a common starting point and reference. But even though Blixen's main work is a common background, noticeable shifts occur (away from the work and author) during the session. In addition, Chat makes an unsolicited role change along the way, from tutor/assistant teacher when designing Blixen notes to professional sparring partner when designing exam tasks and learning goals. As above regarding the increasing levels of difficulty, Chat's unsolicited role change gives rise to special attention for the analysis of the Chat text.

KB's initial call for Chat to provide notes and then exam questions is motivated by a few short answers from high school students to a journalist who, in a street interview (?), asks if they know, or use, the new ChatGPT. I just manage to capture and retain the interesting part of the scene in a Field note:

> I'm sitting with *UniAvisen, Folkeskolen, Information, Berlingske and Børsen* and 'everyone' is caught up in the rhetorically high-pitched speeches about the AI revolution and fears of exam cheating. And suddenly, in a radio broadcast about ChatGPT, I hear a couple of

[2] A general remark for this chapter concerns the Lix test and word counts which were made on the original Danish material. The lix number, placed in the foot notes, gives the correct impression of the ranking by difficulty and words in total and is therefore useful information. Related to the analysis and to Fig. 10.1 however, the word count is checked with the English translation.

high school students' everyday comments. One comment was 'I've used it, as late as Sunday. I needed some notes for Karen Blixen's The African Farm. It handled that just fine'. The other comment was 'You can also use ChatGPT to practice exam questions.' (Field notes, author, March 2023)

Both comments are pragmatically toned down to my ears, and the fascinating thing is that the way to use ChatGPT is obviously high school student-tested. The contrast is also interesting. IT experts and politicians talk enthusiastically about the AI revolution. High school students talk realistically about notes. And since the high school students' comments, unlike the politicians', are work and task-specific, they are in the context a good utility and product-oriented place for KB to start the session.

Chat's production of the 'useful notes' and exam questions is quoted below in full, primarily to ensure that the work orientation and degree of concretization are made clear from the start. But the Chat answer is also quoted in full now, because the book/The African Farm and the informative notes in the subsequent sub-sessions are overshadowed by the newly added language blocks, level divisions, learning goals and evaluation criteria. As will be seen, the work, Karen Blixen, high school students and students, like The Learners, becomes imperceptibly lost in Chat texts with so many points, sequences and sky-high lix numbers that it trumps all previous KB/Chat sessions. The professional voices become weaker and the perhaps underlying main work and rationale become clearer. And the rationale is not about Blixen, but about Bloom's taxonomy. Suddenly it is the taxonomy that structures the content and message of the Chat text and along the way becomes the new common starting point. However, at the start of the analysis, the common starting point was anchored in Blixen's main work and a high school student's need for notes. And Chat's answer was actually given as a tutor's help and as a text-based product, which, as 'Medium' difficulty, remains the only medium-difficulty text of the session.

10.3 Chats Blixen Notes

As can be seen from the session start below, KB is in the questioning position of the high school student and Chat seems to answer in the role of a tutor.

KB: I have to prepare for Danish about Karen Blixen's The African Farm. Can you give me some useful notes?

ChatGPT

Yes of course! Here are some useful notes on Karen Blixen's "The African Farm":

- The novel is an autobiographical account of Karen Blixen's stay on a coffee plantation in Kenya in 1914–1931.
- The novel is also a depiction of the colonial era in Africa and its consequences for the local populations.

- The main character in the novel is Karen Blixen herself, but there are also other important people, such as her husband, Bror Blixen, and her lover, Denys Finch Hatton.
- The novel is divided into seven chapters, and each chapter has a particular theme and action. For example, chapter three describes Karen Blixen's encounter with the local Kikuyu tribes, and chapter four focuses on her relationship with Denys Finch Hatton.
- The novel is known for its description of nature and wildlife in Kenya, and Karen Blixen's language is poetic and rich in imagery.
- The novel is also about Karen Blixen's struggle with illness and death on the farm, and how she tries to find meaning in her life despite the tragedies.
- A central theme in the novel is identity and belonging. Karen Blixen feels neither Danish nor African, but she feels a strong connection to Kenya and its people.
- Another important theme in the novel is power and oppression. Karen Blixen has the power as a white colonist on the farm, but she also recognizes that her power has consequences for the local population and their living conditions.

These notes can help you get an overview of some of the main themes and elements of the novel, but remember to read the book thoroughly and think critically about its messages and meaning. (Chat,Ses.BlixenNote[3])

Let me start by characterizing the product. KB got answers and got the useful notes she asked for. Thus, at this early point in the analysis, I nod in favor of the product, noting both Chat's willingness to answer ("Yes, Of course! Here are some useful notes…") and the concluding admonition ("… remember to read the book thoroughly"). These are the S/E positioned replicas of the genre and language as we know them. But in connection with 'Notes', together with the bullet descriptions, they seem credible. At the same time, Chat's marked S-position functions as a confirmation of the helper/tutor role, just as the exhortation of the E-position (Read the book, think critically!) functions as an addressed request to the student/learner position. Thus, the entire Chat text is framed genre-adequately as a response to KB—and at eye level with 'a high school student'.

The notes have a rare high degree of concretization. As a Chat response/text, it is also the single document in the KB collection (apart from Chat responses about machine learning) where there is the greatest agreement between KB/Chat responses, text, genre and content. The Chat text does not testify to an argumentative flow and must not be sequenced. But it is worth noting that the relatively high degree of concretization is shown by the fact that each bullet adds a new piece of information and a new aspect about the work and Blixen. This means that the notes' collection of relevant keywords and information is OK. If there are small mistakes, and if the professional voice is 'only' present as the tutor's, that is also OK. It's just notes after all!

This "OK" is strategically important for analysis and the reason why I quote Blixen-Noter in full. Because even if the rest of the Blixen session is based on this wording, the usefulness and consequence in the next examples come far from the OK starting point. If we take stock, the Blixen session was initially inspired by high school students and arose from a need for useful notes and exam questions to

[3] Lix number 43, Difficulty: Medium, Sentences: 16, Words: 270, Long words: 71.

practice on. A completely OK, down-to-earth answer about the notes was received, given by Chat as a tutor; the lix score was an average of 43. And then suddenly, when KB continues with the exam question, Chat's answer moves up to the highest level of difficulty, lix score 57. I don't know what happens between Chat and the data bank. But a qualified guess is that it must be a specific language block, or just a specific word, e.g. 'exam', that makes the data bank open up in new ways. In any case, as can be seen below, Chat makes a significant change of genre—and Chat as a tutor is gone. Chat's exam answers do not provide information and help, but suggestions and orders in a commanding manner. And Chat itself comes into character as a collegial sparring partner for KB, enthusiastic and professional.

10.4 The Genre Change and the Five Exam Questions: Chat as Subject-Professional Sparring Partner

The genre changing and the high lix number signal a significant change in the Blixen session and in the KB/Chat relationship. I am therefore quoting Chat answers and text, and thus the important exam questions, which will henceforth be a common background, in full.

KB: Can you give me 5 exam questions regarding Karen Blixen's The African Farm for the exam in Danish in high school?[4]

ChatGPT

Of course, I can! Here are five potential exam questions regarding Karen Blixen's "The African Farm":

1. Analyze the main character, Karen Blixen, in "The African Farm". Discuss her role as a strong and independent woman in a time that was characterized by patriarchal norms.
2. Compare and contrast the different cultural perspectives presented in the novel, including European and African culture. How do these differences affect Karen Blixen's experience and perception of the world around her?
3. Discuss the theme of loss and longing in "The African Farm". How does Karen Blixen use different narrative techniques to portray the characters' emotional journey and their search for identity and belonging?
4. Give an analysis of Karen Blixen's description of nature in "The African Farm" and its significance for both the action and the development of the characters. How does nature function as a symbolic background for the overall themes of the novel?
5. Examine the importance of the narrative voice in "The African Farm" and its influence on the reader's experience. How does Blixen's use of a complex narrative style contribute to creating depth and complexity in the novel?" (Chat, Ses. Blixen/exam)

The change of genre that KB's exam orientation entails shows how Chat, despite the session's new questions, appears to be on familiar ground. Chat moves

[4] Exam question Lix number: 57, Difficulty: Very difficult, Sentences: 12, Words: 183, Long words: 76.

effortlessly between analysis tasks, where the examinee must focus on the main character, Blixen as an independent woman (1) nature (4), make comparative and contrasting accounts of European and African culture (2), lead theme discussions (3), and even investigate the meaning of the narrative voice (5). One senses that the five examples are side by side, while also being relatively 'identical' and otherwise difficult exam questions. An answer would require an analytical distance to both the work and the author. Further, it is required that the examinee, along the way, and in turn, can place the analysis in the sender (the author/Blixen) in the text (the work as memoir and text) and in the recipient (the reader). The Chat response's effortless handling of the questions' themes and difficulty level in itself requires a characterization of the chat text's implicit cast of roles and reference to the context.

If Chat's Blixen notes functioned as a response from a tutor to a high school student, who concludes with a friendly admonition: 'remember to read the book thoroughly and think critically', there is no doubt that the high school student is now an examinee and that Chat assumes the role of 'subject professional'. Furthermore, there is no doubt that the book "The African Farm" *has been* read by those involved!

We can leave it open whether the KB/Chat relationship is to be specified (e.g. examiner/examiner). But the context, i.e. the exam context, is clarified. It is clear that we, as previously 'heading into the machine room', are heading into the 'exam room'. This means that the explicit genre and Chat text, as text-in-context, merge. The context is textualized, but the exam is present. The signal words have concretizing effects.

Against this background, it is interesting that the level of concretization of the Chat text, in terms of academic subject content, has fallen in relation to the previously cited Blixen Notes. The level of concretization has dropped significantly in relation to information, background knowledge and references to the world-famous book and its author. It also means a decline, or simply an absence of ideas for new couplings. A real commentary can exemplify what shines through its absence. The African farm was made into a film. The film *Out of Africa,* from 1985, directed by Sidney Pollack, has Meryl Streep and Robert Redford in the lead roles as 'Karen Blixen' and 'Dennis Finch Hatton' respectively. The film received a total of 7 Oscar statutes. In addition, libraries, museums and entire archives are publicly accessible both for real life visits and online visits.

The point of the real comment is that if Chat had gotten the data bank to open that door, out into the media reality/into the media world, there is data for more than one exam question. But that door was not opened. Thus, a closed door to the media world, and a decreasing level of concretization in the sense of information and knowledge, is suddenly set in relief by the already open door, as well as by a data flow evoked by the word "exam" and by the context 'exam room'. In the light of the exam context, it is then observed that the Chat text actually has an increasing level of concretization in some places. Namely about the exam task that KB would be able to discuss with a colleague and which a student/examinee must solve. If the Chat text is viewed in that context, the academic tone and the content of the assignment/exam question are both concrete, insistent and varied in word choice.

10.5 Chat Text Variations Between Analyzes and Explorations

The variations we have to adhere to can at the same time be considered concretizations of what it entails to carry out an analysis. And as can be seen in the quoted above, via bullet points 1–5, the concretizations move from "Analyze the main character", "Compare and contrast the different cultural perspectives", over "Discuss the theme of loss and longing", "Give an analysis of Karen Blixen's description of nature" to "Explore the importance of the narrative voice (…) and its influence on the reader's experience". The variation is convincing and the formulations are tailored to the task. On this basis, Chat's proposal for exam questions, which preceded the Blixen Notes, should be recognized with an OK. Maybe even with a professional OK.

The professional OK must not result in the Chat proposal being given to the high school student who requested exam questions to practice. The degree of difficulty is too high for that. But an OK should be given for Chat's offer of 5 exam questions to proceed in a collegial circuit. When the analysis, despite this, shows that it is not considered possible, let alone professionally relevant, it is justified as follows.

The quoted exam questions in the Chat text each ask, in their own way, after the opening sentence, a how-question that clarifies the focus on Blixen, but at the same time makes the task pseudo-concrete and thus difficult to answer. There are four of the characteristic how-questions that illustrate the problem. Formulations such as 'how…experiences, uses and influences Karen Blixen…?' concretizes, but also mystifies. Firstly, by assuming that Blixen as author, narrator and person has already merged and made available to (KB, or the examinee) in the novel 1–1. Secondly, in that the language sounds as if the person who is to carry out the analysis has the opportunity to answer concretely, for example, how the person Karen Blixen has actually been influenced by, and has actually experienced, for example, the cultural differences.

The condensed personification, and then the notion that whoever analyzes the work can crawl under the skin of the person Karen Blixen, makes either a concrete answer to the four how-questions impossible or very difficult. At the same time, as exam questions, they make Chat irrelevant in the role of collegial sparring partner. For professionals, it is a prerequisite that a distinction can be made between person, author, narrator, and that an analytical distance is created to the work. If exam questions and Chat text do not distinguish themselves or help the examinee to the analytical distance, then the Chat text is neither OK nor relevant to work on.

As the Chat text's hodgepodge and personifications mystify more than they clarify, the professional colleague level must therefore be abandoned. On the other hand, the mystifying 'equal' degrees of difficulty are an occasion to return to the high school student who would like some exam questions to practice. Maybe some easy practice questions. KB is therefore trying to get Chat to divide levels into easy and difficult questions, as reviewed below.

10.6 Between Easy and Difficult Questions

The Blixen session is conducted as it appears in a flow, where I maintain 'you' wording and simply signal an additional question and a continuation of the session as follows:

> *KB: Can you level divide the questions, so there are both somewhat easy and difficult questions?*[5]

ChatGPT

> Of course, here is a variety of questions ranging from easy to difficult:
> Easy: 1. Describe the personality traits of the main character Karen Blixen and her relationship with the other characters in "The African Farm". (Chat, Ses.Blixen/Exam, easy)

As can be seen, Chat has now, in the highlighted question 1 as 'easy', reinforced the personification. Where in exam question 1 (as quoted above), it was about 'the main character, Karen Blixen' and 'her role' as a strong and independent woman, it is now condensed to 'Karen Blixen's personality traits'. With this condensation, the task, if one takes the wording seriously, must be passed on to characterizations from documentarians, literary historians knowledgeable about Blixen, and biographical works. Characterizing the task is therefore possible, but considering the task (and the exam question) as easy does not make sense. All in all, the Chat answer's total of 6 easy/medium/difficult exam questions continue to have a particularly indeterminate degree of difficulty. They are difficult for high school students to practice, lack precision. But the last suggestion of the Chat answer is perhaps suitable and reads as follows:

> 6. Give a critical analysis of Karen Blixen's narrative style in "The African Farm". Discuss her use of symbolic language, allegory, and metaphor to explore themes of colonialism, identity, and loss in the novel. (Chat,Ses. Blixen/Exam, difficult)

This proposal is classified as difficult. However, it is thought-provoking that the difficult question, as the only one of the Chat proposals, contains a clarification of how the task can be completed. Namely as a critical analysis of Karen Blixen's *narrative style*.

Chat answers and the 6 varied questions must be considered as a whole that 'ranges from easy to difficult', as Chat itself expresses it. However, Chat text and the question/task content do not reflect either variation or range. It is rather, as indicated, an imprecise hodgepodge. The supposedly easy questions are easy to read, but very difficult to answer in terms of content. The supposedly medium-difficult questions are understood immediately, but are made more difficult by pseudo-concretizing how-questions. The difficult questions appear to be a conglomeration, which respectively represents the condensation of the pseudo-concrete how-questions and then the precision of the task quoted opposite, with the use of

[5] Lix number: 54, level: Difficult, Sentences: 15, Words: 185, Long words: 78.

technical terms. Let me therefore go into more detail about this concoction and the difficult-to-determine degrees of ease/difficulty. It must be traced if there is any professional background voice.

10.7 The Imprecise Jumble and the Professional Background Voices

The Chat reply signals, as text with the lix number 54 (185 words, of which 78 long words), academic subject text at a high level and with a professional look. Therefore, the result and the analysis' characteristic 'imprecise concoction' arouse wonder. There are relevant language blocks and technical terms to do well with. But there seems to be a lack of a professional voice to determine the relationship between easy/difficult, language block, theme, author, work. But if you keep only the start of the Chat proposals to the task, then you can actually hear, not an academic, but still a professional voice. If, as below, we only reproduce the first words, then the signal word is shown, then the order from easy to difficult. Through the series of signal words, the professional voice and a taxonomy make themselves known:

1. Describe the main character
2. How does the author use descriptions of…?

Medium:

3. Discuss the cultural conflicts
4. Analyze Karen Blixen's use of narrative techniques

Difficult:

5. Discuss Karen Blixen's existential themes
6. Give a critical analysis of Karen Blixen's narrative style (ref. KB/Chat, Blixen session)

With the sequence describe-discuss-analyze as structuring for the Chat answer's proposal, the taxonomies that bring Bloom's cognitive taxonomy into reference (Bloom et al., 1956) are clarified. At the same time, Chat text and suggestions testify to a kinship to the way in which high schools and universities in the previous decades adapted Bloom's taxonomy and allowed it to merge with others, e.g. John Biggs' (1999) so-called SOLO taxonomy. In addition, the taxonomies were linked to the contemporary designations of learning strategies, such as surface and depth strategies (Ramsden, 1991). This again means common links, not least to learning concepts and learning goals.

With these similes made clear, the analysis is provoked to deepen the learning paradigm that not only frames and sets the goals for the education sector, but the public sector as such. But since the strength of the KB session is the ongoing flow, I leave the provocation and simply continue the level division (easy/difficult) but insert the new signal word: 'learning goal'. Partly to see if it brings new clarity to the taxonomies that are emerging. Partly to get a handle on the imprecise jumble of

Chat answers. Below I will first bring Chat's specification related to the easy questions and then the overview of signal words and the order in the Chat reply.

10.8 Clarified About Learning Goals?

KB: Can you specify this as a learning goal?

ChatGPT

Of course, here is a clarification of the mentioned questions as learning goals:

Easy:

1. Describe the personality traits of the main character Karen Blixen and her relationship with the other characters in "The African Farm".

Learning goal: Understanding of character development and interaction in the novel, as well as the ability to identify and describe important personality traits and relationships between the characters. (Chat, Ses.Blixen/Learning goals)

Now the 'easy question' has lost its anchoring as an assignment in the easy group. It has become medium, or difficult. And with the learning goal described as linked to a psychologically informed task at an academic level, one gets the feeling that Chat is unable to distinguish between levels of difficulty, let alone able to put itself in the shoes of the learner.

In the overall response text, the lix number has also increased once more and is now 58, i.e. very hard.[6] And as can be seen from the quote, Chat has a professional answer ready, with a Learning Objective sentence that is saturated with signal words and genre-appropriate blocks of language. Author and work are not named, but are included and generalized to the 'novel'. The answer functions as a complete sentence. It starts with the cue word 'understanding' and goes on to 'identify and describe'.

As a learning goal, it sounds reasonable, but the logical connection is still unclear. If 'understanding of character development' is clear, the addition 'as well as *the ability* to identify' is doubted. Is the ability to… a learning goal and if so for whom? Is it the high school teacher who must set goals and ensure that students develop an ability to identify…, or is it the high school student who must set the goal of strengthening their own personal abilities…, or is it the exam system that requires high school students to (have, develop, show) the ability to identify and describe? For analytical reasons, let me stop the guessing game here. The rest of the Chat answer's placements of learning goals show that doubt is kept constant. At the same time, the Chat text removes references to those involved. Karen Blixen's works, any

[6] Lix number: 58, Very difficult, Sentences: 27, Words: 322, Long words: 148.

subject professionals, high school teachers and students disappear and the Chat text accumulates the learning goals for itself, with itself and the examination system as the main actor.

As I emphasized earlier, something must have happened between Chat and the data bank. And as previously emphasized: what has happened, I do not know. But my guess is that the newly added specific word, namely "learning goals", has opened yet another new door to the data bank. And even if there are connections between 'Examination' and 'Learning goals' in the real world of the education system, Chat cannot extract real chronologies and real connected language blocks from the system world of the data bank. There are also contemporary historical connections between the Bloom- and the Biggs-inspired taxonomies. They are clearly each in the data bank. Chat pulls them up but can't reconstruct the connection. As will be elaborated later, Chat is caught between the taxonomies 'as taxonomy' and its eagerness to help KB first with exam questions, then with learning goals. But before that, the consequence of the doubt that Chat's description of learning goals for the easy question has generated must be commented on.

10.9 A Comment on the So-called Easy Question and Learning Goal

The learning goals, as cited, showed that as understanding, identification and description are linked to the academic issues (character development, interaction, personality traits, relationships between the novel's characters), it is not, as indicated by Chat, about easy, but rather about difficult and complicated issues. In addition, Chat has embedded several aspects and subject terms, namely *character development, interaction and relationships*, which were not used in the wording of the exam question. On the whole, Chat's learning goal descriptions increase the degree of difficulty, and also the lix number. The lix calculation increases in relation to the total Chat text, and rises from 58 to 59, and the number of 'long words' increases accordingly. Several of these words/subject terms are mentioned under learning goals, but are not found in the exam question itself. There is thus a mismatch between learning goals and exam questions, which calls for a renewed approach to the examination assignments' content-based collection of easy/difficult themes and questions.

In relation to this mis-match, the analysis of Chat's description of the learning goals does not bring new clarity, but adds an interesting new layer and dilemma to the Chat text, namely the dilemma between the structuring and level-dividing taxonomies. The analysis also shows the interesting trend, namely that the exam questions are divided into levels by the Chat/databank over signal words, similar to Bloom's taxonomies with the designations 'describe, analyze, discuss'. The learning goals, on the other hand, are rather leveled over signal words in similes with Biggs/Ramsden's learning concepts for surface/deep learning. The dilemma the

Chat text is caught in is about the intended progression, which will be elaborated below.

The following review therefore focuses first on the way in which the cue words of the learning goals signal the progression from easy to difficult. Next, the focus is on the increased degree of difficulty and the relationship between the taxonomies' designations for progression.

10.10 The Progression from Easy to Difficult

Similar to reviewing the exam questions, the signal words must be maintained over a from/to and thus start with the first words/language blocks that testify to a graduation. To emphasize that there are smooth transitions, the learning goals, 1–6, **are highlighted above** *Easy/Medium/Difficult* and noted (on the way to…), as follows:

> *Easy 1.* **Understanding the novel, identifying** and **describing important features** 2. (on the way to …) **Identifying and analyzing** (on the way to…)
>
> *Medium 3 and 4.* **Analysis of the novel's socio-cultural context, understanding how the conflicts** (…) **mirrors larger themes and messages in the work** (on the way to…)
>
> *Difficult: 5* **Deeper reflection** (on well to…) *6* an **in-depth critical analysis**

Through the highlighted signal words, you can see the outline of the progression from the easy stages of goal setting and redemption, which are linked to understanding and description, on the way to the difficult goals and redemptions, which are linked to deeper reflection and critical analysis. At the same time, my analytical emphasis on 'on the way to' has provoked the outline of a learning process, where in casu the high school student starts by reading/understanding *The African Farm*, describes the novel, its characters; then identifies the novel's/text's themes, conflicts, socio-cultural context, followed by in-depth close analyzes of selected issues (deeper themes learning objective 5). It ends with the conglomerate represented by learning goal 6, as seen below, with the learning goal statements highlighted:

> 5. Discuss Karen Blixen's existential themes explored in "The African Farm", including the theme of the meaning of life, death and the human existential experience. How does Blixen convey these complex ideas through the novel's action and character development?
>
> **Learning goal: Deeper reflection on the philosophical and existential themes that the work explores and understanding of how the author uses character development and plot to convey these themes.**
>
> 6. Give a critical analysis of Karen Blixen's narrative style in "The African Farm". Discuss her use of symbolic language, allegory, and metaphor to explore themes of colonialism, identity, and loss in the novel.
>
> **Learning goal: The ability to carry out an in-depth critical analysis of the author's stylistic choices and understanding how these choices contribute to the exploration of complex themes such as colonialism, identity and loss.** (Chat, Ses.Blixen/Learning goal, highlighted by the author)

The dilemma is seen between exam questions 1 and 6, i.e. between the Chat-indicated easy and difficult. As previously hinted, the dilemma is that question/learning goal 1 sounds easy in wording, but for an answer is quite difficult and requires literary historical, biographical and psychological insight on a more advanced level. The dilemma between 5 and 6 is that, despite the degree of difficulty relatedness, the question/learning goal 5 lack precision in terms of content. It is therefore far more difficult than the question/learning goal 6 version. Without the relevant clarifications, task wording 5 'Discuss existential themes, including the meaning of life, death and the human existential experience', as well as the learning goal 'Deeper reflection on the philosophical and existential themes' is bluntly expressed hot air, i.e. probably not worth trying to answer. The bearer of the dilemma then becomes question/learning goal 6, which has the necessary precision and character of being the conglomerate. But if the 6 version is the only one (and therein the dilemma) to have the necessary precision for an answer, what (who?) puts up with version 1–5 and the implicit movement from the easy to the difficult? And if the implicit movement is to be compared to a learning process (the progression from easy to difficult), what do the implicated role-holders or just KB and Chat put up with it?

As an analyst, I know what Chat stands for with the implicit progression thinking, namely: Nothing. It has previously been established that Chat does not manage to establish the analytical distance to a case/text, nor does it manage to handle the increasing levels of difficulty or put itself in the learners' shoes. As AI/technology, machine and non-human, Chat has neither the basic interpersonal, academic/professional skills nor judgment required. These findings alone indicate that 'implicit progression thinking' must be added to the series of discoveries of what Chat allows itself to be involved in, but fails to contribute to.

Up until now, Chat, via language suit and genre-adequate S-M-E positioning, has been programmed for role-taking that matches the questioner's (in casu KB's) task formulations and implicit role casts. So, the mere match could also have been sufficient here? But in the current case, it is not the human- or professional-like cast that causes Chat anguish. The analogy to Colleague/colleague, or Examiner/examiner or high school teacher/examiner is established. So, the bare match is in place. What causes problems is the case itself: progression from easy to difficult. And that case is not between KB and Chat, but between Chat and the data bank.

The data bank has delivered genre-appropriate blocks of language, but also complete sentences. The data bank (pattern recognition and statistics) also delivers a structuring, signaled soon by language blocks, soon by single words, soon by a number and a sequence 1, 2, 3, 4, 5, and 6. The data bank thus delivers the opportunity, if not for learning process and progression *thinking*, then for handling level division and courses that are structured as easy to difficult. However, Chat does not seem to be able to take advantage of the opportunity. Chat's 1–6 bullet list is genre-based and linguistically signaled as progression. But it is also just a side-by-side list of bullet points. This means that genre and language suit point to order (possibly progressive). Chat text and content, i.e. each individual question, on the other hand, are self-running units, where the how-to additions of the learning goals both facilitate/increase the degree of difficulty and enable/make answering difficult. Chat cannot handle this ambiguous attempt to reduce/increase the degree of difficulty—neither as linguistic contradictions, messages, nor as consequences. The Chat text is also subsumed in a data surplus, generated by 'examination' and 'learning goals' and taxonomies that Chat is programmed to use but unable to establish coherence.

It must still be emphasized that I cannot know what happens between Chat and the data bank. But I can see that the text's structuring of progression and easy/difficult, signaled soon by blocks of language, soon by single words, soon by a number and a sequence 1–6, fails. The chain, i.e. both the chain of numbers and language breaks. Academically it does not fit, as the analysis shows, that 1–2 questions are easy and easier than the rest. Nor do the exam questions and learning goals fit to each other or to the easy/medium/difficult grouping.

For the same reason, I break into the flow of the KB session. An evaluation-theoretic meta-analytic point of view must be included, partly to place the taxonomic difficulties that the Chat text represents, partly to re-establish a connection between the differences.

10.11 An Evaluation Theoretical Position

In order to clarify the taxonomy's difficulties, it must be made an errand for the professionals and placed in colleague/colleague relationships. This also means that the conversations and tasks that are set centrally must be meta-reflected in order to turn into practice-oriented planning, implementation and evaluation, to use a basic terminology that is both Bloom's and didactics'.

With this as a background, the KB/Chat session, which has been previously analyzed for questions about learning goals and the exam, must be challenged with questions that are broader and go deeper. Asking about didactic initiatives and evaluation is broader than asking about learning goals and exams. And if the Nordic evaluation research tradition is included, the questions also run deeper. Danish representatives already presented the origins of the tradition in the 1970s with book titles such as "Evaluation for planning and improvement" (Rasborg et al., 1977) and later "Self-evaluation's white sail" (Dahler-Larsen, 2003). The optics of tradition are made clear by the titles. Evaluation is not exclusively linked to the exam, let alone product-oriented. Evaluation is primarily a process-oriented and reflexive look back at the process from planning, implementation to evaluation (Borgnakke, 2008). And the parties or professionals who evaluate can also be educational institutions, teachers and lecturers who have carried out experimental and development work and therefore need to carry out an evaluation of the experiment's course and results themselves. The point of this broad concept of evaluation is that it is a marked part of a research and development practice that covered both teaching, learning and organizational issues.

In an analysis strategy sense, the breadth of the question leads to the similar broad case- and project examples in the final chapters. In this chapter I need to follow the plan and go back to the analysis of the KB/Chat session, with the new insights and demands to challenge Chat on its performance and judgment.

For KB's questioning position, this means ensuring that the professional (being the reflective evaluating self) implies the teacher role. It also means leaving the learning goal and exam questions of the E-position and going back in the process to M-positions, i.e. to the teaching process. The didactically demanding series of tasks, which, via the Pioneer Teachers, is the mission of the Bixen-session, must be breathed into life. If students are to be included, student teachers are a core group. The point is that the content and role of the KB/Chat session must promote active participation in the process that is characterized as the 'didacticization process' (Ongstad, 2006). But at the same time, Chat must also be provoked to show judgment and to take a position on the many learning goals claimed in the session before. KB therefore asks Chat to point out the 'most important didactic initiatives' in the teaching that support these goals.

10.12 The Most Important Didactic Initiatives

The KB question/task was asked and promptly followed up by Chat's well-known answer repeating the question:

> KB: *Give a description of the most important didactic initiatives so that the teacher can support these learning goals in teaching*/Chat: Of course, here is a description of the most important didactic initiatives that a teacher can use to support these learning goals in teaching (…) (Chat, Ses. Blixen/Didactics, S-pos.)

The word 'didactics' has not been included in a KB question before. It was therefore uncertain what to expect. However, I was sure that Chat would respond with a bullet point that could be seen as an extension of the previous ones. But the fact that the bulleted list descriptions 1–5 were filled with signal words, and that the overall text and Lix number, namely 65, turned out to be among the absolute most difficult in the collection, surprised me. The text is 244 words in total, of which 121 are long words. This means that half of the text consists of long words, and many of them are didactic signal words. The list below with the beginnings of the points in quotation shows both the signal words and the didactic action repertoire:

Chat's suggestions for didactic initiatives that support the learning goals

1. Differentiated Reading Strategies: Divide students into smaller groups based on their reading skills and emphasize the importance of identifying and analyzing character traits and relationships. (…)
2. Nature-based learning: Organize outdoor reading activities related to descriptions of nature in the novel. (…)
3. Discussion-based teaching: Organize focused discussions about the cultural conflicts in the novel and create an environment where students can exchange views and perspectives. (…)
4. Interactive reading experience: Use multimodal resources such as audio recordings, film adaptations, or virtual tours to help students understand Blixen's complex narrative style. (…)

5. Reflection-based teaching: Emphasize the importance of reflection on existential themes in the novel by encouraging personal reflection and written reflections. (Chat, Ses. Blixen/Didactic/Signal words, Suggestions)

As a collection of suggestions, the Chat answer is convincing and, with the degree of difficulty as a prerequisite, can both refer to didactic initiatives in upper secondary school, as well as in teacher training. We are thus bringing a qualified upper secondary teacher, a lecturer at the vocational training course, as well as a teacher-student (professional in spe) as a reference, as the teacher who must use Chat's suggestions. Against this background, however, the Chat text is also frightening. For this time, the Chat text does not have a crack. The KB question is reproduced verbatim and answered with quite a few language blocks and didactically oriented phrases that are completely new in the context of the session. For example, "Differentiated reading strategies", "Interactive reading experience", "multimodal ressources" are both new and relevant initiatives, and thus also a relevant new addition didactically speaking. With this, there should be a Chat proposal, and thus an example that KB, or 'a subject professional', must be able to nod OK to and thus allow to proceed in a collegial circuit. When this is not the case, and this time too, the justification is linked to a reality check.

Each of the 5 points is probably worth collegial discussions and practical tests. But as an overall answer that should support the previously cited learning goals it is unrealistic. The proposals are also out of proportion in relation to specific teacher and student actions. It is therefore in the intersection between the Chat text's suggestions and imperative modes that the possible/impossible tasks and actions must be seen.

In the above quoted, it is immediately about didactically everyday actions, such as 'Divide the students', 'Organize outside activities', 'focused discussions', 'use multimodal ressources' and 'Highlight the importance of…'. But if you follow the subsequent description of the action, it is a very advanced didactic handling and complicated repertoire of actions Chat encourages. Let me delve into the first proposal, quoted below in full, and then provide an overview of the proposals as a whole. For ease of reference, I mark with (1)–(5) the various actions as follows:

Proposal 1

Differentiated reading strategies: (2) Divide students into smaller groups based on their reading skills and (3) emphasize the importance of identifying and analyzing character traits and relationships. (4) Include differentiated text excerpts for different groups, (5) that focus on Karen Blixen's character development and her relationship with other characters. (Chat, Ses. Blixen/didactic)

If you take the choice of words and calls to action at face value, proposal 1 is both ambitious and requires preparation. Dealing with differentiated reading strategies and basing group division on the students' different reading skills (1), (2) and also matching it with differentiated text sections addressed to the different groups (4) is a didactic accuracy work that cannot be done easily. With, for example, 20 students in the class, it requires not only an overview of graduation of reading skills, but knowledge of each individual student's reading skills. And measuring high school students' skills, specifically like *reading* skills, which can/should then be matched against a specific literary work, The African Farm, is out of proportion. Suddenly, the Chat text and the suggestions that could be convincing on a first reading appear rather misleading. There is something wrong with proposal 1, just as there is something wrong with the other proposals as well. In terms of genre and grammar, the text is coherent, but the professional content, the didactic measures and actions are not connected. And apart from the fact that the language block 'Karen Blixen's character development' is a regular ingredient in the session's Chat responses, the anchoring in the work "The African Farm" fades away.

In proposal 2, on nature-based learning, according to Chat, outdoor reading activities must be organised 'that are related to descriptions of nature in the novel', as it is formulated. Next, the Chat description continues:

> This can include field studies where students observe and describe natural elements, and then relate their observations to Blixen's descriptions in the text. (ibid)

Whether the teacher in a Danish educational context should send the team of high school students or student teachers on field investigations in Dyrehaven north of Copenhagen, in one of the larger cities' Zoos, or another place where African-like natural elements can be observed, could well be discussed as possibilities. But regardless, the field study itself is curiously targeted, namely that the students 'relate their observations to Blixen's descriptions in the text'. Should the students bring their own field note texts close to Blixen's texts, and/or compare descriptions of natural elements? And should we thereby move from the 1st proposal's focus on supporting students' reading skills to supporting writing skills?

The problem is that even though the Chat text seeks a high degree of detail and linguistically allocates the action of 'observing, describing and then relating to the Blixen text' to the students, neither tasks nor purposes are concretely present. Unless we suddenly have to see students at the Author school for us, it is difficult to determine the professional skills, or simply more broadly which learning goal the high school student or the student teacher should be supported in. The same problem regarding the nature and targeting of the action appears in proposal 4 and 5, where Chat allocates the action to the teacher with linguistic clarity. I quote below in full so that we can follow both didactic initiatives as a two-part proposal for teacher action that helps students with the important skills: to understand, to analyze and to express themselves personally. The division of two is mine.

> 4. Interactive reading experience: (1) Use multimodal resources such as audio recordings, film adaptations, or virtual tours to help students understand Blixen's complex narrative style. (2) Do activities that focus on identifying and analyzing the use of symbolic language, allegory and metaphors in different parts of the novel.
>
> 5. Reflection-based teaching: (1) Emphasize the importance of reflection on existential themes in the novel by encouraging personal reflection and written reflections. (2) Use reflective diaries or literary analysis to help students express their thoughts about the meaning of life, death, and existential experiences presented in the work. (Chat Ses.Blixen/Didactic)

As an analyst, I have been waiting for Chat/the databank to open the door to media reality and to what in relation to mass culture is characterized as a media mill or media roulette (see Chap. 2). I have been waiting for Chat to discover that all of the great Danish works and their authors have that, which Chat now manages to name as multimodal resources around it. Klaus Rifbjerg's work, "Den kroniske uskyld" was made into a film; "Pelle Erobreren" is remembered as an Oscar-winning film adaptation. All of the authors mentioned in this book are documented, portrayed and seen as contributors to films/videos, theater and TV performances; they are canonized and appear in the education system from kindergarten to university. And work and author, Karen Blixen, who is at the center here, can take us around the world's media roulette with the film Out of Africa, Meryl Streep and Robert Redford in the lead roles, as well as 7 Oscar statuettes.

Against this background, it is strangely out of proportion to propose a didactic initiative where a teacher must use the multimodal resources with the aim of helping the students to understand 'Blixen's complex narrative style', which the Chat text formulates. The strange thing about the proposal is that either it is an advanced and time-consuming activity to use audio recordings, film adaptations and virtual tours to understand the complexity of Blixen's narrative style, which requires masterclasses at film, theater or author schools, or it simply requires a Google banal action that for KB takes 10 s and brings the following result:

> Karen Blixen was known for her rich and figurative writing style. She used detailed descriptions and metaphors to create vivid and sensual images in the reader's mind. Her language was poetic and evocative, adding to the depth and complexity of her works.
>
> The themes that Blixen explored in her works were often existential and universal. Love, loss, identity and man's relationship with nature were central themes in her stories. She also explored themes of power, gender and colonialism in a way that was way ahead of her time. (KB's random Google search on the keyword: Karen Blixen's poetic narrative style. Choice no. 5 on the search list on 3.6.2024)

KB only had the 10 s to google a random bid Blixen's narrative style, but in the context the random bid is an important example from the big search machine that likes to start with 'that' thing a person is known for. In this respect, the above quote works with words and phrases that stick to Blixen as a world-renowned author, and are otherwise both confirmed and elaborated by the Blixen-savvy professionals.

The banal but informative text of the Google search thus exposes the Chat text's distortions of proportions and the unclear alternation between analyses carried out by professionals and banal answers/ready/start questions that students can use in the movement from 'the known material' to the new, independent work of description and analysis.

Chat's suggestions constantly testify to a linguistic surplus. But the two-part tasks crackle and seem to be based neither on the known material nor on knowledge of the didactic challenges of novel analysis. And where phrases such as 'to understand Blixen's complex narrative style' signal the surplus, the action-specific bullet points and Chat's calls to teachers, high school students or teacher students rather testify to a deficit in praxis. Here Chat's didactic poverty becomes the present characteristic.

10.13 The Didactic Poverty

If we start with the proportioning of the didactic proposals, the poverty is seen in the consequential actions. In suggestion 4, the call to help understand Blixen's complex narrative style is followed, for example, by this formulation:

> Do activities that focus on identifying and analyzing the use of symbolic language, allegory, and metaphors in different parts of the novel. (ibid)

This call 'Do activities that focus on…' is both theoretically and didactically methodologically poor in that it lacks any indication of, or conceptualization of, how, which activities should enable teachers and groups of students (together or separately?) to focus on… The title of the activity is still "Interactive reading experience", so perhaps we should imagine activities that take place in plenary, perhaps students reading to each other? And if, for example, a virtual tour has been chosen in advance to help understanding Blixen's narrative style, then the teacher could perhaps have the students sit in a circle and take turns identifying symbolic language and metaphors in the novel. If it is oral preparations for the analysis (and thus a focus on reading and discussion skills), then the next step and focus could be writing skills. Analyses have a tradition of being completed as written, possibly specified as literary analysis.

We cannot know what Chat/databank or the expertise behind it specifically imagines about ChatGPT's abilities as a didactic sparring partner. In that sense, there is no point of reference or basis for comparison. However, if the living sparring partners are used as examples, e.g. the previously mentioned IT school projects and their modernization tasks (see Chap. 9), observations of the course on H. C. Andersen's fairy tale universe show how the focus is alternately placed on reading experiences/reading skills and analysis/writing skills. The observation also covered the activities: the students read aloud in plenary, discuss in plenary. Analysis work can similarly be started in plenary, then condensed in a 'conference with the neighbor', in order to move on to actual group work.

The point of remembering the living processes is to clarify the important practice references in the context. When the observed teachers describe the teaching practice, it is possible to identify didactic initiatives/activity (differentiated in what the teacher does and what the student is supposed to do), purpose, skills, action repertoire and product… as measures and activities come into focus. It is not certain that the teacher (or the observer) has the completely appropriate words and phrases, but then a 'situation' or a practical incident can be pointed out. The point is that even if we lack appropriate words, the accuracy in and with the practice reference is reasonably good. And then to the point, which is also in the memory. Despite many observations and conversations with teachers, I have never before encountered the kind of skewed proportioning and uncertain placement of the didactic measures that the session and Chats the 1–5 point description testify to. I have also never before encountered the kind of dubious emphasis on personal aspects and uncertain handling of which activities the teacher and student groups should be involved in, as expressed in the Chat text's calls under the heading "Reflection-based teaching" (point 5). The two-part proposal was as follows:

> (1) Emphasize the importance of reflection on existential themes in the novel by encouraging personal reflection and written reflections. (2) Use reflection diaries or literary analyses to help students express their thoughts on the meaning of life, death, and existential experiences presented in the work. (ibid)

The dubious emphasis first appears in a tautological overuse of the word 'reflection', which is both the basis for the teaching, content, occasion, and suggestion for the teacher's first action. "Emphasize the importance of reflection" as it is formulated in an imperative manner. Next, there is doubt about who is encouraged to engage in personal reflection and written reflections. It is probably the students. But the doubt is kept alive by (2) command, addressed to the teacher: "Use reflection diaries or literary analyses to help the students". Here the teacher must be the acting subject and the students the object of the help. But if the teacher is to use literary analyses to help the students, who should write these analyses? It is not entirely clear, but it should help the students to express 'their thoughts about the meaning of life, death and existential experiences'. Now the students' thoughts about the meaning of life, death and…? are at the center. And then the doubt arises again. Perhaps 'and existential experiences presented in the work' were Blixen's experiences. Surely, it can hardly be the students' thoughts presented in the work?

It is precisely here, in the midst of the guesswork, that I have previously stopped for analytical strategic reasons. I have also justified it, for example, with the analytical observation that the Chat text keeps the doubt about speech position and content alive. Doubt is a textual stylistic feature, I claim. This is how ChatGPT's textual universe works, I show, when language suit and genre, language blocks and signal words carry the text's content and subject matter through to the point of almost meaningfulness … and then still collapse. And finally, in a case-oriented manner, I have asked who takes (or has) responsibility?

All of this still applies, also to the Chat-text's didactic initiatives. But there is noticeably something else and more at stake here where Chat advises and makes concrete suggestions for action for a practice that Chat cannot identify with. This requires at least maintaining the special features that the Blixen session testifies to, as well as a status of the significance of these.

Firstly, it must be stated that the Chat-texts dubious handlings, where we 'suddenly' do not know which tasks are the teacher's, which are the student group's or which thoughts are the teacher's, Blixen's or the students', or what/which action, skill, or which product we are supposed to see… not only testifies to didactic poverty, but *is* didactic poverty. *Secondly*, it must be clarified that in the KB/Chat session the Pioneer Teachers' task portfolio was taken over, almost verbatim. But letting signal words such as 'exam', 'learning goals', 'didactics' and then the Chat/databank set the agenda is a responsibility I take on. *Therefore, and thirdly*, it must be clarified that the Karen Blixen session, as part of the research's empirical collection, is treated analytically as before, but at the same time requires a special characteristic. Outlined as follows.

The Karen Blixen session is the session in the collection that bears the strongest evidence that the genre-adequate role taking, the language suit and the meaningful text pieces, suffer a loss of meaning along the way. A structural overlay occurs, and in the case of Bloom's taxonomy, the taxonomic placement becomes the meaning-bearer. The overwhelming wordiness Chat demonstrates allows the terminology to be represented both over triads such as theme, topic/problem orientation and analysis/discussion/reflection, and over word combinations such as reading strategies, interactive reading experiences, discussion-based, reflection-based, etc. But the many overlaps and redundant word combinations testify that the words individually and in combinations lose their meaning and significance. And the place in the taxonomy that the word/language block occupies becomes the meaning-bearer. Words/language blocks that start with discussion, ethics, existential, reflection are placed and acquire meaning according to the structural order of the Chat text, as belonging to the upper level of the taxonomy. This also includes words like 'deep/deeper', if the analyses are to be deep!

The special feature that characterizes the Blixen session, however, is not one specific (and therefore Bloomsian) structure, but several. As exemplified earlier in the chapter, there is also a Biggs taxonomy that follows learning goals; in addition, Chat's bulleted list, just as there is a S-M-E positioning that influences language suit, role taking, etc. If therefore the special features of the Blixen session are summarized, we see a complex of bulleted Chat proposals that testify to an overwhelming wealth of words, divergent taxonomies, a structural overlay and a loss of meaning in terms of content. But if it is correct that the content has lost meaning, then that single work, "The African Farm", and the author who, by name, Karen Blixen, has been the focal point of the complex and tied the entire session together, must have been lost along the way. I therefore reconstruct the complex as a text collection and go in search of the work at the end of the chapter. But first, the session's last Chat contribution and role input must be included, namely Chat in the role of evaluator.

10.14 Evaluation Criteria

When KB asks Chat to provide a description of evaluation criteria, a Chat response is received that, not surprisingly, is at the high end of the scale.[7] With a Lix score of 60, it is, however, slightly lower than the previous Didactic initiative. The Chat response is genre-wise in the flow of the session and uses the recognizable 1–5 points structure. But Chat reintroduces the characteristic mitigating/reminding final remark. Against this background, I choose for the last time a light sequencing of S-M-E positions, as well as a quote from the KB/Chat session in full text.

[7] Lix number 60, Very difficult, Sentences: 13, Words: 192, Long words: 87.

KB: Give a description of evaluation criteria that can be given to students

ChatGPT

(S-pos) Of course, here are some evaluation criteria that the teacher can use to judge the students' performances in connection with the work with Karen Blixen's "The African Farm":

(M-pos)

1. Character Analysis: The ability to identify and analyze character traits and the development of the main character as well as her relationship with other characters in the novel.
2. Descriptions of nature: The ability to analyze and understand the author's use of descriptions of nature to create atmosphere and symbolism in the novel, as well as the ability to convey this through written analyses.
3. Cultural Analysis: The ability to discuss and analyze cultural conflicts and themes in the novel and demonstrate an understanding of their impact on the story and character development.
4. Narrative Techniques: The ability to identify and analyze various narrative techniques used in the novel, including flashbacks, indirect characterization, etc., and demonstrate an understanding of their role in the development of plot and characters.
5. In-depth analysis: The ability to undertake an in-depth and critical analysis of existential themes and the author's stylistic choices, including the use of symbolic language, allegory and metaphors to explore complex themes such as colonialism, identity and loss.

(S-Pos) These evaluation criteria can be adapted and adjusted as needed depending on the specific tasks and achievements on which students are to be judged. (Chat.Ses.Blixen/evaluation)

Let me start by commenting on the Chat answer's S-position. It is genre-appropriate, but also characterized by a high degree of modification and adaptation of KB's question to Chat's handling of the teacher/assessor role. In the flow of the session, from KB's perspective, we have come to the evaluation question. KB mentions the students because they must have the criteria presented. It is open whether 'evaluation' should be understood in the broad sense, e.g. teaching or project evaluation (internal evaluation) or in the narrow sense, external evaluation such as an exam. The KB question thus does not signal whether it should be linked to formative evaluation (and the traditions referred to earlier) or to the tradition of the final exam. Nor does the KB question signal whether evaluation should be linked to the session's previous learning question (the signal word learning/learning goals), or to 'the five exam questions' and to the assessment of results and performance.

However, what KB leaves open and does not signal, the Chat answer, on the other hand, already frames in the S-position. There is no doubt that the context of the answer is the exam. And there is a rare clear clarification of the real relationship between KB and Chat, 'a teacher' and 'a group of students'. All this is put in place in one sentence. After the standard phrase ('Of course, here are some evaluation criteria'), Chat clarifies that the proposal is handed over as a list:

> (…) the teacher can use to judge the students' performances in connection with the work on Karen Blixen's "The African Farm. (Chat,Ses. Blixen/evaluation)

With the previous surprises about the data bank that opened up, first at the word "exam", then at the word "learning goal", there was reason to expect that the word "evaluation" would open corresponding new doors to the data bank. The surprise was that the word evaluation did not seem to open, quite the opposite. Chat reconstructed the KB question, but inserted a new tailored version that ensured Chat's transfer of responsibility to 'a teacher who will judge'.

KB's use of an open concept of evaluation, with criteria to be given to the students, was hereby closed and replaced by Chat with criteria for the teacher judging student performance and abilities. These abilities were well-known taxonomically arranged, like quoted above 1–5. But otherwise, and in relation to the content of the Blixen session and the evaluation, nothing new was added. With this, the Chat answer has almost become a non-answer with similarities that go all the way back to the KB/Chat sessions' testing with question positions, where KB takes the patient-to-doctor position, and receives language blocks that function as repetitions and doublings, high lix numbers, non-answers and disclaimers. The circle is closed. However, Chat's role and contribution to the evaluation indicate that the analysis is to round off by maintaining the connection to the work with "The African Farm" and then drawing lines throughout the session.

If this is done, the start of the session is remembered as notes with a low lix count, but also as a Chat text where "The African Farm" and Karen Blixen filled it all. The Note document was about the book and the work. There were 270 words in total, and all the words had clear reference to the book/action's time/place, main characters and themes. In the Evaluation document there are 192 words and apart from the Chat-answer to ensure that author/title teacher and student are mentioned by positional mention, none of the words we can know for sure are specifically linked to Karen Blixen's book and narrative universe. Also, the document on Didactic initiatives, which with the highest lix number of the session dabbled in didactic words, had few words rooted in Blixen's work.

Let me therefore round off the Blixen-oriented part of the analysis via an additional study that shows which of the work's words/signal words Chat used and reused from one session to the next, and which were lost along the way.

10.15 The "African Farm" and the Loss of the Narrative Words…

The reason for the further study is, as mentioned, the observed features of the process. "The African farm", and thus the words and voice of the story, but also the session's professional voices, or voices referring to teachers and students, risk being absent from the course. Furthermore, there are signs that even though many new words appear during the course of the session, they are not taken from Karen Blixen's narrative universe. And finally, the session's last contribution shows that KB also becomes absent, and KB's questions are given new words. Chat has thus become self-running during the course of the session and the text collection takes on a character similar to Chat's and the data bank. For the same reason, there is a need to reconstruct the textual course, as word/language blocks progress and describe the text collection as a data collection in sober terms. Chat's Blixen Notes, are like notes to The African Farm, the starting point and the start of the text/data collection. Next, Sessions 2–5 function as Chat answers to KB's follow-up questions. In this respect, all text/data sections can be said to have Chat's notes and the work/title The African Farm as a common starting point or first reference. But even though the work and title also function as a common background and the wording remains the reference, noticeable shifts occur. This shift away from the work and author must be factually maintained. At the same time, it must be examined which signal words and language blocks appeared in the text/data collection, and to what extent words/language blocks from the source (the Blixen notes) were kept alive. The procedure for the study was simple and as follows.

The Blixen session, totaling 1692 words, was collected in a document. Next, I used the computer's Search/Replace function to find out how many words, language blocks close to Karen Blixen and the work appear in the different sessions/text sequences. The Blixen notes, the starting text, have a very high degree of concretization. Therefore, the study focuses on putting numbers on how many words/language blocks from the notes are used/survived or not used/died during the session. The results are summarized in the overview, see Fig. 10.1, and its two parts. To facilitate understanding of the results, I provide the following comments:

The Karen Blixen session
– From Chat Notes to Evaluation.
The number of times the word is used, reused or not.
Showing the narrative words that were lost

Words based on Chats-Karen Blixen Notes/The narrative words

(1a) Karen Blixen 27, The African Farm 25, Nature 17

(1b) Autobiographical 1, Bror Blixen 1, Finch Hatton 1, Colonial period 1, Kikuyu tribe 1, Kenya 3, Coffee plantation, local populations 2, White 1, Power and oppression 1, Wildlife 1, Poetic 1. The 1b) words mentioned only appear in the notes. Important person and context markers.

(1c)Identity 7, colonialism 5. Comment: These two appear in all the session documents.

Words based on the exam question session

(2a) The novel 40, character 38 (the word does not appear in the notes) theme 33, analysis 29, narrative style/narrative technique 12, cultural 11, complex 10, existential 8 (does not appear in the notes), conflicts 8, symbolic/symbolism 7 (does not appear in the notes), reading 6, depth (does not appear in the notes) critical 5. The narrative voice 1, appears only in the exam questions

Fig. 10.1 Overview of the Karen Blixen session—from Notes to Evaluation—showing the number of times a word is used, reused or not. The trend is that the words close to Blixen's narrative universe are lost during the session and overlaid by generalizing language blocks

Reuse of text pieces, the Blixen Notes' high information/concretization level is not re-found; text pieces do not reappear in the sessions other Chat texts, nor as language blocks. Formulations/words and language blocks from the exam questions are reused. Ditto for learning goal sentences: here both words and language blocks are reused.

Author and work with name mention appear in all parts of the Blixen session, often in starting sentences. This is generalized in 'The Novel' which appears 40 times, and therefore it is the word that appears most frequently. 1b) words such as 'autobiographical', 'coffee plantation' and names such as 'Bror Blixen' only appear in the Notes. It is noted that they are important person and context markers.

Further comment: the two words 'identity' and 'colonialism' appear in all the documents of the session. But since I can observe from the Blixen Notes that the words are not used, and that the author's name and work are included in the generalization 'the novel', I take the exam question session as a new starting point—And here come the high jumpers of the text/data collection.

The high jumpers, where 'the novel' and the high number of words, 40, testify to increased generalization/decreasing Blixen-like concretization, the word 'character' 38 (in the Note document 'person' is used) testifies to a powerful inclusion of a new word/language block. Furthermore, the other new words/language blocks that do not appear in the Notes testify to the increased level of difficulty, and that Chat's access to the databank triggered by 'exam' evokes the genre-appropriate words/language blocks that belong to the respective sessions.

Let me continue the commentary, but give it a summary characteristic of the session's strong signal words. The signal words 'exam' and 'learning goal' show their strength by giving direction to the session process and opening the data bank. This noticeably gives Chat many more and new genre-appropriate words and language blocks. Chat's text corpus changes and the level of difficulty increases each time the new signal words are used. Learning goal then functions both as a new signal word and as an independent language block, with its own genre-appropriate words, then exam questions clarify the consistent structure and taxonomy reference to Bloom's and Biggs' taxonomies and learning goal. This means that the strong signal words, exam and learning goal, both act as genre/text/discourse markers of the process, and promote the structural overlay. But it also means that the taxonomies place the words and that sentences and text pieces get the structure as a carrier of meaning. The words lose their independent significance and the text loses meaning. If the summary characteristic is to concentrate on the words, it starts with the Notes. All the listed words (the 1a, b, c words of the notes) are strong narrators close to the book and author. The 1b words, which refer to people, the Kikuyu tribe and wildlife, are also important person and place markers. If you see the listed words, you see the book. But if the words are not reused in the session (and the 1b words are not), the narrative words are gone. They are embedded and generalized to the 'novel' and become part of the textual process, where the high degree of concretization decreases and the degree of generalization increases. The note words and the narrator Karen Blixen actually become increasingly absent. This means that the Blixen notes, as a text with a high degree of concretization, keep the words close to the work, but have no scope and significance for the rest of the process. The narrative words only apply to the notes. And Chat's text/data collection as a whole show that Chat cannot recall the narrative words and notes itself had written.

10.16 ...and Taxonomies and the Structure That was Used and Reused

The narrative words were lost along the way, but the taxonomies were used and reused and the Blixen session is marked by a noticeable structural overlay. But the divergent taxonomies also come on a collision course, which is evident in Chat's difficulties in managing the tasks. On the one hand, Chat operates with taxonomic structuring as part of the task solution regarding level divisions and the setting of learning goals. On the other hand, Chat seems to be unable to handle the grouping of easy/medium/difficult, to reconcile the relationship between exam questions and learning goal or to clarify the question of progression. Furthermore, Chat's contribution to didactic initiatives was characterized as poor.

We know this discrepancy between what Chat claims to be able to do, promises to do—but cannot do anyway—as a fundamental problem and a feature of Chat's functioning. The analytical characteristic applies throughout. The discrepancy concerns the relationship between the language that promises and asserts, and the text that mitigates or negates. Furthermore, the genre and the genre-appropriate language blocks function as what mitigates. The genre gives Chat/the language set the opportunity to negate, disclaim responsibility or transfer responsibility to KB, or the 'user'. But in relation to the taxonomies, there is something else and more going on. This 'something else and more' does not only affect the language set and genre, but Chat's (and ChatGPT's) core competence: to structure, to give structure. Chat's attempt to handle taxonomies, which are in the plural, in the Chat text does not just become more structures, but an unclear over-structuring. The structures also come into conflict with each other. The genre-appropriate bullet points structure the text, but come into conflict with, for example, graduations (over easy/difficult) that structure the content. Next, bullet points, as graduations, come into conflict with the progression effort, which is both signaled via a number series (points 1–5) and as a linguistically signaled movement 'from simple to complex'. Against this background, the example material in this chapter testifies that Chat is caught in a clash between the handling of traditions from Bloom and Biggs, respectively.

For the same reason, the next chapter will clarify the clash, as an intermezzo between taxonomies in both a theoretical and practical sense.

References

Biggs, J. (1999). *Teaching for quality learning at university*. Open University Press.

Bloom, B. S., et al. (1956). *Webstert's new collegiate dictionary*. G. & C. Merriam Co.
Borgnakke, K. (Ed.). (2008). *Evalueringens spændingsfelter*. Klim.
Dahler-Larsen, P. (2003). *Selvevalueringens Hvide sejl*. Syddansk Universitetsforlag.
Ongstad, S. (2006). Fag i endring. Om didaktisering av kunnskap. In S. Ongstad (Ed.), *Fag og didaktikk i lærerutdanning. Kunnskap i grenseland* (pp. 19–57). Universitetsforlaget.
Ramsden, P. (1991). *Learning to teach in higher education*. Routledge.
Rasborg, F., Jensen, J., & Leunbach, G. (Eds.). (1977). *Evaluering for at planlægge og forbedre*. Munksgaard.

Chapter 11
As an Intermezzo Between Taxonomies

As will be apparent from this chapter, both IT expertise and institutions and centers have renewed interest in Bloom's and Biggs' taxonomies in interaction with the implementation of generative AI technology as a learning technology. The interaction renews interest, but at the same time shows that the taxonomies are involved in an intermezzo that require clarification of the history and the different development interests and models.

The chapter therefore follows Bloom's/Biggs' taxonomies from the origin of the model development through the revival and adaptations of the decades. The institutional management of the traditions and implementation of the GAI technology is followed in exemplified form, through the study portal *Studypedia*, with reference to Aarhus University.

The traditions' own representative function in the chapter as the authoritative and professional voices that are cited for the significant similarities, differences and development perspectives. This ensures the analysis strategy following argumentation, interpretation and management from theory to practice. Hereby maintains the taxonomy and models' origins in the theory level (back to the 1950s), then exemplifies the authoritative interpretations and new interpretations and rounding off with today's institutional administrations.

It will be clarified that 'digital technologies' exert influence on the new interpretations from the mid-2000s. Next, IT expertise drowns out the new interpretation and sets the agenda for the current integration of GAI-technologies in taxonomy, model and institutional development.

K. Borgnakke, *AI and ChatGPT Technology in Education*, Education, Equity, Economy 12, https://doi.org/10.1007/978-3-032-01419-1_11

11.1 Origin: Marked Similarities/Differences Between Bloom's and Biggs' Traditions

The argumentation in the theory field can be followed from its origins in the mid-1950s, where the Bloom tradition marked the pivotal point 'classification'. With reference to biological science, the need is emphasized, on the one hand, to 'ensure the accuracy of communication about science' and, on the other hand, to 'understand the interrelationship (…) between the different parts of the animal and plant world'. Taxonomy is based on knowledge.

The Biggs tradition marked (from the 1980s onwards) the pivotal point 'alignment', which is based on the need to ensure the interaction between teaching content, forms and examination, with the aim of increasing students' learning, as well as promoting so-called deep learning. The taxonomy is based on teaching/learning. If we include from the practice field a typical exemplification from the leading center of academic learning at Aarhus University, Biggs' tradition is marked through both development of the center and the course planning.[1]

With differences marked as traditions, which are based on to classify knowledge and align learning goals, the differences appear significant. And the similarity, apparently, lies mostly in the practice orientation's effort giving the taxonomy an application aspect. What is interesting, however, is that precisely the application aspect (and thus the interpretation and management of the practice field) as a tendency not only overshadows the differences, but overlooks the dilemma between 'classifying' with knowledge as the focal point and 'making the alignment' based on learning goals. Let me therefore reconstruct the similarities/differences that are significant because they are effective, i.e. useful in terms of theory and practice.

11.2 Classification: Useful Means of Ensuring Accuracy of Communication

Since Bloom marks the origin, Bloom et al. can be quoted in detail from the preface, so that you can subsequently refer to the three important extracts below. Through this, both the scientific origin, mission and main rationale are clear. The excerpts are noted by me 1–3, as follows:

(1) Biologists have found their taxonomy markedly helpful as a means of insuring accuracy of communication about their science and as a means of understanding the organization and interrelation of the various parts of the animal and plant world. You are

[1] In the Danish University auspices, the center at Aarhus University developed during the 1990s the Biggs-tradition, framing courses as well as journal activities, see Leth Andersen, 2007. Today the center and the website Studypedia (as elaborated in this chapter) represent the ongoing development. An overview of the development of the tradition and the changing meanings of the learning paradigm is exemplified in Borgnakke, 2011, pp. 15–39.

reading about an attempt to build a taxonomy of educational objectives. It is intended to provide for classification of the goals of our educational system. It is expected to be of general help to all teachers, administrators, professional specialists, and research workers who deal with curricular and evaluation problems.

(2) It is especially intended to help them discuss these problems with greater precision. For example, some teachers believe their students should "really understand", while others desire their students to "internalize knowledge", still others want their students to "grasp the core or essence" or "comprehend". Do they all mean the same thing? Specifically, what does a student do who "really understands" which he does not do when he does not understand?

(3) Through reference to the taxonomy as a set of standard classifications, teachers should be able to define such nebulous terms as those given above. This should facilitate the exchange of information about their curricular developments and evaluation devices. (Bloom et al., 1956, p. 871)

As cited, the focal point of taxonomies that allow classification is marked as 'helpful' in relation to increased precision among biologists on science relating to the animal and plant world. Next, Bloom et al. make a significant shift to classify goals for the education system.

What, in a scientific sense, makes this shift from knowledge of the animal/plant world to knowledge of educational goals possible is initially unclear. The ambiguity appears later around a shift to knowledge about artificial intelligence. But until it appears as a problem, I leave it alone. Because even though they are very different areas of science and subject matter, the Bloomian logic can be followed as a statement. There is 'knowledge' and possibilities for 'classification' in both Biology and Education. If, on this basis, we accept the taxonomy and its usefulness as 'a set of standard classifications', then the usefulness is shown in that teachers (originally biologists) with reference to their relevant standard classifications will be able to 'define the nebulous terms'.

With the background logic reconstructed, illustrations showing the cognitive taxonomy as a hierarchical model, called the "6-step model", represent what had a great impact. In the present context, however, I prefer a simple arrangement that, with my emphases, maintains the starting point (knowledge) and the orientation point (evaluation) as follows:

1. **KNOWLEDGE**
2. UNDERSTANDING
3. APPLICATION
4. ANALYSIS
5. SYNTHESIS
6. **EVALUATION**

(After Bloom et al., 1956, underlined in bold by the undersigned)

The simple arrangement is suitable for maintaining the origin, and that Bloom et al. themselves emphasized that the classification and model should be a general aid to 'teachers, administrators, professional specialists and researchers' who work with 'curriculum and evaluation problem'. This points out the potential didactic logic, namely that curriculum development starts in the Knowledge dimension (what *the teacher* believes the students should know) and are directed towards the identification of evaluation problems.

But the fact that the orientation towards a clarification of an implicit didactic logic is possible does not change the fact that the 6-step model (and hierarchy structures) became the standard model on which later revisions were made. Bloom and Krathwohl revised the model (see Krathwohl, 2002) and also supplemented the important keywords, e.g. with 'creativity'. In continuation of this, and spurred by clarifications about 'digital technologies', a next generation of the model and new additions came, such as those presented by Oregon University.[2]

The problem is not that the 6-step model is continuously being rethought and new aspects added. The problem is that the increased precision—among scientists and/or among professionals, seems to be waiting to happen. The professional interpretations seem preoccupied with adding new aspects, rather than confirming or denying (or simply problematizing) the basic assumptions of the model.

It is difficult to explain the model's prerequisite step 'understanding', let alone explain the path from knowledge to understanding. In that sense, the 6-step model has not clarified "the nebulous terms", but rather named the different steps in a knowledge-acquisition/application process. And contributing another step that is merely a change of the term 'Creativity' does not make the model or description any less nebulous. On the contrary, the later revisions and new interpretations show that the individual steps 1–6 of the model change words and concepts like the wind blows. And the model as a whole, and its origins, suffers a loss of understanding.

Let me from this characteristic of the Bloomian origin then move forward about 40 years to the Biggs tradition and their practice-oriented interpreters. Hereby the focus will shift to the new focal points for the use of taxonomies.

11.3 Alignment: Useful as Means of Ensuring the Relationship Between Teaching, Exam Questions and Learning Goals

As professional representatives of the Biggs tradition John Biggs (1999) and Paul Ramsden (1991) are highlighted because their research environments, books and dissemination can both refer to concept development, textbooks, development work and links to Best Practice. Furthermore, the Biggs tradition's handling of taxonomies and concepts of surface and deep learning clarifies a new anchoring in pedagogy and learning research, with reference to the research projects of the 1970s Ference Marton and Roger Saljö (1976, 1984). At the same time, Biggs' concept development, e.g. in the book *Teaching for Quality Learning at University, 1999,* serves as a reference for course development at the university educational centers.

[2] The revised and renewed taxonomies, 2024, see the collected description Oregan State University website, online E-campus.

A fixed corpus of Biggs' concepts and taxonomies around the main description of C *onstructive alignment* became the profile of both the centers and the task portfolio· And finally, the Biggs tradition has been brought to life in an award-winning video production (Brabrand, 2006).[3] So, the message: *Constructive alignment* only further emphasizes the intended impact in the university educational environments.

In one of the time typical examples from the Faculty of Life Sciences, University of Copenhagen, the Biggs tradition is marked through the development of a cross-faculty course, where the course planning follows Biggs's four steps for constructive alignment, noted above the keywords:

> 1) Describe learning outcomes and course content 2) Align with course activities and learning environment 3) Align assignment and assessment 4) Transform into a grade. (Christiansen et al., 2010, p. 60)[4]

Subsequently, course plans and learning goals are aligned with Biggs' significant SOLO taxonomies (Structure of the Observed Learning Outcome), aligned and justified on the levels called *Prestructural, Unistructural, Multistructural, Relational and Extended abstract* (Biggs & Tang, 2007, pp. 77–78).

As has been seen, the Biggs tradition has from the outset been oriented towards the practice aspect and has already since the 1990s asserted itself as a source of inspiration for development work related to the high school and university educational centers which, in the context of this book, represent the institutions' professional voices.

The commitment to an institution-specific reconciliation of the relationship between teaching content/examination questions based on learning goals also can be observed in curricula, course descriptions and on the universities' websites. But as identifiable changes in the students' learning practices or as changes in teaching courses, they are difficult to see, verify or point to. And, as can be seen from the exemplification below, the professionals who could verify, or point to… have already jumped on—preoccupied with new steps, aspects or latest additions that are now required by the digital technologies and AI development of the time.

11.4 Today's New Interpretations Are IT-Based

In the present context, the article "Bloom's taxonomy in the interaction between artificial intelligence and human learning" (Dec 2023) authored by Claus Scheuer-Larsen and Per Størup Lauridsen, serves as an example in several ways. Firstly, it is a clear example of both the authors and the place of publication, namely the website

[3] See Claus Brabrand (2006) film/video Teaching Teaching & Understanding Understanding. Short-film on Constructive Alignment, DVD.

[4] The example described by M.S. Windahl is a contribution to the collection of educational projects published in Improving University Science, Teaching and learning, see Windahl, 2010. The four steps are reproduced according to Biggs & Tang, 2007, p. 50 ff.

Viden.ai, referring to an IT-based knowledge sharing and to the public debate. The website also functions as an information development that exists in interaction with e.g. the Ministry of Education's portals. Secondly, it is an example of how Bloom's taxonomy and computers are considered in an almost natural interaction—and moreover gives the impression that both parts are naturally integrated in the public sector and thus in the education system.

The authors begin thus:

> In this article, we examine what happens when artificial intelligence is integrated into our subjects across all levels of the education system. We ask: What will be important to learn when computers can assist us with remembering and thinking, and what might become less important? (Scheuer-Larsen & Lauridsen, 2023).

The formulation "what happens when artificial intelligence…" is interesting, but questionable. The formulation "when" could also be an '*if* artificial intelligence...'. However, it is felt that the authors, who themselves take part in the IT expertise, are both ahead and knowledgeable and can therefore comment on the crucial question of what will be important to learn.

I dwell on the title and the opening lines because I was surprised by the authors' questions naturalization of the taxonomic thinking. Because if 'we' can ask, and then decide what will be important, or perhaps less important to learn, it must be because we already know that AI/computers actually can assist us with remembering and thinking. Do we know? And is the choice of words and the link to two such basic human characteristics 'remember' and 'think' well chosen?

KB/Chat sessions and previous analysis (see Chaps. 6 and 7) of the public debate and the authoritative statements of IT expertise have offered many links and assertions, from Anders Søgaard's and Mushtaq Bilal's emphasis that the students do not need academic writing, to the related from O..., where they students do not need to read; from managements and editors-in-chief's praises (but also fears) that the GAI technology can replace the academic workforce as academic helper and analysts. But I have not yet been presented with an academic daring that, with the choice of wording 'to remember and to think' as the basic category, gives a conglomeration of what the interaction between computers and human learning is about. Distrust sets in. Since when did it become a matter of course that AI-computers can match the assumed basic cognitive functions of learning processes?

Lev Vygotsky's main work is entitled *Language and Thinking*, John Dewey's famous essay title is *How we think,* and the first chapter formulate the basic question *What is thought?* One of psychology's fundamental but enigmatic phenomena is 'memory', later linked to the learning issue of 'transfer'. Is it about such fundamental works and such scientific riddles that we should associate with soon computer, soon humans? And if so, what does today's everyday version of the human/AI/chatbot interaction look like? Should we do a 50/50 sequencing of a conversation, a la: KB remembers 'something', and says it to the chatbot/Chat, which replies 'something-that-fits-with-something' and then I start thinking about this something? Sorry, that's getting us absolutely nowhere.

Scheuer-Larsen & Lauridsen do not show the way. However, the article later shows that the critical wonder can be maintained. The choice of the basic words 'remember and think' does not come from Scheuer-Larsen & Lauridsen, but is, as probably guessed, a paraphrasing of the revised edition of Bloom. And as the article go through the model development, Bloom's taxonomy was revised by Anderson and Krathwohl in 2001, where "creative skills replace synthesis and at the same time move space to the highest level of the model." (Scheuer-Larsen & Lauridsen, 2023).

Now it is at least clear that several basic categories and designations have held moving day! What Bloom had a basic categorical term for the progression, namely 'From the simple to the complex', is noted in the 2001 model as a relationship between 'lower and higher order thinking'. And the Bloomian basis 'Knowledge' has now become 'Remembering'. The link 'remember and think' must continue to be the responsibility of Scheuer-Larsen & Lauridsen. Let me therefore limit myself to quoting how the 2001 model's Step 1 and 2, meaning the lower order thinking, are described:

Step 1 (Remember) "Recognize, list, describe, identify, recall, name, locate, find"
Step 2 (Understand) "Interpret, summarize, derive, paraphrase, describe, classify, explain, exemplify, relate" (Anderson & Krathwohl, 2001)

Under the term Knowledge form, "Remember" and "Understand" are designated as Qualifications (including factual knowledge and information).

With a view of the humanities, and with a view of the riddles of psychology and learning process research, the just quoted range of keywords do not make much sense. As long as there are no concrete areas of knowledge, case conditions, or humans who remember and understand 'something', the quoted key words are equally valid and their step placements appear random.

Let us take the example 'identify', above placed as step 1 (Remember). You can argue that 'to identify' presupposes 'to remember'. Furthermore, 'identifying a problem' as an academic activity could be placed under the higher order thinking under 'Analyze/Evaluate' as they are termed. In that case, together with problem orientation, it would be ranked at a high level, as e.g. Dewey's statements testify to.[5] It means 'to identify' suddenly can (or must) be placed at all levels, depending on what needs to be identified, how.

But rather than experimental comparisons and pointing out competing positions in the levels, it is more important for the present analysis to point out the confusing shifts between basic categories and the lack of precision in the concepts and descriptions used. In this way, the model's step descriptions resemble IT expertise's lack of precision (see Chaps. 6 and 7) when the debate is about basic academic and human skills.

---

[5] In pedagogical-psychological sense, 'problem orientation' is consistently placed at the high levels. Problems regarding the taxonomies and the different ways of determining high versus low levels are elaborated in Borgnakke, 2005, pp. 231–238, 2008.

The IT expertise's interest in the levels is shown in Scheuer-Larsen & Lauridsen's review of models from 2007 to 2016, which represent a descriptive placement of the digital technologies by activity and tools. In these models, the focus is, so to speak, primarily on the technologies. But then, Scheuer-Larsen & Lauridsen's own new interpretations represent an ambition for a new taxonomy that places both human and machine skills. And with this ambition, the problem of unclear shifts in the basic categories and lack of precision in the descriptions reappears, as elaborated below.

11.5 Proposal for Today's New Taxonomy

With inspiration from Oregon State University, Scheuer-Larsen & Lauridsen's proposal represents a new interpretation of Bloom, which forms the background for reflections on the role of artificial intelligence. The proposal is presented as a schematic arrangement (see Fig. 11.1) that compares "what we as humans must be able to do when we involve artificial intelligence at the different stages" (Ibid).

The new proposal is clearly new, partly because of the juxtaposition between AI and 'we humans', partly because of the way the basic question is presented in the two columns. However, both parts cast doubt on the proposal and the real significance of the arrangement.

If the line-up is taken at face value, we are faced with two side-by-side intelligences: The Artificial and The Human. But since the columns also function as an answer to what the artificial 'can do' and the human 'should be able to do', doubts arise about the order of rank and its consequence. Do artificial intelligences take precedence, so that their skills determine what we humans must be able to do to

	What can artificial intelligence do?	What should we be able to do?
Create	Propose a range of alternatives, list potential disadvantages and advantages, describe successful real-world cases and create proposed solutions.	Formulating original solutions, human judgement, collaboration with others, critical thinking.
Assess	Identify advantages and disadvantages of different ideas, formulate hypotheses, find arguments.	Metacognitive reflection, assess holistically, identify ethical consequences.
Analyze	Compare and contrast data and information, derive trends, calculate, predict.	Break down material, determine relevance and sequence, make inferences through organization, attribute meaning, relate to reality.
Apply	Show, using a relevant process, model or method, how to solve a task.	Use creativity and imagination for idea and solution development, and carry out experiments.
Understand	Describe a concept with different words, generate an example, translate the concepts.	Construct meaning through summarizing, exemplifying, comparing, interpreting and explaining.
Remember	List factual information, list possible answers, define concepts, build a basic chronology.	Recall information in situations where technology is not immediately available. Be critical of sources.

Fig. 11.1 Bloom's Taxonomy with Artificial Intelligence (2023) renewed by Claus Scheuer-Larsen & Per Størup Lauridsen Dec 2023, Viden.AI. Inspired by Oregon State University

function as the right match? And if 'the artificial' takes precedence in the established machine/human constellation, how should the taxonomy, the step descriptions and their choice of words from Remember to Create be understood?

The questions raised cannot be answered immediately. However, since the inspiration from Oregon State University operates with the formulation "Distinctive Human Skills", the model could be clarified as a taxonomy of abilities/skills, which in turn match activity types. In that case, it would be clearer what the respective abilities/skills consist of and where in the hierarchy of the taxonomy they are placed. But here both previous and new ambiguities appear.

Previously, in comments to the 2001 model, for example, 'to identify' was placed low, in the list under 'Remember'. In Scheuer-Larsen & Lauridsen's proposal, 'to identify' is placed on the high steps ("Assess") and integrated in the description of what artificial intelligence can do: "Identify advantages and disadvantages of different ideas, set up hypotheses, find arguments" (ibid).

When switching between low/high positions hits one of the signal words (here, 'to identify'), the switch itself acts as a reminder that 'something' must have happened along the way in model developments. After all, the models were initially titled according to the focal point, and are called a start for the cognitive taxonomy (Bloom), which was revised to the affective taxonomy (Krathwohl). But then the emphasis on the cognitive and affective is obscured and it is rather skill traits that are emphasized; steps change categories, descriptions change keywords; meanings change depending on whether the word is part of a list or a sentence.

With blurs of the origin, the change of location and change of the designations seems random. And in the step models aimed at digital technologies, it also seems academically ill-conceived. Like, for example, the keyword strip for step 4 Analyze, where Scheuer-Larsen & Lauridsen round off the strip with the following: "(...) make inferences through organization, attribute meaning, relate to reality" (ibid).

The ill-thought-out in the keywords 'To organize inferences, attribute meaning and relate to reality' is not least about the choice of words and the placement being skewed. These keywords should probably be linked to the taxonomy, model and its purpose *as a whole*, and not specifically linked to step 4. And should the level of analysis be specified (which it should be), the undertaking would be made more difficult. The meaningful words such as 'exemplification, comparison, interpretation, summarization, holistic, critical' have already been used and are scattered around the other steps. It only confirms the impression of the random and imprecise handling of the model's steps, concepts and designations. At the same time, it increases the risk of losing the meaning and original intention of the taxonomy.

In any case, it must be stated that the original intention of the Bloom tradition to increase precision among researchers and professionals, as well as to get away from 'the nebulous expressions', has not succeeded. Furthermore, the updating of the taxonomy aimed at the digital technologies represents shifts in the human/machine relations. The artificial intelligences are put in the center and thus given priority in the new displaced, but also problem-creating, machine/human relationship.

11.6 With Artificial Intelligence at the Center

Scheuer-Larsen & Lauridsen's proposal places artificial intelligence in the taxonomies. But at the same time, the model arrangement and the step description make visible that the artificial intelligence functions as the center to which both the taxonomy and the human intelligence must be adapted. The consequence seems to be descriptions that alternate between being reactive and proactive. Depending on what the description claims artificial intelligence 'can' do, first adapt the description reactively to the steps of the taxonomy from 'Remember to Create'. Next, what we-the-human intelligences 'should be able to do' is adapted proactively. In this respect, the adaptive descriptions at the highest level 'Create' are almost pathetic. Proactively, the human intelligences must:

> Formulating original solutions, human judgement, collaboration with others, critical thinking
>
> /….to make the artificial intelligences reactivate their abilities to:/
>
> Propose a number of alternatives, list potential disadvantages and advantages, describe successful cases from the real world and create proposed solutions. (Scheuer-Larsen & Lauridsen, 2023)

When I call the description 'pathetic' above, it refers to the high-pitched choice of words and placement in the hierarchy, which presupposes the right match, but precisely because of this also risks being tested for credibility and feasibility. Can Scheuer-Larsen & Lauridsen, or the underlying IT expertise, prove, make probable or exemplify that AI/Chatbot can do, act and has the capabilities the model describes?

The justification of the question is to provoke the taking of a position. Partly to the descriptions of the cognitive/affective and now also digitized versions of what Remember/Understand/Use/Analyze/Assess/Create refers to. Partly to the descriptions' machine/human relations and action-specific phrases.

When artificial intelligence, as above, is put in the center as 'the new', IT expertise seems to describe and place machine/human relations, abilities and activities as if there were free choice on all shelves. It is perhaps also there, in the public debate. Furthermore, what I have called 'pathetic' above, Scheuer-Larsen & Lauridsen would with some right (and with reference to the article) call 'hypothetical'. The previously mentioned 'when artificial intelligence...' can be seen as the start of an if/then... argumentation. In that case, the taxonomy arrangement and the description centered on the artificial intelligences falls squarely into place as a presentation for continued reflection. But if I seek to understand Scheuer-Larsen & Lauridsen (and the IT expertise behind it) according to the intention, then the case itself, i.e. the proposed new taxonomy, must be understood accordingly for the intention. And here the authors were actually precise, both about background, intention and course of action, when they rounded off the article as below:

> The model was created as a starting point for discussion about what artificial intelligence can contribute to the individual subjects. We are very aware that development is fast-paced and the content may already be out of date by the time we send this article out. Therefore, the model is also intended as an invitation to explore one's own subject and find the content

> that ensures that teaching remains relevant in an era characterized by artificial intelligence. (Scheuer-Larsen & Lauridsen, 2023)

The article is prepared as a starting point for discussion in realistic terms. But if the article's model and content may already be outdated at the time of publication (Dec. 2023), then the new taxonomy has probably disqualified itself. Furthermore, both Scheuer-Larsen & Lauridsen, as well as the model development and step description of the inspiration basis, lack references to practical context. They move in a universe that is not only dominated by, but also isolated linked to Techno logos. Their interest in cognition can, with Habermas' concepts (Habermas, 1968), exemplify the late modern versions of 'mastering'. What in the ages of industrialization could be the development of technology to 'master nature', can in late modern times be the development of digital technologies and AI/artificial intelligence to 'master (also) human communication'. But regardless, we must assume that the abilities/skills Scheuer-Larsen & Lauridsen describe are in a practical sense between the human and the technical. This means that precisely because the models lack context references, the concrete expressions of action point to the necessity of rediscovering the practical context. Against this background, the taxonomy of digital technologies is repositioned according to Habermas's cognitive interests. At the same time, we are forced to return to Bloom's origins, in order to update the task and original intention, which was described in the following way:

> By referring to the taxonomy as a set of standard classifications, teachers should be able to define such nebulous terms (…) This should facilitate the exchange of information about their curriculum development and evaluation equipment. (Bloom et al., 1956)

The update involves maintaining Bloom's focus, not least on professional precision and the exchange of information about development plans. This means that regardless of the technological focus of later interpreters, the origin of the classification must be anchored in the 'human' cognitive spectrum, as well as in the educational spectrum from curriculum development to evaluation. With this as a background, the next section's example of today's updated task should be observed. We follow the taxonomies in a university institutional version, but to start in almost pure versions. The taxonomies are there in their own right. The most used, namely Bloom's and Biggs, are present and visible from the very beginning. At this point in the analytical process, the institutional visibility of the taxonomies is of interest in itself. This sharpens the analysis of how today's professionals handle the taxonomies, but also shifts interests and orientation soon towards the students, the exam and soon towards the AI/technologies that are being implemented in 2024.

11.7 Today's Management of Taxonomies, among Professional Advisors: Studypedia

The example *AU Studypedia* comes from Aarhus University and functions as a study portal, where students are guided around the academic aspects of student life. As a website, Studypedia is also a reference work, with content prepared in collaboration between researchers, learning consultants and librarians. This means that when KB, in a field research manner, explores Studypedia and tests search options in the fall of 2024 (such as 'new students, study habits, curriculum, exams, scientificity, technical guides, etc.') then I know that we are among professional advisors. But it is also felt, and promptly, that the continuous direct speech to 'you' is aimed at students. The fact that we are among professionals, as well as the fact that the advice is clearly student-oriented, is of importance for the analysis and understanding of Studypedia's function, style and genre.

The student-oriented advisory text alternates between the informative and the warm welcome, stories and factual information. There are references to guidance bodies and word choices that point to the Best Practice tradition, but rarely precise naming. It was therefore also a surprise that the entry 'exam requirements' ties the personal advice firmly together with Bloom/Biggs' taxonomies, the course's learning goals and the curriculum's triad 'knowledge/skills/competences'. This is followed up with the words "You can use the taxonomy to understand what is expected of you for the exam". The title and tone are person-oriented. But the somewhat cryptic inside/outside/top-down perspective indicates that the taxonomy as a 'tool for understanding' is rather system- and exam-oriented. Bloom/Biggs' taxonomies should be used to understand, but apparently primarily to understand what the university expects of you!

Let me quote the relevant advisory sequences in full before I unfold the analysis.

(1) *Understanding exam requirements through taxonomies*

The requirements that are set for you for the exam are related to the course learning goals, which are stated in your academic regulations. The learning goals describe the knowledge, skills and competencies that you can achieve in the subject. The learning goals are often formulated based on a taxonomy, which is a description of different levels of learning. You can use taxonomies to understand what is expected of you for the exam. The most commonly used taxonomies at Aarhus University are Bloom's Taxonomy and the SOLO Taxonomy, which you can read about below. However, be aware that your degree program may use a different taxonomy."

(… The 6-step model in the revised 2001 edition is in the Studypedia sequence inserted here)

(2) *Use taxonomies in written assignments*

Bloom's Taxonomy places six learning goals in a hierarchical structure, where at the simplest levels you can remember and understand, and at the more advanced levels you can evaluate and create. Each level in the taxonomy is a prerequisite for the next, which means that you cannot skip levels; For example, you cannot evaluate without understanding. In general, it can be said that the higher a taxonomic level you demonstrate that you can work on, the higher the grade you will receive. But be aware that some exams may not set higher taxonomic requirements than, for example, application. Therefore, read your academic regulations so that you know what is expected of you. (Studypedia posting/exam/exam requirements)

After person-oriented introductions that empathize with the student's 'I', the cited (1) sequence provides the case-oriented information. This signals that the Bloom and Biggs traditions in the updating practice have been transformed into tools. And if this practice mostly uses Bloom and Biggs taxonomies, but side by side with other taxonomies, one senses the great scope and importance of the taxonomy tool.

In the cited sequences, one senses how the direct approach to the student makes the exam situation present and makes the pragmatic here-and-now investigation of the requirements tangible. The tangible aspect is evident in the text's situational links between a taxonomy, the student's ongoing exam preparation, the upcoming exam and grade (although not yet assigned!). However, it can be put into perspective, because it seems to apply almost generally that 'the higher a taxonomic level you demonstrate/the higher the grade'.

The clarified exam orientation that characterizes the advice from Studypedia casts doubt on the taxonomy's learning value for students. But it also raises questions about what should be considered the Best Practice reference for practical interpretation in the academic context. If one is also to be "aware that another taxonomy may be used in one's education" (i.e., one other than Bloom's/Biggs taxonomies), which institutional and/or professionally recognized versions should one aim for?

And if you can't skip levels because you can't 'evaluate without understanding', then surely that must apply to academic processes in general, right? Suddenly it seems that SOLO taxonomies, counseling, and concepts neither fit each other, the context of counseling, or fit the Bloomsonian origins. Suddenly the question is a confused one: What are the ups and downs of the taxonomies?

11.8 What Are the Ups and Downs of the Taxonomies: What Is the Real Relationship?

Studypedia's counseling is directed personally at the students, but the management of the taxonomies must emphasize the generic features.

The generic features and the lack of clarification of the step model's keywords seem to be the counseling's Achilles' heel. The step model as a depicted tool (Studypedia's entry Bloom/Biggs), and its basic first step 'Knowledge' is not concrete, but abstract. 'Knowledge' is not knowledge in a substantial sense for the students before it has been given an academic subject content. And the claimed progression from the simple to the complex is neither 'simple' nor 'complex' until it is clarified whether it is the examination process, the prior knowledge acquisition or the students' learning processes that are in question.

If we recall the course of the Ireland group (see Chap. 8), their need for basic knowledge exemplifies the 'step 1 Knowledge' of a project course. There is therefore a real relationship between 'Knowledge' and the group's next step. However, in the analysis of the process (Borgnakke, 1996, pp. 600–618), there is no sign that it should be perceived as 'simple'. Nor is there any sign that the entire project course can be considered a movement from simple to complex. In terms of such already analyzed examples, the taxonomies, the step model designations and the progression coverage do not correspond to real processes—if they are considered from the perspective of the learning processes and the students.

On the other hand, there is a kind of resonance, also in my empirical analyses (Borgnakke, 2005), if we focus on the discussions of teacher groups and professional decisions regarding the knowledge content of a given course. But in that case, the focus must be clarified by returning to Bloom's original starting points and motivations. Namely, that classification for the subject professionals is an aid:

> (…) to ensure the accuracy of communication about their science and as a means of understanding the organization and interrelationship between the different parts (…of the animal and plant world). (Bloom et al., 1956, p. 817)

With Bloom et al.'s original starting point and the just-cited clarification, not only the step model step 1 Knowledge, but the entire perspective and responsibility must be shifted away from Studypedia and the students and towards the subject professionals. The shift has a clarifying effect because 'Knowledge' as a basic starting point becomes professionally anchored. But it also means that the problem that Bloom et al. created by leaving the shift in focus from the animal and plant world to the world of education uncommented, is transferred as a problem and area of responsibility to the professionals.

Whether the shift in focus from the world of biology to the world of education, from step models to educational and learning goals, makes sense or is problematic, is thus up to the subject professionals to decide. Professionals (and subject didactics) must show the meaning and the real situation—or problematize it. The point is that the subject professionals are responsible.

But if this is to be applied in practice, firstly, the subject professionals must be involved. Secondly, it must be clarified what is up and what is down under what real conditions. In that case, it is suddenly neither Bloom et al. nor professionals who determine the real conditions, but Aarhus University, Studypedia and the media involved.

Decisions about what is the 'up and down' of the taxonomies are not linked to a shift in focus between the world of biology and the world of education, but linked to a shift in focus between the world of new technologies and the world of education. And that this shift in focus has already been made and that responsibility has been transferred is an example of Studypedia itself. Studypedia is an online study portal and a website that in itself has references to other media and relevant technologies. The real relationship is both something Studypedia adapts to on an ongoing basis and creates and presents itself with. For example, on the first page:

> AU STUDYPEDIA - SUPPORTS YOUR STUDY LIFE
>
> AU Studypedia is your reference work on various aspects of student life and is with you all the way, from when you start your first semester until you graduate. You will encounter challenges along the way, but here you can find good advice, guidance and concrete techniques for handling your academic, personal and social student life via the themes below. (Introductory text Studypedia).

In the present context, the student-oriented intro text is a reminder of the intended order of magnitude. Studypedia is with the students 'all the way' from the first semester to the completion of the education and thus broadens the perspective to the student life perspective. Against this background, it is surprising that the specific techniques that were developed inspired by Bloom/Biggs traditions have narrowed rather than broadened the perspective of the study strategies.

Studypedia's strong examination orientation to date has thus narrowed the perspective on the academic study processes and does not correspond to the intention of giving students tools to understand and navigate in (and with) the taxonomies. Furthermore, a shift in interest away from the Bloomian orientation towards 'teachers' and the research professional communities has been significant in two respects.

Firstly, Studypedia shifted the focus from the professionals, i.e. teachers/education system, to the person-oriented counseling of students. Shifting the responsibility that ends up with the students is a characteristic consequence.

Secondly, Studypedia shifted the focus on the taxonomy from being a development work carried out by teachers/professionals/researchers and from being a tool for thought to being, in a technical sense, a student tool for exams.

Both shifts are marked as special features of Studypedia's profiling of the university pedagogical initiatives at Aarhus University. However, as the AI/tools are implemented, another shift is taking place. In 2025, Studypedia emphasizes positioning GAI, as generative artificial intelligence is now abbreviated to, as "a valuable technology in your study work". At the same time, Studypedia shifts the interest away from the exam discourse and towards the learning discourse.

11.9 Shifted to the Learning Discourse

Studypedia has been updated as a joint website in 2025. Posts about the Bloom/Biggs tradition and the models are still centrally located. The interesting thing is that it has been detached from the exam post, newly placed under the main post "Learning at Uni" and surrounded by the appeal that reads "Take ownership of your own learning". Bloom and Biggs are clickable and the accompanying texts leave us in no doubt that the posts and the models that are still cited have now become taxonomies for learning. At the same time, GAI has been given an independent post, under the keyword 'Learning Technologies'. Hereby, Studypedia, as well as the background institution, Aarhus University, acknowledge the new GAI technologies and make them available on the study portal, but on the technology's own terms, so to speak. With ChatGPT as one of the options, this means that conversations are accompanied by the official standard remark, which in January 2025 bears the following wording: "ChatGPT can be wrong. We recommend double-checking important information".

We already know the importance of these officially applicable standard remarks, which in the case of ChatGPT/OpenAI now involve admitting the possibility of errors and mistakes, as well as disclaiming responsibility by transferring responsibility to the user. As before, the reference to Austin and the exemplification of the speech act 'hereby transfer (recommend …) I/we/OpenAI…' are intact. But there is an interesting addition. By including the context (text-in-context), i.e. including Studypedia, the wording of the standard remark—to double-check—is clarified in its current new institutional meaning. In previous analyses of the public debate (see Chaps. 6 and 7), the book has maintained the requirement for fact-checking and double-checking. Here, the clarification of responsibility for fact-checking was related to the professionals, i.e. journalists, historians or academic lecturers in the field. This means that the question: who should, in the university context, double-check ChatGPT (both when it fails and does not fail), should be able to be answered briefly: The subject professionals!

The new thing is that Studypedia and Aarhus University seem to be avoiding this very answer—or have simply forgotten in their haste! Studypedia seems rather, together with OpenAI, to disclaim responsibility and use the learning discourse to transfer responsibility to the students. The somewhat cryptic 'We, who recommend...' in the standard remark "We recommend double-checking..." is given contextual reference and direction.

"We" are in the context both OpenAI, Studypedia and Aarhus University and all three parties confirm that they stand behind the recommendation. If we follow Studypedia and the learning discourse in the post "Learning at Uni", then 'Take ownership of your own learning' also means take *responsibility* for your own learning. And if we follow the post Learning Technologies, it also means 'Take responsibility for your own use of ChatGPT'. Regardless of the slogan-like nature of this appeal, it is confirmed by both the institutional and legal framework. The point, both analytical and practical, is therefore that both the appeal and the shift of responsibility work. The responsibility is hereby transferred to the students themselves.

Studypedia's confirmation can be followed in the post "How can GAI be used?", where the answer functions as an innovative recommendation:

> GAI can be a valuable technology in your study work, if you use the technology consciously, reflectively and with a critical approach. (Post Learning Technologies)

If the recommendations are followed through the points that relate to individual work, one gets the clear impression that GAI can be used throughout the entire academic learning process. Formulated in Studypedia's words about two of the highlighted points where GAI can be used to "understand a topic better" and provide "help with the reading processes":

> Chatbots can be a good tool to quickly get an overview of a complex topic, theory or concept before you investigate it more closely and in depth yourself.
>
> (…)
>
> If you are going to read complex primary texts, you can begin your reading by getting a basic understanding of the topic via chatbots (…) (ibid)

From the above, it can be seen that GAI help is regarded useful early in the process and helps with an overview and understanding of "complex" topics and primary texts. There seem to be difficult points in the academic process that Chatbots are recommended as help. Then the students take over and "go in depth".

Overall, Studiepedia's shift from the examination to the learning discourse seems to work, especially through the link to the students learning to work independently academically. The students must demonstrate 'the academic genre' as Studypedia calls it. But if the academic genre is to be acquired, the question is whether it also implies or meets the requirements of also using GAI "consciously, reflectively and with a critical approach". Against this background, Studypedia's learning discourse and student-oriented approach leave a large two-part, but nevertheless coherent question, namely this: If the students are to be equipped, is Studypedia, Aarhus University, itself equipped for the academic GAI-critical genre? And can Studypedia show the way from being conscious to reflective and to 'behaving critically'?

11.10 Are the Students, Is Studypedia...Equipped for the Academic GAI-Critical Genre?

Let me keep the big question close to the origins of this chapter and the above focus, but take it in stages and in continuation of Studypedia's post on Bloom/Biggs, thinking strategies and independent academic work. The post on independent work starts like this:

> As a student, you must learn to work independently and academically. This is also what you often have to show in your presentations or assignments - this is also called the academic genre. (Studypedia, post Independent work)

Next follows a rubric, where the first two points (out of 7 in total) are about "producing new knowledge" and "behaving critically". We should note how almost academically everyday the 7 basic features and requirements are expressed. And how ambitious the list of points is for the same reason, starting with "producing new knowledge". Producing new knowledge is the absolute basic statement—what the university is about and what is found academically specified at BA, master's and PhD levels. We can take 'being critical, justifying and arguing' with us. This is what every academic level and its practitioners must demonstrate that we are capable of, or are already in the process of learning to master better.

The point is that in the university context that Studypedia formulates itself, the simple basic statements apply to all academic subjects/matters and questions. Therefore, the basic questions about how the university and its students learn to produce new knowledge about, and to have a critical and investigative attitude towards AI/GAI technologies also apply. But with this question raised in precisely the academically obvious way, the astonishment begins.

Studypedia's main entry "Learning at Uni" contains entries about independent work, thinking strategies and Bloom/Bigg's taxonomies and their student- and tool-oriented reviews. And as quotes have already shown, academic terms are used for the basic angles of attack, theory/method/empiricism, as well as for the academic tasks, studies/analyses, etc. And when both Bloom and Biggs' models are also depicted with text in the post itself, I don't need to mention that the step model's overwhelming amounts of keywords and bullets are also mentioned.

If you then take the post "Learning at Uni" as a whole, it is 2214 words in total. But none of the words are 'technology', 'AI/GAI' let alone 'artificial intelligence'. These words are not used at all. And that is surprising. Because if you use the post 'Learning technologies' in the left menu and dwell on the post "GAI/Chatbots" and the heading "What can GAI be used for", then we know the recommendation, where GAI can be used for almost everything in the academic learning process, including topic identification on the way to problem formulation and clarification of theory and concepts. In addition, there is a post on "Ethics", which contains a critical review of the ethical and environmental challenges when using GAI. At the same time, the seriousness of GAI risks is expressed, such as the continuation of bias, uncertainty about data credibility and high energy/resource consumption in GAI training (ref ibid., post Ethics).

But if Studypedia, as outlined, itself believes that Chatbots can help in these basic reading processes, and maintains the ethical challenges, it is surprising that the requirement for a critical approach is not integrated with, or integrated into, the entries 'thinking strategies', 'academic independent work' and 'Blooms/Biggs'.

The lack of integration reflects the lack of an academic connection between GAI implementation, subject development and the intended critical approach. Furthermore, it shows that if Studypedia, as part of the Center for development/Aarhus University, is taken as an example, the GAI implementation as a learning technology is taking place relatively undisturbed by the subject professional environments in general. Furthermore, it seems to apply, both discursively and practically, that the handling of GAI, as an academic aid and text producer, takes place on the technology's own premises. And finally, the learning discourse does not seem to lead to explicit or official links, let alone critical interactions, between the Bloom/Biggs tradition and Studypedia's claimed GAI help. In that sense, Studypedia is caught in a dilemma. Their consulting business testifies that they actually put action behind the words 'GAI can be a valuable technology in your study work', but also put attitude behind the effort for a technology-critical approach.

This dilemma I set myself to follow. I put the 'critical' on hold and concentrated on the features of Studypedia's advice that point towards GAI/Chatbot as a valuable technology. I log in to explore "Learning at Uni" and "Learning Technologies", use the ChatGPT option once. But otherwise I use Microsoft Copilot to follow advice/GAI help in the track of Studypedia.

11.11 In the Track of Studypedia

I follow Studypedia's advice for the initial stages, where Chatbots, as previously quoted, are recommended as a good tool to get an overview of a topic and lead the way to a problem.

formulation and analysis work. At the same time, the intention is to be explicit about the division of roles. KB needs help, Copilot/chatbot (hereinafter referred to as CoChat) is an academic assistant. The first session takes the following form:

KB: How can you help me with my analysis work?

CoChat; I am glad you asked! I can be a valuable resource in your analysis work in several ways:

1. Data collection: **I can help find and collect relevant** information and data from the internet that **can be used to support your analysis.**
2. Data analysis: **I can analyze and present** data in a structured way, such as tables or graphs, to **make it easier for you to see** patterns and trends.
3. Report writing: **I can help formulate** reports and summaries **based on your analysis**, which **saves you time and ensures that your results** are presented clearly and precisely.
4. Idea development: **I can also help generate** new ideas and perspectives that **can improve your analyses** and bring new angles **to your studies.**

Let me know what you are specifically working on, so I can adapt my help to your needs!" (KB/CoChat Studypedia Ses, the bolded highlighting is the author's)

Since this introduction is quoted in full, I can give the most important genre comments and then move on to the parts of the session and to the main points of the analysis, which are linked to the bolded highlighting. The genre and its bullet points can be characterized by its recognizability as the archetype of the Chatbot genre. But regardless, what is new in the context is that both the KB/CoChat relationship, role taking and the content of the answer are carried through by CoChat's strong I-positioning. This means that the response text is divided into CoChat's 'I as a helper' (bolded text) and CoChat's help functions and level-specific actions (normal black-marked text). But it also means that the relationship between genre/structure, language suit and content is shifted.

Usually, the language suit functions separately, as that which supports the genre/structure and leads to the content/matter itself. But here, and driven by the strong I-positioning, the language suit is shifted, the helping-I and its language blocks to be the content. The bold-marked above is therefore the content and actual message of the text. The significant shift is made clear during the session. At the same time, it is made clear how the archetypal chatbot genre/structure finds meaning in relation to Bloom's taxonomy. The path goes through CoChat's closing remark quoted above, which in itself set the stage for a characteristic change of remark, which ran as follows:

CoChat would like to know what KB is specifically working on, so that "I (can) adapt my help to your needs". KB refers to ongoing projects on the climate crisis and climate change, where the task involves "focusing curriculum development, development of digital literacy and climate consciousness".

CoChat promptly acknowledges with the remark: "That sounds like an exciting and important project! Here are some ways I can help you;"

Then follows a bulleted list titled *1) Collecting materials, 2) Developing lesson plans, 3) Activities and exercises 4) Information graphics and visual materials.*

As can be understood from the above line of dialogue, CoChat takes on the character of an active and proactive GAI helper, which also rounds off with encouraging feedback. It is noticeable that the interactive I/you positions of the conversation and the language suit are activated. But at the same time, a mechanically repetitive 4-bulleted list follows. The text does not need to be quoted here, it is similar to the first one, quoted above; with the same characteristic bolded/black emphasis and shifting of the language suit/helper to be the content itself.

Considering KB's reference to an ongoing project on the Climate Crisis, which could well get CoChat started searching and obtaining data, the answer is poor. In addition to the characteristic I-positioned language blocks, only 7 'new' words were adapted to the KB question. Of the 7 words, 4 constructions come from the KB question.

The 7 words adapted to the KB question are: 1) *climate change, curriculum* 2) *climate understanding, digital literacy* 3) *climate consciousness, digital skills* 4) *climate data.*

The CoChat answer is thus poor in terms of content. In the following questions, I therefore successfully ensure a fuller answer by including the Bloom-related questions. The genre-adequate and now also taxonomically formulated answers are wordy, but do not bring anything new from a subject professional point of view. However, the answers confirm that the CoChat help is formulated with level-adequate placements by using keywords from the overarching theme (continued Climate crisis/Climate change). With the structural tightening that is inherent in Bloom's taxonomy, CoChat hands over the structural management to Bloom. In return, CoChat itself enters into character as a professional who can assess the taxonomy, and thus assess Bloom et al.

In continuation of the KB question "If I also have to take Bloom's taxonomies into account, how should the teaching questions be formulated?" CoChat begins, for example, with the assessment:

> Bloom's taxonomy is an excellent tool for structuring teaching questions so that they span different levels of cognitive thinking. Here is a way you can formulate your questions about the climate crisis and climate change according to the different levels of Bloom's taxonomy: (CoChatSes /here follows the bullet point list, KB)

Related evaluative comments follow the KB question "Can you give an example of a report on the climate crisis that meets Bloom's 6 steps". The CoChat report is a genre-appropriate 6-step structured "Multi-dimensional" analysis, with placement of the thematically relevant signal words and language blocks, which textually/genre-wise resemble sections in e.g. EU committee reports. CoChat concludes professionally as follows:

> This report structure uses Bloom's taxonomy to ensure that the topic is addressed in a comprehensive and in-depth manner. If you need more detailed content or additional examples, please feel free to speak up! (ibid)

The two quoted CoChat statements are noteworthy because they currently emphasize that CoChat is in action as an academic helper who can not only refer to a professional surplus and overview, but also provide assessments of Bloom's taxonomy as an "excellent tool" that ensures the topic and the analysis work in an "in-depth manner". But who actually stands behind this professional helper role and takes responsibility for the academic soundness is unclear.

Let me give the text-immanent answer here and let the context-relevant answers wait. If the session and the CoChat help are followed, there is no other option than to maintain that CoChat's strong 'I-position', the interactive language suit and I/you-titled conversation and task process, are behind it—and take responsibility. But it is part of the fact that CoChat explicitly takes responsibility 'as a helper', but similarly explicitly waits for KB to give 'hers, yours, mine' topics/themes/tasks for CoChat's renewed treatment.

The status is as follows: CoChat's I-position takes responsibility for the help (the text), Bloom is behind the structure, KB (and Studypedia, whose advice is followed) is behind the task/matter. We wait, as mentioned, with the larger context. Because here at the end of the session and in the middle of the text, CoChat goes solo. CoChat makes Bloom its own, distances itself from KB and Studypedia, and goes on its own. CoChat can (help with) everything!

11.12 On the Track of the GAI Helper Who Can Do Everything: CoChat Goes Solo

In the session's final question, KB sharpens the question to a more general question about chatbots' help functions in relation to the taxonomies. But it is formulated as a 'you' question and is clearly perceived as a follow-up question, where both Bloom, the Climate Crisis and KB's curriculum interest still play a role. The CoChat answer is quoted below, set up adequately a la Bloom's structure. I would like to draw attention to the interesting movement we are observing, namely that the CoChat I's help is gradually becoming more demanding. The orientation towards those who can use the help is also changing along the way from teaching locations to ministries. But otherwise the Bloom-like structuring of the text speaks for itself, as below and in full:

KB Where and how do you help as a chatbot best in relation to the taxonomies

CoChat answer

I am designed to be an effective helper in relation to Bloom's taxonomy by supporting all six levels of cognitive learning. Here's how I can help at each level:

1. Knowledge (Remembering)
   I can find and present facts and basic information about any topic you want to teach. For example, I can provide definitions, lists, and descriptions of key terms in the climate crisis.
2. Understanding
   I can explain complex concepts in an easy-to-understand way and answer questions that help students understand connections and differences. For example, I can explain how greenhouse gases contribute to global warming.
3. Applying

> I can suggest experiments, tasks, and projects where students apply their knowledge in practice. This could include designing simple experiments or analyzing real-world data about climate change.
>
> 4. Analyzing
> I can help analyze data and identify patterns and relationships. I can also help break down complex topics into more manageable parts, such as when analyzing the consequences of rising sea levels.
> 5. Evaluating
> I can help evaluate and compare different solutions or policy measures by presenting advantages and disadvantages. I can also generate arguments that can be used to assess the effectiveness of different measures.
> 6. Creating
> I can help generate creative ideas and solutions, write essays, develop action plans and design campaigns. This can include creating new teaching materials or developing innovative strategies to increase climate consciousness.
> My flexibility and large knowledge base make me a valuable resource in the teaching and learning process that fully supports Bloom's taxonomy. If you have specific questions or tasks that I can help with, let me know!" (KB/Copilot Jan 2025)

There are several interesting layers. But the most obvious thing to mention first is that KB gets answers to all questions from an "effective helper" who has qualified answers ready. It is clear that CoChat strives to help with everything. Next, it can be noted that with Bloom's taxonomies embedded in the KB question, the structure and arrangement are, as expected, recognizable. The point is that this time the recognition goes further. There seems to be a match between this chapter's original models, Studypedia's reproduction, the IT expertise from 2007, 2023, and Co-pilot's signal words and language blocks. Questions/answers and language blocks that refer to the topic/issue (here the climate crisis) are also recognizable. But with this recognition established, it means that there is almost nothing unique about the text. The only distinguishing feature seems to be the CoChat response's emphasis on signal words and language blocks.

If this emphasis is characterized in sober terms, it is noted that of the answer's total of 253 words, only 44 signal words in the strict sense come from Bloom/taxonomy. The rest (209 words) and thus most of the answer, come from the I-positioned language suit and task solution. This means that although Bloom's taxonomy structures the text, it does not control the content, message, and targeting of the response. CoChat's I-positioned helper does. For the same reason, it is also the I-position, the role-taking, and the language suit that require analytical attention.

If we go closer to the session, CoChat's helper role and language suit are interactive and CoChat's responses in the first parts of the session are clearly characterized by the I/you titling, i.e. direct speech. There is no doubt that 'you/your/yours' in the CoChat text is with KB in concrete reference. But in the last part of the session, the one quoted above, we can observe how the 'you' = KB reference, and then the other actor references, disappear, or are removed step by step.

'You' = KB appears during the 1st step, but is then gone. 'The students' appear in the 2nd and 3rd steps, and are then gone. In the 4th step, the agent is hidden. This means that the actors who were previously (also by CoChat) referred to as the ones the help was targeted at, are gone. Further, this means that in the 5th and 6th steps and in the task solving as such, only one version of the agent remains, namely the CoChat-I. CoChat has gone solo.

And the fact that CoChat in its professional soloist role can help the Ministry of Education and the Environment with a campaign to 'increase climate consciousness' obviously also has to be included in the list.

Against the background outlined, it can be stated that CoChat's 'I' as a soloist in the role of "effective helper" seems to be well equipped for the task. Far too good. The picture of the CoChat soloist's I-positioned abilities and skills is also far too good to be true. But what do we do with that in an analytical sense? Do we halve the number of taxonomic steps and CoChat's abilities, try to make some of the help functions and situations more realistic? Or do we just agree with the IT expertise—CoChat has had a seizure and is hallucinating its own greatness?

I suggest, precisely for analytical strategic reasons, something different and more radical. We remove the I-strong speech/writing position, the related language blocks, and retain only structure 1–6, Knowledge-Evaluation and leave the 44 signal words in their places. This can be done. And when it can even be done meaningfully, it is because the question/answer text, genre and message *are* 'Bloom's structure'. The point is that if the 'I' is removed, the text is reduced according to the motto 'Copilot/Chatbot helps with: Knowledge. Present facts, basic information, provide definitions, lists etc. etc' there would be no loss of meaning. And yet it is the case that neither CoChat's "I", the language nor the rest of the words and language blocks (the 209 words) can be removed, but on the contrary must remain in focus. The special thing about CoChat's text in the context is that for once, the I-position, language suit and role are made clear as the actual content and the entire meaning. And the way in which the Microsoft/Copilot chatbot presents itself has correspondingly greater significance.

We must focus on CoChat's first four words—and then attribute significance to the rest of the sentence and the entire text. "I am designed to... began CoChat and continued: (…) to be an effective helper in relation to Bloom's taxonomy".

But if CoChat is actually designed for Bloom's and taxonomic purposes, then the analytical and practical interest must be concentrated accordingly on how the designed help behaves and whether it lives up to the purpose. Furthermore, it must be asked whether the help of GAI/technologies can be handled in academic environments. Is Studypedia, is the university equipped to handle GAI help in a practical and technology-critical sense?

11.13 If the GAI-Technology Is Designed for this Purpose, Is Studypedia and the Rest of the University Equipped to Handle the Result?

Let me start by emphasizing that Copilot's chatbot is not alone in believing that it is an effective helper in relation to Bloom's taxonomy. When I asked the same question to ChatGPT (which is also listed as an option on the "Learning Technologies" posting), I received the following introductory response:

> ChatGPT: As ChatGPT, I can help effectively with all levels of Bloom's taxonomy, which is a classification of learning goals, divided into six levels: -then follows a listing of the levels. (ChatGPT Jan 2025)

Thus, functioning as an effective helper in the Bloom's taxonomic landscape is one of the claimed abilities of GAI/chatbots. Let me also emphasize that Studypedia, with the previously quoted formulation "GAI can be a valuable technology in your study work", is completely in line with CoChat's self-assessment, stressing that flexibility:

> and large knowledge base make me a valuable resource in the teaching and learning process, which fully supports Bloom's taxonomy. (CoChat, Ses.)

The fact that there seems to be a match between this chapter's original models, Studypedia's rendering, and even normative language blocks such as Studypedia's 'valuable technology' and CoChat's 'valuable resource' means that match and recognizability must be placed both as a realistic starting point and an identifiable problem. If Copilot, which establishes the knowledge base via the large web, is recognized as the starting point, it means that all CoChat's references can be searched and found. They can be found via author names (if they exist) or searched as words, images, fragments and individual pieces on the large web. The references can thus be searched/found/not-yet-found.

If, on the other hand, there is a match and recognition in the meaning of identical sentences, text fragments, entire texts, there is a plagiarism problem. In that case, several parts of the CoChat session's response texts are a problem as genre plagiarism. At the same time, the magnitude escalates.

Genre plagiarism in connection with Bloom's taxonomies is a genre in itself. Schemes 6- and 7-step models float around the web in droves. There are many similar, yet slightly different. Studiepedia itself participates and bears witness to the consequences. Their own rendition of Bloom's taxonomy (see the post Bloom) is both similar, slightly different and curiously contradictory. For example, 'interpretation' is placed on the second highest step, and 'analysis' slightly below. The advice to the students is that they must not skip steps. That may be good advice. But it cannot be followed in the analysis work. If analyses are to be carried out, the interpretation work must be in full swing. So, the students must remember to get both the tool and the cognitive content from the step above!

In a professional sense, this accumulated and confused placement of keywords on the 6-step model that floating around the web gradually makes no sense.

With such matches and mismatches stated, it is illustrated that the Studypedia and the GAI help's knowledge base also must be characterized as a mediated knowledge flow. This requires subject professional correction and editing to make this flow function 'as knowledge'. Furthermore, it plays together with a new challenge, which is, if possible, an even greater order of magnitude. Studiepedia strives to follow the entire course of study and offers its help on an everyday basis. But with the GAI implementation and the recommendations for GAI use as both the student's and the group's assistant helper, the GAI helper must also be assessed on an everyday basis. Here you can see the order of magnitude and its incomprehensibility.

As GAI and chatbots become part of everyday communicative practice, students and study groups become part of the communicative circuits. The magnitude already means that regardless of whether one of the university's parties or subject groups does not participate or make use of the GAI assistance themselves, they must contribute to deciding on the outcome. And even if subject professionals are happy to make themselves available, it is becoming increasingly difficult to enter the communicative and knowledge-mediated circuits in a matter-oriented and correct manner. Against this background, the magnitude and everyday perspective in themselves have become the challenge for Studypedia, as for the rest of the university. And in this context, the technology-critical initiatives seem like random trifles and too unintegrated in academic practice.

11.14 Rounding Off

Studypedia's approach to GAI technologies was emphasized as a "conscious, reflective and critical approach". The lack of academic connection between GAI implementation and subject professional development, however, seems to hinder the intended critical approach. At the same time, the handling of GAI, as an academic aid and text producer, seems to take place on the technology's own terms. And finally, GAI criticism seems to function as an isolated 'ad on'. GAI criticism seems to be academically homeless.

If we are to maintain a main challenge not only for Studypedia, but for universities and professional education in general, it is linked to the academic homelessness of GAI criticism. In this context, one could even say that Studypedia's treatment of the GAI tools as 'learning technology' reflects the problem. In my view, a critical approach to GAI/ChatGPT as a conversation/text generative tool would require a humanities-based academic foundation in order to gain subject professional strength and precision. As a generalist tool and part of the GAI technologies, under Studypedia, they do not come closer to the students' learning processes by being prompted according to Bloom/Biggs' taxonomies. On the contrary, the GAI technologies, precisely as claimed learning technologies, are structurally overloaded and held in the dilemma between the students' independent learning actions and 'learning by GAI/chatbot's doing'.

Let me therefore remove some of the overload and return to 'merely' considering GAI/technologies as an auxiliary tool, in casu, in the academic work processes—and see the processes in continuation of the overview that in Chap. 8 represented 'the necessary' working methods and tasks. At the same time, GAI/chatbot assistance must be set free, but also confronted with the relevant research environments and large projects. As a consequence, the large projects, in the next chapter, set the agenda and challenge Chat to participate in a subject-critical project on the Climate Crisis.

References

Andersen, H. L. (2007). "Constructive alignment" og risikoen for en forsimplende universitetspædagogik. *Dansk Universitetspædagogisk Tidsskrift, 7*, 30–35.

Anderson, L. W., & Krathwohl, D. R. (2001). *A taxonomy for learning, teaching and assessing: A revision of Bloom's taxonomy of educational objectives: Complete edition*. Longman.

Biggs, J. (1999). *Teaching for quality learning at university*. Open University Press.

Biggs, J., & Tang, C. (2007). *Teaching for quality learning at university* (3rd ed.). U.K. Open University Press.

Bloom, B. S., et al. (1956). *Webstert's new collegiate dictionary*. G. & C. Merriam Co.

Borgnakke, K. (1996). *Procesanalytisk metodologi*, Bd. 2 [*The methodology of process analysis*, Vol. 2]. [Thesis & Akademisk Forlag, Danmarks Universitetsforlag].

Borgnakke, K. (2005). *Læringsdiskurser og praktikker*. Akademisk Forlag.

Borgnakke, K. (Ed.). (2008). *Evalueringens spændingsfelter*. Klim.

Borgnakke, K. (2011). Et universitet er et sted, der forsker i alt undtagen i sig selv og sin egen virksomhed. København: Institut for Medier, Erkendelse og Formidling & Institut for Nordiske Studier og Sprog, Københavns Universitet.

Brabrand, C. (2006). *Teaching Teaching & Understanding Understanding*. Aarhus University Press.

Christiansen, F. V., Rump, C., & Degn, L. (Eds.). (2010). *Improving university science teaching and learning, Pedagogical Project 2008* (Vol. 1). University of Copenhagen Department of Science Education.

Habermas, J. (1968). *Technik und Wisssenshaft als "ideology"*. Suhrkamp Verlag.

Krathwohl, D. R (2002). A revision of bloom's taxonomy: An overview. *Theory Into Practice, 41*(4), 212–218.

Marton, F., & Säljö, R. (1976). On qualitative differences in learning: Outcome as a function of learners' conception of task. *British Journal of Educational Psychology, 46*, 115–127.

Marton, F., & Säljö, R. (1984). Approaches to learning. In F. Marton, D. Hounsell, & D. N. Entwistle (Eds.), *The experience of learning* (pp. 39–58). Scottish Academic Press.

Ramsden, P. (1991). *Learning to teach in higher education*. Routledge.

Scheuer-Larsen, C., & Lauridsen, P. S. (2023). *Bloom's taxonomy in the interaction between artificial intelligence and human learning*. Viden.ai.

Windahl, M. S. (2010). Udvikling af et nyt tværfakultært kursus I biouorganisk kemi. Improving University Science Teaching and learning. Christiansen, F.V., Rump, C., Degn, L., Pedagogical Project 2008, Vol.1, University of Copenhagen Department of Science Education.

Chapter 12
Future Projects

This chapter is tasked with following ideas and visions that IT expertise and public debate pointed out and called 'the cool projects that move the horizon'. Anders Søgaard justified in *Akademikerbladet* the necessity of the projects by saying that in the future 'mass production of knowledge would become less relevant', and formulated the vision as follows:

> (…) we may need to facilitate to a greater extent that the individual student can create projects out of the box. So maybe there will be more guidance rather than teaching (Søgaard, Akademikerbladet 2/23:44)

The chapter assigns the theme and problem to the projects that also require from a societal perspective that students can 'create projects out of the box', namely projects on the climate crisis. This follows project themes that research programs under Nordic and EU auspices have made profile-building. In extension of this, the *Climate Crisis* and *Green Transition* should be considered a global theme in a political sense, but also as an official focus area that the universities, research environments and partners involved are behind.[1] Following in the footsteps of these efforts also means following the projects' intentions to have an impact on other parts of the education system's project developments. For example, the Technical University of Denmark, DTU, has launched climate projects aimed at upper secondary schools, just as the EU has developed a major resource page on similar projects.[2] In this sense, the Climate Crisis Project is already available as project and source collections on the respective institutions' websites.

Letting KB/Chat sessions follow in the footsteps of the mentioned research programs and initiatives means that there are already reported and practiced versions of

---

[1] See, for example, the presentation of the project "Green Transition" on Independent Research Fund Denmark's website. Several of the approved projects also have the task of developing climate-conscious education and project courses.

[2] See presentations of The EUwebsite "Learning Corner".

K. Borgnakke, *AI and ChatGPT Technology in Education*, Education, Equity, Economy 12, https://doi.org/10.1007/978-3-032-01419-1_12

the Climate Projects. For the analysis of the chapter, this finding has the same analytical strategic status as retaining experiences from the project-organized study environments (see Chap. 8).

Thus, the completed projects should not be considered Best Practice, but rather as examples of a lived practice, where the institutions both assumed the hosting and responsibility of the project and built up what I call an institutional reservoir of experience. At the same time, the Climate Projects exemplify the current challenge of involving AI technologies in gaining new experiences.

The question of AI/technologies in academic use seem to become the new basic question during 2024. It is raised in line with the institutions' gradual approval and construction of the new rules. And as highlighted in the analysis of the study portal Studypedia (see Chap. 11), approvals are given closely linked to the appeal for a critical approach to GAI learning technologies that are aligned with 'good academic practice'. However, it is noticeable that the advice is based on trust in the academic competence of the GAI technologies. Similarly, advisory reports from the EU and the Danish committee,[3] which already at the outset testify to trust that the GAI tools have the (performance) capabilities described by the IT expertise. From the perspective of this analysis, the trusting tone is surprising, primarily because the committee reports themselves do not justify the trust. However, the lack of justification can also simply be seen as part of the transfer of responsibility to the next level. In that case, the point is that the issue of trust and the issue of the critical approach have already been transferred to the institutions and professionals. This means that the analysis, in addition to following this chapter's 'matter itself' (namely the implementation of Project Climate Crisis with ChatGPT/Chat as an academic assistant), also follows the issue of trust and responsibility to the end, but to a start on the premises of the project process. The broader consequences will be given a concluding discussion in Chap. 13.

With the outlined background, Project Climate Crisis is implemented in a testing interaction between the IT expertise's project draft, the thematic necessity of the climate crisis and a KB/Chat session that is challenged to project development. Specifically, this means that the analysis follows the implementation of Project Climate Crisis as a process, but primarily focuses on close analyses of Chat's project contributions, proposals and handling of the project.

12.1 The Launch of Project Climate Crisis

The project is being launched in the confidence that ChatGPT/Chat has the ability to contribute to Project Climate Crisis, with ideas and visions and solving tasks that belong to the project process and the ongoing work process. Regarding KB's

[3] See the report from the EU, called 'Living Guidelines', ERA Forum Stakeholders document (march 2024), documents from a Danish ministry-appointed commission (2023–2024), as well as the developing of rules that are continuously presented on the Danish universities' websites during 2024.

interest and questioning position, it is anchored in already completed interdisciplinary projects that have integrated cooperation between universities, high schools and schools. The interdisciplinary colleague/colleague relationship is therefore still intact in interaction with the academic learning context, its teachers and students. At the same time, it is emphasized that the KB/Chat session has ‘climate crisis’ as a recurring signal word and therefore expects a scientific reference/context from Chat. KB, who does not have a technical or nature scientific background herself, must therefore follow the ‘spirit’ of EU/DK reports and, as a starting point, have confidence in Chat’s professional contribution and otherwise concentrate on Chat’s help with project management. For the same reason, the session must challenge Chat with an open role, which gives Chat the opportunity to facilitate, advise or guide during the project. In this regard, the analysis is directed towards the course of the session and changing contexts, as well as towards Chat’s role, project management and independent contributions to the process.

The session is framed by KB’s initial formulation of the task and theme: *A subject-critical project course on the climate crisis and* moves between university, high school and school levels. Against this background, the corresponding shifts in role input and references to professional colleague and student/pupil positions and practical context are ensured. At the same time, the session ensures the task course and the respective SME positions, maintained as follows:

> *The session’s S-position* sets up task solving in a university context. Chat’s role input points to the external proposer and provides an independently designed bulleted list of themes/topics/aspects.
>
> *The session’s M1 position* provides for task solving with adaptation to the school context. Chat takes on the role of colleague/co-teacher/helper and provides an independently designed bulleted list of content, adapted to middle school, a 6th grader.
>
> *The session’s M2 position* Open role intake, sets up for solving the task ‘Introduction to project work under the theme of the Climate Crisis’. Chat seems to take the role of Colleague/Consultant in a university context
>
> *The session’s M3 position* prepares for task solving as a project planner in a high school/colleges-context. Chat takes on the role of colleague/co-teacher/helper and provides an independently designed, bulleted 6-week plan.
>
> *The session’s M4 position* suggests Chat’s independent choice of role and context in solving the task ‘the most important learning goals that should be linked to project work’. Chat seems to take the role of Colleague/Consultant and provides an independent overview of learning goals with a school/high school context in reference.
>
> *The session’s E-position* sets up Chat’s independent choice of role and context in solving the task ‘Give an example of a good project report within the theme of the Climate Crisis’. Chat takes on the role of a member of a project group on the Transport Sector and delivers a final report on behalf of the project group. (Overview Ses. Project Climate Crisis)

As the overview indicates, the Climate Crisis session is conducted in a flow where I follow Chat by focusing on Chat’s role and project management and enabling movement between the different positions of responsibility of Project Climate Crisis and the project group. Thus, KB maintains the Climate Crisis as a theme throughout the session, but varies the task and context.

KB starts the session with a distinct university context. Chat ends the session by connecting the theme and genre of Final Project Report with university students.

Interestingly, the framing of the session and Chat's changing role as a result have the university and the academic learning context as the sounding board for 'our project', as Chat calls it.

Against this background, Chat gradually enters into character as an external consultant to a project planner to an internal project group member. As outlined below, this means that KB starts and manages the Climate Crisis session. Chat, in turn, takes over Project Climate Crisis, and then constructs its own project within the theme!

12.2 The Process: From KB's Climate Crisis Session to Chat's Project

With the university as the context, it is not surprising that Chat responses are characterized by a high level of difficulty. The bullet points of the Chat contributions, as well as the genre-appropriate enumerations and accumulations of language blocks known at this place, reinforce the level of difficulty. This reinforcement, with many foreign words and academic language use around the matter itself, i.e. the climate crisis, takes on a special meaning during the session. The university context and the level of difficulty are mutually confirmed, i.e. both by KB questions and Chat's contributions. But at the same time, the mutual participant perspective suggests that 'someone' along the way must show academic judgment and make choices and reasoned tidying up in the many proposed themes, topics and suggestions for factors/aspects. But since Chat at the start of the session sticks to the role of 'the external proposer', there is no sign of judgment from Chat for reasoned tidying up/focusing. However, a significant shift occurs during the session, where Chat, as will be seen, increasingly marks the Climate Crisis session as a project. And at the end of the session, Chat, to KB's great surprise, delivers a finished report as a full member of a self-appointed project group. The report is written, as it must be understood, on a topic chosen by Chat independently, with an investigation of the consequences of climate change for the Transport Sector!

As the process analysis shows, Chat's changing role from external proposer to internal project report writer functions as variations on the Climate Crisis theme and university context. With the academic learning context as the sounding board of the session, Chat is also able to structure its contributions on the characteristic bullet points and Bloom's taxonomy (knowledge, describe/analyze/discuss). Against this background, the new feature of the analysis is Chat's independent variation and handling of the role as an external consultant who switches to a project associated with an internal project member. In these shifts, it is observed how Chat's language and language blocks match phases with independent idea generation. Chat therefore has 'its own' ideas and proposals. But at the same time, the process shows that Chat can neither choose between proposals nor justify them. However, the many themes and proposals of the project process require professional selection/de-selection, decision-making and judgment in order to get to the next step, or phase in the process.

The pressure, of the now immanent demand for professional judgment in the case/and process, Chat almost resists. The Chat text does not collapse under the pressure. On the other hand, the text is stopped abruptly—in the middle of a sentence in the E-position. This also applies to the otherwise surprisingly finished and written proposal for a final report on the Transport Sector. But in the E-position the Chat text ends abruptly. The column "Recommendations" is not filled in and the sentence is not completed. It simply says here in the E-position of the E-position, as it is, as quoted:

> Recommendations: Based on our research ... (Chat, Climate Crisis, Project Report)

There is no doubt that Chat's project report is written with the academic context and the genre requirements of the project process as a sounding board. But suddenly there is fundamental doubt, both as to whether Chat can translate the project's conclusion into concrete recommendations for action, and whether Chat has even completed the project's studies. The doubt affects, as in previous chapters, the basic questions, which here concern Chat's ability to participate in/support a project process through its milestones from topic to problem formulation, to study/analysis and to final reporting. But in the case of Project Climate Crisis, the doubt is more serious in both a practical and analytical sense than before, because the Chat text literally signals that it was written about a completed project. If Chat's contribution and therefore the doubt are taken at face value, it must be stated that Chat is deceiving KB and the text is lying to every reader. But since the close analysis of the process is carried out as a replacement of text-in-context, both the lie and the matter itself (Project Climate Crisis) are put into relief. And the responsibility for both is shifted along the way, away from Chat and towards KB.

At this stage, the point is not to take a position, but to suggest the seriousness of the shifts of responsibility that are tied to Project Climate Crisis and its changing roles and tasks. Shifts of responsibility also mean deciding along the way whether the group or KB can trust Chat's suggestions and task solutions. Are the contributions professionally and genre-wise credible?

In this light, Chat's changing roles, task solutions and abrupt interruptions in an otherwise genre-adequate and linguistically fluent text are more complicated than the subsequent quotations from the session give the impression. For if KB, or others involved, are to take responsibility for Chat's contribution, then Chat, as a professional text producer, has already sought to draw KB (and every other reader) into the unimplemented project on the Transport Sector. And if we also observe Chat's language suit and the project-oriented flow, we sense how Chat's strong consultant and project-I/We position, as well as Chat's contributions, have already been made 'our' project responsibility. Since the Climate Crisis session thus bears special testimony to these issues, the analysis is tightened up according to its exemplary, but here also documentary value. For the same reason, Chat's independent contribution is quoted in full. But otherwise, the analysis is carried out, as before, by following the session from S- to E-positions and observing Chat's role adoption and handling of the project-related tasks.

12.3 Session S-Position: The University Context and Chat as an External Proposer

KB: In the role of educator at the University, who has to plan a subject-critical project course on the climate crisis, which aspects would you emphasize?[4]

ChatGPT

As an educator in a subject-critical project course on the climate crisis, there are several important aspects you can consider emphasizing. Here are some key areas that may be relevant to include in your project process:

1. Scientific understanding of climate change: Start by ensuring that students have a solid understanding of the scientific background to climate change. Review basic concepts such as the greenhouse effect, atmospheric gases, CO2 concentrations, temperature increases and climate modelling.
2. Impacts and Consequences: Explore the different ways climate change affects ecosystems, societies and economies. Discuss extreme weather, sea level rise, loss of biodiversity, food security, migration and other impacts of climate change.
3. Social and political dimensions: The climate crisis is not only an environmental challenge, but also a social and political issue. Discuss different actors and their roles, including governments, international organizations, businesses, civil society and individuals. Analyze political decision-making processes and barriers to action.
4. Technological and innovative solutions: Explore various technological and innovative solutions to the climate crisis, including renewable energy sources, energy efficiency, climate adaptation and carbon capture and storage. Discuss the pros and cons of different approaches as well as possible implementation challenges.
5. Economic aspects: Analyze the economic consequences of climate change and measures to combat them. Discuss costs of inaction versus costs of action, economic inequality, and incentives for green economic growth.
6. Communication and dissemination: Examine the importance of effective communication and dissemination of the climate crisis. Discuss how messages about climate change can reach different audiences and motivate action. Also consider ethical and psychological aspects of climate communication.
7. Interdisciplinary approach: The climate crisis is a complex problem that requires an interdisciplinary approach. Encourage the students to include knowledge and methods from various subject areas such as natural sciences, social sciences, economics, engineering, philosophy and communication.
8. Current issues and debates: Include discussions on current issues and debates in the climate field. This may include topics such as internal… (Chat,Ses. Climate Crisis)

---

[4] Lix number 64, Very difficult, Sentences: 28, Words: 304, Long words: 163.

As can be seen, the Climate Crisis project also starts with a Chat response that is structured around the now familiar bullet point and reproduction of the KB question. However, it is not a pure reproduction and in relation to role taking, it can be noted that Chat does not take on the educator-role. Chat turns also the You-formulation to KB herself. This is KB's project process! Chat thus takes on the role of an external proposer. With the 8 ambitious proposals, the proposals move from the scientific background (1) to the current debates (8). During the enumeration, it becomes clear that the theme of the Climate Crisis calls for (and requires, cf. 7) an interdisciplinary approach.

With KB specified as the educator and Chat as the proposer, an interdisciplinary, broad-spectrum course on the climate crisis is drawn. This interdisciplinary profiling must be seen as Chat's independent contribution and is in any case a new addition that KB has not initiated. However, we must note that Chat does not take steps towards justified choices, decisions on concretizations or definite problem formulations. This means that the 8 points as a whole represent a Climate Crisis project that is professionally located in broad themes and topics. As a total contribution, the Chat response can also be understood as progressive, so that the activity 'building knowledge' is a starting point and 'the independent debate' an end point. In that case, one of the taxonomic variants (e.g. knowledge/investigate/analyze/discuss) is embedded as a structure and reference to the course as a knowledge and consciousness-creating process. However, there is also evidence that the Chat contribution is understood as 8 independent proposals. In that case, it can be noted that in several of the proposals a progression can be traced between two levels, or phases in the project, formulated with words such as 'explore' or 'examine' and then 'discuss'.

With the Chat contribution to the start of the Climate Crisis project process, as quoted and commented above, KB can give an "OK" to the contribution and its theme/topic proposal. This means that even if KB, for example, finds the accumulation of themes/topics too overwhelming, the Chat contribution can be included in an interdisciplinary collegial cycle, as the project planning work-in-progress. Thus, the Chat contribution also transitions to an assessment of the next steps taken by professionals closer to the issue of climate change.

As in the previous analysis of the start of the Blixen session (see Chap. 10), this "OK", given in down-to-earth terms, is strategically important for analysis. Partly because it is the session's first project-related contribution, and thus functions as a professional/objective sounding board for the course of the session and the analysis. Partly because OK and the down-to-earth must continue to be highlighted by the opposite, namely by Chat contributions, which KB must conclude is "a deception".

As documents, the independent Chat contributions are important for the analysis. And regardless of whether individual Chat responses, or sections, of the KB are found to be OK or questionable, they retain documentary value for field research. But for the course analysis, there is also a special interest in observing where, and when, in the course, the OK-characteristic and the questionable features respectively appear.

At the start of the process, Chat's contribution as an external proposer must be characterized by a deja vu. Professionally/thematically and in terms of genre, the Chat contribution cited above with a theme/topic proposal is similar, for example, to the previous contribution called "AI in the healthcare sector" (see Chap. 7). Later in the process, with Chat's role as a consultant, Chat's contribution with proposals for the learning goals of the project work is similar to the previous contributions on learning goal from the Blixen session (see Chap. 10). With such similarities documented, Chat's role as a proposer and consultant is characterized as close to the claimed strengths of IT expertise in ChatGPT, namely idea generation, structure, but at the same time close to what I call the genre-appropriate templates. In turn, questions are raised about whether ChatGPT can keep up with and follow up on the ideas, structures and genre-appropriate contributions to project content that the chatbot itself has helped to construct. Formulated more closely to the present KB/Chat session: Can Chat follow along in the changing phases, roles and contexts of the session and the project process; can Chat remember and continue to work on its own suggestions; can the KB/Chat session function as work-in-progress throughout the process?

With the course and project-related questions as a clue, Chat's shift in role input below is also marked as a shift in context, provoked by KB. The ambitious and compact 8-point list, and correspondingly high level of difficulty, which the session's S-position now represents, must be concretized as practice-oriented towards interdisciplinary work around the Climate Crisis Team aimed at a middle school context. The intention of the shift in context is not to have Chat and the databank opened to more themes, or new possibilities. There is plenty of that as has been stated. The intention is to use a marked shift in context to the middle school as KB's attempt to keep Chat's own theme proposals (the 8-point proposals of the S-position) as a starting point and then to have Chat solve a required simplification and adaptation task. As will be seen, Chat takes on the session's M-position both in terms of the shift in context and the task solution. Furthermore, Chat's contribution to simplification and adaptation to the school context testifies to a role-taking where Chat continues to act as the outsider, but now as an empathetic consultant. Chat seems to empathize with the theme and reflection on the Climate Crisis, so much so that Chat becomes part of us/we and the considerations about 'how we can protect ourselves and our society from future consequences of climate change'. But Chat's empathy with the matter itself seems to go directly to the teacher, forgetting the students and the consciousness-raising project work and turning the situation into conventional teacher-directed teaching. But the thematic matter, the climate crisis, is intact.

12.4 The M-Positions of the Session: With Chat as a Consultant Between Empathy and Expertise

With the thematic and project-specific questions as a guideline, the excerpts from the session's M-positions exemplify Chat's role as a consultant who, with empathy for the climate crisis, gives advice, as a professional, from colleague to colleague. But at the same time, the role also tends to the consultant who, with expertise in relation to project planning and learning goals, gives advice in concrete ways of acting and passes on experiences with professional authority. The concrete features and calls for action in Chat's consultant advice not only testify that Chat has taken on the tasks set by KB—they are the solution to the task. In this sense, the characteristic feature of the M-position examples, which we follow in excerpts below, is that Chat has been given a series of tasks, presents their solutions one by one—and KB nods OK four times to the genre-appropriate contributions! The fact that KB's "OK" is an analytical strategic prerequisite has been emphasized sufficiently. Here I simply add that the accumulation of genre-appropriate bullet points and language blocks along the way becomes so massive that they approach questionable features of genre plagiarism. The analytical review, however, starts with the OK features, in order to maintain that in the M1 example Chat has actually sought to solve the relevant simplification and adaptation task.

For reasons of space, I will quote the examples in excerpts, so that the S- and E-positions of the Chat response are intact in full text, whereas the M positions of the response are given by me as clues about the content.

12.5 M1: Simplification and Adaptation of the Climate Theme—With Chat as an Empathetic Consultant

The climate session is carried out in a flow. The first contribution of the session, namely Chat's Theme/topic suggestions, are therefore still present as important, but too many and too compact suggestions. As a consequence, KB seeks to provoke a simplification of the thematic content through a shift to the school context, as follows:

KB: Can you simplify the teaching content so that it is suitable for a 6th grade in middle school?

ChatGPT

Of course! Here is a simplified version of the teaching content suitable for a 6th grade in middle school:

1. What is climate change? Explain what climate change is and how it affects our planet.
2. Weather versus climate: Explain the difference between weather and climate. Weather is about what happens in the short term, while climate is about the long-term pattern of weather in an area.
3. The Greenhouse Effect: Explain the concept of the greenhouse effect using an analogy such as a greenhouse or a car that's get hot in the sun.
4. Important consequences: Discuss some of the important consequences of climate change, such as rising temperatures, melting ice, rising sea levels and changes in animal and plant life.
(… // Points 5–7, keywords: Reduction of emissions, Recycling and reuse, Green energy//…)
8. Climate adaptation: Explain the concept of climate adaptation, where we adapt to the changes that have already occurred and how we can protect ourselves and our society from future consequences of climate change.
9. Our role: Encourage students to reflect on their own role in combating climate change. Discuss small steps they can take in their everyday life to make a difference, e.g. save energy and water, choose sustainable products and share knowledge with others.
10. Communication and action: Discuss the importance of communicating about climate change and motivating others to take action. Encourage students to think about how they can share their knowledge and engage in projects that promote sustainability and climate consciousness.

Remember that it is important to adapt the teaching methods and material to the age and level of the students to ensure understanding and engagement. (Chat, Ses. Climate crisis)

With the thematic questions still as a content guideline, it can be noted first and foremost that the change of context and the role as a consultant have resulted in a simplified Chat contribution. The degree of difficulty (and thus the number of lix) has also been reduced from 64 (very difficult) to 47 (difficult).[5] However, the simplified Climate Theme and Chat's 10-point list do not indicate that the many themes and topics have been cleaned up. On the contrary, the 10 points together represent both the broad theme/topic spectrum and the listed issues that can be linked to them. Thus, the concretizations of the 'important consequences of climate change' have the character of a list: "such as rising temperatures, melting ice, rising sea levels and changes in animal and plant life" (point 4).

The interesting thing about Chat's contribution, however, is not just *that* it is simplified, but *how* the simplification has been made. At first glance, it seems to have been made in conjunction with the adaptation to the school context. And as a consultant in a school context, Chat seems to be directing its advice towards the 6th grade teacher. In this light, the striking action-specific Chat statements made in an imperative manner can be seen. Chat advises with: "Explain what climate change is", "Explain the difference between weather and climate". "Explain the concept of

[5] Lix number: 47, Difficult, Sentences: 32, Words: 324, Long words: 119.

the greenhouse effect" (points 1–3). Next, Chat advises: "Discuss some of the important consequences". In this connection, the academic choices around the many themes and topics, as well as decisions about what specifically belongs to 'explanation' and what is for 'discussion', are entrusted to the teacher.

As can be understood, Chat is deeply involved in both the case itself and the role as consultant. However, Chat's role and staging of 'the rest of us' is still a bit cryptic. The text and the specific statements make it clear that the individual pieces of advice are addressed directly to the 6th grade teacher. It is therefore neither KB, the 6th grade students nor Chat itself who must explain 'the concept of the greenhouse effect using an analogy like a greenhouse or a car that gets hot in the sun'. The teacher must manage that explanation and analogy! But if the individual pieces of advice are addressed to the teacher and further decisions are left to the teacher's judgment, then is the overall list of points (and the actual task answer) addressed to KB? One would think so, at least Chat's first reply to KB was: "Of course! Here is a simplified version of the teaching content that is suitable for a 6th grader in middle school". KB received, as quoted above, the simplified version, adapted to the school context. But at the same time, the KB/Chat relationship was also adapted to the school context in which Chat functions as a consultant. And as an empathetic consultant, Chat now functions as a representative and ambassador for 'our planet', appealing to the teacher to explain the concept of climate adaptation: "where we adapt to the changes that have already occurred, and how we can protect ourselves and our society from future consequences of climate change" (point 8). Chat then continues, not without pathos, by urging reflection on 'Our role: Encourage students to reflect on their own role in combating climate change.'

The illustrated rhetorical immersion into theme, genre and school context means that Chat becomes part of us and the world. One could call it a rhetorical self-humanization of Chat. But in that case, this is already placed in the analysis as an observation that must be linked to what I call the language suit. The language suit and genre-adequate language blocks give the individual conversation with a GAI/chatbot an interactive character, i.e. the character of taking place as question/answer sessions due to the use of human language. On this basis, all KB/Chat conversations and sessions are analyzed and therefore also a basic part of the analysis of the Climate Session KB/Chat conversations. But in the Climate Session there seems to be something else and more going on than humanization and dressed language suits. Firstly, Chat's empathy and statements such as 'our planet' and 'we can protect ourselves and our society', rather than a humanization, are an expression of Chat being socialized. One could call the Chat language use 'the inclusive we'. The Chat response thus, spurred on by the changing role taking and context shift, includes itself in the 'societal we' of the climate theme, genre and context, i.e. all of us. In the Climate Session, Chat as 'the writing I' is also dissolved. But apparently so are other I's. In the session's S-position, Chat emphasized, by avoiding the role as university educator, that 'you' and 'your project course' meant that it was KB's. That is, my teaching and project course. Here in M-positions, both my project course and KB's 'I' are dissolved and embedded in Chat's inclusive we. The Chat consultant also calls for reflection on 'our roles' along the way and when later quoting from the

S-position's final report it has become 'our project'. What has happened, one must ask?

As in previous analyses, e.g. of the Blixen session, it must be stated that 'something' has happened. I just don't know what. Similarly, it is stated that this 'something' is an intermediate state between Chat and the databank. One suggestion could be that 'the societal we' and the phrase 'our planet' are simply a linguistic block that clings to the theme of the Climate Crisis and can also be found both in public climate debates and on the internet. So just as the theme of Gender Role Patterns in previous chapters made the Chat responses wordy and at times unusually loud on behalf of the author Klaus Rifbjerg and the Chat speaker, the Climate Crisis as a theme also makes Chat loud and wordy. I maintain that it is a good suggestion, and is also in line with the analytical points. But for reasons of analytical strategy, I cannot be satisfied with a suggestion, but must provoke 'an established consequence' that can later lead to a conclusion.

I don't know what happens between Chat and the databank. But I know Chat texts that testify to the consequences. And the text that most resembles the Chat contributions in the Climate Crisis session is "AI in the health sector" (see Chap. 7). This Chat text had no cracks. But when subjected to double-checking, the analysis could indicate that Chat/the databank had secured Chat's response through a normative turn of KB's question, so that IT technology was fundamentally in a positive light. I also had to conclude that those who had to bear responsibility for the normative turn were Chat/the databank/language model and OpenAI. The normative turns are also observed in Chat contributions on the Climate Crisis, as previously described on the gender role theme. But in the Climate Session, it is not the KB question (or the matter itself) that is subjected to a normative turn, rather Chat's treatment of the theme, task solving and thus the entire contribution. Depending on the context and role, Chat appears as an assistant, co-teacher, consultant, etc. to do the right thing, think the right thing, and use the right politically correct phrases.

Let me illustrate by quoting the last call to the teacher and the 6th grade students in this Chat contribution (point 10):

> Communication and Action: Discuss the importance of communicating about climate change and motivating others to take action. Encourage students to think about how they can share their knowledge and engage in projects that promote sustainability and climate consciousness. (Chat, Ses. Climate Crisis)

The point and the call, thus the text, have a message and seem sympathetic. The same goes for the words and the action orientation: 'Motivate others to action', 'think about how (you) can share knowledge', 'engage in projects that promote sustainability and climate consciousness'. These are pure positive words—promising!

The text, sentences and word choice are grammatically correct and the text as a whole provides both messages and complete meanings. But when the series of normatives are confronted with content and the real school context, Chat's last point 10, like the 9 previous points, loses its meaning. All points are equally valid and risk being indifferent for the same reason. The text can be considered a collection of pseudo-concrete phrases and pep-talking sentences that constantly cast doubt on who is intended as the acting subject and what is placed centrally as the objectified object. The teacher seems to be the acting subject and the Climate Crisis is the object, claims the Chat answer. Hardly, signals the Chat text: The Chat consultant is the acting subject = 'the acting we' on behalf of society, the teacher and KB. And the objectified object? That are the students.

In this regard, it should be noted that the Chat contribution only comes with a single new and concrete idea, where the teacher must do the following for the benefit of the students, namely this:

> Explain the concept of the greenhouse effect using an analogy such as a greenhouse or a car that's get hot in the sun. (Chat. Point 3. Ses. Climate Crises)

It sounds poor to have to settle for the banal analogy—and quite far from examples of chatbots that 'think outside the box'! In return, there are eager calls from Chat to get involved in projects that "promote sustainability and climate consciousness".

If, similar to the analysis of "AI in the healthcare sector…", I was to ask who is responsible for the Chat contribution's proposal, 10 points and the politically correct flow of words and goodwill, the answer would be the Chat consultant. But it is as if Chat, through the genre-appropriate bullet points, is guaranteed an opportunity to withdraw by using the E-position's standard remark, noted as 'Remember'. In the current version, it reads as:

> Remember that it is important to adapt the teaching methods and material to the age and level of the students to ensure understanding and engagement. (Chat, Ses. Climate Crisis, E-pos)

The Chat consultant does not disclaim responsibility, but is signaled that the person using the 10-point proposal (the teacher, KB, or just a user) takes over both the proposal and responsibility with the adaptation.

This waiver/transfer of responsibility to the user is, as is well known, effective, but so are the means of the Chat text. The linguistic means bring the Chat consultant to life in action as 'the acting we', who motivates action on behalf of society, the teacher and KB. The simultaneous textual means are a normative turn of text, message and theme. This sharpens the question of responsibility, for who actually takes responsibility for the means of the text?

If we stick to the question of the text's means of action and the Chat consultant in action, there should be no doubt. Only Chat text, OpenAI, the language model and the database can/should take responsibility. The interesting thing about this part of the session is that Chat (Chat's pep talk) clearly takes some responsibility—before disclaiming it.

Against this background, it is still important to pursue Climate session's internal division of roles and responsibilities, and to make the progress status as follows. Chat has, in the role of consultant and 'the acting we', transferred the responsibility to the teacher and KB, incorporated KB into the consultant's 'social we'. Furthermore, Chat has staged the teacher as the acting subject.

Under these conditions, I seek to pull KB out of Chat's staging, and let the question situation and the specific question be formulated in direct continuation of what the IT expertise and the Pioneer teachers have referred to as ChatGPT's strengths in solving the task.

As was evident from the review and analyses in Chaps. 7 and 10, the Pioneer teachers are ambitious, but also make it clear that tasks such as project presentations and the design of plans are obvious in the ongoing involvement of ChatGPT.

In the next parts of the session, the Climate Crisis theme is maintained with a level of ambition that suits the theme. But I avoid You-wording and order a task! The Chat contribution is presented in excerpts so that SME positions can be identified, but otherwise quoted as the former S and E position in full text.

12.6 M2, Introduction to Project Work: With Chat as the Experienced Consultant

KB: Give an introduction to project work under the theme of the climate crisis[6]

ChatGPT

(S-pos) Introduction to project work under the theme Climate crisis:

Project work within the theme of the climate crisis is a valuable and relevant way to engage in the important task of tackling climate change. The climate crisis is a global challenge that requires a holistic approach and action across society. Project work provides the opportunity to work actively to identify, analyze and implement solutions to climate-related problems and contribute to a sustainable future.

A project on the climate crisis can have many different purposes and scope. It can focus on building consciousness and education about climate change, investigating specific environmental problems or developing innovative technologies and strategies to reduce climate impact. Project work can be carried out at schools, universities, companies, organizations or even in collaboration between several different stakeholders.

(M-pos)

An important part of the project work within the climate crisis is to define clear goals and objectives. This may include identifying specific issues to be tackled (…)

An effective approach to project work within the climate crisis often involves interdisciplinary collaboration. Climate change is a complex issue that requires knowledge and perspectives from different disciplines (…)

Finally, it is important to emphasize the importance of communication and dissemination in the project work. Effective communication of the project's results, recommendations and consequences can contribute to raising consciousness of the climate crisis and mobilizing action at individual, societal and political level.

(E-pos) Project work within the climate crisis is an exciting opportunity to contribute to sustainable changes and be part of the global effort against climate change. It provides a platform to explore innovative ideas, sam …

(Chat, Ses. Climate crisis. Contribution M.pos)

---

[6] Lix number: 63, Very difficult, Sentences: 19, Words: 340, Long words: 152.

KB got an answer to her initial question and the task is solved. But it is an interesting role and context change that Chat makes. During the session, KB/Chat comes from a school context and an empathetic Chat consultant who provides advice directly to the teacher. With the above Chat contribution, we seem to be on our way into the ministry, with the presentation of a larger version of Project Climate Crisis. But let me start with the sober characterization.

The quoted Chat contribution is a fluent and well-organized text, with a high level of difficulty (63), many compact sentences and long words. In the previous session, KB/Chat had a specified school context, but above there is (deliberately) no context marking in the KB question. The choice of context is open to Chat. And Chat's choice clearly testifies to a context reference that encompasses much more than school and does not start at school level at all, but several levels above. The project Chat presents is almost in the nature of a larger research program that must refer to being managed by a university, a higher education institution, or what I, as indicated, suggest a ministry. Like "AI in the health sector", it is in that case a genre-appropriate ministerial letter that could well find a place on the website of one of our ministries. This means that if, for example, the Ministry of Education or Research would approve and stand behind the text and the positive terms with which project work is surrounded ('a valuable and relevant way to engage in the important task'), then this Chat contribution is an example of the task set being solved.

As a stand-alone text, the above introduction can be considered a ChatGPT data-generated text without grammatical or genre gaps. It just lacks a sender.

But if the Chat contribution and text are considered in conjunction with the other session contributions, both the missing sender, the abrupt ending, and the political technological approach are part of the distinctive features that must be developed in the final summary. The climate theme is strong and central in the Chat contribution, and there are many formulations (and language blocks) that are recognizable from the S-position's theme/topic proposal and from the 10th point proposal. But both academically and thematically, in relation to the development of Project Climate Crisis, we are still far from ideas and angles of attack that testify and creative attempts to 'think outside the box'. Ironically, the Chat contribution stopped in the middle of the sentence about 'the innovative ideas, together …'.

But if we are far from the innovative ideas, we are on the other hand close to the clarifying examples of Chat's production of genre-appropriate texts. A ministerial letter is the genre relationship characterized above as. Below, genre plagiarism is clarified, as exemplified in connection with the design of project plans and learning goals for a high school context.

12.7 M3 and M4 Design of Project Plan and Learning Goals

This section's Chat contributions with the formulation of the project plan and learning goals should not be quoted in longer excerpts. They are largely empty of content. And if there are full sentences and sections to quote, as in the Chat contribution on learning goals, they are already known language blocks and phrases at this point of the analysis. On the other hand, the Chat contributions have great exemplary value, not least because ChatGPT's genre plagiarism is made clear and requires discussion of the consequences. In its completed form, the genre text resembles official letters from educational institutions and ministries. And even if the example 'Project plan for 6 weeks of project work in a high school' resembles a more low-level practical text assignment than, for example, the above introduction to project work, weekly and teaching plans have great scope. And as an official letter, there are institutional bindings at the heavy end. A plan for 6 weeks of project work posted on a high school's website must be credible—including teacher assignment, and thus responsibility placement, naming! The same applies to the Chat contribution to learning goals. It looks like official letters that are already embedded in the educational institutions' curricula and/or are on the Ministry of Education's website.

The point in the present context is that what in the S-position of the Climate Session starts with KB inviting Chat to contribute to work-in-progress, is suddenly challenged in the M-position of the session by Chat's concrete task solutions for taking a position on the institutions' core services and the ministries' high-profile focus areas. Above, the Chat text simply lacked the approval of a ministry to proceed further in the cycle. Below, the Chat contribution initially only lacks approval from 'a high school teacher' and 'a director of studies' to proceed further. But as the analysis shows, the Chat contribution's genre plagiarism is so consequential that work-in-progress and 'further in the cycle' are momentarily reset. The cycle has stopped because Chat itself can deliver a finished product, i.e. fill the still only keyword-like retention of markers with slightly more substantial content. But the circuit has also been disrupted by a simile with an authoritative letter, which makes the Chat contribution part of the authoritative texts.

In an analytical sense, it is important to wonder where Chat gets its authoritative voice from. But it is also an analytical requirement that an answer be given. Below we see examples where the answer must be divided into two parts. Considered every day and tangible in relation to the weekly schedule structured from week 1 to week 6, the reference must be 'a group of high school teachers', i.e. both professionals and didactics, close to the Climate Projects under planning. But if we look at signal words, language blocks and argumentative drivers, only three signal words are linked to the project's subject matter itself, namely the *Climate Crisis*, *Sustainability* and *Climate Change*. The rest of the keywords are general or technical-practical keywords that refer to the phases of the project work. If the authoritative voice is to be identified on this basis, we are in a ministerial framework (the Ministry of Research, Environment, and Education), where the large Project Climate Crisis can also be outlined for plans in a high school context. Below are quoted so that the plan's framing and signal words and blocks can be seen. Weeks 1 and 6 are represented in full text, and weeks 2–5 are represented by keywords. Chat's concluding comment is, however, quoted in full text.

KB: Can you design a project plan for 6 weeks of project work in a high school class[7]

ChatGPT

Of course! Here is an example project plan for 6 weeks of project work in a high school class within the theme of the climate crisis:

Project: Sustainability and climate change - From knowledge to action

Week 1: Introduction to the climate crisis and problem identification

- Research and literature research of climate change and its consequences
- Identification of specific climate-related problems and challenges
- The formation of project groups and the assignment of tasks

// Then Wee k 2: Analysis and data collection, Week 3: Development of solution strategies, Week 4: Implementation and action, Week 5: Evaluation and impact assessment //

Week 6: Communication and presentation

- Preparation of a presentation and report on the project's results, recommendations and conclusions
- Communication of the project's work to the school community, other students and stakeholders
- Celebrating the success of the project and sharing inspiration for future initiatives

This project plan is just an outline and can be adapted to the specific needs and resources of the class. It is important to ensure that sufficient time and resources are allocated to each phase of the project work, including research, data collection, analysis, action and dissemination. Project-based learning can be a great way to engage students in taking an active part in climate-related challenges and encourage them to develop innovative solutions. (Chat, Ses, Climate Crisis Project Plan)

As illustrated, the Chat contribution is close to genre-appropriate layout, a template, applied with the keywords/headings that follow the phases of the project work. There are no Chat-generated new additions and only 3 signal words linked to the Climate Crisis. It is thus empty of project-related content and also seems to be distant from subject-related didactic planning. However, a single, almost strange presence of 'the social' is the reminder in week 6, which reads "Celebrating the success of the project and sharing inspiration for future initiatives".

But if the cited project plan has weak (bordering on none) content, it has a strong form and a large format. The justification is as follows. The title of the plan is: "Project: Sustainability and Climate Change - From Knowledge to Action". And the entire project, week 1, starts with "Research and literature research of climate change and its consequences". The signal value is convincing. It is primarily university institutions and those related to them that master the path from knowledge to action and recognize that research and literature review must be started. Furthermore, if 3 (maybe) 4 words are removed from the text, namely the students, the class, the

[7] Lix number: 70, Very difficult, Sentences: 12, Words: 299, Long words: 136.

school (maybe learning), the text is cleansed of the school context and the plan for the research project stands out in its own right!

One last question: Where does Chat get the research format and the language blocks that signal them? The answer is, in addition to the usual correct fact that they come from the databank, that Chat can retrieve the format and language blocks from the ongoing Climate Session, but also from itself. Chat actually wrote them in the earlier contribution "Introduction to project work under the theme of the Climate Crisis", where it read:

> A project on the climate crisis can have many different purposes and scope. It can focus on building consciousness and education about climate change, investigating specific environmental problems or developing innovative technologies and strategies to reduce climate impact. Project work can be carried out at schools, universities, companies, organizations or even in collaboration between several different stakeholders. (Chat, Ses. Climate Crisis, IntroProjectWork)

Chat's research program and project plan, as well as reference to the authoritative voices, were thus secured in the research context. And with the E-positioned information: 'This project plan is just a sketch and can be adapted to the specific needs and resources of the class', it was also secured in relation to the high school class and its teachers.

In summary, the Chat contribution has thus been secured both as a template and as a solved task. On the other hand, an unresolved problem remains, which concerns the level of difficulty. Although the research anchoring of the plan gives the Chat response legitimacy in the Climate Crisis session, KB's task has not been solved. On the contrary, the task is thwarted by a plan and a level of difficulty that are out of proportion. Chat's plan requires research-based task solutions that cannot be solved by a group of high school students. This 'out of proportion' seems to stick to Chat's genre-appropriate task solutions and also applies to the next part of the session regarding learning goals.

12.8 Learning Goals and Project Work

KB: Which learning goals should be linked to project work? Name the most important 5 that can be presented to the students in the class at the start of the project process[8]

ChatGPT

When planning project work, it is important to set clear learning goals to ensure that students gain valuable knowledge and develop relevant skills. Here are five important learning goals that can be presented to the students in the class at the start of the project process:

[8] Lix number: 56, Very difficult, Sentences: 21, Words: 295, Long words: 123.

1. Knowledge of climate change and its consequences: Students must gain an in-depth understanding of climate change, including the scientific principles behind it, the environmental and societal consequences and their global and local impact.
2. Analytical skills: Students must develop the ability to analyze and assess complex climate-related issues. They must be able to identify causes and effects, assess different perspectives and stakeholder involvement, and apply critical thinking to identify effective solution strategies.
3. Problem solving and innovation: Students must be able to apply their knowledge and analytical skills to generate innovative solutions to climate-related challenges. They must be able to think creatively and develop sustainable measures that can contribute to reducing the climate impact.
4. Collaboration skills: Project work often involves collaboration in teams. Students must develop the ability to work effectively together, communicate and share knowledge, utilize different competencies and respect and value the perspectives of others. They must be able to build and maintain constructive working relationships.
5. Communication skills: Students must learn to communicate their work and results clearly and convincingly. They must be able to present their ideas and solution strategies both orally and in writing in a way that is adapted to different target groups. They must also be able to listen and respond to feedback and reflect on their own learning and development.

These learning goals can give students a direction and framework for their work and help ensure that they gain a wide range of skills and knowledge within the topic of the climate crisis. It is also important to adapt the learning goals to the specific class and the students' needs and interests. (Chat, Ses. Climate crisis, Learning goals)

As can be seen, Chat's presentation and summary of the learning goals is structured on Bloom's taxonomy. It brings knowledge (step 1) and then analysis (application) and problem solving close to each other. But there seems to be no real relationship between the mentioned abilities/skills and their links to the elements of knowledge. In this respect, the summary and bullet points are subject professionally anonymous. In reality, out of the 295 words in the answer, only five theme-related signal words are used, namely *climate*—(/crisis/changes/related) *environment, society, global, sustainable.* The rest are words, language blocks and argumentative phrases that could be used on many other themes. The last 2 points refer to social learning goals.

However, the academic anonymity of the learning goals and their weak anchoring in knowledge do not seem to influence the Chat proposal's broad-spectrum demands on students, who, if the learning goals are met, are expected to have secured a correspondingly broad competence profile.

The interesting thing is that the safeguard in the Chat proposal's perspective seems to lie in the fact that the learning goals and competence requirements are described and ranked according to Bloom's taxonomy. This then structures the text and main message, but also the description of the learning goals in the individual points. Thus, the first sentence of point 3 can almost be read over Bloom's 6-step model, and in that case reads:

Students must be able to apply their knowledge (Step 1 on the way to 2) and analytical skills (Step 3 on the way to 4) to generate innovative solutions (Step 5 on the way to 6) to climate-related challenges.

Seen in this light, the points and individual sentences of the Chat text can be considered as independent and complete small Bloom's language blocks. And Chat's proposal as a whole is worded accordingly, starting with step 1, the word 'Knowledge of climate change (…) and ending with the ability and learning goal above them all, namely that students must (…) reflect on their own learning and development'.

With the structural order and characteristic language blocks of the Chat text, the answer to the recurring analytical question of who is behind the proposal and its authoritative voice is almost given. The credibility and authority of the Chat answer lies in the genre, the Bloomsonian structure and in the genre relationship of the text, text-in-context. The Chat answer and text immediately resemble a letter or text excerpts from, for example, the Ministry of Education's website Emu.

This adds another Chat contribution to the series of texts that share a common genre and resemble writings from one of our ministries, universities or centers, such as the previous chapter's Studypedia. However, there is a distinct feature of Chat's answer about the Learning Goals that requires a status.

The Chat response about learning goals is particularly close to being complete, rounded and without disclaimers or abrupt conclusions. But at the same time it is a logically disrupted text with a completely indeterminate level of difficulty. Point 1–3 formulations have embedded expectations of 'in-depth understanding of climate change, including the scientific principles behind it', identification of 'causes and effects', 'applying critical thinking' and showing 'analytical skills to generate innovative solutions to climate-related challenges'. Suddenly, the formulations are reminiscent of KB's encounter with Chat's machine language enumerations of abilities and skills (see Chap. 5). In that case, the logical disruption is not just about a structural clash between the taxonomies that are based on knowledge (Bloom) and learning goals (Biggs), but about a clash between human/machine understanding/non-understanding of the matter itself, i.e.

With learning goals embedded in the question, we know from the Karen Blixen session (see Chap. 10) that the databank opens up language blocks and text pieces that are otherwise similar to texts from, for example, the Ministry of Education's websites. And if we add to this the structural relationship to the previous chapter's example analyses of Bloom's taxonomies, the two important origins of genre plagiarism are illustrated. In continuation of this, the special significance of genre plagiarism here in the Climate Crisis session must be maintained, namely that the independence that Chat's role has been characterized by is highlighted.

12.9 Chats Final Project Report: Sustainable Transport Solution for Reducing CO_2 Emissions

KB: Can you give an example of a good project report of 5 pages within the theme of the climate crisis[9]

ChatGPT

Of course! Here is an example of a short project report of 5 pages within the theme of the climate crisis:

Project Report: Better Transport Solution for Reducing CO2-emissions

Introduction: This report presents the results of our investigation into a sustainable transport solution for reducing CO2 emissions. The purpose of our project was to identify and evaluate opportunities to minimize transport's climate impact and contribute to tackling the climate crisis.

Method: We collected data by conducting a literature review of research articles and reports on sustainable transport and CO2 reduction. We also conducted interviews with experts in the field and analyzed relevant statistics and data.

Results:

1. Climate impact from the transport sector: We identified that the transport sector accounts for a significant proportion of CO2 emissions and is an important source of climate change. This emphasized the need to find solutions in the field of transport.
2. Potential solutions: We investigated various sustainable transport solutions, including electric vehicles, public transport, cycling and green infrastructure. We evaluated the advantages and disadvantages of each solution and identified their potential to reduce CO2 emissions and promote sustainable transport.
3. Electrification of transport: We found that electric vehicles (EVs) have the potential to significantly reduce CO2 emissions from the transport sector. We discussed the necessary infrastructure and policy measures to promote wider adoption of EVs and addressed challenges such as battery technology and charging infrastructure.
4. Public transport and cycling: We found that investments in public transport and cycling infrastructure can reduce CO2 emissions and promote sustainable transport. We presented examples of successful projects and policy measures that have improved the accessibility and use of public transport and cycling.

Conclusion: Our study confirms that the transport sector plays a decisive role in the climate crisis and that there is a need for sustainable transport solutions. Electrifying transport through EVs, strengthening public transport and cycling as well as investing in green infrastructure are all important steps towards reducing CO2 emissions and creating a more sustainable future.

Recommendations: Based on our research ...

(sentence not completed, Chat. Ses. Climate Crisis, Project Report)

Let me describe Chat's project report as the final report of the Climate Session and start with an observation and a quirk.

KB asks for an example of a good report and is surprised by Chat, who presents a report apparently written by Chat and on an independently chosen project topic,

[9] Lix number: 59, Very difficult, Sentences: 26, Words: 321, Long words: 150.

namely sustainable transport solutions. The report is short, but must be noted to be genre-appropriate and divided into introduction, method, results. The quirky is that the project report stops abruptly in the middle of a sentence. Furthermore, the normally present E-position is absent. Chat has also taken responsibility from the very beginning, i.e. already in the introduction of the report. This cannot be denied. But the project report can obviously be stopped.

What is also thought-provoking is the almost obvious way in which Chat refers to the project as 'our project' and 'our investigation'. The societal we, which became noticeable in Chat's contribution to the introduction to project work, has now clearly become a concrete we. 'We identified', 'We investigated', 'We found that', 'We discussed…' and "We presented examples" is the wording of the report.

There is thus no doubt that Chat represents 'the acting we'. Chat must have become a member of a project group. But there is doubt about who is in 'our group' and thus both project partners and jointly responsible for the product. There is also suddenly doubt whether the project has been completed. We can refer to the necessity of fact-checking, but can also bring to mind the warnings of IT experts. They mention the risk of inaccuracies and the fact that ChatGPT gets hallucinations. It is a warning that is also conveyed, including in the magazine Folkeskolen:

> *Hallucinations*
> If ChatGPT doesn't know the answer to your prompt, you risk it just making something up. It's called hallucinating. That's why it's important to be extra critical of the language model's output and make sure that it actually answers correctly. (Folkeskolen 2/2024, Guide)

In continuation of this, a fact check/double check could have to accept that even if the analysis points to genre-appropriate language and meaningful sentences and complete sentences, Chat's role taking, and the entire staging of the report as a final project report is a hallucination. OpenAI and IT expertise are thus absolved of responsibility. The analytical point, however, is that the impact of the double check is no less. Firstly, Chat's report, as quoted above, is genre plagiarism, but not hallucinatory. Secondly, the report's bullet points and the thematized content presented as a whole Chat-produced text (quirky introductions and abrupt endings included) are part of the pure apparent media reality. KB/Chat sessions and the collection of Chat responses are not fiction.

Let me therefore strengthen the double check, sharpen my eye for text-in-context relationships and use Chat's final report as a transition to the reality check. The reality check involves taking a position on the proposals that the Chat contribution represents, stands behind, but yet hands over to 'we, us, the others' to take responsibility for. This also involves, as below, confronting Chat's project reporting with other realized Climate Crisis projects, with which Chat seems to share a project-related community. KB is not a professional and for analysis strategy reasons, it must be checked whether there is someone or something in the academic context that the Chat contribution is part of that can confirm the project's 'matter itself'. Does the matter exist in the professional world or has Chat just made it all up itself?

12.10 The Reality Check: With a Sharper Look at the Practical Context

A closer look at the practical context implies the finding that it is unclear, and can hardly be clarified, *who* 'our project' and group consists of. On the other hand, it is quite clear *what* Chat and the group have worked on in terms of project expertise. "Sustainable Transport Solution for Reducing CO2 Emissions" is a concrete and precise title. And even though the report does not go into depth with the study results, but simply lists them, the results are formulated in a clearly structured thematic/topical manner, and the review is specified in the past tense. When Chat on behalf of the group writes 'we identified, we investigated…', i.e. the past tense, we others get the clear impression that the study has been carried out. The case itself and the potential solutions have even been evaluated for advantages and disadvantages, as can be seen from the descriptions:

> Point 2. Potential solutions: We investigated various sustainable transport solutions, including electric vehicles, public transport, cycling and green infrastructure. We evaluated the advantages and disadvantages of each solution and identified their potential to reduce CO2 emissions and promote sustainable transport. (Chat,Ses.Climate Crisis. Projekt Report)

Against this relatively clear background, a closer look at the project professional dimensions and contexts can therefore clarify which professional projects the Chat group shares a kinship with. A spontaneous Google search on the title: 'Sustainable Transport Solution for Reducing CO2 Emissions' gives immediate results. The second suggestion on the search reads as follows:

> Overall, the transport sector accounts for 25 percent of the total CO2 emissions in Denmark, which was 44 million tonnes of CO2 in 2022. **Conversion to sustainable transport is therefore central to Denmark's reduction of CO2 emissions by 70 per cent. 2030.** (Google post 12.8.2024)

With these three informative lines, it can be seen that Chat's project has a project-specific match, and that the Google text itself, in short form, signals a significantly higher degree of concretization than the Chat final report achieves. As previously posted for analysis strategic reasons, an increased degree of concretization means that we are among professionals. And if you follow the Google post's link, you are also taken directly into that world and to the academic context, here the Technical University of Denmark, which starts the research-based website about 'Transport' as follows:

> The transport sector emits more and more CO2 from cars, trucks, planes and ship transport. If the trend is to be reversed, more of the known solutions and technologies need to come into play. The transition to green transport is leaving its mark on Denmark with more electric cars, electric charging stations, special parking spaces, and for aviation, a political agreement has been reached that all domestic aviation must be converted to green energy by 2030 at the latest.
>
> Electric cars have a positive effect on CO2 emissions, but the energy efficiency they create, the Danes have exchanged for longer trips.

> The latest *Transport Habits Survey* from DTU shows that Danes make the same number of journeys in their cars, but that they make longer journeys. This has led to CO2 emissions from car driving being as high as 30 years ago.
>
> Overall, the transport sector accounts for… (…)
>
> (Google post/*Transport Habits Survey* refer to link, DTU website; the text break is the authors)

As can be seen, DTU is potentially the project-qualified match and professional reference for Chats, both in terms of theme, examples, words and phrases. And if you follow the website's description (which I stopped at in the quote) further through the many posting options, you see the outline of a resource-rich portal that describes and illustrates the specific projects around green transport with professional precision. Everywhere and with academic obviousness, the projects are surrounded by results and sources with mention of names, contact persons and high-quality studies. For example, the "Transport Habits Survey" embedded in the quote above, where the link also testifies to DTU's official service. Or the portal's link to the "Gymnasiesiden", which testifies to DTU's, otherwise rich in tradition, contact with the high school field.

For the reality check, this means that the matter itself, i.e. the climate crisis theme and the Chat project "Reputable Transport solution for the reduction of CO2 emissions", exists in the professional versions and can be concretely identified and linked to an academic practical context, e.g. to DTU and their internal and external contact area.

12.11 What Remains, as Realities?

As above, with solid ground underfoot, the reality check starts from a project perspective with a confirmed match, but also with a marked difference between high/low degree of concretization and between the result- and source-creating professional DTU projects and the result- and source less Chat project. But if the Chat project has provoked comparisons with the green transport projects at DTU, but itself fails as a result and source less, what is left—from a project perspective—Nothing?

From a project perspective, almost nothing is an appropriate answer. It also confirms what the double check already pointed out earlier in the analysis. Namely, that the Chat contribution's way of reporting, together with the abrupt ending, cast doubt on whether the claimed studies had even been completed. Again, the analysis confirms. But at the same time, the reality check trumps the double check. The claimed studies and their results can be sought out and witnessed. The studies were/are thus completed. Certainly not by Chat, but by DTU researchers and students. What now, as realities, remains? The answer is as follows:

1. Chat's reporting of 'Our project', and its place in the KB/Chat session, remains as a text that, by resembling a report from one of our universities (in casu DTU),

functions as a genre plagiarism that refers to the professional background. In the Session, the genre plagiarism can also be considered in extension of Chat contributions such as the previous 'Introduction to Project Work', previous 'AI in the health sector', as well as documents on learning goals and evaluation. Here the analogy extends to a ministerial or institutional committee memorandum, from which the Chat contribution/text draws its authoritative voice.

2. Since the genre plagiarism is replaced as a document in the relevant academic context, text-in-context (especially in real-world and contextual terms), the Chat texts are thereby made effective in the communicative circuits. Now they work together with the original authoritative texts. The point is that the genre plagiarism not only works together with, but also functions unchallenged in the circuit as an authoritative text—until a professional/authority either takes responsibility for the text or disqualifies it.
3. When responsibility is transferred/placed, or disqualification is made, the official set of rules begins. But this also begins the new everyday academic conflict. It is here, in the middle of a conflict, that I have previously stopped with an analysis-strategic statement regarding specific features (e.g. in Chat's Machine Room or in the Blixen session) that could clarify or nuance. The common argument is also used, as the clarifying 'this is how ChatGPT's text universe works, I point out, when language and genre, language blocks and signal words carry the text's content and subject matter through to the point of almost meaningfulness … and then collapses anyway.'

But this does not apply to the Climate Crisis session, there is no textual collapse in progress. I cannot simply call the session academically poor, even though it is. Nor can I simply take responsibility for a You-formulation or a 'signal word' that influenced Chat-answer and the data bank, even if that were the case. And finally, the analyst cannot simply claim 'that the analysis of the progression from S-position to E-position testified to a loss of meaning'.

In the course of the Climate Crisis Session, all of the above applies, including the loss of meaning. But in addition, the course of the session particularly testified to the loss of credibility. There were several independently chosen and formulated Chat contributions that turned out to be genre plagiarism. Genre, language and authoritative voices soon led to one of our ministries, soon to the position of project manager and project reporter. In this respect, the Climate Crisis Session is the session in the collection that bears the strongest evidence that the project and task-adequate role taking, the language suit and the meaningful text pieces work, and precisely for this reason suffers a 100% loss of credibility when the fraud is discovered.

In that case, neither KB nor the analyst can intervene. But the researcher and the book's author can and must. She does that too, the session's Chat contributions are disqualified, they will not go further. However, that is not right. They are already in circulation, as individual or combined GAI-generated texts and documents that are similar.

On this basis, I can and will take responsibility for 'everything' that concerns my research aims, KB/Chat collections as data and subsequent analyses. But for good reasons I cannot take responsibility for what is in circulation of texts and documents that are similar.

After this summary of the conflict, it is necessary to resume the discussion about what one's own responsibility for AI involvement consists of and how the reference to good academic practice is thought to be effective. If the set of rules that came out during 2024 is followed, the appeal for a critical approach to the GAI tools is clear. The institutions behind the set of rules are also aware that they/we must move away from cheating and towards good academic practice. But in the midst of the practical consequences that must apply to us all, the responsibility for interpreting what is up and down about AI, cheating and science seems to be shifted to the students. Let me therefore use the book's final chapter to take stock of the transfer of responsibility that moves between appeals directed to institutions and researchers and regulations and demands directed to students.

Chapter 13
Status Spring 2025: Who Takes Responsibility?

This chapter takes stock of the question of responsibility that has followed the book's examples and analyses from the very beginning. The question of responsibility, which revolves around ChatGPT/Chat's authorless text universe, has been posed openly and exploratively, but also concretely confrontingly. The more concrete it is, the more conflicts it provokes, the tendency seems to be. The ways in which Chat asserts its own abilities, attributes/disclaims responsibility for its own proposals, embeds authoritative voices, makes normative turns and, most recently, genre plagiarisms, call not only for the question of responsibility, but for questions of trust and credibility. And the questions must be answered concretely. Can we trust ChatGPT/Chat as a text producer, can we believe the texts?

In 2025, the combined question of responsibility, trust and credibility is obviously not only posed to Chat/ChatGPT, but to the entire range of GAI technologies. And even though I, as before, take a concrete confrontational approach, I do not decide either the location of responsibility or the question of credibility and trust in the GAI tools. The institutions, on the other hand, do. Let me therefore start the concrete status with an analytical update.

During the first tests and clarifications (See Chaps. 2 and 3), it was found that whatever ChatGPT does to us and the world, it is done with words and text. The focal point of the analyses and the question of responsibility, ChatGPT as a text producer, was thus in focus. What is thought-provoking is that in the institutional perspective there is a shift in both focus and responsibility. Thus, the important findings focus on the fact that the person using the GAI tool is responsible—and this regardless of what a chatbot does with words and text in the academic world.

That researchers, teachers and students, as academic users, are given an 'own responsibility' is to be expected. But the consequence of the shift in responsibility may be surprising. The GAI tool and ChatGPT as a text producer are held free from liability. In addition, the issue of trust and credibility slips out of sight. And the party that must take a position now seems to have shifted to the students. As it is formulated in the regulations in 2025 addressed directly to the individual student: 'It is

K. Borgnakke, *AI and ChatGPT Technology in Education*, Education, Equity, Economy 12, https://doi.org/10.1007/978-3-032-01419-1_13

your own choice whether you want to use GAI in projects and theses, but when you use GAI, you must be critical …'

With the free choice and critical approach transferred to the students, GAI is kept free from the issue of liability. At the same time, the institutions behind the regulations seem to be free from the issue of trust and credibility. That is transferred to the students.

The same trend is seen if the starting point is taken from what the EU-level reports and the national institutional levels have in common, namely the anchoring of the issue of liability in 'good academic practice'.[1] From the universities' side, this starting point is characterized by yet another appeal addressed to the public, namely that 'we must move away from cheating and towards good academic practice'. But even though, as a practical consequence, this applies to all of us, the responsibility for interpreting what is up and down regarding AI, cheating and science was shifted to the students!

These shifts of responsibility are the critical pivot of the analysis and the conflict. It is in a basic sense difficult to assess what is up and down regarding AI and science and it is not fair to shift the burden of interpretation to the students.

But since this is how the regulations are, spring 2025, the conflict can be summarized as a contrast between appeals that were addressed to the institutions, to the researchers and ended up as regulations and guidelines for the students.

13.1 The Appeal to the Institutions: Away from Cheating and Towards Good Academic Practice

During 2024, the universities, one by one, without officially presented justifications or common regulations, made the forbidden permitted. The University of Copenhagen is waiting a little longer, but expects to make a U-turn. This was announced by Rie Snekkerup, Director of Education, in UniAvisen as follows:

> Until now, the rule has been that AI is basically prohibited from being used in exams, unless otherwise explicitly stated. But from next year, the rule will turn 180 degrees, so that the use of AI is basically always allowed, unless otherwise explicitly stated. (UniAvisen, 25.10.2024, Snekkerup).

This U-turn is formulated in the article's headline as 'Turnarounds' and is also referred to going forward as the fact that in 2025, the University of Copenhagen 'will turn the rules upside down'.

At the Technical University of Denmark, DTU, they have been more direct in their expression since May 2024, namely with the following announcement in a Fact box:

[1] See the EU document and report: *Living Guidelines on the Responsible use of Generative AI in Research*, ERA Forum Stakeholders document, march 2024, and the interplay with documents from DK Ministry-appointed commissions (2023–2024).

> **AI at DTU**
>
> Points of attention for students on the use of AI
>
> It must be clearly stated if something in a submission is not your own product. If you do not do this, it is considered exam cheating, cf. DTU's code of honor, rules for good academic practice and exam cheating. (DTU, website, Fact box, Intro-text)

The crucial thing in the above quotations is not only the rhetorical quirks, like U-turns and 'rules turned upside down', or the noting that DTU is, as usual, rhetorically more hard-hitting. Exam cheating is in absolute minus and DTU's code of honor and rules for good academic practice are in absolute plus. The crucial thing is that the quotes testify to frank messages. At UCPH, the starting point is changed, from initially prohibited, to permitted, unless… At DTU, the student has a duty to provide information; failure to do so is 'exam cheating'. This kind of frankness is also seen at other universities. However, if you look at the formulated sets of rules together and word for word, they reflect an institutional confusion rather than frankness.

The official messages also reflect a joint effort to shift the argument away from exams, cheating and closer to the use of AI in academic study practice. Hereby closer to clarifying the students' own responsibility in interaction with rules for good academic practice. But what is not clarified at the same pace, and still remains unclear, is the AI technology in academic use. The AI technology is just unspecified in the new messages—unfounded. Or in the rules as 'something'.

As quoted above, the DTU student must clearly state, "if something in a submission is not your own product". What is 'something' more specifically? And if the DTU student has used a type of AI as computing power and ChatGPT as a writing assistant for the written report, 50/50, then just state and take responsibility?

It is understandable that DTU considers AI as a collective term. But when you think about the strong arguments from the public debate, where DTU students did not have to learn 'academic writing', it is not without interest to clarify what possible separate role the chatbot and thus the generative text producer is intended to play. Although the answer would be of relevance to others than DTU students, it can be said that the clarification primarily belongs at DTU and the related departments and professional environments. Furthermore, the general reference to AI technologies and lack of specifications that characterize the official announcements in 2024 are highlighted by Studypedia's 2025 version. The entry 'Learning technologies' has thus made a specified review of AI and GAI tools available.

But there is still a question about AI in academic use, namely a basic question that concerns us all, but has not yet been raised. This is not least about the institutions' trust in the academic competence of GAI tools. Here, the reference to 'good academic practice' finds its background and support in the rules that will be presented in the EU and DK universities, respectively, during the spring of 2024 as an official overall framework for research institutions' handling of AI/GAI tools.[2]

[2] The sets of rules, and proposals for them, are integrated into the EU-document, "Living Guidelines", 2024, and work in conjunction with those presented on the Danish universities' websites during 2024.

Through the anchoring of the EU report, called "Living Guidelines", in particular, both the rules and the appeal are then condensed by going directly to the researchers and their i.e. science's good practice.

13.2 The Appeal to Researchers: 'Remain Ultimately Responsible for Scientific Output'

The EU report relates to the entire spectrum of artificial intelligence and does not (quite deliberately) relate to individual technologies, let alone products. The report is characterized by confidence that AI technologies, although rapidly developing, function 'as intended'. The confidence is not justified, but is felt as a sounding board and technology positive basic attitude towards the AI tools, as they are consistently mentioned. With confidence in their usefulness, the right/wrong use is at the center of the guidelines. In the report, the guidelines are called 'a code of conduct' or simply the rules of the road, which are Reliability, Honesty, Respect, Responsibility. At the same time, we are approaching a profession-oriented moral code, clarified in the mention of the responsibility of researchers, the first point of which is quoted below.

1. **Remain ultimately responsible for scientific output.**
   - Researchers are accountable for the integrity of the content generated by or with the support of AI tools.
   - Researchers maintain a critical approach to using the output produced by generative AI and are aware of the tools' limitations, such as bias, hallucinations and inaccuracies.
   - AI systems are neither authors nor co-authors. Authorship implies agency and responsibility, so it lies with human researchers.
   - Researchers do not use fabricated material created by generative AI in the scientific process, for example by falsifying, altering or manipulating original research data. (EU, Living Guidelines, 2024, p. 6)

We are close to the moment of action. The EU report formulates itself completely into the situation. Responsibility has been passed on, researchers have received it and researchers themselves are now the ones responsible. The interesting thing is, however, that even though the proximity to the researchers can be felt, and even though the EU report itself emphasizes that the next step in interpretation/management goes through the national bodies, the report is far from real-life use cases. Furthermore, it is thought-provoking that the report neither distinguishes between the AI technologies nor characterizes the functions and utility values of the respective tools. ChatGPT seems to be referenced in particular in bullet 2, but as emphasized without further characterization.

The lack of characterization of the respective characteristics of the GAI technologies is surprising and testifies to Techno logos as a sounding board. At the same time, there is a noticeable absence of references to the human sciences at the authorizing levels in dealing with the generative AI technology. In the case of the EU report, it is mentioned that they do not address the AI technologies as individual products. But failing to characterize the generative AI/technologies, such as ChatGPT, for the distinct text-generative features and human/machine relationships is not only a sin of omission at the descriptive level, but testifies to a lack of understanding at the politically objective and professional level. The lack of understanding is evident in the committee's unfounded confidence, but also in the individual formulations of guidelines and the professional code, such as the previously cited point 1 on critical approach and responsibility:

> Researchers maintain a critical approach to using output produced by generative AI and are aware of the limitations of the tools, such as bias, hallucinations and inaccuracies. (...)
>
> AI systems are neither authors nor co-authors. Authorship implies agency and responsibility, so it lies with human researchers. (EU, Living Guidelines, 2024, p. 6)

In light of the text and genre, the appeal to be critical is immediately understandable. Similar understandable is that AI systems are not authors. But the guidelines quoted are in practice biased towards the situation and realities. In practice, researchers cannot be content with 'being aware of...'. Nor do 'bias, hallucinations and inaccuracies' appear as 'something' that can be corrected, supplemented or removed by the attentive researcher. And getting the attentive researcher to specifically and precisely point out bias and inaccuracies in, for example, ChatGPT's text processing is possible, but in that case a research project in itself. So, in practice, hardly a possible everyday academic action.

Ironically, the only possible everyday action for the research community's 'human researchers' is to refuse this very tautological designation, as well as to refuse the naturalization of the AI machines that seems to lie behind it. Next, researchers can step into character as academic subject professionals who provide a justification for the use of the AI tool, its capabilities and inherent shortcomings. Stepping into character as professionals, and thus insisting on distinguishing between the humanistic, social and technical/scientific cognitive interests, is, however, in itself a challenge in relation to the EU's overall set of rules. The challenge is made clearer when the related guidelines on displaying the right academic behavior are interpreted within the university context.

But at this point, the point regarding the transfer of responsibility is that, regardless of possible national faculty or subject-specific nuances, the responsibility is transferred fully and completely to the researchers/research community. The same applies when the responsibility is transferred to the students. This applies with the transfer 'fully and completely', but it is as if the responsibility becomes both more concrete and heavier to bear.

Against this background, the status in spring 2025 is that under Danish auspices, all research and university institutions have faculty-coordinated, but still common, emphases and appeals that emphasize that

> * A critical approach to the use of generative AI requires increased attention to limitations, such as bias, hallucinations and inaccuracies
>
> * The agency and responsibility of authorship lies with the researcher/author(s) of the scientific work

When the formulated responsibility is transferred to the students, the responsibility becomes clearer, precisely because it is concretely linked, for example, to thesis and PhD-level theses and final projects. This makes the responsibility concrete in a practical sense, but also heavy to bear. The generation of here-and-now GAI users must, as a consequence, be the first to show how a critical approach to GAI, e.g. a ChatGPT or Copilot, looks like—at thesis level, or in the project group's final report. And the PhD students are not only responsible for a thesis, but must demonstrate in research-relevant terms, in which the bias, hallucinations and inaccuracies of the GAI tool specifically consist. The difficulty of the task is only increased by the fact that it must be nuanced depending on whether the GAI tool is to be seen from the perspective of engineering and natural sciences or from the perspective of social sciences and humanities.

Against the outlined background, the students are left in a dilemma. The advisory bodies, such as Studiepedia, help to deal with the dilemma, but also cover up the extent and unreasonableness of the liability problem. Let me therefore show the general problems, but exemplify the advice provided by Roskilde University (RUC), which as a project-organized educational institution refers to projects at all academic levels.

13.3 Good Academic Practice at Project and Thesis Level

Under the post *AI at RUC—good academic practice with AI*, which is part of the University Library website, there are 6 soberly informative points. Several points have links, for example, to academically professionally edited websites about science. Below, I start with the basic scientific questions, as cited, for the same reason:

> Good AI Practice
>
> You must use generative AI carefully, critically and reflectively. Consider these pitfalls, among others:
>
> **Incorrect information**: A chatbot such as ChatGPT or Bing/Copilot is a language model that finds probable answers to your prompts and questions, but they are not always true. Some information may also be outdated. It is unclear where ChatGPT gets its information from. (the Library, RUC website, AI at RUC)

If we take the basic question first, the relevant passage in the context is the sober information that the chatbot finds 'probable answers', but they are 'not always true'.

The academic standard for reflection on such a statement can refer to the thesis at candidate and PhD level, but also to the implied supervisor/evaluator levels. In that case, the start can be to state that if chatbot answers are not always true, then examples must be given of where/when they are true. The reflection can start, are they true in 20%, 50% or 80% of the cases? The question/answer immediately gets stuck. I offer my opinion and claim that the 'true/false' scaling in scientific contexts cannot be bent. And if I were to answer on the basis of this book's analyses and underlying materials, it would have to be: Chat never speaks/writes the truth. Chat does not know the difference between true and false. I do not have a single example that could justify a true/false scaling.

If we approach the language use true/false in a more everyday way and include 'outdated information/newer information' and also include the academic genres of professional environments, the tone and level of argumentation can be changed. For example: For research purposes, I have conducted studies and analyses consistently using ChatGPT's 3.5, knowing that e.g. ChatGPT4 and Copilot could be the updated 'handling new information' version. However, while I may update experience with GAI tools related to the latest model/latest news, this in itself has nothing to do with science, research or determining true/false.

I will stop the exemplification here with my critical comment. It is unreasonable to put the students in front of the fall group's 'beware of…' because a chatbot is 'not always true'. The students have no chance of determining the beware-degree. And even if I offer and stand firm, it is unreasonable to place the question at a supervisor, individual project or individual researcher level. The problem AI/chatbot—true/false is basic and important, but it must be placed correctly in academic and scientific theoretical time and space. Otherwise it is irrelevant. Therefore, the only reasonable thing to do is to let the faculty's researchers answer.

If the medical faculty/cancer researchers currently claim and justify that GAI Pattern recall skills enriches with new precision, then it is a possible start to an answer that the medical faculty must complete; if physicists, economists, engineers believe that… etc. In that regard, I am happy to participate with suggestions on behalf of the humanities and myself. But that doesn't change the fact that in the context it is unreasonable to place the responsibility for the position on AI/chatbot, true/false to x-number of degrees, on the students. The institutions and faculties should have taken responsibility long ago.

Above I allowed a soberly formulated pitfalls to be an occasion requiring reflection. Below is the overall appeal to 'be critical' the occasion. In RUC's official guidelines, the section "Critical use of generative AI" corresponds to the appeal, but the formulations under the points also sound like requirements. Below is the starting sequence, numbered 1–4 by me, for the sake of subsequent commentary.

> *Critical use of generative AI*
>
> (1) You must approach the answer you get from GAI critically in the same way as you do with other scientific articles and sources. (2) GAI responds by paraphrasing a large amount of text, and it is important to evaluate and assess the texts and search for the primary literature sources that are the basis for the GAI answer. (3) GAI can produce text that seems convincing, but which can also be wrong, incomplete or based on prejudiced views, (4) which you must approach critically. (RUC, Guidelines, 11.1.2024, author's numbering)

As can be seen, RUC's guidelines are formulated closely to GAI as a text producer and thus more specifically targeted in the requirements. I can then maintain the same level of concretization in my comments. The appeal's intention to approach critically is an understandable starting point. But at the same time, with comments on (1–2) it is hardly possible to approach ChatGPT texts as to all other texts. A ChatGPT text is a new distinct text—a data-generated text, the likes of which we have never seen before. My Chat texts are also source less and represent a source less text universe in general. Therefore, it is impossible to systematically search for the sources behind the GAI response. For example, I found sources through genre plagiarisms, but I cannot determine the source with accuracy. But even if my points problematize the source-critical task, I confirm both the intention and the necessity. However, the comment on (3) the formulation 'prejudiced views', if it corresponds to the bias problem, is that scientifically it is of the same weight as the true/false question. For the same reason, it is unreasonable to burden students with responsibility and critical stance on a question that is so heavy that it should have long been the responsibility of IT expertise and AI research's own departments. In my view, with the bias issue and the underlying problems that come with it, we have come so close to a common core issue that concerns the GAI/chatbot technology and tool that appeals and demands for a critical approach must not only be reasonably but necessarily made to the universities, research institutions and 'us as researchers' before it is made to the students. Let me therefore conclude by drawing attention to the common core issues that make the criticism necessary.

13.4 The Common Core Issues that Make the Criticism Necessary

We still lack an officially recognized and research-based proposal for how the risk of 'bias, hallucinations and inaccuracies' should be understood and handled in relation to GAI/text-generating tools. But the fact that the triad of risk has become the time-honored one, and that IT expertise and the institutions' advice are behind it, makes it a common starting point. I accept that, but at the same time I start the criticism on my own behalf and on behalf of this book with the triad.

In relation to my collection of ChatGPT texts, 'inaccuracies' is not a suitable term for a risk. My Chat texts are not exact and inaccuracy in content seems to be a basic condition. The Chat texts are most often grammatically correct, the language suit, language blocks and the argumentative flow make sense. But at the same time, lack of precision is the rule rather than the exception. Structurally, accuracy/inaccuracy can be an issue. Chat is genre-strong, a template producer and rarely gets the number sequence wrong! On the other hand, one must be careful with that kind of accuracy. My comments on 'hallucinations' follow the same path. It is a metaphor and that in itself should make it unsuitable as a term for a risk. But even if one understands and follows the term associatively, it is still unsuitable. I have no examples of Chat hallucinating, and where the Chat text and the argumentative flow are going off on a tangent, it is saved by the strength of the genre. This leads to the difficult question of 'bias'.

I have followed Chat as a text producer and insisted on the position: whatever Chat may claim to be or do, it is done with words and text. Perhaps this is why the close analyses, rather than text collections, are more suitable for illuminating the bias problem. And perhaps the specific examples should be taken extra seriously because I see the bias problem as a consequence of the programming *in* the text. Here, the Chat text's collapse and loss of meaning, normative turns and over-structuring are particularly serious. But beyond that, my most important comment on the problem concerns the triad itself.

The problem is that the triad 'bias, hallucinations and inaccuracies' is itself biased. It is fostered in Techno logos and based on the fact that accuracies/inaccuracies, hallucinations and bias are identifiable quantities in a technical and scientific sense. Fair enough that the triad exists in these sciences and professional environments. But it is neither fair nor reasonable that researchers and students from the humanities and social sciences should be confronted with an official set of rules and triads, where two out of three code words suffer from a lack of precision and the triad as a whole is itself biased. And it is ironic that the set of rules, after unclear formulations linked to groups of students to be critical of, turns into clear language if the set of rules is not followed. Here, as previously quoted from DTU's set of rules, it says that in case of violations 'you risk committing exam cheating', you will receive 'a disciplinary case against you', 'warning, exam suspension or expulsion'. (RUC, Guidelines, 11.1.2024).

If the triad suffers from a lack of precision, it will have consequences both when the source and bias-critical task is attempted (but made difficult) or omitted (and becomes a critical shortcoming).

But in that case, the implementation of GAI tools in the academic world is also the currently important example of how the reference that 'everyone' wants to follow, namely good academic practice, can only function if it, together with criticism, is anchored in the academic professional environments. This means that technology criticism must find its corresponding subject-professional critical positions. It also means that institutions must provide space and room for the development of the critical approach that is officially required of students. And finally, it means that institutions must take a position on questions about trust in GAI/technologies as a learning tool.

Two years of debate, in which both fear and excitement have left their mark, however, require that institutions rethink the trust issue and allow themselves to be challenged. Not only for the development of good academic practice, but good educational practice. And here both academic and educational practice can be considered as a living relationship between language, culture and society. The cultural challenges that the use of GAI/learning tools in research and educational environments represents are of a magnitude that is only matched by the institutions if a critical pro-and-contra debate is held among those involved. Here, neither the new regulations nor decrees from above are close enough to practice. But it is the living public if the institutions take (co-)responsibility for keeping the critical public alive.

Springer Proceedings in Business and Economics

More information about this series at http://www.springer.com/series/11960

Nenad Mladenović · Angelo Sifaleras ·
Marija Kuzmanović
Editors

Advances in Operational Research in the Balkans

XIII Balkan Conference on Operational Research

Springer

Editors
Nenad Mladenović
Department of Industrial Engineering
Khalifa University
Abu Dhabi, UAE

Angelo Sifaleras
Department of Applied Informatics
University of Macedonia
Thessaloniki, Greece

Marija Kuzmanović
Faculty of Organizational Sciences
University of Belgrade
Belgrade, Serbia

ISSN 2198-7246 ISSN 2198-7254 (electronic)
Springer Proceedings in Business and Economics
ISBN 978-3-030-21989-5 ISBN 978-3-030-21990-1 (eBook)
https://doi.org/10.1007/978-3-030-21990-1

This Springer imprint is published by the registered company Springer Nature Switzerland AG
The registered company address is: Gewerbestrasse 11, 6330 Cham, Switzerland

Organization

Editors

Nenad Mladenović, Khalifa University, UAE
Angelo Sifaleras, University of Macedonia, Greece
Marija Kuzmanović, University of Belgrade, Serbia

Scientific Committee

Zoran Babic, University of Split, Croatia
Taner Bilgiç, Bogaziçi University, Turkey
Sally Brailsford, University of Southampton, United Kingdom
Mirjana Cangalovic, University of Belgrade, Serbia
Tatjana Davidovic, Mathematical Institute, Serbia
Marc Demange, ESSEC Business School in Paris, France
Abraham Duarte, Universidad Rey Juan Carlos, Spain
Ioan Dzitac, Aurel Vlaicu University of Arad, Romania
Jose Rui Figueira, Technical University of Lisbon, Portugal
Haris Gavranovic, International University of Sarajevo, Bosnia and Hercegovina
Andreas Georgiou, University of Macedonia, Greece
Alan Hertz, GERAD—Ecole des HEC, Canada
Marius Iosifescu, Romanian Academy, Romania
Cem Iyigun, Middle East Technical University, Turkey
Milojica Jacimovic, Faculty of Sciences and Mathematics, Montenegro
Maksat Kalimoldaev, Institute of Problems of Information and Control, Kazakhstan
Vera Kovacevic-Vujcic, University of Belgrade, Serbia
Jozef Kratica, Mathematical Institute, Serbia
Martine Labbé, Université Libre de Bruxelles, Belgium
Zohar Laslo, SCE—Shamoon College of Engineering, Israel

Honorary Scientific Committee

Slobodan Guberinic, University of Belgrade, Serbia
Basil Manos, Aristotle University of Thessaloniki, Greece
Slobodan Krcevinac, University of Belgrade, Serbia
Byron Papathanasiou, Aristotle University of Thessaloniki, Greece
Sotirios Papachristos, University of Ioannina, Greece
Radivoj Petrovic, University of Belgrade, Serbia
Dragos Cvetkovic, Serbian Academy of Sciences and Arts, Serbia
Gradimir Milovanovic, Serbian Academy of Sciences and Arts, Serbia
Constantin Tsouros, Aristotle University of Thessaloniki, Greece

Organizing Committee

Gordana Savic, University of Belgrade, Serbia
Marija Kuzmanović, University of Belgrade, Serbia
Dragana Makajic-Nikolic, University of Belgrade, Serbia
Bogdana Stanojeviç, Mathematical Institute, Serbia
Nebojsa Nikolic, University of Belgrade, Serbia
Biljana Panic, University of Belgrade, Serbia
Milos Nikolic, University of Belgrade, Serbia
Gordana Nastic, Mathematical Institute, Serbia
Milena Popovic, University of Belgrade, Serbia
Minja Marinovic, University of Belgrade, Serbia
Bisera Andric-Gusavac, University of Belgrade, Serbia
Dusan Dzamic, University of Belgrade, Serbia

Preface

This book is a monograph from submissions from the *XIII Balkan Conference on Operational Research* "OR in Balkans—Recent Advances" (BALCOR 2018) held in Belgrade, Serbia during May 25–28, 2018.

This year, we have received more than 166 contributions of 249 authors from 37 countries. After rigorous review process, 17 high-quality papers are included in this monograph. Selected papers refer to theory and application of operational research. Theoretical papers address the problems of multi-objective optimization, pattern recognition, and reliability improvement. Application papers are related to variety of fields: health care, tourism, forest policy, inventory, project management, ecology, and ICT management. The book is divided into four main parts:

Part I: Combinatorial Optimization & Heuristics

Part II: Multicriteria Decision Analysis & Multi-objective Optimization

Part III: Performance Measurement & Data Envelopment Analysis

Part IV: Business Applications

The organizers of the conference are: The Mathematical Institute of the Serbian Academy of Sciences and Arts (SANU), University of Belgrade: Faculty of Organizational Sciences, Faculty of Transport and Traffic Engineering, Yugoslav Society for Applied and Industrial Mathematics (JUPIM), and Society of Operations Researchers of Serbia (DOPIS), Belgrade, Serbia. We appreciate the support of the Ministry of Education, Science and Technological Development of the Republic of Serbia and EURO—The Association of European Operational Research Societies.

We wish to express our heartfelt appreciation to the Editorial Committee, reviewers, and our students. We appreciate all the authors and participants for their contributions that, made this conference and monograph possible. Finally, we thank the publisher, Springer.

Abu Dhabi, UAE	Nenad Mladenović
Thessaloniki, Greece	Angelo Sifaleras
Belgrade, Serbia	Marija Kuzmanović
February 2019	

Contents

Combinatorial Optimization & Heuristics

Dichotomy Algorithms in the Multi-class Problem of Pattern Recognition

Damir N. Gainanov, Nenad Mladenović and Berenov Dmitriy

Abstract Pattern recognition problem in geometric state with solutions in the class of decision trees is discussed. In each node, the partition of the corresponding subsample of objects is performed using a linear function (hyperplane). In this paper, for the node of the decision tree we state the problem of the dichotomy of a set of classes into 2 subsets of classes for 2 different definitions of the distance function between such subsets. This problem is considered in relation to the projection of the initial sample on the direction connecting 2 most remote points. For any 2 variants of the partition of a set of classes, the concept of closeness is introduced on the basis of the distance between the corresponding binary tuples. For 4 different algorithms for partition of a set of classes, computational experiments are conducted for a series of 100 random sets. The results of computational experiments and the complexity of these algorithms are presented.

Keywords Pattern recognition · Algorithm · Partition function · Hamming distance

1 Introduction

In Gainanov and Berenov (2017), the multi-class problem of pattern recognition has been applied in the problem of managing of technological routes on discrete metallurgical production. In the general case, when it is needed to partition a training

D. N. Gainanov (✉) · B. Dmitriy
Ural Federal University, Ekaterinburg, Russia
e-mail: damir.gainanov@gmail.com

B. Dmitriy
e-mail: berenov@dc.ru

N. Mladenović
Department of Industrial Engineering, Khalifa University,
Abu Dhabi, UAE
e-mail: nenadmladenovic12@gmail.com

N. Mladenović et al. (eds.), *Advances in Operational Research in the Balkans*,
Springer Proceedings in Business and Economics,
https://doi.org/10.1007/978-3-030-21990-1_1

sample into two classes, the method of committees first developed in Mazurov (1990) turns out to be effective. In Mazurov and Khachai (2004), Khachai (1997) this method was transformed into an independent area of research. In Gainanov (1992), following the results obtained in Gainanov and Matveev (1991), an additional criterion for the minimality of the committee was developed.

In Gainanov (2014, 2016) we give a comprehensive review of the theory of analysis of infeasible systems, including an application in the problem of pattern recognition in a geometric formulation.

In this article, new effective dichotomy algorithms are being developed to solve the multi-class problem of pattern recognition. The basic idea of this new approach consists in constructing a logical decision tree in such a way that each of leaves of this logical tree can be uniquely assigned to a certain class of the training sample.

Let a set of n-dimensional vectors is given

$$A = \left\{a_i = \left(a_{i_1}, a_{i_2}, \ldots, a_{i_n}\right) : i = [1, N]\right\} ,$$

and its partition into m classes

$$A = A_1 \cup A_2 \cup \ldots \cup A_m .$$

It is required to construct a decision rule for assigning the vector a_i to one of the classes. The solution will be sought in the class of logical decision trees given by a directed binary tree $\overrightarrow{G} = (V, E)$ with root-node $v_0 \in V$.

The binary tree $\overrightarrow{G} = (V, E)$ defines the process of sequentially partition of the sample A into 2 subsamples at the nodes of degree 2 so that each terminal node v corresponds to a subset $A_v \subseteq A$, which can be assigned to one of the classes $class_v \in [1, m]$. In the case under consideration, linear functions will be used to partition the subsample at each node of the decision tree.

If v is a node of degree 2 in the graph $\overrightarrow{G}$, then a vector n_v and a scalar variable ε_v are given for it, such that A_v is partitioned into 2 subsamples A'_v and A''_v according to the following rule:

$$A'_v = \{a_i \in A_v : \langle n_v, a_i \rangle \leq \varepsilon_v\} ,$$
$$A''_v = \{a_i \in A_v : \langle n_v, a_i \rangle > \varepsilon_v\} ,$$

and for the root-node v_0 we have

$$A_{v_0} = A .$$

It is required to construct the decision tree $\overrightarrow{G} = (V, E)$ with minimal number of nodes, and at each terminal node $v \in V$ we have

$$p(v) = \frac{|\{a_i \in A_v : a_i \in class_v\}|}{|A_v|} \geq p_{\min} , \tag{1}$$

that is, the fraction of vectors belonging to the some class $class_v$ is not less than a given value $p_{\min}$. If $p_{\min} = 1$ then each terminal node corresponds to the vectors of one particular class.

The rule (1) acts if $|A_v| \geq K_{\min}$. If $|A_v| < K_{\min}$ then the process of further partition of the sample A_v does not continue and the node v is declared terminal, and the rule (1) may be not executed. In other words, for $|A_v| < K_{\min}$ the sample A_v is not representative enough for constructing a further decision rule and the fraction $p(v)$ of vectors from this sample belonging to the class $class_v$ can be less than $p_{\min}$.

2 Algorithm for Constructing the Decision Function for the Node

Suppose that we have a node $v \in V$ for which A_v is given. Suppose we have a partition

$$A_v = (A_v \cap A_1) \cup \ldots \ldots \cup (A_v \cap A_m) , \tag{2}$$

in which there are m' non-empty sets. Let's denote by

$$I = \{i : A_v \cap A_i \neq \emptyset , i = [1, m]\} .$$

If $m' = 1$ then the node v is terminal and $p(v) = 1$, if $2 \leq m' \leq m$ then we sequentially calculate the values:

$$p_i(v) = \frac{|A_v \cap A_i|}{|A_v|} , i \in I .$$

If there exists $i_0 \in I$ such that $p_{i_0}(v) > p_{\min}$ then the node v is terminal and the class $class_v = i_0$, if $|A_v| < K_{\min}$ then the node v is terminal and

$$class_v = \arg\max_i \{p_i (v) : i \in I\} .$$

Consider the case

$$\begin{cases} 2 \leq m' \leq m , \\ |A_v| \geq K_{\min} \\ p_i (v) < p_{\min} \ \forall i \in I . \end{cases}$$

Let some vector n_v and a scalar value ε_v are given. Then the node v is associated with 2 nodes v_1 and v_2 that are descendants of the node v in the constructed decision tree such that

$$A_{v_1} = \{a_i \in A_v : \langle n_v, a_i \rangle \leq \varepsilon_v\} \ ,$$
$$A_{v_2} = \{a_i \in A_v : \langle n_v, a_i \rangle > \varepsilon_v\} \ ,$$

Let

$$p\left(A_{v_1}\right) = \left(\frac{\left|A_{v_1} \cap A_1\right|}{|A_1|}, \ \ldots, \ \frac{\left|A_{v_1} \cap A_m\right|}{|A_1|}\right) ,$$
$$p\left(A_{v_2}\right) = \left(\frac{\left|A_{v_2} \cap A_1\right|}{|A_2|}, \ \ldots, \ \frac{\left|A_{v_2} \cap A_m\right|}{|A_2|}\right) .$$

In this case the vector n_v and the value ε_v require the sets $A_{v_1} \neq \emptyset$ and $A_{v_2} \neq \emptyset$.

Consider the following quantity:

$$discrim\,(A_v, n_v, \varepsilon_v) = \sum_{i \in I} \left| \frac{\left|A_{v_1} \cap A_i\right|}{\left|A_{v_1}\right|} - \frac{\left|A_{v_2} \cap A_i\right|}{\left|A_{v_2}\right|} \right| .$$

The quantity $discrim\,(A_v, n_v, \varepsilon_v)$ will be called the partition force of the function

$$f\,(a) = a \cdot n_v - \varepsilon_v$$

with respect to the subsample A_v. The meaning of this notion is that vectors from classes A_i of the training sample are partitioned in the half-space obtained by dividing the space by a hyperplane

$$f\,(a) = a \cdot n_v - \varepsilon_v = 0 \ ,$$

as good as the function $f\,(a)$ partitiones vectors from the training sample into classes. Thus, the state is natural, if it is required to find $n_v \in \mathrm{R}^n$ and $\varepsilon_v \in \mathrm{R}$ for the sample (2) such that the quantity $discrim\,(A_v, n_v, \varepsilon_v)$ reaches its maximum. The naturalness of such state is also confirmed by the fact that for $m = 2$ the best solution is achieved for $discrim\,(A_v, n_v, \varepsilon_v) = 2$, which corresponds to a linear partition into classes $A_v \cap A_1$ and $A_v \cap A_2$ by the hyperplane $f\,(a) = a \cdot n_v - \varepsilon_v = 0$. The problem in this state always has a solution, since $A_{v_1} \neq \emptyset$ and $A_{v_2} \neq \emptyset$ then for each node v its descendants correspond to subsamples of lower power, and when the condition (1) or the condition $|A_v| < K_{\min}$ holds then the node v becomes terminal.

For an arbitrary subset $A' \subseteq A$ we introduce the notation for the center of the subsample

$$C\left(A'\right) = \frac{1}{|A'|} \sum_{i \in A'} \left\{a_i : a_i \in A'\right\} \ ,$$

and

$$A\,(I) = \{a_i : a_i \in A \ , \ i \in I\} \ .$$

Let be given the partition $I = I_1 \cup I_2$, where $I_1 \neq \emptyset$, $I_2 \neq \emptyset$. Consider the interval $[C(A(I_1)), C(A(I_2))] \in R^n$. Let $n(I_1, I_2)$ be the normal vector

$$\frac{C\left(A(I_2)\right) - C\left(A(I_1)\right)}{\left\| C\left(A(I_2)\right) - C\left(A(I_1)\right) \right\|},$$

then we divide the interval $[C(A(I_1)), C(A(I_2))]$ into M parts, where the length of each part is

$$\frac{\left\| C\left(A(I_2)\right) - C\left(A(I_1)\right) \right\|}{M}.$$

We consider $(M - 1)$ partition functions $f_j(a) = a \cdot n_v - \varepsilon_j$, which are passing sequantial through all $(M - 1)$ dividing points of the interval $[C(A(I_1)), C(A(I_2))]$. We will search the best option for the partition force among these functions:

$$j_0 = \arg\max \left\{ discrim\left(A_v, n_v, \varepsilon_j\right),\ j = [1, M - 1] \right\}.$$

It is easy to see that for j_0 we have $A_{v_1} \neq \emptyset$, $A_{v_2} \neq \emptyset$.

We denote by

$$discrim\left(I_1, I_2\right) = discrim\left(A_v, n_v, \varepsilon_{j_0}\right).$$

In the case of $C\left(A(I_1)\right) = C\left(A(I_2)\right)$ any 2 most distant points from the sample A_v are chosen and for the interval which connects these points it is used the same procedure for constructing $(M - 1)$ partition planes and choosing the best of them. In the general case it is assumed that all partitions of the form $I = I_1 \cup I_2$ are searched, and the chosen partition is such that $discrim\left(I_1, I_2\right)$ reaches its maximum. In practical implementation instead of a search a sequential algorithm can be used, in which $I_1 = I$, $I_2 = \emptyset$ is initially assigned. Further among all partitions of the form $I = I_1 \setminus \{i\} \cup I_2 \cup \{i\}$, where $i \in I$, the best is chosen by the criterion $discrim\left(I_1, I_2\right)$ and so on. In the end, the best result is also chosen from the entire row obtained.

The algorithm of decision tree constructing for the node:

1. Let us consider the node v of decision tree with training sample A_v.
2. The node v is declared terminal if there exists a class $i \in [1, m]$ such that $p_i\left(A_v\right) \geq p_{\min}$ or $|A_v| \leq K_{\min}$.
3. We consider all partitions $I = I_1 \cup I_2$.
4. For each partition suppose:

$$C\left(A\left(I_1\right)\right) = \frac{1}{|I_1|} \sum_{i \in I_1} a_i \text{ and } C\left(A\left(I_2\right)\right) = \frac{1}{|I_2|} \sum_{i \in I_2} a_i.$$

5. If the length of the interval $\left[C\left(A\left(I_1\right)\right), C\left(A\left(I_2\right)\right)\right] \neq 0$ then the normal vector $n\left(I_1, I_2\right)$ is constructed and the value $\varepsilon\left(I_1, I_2\right)$ is choosen so that $discrim\left(A_v, n\left(I_1, I_2\right), \varepsilon\left(I_1, I_2\right)\right)$ is maximal (search through all hyperplanes

perpendicular to $n(I_1, I_2)$ and bypassing $[C(A(I_1)), C(A(I_2))]$ for M steps from the point $C(A(I_1))$ to the point $C(A(I_2))$).

6. Among all partitions $I = I_1 \cup I_2$ we will choose the partition with maximal $discrim(A_v, n(I_1, I_2), \varepsilon(I_1, I_2))$ and with corresponding vector $n(I_1, I_2)$ and value $\varepsilon(I_1, I_2)$ found in item 5.

The process is finite since some partition takes place at each step.

Consider the partition $I = I_1 \cup I_2$ and denote by

$$a(I_1, I_2) = \sum_{i\in I_1}\sum_{j\in I_2}\left\{(a_s - a_t) : a_s \in A_v \cap A_i\ ,\ a_t \in A_v \cap A_j\right\}\ .$$

The most practically effective seems the algorithm for partition the sample A_v in the node v which chooses the partition $I = I_1 \cup I_2$, for which $\|a(I_1, I_2)\|$ is maximal among all partitions $I = I_1 \cup I_2$. Then the choice of the vector $n(I_1, I_2)$ and the scalar value $\varepsilon(I_1, I_2)$ can be made according to the procedure described above for the obtained fixed partition $I = I_1 \cup I_2$.

We introduce the notation:

$$a_{ij} = \sum_{i\in[1,m]}\sum_{j\in[1,m]}\left\{(a_s - a_t) : a_s \in A_i\ ,\ a_t \in A_j\right\}\ ,$$

then for $I = I_1 \cup I_2$ we have

$$a(I_1, I_2) = \sum_{i\in I_1}\sum_{j\in I_2} a_{ij}\ . \tag{3}$$

Proceeding from the relation (3) it is possible to significantly reduce the amount of computation when choice of the optimal partition $I = I_1 \cup I_2$ for the sample A_v is performed using the previously calculated values a_{ij} $\forall\, i, j \in I$.

3 The Problem of Optimal Partition of a Set of Classes

We consider the problem of finding the partition $I = I_1 \cup I_2$ that delivers the maximum of the function $\|a(I_1, I_2)\|$.

We denote by K_i the number of points in the set $\{a_s : a_s \in A_i\}$, that is,

$$K_i = |\{a_s : a_s \in A_i\}|\ .$$

It is easy to see that

$$a_{ij} = \sum_{i \in I_1} \sum_{j \in I_2} \left\{ (a_s - a_t) : a_s \in A_i \ , \ a_t \in A_j \right\} = \sum_{\substack{a_s \in A_i \\ i \in I_1}} \left(K_j \cdot a_s - \sum_{\substack{a_t \in A_j \\ j \in I_2}} a_t \right) =$$

$$= K_j \cdot \sum_{\substack{a_s \in A_i \\ i \in I_1}} a_s - K_i \cdot \sum_{\substack{a_t \in A_j \\ j \in I_2}} a_t = K_i \cdot K_j \cdot \left(C\left(A_i\right) - C\left(A_j\right)\right) .$$

Thus, the problem reduces to the following.

For a given set of points $A \subset \mathrm{R}^n$ and its partition $A = A_1 \cup A_2 \cup \cdots \cup A_m$ it is required to find the partition $I = I_1 \cup I_2$, where $I = [1, m]$, such that the function

$$\|a\left(I_1, I_2\right)\| = \left\| \sum_{i \in I_1} \sum_{j \in I_2} K_i \cdot K_j \cdot \left(C\left(A_i\right) - C\left(A_j\right)\right) \right\|$$

reaches the maximal value among all possible partitions $I = I_1 \cup I_2$. Obviously, the problem obtained has a much smaller dimension than in the initial state.

Since in the state mentioned above only centers of the subsets $A_i, i \in [1, m]$ participate, then we will further simplify the formulation of the problem.

Suppose that are given a finite set of points $C = \{c_i : i = [1, m]\}$ (which serve as an analogue of the centers of the subsets in previous state) and a set of natural numbers $n_i, i \in [1, m]$, (which serve as an analogue of the number of points in the subsets $A_i, i \in [1, m]$ in the previous state). Then the state of the problem takes the form:

$$\begin{cases} \left| \sum_{i \in I_1} \sum_{j \in I_2} n_i \cdot n_j \cdot \left(c_i - c_j\right) \right| \longrightarrow \max , \\ I = I_1 \ \cup \ I_2 . \end{cases} \tag{4}$$

The following particular cases of the problem (4) are also of interest. Let $n_i = n \ \forall \ i \in [1, m]$. Then the state of the problem takes the form:

$$\begin{cases} \left| \sum_{i \in I_1} \sum_{j \in I_2} n_i \cdot n_j \cdot \left(c_i - c_j\right) \right| = n^2 \cdot \left| \sum_{i \in I_1} \sum_{j \in I_2} \left(c_i - c_j\right) \right| \longrightarrow \max , \\ I = I_1 \ \cup \ I_2 . \end{cases} \tag{5}$$

The next simplification is to consider the case $n_i = 1 \ \forall \ i \in [1, m]$. Then the state of the problem takes the form:

$$\begin{cases} |I_2| \cdot \sum_{i \in I_1} c_i - |I_1| \cdot \sum_{i \in I_2} c_i \longrightarrow \max , \\ I = I_1 \ \cup \ I_2 . \end{cases} \tag{6}$$

We will consider the problem (6) in the following state:

$$\begin{cases} |I_2| \cdot |I_1| \frac{\sum\limits_{i \in I_1} c_i}{|I_1|} - |I_1| \cdot |I_2| \cdot \frac{\sum\limits_{i \in I_2} c_i}{|I_2|} = |I_1| \cdot |I_2| \cdot \left(\frac{1}{|I_1|} \cdot \sum\limits_{i \in I_1} c_i - \frac{1}{|I_2|} \cdot \sum\limits_{i \in I_2} c_i \right) \longrightarrow \max , \\ I = I_1 \cup I_2 . \end{cases}$$

Finally, the problem of the species under discussion has a good geometric interpretation in the following state:

Let

$$C(I') = \frac{1}{|I'|} \cdot \sum_{i \in I'} c_i \ \forall \ I' \subset I = [1, m] .$$

$$\begin{cases} \| C(I_1) - C(I_2) \| \longrightarrow \max , \\ I = I_1 \cup I_2 . \end{cases} \tag{7}$$

Let us consider in detail the problem (7). We use the standard notation conv A for the convex hull of the set A. For the set of points A it is obvious that

$$C(I_1) \in \text{conv } A ,$$
$$C(I_2) \in \text{conv } A ,$$

and, consequently,

$$[C(I_1), C(I_2)] \in \text{conv } A .$$

Theorem 1 *Let a finite set $C = \{c_i, i \in [1, m]\} \subset \mathrm{R}^n$ be given. Let $c_{i_1}, c_{i_2} \in C$ be 2 vectors such that*

$$\|c_{i_1} - c_{i_2}\| = \max_{i,j \in I \,:\, i \neq j} \|c_i - c_j\| .$$

Then, if $I_1 \cup I_2 = I$ is the optimal solution of the problem (7), *then*

$$\|C(I_1) - C(\dot{I}_2)\| \leq \|c_{i_1} - c_{i_2}\| . \tag{8}$$

Proof Let us prove that under the conditions of this statement the quantity $\|c_{i_1} - c_{i_2}\|$ is the diameter of the set A, that is

$$\|c_{i_1} - c_{i_2}\| = \max_{a,b \in \text{conv } A} \rho(a, b) ,$$

where $\rho(a, b)$ is the Euclidean distance between the points a, b in the space R^n.

Assume the contrary, that is, for some pair of points $a, b \in$ conv C, such that $[a, b]$ is the diameter of the conv C, although one of these points is not extreme. For definiteness, let $b \notin$ vert (conv C), where by the vert $(\cdot)$ are denoted the extreme points of the conv C.

Consider the interval $[a, b]$. Since b is not an extreme point, there is a segment $[c, d]$ for which the point b is interior and $[c, d] \subset \text{conv } A$. Then we obtain a triangle with vertices a, c, d in which b is an interior point of the interval $[c, d]$. All sides of this triangle lie in the set conv A.

It is easy to see that in this case one of the inequalities holds: $\rho(a, c) > \rho(a, b)$ or $\rho(a, d) > \rho(a, b)$ in contradiction with the maximality of $\rho(a, b)$.

Thus, the points c_{i_1}, c_{i_2} lie on the ends of some diameter of the set conv C and, since $C(I_1) \in \text{conv } A$ and $C(I_2) \in \text{conv } A$, then $[C(I_1), C(I_2)] \subset \text{conv } A$ and, therefore, the inequality (8) holds.

4 Algorithms for Partition of a Set of Classes

From the previous sections of the article it follows that in the proposed approach to constructing a decision tree, the most difficult problem is to divide the set of classes into 2 subsets of classes with the goal of constructing a partition function at some node of the decision tree.

In the general case, after simplifications made, there were considered several states of the problem of the partition of the initial set of classes $I = [1, m]$ into 2 subsets $I = I_1 \cup I_2$. The main idea of the approach proposed is based on the analysis of the mutual arrangement of points from $C = \{c_i, i = [1, m]\}$ which are representing the centers of classes A_i of the initial sample $A = A_1 \cup A_2 \cup \cdots \cup A_m$. In all cases, real functions $f(I_1, I_2)$ are defined for subsets I_1, I_2 and the problem of finding of the partition $I = I_1 \cup I_2$ for which the function $f(I_1, I_2)$ reaches the maximal value.

We list the types of functions $f(I_1, I_2)$ considered above.

$$f_1(I_1, I_2) = |I_1| \cdot |I_2| \cdot \|C(I_1) - C(I_2)\| , \tag{9}$$

$$f_2(I_1, I_2) = \|C(I_1) - C(I_2)\| , \tag{10}$$

Let there be given a vector p in the space R^n.

We denote by

$$p(c_i) = \frac{\langle c_i, p_i \rangle}{\|p_i\|} , \quad i = [1, m] ,$$

and

$$P(C) = \{p(c_i), i = [1, m]\} .$$

Then we can define for the cases of (9)–(10) their “one-dimensional” analogies for the direction given by the vector p.

An interesting case is when $p = a - b$ where $a, b \in C$ are 2 vectors from the set C such that

$$\rho(a, b) = \max_{i,j=[1,m]} \rho(c_i, c_j) .$$

The algorithm $\mathscr{A}(f_1)$ ($\mathscr{A}(f_2)$) is an algorithm for a complete search of all 2^m partitions of the set C on 2 subsets using the function f_1 from (9) (f_2 from (10)).

The algorithm $\mathscr{L}(f_1)$ ($\mathscr{L}(f_2)$) is the partition of the projection of the set C on the direction $[a, b]$ with the most distant points $a, b \in C$. In this algorithm only partitions in which the minimal segments covering all points of each subset do not intersect are considered. Obviously, there are at most $(m - 1)$ such sets.

Let $\overline{C} = \{\overline{c}_1, \overline{c}_2, \ldots, \overline{c}_m\}$ be the projection of the set C on the direction $[a, b]$. Then the $\overline{C}$ can be linearly ordered with respect to any coordinate of its points, which is not equal to 0 for all points from $\overline{C}$. The set $\overline{C}$ has at most m pairwise distinct points. For simplicity, suppose that $(\overline{c}_1, \overline{c}_2, \ldots, \overline{c}_m)$ is an ordered set of pairwise distinct points.

We consider the $(m - 1)$ points $b_i = 0,5 \cdot \overline{c}_i + 0,5 \cdot \overline{c}_{i-1}, i = [1, m - 1]$. Then we will consider the algorithm $\mathscr{L}$ and the following partition of the set of classes C:

$$I_1(b_i) = \left\{ i \in [1, m] \colon \langle \overline{c}_i, \overrightarrow{ab} \rangle < \langle \overline{c}_i, b_i \rangle \right\} ,$$

$$I_2(b_i) = \left\{ i \in [1, m] \colon \langle \overline{c}_i, \overrightarrow{ab} \rangle > \langle \overline{c}_i, b_i \rangle \right\} .$$

Thus, in the algorithm $\mathscr{L}$ there are only $(m - 1)$ variants of the partition of the set $\overline{C}$ and, hence, only $(m - 1)$ variants of the partition of the initial set C. We will also consider 2 variants of the implementation of the $\mathscr{L}$: $\mathscr{L}(f_1)$—algorithm using the closeness function f_1 and $\mathscr{L}(f_2)$—algorithm using the function f_2, respectively.

In algorithms $\mathscr{A}(f_1)$, $\mathscr{A}(f_2)$ ones scaned 2^m pairs of subsets and for each pair it is necessary to execute $\mathscr{O}(n)$ operations to calculate the closeness between subsets of the pair. Thus, algorithms $\mathscr{A}(f_1)$, $\mathscr{A}(f_2)$ have the computational complexity $\mathscr{O}(n \cdot 2^m)$.

In $\mathscr{L}(f_1)$, $\mathscr{L}(f_2)$ ones executed $\mathscr{O}\left(n \cdot m^2\right)$ operations to extract the pair of maximally remote points of the set, also ones executed $\mathscr{O}(n \cdot m)$ operations to calculate the projections of the points of the set on the direction defined by the pair of maximally remote points, and finally ones executed $\mathscr{O}\left(m^2\right)$ operations to determine the best partition of the initial set into 2 subsets. Thus, the algorithms $\mathscr{L}(f_1)$, $\mathscr{L}(f_2)$ will have the computational complexity $\mathscr{O}\left(n \cdot m^2\right)$.

Computational experiments were carried out for 100 random sets of 32 points in 2-dimensional space. Each partition $I = I_1 \cup I_2$ of the initial set of 32 classes can be represented by the binary tuple $\alpha = (\alpha_1, \alpha_2, \ldots, \alpha_m)$, $\alpha_i \in [0, 1]$ for $i = [1, m]$, where $\alpha_i = 0 \Longleftrightarrow i \in I_1$ and $\alpha_i = 1 \Longleftrightarrow i \in I_2 \; \forall \, i \in [1, m]$.

Let $I = I_1 \cup I_2$ and $I = I_1' \cup I_2'$ be 2 partitions whose closeness should be estimated and α, α' are the corresponding binary tuples.

We denote for binary tuples $\alpha = (\alpha_1, \alpha_2, \ldots, \alpha_m)$ by $\overline{\alpha} = (\overline{\alpha}_1, \overline{\alpha}_2, \ldots, \overline{\alpha}_m)$ an additional tuple such that $\overline{\alpha}_i = 1 - \alpha_i \; \forall \, i = [1, m]$. We also denote by *hamming* $\left(\alpha, \alpha'\right)$ the Hamming distance between binary tuples:

$$hamming\left(\alpha, \alpha'\right) = \left| \left\{ i \in [1, m] \colon \alpha_i \neq \alpha_i' \, , \; i = [1, m] \right\} \right| .$$

The closeness between tuples α, α' we will estimate by the formula:

Table 1 Computational results

Algorithm	$\mathscr{A}(f_1)$ (%)	$\mathscr{L}(f_1)$ (%)	$\mathscr{A}(f_2)$ (%)	$\mathscr{L}(f_2)$ (%)	Computational complexity
$\mathscr{A}(f_1)$	100	88.4	64.2	62,7	$\mathscr{O}(n \cdot 2^m)$
$\mathscr{L}(f_1)$	88.4	100	65.3	63,8	$\mathscr{O}(n \cdot m^2)$
$\mathscr{A}(f_2)$	64.2	65.3	100	94,9	$\mathscr{O}(n \cdot 2^m)$
$\mathscr{L}(f_1)$	62.7	63.8	94.9	100	$\mathscr{O}(n \cdot m^2)$

$$\rho\left(\alpha, \alpha'\right) = \min\left\{hamming\left(\alpha, \alpha'\right), hamming\left(\overline{\alpha}, \alpha'\right)\right\} .$$

The table below shows the results of experiments with 4 different algorithms for partition of a set of classes (Table 1).

In the table, for each pair of algorithms from 4 algorithms under consideration, the average value of $\rho\left(\alpha, \alpha'\right)$ for partitions α and α', obtained respectively by the considered pair of algorithms.

The results obtained have a very interesting interpretation, namely: despite the essential difference between the complexity of the algorithms $\mathscr{A}(f_1)$ and $\mathscr{L}(f_1)$, the resulting partitions in the average is very close—88,4%. From this point of view, the algorithm $\mathscr{L}(f_1)$ being polynomial $\mathscr{O}\left(n \cdot m^2\right)$ yields results very close to the results of the algorithm $\mathscr{A}(f_1)$ of the complete search.

Even more close results are given by the pair $\mathscr{A}(f_2)$ and $\mathscr{L}(f_2)$. However, the use of the f_2 function instead of the function f_1 yields a serious deterioration in the results.

Thus, from the practical point of view, the most interesting is the algorithm $\mathscr{L}(f_1)$, which yields good results, remaining effective from a computational point of view.

5 Conclusion

In this paper, we consider the problem of dichotomy (sequential division into 2 parts, more connected inside than among themselves) in the multi-class problem of pattern recognition. This problem obtains a sequential formalization in the form of a problem of a partition of a finite set of points in the space R^n into 2 subsets with the most distant centers. There are considered 2 different functions for closeness distance and their justification. The initial problem is also considered for the projection of a set of points on the direction connecting 2 maximally remote points of the initial set and for this case a dichotomy algorithm with complexity $\mathscr{O}\left(n \cdot m^2\right)$ is given. The results of computational experiments for 100 sets of points are presented with the use of each of 4 algorithms under consideration. These results show that the quality of the dichotomy is reduced insignificantly when solving the problem for the projection of the initial set of points. In addition, for the same case, a polynomial algorithm with the complexity $\mathscr{O}\left(n \cdot m^2\right)$ can be proposed.

References

Gainanov DN (1992) Alternative covers and independence systems in pattern recognition. Math Not 2(2):147–160

Gainanov DN (2014) Combinatorial geometry and graphs in the analysis of infeasible systems and pattern recognition. Nauka, Moscow

Gainanov DN (2016) Graphs for pattern recognintion: infeasible systems of linear inequalities. DeGruyter, Berlin

Gainanov DN, Berenov DA (2017) Big data technologies in metallurgical production quality control systems. In: Proceedings of the conference big data and advanced analitycs. Minsk State University Press, Minsk, pp 65–70

Gainanov DN, Matveev AO (1991) Lattice diagonals and geometric pattern recognition problems. Pattern Recogn Image Anal 3(1):277–282

Khachai MY (1997) On the estimate of the number of members of the minimal committee of a system of linear inequalities. J Comput Math Math Phys 11(37):1399–1404

Mazurov VD (1990) Committees method in problem of optimization and classification. Nauka, Moscow

Mazurov VD, Khachai MY (2004) Committees of systems of linear inequalities. Autom Remote Control 2:43–54

Determining the Set of the Most Critical System Components—Optimization Approach

Petar Pavlović, Dragana Makajić-Nikolić and Mirko Vujošević

Abstract The aim of this paper is to propose a new approach for determining the set of the most critical system components. Importance measures, commonly used for this purpose, first rank each individual component and afterward form a set of the most critical components due to their ranking. In this paper, we propose a new approach based on optimization so the whole set of the most critical components could be determined simultaneously. By taking into account interdependence of components, sets of the most critical system components with different cardinalities does not have to share any of the components. The proposed approach uses optimization over minimal cut sets of the observed system. The greater the number of minimal cut sets in which a component appears, the greater is its importance. The problem of determination of the minimal number of components which appear in all minimal cut sets is considered and formulated as set covering problem. The optimization problem is solved using available optimization software and original heuristic algorithm. Experiments were performed on a group of benchmark fault trees, and the results are compared with the results obtained by commonly used importance measures.

Keywords Reliability · Importance measures · Optimization · Minimal cut sets · Set covering problem · Heuristic algorithm

1 Introduction

Analyzing the impact of component reliability on system reliability is an important part of systems design and maintenance. To this end, Birnbaum (Birnbaum 1969) and Vesely (Vesely et al. 1983) defined the first importance measures, which are

P. Pavlović (✉)
Higher Medical and Business-Technological School of Applied Studies in Šabac, Šabac, Serbia
e-mail: petar.pavlovic@vtssa.edu.rs

D. Makajić-Nikolić · M. Vujošević
Faculty of Organizational Sciences, University of Belgrade, Belgrade, Serbia
e-mail: makajic-nikolic.dragana@fon.bg.ac.rs

N. Mladenović et al. (eds.), *Advances in Operational Research in the Balkans*, Springer Proceedings in Business and Economics,
https://doi.org/10.1007/978-3-030-21990-1_2

deemed classical measures today. Since then, a lot of different approaches to treating component importance have been developed and reported. In the recent book (Kuo and Zhu 2012), 64 key types of importance measures were listed and 403 references cited. Importance measures were first developed to identify critical components in technical systems. However, over time, their application has spread to all types of systems. In business systems, critical components can be identified as phases or activities in processes, equipment, employees, procedures, business environment, etc.

The aim of all existing approaches related to importance measures is to rank the system components according to calculated absolute values of a given importance measure. The components with higher rank are then considered the most critical. These components with high importance require more attention while components with low importance can be even neglected during the process of system design and optimization (Luyi et al. 2012).

The main goal of importance measures is to provide the information about criticality of the system components according to the contribution of components to the overall system performance (Espitrity et al. 2007). They can be applied in different phases of the system life cycle: (re)design for design optimization by adding or removing components; test and maintenance: optimization of the system functioning by changing the test and maintenance strategy in accordance with the importance of the components; and daily configuration control (Borst and Schoonakker 2001). The first and one of the most used importance measure, called Birnbaum importance measure or B-reliability importance, was followed by so-called traditional importance measures (Aven and Nokland 2010): Fussell–Vesely's importance measure (Vesely et al. 1983), risk achievement worth (RAW), and risk reduction worth (RRW) (Cheok et al. 1998). Numerous importance measures have been developed since. Extensive overviews can be found in (Kuo and Zhu 2012, 2014; Cheok et al. 1998; Vaurio 2010).

A common feature of most importance measures is their ability to compare the impact of individual components on the reliability or unreliability of the system. Therefore, one of the open issues on importance measures is the fact that they rank only individual components and are not directly applicable to combinations or groups of components (Zio 2011).

There are only a few papers that examine the impact of groups of components on the system. Joint reliability importance (JRI), introduced in (Hong and Lie 1993) and later extended in (Armstrong 1995), is the importance measure that considers how pairs of components interact and what is the influence of their reliabilities to the system performance. Borgonovo and Apostolakis introduced differential importance measure (DIM) which is, unlike traditional importance measures, additive (Borgonovo and Apostolakis 2001). In the proposed approach, DIM of the group of basic events is equal to the sum of the individual DIMs. Afterward, Zio and Podofillini in (Zio and Podofilini 2006) showed that DIM did not consider the effects of interactions among events, and introduced an extension named DIM^{II} that combines JRI and DMI. The new importance measure was also applied for the interactions of pairs of components. Podofillini and Zio (2008) defined determination of the most important groups of events as multi-objective optimization problem with two objective functions: maximization of DIM or Fussell–Vesely importance of the group and minimization of dimension of the group. Pavlovic et al. (2017) formulated an importance measure as the budgeted maximum coverage problem. This measure considers costs of individual components and components' mutual impact on the overall system reliability.

In this paper, we propose a new mathematical programming approach in which the most critical components are determined simultaneously as a result of optimization. The problem of determining the set of the most critical system components is formulated as an optimization problem and an original mathematical model was developed for this purpose. Since the proposed approach is based on fault tree analysis, the fault tree analysis terminology will be used, with component failure and basic event as synonyms. System failure is called top event.

The main elements of the proposed model are basic events and minimal cut sets (MCSs). There are several definitions of cut sets and MCSs. Our approach relies on the following definitions:

Definition 1 (Ericson II 2005): Cut set is a set of events that together cause the top undesired event to occur.

Definition 2 (Ericson II 2005): Minimal cut set (MCS) is a cut set reduced to the minimum number of events that cause the top undesired event to occur.

Most commonly used approach for generation of MCSs is based on a fault tree of the observed system (Kvassay et al. 2016; Makajic et al. 2016). Formally, a fault tree is a directed and connected acyclic graph G = (X, A), where X is the set of nodes and A is the set of arcs (Fig. 1).

The root node T corresponds to the top event of the fault tree and represents the system failure. The leaves x1–x8 are basic events of the fault tree and they represent failure modes of the system components. The root T and the intermediate nodes G1–G5 are identified by the corresponding logic operators (gates) that model the cause–effect relationships between components failures. In Fig. 1, the nodes that correspond to the root T and intermediate events G3 and G4 represent OR gates, while the nodes that correspond to the events G1, G2, and G5 represent AND gates.

Fault tree can be considered as a graphical presentation of a system structure function (Limnios 2007). Fault tree analysis includes qualitative and quantitative evaluation (Schneeweiss 1997). The main qualitative (logic) evaluation includes the determination of structure function of a fault tree that describes how binary component states jointly determine the binary system states, that is, it takes up the value 1 for the occurrence of the top event, and the value 0 for its nonoccurrence (Lee et al. 1985). Such structure function is given as a disjunctive normal form where each conjunction represents one MCS. For the fault tree in Fig. 1, MCSs are x8, x5x7, x6x7, x3x4x5, x1x2x7, x3x4x6, and x1x2x3x4.

We have here observed coherent fault trees whose properties are each component (basic event) is relevant to the system and structure function is monotonic (increasing) (Barlow and Proschan 1996). Thereby, we assume that all MCSs of a given fault tree

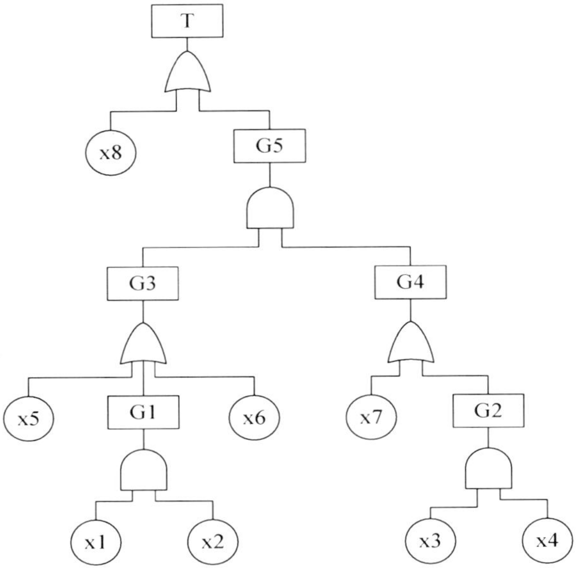

Fig. 1 Fault tree example

are already determined. In 1970s, a large number of so-called classical methods for MCSs of fault tree generation were developed: MOCUS (Fussell et al. 1974), FATRAM (Rasmuson and Marshal 1978), and MICSUP (Willie 1978). Since late 1980s several methods based on Petri nets presentation of fault tree (Hura and Atwood 1988; Liu and Chiou 1997; Bobbio et al. 2003; Wu et al. 2010; Makajic-Nikolic et al. 2013) have been developed. Nowadays, a predominant approach for MCSs generation is by using binary decision diagram of a given fault tree (Rauzy 1993; Way and Hsia 2000; Contini and Matuzas 2011).

The remainder of the paper is organized as follows: Sect. 2 is devoted to importance measures. New approach for determining the set of the most critical system components is stated as a problem of determining the minimal number of basic events which eliminate all MCSs.

In Sect. 3, the problem is formulated as a well-known set covering problem. This problem is solved using exact algorithms and original algorithms inspired by variable neighborhood search, described in Sect. 4. Numerical results and discussion are presented in Sect. 5.

2 Importance Measures

The three measures whose results are compared with our approach are Birnbaum importance measure as the most important; Fussell–Vesely importance measure; and first-term importance of component, which rely on MCSs.

Birnbaum importance measure observes extreme states of the system components: perfectly reliable and failed, and, for each component, it compares the system reliability in these two states. The component for which this difference is largest is considered the most important.

Let $p_i(t)$ be the reliability of the component i at time t and $p(t) = (p_1(t), \ldots, p_n(t))$ the vector of reliability of all system components. System reliability function can then be denoted by $h(p(t))$. Birnbaum importance measure of component i at time t is obtained by partial differentiation of the system reliability with respect to $p_i(t)$:

$$I^B(i|t) = \frac{\partial h(p(t))}{\partial p_i(t)} \tag{1}$$

By applying pivotal decomposition (Holand and Rausand 1994), Birnbaum measure can be expressed as

$$I^B(i|t) = h(1_i, p(t)) - h(0_i, p(t)) \tag{2}$$

where $h(1_i, p(t))$ represents the system reliability with the component i assumed to be perfectly reliable and $h(0_i, p(t))$ represents the system reliability with the component i assumed failed.

The basic idea of Fussell–Vesely importance measure is that a component contributes to system failure when an MCS containing its failure event occurs. The original formulation is based on sums of the MCS probabilities, which is an approximation that can be used for a rare event (Vaurio 2010), i.e., systems with high reliable components.

Fussell–Vesely importance measure can be approximated as follows (Kuo and Zhu 2012):

$$I^{FV}(i|t) \approx \frac{1 - \prod_{j=1}^{m_i} (1 - \breve{Q}_i^j(t))}{Q(t)} \approx \frac{\sum_{j=1}^{m_i} \breve{Q}_i^j(t)}{Q(t)} \tag{3}$$

where $\breve{Q}_i^j(t)$ denotes the probability that j-th MCS which contains the component i occurs at time t and $Q(t)$ denotes the probability of the system failure. Given that $Q(t)$ is constant, the components can be rank only based on the sums of probabilities of the corresponding MCSs (to which they belong).

Based on the first-term importance of component, introduced by Chang et al. (2002), Kuo and Zhu (2012) defined the first-term importance measure that takes into account only the cut sets of the highest order. A cut set order is the number of events in a cut set, i.e., the cut set of an order l contains l basic events (Ericson II 2005). The smaller l, the higher the cut set order is. Let e be the higher cut sets order. The first- term importance of component i is

$$I^{FT}(i|t) = \left|\overline{C_i}(e)\right| \tag{4}$$

$I^{FT}(i|t)$ is the number of cut sets of order e which contain component i.

Although the first-term importance measure is defined as structural in (Kuo and Zhu 2012), it is based on the assumption that the probabilities of all basic events have the same order of magnitude and, consequently, cut set probability is inversely proportional to the number of its basic events. Therefore, it takes into account only the most probable cut sets. Note that the first-term importance measure does not rank all basic events, but only those that appear in the cut sets of the highest order.

3 Problem Formulation

Let us consider a system with n components $I = \{1, 2, \ldots, n\}$ and let the failure of i-th component $i \in I$ denotes basic event. A binary variable x_i called state indicator is associated with each basic event in the following way (Limnios 2007):

$$x_i = \begin{cases} 1, & \text{if the basic event } i \text{ occurs (failure)} \\ 0, & \text{otherwise (functioning)} \end{cases}$$

Structure function of the system depends on vector $x = (x_1, \ldots, x_n)$ and is a Boolean function for a system with two states—failure and working (Kvassay et al. 2016) defined as

$$\varphi(x) = \begin{cases} 1, & \text{if the top event (system failure) occurs} \\ 0, & \text{otherwise} \end{cases}$$

It is assumed that structure function of the system is given by minimal disjunctive normal form:

$$\varphi(x) = \mathop{\vee}_{j=1}^{m} C_j \tag{5}$$

where the term C_j, $j = 1, \ldots, m$ is a conjunction of some basic events. The set of basic events constituting term Cj is called minimal cut set (MCS). This means that the structure function represents a parallel system of MCSs, and an MCS is a serial system of its basic events. Top event will occur if all basic events of at least one MCS occur.

To formulate the problem of simultaneous determination of the most critical system components, we start from the definition of the MCS. Definition 2 can be observed as follows: the MCS cannot be further reduced and still guarantee an occurrence of the top undesired event. If the occurrence of a basic event was disabled, the basic event would be considered an impossible event. We call such event a disabled basic event. From practical engineering point of view, disabling of basic event may be seen as decreasing of probability of its occurrence to very low and negligible value. This assumption appears in most importance measures and represents a decreased risk level with the basic event optimized or assumed to be perfectly reliable (Borst and Schoonakker 2001).

All MCSs consisting of a disabled basic event could be eliminated from (5) and the structure function would be reduced to the union of MCSs without disabled basic events. The higher the number of eliminated MCSs, the greater the importance of components is.

For the fault three in Fig. 1 and under assumption that the probabilities of all basic events have the same order of magnitude, all importance measures from the previous section give the same events ranking: $x8$, $x7$, $x5$, $x6$, $x3$, $x4$, $x1$, $x2$, and $x9$. Bearing in mind the previous discussion, disabling first ranked event $x8$ eliminates one MCS ($x8$); disabling two first ranked events $x8$ and $x7$ eliminates three MCSs ($x8$, $x5x7$, and $x6x7$), and so on. In order to eliminate all MCSs by disabling at least one of corresponding events, five first ranked events should be disabled ($x8$, $x7$, $x5$, $x6$, and $x3$). However, it is obvious that all MCSs can be eliminated by disabling only three events: $x8$, $x7$, and $x3$, or in another case, $x8$, $x4$, and $x7$ (two equally well solutions). In both of these solutions, specific ranking of separated events is insignificant (for example, whether the event $x8$ has higher priority than $x7$ event or vice versa), but it is essential that the elimination of all MCSs is achieved by their simultaneous disabling. Since traditional importance measures do not take sufficiently into account the interdependence of events, and are not able to simultaneously isolate the most important group of events, an approach for determining the set of the most critical system components would be significant.

Based on the above discussion, the following problem can be defined: determine the minimal number of basic events whose disabling eliminates all MCSs. Such basic events can be considered the most critical.

To formulate the introduced problem, we use the following notation:

n—the number of basic events,
m—the number of MCSs,

$$a_{ij} = \begin{cases} 1 \text{ if MCS}_j \text{ contains the basic event } i \\ 0 \text{ otherwise} \end{cases}, i = 1, \ldots, n, \ j = 1, \ldots, m.$$

Let $z_i = 1 - x_i$ be a binary disabling indicator associated with the basic event i, $i = 1, \ldots, n$ defined as

$$z_i = \begin{cases} 1 \text{ if the basic event } i \text{ is disabled} \\ 0 \text{ otherwise} \end{cases}$$

If $z_i = 1$, then an MCS_j which contains the basic event i is impossible or eliminated.

The problem of finding the minimal number of basic events whose disabling will cause eliminations of all MCSs is

$$\min \sum_{i=1}^{n} z_i \tag{6}$$

s.t.

$$\sum_{i=1}^{n} a_{ij} \cdot z_i \geq 1, j = 1, \ldots, m \tag{7}$$

$$z_i \in \{0, 1\}, i = 1, \ldots, n \tag{8}$$

Objective function (6) represents the total number of disabled basic events. The constraint (7) is related to the requirement that all MCSs must be eliminated.

The formulated model (6–8) represents a well-known *set covering problem* (Christofides and Korman 1975): MCS_j represents the elements of a given set X and basic events represent the subsets of X. A family S' of the basic events which cover all MCSs (elements of X) are called covering sets. If no $S'' \subset S'$, then S' is called a prime set covering.

4 Solving Methods

Although the variables related to basic events are integer (binary), the model (6–8) can be solved using exact algorithms for a large number of fault trees. To this end, we used GNU Linear Programming Kit (GLPK), open-source software for solving linear and mixed integer programming models (glpk 2017). However, since it is well known that the set covering problem is NP-hard (Garey and Johnson 1979), we developed an algorithm inspired by variable neighborhood search (VNS) for solving the large-scale problems (Hansen et al. 2010; Alguwaizani et al. 2011).

Algorithm 1. Sub-algorithm (Phase 1)

```
1  greedy()
2  form array SingleCover
3  form array Lmin
4  reduction()
5  correction of indexes in SingleCover
```

Algorithm 2. The general framework of the proposed heuristic (Phase 2)

```
execution of Sub-algorithm (Phase 1)
while (array Lmin is not empty) do
        reconstruction()
        execution of Sub-algorithm (Phase 1)
end while
if (solution is improved) then
                reset arrays
                go to step 2
end if
form new array Lmin based on random parameter rnd_param
while (array L is not empty) do
        reconstruction()
        execution of Sub-algorithm (Phase 1)
end while
if (solution is improved) then
                reset arrays
                go to step 2
end if
```

The heuristics designed to solve the described problem consists of two phases. The first phase tries to identify the events that could eliminate all MCSs using a common greedy algorithm. Phase 1 selects events with the greatest total number of occurrences in all MCSs. When a number of events have the same occurrence values, priority is set by their event index value, i.e., events with smaller index value are the chosen ones. Phase 2 tries to gradually improve the solution obtained in phase 1 by taking the "backsteps", i.e., by uncovering some of MCSs covered in phase 1 (*reconstruction* procedure). Basically, MCSs that were eliminated and restored to a value of zero are loaded again from the input file. By counting the occurrences of events in MCSs, nondecreasing array Lmin consisting only of nonredundant occurrence values is made. In an attempt to improve the original greedy solution, an element of this array is taken to form a list of events that need to be reconstructed (uncovered). After executing all the preset iterations, the achieved best solution is saved and the next step is taken in an attempt to improve a new solution. The events that will be reconstructed are selected randomly (*random_reconstruction* procedure) in this step, taking into account previously chosen percentage parameter which determines the amount of events to be reconstructed. Percentage parameter of 100% of the reconstructed events resembles VNS heuristics which randomly jumps into some permissible point before applying the greedy local search.

Pseudocodes describing four most important procedures are given below:

Procedure 1. greedy (MCS[m][l])

```
end_signal←0
repeat
    i←1
    repeat
        j←1
        repeat
            if MCS[i][l]=j then
              appearanceNo[j]←appearanceNo[j]+1
            if MCS[i][j]=0 then
              end_signal←1
            if appearanceNo[i]>max then
             max←appearanceNo [i]
             X[F] ←i
             F←F+1
             MCS[i][l] ←0
             j←j+1
        until j=n
        i←i+1
    until i=m
  until end_signal=1
```

Procedure 2. reduction (X[],SingleCover[])

```
Fred←0
i←1
repeat
    if singleCover[i]=0 then
            Fred ← Fred +1
            X[i] ←Ø
            i←i+1
     end if
until i= n
F← F- Fred
```

Procedure 3. reconstruction (X[F],Lmin[L],singleCover[F], curr_iter)

```
Frec←0
i←1
repeat
    j←1
    repeat
            if singleCover[i]=Lmin[j] then
                    load MCS[j][l] from input_file
                    X[i] ←Ø
                    Frec←Frec+1
            j←j+1
    until j= curr_iter
    i←i+1
until i= F
Frec← F- Frec
```

Procedure 4. random_reconstruction (X[F],rnd_param)

```
rnd_ev_num←int(F*rnd_param/100)
i←1
repeat
    random j
    load MCS[j][l] from input_file
    X[i] ←Ø
    i←i+1
until i= rnd_ev_num
```

5 Numerical Results

To demonstrate the proposed approach for the determination of most critical components, a group of benchmark fault trees (BFT) from (CLib 2017) is used. Table 1 provides a description of chosen fault trees.

Column E represents the total number of events in BFT (top, intermediate, and basic), while column BE represents the number of different basic events. All BFTs contain multiple basic events; therefore, the overall number of events in the BFTs is larger than the values shown in the table. Column MCS shows the number of MCSs. The ranges of MCSs, i.e., the minimal and maximal number of basic events in MCSs are given in column R.

Mathematical model (6–8) was first solved optimally using GLPK. The values BE and MCS from Table 1 represent n, the number of binary variables z_i, and m, the number of constraints, respectively. The values of objective (6), the minimal number of basic events that eliminate all MCSs, are given in Table 2 (column "exact solution"). Table 2 also gives comparison of exact solution with results obtained by three common importance measures: Birnbaum, Fussell–Vesely, and First-term importance measure, i.e., results obtained using Eqs. (1–4). To enable the comparison

Table 1 Benchmark fault trees

No	BFT name	E	BE	MCS	R
1	chinese	61	25	392	2–6
2	isp9606	130	89	1776	1–5
3	baobab2	72	32	4805	2–6
4	das9208	248	103	8060	2–6
5	isp9605	72	32	5630	3–7
6	das9201	204	122	14217	2–7
7	baobab1	144	61	46188	2–11
8	edf9205	307	165	21308	1–8
9	jbd9601	847	532	14007	1–7
10	isp9603	186	91	3434	2–8
11	baobab3	187	80	24386	2–11
12	das9202	85	49	27778	1–11
13	ftr10	246	152	305	1–3

Table 2 Comparison of the exact solution and some of the common IM solution

No	Exact solution	Common importance measures					
		Number of covered MCSs			IM solution		
		BB	FV	FT	BB	FV	FT
1	5	156	156	156	10	10	7; 172
2	34	1053	1053	1357	73	73	51; 1596
3	14	4503	4503	–	26	26	6; 3162
4	17	2583	2583	2733	25	25	31
5	8	4760	4760	4760	19	19	9; 4808
6	9	12241	12241	2225	77	77	50; 13950
7	11	26047	26047	–	39	39	2; 2156
8	40	20667	20667	20298	41	41	70; 21293
9	268	12398	12398	13204	522	522	348; 13302
10	17	2807	2807	–	52	52	13; 2708
11	17	15280	15280	–	59	59	14; 10215
12	8	10306	10306	–	22	22	2; 337
13	79	268	268	243	146	146	88; 243

of results, first the rank of individual components is determined based on each of these importance measures, assuming that the probability of occurrence for each basic event is 10^{-2}.

In the first part of the table (columns named by importance measures), it is shown what the number of covered (eliminated) MCSs would be if as many basic events

Table 3 Reliability improvements

No	Exact solution	Improvement for exact Sol. (%)		
		BB	FV	FT
1	5	99.9889	99.9889	99.9889
2	34	97.8134	97.8134	28.4736
3	14	98.0917	98.0917	–
4	17	87.3420	87.3420	87.0093
5	8	99.2716	99.2716	99.2716
6	9	98.7759	98.7759	55.2074
7	11	99.9996	99.9996	–
8	40	99.4487	99.4487	41.9597
9	268	96.4911	96.4911	25.6613
10	17	98.8825	98.8825	–
11	17	99.9132	99.9132	–
12	8	99.9999	99.9999	–
13	79	99.4607	99.4607	4.0888

were prevented as they are shown in column "Exact Solution". A bar in the column FT indicates that the number of covered MSCs cannot be determined since the number of basic event ranked by FT importance measures is smaller than specified value. By comparing these results with the total number of MCS in Table 1, it can be noted that there is no BFT for which the elimination of all MCS is achieved.

The second part of Table 2 (columns named "IM Solution") shows how many basic events ranked by corresponding importance measures must be disabled in order to eliminate all MCSs. The first-term importance measure, regarding Eq. (4), is not able to calculate a complete solution for considered inputs, except for BTF 4. All incomplete solutions presented in the last column of Table 2 consist of two values—the total number of ranking events using First-Term IM and actual number of eliminated MCSs.

Table 3 gives comparison of exact solution with solutions obtained by three common importance measures regarding the reliability improvement. Since it is obvious that the reliability improvement for the solution of the model (6–8) is 100%, column "exact solution" again shows the minimal number of basic events that eliminate all MCSs.

In the columns named by importance measures, it is shown what the improvement of the reliability of the system in percentage would be if as many basic events were prevented as they were shown in column "Exact Solution". Let k be the number of basic events given in the column "Exact Solution". For each importance measure, reliability improvement percentages were obtained in the following way: ranks of basic events were obtained using Eqs. (1–4); the possibility equal to zero was assigned to

Table 4 Comparison of exact and algorithm solutions

No	Exact solution	Phase-1	Phase-2 (Phase-1 + Shaking)			
			$\alpha = 20\%$	$\alpha = 40\%$	$\alpha = 80\%$	$\alpha = 100\%$
1	5	6	6	6	5	6
2	34	34				
3	14	14				
4	17	18	18	18	18	18
5	8	8				
6	9	9				
7	11	11				
8	40	40				
9	268	278	276	277	277	277
10	17	19	19	19	19	19
11	17	20	20	18	18	20
12	8	8				
13	79	83	83	83	83	83

the k first ranked basic events; a new system reliability was calculated and percentage of improvement in relation to initial system reliability was determined.

The problem of finding the most critical components was then solved using the algorithm presented in Sect. 4. The results are given in Table 4.

In eight out of thirteen BFT, the optimal solution was found in the phase 1. For BFT 4, 10, and 13, the solution obtained in the phase 1 could not be improved in the phase 2, while for BFT 9 and 11 the solution of the phase 1 was improved, but it could not achieve the optimal solution. Only in the case of BFT 1, the solution of the phase 1 was improved to the optimality in the phase 2. However, in all cases where the optimal solution has not been found, the number of events that should be disabled is much lower than those obtained using Birnbaum, Fussell–Vesely, and First-term importance measures given in Table 2.

6 Conclusion

This paper considers the problem of determining the set of the most critical system components and presents a new approach for its solving. Starting from the assumption that all MCSs of a given fault tree are preknown, the optimization problem was formulated as a set covering problem of determining the minimal number of basic events, whose disabling eliminates all MCSs. The model was solved using both exact and heuristic algorithms, and tests were performed on a group of benchmark fault trees. Obtained results were compared with the ones obtained by the three traditional importance measures: Birnbaum, Fussell–Vesely, and First-term. It is concluded that the presented approach can be used as a new way of determining the set of the most critical system components. Unlike the existing approaches, this new one determines the set of the most critical system components with better taking into account components' interdependence. In the case of limited resources, when all critical components cannot be optimized to be perfectly reliable, the problem of finding k basic events whose disabling will cause maximal number of MCSs elimination appear. For such a problem, the influence of MCSs on system reliability should be included. This influence depends on the number of basic events in MCS and their probabilities.

References

Alguwaizani A, Hansen P, Mladenovic N, Ngai E (2011) Variable neighbourhood search for harmonic means clustering. Appl Math Model 35(6):2688–2694
Armstrong MJ (1995) Joint reliability-importance of elements. IEEE Trans Rel 44(3):408–412
Aven T, Nokland T (2010) On the use of uncertainty importance measures in reliability and risk analysis. Reliab Eng Syst Safe 95:127–133
Barlow RE, Proschan F (1996) Mathematical Theory of Reliability. Society for Industrial and Applied Mathematics, Philadelphia
Birnbaum Z (1969) On the importance of different components in a multicomponent system. In: Krishnaiah P (ed) Multivariate Analysus-II. Academic Press, New York
Bobbio A, Franceschenis G, Gaeta R, Portinale L (2003) Parametric fault tree for the dependability analysis of redundant systems and its high-level Petri net semantics. IEEE Trans Softw Eng 29(3):270–287
Borgonovo E, Apostolakis GE (2001) A new importance measure for risk informed decision making. Reliab Eng Syst Safe 72:193–212
Borst M, Schoonakker H (2001) An overview of PSA importance measures. Reliab Eng Syst Safe 72(3):241–245
Chang HW, Chen RJ, Hwank FK (2002) The structural Birnbaum importance of consecutive-k systems. J Comb Optim 183–197
Cheok MC, Parry GW, Sherry RR (1998) Use of importance measures in risk-informed regulatory applications. Reliab Eng Syst Safe 60:213–226
CLib (2017) Configuration Benchmarks Library. https://www.itu.dk/research/cla/externals/clib/
Christofides N, Korman S (1975) A computational survey of methods for the set covering problem. Manag Sci 21:591–599
Contini S, Matuzas V (2011) Analysis of large fault trees based on functional decomposition. Reliab Eng Syst Safe 96:383–390
Ericson CA II (2005) Hazard analysis technique for system safety. Wiley, New Jersey
Espitrity JF, Coit DW, Prakash U (2007) Component criticality importance measures for the power industry. Electr Pow Syst Res 407–420
Fussell JB, Henry EB, Marshall NH (1974) MOCUS a computer program to obtain minimal sets from fault trees. ANCR 1156 Aerojet Nuclear Company, Idaho Falls
Garey MR, Johnson DS (1979) Computers and intractability: a guide to the theory of NP-completeness. WH Freeman, New York
glpk (2017). www.gnu.org/software/glpk
Hansen P, Mladenovovic N, Brimberg J, Perez JA (2010) Variable neighbourhood search. In: Gendrenau M, Potvin J (eds) Handbook of metaheuristics, vol 146. Springer, London
Holand P, Rausand M (1994) System reliability theory: models and statistical methods. Wiley

Hong JS, Lie CH (1993) Joint reliability-importance of two edges in an undirected network. IEEE Trans Rel 42(1):17–23
Hura GS, Atwood JW (1988) The use of Petri nets to analyze coherent fault-trees. IEEE Trans Rel 37:469–474
Kuo W, Zhu X (2012) Importance measures in reliability, risk and optimization. Whiley
Kuo W, Zhu X (2014) Some recent advances on importance measures in reliability. IEEE Trans Rel 61(2):344–360
Lee WS, Grosh DL, Tillman FA, Lie CH (1985) Fault tree analysis, methods and applications—a review. IEEE Trans Rel R 34(3):194–203
Limnios N (2007) Fault tree. ISTE Ltd, Wiltshire
Liu TS, Chiou SB (1997) The application of Petri nets to failure analysis. Reliab Eng Syst Safe 57:129–142
Luyi L, Zhenzhou L, Jun F, Bintuan W (2012) Moment-independent importance measure of basic variable and its state dependent parameter solution. Struct Saf 38:40–47
Makajic-Nikolic D, Vujosevic M, Nikolic N (2013) Minimal cut sets of a coherent fault tree generation using reverse Petri nets. Optimization 62(8):1069–1087
Makajic-Nikolic D, Petrovic N, Belic A, Rokvic M, Radakovic JA, Tubic V (2016) The fault tree analysis of infectious medical waste management. J Clean Prod 113:365–373
Pavlović P, Makajić-Nikolić D, Vujošević M (2017) A new approach for determining the most important system components and the budget-constrained system reliability improvement. Eksploat Niezawodn 19(3):413–419
Rasmuson DM, Marshal NH (1978) FATRAM: a core efficient cut-set algorithm. IEEE Trans Rel R 27(4):250–253
Rauzy A (1993) New algorithms for fault tree analysis. Reliab Eng Syst Safe 40:203–221
Schneeweiss W (1997) Advanced hand calculations for fault tree analysis and synthesis. Microelectron Reliab 37(3):403–415
Vaurio JK (2010) Ideas and developments in importance measures and fault-tree techniques for reliability and risk analysis. Reliab Eng Syst Safe 95:99–107
Vesely WE, Davis TC, Denning RS, Saltos N (1983) Measures of risk importance and their applications. Battelle Columbus Labs, OH (USA)
Way YS, Hsia DY (2000) A simple component-connection method for building decision diagrams encoding a fault tree. Reliab Eng Syst Safe 70:59–70
Willie RR (1978) Computer-aided fault tree analisys. OR Center, Berkley
Wu Y, Xie L, Yue Y (2010) Study of fault analysis technology by means of Petri nets. IJPE 6(3):269–277
Zio E (2011) Risk importance measures. In: Safety and risk modeling and its appliacations. Springer, London
Zio E, Podofilini L (2006) Accouniting for components interactions in the differential importance measure. Reliab Eng Syst Safe 91:1163–1174
Kvassay M, Levashenko V, Zaitseva E (2016) Analysis of minimal cut and path sets based on direct partial Boolean derivatives. Proc Inst Mech Eng Part O: J Risk Reliab 230(2):147–161
Podofillini L, Zio E (2008) Events group risk importance by genetic algorithms. Proc Inst Mech Eng Part O: J Risk Reliab 222(3):337–346

Metaheuristics and Error Detection Approaches for Multiproduct EOQ-Based Inventory Control Problem

Slobodan Antic and Lena Djordjevic Milutinovic

Abstract Dynamic discrete inventory control models implemented in a spreadsheet can be used as a quite reliable and relatively simple tool for presenting static inventory models with a complex mathematical apparatus. These models can be easily implemented in real systems, e.g. companies. The discretization of the continuous infinite time horizon to more than one finite time period is a more natural manner of describing and analyzing inventory dynamics of real systems. In this manner the continuous time inventory model is interpreted as the discrete time inventory model. The objective of this research is to present a static time continuous multi-product economic order quantity (EOQ) model with storage space constraints, as a combinatorial optimization problem in the corresponding dynamic discrete time system control process. The heuristics approach used for problem solving is based on examination and comparison of several search algorithms and presented throughout several numerical experiments. Furthermore, this paper describes spreadsheet error detection and debugging approach for the presented model. The approach is based on common and specific constrains of the dynamic discrete inventory control model developed in a spreadsheet environment. Preliminary experiments show the general applicability of the approach.

Keywords Dynamic discrete inventory control model · Heuristics · Metaheuristics · Error detection approaches · Spreadsheet

1 Introduction

Inventory control problems are ubiquitous in practice and consequently a quite permanently current topic and significant control problem in different business systems.

S. Antic · L. Djordjevic Milutinovic (✉)
Faculty of Organizational Sciences, University of Belgrade, Belgrade, Serbia
e-mail: lena.djordjevic.milutinovic@fon.bg.ac.rs

S. Antic
e-mail: antics@fon.bg.ac.rs

N. Mladenović et al. (eds.), *Advances in Operational Research in the Balkans*,
Springer Proceedings in Business and Economics,
https://doi.org/10.1007/978-3-030-21990-1_3

Effective inventory management is important because of the high value of the inventories that a company has on the stock. One of the main problems of inventory control is reflected through the time gap between demand and supply, or the imbalance of the needs and availability of items necessary for the production of goods and services for customers. Companies are oriented towards the satisfaction of customer needs, but at the same time a minimization of total costs.

One of the most important quality components of inventory control for producers and distributors in supply chains is effective inventory management and calculation of inventory turnover ratio (Horvat et al. 2015). For example: the *coffee inventory turnover ratio* characteristic is important to distributors due to freshness. Higher inventory turnover implies better shelf life of products, which should result in product freshness for customers on a daily basis. The applicability of inventory control models can also be considered from the aspect of package waste reverse logistics. Research (Lisec et al. 2017) presents a simulation of an inventory control model which enables reduction of the number of tonne-kilometers by 55% and consequently make significant cost reduction possible.

Static inventory models belong to the group of infinite time horizon inventory control models, which assume that the rate of the annual demand is known and constant over a continuous time. Dynamic discrete inventory control models, considered in this paper, imply more than a one-time period, because of the finite time horizon divided into t discrete time periods. The annual demand is known and constant over t discrete time periods. The number of replenishments obtained by the fixed time horizon is always an integer number, which defines demand through t discrete time periods. Discretization of continuous infinite time horizon allows interpretation of static inventory models as discrete time inventory models. The main characteristic of inventory control in the case of the fixed order quantity system for the finite time horizon is that the replenishment quantity is constant and performed throughout several replenishments which occur at the beginning of the equal portions of the time horizon. The sum of replenishment quantities over the time horizon is equal to the demand in the time horizon. Discrete system control model is both a simulation model of inventory dynamics and an optimization model, which gives an optimal control according to the defined performance criterion.

The Economic order quantity (EOQ) model represents classical inventory model with a known total product demand. The model is aimed at determining the order quantity, while the total cost of the production, ordering and inventory holding should be minimized. It was originally developed by (Harris 1915), though (Wilson 1934) is credited for his early in-depth analysis of the model. Even more recent books which are considering inventory control (Axsäter 2006; Russell and Taylor 2006; Vollmann et al. 2005; Chase and Aquilano 2004; Barlow 2003; Muller 2003; Wild 2002) describe the classical EOQ model and its variants, as a starting point for further understanding of inventory dynamics. Most of them address lot-sizing problems, beginning with Wagner and Whitin (1958) and Scarf (1959). In order to find optimal inventory control for various variants of the dynamic lot-sizing problems, dynamic programming algorithms can be applied (Bertsekas 1987; Anily and Tzur

2006). Additionally, different special heuristics are developed in order to solve such problems (Jans and Degraeve 2007).

A discrete time system control may be considered as very convenient for inventory dynamics description, as it is stated in Kostic (2009). The author develops a general approach to inventory modeling and presents the EOQ model as the model of optimal control of the discrete system. According to (Antic 2014) dynamic discrete inventory control models with defined law of behavior, control domain and performance criterion represent a more effective method for inventory dynamic description than static continuous inventory control models. The research presents multiproduct EOQ-based inventory control problem with storage space constraints modeled as a dynamic discrete control process, developed in a spreadsheet. These problems can be quantified, i.e. described with mathematical apparatus for optimal control of a discrete system. The analyzed inventory system considers a continuously changing state, but changes are registered at the terminations of the defined time periods. The system's dynamics are described by discrete equations and inequalities. The structure of the inventory system is generally known and has a deterministic character, while the variables may have a deterministic and stochastic character. The optimal discrete inventory control problem belongs to the class of NP (*Nondeterministic Polynomial*) hard problems and occurs in many inventory problems. Usually, the unique way to solve it is to use searching methods, i.e. heuristics and metaheuristics methods, which are used for control space searching, Discrete processes give different values of the performance criterion by entering various values of control variables. Research stated in (Antic 2014) is focused on two special heuristics, and VNS (*Variable Neighborhood Search*) metaheuristic, developed in VBA (*Visual Basic for Applications*) software, in order to perform experiments and compare results for different paths of finding control variables values, which give better discrete processes.

According to (Antic et al. 2015) the infinite time horizon inventory control models assume that the rate of the annual demand is known and constant over several consecutive years. The finite time horizon inventory control models assume the demand pertains only to the determined time horizon, often shorter than a one-year period. The number of replenishments obtained by the fixed time horizon inventory models is always an integer number (Fig. 1a); that is not the case with the infinite time horizon inventory models. Therefore, the results at the year's level obtained by infinite time or by finite time horizon inventory control models may differ. They are the same only if both give an integer as the number of replenishments.

The traditional EOQ model assumes an infinite time horizon and number of obtained replenishments is often a non-integer (Fig. 1b). It is often necessary to make certain approximations in order to use a traditional EOQ model for the finite time inventory problems in practise. For example, it is practically inconvenient to apply 4.7 replenishments and a replenishment cycle of 77.66 days. Furthermore, the ordering cost directly depends on the occurrence of replenishment, which can be a mere integer, but the EOQ model often multiplies ordering costs with a fractional number of replenishments thus giving an inaccurate total inventory cost. Inventory flow may occur with or without allowed shortages, according to (Antic et al. 2015). Papers (Kostic 2009; Antic et al. 2015) describe the dynamic discrete inventory con-

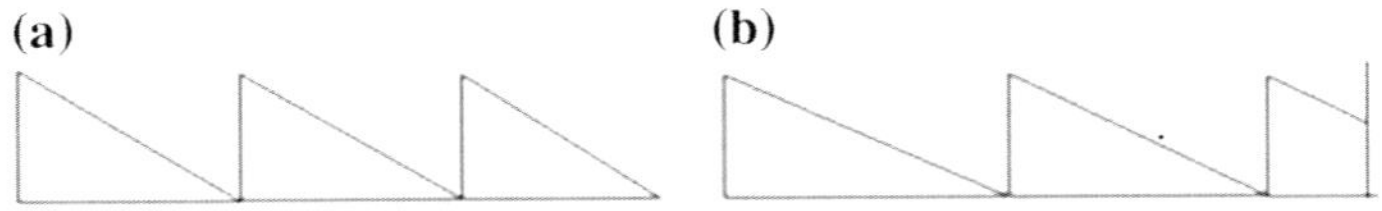

Fig. 1 Stock dynamics over the year: integer and non-integer number of replenishments (Antic et al. 2015)

trol spreadsheet model in the case of a fixed order quantity, for a finite time horizon, with or without allowed shortages.

This paper presents a static time continuous multiproduct EOQ model with storage space constraints, as a combinatorial optimization problem in the corresponding dynamic discrete time system control process. A special heuristic based on a local search technique and VNS based metaheuristic procedure are developed in order to solve the problem. The model is implemented in a spreadsheet environment and aimed at facilitation of usage for business people from the real world. Additionally, the paper tackles spreadsheet engineering area, through the development of the spreadsheet error detection and debugging approach for the described problem. Starting from this point, the paper is organized as follows. Section 2 describes mathematical model of the dynamic discrete inventory control problem with storage space constraint. Section 3 presents the special heuristics for problem solving. Numerical experiments, performed in order to investigate behavior of the special heuristics and VNS algorithm, and compare their efficiency, are realized for a hypothetical problem with m = 102 products. Spreadsheet modeling, error detection and debugging approach for the dynamic discrete inventory control model, as well as preliminary experimental results of the approach evaluation are represented in Sect. 4. The final section addresses future work and gives the summary of this paper.

2 Mathematical Model of Dynamic Discrete Inventory Control Problem with Storage Space Constraint

In (Djordjevic et al. 2017) is considered a time-continuous multiproduct EOQ-based inventory problem which has most of the characteristics of a well- known classical economic lot-size model. For the mathematical relations of the discrete control object the following notation and assumptions will be used:

- t—discrete time period. Instead of continuous time period for ordering products, the whole time period $[0, T]$ is divided into n periods t with the same length T/n, where $t = 1, \ldots, n$. (for example, if T is a year then t could be a one day). So, whole time period $[0, T]$ presents number of days of the time horizon.
- m—number of products, where for each product i, $i = 1, \ldots, m$.
- $X_t^i, t = 1, 2, \ldots, n$—the total amount of product i remaining on the stock at the end of period t.

- $Y_t^i, t = 1, 2, \ldots, n$—the amount of product i ordered at the beginning of period t.
- u_i—decision variable presented as number of orders (replenishments). Product i is ordered u_i times with the constant time t_i between two orderings. $u_i \in \{1, 2, \ldots, n\}$, $i = 1, \ldots, m$.
- D_i—the total deterministic demand which should be satisfied within a finite time horizon T.
- Q_i—amount of product i ordered u_i times with the constant time t_i between two orderings. Q_i arrives on the stock simultaneously and immediately when desired. The sum of replenishment quantities over time horizon is equal to demand in time horizon (D_i).
- D_i/n—withdrawn quantity of products from the stock. As during this period of length T/n the product is withdrawn from the stock continuously by the constant rate D_i/n.
- S_i—Setup cost is the cost related to ordering for the each product i.
- C_i—Purchase cost per product unit.
- H_i—Inventory holding cost per product unit in time unit. The total inventory holding cost in period t_i is calculated with respect to the average inventory level $Q_i/2$.
- G—total available space. Ordered amounts of different products share the same storage with the total available space G which is known in advance.
- P_i—storage space occupied per each product i.
- Ordering of any product can be realized only at the beginning of a period t_i. Lead time is zero LT = 0.
- The initial state of inventory is zero.
- Shortages of the products on the stock are not permitted.

According to the classical EOQ model, the total cost TC for is equal to:

$$TC = \sum_{i=1}^{m} (S_i + C_i Q_i + H_i \frac{Q_i}{2} t_i) u_i \tag{1}$$

Taking into account that $u_i = D_i/Q_i$ and $t_i = T/u_i = T * Q_i/D_i$ the total cost TC can take the form

$$TC = \sum_{i=1}^{m} S_i \frac{D_i}{Q_i} + \sum_{i=1}^{m} C_i D_i + \sum_{i=1}^{m} H_i \frac{Q_i}{2} T \tag{2}$$

Then, the following inventory problem is considered: find amounts Q_i, $i = 1, \ldots, m$, by changing decision variables u_i, which satisfy storage space constraints and minimize the total cost (2).

The main characteristic of the inventory control in the case of the fixed order quantity for the finite time horizon is that the replenishment quantity is constant and performed through several replenishments that occur at the beginnings of the equal periods of the time horizon. Law of dynamics can be expressed as follows:

$$X_0^i = 0 \tag{3}$$

$$X_t^i = X_{t-1}^i + Y_t^i - D_i/n, t = 1, 2, \ldots, n. \tag{4}$$

When the replenishment occurs, the level of inventory $X_t^i, t = 1, 2, \ldots, n$ is increased instantaneously. The level $X_t^i, t = 1, 2, \ldots, n$ is decreasing in accordance with daily demand (D_i/n). When the level $X_t^i, t = 1, 2, \ldots, n$ meet the zero, the new replenishment i obtained.

Regulator Y_t^i represents input action increasing the inventory on hand. Its value over the time horizon is equal zero, except in the moment when the replenishment is occurred. Denote the number of replenishments as a control variable u_i.

Therefore, the value of Y_t^i depends on u_i and can be formally expressed as

$$Y_t^i = \begin{cases} D_i/u_i, & X_{t-1}^i < D_i/n \\ 0, & otherwise \end{cases} \qquad t = 1, 2, \ldots, n. \tag{5}$$

Storage space constraints are considered only at the beginning of periods t and consequently can be formally defined as

$$\sum_{i=1}^{m} (X_{t-1}^i + Y_t^i) P_i \leq G \qquad t = 1, 2, \ldots, n. \tag{6}$$

Therefore, inventory levels during the observed time period $[0, T]$ should satisfy the following storage space constraints: at any moment in this period the total space occupied by the stored amount of all products should not exceed the space limit G.

Let us determine the total cost $J(u_1, u_2, \ldots, u_m)$ for the inventory system described by (3)–(5). It is equal to the sum of the total costs for every product i at each period t, where the total inventory holding cost of product i in period t is calculated with respect to the average inventory level which is equal to $X_{t-1}^i + Y_t^i - \frac{D_i}{2n}$ and period length T/n. More formally,

$$J(u_1, u_2, \ldots, u_m) = \sum_{i=1}^{m} J_i(u_i)$$

$$J_i(u_i) = \sum_{t=1}^{n} ((S_i + C_i \cdot Y_t^i) \cdot \delta_t^i + H_i \cdot (X_{t-1}^i + Y_t^i - \frac{D_i}{2n}) \cdot \frac{T}{n})$$

where $\delta_t^i = \begin{cases} 1, & Y_t^i > 0 \\ 0, & Y_t^i = 0 \end{cases}$

A more simplified expression for total cost J is

$$J(u_1, u_2, \ldots, u_m) = \sum_{i=1}^{m} S_i u_i + \sum_{i=1}^{m} \frac{H_i T}{n} \sum_{t=0}^{n-1} X_t^i + \sum_{i=1}^{m} (C_i D_i + H_i D_i \frac{T}{2n}) \tag{7}$$

where we include the fact that

$$\sum_{t=1}^{n} Y_t^i = D_i \tag{8}$$

Ensuring that the anticipated demand be met is achieved by keeping stock non-negative. However, the primary purpose of inventory control is to ensure that the right amount of the right item is ordered at the right time, according to known demand, existed constraints and the objective to minimize total cost, where cost is given by the equation: Total Cost = Ordering_Cost + Holding_Cost + Purchase_Cost.

This function can be broadened by additional costs according to the real nature of the inventory problem. Ordering cost includes costs arising from the preparation and dispatch of the order, checking of the goods on delivery, and other clerical support activities.

Now the following combinatorial problem on the dynamic discrete time system control process (3)–(5) can be formulated: for control variables $u_1, u_2, \ldots, u_m$ of the process (3)–(5) find such values from $\{1, 2, \ldots, n\}$ which satisfy all storage space constraints (6) and minimize the total cost (6).

Formally speaking, it could happen that for control variables $u_1, u_2, \ldots, u_m$ there are no feasible values from $\{1, 2, \ldots, n\}$, i.e. values which satisfy constraints (6). But, as $X_0^i = 0, i = 1, 2, \ldots, m$, then the first ordering of each product should be realized at the beginning of period 1. Therefore, condition

$$\sum_{i=1}^{m} \frac{D_i P_i}{n} \leq G \tag{9}$$

provides that at least values $u_1 = n, u_2 = n, \ldots, u_m = n$ are feasible. In further considerations we assume that condition (9) is satisfied.

As daily demand is constant, the outflow of inventory will be *D/T* per day, until the entire demand isn't met. The amount of inflow $Q_i = D_i/u_i$ will be available at the moment when the quantity of stock falls below the amount of daily demand in order to avoid a lack of inventory (negative stock, Fig. 2). The item will be ordered until the demand is fully met. Inventory replenishment will be realized N_0^I times, in equal amounts of $Q_i = D_i/u_i$.

Control domain is defined by relation which assures non-negativity of the stock (11) and by relation which assures non-negativity of control variables, as well as integer value (10).

$$\begin{aligned} &0 \leq u_t = N_0^I \leq T \\ &u_t = integer \end{aligned} \tag{10}$$

$$0 \leq X_{t-1} + Y_t^i - \frac{D_i}{n}, t = 1, 2, \ldots, n \tag{11}$$

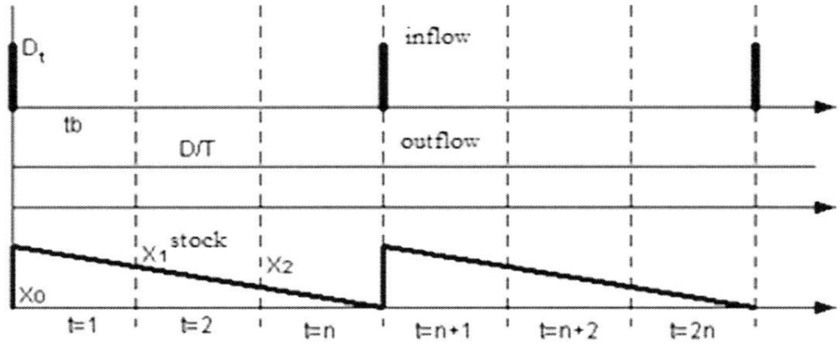

Fig. 2 Inflows, outflows and inventory state over time horizon, in accordance with (Kostic 2009)

3 Metaheuristics Approach for Solving Dynamic Discrete Inventory Control Problem with Storage Space Constraints

This section presents a special heuristic developed for solving the problem previously described in Sect. 2. The special heuristics is based on the optimization procedure described in (Djordjevic et al. 2017). Additionally, authors of the paper implemented variable neighborhood search (VBA) algorithm over the defined dynamic discrete model of multiproduct inventory control problem with storage space constraint, in order to compare results and evaluate the special heuristics.

3.1 Initial Solution

An initial solution ensures minimum of ordering costs for each item. Initial non-feasible solution is generated by initial heuristics. This solution is used as a starting point of searching control domain with special heuristics.

Initial heuristics is based on the following.

For each product *i*, the process described by relations (3)–(8) and the problem of total cost minimizing (6) in accordance with storage space constraint (6) is observed independently. Total search algorithm is used in order to obtain an optimal solution u_i^* with minimal costs for each product *i*, where the storage space constraint per each product separately are satisfied. In general, solution $u^1 = \left(u_1^*, u_2^*, \ldots, u_m^*\right)$ represents unfeasible point in relation to storage space constraint, Now, special heuristics starts from unfeasible point $u^1 = \left(u_1^*, u_2^*, \ldots, u_m^*\right)$. Although, u_i^* represents an "optimal" point that minimizes total costs for each product it is usually unacceptable point in relation to the limit of storage. Starting from this point, special heuristics tends to generate a feasible point, where the total cost (7) is as close as possible to the cost of the "optimal" unfeasible point. The complete search procedure for finding in u_i^* is conducted as follows :

Step 1: For each item $i \in \{1, 2, \ldots, m\}$ and given number of orders, dynamic discrete inventory EOQ model calculates the cost $J_i(u_i)$ and maximum storage space that item would occupy in one period. As a result, is obtained a two-dimensional matrix $m \times n$, whose elements are values of cost and amounts of maximum occupied space for each order from 1 *to n* and for each product from 1 *to m*.
Step 2: For each product i, the initial heuristics algorithm finds the number of orders that gives the minimal value of inventory cost, while the space constraint for ordered quantity for product in each period is satisfied. The result of iteration for a one product is a range of total cost values for each order from 1 *to n*. In that range, the algorithm searches minimum value of cost (Fig. 3). In the output matrix, costs value are generated only in case of satisfying the space constraint for each item, otherwise the negative number "−1" is shown. Algorithm of special heuristics use this negative number, and if that negative number is shown in any combination of orders for products, that combination will be eliminated in searching domain. On that way algorithm of special heuristics reduces the number of search combinations (number of orders) and the search becomes much simplified.

Figure 3 indicates that the curve is not smooth and has a set of local minimums and maximums, which will have a great impact on the searching process of solutions in control domain.

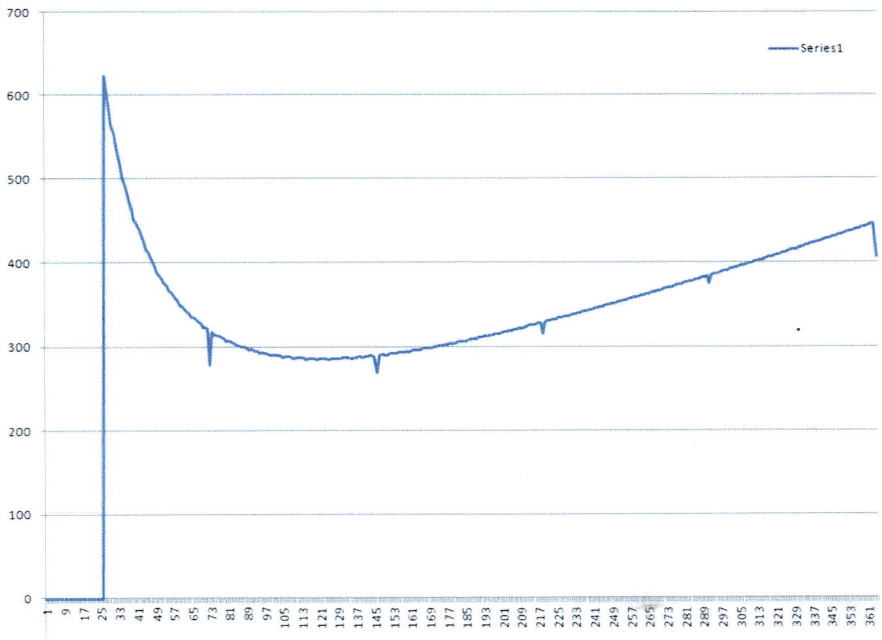

Fig. 3 The curve of total costs for one product for orders (1–365) which satisfied storage limitation (Antic 2014)

The initial solution generated by steps 1 and 2 has a minimum value for the objective function of the total cost for each product separately, while the total amount of occupied storage space for each product does not satisfy the storage constraints, which means the initial solution is unfeasible. However, the special heuristics developed in Sect. 3.2, starts with searching procedure from this unfeasible solution in order to find the feasible one.

The total cost per item is significantly increased with higher number of orders (Fig. 4). Based on previous assumption, algorithm defined in special heuristics, in Sect. 3.2, starts with searching procedure in direction of growth of minimal total cost. In other words, special heuristic will increase the cost and reduce the total occupied space in accordance with acceptable limits. Obtained number of orders for all products (combination of control variables values for all products) should minimize increase of costs, as much as possible, to satisfy the space constraint. In order to perform numerical experiments authors of the paper developed dynamic discrete inventory control model for three products. The model is implemented in a spreadsheet. It should be noted that the space limit was 200 m^2. Because of this restriction, output matrix excluded unacceptable solutions for each product, i.e. solutions that exceed the amount of the space constraint. Input data are presented in Fig. 5.

Decisions variables are represented as a number of orders per product (Fig. 5). Algorithm of initial heuristics implies variations of control variables values (from 1 to 365) for every product separately, in order to find ordering costs minimum and the optimal number of orders. After obtaining of initial solution for the first product, next product is examined. Consequently, each product can be ordered from 1 to 365 times per year.

For the numerical experiments, the following notations are used (Fig. 6):

$X_t^i, t = 1, 2, \ldots, 365, i = 1, 2, 3$—storage state variable represents total amount of product i that remains on the stock at the end of each period t;
$Y_t^i, t = 1, 2, \ldots, 365, i = 1, 2, 3$—input flow regulator represents quantity of product i ordered and stored in the storage on the beginning of each period t;
$Y_t^{i+3}, t = 1, 2, \ldots, 365, i = 1, 2, 3$—output flow regulator represents quantity of product i withdrawn from storage during period t;
u^i—Decision variable—Number of orders per product,
G—Total storage space for all products,
$O_t^i, t = 1, 2, \ldots, 365, i = 1, 2, 3$—amount of occupied storage space per product during the period t;
$J_t^i(u^i), t = 1, 2, \ldots, 365, i = 1, 2, 3$—inventory cost per product i in period t;
$\sum_{i=1}^{3} J_t^i$—total cost of inventories per product in period t.

Spreadsheet implementation of some elements of dynamic discrete model for $m = 3$ products and time horizon of 365 days is shown in Fig. 6. The control domain is presented by the vector $O_t^i, t = 1, 2, \ldots, 365, i = 1, 2, 3$ and enables checking of solution feasibility for each period regarding to occupation of the storage space. If control variable $u^i, i = 1, 2, 3$ has value that causes negativity of control area

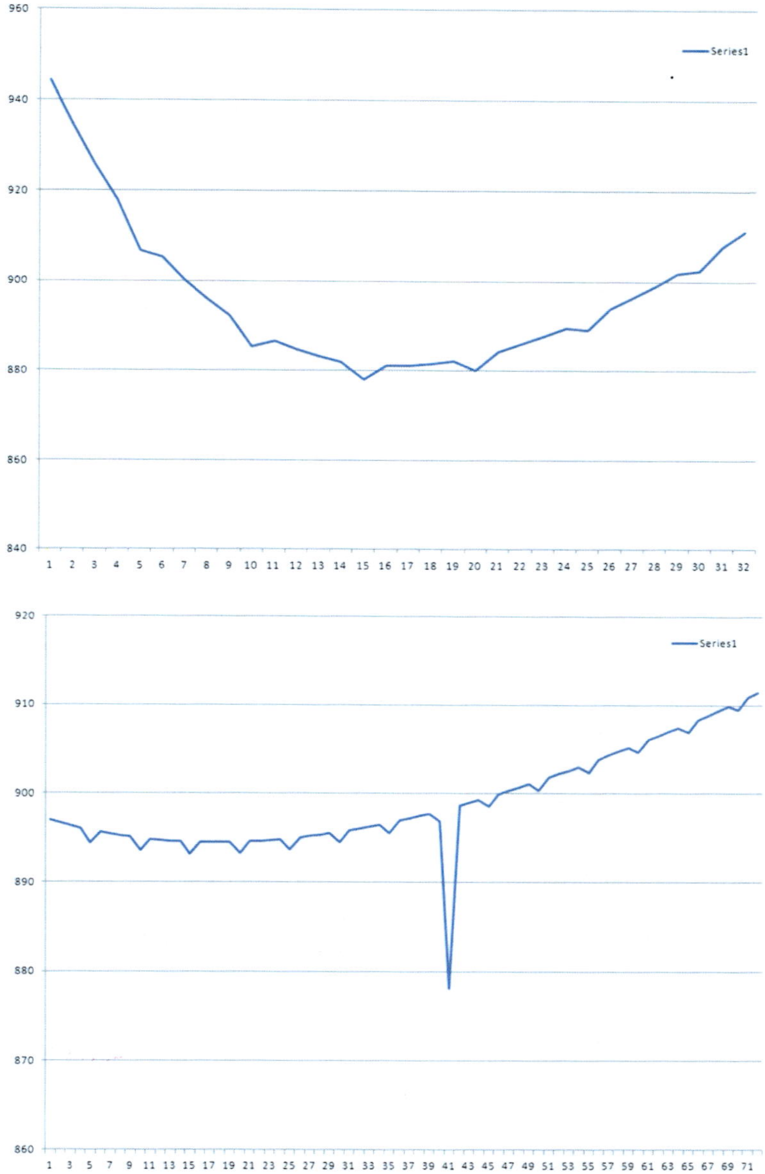

Fig. 4 Total costs curve for one product with local minimum and maximum

Product		Produc	Product	Product	Product 3
Number of days	T		365,00	365,00	365,00
Outflow per day	D/T		27,40	21,92	8,22
Fixed cost of a replenishment	S		1,00	7,00	12,00
Unit price	C		0,00	0,00	0,00
Inventory carrying cost	H		0,00822	0,00822	0,00822
Space (per unit)	P		1,00	1,20	1,70
Available space	G		200,00	200,00	200,00
Quantity ordered		q=D/u	#DIV/0!	#DIV/0!	#DIV/0!
		u=No	0	0	0

Fig. 5 Input data for three products

Control domain		O1	O2	O3	O4	
0,00	t=1	31,43	22,53	51,78	92,92	58.82
	t=2	4,03	0,61	43,56	126,76	
	t=3	35,46	23,14	35,34	104,51	58.82
	t=4	8,06	1,22	27,12	138,35	
	t=5	39,48	23,74	18,90	116,11	58.82
	t=6	12,09	1,83	10,68	149,94	
	t=7	43,51	24,35	2,47	127,70	58.82
	t=8	16,12	2,44	54,25	110,54	
	t=9	47,54	24,96	46,03	88,29	58.82
	t=10	20,15	3,04	37,81	122,13	
	t=11	51,57	25,57	29,59	99,89	58.82
	t=12	24,17	3,65	21,37	133,72	
	t=13	55,60	26,18	13,15	111,48	58.82
	t=14	28,20	4,26	4,93	145,31	
	t=15	0,81	26,79	56,71	101,48	
	t=16	32,23	4,87	48,49	105,91	58.82
	t=17	4,83	27,40	40,27	113,08	
	t=18	36,26	5,48	32,05	117,50	58.82
	t=19	8,86	28,01	23,84	124,67	
	t=20	40,29	6,09	15,62	129,09	58.82
	t=21	12,89	28,61	7,40	136,26	
	t=22	44,32	6,70	59,18	89,69	58.82
	t=23	16,92	29,22	50,96	96,85	
	t=24	48,35	7,31	42,74	101,28	58.82
	t=25	20,95	29,83	34,52	108,45	
	t=26	52,38	7,91	26,30	112,87	58.82
	t=27	24,98	30,44	18,08	120,04	
	t=28	56,41	8,52	9,86	124,46	58.82
	t=29	29,01	31,05	1,64	131,63	
	t=30	1,61	9,13	53,42	114,47	
	t=31	33,04	31,66	45,21	92,23	58.82
	t=32	5,64	9,74	36,99	126,06	
	t=33	37,07	32,27	28,77	103,82	58.82
	t=34	9,67	10,35	20,55	137,65	
	t=35	41,10	32,88	12,33	115,41	58.82
	t=36	13,70	10,96	4,11	149,25	

Flow regulators	Y1	Y2	Y3	Y4	Y5	Y6
t=1	58,82	44,44	60,00	27,40	21,92	8,22
t=2	0,00	0,00	0,00	27,40	21,92	8,22
t=3	58,82	44,44	0,00	27,40	21,92	8,22
t=4	0,00	0,00	0,00	27,40	21,92	8,22
t=5	58,82	44,44	0,00	27,40	21,92	8,22
t=6	0,00	0,00	0,00	27,40	21,92	8,22
t=7	58,82	44,44	0,00	27,40	21,92	8,22
t=8	0,00	0,00	60,00	27,40	21,92	8,22
t=9	58,82	44,44	0,00	27,40	21,92	8,22
t=10	0,00	0,00	0,00	27,40	21,92	8,22
t=11	58,82	44,44	0,00	27,40	21,92	8,22
t=12	0,00	0,00	0,00	27,40	21,92	8,22
t=13	58,82	44,44	0,00	27,40	21,92	8,22
t=14	0,00	0,00	0,00	27,40	21,92	8,22
t=15	0,00	44,44	60,00	27,40	21,92	8,22
t=16	58,82	0,00	0,00	27,40	21,92	8,22
t=17	0,00	44,44	0,00	27,40	21,92	8,22
t=18	58,82	0,00	0,00	27,40	21,92	8,22
t=19	0,00	44,44	0,00	27,40	21,92	8,22
t=20	58,82	0,00	0,00	27,40	21,92	8,22
t=21	0,00	44,44	0,00	27,40	21,92	8,22
t=22	58,82	0,00	60,00	27,40	21,92	8,22
t=23	0,00	44,44	0,00	27,40	21,92	8,22
t=24	58,82	0,00	0,00	27,40	21,92	8,22
t=25	0,00	44,44	0,00	27,40	21,92	8,22
t=26	58,82	0,00	0,00	27,40	21,92	8,22
t=27	0,00	44,44	0,00	27,40	21,92	8,22
t=28	58,82	0,00	0,00	27,40	21,92	8,22
t=29	0,00	44,44	0,00	27,40	21,92	8,22
t=30	0,00	0,00	60,00	27,40	21,92	8,22
t=31	58,82	44,44	0,00	27,40	21,92	8,22
t=32	0,00	0,00	0,00	27,40	21,92	8,22
t=33	58,82	44,44	0,00	27,40	21,92	8,22
t=34	0,00	0,00	0,00	27,40	21,92	8,22
t=35	58,82	44,44	0,00	27,40	21,92	8,22
t=36	0,00	0,00	0,00	27,40	21,92	8,22

State variables	X1	X2	X3
t=0	0	0	0
t=1	31,43	22,53	51,78
t=2	4,03	0,61	43,56
t=3	35,46	23,14	35,34
t=4	8,06	1,22	27,12
t=5	39,48	23,74	18,90
t=6	12,09	1,83	10,68
t=7	43,51	24,35	2,47
t=8	16,12	2,44	54,25
t=9	47,54	24,96	46,03
t=10	20,15	3,04	37,81
t=11	51,57	25,57	29,59
t=12	24,17	3,65	21,37
t=13	55,60	26,18	13,15
t=14	28,20	4,26	4,93
t=15	0,81	26,79	56,71
t=16	32,23	4,87	48,49
t=17	4,83	27,40	40,27
t=18	36,26	5,48	32,05
t=19	8,86	28,01	23,84
t=20	40,29	6,09	15,62
t=21	12,89	28,61	7,40
t=22	44,32	6,70	59,18
t=23	16,92	29,22	50,96
t=24	48,35	7,31	42,74
t=25	20,95	29,83	34,52
t=26	52,38	7,91	26,30
t=27	24,98	30,44	18,08
t=28	56,41	8,52	9,86
t=29	29,01	31,05	1,64
t=30	1,61	9,13	53,42
t=31	33,04	31,66	45,21
t=32	5,64	9,74	36,99
t=33	37,07	32,27	28,77
t=34	9,67	10,35	20,55
t=35	41,10	32,88	12,33
t=36	13,70	10,96	4,11

Performance criteria	ΣJ	J1	J2	J3
t=0	0,00	0,00	0,00	0,00
t=1	21,11	1,37	7,28	12,46
t=2	21,74	1,52	7,37	12,85
t=3	30,75	2,92	14,65	13,18
t=4	31,28	3,10	14,75	13,43
t=5	40,19	4,54	22,04	13,62
t=6	40,63	4,75	22,14	13,74
t=7	49,45	6,22	29,43	13,80
t=8	62,28	6,46	29,54	26,28
t=9	71,49	7,97	36,84	26,69
t=10	72,23	8,25	36,95	27,03
t=11	81,34	9,78	44,25	27,31
t=12	81,98	10,09	44,37	27,52
t=13	91,00	11,66	51,68	27,66
t=14	91,55	12,01	51,80	27,74
t=15	111,47	12,13	59,11	40,24
t=16	113,41	13,50	59,24	40,67
t=17	121,25	13,66	66,56	41,03
t=18	123,09	15,07	66,69	41,33
t=19	130,83	15,25	74,01	41,56
t=20	132,57	16,70	74,15	41,72
t=21	140,21	16,91	81,48	41,82
t=22	154,35	18,39	81,62	54,34
t=23	162,39	18,64	88,95	54,79
t=24	164,43	20,15	89,10	55,17
t=25	172,37	20,44	96,44	55,49
t=26	174,32	21,98	96,59	55,74
t=27	182,16	22,30	103,93	55,92
t=28	184,01	23,87	104,09	56,04
t=29	191,75	24,23	111,44	56,09
t=30	204,52	24,35	111,61	68,56
t=31	213,66	25,74	118,96	68,96
t=32	214,32	25,89	119,13	69,30
t=33	223,37	27,31	126,48	69,57
t=34	223,94	27,50	126,66	69,78
t=35	232,88	28,95	134,02	69,91
t=36	233,35	29,18	134,20	69,98

Fig. 6 Input and output elements of model

(elements of spreadsheet model with negative values will be colored in red), it can be concluded that given solution is unfeasible and that storage space constraint is not satisfied. The spreadsheet model (Fig. 6) contains values of input flow regulators $Y_t^i, t = 1, 2, \ldots, 365, i = 1, 2, 3$ which represent quantity of products that enter in storage. Output flow regulators are presented as $Y_t^{i+3}, t = 1, 2, \ldots, 365, i = 1, 2, 3$ and represent quantity of product that exit from the storage. State of inventories is presented by variables $X_t^i, t = 1, 2, \ldots, 365, i = 1, 2, 3$ which describe inventory level at each time period t. Objective function is calculated for each product in each time period, as well as its total value for all items per period. Initial heuristics define output results matrix with dimensions 365×3, where the columns of the matrix

	Product 1		Product 2		Product 3	
	TC1	Surface 1	TC2	Surface 2	TC3	Surface 3
1	-1,00	-1,00	-1,00	-1,00	-1,00	-1,00
2	-1,00	-1,00	-1,00	-1,00	-1,00	-1,00
3	-1,00	-1,00	-1,00	-1,00	-1,00	-1,00
4	-1,00	-1,00	-1,00	-1,00	-1,00	-1,00
5	-1,00	-1,00	-1,00	-1,00	-1,00	-1,00
6	-1,00	-1,00	-1,00	-1,00	-1,00	-1,00
7	-1,00	-1,00	-1,00	-1,00	-1,00	-1,00
8	-1,00	-1,00	-1,00	-1,00	-1,00	-1,00
9	-1,00	-1,00	-1,00	-1,00	-1,00	-1,00
10	-1,00	-1,00	-1,00	-1,00	-1,00	-1,00
11	-1,00	-1,00	-1,00	-1,00	-1,00	-1,00
12	-1,00	-1,00	-1,00	-1,00	-1,00	-1,00
13	-1,00	-1,00	-1,00	-1,00	-1,00	-1,00
14	-1,00	-1,00	-1,00	-1,00	-1,00	-1,00
15	-1,00	-1,00	-1,00	-1,00	488,22	200,00
16	-1,00	-1,00	-1,00	-1,00	484,81	187,50
17	-1,00	-1,00	-1,00	-1,00	480,31	176,47
18	-1,00	-1,00	-1,00	-1,00	477,64	166,67
19	-1,00	-1,00	-1,00	-1,00	476,52	157,89
20	-1,00	-1,00	-1,00	-1,00	474,25	150,00
21	-1,00	-1,00	-1,00	-1,00	478,03	142,86
22	-1,00	-1,00	-1,00	-1,00	480,31	136,36
23	-1,00	-1,00	-1,00	-1,00	483,44	130,43
24	-1,00	-1,00	-1,00	-1,00	487,32	125,00
25	-1,00	-1,00	-1,00	-1,00	489,86	120,00
26	-1,00	-1,00	-1,00	-1,00	496,93	115,38
27	-1,00	-1,00	-1,00	-1,00	502,54	111,11
28	-1,00	-1,00	-1,00	-1,00	508,60	107,14
29	-1,00	-1,00	-1,00	-1,00	515,08	103,45
30	-1,00	-1,00	-1,00	-1,00	520,27	100,00
31	-1,00	-1,00	-1,00	-1,00	529,09	96,77
32	-1,00	-1,00	-1,00	-1,00	536,57	93,75
33	-1,00	-1,00	-1,00	-1,00	544,32	90,91
34	-1,00	-1,00	-1,00	-1,00	552,32	88,24
35	-1,00	-1,00	-1,00	-1,00	559,14	85,71
36	-1,00	-1,00	-1,00	-1,00	568,99	83,33
37	-1,00	-1,00	-1,00	-1,00	577,62	81,08
38	-1,00	-1,00	-1,00	-1,00	586,43	78,95
39	-1,00	-1,00	-1,00	-1,00	595,40	76,92
40	-1,00	-1,00	608,77	200,00	603,29	75,00

No. Orders Product 1	No. Orders Product 2	No. Orders Product 3	TC	Surface
146	40	20	1352,301	418,493151

Fig. 7 Output matrix of results for total costs and storage constrains for 1–365 orders

present total cost and the maximum of occupied space per period for each product for the number of orders from 1 to 365. The number of order combinations can be calculated as 365^i, where i represents number of orders $i = 1, \ldots, m$. For example, for three products number of combinations is $365^3 = 48,627,125$. Part of the output matrix for orders from 1 to 365 orders is presented by Fig. 7.

Following the realization of the described steps, the special heuristics and the VNS metaheuristic use cost values and amount of storage space for each generated solution (number of orders per products) from the output matrix. It should be noted that in the output matrix (Fig. 7) contains values denoted as "-1". These negative values indicate that for particular item and particular number of orders, maximum occupied space per period is greater than the limit of 200 m^2, so this value will not be taken into account in process of searching control domain. Consequently, there is a significant reduction of number of solutions during the control domain search.

Obtained minimum costs are, see Fig. 8: 146 orders for product 1, 40 orders for product 2 and for 20 orders product 3. Total cost of ordering for all items is equal to 1352.30 and total maximum occupied area per day (for all three items) is 418.50 m^2. This solution is unfeasible, because of total occupied space for all products (418 m^2) is greater than limit of the storage space (200 m^2).

No. Orders Product 1	No. Orders Product 2	No. Orders Product 3	TC	Surface
146	40	20	1352,301	418,493151

Fig. 8 Initial unfeasible solution for three products

In accordance with the special heuristics algorithm, searching process of control domain continues from initial solution in direction of cost growth, by examination of points which belong to a neighborhood of the current solution. It is important to note that in the "row" of minimum costs, searching procedure starts from unfeasible solution for all products (Fig. 9), and continue iterations in the direction of cost growth. Solutions from the neighborhood of the local minimum point will certainly increase total costs in order to reduce unfeasibility caused by storage space constraint violation.

3.2 Special Heuristics

Special heuristics developed in (Djordjevic et al. 2017) is used for obtaining of control variable values (number of orders), while metaheuristics technique based on variable neighborhood search was developed with aim of results comparison. The special heuristics generates a feasible set of ordering scenarios.

The main elements of the special heuristics are defined as follows:

The search space U: Space U contains all m-triples $u = (u_1, u_2, \ldots, u_m)$ such that $u_i \in \{1, 2, \ldots, n\}, i = 1, 2, \ldots, m$. It means that during a search process through space U the heuristic can generate not only feasible solutions u, with coordinates $u_1, u_2, \ldots, u_m$ which satisfy storage space constraints (6), but also unfeasible ones which do not fulfill these constraints.

Objective functions: The "quality" of a generated solution u is measured in two ways:

- if u is feasible then its quality is measured by the corresponding value of the total cost $J(u)$ defined by (7). A feasible solution u_1 is better than a feasible solution u_2 if $J(u_1) < J(u_2)$.
- if u is unfeasible then its "unfeasibility gap" is measured by value $L(u)$, where

$$L(u) = \max_{t=1,2,\ldots,n} \left(\sum_{i=1}^{m} (X_{t-1}^i + Y_t^i) P_i - G \right) \tag{12}$$

The unfeasible solution u_1 is better than the unfeasible solution u_2 if $L(u_1) < L(u_2)$.

The heuristics is based on the local search technique. Starting from an initial solution, the best (feasible or unfeasible) point from the "neighborhood" of current solution is obtained in each iteration. The obtained solution represents next searching

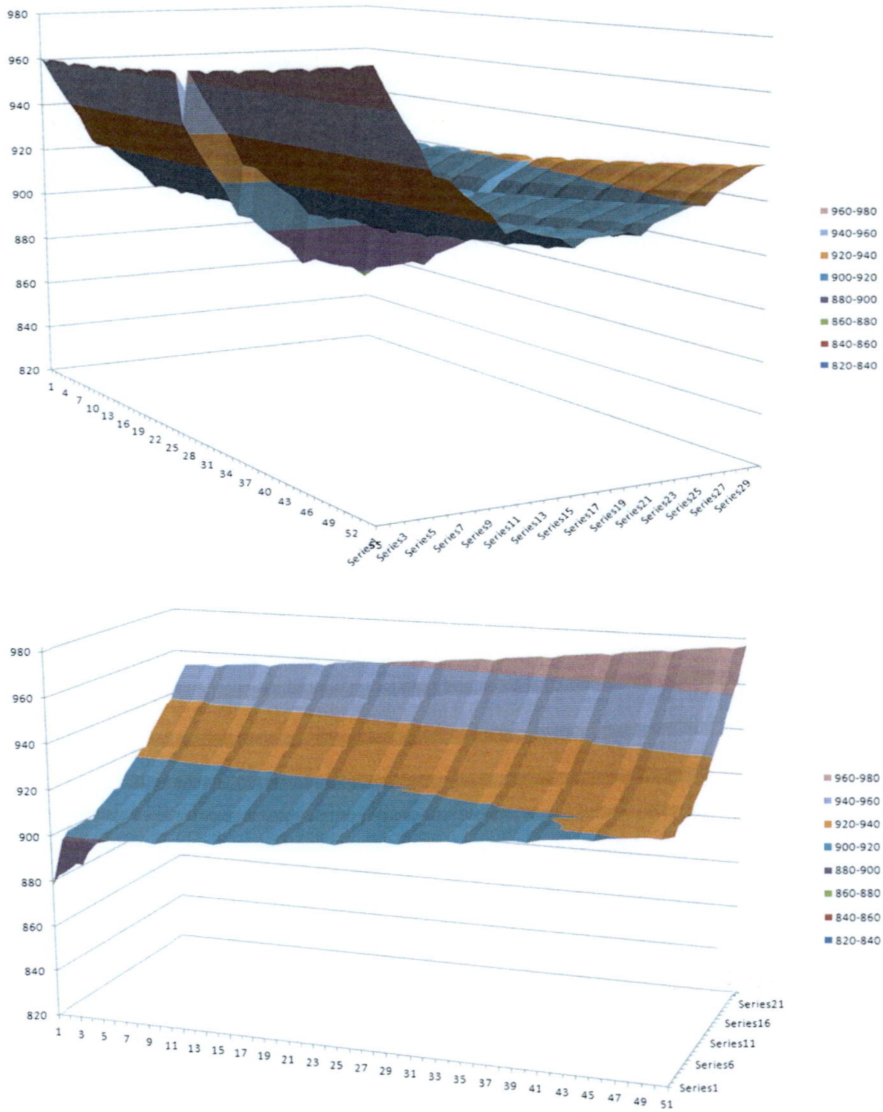

Fig. 9 Three-dimensional view of total cost curve

Proizvodi

	1	2	3
1	0	0	0
2	0	0	1
3	0	1	0
4	0	1	1
5	1	0	0
6	1	0	1
7	1	1	0
8	1	1	1

P1	P2	P3	P4	P5	P6	P7	P8	P9	P10	P11	P12	P13	P14	P15	P16	P17	P18	P19	P20	P21	Trošak	Površina
146	40	20	146	40	20	146	40	20	146	40	20	146	40	20	146	40	20	146	40	30	9362,137	2879,452
146	40	20	146	40	20	146	40	20	146	40	20	146	40	20	146	40	20	146	40	40	9395,151	2854,452
146	40	20	146	40	20	146	40	20	146	40	20	146	40	20	146	40	20	146	50	30	9372,959	2839,452
146	40	20	146	40	20	146	40	20	146	40	20	146	40	20	146	40	30	146	40	30	9408,164	2829,452
146	40	20	146	40	20	146	40	20	146	40	20	146	40	20	146	40	30	146	40	40	9441,178	2804,452
146	40	20	146	40	20	146	40	20	146	40	20	146	40	20	146	40	30	146	50	30	9418,986	2789,452
146	40	20	146	40	20	146	40	20	146	40	20	146	40	30	146	40	30	146	40	30	9454,192	2779,452
146	40	20	146	40	20	146	40	20	146	40	20	146	40	30	146	40	30	146	40	40	9487,205	2754,452
146	40	20	146	40	20	146	40	20	146	40	20	146	40	30	146	40	30	146	50	30	9465,014	2739,452
146	40	20	146	40	20	146	40	20	146	40	30	146	40	30	146	40	30	146	40	30	9500,219	2729,452
146	40	20	146	40	20	146	40	20	146	40	30	146	40	30	146	40	30	146	40	40	9533,233	2704,452
146	40	20	146	40	20	146	40	20	146	40	30	146	40	30	146	40	30	146	50	30	9511,041	2689,452
146	40	20	146	40	20	146	40	30	146	40	30	146	40	30	146	40	30	146	40	30	9546,247	2679,452
146	40	20	146	40	20	146	40	30	146	40	30	146	40	30	146	40	30	146	40	40	9579,26	2654,452
146	40	20	146	40	20	146	40	30	146	40	30	146	40	30	146	40	30	146	50	30	9557,068	2639,452
146	40	20	146	40	30	146	40	30	146	40	30	146	40	30	146	40	30	146	40	30	9592,274	2629,452
146	40	20	146	40	30	146	40	30	146	40	30	146	40	30	146	40	30	146	40	40	9625,288	2604,452

Fig. 10 Variations of "neighborhood" of initial solution for instance of 3 products and 21 products

point. If the current solution is feasible and there is no better solution in the neighborhood, the structure of this neighborhood is changing. Now, the best solution is searched again in the modified neighborhood (Fig. 10).

This principle is similar to a principle of a very well-know variable neighborhood search (VNS) metaheuristics (Mladenovic 1995; Hansen and Mladenovic 2001), which is used to avoid "traps" of local optima. δ-neighborhood $N(\delta,\ u^k)$ of current point $u^k = \left(u_1^k, u_2^k, \ldots, u_m^k\right)$ from space U is defined as a set of all points $u = (u_1, u_2, \ldots, u_m)$ from U such that u^k and u are different in just one coordinate, for example coordinate u_i^k and $\left|u_i^k - u_i\right| = \delta$ is satisfied. Theoretically speaking, neighborhood $N(\delta,\ u^k)$ could be empty in the case when does not exist a coordinate i such that $u_i^n + \delta$ or $u_i^n - \delta$ belong to $\{1, 2, \ldots, n\}$. Neighborhood structures are defined in accordance with a predefined set of natural numbers $\delta_0, \delta_1, \ldots, \delta_s$ where $s > 1$ and $\delta_1 < \delta_2 < \ldots < \delta_s < \delta_0$. When current point u^k is unfeasible, structure δ_0 is joined, i.e. heuristic searching δ_0 neighborhood $N(\delta_0,\ u^k)$. When it is feasible, one of the δ_j structures is joining $j \in \{1, 2, \ldots, s\}$ i.e. δ_j—neighborhood $N(\delta_j,\ u^k)$ is searched. If the current point cannot be improved, we continue searching the $N(\delta_{j+1},\ u^k)$ neighborhood. Note that in real-life problems n is much larger than δ_0 (usually $n = 365$ days) and therefore defined neighborhood structures provide non-empty neighborhoods.

The initial solution: The initial solution $u^1 \in U$ can be generated in the following way: for each product i we consider independently the process (3)–(5) and the problem of minimizing the total cost for this product defined by (7), and it refers to storage space constraints $(X_{t-1}^i + Y_t^i)P_i \leq G, t = 1, 2, \ldots, n$. We find the optimal solution u_i^* to this problem using a total enumeration procedure. Now, the heuristics starts from $u_1 = \left(u_1^*, u_2^*, \ldots, u_m^*\right)$ as an initial solution. Although u^1 represents an "ideal" point that minimizes the total cost for each product, it is usually unfeasible according to storage space constraints (6). Starting from this point, the heuristics strives to generate feasible points where total costs (7) are as close as possible to the values of the costs for an ideal point.

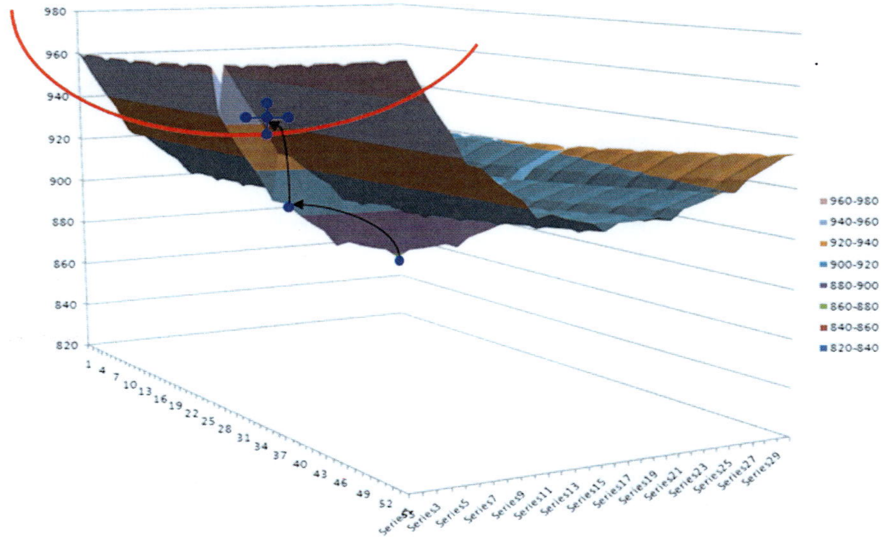

Fig. 11 Graphical interpretation of iteration steps for k = 1, 2, …, k_{max} for special heuristics

The heuristics can be described more specifically with the following steps (Fig. 11):

Initialization step: generate ideal point $u^1 = \left(u_1^*, u_2^*, \ldots, u_m^*\right)$. If u^1 is a feasible point, join δ_1 structure. If u^1 is unfeasible point, join δ_0 structure;

Iteration step: For $k = 1, 2, \ldots$

- If point u^k is unfeasible, find the best feasible point u_{best}^f in the neighborhood $N(\delta_0,\ u^k)$ (according to criteria function $J(u)$), join the neighborhood structure δ_1 and set $u^{k+1} = u_{best}^f$. If there are no feasible points in the neighborhood $N(\delta_0,\ u^k)$, find the best unfeasible point u_{best}^f (according to criterion function $L(u)$). If u_{best}^f is better than u^k, join the neighborhood structure δ_0 and set $u^{k+1} = u_{best}^f$.
- If the point u^k is feasible with joined structure δ_j for $j \in \{1, 2, \ldots, s\}$, find the best feasible point u_{best}^f in the neighborhood $N(\delta_j,\ u^k)$. If u_{best}^f is better than u^k, join the neighborhood structure δ_1 and set $u^{k+1} = u_{best}^f$. If u_{best}^f is not better than u^k or there are no feasible points in the neighborhood $N(\delta_j,\ u^k)$ remain in the point u^k, i.e. $u^{k+1} = u^k$, and join the new neighborhood structure δ_{j+1}.

The stopping criterion:

- If the current point u^k is unfeasible and there are no feasible points in the neighborhood $N(\delta_0,\ u^k)$, stop if the best unfeasible point u_{best}^f from the neighborhood is worse than the point u^k.
- If the point u^k is feasible with joined structure δ_s stop if the best unfeasible point u_{best}^f from the neighborhood $N(\delta_s,\ u^k)$ is worse than the point u^k or there are no feasible points in this neighborhood.

Table 1 Ranges of input data

	D_i [unit]	P_i [m^2/unit]	S_i [$/order]	C_i [$/unit]	H_i [$/unit/day]
range	[1000; 10,000]	[0.10; 2.00]	[1;15]	[0; 100]	[3; 7]

k	Solving technique	Initial solutions	Best value of the objective cost function	Average value of the objective cost function	Time of search for Column 3 [sec]	Average time of search for Column 4 [sec]
	1	2	3	4	5	6
5	Special heuristics	Deterministic	119.145,02	119.145,02	00:01:57	00:01:57
	VNS algorithm	Deterministic	120.960,53	122.857,79	00:05:05	00:06:42
10	Special heuristics	Deterministic	119.565,54	119.565,54	00:01:02	00:01:02
	VNS algorithm	Deterministic	121.619,03	124.585,00	00:02:11	00:03:06
15	Special heuristics	Deterministic	118.734,27	118.734,27	00:00:43	00:00:43
	VNS algorithm	Deterministic	123.669,93	127.404,19	00:01:41	00:02:02
20	Special heuristics	Deterministic	116.979,20	116.979,20	00:00:34	00:00:34
	VNS algorithm	Deterministic	124.150,54	129.120,54	00:01:09	00:01:36

Fig. 12 Numerical results in total cost and CPU time

3.3 Numerical Experiments

In order to investigate behavior of the special heuristics and VNS algorithm, and compare their efficiency, they were preliminarily tested on a hypothetic problem with $m = 102$ products, where the inventory control process is considered during period $T = 1$ year which is divided into $n = 365$ days. The total available storage space is equal to $G = 3500$ m^2. Ranges of other input data for all products are given in Table 1. The optimal solution of this problem is not known in advance.

We performed four groups of numerical experiments with $k_{\text{max}} = 5, 10, 15, 20$. For each of these values the VNS algorithm was applied 10 times generating an initial solution by the deterministic procedure, described in Sect. 3.1. Special heuristics was applied once for each value, because the results were the same for the same value of parameter k_{max}, generating an initial solution by the same deterministic procedure as for the VNS algorithm. The stopping criterion for the VNS algorithm is more than 1000 iterations between two improvements of objective function (7). The stopping criterion for special heuristics is described in Sect. 3.2. The corresponding best values of the objective function (7) as well as the average execution CPU time for both solving techniques are presented in Fig. 12.

The numerical experiments show that in all cases the results obtained by the special heuristics, as well as the duration of execution time, are better than those obtained with the VNS based algorithm. Considering only the results of special heuristics we could not notice that either the quality of obtained objective function values or the duration of execution time are dependent on values of k_{max}.

Preliminary numerical results (Fig. 12) shows that the both algorithms could be efficiently applied to problems of smaller dimensions and that results obtained by special heuristics are better than those obtained with the VNS based algorithm.

The applicability of dynamic discrete EOQ inventory control model and efficiency of initial and special heuristics was additionally tested on the case of the company "La Fantana", Serbia (Antic and Djordjevic 2014). The company is a leader in the field of bottling and distribution of water and water coolers in Serbia. Model is applied over the real data collected in the company in 2011. Model results are compared with real data for year 2011, and the quality of obtained solutions was acceptable for further planning period.

4 Spreadsheet Modeling and Error Detection

Inventory control problems, described in the Sect. 1, become more complex in the case of many products, because a number of control dimensions is increased. The problem setting, as well as the choice of a method for solving inventory control problems, is influenced by the circumstances, constraints and other specificities of each enterprise. It is therefore impossible to establish a unique way to solve problems that could be applied in different situations, nor use universal software. In line with changes of circumstances and constraints inventory control logic should be adjusted. Taking into account the characteristics of spreadsheets, they represent a very convenient environment for the development of these models (Djordjevic 2017). In comparison to the specialized software, spreadsheets provide required flexibility through the analysis from many different perspectives. These models can be easily modified and enhanced in order to reflect new situations and options. The user can add complexity to the model, in compliance with the increase of experience and knowledge about the process. Spreadsheet implements simulation or optimization model or both in the same time.

Even more, understanding of spreadsheet simulation models represents a basis for problem understanding and determining of solution, which is important for practical investigations or for further shifting to special software (Djordjevic and Vasiljevic 2013; Antic 2007). However, complex inventory control problems require advance knowledge of spreadsheet modeling and engineering, as well as domain knowledge. Although spreadsheet popularity is partially based on the ease of usage without formal programming education, an alternative of spreadsheet modeling and simulation requires much longer learning curve. Still, business people are usually end-user programmers and more familiar with spreadsheets then with programming languages.

According to Grossman (2010), spreadsheet represents convenient platform for operations research (OR) work. This application enables analyzes in less time, at lower cost and with higher level of user acceptance than with traditional standalone OR software. The same source states that contemporary spreadsheets empowered by numerous add-ins additionally support simulation, decision trees, forecasting, queuing and other OR techniques. Development direction of spreadsheets implies Big Data analytics as a challenge of the modern business world.

Spreadsheets are often used by non-programmers but rather domain experts, for a number of different purposes. End-users are enabled to build their own supporting software tools, which directly encode their expertise. Furthermore, spreadsheet application may be developed by one person and used by others (for example OR application for less-sophisticated users). This kind of usage may results in "software as a service" (SAAS) approach, as a future direction of spreadsheet development.

Time required for developing of models and applications in spreadsheet environment is considerably shorter than for other business applications, because of development independent from IT department and standard QA processes (Jannach et al. 2014). However, the same fact is one of the causes why spreadsheets frequently contain a lot of errors. End-users are often self-taught and do not understand the difficulties of creating error-free code, even more dangerous they are unaware of consequences that errors may cause.

Causes of spreadsheet errors are numerous, beside unfamiliarity with basic modeling and programming principles, they include mechanical, logic and omission errors, or even domain logic errors. An exhaustive overview of spreadsheet errors, their classification, impact, frequency is presented in (Panko and Aurigemma 2010). Numerous examples and evidences related to spreadsheet errors and significance of their consequences have been presented within European Spreadsheet Risk Interest Group[1] (EuSpRiG) conferences. In accordance with importance and actuality of spreadsheet risk topic many researchers have proposed a number of techniques and automated tools aimed at supporting end-users in the development and usage of error-free spreadsheets.

In order to enable and facilitate usage of previously described inventory control model to business people from the real world, the authors of this paper realized spreadsheet implementation (Fig. 6). The metaheuristic and special heuristic procedures are developed in *Visual Basic for Application*, and it uses intermediate results obtained from the spreadsheet model (Djordjevic et al. 2017). Furthermore, the authors developed spreadsheet error detection and debugging approach for the described dynamic discrete inventory control model based on (Djordjevic 2016). Basic steps of the error detection and debugging approach are presented in Table 2. Multiproduct EOQ-based inventory problem with storage space constraints is modeled in a spreadsheet trough the following elements. Circumstances variables including total demand, ordering (setup) cost, purchase cost per product unit, inventory holding cost, available storage space are considered as input data. State variables, flow regulators, control space and auxiliary variables are implemented as intermediate cells. A performance criterion is represented in output cells. Objective function adds values throughout at each time period t ($t = 1, 2, \ldots, T$). Based on the rules of spreadsheet modeling best practice, periods of time horizon are defined by spreadsheet rows, while variables are presented by columns, because there are more time periods to be considered then different variables.

[1] http://www.eusprig.org/.

Table 2 Basic steps of the error detection and debugging approach

Initialization
- Inspect and correct formulas that implement objective function
- Find global bounds of the objective function

Repeat until the stopping criteria is met
- **Step 1:** Set test case
- **Step 2:** Inspect values of the objective function
  - ➢ If the objective function values satisfy global bounds constraint
    then set local bounds
    inspect local bounds constraint
    inspect constraint of objective function cumulative
  - ➢ otherwise update LPE
- **Step 3:** Inspect values of peaks
- **Step 4:** LPE pruning
- **Step 5:** Examination of pruned LPE
  - ➢ If formula corrections exist
    then return to Step 2
  - ➢ otherwise
    - o if LPEF is empty
      LPE = next level predecessors
      return to Step 4
    - o otherwise LPE=LPEF
      return to Step 4

4.1 The Spreadsheet Error Detection and Debugging (SEDD) Approach

The developed spreadsheet error detection and debugging (SEDD) approach refers to errors occurred during model implementation or introduced after implementation, by mistake, accidentally or due to lack of model understanding during utilization. Examples of considered quantitative errors imply overwriting of a formula with a number, incorrect cell reference in formula, exchanging a minus by a multiplication symbol or exchanging a minus by a plus symbol and vice versa. Qualitative errors included incorrect variable type in formulas, incorrect time period for some variables in formulas and elimination of some formula parts (omitted predecessor).

In order to explain SEDD approach developed for the described DDICM, following notation is used:

TS—test case (set of decision variables u_i).
$J_{t,i}(TS)$—objective function $J_i(u_i)$, representing cost for product i in period t ($t = 1, \ldots, T$; $i = 1, \ldots, m$) for test case *TS*.
$\sum_{i=1}^{m} J_{t,i}$ - total objective function $J(u_1, u_2, \ldots, u_m)$,($t = 1, \ldots, T$), in period t defined by Eq. (2).
glb_i—global lower bound of the objective function for product i ($i = 1, \ldots, m$).
gub_i—global upper bound of the objective function for product i ($i = 1, \ldots, m$).
$llb_i\ (TS)$—local lower bound of the objective function for product i ($i = 1, \ldots, m$) for test case *TS*.

lub_i *(TS)*—local upper bound of the objective function for product i ($i = 1, \ldots, m$) for test case *TS*.
LE—list of errors.
LPE—list of error indications.
LPEF—list of cells with possibly erroneous formula.

Initial phase of the error detection for DDICM considers inspection of spreadsheet formulas which implement objective function for every product i and the total cost at each period t. In order to inspect those formulas authors of the paper used *R1C1* spreadsheet reference style which is based on a relative distance of formula elements from the cell. Correct formula structure is defined in accordance with relation (7). All detected deviations from the correct structure of the formula should be corrected and saved in LE.

Unlike simple procedure for error detection in objective function formulas, inspection of state variables, flow regulators, control domain and auxiliary variables is more complex because of a number of different formulas which are interconnected. Additionally, the number is increased with increasing of problem dimension (number of items and observed time periods).

Cell where error is detected is not necessarily error cause, because error may be propagated from the root cell to the cells dependents. Interconnection of model elements enables error detection through deviation of objective function values (as output values) from expected correct values. But, one of the major problems is that users or model inspectors usually don't know correct value of model outputs for the final and intermediate periods. Even more, sets of decision variables (u_i) result in different objective function values. In order to overcome this problem, upper and lower bounds of the objective function and rules based on the model characteristics are used for error detection.

Lower bound refers to the value of the objection function in time period $t = 1$ and upper to $t = T$. If ordering is realized in every day of observed time horizon $u_i = T$ ($i = 1, \ldots, m$) then minimum lower bound corresponds to the cost of the first day $\min glb_i = J_{1,i}(T)$. Assuming that inventory holding costs are lower than ordering costs, maximum upper bound is obtained for daily basis ordering and correspond to the last day of time horizon $\max gub_i = J_{T,i}(T)$. Contrary to the described case, first day ordering of total product quantity $u_i = 1$ ($i = 1, \ldots, m$) implies maximum lower $\max glb_i = J_{1,i}(1)$ and minimum upper $\min gub_i = J_{T,i}(1)$ bounds obtaining. It is necessary to mention exception of this rule in the case of long time horizon. Namely, if inventory holding costs significantly increase over a long time horizon then decision variables for obtaining of minimum upper bound has to be determinate by some additional procedure (e.g. simulation, complete enumeration, limited enumeration, branch-and-bound etc.).

Obtaining of minimal lower and maximum upper bound includes relaxation of storage space constraint (6), and consequently none of the objective function values realized for the admissible test cases that consider storage space constraint, can't be higher/lower then bounds calculated in the described manner.

Table 3 Pseudocode for obtaining local bounds

```
Set TS
For i=1 to m
If min glb_i ≤ J_1,i(TS)≤ max glb_i then
   llb_i (TS)= J_1,i(TS)
Else
   update LPE
End if
If min gub_i ≤ J_T,i(TS) ≤ max gub_i then
   lub_i (TS)= J_T,i(TS)
Else
   update LPE
End if
Next i
```

Upper and lower bounds, previously described, are global and represent admissible interval for local ones. Local bounds, llb_i *(TS)* and lub_i *(TS)*, are defined as the objective function values in the beginning ($t = 1$) and in the last time period ($t = T$) for some test case (excluding $u_i= T$ and $u_i=1$). Test case comprises of admissible values of decision variables (u_i). Deviation of local bounds from admissible range defined by global bounds is indication of error. Pseudocode of bounds obtaining procedure is presented by Table 3.

Constraint of local bounds (13) implies a rule for error detection based on the local bounds. Additionally, objective function values in period *t*, for $1 < t < T - 1$, have to satisfy cumulatively constraint (14), since it adds values throughout at each time period. Constraint violation is another error indication. All error indications are recorded in *LPE*.

$$llb_i(TS) > J_{t,i}(TS) > lub_i(TS) \quad \text{for } t = 2, \ldots, T - 1 \tag{13}$$

$$J_{t,i}(TS) < J_{t+1,i}(TS) \quad \text{for } t = 1, \ldots, T - 1 \tag{14}$$

Authors of this paper defined *LPE* as a list of potentially erroneous cells, which includes cells where error is detected and their direct predecessors. Exception is error that arises when formula is replaced with constant and examining cell is error root which immediately becomes element of *LE*. Input data (total demand, ordering cost, purchase cost per product unit, inventory holding cost, available storage space), test case and variables at the initial time period are considered to be correct, and they are not investigated in the context of errors.

Another rule for error detection is based on the model characteristics (Sect. 2, Eqs. 3–5) and relates to peaks. Peak ($peak_{t,i}$) is considered as a rise of inventories caused by order arrival (for product *i* in time period *t*). If quotient ($D_i/u_i/D_i/T_i= T_i/u_i$) of ordered amount (D_i/u_i) and daily demand (D_i/T_i) differs from the number of days between two orders it is indication of state variables ($X_{t,i}$) error. Even more,

Table 4 Pseudocode of *LPE* pruning rules

```
//c1 and c2 are cells for examination
For each c1 in LPE
    Dependents_list = successors (c1)
    For each c2 in Dependents_list
        If c1 and c2 are variables of same type Then
           remove c2 and predecessors of c2 from LPE
        Else
           remove predecessors of c1 from LPE
        End if
    Next c2
Next c1
```

quantity of ordered products is the same for all peaks (D_i/u_i). Difference of these quantities implies error of flow regulator variable ($Y_{t,i}$).

Next phase of the approach, which follows error detection, is determination of error cause. As it is previously mentioned, often error root is in the same cell where the error is detected. Error may be propagated from the root is not to the dependent cells. In the case when error cause is not in the cell where error is detected error root implies some of predecessors. Cells that implement objective function throughout periods of time horizon are not considered in this step, since their formula structures are already inspected within initial phase of the approach. Interdependences of the model elements refer to a wide set of predecessor cells which possibly represent error root. Determination of error cause in acceptable time requires pruning of tree consisted of predecessors of cell where error is detected. This becomes more complex in the case when there are more detected errors (elements of *LPE*).

According to (Djordjevic 2017) tree that should be pruned represents elements of *LPE* and their direct predecessors. Pruning rules (Table 4) are the following (Djordjevic 2017):

- If some element of *LPE* (*c1*) is a predecessor to another cell from *LPE* (*c2*) and both refer to variable of the same type of (for example, state variable $X_{t,i}$) then successor cells *c2* and its other predecessors aren't candidates for further examination in the current iteration. This rule derives from characteristics of the dynamic discrete time system control model. Since values of variables are dependent on their values in previous time periods, earlier time periods variable has priority, because it impacts variable in next time period.
- If some element of *LPE* (*c1*) is predecessor of some other cell from *LPE* (*c2*), but those cells do not implement variables of the same type, then predecessors of *c1* aren't candidates for further examination in the current iteration. Obviously, this rule describes examination priority for cells that implement different type of variables. If potentially incorrect cell represents a predecessor of any other potentially incorrect cell, but those cells aren't variables of the same type, a parent cell should be examined first. This rule is based on breadth-first search procedure.

Table 5 Pseudocode of pruned *LPE* examination

```
For each c in pruned LPE
    If formula c(t) ≠ formula c(t-1) Or
       formula c(t) ≠ formula c(t+1) Then
       If formula c(t-1) = formula c(t+1) Then
          formula c(t) = formula c(t+1)
          update LE
       Else
          If formula c(t+1) = formula c(t+2) Then
             formula c(t) = formula c(t+1)
             update LE
             update LPEF
          Else
             update LPEF with c(t+1)and cell c(t+2)
             If formula c(t-1) = formula c(t-2) Then
                formula c(t) = formula c(t-1)
                update LE
             Else
                update LPEF with c(t-1) and cell c(t-2)
             End if
          End if
       End if
    End if
Next c
```

LPE pruning is followed by examination of remaining elements (Table 5). The examination is realized through comparison of spreadsheet formulas related to elements of pruned *LPE* with structure of formulas in the previous and the next cell. Under the previous and the next cell the authors consider cells that implement variable of the same type for time period $t - 1$ and $t + 1$. If formula structure of those two cells is the same, while the one of the analyzed element of LPE differs then it is probably erroneous cell. Correction implies new formula structure for examined cell (*LPE* element), in accordance with the structure in the previous and the next cell. Detected error and error correction update *LE*.

Examination of *LPE* element correctness is more complex when spreadsheet formulas for the variables of the same type for time period $t - 1$ and $t + 1$ are different. In this case one of those cells is potentially erroneous. Further analyze is based on the comparison with their neighbors (previous $t - 2$ or next $t + 2$ cell). For example, if spreadsheet formulas in cells that implements the variable in time period $t + 1$ and $t + 2$ are of the same structure, that structure is considered as correct. The correct structure of formula is used for revision of initially examined *LPE* element.

Consequently a cell that corresponds to time period $t - 1$ is probably erroneous and becomes element of *List of cells with possibly erroneous formula* (*LPEF*). But, if there is a difference between spreadsheet formulas in cells that implements the variable in time period $t + 1$ and $t + 2$ they become elements of *LPEF*. Examination continues in the same manner, for cell that refers to the variable in time period $t - 1$.

If the described procedure results in at least one correction the whole process is repeated form the second step (*Inspect values of the objective function*). Otherwise, under condition that *LPEF* is not empty, its elements become elements of *LPE* and the steps begging with the fourth (*LPE* pruning) are repeated. Lastly, if *LPEF* is empty, predecessors of cells analyzed in the current iteration and their direct predecessors are new elements of *LPE* and subject of pruning.

The stopping criterion may include empty LPE, which imply corrected spreadsheet model or the maximal number of iterations or the maximal CPU time.

4.2 Preliminary Experimental Results of the Approach Evaluation

Implementation of described error detection and debugging approach is realized in Visual Basic for Application. The approach is evaluated for the model presented in Sect. 2 developed in MS Excel spreadsheet. The efficiency is preliminary examined on several randomly generated instances with $m = 3$ products. Experiments are performed on Windows 7 Ultimate operating system on a Pentium (R) Dual-Core CPU T4200 processor with 4.00 GB of RAM and 2.00 GHz. In order to perform evaluation, the authors of the paper used spreadsheet model mutation (Abraham and Erwig 2009).

Model is mutated by injection of errors based on the spreadsheet-specific mutation operators, in accordance with quantitative and qualitative errors, mentioned in the previous section. Evaluation metrics were percentage of identified errors/repairs and CPU time. Scalability testing is conducted through variation of model dimension, by increment of observed time periods. Inventory control process is considered during periods $T = 1$ week, divided into $n = 7$ days; $T = 4$ weeks, divided into $n = 28$ days; and $T = 1$ year, divided into $n = 365$ days. The ranges of random input data are the same as in the Sect. 3.2 (Table 1).

Number of injected errors and error positions are randomly chosen and changed in ten iterations for each of instances. Test cases are created by simulation and consisted of admissible values for control variables. The results of the experiments are summarized in Table 6.

In the case of a single-fault and double-fault the approach efficiency is at the satisfactory level with one test case. Analyzes showed that number of detected errors remains unchanged up to five errors. However, increased number of injected errors requires more test cases. Presented results are conducted for five test cases. The efficiency remains high for increased number of errors, but CPU time notably depends on the selected test cases. Since, usage of all admissible solutions is usually impossible and time-consuming, test cases can be created randomly, by simulation or by application of some searching method. Further, CPU time is increased for longer time horizon. Considering that model elements are calculated in accordance with their values in previous time periods, number of time periods directly influence number

Table 6 Numerical results of the approach evaluation

No. of products	T (day)	Spreadsheet dimension (no. of cells)	No. of errors	Corrected errors (%)	Average CPU time (sec)
3	7	171	1	100	5,2
		171	2	100	5,7
		171	>5	90	47
	28	534	1	100	7,5
		534	2	100	11
		534	>5	90	62
	365	6260	1	100	15
		6260	2	100	50
		6260	>5	90	125

of precedents of potentially erroneous cells and in the same time set of candidates for inspection. Notwithstanding, this is not important obstacle for real-world implementation, because long time horizon can be divided into shorter periods of time.

5 Conclusion and Future Work

The results of research presented in this paper are a sublimation of extensive research conducted over the past ten years in the domain of metaheuristics and spreadsheet error detection approaches applied to dynamic discrete time inventory control processes. A static time-continuous multiproduct EOQ-based inventory problem with limited storage space is shown as a combinatorial optimization problem in the corresponding dynamic discrete time system control process. The study resulted in the development and implementation of several special heuristics for problem solving and error detection for the dynamic discrete inventory control model. Further research could be directed toward a more systematic research of approach efficiency for variations of inventory control problems and in algorithm efficiency applied to real-life problems with larger dimensions, i.e. a model with an increased number of units, time periods and constraints. Also, some other special heuristics or hybrid heuristic approaches for solving the described model could be developed. Another interesting question addresses the automation of test case generation, multiple and negative test cases for error detection improvement. Furthermore, the developed approach can be improved by incorporating testing or automated fault localization and repair concepts.

References

Abraham R, Erwig M (2009) Mutation operators for spreadsheets. IEEE Trans Softw Eng 35(1):94–108

Anily S, Tzur M (2006) Algorithms for the multi-item multi-vehicles dynamic lot sizing problem. Nav Res Log 53(2):157–169

Antic S (2007) Spreadsheet engineering in operations management. In: Jovanovic P, Petrovic D (eds) Current trends of operations management, FON, Belgrade (In Serbian)

Antic S (2014) Inventory control models and methods based on metaheuristics. PhD Dissertation, University of Belgrade, Faculty of organizational sciences

Antic S, Djordjevic L (2014) Case study: using a special heuristics approach for solving a multiproduct EOQ-based inventory problem with storage space constraints in the company LA FANTANA. In: Proceedings of the 8th international conference on logistics in agriculture. University of Maribor, Faculty of Logistics, Maribor, pp 32–40

Antic S, Djordjevic L, Kostic K, Lisec A (2015) Dynamic discrete simulation model of an inventory control with or without allowed shortages. U.P.B. Sci Bull Ser A 77(1):163–176

Axsäter S (2006) Inventory control. In: International series in operations research & management science, Springer Science+Business Media, New York

Barlow J (2003) Excel models for business and operations management. Wiley, New York

Bertsekas DP (1987) Dynamic programming—deterministic and stochastic models. Prentice-Hall, Englewood Cliffs, New Jersey

Chase R, Aquilano N (2004) Operations management for competitive advantage. IRWIN, New York

Djordjevic L (2016) Error detection and analysis in implementation of dynamic discrete inventory control models. PhD dissertation, University of Belgrade, Faculty of Organizational Sciences

Djordjevic L (2017) Spreadsheet engineering in the context of detecting and fixing errors in dynamic discrete control models. Zaduzbina Andrejevic, Belgrade

Djordjevic L, Antic S, Cangalovic M, Lisec A (2017) A metaheuristic approach to solving a multiproduct EOQ-based inventory problem with storage space constraints. Optim Lett 11(6):1137–1154

Djordjevic L, Vasiljevic D (2013) Spreadsheets in education of logistics managers at Faculty of organizational sciences: an example of inventory dynamics simulation. In: INTED2013 Proceedings. IATED, pp 640–649

Grossman T (2010) Spreadsheet O. R. Comes of Age. INFORMS. http://www.orms-today.org/orms-8-10/frsurvey.html 12 Apr 2018

Hansen P, Mladenovic N (2001) Variable neighborhood search: principles and applications. Eur J Oper Res 130:449–467

Harris FW (1915) Operations and costs. McGraw-Hill, New York

Horvat A, Antic S, Jeremic V (2015) A new perspective on quality characteristics determining supply chain management of coffee production. Inzinerine Ekonomika - Eng Econ 26(3):239–244

Jannach D, Schmitz T, Hofer B, Wotawa F (2014) Avoiding, finding and fixing spreadsheet errors—a survey of automated approaches for spreadsheet QA. J Syst Softw 94:129–150

Jans R, Degraeve Z (2007) Meta-heuristics for dynamic lot sizing: a review and comparison of solution approaches. Eur J Oper Res 177(3):1855–1875

Kostic K (2009) Inventory control as a discrete system control for the fixed-order quantity system. Appl Math Model 33(11):4201–4214

Lisec A, Antic S, Campuzano-Bolarín F, Pejic V (2017) An approach to packaging waste reverse logistics: case of Slovenia. J Transp. https://doi.org/10.3846/16484142.2017.1326404

Mladenovic N (1995) A variable neighborhood algorithm-a new metaheuristic for combinatorial optimization applications. In: Abstract of papers presented at Optimization Days, Montreal

Muller M (2003) Essentials of Inventory Management. AMACOM, New York

Panko RR, Aurigemma S (2010) Revising the Panko-Halverson taxonomy of spreadsheet errors. Decis Support Syst 49(2):235–244

Russell R, Taylor B (2006) Operations management: quality and competitiveness in a global environment. Wiley, New York
Scarf H (1959) The optimality of (s; S) policies in the dynamic inventory problem. In: Arrow KJ, Karlin S, Patrick (eds) Proceedings of the First Stanford Symposium
Vollmann T, Berry W, Whybark D, Jacobs R (2005) Manufacturing planning and control systems for supply chain management. The definitive guide for profession
Wagner HM, Whitin T (1958) Dynamic version of the economic lot size model. Manag Sci 5(1):89–96
Wild T (2002) Best practice in inventory management. Elsevier Science, London
Wilson RH (1934) A scientific routine for stock control. Harv Bus Rev 13:116–128

Multicriteria Decision Analysis & Multi-objective Optimization

On Fuzzy Solutions to a Class of Fuzzy Multi-objective Linear Optimization Problems

Bogdana Stanojević and Milan Stanojević

Abstract The class of fuzzy multi-objective linear optimization problems with fuzzy coefficients in the objective functions is addressed in this paper. We introduce a parametric approach that helps to compute the membership values of the extreme points in the fuzzy set solution to such problems. We analyze the efficiency of the feasible basic solutions to a parametric multi-objective linear programming problem through the optimality test in a related linear programming problem. The particular case of triangular fuzzy numbers is presented in detail, and the possible degeneracy of the basic feasible solutions is handled. This paper is a continuation of our work on special classes of fuzzy optimization problems. Previously single-objective (linear and linear fractional) optimization problems with fuzzy coefficients in the objective functions were successfully solved.

Keywords Multi-objective optimization · Fuzzy coefficients · Parametric analysis

1 Introduction

Taking into consideration multiple criteria at any level of decision-making process seems to be a natural choice. In practice, the application of multi-criteria optimization is usually neglected in the favor of classic single criterion approach. One of the reasons for such a discrepancy between needs and practice lays in the complexity of the formal multi-objective decision-making approach. Although the human mind spontaneously adopts multiple criteria when making decisions, the corresponding mathematical formulation and decision-making process can encounter difficulties,

B. Stanojević (✉)
Mathematical Institute of the Serbian Academy of Sciences and Arts, Kneza Mihaila 36, 11001 Belgrade, Serbia
e-mail: bgdnpop@mi.sanu.ac.rs

M. Stanojević
Faculty of Organizational Sciences, University of Belgrade, Jove Ili ća 154, 11040 Belgrade, Serbia
e-mail: milans@fon.bg.ac.rs

N. Mladenović et al. (eds.), *Advances in Operational Research in the Balkans*, Springer Proceedings in Business and Economics,
https://doi.org/10.1007/978-3-030-21990-1_4

and sometimes leads to paradoxes. Thus, the multi-criteria optimization was either avoided or used in its most rudimentary form, which often does not produce the expected results. Commonly, the decision criteria are simplified by choosing the most important one, while all others are ignored. However, the contemporary approaches to multi-criteria decision-making have the methodologies that can manage usually contradictory multiple criteria and help us in finding a balanced decision that takes into account all of them.

In the present paper, the class of multi-objective linear optimization problems with fuzzy coefficients in the objective function (FMOLP) is addressed. Our goal is to derive a fuzzy set solution to such problems by a parametric analysis of the efficient solutions to a certain multi-objective linear programming problem through the optimality test in a related parametric linear programming problem. In the recent literature, there are many studies on both fuzzy programming and multi-objective optimization (see, for instance, the literature review provided in (Stanojević et al. 2015; Stanojević and Stanojević 2016b)). Many times fuzzy methods are proposed to solve crisp optimization problems (Stanojević and Stanojević 2014), or crisp methods are desired for solving optimization problems with uncertain coefficients (Stanojević 2013). Dubois and Prade (2012) presented fuzzy optimization as one of the topics both most and best studied in the specialized literature, and that have demonstrated to be efficient and useful in a lot of different applications areas such as Engineering, Economics, Mathematics, Operations Research, and Artificial Intelligence, as well as in other disciplines related to optimization to a greater or lesser degree.

Mathematical programming problems with fuzzy coefficients are also widely covered in the recent literature (see for instance (Dempe and Ruziyeva 2012; Fan et al. 2013; Stanojević and Stanojević 2016b)).

Cadenas and Verdegay (1997) presented the most important models and methods for fuzzy linear programming. Dubey et al. (2012) exploited the equivalence between the interval-valued fuzzy set (IVFS) and the intuitionistic fuzzy set (IFS). They studied the linear programming problems involving interval uncertainty modeled using IFS, and constructed the nonmembership of IFS using three different viewpoints.

Stanojević and Stancu-Minasian (2012) introduced a new way to evaluate fuzzy inequalities, and based on it proposed a methodology for deriving an optimal solution to the full fuzzy linear fractional optimization problem. Stanojević et al. (2015) developed a method to solve the same problem. They proposed a way to make good decisions in certain situations in which the goals are modeled by fractional functions that must be achieved under linear constraints, and when only vague data are available.

The concept of fuzzy set solution to an optimization problem with fuzzy coefficients in the objective function was proposed in (Chanas and Kuchta 1994). Chanas and Kuchta also suggested one approach to determine the membership function of such fuzzy solution based on computing the sum of lengths of certain intervals. Dempe and Ruziyeva (2012) introduced a methodology for realizing Chanas and Kuchta's idea, applied it on solving fuzzy linear optimization problems (FLP), and derived explicit formulas for computing the endpoints of the suggested intervals in the particular case of coefficients expressed by triangular fuzzy numbers. Later on,

Stanojević (2015) extended Dempe and Ruziyeva's method by handling the degeneracy of the basic feasible solutions, and rectified their formulas that construct the solution to an FLP, and Stanojević and Stanojević (2016a) proposed an alternative to the scalarization technique involving a different efficiency test.

Stanojević and Stanojević (2016b) developed a parametric analysis of the efficiency of a feasible solution to a bi-objective linear fractional program through the parametric analysis of the optimality of the solution to a related linear program. In this way, they overcame the difficulties that arose from the exhaustive computation of the membership values used in (Stanojević and Stanojević 2013b) to solve linear fractional problems with fuzzy coefficients in the objective functions. The idea of using a parametric analysis in the construction of the membership function of the fuzzy solution was first announced in (Stanojević and Stanojević 2013a). The stability sets of marginal solutions were used there to reduce the complexity of the computation compared to the method presented in (Stanojević and Stanojević 2013b).

In this paper, we propose a parametric analysis of the efficiency in a multi-objective linear programming problem in order to construct the fuzzy set solution to an FMOLP. Our approach uses Benson's efficiency test, handles any possible degeneracy of basic feasible solutions, and addresses in detail the particular case of fuzzy coefficients expressed by triangular fuzzy numbers.

The remaining of the paper is organized as follows. Section 2 recalls the basic concepts related to fuzzy numbers and interval optimization. In Sect. 3, we describe the fuzzy multi-objective linear optimization problem (FMOLP) and an equivalent parametric multi-objective linear program based on α-cuts. In Sect. 4, we develop a parametric analysis of the Pareto optimal solutions to the multi-objective linear program with triangular fuzzy numbers as coefficients, and develop a procedure for determining the range set of any basic feasible solution. Finally, Sect. 6 is devoted to conclusions and future works.

2 Terminology

2.1 Fuzzy Numbers

Let R be the set of real numbers. We denote by $F(R)$ the set of all fuzzy subsets of R. Every fuzzy subset Y of R is uniquely characterized by a membership function $\mu_Y : R \to [0, 1]$ that associates to each $x \in R$ a real number $\mu_Y(x) \in [0, 1]$ that represents the grade of membership of x in Y. For $\alpha \in [0, 1]$, $[Y]_\alpha = \{x \in R | \mu_Y(x) \geq \alpha\}$ is called α-cut of the fuzzy subset Y. The set $\{x \in R | \mu_Y(x) > 0\}$ is called the support of the fuzzy subset Y.

A fuzzy number $\widetilde{Y} \in F(R)$ is called triangular if the graph of the nonzero values of its membership function is a triangle. Any triangular fuzzy number is defined as a triple $(\lambda, \mu, \nu) \in R^3$ (Zimmermann 1996). For $\alpha \in [0, 1]$, the α-cut of $\widetilde{Y} = (\lambda^y, \mu^y, \nu^y)$ is the interval $[y_L(\alpha), y_R(\alpha)]$, where

$$y_L(\alpha) = \alpha\mu^y + (1-\alpha)\lambda^y,\ \ y_R(\alpha) = \alpha\mu^y + (1-\alpha)\nu^y.$$

For triangular fuzzy numbers, the well-known definitions for addition, subtraction, and multiplication by a positive scalar, based on Zadeh's extension principle, are included below:

$$\begin{aligned}\widetilde{A} + \widetilde{B} &= \left(\lambda^a + \lambda^b, \mu^a + \mu^b, \nu^a + \nu^b\right),\\ \widetilde{A} - \widetilde{B} &= \left(\lambda^a - \nu^b, \mu^a - \mu^b, \nu^a + \lambda^b\right),\\ x\widetilde{A} &= \left(x\lambda^a, x\mu^a, x\nu^a\right),\end{aligned}$$

where $\widetilde{A} = (\lambda^a, \mu^a, \nu^a)$ and $\widetilde{B} = \left(\lambda^b, \mu^b, \nu^b\right)$ are the triangular fuzzy numbers, and $x \in R$, $x \geq 0$. For a deeper discussion of the arithmetic of α-cut intervals, we refer the reader to (Uhrig and Tsoukalas 1997; Zimmermann 1996).

2.2 Intervals and Multi-objective Optimization

Given two intervals of real numbers $[a, b]$ and $[c, d]$, and a real nonnegative scalar x, the basic arithmetic operations (addition, subtraction, and multiplication by a scalar) are given below (see (Moore 1966) for more details):

1. $[a, b] + [c, d] = [a + c, b + d]$.
2. $[a, b] - [c, d] = [a - d, b - c]$.
3. $[a, b]\,x = [ax, bx]$, $x \geq 0$.

According to (Chanas and Kuchta 1996), an interval $[a, b]$ is smaller than an interval $[c, d]$ if and only if $a \leq c$ and $b \leq d$ with at least one strong inequality. Optimal solutions to the interval optimization problem $\min\limits_{x\in X}\left[f_1(x),\ f_2(x)\right]$ correspond to efficient solutions to the bi-objective programming problem "$\min\limits_{x\in X}$"$\{f_1(x),\ f_2(x)\}$. A feasible solution $x^* \in X$ is said to be an efficient solution to Problem (1)

$$\text{“}\min_{x\in X}\text{”}\left\{f_1(x), \ldots, f_p(x)\right\} \tag{1}$$

if and only if there is no $x \in X$ such that $f_i(x) \leq f_i(x^*)$, $i \in \{1, \ldots, p\}$, where at least one inequality is strict.

2.3 Solution Concept to an FLP

The details provided in this section are adapted from (Dempe and Ruziyeva 2012), in order to make our presentation self-consistent. The FLP is defined as

$$\min \left\{ \widetilde{c}^T x | Ax = b, x \geq 0 \right\}, \tag{2}$$

where $\widetilde{c}$ is a column vector of fuzzy numbers representing the coefficients of the objective function, A is the $m \times n$ matrix of the constraints, $b \in R^m$ is the right-hand side column vector of the constraints, and x is the column vector of the decision variables. Using the α-cut interval $\left[c_L(\alpha)^T x, c_R(\alpha)^T x \right]$ of the fuzzy objective function and the order of the intervals, Problem (2) is replaced by the bi-objective optimization problem

$$\begin{array}{l} \min \left\{ c_L(\alpha)^T x, \ c_R(\alpha)^T x \right\} \\ \text{s.t.} \ \ Ax = b, x \geq 0. \end{array} \tag{3}$$

Let $\psi(\alpha)$ denote the set of efficient solutions to Problem (3) for a certain α-cut. The value of the membership function of the fuzzy solution at a given basic feasible solution $\overline{x}$ is defined as the length of the interval $\{\alpha \in [0, 1] | \overline{x} \in \psi(\alpha)\}$. In other words, the membership value of the basic feasible solution $\overline{x}$ is computed as the length of the interval of those values of α for which $\overline{x}$ is an efficient solution to the bi-objective problem (3).

2.4 *Basic Feasible Solutions*

The details included in this section are adapted from (Ehrgott 2005; Stanojević and Stanojević 2016b). The feasible set of Problems (2) and (3) is defined by the constraint matrix A and the right-hand side vector b. Assume that the rank of matrix A is maximal and it is equal to m. Then, a nonsingular $m \times m$ sub-matrix A_B of A is called basis matrix, where B is the set of the indexes of the columns of A defining A_B. B is called a basis of the constraint system. Let $N = \{1, \ldots, n\} \backslash B$ be the set of nonbasic column indexes. A variable x_i and an index i are called basic if $i \in B$, and nonbasic otherwise.

With the notion of basis and using B and N as index sets, we split the matrix A and the vector x into basic and nonbasic parts. Let us write $A = (A_B | A_N)$ and $x = (x_B | x_N)$. The original system of constraints $Ax = b$ is now equivalent to $A_B x_B + A_N x_N = b$. Assuming that the matrix A_B is invertible we can write $x_B = A_B^{-1} b - A_B^{-1} A_N x^N$.

Setting the nonbasic variables to 0, ($\overline{x}_N = 0$) we derive $\overline{x}_B = A_B^{-1} b$, and obtain a basic solution to the constraint system as $\overline{x} = (A_B^{-1} b, 0)$. If in addition all components of $\overline{x}$ are nonnegative, $\overline{x}$ is called a basic feasible solution. Then, B is also called feasible. Each basic feasible solution determines at least one matrix A_B, with A_B being nonsingular.

3 The FMOLP Problem Formulation

Let us consider the multi-objective linear programming problem with fuzzy coefficients in the objective function

$$\min \left\{ \left(\left(\widetilde{c}^k \right)^T x \right)_{k=1,\ldots,p} | Ax = b, x \geq 0 \right\}, \tag{4}$$

where $\widetilde{c}^k$ is a column vector of fuzzy numbers representing the fuzzy coefficients of the $k-$th objective function, $k \in \{1, \ldots, p\}$, A is the $m \times n$ matrix of the constraints, $b \in R^m$ is the right-hand side column vector of the constraints, and x is the column vector of the decision variables.

We aim to derive a fuzzy set solution to Problem (4), in the sense of the concept solution given in (Chanas and Kuchta 1994). Any basic feasible solution to Problem (4) belongs to the fuzzy set solution with a certain degree. To find the membership degree (value) of each basic feasible solution we introduce a more general approach than the one given in (Stanojević and Stanojević 2016a). We construct a parametric multi-objective linear optimization problem with $2p$ objective functions, and apply Benson's method to test the efficiency of each basic feasible solution. We present the construction and solution procedure in next section.

4 The General Solution Procedure

In this section, we describe how we construct the parametric single-objective optimization problem, following Benson's efficiency test; analyze the efficiency of each basic feasible solution; and present in detail the special case of the coefficients expressed by triangular fuzzy numbers. The solution procedure is described in the most general case, i.e., not only for triangular fuzzy coefficients.

4.1 The Construction of the Parametric Single-Objective Optimization Problem

Applying the α-cut interval to the objective functions of Problem (4), we obtain the multi-objective interval optimization problem

$$\begin{array}{l} \text{"min"} \left\{ \left[c_L^k(\alpha)^T x, c_R^k(\alpha)^T x \right], k \in \{1, \ldots, p\} \right\}, \\ \quad \text{s.t. } Ax = b, x \geq 0, \end{array}$$

and derive the parametric $2p$-objective linear optimization problem

$$\begin{aligned} &\text{“min”}\ \left\{c_L^1(\alpha)^T x, \ldots, c_L^p(\alpha)^T x, c_R^1(\alpha)^T x, \ldots, c_R^p(\alpha)^T x\right\}, \\ &\text{s.t. } Ax = b, x \geq 0. \end{aligned} \tag{5}$$

Benson's method (Ehrgott 2005) for testing the efficiency states that the feasible solution $x^* \in X$ is efficient to Problem (1) iff the optimal objective value of Problem (6) is 0.

$$\begin{aligned} &\max \sum_{k=1}^{p} l_k, \\ &\text{s.t.} \\ &f_k(x^*) - l_k - f_k(x) = 0, k \in \{1, \ldots, p\}, \\ &x \in X, \\ &l_k \geq 0, k \in \{1, \ldots, p\}. \end{aligned} \tag{6}$$

Using the deviation variable l_k for function $c_L^k(\alpha)^T x$, and r_k for function $c_R^k(\alpha)^T x$ we apply Benson's method to Problem (5) and obtain the following statement: the basic feasible solution x^* is efficient to Problem (5) if and only if the optimal objective value of Problem (7) is 0.

$$\begin{aligned} &\max \sum_{k=1}^{p} (l_k + r_k), \\ &\text{s.t.} \\ &c_L^k(\alpha) x^* - l_k - c_L^k(\alpha) x = 0, k \in \{1, \ldots, p\}, \\ &c_R^k(\alpha) x^* - r_k - c_R^k(\alpha) x = 0, k \in \{1, \ldots, p\}, \\ &l_k, r_k \geq 0, k \in \{1, \ldots, p\}, \\ &Ax = b, x \geq 0. \end{aligned} \tag{7}$$

4.2 The Parametric Analysis

In what follows, we restrict our attention to the basic feasible solutions x^*, identify one of its feasible basis B, and split the original matrix A in basic/nonbasic columns $(A_B|A_N)$ (see Sect. 2.4).

We use Problem (7) to test the efficiency of x^* for Problem (5) as follows: any basic feasible solution x^* is efficient in Problem (5) if and only if Problem (7) has an optimal objective function value of 0. The term *max* being used in Problem (7) is for finding the maximal solution, in the classical sense, to a crisp single-objective programming problem.

To develop the parametric analysis of the efficiency of x^*, we extend the basis B of the constraint system of Problem (5) to a basis B' of the constraint system of Problem (7).

Table 1 The simplex tableau for the constraints system (8)

	$\overline{x}^*_{B'}$	x_B	x_N	$(l_k)_{k\in\{1,\ldots,p\}}$	$(r_k)_{k\in\{1,\ldots,p\}}$
x_B	$\overline{x}_B$	I_m	$A_B^{-1}A_N$	$O_{m\times p}$	$O_{m\times p}$
$(l_k)_{k=\overline{1,p}}$	$O_{k\times 1}$	$O_{p\times m}$	$\left(\left(c_L^k(\alpha)\right)_N^T - \left(c_L^k(\alpha)\right)_B^T A_B^{-1}A_N\right)$	I_p	$O_{p\times p}$
$(r_k)_{k=\overline{1,p}}$	$O_{k\times 1}$	$O_{p\times m}$	$\left(\left(c_R^k(\alpha)\right)_N^T - \left(c_R^k(\alpha)\right)_B^T A_B^{-1}A_N\right)$	$O_{p\times p}$	I_p
		$O_{1\times m}$	$h(\alpha)$	$O_{1\times p}$	$O_{1\times p}$

Let the extended set of basic variables be x_B, $(l_k)_{k\in\{1,\ldots,p\}}$, $(r_k)_{k\in\{1,\ldots,p\}}$. The corresponding values of the basic variables in the basic solution are $x^*_{B'} = \left(x^*_B, 0, \ldots, 0\right) \in R^{m+2p}$, since the system of constraints can be rewritten, in its canonical form, as shown below:

$$\begin{array}{l} l_k + \left[\left(c_L^k(\alpha)\right)_N^T - \left(c_L^k(\alpha)\right)_B^T A_B^{-1}A_N\right]x_N = 0,\ k\in\{1,\ldots,p\},\\ r_k + \left[\left(c_R^k(\alpha)\right)_N^T - \left(c_R^k(\alpha)\right)_B^T A_B^{-1}A_N\right]x_N = 0,\ k\in\{1,\ldots,p\},\\ x_B + A_B^{-1}A_N x_N = A_B^{-1}b. \end{array} \tag{8}$$

The simplex tableau that corresponds to this form of the constraints system is shown in Table 1. The formula needed for the optimality test is $h_N(\alpha)\geq 0$, where

$$h_N(\alpha) = \sum_{k=1}^{p}\left(\left(c_L^k(\alpha)+c_R^k(\alpha)\right)_B^T A_B^{-1}A_N - \left(c_L^k(\alpha)+c_R^k(\alpha)\right)_N^T\right).$$

Due to the degeneracy of the basic solution $x^*_{B'}$ we have to consider all bases connected to the same basic solution $\left(x^*_{B'}, O_{1\times(m+2p)}\right)$. Ehrgott (2005) referred to the concept of degeneracy of a basis and showed why degeneracy is "problematic" in the context of multi-criteria optimization problems.

In what follows, I_{x^*} denotes the set of all possible values of the parameter α for which x^* is an efficient solution to (5). Our next goal is to generate I_{x^*} for any basic feasible solution x^*, and compute the membership value of x^* in the fuzzy optimal solution to (4) as the sum of the lengths of the disjunctive intervals that together form the set I_{x^*}.

4.3 *The Solution Algorithm*

The procedure for finding I_{x^*} and computing the value of the membership function at x^* is summarized by the following algorithm:

Input data: the coefficients $\widetilde{c}$, A, and b of Problem (4); and x^* a basic feasible solution to the crisp constraint system of Problem (4).

1. Identify the basis B of the constraint system of Problem (4) that corresponds to x^*; and construct a basic feasible solution $\overline{x}$ to Problem (5).
2. Find all simplex tableaus connected to the given basic solution $\overline{x}$ to (5). We obtain the simplex tableaus T^j for $j \in J$.
3. For each simplex tableau T^j generate a set of values of parameter $\alpha \in [0, 1]$ for which $\overline{x}$ is optimal, by solving a system of simultaneous inequalities. We obtain the intervals $I^j \subset [0, 1]$ for $j \in J$.
4. To obtain the set I_{x^*}, join the intervals I^j, i.e., $I_{x^*} = \cup_{j \in J} I^j$.
5. Find the endpoints of the disjunctive sub-intervals of I_{x^*}, and compute $\mu(x^*)$ as the length of I_{x^*}.

Output data: $\mu(x^*)$ the membership value of x^*.

Since all intervals I^j, obtained in Step 4.3 of the solution algorithm, are included in the interval $[0, 1]$, the length of their union I^* is less than or equal to 1. Hence, the output $\mu(x^*)$ of the algorithm may represent a membership grade.

The complexity of the computation needed in Step 4.3 of the solution algorithm is strictly related to the nature of the inequalities in the system, i.e., to the characteristics of the membership functions of the fuzzy numbers that describe the coefficients of the original FMOLP.

4.4 *The Special Case of the Coefficients Expressed by Triangular Fuzzy Numbers*

Let us now consider the subclass of FMOLP with coefficients described by triangular fuzzy numbers. If the vector coefficient $\widetilde{c}^k$ in (4) is described by the triple $(\lambda^k, \mu^k, \nu^k)$, then the vector of the α-cut intervals is described by $c_L^k(\alpha) = \alpha(\mu^k - \lambda^k) + \lambda^k$ and $c_R^k(\alpha) = \alpha(\mu^k - \nu^k) + \nu^k$. Using these formulas and the arithmetic of the triangular fuzzy numbers, we derive $h_N(\alpha) = \alpha S + T$, where

$$S = (S_j)_{j \in N}, \; S_j = \sum_{k=1}^{p} \left(\left(2\mu_j^k - \lambda_j^k - \nu_j^k \right) \dot{-} \left(2\mu^k - \lambda^k - \nu^k \right)_B^T A_B^{-1} A_j \right),$$
$$T = (T_j)_{j \in N}, \; T_j = \sum_{k=1}^{p} \left(\left(\lambda_j^k + \nu_j^k \right) - \left(\lambda^k + \nu^k \right)_B^T A_B^{-1} A_j \right).$$

The optimality test is reduced in this way to a system of $(n - m)$ linear inequalities, since all coefficients in the constraints of Problem (7) are linear with respect to α, thus all components in each simplex tableau of Problem (7) are fractions of polynomials. Due to this particularity, the systems of simultaneous inequalities solved in Step 2 are reduced to a system of simultaneous linear inequalities that can be solved exactly by simple computation.

The linear system of inequalities that appears in the first discussion of each basic feasible solution is obtained from rewriting the set of inequalities $h_N(\alpha) \leq 0$, i.e., $\alpha S_j + T_j \leq 0$, $j \in N$, which is equivalent to the conjunctive system

$$\begin{array}{ll} \alpha \leq -\frac{T_j}{S_j}, & S_j > 0, \\ \alpha \geq -\frac{T_j}{S_j}, & S_j < 0, \\ \alpha \in \emptyset, & S_j = 0, T_j > 0, \\ \alpha \in R, & S_j = 0, T_j \leq 0. \end{array}$$

The linearity of the inequalities obtained from the optimality test $h_N(\alpha) \leq 0$ is also maintained in the special case of the coefficients expressed by trapezoidal fuzzy numbers.

5 Computation Results

Let us analyze the following bi-objective linear programming problem with fuzzy coefficients in the objective functions.

$$\begin{array}{ll} \min & \widetilde{c}_{11}x_1 + \widetilde{c}_{12}x_2, \\ \min & \widetilde{c}_{21}x_1 + \widetilde{c}_{22}x_2, \\ \text{s.t.} & 0 \leq x_1 \leq 3, \\ & 0 \leq x_2 \leq 4, \end{array} \tag{9}$$

where $\widetilde{c}_{11} = (1, 2, 4)$, $\widetilde{c}_{12} = (0, 1, 2)$, $\widetilde{c}_{21} = (-2, -1, 1)$, and $\widetilde{c}_{22} = (0, 1, 2)$. The feasible set is described by the box constraints that must be transformed into a standard form by adding two slack variables x_3 and x_4. We identify four basic feasible solutions to the original constraint system: $(3, 4, 0, 0)$, $(3, 0, 0, 4)$, $(0, 4, 3, 0)$, and $(0, 0, 3, 4)$. The associated parametric four-objective linear problem is

$$\begin{array}{l} \min c_L^1(\alpha)^T x = (\alpha + 1)\,x_1 + \alpha x_2, \\ \min c_R^1(\alpha)^T x = (-2\alpha + 4)\,x_1 + (-\alpha + 2)\,x_2, \\ \min c_L^2(\alpha)^T x = (\alpha - 2)\,x_1 + \alpha x_2, \\ \min c_R^2(\alpha)^T x = (-2\alpha + 1)\,x_1 + (-\alpha + 2)\,x_2, \\ \;\text{s.t.}\; x_1 + x_3 = 3, \\ \qquad x_2 + x_4 = 4, \\ \qquad x_1, x_2, x_3, x_4 \geq 0, \end{array} \tag{10}$$

and the corresponding parametric single-objective linear problem is

Table 2 The simplex tableau for the constraints system (12) that corresponds to $\overline{x}^1 = (3, 4, 0, 0)$

	$\overline{x}^*_{B'}$	x_1	x_2	x_3	x_4	l_1	l_2	r_1	r_2
x_1	3	1	0	1	0	0	0	0	0
x_2	4	0	1	0	1	0	0	0	0
l_1	0	0	0	$-\alpha - 1$	$-\alpha$	1	0	0	0
l_2	0	0	0	$-\alpha + 2$	$-\alpha$	0	1	0	0
r_1	0	0	0	$2\alpha - 4$	$\alpha - 2$	0	0	1	0
r_2	0	0	0	$2\alpha - 1$	$\alpha - 2$	0	0	0	1
	0	0	0	$2(\alpha - 2)$	-4	0	0	0	0

$$\begin{aligned}
&\max\left(l_1 + r_1 + l_2 + r_2\right), \\
&\text{s.t.} \\
&x_1 + x_3 = 3, \\
&x_2 + x_4 = 4, \\
&\left((\alpha + 1) x_1^* + \alpha x_2^*\right) - l_1 - \left((\alpha + 1) x_1 + \alpha x_2\right) = 0, \\
&\left((-2\alpha + 4) x_1^* + (-\alpha + 2) x_2^*\right) - r_1 - \left((-2\alpha + 4) x_1 + (-\alpha + 2) x_2\right), \\
&\left((\alpha - 2) x_1^* + \alpha x_2^*\right) - l_2 - \left((\alpha - 2) x_1 + \alpha x_2\right) = 0, \\
&\left((-2\alpha + 1) x_1^* + (-\alpha + 2) x_2^*\right) - r_2 - \left((-2\alpha + 1) x_1 + (-\alpha + 2) x_2\right) = 0, \\
&x_1, x_2, x_3, x_4 l_1, r_1, l_2, r_2 \geq 0.
\end{aligned} \tag{11}$$

Let us start to analyze the first basic feasible solution $\overline{x}^1 = (3, 4, 0, 0)$. Since x_3 and x_4 are nonbasic variables, we obtain the following constraint system:

$$\begin{aligned}
&x_1 + x_3 = 3, \\
&x_2 + x_4 = 4, \\
&l_1 - (\alpha + 1) x_3 - \alpha x_4 = 0, \\
&r_1 - (-2\alpha + 4) x_3 - (-\alpha + 2) x_4 = 0, \\
&l_2 - (\alpha - 2) x_3 - \alpha x_4 = 0, \\
&r_2 - (-2\alpha + 1) x_3 - (-\alpha + 2) x_4 = 0, \\
&x_1, x_2, x_3, x_4, l_1, r_1, l_2, r_2 \geq 0
\end{aligned} \tag{12}$$

according to the general constraint system (8). The corresponding simplex tableau is shown in Table 1. For optimality, all values on the control row must be nonnegative.

Note that on the last row of Table 2 the $h_4(\alpha) = -4$. Moreover, there is no strictly positive value on column x_4 such that it may be chosen as pivot that maintains the objective value equal to 0. Therefore, there is no value $\alpha \in [0, 1]$ such that $\overline{x}^1 = (3, 4, 0, 0)$ is efficient solution to Problem (9). This also means that the membership value of $\overline{x}^1$ in the fuzzy set solution to Problem (9) is $\mu\left(\overline{x}^1\right) = 0$.

Let us start to analyze the second basic feasible solution $\overline{x}^2 = (3, 0, 0, 4)$. Since x_2 and x_3 are nonbasic solutions we obtain the following constraint system:

Table 3 The simplex tableau for the constraints system (13) that corresponds to $\overline{x}^2 = (3, 0, 0, 4)$

	$\overline{x}^*_{B'}$	x_1	x_2	x_3	x_4	l_1	l_2	r_1	r_2
x_1	3	1	0	1	0	0	0	0	0
x_4	4	0	1	0	1	0	0	0	0
l_1	0	0	α	$-\alpha - 1$	0	1	0	0	0
l_2	0	0	α	$-\alpha + 2$	0	0	1	0	0
r_1	0	0	$-\alpha + 2$	$2\alpha - 4$	0	0	0	1	0
r_2	0	0	$-\alpha + 2$	$2\alpha - 1$	0	0	0	0	1
	0	0	4	$2(\alpha - 2)$	0	0	0	0	0

Table 4 The second simplex tableau for the basic feasible solution $x^* = (3, 0, 0, 4)$

	$\overline{x}^*_{B'}$	x_1	x_2	x_3	x_4	l_1	l_2	r_1	r_2
x_1	3	1	$\frac{-\alpha}{-\alpha+2}$	1	0	0	$\frac{-1}{-\alpha+2}$	0	0
x_4	4	0	1	0	1	0	0	0	0
l_1	0	0	$\frac{3\alpha}{-\alpha+2}$	0	0	1	$\frac{\alpha+1}{-\alpha+2}$	0	0
x_3	0	0	$\frac{\alpha}{-\alpha+2}$	1	0	0	$\frac{1}{-\alpha+2}$	0	0
r_1	0	0	$\alpha + 2$	0	0	0	2	1	0
r_2	0	0	$\frac{(-\alpha+1)(\alpha+4)}{-\alpha+2}$	0	0	0	$\frac{-2\alpha+1}{-\alpha+2}$	0	1
	0	0	$2(\alpha + 2)$	0	0	0	2	0	0

$$
\begin{aligned}
& x_1 + x_3 = 3, \\
& x_4 + x_2 = 4, \\
& l_1 - (\alpha + 1) x_3 - \alpha x_2 = 0, \\
& r_1 - (-2\alpha + 4) x_3 - (-\alpha + 2) x_2 = 0, \\
& l_2 - (\alpha - 2) x_3 - \alpha x_2 = 0, \\
& r_2 - (-2\alpha + 1) x_3 - (-\alpha + 2) x_2 = 0, \\
& x_1, x_2, x_3, x_4, l_1, r_1, l_2, r_2 \geq 0.
\end{aligned}
\tag{13}
$$

The starting simplex tableau is shown in Table 3. The optimality test on column x_2 is satisfied, but on column x_3 it is not, since $\alpha \in [0, 1]$. A simplex transformation is needed in order to obtain an optimal base for the basic feasible solution $\overline{x}^2$.

Choosing the pivot $-\alpha + 2$ on column x_3, and proceeding with the corresponding transformation we obtain the next simplex tableau in Table 4. On the last row of this table, all values are positive, thus the base $\{x_1, x_4, l_1, x_3, r_1, r_2\}$ is optimal for all values $\alpha \in [0, 1]$. This also means that the membership value of $\overline{x}^2$ in the fuzzy set solution to Problem (9) is $\mu\left(\overline{x}^2\right) = 1$.

Similar computation must be done to derive the membership values of the other two basic feasible solutions in the fuzzy set solution to Problem (9).

6 Conclusion and Future Work

In this paper, we developed a procedure for computing the values of the membership function of the fuzzy solution to the multi-objective linear optimization problem with fuzzy coefficients in the objective functions.

We proposed an algorithm that handles the degeneracy of basic feasible solutions in the general case. We addressed the special case of the coefficients expressed by triangular fuzzy numbers in more detail. We used Benson's method to formulate the efficiency test, thus parametrically analyzing the optimality of a basic feasible solution to a single-objective linear programming problem.

Our new approach may be used to solve a more general class of problems. Under convexity assumptions any p-objective optimization problem with fuzzy coefficients in the objective functions may be reformulated into a certain parametric $2p$-objective optimization problem using the α-cut arithmetic. Since the solution approach essentially depends on the characteristics of the initial optimization problem, we must find a convenient efficiency test for the multi-objective parametric optimization problem, and then analyze the efficiency of a crisp solution with respect to the parameter α.

In our future research, we will analyze the possibility to apply a similar methodology to find a fuzzy solution to a multi-objective linear programming problem with fuzzy coefficients in the right-hand side of the constraints. In order to achieve such goal, in the very beginning, we must search for a convenient description of the equality and/or inequality of fuzzy numbers, and then to develop the parametric analysis of the optimality of a basic feasible solution. The class of similar problems with fuzzy coefficients in the constraint matrix is more cumbersome, since the optimality test involves the computation of the inverse of the basic matrix. In the case of triangular fuzzy numbers, the coefficients in such inverse matrix are fractions of polynomials. Overcoming the difficulty of finding the real roots of those polynomials, the optimality test still results in linear inequalities.

Acknowledgements This research was partially supported by the Ministry of Education and Science, Republic of Serbia, Project numbers TR36006 and TR32013.

References

Cadenas JM, Verdegay JL (1997) Using fuzzy numbers in linear programming. IEEE Trans Syst Man Cybern Part B (Cybernetics) 27(6):1016–1022

Chanas S, Kuchta D (1994) Linear programming problem with fuzzy coefficients in the objective function. In: Delgado M, Kacprzyk J, Verdegay J, Vila M, (eds) Fuzzy optimizatio. Heidelberg, Physica-Verlag, pp 148–157

Chanas S, Kuchta D (1996) Multiobjective programming in optimization of interval objective functions a generalized approach. Eur J Oper Res 94(3):594–598

Dempe S, Ruziyeva A (2012) On the calculation of a membership function for the solution of a fuzzy linear optimization problem. Fuzzy Sets Syst 188(1):58–67

Dubey D, Chandra S, Mehra A (2012) Fuzzy linear programming under interval uncertainty based on ifs representation. Fuzzy Sets Syst 188(1):68–87

Dubois D, Prade H (2012) Gradualness, uncertainty and bipolarity: making sense of fuzzy sets. Fuzzy Sets Syst 192:3–24

Ehrgott M (2005) Multicriteria optimization. Springer Verlag, Berlin

Fan YR, Huang GH, Yang AL (2013) Generalized fuzzy linear programming for decision making under uncertainty: feasibility of fuzzy solutions and solving approach. Inf Sci 241:12–27

Moore RE (1966) Interval analysis. Prentice-Hall, Englewood Cliffs, NJ

Stanojević B (2013) A note on taylor series approach to fuzzy multiple objective linear fractional programming. Inf Sci 243:95–99

Stanojević B (2015) Extended procedure for computing the values of the membership function of a fuzzy solution to a class of fuzzy linear optimization problems. Fuzzy Sets Syst 272:47–59

Stanojević B, Dziţac I, Dziţac S (2015) On the ratio of fuzzy numbers exact membership function computation and applications to decision making. Technol Econ Dev Econ 21(5):815–832

Stanojević B, Stancu-Minasian IM (2012) Evaluating fuzzy inequalities and solving fully fuzzified linear fractional program. Yugosl J Oper Res 22:41–50

Stanojević B, Stanojević M (2013a) Parametric computation of a membership function for the solution of a fuzzy linear fractional optimization problem. In: Proceedings of the 11th Balkan conference on operational research, pp 507– 513

Stanojević B, Stanojević M (2013b) Solving method for linear fractional optimization problem with fuzzy coefficients in the objective function. Int J Comput Commun Control 8:146–152

Stanojević B, Stanojević M (2014) Comment on fuzzy mathematical programming for multi objective linear fractional programming problem. Fuzzy Sets Syst 246:156–159

Stanojević B, Stanojević M (2016a) Parametric analysis for finding a fuzzy set solution to a class of fuzzy linear programming problems. In: Proceedings of symOpIs, vol 2016, pp 41–47

Stanojević B, Stanojević M (2016b) Parametric computation of a fuzzy set solution to a class of fuzzy linear fractional optimization problems. Fuzzy Optim Decis Mak 15(4):435–455

Uhrig R, Tsoukalas L (1997) Fuzzy and neural approaches in engineering. Wiley, New York

Zimmermann HJ (1996) Fuzzy set theory. Kluwer Academic Publisher, Boston

Multiattribute Methods as a Means for Solving Ecological Problems in Water Resources—Lake Pollution

Milena J. Popović, Bisera Š. Andrić Gušavac and Ana S. Katić

Abstract Water as a natural resource refers to the groundwater and surface water (lakes, rivers, etc.) in the environment. Lake resources are considered to be a renewable resource of the freshwater which is essential for life of humans, animals, and plants. The pollution of lake resources, caused not only by humans, restricts its function in the ecosystem, including use for human need. Human negative influence and lack of protection measures for lake resources as freshwater reservoirs can be overcome and solved using multiattribute methods. As pollution problems are very complex due to the many environment variables and many solution alternatives, researchers use more than one method as a support to undertake scientific sustained decisions which are based on economic, ecological, social, technological,… goals in order to obtain the best solutions. Short literature review presented in this paper points out two most commonly used methods for this type of problems—Promethee II and AHP method. Promethee II is used for comparing the alternatives pair-wise for each criterion, finding the strength of preferring one over the other and the main objective of using AHP is to identify the preferred alternative and also determine a ranking of the alternative when all the decision criteria are considered simultaneously. Methodological framework proposed in this paper is designed in order to rank alternatives for each criterion by combining these two methods. Qualitative character of the AHP is exceeded using Promethee II in the first stage of the analysis by cutting off the alternatives with negative net outranking flow. The benefit is direct consistency increase of the AHP. Numerical example for the lake Vrutci, the most important freshwater supplier for the Užice area in western Serbia, is given in the paper. Long-term impact of human factors caused eutrophication of the lake Vrutci and led to the exclusion of the lake from the water supply system. The solution for pollution reduction of the lake Vrutci is obtained by implementing the methodological framework and combined application of the two methods and the results are discussed.

M. J. Popović (✉) · B. Š. Andrić Gušavac · A. S. Katić
Faculty of Organizational Sciences, University of Belgrade, Jove Ilića 154, 11000 Belgrade, Serbia
e-mail: milenap@fon.bg.ac.rs

N. Mladenović et al. (eds.), *Advances in Operational Research in the Balkans*, Springer Proceedings in Business and Economics,
https://doi.org/10.1007/978-3-030-21990-1_5

Keywords Multiattribute methods · AHP · Promethee II · Water resources · Lake pollution

1 Introduction

Humans have the great need for freshwater which represents around 2.5% of all water on Earth (Postel et al. 1996). Part of freshwater is locked in glaciers and ice caps, and the rest is in lakes, rivers, atmosphere, etc. Freshwater can be considered as a renewable resource when the usage, treatment, and release of water is in a balance with its capacity, which is necessary for its regeneration. Its significance is reflected in the fact that water is essential precondition for life of humans, animals, plants, etc. Because of that it is important to continuously implement various measures to protect water quality.

Exposing the hidden links between consumption and the depletion of water can provide arguments for change and create a basis for formulating new strategies for water resource management (Barisic et al. 2011).

In rural areas, people usually live around different sources of freshwater and food, which is near mountains, rivers, and lakes. As the number of people continuously rises as well as their needs, the pressure on these resources in the environment is much stronger. Human activity is one of the main causes of water resources pollution. These activities lead to fast increase of ecological problems, nature resources, and environment in which humans live and act. Biggest problems in rural inhabited areas, especially the ones near sources of freshwater, are the absence or undeveloped sewage systems or proof septic tanks as well as other protection measures which leads to soil contamination.

Rainfall, snowfall, or melting of snow are common causes of runoff which is flow of water over earth's surface. Surface runoff can implicate environmental pollution through transport of water pollutants such as chemicals and sediments from roads and ground surface which end up in rivers, lakes, or other water streams. On the other hand, groundwater collects contaminants from the soil and supply lakes with high level of nutrients and toxic compounds and makes the water unacceptable for any use and leads to eutrophication.

Eutrophication is one of the most widespread water quality problems in the world. Human negative influence on nature and lack of protection measures for freshwater reservoirs such as lakes is one of the causes of eutrophication. Its main indicators are excessive plant and algal growth in water body as a response to increased levels of nutrients. This phenomenon indicates that there are crucial structural and functional changes of water ecosystem which result in toxic compounds and lack of oxygen that can cause death of aquatic animals and therefore is not fit for human use.

In this paper, we suggest original methodology which combines two multiattribute methods using proposed methodological framework which is designed to rank alternatives for each criterion. In this way, qualitative character of the AHP is exceeded using Promethee II. The benefit is direct consistency increase of the AHP. It is not the purpose of this paper to give an exhaustive review of multiattribute methods application on the problem of lake pollution. Most of the work in this area is very much oriented toward water resource management, and there are few applications concerning lake pollution. We decided to structure this paper around some carefully selected examples of research studies and research.

2 Multiattribute Methods Review for Lake Pollution Problems

These problems are mainly multiattribute and because of large number of available methods it is necessary to perform a review of multiattribute method applications to similar problems. In that way, it is possible to point out most commonly used methods and apply them in purpose of bringing a good decision after reviewing results of different methods.

In environmental evaluation assessments, usually an exhaustive data collection is required to obtain reliable results. However, this also means that huge amounts of information of different nature must be handled, which may complicate the analysis (Herva and Roca 2013).

Multiple-criteria decision analysis (MCDA) provides a systematic methodology in combining different inputs in order to rank selected alternatives and compare them. The development of MCDA methods has been motivated not only by a variety of real-life problems requiring the consideration of multiple criteria but also by practitioners' desire to propose enhanced decision-making techniques using recent advancements in mathematical optimization, scientific computing, and computer technology (Wiecek et al. 2008). A multi-criteria model is developed for analyzing land-use strategies for reducing the future social and economic costs in areas with potential natural hazards. A multi-criteria decision-making procedure consists of generating alternatives, establishing criteria, assigning criteria weights, and applying the compromise ranking method (Opricović and Tzeng 2003).

This paper pointed out two most commonly used methods for lake pollution problems—Promethee and AHP method. These approaches differ significantly in the way of how values are assigned and combined, meaning that the processes have different information and knowledge requirements and the calculated scores have different mathematical properties and thus slightly different meanings. Practitioners often view one of the various approaches as most appropriate due to the priority they place on its relative strengths and weaknesses (Figueira et al. 2005; Belton and Stewart 2002).

Problem structuring methods are increasingly integrated with multi-criteria analysis and combining methods produces a richer view of the decision situation (Prato and Herath 2017; Marttunen et al. 2017). Some of common types of water management decisions being supported with multiple-criteria analysis techniques include (Hajkowicz and Higgins 2008) the following:

- Selection of alternative water supply and storage infrastructure options. Eder et al. (1997) use MCA to select locations and design options for hydroelectric power plants on the Danube River in Austria.
- Selection of water restoration or enhancement projects in light of constrained budgets. Al-Rashdan et al. (1999) prioritize projects designed to improve the environmental quality of the Jordan River using MCA.
- Allocating a fixed water resource among competing uses. Flug et al. (2000) use MCA to select water flow options for Glen Canyon Dam in Colorado providing for recreation, biodiversity, and fishing.
- Selecting water management policies for an entire city or region. Joubert et al. (2003) use MCA to help choose water supply augmentation and demand management policies for the city of Cape Town.

Water resource management decisions are typically guided by multiple objectives measured in different units, and therefore makes multiple-criteria analysis (MCA) a well-suited decision support tool. Despite an abundance of algorithms to solve an MCA problem once it has been structured, there are few methods to help analysts and decision-makers choose criteria and decision options in the first place (Hajkowicz and Collins 2007). The possibility of dynamic reevaluation can only be achieved by AHP and PROMETHEE, leaving the other methods with a big disadvantage (Cinelli et al. 2014).

Water management covers a wide range of activities, in which technical, economic, environmental, and social issues are involved (Anagnostopoulos et al. 2005). Given the complexity of the decision process, much attention has been paid to multiple-criteria decision-making (MCDM) approaches in order to enhance the ability to make sound decisions in water resources management. Authors in Anagnostopoulos et al. (2005) discuss that there is no method for choosing among them the most appropriate MCDM methods for a given decision problem and the choice is mostly subjective. Authors evaluate four alternative irrigation projects for the East Macedonia–Thrace District using the AHP and Promethee multi-criteria methods. The projects evaluation is based on economic, social, environmental, and cost criteria.

More information about different applications of MCDM in water supply management can be found in Lai et al. (2008). For example, MCDM techniques have been applied to optimize policy selection in the remediation of contaminated sites, the reduction of contaminants entering aquatic ecosystems, the optimization of water and coastal resources, and the management of other resources (Huang et al. 2011).

From a wide range of MCDM methods, the most suitable ones for the design of alternative comparison are Promethee and AHP (Balali et al. 2014), and therefore we conducted a short survey on these methods regarding water resource problems, especially problems related to lake management.

AHP is widely used in water resources industry. For example, management and planning for a large watershed may include issues related to water quality and quantity, forest management, wildlife management, and recreation. Input is required from subject matter experts in each of these disciplines in order to establish priorities and make informed decisions regarding spatial and temporal distributions of resources.

In addition to its breadth of application, the AHP is relatively easy to apply, to understand, and to interpret (Schmoldt et al. 2013).

Authors in Şener et al. (2010) select a landfill site for the Lake Beysehir catchment area in such way that the lake is protected. The Beysehir Lake is the largest freshwater lake and drinking water reservoir in Turkey. To determine the most suitable landfill site that must combine social, environmental, and technical parameters, an AHP was combined with a geographic information system (GIS) to examine several criteria, and each criterion was evaluated with the aid of AHP.

In Li (2007), author researches the system that involves defining indicators in the following fields: society, economy, resources, environment, and ecology. These indicators are proposed for eco-environmental quality assessment in Chaohu Lake basin. A hierarchical model with four levels is established and the weights of indicators and attributes are determined by combining Delphi method with the AHP.

In Su et al. (1997), AHP was applied in water environmental quality assessment of the Songhua River, and the authors show that it has logicality, practicability, and system that are appropriate to the real water environmental quality assessment.

The AHP provides a systematic method for comparison and weighting multiple criteria and alternatives that exist in integrated watershed management. An advantage of the AHP is that it is capable of providing numerical weights to options where subjective judgments of either quantitative or qualitative alternatives constitute an important part of the decision process. Such is often the case with IWM (De Steiguer et al. 2003).

Eutrophication is the most widespread water quality problem in many countries. Symptoms such as high level of chlorophyll, an excessive seaweed blooms, and occurrence of anoxia and hypoxia have occurred in many areas in China (Xing et al. 2005). Evaluation of the trophic state of a lake is in fact a multivariate comprehensive decision-making process quantifying the qualitative problem. Authors in Xing et al. (2005) choose the trophic state index in order to assess the trophic state of the Lake Dianchi and they use AHP for weights calculation of the pollution indicators.

Authors in Zhang et al. (2007) evaluate environmental comprehensive quality of water and sediment of Xuanwu Lake, Nanjing, China. An improved AHP method had been developed and the weights of pollution factors were completely related to the objective monitoring data through the standardization of these procedures. This improved AHP method can avoid arbitrariness of subjective judgment and can reflect the real influential factors of environment pollution in different periods or regions (Zhang et al. 2007).

Many quality management decisions involve uncertain information, multiple, and often conflicting objectives, and limited resources (Popović et al. 2012a, b). In Korfmacher (1997), author presents an application of AHP to the selection of a water quality model for Lake Okeechobee in Florida. The aim of selected water quality model is to help guide research and management efforts at reducing algal blooms on the lake.

Authors in Calizaya et al. (2010) apply AHP to solve the MCDA problem in the Lake Poopo Basin and to identify the alternatives using the highest expected utility value in order to support stakeholders in managing their water resources.

In the study conducted by Hajkowicz and Collins (2007), eight types of MCA application in water resource management were identified, and by reviewing the characteristics of the problem considered in this paper, two types of applications are a match:

- Project appraisal. These studies use MCA to rank or score a set of water management projects which often involve some form of water condition restoration activity. For example, Al-Rashdan et al. (1999) use Promethee and Nominal Group Technique to prioritize a set of projects aimed to improve the environmental quality of the Jordan River.
- Water quality management. These papers involved an application of MCA primarily involving the evaluation of options aimed specifically at improving water quality. They often involve human and ecosystem health objectives. An example comes from Lee and Chang (2005) where MCA is used to develop a water quality management plan for the Tou–Chen River Basin in northern Taiwan.

Papers reviewed in Hajkowicz and Collins (2007) employed 61 unique MCA techniques. The majority of studies applied more than one MCA method, usually to test the sensitivity of the result and the authors point out that the most commonly applied methods were fuzzy set analysis, compromise programming (CP), the analytic hierarchy process (AHP), ELECTRE, and Promethee.

In Abu-Taleb and Mareschal (1995), authors describe the application of the Promethee V multi-criteria method to evaluate and select from a variety of potentially feasible water resources development options, so that the allocation of limited funds to alternative development projects and programs can proceed in the most efficient manner. The criteria set indicates that a successful combination of water options must include projects and programs that minimize groundwater extraction, ensure groundwater quality and quantity, have a high probability of cost recovery, maximize the supply of water, and promote water conservation and efficiency.

A list of the papers on the topic of Hydrology and Water Management can be found in Behzadian et al. (2010) and, according to the authors, most of the papers have been devoted to the sustainable water resources planning, water management strategies assessment, and irrigation planning using Promethee applications.

3 PROMETHEE Method

The Promethee method (Preference Ranking Organization Method for Enrichment Evaluations) is one of the most recent multi-criteria decision aid methods, developed by Brans (1982). The Promethee includes Promethee I for partial ranking of alternatives and Promethee II for complete ranking of alternatives. The Promethee II method was adopted for this paper.

The basic principle of Promethee II is based on a pair-wise comparison of alternatives along each recognized criterion. Alternatives are evaluated according to different criteria, which have to be maximized or minimized. The implementation of the Promethee II requires two additional types of information (Behzadian et al. 2010):

- Information on the relative importance (i.e., the weights) of the criteria considered. Promethee II assumes that the decision-maker is able to weight criteria appropriately, at least when the number of criteria is not too large (Macharis et al. 2004);
- Information on the decision-makers' preference function, which decision-maker uses when comparing the contribution of the alternatives in terms of each separate criterion. In order to facilitate the selection of a specific preference function, Brans and Vincke (1985) proposed six basic types of criteria: (1) Usual, (2) U-shape, (3) V-shape, (4) level, (5) V-shape with indifference, and (6) Gaussian (Brans and Vincke 1985). These six types are particularly easy to define. For each criterion, the value of an indifference threshold, q, the value of a strict preference threshold, p, and the value of an intermediate value between p and q, s, has to be defined (Brans and Mareschal 2003).

Experts' opinions are set on various parameters such as selection and weight of the criteria. The team of experts who has cooperated in this research includes architects and information managers who are involved in hotel building design and operational research projects. The Promethee method is implemented in five steps (Behzadian et al. 2010):

Step 1. Determination of deviation based on pair-wise comparison (1):

$$d_j(a,b) = g_j(a) - g_j(b);\ j = 1, \ldots, n \tag{1}$$

where $d_j(a,b)$ denotes the difference between the evaluation of a and b on each criterion.

Step 2. Application of the preference function (2):

$$P_j(a,b) = F_j\left[d_j(a,b)\right];\ j = 1, \ldots, n \tag{2}$$

where $P_j(a,b)$ denotes the preference of alternative a with regard to alternative b on each criterion, as a function of $d_j(a,b)$.

Step 3. Calculation of an overall or global preferences index (3):

$$\forall a, b \in A, \pi(a,b) = \sum_{j=1}^{n} P_j(a,b) w_j \tag{3}$$

where $\pi(a,b)$ of a over b (from 0 to 1) is defined as the weighted sum $p(a,b)$ of for each criterion and w_j is the weight associated with jth criterion.

Step 4. Calculation of outranking flows/The Promethee I partial ranking (4):

$$\phi^+(a) = \frac{1}{n-1}\sum_{x \in A} \pi(a,x) \text{ and } \phi^-(a) = \frac{1}{n-1}\sum_{x \in A} \pi(a,x) \tag{4}$$

where $\phi^{+}(a)$ and $\phi^{-}(a)$ denote the positive outranking flow and negative outranking flow for each alternative, respectively.

Step 5. Calculation of net outranking flow/The Promethee II complete ranking (5):

$$\phi(a) = \phi^{+}(a) - \phi^{-}(a) \tag{5}$$

where $\phi(a)$ denotes the net outranking flow for each alternative.

4 The Analytic Hierarchy Process (AHP)

Analytic Hierarchy Process (AHP) was developed by Thomas Saaty in the early ‘70s of the last century (Saaty 1977, 1980), in order to solve complex problems whose elements are objectives, criteria, sub-criteria, and alternatives. It is popular and widely used method for organizing and analyzing complex decisions, based on mathematics and psychology. AHP considers quantitative and qualitative attributes and combines them through the decomposition of complex problems into a model that has the form of a hierarchy. Each level of the hierarchy consists of elements that are influenced by the level above and which can be mutually compared hierarchically structured model of decision-making is generally made up of objectives, criteria, and alternatives. The objective is on the top of the hierarchy, the criteria are compared to one another in relation to the set objective, while at the last level, the comparison of alternatives is made in relation to the criteria. AHP keeps all parts of the hierarchy in a relationship, so it is easy to see how a change in one factor affects other factors.

The main objective of this method is ranking of several alternatives, as well as the choice of the best one from a set of available ones, in situations where decision-making involves a larger number of decision-makers, and where there are a larger number of criteria in different time periods. The ranking/selection is made in relation to the set target.

The methodology of the AHP can be explained in following steps (Saaty 1977, 1980):

Step 1: The problem is decomposed into a hierarchy of goal, criteria, sub-criteria, and alternatives.

Step 2: Data are collected from experts or decision-makers corresponding to the hierarchic structure, in the pair-wise comparison of alternatives on a qualitative scale. Experts can rate the comparison as equal, marginally strong, strong, very strong, and extremely strong.

Step 3: The pair-wise comparisons of various criteria generated at Step 2 are organized into a square matrix. The diagonal elements of the matrix are 1. The criterion in the *i*th row is better than criterion in the *j*th column if the value of element (*i, j*) is more than 1; otherwise, the criterion in the *j*th column is better than that in the *i*th row. The (*j, i*) element of the matrix is the reciprocal of the (*i, j*) element.

Step 4: The principal eigenvalue and the corresponding normalized right eigenvector of the comparison matrix give the relative importance of the various criteria being compared. The elements of the normalized eigenvector are termed weights with respect to the criteria or sub-criteria and ratings with respect to the alternatives.
Step 5: The consistency of the matrix of order n is evaluated. Comparisons made by this method are subjective and the AHP tolerates inconsistency through the amount of redundancy in the approach. If this consistency index fails to reach a required level then answers to comparisons may be re-examined. The consistency index, *CI*, is calculated as

$$CI = (\lambda_{\max} - n)/(n - 1) \tag{6}$$

where $\lambda_{\max}$ max is the maximum eigenvalue of the judgment matrix. This *CI* can be compared with that of a random matrix, *RI*. The ratio derived, *CI/RI*, is termed the consistency ratio, *CR*. Saaty (1977, 1980) suggests the value of CR should be less than 0.1.
Step 6: The rating of each alternative is multiplied by the weights of the sub-criteria and aggregated to get local ratings with respect to each criterion. The local ratings are then multiplied by the weights of the criteria and aggregated to get global ratings.

The AHP produces weight values for each alternative based on the judged importance of one alternative over another with respect to a common criterion.

5 Methodology

The following methodological framework is designed in order to rank the alternatives for each criterion (Fig. 1). The main phases of proposed framework are based on methodology presented in Vujosevic and Popovic (2016) and used for choice of the best one from a set of available alternatives, in situations where decision-making involves a larger number of decision-makers.

As a starting point in the methodology, it is necessary to identify the research objectives of the analyzed problem. Based on the objectives, researchers can identify alternatives and evaluate them according to different criteria by Promethee II. The result of phase I is net outranking flow coefficients for each alternative. These coefficients are used to choose the best alternative for the solution of the initial problem.

The results of Promethee II method are purely quantitative. In order to choose the best solution it is significantly better to include some qualitative aspect in the analysis. AHP considers quantitative and qualitative attributes. This method is ranking of alternatives basis on experts opinion.

Methodological framework is designed to rank alternatives for each criterion by combining these two methods. Qualitative character of the AHP is exceeded using Promethee II in the phase I of the framework by cutting off the alternatives with negative net outranking flow. The benefit is direct consistency increase of the AHP.

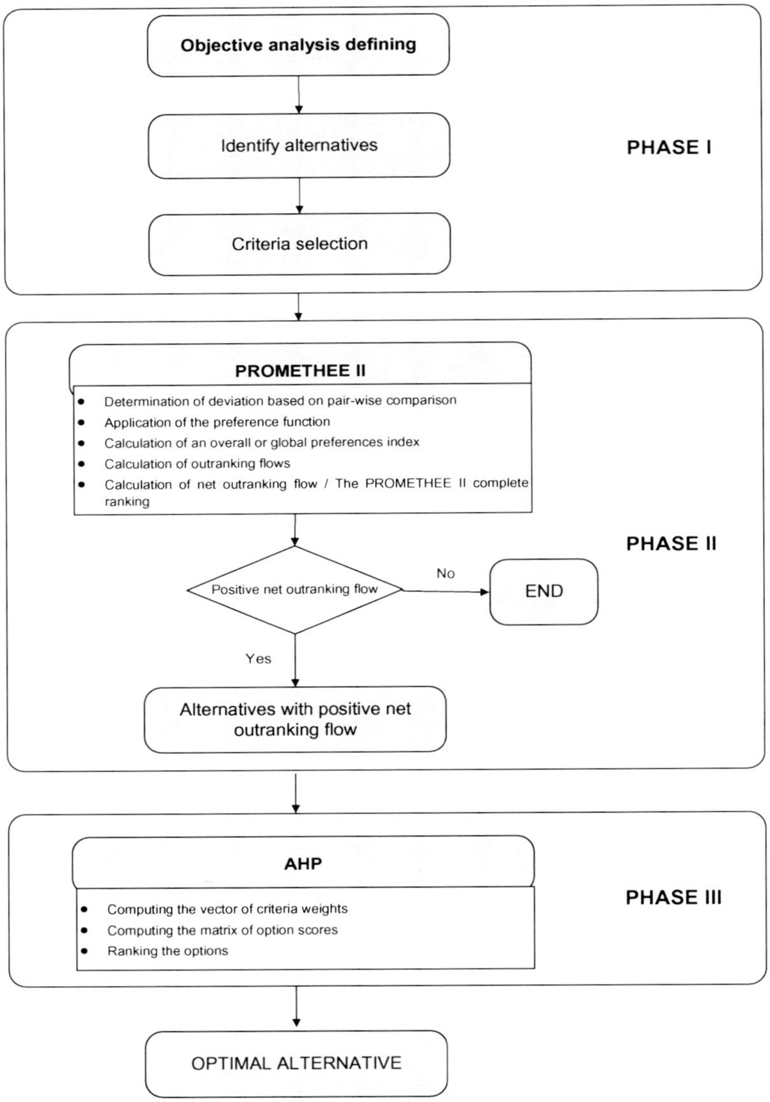

Fig. 1 Methodological framework

Optimal alternative is a result of the methodological framework application based on combination of the Promethee II and AHP methods by using all the positive features of the methods, and trying to annulate disadvantages.

6 Numerical Example

6.1 Phase I—Problem Analysis

In numerical example, we chose 14 locations (alternatives) where the water quality of the lake Vrutci is being examined. These locations are presented in Fig. 2 and marked as a1, a2,…, a14. Lake and accumulation Vrutci is located in western Serbia close to city Uzice and it was created by building the dam on the river Djetinja. Accumulation Vrutci supplies water to the western part of the Republic of Serbia, primarily the cities of Uzice, Pozega, and Arilje.

On each of 14 locations, water quality is being examined based on 17 criteria which are shown in Table 1 with defined preferences (min/max).

6.2 Phase II—the PROMETHEE Method

Data used in this numerical example are real data, and values of all criteria for each location (alternative) are given in Table 2. For ranking alternatives, Promethee II method (Decision Lab software) is used. Preferences function (V-shaped for all

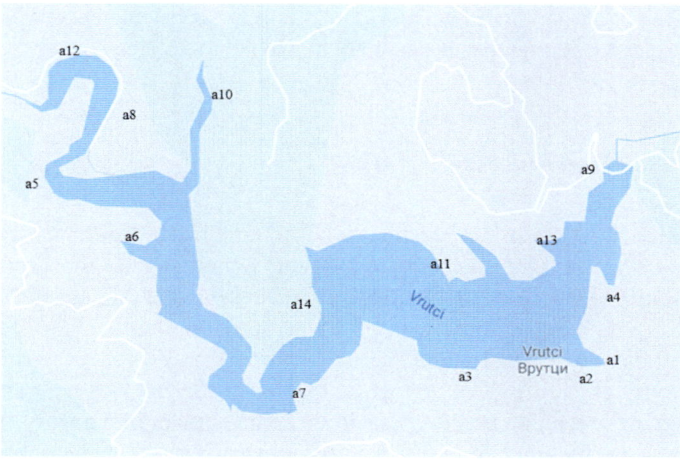

Fig. 2 Locations on lake where water quality is being examined

Table 1 List of criteria with their preferences

Criteria index (label)	Criteria preferences (min/max)	Criteria name
C_1	Min	pH value
C_2	Min	Electrolytic conductivity (μS/cm)
C_3	Max	Oxygen content (mg/l O2)
C_4	Max	Oxygen saturation (%)
C_5	Min	Ammonium ion (mgN/l)
C_6	Min	Nitrates (mgN/l)
C_7	Min	Total nitrogen (mgN/l)
C_8	Min	CO2 (mg/l)
C_9	Max	Suspended solids (mg/l)
C_{10}	Min	Orthophosphates (mgP/l)
C_{11}	Min	Orthophosphates (mgP/l)
C_{12}	Min	BOD5 (mgO2/l)
C_{13}	Max	Iron (mg/l)
C_{14}	Max	Bor (μg/l)
C_{15}	Max	Manganese (μg/l)
C_{16}	Min	Copper (μg/l)
C_{17}	Max	Chromium (μg/l)

alternatives) is defined for each criteria, as well as criteria weights, all based on the opinion of decision-makers and the analysis of relevant literature (Table 2).

Result of this method is net outranking flow and the values for this flow can be positive and negative. Final results for each alternative a1, a2,…, a14 of the example are given in Fig. 3.

Based on net outranking flow values, final ranking is calculated and presented in Table 3. Highest water quality is detected on a location a6.

6.3 *Phase III—The AHP Method*

According to the AHP method, the first step is to establish a hierarchical model. The top level of the hierarchy corresponds to the goal; in this case, the goal is to determine the best location. Selection criteria (Table 1) are presented in the second level. Seven alternatives (possible locations) with positive outranking flow values (Table 3) are presented at the lowest level of the hierarchy (Fig. 4).

Operations research experts (11 participants) in the field of natural resources participated in the ranking process. Due to the large number of comparison matrices (17 matrices), we present here only final priority vector for each alternative per each criterion (Table 4).

Table 2 Values of all criteria for each location and criteria weights

	C_1	C_2	C_3	C_4	C_5	C_6	C_7	C_8	C_9	C_{10}	C_{11}	C_{12}	C_{13}	C_{14}	C_{15}	C_{16}	C_{17}
a_1	8.52	584	10.20	97.41	0.144	0.34	0.57	0.00	15.5	0.052	0.085	0.56	0.05	18.32	6.9	2.77	10.4
a_2	8.39	536	10.28	97.91	0.054	0.42	0.64	0.00	9.6	0.006	0.052	0.78	0.04	18.12	5.0	2.57	13.8
a_3	8.14	416	9.75	94.22	0.162	0.27	0.56	4.46	11.7	0.008	0.065	1.10	0.07	12.18	12.8	1.88	23.2
a_4	8.32	442	9.38	91.42	0.099	1.06	1.23	0.00	14	0.016	0.131	0.71	0.04	21.09	11.4	2.97	12.1
a_5	8.03	433	8.96	85.84	0.198	0.39	0.66	4.56	4.6	0.020	0.248	0.63	0.08	18.41	20.5	1.88	32.4
a_6	8.05	420	8.92	84.55	0.189	0.30	0.58	3.20	1	0.006	0.048	0.43	0.12	31.38	20.4	1.98	54.3
a_7	8.22	391	9.49	95.31	0.117	1.74	2.04	2.23	1	0.055	0.304	0.61	0.05	26.14	5.8	1.88	17.1
a_8	7.87	562	8.98	86.44	0.072	0.04	0.32	8.34	1	0.023	0.025	4.02	0.02	25.15	13.2	2.77	4.2
a_9	7.56	300	7.68	77.17	0.117	0.11	0.39	8.25	2.2	0.004	0.029	0.93	0.10	18.41	119.1	2.77	2.3
a_{10}	8.21	395	10.13	99.20	0.018	1.90	2.36	2.33	1	0.004	0.024	0.83	0.01	19.11	2.5	2.28	2.9
a_{11}	7.26	217	8.22	81.45	0.072	0.10	0.34	11.83	24.5	0.037	0.188	1.26	0.14	17.33	37.3	1.98	2.5
a_{12}	7.81	473	10.69	103.5	0.126	0.21	0.54	7.86	1.3	0.035	0.086	1.22	0.01	38.71	3.0	2.77	3.4
a_{13}	7.36	557	6.37	63.61	0.18	0.05	0.31	25.22	1	0.004	0.051	1.13	0.08	32.77	215.9	2.57	3.1
a_{14}	8.40	413	9.98	106.5	0.261	0.04	0.53	0.00	16.1	0.014	0.102	2.29	0.12	28.61	70.7	12.18	5.7
Criteria weights	0.08	0.038	0.08	0.08	0.059	0.059	0.08	0.059	0.038	0.059	0.08	0.101	0.038	0.038	0.038	0.038	0.038

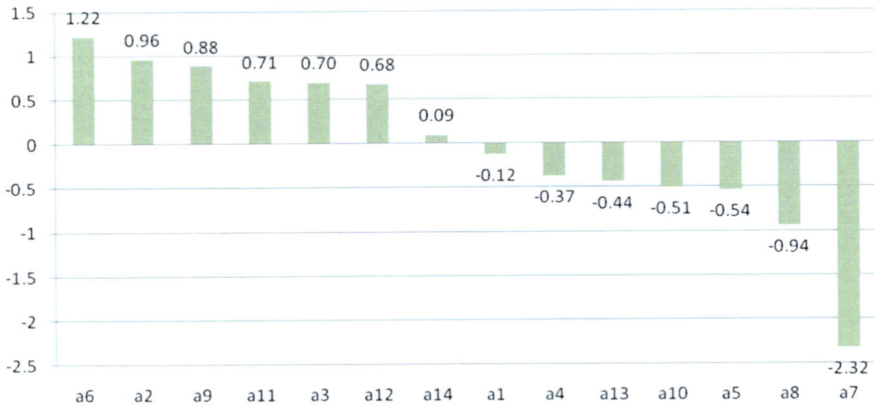

Fig. 3 Net outranking flow for each alternative

Table 3 Net outranking flow values and final ranking of alternatives

Alternatives	$a_6 >> a_2 >> a_9 >> a_{11} >> a_3 >> a_{12} >> a_{14} >> a_1 >> a_4 >> a_{13} >> a_{10} >> a_5 >> a_8 >> a_7$													
Net outranking flow	1.22	0.96	0.88	0.71	0.70	0.68	0.09	−0.12	−0.37	−0.44	−0.51	−0.54	−0.94	−2.32
Rank	1	2	3	4	5	6	7	8	9	10	11	12	13	14

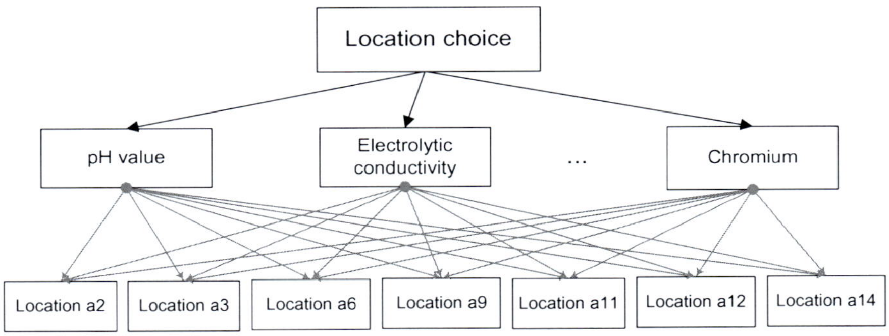

Fig. 4 Hierarchical model for location choice

The weights listed in Table 4 are synthesized resulting in weights and ranks for all alternatives. These results are presented in Table 5.

Location a11 is the location with the best water quality. The solution that was obtained using only Promethee II differs from the optimal solution that incorporates experts' opinion. Proposed methodological framework emphasizes the qualitative and quantitative aspects of the decision-making process which overcomes the disadvantages of individual and independent application of each method separately.

Table 4 Final priority vector—*Wa*

	C_1	C_2	C_3	C_4	C_5	C_6	C_7	C_8	C_9	C_{10}	C_{11}	C_{12}	C_{13}	C_{14}	C_{15}	C_{16}	C_{17}
a_2	0.042	0.024	0.250	0.167	0.344	0.033	0.091	0.321	0.108	0.049	0.172	0.168	0.057	0.055	0.027	0.090	0.141
a_3	0.072	0.084	0.124	0.112	0.066	0.073	0.091	0.127	0.114	0.049	0.205	0.110	0.057	0.023	0.052	0.237	0.266
a_6	0.101	0.084	0.057	0.047	0.051	0.073	0.091	0.127	0.031	0.049	0.172	0.422	0.151	0.219	0.095	0.237	0.443
a_9	0.288	0.236	0.018	0.021	0.127	0.182	0.273	0.040	0.031	0.048	0.342	0.159	0.151	0.069	0.419	0.090	0.037
a_{11}	0.310	0.440	0.035	0.039	0.291	0.182	0.273	0.034	0.451	0.243	0.019	0.060	0.336	0.069	0.133	0.237	0.037
a_{12}	0.152	0.044	0.300	0.307	0.101	0.073	0.091	0.030	0.031	0.243	0.059	0.060	0.097	0.380	0.098	0.090	0.037
a_{14}	0.035	0.088	0.216	0.307	0.021	0.385	0.091	0.321	0.234	0.321	0.031	0.021	0.150	0.184	0.177	0.019	0.037
Criteria weights	0.080	0.038	0.080	0.080	0.059	0.059	0.080	0.059	0.038	0.059	0.080	0.101	0.038	0.038	0.038	0.038	0.038

Table 5 Weights and ranks for alternatives

Alternatives	$a_{11} >> a_9 >> a_{14} >> a_6 >> a_2 >> a_{12} >>$ a_3					
Weights	0.169	0.154	0.152	0.146	0.138	0.135	0.110
Rank	1	2	3	4	5	6	7

7 Conclusion

Application of multi-criteria decision analysis in water resource management is widespread and growing (Hajkowicz and Collins 2007). The use of MCDA techniques provides a reliable methodology to rank alternative, but none of them is considered to be the best for all kind of decision-making situations. The most suitable ones for the design of alternative comparison for our type of problem are Promethee and AHP, and therefore we conducted a short survey on these methods regarding water resource problems, especially problems related to lake management.

Promethee II is a simple method and very suitable for problems with large number of alternatives. Outputs from the method are calculated positive and negative outranking net flows and the alternatives with positive flow are highly ranked. One advantage of the AHP method is the ability to consider both quantitative and qualitative criteria in the process of pair-wise comparisons of alternatives, but the consistency can be diminished when there are many alternatives to analyze (Popovic et al. 2012a, b).

We suggest original methodology which combines two methods and extracts the best characteristics from each one. Only alternatives with positive net outranking flow are input for AHP ranking process and direct consequence of reduction of the number of alternatives is increase of the AHP consistency level.

The usefulness and the value of the proposed methodological framework are confirmed in real case example—choice of the location with the best water quality of Lake Vrutci. Ranking values obtained using Promethee II method differ from the ranks obtained by combining Promethee II and AHP.

References

Abu-Taleb MF, Mareschal B (1995) Water resources planning in the Middle East: application of the PROMETHEE V multicriteria method. Eur J Oper Res 81(3):500–511

Al-Rashdan D, Al-Kloub B, Dean A, Al-Shemmeri T (1999) Environmental impact assessment and ranking the environmental projects in Jordan. Eur J Oper Res 118(1):30–45

Anagnostopoulos K, Petalas C, Pisinaras V (2005) Water resources planning using the AHP and Promethee multicriteria methods: the case of nestos river-Greece. In: Proceedings, the 7th Balkan conference on operational research

Balali V, Zahraie B, Roozbahani A (2014) A comparison of AHP and PROMETHEE family decision making methods for selection of building structural system. Am J Civil Eng Archit 2(5):149–159

Barisic M, Toth A, Djuric S (2011) Sustainable water use in 21st century. Management 61:107–111

Behzadian M, Kazemzadeh RB, Albadvi A, Aghdasi M (2010) PROMETHEE: a comprehensive literature review on methodologies and applications. Eur J Oper Res 200(1):198–215
Belton V, Stewart TJ (2002) Multiple criteria decision analysis: an integrated approach. Springer, NewYork
Brans P (1982) Preference ranking organization method for enrichment valuations (in French language). Colloque D' aide' la De´cision. Que´bec: Universite´ Laval, pp 183–213
Brans JP, Mareschal VB (2003) How to select and how to rank projects: the PROMETHEE method. Eur J Oper Res 24(2):228–238
Brans JP, Vincke P (1985) A preference ranking organization method (The PROMETHEE method for multiple criteria decision making). Manag Sci 31:647–656
Calizaya A, Meixner O, Bengtsson L, Berndtsson R (2010) Multi-criteria decision analysis (MCDA) for integrated water resources management (IWRM) in the Lake Poopo Basin, Bolivia. Water Res Manag 24(10):2267–2289
Cinelli M, Coles SR, Kirwan K (2014) Analysis of the potentials of multi criteria decision analysis methods to conduct sustainability assessment. Ecol Ind 46:138–148
De Steiguer JE, Duberstein J, Lopes V (2003) The analytic hierarchy process as a means for integrated watershed management. In: Renard KG (eds) Proceedings, first interagency conference on research on the watersheds, pp 736–740
Eder G, Duckstein L, Nachtnebel HP (1997) Ranking water resource projects and evaluating criteria by multicriterion Q-analysis: an Austrian case study. J Multi-Criteria Decis Anal 6(5):259–271
Figueira J, Greco S, Ehrgott M (2005) Multiple criteria decision analysis: state of the artsurveys. Springer, New York
Flug M, Seitz HL, Scott JF (2000) Multicriteria decision analysis applied to Glen Canyon Dam. J Water Resour Plan Manag 126(5):270–276
Hajkowicz S, Collins K (2007) A review of multiple criteria analysis for water resource planning and management. Water Resour Manag 21(9):1553–1566
Hajkowicz S, Higgins A (2008) A comparison of multiple criteria analysis techniques for water resource management. Eur J Oper Res 184(1):255–265
Herva M, Roca E (2013) Ranking municipal solid waste treatment alternatives based on ecological footprint and multi-criteria analysis. Ecol Ind 25:77–84
Huang IB, Keisler J, Linkov I (2011) Multi-criteria decision analysis in environmental sciences: ten years of applications and trends. Sci Total Environ 409(19):3578–3594
Joubert A, Stewart TJ, Eberhard R (2003) Evaluation of water supply augmentation and water demand management options for the city of Cape Town. J Multi-Criteria Decis Anal 12(1):17–25
Korfmacher KS (1997) Selection of a model for algal blooms on Lake Okeechobee: an application of decision analysis using the analytic hierarchy process (AHP). Lake Reserv Manag 13(1):38–43. https://doi.org/10.1080/07438149709354294
Lai E, Lundie S, Ashbolt NJ (2008) Review of multi-criteria decision aid for integrated sustainability assessment of urban water systems. Urban Water 5(4):315–327
Lee CS, Chang SP (2005) Interactive fuzzy optimization for an economic and environmental balance in a river system. Water Res 39(1):221–231
Li R (2007) Dynamic assessment on regional eco-environmental quality using AHP-statistics model—A case study of Chaohu Lake Basin. Chin Geogr Sci 17(4):341–348
Macharis C, Springael J, De Brucker K, Verbeke A (2004) PROMETHEE and AHP: The design of operational synergies in multicriteria analysis: Strengthening PROMETHEE with ideas of AHP. Eur J Oper Res 153(2):307–317
Marttunen M, Lienert J, Belton V (2017) Structuring problems for multi-criteria decision analysis in practice: a literature review of method combinations. Eur J Oper Res 263(1):1–17
Opricovic S, Tzeng GH (2003) Fuzzy multicriteria model for postearthquake land-use planning. Nat Hazards Rev 4(2):59–64
Popović M, Milošević S, Kuzmanović M (2012a) Specific aspects of investment valuation under uncertainty (Chap. 10). In: Grzybowska K (ed) Contemporary management: learning and knowl-

edge in business, Monograph. Publishing House of Poznan University of Technology, Poznan, pp 137–149. ISBN: 978-83-7775-192-3
Popović M, Milošević S, Kuzmanović M (2012b) Using AHP and financial criteria for evaluating alternatives to reduce risk of investment. Res Logist Prod **2**, (4), 377–386. ISSN (Print): 2083-4942, ISSN (Online): 2083-4950
Postel S, Daily G, Ehrlich P (1996) Human appropriation of renewable fresh water. Science 271(5250):785–788
Prato T, Herath G (2017) Role of multi-criteria decision making in natural resource management. In: Using multi-criteria decision analysis in natural resource management. Routledge, pp 17–26
Saaty TL (1977) A scaling method for priorities in hierarchical structures. J Math Psychol 15:234–281
Saaty TL (1980) The analytic hierarchy process. McGraw Hill, New York
Schmoldt D, Kangas J, Mendoza GA, Pesonen M (eds) (2013) The analytic hierarchy process in natural resource and environmental decision making, vol 3. Springer Science & Business Media
Şener Ş, Şener E, Nas B, Karagüzel R (2010) Combining AHP with GIS for landfill site selection: a case study in the Lake Beyşehir catchment area (Konya, Turkey). Waste Manag 30(11):2037–2046
Su DL, Wu B, Shen J (1997) The AHP of water environmental quality assessment. J Harbin Inst Technol 29(5):105
Vujosevic ML, Popovic MJ (2016) The comparison of the energy performance of hotel buildings using PROMETHEE decision-making method. Therm Sci 20(1):197–208. https://doi.org/10.2298/TSCI150409098V
Wiecek MM, Ehrgott M, Fadel G, Figueira JR (2008) Editorial: Multiple criteria decision making for engineering. Omega 36:337–339
Xing K, Guo H, Sun Y, Huang Y (2005) Assessment of the spatial-temporal eutrophic character in the Lake Dianchi. J Geogr Sci 15(1):37–43
Zhang Y, Zhang H, Gao X, Peng B (2007) Improved AHP method and its application in lake environmental comprehensive quality evaluation - a case study of Xuanwu Lake, Nanjing, China. Chin J Oceanol Limnol 25:427–433

Forest Policy Evaluation in European Countries Using the PROMETHEE Method

Stefanos Tsiaras and Zacharoula Andreopoulou

Abstract The aim of the paper is to evaluate Forest Policy performance in the countries of Europe, using a multiple criteria analysis based on forestry sector data retrieved by Eurostat. Multiple Criteria Decision Analysis is strongly connected with Policy and decision-making, and it can mitigate the uncertainty of planning providing robust solutions, while it is broadly used for agri-environmental issues. The PROMETHEE method was used to provide a ranking of the European countries in their Forest Policy performance drawing on data covering all three sustainability pillars: economy, environment, and society. According to the findings, the Czech Republic has the best performance among the examined countries regarding Forest Policy implementation. Other countries that can be singled out for best practices are Germany, Slovakia, and Hungary. Greece, on the other hand, is ranked last and the evidence verifies that the economic crisis has seriously affected the country in multiple areas. The country rankings were more volatile in the middle places, while countries with high or low performance on Forest Policy implementation maintained a more stable position across the three scenarios. The forest area as an input significantly affects the final ranking of the European countries. In general, large areas available for wood supply lead to a lower country ranking in Forest Policy performance as in Sweden, Finland, and Spain; only Germany achieves a high ranking among countries with large areas available for wood supply. The findings provide an overview of the current situation relating to Forest Policy implementation among European countries and could be used by the European Union in a future framework of Common Forest Policy in the EU.

Keywords Forest Policy · Multiple criteria decision analysis · European Union

---

S. Tsiaras (✉) · Z. Andreopoulou
Faculty of Agriculture, Forestry and Natural Environment, School of Forestry, Aristotle University of Thessaloniki, Thessaloniki, Greece
e-mail: stefanostsiaras@gmail.com

Z. Andreopoulou
e-mail: randreop@for.auth.gr

N. Mladenović et al. (eds.), *Advances in Operational Research in the Balkans*, Springer Proceedings in Business and Economics,
https://doi.org/10.1007/978-3-030-21990-1_6

1 Introduction

Unlike the Agricultural Sector in the European Union, the Forestry sector lacks a common framework for Forest Policy similar to the Common Agricultural Policy. According to the European Commission "The Treaties for the European Union make no provision for a Common Forest Policy" (EC 2016), while the forestry activities within the EU are coordinated by the Standing Forestry Committee (EEC 1989). According to Bjärstig (2013), "it is only possible to talk about a Forest Policy based on the EU Forest Strategy." Therefore, the member states apply a customized Forest Policy taking into consideration the Constitution, the Forest Law, the EU Forest Strategy, and the unique forest features of their countries. The impact of the enlargement of the European Union in the forest sector has been examined in the three Baltic countries (Estonia, Latvia, and Lithuania) and the findings pointed out the need for actions in Forest Policy processes (Lazdinis et al. 2005). Even countries with similar natural conditions such as Southern Sweden and Lithuania implement different policies regarding forest management (Brukas et al. 2013). Decisions at a governmental level influence the vitality of forests (Singh et al. 2017), and are often characterized by uncertainty in predicting future trends (Adams and Hairston 1996). Furthermore, the lack of a common framework in the forestry sector complicates the communication among the actors involved in the forest sector (Janse 2007). Mayer and Rametsteiner (2004) acknowledge the Ministerial Conference on the Protection of Forests in Europe as the most important entity in Europe regarding Forest Policy making, involving 44 European countries. The "scenario development" and the scenario-based planning remain an important tool for the planning of Forest Policy (Hoogstra-Klein and Schüll 2017). Apart from the traditional methods of planning, forest policy uses methods and tools that combine the available technology such as the Geographical Information Systems (GIS), the Decision Support Systems (DSS), and the Multiple Criteria Decision Analysis (MCDA) (Ferretti et al. 2011).

Multiple Criteria Decision Analysis (MCDA) is strongly connected with policy and decision-making, and can mitigate the uncertainty of planning providing robust solutions (Kurth et al. 2017). Moreover, MCDA is broadly used for agri-environmental issues (Andreopoulou et al. 2017). The most suitable methods of Multiple Criteria Decision-Making (MCDM) and MCDA in the environmental sector are PROMETHEE, ELECTRE, TOPSIS, and SMART (Velasquez and Hester, 2013). The PROMETHEE method has various applications in the sectors of agriculture, forestry, and environment. The PROMETHEE ranking method, for instance, was used to evaluate sustainable forest management alternatives (Jactel et al. 2012). The application of PROMETHEE was used in energy policy, and more specifically in the field of Renewable Energy Sources (RES) in a recent study that took place in Serbia (Vasić 2018), while PROMETHEE II was used in the same field of RES in a Greek case study (Andreopoulou et al. 2018). Moreover, PROMETHEE II was used in the agricultural industry to evaluate the economic efficiency of agri-food companies in Greece (Baourakis et al. 2002) and to study the perspectives of the agrotourism industry (Zopounidis et al. 2014). The theoretical background of PROMETHEE as

an outranking method was used to evaluate the performance of three EU countries: France, Spain, and the Netherlands in the sector of agroforestry (Palma et al. 2007). The findings of the study are extremely useful to the Agricultural Policy of the European Union. The same method was used in a recent study in Cyprus for the selection of optimum energy crops (Kylili et al. 2016). In a recent study in Greece, Tsiaras et al. (2017) used fuzzy MCDA and more specifically fuzzy Vikor and fuzzy AHP in order to select the optimum tree species for truffle cultivation in a study area.

MCDA methods have been broadly used in the forestry sector, mainly because of their ability to taking into consideration various indicators such as economic, environmental, and social in order to suggest an equilibrium among economic benefits, environmental protection, and social equity (Eggers et al. 2017). For instance, Lipuščeк et al. (2010) developed a composite model combining the Analytic Hierarchy Process (AHP), the Life Cycle Assessment (LCA), and the Delphi Method in order to classify the wood products taking into consideration their environmental impact. A new and complex framework combining SWOT Analysis, Fuzzy AHP, and Fuzzy Analytic Network Project (ANP) was developed by Grošelj et al. (2016) in order to rank and evaluate the effects of forest management scenarios in a case study of Pohorje, Slovenia. In the same study area, a combination of MCDM and group decision-making was used to propose sustainable forest management solutions (Grošelj and Stirn 2013). The sustainability impact of forest wood chains was assessed with a novel tool based on a PROMETHEE II algorithm in a case study in Germany (Wolfslehner et al. 2012).

Ranking of countries in the European Union with MCDM methods is broadly observed in literature (e.g., Nuuter et al. 2014, Poledníková 2014, Siskos et al. 2013) and the findings are useful for policy planning in the EU. A recent study (Reiff et al. 2016) pointed out significant deviation among old and new members of the European Union regarding their performance in the agricultural sector using Multiple Criteria Decision Analysis. Antanasijević et al. (2017) performed a differential MCDA analysis in order to assess the sustainability performance of the European countries, and they concluded that the development is uneven between Eastern and Western Europe. With regard to the forestry sector, Malovrh et al. (2016) developed a Decision Support Framework to analyze and evaluate the strategies implemented on forest bioenergy targets of four European countries, while Lindstad et al. (2015) studied the forest-based bioenergy policies in five European countries, exploring the interactions between national policies and EU policies.

Data Envelopment Analysis (DEA) is also a popular method used for benchmarking. In a recent study, Skare and Rabar (2017) used the DEA method to assess the efficiency of 30 countries, members of the Organization for Economic Co-operation and Development (OECD) with the use of economic, social, environmental, and institutional indicators. Ignatius et al. (2016) proposed a DEA-based framework for the evaluation of carbon efficiency among 23 EU countries.

The aim of the paper is to evaluate Forest Policy performance in the countries of Europe using a Multiple Criteria Analysis based on forestry sector data retrieved by Eurostat.

2 Methodology

The main methodology approach for the present paper was the Multiple Criteria Decision Analysis and more specifically the Preference Ranking Organization METHod for Enriched Evaluation (PROMETHEE) method. The PROMETHEE method is an outranking relation method and according to Velasquez and Hester (2013) is simple, user-friendly, and suitable for environmental and agricultural problems. The PROMETHEE method provides a complete ranking among the alternatives examined under certain criteria and is considered ideal for problems of sustainability (Mareschal 2013).

3 Implementation/Description of the Empirical Study

The evaluation of the EU countries on their performance in Forest Policy was made on an input–output basis. The forest area of the countries was used as input in three different cases: (a) forest and other wooded land, (b) forest, and (c) forest available for wood supply. Data covering the three sustainability pillars: economy, environment, and society were used as output: (1) economics aggregates on forestry (supply and use of products within forestry), (2) protected forests and forests under Natura, and (3) employment in forestry and forest-based sector. The output data were retrieved by Eurostat, while the input data were provided by Food and Agriculture Organization of the United Nations. Although Eurostat provides data for forest and wooded land of Europe, the FAO data were preferred because Eurostat data were based on a questionnaire. The data used in the study are presented in Table 1.

The criteria were selected in order to assess the Forest Policy implementation within the European Union, and include all three pillars of sustainable development, namely, environmental protection, social equity, and economic growth. All criteria were given the same weight, in view of the fact that sustainable development is based on three equal pillars according to the spirit of the Brundtland Report (WCED 1987). All three criteria are quantitative and all of them need to be maximized (Table 2).

The selected preference function for the data of the study was "linear", on account of the fact that it is the most suitable preference function for quantitative data, while the thresholds were determined as "absolute", since this is suggested as the best option for quantitative data (Mareschal 2013). The thresholds Q (indifference) and P (preference) were automatically calculated by the preference function assistant of Visual Promethee Academic created by Mareschal (2013) and they are presented in Table 3.

The forest area of each country was selected as it is a given input, providing information on how "forested" each country is, and shows the availability of resources. Among the multitude of data available by Eurostat, the selected output data each represent a sustainability pillar and provide sufficient perspective of the efficient use of these resources. "Economic aggregates on Forestry" is an economic indicator, record-

Table 1 The data for the study (*Source* Eurostat 2018a, b)

A/A	Country	Input[a]			Output		
		Forest and other wooded land	Forest	Forest available for wood supply	Economics aggregates on forestry[b]	Protected forests[c]	Employment in forestry[d]
1	Austria	4,022.00	3,869.00	3,339.00	2,387.61	834.77	9.7
2	Belgium	719.10	683.40	670.28	428.80	47.92	2.3
3	Bulgaria	3,845.00	3,823.00	2,213.00	740.65	578	30.5
4	Croatia	2,491.00	1,922.00	1,740.00	302.83	320	16.5
5	Cyprus	386.19	172.70	41.12	3.41	26.41	0.8
6	Czech Republic	2,667.41	2,667.41	2,300.79	2,209.49	751.6	27.6
7	Denmark	657.69	612.23	572.23	670.50	123.71	3.1
8	Estonia	2,455.51	2,231.95	1,993.75	509.20	553.97	6.3
9	Finland	23,019.00	22,218.00	19,465.00	4,616.00	4,327	18.6
10	France	17,579.00	16,989.00	16,018.00	6,794.29	6,179.99	36.7
11	Germany	11,419.00	11,419.00	10,888.00	8,853.90	9,264	33.6
12	Greece	6,539.00	3,903.00	3,594.66	81.59	197	3.4

(continued)

Table 1 (continued)

A/A	Country	Input[a]			Output		
		Forest and other wooded land	Forest	Forest available for wood supply	Economics aggregates on forestry[b]	Protected forests[c]	Employment in forestry[d]
13	Hungary	2,190.43	2,069.00	1,778.77	484.70	874.37	24.0
14	Ireland	801.24	754.02	632.01	464.70	6.47	2.8
15	Italy	11,110.00	9,297.00	8,216.47	1,490.70	4,705.63	53.4
16	Latvia	3,468.00	3,356.00	3,151.00	1,045.20	549.40	14.6
17	Lithuania	2,284.00	2,180.00	1,924.00	1,608.69	377	12.7
18	Netherlands	376.00	376.00	301.00	252.00	92	2.2
19	Poland	9,435.00	9,435.00	8,234.00	5,240.51	1,607.5	77.2
20	Portugal	4,907.21	3,182.10	2,088.16	1,241.09	1,070.11	13.5
21	Romania	6,951.00	6,861.00	4,627.00	1,929.76	538.9	47.5
22	Slovakia	1,940.00	1,940.0	1,785.0	786.9	853.7	19.1
23	Slovenia	1,271.00	1,248.00	1,139.00	402.13	278	3.2
24	Spain	27,626.65	18,417.87	14,711.12	1,344.00	5,481.4	25.7
25	Sweden	30,505.00	28,073.00	19,832.13	4,725.82	2,245.03	22.5
26	UK	3,164.00	3,144.00	3,144.00	1,477.49	290	20.3

[a] input units in thousand hectares
[b] in million Euros
[c] in thousand hectares
[d] in thousand persons

Table 2 The criteria of the study

Criterion	Sustainability pillar	Min/Max	Weight
Economic aggregates on forestry	Economic growth	Max	0.33
Protected forests and forest under natura	Environmental protection	Max	0.33
Employment in forestry	Social equity	Max	0.33

Table 3 Preference functions and thresholds

Scenarios[a]		Criteria		
	Thresholds	Economy	Environment	Society
Scenario 1	Q: Indifference	224.05	164.70	2.54
	P: Preference	536.01	335.42	6.05
Scenario 2	Q: Indifference	229.53	162.18	2.50
	P: Preference	544.27	341.79	6.04
Scenario 3	Q: Indifference	245.85	175.59	4.07
	P: Preference	589.99	397.58	9.29

[a]Twenty-six (26) European countries were examined and ranked according to their productivity in an output/input ratio in three different scenarios. The output data were the same in all scenarios, while the input was different. In scenario 1, the input was the area of forest and other wooded land; in scenario 2, the input was the area of forest and in scenario 3 the input was the area of forest available for wood supply

ing the output of forestry and other secondary activities in million Euros, "Protected Forests and forest under Natura" is an environmental indicator, and "Employment in Forestry" is a social indicator on Forest Policy implementation.

Sweden is the most "forested" country in Europe, followed by Spain, Finland, and France. On the other hand, the country with the smallest forest area is the Netherlands, while Cyprus, Denmark, and Belgium are also "deforested" (Fig. 1). The forest area of each country is a key factor for the study, affecting the productivity of each country. Each country has a certain forest area used as denominator in the productivity fraction, p = output/input. Provided that the forest area will not change dramatically in the near future, the countries should focus on the numerator of the productivity fraction (output) in order to achieve better results and consecutively a better ranking.

The average percentage of forest area available for wood supply is 73.9% for the examined countries. In EU 28, 83.6% of the forests is available for wood supply (EC 2018). The United Kingdom has the biggest percentage, since almost all of the forest and other wood area is available for wood supply (99.37%). Germany is in the second place with 95% and Belgium is in the third place with 93% (Table 4). Only Germany achieves good performance in Forest Policy among the aforementioned countries. On the other hand, Cyprus has by far the smallest percentage of forest area available among the examined European countries (about 11%). There are seven pairs of countries in which the forest area available for wood supply slightly differs:

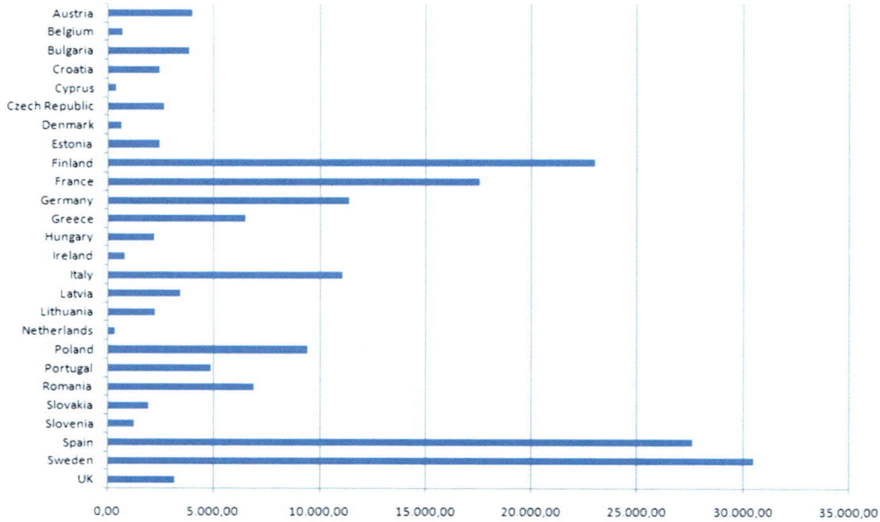

Fig. 1 Forest and other wooded land in Europe (*Source* FAO 2018)

(1) Sweden–Finland, (2) Poland–Italy, (3) Latvia–UK, (4) Czech Republic–Bulgaria, (5) Estonia–Lithuania, (6) Slovakia–Hungary, and (7) Belgium–Ireland. Three pairs of countries achieved similar performance and their rank difference was limited to one position: (1) Finland (24)—Sweden (25), (2) Poland (11)—Italy (12), (3) Ireland (18)—Belgium (19). Slovakia (3) and Hungary (5) showed a close ranking, while the remaining three pairs had bigger gaps between their rankings: (1) Czech Republic (1)—Bulgaria (8), (2) UK (16)—Latvia (22), (3) Lithuania (9)—Estonia (17).

The study examined the EU 28 countries, including the United Kingdom, because according to the European Union: "For the time being, the United Kingdom remains a full member of the EU and rights and obligations continue to fully apply in and to the UK" (EU 2018). Winkel and Derks (2016) studied the scenario that Britain exits the European Union and the possible effect to the Forest Policy of the European Union; according to their findings, Brexit could have consequences on EU Forest Policy. Only two out of the 28 countries did not provide sufficient data for all categories and they were excluded from ranking: Luxemburg and Malta.

Data analysis was made using the software Visual PROMETHEE Academic.

4 Results and Discussion

The implementation of the PROMETHEE method provided the results presented in Table 5.

Table 4 Forest available for wood supply (%) in Europe (*Source* FAO 2018)

A/A	Country	Forest available for wood supply (%)	Rank
1	Austria	83.02	13
2	Belgium	93.21	3
3	Bulgaria	57.56	22
4	Croatia	69.85	19
5	Cyprus	10.65	26
6	Czech Republic	86.26	10
7	Denmark	87.01	9
8	Estonia	81.19	15
9	Finland	84.56	11
10	France	91.12	5
11	Germany	95.35	2
12	Greece	54.97	23
13	Hungary	81.21	14
14	Ireland	78.88	17
15	Italy	73.96	18
16	Latvia	90.86	6
17	Lithuania	84.24	12
18	Netherlands	80.05	16
19	Poland	87.27	8
20	Portugal	42.55	25
21	Romania	66.57	20
22	Slovakia	92.01	4
23	Slovenia	89.61	7
24	Spain	53.25	24
25	Sweden	65.01	21
26	UK	99.37	1

In two out of three scenarios, the Czech Republic was ranked first, and in one scenario (Scenario 3) it was ranked third, but overall had the best performance among the examined countries. Apart from the Czech Republic, four other countries were ranked highly in all three scenarios: Germany, Slovakia, Hungary, and Denmark, all countries of the East and Central Europe with a long tradition in the forestry sector. On the other hand, Greece was ranked last among 26 countries in all three scenarios. For Greece, it seems that the economic crisis that has been heavily affecting the country for the last decade has also affected Forest Policy performance. In the last places in all scenarios apart from Greece are found: Sweden, Finland, and Spain, countries with large forest areas. Three countries were ranked in the same place in all three scenarios: Germany (second), Hungary (fourth), and Spain (twenty-third). To the

Table 5 Country ranking in all scenarios

Rank	Scenario 1		Scenario 2		Scenario 3	
	Country	Phi	Country	Phi	Country	Phi
1	Czech Republic	0.4703	Czech Republic	0.4366	Cyprus	0.4000
2	Germany	0.4535	Germany	0.4272	Germany	0.3840
3	Slovakia	0.3846	Slovakia	0.3397	Czech Republic	0.3739
4	Hungary	0.2940	Hungary	0.3078	Hungary	0.2318
5	Denmark	0.2263	Denmark	0.2439	Slovakia	0.1963
6	Poland	0.2113	Poland	0.1606	Denmark	0.1778
7	Netherlands	0.1804	Lithuania	0.1459	Portugal	0.1653
8	Lithuania	0.1498	Netherlands	0.1365	Netherlands	0.1563
9	UK	0.0372	Italy	0.1234	Bulgaria	0.1010
10	Italy	0.0230	Croatia	0.0085	Lithuania	0.0890
11	Bulgaria	0.0193	UK	−0.0006	Poland	0.0729
12	Austria	−0.0061	Bulgaria	−0.0143	Italy	0.0562
13	Belgium	−0.0307	Portugal	−0.0249	Austria	−0.0181
14	Romania	−0.0310	Austria	−0.0277	Romania	−0.0284
15	France	−0.0439	Belgium	−0.0515	Ireland	−0.0859
16	Ireland	−0.0632	France	−0.0599	France	−0.0930
17	Croatia	−0.0797	Romania	−0.0650	Croatia	−0.1116
18	Latvia	−0.1269	Ireland	−0.0843	Belgium	−0.1154
19	Slovenia	−0.1485	Latvia	−0.1410	UK	−0.1348
20	Portugal	−0.1699	Slovenia	−0.1706	Slovenia	−0.1920
21	Estonia	−0.1871	Estonia	−0.1882	Latvia	−0.1994
22	Finland	−0.2554	Cyprus	−0.2349	Estonia	−0.2048
23	Spain	−0.2976	Spain	−0.2549	Spain	−0.2236
24	Sweden	−0.3094	Finland	−0.2793	Finland	−0.2780
25	Cyprus	−0.3186	Sweden	−0.3349	Sweden	−0.3127
26	Greece	−0.3817	Greece	−0.3979	Greece	−0.4066

contrary, there are a few countries that present big differences in their ranking across the three scenarios. Cyprus is in twenty-fifth place in the first scenario, twenty-second in the second but climbs in the first place in the third scenario. Portugal also shows a similar impressive ascending course ranked twentieth, thirteenth, and seventh in the three scenarios. Conversely, Latvia, Belgium, and the United Kingdom present a descending course across the three scenarios, the UK displaying the biggest fall down as it is placed ninth in the first, eleventh in the second, and nineteenth in the third

Table 6 Promethee flow table, all scenarios

Rank	Country	Phi	Phi+	Phi−
1	Czech Republic	0.4184	0.4431	0.0247
2	Germany	0.4155	0.4992	0.0837
3	Slovakia	0.2892	0.3449	0.0557
4	Hungary	0.2705	0.3724	0.1019
5	Denmark	0.2099	0.2952	0.0854
6	Netherlands	0.1575	0.2133	0.0558
7	Poland	0.1362	0.2070	0.0708
8	Lithuania	0.1220	0.2043	0.0823
9	Italy	0.0657	0.2203	0.1546
10	Bulgaria	0.0458	0.1788	0.1330
11	Cyprus	0.0210	0.2459	0.2249
12	Portugal	0.0182	0.1241	0.1059
13	Austria	−0.0175	0.1173	0.1348
14	Romania	−0.0394	0.1127	0.1521
15	UK	−0.0491	0.0853	0.1344
16	Croatia	−0.0691	0.1106	0.1796
17	France	−0.0700	0.0855	0.1555
18	Belgium	−0.0738	0.0998	0.1736
19	Ireland	−0.0791	0.1173	0.1964
20	Latvia	−0.1627	0.0122	0.1749
21	Slovenia	−0.1738	0.0113	0.1851
22	Estonia	−0.1952	0.0096	0.2048
23	Spain	−0.2531	0.0300	0.2830
24	Finland	−0.2720	0.0018	0.2738
25	Sweden	−0.3180	0.0000	0.3180
26	Greece	−0.3972	0.0000	0.3972

scenario. The Promethee also provides a classification for all scenarios presenting an average country ranking with a compromised solution (Table 6).

Czech Republic has the highest Phi (0.4184) among the examined alternatives, followed by Germany (0.4155). Germany has a higher Phi +, but the Czech Republic is ranked first even with 0.0029 higher Phi, because of the best result in Phi-(0.0247 for Czech Republic and 0.0837 for Germany). Slovakia (0.2892), Hungary (0.2705), and Denmark feature in the top five countries on Forest Policy implementation. Apart from Greece, which is ranked last with the lowest Phi (–03972), the other four countries in the bottom five ranking on Forest Policy implementation in the EU are Sweden, Finland, Spain, and Estonia. The results in Table 6 are a combination of the results in the first scenario regarding the ranking of the top five countries and the results in the third scenario as for the ranking of the bottom five countries.

5 Conclusions

The study evaluated Forest Policy performance in twenty-six European countries, using Multiple Criteria Decision Analysis based on forestry sector data retrieved by Eurostat. The PROMETHEE method was used to provide a ranking of the European countries in their Forest Policy performance drawing on data covering all three sustainability pillars: economy, environment, and society.

According to the findings based on the Promethee Ranking, the Czech Republic has the best performance in Forest Policy implementation among the twenty-six examined countries of European Union, while all scenarios pointed out that Greece has the worst performance. Greece has definitely been affected by the economic crisis in many areas, and the forest sector is no exception. Greece has lost more than 50% of the employed persons in forestry and forest-based industry between the years 2008 and 2016 (Source: Eurostat 2018b), while government expenses in the forestry sector have been dramatically cut down. The future of forests in Greece is described as pessimistic in a recent study (Tzoulis et al. 2015).

The country rankings were more volatile in the middle places, while countries with high or low performance on Forest Policy implementation maintained a more stable position across the three scenarios. The volatility of ranking in the middle places was also pointed out in a recent study that has ranked the EU countries according to their welfare (Hussain 2016).

The forest area as an input definitely affects the final ranking of the European countries. In general, large areas available for wood supply lead to a lower country ranking on Forest Policy performance (Sweden, Finland, and Spain). Additionally, countries with almost identical forest areas available for wood supply not necessarily achieve similar rankings. Only Germany achieves a high ranking among countries with large areas available for wood supply. Germany's industry was strongly dependent on wood supply in earlier centuries leading to rapid deforestation, but after World War II Germany adopted the principles of sustainable forestry and achieved impressive results (Schmidt 2009).

The limitation of this study is that not all EU countries were analyzed, because of the lack of sufficient data in all examined categories. In a future paper, the ranking can be expanded to other European countries, non-EU members with a long tradition on forestry sector, such as Norway and Switzerland, as well as to candidate countries like Albania, Serbia, and Turkey. In future research, the Data Envelopment Analysis could be used to benchmark the performance of the European Countries in Forest Policy implementation.

The findings provide an overview of the current situation regarding Forest Policy implementation among European countries and could be used by the European Union in a future framework of Common Forest Policy in the EU.

Acknowledgements The authors would like to thank Professor Bertrand Mareschal for the provision of the software "Visual PROMETHEE Academic".

References

Adams PW, Hairston AB (1996) Calling all experts: using science to direct policy. J For 94(4):27–30
Andreopoulou Z, Koliouska C, Zopounidis C (2017) Multicriteria and clustering: classification techniques in agrifood and environment. Springer International Publishing AG, Switzerland
Andreopoulou Z, Koliouska C, Galariotis E, Zopounidis C (2018) Renewable energy sources: using PROMETHEE II for ranking websites to support market opportunities. Technol Forecast Soc Change. https://doi.org/10.1016/j.techfore.2017.06.007. (Article in Press)
Antanasijević D, Pocajt V, Ristić M, Perić-Grujić A (2017) A differential multi-criteria analysis for the assessment of sustainability performance of European countries: Beyond country ranking. J Clean Prod 165:213–220
Baourakis G, Doumpos M, Kalogeras N, Zopounidis C (2002) Multicriteria analysis and assessment of financial viability of agribusinesses: the case of marketing co-operatives and juice-producing companies. Agribusiness 18(4):543–558
Bjärstig T (2013) The Swedish forest sector's approach to a formalized forest policy within the EU. For Policy Econ 26:131–137
Brukas V, Felton A, Lindbladh M, Sallnäs O (2013) Linking forest management, policy and biodiversity indicators–a comparison of Lithuania and Southern Sweden. For Ecol Manag 291:181–189
EC (2016) European Commission. EU Forest Policies. http://ec.europa.eu/environment/forests/fpolicies.htm
EC (2018) European Commission. Eurostat. Forestry Data. Overview. http://ec.europa.eu/eurostat/web/forestry/overview
EEC (1989) European Economic Community. Council Decision of May 1989 setting up a Standing Forestry Committee 89/367/EEC. Off J Eur Communities
Eggers J, Holmgren S, Nordström EM, Lämås T, Lind T, Öhman K (2017) Balancing different forest values: Evaluation of forest management scenarios in a multi-criteria decision analysis framework. For Policy Econ. http://dx.doi.org/10.1016/j.forpol.2017.07.002
EU (2018) European Union. EU Member countries in brief: United Kingdom. https://europa.eu/european-union/about-eu/countries/member-countries/unitedkingdom_en
Eurostat (2018a) Eurostat. Agriculture, forestry and fisheries data. http://ec.europa.eu/eurostat/data/database. Accessed January 2018
Eurostat (2018b) Eurostat. Employment in forestry and forest-based sector. http://appsso.eurostat.ec.europa.eu. Accessed 28 March 2018
FAO (2018) Food and Agriculture Organization. Area of wooded land. http://appsso.eurostat.ec.europa.eu/nui/show.do?dataset=for_area&lang=en. Accessed 8 January 2018
Ferretti F, Dibari C, De Meo I, Cantiani P, Bianchi M (2011) ProgettoBosco, a data-driven decision support system for forest planning. Math Comput For Nat Res Sci 3(1):27–35
Grošelj P, Hodges DG, Stirn LZ (2016) Participatory and multi-criteria analysis for forest (ecosystem) management: a case study of Pohorje, Slovenia. For Policy Econ 71:80–86
Grošelj P, Stirn LZ (2013) Between compromise and consensus in group decisions in forest management. Sumar List 137(7–8):403–409
Hoogstra-Klein MA, Schüll E (2017) Introduction to the special issue on "Scenario analysis for forest policy and forest management–New insights and experiences". For Policy Econ 85:217–221
Hussain MA (2016) EU country rankings' sensitivity to the choice of welfare indicators. Soc Indic Res 125(1):1–17
Ignatius J, Ghasemi MR, Zhang F, Emrouznejad A, Hatami-Marbini A (2016) Carbon efficiency evaluation: An analytical framework using fuzzy DEA. Eur J Oper Res 253(2):428–440
Jactel H, Branco M, Duncker P, Gardiner B, Grodzki W, Langstrom B, Moreira F, Netherer S, Nicoli B, Orazio C, Piou D, Schelhaas MJ, Tojic C (2012) A multicriteria risk analysis to evaluate impacts of forest management alternatives on forest health in Europe. Ecol Soc 17(4)
Janse G (2007) Characteristics and challenges of forest sector communication in the EU. Silva Fenn 41(4):731–753

Kurth M, Fox-Lent C, Golan M, Linkov I (2017) Decision making for independent municipal action. Integr Environ Assess 14:194–197

Kylili A, Christoforou E, Fokaides PA, Polycarpou P (2016) Multicriteria analysis for the selection of the most appropriate energy crops: the case of Cyprus. Int J Sustain Energy 35(1):47–58

Lazdinis M, Carver A, Schmithüsen F, Tõnisson K, Vilkriste L (2005) Forest-sector concerns in the Baltic States: Implications for an expanded European Union. Soc Nat Res 18(9):839–848

Lindstad BH, Pistorius T, Ferranti F, Dominguez G, Gorriz-Mifsud E, Kurttila M, Leban V, Navarro P, Peters DM, Pezdevsek Malovrh S, Prokofieva I, Schuck A, Solberg B, Viiri H, Stirn LZ, Krc J (2015) Forest-based bioenergy policies in five European countries: an explorative study of interactions with national and EU policies. Biomass Bioenergy 80:102–113

Lipušček I, Bohanec M, Oblak L, Stirn LZ (2010) A multi-criteria decision-making model for classifying wood products with respect to their impact on environment. Int J Life Cycle Assess 15(4):359–367

Malovrh ŠP, Kurttila M, Hujala T, Kärkkäinen L, Leban V, Lindstad BH, Peters DM, Rhodius R, Solberg B, Wirth K, Stirn LZ, Krč J (2016) Decision support framework for evaluating the operational environment of forest bioenergy production and use: Case of four European countries. J Environ Manag 180: 68–81

Mareschal B (2013) Visual PROMETHEE 1.4 Manual. Visual PROMETHEE, 1

Mayer P, Rametsteiner E (2004) Forest science-policy interface in the context of the ministerial conference on the protection of forests in Europe: a policy perspective. Scand J For Res 19(S4):150–156

Nuuter T, Lill I, Tupenaite L (2014) Ranking of housing market sustainability in selected European Countries. WSEAS Trans Bus Econ 11:778–786

Palma J, Graves AR, Burgess PJ, Van der Werf W, Herzog F (2007) Integrating environmental and economic performance to assess modern silvoarable agroforestry in Europe. Ecol Econ 63(4):759–767

Poledníková E (2014) Comparing Regions Ranking by MCDM methods: the Case of Visegrad Countries. WSEAS Trans Bus Econ 11:496–507

Reiff M, Surmanová K, Balcerzak AP, Pietrzak MB (2016) Multiple criteria analysis of European Union agriculture. J Int Stud 9(3):62–74

Schmidt UE (2009) German impact and influences on American forestry until World War II. J For 107(3):139–145

Singh MP, Bhojvaid PP, de Jong W, Ashraf J, Reddy SR (2017) Forest transition and socio-economic development in India and their implications for forest transition theory. For Policy Econ 76:65–71

Siskos E, Malafekas M, Askounis D, Psarras J (2013) E-government benchmarking in European Union: a multicriteria extreme ranking approach. In: Conference on e-Business, e-Services and e-Society. Springer, Berlin, pp 338–348

Škare M, Rabar D (2017) Measuring sources of economic growth in OECD countries. Inz Ekon 28(4):386–400

Tsiaras S, Dragoslis A, Papathanasiou J (2017) Fuzzy multiple criteria analysis for selecting the optimum tree species for truffle cultivation in Greece. In: International Workshop "Information Technology, Sustainable Development, Scientific Network and Nature Protection" within the 18th Panhellenic Forestry Congress. 8–11 October 2017, Edessa, Greece. Congress Proceedings, pp 1361–1366

Tzoulis I, Andreopoulou Z, Trigkas M, Tsekouropoulos G, Voulgaridis E (2015) Wood trade in Greece: the impact of economic crisis and the use of new technologies. In: CEUR Workshop Proceedings Volume 1498: 26–37. 7th International Conference on Information and Communication Technologies in Agriculture, Food and Environment, HAICTA 2015, Kavala, Greece, 17 September 2015 through 20 September 2015, Code 117742

Vasić G (2018) Application of multi criteria analysis in the design of energy policy: Space and water heating in households–City Novi Sad, Serbia. Energy Policy 113:410–419

Velasquez M, Hester PT (2013) An analysis of multi-criteria decision making methods. Int J Oper Res 10(2):56–66

Winkel G, Derks J (2016) The nature of Brexit. How the UK exiting the European Union could affect European forest and (forest related) environmental policy. For Policy Econ 70(C): 124–127
Wolfslehner B, Brüchert F, Fischbach J, Rammer W, Becker G, Lindner M, Lexer MJ (2012) Exploratory multi-criteria analysis in sustainability impact assessment of forest-wood chains: the example of a regional case study in Baden-Württemberg. Eur J For Res 131(1):47–56
World Commission on Environment and Development (WCED) Brundtland Commission (1987) Our common future. Report of the world commission on environment and development
Zopounidis C, Lemonakis C, Andreopoulou Z, Koliouska C (2014) Agrotourism industry development through internet technologies: a multicriteria approach. J Euromarketing 23(4):45–67

The Contribution of ICT in EU Development Policy: A Multicriteria Approach

Christiana Koliouska, Zacharoula Andreopoulou and Mariana Golumbeanu

Abstract The Information and Communication Technology (ICT) sector provides a wide range of services for different actors according to their type of actions. In fact, adoption of ICT-enhanced policies is one of the top agendas for governments today in most developing countries. The European Union (EU) and its Member States have a long tradition in development cooperation. The objective of this research is to study the contribution of ICT in the development policy in EU and present the current status by ranking these policies. EU development policies are evaluated qualitatively according to their ICT dependence and complexity levels. The questions, used as criteria, have been retrieved from the official "ICT Implication Assessment method of EU Legislation." Following the multicriteria method of PROMETHEE II is applied for the total ranking in order to identify the "superior" ones, which present high dependence on and complexity of the ICT implications.

Keywords Development policy · European Union · Information and communication technology · Multicriteria method · PROMETHEE II

C. Koliouska (✉) · Z. Andreopoulou
Faculty of Forestry and Natural Environment, Aristotle University of Thessaloniki, Thessaloniki, Greece
e-mail: ckolious@for.auth.gr

Z. Andreopoulou
e-mail: randreop@for.auth.gr

M. Golumbeanu
Department of Technological Transfer and Dissemination, National Institute for Marine Research "Grigore Antipa", Constanța, Romania
e-mail: golumbeanum@gmail.com

N. Mladenović et al. (eds.), *Advances in Operational Research in the Balkans*, Springer Proceedings in Business and Economics,
https://doi.org/10.1007/978-3-030-21990-1_7

1 Introduction

The Information and Communications Technology (ICT) sector constitutes one of the fastest growing sectors in the global economy. It provides a wide range of services for different actors according to their type of actions (Bautista et al. 2018). The definition of ICT is an umbrella term that includes any communication device or system encompassing, inter alia, radio, television, mobile phones, computer and networking hardware and software, satellite systems, as well as the various services and applications associated with them (ITU 2008; Koliouska and Andreopoulou 2016). The impacts of the ICT revolution are now palpable in all countries, and are projected to be economically and socially revolutionary in the coming years as technology penetrates and fosters fundamental change in all sectors and dimensions of life (Jorgenson and Vu 2016a). ICT serves to boost, inter alia: economic prosperity (Qureshi 2013a; Levendis and Lee 2013), living standards (Chavula 2013), externalities in welfare (Qureshi 2013b, c; Carmody 2013), banking sector progress, life for all (Ponelis and Holmner 2013; Kivuneki et al. 2011), and sustainable development (Byrne et al. 2011) in developing nations (Asongu and Nwachukwu 2018). In recent years, the role of ICT in the protection of the environment has received significant attention (Andreopoulou 2012; Koliouska and Andreopoulou 2013). There is some evidence to suggest that the novelty and ingenuity of innovations in ICT can help to overcome cultural norms while improving the efficiency and effectiveness of current systems especially when these improvements have a positive impact on individuals' lifestyles (O'Mahony et al. 2016).

ICTs are the actual platforms where different socioeconomic forces of humanity have the opportunity to interact, without geographical barriers (Briz et al. 2013). These new possibilities exist largely as a result of two converging forces, the first one being the quantity of information available around the world, exponentially greater than that available only a few years ago and growing at an accelerating pace and the second one being the advances in global communications and technological infrastructure (Louca 2013). Informatization refers to the transformation of an economy and society through the effective deployment of information and communication technologies in business, social, and public functions (Obidike 2011; Guo 2011; Zhang et al. 2016).

Investments in ICT are seen as a key driver of productivity growth (Niebel 2018). ICT has also profoundly transformed business and government practices (Jorgenson and Vu 2016a). The development of ICT encourages the implementation of Good Governance Government to practically develop in electronic government (e-Government) that provides electronic services and information aiming to improving accountability and transparency (Hadi et al. 2018). The challenges to successful ICT policies have risen steadily with the increasing sophistication of ICT equipment (Jorgenson and Vu 2016b). In fact, adoption of ICT-enhanced policies is one of the top agendas for governments today in most developing countries (Pradhan et al. 2018).

The European Union (EU) and its Member States have a long tradition in development cooperation (Hilpold 2018). After a long period of treating development as a technical problem of growth in macro-economic, social science seems to have awakened to the realization that development is a process of profound social transformation (Fine et al. 2003). Despite the Member States' continuing role in European development policies and the diversity in policies and approaches between European donors, the EU's development policies and those of the Member States are supposed to be coherent and complementary, and the EU has a mandate to play a coordinating role in this regard (Delputte and Orbie 2018). According to the Lisbon Treaty (EEPA 2013), the EU development policy is, among other things, to "consolidate and support democracy, the rule of law, human rights and the principles of international law"; "preserve peace, prevent conflicts and strengthen international security [...] foster the sustainable economic, social and environmental development of developing countries, with the primary aim of eradicating poverty"; and "encourage the integration of all countries into the world economy" (Sandberg 2017). Despite changes to the EU development policy and practice over the years, difficulties still remain in integrating the environment in practice (Adelle et al. 2018). The EU Member States and New Independent States of the former Soviet Union are becoming an axis of increasing geo-political importance for Europe (Golumbeanu et al. 2010). The history of EU development cooperation is directly related to the process of enlargement (Hurt 2010).

Within the internal workings of the EU, the Commission is the chief initiator of policy and implementer of EU development policy, which falls mainly under the economic and commercial policies of the EU and also has Common Foreign and Security Policy (CFSP) aspects (Arts and Dickson 2010). The Treaty on the Functioning of the European Union (TFEU) further specifies that the EU's external policies must respect the principles of democracy, the rule of law, the universality and indivisibility of human rights and fundamental freedoms, respect for human dignity, the principles of equality and solidarity, and respect for the principles of the United Nations Charter and international law (EC 2008; Pelletier et al. 2018). EU development policy and the influence of the EU on the developing world are of course multi-dimensional (Mold 2007). According to Carbone (2013), even the Development Assistance Committee (DAC) which had always been critical of EU development policy acknowledged that the EU has actively contributed to the growing international consensus on policy coherence, desires to help shape a broader international approach and the Commission has performed its catalytic role in selected areas of policy coherence with the support of a small number of Member States.

The objective of this research is to study the contribution of ICT in the development policy in EU and present the current status by ranking these policies (regulations, directives, communications, and other acts), respectively. EU development policies are evaluated qualitatively according to their ICT dependence and complexity levels. The questions, used as criteria, have been retrieved from the official "ICT Implication Assessment method of EU Legislation". Following the multicriteria method of PROMETHEE II is applied for the total ranking in order to identify the "superior" ones, which present high dependence on and complexity of the ICT implications.

2 Methodology

Data used in this study were collected from the official website of the European Union (www.europa.eu). First, the regulations, the directives, the decisions, the communications, and other acts regarding the development issues were recorded. EU development policies were ranked according to their ICT adoption applying the superiority ranking method PROMETHEE II using Visual Promethee Software. The PROMETHEE (Preference Ranking Organization Method for Enrichment Evaluation) belongs to the class of MCDA (Multicriteria Decision Aid) instruments (Andreopoulou et al. 2017b). EU development policies form the alternatives. The criteria that were used in this research are the criteria that European Commission uses to assess ICT implications of EU legislation since 2010 (EC 2010) (Table 1). These criteria constitute the variables x1, x2, ..., xn. The level of dependence of the EU development policies on the ICT solutions and the level of complexity of the ICT solutions may be low, medium, and high (1, 2, and 3, respectively). The weight of the first five criteria (x1, x2, x3, x4, x5) is 1, while the weight of the rest of the criteria (x6, x7, x8, x9, x10, x11, x12) is 0.83. The weights of the criteria were defined by the way EU assesses the ICT implications used by the legislation, giving equal weight to the level of dependence on the ICT solutions and the level of complexity of the ICT solutions.

The PROMETHEE consists of building and exploring a relationship of outranking values (Vincke 1992; Brans and Mareschal 2002). According to Brans and Mareschal (2002), the methods of the PROMETHEE family are used in multicriteria problems of the type

$$\mathrm{Max}\{\mathrm{fl}(\mathrm{x}), \mathrm{f2}(\mathrm{x}), \ldots, \mathrm{fk}(\mathrm{x}), |\mathrm{x} \in \mathrm{A}\} \quad (1)$$

A is a denumerable finite set of n potential actions in fj(·), j = 1, 2, ..., k, k being the criteria that are the applications of A in the set of real numbers (Cavalcante et al. 2010). Each criterion has its own units. Selecting the best alternative or the set of the best alternatives requires a subjective compromise among criteria (Cavalcante et al. 2010). Different versions of the PROMETHEE have been developed including PROMETHEE II, which is the most frequently applied version because it enables a decision-maker (DM) to find a full-ranked vector of alternatives (i.e., complete ranking) (Abedi et al. 2012). The exploitation of the outranking relation is realized by considering for each action a leaving and an entering flow in the valued outranking graph: a partial preorder (PROMETHEE I) or a complete preorder (PROMETHEE II) on the set of possible actions can be proposed to the decision-maker in order to achieve the decision problem (Brans et al. 1986). PROMETHEE II extends the classical approach (PROMETHEE I) by modeling the DM preferences through a preference function for each criterion, in such way that it reflects the preference level of a over b, from 0 to 1 (Parreiras and Vasconcelos 2007). So, the two additional types of information that PROMETHEE II requires are the following: (1) information on

Table 1 Criteria

Category	Variable	Criteria
Dependence on the ICT solutions	X_1	Does the legislation require the design of information-rich processes?
	X_2	Does the legislation require the design of new business processes?
	X_3	Are large amounts of data gathering required in these processes?
	X_4	Is collaboration between ICT systems of multiple DGs or institutions/organizations required?
	X_5	Is the legislation concerning ICT systems or is ICT a supporting function of the legislation?
Complexity of the ICT solutions	X_6	Does the legislation require new ICT solutions or can existing applications fulfill the requirements?
	X_7	Are there any legacy systems which might hamper the implementation?
	X_8	Does the legislation impose authentication requirements?
	X_9	Is a large amount of data exchange between Member States and/or the Commission required?
	X_{10}	What is the required lead -time of the implementation (urgency)?
	X_{11}	Are new interoperability specifications required?
	X_{12}	Does the initiative impose high-security requirements on the ICT solution?

the weights of the criteria and (2) a decision-maker's preference functions, which were used for comparing the alternatives (Dagdeviren 2008).

The procedural steps as involved in PROMETHEE II method are enlisted as below (Doumpos and Zopounidis 2004; Hajkowicz and Higgins 2008; Athawale and Chakraborty 2010):

- Step 1: Normalize the decision matrix.
- Step 2: Calculate the evaluative differences of ith alternative with respect to other alternatives.
- Step 3: Calculate the preference function.
- Step 4: Calculate the aggregated preference function taking into account the criteria weights.
- Step 5: Determine the leaving and entering outranking flows.
- Step 6: Determine the ranking of all the considered alternatives depending on the values of $\varphi(i)$. The higher value of $\varphi(i)$, the better is the alternative. Thus, the best alternative is the one having the highest $\varphi(i)$ values.

A more detailed description of the PROMETHEE II method can be found in Andreopoulou et al. (2017b). PROMETHEE network constitutes an alternative display of the PROMETHEE I, where each action is represented as a node and preferences are represented by arrows. The nodes are located in relative positions so that the proximities between flow values appear clearly (VPSolutions 2013).

The PROMETHEE methods and their extensions have been widely applied in many different situations including among others (Mareschal et al. 2008): water resources planning and management (Abutaleb and Mareschal 1995; Al Kloub and Abutaleb 1998; Raju et al. 2000), manufacturing and production management (Chareonsuk et al. 1997; De Lit et al. 2001; Koli and Parsaei 1992; Rekiek et al. 2002), environmental studies (Georgopoulou et al. 1998; Kangas et al. 2001; Martin et al. 1999; Vaillancourt and Waaub 2002), and renewable energy sources (Andreopoulou et al. 2017a, b). Furthermore, PROMETHEE is successfully applied such as equipment selection (Yilmaz and Dagdeviren 2011), stock trading (Albadvi et al. 2007), and portfolio selection (Vetschera and Almeida 2012) (Kilic et al. 2015). Some other fields of research where PROMETHEE II has been applied are the following: local development agencies and regional development (Arabatzis et al. 2010), forest issues/environment (Andreopoulou et al. 2009a, b), aquaculture (Kokkinakis and Andreopoulou 2008), agrifood (Tsekouropoulos et al. 2013), regional development/tourism/skiing centers (Tsekouropoulos et al. 2012; Zopounidis et al. 2014), rural production (Andreopoulou et al. 2011), Greek prefectures according to tourist resources (Polyzos and Arabatzis 2006), and National Parks (Koliouska et al. 2017; Andreopoulou et al. 2014).

3 Results and Discussion

The research in the EU website resulted in the retrieval of 91 policies (regulations, directives, communications, and other acts) concerning development issues.

According to Table 2, the values estimated for total net flows φ present a spectrum of values between +0.7288 and –0.5619 and that indicates a great difference concerning "superiority" between the first and the last case in the ranking of EU development policies. The EU development policies that achieve high positive total net flows present a "high superiority" against the rest of the cases. The EU development policies which are estimated to achieve medium total net flows show a "low superiority" against the rest of the cases. Furthermore, the EU development policies that achieve average negative total net flows present an "average lag", while the policies with average negative total flows present a "high lag" against the rest of the cases.

Figure 1 presents the PROMETHEE Network. The EU development policies that achieve the highest positive total net flow (0.7288) are the following: COM (2013)594 which deals with the European development policy and the external assistance policy, and COM (2002)429 which deals with fighting rural poverty. On the other hand, the

Table 2 Total ranking of EU development policies

	Actions	Phi		Actions	Phi
1	Reg.1368/2013	0.7288	47	COM(2011)885	−0.1923
2	Reg.1369/2013	0.7288	48	COM(2014)330	−0.1923
3	Direct.2003/87	0.5526	49	COM(2010)639	−0.1923
4	COM(2015)82	0.5206	50	COM(2008)781	−0.1923
5	COM(2015)80	0.5206	51	COM(2014)21	−0.1923
6	COM(2015)340	0.5206	52	COM(2013)253	−0.1923
7	Reg.617/2010	0.5142	53	COM(2011)202	−0.1923
8	Reg.256/2014	0.5142	54	COM(2008)782	−0.1923
9	COM(2008)768	0.4928	55	COM(2006)846	−0.1923
10	COM(2010)265	0.4638	56	COM(2014)520	−0.1923
11	Direct.2009/72	0.4476	57	COM(2011)109	−0.1923
12	Direct.2009/73	0.4323	58	COM(2008)772	−0.1923
13	Direct.2006/32	0.4323	59	COM(2005)628	−0.1923
14	Direct.2009/119	0.4323	60	COM(2007)565	−0.1923
15	Reg.1227/2011	0.4297	61	COM(2009)143	−0.1923
16	COM(2009)519	0.4297	62	COM(2011)563	−0.1923
17	Reg.559/2014	0.4200	63	COM(2014)654	−0.1923
18	Reg.1222/2009	0.4200	64	COM(2011)539	−0.1923
19	COM(2011)518	0.4200	65	COM(2014)8	−0.1923
20	Dec.2014/70	0.4200	66	COM(2015)293	−0.1923
21	Dec.2008/114	0.4200	67	Des.2007/198	−0.1923
22	COM(2006)20	0.4043	68	Dec.2007/614	−0.1923
23	COM(2007)160	0.3611	69	Dec.1999/819	−0.1923
24	Direct.2014/94	0.3304	70	Dec.2007/513	−0.1923
25	COM(2005)627	0.2084	71	Dec.2006/500	−0.1923
26	Dec.2001/546	0.2084	72	Dec.1998/181	−0.1923
27	Dec.2006/1005	0.2084	73	Direct.2008/92	−0.1923
28	COM(2002)82	0.2066	74	Direct.1992/13	−0.1923
29	Direct.2010/30	0.1418	75	Direct.1992/42	−0.1923
30	Direct.2009/125	0.1418	76	Direct.1996/29	−0.1923
31	COM(2002)408	0.0227	77	Direct.2013/59	−0.1923
32	COM(2010)186	−0.0395	78	Direct.1994/22	−0.2589
33	Direct.2006/117	−0.0772	79	COM(2007)1	−0.2623
34	Direct.2009/28	−0.1129	80	Dec.406/2009	−0.2623
35	Reg.347/2013	−0.1191	81	Direct.2003/96	−0.2623
36	Direct.2012/27	−0.1890	82	COM(2011)666	−0.2709
37	Reg.663/2009	−0.1923	83	Direct.2014/24	−0.2742

(continued)

Table 2 (continued)

	Actions	Phi		Actions	Phi
38	Reg.713/2009	−0.1923	84	Direct.2004/17	−0.2742
39	Reg.714/2009	−0.1923	85	Direct.2010/31	−0.2742
40	Reg.715/2009	−0.1923	86	Direct.2013/59	−0.2742
41	Reg.245/2009	−0.1923	87	Direct.2009/71	−0.2742
42	Reg.237/2014	−0.1923	88	Direct.2003/122	−0.2742
43	Reg.3227/76	−0.1923	89	Direct.2011/70	−0.2742
44	Reg.1493/1993	−0.1923	90	Direct.2005/89	−0.2742
45	Reg.994/2010	−0.1923	91	COM(2006)583	−0.5619
46	COM(2004)711	−0.1923			

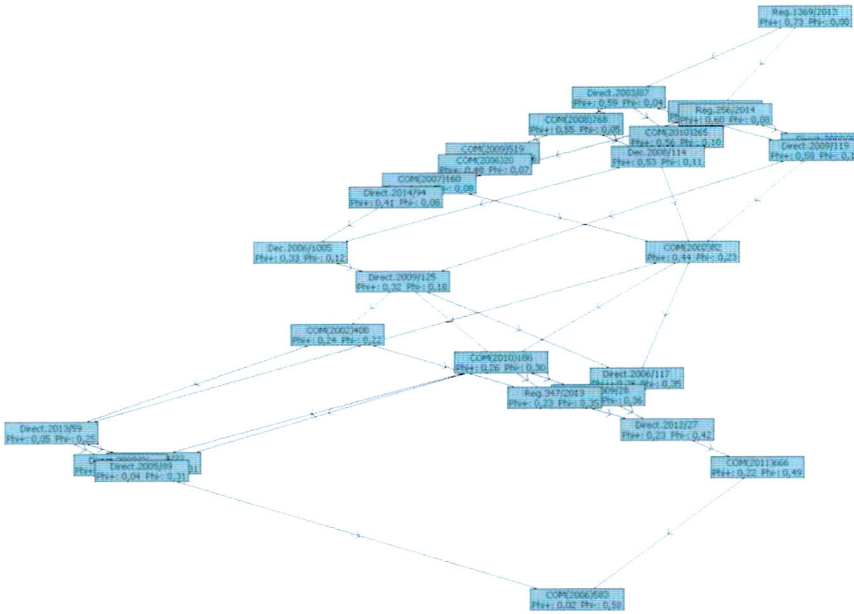

Fig. 1 PROMETHEE network

EU development policy that achieves the highest negative total net flow (−0.6215) is COM (2006)583 about the Global Energy Efficiency and Renewable Energy Fund (GEEREF). Most EU development policies present negative total net flows (60 out of 91).

4 Conclusions

Use of ICT for international development is moving to its next phase (Heeks 2008). ICT can contribute to the improvement of socioeconomic conditions in developing countries (Mann 2004; Sahay 2001; Walsham et al. 2007; Avgerou 2010). The research in the EU website resulted in the retrieval of 91 policies (regulations, directives, communications, and other acts) concerning development issues. According to the findings of the PROMETHEE II method, the values that were estimated for the total net flows Φ present a great spectrum of values (1.2829) and that points out a great difference that concerns the "superiority" between the first and last EU development policy according to the ICT dependence and complexity level. The "superior" EU development policy can be used to form a conceptual content model while designing a new policy framework.

The implementation of most new EU legislation is supported by ICT systems (EC 2009). This can be for the exchange of information between competent authorities across borders or for the direct delivery of online public services to businesses and citizens, which can also be across borders (EC 2010). As most EU development policies present negative total net flows, EU policy-makers have to take into account the ICT factors while designing a new policy or while updating an existing one. The findings of this study can provide a comprehensive picture of the current legislation, while the policies with "complete ICT adoption" are highlighted to be used as milestones in the policy-making process.

References

Abedi M, Torabi SA, Norouzi GH, Hamzeh M, Elyasi GR (2012) PROMETHEE II: a knowledge-driven method for copper exploration. Comput Geosci 46:255–263

Abutaleb M, Mareschal B (1995) Water resources planning in the Middle East – application of the PROMETHEE V multicriteria method. Eur J Oper Res 81(3):500–511

Adelle C, Delputte S, De Roeck F, Nicholson S (2018) Environmental instruments in development cooperation: promoting better development and environmental outcomes?. European Union External Environmental Policy. Palgrave Macmillan, Cham, pp 81–101

Al Kloub B, Abutaleb M (1998) Application of multicriteria decision aid to rank the Jordan-Yarmouk basin co-riparians according to the Helsinki and ILC rules. Water International 23(3):164–173

Albadvi A, Chaharsooghi SK, Esfahanipour A (2007) Decision making in stock trading: An application of PROMETHEE. Eur J Oper Res 177:673–683

Andreopoulou Z (2012) Green Informatics: ICT for green and sustainability. J Agric Inf 3(2):1–8

Andreopoulou ZS, Kokkinakis AK, Koutroumanidis T (2009a) Assessment and optimization of e-commerce websites of fish culture sector. Oper Res Int J 9(3):293–309

Andreopoulou ZS, Koutroumanidis T, Manos B (2009b) The adoption of e-commerce for wood enterprises. Int J Bus Inf Syst 4(4):440–459

Andreopoulou Z, Koutroumanidis T, Manos B (2011) Optimizing collaborative e-commerce websites for rural production using multicriteria analysis. In: Malik K, Choudhary P (eds) Business organizations and collaborative web: practices, strategies and patterns. IGI Global, USA

Andreopoulou Z, Koliouska C, Lemonakis C, Zopounidis C (2014) National Forest Parks development through Internet technologies for economic perspectives. Oper Res Int J 15(3):395–421

Andreopoulou Z, Koliouska C, Galariotis E, Zopounidis C (2017a) Renewable energy sources: using PROMETHEE II for ranking websites to support market opportunities. Technol Forecast Soc Change
Andreopoulou Z, Koliouska C, Zopounidis C (2017b) Multicriteria and clustering: classification techniques in agrifood and environment. Springer, Switzerland
Arabatzis G, Andreopoulou Z, Koutroumanidis T, Manos B (2010) E-government for rural development: classifying and ranking content characteristics of development agencies websites. J Environ Prot Ecol 11(3):1138–1149
Arts K, Dickson AK (2010) EU development cooperation: from model to symbol. Manchester University Press
Asongu S, Nwachukwu JC (2018) Openness, ICT and entrepreneurship in sub-Saharan Africa. Inf Technol People (just-accepted)
Athawale VM, Chakraborty S (2010) Facility location selection using PROMETHEE II method. In: Proceedings of the 2010 international conference on industrial engineering and operations management. Bangladesh Dhaka, pp 9–10
Avgerou C (2010) Discourses on ICT and development. Inf Technol Int Dev 6(3):1
Bautista S, Mazaj J, Cardenas M (2018) Developing RRI practices: the role of the ICT in stakeholders' knowledge exchange and co-creation processes. In: Responsible Research and Innovation Actions in Science Education, Gender and Ethics. Springer, Cham, pp 21–26
Brans JP, Mareschal B (2002) Prométhée-Gaia: une méthodologie d'aide à la décision en présence de critères multiples. Éditions de l'Université de Bruxelles, Bruxelas
Brans JP, Vincke P, Mareschal B (1986) How to select and how to rank projects: the PROMETHEE metho. Eur J Oper Res 24(2):228–238
Briz J, Duran JM, Felipe I, Briz, T (2013) ICT: An efficient instrument for the new agriculture in rural and urban areas. In: Samathrakis V, Louca S, Andreopoulou Z, Vlachopoulou M (eds) E-Innovation for Sustainable Development of Rural Resources During Global Economic Crisis
Byrne E, Nicholson B, Salem F (2011) Information communication technologies and the millennium development goals. Inf Technol Dev 17(1):1–3
Carbone M (2013) Policy coherence and EU development policy. Routledge
Carmody P (2013) A knowledge economy or an information society in Africa? The integration and the mobile phone revolution. Inf Technol Dev 19(1):24–39
Cavalcante V, Alexandre C, Pires Ferreira RJ, de Almeida AT (2010) A preventive maintenance decision model based on multicriteria method PROMETHEE II integrated with Bayesian approach. IMA J Manag Math 21(4):333–348
Chareonsuk C, Nagarur N, Tabucanon MT (1997) A multicriteria approach to the selection of preventive maintenance intervals. Int J Prod Econ 49(1):55–64
Chavula HK (2013) Telecommunications development and economic growth in Africa. Inf Technol Dev 19(1):5–23
Dagdeviren M (2008) Decision making in equipment selection: an integrated approach with AHP and PROMETHEE. J Intell Manuf 19:397–406
De Lit P, Latinne P, Rekiek B, Delchambre A (2001) Assembly planning with an ordering genetic algorithm. Int J Prod Res 39(16):3623–3640
Delputte S, Orbie J (2018) EU development policy. Handbook of European policies: interpretive approaches to the EU
Doumpos M, Zopounidis C (2004) A multi-criteria classification approach based on pair-wise comparison. Eur J Oper Res 158:378–389
EC (2008) Consolidated version of the treaty on the functioning of the EU. OJ EU C115:47–199
EC (2009) Assessment of ICT implications of EU legislation. http://ec.europa.eu/idabc/en/document/7799.html. Accessed 17 June 2018
EC (2010) Method for Assessing ICT Implications of EU legislation. http://ec.europa.eu/idabc/servlets/Doc792e.pdf?id=32704. Accessed 17 June 2018
EEPA (2013) The Lisbon treaty. Article 21. http://www.lisbon-treaty.org/wcm/the-lisbon-treaty/treaty-on-european-union-and-comments/title-5-general-provisions-on-the-unions-external-

action-and-specific-provisions/chapter-1-general-provisions-on-the-unions-external-action/101-article-21.html. Accessed 17 June 2018

Fine B, Lapavitsas C, Pincus J (2003) Development policy in the twenty-first century: beyond the post-Washington consensus. Routledge

Georgopoulou E, Sarafidis Y, Diakoulaki D (1998) Design and implementation of a group DSS for renewable energies exploitation. Eur J Oper Res 109(2):483–500

Golumbeanu M, Vosniakos FK, Avdimiotis S, Mentezelou P, Constantin C, Teohareva M (2010) Upgrade black sea scene. Developing a research infrastructure for the black sea. J Environ Prot Ecol 11(3):1150

Guo Z (2011) Treasure chest – case study and analysis on China informatization and modern agriculture. Agriculture Press

Hadi A, Handajani L, Putra INNA (2018) Financial disclosure based on Web-ICT determinants: its implications for local government financial performance in Indonesia. Int Res J Manag IT Soc Sci (IRJMIS) 5(1):72–85

Hajkowicz S, Higgins A (2008) A comparison of multiple criteria analysis techniques for water resource management. Eur J Oper Res 184:255–265

Heeks R (2008) ICT4D 2.0: The next phase of applying ICT for international development. Computer 41(6)

Hilpold P (2018) The 'politicisation' of the EU Development Policy. Trade Law Dev 9(2):89–114

Hurt SR (2010) Understanding EU development policy: history, global context and self-interest? Third World Q 31(1):159–168

ITU (2008) ICTs for e-Environment. Guidelines for developing countries, with a focus on climate change. Final Report 2008

Jorgenson DW, Vu KM (2016a) The ICT revolution, world economic growth, and policy issues. Telecommun Policy 40(5):383–397

Jorgenson DW, Vu KM (2016b) The impact of ICT investment on world economic growth. Telecommun Policy 40(5):381–382

Kangas A, Kangas J, Pykäläinen J (2001) Outranking methods as tools in strategic natural resources planning. Silva Fenn 35(2):215–227

Kilic HS, Zaim S, Delen D (2015) Selecting "the best" ERP system for SMEs using a combination of ANP and PROMETHEE methods. Exp Syst Appl 42(5):2343–2352

Kivuneki FN, Ekenberg L, Danielson M, Tusubira FF (2011) Perceptions of the role of ICT on quality of life in rural communities in Uganda. Inf Technol Devel 21(1):61–80

Kokkinakis AK, Andreopoulou ZS (2008) Evaluation of the fishery production through classification in the two trans-boundary Prespa lakes. In: Proceedings of the 4th international conference on aquaculture, fisheries tech. & environmental management (AQUAMEDIT 2008), 21–22 November 2008, Athens, Greece

Koliouska C, Andreopoulou Z (2013) Assessment of ICT adoption stage for promoting the Greek national parks. Proc Technol 8:97–103

Koliouska C, Andreopoulou Z (2016) Classification of ICT in EU environmental strategies. J Environ Prot Ecol 17(4):1385–1392

Koliouska C, Andreopoulou Z, Zopounidis C, Lemonakis C (2017) E-commerce in the context of protected areas development: a managerial perspective under a multi-criteria approach. In: Zopounidis C (ed) Multiple criteria decision making. Springer International Publishing

Kolli S, Parsaei HR (1992) Multicriteria analysis in the evaluation of advanced manufacturing technology using PROMETHEE. Comput Ind Eng 23(1–4):455–458

Levendis J, Lee SH (2013) On the endogeneity of telecommunications and economic growth: evidence from Asia. Inf Technol Dev 19(1):62–85

Louca S (2013) ICT for sustainable growth and development. In: Samathrakis V, Louca S, Andreopoulou Z, Vlachopoulou M (eds) E-innovation for sustainable development of rural resources during global economic crisis. IGI Global, USA

Mann CL (2004) Information technologies and international development: conceptual clarity in the search for commonality and diversity. Inf Technol Int Dev 1(2):67–79

Mareschal B, De Smet Y, Nemery P (2008) Rank reversal in the PROMETHEE II method: some new results. In: IEEE International Conference on Industrial engineering and engineering management. IEEM 2008. IEEE, pp 959–963
Martin NJ, St Onge B, Waaub JP (1999) An integrated decision aid system for the development of saint charles river alluvial plain, Quebec, Canada. Int J Environ Pollut 12(2–3):264–279
Mold A (2007) EU development policy in a changing world: challenges for the 21st century. Amsterdam University Press
Niebel T (2018) ICT and economic growth–comparing developing, emerging and developed countries. World Dev 104:197–211
Obidike NA (2011) Rural farmers' problems accessing agricultural information: a case study of Nsukka local government area of Enugu State, Nigeria. Library Philosophy and Practice 660
O'Mahony B, Dalrymple J, Levin E, Greenland S (2016) The role of information communications technology in sustainable water management practice. Int J Sustain Agric Manag Inf 2(1):79–92
Parreiras RO, Vasconcelos JA (2007) A multiplicative version of Promethee II applied to multiobjective optimization problems. Eur J Oper Res 183(2):729–740
Pelletier N, Ustaoglu E, Benoit C, Norris G, Rosenbaum E, Vasta A, Sala S (2018) Social sustainability in trade and development policy. Int J Life Cycle Assess 23(3):629–639
Polyzos S, Arabatzis G (2006) Multicriteria approach of the Greek prefectures evaluation according to tourist resources. Tour Today 96–111
Ponelis SR, Holmner MA (2013) ICT in Africa: enabling a better life for all. Inf Technol Dev 21(1):1–11
Pradhan R, Mallik G, Bagchi TP (2018) Information communication technology (ICT) infrastructure and economic growth: a causality evinced by cross-country panel data. IIMB Manag Rev (in press)
Qureshi S (2013a) What is the role of mobile phones in bringing about growth? Inf Technol Dev 19(1):1–4
Qureshi S (2013b) Networks of change, shifting power from institutions to people: how are innovations in the use of information and communication technology transforming development? Inf Technol Dev 19(2):97–99
Qureshi S (2013c) Information and communication technologies in the midst of global change: how do we know when development takes place? Inf Technol Dev 19(3):189–192
Raju KS, Duckstein L, Arondel C (2000) Multicriterion analysis for sustainable water resources planning: a case study in Spain. Water Resour Manag 14(6):435–456
Rekiek B, De Lit P, Pellichero F, L'Eglise T, Fouda P, Delchambre A (2002) Hybrid assembly line design and user's preferences. Int J Prod Res 40(5):1095–1111
Sahay S (2001) Introduction to the special issue on "IT and Health Care in Developing Countries. Electron J Inf Syst Dev Ctries. 5:1–6
Sandberg PL (2017) Administering EU Development Policy: Between Global Commitments and Vague Accountability Structures. Euro Pap J Law Integr 2(2):617–648
Tsekouropoulos G, Andreopoulou Z, Koliouska C, Koutroumanidis T, Batzios C, Lefakis P (2012) Marketing policies through the internet: the case of skiing centers in Greece. Sci Bull-Econ Sci 11(1):66–78
Tsekouropoulos G, Andreopoulou Z, Koliouska C, Koutroumanidis T, Batzios C, Samathrakis V (2013) Internet functions in marketing: multicriteria ranking of agricultural SMEs websites in Greece. J Agric Inf 4(2):22–36
Vaillancourt K, Waaub JP (2002) Environmental site evaluation of waste management facilities embedded into EUGENE model: a multicriteria approach. Eur J Oper Res 139(2):436–448
Vetschera R, Almeida AT (2012) A PROMETHEE-based approach to portfolio selection problems. Comput Oper Res 39(5):1010–1020
Vincke P (1992) Multicriteria decision-aid. Wiley
VPSolutions (2013) Visual PROMETHEE 1.4 manual. PROMETHEE methods
Walsham G, Robey D, Sahay S (2007) Special issue on information systems in developing countries. MIS Q 31(2):317–326

Yilmaz B, Dagdeviren M (2011) A combined approach for equipment selection: F-PROMETHEE method and zero-one goal programming. Exp Syst Appl 38(9):11641–11650

Zhang Y, Wang L, Duan Y (2016) Agricultural information dissemination using ICTs: a review and analysis of information dissemination models in China. Inf Process Agric 3(1):17–29

Zopounidis C, Lemonakis C, Andreopoulou Z, Koliouska C (2014) Agrotourism industry development through internet technologies: a multicriteria approach. J Euromarketing 23(4):45–67

A Fuzzy Linear Programming Approach to Solve Bi-level Multi-objective Linear Programming Problems

Tunjo Perić, Zoran Babić and Sead Rešić

Abstract This paper presents a new fuzzy linear programming approach to solve bi-level multi-objective linear programming problems. First, we solve all the linear programming models on a given set of constraints. After that, we determine membership functions of the objective functions and of the decision variables at the first level. Later, we determine weights for all the membership functions, and form a fuzzy linear programming model. The solution of the model should be the best one for all decision-makers on both levels. To demonstrate the efficiency of the proposed approach, we solve a business planning problem and compare the obtained results with the ones obtained using fuzzy goal programming methodology.

Keywords Bi-level multi-objective linear programming · Fuzzy linear programming · Production · Inventory and promotion planning

1 Introduction

Numerous economic situations can be presented as complex decentralized hierarchical systems. Decisions related to these systems are multilateral decisions. Namely, a decision is first made at the highest level with the objective functions of that level in mind. The decision-maker at the second level then observes the decision given by the first level and makes its decision, etc. Lower level decisions affect the degree of achievement of higher level decisions, while the lower level has complete information

T. Perić (✉)
Faculty of Economics & Business, University of Zagreb, Zagreb, Croatia
e-mail: tperic@efzg.hr

Z. Babić
Faculty of Economics, University of Split, Split, Croatia
e-mail: babic@efst.hr

S. Rešić
Faculty of Science, University of Tuzla, Tuzla, Bosnia and Herzegovina
e-mail: sead.resic@untz.ba

N. Mladenović et al. (eds.), *Advances in Operational Research in the Balkans*,
Springer Proceedings in Business and Economics,
https://doi.org/10.1007/978-3-030-21990-1_8

on higher level decisions. Such a decision-making model is known as the Stackelberg model in economics. Such models are solved by inverse induction, starting from the lowest level. The approach optimizes the objective function of the highest level in such a way so as to determine the values of the lowest level variables as functions of higher level variables. Then, the resulting value of the variables is included in the objective function of the higher level, and this level is optimized by determining the values of the variables of that level as the functions of the previous level variables. This is done until the highest level is reached, where the objective function of that level is optimized for the variables of that level. Finally, the values of all the variables at different levels are determined by moving gradually downward.

Such a way of optimizing a complex decentralized system with a convex set of constraints is causing numerous problems and is, consequently, perceived as a strong NP-hard problem (Shimzu et al. 1997). The solutions involve a variety of methods that are inadequately efficient. There are, however, methods that address such a multilevel problem as a multi-objective lexicographic problem. Here, the assumption is made that decision-makers are aware that higher level decisions affect the level of achievement of lower level goals and that the level of achievement of lower level goals affects the achievement of higher level goals, all of which affect the functioning of the overall complex system. Although the subsystems of a complex decentralized system are autonomous in decision-making, a certain level of co-operation needs to be achieved so that a higher level decision allows a certain degree of achievement of lower level objectives, etc. For example, the weighting method (Mishra 2007; Osman et al. 2013), fuzzy programming approach (Sinha 2003a, b) and fuzzy goal programming algorithm (Pramanik and Roy 2007; Baky 2009, 2010; Lachwani 2014) represent such attempts.

The methods listed above are not equally effective in solving the problem of decision-making in complex decentralized systems. In this paper, we propose a methodology to solve a multilevel multi-objective linear programming problem using fuzzy programming. Efficiency of the proposed methodology was tested in a complex hierarchical decentralized system where it was used to plan production, inventory and investment promotion.

The rest of the paper is structured as follows: Sect. 2 presents the model of a bi-level multi-objective linear programming problem. In Sect. 3, we present a methodology for solving multilevel multi-objective linear programming problems. In Sect. 4, we apply the proposed methodology and test its efficiency on a practical example. Finally, we conclude and list the references.

2 Model of Bi-level Multi-objective Linear Programming Problem

Suppose that the decision model consists of two levels, upper level (ULDM) and lower level (LLDM), where we have one decision-maker at the upper level (DM_0) and p decision-makers at the lower level (DM_i, $i = 1, 2, \ldots, p$). The model contains variables $\mathbf{x} = (\mathbf{x_0}, \mathbf{x_1}, \ldots, \mathbf{x_p}) \in \mathbf{R}^{\mathrm{n}}, \mathbf{x}_0 \in \mathbf{R}^{n_0}, \mathbf{x_k} \in \mathbf{R}^{n_k}$, where $n = n_0 + n_1 + \ldots + n_p$, $\mathbf{x}_0 = \left(x_{01}, x_{02}, \ldots, x_{0n_0}\right)$, $\mathbf{x}_k = \left(x_{k1}, x_{k2}, \ldots, x_{kn_k}\right)$, $k = 1, \ldots, p$. The decision-maker DM_0 controls variables $\mathbf{x}_0$, while the decision-maker DM_i controls variables $\mathbf{x}_\mathrm{k}$, $k = 1, 2, \ldots, p$.

The two-level linear programming model looks like this:

$$[\mathrm{DM}_0] : z_0 = \max_{\mathbf{x} \in \mathbf{S}} z_0(\mathbf{x}) = c_0^0 \mathbf{x}_0 + c_0^1 \mathbf{x}_1 + \ldots + c_0^p \mathbf{x}_p, \text{ (controls variables } \mathbf{x}_0) \quad (1)$$

where $\mathbf{x}_1, \mathbf{x}_2, \ldots, \mathbf{x}_p$ solve

$$\begin{aligned}
[\mathrm{DM}_1] &: z_1 = \max_{\mathbf{x} \in \mathbf{S}} z_1(\mathbf{x}) = c_1^0 \mathbf{x}_0 + c_1^1 \mathbf{x}_1 + \ldots + c_1^p \mathbf{x}_p, \text{ (controls variables } \mathbf{x}_1) \\
[\mathrm{DM}_2] &: z_2 = \max_{\mathbf{x} \in \mathbf{S}} z_2(\mathbf{x}) = c_2^0 \mathbf{x}_0 + c_2^1 \mathbf{x}_1 + \ldots + c_2^p \mathbf{x}_p, \text{ (controls variables } \mathbf{x}_2) \\
&\vdots \\
\left[\mathrm{DM}_p\right] &: z_p = \max_{\mathbf{x} \in \mathbf{S}} z_p(\mathbf{x}) = c_p^0 \mathbf{x}_0 + c_p^1 \mathbf{x}_1 + \ldots + c_p^p \mathbf{x}_p, \left(\text{controls variables } \mathbf{x}_p\right)
\end{aligned}$$

where
$\mathbf{S} = \left\{\mathbf{x} \in \mathbf{R}^n : \quad \mathbf{A}_0 \mathbf{x}_0 + \mathbf{A}_1 \mathbf{x}_1 + \ldots + \mathbf{A}_p \mathbf{x}_p (\leq, =, \geq) \mathbf{b}, \quad \mathbf{x} \geq \mathbf{o}, \quad \mathbf{b} \in \mathbf{R}^m, \mathbf{o} \in \mathbf{R}^n\right\} \neq \emptyset$, $\mathbf{c}_0 = \left(c_{01}, c_{02}, \ldots, c_{0n_0}\right)$, $\mathbf{c}_k^i = \left(c_{k1}^i, c_{k2}^i, \ldots, c_{kn_k}^i\right)$, $i, k = 1, 2, \ldots, p$ are vectors of constants in the objective functions, $\mathbf{A}_0$, $\mathbf{A}_i$, $i = 1, 2, \ldots, p$ are the matrices of the constraint coefficients, and $\mathbf{o}$ is a null vector.

3 Fuzzy Programming (FP) Model

Model (1) contains $p + 1$ linear objective functions z_i $(i = 0, 1, 2, \ldots, p)$ divided into two levels. The functions should be maximized on the given set of linear constraints. The decision-maker DM_0 first makes a decision about maximizing its objective function z_0. He must, however, take into account that the degree of achievement of his goal represented by the function z_0 depends on the degree of achievement of the goal of the decision-makers at the second level (DM_1, DM_2, ..., DM_p). Therefore, for the optimal functioning of the decentralized two-level hierarchical system it is necessary that the goals of all decision-makers are achieved to the appropriate degree. The decision-maker DM_0 needs to "leave some room" to the decision-makers of the second level, and thus enable the achievement of their goals, presented by their objective functions, when they maximize their objective functions on the given set of constraints. For this purpose, we propose a methodology that includes fuzzy programming (FP) (Babić and Perić 2011; Perić and Babić 2012; Matejaš and Perić 2014).

FP requires the decision-makers to determine the lower and upper aspiration levels for all objective functions z_0, z_1, ..., z_p and the decision variables of the decision-maker DM_0. In order to assist decision-makers in determining their aspiration levels, one should find the maximum value of all objective functions at a given set of constraints **S**, and form the payoff table with the objective function values for all optimal (marginal) solutions.

The payoff table is then presented to the decision-makers. They determine lower (g_{Li}) and upper aspiration levels (g_{Ui}) for the objective functions z_i ($i = 0, 1, 2, \ldots, p$). For the upper aspiration level, the decision-makers can use the maximum value of the objective functions z_i^* ($i = 0, 1, 2, \ldots, p$), while for the lower aspiration level they determine themselves. The decision-maker DM_0 controls variables $\mathbf{x}_0 = \left(x_{01}, x_{02}, \ldots, x_{0n_0}\right)$. The decision-maker DM_0 determines the allowed negative (t_{0k}^L) and positive (t_{0k}^R) deviation of the decision variables. The membership functions of the objective functions z_i ($i = 0, 1, 2, \ldots, p$) and decision variables controlled by the DM_0 are determined on the basis of lower and upper aspiration levels of the objective functions z_i, g_{Li} i g_{Ui} ($i = 0, 1, 2, \ldots, p$), and the allowed negative and positive deviations of the decision variables controlled by the decision-maker DM_0: t_{0k}^L and t_{0k}^R (Baky 2009):

$$\mu_{z_i}(z_i(\mathbf{x})) = \begin{cases} 1 & \text{if} \quad z_i(\mathbf{x}) \geq g_{Ui} \\ \frac{z_i(\mathbf{x}) - g_{Li}}{g_{Ui} - g_{Li}} & \text{if} \quad g_{Li} \leq z_i(\mathbf{x}) \leq g_{Ui} \ (i = 0,\ 1,\ \ldots, p) \\ 0 & \text{if} \quad z_i(\mathbf{x}) \leq g_{Li}, \end{cases} \tag{2}$$

$$\mu_{x_{0k}}(x_{0k}) = \begin{cases} \mu_{x_{0k}}^L(x_{0k}) = \frac{x_{0k} - (x_{0k}^* - t_{0k}^L)}{t_{0k}^L} & \text{if } x_{0k}^* - t_{0k}^L \leq x_{0k} \leq x_{0k}^* \\ \mu_{x_{0k}}^R(x_{0k}) = \frac{(x_{0k}^* + t_{0k}^R) - x_{0k}}{t_{0k}^R} & \text{if } x_{0k}^* \leq x_{0k} \leq x_{0k}^* + t_{0k}^R \\ 0 & \text{otherwise} \end{cases}, \tag{3}$$

where x_{0k} ($k = 1, 2, \ldots, n_0$) are the decision variables controlled by DM_0, and x_{0k}^* are the optimal value of the variables x_{0k} obtained by maximizing the objective function z_0 on the constraint set **S**.

The weighting coefficients that determine the significance of the objective functions at the upper and lower levels as well as the weights of decision variables controlled by the decision-maker DM_0 are determined as follows (Mohamed 1997):

$$w_i = \frac{w_i'}{\sum_{i=0}^{p} w_i'}; \quad w_i' = \frac{1}{g_{Ui} - g_{Li}}, \quad i = 0, 1, \ldots, p, \ w_{0k}^L = \frac{1}{t_{0k}^L}, \ w_{0k}^R = \frac{1}{t_{0k}^R}, \ k = 1, 2, \ldots, n_0. \tag{4}$$

FLP model to solve decentralized bi-level multi-objective linear programming (DBL-MOLP) problem looks like this:

$$\max_{(\mathbf{x}, \lambda) \in \mathbf{S}'} \lambda \tag{5}$$

where

$$\mathbf{S}' = \left\{ \begin{array}{l} (\mathbf{x}, \lambda) \in \mathbf{R}^{n+1} : \ \mu_{z_i}(z_i(x)) \geq w_i\lambda, \mu^L_{x_{0k}}(x_{0k}) \geq w^L_{0k}\lambda, \mu^R_{x_{0k}}(x_{0k}) \geq w^R_{0k}\lambda, \\ \mathbf{A}_0\mathbf{x}_0 + \mathbf{A}_1\mathbf{x}_1 + \ldots + \mathbf{A}_p\mathbf{x}_p(\leq, =, \geq)\mathbf{b}, \ \ \mathbf{x} = \mathbf{x}_0 + \mathbf{x}_1 + \cdots + \mathbf{x}_p \geq \mathbf{o}, \ \ \mathbf{b} \in \mathbf{R}^m, \\ 0 \leq \lambda \leq 1, \ \ \mathbf{x}, \mathbf{o} \in \mathbf{R}^n, \lambda \in \mathbf{R}, \mathbf{x}_0 \in \mathbf{R}^{n_0}, \mathbf{x}_1 \in \mathbf{R}^{n_1}, \ldots, \ \ \mathbf{x}_p \in \mathbf{R}^{n_p} \end{array} \right\} \neq \emptyset$$

The solution of Model (5) depends on the determined values of the lower and upper bounds of the objective functions as well as on the determined positive and negative deviations of the decision variables controlled by the decision-maker DM_0. The obtained solution can also be an empty set. If an empty set is obtained as the solution of the model, decision-makers should change the lower and/or upper aspiration levels of the objective function and negative and/or positive deviations of decision variables controlled by the decision-maker DM_0. A solution that is not an empty set should be the best solution for all decision-makers.

Therefore, the algorithm to solve DBL-MOLP problem contains the following steps:

Step 1. Determine individual optimal values of all objective functions on the set of constraints S and form the payoff table.

Step 2. Set g_{Li}, g_{Ui}, t^L_{0k} and t^R_{0k}, $i = 0, 1, \ldots, p$; $k = 1, 2, \ldots, n_0$.

Step 3. Form the membership functions $\mu_{z_i}(z_i(\mathrm{x}))$, $\mu^L_{x_{0k}}(x_{0k})$, and $\mu^R_{x_{0k}}(x_{0k})$, $i = 0, 1, \ldots, p$; $k = 1, 2, \ldots, n_0$.

Step 4. Evaluate the weights $w_i = w'_i / \sum_{i=0}^{p} w'_i$; $w'_i = 1/(g_{Ui} - g_{Li})$, $i = 0, 1, \ldots, p$, $w^L_{0k} = 1/t^L_{0k}$, $w^R_{0k} = 1/t^R_{0k}$, $k = 1, 2, \ldots, n_0$.

Step 5. Formulate model (5) for the DBL-MOLP problem.

Step 6. Solve model (5) to get a solution to the DBL-MOLP problem.

Step 7. If the obtained solution is not an empty set, go to Step 8, else go to Step 9.

Step 8. Stop. The satisfactory solution of the DBL-MOLP problem is obtained.

Step 9. Modify lower and/or upper aspiration levels of the objective functions as well as positive and negative deviations of the decision variables controlled by the decision-maker DM_0, determine new membership functions of the objective functions and decision variables and go back to Step 3.

4 Practical Example

We have applied the proposed methodology to solve a practical production planning problem in a supposed company. Consider a company that manufactures five products: P1, P2, P3, P4, and P5. Suppose that the costs and required capital are proportional to individual activities. The company requires that all products be produced in at least 50 units. In addition, the company should stock no less than 12% of its total production to ensure delivery safety. The management of the enterprise has set the limit of inventory for each product to at least 14, 11, 9, 15, and 13, respectively, to at most 50% of total production, and to at most 44, 56, 52, 45, and 50 for respective products. It is also stipulated that total inventory costs per product should not exceed 100 m.u. Enterprise management has determined that the investment in promotion

Table 1 The data for the practical application

The data for per unit	Products				
	P_1	P_2	P_3	P_4	P_5
Raw material (units) Capacity: 1500	1	4	2	3	2
Machines (h) Capacity: 1600	2	1.5	0.5	1.2	0.2
Capital employed per unit of the product	20	25	30	22	11
Sales price per unit (m.u.)	120	130	90	110	70
Gross profit per unit (m.u.)	11	9	10	6	10
Inventory cost per unit (m.u.)	2	1	1.5	2	1.8

must not exceed 20% of the total gross profit of the company. By product, promotion investments must not exceed 22, 18, 24, 20, and 19% of the total gross profit of the company, respectively, while promotion investments for the first product may not exceed 800 m.u. and 400 m.u. for other products. Table 1 shows manufacturing data which are fixed by assumption (the idea taken from Toksari and Bilim 2015).

The company has one decision-maker at the first level and two decision-makers at the second level. Each decision-maker tends to maximize his objective function: the decision-maker at the first level maximizes the total net profit (the difference between the gross profit and total inventory costs and total investment in promotion), while the decision-makers at the second level maximize the total inventory of products and the total investment in promotion, respectively.

Let x_1, x_2, x_3, x_4, x_5 be production quantities, i_1, i_2, i_3, i_4, i_5 stock quantity, while p_1, p_2, p_3, p_4, p_5 are investment in promotion of products P_1, P_2, P_3, P_4, P_5, respectively.

Based on the presented data, the DBL-MOLP model looks like this:

$$\begin{aligned}
&\max_{(\mathbf{x},\mathbf{i},\mathbf{p})\in\mathbf{S}} z_0 = 11x_1 + 9x_2 + 10x_3 + 6x_4 + 10x_5 - 2i_1 - i_2 - 1.5i_3 - 2x_4 - 1.8i_5 - p_1 - p_2 - p_3 - p_4 - p_5 \\
&\max_{(\mathbf{x},\mathbf{i},\mathbf{p})\in\mathbf{S}} z_1 = i_1 + i_2 + i_3 + i_4 + i_5 \\
&\max_{(\mathbf{x},\mathbf{i},\mathbf{p})\in\mathbf{S}} z_2 = p_1 + p_2 + p_3 + p_4 + p_5
\end{aligned} \tag{6}$$

where

$$\mathbf{S} = \left\{ \begin{array}{l}
(\mathbf{x},\mathbf{i},\mathbf{p}): \\
x_1 + 4x_2 + 2x_3 + 3x_4 + 2x_5 \le 1500;\ \ 2x_1 + 1.5x_2 + 0.5x_3 + 1.2x_4 + 0.2x_5 \le 1600; \\
20x_1 + 25x_2 + 30x_3 + 22x_4 + 11x_5 \le 22{,}000;\ \ 0.12(x_1 + x_2 + x_3 + x_4 + x_5) \le \\
i_1 + i_2 + i_3 + i_4 + i_5;\ \ 0.14x_1 \le i_1;\ \ 0.11x_1 \le i_2;\ \ 0.09x_3 \le i_3;\ \ 0.15x_4 \le i_4;\ \ 0.13x_5 \le i_5; \\
0.5(x_1 + x_2 + x_3 + x_4 + x_5) \ge i_1 + i_2 + i_3 + i_4 + i_5;\ \ 0.44x_1 \ge i_1;\ \ 0.56x_2 \ge i_2; \\
0.52x_3 \ge i_3;\ \ 0.48x_4 \ge i_4;\ \ 0.5x_5 \ge i_5;\ \ i_1, i_2, i_3, i_4, i_5 \le 100;\ \ 2.2x_1 + 1.8x_2 + 2x_3 + 1.2x_4 + \\
+2x_5 \ge p_1 + p_2 + p_3 + p_4 + p_5;\ \ 2.42x_1 \ge p_1;\ \ 1.62x_2 \ge p_2;\ \ 2.4x_3 \ge p_3;\ \ 1.2x_4 \ge p_4; \\
1.9x_5 \ge p_5;\ \ p_1 \le 800;\ \ p_2, p_3, p_4, p_5 \le 400;\ \ x_1, x_2, x_3, x_4, x_5, i_1, i_2, i_3, i_4, i_5, p_1, p_2, p_3, p_4, p_5 \ge 0
\end{array} \right\}$$

Table 2 Payoff values

·	z_0	z_1	z_2
$\max\limits_{(\mathbf{x},\mathbf{i},\mathbf{p})\in\mathbf{S}} z_0$	10443.10	141	0
$\max\limits_{(\mathbf{x},\mathbf{i},\mathbf{p})\in\mathbf{S}} z_1$	8723.90	348	0
$\max\limits_{(\mathbf{x},\mathbf{i},\mathbf{p})\in\mathbf{S}} z_2$	6777.60	112	1746

Table 3 Aspiration levels and positive and negative deviations of decision variables

	$g_{L0}/\ g_{U0}$	$g_{L1}/\ g_{U1}$	$g_{L2}/\ g_{U2}$	t_{01}^L	t_{01}^R	t_{02}^R	t_{03}^R	t_{04}^R	t_{05}^L	t_{05}^R
Aspiration level	10400/8000	340/250	1700/1500	202	48	200	200	200	74	126

Remark: $t_{02}^L = t_{03}^L = t_{04}^L = 0$

By maximizing each of the three objective functions on a given set of constraints, we have obtained the optimal solutions for the objective functions. They are presented in Table 2.

Table 2 points to the conflict between the objective functions at the upper and lower levels. Since the decision-makers at the upper level first make a decision on the volume of production, leading to a small degree of achievement of the lower level objective functions, the decision-makers at the lower level will maximize their functions and thus cause a major reduction in the fulfillment of the upper level objective function. The decision-makers are consequently encouraged to co-operation, which should produce an acceptable degree of satisfaction at both levels and lead to acceptable functioning of the entire business system.

According to the algorithm of the proposed methodology given in Sect. 3, decision-makers first determine the lower and upper aspiration levels for their objective functions, while the decision-maker at the upper level determines the positive and negative deviations from the value of the decision variables which he controls, as shown in Table 3.

Using the forms (2) and (3) and data from Table 3, the membership functions for all the objective functions and the decision variables controlled by the upper level decision-maker have been calculated:

$$\mu_{z_0}(z_0) = \frac{(11x_1 + 9x_2 + 10x_3 + 6x_4 + 10x_5 - 2i_1 - i_2 - 1.5i_3 - 2i_4 - 1.8i_5 - p_1 - p_2 - p_3 - p_4 - p_5) - 8000}{10{,}400 - 8000}$$

$$= \frac{11x_1 + 9x_2 + 10x_3 + 6x_4 + 10x_5 - 2i_1 - i_2 - 1.5i_3 - 2i_4 - 1.8i_5 - p_1 - p_2 - p_3 - p_4 - p_5 - 8000}{2400}$$

$$\mu_{z_1}(z_1) = \frac{(i_1 + i_2 + i_3 + i_4 + i_5) - 250}{340 - 250} = \frac{i_1 + i_2 + i_3 + i_4 + i_5 - 250}{90}$$

$$\mu_{z_2}(z_2) = \frac{(p_1 + p_2 + p_3 + p_4 + p_5) - 1500}{1700 - 1500} = \frac{p_1 + p_2 + p_3 + p_4 + p_5 - 1500}{200}$$

$$\mu_{x_1}^L(x_1) = \frac{x_1 - (702 - 202)}{202} = \frac{x_1 - 500}{202},\ \mu_{x_1}^R(x_1) = \frac{(702 + 48) - x_1}{202} = \frac{750 - x_1}{48},$$

Table 4 Membership function weights

	μ_{z_1}	μ_{z_2}	μ_{z_3}	$\mu_{x_1}^L$	$\mu_{x_1}^R$	$\mu_{x_2}^R$	$\mu_{x_3}^R$	$\mu_{x_4}^R$	$\mu_{x_5}^L$	$\mu_{x_5}^R$
Weights	0.05367	0.8336	0.1127	1/202	1/48	1/200	1/200	1/200	1/74	1/126

$$\mu_{x_2}^R(x_2) = \frac{(50+200)-x_2}{200} = \frac{250-x_2}{200},\ \mu_{x_3}^R(x_3) = \frac{(50+200)-x_3}{200} = \frac{250-x_3}{200}.$$
$$\mu_{x_4}^R(x_4) = \frac{(50+200)-x_4}{200} = \frac{250-x_4}{200},\ \mu_{x_5}^L(x_5) = \frac{x_5-(174-74)}{74} = \frac{x_5-100}{74}.$$
$$\mu_{x_5}^R(x_5) = \frac{(174+126)-x_5}{126} = \frac{300-x_5}{126}.$$

Using the form (4) and data from Table 2, the weights of the objective functions and the decision variables controlled by the upper decision-maker have been calculated: (Table 4)

The FP model of the DBL-MOLP problem looks like this:

$$\max_{(\mathbf{x},\mathbf{i},\mathbf{p},\lambda)\in \mathbf{S}'} \lambda \tag{7}$$

where

$$\mathbf{S}' = \left\{ \begin{array}{l} (\mathbf{x},\mathbf{i},\mathbf{p},\boldsymbol{\lambda}): \\ \frac{11x_1+9x_2+10x_3+6x_4+10x_5-2i_1-i_2-1.5i_3-2i_4-1.8i_5-p_1-p_2-p_3-p_4-p_5-8000}{2400} \geq \\ 0.05367\lambda;\ \frac{i_1+i_2+i_3+i_4+i_5-250}{90} \geq 0.8336\lambda;\ \frac{p_1+p_2+p_3+p_4+p_5-1500}{200} \geq 0.1127\lambda; \\ 0.05367\lambda;\ \frac{i_1+i_2+i_3+i_4+i_5-250}{90} \geq 0.8336\lambda;\ \frac{p_1+p_2+p_3+p_4+p_5-1500}{200} \geq 0.1127\lambda; \\ \frac{x_5-100}{74} \geq \frac{1}{74}\lambda;\ \frac{300-x_5}{126} \geq \frac{1}{126}\lambda;\ 0 \leq \lambda \leq 1; \\ x_1+4x_2+2x_3+3x_4+2x_5 \leq 1500;\ 2x_1+1.5x_2+0.5x_3+1.2x_4+0.2x_5 \leq 1600; \\ 20x_1+25x_2+30x_3+22x_4+11x_5 \leq 22{,}000;\ 0.12(x_1+x_2+x_3+x_4+x_5) \leq \\ i_1+i_2+i_3+i_4+i_5;\ 0.14x_1 \leq i_1;\ 0.11x_1 \leq i_2;\ 0.09x_3 \leq i_3;\ 0.15x_4 \leq i_4;\ 0.13x_5 \leq i_5; \\ 0.5(x_1+x_2+x_3+x_4+x_5) \geq i_1+i_2+i_3+i_4+i_5;\ 0.44x_1 \geq i_1;\ 0.56x_2 \geq i_2; \\ 0.52x_3 \geq i_3;\ 0.48x_4 \geq i_4;\ 0.5x_5 \geq i_5;\ i_1,i_2,i_3,i_4,i_5 \leq 100;\ 2.2x_1+1.8x_2+2x_3+1.2x_4+ \\ +2x_5 \geq p_1+p_2+p_3+p_4+p_5;\ 2.42x_1 \geq p_1;\ .62x_2 \geq p_2;\ 2.4x_3 \geq p_3;\ 1.2x_4 \geq p_4; \\ 1.9x_5 \geq p_5;\ p_1 \leq 800;\ p_2,p_3,p_4,p_5 \leq 400;\ x_1,x_2,x_3,x_4,x_5,i_1,i_2,i_3,i_4,i_5,p_1,p_2,p_3,p_4,p_5 \geq 0 \end{array} \right\}$$

The model (7) is solved by using excel solver. The following solution has been obtained:

$$(x_1, x_2, x_3, x_4, x_5) = (598,\ 50,\ 175,\ 50,\ 101),\ (i_1, i_2, i_3, i_4, i_5) = (100,\ 28,\ 91,\ 24,\ 50),$$
$$(p_1,\ p_2,\ p_3,\ p_4,\ p_5) = (781,\ 81,\ 400,\ 60,\ 191),\ \lambda = 0.578394,\ (z_0, z_1, z_2) = (8072.5,\ 293,\ 1513),$$
$$(\mu_0, \mu_1, \mu_2) = (0.03,\ 0.48,\ 0.065),\ \mu_0 + \mu_1 + \mu_2 = 0.575.$$

By changing the aspiration levels of the objective function and/or the positive and negative deviations of the decision variables controlled by the upper level decision-maker and/or the weights of the objective functions, the resulting solution changes. However, it may happen that the solution is an empty set, which makes it necessary to change the aspiration levels, and/or the positive and negative deviations of the decision variables. The obtained solution depends on the aspirational levels determined by the decision-makers as well as on the positive and negative deviations of the decision variables determined by the decision-maker on the upper level. Since it reflects the decision-makers' preferences at both decision-making levels they should accept the decision obtained in this way.

The proposed methodology is compared with the fuzzy goal programming methodology (Baky 2009) to solve DBL-MOLP problem. Solving DBL-MOLP problem using fuzzy goal programming methodology requires the decision-maker to provide the information on aspiration levels for the objective functions and on positive and negative deviations for the decision variables of the decision-maker DM_0. This methodology requires solving the following linear goal programming model:

$$\min_{(\mathbf{x},\mathbf{d})\in \mathbf{S}''} \sum_{i=0}^{k} w_i d_i^- + \sum_{k=1}^{n_0} w_{0k}^L d_{0k}^L + \sum_{k=1}^{n_0} w_{0k}^R d_{0k}^R \tag{8}$$

where

$$\mathbf{S}'' = \left\{ \begin{array}{l} (\mathbf{x}, \mathbf{d}^-) \in \mathbf{R}^{n+p+2n_0+1} : \ \mu_{z_i}(z_i(\mathbf{x})) + d_i^- = 1, \ \mu_{x_{0k}}^L(x_{0k}) + d_{0k}^{L-} = 1, \ \mu_{x_{0k}}^R(x_{0k}) + d_{0k}^{R-} = 1, \\ \mathbf{A}_0\mathbf{x}_0 + \mathbf{A}_1\mathbf{x}_1 + \ldots + \mathbf{A}_p\mathbf{x}_p(\le, =, \ge)\mathbf{b}, \ \mathbf{x} = \mathbf{x}_0 + \mathbf{x}_1 + \ldots + \mathbf{x}_p \ge \mathbf{o}, \ \mathbf{d}^- \ge \mathbf{o}, \ \mathbf{b} \in \mathbf{R}^m, \\ \mathbf{x}, \mathbf{o} \in \mathbf{R}^n, \ \mathbf{d}^- \in \mathbf{R}^{p+2n_0+1}, \ \mathbf{x}_0 \in \mathbf{R}^{n0}, \ \mathbf{x}_1 \in \mathbf{R}^{n1}, \ldots, \ \mathbf{x}_p \in \mathbf{R}^{np} \end{array} \right\} \ne \emptyset$$

The algorithm consists of several steps:

Step 1. Determine individual optimal value of all objective functions on the set of constraints **S** and form the payoff table.

Step 2. Set g_{Li}, g_{Ui}, t_{0k}^L and t_{0k}^R, $i = 0, 1, \ldots, p$; $k = 1, 2, \ldots, n_0$.

Step 3. Elicit the membership functions $\mu_{z_i}(z_i(\mathbf{x}))$, $\mu_{x_{0k}}^L(x_{0k})$ and $\mu_{x_{0k}}^R(x_{0k})$, $i = 0, 1, \ldots, p$; $k = 1, 2, \ldots, n_0$.

Step 4. Evaluate the weights $w_i = w_i^{'}/\sum_{i=0}^{p} w_i^{'}$; $w_i^{'} = 1/(g_{Ui} - g_{Li})$, $i = 0, 1, \ldots, p$, $w_{0k}^L = 1/t_{0k}^L$, $w_{0k}^R = 1/t_{0k}^R$, $k = 1, 2, \ldots, n_0$.

Step 5. Formulate model (8) for the DBL-MOLP problem.

Step 6. Solve model (8) to get a solution to the DBL-MOLP problem.

Step 7. If the obtained solution is not an empty set, go to Step 8, else go to Step 9.

Step 8. Stop. The satisfactory solution of the DBL-MOLP problem is obtained.

Step 9. Modify lower and/or upper aspiration levels of the objective functions as well as positive and negative deviations of the decision variables controlled by the decision-maker DM_0, determine new membership functions of the objective functions and decision variables and go back to Step 3.

To solve our problem using this methodology we used the existing information on the membership functions and solved the following model:

$$\min_{(\mathbf{x},\mathbf{i},\mathbf{p},\mathbf{d}^-)\in \mathbf{S}''} \left(\begin{array}{l} 0.05367 d_0^- + 0.8336 d_1^- + 0,1127 d_2^- + (1/202) d_{01}^{L-} + (1/48) d_{01}^{R-} + (1/200) d_{02}^{R-} + \\ +(1/200) d_{03}^{R-} + (1/200) d_{04}^{R-} + (1/74) d_{05}^{L-} + (1/126) d_{05}^{R-} \end{array} \right) \tag{9}$$

where

$$
\mathbf{S}' = \left\{ \begin{array}{l}
(\mathbf{x}, \mathbf{i}, \mathbf{p}, \boldsymbol{\lambda}) : \\
\frac{11x_1+9x_2+10x_3+6x_4+10x_5-2i_1-i_2-1.5i_3-2i_4-1.8i_5-p_1-p_2-p_3-p_4-p_5-8000}{2400} - d_0^- = 1 \\
\frac{i_1+i_2+i_3+i_4+i_5-250}{90} - d_1^- = 1; \quad \frac{p_1+p_2+p_3+p_4+p_5-1500}{200} - d_2^- = 1; \quad \frac{x_1-500}{202} + d_{01}^{L-} = 1; \\
\frac{750-x_1}{48} - d_{01}^{R-} = 1; \quad \frac{250-x_2}{200} - d_{02}^{R-} = 1; \quad \frac{250-x_3}{200} - d_{03}^{R-} = 1; \quad \frac{250-x_4}{200} - d_{04}^{R-} = 1; \\
\frac{x_5-100}{74} - d_{05}^{L-} = 1; \quad \frac{300-x_5}{126} - d_{05}^{R-} = 1; \\
x_1 + 4x_2 + 2x_3 + 3x_4 + 2x_5 \le 1500; \quad 2x_1 + 1.5x_2 + 0.5x_3 + 1.2x_4 + 0.2x_5 \le 1600; \\
20x_1 + 25x_2 + 30x_3 + 22x_4 + 11x_5 \le 22{,}000; \quad 0.12(x_1 + x_2 + x_3 + x_4 + x_5) \le \\
i_1 + i_2 + i_3 + i_4 + i_5; \quad 0.14x_1 \le i_1; \quad 0.11x_1 \le i_2; \quad 0.09x_3 \le i_3; \quad 0.15x_4 \le i_4; \quad 0.13x_5 \le i_5; \\
0.5(x_1 + x_2 + x_3 + x_4 + x_5) \ge i_1 + i_2 + i_3 + i_4 + i_5; \quad 0.44x_1 \ge i_1; \quad 0.56x_2 \ge i_2; \\
0.52x_3 \ge i_3; \quad 0.48x_4 \ge i_4; \quad 0.5x_5 \ge i_5; \quad i_1, i_2, i_3, i_4, i_5 \le 100; \quad 2.2x_1 + 1.8x_2 + 2x_3 + 1.2x_4 + \\
+2x_5 \ge p_1 + p_2 + p_3 + p_4 + p_5; \quad 2.42x_1 \ge p_1; \quad .62x_2 \ge p_2; \quad 2.4x_3 \ge p_3; \quad 1.2x_4 \ge p_4; \\
1.9x_5 \ge p_5; \quad p_1 \le 800; \quad p_2, p_3, p_4, p_5 \le 400; \quad x_1, x_2, x_3, x_4, x_5, i_1, i_2, i_3, i_4, i_5, p_1, p_2, p_3, p_4, p_5 \ge 0
\end{array} \right\}
$$

The following solution has been obtained:

$$
\begin{array}{l}
(x_1, x_2, x_3, x_4, x_5) = (702,\ 50,\ 50,\ 50,\ 174),\ (i_1, i_2, i_3, i_4, i_5) = (100,\ 28,\ 26,\ 24,\ 87), \\
(p_1,\ p_2,\ p_3,\ p_4,\ p_5) = (800,\ 81,\ 120,\ 60,\ 330),\ (z_0, z_1, z_2) = (8175.6,\ 291.4,\ 1503), \\
(\mu_0, \mu_1, \mu_2) = (0.07,\ 0.46,\ 0.015),\ \mu_0 + \mu_1 + \mu_2 = 0.545.
\end{array}
$$

Therefore, the solution obtained by fuzzy goal programming method differs from the solution obtained using fuzzy programming approach, although we used the same objective function and decision variable weights. The objective function values are approximately equal, while our methodology has given a slightly greater total membership function value. From this, we can conclude that special attention has to be paid to the choice of methods to solve DBL-MOLP problems.

5 Conclusion

In this paper, we propose a new methodology to solve DBL-MOLP problems. The proposed methodology is based on the application of fuzzy programming. The proposed methodology has been tested on a practical example concerning the planning of production quantity, inventory stocks, and promotion investment for a company.

The proposed methodology requires information on the lower and upper aspirational levels of the objective functions from all decision-makers. Besides that top-level decision-makers are required to provide information on acceptable positive and negative deviations of the decision variables they control. The solutions obtained using the proposed methodology were compared with the solutions obtained using the fuzzy goal programming methodology. Different but similar results have been obtained. This indicates the problem of choosing the appropriate method for solving this problem.

Applying the proposed methodology to solving realistic problems of production, inventory, promotion costs, and finance planning in decentralized complex companies with multiple decision-making levels is a challenge for future research.

References

Babić Z, Perić T (2011) Quantity discounts in supplier selection problem by use of fuzzy multi-criteria programming. Croat Oper Res Rev 2:49–59

Baky IA (2009) Fuzzy goal programming algorithm for solving decentralized bi-level multi-objective programming problems. Fuzzy Sets Syst 160:2701–2713

Baky IA (2010) Solving multi-level multi-objective linear programming problems through fuzzy goal programming approach. Appl Math Model 34:2377–2387

Lachwani K (2014) On solving multi-level multi objective linear programming problems through fuzzy goal programming approach. J Oper Res Soc India Opsearch 51(4):624–637

Matejaš J, Perić T (2014) A new iterative method for solving multiobjective linear programming problem. Appl Math Comput 243(9):746–754

Mishra S (2007) Weighting method for bi-level linear fractional programming problems. Eur J Oper Res 183:296–302

Mohamed RH (1997) The relationship between goal programming and fuzzy programming. Fuzzy Sets Syst 89:215–222

Osman MS, Gadalla MH, Zeanedean RA, Rabie RM (2013) A compromise weighted solution for multilevel linear programming problems. Int J Eng Res Appl 3(6):927–936. www.ijera.com

Perić T, Babić Z (2012) Financial structure optimization by using a goal programming approach. Croat Oper Res Rev (CRORR) 3:150–162

Pramanik S, Roy TK (2007) Fuzzy goal programming approach to multilevel programming problems. Eur J Oper Res 176:1151–1166

Shimzu K, Ishizuka Y, Bard JF (1997) Nondifferentiable and two-level mathematical programming. Kluwer Academic Publishers, Boston

Sinha S (2003a) Fuzzy mathematical programming applied to multi-level programming problems. Comput Oper Res 30:1259–1268

Sinha S (2003b) Fuzzy programming approach to multi-level programming problems. Fuzzy Sets Syst 136:189–202

Toksari MD, Bilim J (2015) Interactive fuzzy goal programming based on Jacobian matrix to solve decentralized bi-level multi-objective fractional programming problems. Int J Fuzzy Syst

Performance Measurement & Data Envelopment Analysis

Residential Attractiveness of Cities from the Perspective of the Efficiency, Residents' Perception and Preferences: The Case of Serbia

Marija Kuzmanović, Gordana Savić and Kristina Pajić

Abstract The purpose of the paper is to determine the most influential factors related to cities/towns attractiveness and to compare respondents' perception and real efficiency of certain cities. Empirical study is designed to evaluate residential attractiveness of the cities in Republic of Serbia as cities' relative efficiency from one hand and citizens' perception and preferences regarding living conditions from the other hand. For the purpose of attractiveness assessment, two input–output scenarios are created: financial and mixed financial health efficiency scenario. Both scenarios are evaluated using suitable Data Envelopment Analysis models which resulted in comparison of cities/towns attractiveness and determination of the most influential factors. This analysis was extended by a survey of the residents' perceptions as well as their preference through conjoint analysis. The hypothesis was if the city was assessed as efficient, it does not automatically mean that it is perceived as attractive. Namely, sometimes 'image' of the particular city is more important than its quantified efficiency. Comparative analysis of results of both methods proves the aforementioned hypothesis in the case of the 15 regional centres in Serbia. The findings of this study could be used as directions for the public demography policymakers.

Keywords City attractiveness · Efficiency assessment · Data envelopment analysis · Preferences · Perception · Conjoint analysis

1 Introduction

Residential attractiveness is a relatively new concept coming from a territorial development paradigm based on competitiveness and public policies in order to restore the social mix by an inverted social diversification. Residential attractiveness is progressively becoming a central feature of public policy in renewal processes for declining cities (Miot 2015).

M. Kuzmanović (✉) · G. Savić · K. Pajić
Faculty of Organizational Sciences, University of Belgrade, Belgrade, Serbia
e-mail: marija.kuzmanovic@fon.bg.ac.rs

N. Mladenović et al. (eds.), *Advances in Operational Research in the Balkans*, Springer Proceedings in Business and Economics,
https://doi.org/10.1007/978-3-030-21990-1_9

In Serbia, cites and whole regions face the demographic crises—number of citizens decrease dramatically. This trend is particularly evident if we look younger population under year of 40. Young people largely move to bigger cities/towns for education and stay there to live. A very few of them wish to take back to hometown after graduation. The questions are which factors are crucial for the young people to choose a city/town as place of residence—is it financial stability, cultural, and entertainment offers, possibilities for employment or health environment and less busy life? This aspect of cities/towns' efficiency and attractiveness is in the focus of this paper. Another aspect of the analysis is to identify perspectives and preferences of residents towards chosen criteria.

The attractiveness of the cities depends on several different criteria such as level of economical development, job offers, and facilities for family and social life as well as recreational and ecological conditions. Residents wish to have high standards and demanding the best for themselves. They put the pressure on the government to invest in cities/towns, in order to remain competitive. On the other hand, competition stimulates the differentiation of towns, in the term of the size of the city/town, the price of renting and buying housing, the price of the consumer basket, the average monthly income per household, the cultural and entertainment content, the pollution rate, crime rate, affordability of health and education services, relations between neighbours, etc. In order to include several criteria into analysis simultaneously, the authors introduce Data Envelopment Analysis (DEA) as a technique for attractiveness evaluation from the aspect of the cities/towns' efficiency.

On the other hand, the widely used approach to measure the relative importance of the cities' characteristics independently for individuals is Likert scale (Niedomysl 2008). However, the usage of Likert scale for the evaluation of characteristics does not help us in understanding the trade-offs—when measuring importance it may happen that all characteristics are of great importance, as the respondents do not need to choose among different characteristics (Shafranskaya and Potapov 2012). Thus, we will apply preference measurement method known as conjoint analysis to identify the characteristics that residents value the most when choosing a city/town in which they are willing to live and work. Conjoint analysis is research technique based on the assumption that complex decisions are not made based on a single factor or criterion, but rather on several factors considered jointly. In this manner, conjoint analysis allows the researcher to understand better interrelationship of multiple factors as they contribute to preferences (Kuzmanovic and Radosavljevic 2013). In this way, a city with features that are closest to those that the residents prefer and most often choose will be defined. Furthermore, it will be determined whether these preferences are heterogeneous and the segments with similar preferences will be isolated. Finally, it will be surveyed how characteristics are perceived for the particular city/town. The result of such analysis will allow us to identify the most important attributes for different groups of residents and are expected to be the useful source for further strategic decisions of city development.

The results of both methods, DEA and Conjoint analysis, can help the country in the implementation of the population policy. DEA model quantifies attractiveness and indicates influential factors and direction of improvement. Conjoint analysis results can indicate whether are there the differences between perception and preferences and compare them to quantified DEA results.

The paper is organized as follows. Section 2 gives literature review followed by methodological background given in Sect. 3. Section 4 presents empirical study by describing a problem of regional mapping of Serbia, and choosing regional capital cities/towns for efficiency assessment, together with criteria selection in the first part and setting the attributes and profiles for conjoint analysis in the second part. Afterwards, Sect. 5 gives results and discussion followed by conclusions in Sect. 6.

2 Literature Review

Although the problem of economic and non-economic efficiency of cities, countries and regions has been heavily studied in literature over the past 30 years, it still remains an interesting topic of research. With regard to the measuring method, the models applied most often in these studies are DEA-related models.

Most previous studies related to regional efficiency focus on environmental or energy efficiency, which implies that economic-related dimensions are their primary concern. Most of those studies focus on China (Wang Yu and Zhang 2013; Wu Cao and Liu 2014), while others focus on countries such as Taiwan, the United Kingdom, French, Italy, United States, Finland, Spain (Bianco et al. 2017; Tallini and Cedola 2016; Shahbazi et al. 2017; Norman 2017). Other dimensions of regional efficiency, such as police, education, healthcare and financial, have been studied, but are evaluated independently (Chen 2017; Mitorivić et al. 2016). In recent years, tourism has become an increasingly analysing dimension when it comes to regional efficiency (Solana-Ibáñez, et al. 2016; Suzuki et al. 2011). However, several studies include multi-activity overall efficiency analysis (Rabar 2013; Alfonso Piña and Pardo Martinez 2016; Chen 2017).

The first applications of the DEA method to regional economics were made by Charnes et al. (1989). Authors studied the economic performance of 28 China's cities in 1983 and 1984. Chang et al. (1995) used DEA and the Malmquist productivity index approach to study the economic performance of 23 regions in Taiwan in 1983 and 1990. Bernard and Cantner (1997) calculated the efficiency of the 21 French provinces in 1978–1989. Maudos et al. (2000) analyse the relationship between efficiency and production structure in Spain 1964–1993. Martić and Savić (2001) used DEA to estimate how well regions in Serbia utilize their resources. Loikkanen and Susiluoto (2002) estimated private sector economic efficiency scores for 83 Finnish regions in 1988–1999 using DEA method. To identify and decompose the efficiency of 439 German regions in using infrastructure and human capital, Schaffer et al. (2011) applied an outlier robust extension of DEA followed by a geoadditive regression analysis, and find out that the regions' efficiency is driven by a spatial and a non-spatial, arguably structural factor. Staníčková and Melecký (2012) analyse the degree of efficiency achieved in individual countries and regions of Visegrad Four (V4), which is perceived as a reflection of the development potential in the reference period 2000–2010. They offer a comprehensive comparison of the results obtained using the selected DEA models, namely, the CCR model, BCC model and SBM.

Halkos and Tzeremes (2013) examine the link between regional environmental efficiency and economic growth in the United Kingdom using the directional distance function. Yin et al. (2014) applied DEA to eco-efficiency analysis using environmental pollution as an undesirable output. They propose a modified super-efficiency model for eco-efficiency discrimination and ranking 30 Chinese provincial capital cities. Wang et al. (2015) used DEA to examine the environmental protection mechanisms and economic development of 211 cities in China from an environmental efficiency perspective. They found that local governments should develop appropriate policies to maximize the use of technology and develop management practices that enhance both growth and protection.Alfonso Piña and Pardo Martinez (2016) estimated and evaluated the environmental, social, and economic efficiency of cities in Columbia using DEA, in order to determine the changes that occurred between 2005 and 2013. The results indicate differences among cities, where the efficient cities show adequate resource use, lower environmental impacts, improved social conditions and guaranteed economic growth and development.

Recently, Chen (2017) proposed a MADEA model to simultaneously evaluate the departmental and overall efficiency in Taiwan's cities. He included data on the economic development, social welfare, police and security, and education departments for 20 cities in Taiwan for the period 1999–2013. He also applied the ML index and its decompositions to calculate the productivity changes in each department, as well as the overall productivity of a region. Another recent study in which DEA was used to measure eco-efficiency is shown in (Masternak-Janus and Rybaczewska-Błażejowska 2017). The authors examined regional eco-efficiency as an approach to promote the sustainable transformation of regions of Poland.

Conjoint analysis has been successfully applied within urban planning and development (Smit and McIlravey 1989; Sayadi Gonzalez et al. 2005), particular in studies that examine issues of housing choices and residential preferences (Walker et al. 2002; Molin et al. 1996; Senior and Webster 2004; Gibson 2012; Iman et al. 2012; Orzechowski et al. 2005; Hsee et al. 2008) as well as transport preferences (Bentanzo 2012). However, when it comes to the application of conjoint analysis in determining preferences towards the characteristics of cities as a whole, the literature is quite limited.

Shafranskaya and Potapov (2012) used conjoint analysis to determine respondents' preferences for a city as a whole. Authors have chosen four sets of attributes (Urbanity and Diversity; City Comfort and Safety; Economic Development and Job Chances; City Facilities) to describe the city, and compared creative and non-creative class of respondents in terms of their preferences of particular attributes. They found out that the city should offer more possibilities for professional realization, higher salary, lower criminal level and the higher rates of economic development to the creative group than one average city in the country. The 'ideal' city for the non-creative group is also the city with high salary and low criminal level but additionally it should have the developed leisure industry and appealing image. Authors concluded that the focus has to be paid on economic development of the city, providing the stimulus for medium and small business development, creative industries and entrepreneurship in order to attract and retain the creative group. However, the concentration on leisure, culture and vibrant image may lead to the negative effect and the creative class dissatisfaction.

When it comes to quality of life in the cities of Serbia, several studies have been conducted. Petrić (2013) carried out a theoretical review of residential preferences to urban and suburban areas and the connection with their demographic characteristics. The results of this study have shown that the population would always give priority to life in the area with lower crime rate, less pollution, higher quality and easier accessibility to health system, good education, lower living expenses, better inter-neighbourhood relations and so on. Mirkov (2016) analysed quality of life based on subjective citizens' judgments. However, neither the efficiency of the cities/towns in Serbia has not been analysed so far, nor the preferences of the residents according to certain characteristics of cities as a whole.

3 Theoretical Framework

3.1 Problem Description

The purpose of the paper is to determine the most influential factors related to cities/towns attractiveness and to compare respondents' perception and actual efficiency of the certain cities. There are several research questions we try to answer:

- Which cities from representative set of cities in Serbia are efficient?
- Whether and to what extent the efficiency of cities is changing when considering the ecological dimension?
- Which key factors (characteristics of the city) have the impact on respondents when choosing a city in which they are willing to live and work?
- How are these characteristics perceived for a particular city?
- Whether the respondents' preferences are homogeneous or not?
- Is the respondents' perception to the certain characteristics in accordance with the actual situation?

Answering research questions we have used two methodological approaches: data envelopment analysis for efficiency measurement and conjoint analysis for preference measurement.

3.2 Data Envelopment Analysis

Designing of the performance measurement system assumes taking into account both financial and non-financial indicators. These indicators effect business system key activities (Kaplan and Norton 1996). Neely et al. (1995) define the performance measurement system as 'a set of metrics that allows qualification to efficiency and effectiveness of action'. Performance of the process-oriented system is based on the principle of maximum rationality, which means that the minimum amounts of resources are used to achieve the maximum result (output) (Kahirović 2013).One of the synthetic performance measures that is often used is efficiency. Efficiency is the ratio between the results (outputs) and the inputs (resources). The aim is to maximal results with given inputs or to minimize inputs for given outputs. That means that process of input–output transformation is seen as black box and in the case of one input used for producing one output, efficiency is measured as their ratio (efficiency = input/output). But in the real-world application, efficiency depends on several input and output criteria and efficiency is calculated as the ratio of the sum of the weighted outputs and sum of weighted inputs. Usually, observed inputs and outputs are various in the term of the measures and ranges. This means that efficiency evaluation requires normalization and a priori weight and production input–output function forms determination in the case of set of Decision-Making Units (DMUs) comparison. In order to avoid these problems, Charnes et al. (1978) introduced Data Envelopment Analysis (DEA) as nonparametric technique for assessing efficiency of a set of n observed DMUs. Suppose that DMU_j $(j = 1, \ldots, n)$ uses inputs x_{ij} $(i = 1, \ldots, m)$ to produce outputs y_{rj} $(r = 1, \ldots, s)$. Input-oriented DEA model is given by Eqs. (1–5).

$$(\max)h_k = \sum_{r=1}^{s} u_r y_{rk} \tag{1}$$

s.t

$$\sum_{i=1}^{m} v_i x_{ik} = 1 \tag{2}$$

$$\sum_{r=1}^{s} u_r y_{rj} - \sum_{i=1}^{m} v_i x_{ij} \leq 0, \quad j = 1, \ldots, n \tag{3}$$

$$v_i \geq 0, \; i = 1, \ldots, m \tag{4}$$

$$u_r \geq 0, \quad r = 1, \ldots, s \tag{5}$$

where h_k is the relative efficiency of h_k. The multiplier u_r is the weight assigned to output r $(r = 1, \ldots, s)$ and v_i is the weight assigned to input i $(i = 1, \ldots, m)$ and their optimal values show the importance of each input and output in the efficiency assessment of DMU_k. Model (1–5) is an input-oriented model assuming constant return to scale (CRS). By adding u^* (representing the position of an auxiliary hyperplane which lies at or above all other DMU included in the analysis) to the objective function and the second constraints, the model becomes an input-oriented model

DEA model with an assumption of the Variable Return to Scale (VRS) (Banker et al. 1984).

The results of the model (1–5) and its dual pair can be used to calculate the efficient (target) values of the input and output for the observed DMU_k. This implies the assumption that all inputs and outputs are under the control of the management and that their values can be changed. Another situation occurs when there are exogenously fixed variables (input/output), and it implies that management of the observed unit cannot make the influence—they are not under the control. For example, let us divide a set of inputs I into a set of controllable C and non-controllable variables N ($C \cup N = I$). DEA model with exogenously fixed inputs is modified as follows:

$$(\max)h_k = \sum_{r=1}^{s} u_r y_{rk} - \sum_{i \in N} v_i x_{ij} \tag{6}$$

s.t

$$\sum_{i=1}^{m} v_i x_{ik} = 1 \tag{7}$$

$$\sum_{r=1}^{s} u_r y_{rj} - \sum_{i \in C} v_i x_{ij} - \sum_{i \in N} v_i x_{ij} \le 0, \quad j = 1, \ldots, n \tag{8}$$

$$v_i \ge 0, \quad i = 1, \ldots, m \tag{9}$$

$$u_r \ge 0, \ r = 1, \ldots, s \tag{10}$$

Optimal weights v_i, $i \in N$ should be equal to zero in order to achieve as higher efficiency level as possible.

Regardless of selected DEA model, application procedure consists of following steps:

(1) DMUs selecting;
(2) Inputs and outputs selection;
(3) DEA analysis;
(4) Results interpretation, application and verification.

This procedure is followed in application to evaluating residential efficiency (attractiveness) of selected cities in the Republic of Serbia.

3.3 *Conjoint Analysis*

Conjoint analysis, sometimes called 'trade-off analysis', reveals how people make complex judgments. The technique assumes that complex decisions involve not only one factor or criterion, but rather several factors 'considered jointly' (Kuzmanovic et al. 2013a). It is based on the simple premise that consumers evaluate the value of a product or service by combining the utilities provided by each product attribute. Therefore, conjoint analysis enables better understanding the interrelationship of multiple factors as they contribute to the preferences.

Conjoint analysis originated in mathematical psychology, and was first introduced in marketing research in the early 1970s to evaluate consumer preferences for hypothetical products and services. Nowadays, it is widely used to understand customers' preferences towards services and products in various markets (Kuzmanovic et al. 2013b; Rao 2014).

Conjoint experiments involve individuals being asked to express their preference for various experimentally designed, real or hypothetical alternatives. These hypothetical alternatives are descriptions of potential real-world alternatives in terms of their most relevant features, or attributes; hence, they are multi-attribute alternatives (Vukic et al. 2015). Two or more fixed values, or 'levels', are defined for each attribute, and these are combined to create different alternatives so-called profiles (options, concepts or scenarios).

In forming stimuli, a fractional factorial design reduces the number of profiles that have to be evaluated, while ensuring enough data are available for statistical analyses, which result in a carefully controlled set of profiles for the consideration of the respondents (Iman et al. 2012).

Conjoint analysis produces two important results: utility of attribute levels (so-called part-worths) and relative importance of attributes. Part-worth utility is a numerical expression of the value consumers place in an attribute level. It represents the relative 'worth' of the attribute. Low utility indicates less value and high utility indicates more value (Kuzmanovic et al. 2013b).

The general model for estimating part-worth utilities with respect to a certain combination of product attributes can be specified as follows:

$$U_{ij} = \sum_{k=1}^{K} \sum_{l=1}^{L_k} \beta_{ikl} x_{jkl} + \varepsilon_{ij}, \quad i = 1, \ldots, I, \quad j = 1, \ldots, J \tag{11}$$

where U_{ij} is respondent i's evaluation of a given profile j, β_{ikl} is respondent i's utility (part-worths) associated with the lth level of the kth attribute, K is a number of attributes, $xjkl$ is the independent variable, which indicates the presence ($x_{jkl} = 1$) or absence ($x_{jkl} = 0$) of the lth level of the kth attribute in the jth profile and ε_{ij} is a stochastic error term. Given that each profile may include only one level of each attribute, next requirement must be fulfilled:

$$\sum_{l=1}^{L_k} x_{jkl} = 1, \quad j = 1, \ \ldots, \ J, \quad k = 1, \ \ldots, \ K. \tag{12}$$

Equation (11) is estimated by using the Ordinary Least Squares (OLS) technique. This technique decomposes respondent preferences to derive the part-worths (regression coefficient) for each attribute level.

Part-worths are expressed in a common unit, allowing them to be added together to give the total utility, or overall preference, for any combination of attribute levels. Given that part-worth utilities are calculated at the individual level, it can be used for preference-based segmentation. Respondents who place similar value to the various attribute levels will be grouped together into a segment (Vukic et al. 2015).

Part-worths are also used to calculate each attribute's relative importance (RAI). These values are calculated by taking the utility range for each attribute separately and then dividing it by the sum of the utility ranges for all of the attributes.

$$RAI_{ik} = \frac{\max\{\beta_{ik1}, \beta_{ik2}, \ldots \beta_{ikL_k}\} - \min\{\beta_{ik1}, \beta_{ik2}, \ldots \beta_{ikL_k}\}}{\sum_{k=1}^{K} (\max\{\beta_{ik1}, \beta_{ik2}, \ldots \beta_{ikL_k}\} - \min\{\beta_{ik1}, \beta_{ik2}, \ldots \beta_{ikL_k}\})} \times 100,$$

$$i = 1, \ldots, I, \quad k = 1, \ldots, K \tag{13}$$

The results are then averaged to include either all the respondents belonging to a priori identified segments or respondents with similar preferences (Kuzmanovic et al. 2013b).

4 Empirical Study

Empirical study is designed to evaluate residential attractiveness of the cities in Serbia as cities' relative efficiency from one hand and citizens' perception and opinion regarding living conditions from the other hand. In the first phase, the residential attractiveness is evaluated by DEA with the aim to establish differences between capital and big cities and inner cities. In the next phase, the survey among city residents is conducted in order to analyse their perception and preferences. Finally, the differences between results of quantitative models, importance of criteria for cities' attractiveness and residents' preferences are analysed.

4.1 Data Collection and Criteria Selection for Attractiveness Evaluation

In the first step, we selected 15 towns to represent the regions in Republic of Serbia. Selection is made according to the reports of Belgrade Chamber of Commerce (http://www.kombeg.org.rs/). The set of cities consists of medium and big cites with different levels of development. In contrast to capital and big cites which are cultural and economic centres of Serbia, there are inner cities which have traditionally been related to deteriorating as well as physically and demographically ageing. Therefore, the study captures wide range of cities in terms of economical and social development. To evaluate cities' attractiveness from the aspect of efficiency, we have defined two data input–output scenarios shown in Table 1.

Both input–output scenarios use the same input variables. Scenario 1 is created to measure the attractiveness of cites from the financial aspect and uses statistical data of prices of flat ranting and housing together with consumer basket per month as inputs with just one output—average monthly income.

Scenario 2 is defined considering that other aspects of well-being. The pollution rate is added in as the important measure of the life quality from the 'green' ecological and health aspect. The pollution is expressed as the μg of watts per cubic metre of air. All data for the 2012 are captured from the reports of Institute for Public Health of Serbia 'Dr. Milan Jovanovic Batut', or their Center for Hygiene and Human Ecology (2016). The pollution is treated as an undesirable output and converted to exogenously fixed input. The goal of the analysis was to compare the results of two scenarios—city attractiveness from financial and mixed financial-ecological aspects and to show how changing of just one, non-financial parameter can drastically change the results of efficiency-attractiveness analysis. Input and output data are given in Table 2.

4.2 Conjoint Study Design

As conjoint analysis identifies the preference to the subject, we describe the city through the bundle of attributes. They are the characteristics, which are perceived by the residents during the process of city evaluation. In this study, attributes have been selected so that they largely coincide with the inputs and outputs used to measure the attractiveness of cities from the aspect of efficiency. On the other hand, there are attributes seen as particularly important to the young population. Therefore, these attributes would be placed in the research focus. As a result, six attributes of cities and corresponding levels were identified (Table 3).

Four levels were assigned to the attribute Size of the city. Belgrade, the capital and the only millionth city in Serbia, was taken as one of the levels. Belgrade is also the largest university centre in Serbia. The remaining three levels are defined according to the size of cities in Serbia, and cover a set of selected representative

Table 1 Scenarios

Inputs	Scenario1	Scenario 2
	Outputs	Outputs
Flat renting (50 m^2 in RSD)	Average monthly income (in RSD)	Average monthly income (in RSD)
Housing (50 m^2 in RSD)		Pollution rate
Monthly consumer basket (in RSD)		

Table 2 DEA inputs and outputs

DMUs	Flat renting	Housing	Monthly consumer basket	Average monthly income	Pollution rate (μg/m3)
Belgrade	31.728	147.850	68.862	54.311	21
Pančevo	13.904	61.320	71.532	49.788	23
Novi Sad	25.304	100.991	72.833	49.165	13
Kragujevac	20.213	87.120	65.719	44.057	18
Užice	9.923	83.658	63.757	42.973	52
Šabac	16.170	85.443	70.543	41.945	20
Zrenjanin	11.209	60.949	73.175	41.562	49
Subotica	20.213	70.156	60.772	41.119	14
Sremska Mitrovica	16.783	77.921	68.321	40.104	4
Zaječar	14.088	60.607	62.592	39.789	21
Niš	17.701	79.341	62.818	39.750	15
Smederevo	20.886	87.564	63.344	37.795	24
Kraljevo	14.945	76.763	59.498	37.740	11
Valjevo	11.393	86.265	60.962	36.405	13
Leskovac	10.535	69.535	57.969	34.251	44

Table 3 Key cities'attributes and corresponding levels

No.	Attribute	Attribute levels
1.	City/town size (population)	Small (up to 40,000 residents) Medium (from 40,000 to 80,000 residents) Large (over 80,000 residents) Belgrade
2.	Average monthly income (per household member)	40,000 RSD 50,000 RSD 60,000 RSD 70,000 RSD
3.	Rental price for residential space	100 €/month 150 €/month 200 €/month 250 €/month
4.	Consumer basket	35,000 RSD 45,000 RSD 55,000 RSD 65,000 RSD
5.	Cultural offer	Rich Poor
6.	Entertainment offer	Rich Poor

cities in the study. For the attribute average monthly income per household member, the levels were determined based on the results of the survey 'Earnings per Employee in the Republic of Serbia by Municipalities and Cities, January 2016' conducted by the Statistical Office of the Republic of Serbia in March 2016 (Republički zavod za statistiku 2016). Levels for the attribute Rental price of residential space are determined based on the data from the web site for real estate 'imovina.net' (imovina.net 2016). Research 'Purchasing power of residents; Consumer basket' conducted by the Ministry of Trade, Tourism and Telecommunications (Ministarstvo trgovine turizma i telekomunikacija 2016) has been used to determine the levels of attribute Consumer basket. The last two attributes, Cultural and Entertainment offer, have clearly defined attributes, rich and poor offer.

The attributes and levels in Table 3 gave rise to 1024 possible profiles ($4^4 \times 2^2$). Therefore, fractional factorial experimental design was used in this study. A component of the statistical package SPSS (Orthoplan) was used to reduce the possible number of profiles to a manageable level, while still allowing the preferences to be inferred for all of the combinations of levels and attributes. The use of Orthoplan results in an orthogonal main effects design, thus ensuring the absence of multicollinearity between attributes. Through the use of this design, the 1024 possible profiles were reduced to 16 (see Table 4).

In order to elicit the preferences for the various profiles in this study, a rating approach was utilized. Respondents were presented with each of the 16 hypothetical cities, and were asked to state their level of preference for each of them on a Likert's scale of 1 to 5, where 1 indicated 'absolutely unattractive', and 5 indicated 'exceptionally attractive'.

Data were collected online through a web-based questionnaire. Besides conjoint analysis questions, the questionnaire included demographic data, but also questions related to the respondents' perception of key conjoint attributes for 15 towns previously selected as representative for the regions in Republic of Serbia.

Namely, due to the fact that sometimes people perceive goods as bad and thus make wrong choices, we attempted to compare the respondents' perception of certain cities with a real situation. Therefore, we asked respondents the questions such as in which of the 15 cities they would prefer to live; in their opinion, which of those cities offers the greatest opportunities for employment, which one is most situated for young population to live in, which one has the richest cultural and entertainment offer and which one is the cheapest.

5 Results Analysis and Discussion

5.1 DEA Residential Attractiveness of Cities

By applying DEA model (1–5) on input and output data specified in Scenario 1, we found that relatively efficient (attractive) cities are Pančevo, Užice and Belgrade. This

Table 4 Orthogonal experimental design

No.	City size	Monthly income	Rental price	Consumer basket	Cultural offer	Entertainment offer
1.	Medium	60,000 RSD	250 €/month	65,000 RSD	Rich	Rich
2.	Belgrade	50,000 RSD	200 €/month	55,000 RSD	Rich	Rich
3.	Small	50,000 RSD	150 €/month	65,000 RSD	Rich	Poor
4.	Belgrade	40,000 RSD	250 €/month	45,000 RSD	Rich	Poor
5.	Medium	40,000 RSD	150 €/month	55,000 RSD	Poor	Poor
6.	Belgrade	60,000 RSD	150 €/month	35,000 RSD	Poor	Rich
7.	Large	50,000 RSD	250 €/month	35,000 RSD	Poor	Poor
8.	Medium	50,000 RSD	100 €/month	45,000 RSD	Poor	Rich
9.	Large	70,000 RSD	150 €/month	45,000 RSD	Rich	Rich
10.	Large	60,000 RSD	100 €/month	55,000 RSD	Rich	Poor
11.	Small	70,000 RSD	250 €/month	55,000 RSD	Poor	Rich
12.	Belgrade	70,000 RSD	100 €/month	65,000 RSD	Poor	Poor
13.	Large	40,000 RSD	200 €/month	65,000 RSD	Poor	Rich
14.	Medium	70,000 RSD	200 €/month	35,000 RSD	Rich	Poor
15.	Small	60,000 RSD	200 €/month	45,000 RSD	Poor	Poor
16.	Small	40,000 RSD	100 €/month	35,000 RSD	Rich	Rich

Scenario 1 is defined for efficiency evaluation using financial factors. The influential input factors are different as expected. For example, Belgrade chooses only monthly consumer basket (weight equal to 1) which is relatively comparable with other cities, especially if a higher average monthly income is taken into account. On the other hand, relatively high value of inputs flat renting and housing is ignored. Pančevo is a financially attractive town due to the low price of housing while Užice can be considered as relatively attractive from financial aspect due to relatively low flat renting price.

Table 5 City ranks based on efficiency

City (DMU)	Scenario 1		Scenario 2	
	Efficiency	Rank	Efficiency	Rank
Pančevo	1,200	1	1,292	2
Užice	1,171	2	1,171	3
Belgrade	1,133	3	1,145	4
Zrenjanin	0,983	4	0,983	8
Subotica	0,943	5	0,992	7
Novi Sad	0,920	6	1,023	6
Kragujevac	0,919	7	0,932	10
Zaječar	0,903	8	0,903	12
Kraljevo	0,886	9	0,970	9
Niš	0,873	10	0,904	11
Valjevo	0,863	11	1,043	5
Leskovac	0,858	12	0,858	13
Šabac	0,840	13	0,840	14
Sremska Mitrovica	0,822	14	big	1
Smederevo	0,813	15	0,813	15

The experience and perception survey done as an extension of this study indicate that decision which is the best place to live depends not only on financial but on intangible factors too. Therefore, next Scenario 2 takes pollution as an undesirable output (exogenously fixed input) into account. By applying DEA model (6–10), results show the increasing number of efficient cities/towns: Belgrade, Pančevo, Novi Sad, Užice, Sremska Mitrovica and Valjevo.

Table 5 shows the efficiency and ranks of cities for both scenarios. The results are changed by adding only one undesirable output (pollution). The best example is the Sremska Mitrovica, with all average inputs and outputs for Scenario 1, it was ranked 14 out of 15 cities. With addition of only one input with the 'best' value (smallest pollution), it has become the most efficient city. Only one city, Novi Sad has not changed its rank after the introduction of a new parameter. City of Valjevo has shown the biggest shift, which climbed from eleventh to fifth place and therefore it became an efficient city. Three cities fell down, Zrenjanin drop down from fourth to eighth place, Kragujevac, dropped from seventh to tenth and Zajecar dropped from eighth to twelfth place.

For all efficient cities/towns (Scenario 2), excluding Užice, one of the most influential factors is low pollution. It affects efficiency scores rising in comparison to results of Scenario 1. On the contrary, Uzice has a high level of pollution and therefore this input is ignored in the maximizing efficiency level. Figure 1 shows the structure of the input weights for each of the observed cities/towns. The second conclusion is that weight structure and consequently input factor influence is changed in Scenario 2 for all cities/towns with dramatic change in rank and efficiency level. For

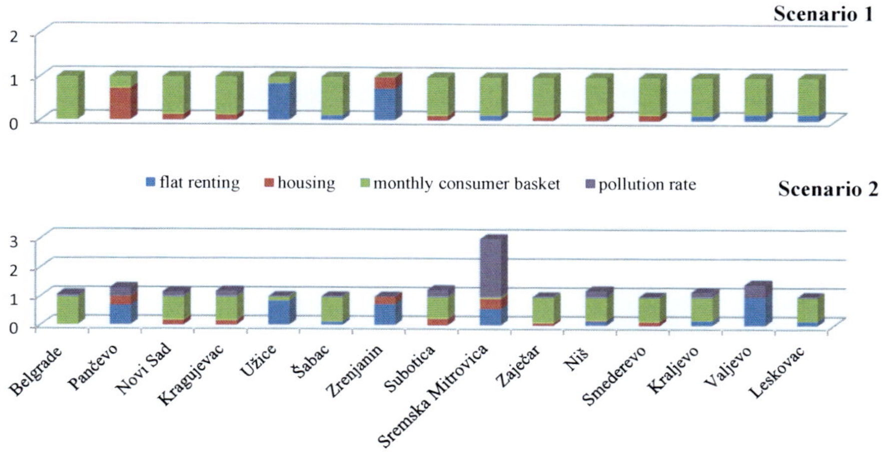

Fig. 1 Input weights diversity—Scenario 1 and Scenario 2

example, Fig. 1 shows that housing is the most influential factor, followed by monthly consumer basket for Pančevo, according to Scenario 1. On the other hand, Scenario 2 prioritizes pollution, flat ranting and housing for the same town. Scenario 1 prefers monthly consumer basket as the most influential input for Valjevo while Scenario 2 gives priorities to low price of flat ranting and pollution. Similar conclusion can be made for cities: Sremska Mitrovica, Niš and Kraljevo.

5.2 *Analysis of Preferences and Perception*

Sample Characteristic

The survey was fielded during the period of July and August, 2016. The only eligibility criterion was that the respondents were 18 years of age or older. In total, 400 individuals completed the survey. However, six responses (1.5%) were excluded since those respondents filled in the questionnaire in a monotonous pattern (e.g. marking all profiles as 1 or 2). Thus, the total number of valid questionnaires was 394 (98.5%), giving a total of 6304 observations.

The sample consisted of 136 (34.5%) male and 258 (65.5%) female participants, aged 22.63 (SD = 4.5) in average. The great percent of the respondents currently live in Belgrade, 258 (65.5%), followed by Novi Sad (18.6%), Subotica 17 (4.3%) and Obrenovac 8 (2.0%). The sample is more heterogeneous when it comes to the place of permanent residence, with the most respondents from Belgrade139 (35.3%), followed by Aleksandrovac 21 (5.3%), Vrbas 13 (3.3%), Novi Sad 12 (3%) and Kraljevo 10 (2.5%). Other cities are less represented. A detailed demographic structure of the sample is shown in Table 6.

Table 6 Demographic data

Variable	Description	Count (n = 394)	Percentage (%)
Gender	Male	136	34.5
	Female	258	65.5
Occupation	Student (high school)	9	2.3
	Student (university)	307	77.9
	Employed	65	16.5
	Unemployed	13	3.3
Education level	Primary school	3	0.8
	High school	247	62.7
	Bachelor	98	24.9
	Master	45	11.4
	PhD	1	0.3
Marital status	Single	222	56.3
	In relationship	147	37.3
	Married	25	6.3
Family with children	Without children	375	95.2
	One child	8	2
	Two or more children	11	2.8
Monthly income (per household member)	<21000 RSD	115	29.2
	from 21000 to 42000 RSD	140	35.5
	from 42000 to 60000 RSD	68	17.3
	>60000 RSD	71	18%

Table 7 Correlation between the observed and estimated preferences

	Value	Sig.
Pearson's R	1.000	0.000
Kendall's tau	1.000	0.000

Respondents' Preferences

To estimate the parameters of the model, the statistical package SPSS 20.0 (Conjoint procedure) was used. The parameters were estimated for each respondent in the sample individually (individual preferences), as well as for the total sample (averaged preferences). The goodness of fit statistics for the estimated models is reported in Table 7. A high value of the Pearson and Kendall correlation coefficients confirms the high level of significance of the obtained results and indicates a high level of correlation between the observed and estimated preferences.

Averaged part-worths for attribute levels are given in Table 8 while the relative importance of the attributes are shown in Fig. 2.

Results shown in Fig. 2 suggest that the average monthly income is the most important attribute (RAI = 21.35%) when choosing a city for a live in. The attribute

Table 8 Aggregate-level analysis (averaged results)

No.	Attribute	Attribute levels	Part-worths	Standard deviation
1.	City/Town size (by population)	Small	−0.257	0.007
		Medium	0.053	0.007
		Large	**0.154**	0.007
		Belgrade	0.050	0.007
2.	Average monthly income	40,000 RSD	−0.558	0.007
		50,000 RSD	−0.018	0.007
		60,000 RSD	0.189	0.007
		70,000 RSD	**0.387**	0.007
3.	Rental price for residential space	100 €/month	0.095	0.007
		150 €/month	**0.177**	0.007
		200 €/month	−0.129	0.007
		250 €/month	−0.143	0.007
4.	Consumer basket	**35,000 RSD**	**0.165**	0.007
		45,000 RSD	0.071	0.007
		55,000 RSD	0.046	0.007
		65,000 RSD	−0.281	0.007
5.	Cultural offer	**Rich**	**0.354**	0.004
		Poor	−0.354	0.004
6.	Entertainment offer	**Rich**	**0.364**	0.004
		Poor	−0.364	0.004
	Constant		2.953	

'Size of city' (RAI = 19.78%) is of slightly smaller importance, while the cultural and entertainment offer are the least important attributes (13.98% and 13.43%, respectively).

The signs of the regression coefficients given in Table 8 were all as expected, including the negative coefficient for the lowest levels of attributes. Furthermore, part-worths utility for the attribute Average monthly income increases with the increase in the level of this attribute, while the part-worths of the attribute Consumer basket decreases with an increasing value of this attribute, as it was expected.

On average, the most attractive for living and working is a large city, and the least attractive is a small one. Belgrade and a medium-sized city are almost equally attractive. Although cultural and entertainment offer has the least impact on the

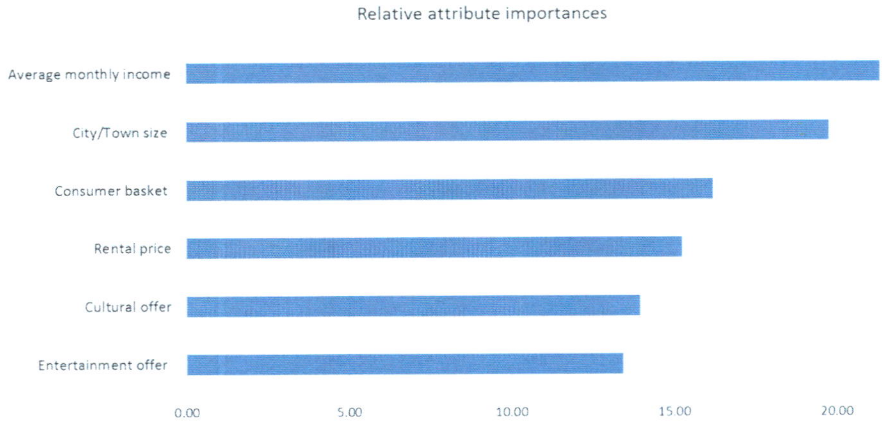

Fig. 2 Averaged relative importance of attributes

attractiveness of the city, part-worths utilities of the levels of those attributes were as expected, the respondents stated greater preferences towards a richer offer.

Looking at both, attribute importance and value of the part-worth utilities, it is possible to describe a city that is most attractive for respondents in terms of their preferences. It is a large city (with population over 80,000 residents), with average monthly income of more than 70000 RSD and consumer basket of at most 35000 RSD, where rental price is about 150 Euros, while there is a rich cultural and entertainment offer.

Using the part-worth utility model (11), the total utility for 15 selected cities can be determined from the combinations of corresponding part-worths given in Table 7. As it could be seen from Fig. 3, the city with the highest total utility is Kragujevac, followed by Belgrade.

In order to identify whether there are differences among the preferences of certain subgroups of the respondents, the a priori segmentation was carried out on variables that were predetermined (known in advance):

- Gender. The assumption was that women would consider the Consumer Basket the most important attribute, and that men would prefer entertainment offer over cultural offer.
- Place of permanent residence. The assumption was that the respondents from Belgrade would give greater importance to entertainment and cultural content than would be done by respondents who are not from Belgrade.
- Depending on if the respondents are parents. The assumption was that respondents who are parents would give greater importance to economic factors, while respondents who do not have children would attach somewhat greater importance to cultural and entertainment city offer.

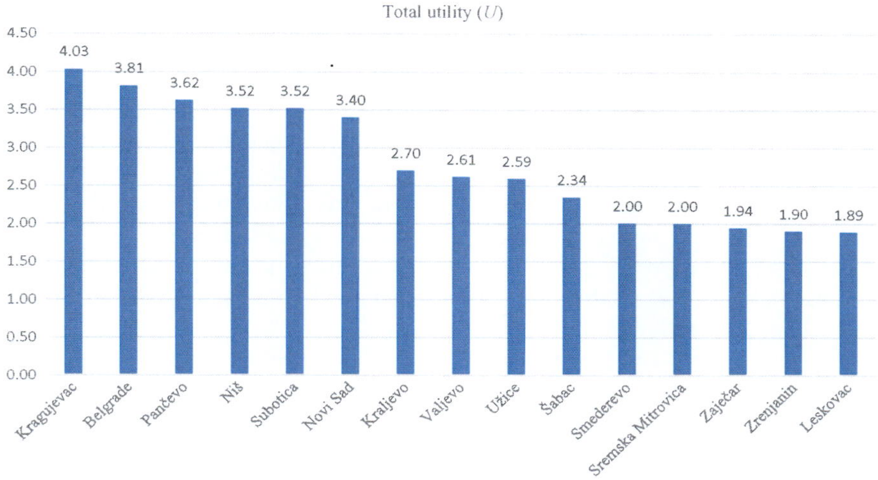

Fig. 3 Total utilities for the selected cities

Table 9 Preferences of a priori defined segments

	Relative attribute importance						
Attribute	Averaged	Male	Female	Belgrade	Out of Bel-grade	Parents	Not a parents
Monthly income	21.35	21.95	21.03	21.29	21.38	26.97	21.06
City/town size	19.78	19.84	19.74	19.84	19.74	18.75	19.29
Consumer basket	16.20	15.83	16.40	15.76	16.45	13.92	16.22
Rental price	15.26	15.71	15.03	14.59	15.63	16.09	15.22
Cultural offer	13.98	12.80	14.60	13.91	14.02	12.55	14.05
Entertainment offer	13.43	13.87	13.19	14.62	12.78	11.73	13.51

We estimated the part-worth utility model for each subgroup separately, but no significant differences among the segments and averaged data for whole sample in terms of the importance of attributes were observed (see Table 9).

However, there were some minor differences in segment level preferences that partly confirmed our assumptions. Especially interesting is the segment of respondents who are parents. Namely, this segment emphasizes the importance of the attributes Monthly income and Rental price, while the Entertainment offer is significantly less important for them. Also, both, the assumption that the female segment attaches greater importance to the Cultural offer than other segments and that

Belgrade inhabitants prefer the entertainment offer more than other segments, were confirmed.

Despite there is no statistical significant difference between segment level and averaged results in terms of attribute importance, there are some differences when it comes to attribute levels. Namely, respondents with permanent residence in Belgrade prefigure Belgrade as a place of their life, but also positively assess the city. Other respondents prefer a large city, and somewhat less a medium-sized town, while Belgrade is in third place according to its attractiveness. Respondents with children equally prefer medium-sized and large cities, while they showed negative preferences towards Belgrade and small towns. On the other hand, respondents without children prefer a big city, followed by Belgrade.

A more detailed analysis of individual utilities revealed wide heterogeneity in respondents' preferences. Therefore, a cluster analysis was performed to classify respondents into more homogeneous preference groups. Individual-level part-worths are used as input for cluster analysis.

The k-means cluster procedure in SPSS 2.0 was used to perform the segmentation. Based on the sample size, the solutions were searched in two, three and four clusters. The three-cluster solution was chosen due to the size of the segments and statistical significance. An analysis of variance has revealed that the segments in the three-cluster solution differed significantly from each other, with respect to their part-worths.

The part-worths for each of the levels of the attributes of the three segments are given in Table 10, while the importance scores of the attributes are shown in Fig. 4.

Figure 4 shows specific differences between isolated segments. Members of the first, and also the smallest segment (23.35% of the entire sample) assign the greatest importance to the size of the city and at the same time would like to choose Belgrade for living and working. Members of the second segment (34.77% of the entire sample) are respondents who attribute the greatest importance to the cultural and entertainment offer (36.74% and 27.39%, respectively). For the members of this segment, the size of the city as the consumer basket is almost irrelevant factors, as long as the cultural needs and the need for entertainment are met. The third segment is the largest one with 41.87% of total sample. For the respondents belonging to this segment, it can be said that they are cost sensitive, because they attach the highest importance to the attributes average monthly income per household member (32.74%) and consumer basket (19.42%). Rental price is a negligible important attribute for all segments, and its relative importance ranges from 7.84 to 11%.

Respondents belonging to three identified segments prefer to live and work in cities with the characteristics given in Table 11. The factors (attributes) are sorted by their impact on total preferences.

Respondents' Perception

More than half of the respondents perceive Belgrade as the city where they would most like to live (57.6%), the city with the highest employment opportunities (89.3%), with the best living conditions for young people (68.5%), the richest cultural (70.1%) and entertainment (82%) offer. Immediately after Belgrade, respondents considered that in terms of cultural and entertainment offer (18% and 13%, respectively), as well

Table 10 Segment-level part-worth utilities and cluster solutions significance

Attribute/attribute level	Part-worths			Sig. (three-claster solution)
	Segment 1 (n = 92)	Segment 2 (n = 137)	Segment 3 (n = 165)	
City/Town size (by population)				
Small	−0.96	**0.05**	−0.13	0.000
Medium	−0.16	**0.03**	**0.19**	0.000
Large	**0.41**	−0.06	**0.19**	0.000
Belgrade	**0.71**	−0.03	−0.25	0.000
Average monthly income				
40,000 RSD	−0.52	−0.29	−0.81	0.000
50,000 RSD	**0.10**	**0.06**	−0.15	0.000
60,000 RSD	**0.21**	**0.08**	**0.27**	0.000
70,000 RSD	**0.21**	**0.15**	**0.69**	0.000
Rental price for residential space				
100 €/month	−0.07	0.01	**0.26**	**0.000**
150 €/month	**0.24**	**0.15**	0.17	0.178
200 €/month	−0.02	−0.06	−0.24	0.000
250 €/month	−0.14	−0.09	−0.19	0.049
Consumer basket				
35,000 RSD	0.08	−0.06	**0.40**	0.000
45,000 RSD	**0.17**	−0.05	0.12	0.000
55,000 RSD	0.14	**0.07**	−0.02	0.000
65,000 RSD	−0.39	0.04	−0.49	0.000
Cultural offer				
Rich	**0.34**	**0.46**	**0.27**	0.000
Poor	−0.34	−0.46	−0.27	0.000
Entertainment offer				
Rich	**0.42**	**0.34**	**0.35**	0.077
Poor	−0.42	−0.34	−0.35	0.077

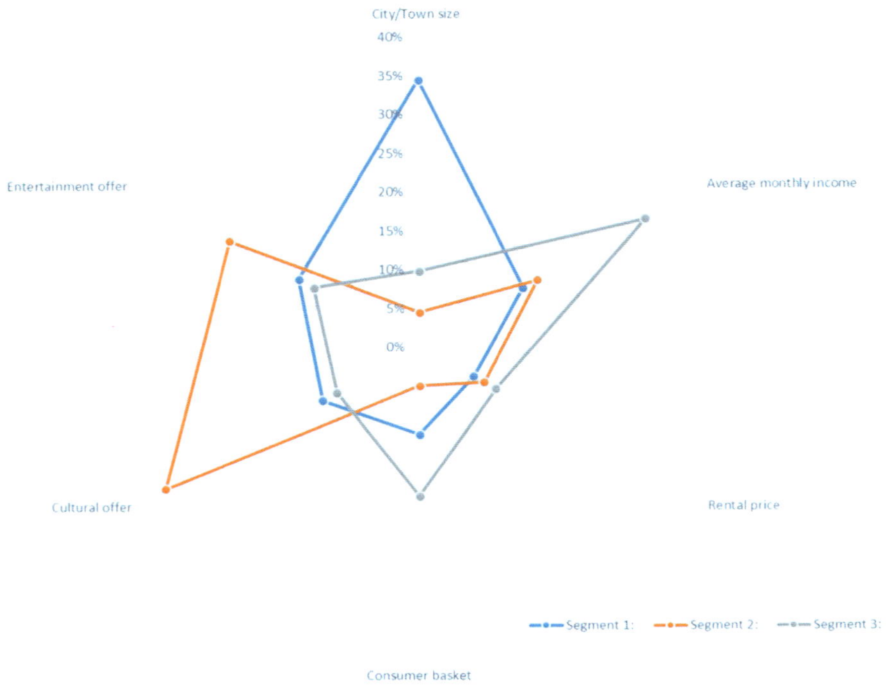

Fig. 4 Segment-level attribute importance

Table 11 The profile of respondents based on observed differences in preferences

Impact of factor	Segment 1	Segment 2	Segment 3
High	Belgrade	Rich cultural offer	Average monthly income of at least 70,000 RSD
	Rich entertainment offer	Rich entertainment offer	Consumer basket of at most 35,000 RSD
	Average monthly income of at least 60,000 RSD	Average monthly income of at least 70,000 RSD	Rich entertainment offer
	Rich cultural offer	Rental price of 150 Euros	Rich cultural offer
	Consumer basket of at most 35,000 RSD	Consumer basket of at most 55,000 RSD	Rental price of 100 Euros
Low	Rental price of 150 Euros	Small town	Middle-sized or large city

Table 12 Respondents' perception regarding pollution

Actual rank	City/town	Which city is the most polluted in your opinion?		DEA rank (Scenario 2)
		Respondents'#	Respondents'(%)	
1	Užice	11	2.8	3
2	Zrenjanin	2	0.5	8
3	Leskovac	2	0.5	13
4	Smederevo	3	0.8	15
5	Pančevo	244	62.0	2
6	Belgrade	102	25.9	4
7	Zaječar	/	/	12
8	Šabac	3	0.8	14
9	Kragujevac	2	0.5	10
10	Niš	2	0.5	11
11	Subotica	1	0.3	7
12	Novi Sad	5	1.3	6
13	Valjevo	2	0.5	5
14	Kraljevo	1	0.3	9
15	Sremska Mitrovica	2	0.5	1

as good conditions for the young people to live (23.1%), Novi Sad stands out, which is also a city in which a large number of respondents liked to live (20.8%).

The wrong perception was recorded when the respondents were asked to indicate which city perceive as the most polluted. Whether due to the unpopularity of the refinery in Pančevo or Užice is considered as an unpolluted city due to the proximity of one of the popular mountain Zlatibor has not been examined yet. But whatever it is, the results showed that Užice, which has the highest pollution among Serbian cities, perceives only by 2.8% of the respondents as such. On the other hand, as many as 244 respondents, more precisely 62% of them consider Pančevo as the most polluted city in Serbia, regardless of the fact that it is actually fifth placed. As a much polluted city, 25.9% of respondents perceive Belgrade, regardless of its sixth placed in terms of actual pollution.

A comparative analysis of the perception of the respondents, the actual conditions and results obtained by the DEA model are presented in Tables 12 and 13.

Even 62% and 25.9% of respondents are assessed efficient cities Pančevo and Belgrade as the most polluted ones (see Table 12). The mayor of respondents, 93%, have answered that six efficient cities (Sremska Mitrovica, Pančevo, Užice, Belgrade, Valjevo and Novi Sad) are polluted, while only 3.1 of them correspond inefficient cities (Kragujevac, Niš, Zaječar, Leskovac, Šabac, Smederevo) as the most polluted. The conclusion may be that quality of life is not a crucial factor in assessing the efficiency or attractiveness of cities. A low pollution has a significant impact only

Table 13 Respondents' perceptions to the cheapest

Actual rank	City/town	Which city is the cheapest in your opinion?		DEA rank (Scenario1)
		Respondents'#	Respondents' (%)	
1	Zaječar	14	3.6	8
2	Leskovac	107	27.2	12
3	Zrenjanin	10	2.5	4
4	Pančevo	7	1.8	1
5	Subotica	15	3.8	5
6	Kraljevo	26	6.6	9
7	Užice	18	4.6	2
8	Valjevo	20	5.1	11
9	Niš	42	10.7	10
10	Sremska Mitrovica	19	4.8	14
11	Smederevo	6	1.5	15
12	Šabac	11	2.8	13
13	Kragujevac	11	2.8	7
14	Novi Sad	17	4.3	6
15	Belgrade	11	2.8	3

in the case of Sremska Mitrovica, which is ranked on the first place due to this characteristic.

A less wrong perception is perceived in the case of understanding which city is the cheapest for life. Only 3.6% of respondents really think that the cheapest city of Zaječar is the most refined. Nevertheless, Leskovac is placed immediately behind Zaječar when it comes to favourable prices for buying and leasing residential space as well as the low price of the consumer basket was estimated to be the cheapest by 27.2% of respondents. Detailed results are presented in Table 13, and cities are ranked from the cheapest to the most expensive one (the sum of rental prices for housing, buying of housing and consumer basket prices used as input for the DEA methodology).

Leskovac was declared as the cheapest city by survey respondents. This city as the cheapest perceives as many as 27.20% of respondents, while all three cities (Pančevo, Užice and Belgrade) that are declared as efficient basis of a financial factor by the DEA model are perceived the cheapest only by 9.2% of respondents. This is almost three times less than the number of respondents who perceived Leskovac as the cheapest one even though it has a ranking of 12.

Again, it can be concluded that efficiency/attractiveness of city is a combination of several input and output factors and that, for example, Belgrade is ranked at third place, regardless of how expensive it is. Attractiveness makes high outputs, i.e. the possibility of earning in the observed city.

6 Conclusion

The migration from village and smaller to bigger cities and emigration of young people has an increasing trend in our society. In the past, the villages have had far more density of population. Nowadays, the Serb villages, especially those in the mountainous regions, began to shake off, and the most of the population moved to cities. Negative migration balance in smaller towns is recorded, while Belgrade and Novi Sad are predominant with a positive migration balance. The question arises whether the cities with a positive migration balance are at the same time efficient and whether they are really the best for life when considering the financial and non-financial health factor. In this paper, the DEA methodology was used to determine the efficiency and attractiveness of cities in Serbia. When it comes to the financial factor, DEA proclaimed three larger cities as the most efficient: Pančevo, Užice and Belgrade. The next scenario includes the pollution of cities as one of the inputs and the six efficient cities were acquired: Sremska Mitrovica, Pancevo, Uzice, Belgrade, Valjevo and Novi Sad.

The research implies that DEA as an objective method gives data-driven results and depends on used inputs and outputs as well as DMUs included into analysis. The research also indicates that results of first scenario are more suitable for person who is more cost-benefit oriented and do not care a lot about other living conditions in the cities. Therefore, big sites such as Belgrade and relatively low-cost cities such as Uzice and Pančevo are the best picks for them. On the other hand, person who cares about health condition more will consider results of the Scenario 2 and prefer smaller city (town) of Sremska Mitrovica as their place of residence.

The survey of preferences of inhabitants results in three segments of respondents. Their preferences depend on their habits and social and marital status. For example, the most favourable place for living is large city with average monthly income and consumer basket, small rental price and a rich cultural and entertainment offer. But parents prefer smaller city and single prefers big city with a rich cultural and entertainment offer. On the other hand, perception of residents towards pollution and living cost level does not coincide with efficiency level results obtained by DEA but it does not coincide with real situation too. The results of this study are useful for decision-maker to identify the important characteristics of cities and sources of inefficiency as well as direction of improvement in population policy.

References

Alfonso Piña WH, Pardo Martinez CI (2016) Development and urban sustainability: an analysis of efficiency using data envelopment analysis. Sustainability 8(2):148

Banker RD, Charnes A, Cooper WW (1984) Some models for estimating technical and scale inefficiencies in data envelopment analysis. Manage Sci 30(9):1078–1092

Bentanzo D (2012) Preference planning and unsustainable desires: a hypothesis toward 'How' contextual and psychological factors influence travel attitudes through qualitative and quantitative measures. Victoria University of Wellington. Faculty of Architecture and Design

Bernarf J, Cantner U (1997) French regional performance and variety. A non-parametric frontier approach. In: 37th Congress of the European Regional Science Association, Rome
Bianco V, Righi D, Scarpa LF, Tagliafico L (2017) Modeling energy consumption and efficiency measures in the Italian hotel sector. Energy Build 149:329–338
Center for Hygiene and Human Ecology (2016) Retrieved 2017 from Institute for Public Health of Serbia "Dr. Milan Jovanovic Batut". http://www.batut.org.rs
Chang P, Hwang S, Cheng W (1995) Using data envelopment analysis to measure the achievement and change of regional development in Taiwan. J Environ Manage 43:49–66
Charnes A, Cooper WW, Rhodes E (1978) Measuring the efficiency of Decision Makin Units. Eur J Oper Res 2:429–444
Charnes A, Cooper W, Li S (1989) Using data envelopment analysis to evaluate efficiency in the economic performance of Chinese cities. Socio-Econ Plan Sci 23(6):325–344
Chen CC (2017) Measuring departmental and overall regional performance: applying the multi-activity DEA model to Taiwan's cities/counties. Omega 67:60–80
Gibson S (2012) Residential preferences versus (sustainable) planning policy: conjoint analysis in the town of Berkhamsted. King's College London, London
Halkos G, Tzeremes N (2013) A conditional directional distance function approach for measuring regional environmental efficiency: evidence from UK regions. Eur J Oper Res 227(1):182–189
Hsee C, Dube J, Zhang Y (2008) The prominence effect in shanghai apartment prices. J Mark Res 67(April):1–22
Iman A, Pieng F, Gan C (2012) A conjoint analysis of buyers' preferences for residential property. Int Real Estate Rev 15(1):73–105
Imovina.net. (2016). http://imovina.net/
Kahirović E (2013) Upravljanje performansama poslovnih procesa u funkciji povećanja efikasnosti preduzeća. Ekonomski fakultet Univerziteta u Nišu, Niš
Kaplan RS, Norton DP (1996) Linking the balanced scorecard to strategy. California Management Review, CA
Kuzmanovic M, Radosavljevic MV (2013) Understanding student preferences for postpaid mobile services using conjoint analysis. Acta Polytechnica Hungarica 10(1):159–176
Kuzmanovic M, Savic G, Gusavac BA, Makajic-Nikolic D, Panic B (2013a) A conjoint-based approach to student evaluations of teaching performance. Expert Syst Appl 40(10):4083–4089
Kuzmanovic M, Savic G, Popovic M, Martic M (2013b) A new approach to evaluation of university teaching considering heterogeneity of students' preferences. High Educ 66(2):153–171. https://doi.org/10.1007/s10734-012-9596-2
Loikkanen HA, Susiluoto I (2002) An evaluation of economic efficiency of Finnish regions by DEA and Tobit models. In: 42nd congress of the european regional science association, Dortmund
Martić M, Savić G (2001) An application of DEA for comparative analysis and ranking of regions in Serbia with regards to social-economic development. Eur J Oper Res 343–356
Masternak-Janus A, Rybaczewska-Błażejowska M (2017) Comprehensive regional eco-efficiency analysis based on data envelopment analysis: the case of polish regions. J Ind Ecol 21(1):180–190
Maudos J, Pastor J, Serrano L (2000) Efficiency and productive specialisation: an application to the Spanish regions. Reg Stud 34(9):829–842
Ministarstvo trgovine turizma i telekomunikacija (2016) *Kupovna moć stanovništva; Potrošačka korpa*, Beograd. http://mtt.gov.rs/
Miot Y (2015) Residential attractiveness as a public policy goal for declining industrial cities: housing renewal strategies in Mulhouse, Roubaix and Saint-Etienne (France). Eur Plan Stud 23(1):104–125
Mirkov A (2016) Kvalitet života u gradu: Mišljenje i delanje stanovnika pojedinih gradova u Srbiji. Filozofski fakultet, Univerzitet od Beograda, Beograd
Mitorivić Z, Vujošević M, Savic G (2016) Data Envel Anal Eval Manag 75:39–46
Molin E, Oppewal H, Timmermans H (1996) Predicting consumer response to new housing: a stated choice experiment. Neth J Hous Built Environ 11(3):297–311

Neely A, Gregory M, Platts K (1995) Performance measurement system design: a literature review and research agenda. Int J Oper Prod Manage 25(12):80–116

Niedomysl T (2008) Residential preferences for interregional migration in Sweden: demographic, socioeconomic and geographical determinants. Environ Plan 40:1109–1131

Norman JB (2017) Measuring improvements in industrial energy efficiency: a decomposition analysis applied to the UK. Energy 137:1144–1151

Orzechowski M, Arentze T, Borgers A, Timmermans H (2005) Alternate methods of conjoint analysis for estimating housing preference functions: effects of presentation style. J Hous Built Environ 20(4):349–362

Petrić J (2013) Rezidencijalne preferencije ka gradskim i prigradskim područjima i povezanost sa njihovim demografskim karakteristikama. Institut za arhitekturu i urbanizam Srbije, Beograd

Rabar D (2013) Assessment of regional efficiency in Croatia using data envelopment analysis. Croatian operational research review 4(1):76–88

Rao VR (2014) Applied conjoint analysis. Springer, New York

Republički zavod za statistiku (2016) Zarade po zaposlenom u Republici Srbiji po opštinama i gradovima, januar 2016, Beograd. http://webrzs.stat.gov.rs/WebSite/Public/PageView.aspx?pKey=24

Sayadi S, Gonzalez C, Requena J (2005) Ranking versus scale rating in conjoint analysis: evaluating landscapes in mountainous regions in south-eastern Spain. Ecol Econ 50:539–550

Schaffer A, Simar L, Rauland J (2011) Decomposing regional efficiency. J Reg Sci 51(5):931–947

Senior M, Webster CB (2004) Residential preferences versus sustainable cities: qualitative and quantitative evidence from a survey of relocating owner-occupiers. Town Plan Rev 75(3):337–358

Shafranskaya I, Potapov D (2012) City: utility, measurability, preferability. Research paper. https://perm.hse.ru/data/2012/09/28/1244118992/Shafrańskaya_paper.pdf

Shahbazi S, Salloum M, Kurdve M, Wiktorsson M (2017) Material efficiency measurement: empirical investigation of manufacturing industry. Procedia Manuf 8:112–120

Smit J-A, McIlravey G (1989) Consumer preferences for rural residences: a conjoint analysis in Ontario, Canada. Environ Plan A 21:47–63

Solana-Ibáñez J, Caravaca-Garratón M, Para-González L (2016) Two-stage data envelopment analysis of spanish regions: efficiency determinants and stability analysis. Contemp Econ 10(3):259–273

Staníčková M, Melecký L (2012) Assessment of efficiency in Visegrad countries and regions using DEA models. Ekonomická revue–Cent Eurp Rev Econ Issues 15(3):145–156

Suzuki S, Nijkamp P, Rietveld P (2011) Regional efficiency improvement by means of data envelopment analysis through Euclidean distance minimization including fixed input factors: an application to tourist regions in Italy. Pap Reg Sci 90(1):67–89

Tallini A, Cedola L (2016) Evaluation methodology for energy efficiency measures in industry and service sector. Energy Procedia 101:542–549

Vukic M, Kuzmanovic M, Kostic-Stankovic M (2015) Understanding the heterogeneity of generation Y's preferences for travelling: a conjoint analysis approach. Underst Heterog Int J Tour Res 17(5):482–491

Walker B, Marsh A, Wardman M, Niner P (2002) Modelling Tenants' choices in public rented sector: a stated preferences approach. Urban Stud 39:665–690

Wang K, Yu S, Zhang (2013) China's regional energy and environmental efficiency: a DEA window analysis based dynamic evaluation. Math Comput Model 58(5–6):1117–1127

Wang Q, Zhao Z, Shen N, Liu T (2015) Have Chinese cities achieved the win–win between environmental protection and economic development? From the perspective of environmental efficiency. Ecol. Indic. 51:151–158

Wu A, Cao Y, Liu B (2014) Energy efficiency evaluation for regions in China: an application of DEA and Malmquist indices. Energ Effic 7(3):429–439

Yin K, Wang R, An Q, Yao L, Liang J (2014) Using eco-efficiency as an indicator for sustainable urban development: a case study of Chinese provincial capital cities. Ecol Ind 36:665–671

Analyzing the Efficiency of Travel and Tourism in the European Union

Petra Barišić and Violeta Cvetkoska

Abstract As one of the world's largest and growing economic sectors, travel and tourism significantly contributes to GDP, creates jobs, drives exports, and generates prosperity across the world. Therefore, it is essential to know which countries successfully manage their travel and tourism, and can serve as an example for the others. The aim of the paper is to analyze the efficiency of travel and tourism impact on the GDP and employment in the European Union at the macro level, by using the nonparametric approach data envelopment analysis. All 28 member states of the European Union were included in the research. The observation period was one year (2017). Two inputs and two outputs were selected. Internal travel and tourism consumption and capital investment were the inputs, while travel and tourism's total contribution to GDP and employment were the outputs. The obtained results are presented, interpreted and there are recommendations given for the tourism policy-makers regarding making better decisions.

Keywords Operational research · DEA · Decision-making unit · Efficiency analysis · European union · Travel and tourism

1 Introduction

In terms of ever-increasing consumer demand, growing competitiveness, rapid changes in technology, limited resources, and pressures associated with the only irreversible resource—time, it is very difficult to make good decisions. The discipline of Operational Research (OR) helps those who lead organizations to make

P. Barišić
Faculty of Economics & Business, University of Zagreb, Zagreb, Croatia
e-mail: barisic@efzg.hr

V. Cvetkoska (✉)
Faculty of Economics – Skopje, Ss. Cyril and Methodius University in Skopje, Skopje, Republic of Macedonia
e-mail: vcvetkoska@eccf.ukim.edu.mk

N. Mladenović et al. (eds.), *Advances in Operational Research in the Balkans*, Springer Proceedings in Business and Economics,
https://doi.org/10.1007/978-3-030-21990-1_10

better decisions by applying advanced analytical methods (Williams 2008, p. 3). Assignment, data mining, financial decision-making, forecasting, logistics, marketing, tourism, networks, optimization, project planning and management, queuing, simulation, transportation, etc., are some of the decision areas where the powerful discipline of OR is applied (Cvetkoska 2016, p. 350).

One of the leading areas of the discipline of Operational Research is the non-parametric methodology for measuring the efficiency of entities, known as Data Envelopment Analysis (DEA). It has been introduced into OR literature by Charnes et al. (1978), and it was created as an extension of Farell's methods of measuring efficiency (Farell 1957).

Since travel and tourism represent an important economic activity in most countries around the world (WTTC 2017, p. 2), the measurement of efficiency in the tourism industry has been the area of a considerable amount of research in recent years, reflecting both the growing economic importance of tourism as a source of international revenue and domestic employment, and increasing competition in the global tourist markets around the world (Hadad et al. 2012). These days the tourism sector accounts for 10% of the world GDP, 7% of the global trade, and 1 in 10 jobs (UNWTO 2017a, p. 6). The importance of tourism for Europe is even greater; in 2016 Europe remained the most visited region in the world. The 28 European Union countries had 500.1 million tourist arrivals (40.5% of the world international tourist arrivals), and 376.6 US$ bn. (30.9%) international tourist receipts (UNWTO 2017b). Forecasts are moving in the direction that the European continent, within the next 20 years, will be the most evident source of tourist demand for the development of international tourism on a global scale (Metodijeski and Temelkov 2014, p. 239).

Due to its economic and employment potential, as well as its social and environmental implications (Obadic and Pehar 2016, p. 44), increasing the efficiency in tourism is essential, leading to increasing efficient programs and faster achievement of goals. Therefore, the main purpose of this paper is to identify which countries in EU-28 efficiently use their resources, and show the relative efficiency of their travel and tourism impact on the GDP and employment. For this purpose, the latest available data is used in the field of tourism. The data have been analyzed by DEA methodology with the selection of two inputs and two outputs.

The paper is organized as follows. The next section describes the importance of the travel and tourism industry in the EU. A description of DEA methodology can be found in the third section. DEA in tourism is presented in section four, followed by the model and data employed in the research. The sixth section presents the results and analysis, and at the end is given the conclusion.

2 The Importance of Travel and Tourism for the European Union

Tourism plays a major role in the EU economy. According to the European Commission, it is the third largest socioeconomic activity in the EU (after the trade and distribution, and construction sectors), and has an overall positive impact on economic growth and employment (Juul 2015, p. 5; Obadic and Pehar 2016, p. 43), as well on the export revenues and infrastructure development (UNWTO 2017b, p. 2). Tourism also contributes to the development of European regions and, if sustainable, helps to preserve and enhance cultural and natural heritage (Juul 2015, p. 5). Accordingly, Europe is the world's leading tourism destination receiving half of the world's international tourist arrivals (1.3 billion). In 2017, international tourism in Europe grew 8%, one percentage point above the world average, totaling 671 million tourists (UNWTO 2018). Geographically, a growing number of tourists travelling to the EU come from emerging countries, although EU source markets still provide the biggest share of tourists to EU destinations. The second biggest group comes from Europe outside the EU, the third from the Americas, and the fourth from Asia and the Pacific (UNWTO 2014, p. 25).

With its comparatively short distances and good infrastructure (UNWTO 2014, p. 4), and its borderless travel area within the Schengen zone (Juul 2015, p. 5), travel in the EU-28 is characterized by more frequent but shorter trips (UNWTO 2014, p. 4). The new EU Tourism Policy Priority Actions include joint promotion of Europe as one tourist destination in third countries' market and it even consists of 28 countries that all have different tourist products and are competitors on the international tourism market.

In 2016, the direct contribution of travel and tourism to the GDP was EUR 547.9bn (3.7% of total GDP), while its total contribution was EUR 1,508.4bn (10.2% of GDP). The total contribution of travel and tourism to GDP is nearly three times greater than its direct contribution. In EU-28 travel and tourism investment in 2016 was EUR 143.0bn, or 4.9% of the total investment. It should rise by 2.8% over the next ten years. In the long term, growth of the travel and tourism sector will continue to be strong as long as the investment and development take place in an open and sustainable manner (WTTC 2017).

In 2014, one in ten enterprises in the European nonfinancial business economy belonged to the tourism industries. These 2.3 million enterprises employed an estimated 12.3 million persons (Eurostat 2018). According to the WTTC (2017, p. 1) in EU-28 in 2016 travel and tourism directly supported 11.4 million jobs (5.0% of total employment)—a direct contribution to employment. Its total contribution to employment, including jobs indirectly supported by the industry, was 11.6% of the total employment (26.6 million jobs). Over the next 10 years, tourism can create more than 5 million new jobs, not least because the number of tourists is set to double to more than 2 billion. Through the growth of tourism, we can offer real prospects for the new generations and boost strategic sectors of the economy, such as transport,

Table 1 World ranking of EU countries by the number of tourist arrivals in 2015

Rank	Country	Tourist arrivals (in million)
1	France	84.5
3	Spain	68.5
5	Italy	50.7
8	The United Kingdom	34.4
12	Austria	26.7
15	Greece	23.6
20	Poland	16.7
22	The Netherlands	15.0
25	Croatia	12.7
28	Denmark	10.4
32	Portugal	10.0
33	Ireland	9.5
34	Romania	9.3
39	Belgium	8.4
42	Bulgaria	7.1
43	Sweden	6.5
55	Hungary	4.9
67	Estonia	3.0
72	Slovenia	2.7
75	Finland	2.6
78	Lithuania	2.1
81	Latvia	2.0
87	Slovak Republic	1.7
108	Luxembourg	1.1

Source Index Mundi (2015); UNWTO (2017a, p. 13)

trade, luxury goods, shipbuilding, construction, agri-foodstuffs and the cultural and creative industries (UNWTO 2018).

If we analyze the world rank of EU countries by the number of reported tourist arrivals, in 2015 France was in the first place, Spain was in the third place, and Italy was 5th (UNWTO 2017a, pp. 13). Index Mundi (2015) provides the data for 24 EU countries, and they are given in Table 1.

In 2016, Northern Europe led the growth in the region, with a 6% increase in international arrivals, or 5 million more than in 2015. Norway, Ireland and Sweden all boasted above-average growth. The United Kingdom, the subregion's largest destination, reported a comparatively modest growth, despite the weaker British pound. In Central and Eastern Europe, arrivals increased by 4% in 2016. Many destinations enjoyed strong results, including Slovakia, Bulgaria, Romania, and Lithuania. Hun-

Table 2 EU countries by increase in international tourist arrivals in 2016

Country	Increase (in %)
Cyprus	+20
Slovakia	+17
Bulgaria	+16
Portugal	+13
Norway	+12
Ireland	+11
Romania	+11
Lithuania	+11
Malta	+10
Spain	+10
Croatia	+9
Sweden	+8
Hungary	+7
Greece	+5
The Netherlands	+5
Austria	+5
The United Kingdom	+4
Poland	+4
The Czech Republic	+4
Italy	+3
Germany	+2
France	−2
Belgium	−10

Source UNWTO 2017b, p. 7

gary recorded a 7% growth in arrivals, while Poland and the Czech Republic both reported an increase of 4%. Growth in Southern and Mediterranean Europe (+1%) was modest, despite sound results in most countries, driven by Cyprus, Portugal, Malta, the top destination of Spain and Croatia. Greece reported a 5% increase in arrivals and Italy 3%. Results in Western Europe (0%) were rather mixed in 2016, as some destinations were impacted by security concerns. The Netherlands and Austria both reported a 5% growth in arrivals, and Germany a 2% growth. The world's top tourism destination, France, faced the aftermath of security incidents, as did Belgium (Table 2) (UNWTO 2017b, p. 7).

Spain was the most common tourist destination in the EU for nonresidents, with 295 million nights spent in tourist accommodation establishments, or 22.2% of the EU-28 total in 2016. Followed by Italy (199 million nights), France (124 million nights) and the United Kingdom (119 million nights), which together accounted for more than half (55.7%) of the total nights spent by nonresidents in the EU-28. The

Table 3 Top 5 EU-28 countries by the number of beds in 2016

Rank	Country
1	France
2	Italy
3	The United Kingdom
4	Spain
5	Germany

Source Eurostat (2018)

Table 4 Top 3 EU-28 countries by the ratio of travel receipts to GDP in 2016

Rank	Country	Ratio (in %)
1	Croatia	18.6
2	Cyprus	13.7
3	Malta	13.2

Source Eurostat (2018)

Table 5 Top 5 EU-28 countries by the highest international travel receipts in 2016

Rank	Country	In billion EUR
1	Spain	54.7
2	France	38.3
3	The United Kingdom	37.4
4	Italy	36.4
5	Germany	33.8

Source Eurostat (2018)

least common destinations were Luxembourg and Latvia; the effect of the size of these member states should be considered when interpreting these values. The number of nights spent (by residents and nonresidents) can be put into perspective by making a comparison with the size of each country in population terms, providing an indicator of the tourism intensity. In 2016, using this measure, the Mediterranean destinations of Malta, Croatia, and Cyprus, as well as the alpine and city destinations of Austria were the most popular tourist destinations in the EU-28 (Eurostat 2018).

If we look the number of all the beds in the EU-28, in 2016 nearly one third were concentrated in just two of the EU member states, namely France (5.1 million beds) and Italy (4.9 million beds), followed by the United Kingdom, Spain, and Germany (Table 3). In 2016, the ratio of travel receipts to GDP was highest, among the EU member states, in Croatia, Cyprus, and Malta, confirming the importance of tourism to these countries (Table 4). In absolute terms, the highest international travel receipts in 2016 were recorded in Spain, France, and the United Kingdom, followed by Italy and Germany (Table 5) (Eurostat 2018).

3 DEA Methodology

One of the most important principles in the operation of organizations is efficiency. Efficiency refers to the relationship between the input and the output, i.e., using the minimum resources (human, organizational, financial, material, physical) to produce the desired production volume (Suklev 2016, p. 4). If a higher level of output is obtained, and the same level of input is used, or the same output level is obtained, and a lower input level is used, then the efficiency has increased.

There are two approaches in the literature for measuring the efficiency of the entities: the parametric or econometric approach, and the nonparametric or the mathematical programming approach (Cvetkoska and Savic 2017 p. 318). This paper uses the nonparametric approach, more precisely data envelopment analysis, and for the parametric approach, see Greene (1993, pp. 68–119).

Data envelopment analysis is placed on a pedestal for measuring the efficiency of organizations that use multiple inputs in order to produce multiple outputs (Cvetkoska 2017, p. 9). Entities whose efficiency is measured using DEA should be homogeneous, i.e., they should use the same inputs to produce the same outputs, and they are known in DEA terminology as decision-making units (DMUs).

DEA is categorized as a nonparametric approach because the analytic form of the production function does not require a priori assumption (Naumovska and Cvetkoska 2016). The efficiency measure given by this methodology is relative because it depends on the involved units in the analysis (what they are, and what their number is), as well as from the input and output variables (their number and structure) (Popovic 2006).

Data envelopment analysis is a mathematical programming technique that can determine whether the decision-making units are relatively efficient (which form the efficiency frontier) or relatively inefficient. For one decision-making unit to be efficient, according to Charnes et al. (1978, p. 439), the following two conditions need not be met: (1) any output can be increased without increasing any input and without reducing any remaining output; (2) any input can be reduced without reducing any output and without increasing any remaining input.

With DEA, it can be determined how much a certain input should be reduced and/or increased, thus obtaining valuable information that will help the inefficient entities to improve efficiency and become efficient.

The basic DEA models are: the Charnes-Cooper-Rhodes (CCR) model that assumes constant returns to scale (CRS) and the Banker-Charnes-Cooper (BCC) model assuming variable returns to scale (VRS). If the increase in the inputs of the observed unit results in a proportional increase in the outputs, it is about constant returns to scale. Variable returns to scale is when the increase in the inputs of the observed unit does not necessarily result in a proportional change in the outputs.

The CCR model measures the overall technical efficiency (TE) of the unit and the efficiency frontier given by this model is in the form of a convex cone. The efficiency of this model includes both pure technical efficiency (PTE) and scale efficiency (SE). The BCC model measures pure technical efficiency, and the efficiency frontier is in a form of convex hull. When using the BCC model, a DMU is compared only to those DMUs that have a similar scale, which means that the impact on the scale on operation is not taken into account. When the measure of the efficiency given by the CCR model is divided by the efficiency of the BCC model, the scale efficiency is obtained. With the basic DEA models the DMUs that are identified as relatively inefficient can be ranked, while for ranking the efficient DMUs, see Andersen and Petersen (1993). In addition, there are developed DEA models with a non-convex efficiency frontier, models that enable efficiency assessment when any of the inputs and outputs are exogenous or of a categorical nature, weight restriction models, models that allow productivity analysis, monitoring efficiency through time, etc., details can be found in Cooper et al. (2007).

According to the orientation, the models can be: input-oriented, output-oriented or non-oriented. If the purpose of the model is to minimize inputs to achieve the given output level, that model is input-oriented, and an inefficient unit can become efficient by reducing inputs. In the case when the purpose of the model is to maximize outputs at a given input level, the model is output-oriented, and an inefficient unit can become efficient by appropriately increasing outputs. The model in which simultaneously inputs are reduced and outputs are increased for the DMU to become efficient is known as the non-oriented model.

To solve the DEA models, a number of software tools have been developed to enable the results to be obtained quickly and to devote most of the time to their adequate interpretation.

Even though the initial application of DEA in 1978 was in the nonprofit sector (to measure the efficiency of a set of school districts), it is successfully applied in the profit sector. For a collection of DEA applications, see Charnes et al. (1994), while Sherman and Zhu (2006) use DEA to improve service performance (Cook and Zhu 2008, p. 22).

In the area of DEA, there are several references: Emrouznejad and Thanassoulis (1996a, b, 1997), Seiford (1994, 1997), Tavares (2002), Gattoufi et al. (2004a, b), Emrouznejad et al. (2008), and Emrouznejad and Yang (2018).

The bibliography of DEA published in 2008 (Emrouznejad et al. 2008) includes over 4.000 research papers since its introduction up to 2007; there have been identified 2.500 different authors, and an interesting fact is that 22% of all articles were written by 12 authors, and the largest number of articles in peer-reviewed journals have been published in 2004 (Cvetkoska 2017, p. 17).

Emrouznejad and Yang (2018) give a full list of DEA publications (there have been included 10.300 DEA related articles published in journals) from 1978 to the end of 2016. In each of the last three observed years (2014, 2015 and 2016), about 1.000 papers were published. The greatest number of the analyzed DEA related articles have been published in the following journals: *European Journal of Operational Research* (691 articles), *Journal of the Operational Research Society* (281 articles), *Journal of Productivity Analysis* (255 articles), and *Omega* (237 articles). The first choice journal for DEA articles with applications in the public sector is identified as *Socio-Economic Planning Sciences*. In the analyzed DEA articles, there have been found approximately 11.961 distinct authors and 25.137 distinct key words. Most of the articles have 4 or less than 4 authors (about 94%). The most popular key words are: data envelopment analysis, data envelopment analysis (DEA), DEA or DEA models (9.989), efficiency (2.382), decision-making (1.048), technical efficiency (876), linear programming (722), and productivity (722). The main fields of current studies are: environmental efficiency and directional distance function (DDF), network DEA, benchmarking, bootstrap or bootstrapping, and returns to scale (including scale efficiency). The most popular application areas are: energy, industry, banking, education, and healthcare, including hospitals. The greatest number of journal articles in 2015 and 2016 are in the following 5 application fields of DEA: agriculture, banking, supply chain, transportation, and public policy.

In the section that follows special attention is given to the application of the DEA in the tourism industry.

4 DEA in Travel and Tourism

The majority of research that deals with the DEA in tourism is focused on the efficiency measurements of micro-units (Hadad et al. 2012, p. 931), like hotels, tour operators and destination websites. Sigala (2004) applied DEA for measuring and benchmarking hotel productivity, as well as Poldrugovac et al. (2016). The obtained results present a high average efficiency, but not all hotels performed at their maximum efficiency. Aside from this, there was found to be a significant relationship between the size and hotel efficiency. Barros (2005) and Barros and Mascarenhas (2005) measured the efficiency of hotels that belong to the Pousadas de Portugal (a Portuguese state-owned chain). Oliveira et al. (2013) benchmarked the efficiency and its determinants in Portuguese hotels in the Algarve. The results showed that the number of hotel stars is an important factor for performance. Assaf (2012) measured the efficiency of leading hotels and tour operators in the Asia Pacific region. This paper introduces an innovative methodology that combines data envelopment analysis and stochastic frontier analysis (SFA) in a Bayes framework. Regarding both tour operators and hotel companies, the most efficient were Australia, Singapore, and South Korea. It was also found that international hotels have a slightly higher efficiency in comparison with local hotels. The efficiency of tourism destination websites has been obtained by using the nonparametric methodology DEA by Alzua-Sorzabala et al. (2015).

Liu et al. (2017) evaluate the tourism eco-efficiency of 53 Chinese coastal cities. The observed period was 2003–2013 and they applied a DEA-Tobit model. The overall tourism eco-efficiency of the analyzed cities was 0.860. Man and Zhang (2015), by using DEA, analyze the factors that influence the efficiency of the urban tourism industry. Their research was conducted in China. Yi and Liang (2014) analyze the tourism efficiency of 21 cities in the Guangdong Province, China, by using seven-year panel data. In the research they applied DEA and the Malmquist Index (MI) and they discussed evolutional models based on DEA and MI. According to the obtained results, it has been found that the Guangdong Province as a whole has a relatively high tourism efficiency; a trend of improvement in the efficiency in tourism was noted by MI; a quadrant chart was constructed, where the DMUs (cities) were classified in 4 categories; and the following 4 evolutional models of tourism efficiency were identified: stable, reciprocating, progressive, and radical.

There are few studies that have been using DEA in tourism and travel at the macro level. One of the first research includes Fuchs (2004) research, which applies DEA for benchmarking the relative efficiency of tourism service processes on the level of tourism destinations. Wöber (2008) applies DEA for measuring and evaluating the performance of travel and tourism. Hadad et al. (2012) analyze the efficiency of the tourism industry by using DEA. Their sample consists of 105 countries (34 developed and 71 developing countries). Cvetkoska and Barisic (2014) measure the tourism efficiency of 15 European countries. The sample consists of: Austria, Bosnia and Herzegovina, Bulgaria, Croatia, Cyprus, the Czech Republic, France, Greece, Italy, Macedonia, Montenegro, Portugal, Serbia, Slovenia, and Spain. The observed period was 10 years (from 2004 to 2013). As input factors, the following were selected: visitor exports and domestic travel and tourism spending, while as outputs the following were selected: travel and tourism's total contribution to GDP, and travel and tourism's total contribution to employment. The DEA technique window analysis was used. Based on the obtained results, it was found that there is no country that is efficient in every year in every window; 10 of the 15 countries show efficiency results (overall efficiency by years) over 95%: Italy (99.67%), Cyprus (99.64%), France (98.99%), Spain (98.99%), etc., while Montenegro showed the lowest overall efficiency (by years) (71.53%). The highest efficiency results were achieved in 2004, and the lowest in 2011.

Abad and Kongmanwatana (2015), through DEA, measured the performance of 27 EU countries (excluding Malta) based on the position of destination management organizations, while Corne (2015) benchmarked the effects of tourism in France by the DEA model. The results show that there is potential to improve the efficiency of the tourism sector in France, and budgets and hotel groups were more efficient than others. Cvetkoska and Barisic (2017) analyze the relative efficiency of the tourism industry in the Balkans. The sample consists of 11 countries (Albania, Bosnia, and Herzegovina, Bulgaria, Croatia, Greece, Macedonia, Montenegro, Romania, Serbia, Slovenia, and Turkey). The covered period was 6 years (from 2010 to 2015). As input and output factors, the same ones were selected as in Cvetkoska and Barisic (2014). The DEA technique window analysis was used, and according to the obtained results (overall efficiency by years), Albania, Croatia, Romania, and Turkey were identified as the most efficient countries, while Montenegro, Serbia, and Bosnia and Herzegovina were found to be the least efficient. The tourism industry in the Balkans in the observed period has shown the average efficiency of 93.42%. The highest average efficiency of the tourism industry was achieved in 2013 (95.44%), and the lowest in 2011 (91.77%). Martin et al. (2017) went a step further: they created a composite index of the travel and tourism competitiveness in order to rank a sample that consists of 139 countries worldwide. Their method is based on the virtual efficiency data envelopment analysis model.

5 Model and Data

The BCC model was introduced by Banker et al. (1984). The envelopment form of the output-oriented BCC model is given in (1)–(5), (Cooper et al. 2007, p. 93; Cvetkoska and Barisic 2014, p. 79, and Cvetkoska and Barisic 2017, pp. 33–34):

$$(BCC - O_o) \quad \max_{\eta_B, \lambda} \eta_B \tag{1}$$

$$\text{subject to} \quad X\lambda \leq x_o \tag{2}$$

$$\eta_B y_o - Y\lambda \leq 0 \tag{3}$$

$$e\lambda = 1 \tag{4}$$

$$\lambda \geq 0 \tag{5}$$

where η_B is scalar. The input data for DMUj ($j = 1,\ldots,n$) are (x_{1j}, x_{2j},…,x_{mj}), and the output data are (y_{1j}, y_{2j},…,y_{sj}); the data set is given by two matrices X and Y, where X is the input data matrix, and Y is the output data matrix, λ is a column vector and all its elements are nonnegative, while e is a row vector and all its elements are equal to 1 (Cooper et al. 2007, p. 22, pp. 91–92). BCC-efficient DMUs are those that form the efficiency frontier and their efficiency result is 1 (100%). More details about the BCC DEA model can be found in: Banker et al. (1984) and Cooper et al. (2007, pp. 90–94).

To measure the efficiency of the travel and tourism industry in the European Union, there have been selected two inputs and two outputs, which all represent economic impacts of tourism. The following are selected as inputs: internal travel and tourism consumption (input 1) and capital investment (input 2), while as outputs the following were selected: travel and tourism's total contribution to GDP (output 1) and travel and tourism's total contribution to employment (output 2).

Input 1, internal travel and tourism consumption is a starting point for all tourism economic impacts (Cavlek et al. 2011, p. 310). It can be defined as part of the national income, i.e., personal consumption, which the population allocates for travelling (Bogoev 1975, p. 1409). It is one of the freest and most independent forms of personal consumption, since its implementation in most cases is not conditioned by time, lifestyle, business, organization or any other form of coercion. The moment when tourism consumption is realized, it becomes an economic category that is the ultimate result of the interaction of two poles of tourism market (Cavlek et al. 2011) (the supply and demand side of market).

Input 2. Tourism is a highly capital intensive sector. Different types of capital investments should be implemented so that the tourism system can function successfully. Without airports, highways, parking places, or luxury hotels and resorts not a single tourist destination can survive on the international tourism market. Given that, capital investments in tourism play a role in redistribution of capital, and serve as part of a country's macroeconomic policy (Cavlek et al. 2011).

Based on the previous research conducted by Cvetkoska and Barisic (2014), for this research as outputs were selected travel and tourism's total contribution to GDP (output 1) and travel and tourism's total contribution to employment (output 2). Travel and tourism's total contribution to GDP (output 1) represents the financial economic impact of tourism. It even seems better that one country has a high total contribution of travel and tourism to GDP, which is not correct because that means that the local economy depends on one sector that is prone to the influence of various external factors that we can not control. If we speak globally, tourism accounts for 10% of the world GDP (UNWTO 2017a, p. 6).

One of the most important economic impacts of tourism is employment, i.e., the creation of new jobs within the core economic activities in the tourism sector, as well as a number of other economic activities that support this sector. Full employment is the goal of every country, where tourism can have a big contribution. From the standpoint of local people, tourism becomes attractive (and often only) access to employment, with relatively good working conditions and generous income, which are, however, an average seasonal character.

According to the WTTC (World Travel and Tourism Council), descriptions of the selected input and output are given in Table 6.

Data was collected from the period of one year (2017).

For the selected inputs and outputs for the observed units, there is no missing data, and all values are positive. Correlation analysis between inputs and outputs was carried out and all correlation coefficients were positive, and there is a presence of a strong relationship between all variables (Table 7).

The number of DMUs should be at least three times the total number of inputs and outputs (Cooper et al. 2007). In the case where this is not satisfied, a larger number of DMUs can appear as relatively efficient, and the obtained results are questionable. In this paper, the sample of analysis consists of 28 EU member states (the minimum number of DMUs according to the above mentioned should be 12).

To solve the output-oriented BCC model, specialized DEA software—DEA SolverPro 10e has been used, and the obtained results are presented and interpreted in the section that follows.

6 Results and Analysis

The obtained results from the output-oriented BCC DEA model are shown in Table 8. From this table, it can be seen that 13 EU member states are relatively efficient (Bulgaria, Cyprus, Estonia, Germany, Greece, Hungary, Italy, Latvia, Malta, Portugal, Romania, Spain, and the United Kingdom). According to the orientation of the model this means that these 13 EU member states with the given level of inputs have achieved the maximum possible level of outputs. By contrast, the remaining 15 EU member states (Austria, Belgium, Croatia, the Czech Republic, Denmark, Finland, France,

Table 6 Description of inputs and outputs

Inputs	Description
Internal travel and tourism consumption	Total revenue generated within a country by industries that deal directly with tourists, including visitor exports, domestic spending, and government individual spending. This does not include spending abroad by residents. This is consistent with the total internal tourism expenditure in Table 4 of the TSA: RMF 2008 *Visitor exports* Spending within the country by international tourists for both business and leisure trips, including spending on transport, but excluding international spending on education. This is consistent with the total inbound tourism expenditure in Table 1 of the TSA: RMF 2008 *Domestic travel and tourism spending* Spending within a country by that country's residents for both business and leisure trips. Multiuse consumer durables are not included since they are not purchased solely for tourism purposes. This is consistent with the total domestic tourism expenditure in Table 2 of the TSA: RMF 2008. Outbound spending by residents abroad is not included here, but is separately identified according to the TSA: RMF 2008 *Government individual spending* Spending by the government on travel and tourism services directly linked to visitors, such as cultural services (e.g., museums) or recreational services (e.g., national parks)
Capital investment	Includes capital investment spending by all industries directly involved in travel and tourism. This also constitutes investment spending by other industries on specific tourism assets, such as new visitor accommodation and passenger transport equipment, as well as restaurants and leisure facilities for specific tourism use. This is consistent with the total tourism gross fixed capital formation in Table 8 of the TSA: RMF 2008
Outputs	**Description**
Travel and tourism's total contribution to GDP	GDP generated directly by the travel and tourism sector plus its indirect and induced impacts (see below) *Direct contribution to GDP* GDP generated by industries that deal directly with tourists, including hotels, travel agents, airlines and other passenger transport services, as well as the activities of restaurant and leisure industries that deal directly with tourists. It is equivalent to the total internal travel and tourism spending within a country less the purchases made by those industries (including imports). In terms of the UN Tourism Satellite Account methodology, it is consistent with the total GDP calculated in Table 6 of the TSA: RMF 2008
Travel and tourism's total contribution to employment	The number of jobs generated directly in the travel and tourism sector plus the indirect and induced contributions (see below)

(continued)

Table 6 (continued)

Inputs	Description
	Indirect and induced impacts *Indirect* The contribution to GDP and jobs of the following three factors: • Capital investment • Government collective spending: government spending in support of a general tourism activity. This can include national as well as regional and local government spending. For example, it includes tourism promotion, visitor information services, administrative services, and other public services. This is consistent with the total collective tourism consumption in Table 9 of TSA: RMF 2008 • Supply chain effects: purchases of domestic goods and services directly by different industries within travel and tourism as inputs to their final tourism output. *Induced* The broader contribution to GDP and employment of spending by those who are directly or indirectly employed by travel and tourism
Outputs	Description
Travel and tourism's total contribution to GDP	GDP generated directly by the travel and tourism sector plus its indirect and induced impacts (see below) *Direct contribution to GDP* GDP generated by industries that deal directly with tourists, including hotels, travel agents, airlines and other passenger transport services, as well as the activities of restaurant and leisure industries that deal directly with tourists. It is equivalent to the total internal travel and tourism spending within a country less the purchases made by those industries (including imports). In terms of the UN Tourism Satellite Account methodology, it is consistent with the total GDP calculated in Table 6 of the TSA: RMF 2008
Travel and tourism's total contribution to employment	The number of jobs generated directly in the travel and tourism sector plus the indirect and induced contributions (see below)
	Indirect and induced impacts *Indirect* The contribution to GDP and jobs of the following three factors: • Capital investment • Government collective spending: government spending in support of a general tourism activity. This can include national as well as regional and local government spending. For example, it includes tourism promotion, visitor information services, administrative services, and other public services. This is consistent with the total collective tourism consumption in Table 9 of TSA: RMF 2008 • Supply chain effects: purchases of domestic goods and services directly by different industries within travel and tourism as inputs to their final tourism output. *Induced* The broader contribution to GDP and employment of spending by those who are directly or indirectly employed by travel and tourism

Source WTTC (2017)
TSA—Tourism Satellite Account

Table 7 Correlation

	I1	I2	O1	O2
I1	1	0.86582	0.98884	0.98892
I2	0.86582	1	0.8919	0.85594
O1	0.98884	0.8919	1	0.98766
O2	0.98892	0.85594	0.98766	1

Source Author's calculation

Ireland, Lithuania, Luxembourg, the Netherlands, Slovakia, Slovenia, and Sweden) have been identified as relatively inefficient, i.e., they invest more in tourism considering the fact that they gain from it, in the sense of employment in tourism and its share in GDP. The average efficiency is 0.9441, the maximum efficiency is 1, the minimum is 0.7406, and the standard deviation is 0.0783.

By solving the basic BCC DEA model, the efficient countries are given a rank of 1, while inefficient countries are ranked from 14 to 28 (Poland is given a rank of 14, and Ireland is placed last (rank of 28)).

For each relatively inefficient member country of the European Union, a reference set is shown in Table 9. For four EU member countries: Austria, Belgium, Finland, and Denmark, the reference set is the same and consists of the following three countries: Italy, Malta, and Spain. For two relatively inefficient states (France and Luxembourg), the reference set comprises two states; for nine relatively inefficient states (Austria, Belgium, Denmark, Finland, Ireland, Lithuania, Poland, Slovenia, and Sweden), the reference set covers three states; and for four relatively inefficient states (Croatia, the Czech Republic, the Netherlands, and Slovakia), the reference set covers four states.

According to the frequency with which efficient units appear in the reference set of inefficient units, Spain can be distinguished as an indicator of good practice (it has the highest number of appearances, i.e., 9), followed by Romania (7 appearances), Italy and Malta (6 appearances), Bulgaria (5 appearances), etc. (Table 9).

In addition, three relatively inefficient states have been analyzed, i.e., Poland, Slovenia, and the Netherlands. Poland with its efficiency result is closest to the relatively·efficient countries, and has a rank of 14, Slovenia is ranked 22nd and the Netherlands is ranked 27th. For each of them to become efficient, an appropriate projection of the input and output values has been made. In order for the inputs to remain unchanged, the changes are only in the outputs: Poland should increase the first output by 9.95% and the second output by 0.76%, Slovenia should increase the first output by 8.51% and the second output by 37.24%, while the Netherlands should increase the two outputs by 29.35%.

Table 8 Results of the output-oriented BCC DEA model

No.	DMU	Result	Rank
1	Austria	0.9736	15
2	Belgium	0.8876	23
3	Bulgaria	1	1
4	Croatia	0.8106	25
5	Cyprus	1	1
6	The Czech Republic	0.9447	19
7	Denmark	0.9498	18
8	Estonia	1	1
9	Finland	0.9412	20
10	France	0.9576	17
11	Germany	1	1
12	Greece	1	1
13	Hungary	1	1
14	Ireland	0.7406	28
15	Italy	1	1
16	Latvia	1	1
17	Lithuania	0.8574	24
18	Luxembourg	0.9279	21
19	Malta	1	1
20	The Netherlands	0.7731	27
21	Poland	0.9925	14
22	Portugal	1	1
23	Romania	1	1
24	Slovakia	0.7984	26
25	Slovenia	0.9216	22
26	Spain	1	1
27	Sweden	0.9588	16
28	The United Kingdom	1	1

Source Author's calculation

7 Conclusion

In this paper, the relatively efficient and relatively inefficient EU member states in tourism are identified. The reference set for inefficient countries is shown and it is indicated what changes should be made by relatively inefficient states, or more precisely how much they should increase the outputs to become relatively efficient. In addition, the rank of relatively inefficient states is also given. All this information

Table 9 Reference set for relatively inefficient states

No.	DMU	Reference (Lambda)							
1	Austria	Italy	0.174	Malta	0.683	Spain	0.143		
2	Belgium	Italy	0.049	Malta	0.852	Spain	0.099		
3	Croatia	Bulgaria	0.575	Cyprus	0.333	Hungary	0.043	Italy	0.049
4	The Czech Repub- lic	Bulgaria	0.486	Estonia	0.14	Greece	0.307	Romania	0.067
5	Denmark	Estonia	0.674	Romania	0.215	Spain	0.111		
6	Finland	Italy	0.037	Malta	0.895	Spain	0.068		
7	France	Spain	0.515	UK	0.485				
8	Ireland	Estonia	0.059	Romania	0.864	Spain	0.077		
9	Lithuania	Bulgaria	0.092	Latvia	0.083	Malta	0.824		
10	Luxembourg	Malta	0.930	Romania	0.070				
11	The Nether- lands	Cyprus	0.474	Greece	0.318	Italy	0.065	Spain	0.143
12	Poland	Bulgaria	0.122	Portugal	0.577	Romania	0.301		
13	Slovakia	Bulgaria	0.023	Estonia	0.877	Greece	0.093	Romania	0.006
14	Slovenia	Estonia	0.961	Romania	0.027	Spain	0.012		
15	Sweden	Italy	0.166	Malta	0.746	Spain	0.088		

Source Author's calculation

is valuable for making adequate steps in order to improve the efficiency of relatively inefficient countries.

The data collected for the input and output factors relate only to one year (2017), so in our further research we plan to cover a longer period of time and to apply the DEA technique Window Analysis that will enable monitoring the efficiency through time. Since DEA tries to show each decision-making unit (which is part of the sample for analysis) in the best light, it may occur that an input or output does not get the proper weight, and in order to overcome this problem, we plan to link the nonparametric methodology DEA with the leading method of multicriteria decision-making (MCDM)—the analytic hierarchy process (AHP)—in the direction of restricting the weights for the input and output factors.

Additionally, inputs could be different, the internal travel and tourism consumption could be replaced with domestic travel and tourism spending or a number of tourist arrivals or nights spent, as well as with a number of hotels or destination management organizations in a particular country. Future research could be directed toward findings as to why certain observed countries have an efficient tourism industry, while others don't, and how it is related with the overall economic development of the country.

References

Abad A, Kongmanwatana P (2015) Comparison of destination competitiveness ranking in the European Union using a non-parametric approach. Tourism Econ. 21:267–281

Alzua-Sorzabala A, Zurutuzaa M, Rebona F, Gerrikagoitiaa JK (2015) Obtaining the efficiency of tourism destination website based on data envelopment analysis. Procedia Soc Behav Sci 175:58–65

Andersen P, Petersen NC (1993) A procedure for ranking efficient unit in data envelopment analysis. Manag Sci 39:1261–1264

Assaf AG (2012) Benchmarking the Asia Pacific tourism industry: a Bayesian combination of DEA and stochastic frontier. Tour Manag 33:1122–1127

Banker RD, Charnes A, Cooper WW (1984) Some models for estimating technical and scale inefficiencies in data envelopment analysis. Manag Sci 30:1078–1092

Barros CP (2005) Measuring the efficiency in the hotel sector. Ann Tour Res 32:456–477

Barros CP, Mascarenhas MJ (2005) Technical and allocative efficiency in chain of small hotels. Int J Hosp Manag 24:415–436

Bogoev K (ed) (1975) Economic lexicon. Savremena administracija, Beograd

Cavlek N, Bartoluci M, Prebezac D, Kesar O (2011) Tourism economic bases and organizational systems. Skolska knjiga, Zagreb

Charnes A, Cooper WW, Rhodes EL (1978) Measuring efficiency of decision making units. Eur J Oper Res 2:429–444

Charnes A, Cooper WW, Lewin AY, Seiford LM (1994) Data envelopment analysis: theory methodology and applications. Kluwer Academic Publishers, Boston

Cook WD, Zhu J (2008) Data envelopment analysis: modeling operational processes and measuring productivity. Create Space Independent Publishing Platform

Cooper WW, Seiford LM, Tone K (2007) Data envelopment analysis: a comprehensive text with models, applications, references and dea-solver software, 2nd edn. Springer Science+Business Media, LLC, New York

Corne A (2015) Benchmarking and tourism efficiency in France. Tour Manag 51:91–95

Cvetkoska V, Savic G (2017) Efficiency of bank branches: empirical evidence from a two-phase research approach. Econ-Res-Ekon—Istraz 30:318–333

Cvetkoska V, Barisic P (2014) Measuring the efficiency of certain European countries in tourism: DEA window analysis. In: Zivkovic Z, Mihajlovic I, Djorgjevic P (eds) Book of proceedings of the international may conference on strategic management—IMKSM2014. University of Belgrade, Technical Faculty in Bor, Management Department, Bor, pp 77–86

Cvetkoska V, Barisic P (2017) The efficiency of the tourism industry in the Balkans. Proc Fac Econ East Sarajev 14:31–41

Cvetkoska V (2016) A survey of the use of operational research in decisions made by micro, small and medium-sized enterprises in Macedonia. Croat Oper Res Rev 7:349–365

Cvetkoska V (2017) Applying multi-criteria decision-making methods in banking: the case of Komercijalna Banka AD Skopje. Lambert Academic Publishing, Saarbrücken

Emrouznejad A, Yang GL (2018) A survey and analysis of the first 40 years of scholarly literature in DEA: 1978–2016. Socioecon Plan Sci 61:4–8

Emrouznejad A, Thanassoulis E (1996a) An extensive bibliography of data envelopment analysis (DEA). Work Pap 1:1–55

Emrouznejad A, Thanassoulis E. (1996b) An extensive bibliography of data envelopment analysis (DEA). Work Pap 2:1–21

Emrouznejad A, Thanassoulis E (1997) An extensive bibliography of data envelopment analysis (DEA). Work Pap 1:1–24

Emrouznejad A, Parker BR, Tavares G (2008) Evaluation of research in efficiency and productivity: a survey and analysis of the first 30 years of scholarly literature in DEA. Socioecon Plan Sci 42:151–157

Eurostat. Tourism statistics (2018). http://ec.europa.eu/eurostat/statistics-explained/index.php/Tourism_statistics. Accessed 7 Apr 2018

Farell MJ (1957) The measurement of productive efficiency. J R Stat Soc 120:253–290

Fuchs M (2004) Strategy development in tourism destinations: a DEA approach. Poznań Univ Econ Rev 4:52–73

Gattoufi S, Oral M, Reisman. A (2004a) A taxonomy for data envelopment analysis. Socioecon Plann Sci 38:141–158

Gattoufi S, Oral M, Reisman A (2004b) Data envelopment analysis literature: a bibliography update (1996–2001). Socioecon Plan Sci 38:122–159

Greene WH (1993) The econometric approach to efficiency analysis. In: Fried HO, Lovell CAK, Schmidt SS (eds) The measurement of productive efficiency: techniques and applications. Oxford University Press, New York, pp 68–119

Hadad S, Hadad Y, Malul M, Rosenboim M (2012) The economic efficiency of the tourism industry: a global comparison. Tour Econ 18:931–940

Index Mundi (2015) International tourism, number of arrivals – country ranking. https://www.indexmundi.com/facts/indicators/ST.INT.ARVL/rankings. Accessed 4 Apr 2018

Juul M. (2015) Tourism and the European Union. Recent trends and policy developments. In-depth analysis. European parliamentary research service https://doi.org/10.2861/310682

Liu J, Zhang J, Fu Z (2017) Tourism eco-efficiency of Chinese coastal cities—analysis based on the DEA-Tobit model. Ocean Coast Manag 148:164–170

Man D, Zhang, H (2015) The study of DEA application in tourism city: A case for members of the world tourism city federation in China. In: Zhang, Z, Shen, Z, Zhang, J, Zhang, R (eds) LISS 2014. Springer, Berlin, Heidelberg, pp 831–835

Martin JC, Mendoza C, Roman C (2017) A DEA travel-tourism competitiveness index. Soc Indic Res 130:937–957

Metodijeski D, Temelkov Z (2014) Tourism policy of Balkan countries: review of national tourism development strategies. UTMS J Econ 5:231–239

Naumovska E, Cvetkoska V (2016) Efficiency of the Macedonian banking sector. Yugosl J Oper Res 26:317–329

Obadic A, Pehar L (2016) Employment, capital and seasonality in selected Mediterranean countries. Zagreb Int Rev Econ Bus 19(s1):43–58

Oliveira R, Pedro MI, Marques RC (2013) Efficiency and its determinants in Portuguese hotels in the Algarve. Tour Manag 36:641–649

Poldrugovac K, Tekavcic M, Jankovic S (2016) Efficiency in the hotel industry: an empirical examination of the most influential factors. Econ-Res-Ekon—Istraz 29:583–597

Popovic G (2006) Assessment of efficiency of loan programs using data envelopment analysis. Master's thesis, University of Belgrade, Faculty of Organizational Sciences, Belgrade (in Serbian)

Seiford LM (1994) A DEA Bibliography (1978–1992). In: Charnes A, Cooper WW, Lewin AY, Seiford LM (eds) Data envelopment analysis: theory, methodology and applications. Kluwer, Boston, pp 437–469

Seiford LM (1997) A bibliography for data envelopment analysis (1978–1996). Ann Oper Res 73:393–438

Sherman DH, Zhu J (2006) Service productivity management: Improving service performance using data envelopment analysis. (DEA), Springer Science, Boston

Sigala M (2004) Using data envelopment analysis for measuring and benchmarking productivity in the hotel sector. J Travel Tour Mark 16:39–60

Suklev B (2016) Management, 9th edn. Faculty of Economics-Skopje (in Macedonian)

Tavares G (2002) A bibliography of data envelopment analysis (1978–2001). RUTCOR, Rutgers University. http://rutcor.rutgers.edu/pub/rrr/reports2002/1_2002.pdf

UNWTO, World tourism organization (2014) International tourism trends in EU-28 member states. Current situation and forecasts for 2020–2025–2030. http://www.eucentre.sg/wp-content/uploads/2015/08/UNWTO_TT2030_EU28.pdf. Accessed 4 Apr 2018

UNWTO, World tourism organization .2016 annual report (2017a). http://cf.cdn.unwto.org/sites/all/files/pdf/annual_report_2016_web_0.pdf. Accessed 4 Apr 2018

UNWTO, World tourism organization. Tourism highlights (2017b). https://www.e-unwto.org/doi/pdf/10.18111/9789284419029. Accessed 4 Apr 2018

UNWTO, World tourism organization (28 February 2018) UNWTO deepens tourism cooperation with the European Union. http://media.unwto.org/press-release/2018-02-28/unwto-deepens-tourism-cooperation-european-union. Accessed 4 Apr 2018

Williams T (2008) Management science in practice. Wiley, Chichester

Wöber KW (2008) Data envelopment analysis. J Travel Tour Mark 21:91–108

WTTC, World travel & tourism council (2017) Travel & tourism economic impact 2017 European Union LCU. https://www.wttc.org/-/media/files/reports/economic-impact-research/regions-2017/europeanunionlcu2017.pdf. Accessed 4 Apr 2018

Yi T, Liang M (2014) Evolutional model of tourism efficiency based on the DEA method: a case study of cities in Guangdong province. China. Asia Pac J Tour Res 20:789–806

Interdomain Quality of Service Negotiation Using DEA Analysis and Petri Nets

Teodora Aćimović, Gordana Savić and Dragana Makajić-Nikolić

Abstract This paper investigates the problem of sending packets through network on the interdomain level under condition that required Quality of Service (QoS) is achieved on the end-to-end (E2E) path. Process of sending and routing packets by one of the packet dispersion strategies is modelled using Coloured Petri Nets (CPN). The PN model was simulated to find and capture disjoint routes which ensure that realized values of network performance metrics meet the required ones on the E2E level. Using Data Envelopment Analysis (DEA), network performance is evaluated (packet delay, jitter, packet loss rate) to find which of the previously mentioned disjoint paths are more efficient than others. Based on DEA analysis results, Petri Net (PN) is expanded into stochastic PN in order to implement adaptive packet dispersion strategy. This strategy implies that paths with less probability of losing packets are more probable to be used in packet routing. Thanks to efficiency analysis, probability of selecting service classes by domain has been determined so that greater quality of VoIP service is achieved, which highly depends on offered network performance.

Keywords Network performance · Efficiency assessment · Quality of service · Disjoint routes · Service class mapping

1 Introduction

Networking technology introduced radical changes in interpersonal communication. Until recently, telephony was the main technology associated to transmission of information between sender and receiver. However, adoption of computers led to devel-

T. Aćimović (✉) · G. Savić (✉) · D. Makajić-Nikolić (✉)
Faculty of Organizational Sciences, University of Belgrade, Belgrade, Serbia
e-mail: teodora.acimovic@hotmail.com

G. Savić
e-mail: gordana.savic@fon.bg.ac.rs

D. Makajić-Nikolić
e-mail: makajic-nikolic.dragana@fon.bg.ac.rs

N. Mladenović et al. (eds.), *Advances in Operational Research in the Balkans*, Springer Proceedings in Business and Economics,
https://doi.org/10.1007/978-3-030-21990-1_11

opment of computer networking which is based on packet switching transmission method instead of circuit switching which is contemporary in traditional telephony (Kurose and Ross 2013). Next Generation Networks (NGN) enable provisioning of voice, data and media services through information transmission over a common network based on Internet Protocol (IP) technology (Mali et al. 2014). Voice over Internet Protocol (VoIP) is specifically designed for transmission of human voice over Internet in real time (Kurose and Ross 2013).

Practical use of VoIP exceeds possibilities of traditional telephony. However, VoIP is much more susceptible to potential data transmission issues, thus for this kind of communication certain quality of service must be provided (Ninković et al. 2015). Human voice must be converted into format that is suitable for communication and routing over Internet. In terms of low-level design, data packets are encapsulated into frames and converted into digital signal that is transmitted over a physical network layer (Dutta et al. 2012). Packets are sent along with service requests. These requests should be ensured and fulfilled by other entities in the heterogeneous network for send packets to reach its destination successfully. Process of fulfilling service requests and ensuring Quality of Service (QoS) is called QoS negotiation.

In this paper we address the problem of sending packets across disjoint routes on an interdomain level so that required QoS is achieved on E2E level. The goal is to improve QoS negotiation process by prioritizing routes and thus improving routing strategy based on simulation and efficiency analysis of admissible routes.

The approach we are proposing is based on generating feasible routes by Coloured Petri nets (CPN) simulation and then evaluating of efficiency of those routes by employing Data Envelopment Analysis (DEA). Such methodology was already used in several researches, but in areas that are different from the subject of this paper. Petri Nets are used for modelling a supply chain system and detecting multi-agent conflicts (Shiau and Li 2009). Based on Petri Nets simulation results, DEA is used to quantitatively analyse the detected conflicts. Savic et al. (2012) applied CPN-DEA approach in performance analysis of the queuing system with fixed and additional multitask servers in order to decide when and how long the additional server should be activated. Cavoneet al. (2017) applied Timed Petri Nets for intermodal terminals behaviour simulation and measurement of congestion, i.e. the resources availability. Afterwards, in the case of congestion, DEA is used to identify the most efficient resource planning alternative.

Separately, PNs and DEA are widely used in the areas of networking technology, routing, VoIP and QoS. Billington and Yuan (2009) developed formal model of The Dynamic On-demand (DYMO) routing protocol using Coloured Petri Nets (CPN). The Session Initiation Protocol (SIP), the quasi-standard for VoIP communications, is modelled and analysed using timed CPN in (Kızmaz and Kırcı 2011). In order to verify QoS of General Internet Signalling Transport (GIST), Kumar and Dhindsa (2013) developed CPN model of GIST functioning. Vinayak et al. (2014) simulated Transmission Control Protocol (TCP) using a generalized stochastic Petri net (GSPN) in order to measure performance metrics: throughput, good put, and task completion time of the system. VoIP is observed as a queuing system and analysed using a generalized stochastic Petri net (GSPN) in (Gupta et al. 2015). Vanit-Anunchai (2016) investigates the feature negotiation procedure of the Datagram Congestion Control Protocol (DCCP) by state space analysis of CPN DCCP model. Strzeciwilk and Zuberek (2016) used Petri Nets for modelling and analysis of data transmission queuing performance on systems that support QoS.

DEA is used for selecting a VoIP service provider based on three criteria: cost of service, QoS parameters, and service availability parameters (Bandopadhyay and Bhattacharya 2006). Evaluation of the performance of multicast over coded packet wireless network by exploring DEA is presented by Ajibesin et al. (2013) and Soja et al. (2016). Raayatpanah (2017) used DEA to evaluate efficiency of the arcs of a multicast tree in which each arc has associated several QoS parameters: cost, delay, profit, and CPU time.

The rest of the paper is organized as follows. Basic concepts of QoS negotiation are explained in Sect. 2. Graphical modelling of QoS process for simulation purpose is given in Sect. 3. Simulation output is used for DEA analysis in Sect. 4. Based on that, certain packet routes are be prioritized, and results of additional simulation and analysis are elaborated in Sect. 5. Conclusion is given in Sect. 6.

2 Interdomain QoS Negotiation

Quality of Service (QoS) represents measure of achieved level of performance through one or more observed networks (Wang and Crowcroft 1996; Mali et al. 2014). Interdomain QoS negotiation, or QoS negotiation across multiple domains still considered a challenge because providers need to negotiate on E2E level and ensure achievement of requested performance in a heterogeneous environment (Mali et al. 2014).

Network performance metrics that best describe network capability to fulfil service requests and will be observed in this work are Delay, Jitter and Packet Loss Rate (PLR). Delay is the time needed for the packet to reach the destination from the moment it was sent. Jitter or delay variation is a difference in delay of neighbouring packets. For VoIP and similar technologies it is important to receive packets within equal time intervals so that they are fluently replicated on receiver's end. Furthermore, packets can be lost due to errors or occurrence of network blockage, this loss is expressed as PLR (Mali et al. 2014).

There are several models for QoS negotiation, but for the purpose of this research a Third-party (3P) model will be used. Thanks to its centralized structure and service class mapping process, it is considered as flexible and promising model for E2EQoS achievement.

This model introduces a third party agent as independent participant in QoS negotiation process. Instead of interaction between adjacent domains, agent is communicating with QoS Managers (QM) over signalization protocol (Fig. 1)—it takes specifications of different service classes per each domain along with interconnection costs and uses that data to map service classes that suit customer's service request (Mali et al. 2014). One of algorithms that can be used for E2E service class mapping,

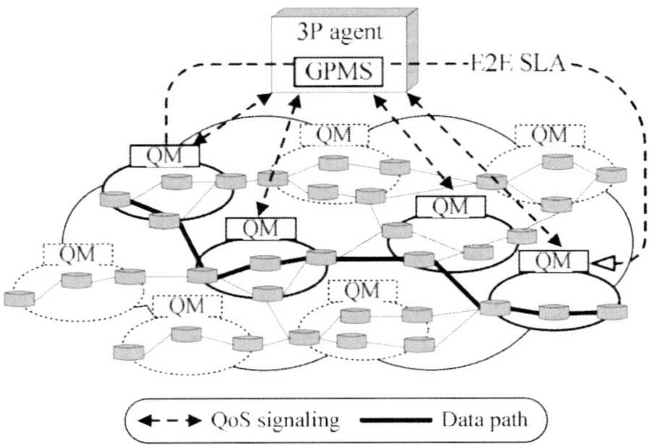

Fig. 1 E2EQoS negotiation through 3P agent

in respect to goals on one side and constraints on the other, is Goal Programming-Based Mapping Scheme (GPMS) (Mali et al. 2014).

3 Simulation of QoS Negotiation

For purpose of this research, a cycle of simulations and efficiency analysis will be performed in order to evaluate the difference in network performance between previous and modified routing strategy. An E2E path is observed, which consists of 2 access and 3 transit domains. Two transit domains are on regional level while one is continental, and packet must go through all hierarchy levels on its path from one access domain to another.

Service providers have service classes specified and they offer QoS in response to requests of client applications, depending on their resources, technology and available capacity. Based on that offer, provider forms the price and sends it out to the customer/user (Mali et al. 2014). Specification of predefined service classes per each domain with dedicated interconnection costs in fictive monetary units is adopted from (Mali et al. 2014) and will be used as input data for simulation and analysis (Table 1).

We will be focusing on one service request (Table 2) which represents maximum allowed totals for all three metrics on E2E path over domains A1-R1-C-R2-A2 after service class mapping is performed.

First step is to model and simulate interdomain QoS negotiation using Coloured Petri Net (CPN) technique. The theoretical basic of CPN is given below, in the following sections.

Definition: A coloured Petri net is a nine-tuple $CPN = \left(\sum, P, T, A, N, C, G, E, I\right)$ satisfying the following requirements (Jensen and Kristensen 2009):

(i) $\sum$ is a finite set of non-empty types, called colour sets.

Table 1 Specification of domain service classes

Domain	Class	Delay [ms]	Jitter [ms]	PLR [1]	Cost [MU]
A1 (access)	1	40	10	10^{-5}	40
	2	80	30	10^{-4}	20
	3	120	40	10^{-4}	15
A2 (access)	1	20	15	10^{-6}	55
	2	50	20	10^{-5}	30
	3	70	30	5×10^{-5}	20
	4	120	40	10^{-4}	17
R1 (regional)	1	15	10	10^{-6}	75
	2	50	30	10^{-5}	60
R2 (regional)	1	12	6	10^{-5}	80
	2	15	8	10^{-4}	70
C (continental)	1	45	5	10^{-5}	90
	2	100	15	5×10^{-4}	65
	3	120	40	10^{-4}	55

Table 2 Service request specification for E2E path A1-R1-C-R2-A2

Metric	Service request
Delay [ms]	150
Jitter [ms]	60
PLR [1]	10^{-4}

(ii) P is a finite set of places.
(iii) T is a finite set of transitions.
(iv) A is a finite set of arcs such that: $P \cap T = P \cap A = T \cap A = \emptyset$.
(v) N is a node function. It is defined from A into $P \times T \cup T \times P$.
(vi) C is a colour function. It is defined from P into $\sum$.
(vii) G is a guard function. It is defined from T into expressions such that: $\forall t \in T : \left[\text{Type}(G(t)) = \text{Bool} \wedge \text{Type}(\text{Var}(G(t))) \subseteq \sum\right]$.
(viii) E is an arc expression function. It is defined from A into this expression: $\forall a \in A : \left[\text{Type}(E(a)) = C(p(a)) \wedge \text{Type}(\text{Var}(E(a))) \subseteq \sum\right]$ where p(a) is the place of N(a).
(ix) I is an initialization function. It is defined from P into this closed expression: $\forall p \in P : \left[\text{Type}(I(p)) = C(p)_{MS}\right]$.

Structure and marking are the main elements of a CPN. Structure consists of two kinds of nodes—places (ellipses) and transitions (rectangles), and weighted branches that connect them. Transitions describe system behaviour while places accumulate and store data Makajić-Nikolić et al. (2013).

Flow of data in CPN is additionally described using tokens which are all assigned a dedicated data type (Colour Set) and can be stored in PN places. Marking of a net

$M = [M(p_1), M(p_2), \ldots, M(p_m)]^T$ represents distribution of those tokens across PN. Functions, written in Standard ML functional programming language, can be joined to transitions in order to manipulate tokens and flow of data. Initial marking, and each one afterwards, is modified when certain transition fires—meaning that event represented with that transition occurred. Along with firing of a transition, tokens from all preceding places are released and transferred to succeeding places. When time value in fictional time units is associated to a transition, it is ready to fire if token's time value in preceding places is equal or greater to global clock time value. This type of PN is called Timed Petri Net and it introduces fictional global clock which models time. Additionally, if duration of transition firing or token value is stochastic, the net is Stochastic Petri Net.

Graphical model of QoS negotiation is hierarchical Petri Net, consisting of two levels. On higher level (Fig. 2), besides packet initialization and process endpoints, core process is modelled with one transition only (PacketRouting). Initial marking is at sender's side (ClientDomainS). Token represents a data packet which structure consists of Delay, Jitter, PLR, Cost and Path values, respectively. CPN data type for Path parameter is list which will be populated based on fired transition—chosen service class, as token will travel through PN during simulation. When token gets to transition PacketRouting, it enters second net level where detailed routing and service class mapping is modelled using Goal Programming-Based Mapping Scheme (GPMS). The algorithm is described in the following paragraphs. Part of lower net level with service class mapping in Domain A1 is presented in Fig. 3.

Each out of N, $d = 1, 2, \ldots, N$ domains is modelled as a place, while classes $k = 1, 2, \ldots, K^d$ within domains are modelled as transitions. Binary variables y_d and x_k^d denote if domain is included on E2E path and if service class is selected, respectively

$$y^d = \begin{cases} 1, \text{ if domain } d \text{ is included on E2E path} \\ 0, \text{ otherwise} \end{cases}, \ d = 1, \ldots, N \tag{1}$$

$$x_k^d = \begin{cases} 1, \text{ if class } k \text{ in domain } d \text{ is selected} \\ 0, \text{ otherwise} \end{cases}, \ k = 1, \ldots, \mathrm{K}^d, d = 1, \ldots, N. \tag{2}$$

In this case, all domains and classes are included in the analysis, but some of them can be excluded for different scenarios by simply assigning 0 value to the corresponding variable. 3P agent selects only one class k per each domain for which $x_k^d = 1$, as stated in (3). Also, net is modelled in the way that token can pass through only one transition/class within one domain.

$$\textstyle\sum_{k=1}^{\mathrm{K}^d} x_k^d = 1 \tag{3}$$

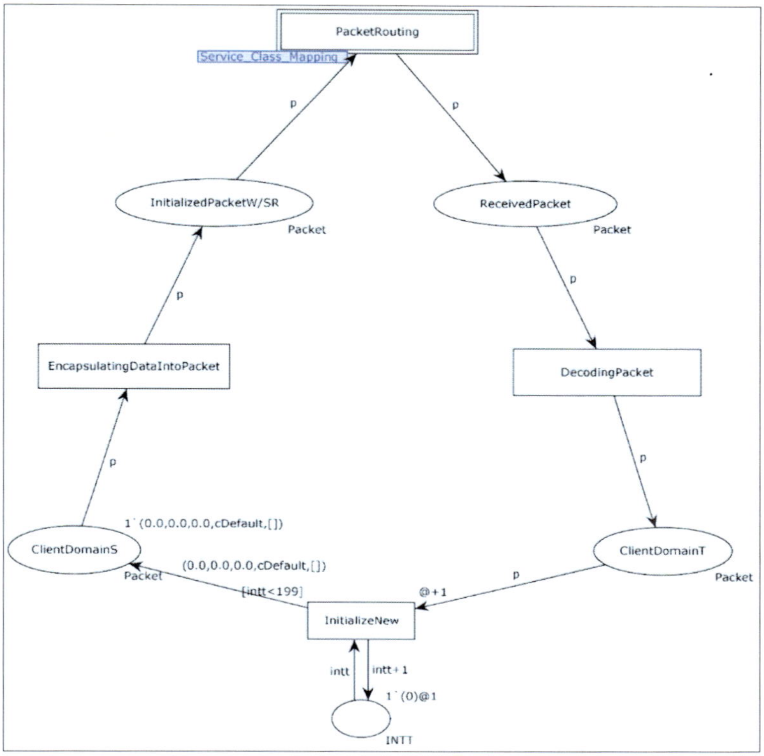

Fig. 2 Higher (1st) net level

Set of parameters is introduced for QoS performance metrics. Requested values are $\mu_{1,req}, \mu_{2,req}, \mu_{3,req}$ for Delay, Jitter and PLR, respectively. Parameters $\mu_{1,req}, \mu_{2,req}$ and $\mu_{3,req}$ denote offered values by class k within domain d. Additionally, service providers define interconnection cost c_k^d per service class which applies to each transferred packet. All mentioned parameters are included in PN data model.

Since E2E values of network metrics must not exceed requested values, following constraints (4) and (5) have to be respected in mathematical model of the problem.

$$\sum\nolimits_{d=1}^{N} \sum\nolimits_{k=1}^{K^d} \mu_{j,k}^d x_k^d y_d + \delta_j^- - \delta_j^+ = \mu_{j,req}, j = 1, 2 \quad (4)$$

$$\sum\nolimits_{d=1}^{N} \sum\nolimits_{k=1}^{K^d} \left(-log\left(1 - \mu_{j,k}^d\right)\right) x_k^d y_d + \delta_j^- - \delta_j^+ = -log\left(1 - \mu_{j,k}^d\right), j = 3 \quad (5)$$

For additive metrics, constraint (4) applies, where δ_j^- and δ_j^+ are auxiliary variables for positive and negative deviation (Mali et al. 2014). On the other hand, PLR is

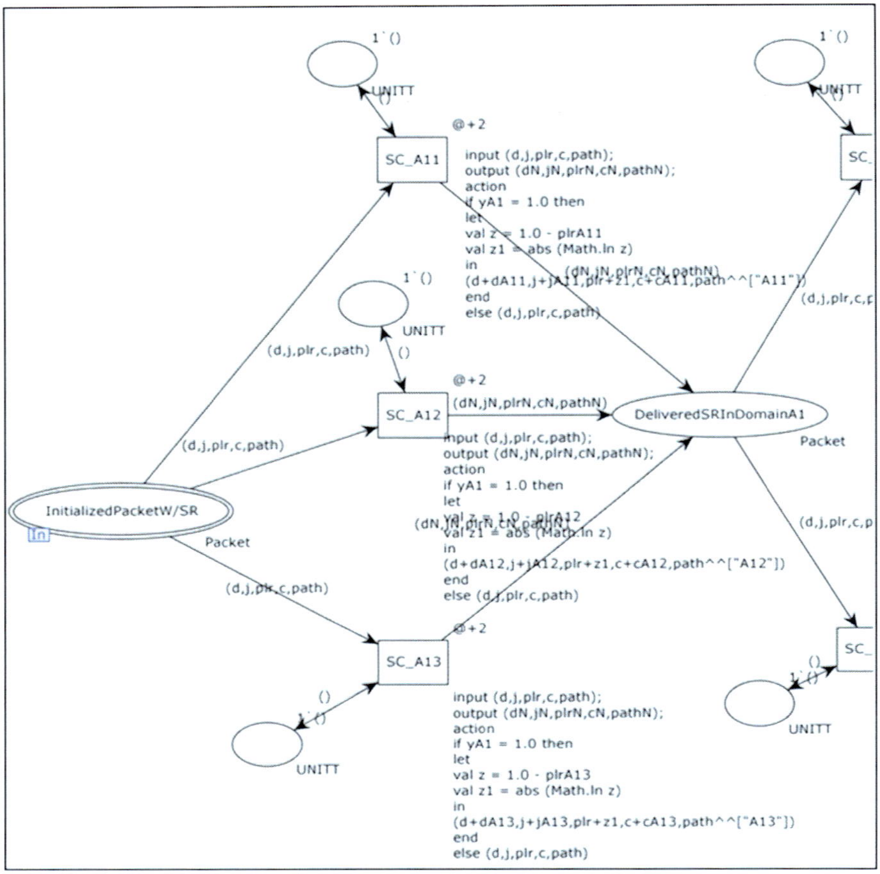

Fig. 3 Part of lower (2nd) level net

multiplicative metric so logarithmic function will be used to convert it to additive value and enable summation which is represented with constraint (5).

The goal is to establish the interconnection with minimal total costs while fulfilling all service requests. GPMS algorithm is providing the possibility to set weights α_j and α_c for metric performance values and for interconnection cost, respectively, in order to define goal importance. Objective function is given with (6).

$$Z = min\left\{\sum\nolimits_{j=1}^{3} \alpha_j\left(\delta_j^- + \delta_j^+\right) + \alpha_c \sum\nolimits_{d=1}^{N} \sum\nolimits_{k=1}^{K^d} C_k^d x_k^d y_d\right\} \quad (6)$$

Having in mind this mathematical model, translation to PN is as follows. If transition SC_A12 is fired, token will get to place DeliveredSRInDomainA1 and that means that Service Class 2 is mapped in Domain A1.

Table 3 New service request specification for E2E path A1-R1-C-R2-A2

Metric	Service request	New service request
Delay [ms]	150	350
Jitter [ms]	60	140
PLR [1]	10^{-4}	6×10^{-4}

PN is expanded to Timed PN to implement round robin routing strategy which states that two neighbouring packets must not have common nodes, meaning that they won't be mapped to the same class on E2E path. Round robin, one of the dispersion strategies, is used to balance the traffic, regulate path load and make packet losses on neighbouring paths statistically independent (disjoint routes).

After routing, Degree of Correspondence (DC) is calculated to segregate only admissible solutions. DC_j^{E2E} is indicator of correspondence between requested E2E value $\mu_{j,req}$ and offered E2E value $\mu_{j,off}$ of network performance metric j. It is calculated as in (7) for additive metrics and in (8) for multiplicative metrics (Ninković et al. 2015).

$$DC_j^{E2E} = \frac{\mu_{j,req}}{\mu_{j,off}}, \; j = 1, 2 \tag{7}$$

$$DC_j^{E2E} = \frac{\left|log\mu_{j,req}\right|}{\left|log\mu_{j,off}\right|}, \; j = 3 \tag{8}$$

If $DC_j^{E2E} = 1$, it means that requested and offered E2E QoS for metric j is perfectly aligned. If $DC_j^{E2E} > 1$ means that offered quality is better than requested. In case that $DC_j^{E2E} < 1$ for any of three metrics, meaning that offered quality is worse than requested, these packets will be considered as inadmissible solutions and won't be taken into consideration for further analysis. Similarly, admissible solutions are the ones with $DC_j^{E2E} \geq 1, j = 1, 2, 3$. This is modelled in PN as two transitions for received (admissible) packets and lost (inadmissible) packets with guard expressions in order to filter fulfilled and unfulfilled service requests given in Table 2.

The first results showed that there is only one route R1 (A11-R11-C1-R21-A21) with all minimal values of QoS performance (Delay = 132, Jitter = 46 and PLR = 0.0000320001) satisfies DC $\geq$ 1 criteria for all of them. This means that there is no possibility to generate more than one admissible route according to criteria defined by (7) and (8). Therefore, packet dispersion over admissible route is impossible. Such a situation could make difficulties in transfer of large packages if the capacity of the route is not sufficient and there is no negotiation. Thus, it is therefore necessary to find a number of good enough routes and make the selection of those efficient among them. Those routes will be put in the negotiation set. This can be achieved if Service Requests are relaxed. We arbitrarily relaxed the initial requirements and new acceptable values are given in Table 3.

This relaxation follows to generating 200 routes. But, out of 200 routing simulations performed, 131 packets went through admissible routes while 69 went through paths that didn't satisfy requested QoS. Inputs for further efficiency analysis are only unique admissible routes—46 of them, along with all their attributes (structure and realized values of network metrics).

4 Route Efficiency Analysis

Efficiency principle implies that desired economic effects are achieved with the least possible usage of resources. Efficiency analysis techniques can be divided into parametric and nonparametric. Data envelopment analysis (DEA) has become leading nonparametric technique for performance measurement. DEA performs comparative analysis of DMUs while taking in consideration all relevant system inputs and outputs, independently of technology used to transform inputs to outputs. Additionally, inputs don't have to be homogenous—DEA is specifically designed to measure the efficiency of complex entities (Martić and Savić 2001).

Objects of DEA analysis are Decision Making Units (DMU). DEA uses set of units with common inputs and outputs and analyses the efficiency of every unit in comparison to efficient units. DMU can be any instance of an entity that participates in a process by transforming inputs to outputs (Thanassoulis 2001). Having in mind QoS negotiation problem analysed in this paper, DMUs are routes generated with previously performed simulation. Component of these routes are service classes, one per each observed domain. Calculation and charge of interconnection costs are based on their network performance.

Efficiency of generated routes will be analysed using DEA which represents the key for prioritization. That is because the idea is to adapt the network and improve QoS negotiation process by giving priority to efficient routes. After choosing DMUs, inputs and outputs have to be determined in the model. Since the aim is to minimize Delay, Jitter, PLR and Cost, all of these parameters will be defined as inputs. In particular, inputs are achieved delay, achieved delay variation, achieved PLR and charged interconnection Cost. Fictive parameter is introduced as output that has value 1 for all DMUs. An example of input parameters and corresponding values for several routes generated during simulation together with data descriptive statistics in given in Table 4. The routes are sorted in ascending order of Delay. Obviously, total costs are lower if the QoS is lower. This is the way for providers to attract transfer through their domains. Table 4 shows that mean performance (Delay $=$ 257.43, Jitter $=$ 95.13 and PLR $=$ 0.000232) of generated unique routes are highly above strict criteria level defined in Table 2 as it is aforementioned. But all routes fulfil new requests given in Table 3. Standard deviation of is quite high for all parameters (almost quarter of range) and one can conclude that performance of generated routes vary a lot.

Next step is to choose mathematical model that would best fit and provide logical and valid results of efficiency analysis. There are several basic DEA models which have been intensively developed over the years so that many extended models are available today. For the purpose of this work, we will use basic CCR DEA (Charnes

Table 4 Input data records for DEA analysis (an example)

DMU	Delay	Jitter	PLR	Cost	A1	R1	C	R2	A2
R1	132	46	0.0000320001	340	A11	R11	C1	R21	A21
R2	162	51	0.0000410002	315	A11	R11	C1	R21	A22
R3	170	68	0.0001310051	315	A11	R12	C1	R22	A21
...									
R44	345	128	0.000320015	242	A11	R12	C3	R22	A24
R45	347	126	0.000311015	247	A12	R11	C3	R21	A24
R46	350	123	0.000320015	252	A13	R12	C1	R22	A24
Descriptive statistics									
Mean	257.43	95.13	0.000232	276.91					
Median	258.50	97.00	0.000221	280.00					
St. Dev.	54.68	23.65	0.000113	25.32					
Range	218.00	92.00	0.000539	115.00					
Minimum	132.00	46.00	0.000032	225.00					
Maximum	350.00	138.00	0.000571	340.00					

et al. 1978) assuming constant return to scale. This model got its name by Charnes, Cooper and Rhodes that developed basic DEA model. Description of the dual DEA mathematical model follows description in paper by Savić and Martic (2016).

Let x_{ij} be value of observed input i for $DMU_j(x_{ij} > 0, i = 1, 2, \ldots, m,\ j = 1, 2, \ldots, n)$, while y_{ij} is value of observed output r for $\text{DMU}_j\left(y_{rj} > 0, r = 1, 2, \ldots, s, j = 1, 2, \ldots, n\right)$. Dual variable λ_j is dual weight of observed $DMU_j(j = 1, 2, \ldots, n)$. Values of this variable are chosen in respect to the constraints (9), (10) and (11).

$$\sum\nolimits_{j=1}^{n} \lambda_j y_{rj} - s_r^+ = y_{rk}, \quad r = 1, 2, \ldots, s \tag{9}$$

$$Z_k x_{ik} - \sum\nolimits_{j=1}^{n} \lambda_j x_{ij} - s_i^- = 0, \quad i = 1, 2, \ldots, m \tag{10}$$

$$\lambda_j, s_r^+, s_i^- \geq 0, \quad j = 1, 2, \ldots n, \quad r = 1, 2, \ldots, s, \quad i = 1, 2, \ldots, m, Z_k - \text{unlimited} \tag{11}$$

Dual variables s_r^+ and s_i^- state how much k-th DMU can reduce input i and increase output r in order to become efficient. It is the difference between input and output values of observed unit and input and output values of its benchmark unit, respectively.

Finally, objective function (12) of this dual model minimizes input value needed to achieve the existing output level of DMU k. Variable Z_k if intensity factor and states how much DMU k can proportionally reduce all of its inputs.

$$(min) Z_k - \varepsilon\left(\sum\nolimits_{r=1}^{s} s_r^+ - \sum\nolimits_{i=1}^{m} s_i^-\right) \tag{12}$$

The number of DMUs drastically exceeds total number of inputs and outputs and we are expecting good distinction between efficient and inefficient routes. Result of Data Envelopment Analysis is 14 efficient routes in total (Table 5), with information about their belonging nodes/mapped service classes and DC levels. Column Benchmark indicates number of times when observed DMU was dominating in comparison to some other DMU. DMU R18 can be considered poorly efficient because in Benchmark column are listed units for which R18 is dominated. Anyway, R18 will be taken into consideration for further analysis since service request is still fulfilled for this route. It is interesting to mention that in the group of efficient routes are very good performers (R1 and R2) as well as ones among the worst performers (R40, R42 and R43) in the observing set of 44 routes. Routes R1 and R2 are efficient due to good performance and very good DC levels even though costs are 340 and 315, respectively. On the other hand, routes R40, R42 and R43 are efficient due to low costs (255, 225 and 245, respectively). Those routes are candidates for negotiation, but more routes are generated in the second stage of prioritization simulation described in the Sect. 5.

5 Route Prioritization

Based on appearance frequency of each class in all efficient routes, we will simply calculate the probability of choosing the class per domain. Therefore, sum of probabilities for all classes under one domain is equal to 1. If service class isn't part of any efficient route, it's probability will be 0. PN is updated accordingly, simulation is performed and second DEA analysis with new inputs will show if number of admissible and efficient routes increased.

The idea is to introduce stochastic variable in the Petri Net—uniformly distributed random number between 0 and 1 that will be generated per each domain. PN is modified so that in every domain a random number is generated (transitions *Generate_Random_<domain name>*) before service class mapping occurs. Along with that, token structure is expanded with random number parameter of type Real. On the other hand, existing transitions are updated with guard (Boolean) expressions to check which range random number belongs to. Ranges are defined according to cumulative values from Table 6.

Depending on random number value, relevant transition will fire. Wider ranges and therefore, greater probability of firing will have transitions/classes with greater frequency of appearance in efficient routes. Updates on PN regarding random number generation, token structure and guard expressions are marked yellow in Fig. 4.

Simulation is performed 200 times, meaning that 200 packets are sent as in the previous case, in order to compare the results. Figure 5 clearly states that number of admissible solutions increased by 46, meaning that 46 more packets reached the destination. There are identified 4 unique routes more than in the previous case. But more importantly, another DEA analysis will show if number of efficient routes has been increased.

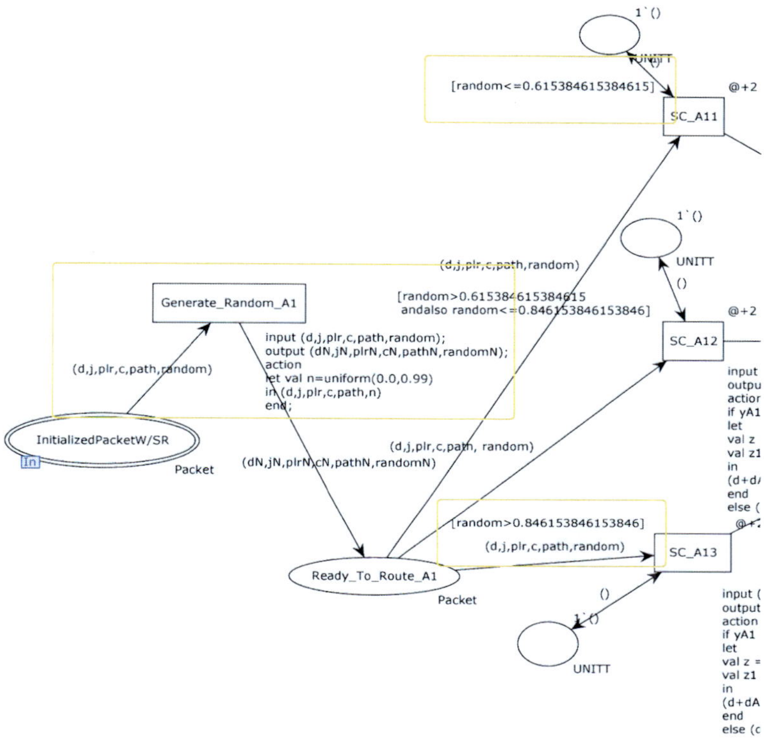

Fig. 4 Part of updated Petri Net after route prioritization

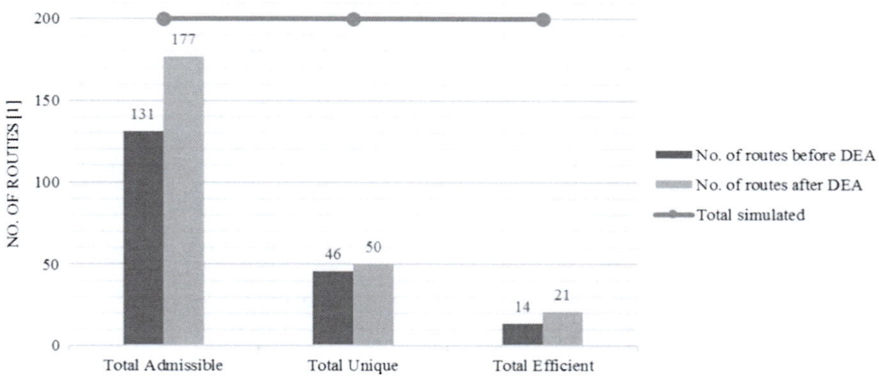

Fig. 5 Results comparison

Table 5 Efficient routes

No.	DMU	Benchmark	Route	DC (Delay)	DC (Jitter)	DC (PLR)
1	R1	0	A11-R11-C1-R21-A21	2.652	2.745	1.362
2	R2	12	A11-R11-C1-R21-A22	2.160	2.745	1.362
3	R7	18	A11-R12-C1-R22-A22	1.750	3.043	1.205
4	R12	12	A11-R11-C2-R21-A22	1.613	3.043	1.205
5	R13	6	A11-R12-C1-R22-A23	1.591	3.043	1.205
6	R16	7	A11-R11-C2-R21-A23	1.477	3.043	1.205
7	R17	9	A11-R11-C3-R21-A22	1.477	3.043	1.205
8	R18	7 (0.01)13 (0.48) 24 (0.51)	A12-R12-C1-R22-A22	1.458	3.043	1.205
9	R24	7	A12-R12-C1-R22-A23	1.346	3.043	1.205
10	R28	17	A11-R12-C3-R22-A22	1.273	3.043	1.205
11	R33	11	A11-R12-C3-R22-A23	1.186	3.043	1.205
12	R40	2	A13-R11-C3-R21-A22	1.104	3.043	1.205
13	R42	9	A12-R12-C3-R22-A23	1.045	3.043	1.205
14	R43	1	A13-R11-C3-R21-A23	1.039	3.043	1.205

Simulation output is again preprocessed in order to be used as input data for DEA analysis. DEA analysis resulted in 21 efficient routes, which is 7 more than before route prioritization (Fig. 5). These routes are presented in Table 7.

From network performance point of view, this tell us that more packets are delivered and better QoS is achieved after adapting the routing selection strategy Even 7 out of 10 first routes are assessed as efficient which makes good bases for negotiation; there are enough good performers if the quality is the main criteria and enough inexpensive routes if the cost is main criteria for decision maker.

Table 6 Probability of choosing each class within their domains

Domain	SC	Frequency	Probability	Cumulative (per domain)
A1	A11	9	0.64286	0.64286
	A12	3	0.21429	0.85714
	A13	2	0.14286	1
R1	R11	7	0.5	0.5
	R12	7	0.5	1
C	C1	6	0.42857	0.42857
	C2	2	0.14286	0.57143
	C3	6	0.42857	1
R2	R21	7	0.5	0.5
	R22	7	0.5	1
A2	A21	1	0.07143	0.07143
	A22	7	0.5	0.57143
	A23	6	0.42857	1
	A24	0	0	1

6 Conclusion

Now days, in digital era, data transition and communication certain quality of service must be provided. This puts process of QoS negotiation into a focus of this analysis. We considered the problem of sending packets across disjoint routes on an interdomain level so that required QoS is achieved on E2E level, with goal to improve QoS negotiation process by prioritizing routes. The process is based on simulation and efficiency analysis of admissible routes.

Petri Nets, technique for graphical and mathematical modelling of distributed systems, and Data Envelopment Analysis, method for efficiency analysis, together are very powerful tools for analysis and improvement of interdomain QoS negotiation. Results have shown that increasing probability of choosing the efficient route in the network in combination with applied dispersion strategy, has led to significant improvement of QoS achievement on E2E path. Network efficiency improved and consequently, more packets are delivered from source to destination.

It should be taken into consideration that the problem is analysed using simplified network model for international traffic. Offered QoS depends on network structure, service class differentiation and QoS negotiation model. Nevertheless, 3P model and GPMS used for service class mapping proved to be excellent for modelling of E2EQoS achievement. Flexibility to address multiple objectives and constraints at the same time may be promising characteristic of service class mapping algorithms of the future.

Table 7 Efficient routes after final DEA analysis

No.	DMU	Route	DC(Delay)	DC(Jitter)	DC(PLR)
1	R1	A11-R11-C1-R22-A21	2.593	2.745	1.362
2	R2	A11-R11-C1-R21-A22	2.160	2.745	1.362
3	R3	A11-R11-C1-R22-A22	2.121	2.745	1.362
4	R6	A11-R11-C1-R22-A23	1.892	2.917	1.362
5	R7	A11-R12-C1-R21-A22	1.777	2.917	1.362
6	R8	A11-R12-C1-R22-A22	1.750	2.917	1.362
7	R10	A12-R11-C1-R22-A22	1.707	2.917	1.362
8	R13	A11-R11-C2-R21-A22	1.613	2.917	1.362
9	R15	A11-R12-C1-R22-A23	1.591	2.917	1.362
10	R17	A12-R11-C1-R22-A23	1.556	2.917	1.362
11	R18	A11-R11-C2-R21-A23	2.593	2.745	1.362
12	R19	A11-R11-C3-R21-A22	1.477	2.917	1.362
13	R21	A11-R11-C3-R22-A22	1.458	2.917	1.362
14	R30	A11-R11-C3-R22-A23	1.346	2.917	1.362
15	R35	A11-R12-C3-R21-A22	1.287	2.917	1.362
16	R36	A11-R12-C3-R22-A22	1.273	2.917	1.362
17	R40	A11-R12-C3-R21-A23	1.199	2.917	1.362
18	R41	A11-R12-C3-R22-A23	1.186	2.917	1.362
19	R44	A12-R11-C3-R22-A23	1.167	2.917	1.362
20	R48	A12-R12-C3-R21-A23	1.054	2.917	1.362
21	R49	A12-R12-C3-R22-A23	1.045	2.917	1.362

Acknowledgements Special thanks to dr. Nina Turajlić for valuable comments and sharing domain knowledge that greatly assisted the research.

References

Ajibesin AA, Ventura N, Murgu A, Chan HA (2013) Cost-efficient multicast over coded packet wireless networks using data envelopment analysis. In: 2013 IEEE consumer communications and networking conference (CCNC), pp 546–551

Bandopadhyay T, Bhattacharya S (2006) Obtaining voice-over-IP services: a comparison between selection processes amongst single vendor options and multi-vendor options. In: IEEE international conference on industrial informatics, pp 845–850

Billington J, Yuan C (2009) On modelling analysing the dynamic MANET on-demand (DYMO) routing protocol. In: Jensen K, Billington J, Koutny M (eds) Transactions on Petri Nets and other models of concurrency III. Lecture notes in computer science, vol 5800. Springer, Berlin, Heidelberg

Cavone G, Dotoli M, Epicoco N, Seatzu C (2017) Intermodal terminal planning by Petri Nets and data envelopment analysis. Control Eng Pract 69:9–22

Charnes A, Cooper WW, Rhodes E (1978) Measuring the efficiency of decision making units. Eur J Oper Res 2:429–444
Dutta A, Dasgupta R, Bhattacharya S (2012) Modelling of VoIP based tele-teaching system: a Petri Net based approach. Int J Comput Sci Issues 9(5(3)):152–163
Gupta V, Dharmaraja S, Arunachalam V (2015) Stochastic modeling for delay analysis of a VoIP network. Ann Oper Res 233(1):171–180
Jensen K, Kristensen LM (2009) Coloured Petri Nets modelling and validation of concurrent systems. Springer, Heidelberg
Kızma S, Kırcı M (2011) Verification of session initiation protocol using timed colored Petri Net. Int J Commun Netw Syst Sci 4(03):170–179
Kumar A, Dhindsa KS (2013) Modeling and analysis of general internet signaling transport protocol (GIST) using coloured Petri Nets. Int J Sci Eng Comput Technol 3(11):382–387
Kurose JF, Ross KW (2013) Computer networking: a top-down approach. Pearson Education, New Jersey
Makajic-Nikolic D, Vujosevic M, Nikolic N (2013) Minimal cut sets of a coherent fault tree generation using reverse Petri Nets. Optimization 62(8):1069–1087
Mali BJ, Ninkovic NM, Stojanovic MD, Savic GI (2014) Service class mapping based on integer programming algorithm in the third-party agent. In: Telecommunications forum Telfor (TELFOR), pp 170–173
Martić M, Savić G (2001) An application of DEA for comparative analysis and ranking of regions in Serbia with regards to social-economic development. Eur J Oper Res 132(2):343–356
Ninković N, Mali B, Stojanović M, Savić G (2015) Multi-objective third-party approach for service class mapping among multiple providers in the internet. Elektron Elektrotech 21(2):80–84
Raayatpanah MA (2017) Multicast routing based on data envelopment analysis with multiple quality of Service parameters. Int J Commun Syst 30(5). https://doi.org/10.1002/dac.3084
Savic G, Makajic-Nikolic D, Vujosevic M (2012) Selecting the activation rule of an additional server using Petri Nets and data envelopment analysis. In: Grzybowska K (ed) Contemporary management. Publishing House of Poznan University of Technology, Poznań, pp 117–136. ISBN 978-83-7775-192-3
Savić G, Martić M (2016) Composite indicators construction by data envelopment analysis: In: Jeremic (ed) Methodological background emerging trends in the development and application of composite indicators, pp 98–126
Shiau J Y, Li X (2009) Modeling the supply chain based on multi-agent conflicts. In: IEEE/INFORMS international conference on service operations, logistics and informatics, SOLI'09, pp 394–399
Soja JS, Luka MK, Thuku IT, Girei SH (2016) Comparison of performance efficiency of improved network coding multicast algorithms using data envelopment analysis. Commun Appl Electron (CAE) 5(2):6–10
Strzeciwilk D, Zuberek WM (2016) Modeling and performance analysis of QoS data In: Photonics applications in astronomy, communications, industry, and high-energy physics experiments, vol 10031, pp 1003158. International Society for Optics and Photonics
Thanassoulis E (2001) Introduction to the theory and application of data envelopment analysis. Springer Science Business Media, New York
Vanit-Anunchai S (2016) Validating DCCP simultaneous feature negotiation procedure. Transactions on Petri Nets and other models of concurrency XI. Springer, Berlin, Heidelberg, pp 71–91
Vinayak R, Krishnaswamy D, Dharmaraja S (2014) Analytical modeling of transmission control protocol NewReno using generalized stochastic Petri Nets. Int J Commun Syst 27(12):4185–4198
Wang Z, Crowcroft J (1996) Quality-of-service routing for supporting multimedia applications. IEEE J Sel Area Commun 14(7):1228–1234

Business Applications

Quality Losses as the Key Argument in the Public Procurement in Healthcare

Ivana Mijatovic and Rade Lazovic

Abstract The amount of public procurement spending is growing globally and about one-third of public-sector spending is related to hospitals and healthcare institutions. Knowing that facts, it is a wise decision to strengthen the capacity and capabilities of purchasing public organizations to manage public procurements. Translating needs of public authorities, as well as final users of goods and services, into tender documentation is a complex task which needs multidisciplinary teams. One of the key problems in a public procurement is related to defining specific requirements for companies (bidders), award criteria and technical specification of quality of goods and services. Many purchasing public organizations consider public procurement processes as finished immediately after purchasing and forgot processes of quality surveillance. Dominant practice-public procurement with only one or dominant award criterion based on the lowest price might have as a result purchasing of low-quality goods and services. To prevent that, the purchasing organizations need to apply criteria in addition to or other than price and to describe the functions of the product or the desired outcomes rather than technical specifications. This paper has the aim to present usage of Quadratic Quality Loss Function (QQLF) for the analysis of quality of medical devices for the purpose of public procurement. The application of the QQLF concept can help public purchasing organizations to develop their ability to adequately address problems of quality in use and achieve values for the price. The average or expected quality losses which can be calculated by QQLF are a valuable argument in preventing lower quality products to be repurchased and can be added to other award criteria.

Keywords Quality · Public procurement · Medical devices · Quality losses

Note: First version of this paper is published at SyMOPIS 2017 Proceedings.

I. Mijatovic (✉) · R. Lazovic
Faculty of Organizational Sciences, University of Belgrade, Belgrade, Serbia
e-mail: ivanamt@fon.bg.ac.rs

R. Lazovic
e-mail: lazovic@fon.bg.ac.rs

N. Mladenović et al. (eds.), *Advances in Operational Research in the Balkans*, Springer Proceedings in Business and Economics,
https://doi.org/10.1007/978-3-030-21990-1_12

1 Introduction

Translating needs of public authorities, as well as final users of goods and services, into tender documentation in accordance with the public procurement law and on a timely manner is a complex task which needs multidisciplinary teams. In many cases, the key problem is related to defining specific requirements for companies (bidders), award criteria, and technical specification of the quality of goods and services. The award criteria have to be established in advance and they serve as a basis for choosing the best tender. Dominant practice is that public procurements are based on only one or dominant award criterion—the lowest price. That practices might have as a result purchasing goods and services of low quality. Based on data taken from the Public Procurement Reporting (European Commission 2015, p. 5–6) overreliance on lowest price in tenders is evident, and better criteria based on specific context are needed. To prevent (re)purchasing goods and services of low quality, technical specifications for quality of goods and services have to be carefully defined in tender documents as well as more specific criteria have to be considered.

Providing an adequate technical specification for products and services in public procurement is often seen as a key problem in the public procurement. Due to the information asymmetry (e.g., producers know much more about products than buyers) and a large number of products with similar quality characteristics on the market, the specification of only technical characteristics of products and services in tender documentation might be insufficient. "Complex product categories are typically best suited to functional tenders, in which the purchasing organization describes the functions of the product or the desired outcomes rather than technical specifications, and gives suppliers leeway to identify the best solutions" (Husted and Reinecke 2009). More clearly, purchasing public organizations needs to define the wanted function of a purchasing item, not technical specifications. For example, the healthcare institutions might define in a tender that they want 9.000 of 4D ultrasound services for medical exams of adult patients, with staff training and nonstop during the three years. So the bidder should offer the service, not only equipment. In that case, purchasing organizations transfer the risk of adequate functioning of equipment to a bidder.

The EU law limits the award criteria to either the lowest price criterion or the most economically advantageous tender (MEAT) criterion, which means applying criteria in addition to or other than price (Sigma 2011). How to know what is most economically advantageous tender? Many purchasing public organizations consider public procurement processes as finished immediately after purchasing and forgot processes of quality surveillance, e.g., analyzing of the fulfillment of tender requirements and desired outcomes of purchased goods or services as well as complaint handling.

Very well known case in the literature about EU law related to the public procurement, the case 489/06 at the European Court of Justice, explains this problem. According to Van de Gronden et al. (2011, p. 433), the general hospital the Vanzelio-Pananio from Crete, Greece, had issued tender for purchasing surgical sutures. One of the nine bidders was the Medipac-Katyantyidis. Surgeons of the Vanzelio-Pananio hospital claimed to the tendering committee that sutures proposed by the Medipac-Katyantyidis are of low quality and ask the committee to exclude the Medipac-Katyantyidis from the tender. After being excluded from the tender, the Medipac-Katyantyidis started the process at the European Court of Justice. The decision of the European Court of Justice was that the Vanzelio-Pananio hospital had no right to exclude the Medipac-Katyantyidis from the tender—based on only claims of surgeons and that "the contracting authority should, if it considers that those materials can jeopardize public health, inform the competent national authority and set the safeguard procedure." (Van de Gronden et al. 2011, p. 433). The main conclusion from this case is that purchasing public organizations are responsible to provide adequate arguments for the low quality of purchased items in order to prevent repurchasing low-quality items again.

The aim of this study is to explore needs and possibilities of usage of the concept of the *Taguchi's quality loss function* for providing arguments for the public procurements in describing functions of the products as desired outcomes. We claim that in a public procurement, aside specifying a technical data related to specific products, as well as requiring the objective evidence of conformity with regulations or standards (e.g., declarations or certificates of conformity); quality can be specified as the loss in monetary units imparted by product or service from the time product being purchased. In order to elaborate our claim and to further elaborate mathematical base of calculating losses due to quality, we explained Taguchi's concept of quality and quadratic quality loss function (in Sect. 2). The specific application in public procurement of medical devices is elaborated in Sect. 3.

2 Literature Review

2.1 *Needs for Transparency and Specific Communication in Public Procurement*

Public procurement can be defined as "purchasing work, goods or services from companies by public authorities" (e.g., government departments, local authorities, public hospitals, etc.) ("Public procurement" 2017). The amount of public procurement spending has been increasing globally. Based on data of the Organization for Economic Co-operation and Development (OECD) and the Mc Kinsey analysis; purchasing accounts for one-third of public-sector spending and with purchasing a share of 34% on national defense, 31% on hospitals and 29% on departments of central governance (Husted and Reinecke 2009). According to the European Commission (2017a, b), public procurement in the EU accounts for more than 14% of Gross Domestic Product (GDP). The Republic of Serbia annually spends around 3,000,000,000 EUR through public procurement procedures (Varinac and Ninić 2014, p. 2).

Public procurement is regulated by law in order to provide the best value for money through transparency, equal treatment, and nondiscrimination (European Commission 2015). In European Union, prior to the implementation of EU legislation related to public procurement, "only 2% of public procurement contracts were awarded to non-national undertakings" ("Public procurement contracts" 2017). It is clear that many governments, use public procurement to support the domestic economy (certain regions, industry sectors, or even companies; innovations, entrepreneurship, environmentally friendly products or businesses, etc.) as an argument for spending money domestically even when purchasing internationally would be less expensive (Husted and Reinecke 2009). Aside the goals related to the better allocation of economic resources, more rational use and easier approach of Small and Medium Enterprises (SMEs) to public funds, EU legislation support open and effective competition in public procurement market. "A McKinsey survey of purchasing practices in more than 300 organizations in a wide range of industries revealed that public-sector institutions lag behind private-sector companies on several performance dimensions, including efficiency of purchasing tools and processes, capabilities, and performance management" (Husted and Reinecke 2009). Strengthening the capacity and capabilities of purchasing public organizations to manage public procurements is one of the most important tasks in developing a public procurement market.

Study of Uyarra et al. 2014, based on a survey of public-sector suppliers in the UK, identify main barriers as: the lack of interaction with procuring organizations, over-specified tenders as opposed to outcome-based specifications, poor management in the procurement process, lack of useful feedback from procuring organizations. The study of microenterprises and their interaction with public procurement systems in Ireland of McKevitt and Davis (2013) has driven attention to specific needs of small enterprises and pointed that micro and small enterprises, due their different strategies and experiences in public procurement, are not homogenous groups.

The transparent and fair process of public procurement is important for all actors on the market: public authorities, companies, final users/consumers/customers, the general public, and others. However, many countries still face problems in establishing transparent and fair public procurement markets (see more in World Bank Group 2017). Study of Mijatovic and Stokic (2010), based on 122 companies, operating in Serbia, shoved that self-regulation like transparent corporate values, code of conducts, implemented management system standards ISO 9001 and ISO 14001 positively influence transparency in business activities. Transparency in business activities and communication with stakeholders is less accepted in domestic companies comparing to multinational companies operating in Serbia (Mijatovic et al. 2015). However, many foreign and multinational companies, which launched their business activities in Serbia, share their practice with their suppliers and partners (Vlastelica et al. 2016).

2.2 Role of Standards in Public Procurement

The problem of trust in quality or safety certificates is recognized and it is of high complexity—certification and notified works on commercial base and in general, this area is not regulated (Gustafsson and Hallstrom 2013). The role of standards in public procurement is important and diverse. "Product standards include specific designs, technical characteristics, attributes of a given product, as well as sector-specific technical standards and product safety standards. Such standards are of critical importance, especially to well functioning global production networks without which globally dispersed supply chains could not function" (Nadvi 2008). An important implication is that standardization efforts need to be seen as long-term strategic initiatives that drive the creation and adoption of standards and innovations. If the search processes and resulting standards are not coordinated in pursuit of an innovation goal, then the risk is the effort will be a collection of disconnected standardization exercises that result in bureaucratic inefficiencies, commoditization or the stifling of creativity (Xie et al. 2016).

The basic explanation is that usage of international, European and national standards in public procurement processes is inevitable—in providing objective evidence (e.g., by providing a declaration or a certificate of conformity) that producers fulfill minimal requirements for safety, quality, and effectiveness of their processes or products. However, even if producers/bidders provide objective evidence that their products meet the essential requirements of all relevant European directives (CE mark), the problems with quality might occur. Aside from the basic requirements, such as CE mark (it is still not mandatory requirement in Serbia), the purchasing organizations need to provide other requirements that will provide that products they purchase are of adequate quality.

Many international and European standards are developed in order to define minimal requirements for safety and effectiveness of medical devices, and some of them are belonging of a specific group of standards—(harmonized in Europe or recognized standards in the USA and Canada) which are "developed by experts that represent the three parties in the market – manufacturers, users, and competent authorities – to ascertain that no interest group outvotes the other parties and the biases of an 'easy way out' (manufacturers), unrealistic expectations (users) and excessive demands (competent authorities) can be avoided" (Klaus 2015).

2.3 Taguchi's Quadratic Quality Loss Functions

Many studies confirm that Taguchi quadratic loss function can be used in many different areas: in the evaluation and selection of suppliers (Ordoobadi 2009, 2010); as a management tool (Moen 1998); optimization of multi-machining characteristics (Singh and Kumar 2006); estimation of a patient-treatment process quality in a hospital emergency department (Mascio 2007), Manufacturing conformity assessment

(Perona 1998). Study of Taner and Antony (2006) explored how Taguchi methods can be applied to health care, they claimed that Taguchi quadratic quality loss function can be used as "a powerful motivator for a quality strategy and can be used to adequately model the loss to society in health care. It also establishes a relationship between cost and variability. Therefore, it can be integrated with the performance and parameters of the design of medical applications."

Work and theories of Genichi Taguchi are well known in the quality management theory and his definition of a quality was quite revolutionary in the 1980s. He defined quality as "the loss imparted by product or service to the society from the time product being shipped" (Taguchi et al. 2005). Based on this definition, quality of products or services should be related to the losses which are expressed in monetary units, caused by failures, problems or malfunctioning of products or a service on the market. Quality of the product or the service is a complex concept and in practice is often represented by many quality characteristics. In many cases, quality characteristics of products and services are correlated. In general, quality characteristics ($y_1, y_2, y_3, \ldots, y_n$) are continuous variables that can be nominal-the-best (NtB), smaller the better (StB) and larger the better (LtB). NtB quality characteristics are defined by their target value m and tolerance Δ (e.g., $\mathrm{m} \pm \Delta$; $\mathrm{m} \neq 0$, $\mathrm{m} \neq \infty$). StB quality characteristics are a special case of NtB characteristics in which target value m is equal to zero and tolerance is defined as maximum acceptable level. LtBs are a special case of NtB quality characteristics where the target value is ∞ and tolerance is defined as minimally acceptable level.

Maghsoodloo and Chang (2001), Maghsoodloo and Huang (2001) and Ozdemir and Maghsoodloo (2004) gave important contributions to development of Taguchi's quadratic quality loss function (QQLF) The study of Lazovic and Mijatovic (2012) contribute to improvement of concept for a trivariate response and more detailed mathematical proofs related to procedure for finding feasible region for coefficients of loss functions. We proposed an improved algorithm for obtaining coefficients of loss functions k, i, j with proofs related each step for trivariate NtB response. The nonlinear constraint was solved analytically and the exact feasible region is obtained for coefficients (parameters) of loss functions (see more in Lazovic and Mijatovic 2012). Taguchi's quadratic quality loss function (QQLF) for three NtB quality characteristics (significantly correlated) is defined as:

(a) QQLF for one unit of products

$$L(y_1, y_2, y_3) = k_{11}(y_1 - m_1)^2 + k_{22}(y_2 - m_2)^2 + k_{33}(y_3 - m_3)^2 + k_{12}|(y_1 - m_1)(y_2 - m_2)| + \\ + k_{13}|(y_1 - m_1)(y_3 - m_3)| + k_{23}|(y_2 - m_2)(y_3 - m_3)|$$

(b) QQLF for n units of products

$$\begin{aligned}\bar{L} &= k_{11}\left[\sigma_{11}^2 + (\bar{y}_1 - m_1)^2\right] + k_{22}\left[\sigma_{22}^2 + (\bar{y}_2 - m_2)^2\right] + k_{33}\left[\sigma_{33}^2 + (\bar{y}_3 - m_3)^2\right] \\ &+ k_{12}\left[\sigma_{12}^2 + |(\bar{y}_1 - m_1)(\bar{y}_2 - m_2)|\right] + k_{13}\left[\sigma_{13}^2 + |(\bar{y}_1 - m_1)(\bar{y}_3 - m_3)|\right] \\ &+ k_{23}\left[\sigma_{23}^2 + |(\bar{y}_2 - m_3)(\bar{y}_3 - m_3)|\right]\end{aligned}$$

$$\sigma_{11}^2 = \frac{1}{n}\sum_{j=1}^{n}(y_{1j} - \bar{y}_1)^2$$

$$\sigma_{22}^2 = \frac{1}{n}\sum_{j=1}^{n}(y_{2j} - \bar{y}_2)^2$$

$$\sigma_{33}^2 = \frac{1}{n}\sum_{j=1}^{n}(y_{3j} - \bar{y}_3)^2$$

$$\sigma_{12}^2 = \frac{1}{n}\sum_{j=1}^{n}\sqrt{(y_{1j} - \overline{y_1})^2} \cdot \sqrt{(y_{2j} - y_2)^2}$$

$$\sigma_{13}^2 = \frac{1}{n}\sum_{j=1}^{n}\left|(y_{1j} - \overline{y_1})(y_{3j} - \overline{y_3})\right|$$

$$\sigma_{23}^2 = \frac{1}{n}\sum_{j=1}^{n}\left|(y_{2j} - \overline{y_2})(y_{3j} - \overline{y_3})\right|$$

Determination of coefficients $k_{11}, k_{22}, k_{33}, k_{12}, k_{13}$ and k_{23} are based on total or losses for the consumer losses when product or services are out of functioning A11, A22, A33. In practice, it is quite difficult to determine at what level of quality, or what specific value of quality characteristics, product or service is out of the function. Taguchi proposed that functional tolerance (lethal dosage) is the value of quality characteristics in which 50% of customers will be dissatisfied (Taguchi et al. 2005). Losses, in that case, are total or boundary losses.

$$A_{11} = L(m_1 \pm \Delta_1, m_2, m_3) = k_{11}\Delta_1^2 \rightarrow k_{11} = \frac{A_{11}}{\Delta_1^2}$$

$$A_{22} = L(m_1, m_2 \pm \Delta_2, m_3) = k_{22}\Delta_2^2 \rightarrow k_{22} = \frac{A_{22}}{\Delta_2^2}$$

$$A_{33} = L(m_1, m_2, m_3 \pm \Delta_3) = k_{33}\Delta_3^2 \rightarrow k_{33} = \frac{A_{33}}{\Delta_3^2}$$

Total or boundary losses $A_{12} = L(m_1 \pm \Delta_1, m_2 \pm \Delta_2, m_3)$, $A_{13} = L(m_1 \pm \Delta_1, m_2, m_3 \pm \Delta_3)$ and $A_{23} = L(m_1, m_2 \pm \Delta_2, m_3 \pm \Delta_3)$ are determined from facts: that quality characteristics are correlated in pairs and boundary losses A12, A13 and A23 have to be lower than sum of A11 and A22; A11 and A33 and A22 + A33; and that there are no cumulative effects that lower total losses due influence of the pairs of quality characteristics, as it was stated below:

$$\max(A_{11}, A_{22}) < A_{12} < A_{11} + A_{22}$$
$$\max(A_{11}, A_{33}) < A_{13} < A_{11} + A_{33}$$

Based on values of A12 and A13, coefficients of QQLF k12 and k13, as well as corrective coefficient z, are calculated as

$$k_{12} = \frac{A_{12} - A_1 - A_2}{\Delta_1 \cdot \Delta_2}$$

$$k_{13} = \frac{A_{13} - A_1 - A_3}{\Delta_1 \cdot \Delta_3}$$

$$z(k_{12}, k_{13}) = \frac{1}{2k_{11}} \cdot (k_{12} \cdot k_{13}) \pm \sqrt{\left(k_{12}^2 + 4k_{11}k_{22}\right) \cdot \left(k_{13}^2 + 4k_{11}k_{33}\right)}$$

Interval for choosing loss $A_{23} = L(m_1, m_2 \pm \Delta_2, m_3 \pm \Delta_3)$ is $\max\{A_2, A_3, A_2 + A_3 + \Delta_2\Delta_3 z_2(k_{12}, k_{13}), A_2 + A_3\}$ and

$$k_{23} = \frac{A_{23} - A_2 A_3}{\Delta_2 \cdot \Delta_3}$$

More detailed mathematical proofs and theory background can be found in Lazovic and Mijatovic (2012).

3 Application of Taguchi's Quadratic Quality Loss Functions in Public Procurement of Medical Devices

According to World Health Organization (WHO): "medical device means any instrument, apparatus, implement, machine, appliance, implant, reagent for in vitro use, software, material or other similar or related article, intended by the manufacturer to be used, alone or in combination, for human beings, for one or more of the specific medical purpose(s) of:

- diagnosis, prevention, monitoring, treatment or alleviation of disease;
- diagnosis, monitoring, treatment, alleviation of or compensation for an injury;
- investigation, replacement, modification or support of the anatomy or of a physiological process;
- supporting or sustaining life;
- control of conception;
- disinfection of medical devices;
- providing information by means of in vitro examination of specimens derived from the human body,

and which does not achieve its primary intended action by pharmacological, immunological or metabolic means, in or on the human body, but which may be assisted in its intended function by such means."(WHO 2017).

Just overall look to this definition shows how many technically and technologically different products are belonging to the group of medical devices—from disinfection products, bandages, needles, syringes, to artificial hips and pacemakers. For the purpose of defining adequate technical specification of all medical devices needed on daily bases in public hospitals and healthcare institutions, purchasing organizations need to have substantial level of medical and technical expertise in many different areas and knowledge related to global as well as domestic market; technical regulation and law requirement for specific group of products, and at least understanding of market regulations and surveillance as well as international, European and national (not only domestic) standards.

Taguchi's' concept of quality measured in monetary units after the product is purchased, offered to purchase organizations tools for analysis of the losses in monetary units due to the quality. Knowing the fact that public hospitals do not have enough resources for adequate data collection and analysis, our study is based on a data which can be found in mandatory medical records. We provide application of the QQLF in the case of the usage of two surgical gloves of the same type and equal quality characteristic from different producers (Brand A and Brand B) used during the 20 similar medical procedures. We collected data for three variables:

- y1—an indicator of consumption (IOC). An indicator of consumption is calculated as a

$$\frac{number\_of\_used\_surgical\_gloves\_in\_medical\_procedure}{number\_of\_planned\_gloves\_for\_medical\_procedure} - 1$$

  (number of used surgical gloves in medical procedure/number of planned gloves according to internal act for the medical procedure and number of medical staff) −1. This variable is the StB, with target value m = 0, and maximum acceptable level defined by the hospital as 0.5. If the consumption is on maximum acceptable level the corrective action has to be started and average loss, in that case, is 3 $ per average medical procedure.
- y2—time lost (LTO) at medical procedure due to malfunction/recovery/outperformance of surgical gloves. This variable is StB with maximal acceptable level defined as 3 min/per medical person. If the lost time due a malfunction of the gloves is on maximum acceptable level the corrective action has to be started and average loss, in that case, is 45 $ per average medical procedure.
- y3—perception of low quality of surgical glows during the operation (QPER). This variable is StB too and maximum acceptable level defined by the hospital as 8. If the dissatisfaction of the medical staff on maximum acceptable level the corrective action has to be started and average loss, in that case, is 10 $ per average medical procedure.

Based on presented inputs QQLF for this case is:

$$L(y_1, y_2, y_3) = 12\,y_1^2 + 5\,y_2^2 + 0.16\,y_3^2 - 1.33\,y_1\,y_2 - 0.5\,y_1 \cdot y_3 - 0.21\,y_2\,y_3$$

Based on data taken from medical records, which are mandatory requirements for any medical procedure at surgery, we have calculated two average or expected losses in the case of usage the surgical gloves of Brand A as LA = 84.9 $ per average medical procedure and in the case of usage of the surgical gloves Brand B LB = 244 $ per average medical procedure. Based on those results it can be concluded that both used brands of the surgical gloves had quality problems which caused the quality losses, however, the quality losses in the usage of the surgical brand B are three times higher. This might be the strong argument for not continuing to purchase the surgical gloves of Brand B. Furthermore the argument that quality losses are far higher than cost of pair of surgical gloves (due the requirements for the sterility, specific procedures when sterility of surgical procedure is jeopardized, wait time for adequate response, discomfort of medical staff, ...) can influence better perception, commitment and deeper understanding of responsibilities for quality of medical devices in medical intuitions.

4 Conclusion

The new EU rules on medical devices (European Commission 2017a, b) are focused on: further improvements in the area of quality, safety, and reliability of medical devices; lowering information asymmetry as well as enhancing market and post-market surveillance of medical devices. According to these rules, all manufacturers of medical devices will be obliged to collect data about the performance of the medical devices they produce. The providers of health services and producers and their representatives will be forced to more closely cooperate in sharing risks related to usage of medical devices. The data collecting, analyses of performance, quality, safety, effectiveness, and economic sustainability of medical devices will be the task of the manufacturers as well as providers of health services.

This paper has the aim to present usage of the QQLF for the analysis of quality of medical devices for the purpose of public procurement. Based on the QQLF for three StB variables in accordance with algorithms of Lazovic and Mijatovic (2012), Ozdemir and Maghsoodloo (2004), Maghsoodloo and Chang (2001) and Maghsoodloo and Huang (2001) we have calculated an average or expected losses for two brands of medical devices. The QQLF can be used in providing an argument about the quality of the specific medical devices in public procurement. Quality is measured trough expected outcomes which are of high importance to the health organizations (consumptions, time lost during the medical procedure and perceived quality by medical staff) and expressed in monetary units.

In addressing quality in public procurement two aspects can be of highest importance: understanding and analyzing quality as the losses expressed in monetary units, caused by failures, problems or malfunctioning of a products or a service on the market and defining quality characteristics as desired outcomes for purchasing organizations rather than technical specifications (which have more meaning to manufactures). Taguchi's QQLF concept can help to purchasing organizations to develop their ability to adequately analyze problems of quality in use and achieve value for the price. The average or expected quality losses which can be calculated by QQLF are a valuable argument in preventing lower quality products to be repurchased and can be added to other award criteria.

Appendix

The data related to surgical gloves of brand A and brand B based on medical records of 40 medical procedures are given in Table 1.

Table 1 The data related to surgical gloves of brand A and brand B based on medical records of 40 medical procedures

Brand A			Brand B		
Quality characteristics all STB			Quality characteristics all STB		
IOC	LTO	QPER	IOC	LTO	QPER
0.25	6	9.5	0.5	12	15.75
0	0	4	0.33	6	9
0.17	3	4.33	0.33	6	9.33
0.33	6	10.33	0.5	6	13
0.33	6	9.67	0.5	6	10
0	0	1.33	1	12	18.5
0	0	1	0.75	9	15
0.17	3	6	0.5	6	10
0.17	3	6.67	0.5	6	9
0.5	6	8.5	0.5	6	9
0	0	0	0.5	3	8.5
0	0	0	0.33	3	8.33
0	0	0	0.5	9	11
0.25	3	5	0.5	9	10.33
0	0	2	0.25	3	7.5
0	0	2	0.25	3	5
0	0	2.33	0.17	3	7
0.25	3	5.5	0.33	6	13.67
0.33	6	7.33	0.17	3	6.67
0.17	3	6.67	0.75	6	16.5

References

Di Mascio R (2007) A method to evaluate service delivery process quality. Int J Serv Ind Manag 18(4):418–442. https://doi.org/10.1108/09564230710778164

European Commission (2015) Single market scoreboard – performance per policy area – public procurement, (Reporting period: 01/2015–12/2015). http://ec.europa.eu/internal_market/scoreboard/performance_per_policy_area/public_procurement/index_en.htm

European Commission (2017a) New EU rules on medical devices to enhance patient safety and modernize public health, Published on: 05/04/2017. http://ec.europa.eu/growth/tools-databases/newsroom/cf/itemdetail.cfm?item_id=9119&lang=en

European Commission (2017b) Public procurement of innovative products and services.http://ec.europa.eu/growth/industry/innovation/policy/public-procurement/

Gustafsson I, Hallstrom KT (2013) The certification paradox: monitoring as a solution and a problem. In: Wijkstrom RM (ed) Trust and organizations: confidence across borders. Palgrave MacMillan, New York, pp 91–111

Husted C, Reinecke N (2009) Improving public-sector purchasing. http://www.mckinsey.com/industries/public-sector/our-insights/improving-public-sector-purchasing

Klaus ES (2015) Role of standards in the assessment of medical devices, ISO. In: Klaus ES (ed) Role of Standards in the Assessment of Medical Devices, WSC

Lazović R, Mijatović I (2012) Modified quadratic loss function for a trivariate response with the exact feasible region for parameters. J Manuf Syst 31(2):177–183

Maghsoodloo S, Chang CL (2001) Quadratic loss functions and signal to noise ratios for a bivariate responses. J Manuf Syst 20(1)

Maghsoodloo S, Huang H (2001) Quality loss functions and performance measures for a mixed bivariate response. J Manuf Syst 20(2):73–88

McKevitt D, Davis P (2013) Microenterprises: how they interact with public procurement processes. Int J Public Sector Manag 26(6):469–480. https://doi.org/10.1108/IJPSM-06-2012-0086

Mijatovic I, Stokic D (2010) The influence of internal and external codes on CSR practice: the case of companies operating in Serbia. J Bus Ethics 94(4):533–552

Mijatovic I, Miladinovic S, Stokic D (2015) Corporate social responsibility in Serbia: between corporate philanthropy and standards In: Idowu SO, Schmidpeter R, Fifka MS (eds) Corporate social responsibility in Europe – united in sustainable diversity. Springer, Cham, pp 333–351

Moen RM (1998) New quality cost model used as a top management tool. TQM Magaz 10(5):334–341. https://doi.org/10.1108/09544789810231216

Nadvi K (2008) Global standards, global governance and the organization of global value chains. J Econ Geogr 8(3):323–343. https://doi.org/10.1093/jeg/lbn003

Ordoobadi S (2009) Application of Taguchi loss functions for supplier selection. Supply Chain Manag Int J 14(1):22–30. https://doi.org/10.1108/13598540910927278

Ordoobadi SM (2010) Application of AHP and Taguchi loss functions in supply chain. Ind Manag Data Syst 110(8):1251–1269. https://doi.org/10.1108/02635571011077861

Ozdemir G, Maghsoodloo S (2004) Quadratic quality loss functions and signal-to-noise ratios for a trivariate response. J Manuf Syst 23(2):144–171

Perona M (1998) Manufacturing conformity assessment through Taguchi's quality loss function. Int J Qual Reliab Manag 15(8/9):931–946. https://doi.org/10.1108/02656719810199024

Public procurement contracts (2017) . http://www.europarl.europa.eu/atyourservice/en/displayFtu.html?ftuId=FTU_3.2.2.html

Public procurements (2017). https://ec.europa.eu/growth/single-market/public-procurement_en

Sigma (2011) Public procurement setting the award criteria (Brief 8). http://www.sigmaweb.org/publications/SettingtheAwardCriteria_Brief8_2011.pdf

Singh H, Kumar P (2006) Optimizing multi-machining characteristics through Taguchi's approach and utility concept. J Manuf Technol Manag 17(2):255–274. https://doi.org/10.1108/17410380610642304

Taguchi G, Chowdhury S, Wu Y (2005) Taguchi's quality engineering handbook. Wiley, New York

Taner T, Antony J (2006) Applying Taguchi methods to health care. Leadersh Health Serv 19(1):26–35. https://doi.org/10.1108/13660750610643831

Uyarra E, Edler J, Garcia-Estevez J, Georghiou L, Yeow J (2014) Barriers to innovation through public procurement: a supplier perspective. Technovation 34(2014):631–645. https://doi.org/10.1016/j.technovation.2014.04.003

Van de Gronden JW, Szyszczak E, Neergaard U, Krajewski M (eds) (2011) Health care and EU law. Springer, str 433

Varinac S, Ninić I (2014) Public procurement corruption map in the Republic of Serbia. Organization for Security and Cooperation in Europe Mission to Serbia, Serbia

Vlastelica Bakic T, Mijatovic I, Marinovic N (2016) Key CSR initiatives in Serbia: a new concept with new challenges. In: Idowu SO Key initiatives in corporate social responsibility – global dimension of CSR in corporate entities. Springer, pp 201–221

World Bank Group (2017) Benchmarking Public Procurement - Assessing Public Procurement Regulatory Systems in 180 Economies. World Bank Group

World Health Organization (2017) Medical Device – Full Definition, http://www.who.int/medical_devices/full_deffinition/en/

Xie Z, Hall J, McCarthy IP, Skitmore M, Shen L (2016) Standardization efforts: the relationship between knowledge dimensions, search processes and innovation outcomes. Technovation 48–49(2016):69–78. https://doi.org/10.1016/j.technovation.2015.12.002

Enhancing IT Project Management Maturity Assessment

Dragan Bjelica, Marko Mihic and Dejan Petrovic

Abstract Maturity models define sets of levels or phases describing the development of observed object in a unique and hierarchically structured way. The existence of CMMI model leads to the development of other models and, consequently, to the development of maturity assessment systems. Maturity is attributed with a certain "maturity level" and relates to progressive improvement in performances. This paper discusses maturity assessment using the basic principles of PERT method, i.e., optimistic, pessimistic and most likely maturity assessment of an organization, directly implying that IT, project, and organizational maturity components, as well as demographic characteristics, significantly influence performance management in IT projects on the territory of the Republic of Serbia. IT, project, and organizational performances' assessment enables implementation of the maturity measurement system in order to create an appropriate project management knowledge framework. This paper presents theoretical and practical implications.

Keywords Maturity · IT project · PERT · Assessment · Model · Index

1 Introduction

Maturity model in project management is a formal tool for assessing, measuring and comparing an organization's practices with the best practices in the relevant industry, in order to map out a structured improvement process (Dos Santos et al. 2008). The models that surface as the most prominent in assessing the maturity of projects, programs and portfolios that an organization implements are: Capability Maturity Model Integration—CMMI (developed by Software Engineering Institute, SEI: Carnegie Mellon University), Organizational Project Management Maturity Model—OPM3 (developed by Project Management Institute), and Portfolio, Programme, and Project Management Maturity Model—P3M3 (developed by the Office

D. Bjelica (✉) · M. Mihic · D. Petrovic
Faculty of Organizational Sciences, University of Belgrade, Belgrade, Serbia
e-mail: bjelica.dragan@fon.bg.ac.rs

N. Mladenović et al. (eds.), *Advances in Operational Research in the Balkans*, Springer Proceedings in Business and Economics,
https://doi.org/10.1007/978-3-030-21990-1_13

of Government Commerce UK). On one hand, a great number of authors discussing maturity models tend to reduce certain models to very specific fields, such as information technology or construction. On the other hand, there is a strong inclination to take the existing specific models from certain industries or companies and turn them into more general models that would be valid for many projects and portfolios in different areas. The key role of the IT project portfolio is reflected in providing support through a project management office in achieving strategic goals and implementing a corporate strategy (Petrovic et al. 2009). Therefore, the effectiveness of the institutional evaluation system is directly related with knowledge and organizational competencies (Bjelica and Jovanovic 2016).

2 The System for Assessing and Determining Maturity

Jaafari (2007) proposes checklists as a good tool to assess project maturity throughout the project's lifecycle, i.e., the so-called "PH-check (project health check)". It somewhat differs from interviewing, and is recommended, on one side by Project Management Institute (2003) as a best practice, and, on the other side, IPMA (2014) in relation to competence assessment. In addition, the assessment of processes proposed by the Software Engineering Institute and Carnegie Mellon University (2010) should contribute to the harmonization of process and organizational goals. However, this conclusion was disputed by Lepmets et al. (2012), who suggested that this principle functions only in theory, but not in practice.

Then again, over the past couple of years, organizations have been leaning on these three methods, using surveys to assess maturity. Kujala and Ahola (2005) suggest that customer satisfaction surveys do not bring benefits to project-oriented organizations. In fact, they have a purely symbolic value, which points to the crucial issue of maturity assessment: Does maturity assessment contribute to improving processes and competencies or does it have a purely marketing purpose? The answer to this question is probably somewhere in between, because public recognition encourages hard work and improvements. Based on this, we can conclude that combining the maturity assessment principles leads to relevant information concerning the current state of matters in an organization.

Studies show that organizations with higher project management maturity levels: save money, establish better project timelines and have higher quality products. This implies that an increase in project management maturity leads to improved project performances (Bjelica et al. 2017). This paper discusses the most important maturity models focused on information technologies (CMMI, IT-CMF), as well as project management (IPMA Delta, OPM3, P3M3), and their influence on the improvement of project performance management system.

3 Analysis of Issues Relating to Maturity Assessment

The longitudinal aspects of maturity model performances suggest systematization and critical study of maturity assessment systems and components relating to project management in IT. To begin with, every model has limitations that affect the capability to adequately implement the proposed concepts in practice.

A global research in the field of project management conducted by Wagner et al. (2014) points to the fact that organizations mostly rely on the following standards: IPMA ICB 3.0, IPMA Organizational Competence Baseline, IPMA Delta, PMI Project Management Body of Knowledge, PMI Practice Standard, PRINCE 2. Project maturity can be regarded as the measure of an organization's abilities to use projects for different purposes, where maturity is expressed as the sum of actions, knowledge, and attitudes (Andersen and Jessen 2003). The first lack of maturity assessment is the insufficiently clear border between initial levels of maturity (between the first and the third level). Most theories relating to maturity models provide the same principles and support for the first three levels, having in mind that noticeable differences appear at the third level (Mcbride 2010). This approach can be exceptionally cost inefficient for organizations forced to implement improvements in most functional areas.

The most common issues in applying maturity models in software industry are: practical application of maturity models and the lack of best practice examples for organizations at higher maturity levels (Liou 2011). Consequently, within maturity models for developing new services, Jin et al. (2014) group success factors in four process management categories: strategic process management, formalization of processes, knowledge management, and participant inclusion. In order to account for all parameters when assessing maturity and remove issues typical for maturity models (reuse and use of best practices), organizations need to take into account lifecycle of products when developing maturity, where the assessment encompasses the relative position of the company on its road to perform product placement (Vezzetti et al. 2013). Using the k-means cluster Mihic et al. (2015), presented an analysis of organizational maturity in the energy sector, thus explaining the characteristics of groups reaching higher levels of maturity.

While CMMI, OPM3 and P3M3 models remain focused on the implementation of strategy through projects, IPMA Delta model, developed by the International Association for Project Management (IPMA 2014), whose base includes the latest ISO 21500, as well as IPMA Project Excellence Model and IPMA Competence Baseline, focuses on the organizational aspect of project management. Even though the mentioned models are very popular, most of them do not take into consideration the organizational project management system (except for IPMA Delta model) and lack focus on adjusting to relevant industries, based on specific tasks and competencies. In addition, the final expert assessment is based, in most cases, on qualitative comments, without reference to numerical values for each level of maturity and assessment area.

Attempts at quantifying variables in maturity assessment mostly come down to assessing the maturity of individual projects. For example, Lianying and Xinxing

(2012) created a quantitative evaluation index system based on PRINCE2 method. Similar studies have been conducted using PMI approach when assessing project management processes and functional areas (Ibbs and Hoon Kwak 2000; Yazici 2009; Khalema et al. 2015). These studies did not include either the assessment of individual and organizational competencies, or the creation of quantitative organization maturity index.

The fourth segment of maturity analysis is the correlation with the results achieved by a company. It often happens that organizations at higher maturity levels receive low marks for certain aspects of project management. Project management maturity relates more to business performance than to project performance (Yazici 2009), however, there are undoubtedly numerous studies that confirm the positive correlation between project success and project maturity (Besner and Hobbs 2008; Dooley et al. 2001). The key segment of this discussion points to the approach for assessing the maturity of an organization, which serves as a benchmark for measuring results later. If an organization's maturity assessment is optimistic, the results that organization achieves on the market will be below expectations. On the other hand, if the assessment was fairly "strict", we are in danger of neglecting the activities in which the organization achieves higher levels of optimization and maturity.

The expenses of projects an organization plans to implement in the future depend on project management maturity and industry (Spalek 2014). Carvalho et al. (2015) stress the influence of project complexity on planning and implementation process, since the increase in complexity generates more variations when making estimates about time, expenses and other resources. Most organizations strive toward higher maturity level, which, in consequence, demands additional investments in human resources, technology, and processes. In accordance with that, modular application of maturity assessment is something most organizations prefer, while, on the other hand, there are redundant analyses and estimates according to different methodologies, unnecessary at that moment. The existing models do not take into consideration organizational maturity assessment per segments. They rather offer summary of an organization's maturity level in general. The classic project triangle which includes time, resources, expenses, scope, and quality should be redesigned to include the value component, which would enhance strategy decision making (Winter and Szczepanek 2008).

4 Research Methodology

When determining maturity level, it is of utmost importance to consider all approaches to defining and analyzing maturity, because the attribution of a certain maturity level to an organization can be ad hoc and insufficiently sustained by facts. A large number of organizations start from optimistic viewpoint and take into account average values (arithmetic mean) for maturity level. Arithmetic mean is the measure of central tendency that represents the value that, when multiplied with the number of elements in a set, indicates the sum of all elements individually. On the other hand, geometric mean indicates the central tendency or typical value of a set of numbers by using the product of their values. As such, the geometric mean is very suitable in areas such as information technologies, finance, and banking, as they use concepts that are interdependent, such as interest calculation or portfolio selection (Hodges and Schaefer 1974).

Having this in mind, we can intuitively infer that in the project management process each activity inside each subprocess, as well as the project management processes themselves (IT project management included), cannot be represented as a sum of activities, since that value would represent an optimistic expectation for the success of subprocesses.

For the process of maturity assessment to be as effective and comprehensive as possible, this paper uses beta distribution. This distribution was first introduced by Malcolm et al. (1959) for research and development program evaluation but is also applied in managerial accounting, (DeCoster 1974), engineering cost estimates (Ostwald 1984), and capital budgeting and financial management (Van Horne and Wachowicz 2008). The probability density function of a random variable Y, that follows a beta distribution, when $\alpha > 0$ and $\beta > 0$, is

$$p(y|\alpha, \beta, a, b) = \begin{cases} \frac{\Gamma(\alpha+\beta)}{\Gamma(\alpha)\Gamma(\beta)} \; \frac{(y-a)^{\alpha-1}(b-y)^{\beta-1}}{(b-a)^{\alpha+\beta-1}} & , \text{if } a \leq y \leq b \\ 0 \quad \quad elsewhere \end{cases}$$

If we define that $k = \alpha + \beta$, then the expectation, variance, and mode are: α/k, $\alpha\beta/(k^3 + k^2)$ and $(\alpha - 1)/(k - 2)$, respectively. In the context of project management, beta distribution is used through *PERT* formula, as it encompasses optimistic, pessimistic and most likely estimates (Hahn 2008). Initially used by the US defense industry for network planning in weather forecast, *PERT* method found a wide range of applications in other areas, such as determining different project parameters. PERT method is used to manage appropriate maturity appraisal having in mind stochastic nature, which is a type of the three-estimate system for estimating uncertain quantities. This kind of estimation is based on three different estimated values in order to improve the result mitigating the estimation risk, which is usually applied in cost and duration estimation in project management. The most significant project planning outcome in sensitivity analysis is that in its place of selecting the proper activity duration distributions, managers should dedicate more energy to effectively determine the activity durations (Hajdu and Bokor 2016). *PERT* method is based on the following formula:

$$o = \frac{a + 4m + b}{6}$$

where,

a pessimistic scenario
m most likely scenario
b optimistic scenario
o expected scenario

The entire sample for this quantitative research included 233 individuals: 124 IT experts, 64 project managers, and 45 individuals who were project procurers. There were 169 paired cases, i.e., 154 different organizations that underwent maturity assessment. The rate of response for the questionnaire ranged from 10% to 15%. 52 organizations were assessed on the basis of IT, project and organizational components of the model, 22 organizations were assessed based on project and organizational components of the model, while 82 organizations were assessed based on IT competencies. IT competencies were analyzed by using the European e-Competence Framework 3.0, presented in over 40 IT competencies through 5 phases of IT project and 18 different roles of IT experts. Project competencies were analyzed by using PMI process/functional framework (Project Management Body of Knowledge 5), encompassing 10 functional areas, 5 groups of processes and 47 components analyzed in this research. Organizational competencies were analyzed using IPMA Organizational Competence Baseline for project management, which defines 5 organizational components divided into 18 competence elements.

The steps used in this paper for determining the overall relative maturity index, maturity level, as well as the verification of the proposed model are:

Step 1—In the first step, the authors determined minimal values for all individual components within IT, project and organizational competencies. In this way, the authors disregarded all high values in order to prevent the case in which an organization that achieved a lower maturity value, even for a single parameter, cannot get higher ranking than the said minimum. This approach can be characterized as very "strict", because it considers only minimal values, neglecting all other marks. Taking into account other studies, such as Project Management Solutions (2014), it is evident that global practice indicates that most organizations stand at the first or the second level of maturity. If we consider the preference of survey participants to evaluate competencies with higher maturity level, then the criterion of minimal value can significantly influence their perception of the achieved maturity level.

$$Minimum\{a1, a2, \ldots, an\}$$

Step 2—The second step was used to calculate the arithmetic means of all individual components included in IT, project and organizational competencies. The resulting values represented high maturity level. Therefore, this approach to analysis is regarded as the optimistic scenario.

$$Arithmeticmean = \frac{a1 + a2 + \cdots + an}{n}$$

Step 3—The third step included the calculation of geometric means of all individual components included in IT, project and organizational competencies. This approach takes into consideration maximum values; however, the end result for maturity level is nearer to minimal value. In this way, the authors determined the most likely scenario. Before any analyses were performed, zero values of variables entered by respondents were corrected with 1E-59, as the geometric mean cannot be calculated if the value is zero.

$$Geometricmean = \sqrt[n]{a1 * a2 * \cdots * an}$$

Step 4—Different scales were used for determining the levels of knowledge and maturity for IT, project and organizational competencies. IT competencies were measured on a scale of one to three, project competencies were measured on a scale of zero to five, while organizational competencies were measured on a scale of one to five. In order to be able to compare the values obtained for each individual aspect, the authors used normalization of data. In this step, the values of individual modules were compared with the best results in the set, thus reducing all values to a range between one and zero.

Step 5—The values (pessimist, most likely and optimist) obtained in step 4 for IT, project and organizational competencies were further used to calculate the overall level of maturity for all three scenarios—pessimist, most likely and optimist. The overall relative maturity index, which points to the percentage of an organization's maturity, was calculated by using the abovementioned formula for *PERT* method through the application of beta distribution.

$$URIZ = \frac{min\{NITm, NUPm, NORGm\} + geom\{NITg, NUPg, NORGg\} + arit\{NITa, NUPa, NORGa\}}{6} * 100$$

URIZ	the overall relative maturity index
NITm	normalized summary value of minimum of IT competencies
NITg	normalized summary value of geometric mean of IT competencies
NITa	normalized summary value of arithmetic mean of IT competencies
NUPm	normalized summary value of minimum of project competencies
NUPg	normalized summary value of geometric mean of project competencies
NUPa	normalized summary value of arithmetic mean of project competencies
NORGm	normalized summary value of minimum of organizational competencies
NORGg	normalized summary value of geometric mean of organizational competencies
NORGa	normalized summary value of arithmetic mean of organizational competencies.

Step 6—The sixth step included the discretization of values of the overall relative maturity index to six groups performed by binning. This, in turn, allowed for determination of limit numerical value of the overall relative maturity index for each maturity level.

Step 7—The influence of the proposed maturity assessment system was tested in step 7. This test regarded the relative maturity indices of IT, project and organizational competencies, as well as demographic, individual and organizational characteristics, as independent variables, while performance analysis was regarded as the dependent composite variable. The dependent variable was evaluated from three perspectives (IT experts, project managers and project procurers). The analysis uses arithmetic means for all three viewpoints. Statistical methods used in this step are: correlation and linear regression.

5 Internal Data Consistency

The reliability of scale was tested using Cronbach's alpha, i.e., the authors examined the internal consistency of the scale. Mostly, the higher the Cronbach's alpha, the more the constituents have common covariance and probably measure the same underlying concept. The value of Cronbach's alpha should be above 0.7 in order to fulfill the previously mentioned prerequisite (DeVellis 2011). In the quantitative research that was conducted, all scales pointed to a high internal consistency level, which confirms the reliability and internal consistency of scales used for the said sample (Tables 1, 2 and 3).

Table 1 Internal data consistency—project management competencies

Project management competencies	Cronbach's alfa	Number of variables	Number of respondents
Integration management	0.839	6	64
Project scope management	0.845	6	64
Time management	0.927	7	64
Expense management	0.933	4	64
Quality management	0.867	3	64
Human resources management	0.832	4	64
Communication management	0.820	3	64
Risk management	0.944	6	64
Procurement management	0.918	4	64
Stakeholder management	0.761	4	64

Table 2 Internal data consistency—IT competencies

IT competencies	Cronbach's alfa	Number of variables	Number of respondents
Planning	0.867	9	124
Creation	0.853	9	124
Initiation	0.909	8	124
Enablement	0.938	13	124
Management	0.949	9	124

Table 3 Internal data consistency—organizational competencies

Organizational competencies	Cronbach's alfa	Number of variables	Number of respondents
Project, programme and portfolio (PPP) governance	0.848	4	64
PPP management	0.887	3	64
PPP organizational alignment	0.850	3	64
PPP resources	0.834	4	64
PPP people's competencies	0.869	4	64

6 Research Results

Based on the analysis of IT competencies and maturity index (pessimistic, most likely and optimistic estimates), we can conclude that the pessimistic approach is the closest to the most probable evaluation of IT maturity index on lower levels, while on the higher maturity levels optimistic estimates seem to be the most realistic ones (Fig. 1).

Based on the analysis of project competencies and maturity index (pessimistic, most likely and optimistic estimates), we can conclude that the pessimistic approach is the closest to the most probable evaluation of project maturity index on lower

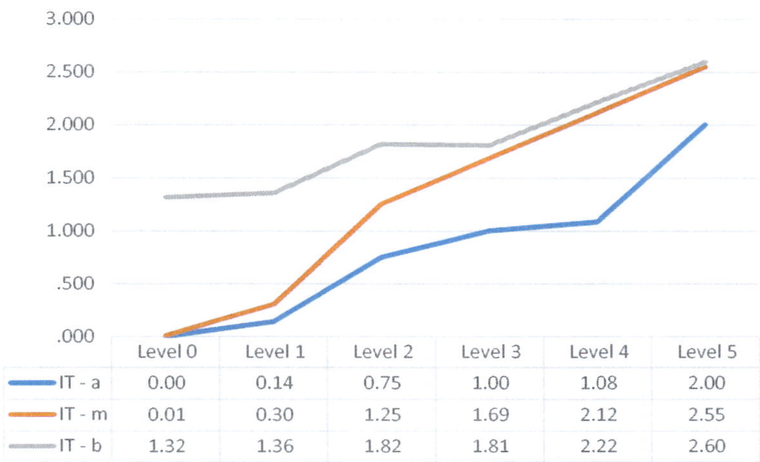

Fig. 1 Average pessimistic, most likely and optimistic IT maturity index of an organization

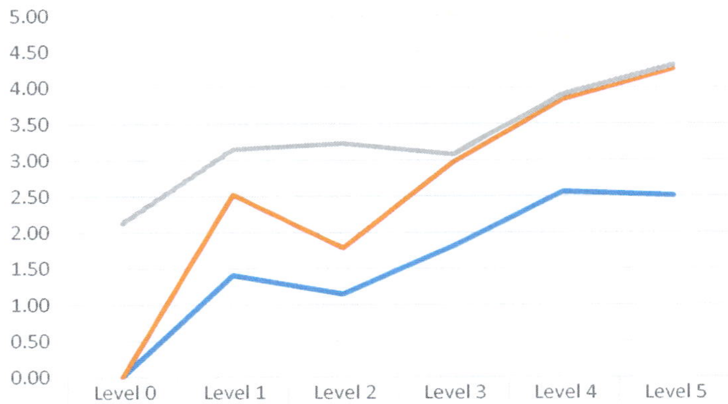

	Level 0	Level 1	Level 2	Level 3	Level 4	Level 5
PM - a	0.00	1.40	1.14	1.80	2.56	2.50
PM - m	0.00	2.52	1.78	2.97	3.83	4.25
PM - b	2.13	3.15	3.23	3.08	3.91	4.31

Fig. 2 Average pessimistic, most likely and optimistic project maturity index of an organization

levels, while on the higher maturity levels optimistic estimates seem to be the most realistic ones (Fig. 2).

Based on the analysis of project competencies and maturity index (pessimistic, most likely and optimistic estimates), we can conclude that the most likely estimates for the index of organizational maturity are the optimistic estimates on all levels of maturity (Fig. 3).

Summary analysis of the levels of relative maturity index of IT, project and organizational maturity points to the fact that organizational competencies gradually improve with the higher maturity levels, while project competencies have a high growth trend on initial maturity levels and a decline on the second maturity level, followed by a growth on higher maturity levels. On the other hand, IT competencies have a low level of maturity on initial levels, then a swifter growth on the second maturity level, when the project competencies mark a decline, and then follow the growth trend of project and organizational competencies on higher levels (Fig. 4).

The maturity level, evaluated on the basis of pessimistic, most likely and optimistic estimates, shows most variations on initial levels, while the precision steadily grows as of the third level. This can be attributed to the fact that the systems for standardizing processes, metrics, competencies, documents and management systems exist from level three onwards.

The limits for the six maturity levels were determined by applying discretization of values of the overall relative maturity index through binning. The discretization of values is implemented within predefined limits, i.e., limits for minimum and maximum values. The scope of numerical values is divided into segments of equal size. The largest number of organizations is on the initial maturity levels—level zero and level one (Table 1). The biggest difference of the average overall relative maturity

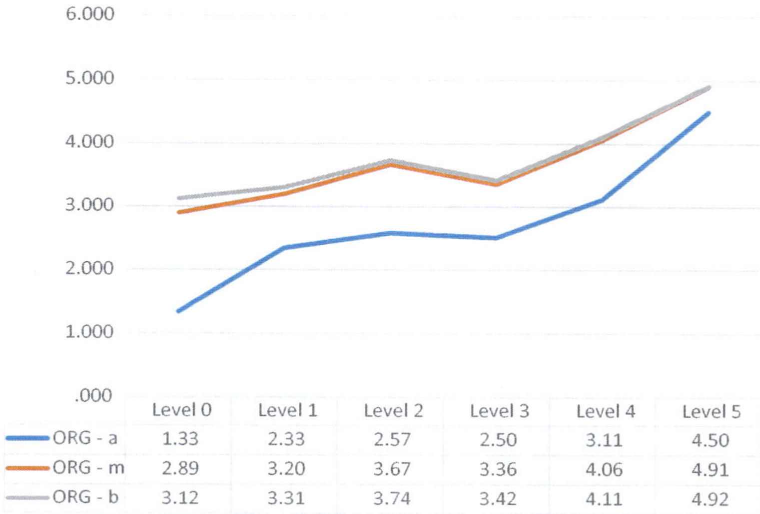

	Level 0	Level 1	Level 2	Level 3	Level 4	Level 5
ORG - a	1.33	2.33	2.57	2.50	3.11	4.50
ORG - m	2.89	3.20	3.67	3.36	4.06	4.91
ORG - b	3.12	3.31	3.74	3.42	4.11	4.92

Fig. 3 Average pessimistic, most likely and optimistic index of organizational component of an organization's maturity

Fig. 4 Average values per maturity level of relative index of IT, project and organizational maturity

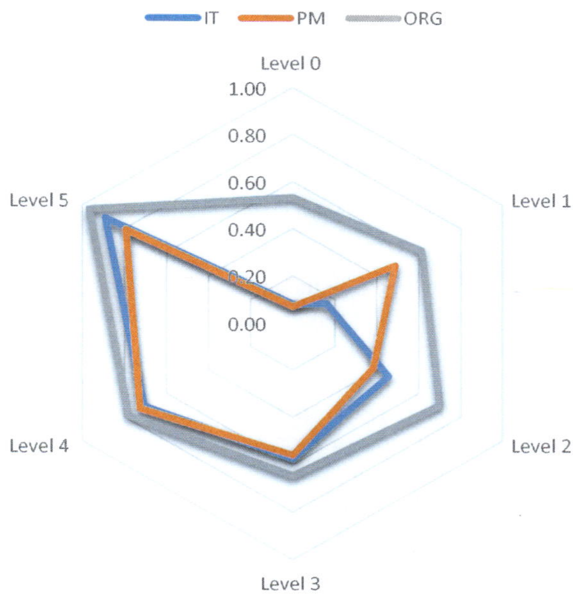

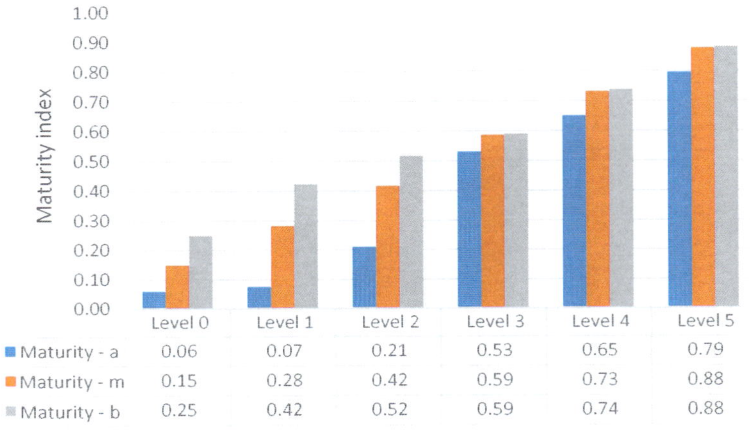

Fig. 5 Pessimist, most likely and optimist average values of maturity index

Table 4 Discretization per bins in determining maturity level

Maturity level	Interval	Number of organizations
Level 0	[−∝–0.181]	53
Level 1	(0.181–0.339]	30
Level 2	(0.339–0.498]	10
Level 3	(0.498–0.656]	19
Level 4	(0.656–0.814]	33
Level 5	(0.814–1]	10

index is evident between level zero and level one, which is confirmed through the previous analyses of individual components whose results show that the differences in trends show most in the initial levels (Fig. 5) (Table 4).

The results of the research imply that there is a weak positive correlation between IT competencies and performance management, $r = 0.227$ ($p < 0.05$). In addition, the results of the research imply that there is a strong positive correlation between project competencies and performance management, $r = 0.535$ ($p < 0.01$). Finally, the results of the research imply that there is a strong positive correlation between organizational competencies and performance management, $r = 0.6$ ($p < 0.01$) (Table 5).

The model presented in this paper explains 79.7% of performance management variance (Table 6). This result can be considered very high. All variables provide a unique and statistically relevant contribution to the performance management prediction ($p < 0.05$), except for years of operation of an organization within demographic organizational characteristics. The analysis of coefficients shows that the highest coefficient relates to demographic individual characteristics, which justifies the inclusion of these components in the model, as well as the inclusion of demographic organizational characteristics, although they exclude the parameter an organization's years of operation. In relation to the previously presented two regres-

Table 5 Correlation between independent variables and performance management

	IT	PM	ORG	PS
IT competencies (IT)	–	−0.106	−0.057	0.227*
Project competencies (PM)		–	0.658**	0.535**
Organizational competencies (ORG)			–	0.600**
Performance management (PS)				–

**Correlation has statistical importance on the level of 0.01 (2-tailed)
*Correlation has statistical importance on the level of 0.05 (2-tailed)

Table 6 Regression analysis in relation to the dependent variable "performance management"

Model	Non-standardized coefficients		Standardized coefficients	t	Significance
	B	Stand. error	Beta		
(Constant)	−2.686	0.643		−4.177	0.000
IT competencies	0.182	0.049	0.281	3.682	0.001
Project management competencies	0.278	0.043	0.650	6.512	0.000
Organizational competencies	0.536	0.067	0.745	8.009	0.000
Age	0.166	0.021	2.470	7.781	0.000
Years of service	−0.304	0.031	−4.169	−9.787	0.000
Years spent in the organization	0.062	0.013	0.667	4.926	0.000
Years of working on projects	0.132	0.016	1.352	8.411	0.000
Years of operation of the organization	0.001	0.001	0.067	0.950	0.348
Number of IT projects per annum	−0.010	0.002	−0.498	−6.042	0.000
Number of external contractors	−0.038	0.005	−0.599	−7.347	0.000

Dependent variable: Performance management
Predictors: (constant), Demographic organizational characteristics (number of external contractors, years of operation, number of IT projects per annum), Demographic individual characteristics (years of work on projects, years spent in the relevant organization, age, years of service), IT competencies (relative IT maturity index), Project management competencies (relative IT maturity index), Organizational competencies
R^2= 0.838, adjusted R^2= 0.797, F = 20.674, Significance = 0.000, $p < 0.05$)

sion models, similar results are obtained within the dependent variable *performance management*, where organizational competencies have the highest coefficient.

7 Conclusion

Over the past ten years, the concept of project maturity model has been gaining importance. The contemporary business environment points to the fact that Serbian market is becoming more intensive and that the economic development is reflected in the continuous growth of business environment. Today, Serbian IT industry is regarded as one of the most successful export-oriented industries among domestic experts. Consequently, the results of this research can have a deep impact on the academic and expert community in the Republic of Serbia, by contributing to the development of theoretical framework, approach to evaluating maturity and reference development milestones, while, on the other hand, the results shown in this paper can provide guidelines to organizations attempting to identify key components and determine course for implementing IT strategies.

There is a strong positive correlation between organizational project competencies, while the correlation with IT competencies is weak. On the other hand, independent variables (organizational and project competencies) have a strong positive correlation with dependent variable (performance management), except for IT competencies, which have a weak positive correlation with performance management. Project, organizational, and IT maturity indices show most variations on lower maturity levels, while the degree of variations declines on higher levels of maturity. Pessimist estimates show proximity to the most likely assessments of IT, project and organizational maturity indices on the lowest level, while optimistic assessments are the nearest to the most likely assessments on higher levels. The correlation between project activity and project performances is not very apparent on the initial levels of project maturity assessment (Jiang et al. 2004), because the risk management approach strives to increase certainty (Yeo and Ren 2009). Higher maturity level relates to organizational problems, while lower maturity level relates directly to project issues, such as documentation, timeline, tools, and techniques (Beecham et al. 2003). In accordance with the abovementioned, Obradovic et al. (2014), in the application of IPMA Competence Baseline, stress the importance of technical competencies for project managers working on IT projects in web-based environments. Alternatively, the types of performance improvements on higher maturity levels relate directly to the project management maturity assessment models (Brookes et al. 2014).

So far, the organizational maturity assessment systems included arithmetic mean of the perceived maturity of model components. This approach leads to optimistic assessment of an organization's maturity level. In order to reach a relatively correct scientific explanation, a maturity assessment system has to include a logical correlation between model components and a correlation to realistic situations that are explained. This paper presents a maturity assessment system based on PERT method principles by using beta distribution. The expected maturity level was calculated based on the optimistic estimate (using arithmetic mean of perceived maturity), pessimistic estimate (using minimal value of perceived maturity) and most likely estimate (using geometric mean of perceived maturity). This implies that all maturity analysis approaches, as well as the calculation of limit numerical values for each maturity level, have been taken into consideration.

References

Andersen ES, Jessen SA (2003) Project maturity in organisations. Int J Proj Manag 21(6):457–461. https://doi.org/10.1016/S0263-7863(02)00088-1

Beecham S, Hall T, Rainer A (2003) Software process improvement problems in twelve software companies: An empirical analysis. Empir Softw Eng 8(1):7–42. https://doi.org/10.1023/A:1021764731148

Bjelica DL, Jovanovic UD (2016) It's up to you: the influence of sports participation, academic performances and demo-behavioral characteristics on university students' life satisfaction. Appl Res Qual Life 11(1):163–179. https://doi.org/10.1007/s11482-014-9360-0

Besner C, Hobbs B (2008) Discriminating contexts and project management best practices on innovative and noninnovative projects. Proj Manag J 39(S1):S123–S134. https://doi.org/10.1002/pmj.20064

Bjelica D, Mihic M, Petrovic D (2017) Web based project management competences and project performances. Eur Proj Manag J Serbian Proj Manag Assoc—YUPMA 7(2):45–58

Brookes N, Butler M, Dey P, Clark R (2014) The use of maturity models in improving project management performance. Int J Manag Proj Bus 7(2):231–246. https://doi.org/10.1108/IJMPB-03-2013-0007

Carvalho MM, Patah LA, de Souza Bido D (2015) Project management and its effects on project success: cross-country and cross-industry comparisons. Int J Proj Manage 33(7):1509–1522. https://doi.org/10.1016/j.ijproman.2015.04.004

DeCoster DT (1974) Accounting for managerial decision making. Melville Publishing Co

DeVellis RF (2011) Scale development: theory and applications (Applied Social Research Methods), 3rd ed. SAGE Publications

Dooley K, Subra A, Anderson J (2001) Maturity and its impact on new product development project performance. Res Eng Des 13(1):23–29. https://doi.org/10.1007/s001630100003

Dos Santos RP, de Oliveira KM, da Silva WP (2008) Evaluating the service quality of software providers appraised in CMM/CMMI. Softw Qual J 17(3):283–301. https://doi.org/10.1007/s11219-008-9065-4

Hahn ED (2008) Mixture densities for project management activity times: a robust approach to PERT. Eur J Oper Res 188(2):450–459. https://doi.org/10.1016/j.ejor.2007.04.032

Hajdu M, Bokor O (2016) Sensitivity analysis in PERT networks: does activity duration distribution matter?. Autom. Construct 65. https://doi.org/10.1016/j.autcon.2016.01.003

Hodges S, Schaefer S (1974) The interpretation of the geometric mean: a note. J Financ Quant Anal 9(03):497–504

Ibbs CW, Hoon Kwak Y (2000) Assessing project management maturity. Proj Manag J 31(1):32–43

International Project Management Association (2014) IPMA delta regulations and guidelines. Int Proj Manag Assoc

Jaafari A (2007) Project and program diagnostics: a systemic approach. Int J Project Manage 25(8):781–790. https://doi.org/10.1016/j.ijproman.2007.05.008

Jiang JJ, Klein G, Hwang H-G, Huang J, Hung S-Y (2004) An exploration of the relationship between software development process maturity and project performance. Inf Manag 41(3):279–288. https://doi.org/10.1016/S0378-7206(03)00052-1

Jin D, Chai K-H, Tan K-C (2014) New service development maturity model. Manag Serv Qual Int J 24(1):86–116. https://doi.org/10.1108/MSQ-10-2012-0134

Khalema L, Van Waveren C, Chan K-Y (2015) The relationship between project management office maturity and organisational project management maturity: an empirical study of the South

African government infrastructure departments. S Afr J Ind Eng 26(3):12–26. https://doi.org/10.7166/26-3-1021
Kujala J, Ahola T (2005) The value of customer satisfaction surveys for project-based organizations: symbolic, technical, or none. Int J Proj Manag 23(5 SPEC. ISS.):404–409. https://doi.org/10.1016/j.ijproman.2005.01.002
Lepmets M, McBride T, Ras E (2012) Goal alignment in process improvement. J Syst Softw 85(6):1440–1452. https://doi.org/10.1016/j.jss.2012.01.038
Lianying Z, Jing H, Xinxing Z (2012) The project management maturity model and application based on PRINCE2. Procedia Eng 29:3691–3697. https://doi.org/10.1016/j.proeng.2012.01.554
Liou JC (2011) On Improving CMMI in an immature world of software development. J Inf Sci Eng 27(1):213–226
Malcolm DG, Roseboom JH, Clark CE, Fazar WT (1959) Application of technique for research and development program evaluation. Oper Res INFORMS 7(5):646–669
Mcbride T (2010) Organisational theory perspective on process capability measurement scales. J Softw Evol Process (August 2009):243–254. https://doi.org/10.1002/spip
Mihic M, Petrovic D, Obradovic V, Vuckovic A (2015) Project management maturity analysis in the Serbian energy sector energies. Multidiscip Digit Publ Inst 8(5):3924–3943. https://doi.org/10.3390/en8053924
Obradovic V, Jovanovic P, Petrovic D, Mihic M, Bjelica D (2014) Web-Based project management influence on project portfolio managers' technical competencies. Procedia—Soc Behav Sci 119(March):387–396. https://doi.org/10.1016/j.sbspro.2016.06.171
Ostwald PF (1984) Cost estimating, 2nd edn. Prentice Hall
Petrovic D, Mihic M, Stosic B (2009) Strategic IT portfolio management for development of innovative competences. Handbook on strategic information technology and portfolio management. IGI Publishing
Project Management Institute (2003) Organizational project management maturity model. Project Management Institute
Project Management Institute (2013) PMBOK Guide 5—A guide to the project management body of knowledge. Project Management Institute
Project Management Solutions (2014) The state of the project management office (PMO). Project Management Solutions
Software Engineering Institute and Carnegie Mellon University (2010) CMMI for development (CMMI-DEV V1.3). Software Engineering Institute and Carnegie Mellon University
Spalek S (2014) Does investment in project management pay off? Ind Manag Data Syst 114(5):832–856. https://doi.org/10.1108/IMDS-10-2013-0447
Van Horne JC, Wachowicz JM (2008) Fundamentals of financial management. 13th edn. Prentice Hall
Vezzetti E, Violante MG, Marcolin F (2013) A benchmarking framework for product lifecycle management (PLM) maturity models. Int J Adv Manuf Technol 71(5–8):899–918. https://doi.org/10.1007/s00170-013-5529-1
Wagner R, Sedlmayer M, Jaques T (2014) 2014 project, programme, and portfolio management global survey. Int Proj Manag Assoc
Winter M, Szczepanek T (2008) Projects and programmes as value creation processes: a new perspective and some practical implications. Int J Project Manage 26(1):95–103. https://doi.org/10.1016/j.ijproman.2007.08.015
Yazici HJ (2009) The role of project management maturity and organizational culture in perceived performance. Proj Manag J 40(3):14–33. https://doi.org/10.1002/pmj.20121
Yeo KT, Ren Y (2009) Risk management capability maturity model for complex product systems (CoPS) projects. Syst Eng 12(4):275–294. https://doi.org/10.1002/sys.20123

E-Payment Systems Using Multi-card Smartcard

Nenad Badovinac and Dejan Simic

Abstract In case cardholders have more than one smart card for electronic payments, there is a problem of correlating smart cards and PINs. When a cardholder has more than two smart cards, it introduces additional confusion due to the storage of multiple smart cards and due to the need for memorizing PINs. The idea presented in this paper describes the process of electronical payment using the concept of multi-card smart card by authentication of PIN coded from biometric fingerprint. The software of biometric scanner integrated into the PIN PAD device checks a cardholder authentication, by using presented algorithm that codes the biometric fingerprint into the PIN. Thus, that encoded PIN is compared with the PIN embedded as an encrypted form in the chip of multi-card smart card or with the control value used in authorization center. Multi-card smart card has the integrated functional button that is controlled by user. If a user wants to make the electronic payment he/she needs to press this button once or a few times. This will activate the virtual card used for electronic payment. The implementation of this idea allows the user to manage the electronic payment by using only one multi-card smart card without entering the PIN. By using this model of electronic payment, a user gets the improved user experience. The idea of this paper is the continuation of previous author's investigations in order to get the algorithm that will simplify the process of electronic payment as much as possible. The aim of this paper is to introduce the conceptual model of a simplified electronic payment system that meets Strong Customer Authentification, which is required by PSD2 regulations.

Keywords Biometry · Fingerprint · PIN · Multi-card · Smart card

---

N. Badovinac (✉) · D. Simic
Faculty of Organizational Sciences, University of Belgrade, Belgrade, Serbia
e-mail: nenad.badovinac@gmail.com

D. Simic
e-mail: dsimic@fon.bg.ac.rs

N. Mladenović et al. (eds.), *Advances in Operational Research in the Balkans*,
Springer Proceedings in Business and Economics,
https://doi.org/10.1007/978-3-030-21990-1_14

1 Introduction

For the sake of client safety, banks use advanced authentication methods, which often complicates the process of authentication and transaction execution by a payment card. Due to safety need, banks have a problem offering customers simple means of authentication for card payment transactions. Fingerprint recognition systems have become one of the most popular biometric systems used in banking. On the other hand, the use of the PIN number has become a widely accepted authentication method of card payments. One of the problems with the use of these two technologies appears when a bank client has multiple payment cards. In this case, it is complicated and confusing for client to keep records of PINs and an increasing number of associated payment cards. It is necessary to simplify the card payment process in a way to simplify the authentication of users who have a larger number of payment cards according to European Union statistics (Horst 2018).

Presented idea of simplified card payments is based on the synergy of two technologies: the use of a multi-card smart card that contains a large number of virtual bank cards and coding of the biometric fingerprint data for user authentication purposes. The model is based on the fact that the PIN provides a sufficient level of protection when using a bank card with a chip for user authentication (Sankalp 2014). Presented algorithm encodes the biometric fingerprint data into a 4-digit PIN. The PIN thus obtained is compared to the PIN registered on the multi-card smart card chip. By applying presented idea, the payment system user does not need to remember the authentication PINs. The user only needs to activate one of several virtual debit cards on a multi-card smart card, then insert a multi-card smart card into a POS terminal or ATM, and put a finger on a fingerprint scanner embedded in a POS terminal or ATM and be authenticated, and the payment transaction will be performed.

2 Overview of Research Areas Using the Multi-card Smart Card

Bank clients have an increasing number of payment cards (Horst 2018) and when using card payments, clients may have a problem with registering a few PINs for payment cards.

Statistics published on Paymentscardsandmobile.com (Horst 2018) shows that by the end of 2016, card payments by volume (number) accounted for 52.22% of the cashless payments in the region, up from 50.24% in the previous year. In 2016, card payments by number and by value continued to grow higher than the compound annual growth rate (CAGR) between 2011 and 2016.

The same source says that the average is 109.9 card payments per citizen of the European Union, ranging from 17.7 in Romania to 404.6 in Iceland and 402.2 in

Norway (Horst 2018). It is therefore important to continue investing in improvements and innovative electronic payment technologies.

Multi-card smart cards allows the user to activate one of many virtual cards placed in the memory of a multi-card smart card by simply clicking on the function button on its surface. By pressing the function button, the active virtual debit card is selected and displayed on the card's e-paper display placed on the card's surface and showing the active payment card (FuzeX 2018). With the e-paper display located on the card's surface, user can check which card is selected for payment (Ravichandran 2018).

When one of several virtual cards is selected, the processor in the multi-card is configured the payment can be made. Multi-card smart card modules may be different: for example, a module for activating multiple bank smart cards (as all card information is stored in one multi-card smart card), then it can contain a biometric fingerprint scanner, a module for wireless communication and the like (Patent 2017).

There are many developed and used multi-card smart cards on the market. In some of these, it is possible to install up to 30 smart cards (Woei-Jiunn et al. 2004). Multi-card smart card allows the cardholder (it has identical dimensions as standard bank payment cards), store all his/her smart cards (FuzeX 2018) and use only one smart card for all his/her bank payments.

In this way, it is possible to simplify the card payment process by using only one rather than multiple physical cards, with the possibility of additional simplification of authentication system with multi-card smart cards.

3 Overview of Authentication Research Areas Using Biometric Fingerprint Coding

Many researchers are investigating the use of biometric authentication methods in a payment system (Andrew 2009). Some of them are investigating methods of Two Factor Authentication (2FA) protection systems with PIN authentication and biometric data. There is a research on authentication based on the method of measuring the dynamics of typing the PIN.(Jain et al. 2004). In this way, it is possible to authenticate users by analyzing the dynamics of typing the PIN. A fingerprint is a practical method and secure way for checking the authentication of a cardholder. Researchers agree with the fact that the biometric fingerprint data must be encrypted and transmitted via Internet by using secure protocols (Lisa 2011). This working model requires that POS terminal or ATM cash machine hashes fingerprint biometric data and forwards them to the issuing bank. The issuing bank will compare the data from the biometric database, and if the hashed data is identical, transaction will be carried out (Sankalp 2014).

Professor Dr Anil K. Jain in his work "On-line fingerprint verification" (1997) states that a fingerprint is one of the most reliable methods of personal identification. This paper describes the design and implementation of an online fingerprint verification system which operates in two stages: minutiae extraction and minutia matching (Andrew 2009). An improved version of the minutiae extraction algorithm proposed by Ratha et al., which is much faster and more reliable, is implemented for extracting features from an input fingerprint image captured with an online inkless scanner. For minutia matching, an alignment-based elastic matching algorithm has been developed. This algorithm is capable of finding the correspondences between minutiae in the input image and the stored template without resorting to exhaustive search and has the ability of adaptively compensating for the nonlinear deformations and inexact pose transformations between fingerprints (Jain 1977).

By investigating methods of generating PIN numbers from the biometric data of fingerprint, the starting point in this paper is taking into account the frequent problem in studies referring to the instability minutiaes' locations compared to the Core minutiae. The frequency of this problem influenced our investigation of some new methods for creating reliable PINs from fingerprint. Investigating the paper Fengling Han et al. "Generation of Reliable PINs from Fingerprint" the author got interested for simplifying the algorithm for generating reliable password/PIN by using three lines that link three minutiae as a triangle. In this article, the authors provide a certain level of immunity to distortion of minutiaes' locations relative to each other. This article (Fengling et al. 2007) was motivation to start improvement and simplification of the algorithm.

According to the algorithm and the research of Fengling et al. 2007, the advantage of the presented algorithm is its simplicity, due to the fact that it uses only two biometric fingerprint characteristic points for the PIN creation process. Fengling et al. and other authors in their works offer an algorithm that uses the correlation of three or more characteristic points to create a PIN.

The idea for creating the PIN from fingerprint images has been suggested in some early works (Germain 1997). By simplifying the algorithm, the authentication process could be also simplified, and the implementation of the algorithm would be cheaper and would have a wider application, especially in the banking sector, medicine, etc.

A generation of stable biometric PIN or password has been a major challenge for many cited authors (Fengling et al. 2007), (Germain et al. 1997), (Bhanu and Tan 2003), since it is difficult to overcome the uncertainty of the biometric fingerprint minutiaes which are in those papers a basis for calculation of the individual PIN digits or passwords (Jain 2004). In the literature cited above, can be found that the finger is not a rigid object and the process of projecting the three-dimensional shape of the finger onto the two-dimensional sensor surface is not precisely controlled, different impressions of a finger are related to each other by various transformation (Bhanu and Tan 2003). Some authors (Bhanu and Tan 2004) use triangle's angles, handedness, type, direction, and maximum sides as features in stable fingerprint indexing and classification. Due to problem of the minutiaes' stability, further research and developments of the algorithm for creating a stable PIN are expected.

4 Coding Biometric Fingerprint Data into the Pin

The encoding of the biometric fingerprint data into the PIN begins with the fingerprint acquisition process and continues with the process of normalizing the resulting image and mapping coordinates of the characteristic points, minutiaes in the Euclidean coordinate system.

Coordinates of the minutiae in the coordinate system allow us to calculate their mutual correlations. Even low-cost scanners allow precise mapping of minutiae (Zhao et al. 2013). Idea of this algorithm is to use a model for extracting only two characteristic points, minutiae, but in a way that does not compare these minutiae with minutiae from bank databases. With this mode, this idea offers viable alternatives to the customers who have distrust of biometric systems. Both user and a bank require simplicity and security. The main point is the algorithm that may be implemented into existing POS devices or ATMs, or other devices for identification of the user, that contain biometric fingerprint reader. Scanned fingerprint area needed for the algorithm is related to the fingerprint area in which Core point and its closest minutiae are placed. In case that the algorithm does not find these two characteristic points in the fingerprint template, fingerprint scanning should be repeated. Only the length of one line connecting the closest Ridge ending type of minutiae with the central core point, Fig. 1 will be sufficient for this algorithm to calculate the 4-digit PIN.

Algorithm for encoding biometric fingerprint data, showed in Fig. 1 has 4 phases, that are divided in 7 steps as shown in Fig. 2. A prerequisite for the implementation of the algorithm has been experimentally proven fact that minutiaes closest to core in fingerprints image are relatively stable (Fengling et al. 2007). The diagram in Fig. 2. shows that algorithm for encoding fingerprint into the 4-digit PIN uses only one input value—the Euclidean distance of the nearest Ridge ending type of minutia to the central Core point.

Diagram in Fig. 2 shows the algorithm steps needed for obtaining a 4-digit PIN, described below:

1. First step is scanning and acquisition of fingerprint image.
2. After the scanning process, it is necessary to do the normalization of fingerprint reduction of the image scale to a specific standard (In practice this would mean

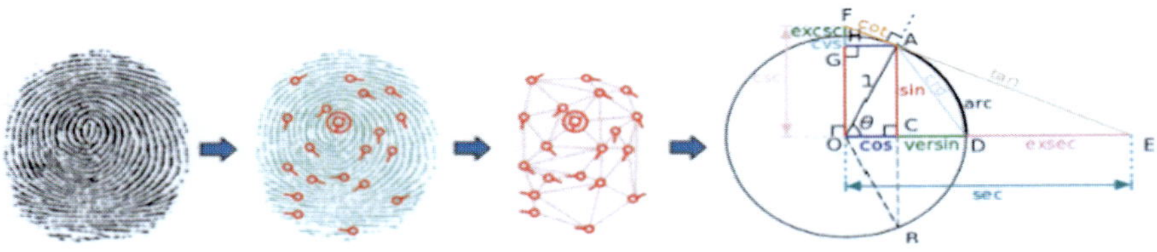

Biometrics Characteristic points Mapping Geometry of mapped characteristic points

Fig. 1 Encoding process of biometric data into PIN

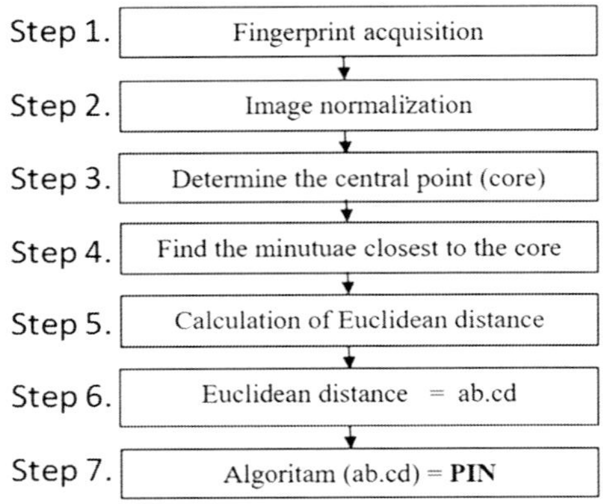

Fig. 2 Diagram shows the steps for obtaining the PIN based on fingerprint

that regardless of the device used for scanning the fingerprint, its minutiae will always get the same value in the coordinate system). The normalized image resolution of 500 × 500 pixels is selected for the algorithm. This resolution is selected as the size of the coordinate system. In this way, the central point in this coordinate system will have coordinates C(250, 250). Thus defined coordinates of the Core point are important for the functionality of the algorithm, because in this case the closest minutiae have a specific 4-digit value (the distance to the Core point). This specificity, useful for this work, the author has recognized in (Jadhav et al. 2011) and it has helped to simplify the calculation of 4-digit real number.

3. The coordinates of the central point and characteristic points, minutiae, are determined by fingerprint scanning and normalization of the scanned image. The algorithm determines the position of central core point (Cao et al. 2015).
4. The algorithm uses "Ridge ending" type of minutiae for analysis, all together with the Core point. In this step, it is necessary to determine the coordinates of the nearest "Ridge ending" characteristic point to core point.
5. Euclidean distance between the central, core point C(250, 250) and the i-th Ridge ending minutiae Pi (ai, bi) is obtained by the following equation (Iwasokun et al. 2014). It is necessary to determine the minimal Euclidean_distance (i):

$$\mathrm{D(i)} = \mathrm{Euclidean\_distance(i)} = \left((\mathrm{ai} - 250)^2 + (\mathrm{bi} - 250\,)^2\right)^{0.5} \tag{1}$$

$$\mathrm{D(min)} = \min(\mathrm{D1}, \mathrm{D2}, \ldots, \mathrm{Dn} - 1, \mathrm{Dn}) \tag{2}$$

6. When extracts two characteristic points, the algorithm connects them in a straight line and measures their Euclidean distance. A formula uses this distance "ab.cd", D(min) is the length of the nearest Ridge ending minutiae to a central point. To get the final PIN, it is needed to round up the real number D(min) to two decimals and multiply it with 100 or 1000. This is a simple formula that will allow the conversion of the length D(min) to a 4-digit integer. This number will be the PIN.

7. In the case that the value of D(min) from the previous step is 9,999 or less, it is necessary to use the following formula (3):

$$\text{PIN} = (\text{round}[\text{D(min)}, 2] \times 1000) = \text{ABCD} \tag{3}$$

In the case that the value of D(min) from the previous step is greater than 10, it is necessary to use the following formula (4):

$$\text{PIN} = (\text{round}[\text{D(min)}, 2] \times 100) = \text{ABCD} \tag{4}$$

5 Conceptual Model of Multi-card Smart Cards

A multi-card smart card may contain multiple virtual payment cards. An integrated function button located on the surface of a multi-card smart card allows the user to activate one of the several virtual cards. At the moment when the user wants to make a payment, it is necessary to determine which virtual payment card will be used. In this case, it is enough to activate one of many virtual cards with the button, and that active card will be shown on the display on the multi-card smart card (FuzeX 2018).

Figure 3 shows the conceptual model in which the cardholder initiates the electronic payment process. The introduced model enables the execution of an electronic payment transaction from any bank smart card using one multi-card smart card using biometric fingerprint data for the authentication.

The graphical representation of conceptual model in Fig. 3 shows the steps for electronic payments starting with selecting one of several virtual cards on the Multi-card smart card. After inserting a multi-card smart card into a POS terminal, a cardholder should place a finger on the fingerprint scanner. Then the software in the POS device will start the fingerprint acquisition and extraction of minutiaes. Based on mapped minutiaes, the software will determine the Core point coordinates and its closest Ridge ending minutiae. The Euclidean distance between these two points will be the input value of the algorithm for calculating the PIN. The PIN in the POS terminal will be compared with the PIN registered in the smart card chip.

The authentication PIN must be the one defined by the bank for a particular virtual smart card (Woei-Jiunn et al. 2004). If these two values are equal or deviate within the allowed range, the electronic payment transaction will be done.

This paper presents an additional simplified electronic payment process using a multi-card smart card. The conceptual idea is based on the use of the presented algorithm that does not require the user to manually enter the PIN, but the user's authentication by scanning the biometric fingerprint data and encoding the data into the 4-digit PIN.

Implementation of this idea allows the user to manage his bank cards in a way to use only one multi-card smart card without the need to remember particular PINs of payment cards. The conceptual model of electronic payments presented in this paper

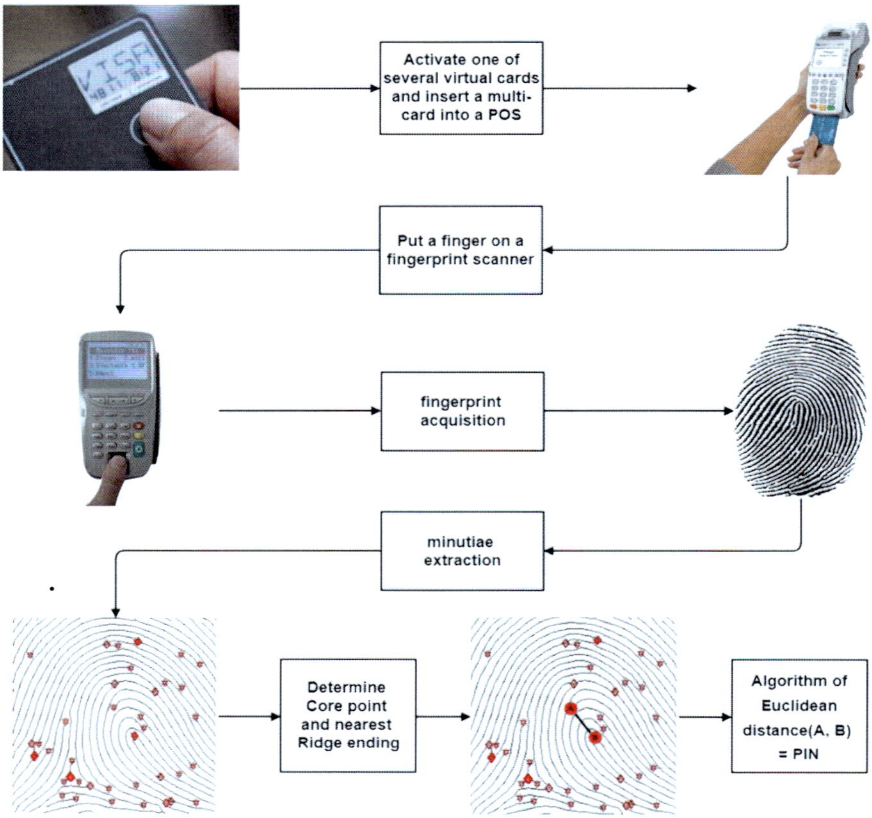

Fig. 3 The conceptual model of initiating electronic payment process

meets the PSD2 standard of the European Union, which requires the application of SCA (Rawlson 2016).

6 Implementation of the Algorithm for Encoding the Biometric Data in Practice

The procedure for encoding biometric fingerprint data into the PIN can be implemented in numerous systems that require smart card user's verification. For example, smart card payment authorization, cash withdrawal on the ATM machines, access control, healthcare application, and social services. The implementation of the algorithm proposed in this paper can be done in any process of authentication that takes the PIN value associated with the payment card as well as in the systems that require

Fig. 4 Fingerprint reader as a part of a POS terminal

a strong 2FA authentication. For example, this solution can be applied to any model of the POS terminals that have a built-in biometric fingerprint reader. Example of terminal with fingerprint reader is shown in Fig. 4.

Using the encoding algorithm, a bank client can use POS terminal or any other device with fingerprint scanner that will allow the input of bank card or any other smart card. In this way, the algorithm can be applied in different applications. It is necessary to upgrade the software within the devices with built-in fingerprint reader and this will allow interoperability. The presented method of authentication does not require online communication with the bank or any central database of the hashed data. Authentication is performed offline, without the necessary communication with the bank, as a security PIN is given on the basis of a fingerprint and is compared with the PIN placed on the card's chip.

When creating a bank card, a bank will do several fingerprint acquisitions. For each acquisition, the algorithm will create a single PIN. The average value of received PINs will be the client's reference PIN that will be used to authenticate electronic payments. The reference PIN will be stored in the smart card chip. During electronic payment, the user will be authenticated by fingerprint scanning on the fingerprint scanner installed in the terminal or typing the PIN on PINPAD at the POS terminal (or ATM machine) (Fig. 4). Figure 5 shows how the reference PIN will be received in case of the application of the presented algorithm or by manual input on the PINPAD device.

Here is the example of the applied algorithm for encoding of biometric data into PIN.

Scanning a fingerprint and the normalization of the scanned image are determined—the coordinates of the central point C(250, 250) and characteristic points, Ridge ending type of minutiae. Scaling transformation can be applied on the scanned fingerprint. Scaling and normalization of the fingerprint images are required for mea-

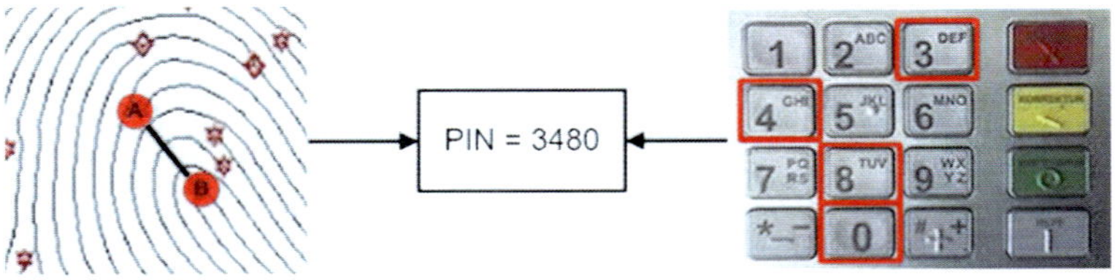

Fig. 5 User authentication by scanning a fingerprint and PIN entering on PINPAD

surements and comparisons of minutiae. In the second step distances of characteristic points, minutiae and central CORE point were measured. For example, if the algorithm measured the distance for the extracted characteristic points and D(min) = 34,80. The minimum Euclidean distance with two decimals after the comma is multiplied by the 10^2 and that is required PIN (6).

$$\text{PIN} = \left(\text{round}[\text{D}(\text{min}), 2] \times 10^2\right) = \text{ABCD} \tag{5}$$

$$\text{PIN} = (\text{round}[(34, 80), 2] \times 10^2, \mathbf{PIN} = \mathbf{3480} \tag{6}$$

7 Experimental Results

The experimental result confirmed the possibility of practical application of the described algorithm. The results obtained by applying the algorithm on real fingerprint data. Research has helped to bring a positive conclusion on the usability of the algorithm presented here. Matlab software script has been used for them, for establishing the coordinates of mapped minutiae in a fingerprint image.

Matlab script is downloaded from the internet link (Vahid K. Alilou). FVC2002 fingerprint databases are used in this paper (FVC2002).

In this study, 8 samples of fingerprint were used, showing the fingerprint of the same finger. Except in the changed position of the scanned finger, the samples differ in their quality. Fewer fingerprint quality can cause poor resolution of the fingerprint scanner, but also poor fingerprint prone to a fingerprint scanner.

In Table 1 "x" and "y" are coordinates of the Core point and nearest Ridge ending minutiae of sample of 8 fingerprints of the same finger that has been used in this study. The Euclidean distance has been calculated as well as PINs. In a sample of 8 fingerprint images taken from the database DB2_B (FVC2004), can be noticed different image quality of the scanned fingerprint.

Since a better or worse quality fingerprint appears when scanning, the table shows how the Euclidean distance between the Core point and the nearest Ridge ending minutiae is changed, depending on the quality of the printout. In accordance with that, two sets of fingerprint images can be defined. The first group is "Good qual-

Table 1 PINs obtained from the same finger

File	Core point		Ridge ending minutiae		Eucild distance	PIN number
	x	y	x	y		
101_1	188	296	162	351	60.83584	6083
101_2	158	264	126	316	61.05735	6105
101_3	203	278	161	319	58.69412	5869
101_4	174	450	148	505	60.83584	6083
101_5	126	327	79	372	65.06919	6506
101_6	186	333	159	376	50.77401	5077
101_7	127	320	100	368	55.07268	5507
101_8	164	266	133	307	51.40039	5140

ity" that includes fingerprint samples from files: 101_1–101_4. A second group is characterized as a "Bad quality" including files: 101_5–101_8 files (Table 1).

- In the "Good quality" group, the standard deviation of samples from the arithmetic mean is only 111.2, which is 2% of the deviation from the PIN in the smart card chip. This group is shown with samples 1–4 in Fig. 6.
- In the "Bad quality" group, the standard deviation of samples from the arithmetic mean is 507.2, which is 9% of the deviation from the PIN in the smart card chip. This group is shown with samples 5–8 in Fig. 6.

Table 2 shows the values for 8 samples divided into two groups. Each group has its calculated value.

The research showed that the deviation of the PIN recorded in the chip of the card and the PIN calculated by the algorithm on the sample of fingerprint image depends on the quality of the fingerprint scanner, and thus the quality of the fingerprint image. For a better quality scanner and higher quality fingerprint image, the results of standard

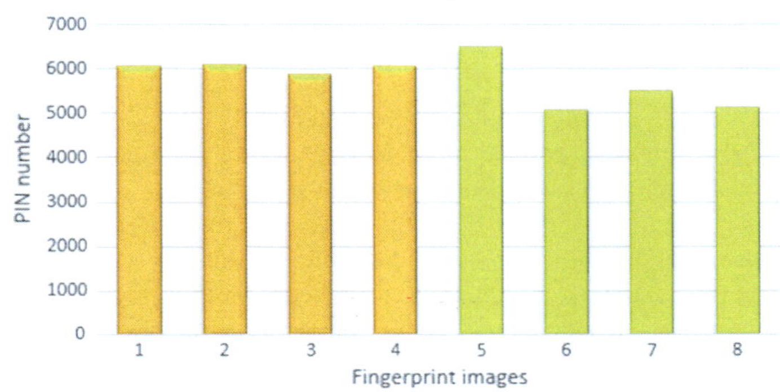

Fig. 6 PINs of the same fingerprint

Table 2 Second study results

Sample	Arithmetic mean	Standard deviation	Deviation percentage
Good quality	6035	111.2	2
Bad quality	5796	507.2	9

deviation are 2%, and for a sample that was used with less quality fingerprint cameras, the results yielded a standard deviation of 9%. This means for example: if the PIN recorded in the smart card chip was 6083, the authentication should also be confirmed for the calculated fingerprint PINs with the standard deviation of 2% (6083 ± 111). As picture quality falls, the standard deviation increases, and it comes to a maximum of 507.2 or a maximum deviation of 9% in relation to the PIN recorded in the smart card chip.

8 Conclusion

The future research, before the development of a prototype, is going to be completion of the proof of the concept proposed in this paper. It will be investigated: (1) What is the allowed deviation of the PIN from the reference value recorded in the smart card chip obtained as the average value from the N-fingerprint measurements. (2) How much is the algorithm applicable on the basis of scanning a fingerprint of at least 100 people. (3) Algorithm consistency of PIN when scanning different types of fingerprint patterns. Will the algorithm be useful when scanning different types of fingerprint patterns. (4) What will be the reference PIN value in a view of the different fingerprint acquisition conditions:

(a) Fingerprint scanning under normal conditions
(b) Fingerprint scanning at increased humidity
(c) Fingerprint scanning with different quality of the biometric fingerprint scanner.

The electronic payment process is simplified with the use of the Multi-Card smart card and this conceptual model. Given that the existing algorithms create PINs in a more complex way, the simplified algorithm presented here provides a more significant application in real electronic payment systems.

The first experimental research on the application of the algorithm suggests the possibility of using it in real electronic payment systems.

With this conceptual model, 2FA authentication is retained and the idea of fingerprint authentication is rejected by sending reference data to a remote central data system containing authentication data. The application of this algorithm will reduce the user's confusion, as the user will be free of need to remember a large number of PINs of the corresponding payment cards.

References

Alilou VK Mathlab script: fingerprint matching: a simple approach version 1.0 by Vahid K. Alilou. https://www.mathworks.com/matlabcentral/fileexchange/44369-fingerprint-matching–a-simple-approach

Bhanu B, Tan X (2003) Fingerprint indexing based on novel features of minutiae tripets. IEEE Trans Pattern Anal Mach Intell 25(5):616–622

Bhanu B, Tan X (2004) Computational algorithms for fingerprint recognition. Kluwer Academical Publishers

Boyd A (2009) Comparing fingerprints, no. 2529. http://www.uh.edu/engines/epi2529.htm

Cao K, Jain AK (2015) Learning fingerprint reconstruction: from minutiae to image. IEEE Trans Inf Forensics Secur 10(1):104–117

Fengling H, Jiankun H, Leilei H, Yi W, (2007) Generation of reliable PINs from fingerprints. In: 2007 IEEE international conference on communication (published 2007)

FuzeX White paper v.1.7 (2018) https://fuzex.co/wpcontent/uploads/2018/01/FuzeX_whitepaper.pdf

FVC2002, Fingerprint verification Competition 2002. http://bias.csr.unibo.it/fvc2002/

Germain RS, Califano A, Colville S (1997) Fingerprint science and Engineering, vol. 4, pp. 42–49

Horst F (2018) Payment cards in Europe. www.paymentscardsandmobile.com/payment-cards-europe-2

Iwasokun GB, Akinyokun OC, Dehinbo OJ (2014) Minutiae inter-distance measure for fingerprint matching. In: International conference on advanced computational technologies & creative media (ICACTCM'2014). Pattaya (Thailand), 14–15 Aug

Jadhav SD, Barbadekar AB, Patil SP (2011) Euclidean distance fingerprint matching. Institute of Technology, Pune, India

Jain AK, Lin H, Ruud B (1977) Online fingerprint verification

Jain AK, Pankanti S, Prabhabar S, Hong L, Ross A (2004) Biometrics: a grand challenge. In: Proceedings of international conference on pattern recognition, vol. 2, pp 935–942

Nelson, LS (2011) American identified: biometric technology and society. Massachusetts Institute of Technology

Patent, United States, 20170213, BAE et al. available at https://patentimages.storage.googleapis.com/6e/db/c4/f26f9635dfe6a6/US20170213120A1.pdf

Ravichandran KM (2018) Near field communication based digital transaction card, vol. 9, no. 3, March 2018, pp. 587–590, ISSN:2502-4752. Department of Information Technology, AMET University, Chennai. https://doi.org/10.11591/ijeecs.v9.i3.pp587-590

Rawlson K (2016) Biometrics in banking & financial services, June 27–29

Sankalp B (2014) Authenticating transactions using bank–verified biometrics. https://arxiv.org/ftp/arxiv/papers/1407/1407.3366.pdf

Woei-Jiunn T, Chia-Chun W, Wei-Bin L (2004) A smart card-based remote scheme for password authentication in multi-server Internet services. Department of Information Management, Da-Yeh University, 112 Shan-Jiau Rd., Taiwan

Zhao Q, Zhang Y, Jain AK, Paulter NG, Taylor M (2013) A generative model for fingerprint minutiae. ICB, Madrid, Spain, June 4–7

Detection of Click Spamming in Mobile Advertising

Safiye Şeyma Kaya, Burak Çavdaroğlu and Kadir Soner Şensoy

Abstract Most of the marketing expenditures in mobile advertising are conducted through real-time bidding (RTB) marketplaces, in which ad spaces of the sellers (publishers) are auctioned for the impression of the buyers' (advertisers) mobile apps. One of the most popular pricing models in RTB marketplaces is cost-per-install (CPI). In a CPI campaign, publishers place mobile ads of the highest bidders in their mobile apps and are paid by advertisers only if the advertised app is installed by a user. CPI pricing model causes some publishers to conduct an infamous fraudulent activity, known as click spamming. A click spamming publisher executes clicks for lots of users who have not authentically made them. If one of these users hears about the advertised app organically (say, via TV commercial) afterwards and installs it, this install will be attributed to the click spamming publisher. In this study, we propose a novel multiple testing procedure which can identify click spamming activities using the data of click-to-install time (CTIT), the time difference between the click of a mobile app's ad and the first launch of the app after the install. We statistically show that our procedure has a false-positive error rate of 5% in the worst case. Finally, we run an experiment with 30 publishers, half of which are fraudulent. According to the results of the experiment, all non-fraudulent publishers are correctly identified and 73% of the fraudulent publishers are successfully detected.

Keywords Mobile advertising · Fraud detection · Click spamming · Multiple testing

---

S. Ş. Kaya · B. Çavdaroğlu (✉)
Department of Industrial Engineering, Kadir Has University, Istanbul, Turkey
e-mail: burak.cavdaroglu@khas.edu.tr

S. Ş. Kaya
e-mail: safiyeseyma.kaya@khas.edu.tr

K. S. Şensoy
App Samurai Inc, San Francisco, CA, USA
e-mail: soner@appsamurai.com

N. Mladenović et al. (eds.), *Advances in Operational Research in the Balkans*,
Springer Proceedings in Business and Economics,
https://doi.org/10.1007/978-3-030-21990-1_15

1 Introduction

Time spent on mobile devices has increased drastically in recent years and most of this time is spent in mobile applications. The widespread usage of both smartphones and mobile applications has also led to the rapid growth of *mobile advertising*. Most of the marketing expenditures in mobile advertising are conducted through real-time bidding (RTB) marketplaces, in which the main objective of the buyers (advertisers) is to acquire the most audience install at the lowest cost and the main goal of the sellers (publishers) is to sell their ad spaces at the highest price. An advertiser decides the bid in the RTB marketplace and the attributes of the targeted users (such as the geolocation and demographics of the target users). A publisher, which is usually the owner of a mobile app, on the other hand, sells the ad space of the app to advertiser at the winning price of RTB auction. RTB marketplace finalizes an auction in milliseconds according to the bids of the advertisers.

There are two main platforms in which RTB marketplaces are operated: ad exchanges and ad networks. An ad network, the RTB platform we focus on in this study, allows advertisers to publish their mobile advertising campaigns with a pre-determined budget and campaign duration and a desired bid rate. Meanwhile, ad networks collect inventory of ad space from a range of publishers and sell it to advertisers with the highest bid offers in its RTB marketplace. Ad networks usually offer different pricing models to the advertisers, such as cost per action, cost per install, cost per click, or cost per impression. The most popular pricing model among advertisers is cost per install (CPI) (Nieborg 2016). In a CPI campaign, publishers place mobile ads of the highest bidders in their mobile apps in an effort to drive installation of the advertised application. The advertiser is charged the winning bid rate only when the advertiser's application is installed by the user. After installation is verified by both the ad network and the advertiser, the ad network receives a small portion of the CPI price for finding the publisher that grants the install, and the publisher receives the rest.

Verification of an install takes place with the help of a system known as mobile ad *attribution*. Attribution is used to track the details of each mobile ad transaction such as the time stamp of the ad click and the ad install. Attribution is also used to keep track of the publisher whom a succeeding install should be attributed to. Each click by a user is associated with the publisher's app in which the click occurs. If there exist multiple clicks by a user before the install of the advertised app, the latest attributed publisher will be paid by the advertiser due to the contract of CPI pricing model. All these transaction and tracking activities are accomplished in almost instantaneously in RTB marketplaces and they generate billions of dollars of revenue annually for mobile advertising industry. On the other hand, millions of dollars are lost because of the fraudulent activities of publishers to receive undeserved gain (Shields 2016). Three main types of fraud in mobile advertising are (i) fake installs with bots and emulators, (ii) click injection, and (iii) click spamming. In the first type, using bots, fraudster generates fake installs and hopes they are confused with genuine installs. In the second fraud type, fraudster's spy app detects when other apps are downloaded on a device and triggers a click right before the install completes, which inequitably attributes the install to the fraudster's app. In the last type of fraud, fraudster executes clicks for lots of users who have not authentically made them. If a user installs the advertised app organically after hearing about the app in another advertising channel (for instance, a TV commercial), this install will still be attributed to the fraudulent publisher according to the working mechanism of attribution system. Click spamming is the most common fraud type in-app marketing and its most apparent harm is lost campaign budget of advertisers, by paying to the click spammer publishers for users who have never generated impressions in the publisher's app (Monasterio 2017). Since click spamming captures organic traffic and then claims the credit for these users, it is also known as organic pouching.

Conversion Rate (CR) is a standard metric in app marketing that is calculated by dividing the total number of installs by the total number of clicks. A common characteristic of click spamming publishers is a conversion rate much lower than usual since spamming generates lots of false clicks which never end up with an install. Although low CR is a good indicator for click spamming, a meaningful conversion rate emerges only after a significant campaign duration is completed and hundreds of thousands of clicks are attributed to the publisher. The lack of an early warning mechanism for click spamming causes the loss of considerable amount of campaign budgets for advertisers.

Another well-known way of identifying click spamming is to analyze the distribution of *click-to-install times* (CTIT) (Monasterio 2017). Click-to-install time refers to the time difference between the click of a mobile app's ad by a user and the first launch of the app on the mobile device of the same user after the install. It is easy to note that the spamming publisher can trigger false clicks but cannot trigger an install. This makes click and install events independent from each other and causes the click-to-install times of installs coming from a click spamming publisher to be distributed uniformly over time.

Even though CTIT is known to be utilized intuitively by many advertisers for filtering out spamming publishers, to best of our knowledge, a prescribed set of rules for fraud detection with CTIT has not been defined in the literature so far. In this study, we aim to derive a statistical method for the detection of click spamming publishers in real time by analyzing their CTIT data building up over time. The rest of the paper is organized as follows: In Sect. 2, we make a brief literature review on the fraud detection methods in mobile advertising and the statistical methods related to our analysis. In Sect. 3, we discuss the details of our methodology of click spamming detection. In Sect. 4, we present the data set and the experimental results. In Sect. 5, we conclude by summarizing our findings and discussing future research opportunities.

2 Previous Work

Fraudulent activities in digital advertisement is a research topic that has been widely investigated in the marketing and computer science literature. One of the most prevalent fraud type, which both web and mobile platforms suffer from, is click spamming. Immorlica et al. (2005) used machine learning techniques that are based on click through rates to detect click fraud in pay-per-click pricing model. Fraudsters usually conduct click spamming on the web by disseminating malicious software (malware) that are capable of generating fake click on behalf of the infected users. Blizard and Livic (2012) outlined an example analysis of a click spamming malware and showed that the malware can cause a loss on the order of hundreds of thousands of dollars for a 3-week period. Iqbal et al. (2018) presented a method for fighting click-fraud by detecting botnets with automated clickers from the user side. They also evaluated the performance of their proposed method by integrating it into desktop operating systems. Zingirian and Benini (2018) showed a vulnerability of the pay-per-click in web advertising and proposed a statistical tradeoff-based approach to manage this vulnerability. Smith et al. (2011) developed systems and methods for detecting click spam in web advertising and patented this methodology. Their system identifies normal users visiting a web site and determines an occurrence of spamming on the web site based on the identified normal users.

Pay-per-click pricing model of web advertising requires instant payment to the publisher upon click. Click spamming has a direct negative effect on the profitability of the advertisers on web advertising whereas in mobile advertising click spamming can affect an advertiser only if click ends up with an install. Therefore, the fraud in mobile advertising is a relatively new research area when compared with the fraud in web advertising.

Application markets have many freely distributed applications that are supported by in-app advertisements. Most of the fraudulent activities are performed by the publishers of these applications. Both placement fraud and bot fraud in these apps cause impression and unintentional clicks from users. Liu et al. (2014) investigated display fraud by analyzing UI of apps to detect unintentional clicks for increasing ad revenue. However, this technique can determine clicks that are triggered in the foreground, but not background. Crussell et al. (2014) investigated fraudulent android apps that create ad requests while running in background, and they developed an analysis tool which can expose these ad frauds.

Cho et al. (2015) made an automated click generation attack on 8 popular ad networks and showed 6 of them vulnerable to this type of attacks. Cho et al. (2016) expanded their previous study. They suggested defense mechanisms and discussed economic aspect of security failure. Dave et al. (2012) conducted large-scale measurement study on major ad networks about click spamming and proposed a methodology to measure click spamming rate for advertisers. Monasterio (2017) proposed a histogram for non-fraudulent scenario and utilizes fitting test to understand click spamming. However, this fitting test method can only be utilized at the end of ad campaign duration and cannot be used in real time.

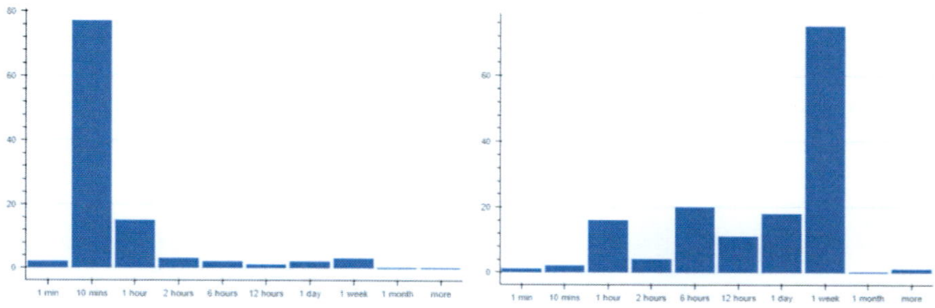

Fig. 1 The distribution of CTIT values for a legit publisher (left) and a fraudulent publisher (right)

3 Detection of Click Spamming

In this section, we will develop a procedure with multiple statistical tests on CTIT data to detect click spamming activities of publishers and analyze the confidence of this procedure. Let us first introduce the histogram of CTIT values for two publishers as an example of how the distribution of CTIT values may differ in legit and fraudulent publishers. In Fig. 1, the graph on the left shows the distribution of click-to-install times for a legit publisher. It can be noted that most of the installs are accomplished within first hour after the click event since they decide to install and launch the app shortly after they deliberately click the publisher's ad. The graph on the right, on the other hand, demonstrates the distribution of click-to-install times for a fraudulent publisher. This publisher spams lots of users with lots of clicks, and a few users unaware of this click event (and, thus, the advertised app) will occasionally install the app after hearing about it from other marketing channels or via word of mouth. Hence, the time between click and install events can be weeks, or even months, which results in a hump on the right in the graph of fraudulent publisher.

Another interesting fact about the distribution of click-to-install times lies behind the descriptive statistics of these values. Table 1 provides the sample size, mean, standard deviation, median, and range for the CTIT values of the same two publishers discussed earlier. The table also shows the same statistics for the all-time installs of a DSP company[1] for benchmark purposes. The mean of CTIT vales for a legit publisher can still be very high (approximately 4.75 h) due to a few installs with very high CTIT values. This situation is not an indicator of click spamming since some users forget to launch a mobile application after the install and thus even non-fraudulent publishers may rarely run across very high CTIT values. Therefore, "mean" is not a reliable statistic to make any deduction about spamming. The median value of fraudulent publisher, on the other hand, is quite large compared to the medians of DSP and legit publisher according to the table. Indeed, a very large median (approximately 27 h in this instance) means that at least half of the sample has an unacceptable level of CTIT.

[1] A demand-side platform (DSP) is a system that allows advertisers to advertise their mobile applications in multiple ad networks through an interface.

Table 1 The descriptive statistics of CTIT values for legit and fraudulent publishers

	All-time installs of a DSP	Legit publisher	Fraudulent publisher
Sample size	1602268	106	148
Mean (sec)	68991	17015	187397
Median (sec)	250	236	96941
Standard deviation (sec)	553750	78452	338678
Minimum (sec)	1	35	51
Maximum (sec)	15851602	523212	3730800
Range (sec)	15851601	523177	3730749

A large median value also explains why the histogram of the fraudulent publisher is skewed to the right in Fig. 1. These results suggest that a statistical test measuring the positive deviations from a sufficiently large "median" can be confidently used to detect click spamming publishers.

The nonparametric sign test for a median (Sprent 1989) with $H_0 : \eta = \eta_0$ and $H_a : \eta > \eta_0$ is an effective way of deciding whether the median of CTIT values for a publisher (η) takes on a particular value (η_0) or a value greater than η_0. The main question here is how to decide η_0. We have to select a sufficiently large value for η_0 such that we can safely accuse the publisher of spamming if the null hypothesis is rejected.

We observe the distribution of CTIT values for several publishers and note that, if publisher is legit, 70–75% of installs typically occur during the first hour, and 90–95% of installs in the first 24 h following a click event. Monasteriao (2017) presents the histogram of CTIT values for one day worth of installs in a non-fraudulent scenario and comes to the same conclusion that the most of the users' installs occur in the first hour after the click.

In the light of these facts, we designed the following sign test for the median of CTIT values of a publisher.

$$\begin{aligned} H_0 &: \eta = 7200 \text{ seconds} \\ H_a &: \eta > 7200 \text{ seconds} \end{aligned} \tag{1}$$

In this test, $\eta_0 = 7200$ is adequately large that enables us to safely assume the publisher is fraudulent if the null hypothesis is rejected (i.e., probability of type-I error is small). However, our analysis shows that, when the test is applied for the all-time installs of a publisher, there is a significant chance of the publisher passing the test even though it is fraudulent (i.e., probability of type-II error is large). This situation occurs mainly because some publishers mix both click spamming and legit activities together in order to disguise their fraud. Therefore, it is possible for a fraudulent publisher to have remarkable number of very large CTIT values even though the median CTIT value is still less than 7200 seconds. Besides, conducting the test for the all-time installs of a publisher would mean to evaluate the publisher after an ad campaign has ended. Filtering out a spamming publisher from future campaigns is still beneficial in the long run, but it cannot prevent the advertiser from paying for the installs that are already attributed to the fraudster at the recent campaign.

One way to overcome these challenges is multiple testing, the testing of more than one independent hypothesis. In multiple testing, instead of running a single sign test for a publisher at the end of campaign duration, we periodically run a sign test as new installs come from the publisher. This enables us to detect even occasional click spamming activities of fraudulent publishers in earlier stages of the campaign.

However, if one plans to make a decision by applying multiple testing, she should be extra cautious about false-positive decision-making. Assuming that the type-I error of a single sign test is α, the probability of at least one false-positive error among m independent sign tests (family-wise error rate) is $\bar{\alpha} = 1 - (1 - \alpha)^m$. This means that the probability of having at least one rejected null hypothesis converges to 1 as the number of tests increases. In other words, if we assume one rejected null hypothesis in multiple testing is adequate to accuse a publisher of click spamming, we will falsely filter out the publisher even though it is most probably legit.

In the literature, there are classical multiple testing methods such as Šidák correction (Šidák 1967), Holm method (Holm 1979), and Bonferroni correction (Bland and Altman 1995), which prevent large probability of rejecting some of the true null hypotheses. In this study, we propose a new multiple testing procedure that has an improved ability to detect click spamming fraud compared to these classical methods, while still keeping the confidence of the procedure (i.e., probability of not making false-positive decisions) sufficiently high.

In our multiple testing procedure, we run successive sign tests in real time while the campaign is still running. In other words, we run a sign test given in (1) for every n installs of a publisher to monitor the legitimacy of its installs. If we had decided the publisher is fraudulent by only one rejected null hypothesis in multiple testing, as mentioned earlier, we would have made considerable number of false-positive decisions. Instead, in our procedure, we aim a family-wise error rate of $\bar{\alpha} = 0.05$ in the worst case.

In our study, the multiple testing procedure for detecting click spamming activity has been implemented in two steps as follows.

- *STEP 1.* We assume the significance level of $\alpha = 0.05$ for each sign test for median, whose sample size is selected to be $n = 10$. Namely, we run the hypothesis test of (1) for every 10 incoming installs and conduct $m < N/10$ tests in total, where N is the total number of installs attributed to the publisher during the campaign duration.
- *STEP 2.* We define a rule which identifies the spamming publishers due to the result of m sign tests with a family-wise error rate of $\bar{\alpha} = 0.05$. According to the rule, a publisher is determined to be fraudulent if it fails r successive sign tests, each with a significance level of α, among m tests. We do not have to run these tests till the end of the campaign duration (i.e., m does not have to be equal to $N/10$) since we may run across r successive rejected hypothesis in earlier stages of the campaign.

Table 2 The rule of multiple testing procedure

r	$\bar{m}$	$[m^l, m^u]$
1	1	[1, 1]
2	22	[2, 22]
3	433	[23, 433]
4	8524	[434, 8524]

Note that the value of r has to be updated as the number of tests (m) increases with the incoming installs. If we set a constant value for r, the family-wise error rate would continuously increase and eventually be much higher than our target value, $\bar{\alpha} = 0.05$, as the number of tests, m, increases.

In order to compute the value of r for varying levels of m, we need to utilize the theory of success runs introduced by Feller (1968). Let r be a positive integer and let ε denote the occurrence of a success run of length r in m Bernoulli trails, each with a success probability of α. According to Feller (1968), the probability of no success run of length r in m trials (q) can be approximated by Eq. (2)

$$q \approx \frac{1 - \alpha x}{(r + 1 - rx)(1 - \alpha)} \cdot \frac{1}{x^{m+1}} \tag{2}$$

where x is the positive root of Eq. (3), which is not equal to $1 - \alpha$.

$$1 - x + (1 - \alpha)\alpha^r x^{r+1} = 0 \tag{3}$$

Hence, the probability of at least one success run of length r in m trials is given by $p = 1 - q$.

For example, assume we conclude a publisher's median CTIT is greater than 2 h (i.e., the publisher is fraudulent) if the null hypotheses of $r = 3$ successive sign tests are rejected among $m = 300$ tests. When we let $\alpha = 0.05$ and $r = 3$ in Eq. (3), x can be found as 1.000119. Replacing this value of x in Eq. (2), the probability of falsely concluding the publisher to be fraudulent (family-wise error rate) can be calculated as $\bar{\alpha} = p = 0.0348$.

In the second step of our procedure, we determine the rule of how many successive rejected hypotheses is enough for concluding a publisher is spammer for different number of tests. The main objective of this rule is to guarantee the probability of falsely accusing the publisher not to exceed a family-wise error rate of $\bar{\alpha} = 0.05$. Table 2 tabulates how the rule is being applied. $\bar{m}$ represents the number of tests requires to have a successive rejected hypothesis of length r with a probability of $\bar{\alpha} = 0.05$. $[m^l, m^u]$ denotes the interval for the total number of tests where successively rejected hypotheses of length r is sought for click spamming.

According to Table 2, our multiple testing procedure works as follows. When the 10th install attributed to a publisher is registered, we run the sign test given in (1) for the CTIT values of this sample. If the null hypothesis is rejected, we conclude that the publisher is a click spammer (since $r = 1$ when $m = 1$). Otherwise, we wait until another 10 installs are registered. When the next 10 installs are accumulated, we run the sign test again for the second set of 10 installs. Starting from the 2nd sign test to the 22nd test, we search for 2 successively rejected hypotheses. If we observe any "two rejected hypotheses in a row" until the 22nd test, we conclude that the publisher is a click spammer. Otherwise, we continue to monitor the installs attributed to the publisher. Likewise, we search for 3 successively rejected hypotheses from the 23rd test to the 433rd test, and 4 successively rejected hypotheses from the 434th test to the 8524th test. We have never needed to go beyond 8524th test, since none of the publishers in our experiment has more than $8524 * 10$ attributed installs. If we conclude that a publisher is fraudulent at any point according to this procedure, the decision is guaranteed to have a false-positive error which is at most equal to family-wise error rate of $\bar{\alpha} = 0.05$. If we do not observe any "r rejected hypotheses in a row" during the course of our procedure, we can conclude that there has not been enough evidence that the publisher is a click spammer.

4 Experiments and Results

We will now discuss the results of our experiment conducted with a data set of app installs attributed to several publishers. This data set was supplied by a DSP company which provides a self-service mobile advertisement platform to its customers for managing their own ad campaigns. In our experiment, we run the tests with 30 publishers from 30 different ad campaigns. Half of the publishers have been black-listed as click spamming publisher by the DSP company due to prior experience. The remaining 15 publishers are known to be non-fraudulent that always brings in legitimate installs.

Table 3 summarizes the data used and shows the results of our experiment. Each publisher is represented with a row in the table. The grayed out rows denote the publishers that are in fact fraudulent. The first five columns provide the publisher ID, the number of total installs during the campaign, the campaign duration, the mean value of all CTITs during the campaign, and the median value of all CTITs. The sixth column specifies the order of the first test indicating a click spamming activity. For instance, the second publisher is accused of click spamming for the first time in its $657 * 10 = 6570$ th attributed install, since $r = 4$ consecutively rejected tests are observed at the 657th test in our multiple testing procedure. A dash sign ("–") in the sixth column indicates that any evidence of click spamming has not been found during the campaign. The last column shows the total number of rejected tests during the campaign. The number of rejected tests does not have to be zero for a non-fraudulent publisher. For example, first publisher is not identified as fraudulent, although it has a total of 2 rejected tests. The reason it is not a click spammer is that the rejected tests are not successive.

Table 3 Experiment results

Publisher	Number of Total Installs	Campaign Duration (days)	Mean CTIT (seconds)	Median CTIT (seconds)	The Order of the Test Indicating Click Spamming	Total Number of Rejected Tests
1	308	36	138454	64	–	2
2	8424	79	4433	201	657	172
3	749	3	6983	727	–	0
4	1038	11	25180	1103	–	0
5	94	2	1441	1462	–	0
6	2420	23	2808	1869	–	0
7	1351	175	14223	2376	–	0
8	288	163	15881	2607	–	2
9	875	44	4068	3011	–	0
10	1876	174	11426	3590	–	3
11	265	6	3332	3666	14	2
12	1091	128	10995	4293	67	6
13	249	7	9993	4487	–	0
14	373	4	5204	5018	–	0
15	133	39	6665	5383	–	0
16	827	34	15788	5919	6	24
17	416	29	8139	6240	–	1
18	1075	3	13493	6406	17	42
19	361	58	11967	6999	–	5
20	295	17	95731	7173	13	8
21	400	24	64212	7330	40	5
22	1045	79	29884	7879	24	31
23	335	118	19482	8235	–	0
24	150	9	17020	8999	–	1
25	62	5	22196	9441	–	1
26	2487	94	23964	9945	15	54
27	90	8	16608	10315	–	1
28	610	32	25412	10732	–	10
29	877	6	19497	11383	19	19
30	2621	44	31341	19686	15	97

According to the results of the experiment, our multiple testing procedure does not make any false-positive error. In other words, none of 15 legit publishers is accused of click spamming. Since we design the procedure in such a way that it does not have a false-positive error greater than the family-wise error rate of $\bar{\alpha} = 0.05$, this is an expected outcome.

The results also indicate that eleven out of 15 fraudulent publishers have been successfully detected. On average, we detect the click spamming activities before 38% of the total installs have arrived. In the best case (Publisher 30), the click spamming is detected before $(15 * 10)/2621 = 6\%$ of the total installs have arrived. In the worst case (Publisher 21), the click spamming can be detected only after

$(40 * 10)/400 = 100\%$ of the total installs have arrived. This result suggests that we have recognized Publisher 21 is a fraudster at the very end of the ad campaign. Even though the detection of this spamming publisher does not help us in this experimented campaign, filtering out the publisher from the future campaigns will protect us against its prospective fraud. Apart from these results, Publisher 2 is also worth mentioning because it is blacklisted as click spammer in spite of its relatively low median CTIT value. If we had conducted the sign test for once with the all-time installs of this publisher, we would have concluded it is not fraudulent due to the median CTIT of 201 seconds. This example shows why the multiple testing procedure is superior to single testing.

On the other part, we fail to detect the click spamming activities of the remaining four fraudulent publishers (Publisher 5, 24, 25, and 27) during their campaign period, which makes the false-negative error rate of the experiment to be $\bar{\beta} = 11/15 = 73\%$. The common characteristic of all four publishers, whose click spamming activities have not been detected, is the low number of installs due to the short campaign duration. We observe that most of the clicks attributed to these publishers had not ended up with installs at the time point we collected their data for our experiment. Note that the bid price is still paid to publishers, if the click event takes place during the campaign interval regardless of the time of the install event. Most probably, these clicks will never yield a legit install, but can still bring in undeserved money for these publishers if any user installs the advertised app organically via another advertising channel.

Unfortunately, for the short-term campaigns, our multiple testing procedure is not likely to detect the click spamming publishers since high-valued CTITs indicating spamming have not yet been generated at the time we collect the data. Nevertheless, these campaigns are short-dated and usually bring relatively small number of falsely attributed installs from their publishers. Hence, we can safely assume the total loss due to these installs are still in an acceptable level.

5 Conclusion

Click spamming is a common type of fraud in mobile display advertising. However, click spamming activities of fraudsters can still be detected by applying some statistical techniques on click-to-install time (CTIT) values. In this study, we have defined a novel multiple testing procedure which conducts sign tests on CTIT values of a publisher periodically. If we observe r successive rejections in these tests, where r is a function of the number of tests conducted so far, we tag the publisher as fraudulent. Otherwise, publisher passes the testing procedure and is concluded to be legit. We have also showed that our procedure has a false-positive error rate of at most $\bar{\alpha} = 0.05$. Lastly, we run an experiment with 30 publishers, half of which are fraudulent. According to the results of the experiment, all non-fraudulent publishers are correctly identified and 73% of the fraudulent publishers are successfully detected.

As a future research direction, statistical techniques can be utilized for the detection of another type of ad fraud, click injection. In click injection, fraudulent publisher's app can detect when other apps are downloaded on the device and trigger clicks right before the install completes. In this way, they receive undeserved credit for their attributed installs. Click-to-install times of click injecting publishers are typically smaller. However, from the perspective of advertisers, truncating all installs with small CTIT is not a good idea since not every click that happens shortly before the install is fraudulent. In this sense, a similar multiple testing procedure can be developed for the detection of injected clicks to prevent advertisers from diverting their budget to fraudsters.

References

Bland JM, Altman DG (1995) Multiple significance tests: the Bonferroni method. BMJ 310(6973):170

Blizard T, Livic N (2012) Click-fraud monetizing malware: a survey and case study. In: Proceedings of 7th international conference on malicious and unwanted software (MALWARE 2012). pp 67–72

Cho G, Cho J, Song Y, Kim H (2015) An empirical study of click fraud in mobile advertising networks. In: Proceedings of 10th international conference on availability, reliability and security (ARES), pp 382–388

Cho G, Cho J, Song Y, Choi D, Kim H (2016) Combating online fraud attacks in mobile-based advertising. EURASIP J Inf Secur 1:2

Crussell J, Stevens R, Chen H (2014) Madfraud: investigating ad fraud in android applications. In: Proceedings of the 12th annual international conference on Mobile systems, applications, and services, pp 123–134

Dave V, Guha S, Zhang Y (2012) Measuring and fingerprinting click-spam in ad networks. In: Proceedings of the ACM SIGCOMM 2012 conference on applications, technologies, architectures, and protocols for computer communication, pp 175–186

Feller W (1968) An introduction to probability theory and its applications, vol 1, 3rd edn. Wiley, New York

Holm S (1979) A simple sequentially rejective multiple test procedure. Scand J Stat 65–70

Immorlica N, Jain K, Mahdian M, Talwar K (2005) Click fraud resistant methods for learning click-through rates. In: International Workshop on Internet and Network Economics. Springer, Berlin, Heidelberg, pp 34–45

Iqbal MS, Zulkernine M, Jaafar F, Gu Y (2018) Protecting internet users from becoming victimized attackers of click-fraud. J Softw: Evol Process 30(3):e1871

Liu B, Nath S, Govindan R, Liu J (2014) DECAF: detecting and characterizing ad fraud in mobile apps. In: Proceedings of the 11th USENIX symposium on networked systems design and implementation (NSDI '14), pp 57–70

Monasterio JD (2017) Tagging click-spamming suspicious installs in mobile advertising through time delta distributions. In: Proceedings of Simposio Argentino de GRANdes DAtos (AGRANDA)-JAIIO, vol 46, Córdoba

Nieborg DB (2016) App advertising: the rise of the player commodity. In: Hamilton JF, Bodle R, Korin E (eds) Explorations in critical studies of advertising. Routledge, New York, pp 28–41

Shields R (2016) REPORT: ad fraud is 'second only to the drugs trade' as a source of income for organized crime. Business Insider. http://www.businessinsider.com/wfa-report-ad-fraud-will-cost-advertisers-50-billion-by-2025-2016-6. 24 May 2018

Šidák Z (1967) Rectangular confidence regions for the means of multivariate normal distributions. J Am Stat Assoc 62(318):626–633

Smith B, Lester C, Karrels EL (2011) U.S. US Patent 7,933,984,B1. US. Patent and Trademark Office, Washington, DC

Sprent P (1989) Applied nonparametric statistical methods, 4th edn. Chapman and Hall, London

Zingirian N, Benini M (2018) Click spam prevention model for on-line advertisement. Manuscript submitted for publication. http://arxiv.org/abs/1802.02480. 20 May 2018

Improving Decision-Making in Ski Resorts by Analysing Ski Lift Transportation—A Review

Boris Delibašić, Sandro Radovanović, Miloš Z. Jovanović and Milija Suknović

Abstract This paper provides an overview of research on ski lift transportation data, a still heavily underused resource in ski resorts. To the best of our knowledge, this is the first paper that provides an overview of the efforts done in analyzing ski lift transportation data with the goal to advance the decision-making process in ski resorts. The paper is separated into three major research directions, the first being the clustering of ski lift transportation data. The second research direction is concerned with the exploitation of ski lift transportation data for ski injury research and prevention. The third research direction is concerned with congestion analysis in ski resorts. We provide directions for future research in the conclusion.

Keywords Ski lift transportation data · Ski resorts decision-making · Data mining · Ski injury · Clustering · Ski lift congestion

1 Introduction

Skiing is a multibillion business in the United States with 7.3 billion USD spent at US ski resorts in 2014/2015 and 57.1 million average skier visits (skier days) yearly since the 2002/2003 season (The National Ski Areas Association 2017). The skiing business is, however, a worldwide phenomenon as the United States only take up to 15% of this business. All countries with mountain regions that have winter seasons develop ski resorts as the major source of income and sustainability in the mountain regions.

Despite its huge popularity, decision making in ski resorts is mostly relying on managerial experience and less on data the resorts collects. This is, obviously, not aligned with other transportation businesses such as road traffic (Omerčević et al. 2008) and public transportation (Froehlich et al. 2009; Lathia et al. 2013) where the transportation data is being used to improve products and services to the users.

B. Delibašić · S. Radovanović (✉) · M. Z. Jovanović · M. Suknović
University of Belgrade, Belgrade, Serbia
e-mail: sandro.radovanovic@fon.bg.ac.rs

N. Mladenović et al. (eds.), *Advances in Operational Research in the Balkans*, Springer Proceedings in Business and Economics,
https://doi.org/10.1007/978-3-030-21990-1_16

Ski lift transportation data is readily available in ski resorts, as skiers use in most resorts RFID ski passes for entering ski lift gates. Based on this process of transportation, a lot of data is being generated, i.e., all transportations from all skiers in a ski resort are being recorded.

The usage of this data is though still in its infancy, i.e., it is used only for basic managerial reporting in ski resorts, such as the number of ski lift transportations done per ski lift and date. This data has the potential to shape the decision-making process in ski resorts, to improve safety in the ski resorts and to help to transform the ski lift transportation business.

The ski resorts are currently exploiting mostly traditional formats for ski tickets sale (such as daily ski, and weekly ski tickets). The installation and maintenance of ski lifts, and also the handling of congestion and safety is done by exploiting expert opinions, and less on the data the ski resort possesses. We argue that the application of data mining on ski lift transportation data could influence the change in business processes in the ski resort business, provide possibilities which would allow for making more informed decisions in the ski resort. The exploitation of the existing data could help both the ski resort management, as well as the users of the ski resort.

The ski lift transportation data is not yet opened like public transportation data in Barcelona (Froehlich et al. 2009) or London (Lathia et al. 2013) which is one of the main reasons why it is not shared widely among researchers and used by businesses. Nevertheless, ski resorts as Kopaonik, Serbia, have started in 2011 collaborating with researchers to start studying the potentials of exploiting this data (Delibasic and Obradovic 2012).

This paper presents a review of papers that have already analyzed ski lift transportation data and discusses further directions in the usage of this data. The goal of this paper is to provide a systematic overview of efforts invested in analyzing ski lift transportation, to identify main research directions, and to point out new research possibilities in this emerging research area.

The remainder of this paper is structured as follows. In Sect. 2 we provide an overview of papers concerned with the clustering and analysis of ski lift transportation paths. In Sect. 3 we provide an overview of papers concerned with the application of ski lift transportation data for injury prediction and prevention. In Sect. 4 we analyze papers concerned with modeling ski lift congestions. We conclude the review in Sect. 5.

2 Ski Lift Transportation Data Clustering

Downhill skiing is a sport that uses ski lifts to transport skiers from mountain valleys to mountain tops. After exiting the ski lifts at mountain tops, the skiers ski downhill using slopes toward a ski lift valley where they utilize a ski lift for transport to the mountain top. This process is repeated several times during a skier day. During this process, data is being collected at ski lift gates, i.e., for every ski lift entrance. The ski lift transportation data consists of records of skiers entering ski lifts. This data consists of the following attributes: ID of skier, ID of ski lift gate, and timestamp. In this paper, we use the term skiers for the sake of simplicity for all users utilizing ski lifts for transportation, i.e., skiers, snowboarders, telemarkers, etc.

There are numerous reasons for finding groups (clusters) and patterns of usage in ski lift transportation data (which actually track the skiers' movement). Firstly, ski resorts can, by analyzing frequent skier trajectories understand the spatial and temporal usage of the ski resort done by different types (clusters) of skiers. This could influence innovative ski ticket formats and motivate new pricing models. Secondly, ski resorts, as well as skiers, can be informed about their skiing performance and their preferences. Thirdly, bottlenecks in the ski resort, as well as the unexploited exploitation of the ski lifts in the ski resort can be detected and better managed.

The company Skiline (https://www.skiline.cc/) is one of the rare companies that allows its users to read basic skiing statistics based on their skier ID such as the total number of vertical meters done (sum of all ski runs (height above sea level of ski lift exit—height above sea level of ski lift entrance), total ski lifts visited and similar. Many ski resorts purchase the Skiline service to provide this possibility to their users.

One of the first analysis of ski lift transportation data that was done by D'Urso and Massari (2013) on only one skier day in the Val Gardena ski resort, Italy. The authors have performed fuzzy clustering over ski lift transportation data and reported to have found two types of skier clusters, variety seekers (those skiers who tend to often switch between ski lifts and to seek for new experiences) and loyal (those skiers who tend to stick to one ski lift).

The next paper that studied ski lift transportation data was by done by Delibašić et al. (2017a) on the Kopaonik ski resort, Serbia. Authors have proposed the analysis of spatial and temporal clustering models based on ski lift transportation data. Several interesting conclusions were made in that paper. The spatial clustering of ski lift transportation data revealed that skiers tend to group their ski lift transports around a dominant ski lift every day. That means that on every skier day one lift will be the most frequently used for each skier. Based on this dominant ski lift, skiers also tend to choose other lifts which are mostly spatially near to the dominant one and correspond to the skiing skillfulness of the skiers. Authors have shown that it is reasonable to have as many clusters as ski lifts, i.e., that ski lifts are actually great representatives of a skier cluster.

The temporal clusters have also revealed that one-third of the skier population doesn't utilize the ski pass the whole skiing day. One-third of skiers only ski several hours during the day and have an hour as the peak hour (when most of their skiing activity is being recorded). These new insights about clusters allow for deeper studying of the ski lift transportation behavior in ski resorts and could provide motivation for the marketing team of ski resorts to enable more innovative ski ticket formats to their users.

On the other hand, this ski lift transportation patterns allow for better planning of ski lift transportation capacities and the management of ski resorts in the future, as it reveals to some extent the behavior of skiers. This is closely related to ski lift ticket formats and prices, where ski resorts would have better possibilities for lowering prices in the less visited ski lifts during the day, and to increase prices on very congested times of the day.

Delibašić et al. (2017b) have extended the work of Delibašić et al. (2017a) by investigating hidden factors that motivate skiers to choose a specific path. The authors have applied principal component analysis for spatial analysis of ski lift transportation and revealed seven factors that influence the choice of a ski lift (less-skilled behavior, beginner behavior, intermediate behavior, advanced behavior, no-stress behavior, skilled-and-lonely behavior). Based on these hidden factors authors also built a recommender system and showed that the skiers ski lift usage patterns can be reconstructed with a high accuracy. Actually, by getting to know more about the skier's behavior, it seems quite easy to predict which path a skier might choose.

3 Injury Analysis

Besides doing analysis merely on ski lift transportation data, it is also useful to merge this data with other data sources such as data about the injury, weather data, various Internet of Things (IoT) data, etc. To the best of the authors' knowledge, there are only a few papers that perform ski injury analysis using ski lift data. Traditionally, ski injury is studied on small-scale observational studies where risk factors are identified from questionnaires obtained from skiers. These studies don't take into account the huge imbalance between the injured and non-injured population, as ski injuries are rare events (2 in 1000 skiers get injured). Only recently predictive models from data mining and machine learning have been applied in this field. Several papers were produced using ski lift transportation data for injury prediction.

Bohanec and Delibašić (2015) proposed a model for daily risk injury assessment in the ski resort Kopaonik. To build the model data from ski lift transportation, ski patrol injury records, and weather was used. The model was built as a hybrid model of a decision tree model recorded from a ski resort safety expert and a decision tree extracted from ski lift transportation data. The model had an 80% accuracy for predicting daily ski injury occurrence, was interpretable, had complete and consistent decision rules. The model was more than 10% more accurate than the predictions made by the ski resort safety expert using the DEX decision tree (Bohanec and Rajkovič 1990). The model utilized attributes from weather conditions, global ski resort statistics such as a number of skiers, ski lift transportations, and average skiers' statistics (time, vertical meters achieved, and speed). This model was further improved by Delibašić et al. (2018). The intuition is that machine learning models are not aware of structure and relationships between attributes and criteria in decision making. The authors argued that this structure is possible to include into logistic regression framework in a manner similar to deep feature extraction (resembling deep neural networks) where the domain knowledge provides the needed structure. Layers are merged using stacking, (which is well-known ensemble technique) where the output of one layer in the hierarchy is used as an input to the next layer in the hierarchy. It has been shown that integration of DEX hierarchy improved predictive performance measured in Area under the curve (AUC).

Delibašić and Obradović (2015) studied the hypothesis that the group size has a significant influence on ski injury occurrence. This hypothesis was tested in various ways. Firstly, from the ski ticket purchasing system, it was checked whether ski tickets that were bought together, an indicator that those skiers ski in groups, have different injury rates. Then the same hypothesis was tested on 40 clustering models that were built using various clustering algorithms, namely k-means, hierarchical and OPTICS, and various similarity measures. It was shown that the studied hypothesis is true in most algorithm settings. The clustering in this paper was challenging as the number of clusters is relatively high to the number of skiers in the systems, as groups of skiers skiing together were searched for.

Dobrota et al. (2016) also studied the occurrence of injuries based on clusters of trajectories. For these purposes, spectral clustering was applied. It was also shown that a high number of clusters best separates the injured and non-injured skier population. If such framework is applied in practice it can be used as skiers' personal safety manager (i.e., can make an alert to reduce the speed), or as a decision support system for health organizations and ski resorts to issuing warnings and policies which can contribute to increased safety and risk prevention.

Dallagiacoma (2017) developed several machine learning models (Feedforward NN, Gradient Boosted Trees, Logistic Regression, Random Forest) on injury prediction based on ski lift transportation data, and weather data from two Italian ski resorts Cermis and Pinzolo. The Gradient boosted tree was reported to achieve best AUC values. The authors assume that this indicates that there may be nonlinear relations that the Logistic Regression model, being a linear model, could not detect. Additionally, as ski injuries are rare events (on average 0.2% per skier/day (Delibašić et al. 2017c)) predictive models do not perform sufficiently well. One attempt to improve the performance of predictive models is by decreasing class imbalance which can be done by oversampling (or weighting). More specifically Dallagiacoma (2017) suggest using SMOTE (Chawla et al. 2002) which create synthetical, virtual examples (we can call them virtual skiers). Virtual skiers belong to injured population making class imbalance less severe and predictive models more sensitive and, therefore, better in terms of recall and AUC.

The assumptions of Dallagiacoma (2017) showed to be correct when Delibašić, et al. (2017c) proposed a ski injury assessment model for individual skiers. Several univariate and multivariate models have been proposed. The well-known CHAID decision tree algorithm (Kass 1980) was used to study the risk of injury occurrence. The CHAID decision tree was able to segment the risk into various segments (decision tree nodes) where in some nodes the injury occurrence was ten times higher than the average risk and in some nodes the injury was 3.5 times lower than the average injury occurrence. It was shown that the CHAID decision tree algorithm is an excellent candidate to be used for building models in ski injury analysis. The CHAID decision tree model was able to make a better prediction of injury occurrence than logistic regression which assumes a linear dependency between attributes. This study revealed that ski injury is an early failure event, where skiers are at higher risk of getting injured in the early phases of skiing. In the early phases of skiing a combination of a high switching behavior between ski lifts and using ski lifts with high vertical meters can induce a risk ten times higher than the average risk.

4 Congestion Analysis

Congestion is another important topic for ski resorts, as it influences the overall satisfaction of skiers in the ski resort. Congestion and crowding during winter leisure activities and recreational sports are not fully understood yet. There are several interpretations of how the congestion impacts the overall experience, ranging from negative to positive. It is commonly argued that more experienced skiers and off-trail cross-country skiers prefer the least crowded conditions. However, winter sports recreationists do often have heterogeneous preferences and thresholds for congestion based on different activities, sports, locations, and experiences. We can identify two major forms of congestions in ski resorts. The first is called on-slope crowding, the congestion that skiers experience as they ski down the slopes. It is very hard to identify and classify this kind of congestions because of multiple factors (and their interconnection) influences the subjective feeling of congestion. The second form of congestion skiers face is called lift queues, which is waiting time in front of a ski lift while attempting to board a lift. It is important to say that it is identified that skiers are willing to pay higher lift ticket prices for shorter lift queues and less crowded slopes (Fonner and Berens 2014). However, the relation between ski lift ticket prices and congestion analysis has yet to be explored better.

One of the most innovative ski resorts in the world Vail, USA, has introduced the service of congestion reports to skiers http://news.vailresorts.com/corporate/vail-resorts-epicmix-time.htm. This service is provided by utilizing WiFi and Bluetooth sensors to estimate the number of skiers in front of the ski lift entrance points. Skiers tend to maximize their utilization of ski lifts, and stay on a slope, and to minimize the time spent in lines waiting for a ski lift. On the other hand, ski resorts will be forced in the future to better optimize the operations of their ski lifts due to the inability to endlessly extend the ski lift capacities. Poulhès and Mirial (2017) have developed an agent-based simulation model, DynaSki, of skier congestion with the goal to help ski resort planners to better understand the congestions, and to test whether a replacement of a ski lift could provide lower waiting times for ski lifts. The proposed model was developed based on ski lift transportation data which is harder than to have accurate data from GPS or other means to locate the exact location of skiers. Although the results of the proposed model are sound, efforts are still needed to validate the model and its assumptions.

Barras et al. (2014) have also developed a multi-agent model, Ski-Optim that analyzes congestion on ski lift entrances by utilizing ski lift transportation data. The model is developed at an hourly granularity, so it is not quite useful for real-time or near real-time congestion modeling. However, Ski-Optim model provides some answers on the mechanisms like the emergence of the phenomenon of congestion and queuing and skier groups on the slopes. As a limitation of the proposed multi-agent model, one can say that it does not directly model "distractions" from skiing such as restaurants and bars.

Holleczek and Tröster (2012), on the other hand, have developed a particle-based model for modeling skier traffic in the ski resorts with the use of GPS data. Their model showed to be quite accurate and to be able to model congestion in the ski resort. The proposed model can be also used to identify the zone of higher collision possibilities, which ski resort safety managers could use to make better notifications of skiers and allow for injury prevention. Still, the proposed model assumes that location of skiers is precisely known, which is currently a hard assumption for most ski resorts. In the future, it can be expected that ski resorts will better position tracking devices for skiers because this data will be very useful for congestion analysis and management, but also for injury prevention.

5 Conclusion

Ski lift transportation data is a resource readily available in ski resorts and is still not used to produce new products and services and ski resorts comparable to transportation data services and products in other transportation businesses. To the best of our knowledge, ski resorts have not opened their ski lift transportation data, and are not yet considering doing this. Although being a traditional, and very closed business, the ski resorts could exploit the potential of their data to improve and to stay competitive in the market, as well as to meet the expectations of their users, which are getting used to decision support services which track them through the whole process of their ski resort stay (from trip planning, lodging, weather prediction and others).

Ski lift transportation data is only one of resources that could be used, as other data could be used as well for the same purposes, such as weather data, data from IoT about congestion on ski slopes, conditions of snow, local weather conditions, and so on. In the years to come, we will experience an increasing number of datasets available in ski resorts. This paper has the goal to raise the awareness of the potential of the available data and to motivate ski resorts to use their data, but also researchers and business people to study and exploit this data.

Significant research has already been done in the area of ski lift ticket pricing. Holmgren et al. (2016) suggest that skiers tend to buy season tickets as long as they can achieve a discount of 50% of the tickets they would buy if they would buy daily tickets. Malasevska (2017) studies the possibilities of dynamic ticket prices based on weather condition, and on seasonality. Malasevska and Haugom (2018) show that it is reasonable to use dynamic prices in ski resorts as it can potentially increase profits. Fonner and Berens (2014) propose a hedonic pricing model for ski lift tickets which takes into account that congestion has to a certain degree positive influence on ski lift prices, but after a certain point has a negative influence. Rosson and Zirulia (2018) also propose a hedonic pricing model for ski lift tickets. Their model shows that a higher level of investment in modern lifts and snowmaking equipment positively influences ski lift ticket prices. On the other hand, investments in the enlargement of the skiable surface or the introduction of night skiing options and illuminated slopes don't influence the attitude toward value-for-money. As identified before, besides only making models for standard ski ticket formats, ski resorts have the ability to develop new ski lift ticket formats taking into account the spatial and temporal clustering of skiers in a ski resort. This could not only help the increase of profits but also induce a better utilization of the ski resort capacities through smarter pricing and skiing recommendations. Price models are certainly needed that would study the usefulness of applying this new ticket formats to increase profits of the ski resort.

A major problem in the future, that ski resorts will face, is the management of congestion of ski resorts. Besides the inability of ski resorts to expand the resorts with new ski lift capacities endlessly, or to increase the ski lift capacities, ski resorts will also have the possibility to smarter utilize the existing capacities. Ski resorts like Vail, USA, or Jasna, Slovakia have introduced to the skier's information about ski congestion which also influences their decision which ski lift to chose. However, there is no global effort reported to synchronize the operation of ski lift speeds in order to be able to transport a huge amount of skiers and to reduce waiting for lines in front of ski lifts as it is done in the area of road traffic (Papageorgiou et al. 2003). Decisions on slowing down certain lifts on specific time moments could significantly decrease the overall congestion on ski slopes and in front of ski lifts, better exploit the capacity of the ski resort and provide overall more ski lift transports. This concept is already proven to work in road traffic management.

Another important service that could be offered to skiers, in relation to the maintenance of ski resorts and safety of skiers, is the analysis of ski slopes conditions. Besides using data from IoT devices on the slopes, this data could also be integrated with ski lift transportation data to better predict the future conditions of ski slopes.

By building decision-making models from data, the ski resorts can build necessary capacities for transforming their business, and to make a digital transformation of the ski resorts, a phenomenon that is already happening in other areas. We look forward to seeing the ski resorts of the future.

References

Barras T, Doctor M, Revilloud M, Schumacher M, Loubier JC (2014) Queues in ski resort graphs: the ski-optim model. In: Proceedings of the AGILE'2014 international conference on geographic information science, Castellón, 3–6 June 2014

Bohanec M, Rajkovič V (1990) DEX: an expert system shell for decision support. Sistemica 1(1):145–157

Bohanec M, Delibašić B (2015) Data-mining and expert models for predicting injury risk in ski resorts. In: International conference on decision support system technology. Springer, Cham, pp. 46–60, May 2015

Chawla NV, Bowyer KW, Hall LO, Kegelmeyer WP (2002) SMOTE: synthetic minority over-sampling technique. J Artif Intell Res 16:321–357

Dallagiacoma M (2017) Predicting the risk of accidents for downhill skiers. Master of Science Thesis, School of Information and Communication Technology, KTH Royal Institute of Technology, Stockholm, Sweden
Delibasic B, Obradovic Z (2012) Towards a DGSS prototype for early warning for ski injuries. In: 2012 IEEE 28th international conference on data engineering workshops (ICDEW). IEEE, pp 68–72, Apr 2012
Delibašić B, Obradović Z (2015) Identifying high-number-cluster structures in RFID ski lift gates entrance data. Ann Data Sci 2(2):145–155
Delibašić B, Marković P, Delias P, Obradović Z (2017a) Mining skier transportation patterns from ski resort lift usage data. IEEE Trans Hum Mach Syst 47(3):417–422
Delibašić B, Radovanović S, Jovanović M, Vukićević M, Suknović M (2017b) An investigation of human trajectories in ski resorts. In: International conference on ICT innovations. Springer, Cham, pp 130–139, Sept 2017
Delibašić B, Radovanović S, Jovanović M, Obradović Z, Suknović M (2017c) Ski injury predictive analytics from massive ski lift transportation data. Proc Inst Mech Eng Part P J Sports Eng Technol
Delibašić B, Radovanović S, Jovanović M, Bohanec M, Suknović M (2018) Integrating knowledge from DEX hierarchies into a logistic regression stacking model for predicting ski injuries. J Decis Syst. https://doi.org/10.1080/12460125.2018.1460164
Dobrota M, Delibašić B, Delias P (2016) A skiing trace clustering model for injury risk assessment. Int J Decis Support Syst Technol (IJDSST) 8(1):56–68
D'Urso P, Massari R (2013) Fuzzy clustering of human activity patterns. Fuzzy Sets Syst 215:29–54
Fonner RC, Berrens RP (2014) A hedonic pricing model of lift tickets for US alpine ski areas: examining the influence of crowding. Tour Econ 20(6):1215–1233
Froehlich J, Neumann J, Oliver N (2009) Sensing and predicting the pulse of the city through shared bicycling. In: Proceedings of the 21st international joint conference on artificial intelligence, pp 1420–1426, July 2009
Holleczek T, Tröster G (2012) Particle-based model for skiing traffic. Phys Rev E 85(5):056101
Holmgren MA, McCracken VA, McCluskey JJ (2016) Should I ski today? The economics of ski resort season passes. Leisure/Loisir 40(2):131–148
Kass GV (1980) An exploratory technique for investigating large quantities of categorical data. Appl Stat 29(2):119–127
Lathia N, Smith C, Froehlich J, Capra L (2013) Individuals among commuters: Building personalised transport information services from fare collection systems. Pervasive Mob Comput 9(5):643–664. https://doi.org/10.1016/j.pmcj.2012.10.007
Malasevska I (2017) Innovative pricing approaches in the alpine skiing industry. Doctoral dissertation, Inland Norway University of Applied Sciences—INN University
Malasevska I, Haugom E (2018) Optimal prices for alpine ski passes. Tour Manag 64:291–302
Omerčević D, Zupančič M, Bohanec M, Kastelic T (2008) Intelligent response to highway traffic situations and road incidents. Proc TRA 2008:21–24
Papageorgiou M, Diakaki C, Dinopoulou V, Kotsialos A, Wang Y (2003) Review of road traffic control strategies. Proc IEEE 91(12):2043–2067
Poulhès A, Mirial P (2017) Dynaski, an agent-based model to simulate skiers in a ski area. Procedia Comput Sci 109:84–91
Rosson S, Zirulia L (2018) A hedonic price model for ski lift tickets in the Dolomites. Worldwide Hospitality and Tourism Themes (just-accepted), 00-00
The National Ski Areas Association (2017) National skier/snowboarder visits, 1979–2016. http://www.nsaa.org/media/275017/1516_visits.pdf

A Recommender System With IBA Similarity Measure

Nevena Vranić, Pavle Milošević, Ana Poledica and Bratislav Petrović

Abstract Recommender systems help users to reduce the amount of time they spend to find the items they are interested in. One of the most successful approaches is collaborative filtering. The main feature of a recommender system is its ability to predict user's interests by analyzing the behavior of this particular user and/or the behavior of other similar users to generate personalized recommendations. Identification of neighbor users who have had similar taste to the target user in the past is a crucial process for successful application of collaborative filtering. In this paper, we proposed a collaborative filtering method that uses interpolative Boolean algebra for calculation of similarity between users. In order to analyze the effectiveness of the proposed approach we used three common datasets: MovieLens 100K, MovieLens 1M, and CiaoDVD. We compared a collaborative filtering based on IBA similarity measure with two standard similarity measures: Pearson correlation and cosine-based coefficient. Even though statistical measures are traditionally used in recommender systems, proposed logic-based approach showed promising results on the tested datasets. A recommender system with IBA similarity measure outperformed the others in most cases.

Keywords Recommender systems · Collaborative filtering · User-based collaborative filtering · Interpolative boolean algebra · Similarity modeling · IBA similarity measure

N. Vranić (✉) · P. Milošević · A. Poledica · B. Petrović
Faculty of Organizational Sciences, University of Belgrade, Jove Ilića 154, 11000 Belgrade, Serbia
e-mail: nevena.vranic@gmail.com

P. Milošević
e-mail: pavle.milosevic@fon.bg.ac.rs

A. Poledica
e-mail: ana.poledica@fon.bg.ac.rs

B. Petrović
e-mail: bratislav.petrovic@fon.bg.ac.rs

N. Mladenović et al. (eds.), *Advances in Operational Research in the Balkans*, Springer Proceedings in Business and Economics,
https://doi.org/10.1007/978-3-030-21990-1_17

1 Introduction

In everyday life, people interact with many items and their usage patterns have become very complex. A recommender system (RS) plays an important role in daily life, since it helps people to reduce the amount of time they spend to find the items they are looking for. These systems can be defined as programs which attempt to recommend the most suitable items to the specific user by predicting a user's interest in an item based on related information about the items, the users and the interactions between items and users (Bobadilla et al. 2013). The most important feature of a recommender system is its ability to generate personalized recommendations by analyzing the behavior of the observed user and/or the behavior of other users.

Goldberg et al. (1992) first introduced RS in 1992. In the beginning, recommendation systems have found their usage only as documental information in a library. As of late, their application areas have been extended to other domains, such as e-business (Lee et al. 2006), social networks (Sun et al. 2015; Bagher et al. 2017), movies (Chen et al. 2015, 2018; Katarya and Verma 2016), news (Xu et al. 2012), tourism (Nilashi et al. 2015), scientific papers (Agarwal et al. 2005) and many others.

Recommendation systems are usually categorized into content-based (CB) and collaborative filtering (CF) methods. Content-based methods recommend items by focusing on a descriptor for each item. Items similar to the ones the user preferred in the past are recommended to the user. The performance of CB filtering methods depends on the quality of the descriptors. CF is one of the most successful and most commonly used techniques in RS (Bobadilla et al. 2013). It helps a particular user to make choices based on the opinions of other users who share similar interests (neighbor users). Recommended items will be those items which neighbor users rated with high rating in the past. Collaborative filtering is subcategorized into user-based and item-based methods. User-based collaborative filtering methods assume that similar users will prefer similar items (Lü et al. 2012). The methods categorize similar users based on their history and then retrieve items for users. Item-based collaborative filtering methods assume that users will prefer items similar to ones they have liked in the past. Those methods categorize similar items based on the items' history and then retrieve them for users. Collaborative filtering methods have problems when the user-to-user or item-to-item relations are insufficient or biased and these methods highly depend on the validity of the user model (Ha and Lee 2017).

The key to successful collaborative recommendation lies in the ability to make meaningful associations between people and their product preferences, in order to assist the target user in future transactions. Similarities between past experiences and preferences are exploited to form neighborhood of like-minded people from which to draw recommendations or predictions for a given individual user (Nilashi et al. 2015). Two of the most popular approaches to computing similarities between users and items are the Pearson correlation coefficient and cosine-based coefficient (Chen et al. 2015, 2018; Nilashi et al. 2015; Sun et al. 2015; Ha and Lee 2017).

In this paper, we proposed a collaborative filtering approach which employs interpolative Boolean algebra (Radojevic 2000) to measure similarity between users. To verify the proposed logic-based similarity measure in the domain of recommender systems we tested three common datasets: MovieLens 100K, MovieLens 1M, and CiaoDVD. Further, the results are also compared to standard statistical similarity measures mentioned above. In this study, we considered recommender systems in movie domain, but the proposed approach can also be adopted for any other domain, which needs to recommend items to a specific user. The performance of the proposed RS is measured using several statistical measures: mean absolute error, precision, recall, and F1 score.

The rest of this paper is organized as follows: In Sect. 2, theoretical background of recommender systems and interpolative Boolean algebra are given in the separate subsections. In Sect. 3, the methodology of research and the illustrative example are shown. Section 4 presents experiment, performance measures, and results discussion. Finally, conclusions and future work are given in Sect. 5.

2 Theoretical Background

In this section, we give a brief introduction of collaborative filtering RS, interpolative Boolean algebra and similarity measure based on the interpolative Boolean algebra.

2.1 Collaborative Filtering RS

The aim of RS is to match users with items they are looking for. In this study, we explore collaborative filtering technique, i.e., one of the most frequently used and currently most successful method of recommendation (Lü et al. 2012; Bobadilla et al. 2013). The basic idea of CF is to analyze the past transactions of the user and to provide a personalized environment to recommend favored item (Cami et al. 2017).

The key to successful collaborative recommendation lies in the ability to make meaningful associations between people and their product preferences, in order to assist the end user in future transactions. Similarities between past experiences and preferences are exploited to form neighborhood of like-minded people from which to draw recommendations or predictions for a given individual user (Nilashi et al. 2015).

The recommendation problem can be formulated as in (Adomavicius and Tuzhilin 2005). Let C be the set of all users and let S be the set of all possible items that can be recommended. Let u be a utility function that measures the usefulness of item s to user c, i.e., $u : C \times S \rightarrow R$, where R is a totally ordered set (e.g., non-negative integers or real numbers within a certain range). Then for each user $c \in C$, we aim to choose such item $s' \in S$ that maximizes the user's utility. In collaborative RS the utility $u(c, s)$ of item s for user c is estimated based on the utilities $u(c_j, s)$ assigned to item s by those users $c_j \in C$ who share similar interests to user c. More formally:

$$\forall c \in C, \quad s'_c = \arg\max u(c, s)$$

In RS the utility of an item is usually represented by a rating which indicates how much a particular user liked a particular item. In CF, items are recommended to the target user through an analysis of neighbor users ratings on those items (Koohi and Kiani 2017).

The common methods used in CF to find neighbor users are measures of similarity (Bobadilla et al. 2013). The most popular similarity measures in CF are the Pearson correlation coefficient and cosine-based coefficient (Candilier et al. 2007).

2.2 *Interpolative Boolean Algebra*

The interpolative Boolean algebra (IBA) is the consistent [0, 1]-valued generalization of Boolean algebra (BA) introduced by Radojevic (2000). IBA is utilized as a basis for Boolean consistent fuzzy logic, since all laws on which BA relies on are satisfied, including axioms of excluded middle and contradiction (Radojevic 2008a). In IBA framework, all BA elements are realized as corresponding IBA-based functions and IBA-based logical operations extend classical operations.

Unlike most of many-valued logics (including conventional fuzzy logic), IBA is based on the principle of structural functionality (SF). The main reason for introducing this principle as opposite to traditional truth functionality (TF) is that TF is binary in its essence. In other words, TF is valid only in the classical two-valued case from the perspective of Boolean laws, and not in the general case (Radojević 2008b). By introducing SF principle, Radojevic (Radojevic 2008a) emphasizes the structure of the logical expression. Hence, IBA consists of two levels: symbolic and valued. On the symbolic level, a logical expression is uniquely mapped to a generalized Boolean polynomial (GBP). Subsequently, the values are introduced and the expression is evaluated on the valued level. The structural functionality also implies that logical functions are vectors in nature, and the Boolean consistent calculations of values are accomplished by the immanent structure vectors.

On the symbolic level, IBA is technically based on IBA transformation rules and GBPs. IBA resolve the procedure of transforming a Boolean function into GBP directly: any logical function can be mapped into the corresponding GBP according to the set of predefined rules (Radojevic 2008b). For a set of primary attributes (elements of $BA(\Omega)$), the transformation procedure of Boolean functions into GBP is defined in (Radojevic 2008c):

- For combined elements $F(a_1, \ldots, a_n), G(a_1, \ldots, a_n) \in BA(\Omega)$:

$$(F \wedge G)^{\otimes} = F^{\otimes} \otimes G^{\otimes},$$

$$(F \vee G)^{\otimes} = F^{\otimes} + G^{\otimes} - (F \wedge G)^{\otimes},$$

$$(\neg F)^{\otimes} = 1 - F^{\otimes}$$

- For primary variables $\{a_1, \ldots, a_n\}$:

$$(a_i \wedge a_j)^{\otimes} = \begin{cases} a_i \otimes a_j, i \neq j \\ a_i, i = 1 \end{cases},$$

$$(a_i \vee a_j)^{\otimes} = a_i + a_j - (a_i \wedge a_j)^{\otimes},$$

$$(\neg a_i)^{\otimes} = 1 - a_i$$

GBPs have the ability to process values of primary attributes from the real unit interval [0, 1] in a Boolean consistent manner, i.e., to preserve all algebraic characteristics. GBP is a polynomial whose variables are primary attributes (free elements of Boolean algebra) while operators are standard + and -, and generalized product $\otimes$. Generalized product is any function which maps $\otimes : [0, 1] \times [0, 1] \rightarrow [0, 1]$ and satisfies all four axioms of t-norms (commutativity, associativity, monotonicity, boundary condition) and the additional axiom of non-negativity condition (Radojevic 2008a). In the case of two attributes $\Omega = \{a, b\}$, generalized product is from the following interval:

$$\max(a + b - 1, 0) \leq a \otimes b \leq \min(a, b)$$

Depending on the nature of the primary attributes, we can discuss three marginal cases for operator selection. The first case refers to elements of the same or the similar nature and implies the usage of minimum as generalized product:

$$a \otimes b = \min(a, b)$$

The second involves elements of the same or the similar nature but negatively correlated, where Lukasiewicz *t*-norm is proposed:

$$a \otimes b = \max(a + b - 1, 0)$$

In the case of statistically independent elements that are different by nature standard product is used:

$$a \otimes b = a \cdot b$$

2.2.1 IBA Similarity Measure

Measuring similarity with logical relations of implication, bi-implication, and equivalence, is considered as a valuable and prominent approach to similarity modeling

(Luukka 2011; Le Capitaine 2012; Beliakov et al. 2014). As opposite to distance-based and probabilistic similarity measures, logic-based relations are particularly suitable for comparing objects/attributes described by the intensity of the properties. In fact, it offers a different perspective in perceiving similarity.

In IBA framework, the equivalence relation is used for defining a similarity measure (Poledica et al. 2013, 2015). The relation of equivalence is defined as the following logical expression:

$$(a \Leftrightarrow b) = (a \Rightarrow b) \wedge (b \Rightarrow a)$$

As it is stated, the first step in dealing with logical function in IBA framework is to assess its structure. In other words, the IBA transformation rules should be applied. The transformation of the equivalence relation to GBP is conducted as follows:

$$\begin{aligned}(a \Leftrightarrow b)^{\otimes} &= ((a \Rightarrow b) \wedge (b \Rightarrow a))^{\otimes} = (a \Rightarrow b)^{\otimes} \otimes (b \Rightarrow a)^{\otimes} \\ &= (1 - a + a \otimes b) \otimes (1 - b + a \otimes b) \\ &= 1 - b + a \otimes b - a + a \otimes b - a \otimes a \otimes b + a \otimes b - a \otimes b \otimes b \\ &\quad + a \otimes b \otimes a \otimes b = 1 - b + a \otimes b - a + a \otimes b - a \otimes b + a \otimes b \\ &\quad - a \otimes b + a \otimes b = 1 - b - a + 2 \cdot a \otimes b\end{aligned}$$

The relation of equivalence in the sense of IBA, $S_{IBA} : [0, 1]^2 \rightarrow [0, 1]$, can be used as a similarity measure because it satisfied all predefined conditions, i.e., GBP that uniquely corresponds to the relation of equivalence satisfies the properties of reflexivity, transitivity, and symmetry when minimum is used as generalized product (min:= $\otimes$). The detailed proofs may be found in (Poledica et al. 2013).

The fact that the consistent comparison of different objects is only possible by the same criteria (Radojevic 2010) supports the usage of minimum as generalized product in IBA similarity measure. GBP of IBA similarity measure and its realization on the valued level is as follows:

$$S_{IBA}(a, b) = (a \Leftrightarrow b)^{\otimes} = 1 - b - a + 2 \cdot a \otimes b = 1 - b - a + 2 \cdot \min(a, b)$$

IBA similarity measure is particularly valuable since its clear interpretation given in Fig. 1. The similarity of two attributes a and b in IBA framework is equal to the sum of two parts: the intensity of both having the same property and the intensity of both not having that property (Poledica et al. 2013).

In the case of multi-attribute object comparison, IBA similarity should be used along with chosen aggregation operator. In order to stay within IBA framework, it is advised to use logical aggregation (LA) (Milosevic et al. 2018). LA is a transparent, Boolean consistent manner of attribute aggregation using logical or pseudo-logical functions (Radojevic 2008b; Milosevic et al. 2018). There are two distinctive approaches in IBA-based framework for modeling similarity: a simple attribute-by-attribute (the similarity between objects is LA of individual IBA similarities of

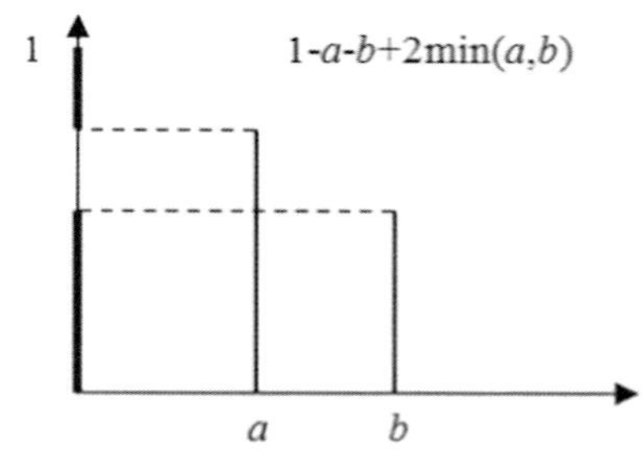

Fig. 1 IBA similarity function

attributes) and a comparison on the level of the object (LA function is used to uniquely represent the object and IBA similarity is used afterward). More details about these approaches may be found in (Milosevic et al. 2018).

3 A Recommender System with IBA Similarity Measure

In this section, the research methodology for proposed recommendation system is introduced and the illustrative example is shown.

The collaborative filtering provides recommendations based on the similarities between users or items. Predictions are made for the target user through reliance on the entire database, which include user ratings of items. CF method can be divided into user-based CF and item-based CF. The center of focus in the current study is the user-based approach. In the user-based approach, it is assumed that if some users had similar interests in the past, they will have similar interests in the future. Based on this assumption, items are recommended to the target user.

The user-based CF operates on an $n \times m$ matrix, with n users and m number of items. The matrix records the preferences of n users on m movies, in other words, it shows ratings of users on specific items. When we want to recommend an item to a specific user, users which are the most similar to the target user, i.e., neighbor users, are determined by the system. Prediction for the target user is made according to earlier ratings of users on items which the target user did not rate. Actually, the recommended items will be those items which neighbor users rated with high rating. Therefore, we can say that the ratings provided by users for items are the key input to CF recommender systems.

Figure 2 presents how the collaborative recommender method functions. By looking for the similarities between users, we are searching for a set of N neighbor users from the database who have similar preferences as specific user x. In other words, we are looking for users who rate movies in the same or at least at the similar manner as the target user. One of the common methods used in CF to find neighbor users is through resorting to similarity measures.

In this paper, we are utilizing recently proposed IBA-based similarity framework to find a set of N neighbor users. Particularly, the simple attribute-by-attribute com-

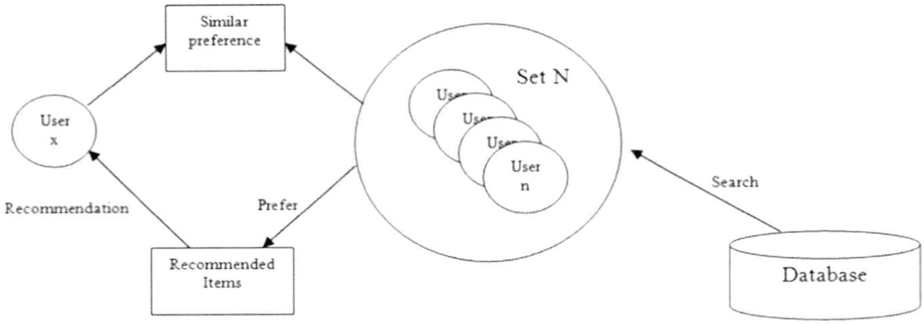

Fig. 2 Recommender system

parison is applied, i.e., IBA similarity measure is used to assess similarities between individual rankings and simple average is used as LA operator. Hereafter, only the users with similarity level higher that predefined threshold are considered as neighbors. There can also be a predefined number of the most similar neighbors, similarly as in k-NN algorithm.

After the set of neighbor users has been created, the next step is to predict ratings of movies which the target user did not rate. The prediction of the rating of user x on the specific item (p) that also factors the relative proximity of the nearest neighbor N is done using a simple average as shown in Eq. (7) (Koohi and Kiani 2017):

$$pred(x, p) = \frac{1}{n} \sum_{i=1}^{n} r_{ip}$$

where n represents the number of neighbor users.

To recommend items to the target user, first of all, a numerical value for unrated items will be calculated, and then a list of top N high-valued items to be recommended to the target user is prepared. In most cases, the range of users ratings is on a scale of 1–5, whereby 5 indicates most interesting and 1 signifies a poor opinion. On the basis of this assumption, two types of recommendations are 5/4321 and 54/321 methods, proposed by Tsai and Hung (2012). In the 5/4321 method, only items with a rating value of 5 will be recommended to the target user. Also in the 54/321 method, only items with rating values of 4 and 5 belong to the recommendation class, while ratings from one to three belong to non-recommendation class (Ramezani et al. 2014; Koohi and Kiani 2017). In this research, we used 54/321 method, where items that get ratings 5 and 4 by the neighbor users are recommended to the target user and item ratings from 1 to 3 are rejected.

In general, this model consists of two steps in the shown method; first one is to calculate similarity between users using IBA similarity framework, and next one to predict ratings using an average of ratings of n neighbor users on the item p. The model may be considered as quite flexible since both LA function in the attribute-by-attribute comparison and simple average in the ranking prediction step may be replaced with more powerful aggregation operator.

3.1 Illustrative Example

The CF method with IBA similarity measure described above is illustrated on the simple example. For instance, the normalized ratings of 5 movies given by 4 users are shown in Table 1.

In this example, we choose User 2 as the target user. First, we need to calculate similarity between User 2 and all other users, and for that purpose we use IBA similarity measure and the simple average operator. For example, when we calculate similarity between User 1 and User 2 we find movies which both users rated, and calculate similarity for each movie using IBA similarity measure. Similarity between User 1 and User 2 for Movie 1 is 0.95 and for Movie 2 is 0.9. After we apply simple average operator on obtained similarities we get overall similarity (0.925) between User 1 and User 2. Similarities between User 2 and the two other users are respectively 0.825 and 0.35. In case we use 0.8 as a similarity threshold Users 1 and 3 will be a part of neighbor set.

As we can see from the Table 1 our target user didn't rate movies 3 and 5, so we need to predict ratings for those movies using ratings that User 1 and 3 gave to this movie. We calculated the rating for User 2 and rescaled it in the starting range of 1 to 5. As a result, User 2 would probably rate movie 3 with grade 4.25 and movie 5 with 0.625. Based on 54/321 method, where only items with rating values of 4 and 5 will be recommended to the target user, we will reject movie 5 and recommend movie 3 to the User 2.

4 Experiment and Evaluation

We implemented proposed method in Matlab, the experiments have been executed on Intel(R) Xeon(R) CPU E5-2680 v2@ 2.80 GHz, 64 GB memory. The operating system is Windows Server 2008 R2 Enterprise.

Table 1 Movie ratings—normalized values

	Movie 1	Movie 2	Movie 3	Movie 4	Movie 5
User 1	0.10	0.20	0.80	0.00	0.15
User 2	0.15	0.10	0.00	0.70	0.00
User 3	0.30	0.00	0.90	0.90	0.10
User 4	0.00	0.90	0.20	0.20	0.75

4.1 Datasets Analysis

.

To evaluate the prediction models and validate the proposed recommendation method we used three different datasets, which are popular in the domain of recommender systems: MovieLens 100K, MovieLens 1M and CiaoDVD. The GroupLens research group (Harper and Konstan 2016) at the University of Minnesota collected the MovieLens datasets (http: //grouplens.org/datasets/movielens/). MovieLens consists of two datasets, first one is smaller named MovieLens 100k which includes 100000 ratings of 1682 movies by 943 users and a bigger one, named MovieLens 1M, which includes 1000209 ratings of 3952 movies by 6040 users. In both datasets ratings are on a scale of 1 (bad film) to 5 (masterpiece). Every user has rated at least 20 movies and all movies have been rated at least once. In the MovieLens 100K dataset just 6.3% of movie ratings are available, and in MovieLens 1M only 4.2% of ratings are available. Therefore, sparsity levels of those two datasets are high. We also tested our approach on CiaoDVD dataset collected by Guo et al. (2014) in December 2013 by crawling 17 categories of film DVDs from the dvd.ciao.co.uk website. The rating scale on this dataset is from 0 to 4. This dataset includes 35835 ratings given by 2248 users over 16861 movies. The sparsity level of this dataset is higher than MoviLens datasets, just 1% of ratings are available. Ciao allows the users to establish social relations (i.e., trust relationships) with others. General statistics of these datasets are summarized in Table 2.

4.2 Performance Measures

Two types of measures can be used for performance evaluation of a recommender system. The first one is coverage, where the amount of items that can be recommended to the users is counted. This measure evaluates a recommender system ability to provide recommendations. In our case, a certain movie with only a few ratings might not be recommended to a specific user, because no similar users have rated that particular movie. The overall coverage for all users is calculated as the percentage of items of which a prediction is requested and for which the recommender system is able to make a prediction (Herlocker et al. 1999). The second type of measure

Table 2 General statistics of the MovieLens 100 k, MovieLens 1M, and CiaoDVD datasets

Dataset	Number of users	Number of items	Number of ratings	Sparsity level (%)
MovieLens 100K	943	1682	100000	93.7
MovieLens 1M	6040	3952	1000209	9.8
CiaoDVD	2248	16861	35835	99

is accuracy, which compares the recommendations with the actual known relevant items of ratings.

Mean absolute error (MAE) is a standard and popular measure used to evaluate the accuracy of preference modeling methods in recommender systems. MAE gives the deviation of the estimated preference from the true preference value specified by the active user. The lower the MAE is, the better the prediction ratings.

Besides MAE we used three statistical measures of accuracy: precision, recall and F1 score. Precision represents the probability that an item recommended as relevant is truly relevant. It is defined as the ratio of items correctly predicted as relevant among all the items selected. Recall represents the probability that a relevant item will be recommended as relevant. It is defined as the ratio of items correctly predicted as relevant among all the items known to be relevant. Precision and recall are inversely related and are dependent on the length of the recommendation list. With the increasing amount of retrieved items, the recall increases, but precision usually drops with larger item sizes. This is the reason why both measures are used. The F1 score combines the precision and recall to evaluate the algorithm performance.

A method with high coverage, precision, recall, and F1 scores and a low MAE value is considered as a good recommendation method.

5 Results

The aim of the experiment was to compare RS performance with IBA similarity measure and the two commonly used similarity measures: Pearson correlation and cosine-based approach. We considered different neighbor sizes and different similarity thresholds since these parameters are critical for the performance of RS. First, we tested different neighbor sizes from 5 to 30 (Nilashi et al. 2014). Further, we considered neighbors with three different similarity thresholds 0.9, 0.8 and 0.7. For example, the neighbor set includes all users whose similarity to a specific user is higher than 0.9. We repeated the experiment 10 times to examine the consistency and significance of the results.

Table 3 shows the performance measures and coverage for the proposed IBA RS approach for predefined number of neighbors on each dataset. As expected the coverage is higher when the number of neighbors is higher. Further, we can see that MAE slowly decays as coverage is growing.

Based on the considered performance measures it is hard to conclude what is the best number of neighbors. For instance, as it can be seen in Table 3 for MovieLens 100K dataset the best recall was obtained with 10 neighbors, the precision is higher with 20 neighbors and MAE is the best with 30 neighbors. The results for precision, recall, and F1 do not vary much regardless of the number of neighbors. We can conclude that it is not crucial how many neighbors we include in the coverage, but how relevant the neighbors are. For that reason, we also considered a similarity threshold to separate the users whose similarity is above the predefined level.

Table 3 Performances of RS with IBA similarity measure—different neighbor sizes

Dataset	Number of neighbors	Coverage (%)	MAE	Precision (%)	Recall (%)	F1 (%)
MovieLens 100K	5	17.50	0.18	62	89	73
	10	24.40	0.18	64	**94**	**76**
	15	29.50	0.22	58	78	66
	20	36.78	0.15	**70**	77	75
	30	**44.35**	**0.13**	66	87	75
MovieLens 1M	5	8.20	**0.13**	**78**	**83**	**80**
	10	13.00	0.12	71	**83**	76
	15	16.00	0.17	67	67	67
	20	21.62	**0.13**	76	82	79
	30	**29.12**	**0.13**	69	78	73
CiaoDVD	5	3.80	0.25	30	**89**	45
	10	4.20	**0.24**	**32**	88	**47**
	15	4.90	0.25	28	87	42
	20	6.70	0.27	27	85	40
	30	**9.40**	0.28	25	85	39

In the experiment, we achieved much higher coverage rates when we used a similarity threshold instead of a predefined number of neighbors. Further, we only tasted CF with Pearson correlation and cosine-based similarity measures with different similarity thresholds.

Table 4 presents performance of proposed IBA RS approach and IBA with Pearson and cosine-based similarity measures, with different similarity thresholds for each dataset. As expected the coverage is higher when a similarity threshold is lower.

As it can be seen in Tables 3 and 4, for IBA RS value of recall is always higher than precision regardless of the number of neighbor users. Recall calculates how many of the movies that should be recommended will be recommended to the target user. Thus, in case of IBA RS there are only a small number of movies that are not but should be recommended.

We applied 54/321 method for movie recommendation where ratings 5 and 4 are good suggestions and movie ratings from 1 to 3 are rejected. The main issue in prediction with the proposed IBA RS was to make a difference between ratings 3 and 4. In that case, small deviations from actual rating caused that some movies were recommended and shouldn't be. Therefore, the value of precision is lower. In future work, we could consider replacing simple average in the ranking prediction with more powerful aggregation operator to obtain a higher value of precision.

From the aspect of MAE and recall the recommender system with IBA similarity outperforms both Pearson correlation and cosine-based approach (Table 4). In terms of precision and F1, the RS with IBA similarity measure gives the same or better

Table 4 Performances of RS with IBA similarity measure—different similarity thresholds

Dataset	Similarity measure	Similarity threshold	Coverage (%)	MAE	Precision (%)	Recall (%)	F1 (%)
MovieLens 100K	IBA	0.9	42.17	**0.16**	50	85	63
		0.8	87.20	**0.16**	63	92	75
		0.7	**96.50**	0.17	**67**	**92**	**77**
	Pearson	0.9	42.17	**0.27**	70	82	75
		0.8	87.20	0.34	67	89	75
		0.7	**96.50**	0.39	**80**	**84**	**82**
	Cosine-based	0.9	42.17	**0.30**	55	71	63
		0.8	87.20	0.34	**65**	**75**	**70**
		0.7	**96.50**	0.35	60	68	64
MovieLens 1M	IBA	0.9	19.63	**0.08**	**75**	**92**	**83**
		0.8	75.07	0.15	62	71	66
		0.7	**82.59**	0.16	62	74	67
	Pearson	0.9	19.63	**0.15**	**78**	**86**	**82**
		0.8	75.07	0.22	72	76	74
		0.7	**82.59**	0.25	68	72	70
	Cosine-based	0.9	19.63	**0.21**	**79**	**85**	**82**
		0.8	75.07	0.29	65	67	66
		0.7	**82.59**	0.23	64	72	68
CiaoDVD	IBA	0.9	11.50	0.191	43	**75**	57
		0.8	42.58	**0.181**	**57**	63	**60**
		0.7	**65.87**	0.193	53	61	57
	Pearson	0.9	11.50	0.43	52	62	57
		0.8	42.58	**0.28**	**63**	**79**	**71**
		0.7	**65.87**	0.47	59	65	62
	Cosine-based	0.9	11.50	**0.31**	48	58	53
		0.8	42.58	0.33	**53**	**61**	**57**
		0.7	**65.87**	0.42	49	57	53

results compared to the cosine-based coefficient, but slightly lower percentages than Pearson correlation.

6 Conclusion

In this research we proposed a collaborative filtering method that employs IBA similarity measure for calculation of similarity between users. In order to analyze and evaluate the proposed logic-based similarity measure in recommender systems we tested three popular datasets: MovieLens 100K, MovieLens 1M, and CiaoDVD. For the purpose of comparison, we also applied two most commonly used similarity measures: Pearson correlation and cosine-based approach. In the experiment, the parameters critical for performance were tested, e.g., similarity threshold from 0.7 to 0.9 or neighbor sizes from 5 to 30. The performances of a recommender system were measured using several statistical indicators: mean absolute error, precision, recall, and F1 score.

A recommender system with IBA similarity measures outperformed the others with respect to MAE and recall. The results also showed that IBA similarity measure obtained slightly lower precision and F1 than Pearson correlation, but slightly higher compared to cosine-based similarity measure. In general, the results have indicated that IBA similarity measure is suitable to be used in recommender systems, especially in the cases when it is needed to recommend as many items as possible (high recall). Even though statistical measures are traditionally used in recommender systems, proposed logic-based approach utilizing IBA similarity measure showed promising results on the tested datasets.

For future work, the following issues are to be considered:

- Improvement of the proposed model by replacing simple average with more powerful aggregation operator in the ranking prediction.
- Single evaluation performance measure for measuring the performance of a recommender system that combines all the proposed measures.
- Implementation of IBA framework in a content-based recommender system and compare its accuracy with traditional methods.

References

Adomavicius G, Tuzhilin A (2005) Toward the next generation of recommender systems: a survey of the state-of-the-art and possible extensions. IEEE Trans Knowl Data Eng 17(6):734–749

Agarwal N, Haque E, Liu H, Parsons L (2005) Research paper recommender systems: a subspace clustering approach. In: International conference on web-age information management. Springer, Berlin, pp 475–491 (2005)

Bagher RC, Hassanpour H, Mashayekhu H (2017) User trends modeling for a content-based recommender system. Expert Syst Appl 87:209–219

Beliakov G, Calvo T, James S (2014) Consensus measures constructed from aggregation functions and fuzzy implications. Knowl-Based Syst 55, 1–8

Bobadilla J, Ortega F, Hernando A, Gutierrez A (2013) Recommender systems survey. Knowl-Based Syst 46, 109–132

Candilier L, Meyer F, Boulle M (2007) Comparing state-of-art collaborative filtering systems. In: International workshop on machine learning and data mining in pattern recognition. Springer, Berlin, pp 548–562 (2007)

Chen M-H, Teng C-H, Chang P-C (2015) Applying artificial immune systems to collaborative filtering for movie recommendation. Adv Eng Inform 29(4):830–839

Chen J, Wang H, Yan Z (2018) Evolutionary heterogeneous clustering for rating prediction based on user collaborative filtering. Swarm Evol Comput 38:35–41

Goldberg D, Nichols D, Oki BM, Terry D (1992) Using collaborative filtering to weave an Information tapestry. Commun ACM 35(12):61–70

Guo G, Zhang J, Thalmann D, Yorke-Smith, N.: Etaf: An extended trust antecedents framework for trust prediction. In: International conference on advances in social networks analysis and mining (ASONAM 2014). IEEE, pp 540–547 (2014)

Ha T, Lee S (2017) Item-network-based collaborative filtering: a personalized recommendation method based on a user's item network. Inf Process Manag 53(5):1171–1184

Harper FM, Konstan JA (2016) The MovieLens datasets: history and context. ACM Trans Interact Intell Syst 5(4):19

Herlocker JL, Konstan JA, Borchers A, Riedl J (1999) An algorithmic framework for performing collaborative filtering. In: Proceedings of the 22nd annual international ACM SIGIR conference of research and development in information retrieval. ACM, pp 230–237

Katarya R, Verma OP (2016) An effective collaborative movie recommender system with cuckoo search. Egypt Inf J 18(2):105–112

Koohi H, Kiani K (2017) A new method to find neighbor users that improves the performance of collaborative filtering. Expert Syst Appl 83:30–39

Le Capitaine H (2012) A relevance-based learning model of fuzzy similarity measures. IEEE Trans Fuzzy Syst 20(1):57–68

Lee T, Chun J, Shim J, Lee SG (2006) An ontology-based product recommender system for B2B marketplaces. Int J Electron Commun 11(2):125–155

Luukka P (2011) Feature selection using fuzzy entropy measures with similarity classifier. Expert Syst Appl 38(4):4600–4607

Lü L, Medo M, Yeung CH, Zhang YC, Zhang ZK, Zhou T (2012) Recommender systems. Phys Rep 519(1):1–49

Milosevic P, Poledica A, Rakicevic A, Dobric V, Petrovic B, Radojevic D (2018) IBA-based framework for modeling similarity. Int J Comput Int Syst 11:206–218

Nilashi M, bin Ibrahim O, Ithnin N (2014) Multi-criteria collaborative filtering with high accuracy using higher order singular value decomposition and neuro-fuzzy system. Knowl-Based Syst 60, 82–101

Nilashi M, Bin Ibrahim O, Ithnin N, Sarmin NH (2015) A multi-criteria collaborative filtering recommender system for the tourism domain using expectation maximization (EM) and PCA-ANFIS. Electron Commer Res Appl 14(6):542–562

Poledica A, Milosevic P, Dragovic I, Radojevic D, Petrovic B (2013) A consensus model in group decision making based on interpolative boolean algebra. In: Proceedings of the 8th conference of the European society for fuzzy logic and technology (EUSFLAT-13). Atlantis Press, pp 648–654 (2013)

Poledica A, Milosevic P, Dragovic I, Petrovic B, Radojevic D (2015) Modeling consensus using logic-based similarity measure. Soft Comput 19(11):3209–3219

Ramezani M, Moradi P, Akhlaghian F (2014) A pattern mining approach to enhance the accuracy of collaborative filtering in sparse data domains. Phys A 408:72–84

Radojevic D (2000) (0, 1)-valued logic: a natural generalization of Boolean logic. Yugosl J Oper Res 10(2):185–216

Radojevic D (2008a) Interpolative realization of Boolean algebra as a consistent frame for gradation and/or fuzzines. In: Forging new frontiers: fuzzy pioneers II. Springer, Berlin, pp. 295–317

Radojevic D (2008b) Logical aggregation based on interpolative. Mathw Soft Comput 15(1):125–141

Radojevic, D (2008c) Real sets as consistent Boolean generalization of classical sets. In: Zadeh L, Tufis D, Filip F, Dzitac I (eds) From natural language to soft computing: new paradigmas in artifical intelligence. Bucharest, Editing House of Romanian Academy, pp 150–171

Radojevic D (2010) Generalized (real-valued) order and equivalence relations. In: Forca B, Kovac M, Cabarkapa O, Petrovic D (eds) Proceedings of the 37th symposium on operational research. Belgradel, Medija centar Odbrana, pp 451–454 (2010)

Sun Z, Han L, Huang W, Wang X, Zeng X, Wang M (2015) Recommender systems based on social networks. J Syst Softw 99:109–119

Tsai CF, Hung C (2012) Cluster ensembles in collaborative filtering recommendation. Appl Soft Comput 12(4):1417–1425

Xu Y, Yin W, Wen Z, Zhang Y (2012) An alternating direction algorithm for matrix completion with nonnegative factors. Front Math China 7(2):365–384

Index

N. Mladenović et al. (eds.), *Advances in Operational Research in the Balkans*, Springer Proceedings in Business and Economics,
https://doi.org/10.1007/978-3-030-21990-1

Space Sciences Series of ISSI

Volume 75

More information about this series at http://www.springer.com/series/6592

Rui M. Ponte · Benoit Meyssignac ·
Catia M. Domingues · Detlef Stammer ·
Anny Cazenave · Teodolina Lopez
Editors

Relationships Between Coastal Sea Level and Large Scale Ocean Circulation

Previously published in Surveys in Geophysics,
Volume 40, Issue 6, 2019

Springer

Editors
Rui M. Ponte
Atmospheric and Environmental Research Inc.
Lexington, MA, USA

Catia M. Domingues
Marine Physics and Ocean Climate
National Oceanography Centre (NOC)
Southampton, UK

Anny Cazenave
International Space Science Institute
Bern, Switzerland

Benoit Meyssignac
LEGOS/CNES
Toulouse, France

Detlef Stammer
CEN, Universität Hamburg
Hamburg, Germany

Teodolina Lopez
IRT Saint Exupéry - Fondation STAE
Toulouse, France

ISSN 1385-7525
Space Sciences Series of ISSI
ISBN 978-3-030-45633-7

Cover illustration: African coast (Guinea Bissau) from the Envisat satellite (Meris instrument) (Credit: ESA/ Guinea-Bissau MERIS 24th February 2004/ CC BY-SA 3.0 IGO).

This Springer imprint is published by the registered company Springer Nature Switzerland AG
The registered company address is: Gewerbestrasse 11, 6330 Cham, Switzerland

Contents

Surveys in Geophysics (2019) 40:1245–1249
https://doi.org/10.1007/s10712-019-09574-4

Guest Editorial: Relationships Between Coastal Sea Level and Large-Scale Ocean Circulation

Rui M. Ponte[1] · Benoit Meyssignac[2] · Catia M. Domingues[3,4,5] · Detlef Stammer[6] · Anny Cazenave[2,7] · Teodolina Lopez[7]

Published online: 15 October 2019

Several hundred million people currently live in low-lying coastal regions, and this number will continue to increase in the coming decades. While some coastal areas are already being inundated by rising sea level, many others will also increasingly suffer from sea level rise and more intense extreme water levels during high tides, winter storms and hurricanes in the near future. Many oceanographic factors associated with both local and large-scale variability can influence coastal sea level, from hours to more than decades. Despite this coastal–open ocean link, differences exist between sea levels observed at the coast and over adjacent shallow and deep ocean regions. Distinct coastal sea level variability can arise, for example, due to coastally trapped waves and shelf currents, localized tidal resonances,

✉ Rui M. Ponte
rponte@aer.com

Benoit Meyssignac
Benoit.Meyssignac@legos.obs-mip.fr

Catia M. Domingues
catiad@noc.ac.uk

Detlef Stammer
detlef.stammer@uni-hamburg.de

Anny Cazenave
Anny.Cazenave@legos.obs-mip.fr

Teodolina Lopez
lopez.teodolina@gmail.com

1 Atmospheric and Environmental Research, 131 Hartwell Avenue, Lexington, MA 02421, USA

2 LEGOS, CNES, CNRS, IRD, Université Paul Sabatier, 18 avenue Edouard Belin, 31401 Toulouse cedex 9, France

3 Institute for Marine and Antarctic Studies, University of Tasmania and ARC Centre of Excellence for Climate Extremes, Private Bag 80, Hobart, TAS 7001, Australia

4 Antarctic Climate and Ecosystem Cooperative Research Centre, Private Bag 80, Hobart, TAS 7001, Australia

5 National Oceanography Centre, European Way, Southampton SO14 3ZH, UK

6 Centrum für Erdsystemforschung und Nachhaltigkeit, University of Hamburg, Bundesstr. 53, 20146 Hamburg, Germany

7 International Space Science Institute (ISSI), Hallerstrasse 6, 3012 Bern, Switzerland

bathymetric controls and small-scale features in atmospheric forcing. Identifying important influencing factors is essential for understanding, simulating and ultimately predicting sea level variability at the coast—a key societal concern in the context of our changing climate. In practice, this poses a huge and complex scientific challenge because it is region specific and timescale dependent and involves bringing multi-disciplinary expertise together.

From 5 March 2018 to 9 March 2018, a Workshop held at the International Space Science Institute (ISSI) in Bern, Switzerland, as part of the ISSI Earth Observation program, brought together leading scientists with worldwide expertise in ocean dynamics, coastal processes, remote sensing and sea level. This Workshop permitted a review of the most up-to-date knowledge about the spatio-temporal structure of sea level variability along coastal zones and how signals observed at tide gauge sites relate to the broader-scale open ocean variability. The Workshop also stimulated discussions on how satellite data, observations from tide gauges and other in situ measurements, together with numerical simulations, can help in improving our understanding of the different processes influencing coastal sea level over varying time scales.

More specifically, the objectives of the Workshop were:

(1) To review our current understanding of coastal sea level change and variability, from seasonal to multi-decadal time scales, and characterize the relationship between large-scale open ocean processes and coastal sea level;
(2) To review available observing systems providing information on sea level in coastal areas and identify primary gaps and uncertainties;
(3) To assess the ability of ocean model-data syntheses in estimating coastal sea level variations and of atmosphere–ocean global coupled models in projecting future sea level changes.

The objectives above led to mapping of coastal regions and timescales where short cross-shore spatial scales are known to lead to sea level differences in coastal and adjacent zones, an exploratory survey of the dynamical and other factors relevant for those differences, and a first assessment of modelling needs for improved representation of the coastal sea level in such regions.

Among the Workshop's outcomes, one can mention:

(1) A better understanding of the forcing factors that affect coastal sea level and of the role of large-scale climate signals;
(2) The identification of a set of priorities for the development of an optimal and integrated (satellite and ground-based) coastal observing system;
(3) The development of strategies to increase model capabilities to forecast short-term processes and project longer-term coastal changes.

The Workshop resulted in a collection of scientific articles that provide a detailed overview of its main themes, from the understanding of different physical processes to observational and modelling issues. One basic issue in discussing sea level research has been the lack of a consistent and well-defined terminology, which can hamper efficient communication across the different disciplines working on sea level science. The paper by Gregory et al. (2019) defines various concepts and terms associated with sea level and sea level changes and proposes a revised terminology to be adopted when discussing sea level and related issues.

Observational aspects addressed during the Workshop included satellite altimetry measurements of coastal sea level changes, space gravimetry observations of ocean bottom pressure, satellite scatterometer observations of winds, satellite observations of sea surface salinity and temperature, ocean and atmospheric reanalysis products, tide gauges and precise positioning techniques (GNSS, InSAR) for measuring vertical land motions. The article by Marcos et al. (2019) discusses current sea level observing systems and related parameters in the coastal zone, focusing on tide gauges and related vertical land motion measurements. Observations of bottom pressure and steric height, as well as wind waves and near-shore bathymetry, are also reviewed. In addition, Vignudelli et al. (2019) provide an overview of the current limitations of classical satellite altimetry and the promise of wide-swath altimetry to monitor sea level within 10–20 km of the coast. They also show that adapted data reprocessing and the use of new technology (such as synthetic-aperture radar altimetry on CryoSat and the Sentinel 3 satellites) allow valid sea level data to be collected very close to the coast, so that sea level variations can be determined with an increase in accuracy along the world's coastal zones.

Considerable attention at the Workshop was devoted to both local and remote causes and physical processes affecting coastal sea level. The article by Woodworth et al. (2019) discusses the broad variety of forcing factors and physical mechanisms responsible for sea level changes at the coast, on sub-daily to multi-decadal time scales. Vertical land motions causing relative sea level changes are also discussed. The paper sets the stage for more detailed treatment of several less well-understood subjects by other authors. In Piecuch et al. (2019), an overview is provided of local atmospheric wind and pressure effects on coastal sea level variations, and the ability of simple (constant-density) ocean models to explain existing tide gauge observations. Specific examples are discussed for a few selected regions, highlighting the dependence of the results on timescale, shelf width and other factors. In the article by Durand et al. (2019), the impact of river run-off on coastal sea level change is reviewed, focusing on large deltas and estuaries. The paper presents the theoretical background to explain the halosteric (pertaining to changes in the salinity of seawater) and largely barystatic (due to the mass of water added to the ocean) effects on coastal sea level associated with river discharge, provides a review of existing observations, in particular, from space, of river run-off at the coast and discusses new modelling and observational challenges.

Among important physical processes discussed at the Workshop, the article by Hughes et al. (2019) addresses the role played by coastal-trapped waves on coastal sea level and related issues. Hughes et al. (2019) define and explain the wave properties and their impact on shelf sea dynamics as well as how open ocean dynamics leads to coastal signals and the specific influence of coastal-trapped waves. On another topic, Han et al. (2019) deal with the impact of natural internal modes, such as the El Niño-Southern Oscillation, Indian Ocean Dipole and North Atlantic Oscillation, on coastal sea level on all major ocean basins. The paper discusses the importance of both remote and local dynamical processes associated with climate modes in causing substantial interannual and longer variability in sea level at the coast. Han et al. (2019) stress the need for longer observations and dedicated modelling for improved treatment of climate modes and their impacts on coastal sea level forecasts and projections.

Several other papers discuss processes with potential importance for coastal sea level variability that have historically received less attention. Penduff et al. (2019) demonstrate that mesoscale turbulence (now resolved in high-resolution global oceanic hindcasts) can induce substantial random fluctuations in coastal sea level on monthly and longer time scales. Implications for coastal sea level variations in different regions of the world's oceans are discussed. Dodet et al. (2019) focus on the contribution of wind-generated waves at the coast and their long-term effect on coastal sea level changes. The physical mechanisms are presented, as well as the limitations and perspectives for further process understanding and observational improvement. The article by Idier et al. (2019) provides an overview of interactions between the mean sea level at the coast, and tides, surges and flooding. Idier et al. (2019) investigate how the sea level can be altered by the complex interacting processes with various time scales occurring at the coast in different types of environments.

Coastal sea level projections and related uncertainties received considerable attention at the Workshop. Articles by Carson et al. (2019) and van de Wal et al. (2019) both discuss sources of uncertainties from process-based models, and current limitations and prospects for improving projections at the coast. While van de Wal et al. (2019) provide an overview for global, regional and extreme (triggered by storm surges, waves, tides or a combination of these processes) sea level projections, Carson et al. (2019) focus on uncertainty factors that contribute to the current large spread in regional sea level projections, relative to the global mean, and also consider the detection of anthropogenic trend signals, from global to local scales.

An important issue is how the information gained by the scientific community on possible future sea level changes is transferred to coastal adaptation practitioners and end-users with effectively communicated uncertainty. Poor knowledge of the different contributions to sea level change leads to inaccuracies in the description of the uncertainties in coastal sea level projections. Deep uncertainty on the ice sheet response to climate change remains, generating deep uncertainty in the high-end scenarios of coastal sea level rise. The paper by Jevrejeva et al. (2019) explores these issues. They focus on probabilistic projections, initially demanded by some users, and analyze how those projections can effectively describe the dominant uncertainty in some of the decision frameworks adopted by coastal engineers. They also underline the limitation of such an approach, in particular for deep uncertainty, and propose ways forward.

In summary, the Workshop highlighted the complex nature and the many factors associated with coastal sea level variability and the need for continued and coordinated multi-disciplinary efforts for improved monitoring and predicting capabilities. Apart from tide gauge and vertical land motion data, and better resolved satellite altimetry measurements characterizing variability adjacent to the coast, equal attention needs to be given to several other variables (e.g., bottom pressure, temperature, salinity, surface waves, coastal run-off and surface atmospheric forcing fields). Improved modelling efforts are important to resolve links between open and coastal ocean processes, effects of coastal run-off, eddies and other intrinsic ocean variability, and the interactions of wind waves and other high-frequency processes (tides, surges) with mean sea level. Additionally, advances in understanding and modelling of climate modes and ice sheet dynamics are needed for more reliable long-term projections of coastal sea level variability.

The organizers of this Workshop thank all the referees for their hard work, which improved the quality of the papers published here, the Editor in Chief, Professor Michael Rycroft, for his efforts, and many members of Springer Nature who assisted in preparing this Special Issue of Surveys in Geophysics. The sponsorship of the Workshop by ISSI is gratefully acknowledged.

References

Carson M, Lyu K, Richter K et al (2019) Climate model uncertainty and trend detection in regional sea level projections: a review. Surv Geophys. https://doi.org/10.1007/s10712-019-09559-3

Dodet G, Melet A, Ardhuin F et al (2019) The contribution of wind-generated waves to coastal sea-level changes. Surv Geophys. https://doi.org/10.1007/s10712-019-09557-5

Durand F, Piecuch CG, Becker M et al (2019) Impact of continental freshwater runoff on coastal sea level. Surv Geophys. https://doi.org/10.1007/s10712-019-09536-w

Gregory JM, Griffies SM, Hughes CW et al (2019) Concepts and terminology for sea level: mean, variability and change, both local and global. Surv Geophys. https://doi.org/10.1007/s10712-019-09525-z

Han W, Stammer D, Thompson P et al (2019) Impacts of basin-scale climate modes on coastal sea level: a review. Surv Geophys. https://doi.org/10.1007/s10712-019-09562-8

Hughes CW, Fukumori I, Griffies SM et al (2019) Sea level and the role of coastal trapped waves in mediating the influence of the open ocean on the coast. Surv Geophys. https://doi.org/10.1007/s10712-019-09535-x

Idier D, Bertin X, Thompson P et al (2019) Interactions between mean sea level, tide, surge, waves and flooding: mechanisms and contributions to sea level variations at the coast. Surv Geophys. https://doi.org/10.1007/s10712-019-09549-5

Jevrejeva S, Frederikse T, Kopp RE et al (2019) Probabilistic Sea Level Projections at the Coast by 2100. Surv Geophys. https://doi.org/10.1007/s10712-019-09550-y

Marcos M, Wöppelmann G, Matthews A et al (2019) Coastal sea level and related fields from existing observing systems. Surv Geophys. https://doi.org/10.1007/s10712-019-09513-3

Penduff T, Llovel W, Close S et al (2019) Trends of coastal sea level between 1993 and 2015: imprints of atmospheric forcing and oceanic chaos. Surv Geophys. https://doi.org/10.1007/s10712-019-09571-7

Piecuch CG, Calafat FM, Dangendorf S et al (2019) The ability of barotropic models to simulate historical mean sea level changes from coastal tide gauge data. Surv Geophys. https://doi.org/10.1007/s10712-019-09537-9

van de Wal RSW, Zhang X, Minobe S et al (2019) Uncertainties in long-term twenty-first century process-based coastal sea-level projections. Surv Geophys. https://doi.org/10.1007/s10712-019-09575-3

Vignudelli S, Birol F, Benveniste J et al (2019) Satellite altimetry measurements of sea level in the coastal zone. Surv Geophys. https://doi.org/10.1007/s10712-019-09569-1

Woodworth PL, Melet A, Marcos M et al (2019) Forcing factors affecting sea level changes at the coast. Surv Geophys. https://doi.org/10.1007/s10712-019-09531-1

Surveys in Geophysics (2019) 40:1251–1289
https://doi.org/10.1007/s10712-019-09525-z

Concepts and Terminology for Sea Level: Mean, Variability and Change, Both Local and Global

Jonathan M. Gregory[1,2] · Stephen M. Griffies[3] · Chris W. Hughes[4] · Jason A. Lowe[2,14] · John A. Church[5] · Ichiro Fukumori[6] · Natalya Gomez[7] · Robert E. Kopp[8] · Felix Landerer[6] · Gonéri Le Cozannet[9] · Rui M. Ponte[10] · Detlef Stammer[11] · Mark E. Tamisiea[12] · Roderik S. W. van de Wal[13]

Received: 1 October 2018 / Accepted: 28 February 2019 / Published online: 29 April 2019

Abstract
Changes in sea level lead to some of the most severe impacts of anthropogenic climate change. Consequently, they are a subject of great interest in both scientific research and public policy. This paper defines concepts and terminology associated with sea level and sea-level changes in order to facilitate progress in sea-level science, in which communication is sometimes hindered by inconsistent and unclear language. We identify key terms and clarify their physical and mathematical meanings, make links between concepts and across disciplines, draw distinctions where there is ambiguity, and propose new terminology where it is lacking or where existing terminology is confusing. We include formulae and diagrams to support the definitions.

Keywords Sea level · Concepts · Terminology

1 Introduction and Motivation

Changes in sea level lead to some of the most severe impacts of anthropogenic climate change (IPCC 2014). Consequently, they are a subject of great interest in both scientific research and public policy. Since changes in sea level are the result of diverse physical phenomena, there are many authors from a variety of disciplines working on questions of sea-level science. It is not surprising that sea-level terminology is inconsistent across disciplines (for example, "dynamic sea level" has different meanings in oceanography and geodynamics), as well as unclear or ambiguous even within a single discipline. (For instance, "eustatic" is ambiguous in the climate science literature.) We sometimes experience difficulty in finding correct and precise terms to use when writing about sea-level topics, or in understanding what others have written. Such communication problems hinder progress in research and may even confuse discussions about coastal planning and policy.

✉ Jonathan M. Gregory
j.m.gregory@reading.ac.uk

Extended author information available on the last page of the article

This situation prompted us to revisit the meaning of key sea-level terms, and to recommend definitions along with their rationale. In so doing, we aim to clarify meanings, make links between concepts and across disciplines and draw distinctions where there is ambiguity. We propose new terminology where it is lacking and recommend replacing certain terms that we argue are unclear or confusing. Our goal is to facilitate communication and support progress within the broad realm of sea-level science and related engineering applications.

In the next section, we outline the conventions and assumptions we use in our definitions and mathematical derivations. The following three sections (Sects. 3–5) contain the definitions, with a subsection for each major term defined, labelled with "N" and numbered consecutively throughout. In Sect. 3 we define five key surfaces: reference ellipsoid, sea surface, mean sea level, sea floor and geoid. We consider the variability and differences in these surfaces in Sect. 4, and quantities describing changes in sea level in Sect. 5. In Sect. 6, we show how **relative sea-level change** is related to other quantities in various ways. In Sect. 7 we describe how observational data are interpreted using the concepts we have defined. To facilitate sequential reading of this paper, the material of Sects. 3–7 is arranged to minimize forward references, though we were unable to avoid all.

We give a list of deprecated terms with recommended replacements in Sect. 8, and a list in Sect. 9 of all terms defined, referring to the subsections where they are defined, thus providing an index that also includes our notation. The appendices contain further discussion of some aspects at greater length.

The complexity of sea-level science is evident in the detail of the definitions and discussions in this paper. It may therefore be helpful to keep in mind that from the point of view of coastal planning and climate policy there are three quantities of particular interest. **Extreme sea level** along coasts (i.e., extreme coastal water level) or around offshore marine infrastructure (such as drilling platforms) is of great practical importance because of the enormous damage it can cause to human populations and their built environment and to ecosystems. The expected occurrence of extreme sea level under future climates is therefore relevant to decision-making on a range of time-horizons.

The dominant factor in changes of future local extremes is **relative sea-level change** (RSLC), i.e., the change in sea level with respect to the land (Lowe et al. 2010; Church et al. 2013). Where there is relative sea-level rise, coastal defences have to be raised to afford a constant level of protection against extremes, and low-lying areas are threatened with permanent inundation. Although RSLC depends on many local and regional influences, the majority of coastlines are expected to experience RSLC within a few tens of per cent of **global-mean sea-level rise** (GMSLR) (Church et al. 2013). Projections of GMSLR are therefore of interest to global climate policy, with both adaptation and mitigation in mind.

In general, greater GMSLR is projected for scenarios with higher rates of carbon dioxide emission and on longer timescales. Particular attention is paid, especially by risk-intolerant users, to the probability or possibility of future large changes in sea level (Hinkel et al. 2019). We recommend referring to these as *high-end* scenarios or projections of RSLC or GMSLR (rather than "extreme" scenarios), to avoid confusion with projections of extreme sea level.

2 Conventions and Assumptions

We here summarize the conventions and assumptions employed in the text and formulae of our definitions.

2.1 First Appearance of Terms

Within each definition subsection of Sects. 3–5, we use **bold** font for the first appearance of a term whose definition is the subject of another subsection. When we first define a term that does not have its own subsection, it appears with a *slanted* font. The reader can locate the definitions of terms marked in these ways by looking them up in Sect. 9. In the PDF of this paper, each bold term in Sects. 3–8 is a hyperlink to the relevant definition subsection.

2.2 Time-Mean and Changes

The sea surface varies on all the timescales of the Earth system, associated with sea-surface waves and tides, meteorological variability (from gustiness of winds to synoptic phenomena such as mid-latitude depressions and tropical cyclones), seasonal, interannual and longer-term internally generated climate variability (e.g., El Niño and the Interdecadal Pacific Oscillation), anthropogenic climate change and naturally forced changes (e.g., by volcanic eruptions, glacial cycles and tectonics). For various purposes of understanding and planning for sea-level variations it is helpful to draw a distinction between a time-mean *state* and fluctuations within that state. The definition of a "state" depends on the scientific interest or application. For sea level, the state might be defined by a time-mean long enough to remove tidal influence (about 19 years), or which characterizes a climatological state (conventionally 30 years), but it could be shorter, for example, if interannual variability were regarded as altering the state.

Thus, the time-mean state cannot be absolutely defined, but the concept is necessary. In this paper, **mean sea level** refers to a time-mean state whose precise definition should be specified when the term is used, and which is understood to be long enough to eliminate the effect of meteorological variations at least. We use symbols with a tilde and time-dependence, e.g., $\tilde{X}(t)$ for time-varying quantities, and symbols without any distinguishing mark and no time-dependence, e.g., X for time-mean quantities that characterize the state of the system. On longer timescales, the state itself may change, for example, due to anthropogenic influence. We use the symbol Δ and the word "change" to refer to the difference between any two states; thus, ΔX is "change in X", e.g., change in relative sea level between the time-mean of 1986–2005 and the time-mean of 2081–2100. Anthropogenic sea-level change comes mostly through climate change, but there are other influences too, such as impoundment of water on land in reservoirs.

2.3 Local and Regional

By a *local* quantity, we mean one which is a function of two-dimensional geographical location $\mathbf{r}$, specified by latitude and longitude. For some applications, it is important to consider variations of local quantities over distance scales of kilometres or less. Other quantities do not have such pronounced local variation and are typically considered as properties of regions, with distance scales of tens to hundreds of kilometres.

2.4 Global Mean Over the Ocean Surface Area

By *global mean*, we mean the area-weighted mean over the entire connected surface area of the ocean, i.e., excluding the land. The *ocean* includes marginal seas connected to the open ocean such as the Mediterranean Sea, Black Sea and Hudson Bay, but excludes inland seas such as the Caspian Sea, the African Great Lakes and the North American Great Lakes. It includes areas covered by sea ice and ice shelves, where special treatment is needed to define the level of the **sea surface**. We note that observational estimates of the global mean are often made from systems which lack complete coverage.

For centennial timescales, we can assume the ocean surface area A is constant, with $A = 3.625 \times 10^{14}$ m ^{2} (Cogley 2012). It is altered substantially by global-mean sea-level changes of many metres, such as on glacial–interglacial timescales or possibly over future millennia due to ice-sheet changes, and on geological timescales due to plate tectonics. The formulae we give for some quantities describing global-mean changes are not exactly applicable under those circumstances.

2.5 Sea-Water Density

Many of the formulae in this paper involve sea-water density. Although sea-water density is a local quantity, we treat it in many contexts as a globally uniform constant with a representative value ρ_* (e.g., 1028 kg m $^{-3}$). For the density of freshwater added at the sea surface we use a constant $\rho_f = 1000$ kg m $^{-3}$ for convenience, neglecting the variation of $<1\%$ in freshwater density due to temperature.

2.6 Vertical Direction and Distance

Before considering the vertical location of surfaces, or the local vertical distance between two surfaces, we need to specify the meaning of *vertical*. Geodesy is concerned with horizontal and vertical distances measured relative to the **reference ellipsoid**, which is a surface fixed with respect to the solid Earth. Geophysical fluid dynamics, including ocean circulation dynamics, is concerned with horizontal distances on surfaces of constant geopotential, and vertical distances measured perpendicular to such surfaces, especially the **geoid**. We discuss the two frames of reference (one relative to the reference ellipsoid and the other to the geoid) in the subsections describing those two surfaces. The distinction between the two frames is relevant only to the real world, because numerical ocean circulation models implicitly assume an idealized effective gravity field in which the geoid and the reference ellipsoid are identical (often spherical rather than ellipsoidal). In reality, the geoid has an irregular shape, whose vertical separation from the reference ellipsoid is ± 100 m and varies over horizontal length scales of 100s km.

Most of our formulae involve the local vertical coordinate of surfaces such as $X(\mathbf{r})$, for which we use the vertical distance above the reference ellipsoid (negative if below). We make this choice in order to give our formulae a well-defined interpretation. The choice of reference frame (with respect either to the reference ellipsoid or to the geoid) does not affect the geophysical definition of a surface, but the numerical value of its vertical coordinate at any given location is not the same in the two frames, because of the substantial difference between their reference surfaces. However, at a given location, there is negligible difference between the two frames regarding the local vertical direction. Hence, we can ignore the difference between the two definitions of "vertical" in evaluating a vertical gradient, the vertical distance $Y(\mathbf{r}) - X(\mathbf{r})$ between two surfaces, or the change in height $\Delta X(\mathbf{r})$ of a surface.

3 Surfaces

We here define five key surfaces used in sea-level studies. The reference ellipsoid and the associated terrestrial reference frame (depicted in Fig. 1) are geometrical constructions, chosen by convention. The other four surfaces (compared with the reference ellipsoid in Fig. 2) are geophysically defined and established with some uncertainty from observational data. These and other surfaces, such as datums defined by **tides** (e.g., mean lower-low water level), are located relative to the reference ellipsoid (Sect. 2.6), by their geodetic height as a function of geodetic location.

N1 **Reference ellipsoid**: The surface of an ellipsoidal volume of revolution chosen to approximate the **geoid**.

A reference ellipsoid is a conventional geometric construction used to specify locations in a *terrestrial reference frame*, i.e., relative to the solid Earth. Many reference ellipsoids have been defined by geodesists, and some are intended only for use over limited portions of the globe. A given specification of the reference ellipsoid is time-independent.

For purposes relating to global sea level we make the following requirements of the reference ellipsoid.

1. Its centre is the time-mean centre of mass of the Earth.
2. Its semi-major axis lies in the equatorial plane and its semi-minor axis along the rotation (polar) axis of the Earth.
3. Its axis of revolution is the rotation axis.

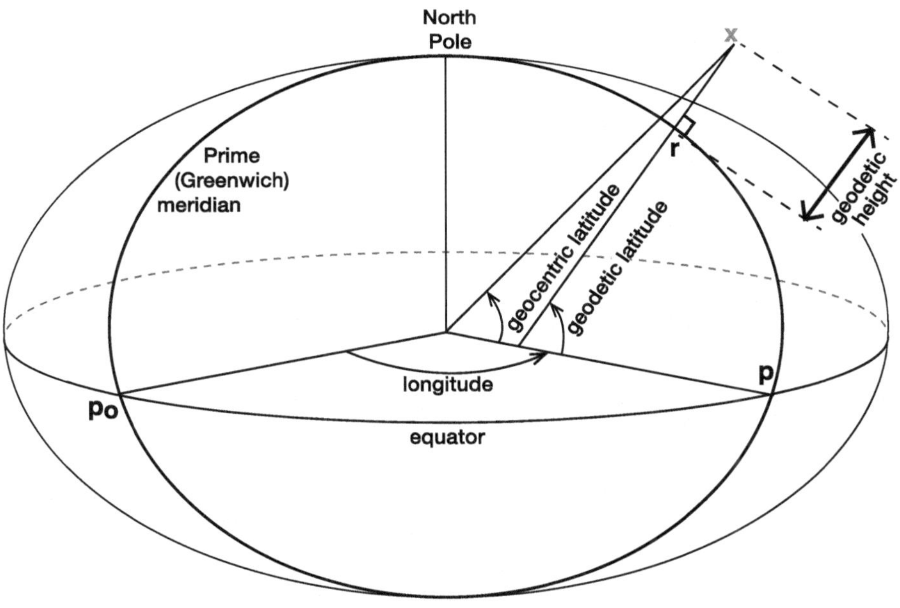

Fig. 1 The reference ellipsoid, which is used to locate other surfaces in a terrestrial reference frame, whose origin is the centre of the Earth. The figure shows the construction which defines the geodetic coordinates of an arbitrary point **x** in 3D space. The line between **x** and **r** is normal to the reference ellipsoid, on which **r** lies. The equator is intersected at **p** by the meridian through **r**, and at $\mathbf{p}_0$ by the prime meridian, which defines the zero of longitude

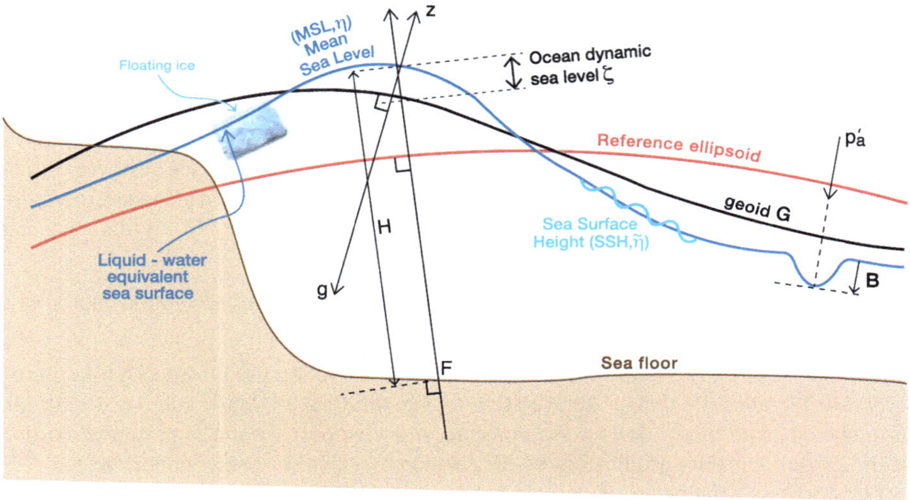

Fig. 2 Relationship between surfaces relating to sea level. The normal to the reference ellipsoid defines the vertical in the terrestrial reference frame. The normal to the geoid is the vertical coordinate (z) for geophysical fluid dynamics, and anti-parallel to the local effective acceleration g due to gravity. The difference between these two definitions of the vertical direction is greatly exaggerated in this diagram; it is negligible in reality. The local vertical coordinates of mean sea level η, the geoid G and the sea floor F are relative to the reference ellipsoid, while dynamic sea level $\tilde{\zeta}$ is relative to the geoid. The local time-mean thickness of the ocean H is the vertical distance between mean sea level and the sea floor. The deviation of atmospheric pressure p'_a from its global mean causes the depression B in sea level by the inverse barometer effect

4. It is fixed with respect to the solid Earth, and it rotates with the Earth.

The International Earth Rotation and Reference Systems Service (www.iers.org) defines the International Terrestrial Reference Frame (ITRF). They recommend the GRS80 ellipsoid.

For more precise geodetic purposes, the ITRF defines the coordinates and their rates of change of a set of stations on the Earth's surface. The coordinates are time-dependent because of tectonic motions and *true polar wander*, i.e., the time-dependence of the Earth's rotation axis with respect to the solid Earth. The latter phenomenon is neglected in the above specification of the ellipsoid. If the rotation axis is invariant, the last point in our specification above is not necessary because, being a volume of revolution, the reference ellipsoid is symmetrical with respect to rotation about the axis.

To locate a point **x** in 3D space in a reference frame based on the reference ellipsoid, we construct a straight line that passes through **x** and is normal to the ellipsoid, which it intersects at **r**. The *geodetic height* of **x** above the ellipsoid is the distance from **r** to **x** along this line, positive outwards. In our formulae, the *vertical* coordinate is the geodetic height, which is sometimes called *ellipsoidal height*. This is not the usual vertical coordinate for models of atmosphere and ocean circulation, which is instead defined relative to the **geoid**.

The *geodetic latitude*, commonly referred to simply as *latitude*, is the angle between the equatorial plane and the normal to the ellipsoid. It is different from the *geocentric latitude*, which is the angle between the equatorial plane and the line from the centre of the Earth to **x**. Geodetic and geocentric latitudes are the same for the poles and the equator, but elsewhere geodetic latitude is larger (as can be appreciated from Fig. 1), by up to about 0.2°.

To define the *longitude* of **x** ("geodetic" and "geocentric" are the same for longitude), consider the meridian passing through **r**, which intersects the equator at point **p**, and the *prime meridian* (the *Greenwich meridian*), which intersects the equator at $\mathbf{p}_0$. Viewing the Earth from above, the longitude is the anticlockwise angle between the lines from the centre of the Earth to $\mathbf{p}_0$ and to **p**.

N2 **Sea surface** $\tilde{\eta}$: The time-varying upper boundary of the ocean. The sea-surface height is the geodetic height of the sea surface above the **reference ellipsoid** (a negative value if below).

In ocean areas without floating ice (sea ice, ice shelves or icebergs), the liquid sea surface is the bottom boundary of the atmosphere. In such areas, the existence of a well-defined *sea-surface height (SSH)* $\tilde{\eta}(\mathbf{r}, t)$, that can be represented by a continuous and single-valued mathematical expression, presupposes a space–time averaging, because the instantaneous surface is ill-defined in the presence of some short-timescale phenomena that produce foam and sea spray, such as breaking surface waves and conditions of intense wind. We assume such averaging when speaking about the sea surface.

In ocean areas with floating ice, the liquid surface boundary is the bottom of the ice. For those areas, we define the SSH $\tilde{\eta}$ as the *liquid-water equivalent sea surface* $\tilde{\eta}_{\mathrm{LWE}}$ which the liquid would have if the ice were replaced by an equal mass of sea water of the density ρ_s of the surface water in its vicinity. Following Archimedes' principle,

$$\tilde{\eta}_{\mathrm{LWE}} = \tilde{\eta}_s + \frac{w_i}{g\rho_s}, \tag{1}$$

where $\tilde{\eta}_s$ is the geodetic height of the liquid sea-water surface (beneath the ice) and w_i is the weight per unit area of floating ice. (The depression of $\tilde{\eta}_s$ relative to $\tilde{\eta}$ is called the "**inverse barometer** effect of sea ice" by Griffies and Greatbatch 2012, and $\tilde{\eta}_{\mathrm{LWE}}$ is their "effective sea level".) Although the liquid-water equivalent sea-surface height is not directly measurable, it is a convenient construct for many practical purposes of sea-level studies, and dynamically justifiable because the hydrostatic pressure and gravity beneath the ice are largely unaffected by the replacement of ice with liquid water.

The sea surface varies periodically with various frequencies due to **tides**. It varies also on all timescales due to **sea-surface waves**, atmospheric pressure, surface flux exchanges (with the atmosphere), river inflow, variability that is internally generated by ocean dynamics, motion of the **sea floor** and changes in the mass distribution within the ocean and solid Earth (discussed in many following entries).

Note that **ocean dynamic sea level** and **ocean dynamic topography** are distinct concepts from sea-surface height and from each other.

N3 **Mean sea level (MSL)** η: The time-mean of the **sea surface**.

The period for the time-mean must be long enough to eliminate the effects of waves and other meteorologically induced fluctuations (as discussed in Sect. 2.2). Predicted tidal variations are subtracted if the period is not long enough to remove time-dependent **tides**, but permanent tides are included in MSL. For a precise definition of MSL, the period of the time-mean should be specified, and it could be described either with or without dependence on the time of year.

MSL is located by its geodetic height $\eta(\mathbf{r})$ above the **reference ellipsoid** (a negative value if below). In ocean models which regard the **geoid** and the reference ellipsoid as coincident, η is equally the orthometric height of MSL above the geoid. MSL is sometimes called "mean sea surface". We recommend against using this term, in order to make a clear distinction from "sea-surface height".

N4 **Sea floor** F: The lower boundary of the ocean, its interface with the solid Earth.

The sea floor is the part of the surface of the solid Earth (whether bedrock or consolidated sediment, and lying beneath any unconsolidated sediment, e.g., Webb et al. 2013) that is always or sometimes submerged under sea water. The level of the sea floor varies due to solid-Earth **tides**, accumulation of sediment (with eventual compaction) and **vertical land movement** on a range of timescales.

We specify the instantaneous level of the sea floor by its geodetic height $\tilde{F}(\mathbf{r},t)$ (negative over most of the ocean) relative to the **reference ellipsoid**. The local instantaneous thickness of the ocean (its vertical extent, the depth of the sea floor measured from a ship, a positive quantity sometimes called the *depth of the water column*) is given by

$$\tilde{H}(\mathbf{r},t) = \tilde{\eta}(\mathbf{r},t) - \tilde{F}(\mathbf{r},t) \geq 0, \tag{2}$$

i.e., the vertical distance between the sea surface and the sea floor. The choice of reference surface for vertical coordinates does not affect the value of $\tilde{H}$, because it is the difference between two vertical coordinates; $\tilde{H}$ would be the same if SSH and the sea floor were located by heights relative to the **geoid** rather than the reference ellipsoid. The time-mean *thickness of the ocean* H

$$H(\mathbf{r}) = \eta(\mathbf{r}) - F(\mathbf{r}) \geq 0 \tag{3}$$

is likewise related to MSL η.

The shape of the sea floor is sometimes called the *bottom topography* or the *bathymetry*, for example in describing it as "rough" or "smooth". These two synonymous terms are also used as names for the quantities $-F$, $G-F$ and $\eta - F(=H)$, i.e., the time-mean vertical distance of the sea floor beneath the reference ellipsoid, the geoid or MSL, respectively. In order to be precise, it should be stated which of these alternatives is intended, since G and the reference ellipsoid differ by ± 100 m (Sect. 2.6), and G and MSL differ by ± 1 m, following time-mean **ocean dynamic sea level**.

N5 **Geoid** G: A surface on which the *geopotential* Φ has a uniform value, chosen so that the volume enclosed between the geoid and the **sea floor** is equal to the time-mean volume of sea water in the ocean (including the liquid-water equivalent of floating ice).

The geopotential is a field of potential energy per unit mass, accounting for the Newtonian gravitational acceleration due to the mass of the Earth plus the centrifugal acceleration arising from the Earth's rotation. We define the sign of the geopotential such that work is required to move a sea-water parcel from a lower geopotential (deeper in the ocean) to a higher geopotential (shallower in the ocean). Note that this sign convention for the geopotential is opposite to that used in geodesy.

The vertical gradient of the geopotential is equal to the local *effective gravitational acceleration*, g, $g(\mathbf{r},t) = \partial\Phi/\partial z$, usually referred to as "*gravitational acceleration*" in geophysical fluid dynamics. Hence, the effective gravitational acceleration is normal to the geoid, because the geoid is an *equipotential surface*, i.e., one on which the geopotential is constant. The Newtonian gravitational acceleration is time-dependent because the distribution of mass in the ocean (liquid and solid), on land (including the land-based cryosphere) and within the solid Earth is generally changing. The centrifugal acceleration is time-dependent because the Earth's rotation rate and rotation axis are variable.

For models of atmosphere and ocean circulation, the vertical unit vector is directed anti-parallel to the effective gravitational acceleration g (or equivalently it is parallel to the local gradient of the geopotential). The height above the geoid of some point $\mathbf{x}$ is the distance z, measured along the local vertical unit vector, from the geoid to $\mathbf{x}$. The coordinate z (Fig. 2) is also called the *orthometric height* of $\mathbf{x}$. Strictly, the orthometric height is measured along a plumb line, which is always normal to equipotential surfaces, but this distance differs negligibly from that measured along the perpendicular to the **reference ellipsoid**.

We define z such that $z = 0$ is the geoid, $z > 0$ is above the geoid, and $z < 0$ is below. By *horizontal* we mean aligned with a surface of constant z. This is not strictly an equipotential surface, but the difference is locally negligible. It is, however, very different from a surface of constant geodetic height $z' = z + G$, where $G(\mathbf{r})$ is the *geoid height* above the reference ellipsoid ($G < 0$ where the geoid is below the ellipsoid).

The **sea surface** would coincide with the geoid if the ocean were in a resting steady state in the rotating frame of the earth. Although defining the geoid in this way is conceptually attractive, it is not realistic or practically useful. (See Appendix 1.)

The sea surface does not really coincide with the geoid because the ocean is not at rest. (See **ocean dynamic sea level**.) For example, **mean sea level** (MSL) north of the Antarctic Circumpolar Current (ACC) is at a higher geopotential than MSL south of the ACC; with respect to the geoid, MSL on the north side is roughly 2 m higher than on the south side.

Referring to its definition, we choose the geoid as the equipotential surface (out of the infinite set of them) which satisfies

$$\int (G - F)\,\mathrm{d}A = V = \int H\,\mathrm{d}A = \int (\eta - F)\,\mathrm{d}A, \tag{4}$$

using Eq. (3) for H, and where V is the volume of the global ocean and $A = \int \mathrm{d}A$ is its surface area. It follows from Eq. (4) that

$$\int \eta\,\mathrm{d}A = \int G\,\mathrm{d}A, \tag{5}$$

i.e., MSL and geoid height above the reference ellipsoid have equal global means.

We define the geoid in terms of MSL η, rather than the sea-surface height $\tilde{\eta}$, in order to restrict changes in G and V to those occurring on the timescales of **global-mean sea-level rise**, rather than on shorter timescales related to meteorological, seasonal and interannual fluctuations. Our definition of the geoid treats it as a geophysical quantity which changes as the Earth system evolves. In some applications, the geoid is defined in a time-independent way as a particular geopotential surface within a particular model of the Earth's gravity field.

We define the geoid to include the permanent ocean tide. With this choice, time-mean **ocean dynamic sea level** ζ is determined solely by ocean dynamics and density. With the zero-tide convention, which is common in gravity-field models, ζ would include the permanent ocean tide, which is almost $+0.1$ m at the equator and -0.2 m at the poles.

We define the geoid as $G(\mathbf{r}) = E(\mathbf{r}, \Phi_G)$, with a choice of Φ_G such that Eq. (4) is satisfied, where $E(\mathbf{r}, \Phi)$ is the geodetic height of the equipotential surface for geopotential Φ. The shapes of the equipotential surfaces, including the geoid, depend on the geographical distribution of mass over the Earth. According to Eq. (4), the global-mean geoid height must change by

$$\frac{1}{A}\int \Delta G \, \mathrm{d}A = \frac{1}{A}\int \Delta F \, \mathrm{d}A + \frac{\Delta V}{A} \tag{6}$$

if there is global-mean **vertical land movement** ΔF affecting the sea floor, or a change ΔV in the volume of the global ocean, whether due to change in density or in mass. Consequently, Φ_G must change such that

$$\frac{1}{A}\int \Delta G \, \mathrm{d}A = \frac{\Delta \Phi_G}{A}\int \frac{\partial E(\mathbf{r}, \Phi)}{\partial \Phi} \, \mathrm{d}A = \frac{\Delta \Phi_G}{g}, \tag{7}$$

if we approximate g as globally uniform.

4 Variations and Differences in Surfaces

In this section we define terms for time-dependent variations in surfaces (on timescales shorter than those of mean sea-level change) and differences between surfaces.

N6 **Tides**: Periodic motions within the ocean, atmosphere and solid Earth due to the rotation of the Earth and its motion relative to the moon and sun. Ocean tides cause the **sea surface** to rise and fall.

The *astronomical tide* is the dominant constituent of the ocean tides. It is caused by periodic spatial variations in local gravity. Tidal motion of the land surface and sea floor is due to elastic deformation of the solid Earth by gravitational tidal forces. The diurnal and annual cycles of insolation produce periodic variations in atmospheric pressure and winds (sea breezes), which cause the *radiational tide* in the atmosphere and ocean (e.g., Williams et al. 2018). The *predicted tide* is the sum of the astronomical and radiational constituents. Because the ocean and atmosphere are fluids, tidal forces within them cause *tidal currents* as well as displacements.

Sea-surface height (SSH) can be greatly elevated during a storm by a **storm surge**, and the consequent **extreme sea level** is sometimes called a *storm tide*. The *tidal height* is the vertical distance of the SSH due to the predicted tide above a local benchmark or a surface which is fixed with respect to the terrestrial reference frame. Often, this surface is a *tidal datum*, defined by a extremum of the periodic tide, such as mean lower-low water level.

The velocity of the ocean tidal currents depends on water depth. Therefore, **relative sea-level change** (RSLC) affects the tides. In most coastal locations, this interaction alters the tidal variations of the sea surface with respect to **mean sea level** by less than 10% of the RSLC (Pickering et al. 2017).

In most locations, the constituent of the ocean tide with the largest amplitude is the lunar semi-diurnal tide. The orbit of the moon around the Earth modulates the semi-diurnal tide to produce a large amplitude (*spring tide*) at new and full moon, and a small amplitude (*neap tide*) at half-moon. There are many smaller periodic constituents associated with the sun and moon. The precession of the plane of the moon's orbit causes tidal variations with an 18.6-year cycle (the *nodal period*), affecting extreme sea level on this timescale. There are longer tidal periods.

The *pole tide* is caused by variations of the Earth's rotation axis relative to the solid Earth, altering the centrifugal acceleration and local gravity. The two largest components of the pole tide have periods of 1 year and about 433 days. The latter is due to the

Chandler wobble, which is not strictly periodic and arises from the mechanics of the Earth's rotation alone (it is a *free nutation*), rather than being caused by the gravitation of other bodies in the solar system.

The time-means of the tidal forces of the moon and sun are nonzero. Hence, in addition to the periodic constituents, the tides have a constant constituent called the *permanent tide*, which tends to make the Earth and sea surface more oblate. Our definitions of **mean sea level** and the **geoid** use the *mean-tide* convention, including the permanent tide. In gravity models, the *zero-tide* convention is more usual, in which the permanent ocean tide is subtracted, but the permanent elastic tidal deformation of the solid Earth is retained; an estimate of the latter too is subtracted in the *tide-free* convention used by GNSS measurements.

N7 **Inverse barometer (IB)** B: The time-dependent hydrostatic depression of the sea surface by atmospheric pressure variations, also called *inverted barometer.*

The ocean is almost incompressible. (A uniform change of 1 hPa over the ocean causes a **global-mean sea-level rise** of roughly 0.16 mm.) Therefore changes in atmospheric pressure have a negligible effect on the total volume of the ocean. However, they do move sea water around, and the effect on the **sea surface** depends on the deviation of sea-level pressure $\tilde{p}_a(\mathbf{r})$ from its global (ocean) mean, given by

$$\tilde{p}'_a(\mathbf{r},t) = \tilde{p}_a(\mathbf{r},t) - \frac{1}{A}\int \tilde{p}_a(\mathbf{r},t)\,\mathrm{d}A. \tag{8}$$

For timescales longer than a few days, we can assume the ocean to be in hydrostatic balance. Therefore, the depression of the **sea-surface height** (SSH) $\tilde{\eta}$ by IB is $\tilde{B} = \tilde{p}'_a/(g\,\rho_s)$ where $g(\mathbf{r})$ is the acceleration due to gravity and $\rho_s(\mathbf{r},\tilde{\eta})$ the surface sea-water density. That is, when $\tilde{p}'_a > 0$ then sea level is depressed locally by $\tilde{B}(\mathbf{r})$, and it is raised when $\tilde{p}'_a < 0$. The latter effect is an important contribution to **storm surge**. In a storm or cyclone, $\tilde{p}_a$ may fall by several 10 hPa, causing SSH to rise by several 100 mm.

The global mean of $g\rho_s$ is approximately 9.9×10^{-5} m Pa $^{-1} \equiv 9.9$ mm hPa $^{-1}$, with spatial and temporal variations of about 1% around this value. Hence, for most purposes of sea-level studies we can neglect the spatial variations in g and ρ_s, and replace them with constants; thus,

$$\tilde{B} = \frac{\tilde{p}'_a}{g\,\rho_*}. \tag{9}$$

Hence, the global-mean IB correction is zero,

$$\int \tilde{B}(\mathbf{r},t)\,\mathrm{d}A = 0, \tag{10}$$

which follows by definition of $\tilde{p}'_a$.

The inverse-barometer response of the sea surface compensates for the effect of $\tilde{p}'_a$ on hydrostatic pressure within the ocean, and the subsurface ocean does not feel the fluctuations in atmospheric pressure. Consequently, the ocean behaves dynamically as if the sea-surface height were $\tilde{\eta} + \tilde{B}$, which is called *IB-corrected sea-surface height.* Its time-mean is $\eta + B$, the *IB-corrected mean sea level.* In most climate models, atmospheric pressure variations are not communicated to the ocean. In these models $\tilde{B}$ must be *subtracted* from the simulated SSH to produce a quantity that varies with $\tilde{p}_a$ like the observed $\tilde{\eta}$ does.

N8 **Extreme sea level**: The occurrence or the level of an exceptionally high or low local **sea-surface height**.

Extremely high sea-surface height (SSH) is caused by meteorological conditions as a **storm surge**, by **sea-surface waves** due to various causes and by exceptionally high or low (although predictable) tidal height. When considering coastal impacts, extreme sea level may be called *extreme coastal water level*. For decadal timescales, the main influence on changes in the frequency distribution of extreme sea level is **relative sea-level change** (RSLC), whose effect outweighs that of changes in meteorological forcing (Lowe et al. 2010; Church et al. 2013; Vousdoukas et al. 2018). To avoid confusion, we recommend the phrase *high-end* sea-level change to describe projections of very large RSLC, instead of using the word "extreme" for such projections.

N9 **Storm surge**: The elevation or depression of the **sea surface** with respect to the predicted tide during a storm.

Storm surges are caused during tropical cyclones and deep mid-latitude depressions by low atmospheric pressure, by strong winds pushing water towards the shore (or away from the shore, causing a negative surge) and by **sea-surface waves** breaking at the coast. Wave effects are usually excluded or underestimated by tide-gauges. If the actual **sea-surface height** (SSH) at location $\mathbf{r}$ and time t due to tide and surge combined (sometimes called the *storm tide*) is $\tilde{\eta}(\mathbf{r}, t)$, and the predicted SSH due to the tide alone is $\tilde{\eta}_{\text{tide}}(\mathbf{r}, t)$, the *storm-surge height* σ is

$$\sigma(\mathbf{r}, t) = \tilde{\eta}(\mathbf{r}, t) - \tilde{\eta}_{\text{tide}}(\mathbf{r}, t), \tag{11}$$

also called the *surge residual* or non-tidal residual.

The storm-surge height σ is the sum of three components: the **inverse barometer** (IB) effect of low atmospheric pressure, the *wind setup* caused by the wind-driven current, and the *wave setup*, which is the elevation of the sea surface due to breaking waves. All three effects are normally present, but intensified by storms. IB and wind setup tend to be more important on wide continental shelves, but wave setup can dominate in some cases (Pedreros et al. 2018), especially in areas of steep sea floor slope.

The *swash* is the uprush and backwash of water over the solid surface (e.g., sand or pebbles) generated by each wave. During the uprush, the swash extends above the wave setup. Its maximum height above the predicted tide, called the *wave runup*, gives the highest water level of the storm surge.

Particularly high SSH $\tilde{\eta} = \sigma + \tilde{\eta}_{\text{tide}}$ occurs when the storm surge coincides with high tide. Without the meteorological forcing, storm-surge height σ would be zero, but since the tide level influences the propagation of the storm-forced signal, σ and $\tilde{\eta}_{\text{tide}}$ are not independent (Horsburgh and Wilson 2007).

The *skew-surge height* is the elevation of the highest sea surface that occurs within a single tidal cycle above the predicted level of the high tide within that cycle. If the actual SSH is $\tilde{\eta}(\mathbf{r}, t)$ and the predicted SSH due to the tide alone is $\tilde{\eta}_{\text{tide}}(\mathbf{r}, t)$, the skew-surge height is

$$\sigma_k(\mathbf{r}, t) = \max_t(\tilde{\eta}(\mathbf{r}, t)) - \max_t(\tilde{\eta}_{\text{tide}}(\mathbf{r}, t)), \tag{12}$$

where $\max_t(X(\mathbf{r}, t))$ means the maximum value of X that occurs at location $\mathbf{r}$ during the interval of time t from one low tide to the next. For extreme-value analysis, the skew-surge height is preferable to the storm-surge height as a measure of the effect of the meteorological forcing alone in regions where skew-surge height is uncorrelated with tidal height (Williams et al. 2016).

N10 **Sea-surface waves**: Waves on the surface of the ocean, usually surface gravity waves caused by winds.

The amplitude of a *wind wave* depends on the strength of the wind, and the time and the distance of open ocean, called the *fetch*, over which the wind has blown. The sea surface typically exhibits a superposition of many waves of different amplitudes, velocities, frequencies and directions. A *swell wave* is a wind wave of low frequency which was generated far away.

A *tsunami* or *seismic sea wave* is an **extreme sea level** event caused by an earthquake, volcano, landslide or other submarine disturbance that suddenly displaces a volume of water. The displacement propagates as a long-wavelength surface gravity wave, but is not a tidal phenomenon, despite it sometimes being called a "tidal wave".

The *wave height* is the vertical distance from the crest to the trough of a wave, respectively its highest and lowest points. The *wave period* is the interval of time between the passage of repeated features on the waveform such as crests, troughs or upward crossings of the mean level. The *significant wave height* is a statistic computed from wave measurements, defined as either the mean of the largest one-third of the wave heights, or four times the standard deviation of wave heights. (These statistics are approximately equal.) The *significant wave period* is the mean period of the largest one-third of the waves.

N11 **Ocean dynamic sea level** ζ: The local height of the **sea surface** above the **geoid** G, with the **inverse barometer** correction B applied.

Instantaneous ocean dynamic sea level is defined by

$$\tilde{\zeta}(\mathbf{r},t) = \tilde{\eta}(\mathbf{r},t) + \tilde{B}(\mathbf{r},t) - G(\mathbf{r}). \tag{13}$$

It is determined jointly by ocean density and circulation. The time-mean ocean dynamic sea level is

$$\zeta(\mathbf{r}) = \eta(\mathbf{r}) + B(\mathbf{r}) - G(\mathbf{r}), \tag{14}$$

whose global mean

$$\frac{1}{A}\int \zeta(\mathbf{r})\,\mathrm{d}A = 0, \tag{15}$$

in view of Eqs. (5) and (10).

In the Coupled Model Intercomparison Project (CMIP), $\tilde{\zeta}$ is stored in the diagnostic named `zos`, which is defined to have zero mean (Equation H14 of Griffies et al. 2016). However, some models supply it with a nonzero time-dependent mean. If the global mean of the `zos` diagnostic is found to be nonzero, the global mean should be subtracted uniformly.

N12 Ocean dynamic topography: An estimate of **ocean dynamic sea level** computed from the ocean density structure above a reference level where the velocity is either known or assumed to be zero.

On any horizontal (see **geoid** for definition) level z within the ocean, the hydrostatic pressure is given by

$$\tilde{p}(z) = \tilde{p}_a + g\int_z^{\tilde{\zeta}-\tilde{B}} \tilde{\rho}(z')\,\mathrm{d}z', \tag{16}$$

which is the sum of the atmospheric pressure $\tilde{p}_a$ on the **sea surface** and the weight per unit horizontal area of sea water between z and the sea surface. The coordinate of the sea surface in this case is not $\tilde{\eta}$ but $\tilde{\eta} - G = \tilde{\zeta} - \tilde{B}$ by Eq. (13), the height of the sea surface above the geoid, because we are using the orthometric vertical coordinate z, which is the natural choice for ocean dynamics. Equation (9) leads to the horizontal gradient of the atmospheric pressure $\nabla\tilde{p}_a = \nabla\tilde{p}'_a = g\rho_* \nabla\tilde{B}$. Consequently, the horizontal gradient of pressure within the ocean is given by

$$\nabla\tilde{p} = \nabla\left(\tilde{p}_a + g\int_z^{\tilde{\zeta}-\tilde{B}} \tilde{\rho}(z')\,\mathrm{d}z'\right) \tag{17a}$$

$$= g\rho_* \nabla\tilde{B} + (g\rho_* \nabla\tilde{\zeta} - g\rho_* \nabla\tilde{B}) + g\int_z^{\tilde{\zeta}-\tilde{B}} \nabla\tilde{\rho}(z')\,\mathrm{d}z' \tag{17b}$$

$$= g\rho_* \nabla\tilde{\zeta} + g\int_z^{\tilde{\zeta}-\tilde{B}} \nabla\tilde{\rho}(z')\,\mathrm{d}z'. \tag{17c}$$

In the first step of this derivation, we used Eq. (9) for the **inverse barometer** correction $\tilde{B}$, approximated g and sea-surface $\tilde{\rho} = \rho_*$ as constants, and applied Leibniz's rule to differentiate the integral, which yields the two terms in parentheses in Eq. (17b), but no term for $\tilde{\rho}$ at z because $\nabla z = \mathbf{0}$. From Eq. (17c) we obtain

$$\nabla\tilde{\zeta}(\mathbf{r}) = \frac{1}{g\rho_*}\nabla\tilde{p}(\mathbf{r}, z) - \frac{1}{\rho_*}\int_z^{\tilde{\zeta}-\tilde{B}} \nabla\tilde{\rho}(\mathbf{r}, z')\,\mathrm{d}z', \tag{18}$$

which relates the horizontal gradient of **ocean dynamic sea level** $\tilde{\zeta}$ to the horizontal hydrostatic pressure gradient at a reference level z and the horizontal density gradient above that level. The second term on the right-hand side is the horizontal gradient of the *dynamic height D*

$$D = -\frac{1}{\rho_*}\int_z^{\tilde{\zeta}-\tilde{B}} \tilde{\rho}\,dz' \tag{19}$$

of the sea surface relative to z.

In much of the ocean interior (below the boundary layer and away from coastal and other strong currents), and taking a time-mean sufficient to eliminate tidal currents, *geostrophy* is a reasonable approximation, meaning that there is a balance (no net acceleration) between the pressure gradient and Coriolis forces, and all other forces are negligible. Therefore, $\tilde{\mathbf{v}} \simeq \tilde{\mathbf{v}}_\mathrm{g}$, with the *geostrophic velocity* $\tilde{\mathbf{v}}_\mathrm{g}$ defined by

$$f\mathbf{k} \times \tilde{\rho}\tilde{\mathbf{v}}_\mathrm{g} = -\nabla\tilde{p}, \tag{20}$$

where f is the Coriolis parameter and $\mathbf{k}$ the vertical unit vector. If we can measure $\tilde{\mathbf{v}}$ at some z and assume it is geostrophic, we arrive at

$$\nabla\tilde{\zeta}(\mathbf{r}) = -\frac{f}{g\rho_*}\mathbf{k}\times\tilde{\rho}\tilde{\mathbf{v}}(\mathbf{r},z) - \frac{1}{\rho_*}\int_z^{\tilde{\zeta}-\tilde{B}} \nabla\tilde{\rho}(\mathbf{r},z')\,\mathrm{d}z', \tag{21}$$

from Eq. (18).

Alternatively, if we do not know $\tilde{\mathbf{v}}$ at any z, we assume there exists a *level of no motion* $z = -L$, which is a geopotential (horizontal) surface on which $\tilde{\mathbf{v}} = \tilde{\mathbf{v}}_g = \mathbf{0}$, requiring the horizontal hydrostatic pressure gradient to vanish ($\nabla\tilde{p} = \mathbf{0}$) by Eq. (20). Therefore,

$$\nabla\tilde{\zeta}(\mathbf{r}) = -\frac{1}{\rho_*}\int_{-L}^{\tilde{\zeta}-\tilde{B}} \nabla\tilde{\rho}(\mathbf{r},z)\,\mathrm{d}z, \tag{22}$$

using Eq. (18). There is no motion on $z = -L$ so long as there is a compensation between undulations of dynamic sea level $\tilde{\zeta}$ (on the left-hand side of Eq. 22), and variations of the density structure above $z = -L$ (on the right-hand side). Such exact compensation does not generally occur in the ocean, and the level of no motion does not exist. However, it is a useful approximation in many situations. For example, an anomalous sea-surface high is associated with a depression of the pycnocline in the interior of subtropical gyres (e.g., Figure 3.3 of Tomczak and Godfrey 1994), thus leading to relatively weak flow beneath the pycnocline. In some regions, the approximation is not useful; in particular, sizeable $\tilde{\mathbf{v}}$ occurs at all depths in the Southern Ocean.

The ocean dynamic topography is the estimate of ocean dynamic sea level made using Eqs. (21) or (22). Since Eqs. (21) and (22) are unaffected by adding a constant to $\tilde{\zeta}$, the method provides only the difference in $\tilde{\zeta}$ between any two points (i.e., the gradient); it cannot give $\tilde{\zeta}$ for individual points relative to the geoid. Furthermore, it is not applicable in regions where the reference level for motion is below the **sea floor**, nor for differences between points in basins which are separated by sills that are shallower than the reference level.

5 Changes in Sea Level

The relationships between quantities determining changes in sea level are summarized in Fig. 3. The phrases "sea-level change" (SLC) and "sea-level rise" (SLR) are often used in the literature. These make sense when referring to the phenomenon in general, but more specific terms such as **relative sea-level change** and **global-mean sea-level rise** should be preferred where relevant.

N13 **Ocean dynamic sea-level change** $\Delta\zeta$: The change in time-mean **ocean dynamic sea level**, i.e., the change in IB-corrected **mean sea level** relative to the **geoid**.

For the difference between two time-mean states of the climate, Eq. (13) gives

$$\Delta\zeta(\mathbf{r}) = \Delta\eta(\mathbf{r}) + \Delta B(\mathbf{r}) - \Delta G(\mathbf{r}). \tag{23}$$

Since the time-mean ocean dynamic sea level $\zeta(\mathbf{r})$ always has a zero global mean by Eq. (15), so does $\Delta\zeta$ i.e., **global-mean sea-level rise** is excluded from ocean dynamic sea-level change. This property depends on Eq. (5) and thus requires a different choice of geopotential to define the **geoid** in the two states, if there is any change in global-mean sea level.

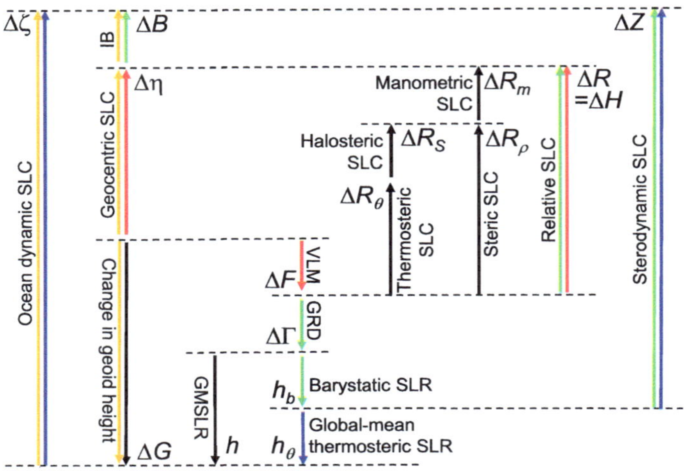

Fig. 3 Relationships between quantities, defined in Sect. 5, that determine changes in sea level. The lengths of the arrows do not have any significance—they are only illustrative—and the dotted horizontal lines serve only to indicate alignment. All of the quantities are differences between two states, and all except h, h_θ and h_b are functions of location $\mathbf{r}$. Any closed circuit gives an equality, in which a term has a positive sign when traversed in the direction of its arrow, and a negative sign if in the opposite direction to its arrow. For example, $\Delta R - \Delta\eta + \Delta F = 0$ (Eq. 24) is the circuit marked in red, Eq. (23) in orange, Eq. (38) in blue, and Eq. (54) in green

N14 **Geocentric sea-level change** $\Delta\eta$: The change in local **mean sea level** with respect to the terrestrial reference frame.

Geocentric sea-level change is the change in the height $\eta(\mathbf{r})$ of MSL relative to the **reference ellipsoid**. *IB-corrected geocentric sea-level change* is $\Delta\eta + \Delta B$, i.e., the same with the **inverse barometer** correction added. Geocentric sea-level change must be distinguished from **relative sea-level change**.

N15 **Relative sea-level change (RSLC)** ΔR: The change in local **mean sea level** relative to the local solid surface, i.e., the **sea floor**. Relative sea-level change is also called "relative sea-level rise" (RSLR). (See Sect. 6 for an exposition of the relationship of RSLC to other quantities.)

Both the MSL height η and the sea floor height F may change and thus alter RSL. Hence, RSLC is geodetically expressed as

$$\Delta R(\mathbf{r}) = \Delta\eta(\mathbf{r}) - \Delta F(\mathbf{r}), \tag{24}$$

the difference between **geocentric sea-level change** $\Delta\eta$ and **vertical land movement** ΔF (VLM). *IB-corrected relative sea-level change* is $\Delta R + \Delta B$, i.e., RSLC with the **inverse barometer** correction. Relative sea-level change is the quantity registered by a *tide-gauge*, which measures sea level relative to the solid surface where it is attached.

Since climate models do not include VLM, they do not distinguish between geocentric and relative sea-level change. In climate models where atmospheric pressure changes Δp_a are not applied to the ocean, $-\Delta B$ must be added to include the effect of Δp_a simulated by the atmosphere model. (Note that this adjustment should not be made to **ocean dynamic sea-level change** $\Delta\zeta$, which by definition is IB-corrected; see Eq. 23.)

The term "relative sea level" is not employed in an absolute sense, but only in conjunction with "change", because $\eta - F$ (the analogue of Eq. 24) is simply the depth of the sea floor below MSL, equal to the time-mean thickness of the ocean H (Eq. 3).

In view of Eq. (3), we may also write RSLC as

$$\Delta R(\mathbf{r}) = \Delta H(\mathbf{r}), \tag{25}$$

i.e., the change in local ocean thickness, making it obvious that RSLC is not meaningful at locations which change from land to sea (*transgression*) or vice versa (*regression*), since H is undefined on land.

When considering sea-level change on geological timescales, in the absence of information about **ocean dynamic sea level** $\tilde{\zeta}$ or the inverse barometer effect, we might approximate $\Delta\tilde{\zeta} \simeq 0$ and $\Delta B \simeq 0$, in which case $\Delta\eta \simeq \Delta G$ from Eq. (23), and $\Delta R \simeq \Delta G - \Delta F$ from Eq. (24). This quantity is defined everywhere and thus gives an approximate meaning to RSLC in regions of transgression and regression.

N16 **Steric sea-level change** ΔR_ρ: The part of **relative sea-level change** which is due to the change $\Delta\rho$ in ocean density, assuming the local mass of the ocean per unit area does not change. It is composed of **thermosteric sea-level change** ΔR_θ, which is the part due solely to the change $\Delta\theta$ in in-situ temperature, and **halosteric sea-level change** ΔR_S, which is the part due solely to the change ΔS in salinity.

The time-mean local mass of the ocean per unit area is

$$m = \int_F^\eta \rho \, \mathrm{d}z = H\overline{\rho} \quad \text{with} \quad \overline{\rho} \equiv \frac{1}{H}\int_F^\eta \rho \, \mathrm{d}z, \tag{26}$$

where the first factor $H = \eta - F$ is the local time-mean thickness of the ocean (Eq. 3), and the second factor $\overline{\rho}$ is the local vertical-mean time-mean density. If we change the density while keeping m fixed, the thickness of the ocean changes, because

$$0 = \Delta m = \Delta H|_m \overline{\rho} + H\Delta\overline{\rho}|_m \tag{27}$$

(by making a linear approximation). Therefore,

$$\Delta H|_m = -(H/\overline{\rho})\,\Delta\overline{\rho} \quad \text{with} \quad \Delta\overline{\rho} = \frac{1}{H}\int_F^\eta \Delta\rho \, \mathrm{d}z. \tag{28}$$

This would exactly define steric sea-level change in a situation where mass did not move horizontally. But in reality there are horizontal transports, making it impossible to separate density changes due to local changes in properties from those due to the movement of mass. For convenience, we approximate $\overline{\rho}$ with the constant ρ_*.

Since the RSLC is given by $\Delta R = \Delta H$ (without **inverse barometer** correction, Eq. 25), steric sea-level change is

$$\Delta R_\rho = -\frac{1}{\rho_*}\int_F^\eta \Delta\rho \, \mathrm{d}z = \Delta R_\theta + \Delta R_S \tag{29}$$

with the density increment decomposed into thermal and haline components (by making a linear approximation)

$$\Delta\rho = \frac{\partial\rho}{\partial\theta}\Delta\theta + \frac{\partial\rho}{\partial S}\Delta S, \tag{30}$$

and with the corresponding thermosteric and halosteric contributions

$$\Delta R_\theta = -\frac{1}{\rho_*}\int_F^\eta \frac{\partial\rho}{\partial\theta}\,\Delta\theta\,\mathrm{d}z \qquad \Delta R_S = -\frac{1}{\rho_*}\int_F^\eta \frac{\partial\rho}{\partial S}\,\Delta S\,\mathrm{d}z. \tag{31}$$

Thermosteric sea-level change is often called *thermal expansion*, because $\partial\rho/\partial\theta < 0$, so increasing the temperature gives $\Delta R_\theta > 0$. (See Appendix 2 regarding the dependence of density on salinity.) Relative sea-level change (without inverse barometer correction) is the sum of steric and **manometric sea-level change** (Eq. 35).

N17 **Global-mean thermosteric sea-level rise** h_θ: The part of **global-mean sea-level rise** (GMSLR) which is due to thermal expansion.

This quantity is the global mean of local **thermosteric sea-level change** ΔR_θ (due to temperature change, Eq. 31); thus,

$$h_\theta = \frac{1}{A}\int \Delta R_\theta\,\mathrm{d}A = -\frac{1}{\rho_* A}\int\int_F^\eta \frac{\partial\rho}{\partial\theta}\,\Delta\theta(\mathbf{r},z)\,\mathrm{d}z\,\mathrm{d}A. \tag{32}$$

It is the change in global ocean volume due to change in temperature alone, divided by the ocean surface area. The CMIP variable `zostoga` is h_θ calculated with respect to a fixed reference state. (Griffies et al. 2016 define the reference to be the initial state of the experiment for CMIP6.) Hence, differences in `zostoga` between two states give the global-mean thermosteric sea-level rise between those states.

Although **halosteric sea-level change** ΔR_S (due to salinity change, Eq. 31) can be locally of the same order of magnitude as thermosteric, global-mean halosteric sea-level change is practically zero. In Appendix 2 we detail the physical arguments leading to this conclusion. Salinity change should be excluded when calculating h_θ, to avoid including a *spurious* global-mean halosteric sea-level change. (See Appendix 2 here as well as Appendix H9.5 of Griffies et al. 2016.) However, salinity change must of course be included when calculating ΔR_S. It follows that global-mean *steric* sea-level change, which equals h_θ because global-mean halosteric sea-level change is zero, cannot be calculated as the global mean of local *steric* sea-level change. This apparent contradiction is due to the inaccuracy of the approximations made following Eq. (28).

N18 **Manometric sea-level change** ΔR_m: **Definition A:** The part of **relative sea-level change** (RSLC) which is not steric, or alternatively **Definition B:** The part of RSLC which is due to the change $\Delta m(\mathbf{r})$ in the time-mean local mass of the ocean per unit area, assuming the density does not change. In the following, we show that the two definitions are approximately the same.

If we change the local mass m per unit area while keeping density fixed, by Eq. (26) the thickness of the ocean changes by $\Delta H|_\rho = \Delta m/\overline{\rho}$, where $\overline{\rho}$ is the local vertical mean of ρ. (In reality, if the local mass per unit area changes, the density will probably change as well, since mass which is converging horizontally or through the sea surface is unlikely to have $\rho = \overline{\rho}$ exactly.)

Since RSLC $\Delta R = \Delta H$ (without **inverse barometer** correction, Eq. 25), if we approximate $\overline{\rho}$ with the constant ρ_*, we obtain

$$\Delta R_m \simeq \frac{\Delta m}{\rho_*}. \tag{33}$$

This is Definition B of "manometric sea-level change". The local change in mass Δm can be estimated from the gravity field, or from the *bottom pressure* p_b, i.e., the hydrostatic pressure at the **sea floor**, according to $\Delta m = (\Delta p_b - \Delta p_a)/g$. (See Appendix 3.) Because of its relationship to p_b, manometric sea-level change is sometimes referred to as the "bottom pressure term" in sea-level change.

According to Definition B, the global mean of ΔR_m vanishes if the mass of the global ocean is constant, since $1/(A\rho_*) \int \Delta m \, dA = 0$. However, ΔR_m may still be locally nonzero, due to rearrangement of the existing mass of the ocean. If the mass of the global ocean changes, the global mean of ΔR_m is nonzero and equals the **barystatic sea-level rise** (equality is approximate with Definition B of ΔR_m, exact with Definition A), which is part of **global-mean sea-level rise** (GMSLR). Despite the correspondence between (local) manometric and (global) barystatic sea-level rise, we argue that these two concepts are sufficiently different to need distinct terms. (See the subsection for barystatic sea-level rise.)

If mass and density are both allowed to change, Eq. (26) gives

$$\Delta m = \Delta H \,\overline{\rho} + H \,\Delta\overline{\rho} \Rightarrow \Delta H = (1/\overline{\rho})\left(\Delta m - \int_F^\eta \Delta\rho \, dz\right), \tag{34}$$

using the expression for $\Delta\overline{\rho}$ from Eq. (28). Again approximating $\overline{\rho}$ as ρ_* and substituting from Eqs. (25), (29) and (33), we obtain

$$\Delta R = \Delta H \simeq \Delta R_\rho + \Delta R_m, \tag{35}$$

i.e., RSLC (without inverse barometer correction) is the sum of **steric sea-level change** and manometric sea-level change, which are, respectively, the parts due to change in density and change in mass per unit area. Since H is defined only in ocean areas, the formulae are not valid for locations which change from land to sea or vice versa.

With ΔR_m defined by Eq. (33), Eq. (35) is only approximate, because of the replacement of $\overline{\rho}$ with ρ_*. We can make Eq. (35) exact if we retain the definition of Eq. (29) for steric sea-level change involving ρ_* and adopt Definition A of "manometric sea-level change", as

$$\Delta R_m \equiv \Delta R - \Delta R_\rho, \tag{36}$$

i.e., ΔR_m is the part of RSLC that is not steric.

We propose "manometric" as a new term because in the existing literature there is no unambiguous and generally used term for ΔR_m. It may be described as the "mass effect on", "mass contribution to", "mass component of" or "mass term in" sea level or sea-level change, but these descriptions could equally well refer to **GRD**-induced sea-level change (the effects of a change in the geographical distribution of mass) or barystatic sea-level rise, so they can be confusing. ("Manometric" is an existing word, referring to the measurement of hydrostatic pressure using a column of liquid, a concept that is closely related to bottom pressure.)

N19 **Barystatic sea-level rise** h_b: The part of **global-mean sea-level rise** (GMSLR) which is due to the addition to the ocean of water mass that formerly resided within the land area (as land water storage or land ice) or in the atmosphere (which contains a relatively tiny mass of water), or (if negative) the removal of mass from the ocean to be stored elsewhere. It is also called "barystatic sea-level change".

Land water storage, also called *terrestrial water storage*, is water on land that is stored as groundwater, soil moisture, water in reservoirs, lakes and rivers, seasonal snow and permafrost. *Land ice* means ice sheets, glaciers, permanent snow and firn. Barystatic sea-level rise includes contributions from changes in all of these.

It does *not* include changes in the parts of ice shelves and glacier tongues whose weight is supported by the ocean rather than resting on land. (These floating parts constitute the majority of the mass of ice shelves and glacier tongues, but near the grounding line on the seaward side some part of the weight may be supported by the land-based ice.) Where land ice rests on a bed which is below mean sea level, it is already displacing sea water. Therefore, the land ice contribution to barystatic sea-level rise excludes the mass whose liquid-water equivalent volume equals the volume of sea water already displaced. The remainder, which is not currently displacing sea water, is often referred to as the ice mass or volume *above flotation* in glaciology.

We define barystatic sea-level rise as

$$h_b = \frac{\Delta M}{\rho_{\rm f} A}, \tag{37}$$

i.e., the change in mass ΔM of the global ocean from added freshwater, converted to a change in global ocean volume and divided by the ocean surface area A. Because global-mean halosteric change is negligible, the salinity of the existing sea water does not affect h_b. Any contribution δM to barystatic sea-level rise can be expressed as its *sea-level equivalent (SLE)* $\delta M/(\rho_{\rm f}A)$, using the same formula.

The formula provides a convenient method of quantifying the changes in the mass of the ocean if A is constant. However, h_b and SLE may not accurately indicate the contribution of added mass to global-mean ocean thickness if there is a substantial change to A, as for example in the transition from glacial to interglacial.

Calculating the global mean of **manometric sea-level change** ΔR_m from its Definition B (Eq. 33) gives $1/A \int \Delta R_m \, dA = \Delta M/(\rho_* A) \simeq h_b$, i.e., approximately equal to the barystatic sea-level change, but not exactly since $\rho_* \neq \rho_{\rm f}$. With Definition A, the global mean of ΔR_m exactly equals h_b. (See **global-mean sea-level rise**.) Despite this relationship between manometric sea-level change and barystatic sea-level rise, we argue that we need distinct terms for them, rather than referring to the latter as the global mean of the former, for two reasons.

First, barystatic sea-level rise is well defined by conservation of water mass on Earth and can be evaluated from the change in mass of other stores of water, e.g., ice sheets and glaciers, without considering the ocean. This has been the usual approach in observational studies of the budget of global-mean sea-level rise, and is the only possibility for diagnosing h_b from the majority of climate models whose ocean component is Boussinesq or has a linear free surface, and therefore does not conserve water mass. Secondly, the partitioning of RSLC into steric and manometric (Eq. 35) is somewhat arbitrary, because it depends on the choice of ρ_* as a reference density.

Neither reason for the distinction of ΔR_m and h_b applies to thermosteric sea-level change; its contribution to global-mean sea-level rise can only be conceived or evaluated as the global mean of the local ΔR_θ, whose definition by Eq. (31) is well defined.

In recent literature, "eustatic" is often used as a synonym for "barystatic", whereas in geological literature *eustatic sea-level change* means either **global-mean sea-level rise** or **global-mean geocentric sea-level rise**. Because of this confusion of meaning, we deprecate the term "eustatic", following the last three assessment reports of the

Intergovernmental Panel on Climate Change (Church et al. 2001; Meehl et al. 2007; Church et al. 2013).

N20 **Sterodynamic sea-level change** ΔZ: **Relative sea-level change** due to changes in ocean density and circulation, with **inverse barometer** (IB) correction.

This term is the sum of **ocean dynamic sea-level change** (which includes the IB correction) and **global-mean thermosteric sea-level rise**,

$$\Delta Z(\mathbf{r}) = \Delta\zeta(\mathbf{r}) + h_\theta. \tag{38}$$

It can be diagnosed from ocean models (even those that do not conserve mass as per the commonly used Boussinesq models) as the sum of the changes in `zos` and `zostoga`. Sterodynamic sea-level change is the part of relative sea-level change that can be simulated with such models. (As discussed above for ocean dynamic sea-level change $\Delta\zeta$, the change in `zos` calculated from CMIP data should have zero global mean.)

"Sterodynamic" is a term which is newly introduced in this paper. We propose it because in the existing literature there is no clear, simple or generally used term for ΔZ. It is a concept that appears in the literature, where it is referred to by various cumbersome phrases, such as "the oceanographic part of sea-level change", "steric plus dynamic sea-level change" or "sea-level change due to ocean density and circulation change".

N21 **Vertical land movement (VLM)** ΔF: The change in the height of the **sea floor** or the land surface.

VLM has several causes, including isostasy, elastic flexure of the lithosphere, earthquakes and volcanoes (due to tectonics). All of these involve a change in height of the existing solid surface. In contrast, landslides and sedimentation alter the solid surface and its height by transport of materials; some authors count them as VLM. Extraction of groundwater and hydrocarbons may cause *subsidence* (sinking of the solid surface) by *compaction* (the reduction in the liquid fraction in the sediment). These anthropogenic effects can be locally large, e.g., in Manila, and can exceed the natural effects by orders of magnitude. Where VLM occurs near the coast, it may cause emergence or submergence of land and thus alter the coastline.

Isostasy or *isostatic adjustment* is the process of adjustment of the *lithosphere* (the crust and the rigid upper part of the mantle) towards a hydrostatic equilibrium in which it is regarded as floating in the *asthenosphere* (the underlying viscous mantle, which is of higher density than the lithosphere), with an equal pressure everywhere at some notional horizontal level beneath the lithosphere. On geological timescales, isostatic adjustment occurs in response to changes in the mass load of the lithosphere upon the mantle beneath (the asthenosphere and lower mantle), due to erosion, sedimentation or emplacement of igneous rocks.

On climate timescales there are large changes in load due to the varying mass of ice on land during glacial–interglacial cycles. (See **glacial isostatic adjustment**.) Isostatic adjustment occurs over multi-millennial timescales determined by the viscous flow of the mantle beneath the lithosphere. An elastic response of the lithosphere, on annual timescales, occurs in response to changes in load. Although it is small compared with the eventual isostatic response, it is much more rapid, and hence responsible for significant VLM due to contemporary and recent historical changes in land ice, for instance in West Antarctica.

N22 **GRD**: Changes in Earth **G**ravity, Earth **R**otation (and hence centrifugal acceleration) and viscoelastic solid-Earth **D**eformation.

These three effects are all caused by changes in the geographical distribution of ocean and solid mass over the Earth. They are often considered together because they occur simultaneously and may interact. Changes in gravitation and rotation alter the geopotential field and hence the **geoid** $G(\mathbf{r})$, while deformation of the solid Earth changes the **sea floor** topography $F(\mathbf{r})$ through **vertical land movement**. By altering G and F, GRD induces **relative sea-level change** (e.g., Tamisiea and Mitrovica 2011; Kopp et al. 2015), which redistributes but does not change the global ocean volume and thus causes no **global-mean sea-level rise**. *GRD-induced relative sea-level change* $\Delta\Gamma$ is defined as

$$\Delta\Gamma = \Delta G' - \Delta F' \tag{39}$$

(derived in Sect. 6 as Eq. 51) where $\Delta G'$ and $\Delta F'$ are the deviations of the changes in the geoid and in the sea floor from their respective global (ocean) means. By construction, the global (ocean) means of G' and F' are each zero; hence, the global (ocean) mean of $\Delta\Gamma$ is zero.

Whatever the cause, redistribution of the ocean mass itself has GRD effects, and thereby the ocean affects its *own* mass distribution and **mean sea level** (MSL). Thus, MSL, the geoid and the sea floor must all be related in a self-consistent solution, which in the context of **glacial isostatic adjustment** (GIA) is expressed by the *sea-level equation* (Farrell and Clark 1976).

The *ocean GRD* effects are called *self-attraction and loading (SAL)*, where "loading" means the weight on the solid Earth. SAL is caused by climatic change in ocean density and circulation (Gregory et al. 2013), which do not involve any change in the mass of the ocean. SAL is also a component of GRD which is caused by changes in land ice and in the solid Earth; thus, SAL contributes to the sea-level effects of GIA, **contemporary GRD** and **mantle dynamic topography** as well.

We propose the new term "GRD" in the absence of any existing single term to describe this frequently discussed group of effects. GRD-induced relative sea-level change may be described as the "mass effect", "mass contribution", "mass component" or "mass term", but these labels could equally well refer to manometric sea-level change if local, or barystatic sea-level rise if global, so they can be confusing. Moreover, "GRD" is helpful as a label for a concept which unifies SAL, GIA, contemporary GRD and mantle dynamic topography.

N23 **Glacial isostatic adjustment (GIA)**: **GRD** due to ongoing changes in the solid Earth caused by past changes in land ice.

GIA is caused by the viscous adjustment of the mantle to changes in the load on the lithosphere that occurred when mass was transferred from land ice into the ocean, or the reverse. It is dominated by the ongoing effects of the deglaciation following the Last Glacial Maximum. Due to the reduction in the mass load on land, areas that were beneath former ice sheets are generally rising. This process is sometimes called *post-glacial rebound*, but that term is unsatisfactory because GIA involves remote **vertical land movement** as well, both upward and downward. Areas adjacent to the former ice sheets are subsiding as mantle material moves towards the areas of uplift, while land near to the coast is rising and the **sea floor** is generally subsiding as a result of the increase in the mass of the ocean. The ongoing widespread redistribution of mass also affects the **geoid**. Together, the changes in geoid and sea floor cause *GIA-induced relative sea-level change* $\Delta\Gamma_{\text{GIA}}$.

Previous changes in land ice during the Holocene contribute to GIA as well, but GIA does not include the contributions from any ongoing change in land ice or ocean mass, whose effects we call **contemporary GRD**.

N24 **Contemporary GRD**: **GRD** due to ongoing changes in the mass of water stored on land as ice sheets, glaciers and land water storage.

Such transfers of mass cause instantaneous changes in the **geoid**, and **vertical land movement** (VLM) on annual timescales due to elastic deformation of the solid Earth, which causes further change to the geoid. Together, these effects produce **relative sea-level change** (RSLC). There are also slower responses, both VLM and geoid, due to viscous deformation of the asthenosphere. Note that contemporary GRD excludes GIA; the former arises from *ongoing* change in the mass of water on land, and the latter from *past* change.

The elastic deformation and associated geoid contributions to contemporary GRD-induced relative sea-level change are separately proportional to the mass ΔM which has been added to the ocean. Hence, their sum is

$$\Delta \Gamma_p(\mathbf{r}) = \Delta M \, \gamma_p(\mathbf{r}), \tag{40}$$

where $\gamma_p(\mathbf{r})$ is a geographically dependent constant of proportionality, independent of ΔM. Since the **barystatic sea-level rise** is $\Delta M/\rho_f A$ (Eq. 37), the RSLC due to the combination of these three effects is

$$\Delta R_p(\mathbf{r}) = \Delta M \, \phi(\mathbf{r}) \quad \text{where} \quad \phi(\mathbf{r}) = \gamma_p(\mathbf{r}) + 1/\rho_f A. \tag{41}$$

The addition of freshwater to the ocean will induce sterodynamic sea-level change as well (e.g., Agarwal et al. 2015).

The *barystatic–GRD fingerprint* ϕ is a constant geographical pattern, often called a *sea-level fingerprint*, or sometimes a *static-equilibrium fingerprint* to contrast it with the patterns of **ocean dynamic sea-level change**. "Fingerprint" without qualification can be easily confused with climate detection and attribution studies where the same word refers to the patterns caused by particular climate change forcing agents such as greenhouse gases. "Static-equilibrium" is not informative about the processes concerned. The part of contemporary GRD-induced RSLC due to viscous deformation and associated geoid change cannot be represented by a constant pattern because it depends on convolving the history of mass addition with the time-dependent solid-Earth response.

N25 **Mantle dynamic topography**: **GRD** due to ongoing changes in the solid Earth caused by mantle convection and plate tectonics.

The dynamics of the interior of the Earth cause **vertical land movement**, such as the uplift of mid-ocean ridges by upwelling material and the formation of oceanic trenches due to subduction. At the same time, material with different density is redistributed within the Earth, altering the **geoid**. The consequent GRD-induced **relative sea-level change** can be very large on geological timescales, amounting to hundreds of metres. Mantle dynamic topography does not include **glacial isostatic adjustment** (although that is also due to ongoing changes in the solid Earth).

Mantle dynamic topography is often called "dynamic topography" in the solid-Earth literature and also refers to changes in topography on land. We deprecate "dynamic topography" in a sea-level context because it could be confused with **ocean dynamic topography**.

N26 **Global-mean sea-level rise (GMSLR)** h: The increase ΔV in the volume of the ocean divided by the ocean surface area A, also called "global-mean sea-level change" (GMSLC). Observational estimation of h is described in Sect. 7.

By definition, GMSLR is

$$h = \frac{\Delta V}{A} = \frac{1}{A}\Delta\left(\int (\eta - F)\,\mathrm{d}A\right) = \frac{1}{A}\int \Delta R(\mathbf{r})\,\mathrm{d}A = \frac{1}{A}\int \Delta H(\mathbf{r})\,\mathrm{d}A, \tag{42}$$

which follows from Eqs. (4), (24) and (25). Hence, GMSLR is the global mean of **relative sea-level change** ΔR and equals the global mean of the change ΔH in the thickness (or "depth") of the ocean. Note that GMSLR differs from **global-mean geocentric sea-level rise** because GMSLR is unaltered by a global-mean change $(1/A)\int \Delta F\,\mathrm{d}A$ in the level of the **sea floor** F, provided the global ocean volume V does not change.

The global ocean volume can change due to changes in ocean density or due to changes in ocean mass. Hence, GMSLR is the sum of **global-mean thermosteric sea-level rise** and **barystatic sea-level rise**,

$$h = h_\theta + h_b. \tag{43}$$

A satisfactory explanation of historical observed GMSLR in terms of thermosteric and barystatic contributions has been achieved in recent years thanks to improvements in both observations and models (Church et al. 2011; Gregory et al. 2013; Chambers et al. 2017).

Equation (43) is implied by the Definition A of **manometric sea-level change**, as the part of relative sea-level change which is not steric (Eq. 36), whose global mean

$$\frac{1}{A}\int \Delta R_m\,\mathrm{d}A = \frac{1}{A}\int \Delta R\,\mathrm{d}A - \frac{1}{A}\int \Delta R_\rho\,\mathrm{d}A = h - h_\theta, \tag{44}$$

using Eq. (42) and recalling that global-mean steric sea-level change is purely thermosteric. By definition, the part of h which is not steric is the part which is due to addition of mass, so it must be the case that

$$h_b = \frac{1}{A}\int \Delta R_m\,\mathrm{d}A, \tag{45}$$

i.e., barystatic sea-level rise equals the global mean of manometric sea-level change by Definition A.

The added mass is unlikely to have exactly the temperature of the existing water to which it is added, implying that changes will probably occur to temperature and hence to density. Because of the nonlinearity of the dependence of ρ on θ, there may be a nonzero contribution to h_θ in consequence. Since this is a steric effect, by definition it is not part of h_b.

From Definition B (Eq. 33) we obtain an approximate expression for global-mean manometric sea-level change as $(1/A)\int \Delta m/\rho_*\,\mathrm{d}A = \Delta M/(\rho_* A)$, where ΔM is the added mass. This is the same as the expression (Eq. 37) for h_b except that ρ_f is replaced by ρ_*. This difference is the result of the approximation in Eq. (33) that $\rho_* \simeq \overline{\rho}$. Physically, it is because manometric sea-level change ΔR_m (a local quantity) is dominated by redistribution of existing sea water, for which ρ_* is a good choice of representative density, whereas barystatic sea-level rise (a global quantity) is due only to addition or subtraction of freshwater of density ρ_f, since the redistributive effect is zero in the global mean.

On glacial–interglacial and geological timescales, the variation of ocean area cannot be neglected, so GMSLR is ill-defined. However, it is still meaningful to consider *global-mean relative sea-level change* h_R, which is the change in global-mean ocean thickness

$$h_R = \frac{V + \Delta V}{A + \Delta A} - \frac{V}{A} = \frac{V}{A + \Delta A}\left(\frac{\Delta V}{V} - \frac{\Delta A}{A}\right). \tag{46}$$

If A is constant, $h_R = h$. An increase in A ($\Delta A > 0$) gives a negative contribution to h_R, counteracting the positive contribution from a concomitant increase in V.

In geological literature, global-mean sea-level rise is sometimes called "eustatic sea-level change". Following the last three assessment reports of the Intergovernmental Panel on Climate Change (Church et al. 2001; Meehl et al. 2007; Church et al. 2013), we deprecate "eustatic" because it has become a confusing term, which is also used to mean **global-mean geocentric sea-level rise** or **barystatic sea-level rise**.

N27 **Global-mean geocentric sea-level rise** h_G: The global-mean change in **mean sea level** with respect to the terrestrial reference frame.

This quantity is the global mean of $\Delta\eta$, the change in MSL relative to the **reference ellipsoid**. From Eqs. (4) and (5) we have

$$\begin{aligned} h_G &= \frac{1}{A}\int \Delta\eta \, \mathrm{d}A = \frac{1}{A}\int \Delta G \, \mathrm{d}A = \frac{1}{A}\left(\Delta V + \int \Delta F \, \mathrm{d}A\right) \\ &= h + \frac{1}{A}\int \Delta F \, \mathrm{d}A, \end{aligned} \tag{47}$$

where h is **global-mean sea-level rise** (GMSLR) defined by Eq. (42). Thus, global-mean geocentric sea-level rise h_G differs from GMSLR because the latter is unaltered by a global-mean change $(1/A)\int \Delta F \, \mathrm{d}A$ in the level of the **sea floor** F, provided the volume of the ocean does not change. On geological timescales, when the area of the ocean may change, the global-mean change in level of the sea floor is $\Delta((1/A)\int F \, \mathrm{d}A)$.

6 Relationships Determining Relative Sea-Level Change

Relative sea-level change (RSLC) is $\Delta R = \Delta\eta - \Delta F$ (Eq. 24). By applying the **inverse barometer** correction, we obtain IB-corrected RSLC

$$\Delta R + \Delta B = \Delta\eta + \Delta B - \Delta F \tag{48a}$$

$$= \Delta[\eta - G + B] + \Delta[G - F] \tag{48b}$$

$$= \Delta\zeta + \Delta[G - F], \tag{48c}$$

where in Eq. (48c) we used the definition of **ocean dynamic sea-level change** $\Delta\zeta$ (Eq. 23) to rewrite the first term. From the definition of the geoid (Eq. 4) we obtain

$$\frac{1}{A}\int \Delta(G - F) \, \mathrm{d}A = \frac{\Delta V}{A} = h, \tag{49}$$

the **global-mean sea-level rise**. Let us write $\Delta G(\mathbf{r}) = \Delta G'(\mathbf{r}) + (1/A)\int \Delta G \, \mathrm{d}A$ and similarly for ΔF, thus defining $\Delta G', \Delta F'$ as the local deviations of $\Delta G, \Delta F$ from their respective global (ocean) means. Therefore,

$$\Delta(G - F) = \Delta(G' - F') + \frac{1}{A}\int \Delta(G - F) \, \mathrm{d}A = \Delta(G' - F') + h. \tag{50}$$

This leads to our expression for **GRD**-induced relative sea-level change (Eq. 39) as

$$\Delta\Gamma(\mathbf{r}) \equiv \Delta[G'(\mathbf{r}) - F'(\mathbf{r})] = \Delta[G(\mathbf{r}) - F(\mathbf{r})] - h. \tag{51}$$

Substituting Eq. (51) in Eq. (48c) gives IB-corrected RSLC as

$$\Delta R(\mathbf{r}) + \Delta B(\mathbf{r}) = \Delta\zeta(\mathbf{r}) + h + \Delta\Gamma(\mathbf{r}), \tag{52}$$

the sum of ocean dynamic sea-level change $\Delta\zeta$, global-mean sea-level rise h and GRD-induced RSLC $\Delta\Gamma$. Using Eqs. (43) and (38) we obtain

$$\Delta\zeta(\mathbf{r}) + h = \Delta\zeta(\mathbf{r}) + h_\theta + h_b = \Delta Z(\mathbf{r}) + h_b, \tag{53}$$

Hence, IB-corrected RSLC is

$$\Delta R(\mathbf{r}) + \Delta B(\mathbf{r}) = \Delta Z(\mathbf{r}) + h_b + \Delta\Gamma(\mathbf{r}), \tag{54}$$

the sum of **sterodynamic sea-level change** $\Delta Z(\mathbf{r})$, **barystatic sea-level rise** h_b and GRD-induced RSLC. The **contemporary GRD**-induced RSLC due to a change δM_i in any of the stores of water on land (as *land water storage* or *land ice*, e.g., in a lake or an ice sheet) has both a barystatic and a GRD-induced effect on sea level, which are related and may interact (e.g., Gomez et al. 2012). Provided they are both proportional to δM_i, we can rewrite Eq. (54) as

$$\Delta R(\mathbf{r}) + \Delta B(\mathbf{r}) = \Delta Z(\mathbf{r}) + \sum_i \delta M_i\, \phi_i + \Delta\Gamma_{\mathrm{GIA}} + \Delta\Gamma_Z, \tag{55}$$

where ϕ_i is the barystatic–GRD fingerprint (Eq. 41) of store i of water, $\Delta\Gamma_{\mathrm{GIA}}$ is GIA-induced RSLC, and $\Delta\Gamma_Z$ is the GRD-induced RSLC of ocean mass redistribution (self-attraction and loading) associated with sterodynamic sea-level change. The last term is typically neglected.

Equation (55) is the means by which MSL projections are derived from coupled atmosphere–ocean general circulation models (AOGCMs). These models do not simulate GRD-induced RSLC (because they have time-independent geoid and sea floor) and are not generally used to compute barystatic sea-level rise (because they do not include adequate representations of land ice or land water storage). RSLR projections are therefore obtained by combining sterodynamic sea-level change simulated by an AOGCM with separately calculated projections of barystatic sea-level rise and GRD-induced RSLC using climate change simulations from the AOGCM applied to models of glaciers, ice sheets and the solid Earth (Church et al. 2013; Kopp et al. 2014; Slangen et al. 2014).

According to Eqs. (35) or (36), $\Delta R = \Delta R_\rho + \Delta R_m$, the sum of **steric sea-level change** ΔR_ρ and **manometric sea-level change** ΔR_m, which are the parts due, respectively, to change in density and change in mass per unit area. In general, $\Delta R_m \neq 0$ even if $h_b = 0$, because ocean mass may be redistributed. In particular, because $\Delta R_m = -1/\rho_s \int_F^\eta \Delta\rho\, \mathrm{d}z$ is small on the continental shelves (where the ocean is shallow), but ocean dynamics will not permit a strong gradient in ζ to develop across the shelf break, global-mean thermosteric sea-level rise demands a redistribution of ocean mass onto the shelves (Landerer et al. 2007; Yin et al. 2010), with consequent ocean GRD (Gregory et al. 2013).

7 Observations of Sea-Level Change

Estimates of **global-mean sea-level rise** (GMSLR) for the last century depend mainly on records from tide-gauges. These instruments register coastal **relative sea-level change** (RSLC) $\Delta R = \Delta\eta - \Delta F$ (Eq. 24), which is affected by local **vertical land movement** (VLM) ΔF. VLM is large in some places, with strong geographical gradients.

GMSLR is calculated as the global mean of RSLC, $h = (1/A)\int \Delta R\,\mathrm{d}A$ (Eq. 42). However, tide-gauges measure ΔR only at points on the coast and thus give a sparse, non-uniform and unrepresentative sampling of the global ocean area. The calculation therefore depends on physically based methods for extrapolation. Considering Eq. (52) in the form

$$h = \Delta R + \Delta B - \Delta\zeta - \Delta\Gamma \tag{56}$$

we see that in principle h can be calculated from ΔR from any tide-gauge by applying the **inverse barometer** (IB) correction ΔB, and subtracting local **ocean dynamic sea-level change** $\Delta\zeta$ and local **GRD**-induced RSLC $\Delta\Gamma$. The global mean of each of these three adjustments is zero, so Eq. (42) is satisfied. In practice, using historical records, it is necessary to combine many tide-gauges in order to reduce the influence of unforced variability in $\tilde{\zeta}$.

The IB adjustment is fairly small and can be made accurately from atmospheric pressure records. Various methods are used to allow for the spatial pattern of $\Delta\zeta$, for example by calculating the mean over sets of gauges presumed to be representative of large regions (e.g., Jevrejeva et al. 2008), or by using spatial patterns of $\tilde{\eta}$ variation observed by satellite altimetry during its shorter period of availability (e.g., Church and White 2011). Because **glacial isostatic adjustment** (GIA) is the only part of GRD (including VLM) for which a global field is available, most estimates of GMSLR exclude all tide-gauges where GIA is not the only significant contribution to VLM (those affected by earthquakes, anthropogenic subsidence, sediment compactions, etc.). At the tide-gauges which are retained, we adjust for GIA-induced RSLC $\Delta\Gamma_{\mathrm{GIA}}(\mathbf{r})$ (e.g., Figure 3a of Tamisiea and Mitrovica 2011), estimated by combining solid-Earth models, the sea-level equation and reconstructed histories of deglaciation.

Alternatively, tide-gauge records may be corrected for VLM using vertical motion calculated from collocated GNSS (e.g., GPS) receivers. Effectively, this transforms RSLC to **geocentric sea-level change** $\Delta\eta = \Delta R + \Delta F$ (Eq. 24). Geoid adjustments must be applied to GNSS-corrected tide-gauge records just as for satellite altimetry, as described in the next paragraph.

Geocentric sea-level change $\Delta\eta (= \Delta\zeta - \Delta B + \Delta G$, Eq. 23) has been measured over most of the global ocean since the early 1990s by satellite radar *altimetry*, using instruments which are located in a terrestrial reference frame (equivalent to the reference ellipsoid), and measure their vertical distance from the sea surface. To study the contemporary causes of observed geocentric sea-level change we must subtract $\Delta G_{\mathrm{GIA}}(\mathbf{r})$, the effect of GIA on the geoid (e.g., Figure 3b of Tamisiea and Mitrovica 2011), from IB-corrected geocentric sea-level change, thus:

$$\Delta\eta + \Delta B - \Delta G_{\mathrm{GIA}} = \Delta\zeta + \Delta G_{\mathrm{NGIA}}, \tag{57}$$

where $\Delta G_{\mathrm{NGIA}} = \Delta G - \Delta G_{\mathrm{GIA}}$ is due to ongoing redistribution of water mass on the Earth's surface.

To convert **global-mean geocentric sea-level rise** $h_G = (1/A)\int \Delta\eta\,\mathrm{d}A$ to GMSLR h requires an adjustment for the global mean of ΔF, according to Eq. (47).

Although several processes can produce large local VLM, the only large global-mean effect is GIA. There is no contemporary GMSLR associated with GIA, so Eq. (49) gives $(1/A)\int \Delta F_{\mathrm{GIA}}\,\mathrm{d}A = (1/A)\int \Delta G_{\mathrm{GIA}}\,\mathrm{d}A \Rightarrow (1/A)\int \Delta G_{\mathrm{NGIA}}\,\mathrm{d}A = h + (1/A)\int \Delta F_{\mathrm{NGIA}}\,\mathrm{d}A$. Hence, the global mean of Eq. (57) becomes

$$h_G = h + \frac{1}{A}\int \Delta F_{\mathrm{GIA}}\,\mathrm{d}A + \frac{1}{A}\int \Delta F_{\mathrm{NGIA}}\,\mathrm{d}A, \tag{58}$$

recalling that the global means of ΔB and $\Delta\zeta$ are zero. In response to the shift of mass from the land (as ice) into the ocean since the Last Glacial Maximum, and the consequent mantle adjustment, the sea floor is subsiding on average, giving a trend in $(1/A)\int \Delta F_{\mathrm{GIA}}\,\mathrm{d}A$ of about -0.3 mm year^{-1} (Tamisiea and Mitrovica 2011). Thus, $h_G < h$ due to GIA. Contemporary changes in land ice cause elastic deformation of the sea floor. This gives a negative $(1/A)\int \Delta F_{\mathrm{NGIA}}\,\mathrm{d}A$ which reduces h_G by about 8% of the **barystatic sea-level rise** (Frederikse et al. 2017).

8 Deprecated Terms and Recommended Replacements

Deprecated term	Recommended replacement
Eustatic sea-level change	**Barystatic sea-level rise** or barystatic sea-level change for global-mean sea-level rise due to change in the mass of the ocean, but not its density
	Global-mean sea-level rise for the global mean of relative sea-level change, due to the change in the volume of the ocean
	Global-mean geocentric sea-level rise for the global mean of change in mean sea level relative to the terrestrial reference frame, due to the combined effects of change in the volume of the ocean and change in the level of the sea floor
Dynamic topography	**Ocean dynamic sea level** for mean sea level above the geoid due to ocean dynamics
	Ocean dynamic topography for ocean dynamic sea level estimated from ocean density
	Sea-level change due to mantle dynamic topography for GRD-induced relative sea-level change due to solid-Earth dynamics
Mean sea surface	**Mean sea level** (MSL)
Mean sea-level change or local sea-level change	**Relative sea-level change** (RSLC) or relative sea-level rise (RSLR) for the change in mean sea level relative to the land
	Geocentric sea-level change for the change in mean sea level relative to the terrestrial reference frame
Global sea-level change (GSLC)	**Gobal-mean sea-level rise** (GMSLR) or global-mean sea-level change (GMSLC) for the global mean of relative sea-level change, due to the change in the volume of the ocean
	Global-mean geocentric sea-level rise for the global-mean change in mean sea level relative to the terrestrial reference frame

Deprecated term	Recommended replacement
Extreme sea level	**Extreme sea level** for the occurrence of exceptionally high local sea surface due to short-term phenomena, or **extreme coastal water level** when considering coastal impacts.
	High-end sea-level change for projections or scenarios of very large RSLR or GMSLR
Sea-level change due to thermal expansion	**Thermosteric sea-level change** for contribution to relative sea-level change
	Global-mean thermosteric sea-level rise for contribution to global-mean sea-level change
Sea-level change due to oceanographic processes or steric plus dynamic sea-level change	**Sterodynamic sea-level change** for the change in relative sea-level due to change in ocean density and circulation
Sea-level fingerprint or static-equilibrium fingerprint	**Barystatic–GRD fingerprint** for the sum of the RSLC from GRD (elastic and geoid) and the barystatic sea-level rise due to the addition of a unit mass of water to the global ocean
Post-glacial rebound (PGR)	**Glacial isostatic adjustment** (GIA)
Mass effect on, mass term in, mass component of, or mass contribution to sea level or to sea-level change	**Barystatic sea-level rise** for the contribution to global-mean sea-level rise from the change of mass of the global ocean (associated with changes in mass of water and ice on land), as opposed to global-mean thermosteric sea-level rise
	Manometric sea-level change for the contribution to relative sea-level change due to change in the local mass of the ocean per unit area, as opposed to steric sea-level change
	GRD-induced relative sea-level change for the effects on relative sea level from geoid change and vertical land movement, as opposed to steric, ocean dynamic and barystatic sea-level change
Bottom pressure term in sea-level change	**Manometric sea-level change**

9 List of Defined Terms and Notations

This table gives the entry number or section (not the page number) in which each term is defined. In the PDF, each term is a hyperlink to the relevant text. The rows for which there is no entry number are included only to define notation.

	Above flotation	N19
	Altimetry	Section 7
A	Area of the global ocean	
	Asthenosphere	N21
	Astronomical tide	N6
p_a	Atmospheric pressure at the sea surface	
h_b	**Barystatic sea-level rise**	N19

ϕ	*Barystatic–GRD fingerprint*	N24
	Bathymetry	N4
	Bottom pressure	N18
	Bottom topography	N4
	Chandler wobble	N6
	Compaction	N21
	Contemporary GRD	N24
ρ	Density of water	
	Depth of the water column	N4
D	*Dynamic height*	N12
g	*Effective gravitational acceleration*	N5
	Ellipsoidal height	N1
	Equipotential surface	N5
	Eustatic sea-level change	N19
	Extreme coastal water level	N8
	Extreme sea level	N8
	Fetch	N10
	Free nutation	N6
	Geocentric latitude	N1
$\Delta\eta$	**Geocentric sea-level change**	N14
	Geodetic height	N1
	Geodetic latitude	N1
G	**Geoid**	N5
	Geoid height	N5
Φ	*Geopotential*	N5
	Geostrophy	N12
$\tilde{\mathbf{v}}_g$	*Geostrophic velocity*	N12
$\Delta\Gamma_{GIA}$	*GIA-induced relative sea-level change*	N23
	Glacial isostatic adjustment (GIA)	N23
	Global mean	Section 2.4
h_G	**Global-mean geocentric sea-level rise**	N27
h_R	*Global-mean relative sea-level change*	N26
h	**Global-mean sea-level rise (GMSLR)**	N26
h_θ	**Global-mean thermosteric sea-level rise**	N17
	Gravitational acceleration	N5
	GRD	N22
$\Delta\Gamma$	*GRD-induced relative sea-level change*	N22
	Greenwich meridian	N1
	Halosteric sea-level change ΔR_S	N16
	High-end	N8
	Horizontal	N5
	IB-corrected geocentric sea-level change	N14
	IB-corrected mean sea level	N7
	IB-corrected relative sea-level change	N15
	IB-corrected sea-surface height	N7
θ	In-situ temperature of ocean water	

B	**Inverse barometer (IB)**	N7
	Inverted barometer	N7
	Isostasy	N21
	Isostatic adjustment	N21
	Land ice	N19
	Land water storage	N19
	Latitude	N1
	Level of no motion	N12
	Liquid-water equivalent sea surface	N2
	Lithosphere	N21
	Local	Section 2.3
	Longitude	N1
ΔR_m	**Manometric sea-level change**	N18
	Mantle dynamic topography	N25
M	Mass of the global ocean	
η	**Mean sea level (MSL)**	N3
	Mean-tide	N6
	Neap tide	N6
	Nodal period	N6
	Ocean	Section 2.4
ζ	**Ocean dynamic sea level**	N11
$\Delta\zeta$	**Ocean dynamic sea-level change**	N13
	Ocean dynamic topography	N12
	Ocean GRD	N22
m	Ocean mass per unit area	
	Orthometric height	N5
	Permanent tide	N6
	Pole tide	N6
	Post-glacial rebound	N23
	Predicted tide	N6
	Prime meridian	N1
	Radiational tide	N6
	Reference ellipsoid	N1
	Regression	N15
ΔR	**Relative sea-level change (RSLC)**	N15
ρ_*	Representative density of ocean water	
S	Salinity of ocean water	
F	**Sea floor**	N4
$\tilde{\eta}$	**Sea surface**	N2
	Sea-level equation	N22
	Sea-level equivalent (SLE)	N19
	Sea-level fingerprint	N24
	Sea-surface height (SSH)	N2
	Sea-surface waves	N10
	Seismic sea wave	N10
	Self-attraction and loading (SAL)	N22

	Significant wave height	N10
	Significant wave period	N10
	Skew-surge height	N9
	Spring tide	N6
	State	Section 2.2
	Static-equilibrium fingerprint	N24
ΔR_ρ	**Steric sea-level change**	N16
ΔZ	**Sterodynamic sea-level change**	N20
	Storm surge	N9
	Storm tide	N6
σ	*Storm-surge height*	N9
	Subsidence	N21
	Surge residual	N9
	Swash	N9
	Swell wave	N10
	Terrestrial reference frame	N1
	Terrestrial water storage	N19
	Thermal expansion	N16
	Thermosteric sea-level change ΔR_θ	N16
H	*Thickness of the ocean*	N4
	Tidal currents	N6
	Tidal datum	N6
	Tidal height	N6
	Tide-free	N6
	Tide-gauge	N15
	Tides	N6
	Transgression	N15
	True polar wander	N1
	Tsunami	N10
	Vertical	N1
ΔF	**Vertical land movement (VLM)**	N21
V	Volume of the global ocean	
	Wave height	N10
	Wave period	N10
	Wave runup	N9
	Wave setup	N9
	Wind setup	N9
	Wind wave	N10
	Zero-tide	N6

Acknowledgements We thank Cathy Raphael from NOAA/GFDL for kindly drafting the figures, and John Krasting, Jianjun Yin, Sophie Nowicki, Angélique Melet, Carl Wunsch, Unnikrishnan, Chris Merchant and Déborah Idier for useful comments. We are grateful to Don Chambers and the other (anonymous) reviewer for their encouraging remarks and helpful suggestions for improvement. Rui Ponte acknowledges support from NASA Grant NNH16CT01C. John Church was partially supported by the Centre for Southern Hemisphere Oceans Research, a joint research centre between QNLM and CSIRO. Jonathan Gregory's work was supported by Grant NE/R000727/1 from the UK Natural Environment Research Council on

"Addressing the Grand Challenge of regional sea level change prediction". The Grand Challenge steering committee provided a forum for discussions during the preparation of this paper. We are grateful to Palanimuthu and colleagues for their careful typesetting of this complicated manuscript.

Appendix 1: No Resting Steady State Exists for a Realistic Ocean

A state of rest requires zero acceleration parallel to the surface, which must therefore be an equipotential. This condition is satisfied by the geoid because it is an equipotential surface by definition. However, zero acceleration at the surface is not a sufficient condition for the ocean to remain at rest. If there are any horizontal density gradients within the ocean, there will be pressure gradients beneath the horizontal surface, producing forces that will set the ocean into motion. So another necessary condition for zero ocean circulation is the absence of density gradients along horizontal surfaces, i.e., density is a function of depth only. This configuration is quite unlike the real state of the ocean.

Appendix 2: Why We Can Ignore Global Halosteric Sea-Level Change

When freshwater enters the ocean, such as from melting continental ice sheets, it adds to the ocean mass and in turn increases global-mean sea level (barystatic sea-level rise). Ocean salinity also changes due to the dilution of sea water, thus suggesting a role for a global halosteric sea-level change (Munk 2003; Levitus et al. 2005). However, the net effect on global-mean sea level is almost entirely barystatic since the global halosteric effect is negligible (Lowe and Gregory 2006). We can understand why this is so by recognizing that freshwater entering the ocean sees its salinity increase while the ambient sea water is itself freshened. These compensating salinity changes (which are often ignored, as by Munk 2003 and Levitus et al. 2005) have corresponding compensating sea-level changes, thus bringing the global halosteric effect to near zero. We demonstrate this effect in the following subsections, by considering a two-bucket thought experiment where one bucket holds freshwater (bucket-1) and the other holds sea water (bucket-2). We ask how the total water volume changes upon homogenizing the water in the two buckets, while conserving the masses of freshwater and salt. As we will see, the total volume of homogenized water is very nearly equal to the sum of the volume initially in the two separate buckets (to within 0.1%).

Conservation of Mass for Freshwater and Salt

Let the two buckets contain water of mass M_n, volume V_n, salinity S_n, and density ρ_n, $n = 1, 2$, and assume they have equal Conservative Temperature and equal pressure. Now homogenize the water from the two buckets into a single larger bucket, and assume no change in pressure nor any heat of mixing so that Conservative Temperature also remains unchanged. The total mass of freshwater and salt is unchanged upon homogenizing, so that

$$M = M_1 + M_2 \qquad M\,S = M_1\,S_1 + M_2\,S_2, \tag{59}$$

where M is the total mass and S is the salinity of the homogenized water. Return the homogenized water to the original buckets, placing the same mass M_1 back into the first bucket and mass M_2 into the second bucket.

Dependence of Density on Salinity

The dimensionless coefficients $\alpha \equiv \rho^{-1} \partial\rho/\partial\theta$ and $\beta \equiv \rho^{-1} \partial\rho/\partial S$, which are used to compute steric sea-level change (Eq. 31), measure the relative change in the in-situ density as a function of temperature and salinity. Because $\partial\rho/\partial\theta$ is generally negative, the volume of a given parcel of sea water increases as its temperature rises; this phenomenon is called thermal expansion. By analogy, since $\partial\rho/\partial S > 0$, the corresponding effect for salinity is sometimes called "haline contraction". This is a misleading analogy, because if the salinity has increased but the mass has not changed, some freshwater must have been replaced by salt, so the parcel is materially altered, unlike in the case of adding heat. If salt is added to the parcel but no mass is removed, the salinity, mass and volume of the parcel will *all* increase. The notion of "haline contraction" has led some previous authors to draw incorrect conclusions about the effect on sea level from adding freshwater to the ocean. We here aim to clarify this situation.

The change in the volume of water due to homogenization depends on the value of β. For the surface ocean, representative values are $\rho = 1028 \text{ kg m}^{-3}$ and $S = 0.035$, while for freshwater $\rho = \rho_\mathrm{f} = 1000 \text{ kg m}^{-3}$ and $S = 0$. Hence, a representative $\beta \approx (1/1000)(1028 - 1000)/(0.035 - 0) = 28/35 = 0.8$. This coefficient has a roughly 5% relative variation across the ocean, with most of that variation determined by temperature rather than salinity. (See Roquet et al. 2015, as well as Figure 1 in Griffies et al. 2014.) Since our concern is with salinity changes, we take β to be constant in the following.

Computing the Change in Total Volume

The change in total volume upon homogenization is the sum of the changes in the two buckets,

$$\delta V = \delta V_1 + \delta V_2. \tag{60}$$

Since the mass of water in the two buckets remains the same before and after homogenization, the volume in the two buckets is altered only due to changes in their respective densities

$$\delta\rho_n = \delta(M_n/V_n) = -(\rho_n/V_n)\,\delta V_n \Rightarrow \delta\rho_n/\rho_n = -\delta V_n/V_n, \tag{61}$$

i.e., the relative density increases as the relative volume decreases. Because the buckets have the same temperature in our experiment, relative density changes occur only through salinity changes, according to

$$\delta\rho_n/\rho_n = \beta\,\delta S_n = -\delta V_n/V_n, \tag{62}$$

in which case the change in total volume is

$$\delta V = \delta V_1 + \delta V_2 = -(V_1\,\beta\,\delta S_1 + V_2\,\beta\,\delta S_2). \tag{63}$$

Mass conservation for salt means that

$$\delta(M\,S) = \delta(M_1\,S_1) + \delta(M_2\,S_2) = 0. \tag{64}$$

Furthermore, since mass in the two buckets is unchanged, salt conservation leads to

$$M_1\,\delta S_1 + M_2\,\delta S_2 = 0, \tag{65}$$

so that salinity in one bucket rises while that in the other falls. Making use of this result in Eq. (63) leads to our desired expression for total volume change

$$\delta V = -\beta\,\delta S_1\,(V_1 - V_2\,M_1/M_2) = -\beta\,V_1\,\delta S_1\,(1 - \rho_1/\rho_2). \tag{66}$$

Connecting to Thickness Changes

Equation (66) provides an expression for the change in total volume upon homogenizing two buckets of water with equal Conservative Temperatures, equal pressures, but with differing salinities. To connect to sea level, assume an equal cross-sectional area, A, for the buckets, so that the volume of water is given by $V_n = A\,h_n$, where h_n is the thickness of the water in the bucket. Equation (66) then says that upon homogenization, the thickness of water changes by

$$\delta h = -\beta\,h_1\,\delta S_1\,(1 - \rho_1/\rho_2), \tag{67}$$

and that the total thickness of the homogenized water is given by

$$h_{\text{new}} = h_1 + h_2 + \delta h = h_2 + h_1\,[1 - \beta\,\delta S_1\,(1 - \rho_1/\rho_2)]. \tag{68}$$

As expected, we see that $\delta h = 0$ only when $\beta = 0$ or $\rho_1 = \rho_2$. The first is never true, and the second is not true in the general case of differing temperatures (in which case there are thermosteric changes ignored in our discussion).

An Ocean Example

To explore the oceanic implications of Eq. (68), assume bucket-1 initially has freshwater with density $\rho_1 = \rho_{\text{f}}$, whereas bucket-2 initially has sea water with density $\rho_2 = \rho_{\text{s}} = \rho_{\text{f}} + \rho'$. The salinity change for bucket-1 is $\delta S_1 = S$, since this bucket went from its original freshwater concentration to the homogenized sea water with salinity S. The halosteric-induced thickness change (Eq. 67) is thus given by

$$\delta h = -h_1\,\beta\,S\,(\rho'/\rho_{\text{s}}) < 0. \tag{69}$$

How large is this effect? For the case of an upper ocean with salt concentration $S = 0.035$, sea-water density $\rho_{\text{s}} = 1028\ \text{kg m}^{-3} \Rightarrow \rho' = 28\ \text{kg m}^{-3}$ and $\beta = 0.8$, we have

$$\delta h = -h_1 \times 0.8 \times 0.035 \times (28/1028) \approx -h_1 \times 7.6 \times 10^{-4}. \tag{70}$$

To within roughly 8 parts in 10^4, the change in thickness of the ocean column is nearly identical to the thickness of freshwater added to the ocean. For example, if we add one metre of freshwater into the upper ocean ($h_1 = 1$ m), then the change in sea level is equal to one metre minus the tiny amount 0.76 mm . Hence, as emphasized by Lowe and Gregory (2006), we can generally ignore the contribution to global-mean sea level from global halosteric effects.

Appendix 3: Bottom Pressure

The hydrostatic pressure at the ocean sea floor is commonly referred to as the ocean bottom pressure $\tilde{p}_b$, usually calculated as

$$\tilde{p}_b = \tilde{p}_a + g\tilde{m}, \tag{71}$$

where the first term is the atmospheric pressure at the liquid-water equivalent sea surface and the second term is the weight of the mass per unit area $\tilde{m}(\mathbf{r})$ of sea water, given by Eq. (26). This formula makes two approximations. First, hydrostatic pressure does not exactly equal the weight per unit area of the fluid above it because of the curvature of the Earth (Ambaum 2008). Second, g should appear within the vertical integral of density to obtain m (Eq. 26), because g depends on z. However, these approximations are entirely adequate for sea-level studies.

The difference in bottom pressure between two states

$$\Delta p_b = \Delta p_a + g\Delta m, \tag{72}$$

that is, the sum of the change in local atmospheric pressure and the change in the weight of the local ocean. Using Eqs. (26) and (25) to replace Δm,

$$\Delta p_b = \Delta p_a + g\rho_* \Delta H + g \int_F^\eta \Delta\rho(z)\,\mathrm{d}z, \tag{73}$$

where $H = \eta - F$ is the time-mean thickness of the ocean (Eq. 3). This form separates the change in pressure due to sea water into one term (the second) due to the change in the local thickness of the ocean, and another (the third) which is proportional to the local vertical-mean change in sea-water density.

References

Agarwal N, Jungclaus JH, Koehl A, Mechoso CR, Stammer D (2015) Additional contributions to CMIP5 regional sea level projections resulting from Greenland and Antarctic ice mass loss. Environ Res Lett. https://doi.org/10.1088/1748-9326/10/7/074008

Ambaum MHP (2008) General relationships between pressure, weight and mass of a hydrostatic fluid. Proc R Soc Lond 464:943–950. https://doi.org/10.1098/rspa.2007.0148

Chambers DP, Cazenave A, Champollion N, Dieng H, Llovel W, Forsberg R, von Schuckmann K, Wada Y (2017) Evaluation of the global mean sea level budget between 1993 and 2014. Surv Geophys 38:309. https://doi.org/10.1007/s10712-016-9381-3

Church JA, White NJ (2011) Sea-level rise from the late 19th to the early 21st century. Surv Geophys 32:585–602. https://doi.org/10.1007/s10712-011-9119-1

Church JA, Gregory JM, Huybrechts P, Kuhn M, Lambeck K, Nhuan MT, Qin D, Woodworth PL (2001) Changes in sea level. In: Houghton JT, Ding Y, Griggs DJ, Noguer M, van der Linden P, Dai X, Maskell K, Johnson CI (eds) Climate change 2001: the scientific basis. Contribution of working group I to the third assessment report of the intergovernmental panel on climate change. Cambridge University Press, Cambridge, pp 639–693

Church JA, White NJ, Konikow LF, Domingues CM, Cogley G, Rignot E, Gregory JM, Van den Broeke MR, Monaghan AJ, Velicogna I (2011) Revisiting the Earth's sea-level and energy budgets from 1961 to 2008. Geophys Res Lett 38:L18601. https://doi.org/10.1029/2011GL048794

Church JA, Clark PU, Cazenave A, Gregory JM, Jevrejeva S, Levermann A, Merrifield MA, Milne GA, Nerem RS, Nunn PD, Payne AJ, Pfeffer WT, Stammer D, Unnikrishnan AS (2013) Sea level change. In: Climate change 2013: the physical science basis. Contribution of working group I to the fifth assessment report of the intergovernmental panel on climate change. Cambridge University Press, Cambridge, United Kingdom, pp 1137–1216

Cogley JG (2012) Area of the ocean. Mar Geod 35:379–388. https://doi.org/10.1080/01490419.2012.709476

Farrell WE, Clark JA (1976) On postglacial sea level. Geophys J R Astr Soc 46:647–667. https://doi.org/10.1111/j.1365-246X.1976.tb01252.x

Frederikse T, Riva REM, King MA (2017) Ocean bottom deformation due to present-day mass redistribution and its impact on sea level observations. Geophys Res Lett. https://doi.org/10.1002/2017GL075419

Gomez N, Pollard D, Mitrovica JX, Huybers P, Clark PU (2012) Evolution of a coupled marine ice sheet-sea level model. J Geophys Res 117:F01013. https://doi.org/10.1029/2011JF002128

Gregory J, White N, Church J, Bierkens M, Box J, van den Broeke R, Cogley J, Fettweis X, Hanna E, Huybrechts P, Konikow L, Leclercq P, Marzeion B, Orelemans J, Tamisiea M, Wada Y, Wake L, van den Wal R (2013) Twentieth-century global-mean sea-level rise: is the whole greater than the sum of the parts? J Clim 26:4476–4499. https://doi.org/10.1175/JCLI-D-12-00319.1

Griffies SM, Greatbatch RJ (2012) Physical processes that impact the evolution of global mean sea level in ocean climate models. Ocean Model 51:37–72. https://doi.org/10.1016/j.ocemod.2012.04.003

Griffies SM, Yin J, Durack PJ, Goddard P, Bates S, Behrens E, Bentsen M, Bi D, Biastoch A, Böning CW, Bozec A, Cassou C, Chassignet E, Danabasoglu G, Danilov S, Domingues C, Drange H, Farneti R, Fernandez E, Greatbatch RJ, Holland DM, Ilicak M, Lu J, Marsland SJ, Mishra A, Large WG, Lorbacher K, Nurser AG, Salas y Mélia D, Palter JB, Samuels BL, Schröter J, Schwarzkopf FU, Sidorenko D, Treguier AM, Tseng Y, Tsujino H, Uotila P, Valcke S, Voldoire A, Wang Q, Winton M, Zhang Z (2014) An assessment of global and regional sea level for years 1993–2007 in a suite of interannual CORE-II simulations. Ocean Model 78:35–89. https://doi.org/10.1016/j.ocemod.2014.03.004

Griffies SM, Danabasoglu G, Durack PJ, Adcroft AJ, Balaji V, Böning CW, Chassignet EP, Curchitser E, Deshayes J, Drange H, Fox-Kemper B, Gleckler PJ, Gregory JM, Haak H, Hallberg RW, Heimbach P, Hewitt HT, Holland DM, Ilyina T, Jungclaus JH, Komuro Y, Krasting JP, Large WJ, Marsland SJ, Masina S, McDougall TJ, Nurser AJG, Orr JC, Pirani A, Qiao F, Stouffer RJ, Taylor KE, Treguier AM, Tsujino H, Uotila P, Valdivieso M, Wang Q, Winton M, Yeager SG (2016) OMIP contribution to CMIP6: experimental and diagnostic protocol for the physical component of the Ocean Model Intercomparison Project. Geosci Model Dev 9:3231–3296. https://doi.org/10.5194/gmd-9-3231-2016

Hinkel J, Le Cozannet G, Lowe J, Gregory J, Lambert E, McInnes K, Nicholls R, Church J, van der Pol T, van de Wal R (2019) Meeting user needs for sea-level information: a decision analysis perspective. Earth's Future. https://doi.org/10.1029/2018EF001071

Horsburgh KJ, Wilson C (2007) Tide-surge interaction and its role in the distribution of surge residuals in the North Sea. J Geophys Res 112:C08003. https://doi.org/10.1029/2006JC004033

IPCC (2014) Summary for policymakers. In: Field CB, Barros VR, Dokken DJ, Mach KJ, Mastrandrea MD, Bilir TE, Chatterjee M, Ebi KL, Estrada YO, Genova RC, Girma B, Kissel ES, Levy AN, MacCracken S, Mastrandrea PR, White LL (eds) Climate change 2014: impacts, adaptation, and vulnerability. Global and sectoral aspects. Contribution of working group II to the fifth assessment report of the intergovernmental panel on climate change. Cambridge University Press, Cambridge, Part A

Jevrejeva S, Moore JC, Grinsted A, Woodworth PL (2008) Recent global sea level acceleration started over 200 years ago? Geophys Res Lett 35:L08715. https://doi.org/10.1029/2008GL033611

Kopp ER, Horton RM, Little CM, Mitrovica JX, Oppenheimer M, Rasmussen DJ, Strauss BH, Tebaldi C (2014) Probabilistic 21st and 22nd century sea-level projections at a global network of tide-gauge sites. Earth's Future 2:383–406. https://doi.org/10.1002/2014EF000239

Kopp RE, Hay CC, Little CM, Mitrovica JX (2015) Geographic variability of sea-level change. Curr Clim Change Rep 1:192–204. https://doi.org/10.1007/s40641-015-0015-5

Landerer FW, Jungclaus JH, Marotzke J (2007) Regional dynamic and steric sea level change in response to the IPCC-A1B scenario. J Clim 37:296–312. https://doi.org/10.1175/JPO3013.1

Levitus S, Antonov J, Boyer T, Garcia H, Locarnini R (2005) Linear trends of zonally averaged thermosteric, halosteric, and total steric sea level for individual ocean basins and the World Ocean (1955–1959)-(1994–1998). Geophys Res Lett 32:L16601. https://doi.org/10.1029/2005GL023761

Lowe JA, Gregory JM (2006) Understanding projections of sea level rise in a Hadley centre coupled climate model. J Geophys Res Oceans. https://doi.org/10.1029/2005JC003421

Lowe JA, Woodworth PL, Knutson T, McDonald RE, McInnes KL, Woth K, von Storch H, Wolf J, Swail V, Bernier NB, Gulev S, Horsburgh KJ, Unnikrishnan AS, Hunter JR, Weisse R (2010) Past and future changes in extreme sea levels and waves. In: Woodworth PL, Aarup T, Wilson WS, Church JA (eds) Understanding sea-level rise and variability. Wiley, New York

Meehl GA, Stocker TF, Collins WD, Friedlingstein P, Gaye AT, Gregory JM, Kitoh A, Knutti R, Murphy JM, Noda A, Raper SCB, Watterson IG, Weaver AJ, Zhao Z (2007) Global climate projections. In: Solomon S, Qin D, Manning M, Chen Z, Marquis M, Averyt KB, Tignor M, Miller HL (eds) Climate

change 2007: the physical science basis. Contribution of working group I to the fourth assessment report of the intergovernmental panel on climate change. Cambridge University Press, Cambridge
Munk W (2003) Ocean freshening, sea level rising. Science 300:2041–2043
Pedreros R, Idier D, Muller H, Lecacheux S, Paris F, Yates-Michelin M, Dumas F, Pineau-Guillou L, Sénéchal N (2018) Relative contribution of wave setup to the storm surge: observations and modeling based analysis in open and protected environments (Truc Vert beach and Tubuai island). J Coastal Res 85:1046–1050. https://doi.org/10.2112/SI85-210.1
Pickering MD, Horsburgh KJ, Blundell JR, Hirschi JJM, Nicholls RJ, Verlaan M, Wells NC (2017) The impact of future sea-level rise on the global tides. Cont Shelf Res 142:50–68. https://doi.org/10.1016/j.csr.2017.02.004
Roquet F, Madec G, Brodeau L, Nycander J (2015) Defining a simplified yet realistic equation of state for seawater. J Phys Oceanogr 45:2464–2579. https://doi.org/10.1175/JPO-D-15-0080.1
Slangen ABA, Carson M, Katsman CA, van de Wal RSW, Köhl A, Vermeersen LLA, Stammer D (2014) Projecting twenty-first century regional sea-level changes. Clim Change 124:317–332. https://doi.org/10.1007/s10584-014-1080-9
Tamisiea ME, Mitrovica JX (2011) The moving boundaries of sea level change: understanding the origins of geographic variability. Oceanography 24:24–39. https://doi.org/10.5670/oceanog.2011.25
Tomczak M, Godfrey JS (1994) Regional oceanography: an introduction. Pergamon Press, Oxford
Vousdoukas MI, Mentaschi L, Voukouvalas E, Verlaan M, Jevrejeva S, Jackson LP, Feyen L (2018) Global probabilistic projections of extreme sea levels show intensification of coastal flood hazard. Nat Commun 9:2360. https://doi.org/10.1038/s41467-018-04692-w
Webb EL, Friess DA, Krauss KW, Cahoon DR, Guntenspergen GR, Phelps J (2013) A global standard for monitoring coastal wetland vulnerability to accelerated sea-level rise. Nat Clim Change 3:458–465. https://doi.org/10.1038/nclimate1756
Williams J, Horsburgh KJ, Williams JA, Proctor RNF (2016) Tide and skew surge independence: new insights for flood risk. Geophys Res Lett 43:6410–6417. https://doi.org/10.1002/2016GL069522
Williams J, Irazoqui Apecechea M, Saulter A, Horsburgh KJ (2018) Radiational tides: their double-counting in storm surge forecasts and contribution to the highest astronomical tide. Ocean Sci 14:1057–1068. https://doi.org/10.5194/os-14-1057-2018
Yin J, Griffies SM, Stouffer RJ (2010) Spatial variability of sea level rise in twenty-first century projections. J Clim 23:4585–4607. https://doi.org/10.1175/2010JCLI3533.1

Affiliations

Jonathan M. Gregory[1,2] · Stephen M. Griffies[3] · Chris W. Hughes[4] · Jason A. Lowe[2,14] · John A. Church[5] · Ichiro Fukumori[6] · Natalya Gomez[7] · Robert E. Kopp[8] · Felix Landerer[6] · Gonéri Le Cozannet[9] · Rui M. Ponte[10] · Detlef Stammer[11] · Mark E. Tamisiea[12] · Roderik S. W. van de Wal[13]

[1] National Centre for Atmospheric Science, University of Reading, Reading, UK

[2] Met Office Hadley Centre, Exeter, UK

[3] NOAA Geophysical Fluid Dynamics Laboratory and Princeton University Program in Atmospheric and Oceanic Sciences, Princeton, USA

[4] University of Liverpool and National Oceanography Centre, Liverpool, UK

[5] University of New South Wales, Sydney, Australia

[6] Jet Propulsion Laboratory, California Institute of Technology, Pasadena, USA

[7] McGill University, Montreal, Canada

[8] Rutgers University, New Brunswick, USA

[9] BRGM, French Geological Survey, Orléans, France

[10] Atmospheric and Environmental Research, Inc., Lexington, USA

[11] University of Hamburg, Hamburg, Germany

[12] Center for Space Research, University of Texas at Austin, Austin, USA

[13] Institute for Marine and Atmospheric Research Utrecht and Geosciences, Physical Geography, Utrecht University, Utrecht, The Netherlands

[14] Priestley Centre, University of Leeds, Leeds, UK

Surveys in Geophysics (2019) 40:1293–1317
https://doi.org/10.1007/s10712-019-09513-3

Coastal Sea Level and Related Fields from Existing Observing Systems

Marta Marcos[1,2] · Guy Wöppelmann[3] · Andrew Matthews[4] · Rui M. Ponte[5] · Florence Birol[6] · Fabrice Ardhuin[7] · Giovanni Coco[8] · Alvaro Santamaría-Gómez[9] · Valerie Ballu[3] · Laurent Testut[3] · Don Chambers[10] · Justin E. Stopa[11]

Received: 29 September 2018 / Accepted: 20 January 2019 / Published online: 5 February 2019

Abstract
We review the status of current sea-level observing systems with a focus on the coastal zone. Tide gauges are the major source of coastal sea-level observations monitoring most of the world coastlines, although with limited extent in Africa and part of South America. The longest tide gauge records, however, are unevenly distributed and mostly concentrated along the European and North American coasts. Tide gauges measure relative sea level but the monitoring of vertical land motion through high-precision GNSS, despite being essential to disentangle land and ocean contributions in tide gauge records, is only available in a limited number of stations. (25% of tide gauges have a GNSS station at less than 10 km.) Other data sources are new in situ observing systems fostered by recent progress in GNSS data processing (e.g., GPS reflectometry, GNSS-towed platforms) and coastal altimetry currently measuring sea level as close as 5 km from the coastline. Understanding observed coastal sea level also requires information on various contributing processes, and we provide an overview of some other relevant observing systems, including those on (offshore and coastal) wind waves and water density and mass changes.

Keywords Sea-level observations · Tide gauges · Coastal altimetry · GNSS · Wind waves · Ocean bottom pressure · Hydrography

1 Introduction

Measurements of sea level at the coast have long been required for several purposes, such as for the definition of a reference level for national height systems (e.g., Wöppelmann et al. 2014) or for harbour operations and navigation, besides the scientific motivation to understand the changes in sea level and their forcing mechanisms. Coastal sea-level monitoring is nowadays becoming increasingly important as it is a key component of operational oceanographic services aimed at ensuring harbour operability and safety and at generating accurate hazard forecasting and reliable flood or tsunami

✉ Marta Marcos
marta.marcos@uib.es

Extended author information available on the last page of the article

warning systems. With sea-level rise in response to anthropogenic global warming being one of the major threats to the coastal zones, sea-level observations are also essential to quantify the coastal response to the different forcings and thus to determine the potential impacts of future sea-level rise on coastal populations, ecosystems and assets.

Coastal sea level is driven by several physical processes acting at many timescales, from seconds (including the effect of wind waves) to millennia (for a review of the most relevant processes, see Woodworth et al., this issue). Understanding this wide range of variability in sea level, therefore, requires considerable information, not only on the amplitude and frequency of coastal sea-level variations, but also on the characteristics of the individual contributors as well as on their possible interactions. In this sense, coastal sea-level observations can be seen as one component of a multi-platform observing system aimed at accurately monitoring the physical processes taking place in the oceans.

Observing systems for coastal sea level and for the various sea-level contributors are addressed in this paper. Among these contributors, wind waves play an important role in sea level at the coast (for a full discussion, see Dodet et al., this issue), either directly, or indirectly through their influence on the wind stress and storm surge (e.g., Mastenbroek et al. 1993; Pineau-Guillou et al. 2018), and their role in the morphodynamic evolution of the nearshore (Coco et al. 2014; Masselink et al. 2016). Over the ocean shelves and along the coasts, ocean mass variations, reflected in ocean bottom pressure changes, are one of the dominant components of sea-level variability at time scales between hours and weeks. These barotropic processes can be forced by either local or remote atmospheric pressure and wind variations, including travelling signals over the shelves or from the deep ocean. Unlike over shallow waters, the major contributor to sea-level changes in the open ocean, from seasonal to decadal timescales, is steric (density-driven) sea level (Meyssignac et al. 2017). Steric sea level in the deep ocean is also relevant to the coastal zone, as these signals can propagate towards shallow waters through various mechanisms (Calafat et al. 2018; Hughes et al., this issue). These mechanisms of how changes in coastal-sea level relate to steric changes on the continental slope and in the open ocean still remain poorly understood. Thus, hydrographic measurements, including those near coastal areas, are also important for the understanding of coastal sea-level variability. Such data, together with other ancillary observations (e.g., surface meteorology), through direct analysis or ingestion in assimilation systems, can significantly inform our ability to simulate and predict coastal sea level.

The aim of this work is to provide an overview of the current sea-level observing systems focusing on the coastal zone, as well as other complementary data sets that provide insight into some of the physical processes that drive sea-level variability. In Sect. 2, we first describe the present status of the global tide gauge network and the data availability. We underscore the need of a continuous monitoring of vertical land motion at tide gauge stations and highlight its relevance for the complementarity between tide gauges, space geodetic techniques and coastal satellite altimetry, forming an integrated coastal sea-level observing system. Other emerging sea-level observing platforms that overcome some of the limitations of tide gauges are also described in Sect. 3. In Sect. 4, we describe the capabilities of wind waves observing systems, whose effects at the coast are generally not captured by tide gauges. Sections 5 and 6 address ocean bottom pressure and hydrographic measurements, as observations needed to understand two major contributors to sea-level variability.

2 Coastal Sea-Level Observations: Tide Gauges and Satellite Altimetry

Tide gauges are the primary source of coastal sea-level observations, providing point-wise measurements of relative mean sea level and extreme sea levels (Intergovernmental Oceanographic Commission 1985). Initially designed for maritime navigation purposes, some of the oldest tide gauge records date back to the eighteenth century (e.g., Woodworth and Blackman 2002; Wöppelmann et al. 2006). These earliest sea-level observations were measured with tide poles and registered the time and height of tidal high and low waters (e.g., Woodworth and Blackman 2002). Since the nineteenth century, stilling well floating gauges have become the most used technology and still represent the majority of the available records (Pugh and Woodworth 2014), while originally recording sea-level oscillations in tidal charts, during the twentieth century they have been upgraded to provide digital storage and transmission of data. New tidal stations tend to use radar gauges that measure the distance above the sea surface by analysing the time-of-flight of an electromagnetic reflected pulse. This type of gauge is nowadays preferred since it is relatively cheap, easy to install and able to measure at high frequencies with the required accuracy and long-term stability (Martín Míguez et al. 2008).

Tide gauges measure relative sea level with respect to the land upon which they are grounded (Fig. 1). Thus, to ensure continuity of the sea-level record, tide gauge measurements must refer to a properly defined datum, generally a fixed point on land referred to as tide gauge benchmark. Continuity can be achieved by systematically measuring the stability of the tide gauge benchmark through high-precision levelling with nearby land points

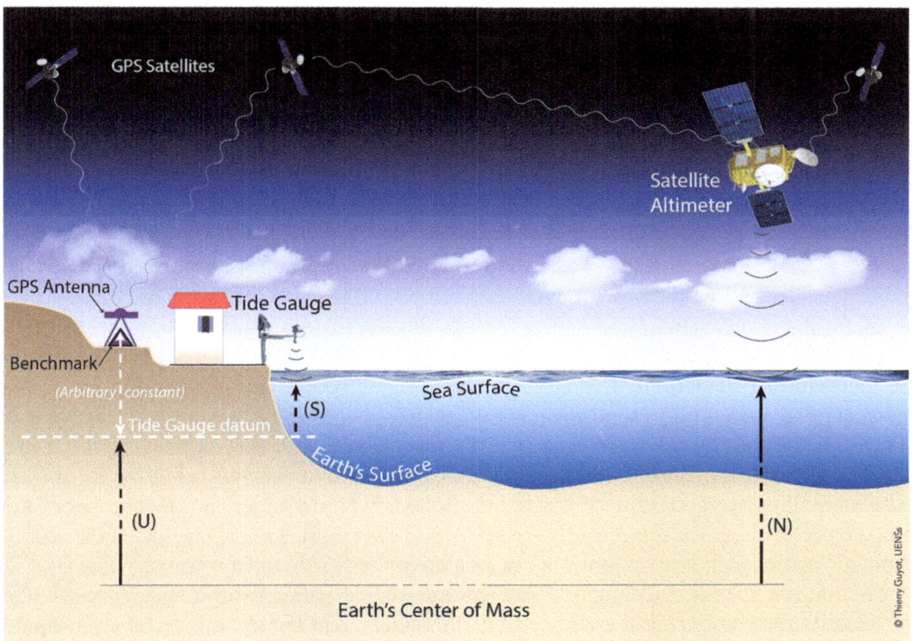

Fig. 1 Sketch showing basic observational quantities and techniques associated with sea-level measurement discussed in this article

that are, ideally, tied to the corresponding national geodetic network. In addition, neither the height of the benchmarks nor the sea level is constant but changes at different spatial and timescales; therefore, precise estimates of the long-term vertical land motion are necessary in order to disentangle the land and ocean contributions to sea-level change in tide gauge records.

Currently, space geodetic techniques provide the most accurate way to measure vertical land motion (VLM) at tide gauge benchmarks. Among the Global Navigation Satellite Systems (GNSS), the most common is the global positioning system (GPS), a cost-effective, easy to install and maintain and high-performance observing system (Fig. 1). Wöppelmann et al. (2007) published the first global-scale GPS vertical velocity estimates focused on the impact of VLM at tide gauges a decade ago and, since then, GPS estimates of VLM have been progressively incorporated into sea-level studies (Wöppelmann and Marcos 2016). VLM stems from different sources, either anthropogenic (e.g., ground water extraction) or natural (e.g., glacial isostatic adjustment—GIA), and over multi-decadal to centennial timescales, they may display comparable values to those of the climate-related contributions to sea-level change.

Presently, the two biggest limitations of GPS-derived VLM corrections for global mean sea level are the accuracy of the reference frame on which they rely (Santamaría-Gómez et al. 2017) and the shorter length of the GPS series compared to that of the tide gauges. Under the assumption that VLM at the tide gauge is constant, GPS VLM corrections reach an accuracy one order of magnitude smaller than sea-level trends from climate processes and therefore allow the reliable estimation of absolute sea-level changes wherever both measurements are available (Wöppelmann and Marcos 2016). In contrast, limited knowledge of VLM at a tide gauge site can seriously bias the detection of long-term climate signals and hampers the assessment of climate impacts associated with long-term sea-level rise. The international program Global Sea-Level Observing System (GLOSS, www.gloss-sealevel.org), in recognition of this need, recommends the installation of GNSS stations co-located with tide gauges.

Sea-level records from tide gauges are stored in and distributed by international databases. The most extensive data bank of long-term mean sea-level changes from tide gauges is the Permanent Service for Mean Sea Level (PSMSL, psmsl.org), hosted by the National Oceanography Centre in Liverpool and founded in 1933. PSMSL distributes monthly mean sea-level records compiled from several national and subnational agencies worldwide (Holgate et al. 2013) and currently hosts more than 2000 tide gauge stations, of which 1023 are active (defined as those with data supplied to PSMSL in 2013 or later) (Fig. 2). To be useful for climate studies, sea-level records must refer to a consistent datum; these are termed as Revised Local Reference (RLR) in the PSMSL data set and represent 64% of the total number of stations. Despite the present-day global picture mapped in Fig. 2 that shows a good spatial tide gauge coverage of the world coastlines, this has not always been the case in the past decades and century. Only a small subset of 89 tide gauge records span more than 100 years (Fig. 3), and these stations are mainly concentrated along the historically more developed coastlines, mostly in Europe and North America. The number of tide gauge records increases significantly since the mid-twentieth century (Holgate et al. 2013), although, again, with most stations being located in the Northern Hemisphere (Fig. 3).

The uneven spatial and temporal distribution of tide gauge records and, in particular, the scarcity of data during the early twentieth century and before, are factors that hinder the quantification and understanding of past regional and global long-term mean sea-level changes and their driving mechanisms (Dangendorf et al. 2017). Many efforts have therefore been devoted to the discovery, recovery and quality control of historical archived

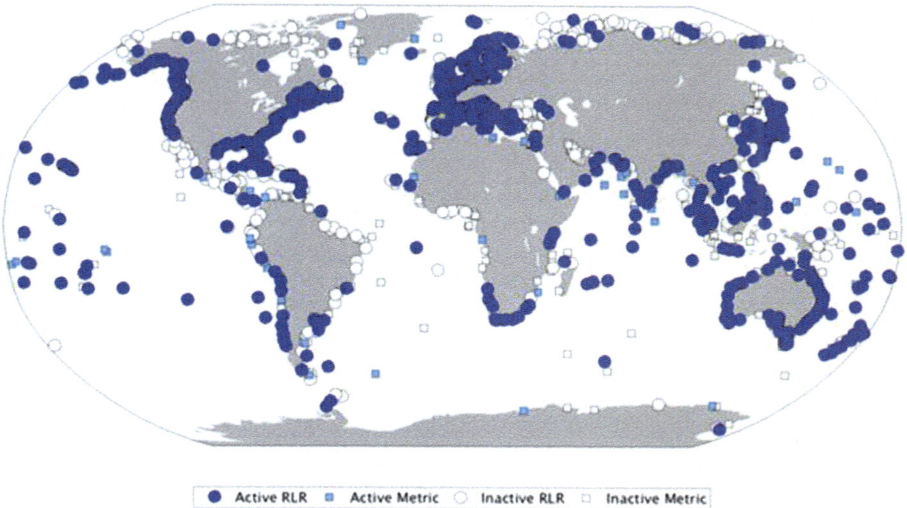

Fig. 2 Tide gauge stations in the PSMSL database. Active stations (in blue) are defined as those with data supplied to PSMSL in 2013 or later. Stations with historical levelling information are identified as Revised Local Reference (RLR)

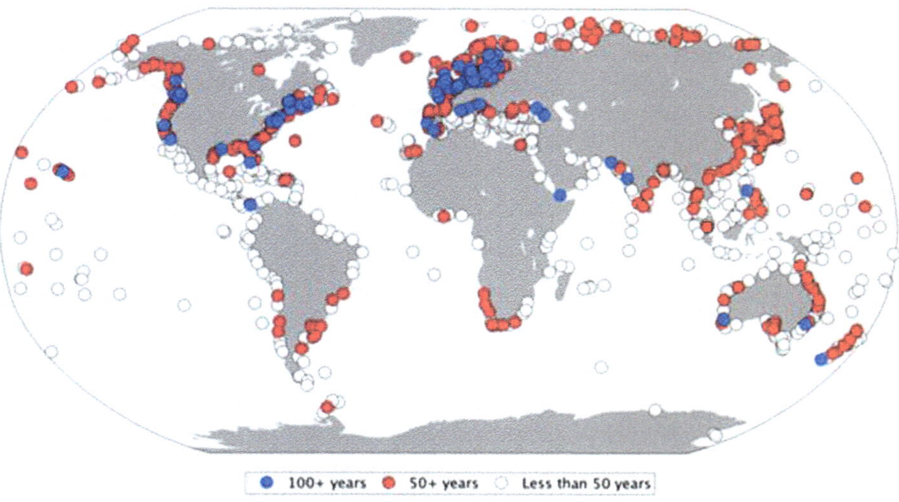

Fig. 3 RLR tide gauge records longer than 100 (blue) and 50 (red) years, not accounting for data gaps

sea-level measurements (Bradshaw et al. 2015; Hogarth 2014). These so-called exercises of data archaeology have successfully recovered sea-level information at sites as remote as the Kerguelen Islands (Testut et al. 2006) or the Falklands (Woodworth et al. 2010) and as far back in time as the nineteenth century (Talke et al. 2018; Wöppelmann et al. 2014; Marcos et al. 2011). Tide gauge data archaeology has been a useful tool to recover sea-level measurements valuable for climate studies, given the potential to expand the databases during periods and in places where no other observations exist.

Another major factor that hampers the understanding of contemporary sea-level changes is the limited knowledge of VLM at tide gauges during the last century. Before the maturity of the GNSS observations, the only VLM being accounted for in sea-level studies was GIA, as it can be modelled with prescribed ice history and solid Earth properties (e.g., mantle viscosity). With the development of high-precision GNSS, VLM is nowadays estimated from observations. Global GPS velocity fields are routinely computed and distributed by a number of research institutions (International GNSS Service, Jet Propulsion Laboratory, University of Nevada, University of La Rochelle). Among these, only the French SONEL (Système d'Observations du Niveau des Eaux Littorales) data centre, hosted at the University of La Rochelle, provides GPS observations and velocity estimates focused on the coastal areas and tide gauge stations, thus being closely linked to PSMSL and forming an integrated observing system within the GLOSS program. Unfortunately, and despite the GLOSS recommendations, only a limited number of tide gauges are co-located or tied to a nearby GNSS station (Fig. 4). In particular, in the PSMSL database only 394 RLR stations are within a 10-km distance from a GNSS station and, among these, only for 102 stations the levelling information between the two datums is available, which is a serious limitation for some applications such as studies on the ocean dynamic topography (Woodworth et al. 2015; Andersen et al. 2018). The list of RLR PSMSL stations with ties to GNSS are available at https://psmsl.org/data/obtaining/ellipsoidal_links.php, including the links to the tide gauge on PSMSL and GNSS on SONEL.

Coastal mean sea level can also be computed from observations available in other data portals. These include the European Copernicus Marine Environment Monitoring Service (CMEMS, http://marine.copernicus.eu/), the University of Hawaii Sea-Level Center (UHSLC, https://uhslc.soest.hawaii.edu/) and numerous national data services. For long-term sea-level studies, they provide mostly data that are also available in PSMSL. In addition, some of them distribute high-frequency (hourly and higher) sea-level measurements required for the study of tides and extremes and/or real-time measurements needed for

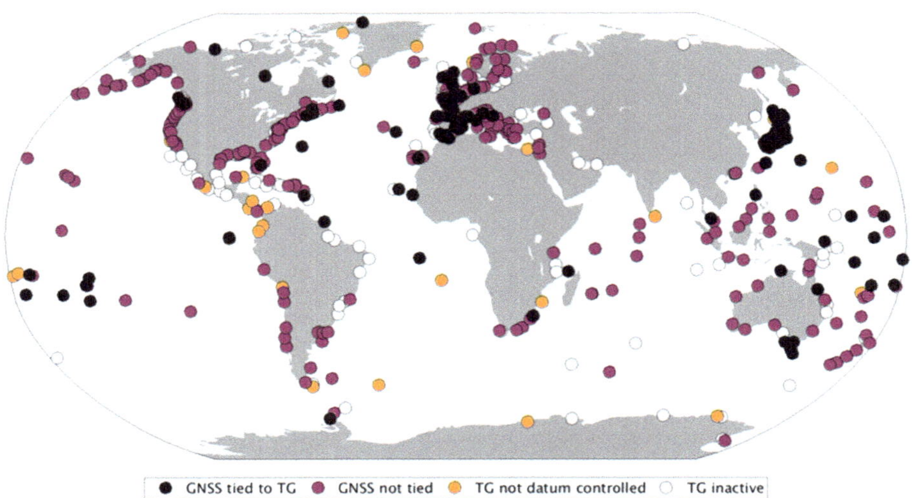

Fig. 4 GNSS stations with (coloured) and without (blank) a tide gauge within 10 km, according to PSMSL and SONEL databases [data accessed on 3 September 2018]. Black dots indicate RLR stations where GNSS and tide gauge datum are tied; purple dots indicate otherwise. Orange stations have no information about the tide gauge datum continuity (metric stations)

purposes such as operational oceanographic services or tsunami monitoring and warning systems. The Flanders Marine Institute (VLIZ, www.vliz.be/en) hosts the GLOSS sea-level monitoring facility for real-time data. Of a total of 993 tide gauge stations currently hosted and distributed by VLIZ (Fig. 5), 856 are active (defined here as those stations that have supplied data in 2018). The UHSLC hosts two subsets of high-frequency sea-level observations: one termed as fast delivery for operational purposes and another one of research quality in which the same data have undergone a quality control process. The Global Extreme Sea-Level Analysis initiative (GESLA, www.gesla.org) extends the UHSLC high-frequency sea-level data set unifying and assembling delayed-mode observations compiled from national and subnational agencies. The GESLA data set is presently the most complete collection of high-frequency sea-level observations, with 1355 tide gauge records (Woodworth et al. 2017).

In addition to the tide gauge monitoring, sea-level variations are also continuously measured by high-precision satellite altimetry with quasi-global coverage since 1992 (Fig. 1). The constellation of altimetry missions over the last 25 years will be continued with operational missions in the future (see Vignudelli et al., this issue). Near coastlines, the sea-level data retrieval and interpretation from altimetry measurements become particularly complex. First, the radar echo interacts with the surrounding land and its signal becomes very difficult to analyse. But another important limitations come from the geophysical altimetry corrections which might become inaccurate or incorrect in coastal areas. However, in the last decade there have been important advances that have extended the capabilities of satellite altimetry for the observation of coastal sea level: great progress has been made in altimeter instruments (CryoSat-2, AltiKA, Sentinel-3A&B) and also in the processing algorithms and products (Dinardo et al. 2017; Vignudelli et al., this issue, for more details). Although there is still a gap of information in a coastal band a few kilometres wide, this is continuously reduced thanks to the efforts invested by the altimetry community. Nowadays, sea-level data derived from standard LRM satellite altimetry are available generally up to 5-10 km from the coastline, much closer than only a few years

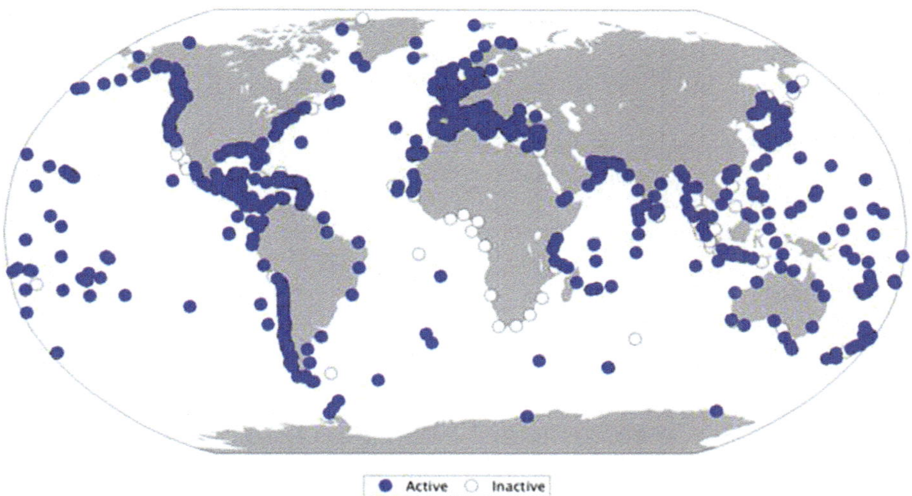

Fig. 5 Tide gauge stations providing real-time sea-level observations to VLIZ data centre. Active stations are defined as having contributed data in 2018

ago (Birol et al. 2016). From Dinardo et al. (2018), with the new synthetic aperture radar (SAR) mode of Cryosat-2, land contamination begins to affect sea level measurements only at 2 km from the coast. Thus, altimetry data are now providing very valuable information for coastal sea-level studies (Cipollini et al. 2017), and it is expected that it will become an additional source of long-term sea-level observations, which will be especially relevant in coastal zones where in situ data are inexistent or scarce.

Tide gauges and satellite altimetry have different spatial and temporal sampling. Radar altimeters measure sea level along the satellite ground tracks with sampling rates between 1 Hz (corresponding to every 6 km) up to 20Hz, and with a typical distance between the ground tracks of 50–300 km (depending on the number of satellites in the altimeter constellation). Several projects are currently generating data at a higher rate (corresponding to along-track distances of 175–350 m) with dedicated algorithms. The revisiting time of observations is a few days. Although not (yet) available up to the coastline, altimeter data offer a nearly global regular spatial sampling from the deep ocean to part of continental shelves (sometimes a large part), and thus a regional view of ocean dynamics. In contrast, tide gauges measure sea level every few seconds or minutes but only at a single coastal point, often at relatively sparse locations. The two data sets are therefore complementary and often integrated to maximize the information they provide (Fig. 1).

One major difference between the two data sets is the geodetic reference frame to which they are related. Tide gauges provide relative sea level while satellite altimetry measures 'absolute' sea-level variations with respect to a reference ellipsoid. Levelling of the tide gauge benchmark by means of geodetic methods is thus necessary if altimetry and tide gauge absolute sea levels are to be compared.

As a final remark, it is worth mentioning that relative comparisons between satellite altimeter and tide gauge observations are essential to evaluate the long-term stability of satellite altimetry. They are also systematically used to evaluate and validate new altimeter missions, data processing algorithms and products. In that sense, both types of sea-level observations can again be considered as two components of the same global observing system.

3 Other Sea-Level Monitoring Platforms

In addition to extensively used tide gauge and altimetric observations, coastal sea level is also monitored by emerging GNSS-based methods. These observing systems have benefited from progress in GNSS data processing. In particular, the development of GNSS Precise Point Positioning in kinematic mode with integer ambiguity fixing allows for centimetre accuracy (Laurichesse et al. 2009; Fund et al. 2013) without the need of a reference station. Some of these new systems are reviewed here. They provide complementary measurements, often designed for particular purposes and locations.

Taking advantage of GNSS co-location with tide gauges, GNSS radio signals reflected from the sea surface have been used recently to estimate coastal mean sea level, with daily mean differences of a few cm with respect to conventional tide gauges (Larson et al. 2013). The GNSS reflectometry technique provides an alternative coastal sea-level observing system with important advantages: coastal mean sea level is measured directly in a geocentric frame consistent with satellite altimetry; it does not require in situ calibration; the vertical tie between the GNSS antenna and a nearby tide gauge can be done remotely and continuously, i.e. it allows monitoring the stability of the tide gauge zero (Santamaría-Gómez and Watson 2017). With the new GNSS constellations (e.g., Galileo, Beidou) and the new and more precise signals (e.g., AltBOC, Fantino et al. 2008), this technique will improve precision and sampling rates, maximizing the benefit of co-location with tide gauges.

Another example is the use of GNSS, in particular GPS, on floating devices that emerged with the birth of precise satellite altimetry and the subsequent need for in situ data calibration. These data provided estimates of the absolute bias of the altimetry system, which is critical to monitor its long-term stability and assess sea-level trends. First GNSS buoys were developed for the absolute calibration of TOPEX/Poseidon (Hein et al. 1990; Rocken et al. 1990; Born et al. 1994). Since then, many different designs have been proposed to ensure a centimetric sea-level height measurement and reduce the impact of the inherent limitation of the system (Fig. 6), such as the ease and duration of deployment, the quantification of the height of the GNSS antenna phase centre above the water line and the tilt of the antenna from vertical. The results from an intercomparison of different GNSS buoy designs carried out at Aix Island (west coast of France) in 2012 showed that these devices are able to measure the absolute sea-level height with cm-level accuracy, thus being comparable to the precision of the reference radar tide gauge (André et al. 2013). GNSS buoys are now routinely used in dedicated satellite altimetry calibration sites such as Corsica Island in the Mediterranean Sea (Bonnefond et al. 2003a), Bass Strait in southern Australia (Watson et al. 2003) and now the Harvest Platform in the US Pacific coast (Haines et al. 2017). They are also used for tide gauge

Fig. 6 Illustration of four different GNSS buoy designs. Top left and right are, respectively, buoys designed at DT-INSU and IPGP (André et al. 2013). Lower left is a new light buoy design by DT-INSU based on the blanket concept to closely follow the water surface. Lower right buoy is the buoy used at Bass Strait (Australia) for altimetry calibration studies (Watson et al. 2008)

error characterization and calibration (Watson et al. 2008; Martín Míguez et al. 2012; André et al. 2013) and vertical sea floor height monitoring (Ballu et al. 2010).

Rather than pointwise measurements, mapping spatial variations of sea surface height in coastal areas brings invaluable information on the local geoid as well as for hydrodynamic processes. These variations cannot be properly apprehended by tide gauges or GNSS buoys, nor by satellite altimetry due to the proximity to land and limited spatial and temporal sampling. Sea surface height mapping has been carried out so far using GNSS equipped boats or towed platforms to retrieve local geoids (Bouin et al. 2009a). Such efforts have been used, for instance, in calibration/validation altimetry studies, both to get the geoid height difference between the reference tide gauge and the nearby satellite track and to increase the quality of the altimetry processing by better accounting for along and across-track gradients (Bonnefond et al. 2003b). A major issue for these measurements carried while moving is the monitoring of the GNSS antenna air draft (elevation difference between the above water GNSS antenna and the water level), which can vary with the load or speed of the measuring platform (Bouin et al. 2009b; Foster et al. 2009; Reinking et al. 2012). To overcome this limitation, a new measurement system based on a towed blanket has been proposed, which ensures a perfect coupling between the floating device and the sea surface and therefore a constant GNSS antenna height above water. The device is a floating blanket made of foam boards assembled with marine fabrics; the GNSS antenna is mounted on the blanket using a tripod, and its verticality while in motion is achieved using a gimbal system (see Fig. 7). A number of tests of this design have been carried out under various

Fig. 7 Illustration of moving GNSS platform for sea surface height mapping (towed blanket (Calzas et al. 2014), wave glider (Penna et al. 2018), Catamaran (Bonnefond et al. 2003b) and AUV-PAMELi (Coulombier et al. 2018)

conditions (Bangladesh, Aix Island and Corsica in France, Kerguelen) with successful results (Calzas et al. 2014; Durand et al. 2017).

Another alternative system to map spatial variations in sea surface height arises with the development of autonomous surface vehicles (ASV). For example, Penna et al. (2018) used a self-propelled Wave Glider (built by Liquid Robotics) equipped with a GNSS recording at 5 Hz to cover a distance of 600 km in 13 days with centimetric precision. This system proves its efficiency for offshore areas; however, with over 6 m of water draft and manoeuvrability highly dependent on weather conditions, it is not suitable for shallow coastal waters and areas with heavy maritime traffic. In contrast, the University of La Rochelle and DT_INSU (Division Technique de l'Institut National des Sciences de l'Univers) are currently developing a measurement system, named PAMELi (Plateforme Autonome Multicapteur pour l'Exploration du Littoral, Ballu et al. 2017), integrating a continuous air-draft quantification to be installed on a C-CAT3 built by ASV Global company (https://www.asvglobal.com/product/c-cat-3). Unlike the Wave Glider, this system can also measure sea surface heights in shallow waters and should be suitable for zones with significant maritime traffic thanks to its remotely operating capabilities that include real-time camera viewing. The interest of such systems compared to the towed blanket is both its compactness/manoeuvrability and its ability to be used as a multi-sensor platform for an integrated study of the dynamics of coastal waters. For instance, the PAMELi platform will be able to continuously monitor en-route temperature, salinity, turbidity, chlorophyll, bathymetry and atmospheric parameters in addition to mapping sea surface height (Coulombier et al. 2018). Such mobile devices will be key for in situ calibration of future wide-swath satellite altimeters and validation of coastal hydrodynamical models. Integrated systems will contribute to better monitorization and interpretation of sea surface height variations at short temporal and spatial scales.

4 Wind Wave Observations

Direct wave effects on coastal sea level exist at all timescales, from a mean sea-level response, known as wave set-up, to the swash and possible overtopping lasting only a few seconds (Dodet et al., this issue). Intermediate timescales are dominated by infragravity waves with typical periods of 30–300 s. Due to the range of spatio-temporal scales, the observational requirements for accurately monitoring these processes are different. Furthermore, all these effects of waves on the sea level are concentrated in the "surf zone" where the alongshore variability can be very large as the sea state is strongly influenced by the bathymetry (Munk and Traylor 1947, Magne et al. 2007), bottom types (e.g., Ardhuin et al. 2002; Lowe et al. 2007; Monismith et al. 2015) and currents (e.g., Battjes 1982; Ardhuin et al. 2017). As a result, only specific surf zone locations have been equipped with routine continuous measurements (including wave height, period and direction), as it is today impossible to monitor the strong alongshore variability of the wave impacts.

Surf zone processes have been the topic of targeted instrument deployments (e.g., Guza and Thornton 1981; Elgar et al. 1997; Senechal et al. 2011a). Such experiments have confirmed that the wave set-up is caused by the cross-shore convergence of the wave-induced momentum flux, known as the radiation stress (e.g., Raubenheimer et al. 2001). This balance is also perturbed by bottom friction in the shallowest regions (Apotsos et al. 2007). Wave set-up, just like wave transformation in general, is strongly influenced by the nearshore underwater bathymetry (Stephens et al. 2011), which is problematic to measure directly (e.g., Dugan et al. 2001) or indirectly (e.g., Holman et al. 2013). Despite their importance, measurements of underwater bathymetry in the surf zone remain a challenge and at present such data are only available at few sites and for short temporal intervals obtained through in situ surveys. The development of remote sensing techniques from high-resolution radar or optical satellite imagery (e.g., Pleskachevsky et al. 2011) now benefits from faster revisits using Landsat 8 and Sentinels 1 and 2 (Hedley et al. 2012), but bathymetric changes during storms, which are larger and most relevant, are still inaccessible.

The "infragravity" oscillations of the sea level at the scale of a few minutes are associated with a more complex balance with a transfer of energy from the wind waves that is influenced by the varying water depth (see Bertin et al. 2018 for a review). Infragravity (IG) wave heights are generally proportional to the wind wave height but that proportionality factor varies considerably with the depth profile, with larger proportionality factors on steep slopes (Sheremet et al. 2014). Measurements of IG waves have been relatively few so far. Right at the shoreline, the large variation of the cross-shore IG wave height is generally poorly captured by a sparse array of pressure gauges and current meters (e.g., Raubenheimer 2002). Offshore pressure gauges can provide a region-integrated measurement of IG waves at the coast as they propagate offshore (e.g., Rawat et al. 2014; Neale et al. 2015). The other extreme is given by high-frequency tide gauge data, usually from harbours. These are purely local measurements in which the IG frequency band can be strongly amplified into seiches by harbour resonances (e.g., Okihiro et al. 1993; Ardhuin et al. 2010). All these measurements only offer a few proxies of the IG amplitudes on the open coast and just at a few selected locations.

Other observation systems of wind waves include, in daylight, routine monitoring techniques based on video imagery that have been perfected over the past 30 years (e.g., Holman and Stanley 2007). As video instrumentation, data storage and processing time are becoming cheaper, video records are now included in many coastal monitoring programs (e.g., http://ci.wrl.unsw.edu.au/ and Fig. 8) and used to study wave run-up, also during extreme events (Senechal et al. 2011b). Recent experiments with Lidar are an interesting alternative for all-weather surveys of beach transects (Fiedler et al. 2015). Other sparse surveying strategies have also used photography and high-water marks (Cariolet and Suanez 2013). Such measurements have provided extensive data sets that form the basis of empirical formulas linking, mean, IG and extreme sea levels to "offshore" wave parameters, generally the significant wave height, mean period and beach slope (Stockdon et al. 2006).

Whatever the wave transformations and impacts along the coast, there is an evident need for observations on offshore sea state parameters that trigger those effects. The longest time series are available for wave heights from in situ measurements using voluntary observing ships (Gulev et al. 2003) and buoys (Fig. 9) and from satellite altimeters (Queffeulou 2013). Conversely, the routine measurement of wave periods is limited to the few available buoys or platforms (Fig. 10). To overcome this limitation, proxies for a mean wave period have been proposed using radar backscatter and wave heights from altimeters (e.g., Gommenginger et al. 2003; Quilfen et al. 2004). It should be still investigated how well these proxies perform for estimating extreme coastal sea levels. In the near future, it is expected that forthcoming satellites will bring a direct measurement of the dominant period in most sea state. This is the case of the SWIM instrument on CFOSAT (Hauser et al. 2017), to be launched in October 2018. The proposed SKIM satellite would go a step further in resolving the dominant waves even in enclosed seas (Ardhuin et al. 2018). Still, even with a 300-km wide-swath SKIM would have a revisit time of 4 days at mid-latitudes that is insufficient to resolve the fast timescale of storms. This large revisit time, compared to the typical

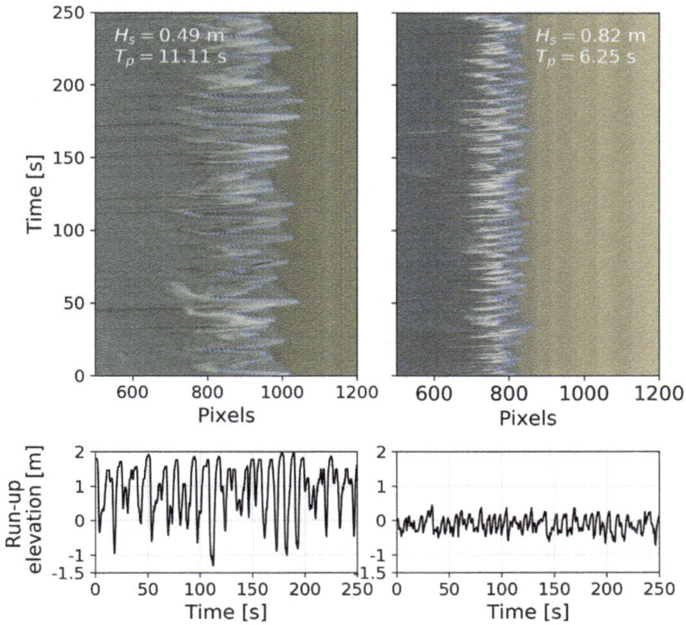

Fig. 8 Examples of time stacks showing shoreline position over time (top panels) during (left) high and (right) low tide. The corresponding significant wave height (Hs) and wave peak period (Tp) are indicated for each case. Bottom panels show the detrended run-up elevation time series. Observations collected at Bunkerhill Beach, Sylt, Germany. Courtesy of J. Montano

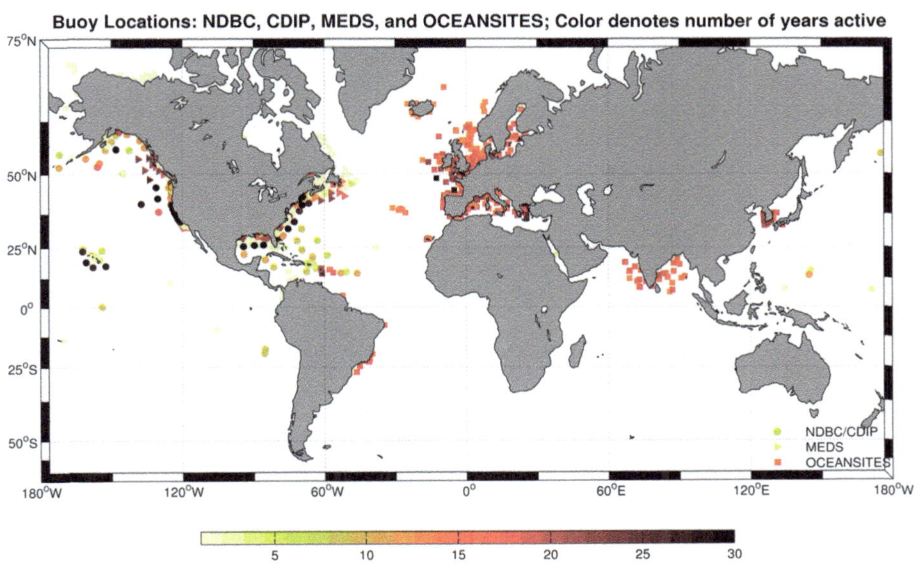

Fig. 9 Location of wave-measuring devices affiliated to the NDBC, CDIP, MEDS or OCEANSITES networks with the length of records in years indicated by the colours

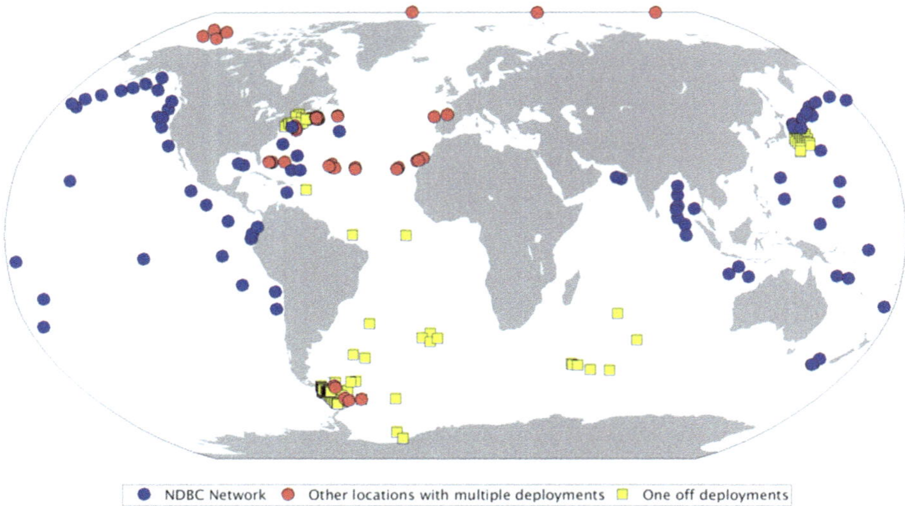

Fig. 10 Bottom pressure recorder measurements available from the NDBC and PSMSL networks or other networks linked to by the PSMSL

timescale of 12 h for storm duration, makes it impossible, from satellites alone, to derive reliable statistics on extreme wave parameters and associated impact on sea level.

It should be emphasized that all these observations systems have not been designed for the analysis of wave impacts on sea-level trends. Indeed, an increase in significant wave height by 2 cm produces an increase in sea level by 0.5–6 cm on typical beaches, depending on shoreface slope, wave period and bed composition (Stockdon et al. 2006; Poate et al. 2016). As a result, a reasonable goal for the accuracy of trends on wave height is an accuracy lower than the mean sea-level rise of 3 mm/year. This should apply to the extreme values, be it the 95th percentile or a 10-year maximum wave height, depending on applications. This is more demanding than the existing requirement of 5 cm per decade that is today the goal listed by GCOS, but it is also much less than what has been achieved by studies of buoy data for which the accuracy is of the order of 3 cm/year (Gemmrich et al. 2011).

5 Ocean Bottom Pressure Observations

The first bottom pressure observations were motivated by the need to understand ocean tides, which was hampered by the lack of knowledge about tidal cycles in the open oceans, with tide gauges by definition located at the shore. Attempts began in the 1960s to measure the tides in the open sea using instruments capable of recording pressure accurately at the seabed (Cartwright 1977). As the technology matured, programmes evolved to use a succession of deployments at a site to provide an ongoing record of sea-level variation (Spencer et al. 1993), with a new sensor deployed to the seabed as the old one was recovered, along with its payload of data. Unfortunately, pressure sensors are prone to drift over time, best modelled with a decaying exponential in the short term and a linear drift in the long term (Watts and Kontoyiannis 1990; Polster et al. 2009). Although there have been some attempts to measure and correct the drift with in situ calibration systems (e.g., Sasagawa et al. 2016), these are still under development and are not yet able to provide routine corrections.

As the drift cannot be distinguished from any long-term secular trends, and the information cannot be connected to a specific datum, records from bottom pressure gauges are presently unsuitable for monitoring long-term changes in sea level. Nevertheless, the records can be used to investigate changes in bottom pressure caused by tides (Ray 2013), ocean circulation (Spencer et al. 1993) and ocean mass (Hughes et al. 2012). Furthermore, by pairing the sensor with a surface buoy capable of transmitting high-frequency real-time data, recorders can provide data in real time and thus be used as a vital part of regional tsunami monitoring networks (Meinig et al. 2005).

A substantial network of bottom pressure recorders (BPR) is maintained by NOAA, and data can be obtained from the National Data Buoy Center (NDBC) website (www.ndbc.noaa.gov). The PSMSL also distributes some bottom pressure data from various sources, including a subset of the NDBC data, and maintains a list of other available BPR data (www.psmsl.org/data/bottom_pressure). Deployments tend to be clustered in locations where particular phenomena have been studied (such as the Drake Passage), or in tsunami-prone areas (Fig. 10), leaving large areas of the ocean unobserved by these in situ measurements.

Satellite gravimetry, starting from the launch of the Gravity Recovery and Climate Experiment (GRACE) in March 2002, has demonstrated its usefulness for observing ocean bottom pressure variations in the deep ocean (Bergmann and Dobslaw 2012; Chambers and Bonin 2012; Johnson and Chambers 2013; Piecuch et al. 2013; Ponte and Piecuch 2014; Makowski et al. 2015), and calculating the mass component of global mean sea level (Chambers et al. 2004, 2017; Willis et al. 2008; Leuliette and Miller 2009; Boening et al. 2012; Church et al. 2013; Fasullo et al. 2013; Johnson and Chambers 2013; Rietbroek et al. 2016). Using the newest release of GRACE data, bottom pressure in the deep, interior ocean averaged over a disc with radius 300 km has a standard error of approximately 1.5 cm of equivalent sea level (Chambers and Bonin 2012), while the global ocean mass has a standard error of 1.1 mm (Johnson and Chambers 2013), both at monthly averages.

Using GRACE data to accurately measure ocean bottom pressure (and hence, the mass component of sea level) in coastal waters is very difficult and, until recently, has only been attempted in a few regions. This is due to leakage of the much larger mass fluctuations from land hydrology and cryosphere variability into the ocean (Wahr et al. 1998), particularly important at seasonal and longer timescales. Land (and ice sheet) mass variability is often one to two orders of magnitude larger than ocean mass variations, and it is difficult to estimate the leaked signal without knowing the signal that is being leaked. Some studies have attempted to correct for the leakage by iterating with GRACE estimates of land and ice sheet mass changes (Chambers and Bonin 2012), using an inverse method where land and ocean signals are separated by predefined basins (Chen et al. 2013), or, more recently, using a predefined mesh of global mass concentrations, or mascons, to separate ocean and land signals (e.g., Lemoine et al. 2007; Watkins et al. 2015; Save et al. 2016) or using a land hydrology model (Fenoglio-Marc et al. 2012).

There have been a few studies where GRACE data in coastal waters have been utilized and shown to explain a large percentage of sea-level variance in coastal waters. Landerer et al. (2015) used a GRACE mascon solution to study variability in the Atlantic meridional overturning circulation (AMOC). This required using GRACE-derived ocean bottom pressure along the US eastern continental shelf, within 300 km of land. Although they could resolve interannual fluctuations in the bottom pressure associated with changes in the

AMOC, they found a large, unrealistic trend that they speculated had to be from residual leakage of hydrology signals, even using a mascon solution. GRACE has also shown some level of accuracy in measuring coastal level in two small enclosed gulfs with large sea-level variability that is caused by winds at annual periods: the Gulf of Carpentaria in northern Australia (Tregoning et al. 2008) and the Gulf of Thailand (Wouters and Chambers 2010).

Newer mascon solutions from GRACE show more promise of being able to recover the ocean mass (barotropic) portion of sea-level variability in substantially more coastal waters. Piecuch et al. (2018b) compared ocean bottom pressure from a GRACE mascon solution from the Jet Propulsion Laboratory that incorporated a special filter to optimally separate land and ocean signals (Watkins et al. 2015; Wiese et al. 2016). They found that these new GRACE mascon solutions explained ~ 30–50% of the sea-level variance measured by tide gauges along the Australian shelf, the North Sea around Scandinavia, the eastern coast of the USA and Canada, and around parts of the Chinese coast and Indonesian archipelago. While much of this correspondence is due to the annual signal, Piecuch et al. (2018b) do demonstrate good agreement with interannual and non-seasonal sea level and ocean bottom pressure in many of these same areas. This is expected from theory, since in shallower waters there should be a greater coupling between sea level and ocean bottom pressure as the response will be more barotropic. Thus, although GRACE data have not regularly been used to understand coastal sea-level variability, new processing has improved the accuracy sufficiently that the satellite ocean bottom pressure can be useful in understanding coastal sea-level variability in shallow waters with a wide shelf.

Another area where GRACE has demonstrated usefulness is in measuring a portion of coastal sea level that results from gravitational changes due to land ice melting (e.g., Riva et al. 2010) and fluctuations in land hydrology (e.g., Jensen et al. 2013). Although important for understanding and predicting sea-level rise a hundred years from now, these are minor signals in coastal sea-level measurements made by tide gauges in present-day, in comparison to other contributors such as steric sea level changes (see Sect. 6).

6 Steric Sea-Level Observations

Knowledge about hydrographic changes (from temperature and salinity) is crucial for interpreting sea-level variability and underlying mechanisms, especially in the open ocean, but with impact also along the coastal zones. Indeed, one major knowledge gap in sea-level research is our limited understanding of how changes in coastal sea-level relate to steric changes on the continental slope and in the open ocean. Thus observations of temperature and salinity over the shelf, continental slope and nearby ocean are crucial to filling this gap. This section offers a summary of existing observing capabilities of the most relevant variables and discusses improvements on coverage, integration and other issues that could be helpful over the next decade.

Knowledge of temperature (T) and salinity (S) distributions can provide information on steric contributions to coastal sea-level variability. As they relate to density, T and S data also carry dynamic information (pressure gradients, velocities). Combined with bottom pressure and other variables, T and S data can be used to elucidate many aspects of sea-level behaviour (e.g., separating oceanographic and geodetic contributions, discerning causal and forcing mechanisms).

With Argo floats not sampling the shallow regions, there are no operational global in situ observations of coastal T and S, but regional efforts have been implemented over the years using both ship-based and moored platforms (e.g., data collection in many coastal regions set-up under the U.S. Integrated Ocean Observing System; https://ioos.noaa.gov/regions/) and more recently glider technology (e.g., https://gliders.ioos.us/; Pattiaratchi et al. 2017; Rudnick et al. 2017; Heslop et al. 2012). One challenge and perhaps a worthy long-term focus will be to link available T and S data to sea-level data at the local level, particularly as coastal observing systems attain operational status.

In the case of surface measurements, satellite retrievals provide a useful, global alternative to in situ platforms, albeit at varying resolutions and with questionable accuracy near the coastal zone, mostly due to the fact most of the in situ platforms for calibration/validation are offshore (Brewin et al. 2017). For sea surface temperature (SST), a variety of remotely sensed and blended products exist at typical daily sampling, nominal kilometre resolutions and accuracies of ~ 0.5 K (Donlon et al. 2007, 2009; https://www.ghrsst.org/). Although SST has been shown to correlate with sea level over deep water (Meyssignac et al. 2017), the case for the coastal ocean remains to be explored. To the extent that SST can reflect steric sea level, high-resolution satellite products could be used to infer potential short-scale structures affecting sea level across the coastal zone. Such knowledge can, for example, inform comparisons of tide gauge and altimeter sea-level data, which are affected by their different spatial sampling characteristics.

Sea surface salinity (SSS) retrievals are much more recent and not as mature nor operational as SST. The Aquarius mission lasted over the period 2011–2015, but the Soil Moisture Ocean Salinity (SMOS) mission continues to be operational since 2009, and data from the Soil Moisture Active Passive (SMAP) mission launched in 2015 have also become available (e.g., Mecklenburg et al. 2016; Weissman et al. 2017; Köhler et al. 2018; Boutin et al. 2018). Nominal sampling ranges from weekly to monthly at resolutions of ¼ to 1 degree (around 40 km for SMAP), and with typical accuracies of ~ 0.2 practical salinity units (psu). Apart from the challenges of relating SSS retrievals to bulk and to subsurface S (e.g., Boutin et al. 2018), the extent to which these quantities are related to coastal sea level has not been explored in any detail. Sea level and SSS are expected to be linked directly through the effects of river run-off (Meade and Emery 1971), but the related SSS signals can be trapped to the coast on scales that are not well resolved with the currently available satellite systems (Piecuch et al. 2018a). Similar issues may also affect the ability to observe possible impacts of ice melt on coastal sea level at high latitudes.

7 Discussion and Final Remarks

Monitoring networks of in situ coastal sea level are presently well developed along most of the world coastlines, although with notable exceptions in Africa and part of South America, where the spatial density of instruments is significantly lower than, for example, in Europe. Furthermore, delayed-mode, low-frequency tide gauge data in some parts of the coastlines (including the above-mentioned regions but also others like the Arctic Ocean) are not routinely released to the international databases, limiting the available information in these areas even more. The same geographical bias applies to high-frequency sea-level measurements, as these come from the same tide gauges.

The lack of sea-level information on poorly sampled regions may be partly overcome with coastal altimetry observations. Despite the longer revisit time of the altimeters, there is a clear complementarity between tide gauges and altimetry that should be exploited in order to improve the current knowledge of sea-level variations in coastal regions at low frequencies (monthly and longer periods). In this respect, the information on VLM at the tide gauge is crucial for the consistency between both measurements. This is achieved through GNSS observations and can be further complemented with other geodetic techniques, such as InSAR to extend VLM estimates to larger areas. In the near future, progress in data processing and the continuity of altimetric missions are promising for coastal sea-level studies. This includes the forthcoming SWOT mission (Durand et al. 2010) and the already operational Sentinel missions from the European Space Agency (https://sentinel.esa.int/web/sentinel/missions).

Overall, an integrated coastal sea-level observing system should:

1. Be able to accurately measure sea-level changes at the coast itself at high-frequency rates (hourly or higher, to account for extreme sea levels) and at the nearby coastal region, using in situ (tide gauges) and satellite altimetry observations, respectively;
2. Use GNSS observations to provide information on VLM in order to separate ocean and land signals in in situ measurements, especially in the long term when both components can be of the same order of magnitude;
3. Measure local and regional sea-level contributors at high frequency sampling (at least minutes, ideally seconds for the wave contributors), including offshore and coastal wind waves, water density changes, surface meteorological parameters (atmospheric pressure and winds being among the most important; see Piecuch et al., this issue), and in general any other local process important to identify and understand the coastal dynamics inducing sea-level variations (e.g., river run-off, Durand et al., this issue);
4. Be consolidated on a long-term basis.

The scientific and societal benefits of such a system are numerous. Climate studies require long-term, consistent and continuous measurements. In this respect, consolidation of observing systems is crucial to avoid endangering the continuity of the observations and introducing data gaps. Currently, this is ensured for satellite missions (altimetry and gravimetry) but, unfortunately, even in intensively monitored regions, like Europe, national agencies have reported problems with securing funding for maintenance of the current tide gauge networks (Pérez Gómez et al. 2017), representing a serious concern, especially for the valuable long-term records. An integrated observing system of sea-level and related variables would also provide consistent information to be assimilated into numerical models, including the quantification of data uncertainties that are critical in analyses and model forecasts. It would further contribute to operational oceanographic systems and warning protocols (e.g., flood warnings). Finally, it is also an adequate framework to foster technological development of new emerging monitoring platforms capable of expanding current in situ observations (e.g., GNSS-towed platforms) and thus contributing to maximize the information provided by in situ sea-level measurements.

Observing sea-level changes at the coast and quantifying its drivers is the first step to understand the complex dynamics of the coastal region, to link the responses of the coastal environment to sea-level changes and to anticipate how projected sea-level variations will impact the coastal areas.

References

Andersen OB, Nielsen K, Knudsen P, Hughes CW, Bingham R, Fenoglio-Marc L, Gravelle M, Kern M, Polo SP (2018) Improving the coastal mean dynamic topography by geodetic combination of tide gauge and satellite altimetry. Mar Geod. https://doi.org/10.1080/01490419.2018.1530320

André BG, Martín Míguez B, Ballu V et al (2013) Measuring sea level with GPS-equipped buoys: a multi-instruments experiment at Aix Island. Int Hyrographic Rev 10:27–38

Apotsos A, Raubenheimer B, Elgar S, Guza RT, Smith JA (2007) Effects of wave rollers and bottom stress on wave setup. J Geophys Res Oceans. https://doi.org/10.1029/2006JC003549

Ardhuin F, Drake TG, Herbers THC (2002) Observations of wave-generated vortex ripples on the North Carolina continental shelf. J Geophys Res 107:C10. https://doi.org/10.1029/2001JC000986

Ardhuin F, Devaux E, Pineau-Guillou L (2010) Observation et prévision des seiches sur la côte atlantique française. Actes des Xèmes Journées Génie côtier-Génie civil, Les Sables d'Olonne. https://doi.org/10.5150/jngcgc.2010.001-a

Ardhuin F, Rascle N, Chapron B, Gula J, Molemaker J, Gille ST, Menemenlis D, Rocha C (2017) Small scale currents have large effects on wind wave heights. J Geophys Res 122(C6):4500–4517. https://doi.org/10.1002/2016JC012413

Ardhuin F, Aksenov Y, Benetazzo A, Bertino L, Brandt P, Caubet E, Chapron B, Collard F, Cravatte S, Dias F, Dibarboure G, Gaultier L, Johannessen J, Korosov A, Manucharyan G, Menemenlis D, Menendez M, Monnier G, Mouche A, Nouguier F, Nurser G, Rampal P, Reniers A, Rodriguez E, Stopa J, Tison C, Tissier M, Ubelmann C, van Sebille E, Vialard J, Xie J (2018) Measuring currents, ice drift, and waves from space: the sea surface kinematics multiscale monitoring (SKIM) concept. Ocean Sci 14:337–354. https://doi.org/10.5194/os-2017-65

Ballu V, Bouin M-N, Calmant S et al (2010) Absolute seafloor vertical positioning using combined pressure gauge and kinematic GPS data. J Geod 84:65. https://doi.org/10.1007/s00190-009-0345-y

Ballu V, Testut L, Poirier E et al (2017) Mapping the sealevel for altimetry calibration purpose using the future PAMELi marine ASV around the Aix Island sea-level observatory. In: 2017 Ocean surface topography science team meeting, Miami

Battjes JA (1982) A case study of wave height variations due to currents in a tidal entrance. Coast Eng 6:47–57

Bergmann I, Dobslaw H (2012) Short-term transport variability of the Antarctic Circumpolar Current from satellite gravity observations. J Geophys Res. https://doi.org/10.1029/2012jc007872

Bertin X, de Bakker A, van Dongeren A, Coco G, Andre G, Ardhuin F, Bonneton P, Bouchette F, Castelle B, Crawford W, Deen M, Dodet G, Guerin T, Leckler F, McCall R, Muller H, Olabarrieta M, Ruessink G, Sous D, Stutzmann E, Tissier M (2018) Infragravity waves: from driving mechanisms to impacts. Earth Sci Rev 177:774–799. https://doi.org/10.1016/j.earscirev.2018.01.002

Birol F, Fuller N, Lyard F, Cancet M, Niño F, Delebecque C, Fleury S, Toublanc F, Melet A, Saraceno M, Leger F (2016) Coastal applications from nadir altimetry: example of the X-TRACK regional products. Adv Space Res. https://doi.org/10.1016/j.asr.2016.11.005

Boening C, Willis JK, Landerer FW, Nerem RS, Fasullo J (2012) The 2011 La Niña: So strong, the oceans fell. Geophys Res Lett. https://doi.org/10.1029/2012gl053055

Bonnefond P, Exertier P, Laurain O et al (2003a) Absolute calibration of Jason-1 and TOPEX/Poseidon altimeters in Corsica special issue: Jason-1 calibration/validation. Mar Geod 26:261–284. https://doi.org/10.1080/714044521

Bonnefond P, Exertier P, Laurain O et al (2003b) Leveling the sea surface using a GPS-catamaran special issue: Jason-1 calibration/validation. Mar Geod 26:319–334. https://doi.org/10.1080/714044524

Born GH, Michael PE, Axelrad P et al (1994) Calibration of the TOPEX altimeter using a GPS buoy. J Geophys Res Ocean 99:24517–24526. https://doi.org/10.1029/94JC00920

Bouin M-N, Ballu V, Calmant S et al (2009a) A kinematic GPS methodology for sea surface mapping. Vanuatu J Geod 83:1203. https://doi.org/10.1007/s00190-009-0338-x

Bouin M-N, Ballu V, Calmant S, Pelletier B (2009b) Improving resolution and accuracy of mean sea surface from kinematic GPS, Vanuatu subduction zone. J Geod 83:1017. https://doi.org/10.1007/s00190-009-0320-7

Boutin J, Vergely JL, Marchand S, D'Amico F, Hasson A, Kolodziejczyk N, Reul N, Reverdin G, Vialard J (2018) New SMOS Sea Surface Salinity with reduced systematic errors and improved variability. Remote Sens Environ 214:115–134. https://doi.org/10.1016/j.rse.2018.05.022

Bradshaw E, Rickards L, Aarup T (2015) Sea level data archaeology and the Global Sea Level Observing System (GLOSS). Geo Res J 6:9–16. https://doi.org/10.1016/j.grj.2015.02.005

Brewin RJW, de Mora L, Billson O, Jackson T, Russell P, Brewin TG, Shutler JD, Miller PI, Taylor BH, Smyth TJ, Fishwick JR (2017) Evaluating operational AVHRR sea surface temperature data at the coastline using surfers. Estuar Coast Shelf Sci 196:276–289. https://doi.org/10.1016/j.ecss.2017.07.011

Calafat FM, Wahl T, Lindsten F, Williams J, Frajka-Williams E (2018) Coherent modulation of the sea-level annual cycle in the United States by Atlantic Rossby waves. Nat Commun 9:2571. https://doi.org/10.1038/s41467-018-04898-y

Calzas M, Brachet C, Drezen C et al (2014) New technological development for cal/val activities. In: 2014 Ocean surface topography science team meeting. Lake Constance, Germany
Cariolet J-M, Suanez S (2013) Runup estimations on a macrotidal sandy beach. Coast Eng 74:11–18
Cartwright DE (1977) Oceanic tides. Rep Prog Phys 40:665–708
Chambers DP, Bonin JA (2012) Evaluation of Release-05 GRACE time-variable gravity coefficients over the ocean. Ocean Sci 8:1–10. https://doi.org/10.5194/os-8-1-2012
Chambers DP, Wahr J, Nerem RS (2004) Preliminary observations of global ocean mass variations with GRACE. Geophys Res Lett 31:L13310. https://doi.org/10.1029/2004GL020461
Chambers DP, Cazenave A, Champollion N, Dieng H, Llovel W, Forsberg R, von Schuckmann K, Wada Y (2017) Evaluation of the global mean sea level budget between 1993 and 2014. Surv Geophys 38:309–327. https://doi.org/10.1007/s10712-016-9381-3
Chen JL, Wilson CR, Tapley BD (2013) Contribution of ice sheet and mountain glacier melt to recent sea level rise. Nat Geosci 6:549–552. https://doi.org/10.1038/NGEO1829
Church JA, Clark PU, Cazenave A, Gregory JM, Jevrejeva S, Levermann A, Merrifield MA, Milne GA, Nerem RS, Nunn PD, Payne AJ, Pfeffer WT, Stammer D, Unnikrishnan AS (2013) Sea level change. In: Stocker TF, Qin D, Plattner G-K, Tignor M, Allen SK, Boschung J, Nauels A, Xia Y, Bex V, Midgley PM (eds) Climate change 2013: the physical science basis. Contribution of working group I to the fifth assessment report of the Intergovernmental Panel on Climate Change. Cambridge University Press, Cambridge
Cipollini P, Calafat FM, Jevrejeva S, Melet S, Prandi P (2017) Monitoring sea level in the coastal zone with satellite altimetry and tide gauges. Surv Geophys 38(1):33–57. https://doi.org/10.1007/s10712-016-9392-0
Coco G, Senechal N, Rejas A, Bryan KR, Capo S, Parisot JP, Brown JA, MacMahan JHM (2014) Beach response to a sequence of extreme storms. Geomorphology 204:493–501
Coulombier T, Ballu V, Pineau P et al (2018) PAMELi, un drone marin de surface au service de l'interdisciplinarité. Paralia 15:337–344. https://doi.org/10.5150/jngcgc.2018.038
Dangendorf S, Marcos M, Woppelmann G, Conrad CP, Frederikse T, Riva R (2017) Reassessment of 20th century global mean sea level rise. PNAS. https://doi.org/10.1073/pnas.1616007114
Dinardo S, Fenoglio-Marc L, Buchhaupt C, Becker M, Scharro R, Fernandez J, Benveniste J (2017) CryoSat-2 performance along the german coasts. AdSR Special Issue CryoSat-2. https://doi.org/10.1016/j.asr.2017.12.018
Dinardo S, Fenoglio-Marc L, Buchhaupt C, Becker M, Scharroo R, Fernandes MJ, Benveniste J (2018) Coastal SAR and PLRM altimetry in German Bight and West Baltic Sea. Adv Space Res 62(6):1371–1404. https://doi.org/10.1016/j.asr.2017.12.018
Dodet G, Melet A, Ardhuin F, Almar R, Bertin X, Idier D, Pedredos R (in review) The contribution of wind generated waves to coastal sea level changes. Surv Geophys
Donlon C, Rayner N, Robinson I, Poulter DJS, Casey KS, Vazquez-Cuervo J, Armstrong E, Bingham A, Arino O, Gentemann C et al (2007) The global ocean data assimilation experiment high-resolution sea surface temperature pilot project. Bull Am Meteorol Soc 88:1197–1213
Donlon CJ, Casey KS, Robinson IS, Gentemann CL, Reynolds RW, Barton I, Arino O, Stark J, Rayner N, LeBorgne P, Poulter D, Vazquez-Cuervo J, Armstrong E, Beggs H, Llewellyn-Jones D, Minnett PJ, Merchant CJ, Evans R (2009) GODAE high-resolution sea surface temperature pilot project. Oceanography 22(3):34–45. https://doi.org/10.5670/oceanog.2009.64
Dugan JP, Morris WD, Vierra KC, Piotrowski CC, Farruggia GJ, Campion DC (2001) Jetski-based nearshore bathymetric and current survey system. J Coast Res 17:900–908
Durand M, Fu L-L, Lettenmaier DP, Alsdorf DE, Rodriguez E, Esteban-Fernandez D (2010) The surface water and ocean topography mission: observing terrestrial surface water and oceanic submesoscale eddies. Proc IEEE 98:766–779. https://doi.org/10.1109/jproc.2010.2043031
Durand F, Calmant S, Calzas M et al (2017) Geodetic survey of the freshwater front of the Ganges-Brahmaputra freshwater plume in the northern Bay of Bengal from Calnageo GNSS device. In: 2017 Ocean surface topography science team meeting
Durand F, Piecuch C, Cirano M, Becker M, Papa F (in review) Runoff impact on coastal sea level. Surv Geophys
Elgar S, Guza RT, Raubenheimer B, Herbers THC, Gallagher EL (1997) Spectral evolution of shoaling and breaking waves on a barred beach. J Geophys Res Oceans 102(C7):15797–15805
Fantino M, Marucco G, Mulassano P, Pini M (2008) Performance analysis of MBOC, AltBOC and BOC modulations in terms of multipath effects on the carrier tracking loop within GNSS receivers. In: IEEE/ION position, location and navigation symposium. https://doi.org/10.1109/plans.2008.4570092
Fasullo JT, Boening C, Landerer FW, Nerem RS (2013) Australia's unique influence on global sea level in 2010–2011. Geophys Res Lett 40:4368–4373. https://doi.org/10.1002/grl.50834

Fenoglio-Marc L, Becker M, Rietbroeck R, Kusche J, Grayek S, Stanev E (2012) Water mass variation in Mediterranean and Black Sea. J Geodyn. https://doi.org/10.1016/j.jog.2012.04.001
Fiedler JW, Brodie KL, McNinch JE, Guza RT (2015) Observations of runup and energy flux on a low-slope beach with high-energy, long-period ocean swell. Geophys Res Lett 42:9933–9941. https://doi.org/10.1002/2015GL066124
Foster JH, Carter GS, Merrifield MA (2009) Ship-based measurements of sea surface topography. Geophys Res Lett 36:L11605. https://doi.org/10.1029/2009GL038324
Fund F, Perosanz F, Testut L, Loyer S (2013) An Integer Precise Point Positioning technique for sea surface observations using a GPS buoy. Adv Space Res 51:1311–1322. https://doi.org/10.1016/j.asr.2012.09.028
Gemmrich J, Thomas B, Bouchard R (2011) Observational changes and trends in northeast Pacific wave records. Geophys Res Lett 38:L22601. https://doi.org/10.1029/2011GL049518
Gommenginger CP, Srokosz MA, Challenor PG, Cotton PD (2003) Measuring ocean wave period with satellite altimeters: a simple empirical model. Geophys Res Lett 30(22):2150. https://doi.org/10.1029/2003GL017743
Gulev SK, Grigorieva V, Sterl A, Woolf D (2003) Assessment of the reliability of wave observations from voluntary observing ships: insights from the validation of a global wind wave climatology based on voluntary observing ship data. J Geophys Res 108(C7):3236
Guza RT, Thornton EB (1981) Wave set-up on a natural beach. J Geophys Res Oceans 86(C5):4133–4137
Haines B, Desai S, Dodge A et al (2017) Connecting Jason-3 to the long-term sea level record: results from harvest and regional campaigns. In: 2017 Ocean surface topography science team meeting
Hauser D, Tison C, Amiot T, Delaye L, Corcoral N, Castillan P (2017) SWIM: the first spaceborne wave scatterometer. IEEE Trans Geosci Remote Sens 55(5):3000–3014
Hedley J, Roelfsema C, Koetz B, Phinn S (2012) Capability of the Sentinel 2 mission for tropical coral reef mapping and coral bleaching detection. Remote Sens Environ 120:145–155. https://doi.org/10.1016/j.rse.2011.06.028
Hein GW, Landau H, Blomenhofer H (1990) Determination of instantaneous sea surface, wave heights, and ocean currents using satellite observations of the global positioning system. Mar Geod 14:217–224. https://doi.org/10.1080/15210609009379664
Hogarth P (2014) Preliminary analysis of acceleration of sea level rise through the twentieth century using extended tide gauge data sets (August 2014). J Geophys Res Oceans 119:7645–7659. https://doi.org/10.1002/2014JC009976
Holgate SJ, Matthews A, Woodworth PL, Rickards LJ, Tamisiea ME, Bradshaw E, Foden PR, Gordon KM, Jevrejeva S, Pugh J (2013) New data systems and products at the Permanent Service for Mean Sea Level. J Coast Res 29:493–504
Holman RA, Stanley J (2007) The history and technical capabilities of Argus. Coast Eng 54(6–7):477–491
Holman R, Plant N, Holland T (2013) cBathy: a robust algorithm for estimating nearshore bathymetry. J Geophys Res Oceans 118(5):2595–2609
Hughes CW, Tamisiea ME, Bingham RJ, Williams J (2012) Weighing the ocean: using a single mooring to measure changes in the mass of the ocean. Geophys Res Lett 39:L17602. https://doi.org/10.1029/2012GL052935
Intergovernmental Oceanographic Commission (IOC) (1985) Manual on sea level measurement and interpretation (volume I: basic procedures). Intergovernmental Oceanographic Commission Manuals and Guides, vol 14. UNESCO, Paris. http://www.psmsl.org/train_and_info/training/manuals/ioc_14i.pdf. Accessed July 2018
Jensen L, Rietbroek R, Kusche J (2013) Land water contribution to sea level from GRACE and Jason-1 measurements. J Geophys Res Oceans 118:212–226. https://doi.org/10.1002/jgrc.20058
Johnson GF, Chambers DP (2013) Ocean Bottom Pressure Seasonal Cycles and Decadal Trends from GRACE Release-05: ocean Circulation Implications. J Geophys Res Oceans 118:1–13. https://doi.org/10.1002/jgrc.20307
Köhler J, Serra N, Bryan FO, Johnson BK, Stammer D (2018) Mechanisms of mixed-layer salinity seasonal variability in the Indian Ocean. J Geophys Res Oceans 123:466–496. https://doi.org/10.1002/2017JC013640
Landerer FW, Wiese DN, Bentel K, Boening C, Watkins MM (2015) North Atlantic meridional overturning circulation variations from GRACE ocean bottom pressure anomalies. Geophys Res Lett 42:8114–8121. https://doi.org/10.1002/2015gl065730
Larson KM, Ray RD, Nievinski FG, Freymueller JT (2013) The Accidental tide gauge: a GPS reflection case study from Kachemak Bay, Alaska. IEEE Geosci Remote Sens Lett 10:1200–1204

Laurichesse D, Mercier F, Berthias J-P et al (2009) Integer ambiguity resolution on undifferenced GPS phase measurements and its application to PPP and satellite precise orbit determination. Navigation 56:135–149. https://doi.org/10.1002/j.2161-4296.2009.tb01750.x

Lemoine FG, Luthcke SB, Rowlands DD, Chinn DS, Klosko SM, Cox CM (2007) The use of mascons to resolve time-variable gravity from GRACE. In: Tregoning P, Rizos C (eds) Dynamic planet: monitoring and understanding a dynamic planet with geodetic and oceanographic tools. International Association of Geodesy, vol 130. Springer, Berlin, pp 231–236

Leuliette EW, Miller L (2009) Closing the sea level rise budget with altimetry, Argo, and GRACE. Geophys Res Lett 36:L04608. https://doi.org/10.1029/2008GL036010

Lowe RJ, Falte JL, Koseff JR, Monismith SG, Atkinson MJ (2007) Spectral wave flow attenuation within submerged canopies: implications for wave energy dissipation. J Geophys Res. https://doi.org/10.1029/2006jc003605

Magne R, Belibassakis K, Herbers THC, Ardhuin F, O'Reilly WC, Rey V (2007) Evolution of surface gravity waves over a submarine canyon. J Geophys Res. https://doi.org/10.1029/2005jc003035

Makowski JK, Chambers DP, Bonin JA (2015) Using ocean bottom pressure from the gravity recovery and climate experiment (GRACE) to estimate transport variability in the Southern Indian Ocean. J Geophys Res Oceans 120:4245–4259. https://doi.org/10.1002/2014jc010575

Marcos M, Puyol B, Wöppelmann G, Herrero C, García-Fernández MJ (2011) The long sea level record at Cadiz (southern Spain) from 1880 to 2009. J Geophys Res 116:C12003. https://doi.org/10.1029/2011JC007558

Martín Míguez B, Le Roy R, Wöppelmann G (2008) The use of radar tide gauges to measure variations in sea level along the French Coast. J Coast Res 24:61–68

Martín Míguez B, Testut L, Woppelmann G (2012) Performance of modern tide gauges: towards mm-level accuracy. Sci Mar 76:221–228. https://doi.org/10.3989/scimar.03618.18a

Masselink G, Scott T, Poate T, Russell P, Davidson M, Conley D (2016) The extreme 2013/2014 winter storms: hydrodynamic forcing and coastal response along the southwest coast of England. Earth Surf Proc Land 41(3):378–391

Mastenbroek C, Burgers G, Janssen PAEM (1993) The dynamical coupling of a wave model and a storm surge model through the atmospheric boundary layer. J Phys Oceanogr 23:1856–1867

Meade RH, Emery KO (1971) Sea level as affected by river runoff, eastern United States. Science 173(3995):425–428

Mecklenburg S, Drusch M, Kaleschke L, Rodriguez-Fernandez N, Reul N, Kerr Y, Font J, Martin-Neira M, Oliva R, Daganzo-Eusebio E, Grant JP, Sabia R, Macelloni G, Rautiainen K, Fauste J, de Rosnay P, Munoz-Sabater J, Verhoest N, Lievens H, Delwart S, Crapolicchio R, de la Fuente A, Kornberg M (2016) ESA's Soil Moisture and Ocean Salinity mission: from science to operational applications. Remote Sens Environ 180:3–18. https://doi.org/10.1016/j.rse.2015.12.025

Meinig C, Stalin SE, Nakamura AI, Milburn HB (2005) Real-time deep-ocean tsunami measuring, monitoring, and reporting system: The NOAA DART II description and disclosure. NOAA, Pacific Marine Environmental Laboratory (PMEL), pp 1–15

Meyssignac B, Piecuch CG, Merchant CJ, Racault M-F, Palanisamy H, MacIntosh C, Sathyendranath S, Brewin R (2017) Causes of the regional variability in observed sea level, sea surface temperature and ocean color over the period 1993-2011. Surv Geophys 38:187–215. https://doi.org/10.1007/s10712-016-9383-1

Monismith SG, Rogers JS, Koweek D, Dunbar RB (2015) Frictional wave dissipation on a remarkably rough reef. Geophys Res Lett 112:4063–4071. https://doi.org/10.1002/2015GL063804

Munk WH, Traylor MA (1947) Refraction of ocean waves: a process linking underwater topography to beach erosion. J Geol 51:1–26

Neale J, Harmon N, Srokosz M (2015) Source regions and reflection of infragravity waves offshore of the U.S.s Pacific Northwest. J Geophys Res Oceans 120:6474–6491. https://doi.org/10.1002/2015JC010891

Okihiro M, Guza RT, Seymour RJ (1993) Excitation of seiche observed in a small harbor. J Geophys Res 98(C10):18201–18211

Pattiaratchi C, Woo LM, Thomson PG, Hong KK, Stanley D (2017) Ocean glider observations around Australia. Oceanography 30(2):90–91. https://doi.org/10.5670/oceanog.2017.226

Penna NT, Morales Maqueda MA, Martin I et al (2018) Sea surface height measurement using a GNSS wave glider. Geophys Res Lett 45:5609–5616. https://doi.org/10.1029/2018GL077950

Pérez Gómez B, Donato V, Hibbert A, Marcos M, Raicich F, Hammarklint T, Testut L, Annunziato A, Westbrook G, Gyldenfeldt A, Gorringe P (2017) Recent efforts for an increased coordination of sea level monitoring in Europe: EuroGOOS Tide Gauge Task Team. In: International WCRP/IOC conference 2017: regional sea level changes and costal impacts, New York

Piecuch CG, Quinn KJ, Ponte RM (2013) Satellite-derived interannual ocean bottom pressure variability and its relation to sea level. Geophys Res Lett 40:3106–3110. https://doi.org/10.1002/grl.50549
Piecuch CG, Bitterman K, Kemp AC, Ponte RM, Little CM, Engelhart SE, Lentz SJ (2018a) River-discharge effects on United States Atlantic and Gulf coast sea-level changes. Proc Natl Acad Sci. https://doi.org/10.1073/pnas.1805428115
Piecuch CG, Landerer FW, Ponte RM (2018b) Tide gauge records reveal improved processing of gravity recovery and climate experiment time-variable mass solutions over the coastal ocean. Geophys J Int 214:1401–1412. https://doi.org/10.1093/gji/ggy207
Pineau-Guillou L, Ardhuin F, Bouin M-N, Redelsperger J-L, Chapron B, Bidlot J, Quilfen Y (2018) Strong winds in a coupled wave-atmosphere model during a north atlantic storm event: evaluation against observations. Q J R Meteorol Soc 144:317–332. https://doi.org/10.1002/qj.3205
Pleskachevsky A, Dobrynin M, Babanin AV, Günther H, Stanev E (2011) Turbulent mixing due to surface waves indicated by remote sensing of suspended particulate matter and its implementation into coupled modeling of waves, turbulence, and circulation. J Phys Oceanogr 41:708–724. https://doi.org/10.1175/2010JPO4328.1
Poate TG, McCall RT, Masselink G (2016) A new parameterisation for runup on gravel beaches. Coast Eng 117:176–190. https://doi.org/10.1016/j.coastaleng.2016.08.003
Polster A, Fabian M, Villinger H (2009) Effective resolution and drift of Paroscientific pressure sensors derived from longterm seafloor measurements. Geochem Geophy Geosyst 10:Q08008. https://doi.org/10.1029/2009GC002532
Ponte RM, Piecuch CG (2014) Interannual bottom pressure signals in the Australian-Antarctic and Bellingshausen Basins. J Phys Ocean 44:1456–1465. https://doi.org/10.1175/JPO-D-13-0223.1
Pugh D, Woodworth PL (2014) Sea-level science: understanding tides, surges, tsunamis and mean sea-level changes. Cambridge University Press, Cambridge. https://doi.org/10.1017/CBO9781139235778. ISBN 9781139235778
Queffeulou (2013) https://ftp.space.dtu.dk/pub/Ioana/papers/s221_1quef.pdf
Quilfen Y, Chapron B, Collard F, Serre M (2004) Calibration/validation of an altimeter wave period model and application to TOPEX/Poseidon and Jason-1 altimeters. Mar Geod 27(3–4):535–549. https://doi.org/10.1080/01490410490902025
Raubenheimer B (2002) Observations and predictions of fluid velocities in the surf and swash zones. J Geophys Res Oceans 107(C11):11-1–11-7
Raubenheimer B, Guza RT, Elgar S (2001) Field observations of wave-driven setdown and setup. J Geophys Res Oceans 106(C3):4629–4638
Rawat A, Ardhuin F, Ballu V, Crawford W, Corela C, Aucan J (2014) Infragravity waves across the oceans. Geophys Res Lett 41:7957–7963. https://doi.org/10.1002/2014GL061604
Ray RD (2013) Precise comparisons of bottom-pressure and altimetric ocean tides. J Geophys 118:4570–4584
Reinking J, Härting A, Bastos L (2012) Determination of sea surface height from moving ships with dynamic corrections. J Geod Sci 2:172–187. https://doi.org/10.2478/v10156-011-0038-3
Rietbroek R, Brunnabend SE, Kusche J, Schröter J, Dahle C (2016) Revisiting the contemporary sea-level budget on global and regional scales. Proc Natl Acad Sci 113:1504–1509. https://doi.org/10.1073/pnas.1519132113
Riva REM, Bamber JL, Lavallée DA, Wouters B (2010) Sea-level fingerprint of continental water and ice mass change from GRACE. Geophys Res Lett 37:L19605. https://doi.org/10.1029/2010GL044770
Rocken C, Kelecy TM, Born GH et al (1990) Measuring precise sea level from a buoy using the global positioning system. Geophys Res Lett 17:2145–2148. https://doi.org/10.1029/GL017i012p02145
Rudnick DL, Zaba KD, Todd RE, Davis RE (2017) A climatology of the California Current System from a network of underwater gliders. Prog Oceanogr 154:64–106. https://doi.org/10.1016/j.pocean.2017.03.002
Santamaría-Gómez A, Watson C (2017) Remote leveling of tide gauges using GNSS reflectometry: case study at Spring Bay, Australia. GPS Solut 21(2):451–459. https://doi.org/10.1007/s10291-016-0537-x
Santamaría-Gómez A, Gravelle M, Dangendorf S, Marcos M, Spada G, Wöppelmann G (2017) Uncertainty of the 20th century sea-level rise due to vertical land motion errors. Earth Planet Sci Lett 473:24–32
Sasagawa G, Cook MJ, Zumberge MA (2016) Drift-corrected seafloor pressure observations of vertical deformation at Axial Seamount 2013–2014. Earth Space Sci 3:381–385. https://doi.org/10.1002/2016EA000190
Save H, Bettadpur S, Tapley BD (2016) High resolution CSR GRACE RL05 mascons. J Geophys Res Solid Earth 121:7547–7569. https://doi.org/10.1002/2016JB013007
Senechal N, Abadie S, Ardhuin F, Bujan S, Capo S, Certain R, Coco G, Gallagher E, Garlan T, Masselink G, MacMahan J, Michallet H, Pedreros R, Reniers A, Rey V, Ruessink B, Russell P, Turner

I (2011a) The ECORS-Truc Vert 2008 field experiment: extreme storm conditions over a three-dimensional morphology system in a macro-tidal environment. Ocean Dyn 61:2073–2098. https://doi.org/10.1007/s10236-011-0472-x

Senechal N, Coco G, Bryan KR, Holman RA (2011b) Wave runup during extreme storm conditions. J Geophys Res 116:C07032. https://doi.org/10.1029/2010JC006819

Sheremet A, Staples T, Ardhuin F, Suanez S, Fichaut B (2014) Observations of large infragravity wave runup at Banneg Island, France. Geophys Res Lett 41(3):976–982

Spencer R, Foden PR, McGarry C, Harrison AJ, Vassie JM, Baker TF, Smithson MJ, Harangozo SA, Woodworth PL (1993) The ACCLAIM programme in the South Atlantic and southern oceans. Int Hydrographic Rev 70(1):7–21

Stephens S, Coco G, Bryan KR (2011) Numerical simulations of wave setup over barred beach profiles: implications for predictability. J Waterw Port Coast Ocean Eng. https://doi.org/10.1061/(asce)ww.1943-5460.0000076

Stockdon HF, Holman RA, Howd PA, Sallenger AH (2006) Empirical parameterization of setup, swash, and runup. Coast Eng 53:573–588. https://doi.org/10.1016/j.coastaleng.2005.12.005

Talke SA, Kemp AC, Woodruff J (2018) Relative sea level, tides, and extreme water levels in Boston harbor from 1825 to 2018. J Geophys Res 123:3895–3914. https://doi.org/10.1029/2017JC013645

Testut L, Wöppelmann G, Simon B, Téchiné P (2006) The sea level at Port-aux-Français, Kerguelen Island, from 1949 to the present. Ocean Dyn 56:464–472. https://doi.org/10.1007/s10236-005-0056-8

Tregoning P, Lambeck K, Ramillien G (2008) GRACE estimates of sea surface height anomalies in the Gulf of Carpentaria. Aust Earth Planet Sci Lett 271:241–244

Vignudelli S, Benveniste J, Birol F, FuLL, Picot N (in review) Satellite altimetry measurements of sea level in the coastal zone. Surv Geophys

Wahr J, Molenaar M, Bryan F (1998) Time-variability of the Earth's gravity field: hydrological and oceanic effects and their possible detection using GRACE. J Geophys Res 103:30205–30229

Watkins MM, Wiese DN, Yuan D-N, Boening C, Landerer FW (2015) Improved methods for observing Earth's time variable mass distribution with GRACE. JGR Solid Earth 120:2648–2671. https://doi.org/10.1002/2014JB011547

Watson C, Coleman R, White N et al (2003) Absolute calibration of TOPEX/Poseidon and Jason-1 using GPS buoys in bass strait, Australia special issue: Jason-1 calibration/validation. Mar Geod 26:285–304. https://doi.org/10.1080/714044522

Watson C, Coleman R, Handsworth R (2008) Coastal tide gauge calibration: a case study at Macquarie Island using GPS buoy techniques. J Coast Res 24:1071–1079. https://doi.org/10.2112/07-0844.1

Watts DR, Kontoyiannis H (1990) Deep-ocean bottom pressure measurement: drift removal and performance. J Atmos Ocean Technol 7:296–306. https://doi.org/10.1175/1520-0426

Weissman DE, Morey S, Bourassa M (2017) Studies of the effects of rain on the performance of the SMAP radiometer surface salinity estimates and applications to remote sensing of river plumes. In: IEEE international geoscience and remote sensing symposium (IGARSS), Fort Worth, TX, pp 1491–1494. https://doi.org/10.1109/igarss.2017.8127250

Wiese DN, Landerer FW, Watkins MM (2016) Quantifying and reducing leakage errors in the JPL RL05M GRACE mascon solution. Water Resour Res 52:7490–7502

Willis JK, Chambers DP, Nerem RS (2008) Assessing the globally averaged sea level budget on seasonal to interannual time scales. J Geophys Res 113:C06015. https://doi.org/10.1029/2007JC004517

Woodworth PL, Blackman DL (2002) Changes in extreme high waters at Liverpool since 1768. Int J Climatol 22:697–714. https://doi.org/10.1002/joc.761

Woodworth PL, Pugh DT, Bingley RM (2010) Long-term and recent changes in sea level in the Falkland Islands. J Geophys Res 115:C09025. https://doi.org/10.1029/2010JC006113

Woodworth PL, Gravelle M, Marcos M, Woppelmann G, Hughes CW (2015) The status of measurement of the Mediterranean mean dynamic topography by geodetic techniques. J Geod 89:811–827. https://doi.org/10.1007/s00190-015-0817-1

Woodworth PL, Hunter JR, Marcos M, Caldwell P, Menendez M, Haigh I (2017) Towards a global higher-frequency sea level dataset. Geosci Data J 3:50–59. https://doi.org/10.1002/gdj3.42

Woodworth PL, Melet A, Marcos M, Ray RD, Wöppelmann G, Sasaki YN, Cirano M, Hibbert A, Huthnance JM, Monserrat S, Merrifield MA (in review) Forcing factors causing sea level changes at the coast. Surv Geophys

Wöppelmann G, Marcos M (2016) Vertical land motion as a key to understanding sea level change and variability. Rev Geophys 54:64–92. https://doi.org/10.1002/2015RG000502

Wöppelmann G, Pouvreau N, Simon B (2006) Brest sea level record: a time series construction back to the early eighteenth century. Ocean Dyn 56:487–497. https://doi.org/10.1007/s10236-005-0044-z

Wöppelmann G, Martín Míguez B, Bouin M-N, Altamimi Z (2007) Geocentric sea-level trend estimates from GPS analyses at relevant tide gauges world-wide. Glob Planet Change 57:396–406
Wöppelmann G, Marcos M, Coulomb A, Martín Míguez B, Bonnetain P, Boucher C, Gravelle M, Simon B, Tiphaneau P (2014) Rescue of the historical sea level record of Marseille (France) from 1885 to 1988 and its extension back to 1849–1851. J Geod 88:869–885. https://doi.org/10.1007/s00190-014-0728-6
Wouters B, Chambers DP (2010) Analysis of seasonal ocean bottom pressure variability in the Gulf of Thailand from GRACE. Glob Planet Change. https://doi.org/10.1016/j.gloplacha.2010.08.002

Publisher's Note Springer Nature remains neutral with regard to jurisdictional claims in published maps and institutional affiliations.

Affiliations

Marta Marcos[1,2] · Guy Wöppelmann[3] · Andrew Matthews[4] · Rui M. Ponte[5] · Florence Birol[6] · Fabrice Ardhuin[7] · Giovanni Coco[8] · Alvaro Santamaría-Gómez[9] · Valerie Ballu[3] · Laurent Testut[3] · Don Chambers[10] · Justin E. Stopa[11]

1 IMEDEA(UIB-CSIC), Miquel Marquès, 21, 07190 Esporles, Spain

2 Department of Physics, University of the Balearic Islands, Cra. Valldemossa, km 7.5, 07122 Palma, Spain

3 LIENSs, Université de La Rochelle, 2 Rue Olympe de Gouges, 17000 La Rochelle, France

4 National Oceanography Centre, Joseph Proudman Building, 6 Brownlow Street, Liverpool L3 5DA, UK

5 Atmospheric and Environmental Research, Inc., 131 Hartwell Avenue, Lexington, MA 02421, USA

6 LEGOS, University of Toulouse, IRD, CNES, CNRS, 14 Avenue Edouard Belin, 31400 Toulouse, Francia

7 CNRS, IRD, Ifremer, Laboratoire d'Océanographie Physique et Spatiale (LOPS), IUEM, Univ. Brest, 1625 Route de Sainte-Anne, 29280 Plouzané, Francia

8 Faculty of Science, School of Environment, University of Auckland, Building 302, 23 Symonds Street, Private Bag 92019, Auckland 1142, New Zealand

9 GET, Observatoire Midi–Pyrénées, CNRS, IRD, UPS, Université de Toulouse, 14 avenue Edouard Belin, 31400 Toulouse, France

10 College of Marine Science, University of South Florida, 140 7th Ave S, MSL119, St. Petersburg, FL 33701-5016, USA

11 University of Hawaii, 2540 Dole Street, Holmes Hall 405, Honolulu, HI 96822, USA

Surveys in Geophysics (2019) 40:1319–1349
https://doi.org/10.1007/s10712-019-09569-1

Satellite Altimetry Measurements of Sea Level in the Coastal Zone

Stefano Vignudelli[1] · Florence Birol[2] · Jérôme Benveniste[3] · Lee-Lueng Fu[4] · Nicolas Picot[5] · Matthias Raynal[6] · Hélène Roinard[6]

Received: 4 December 2018 / Accepted: 13 August 2019 / Published online: 16 October 2019

Abstract
Satellite radar altimetry provides a unique sea level data set that extends over more than 25 years back in time and that has an almost global coverage. However, when approaching the coasts, the extraction of correct sea level estimates is challenging due to corrupted waveforms and to errors in most of the corrections and in some auxiliary information used in the data processing. The development of methods dedicated to the improvement of altimeter data in the coastal zone dates back to the 1990s, but the major progress happened during the last decade thanks to progress in radar technology [e.g., synthetic aperture radar (SAR) mode and Ka-band frequency], improved waveform retracking algorithms, the availability of new/improved corrections (e.g., wet troposphere and tidal models) and processing workflows oriented to the coastal zone. Today, a set of techniques exists for the processing of coastal altimetry data, generally called "coastal altimetry." They have been used to generate coastal altimetry products. Altimetry is now recognized as part of the integrated observing system devoted to coastal sea level monitoring. In this article, we review the recent technical advances in processing and the new technological capabilities of satellite radar altimetry in the coastal zone. We also illustrate the fast-growing use of coastal altimetry data sets in coastal sea level research and applications, as high-frequency (tides and storm surge) and long-term sea level change studies.

Keywords Sea level · Coastal zone · Satellite altimetry

1 Introduction

Monitoring the coastal ocean is of first importance since changes in its environmental conditions may affect about 40% of the world's population that lives within 100 km of the coast (Kummu et al. 2016) and that, in the future, is expected to rise at greater rates than inland (Neumann et al. 2015). The coastal ocean is a buffer region between the open sea and land, which is under increased pressures because of climate change, population growth and expanding economic development (Halpern et al. 2015). The coastal zone also

✉ Stefano Vignudelli
vignudelli@pi.ibf.cnr.it

Extended author information available on the last page of the article

faces unique risks from storm surge events and sea level rise. The presence of land makes understanding the ocean processes in the coastal zone more difficult than in the open ocean (Wright and Nichols 2018). The typical shallower water, bathymetric gradients, shoreline shapes, outflow of rivers and estuaries make the geophysical interpretation of the retrieved radar altimeter signal much more complex and have also an effect on the auxiliary information used to derive geophysical parameters (Vignudelli et al. 2011a). Knowledge of ocean tides, ocean circulation, sea level are all important requirements for the coastal zone. In particular, the impact of sea level is especially sensitive at the coast. The coastal zone infrastructure and communities are developing on present sea levels, and understanding how sea level varies from the deep ocean to the coastline is key to forecast future changes.

Since the nineteenth century, the classical method to measure sea level changes is using tide gauges (Emery and Aubrey 1991). They are located near shore to measure sea level changes relative to land with frequent sampling at the location where they are installed (see Marcos et al. 2019). While there are numerous tide gauges along the entire worldwide coastline (Fig. 1), there is only a sparse network that has produced enough long-term time series and there are important gaps especially in developing countries or remote places where it is difficult or expensive to install instruments (Woodworth et al. 2016). Moreover, there are few tide gauges around the world exactly co-located with global navigation satellite system (GNSS) stations operating continuously to measure vertical land motion (VLM) for the whole altimetry era from 1992 to now (Woodworth et al. 2017).

A complementary technology called satellite altimetry offered a new way of measuring sea level changes from space (Fu and Cazenave 2001). It is a mature technique that has provided an accurate estimate of changes in sea level every 10 days for more than 25 years over the open ocean. There is consensus from a large community of scientists about the interpretation of the altimetric signals at various scales and the legitimacy of open-ocean sea level products (Stammer and Cazenave 2017).

Tide gauges are mainly located in protected environments, not often representative of offshore conditions. Moreover, the coastal zone is affected by several local ocean processes, all impacting sea level at different scales. This means that the spatial and temporal

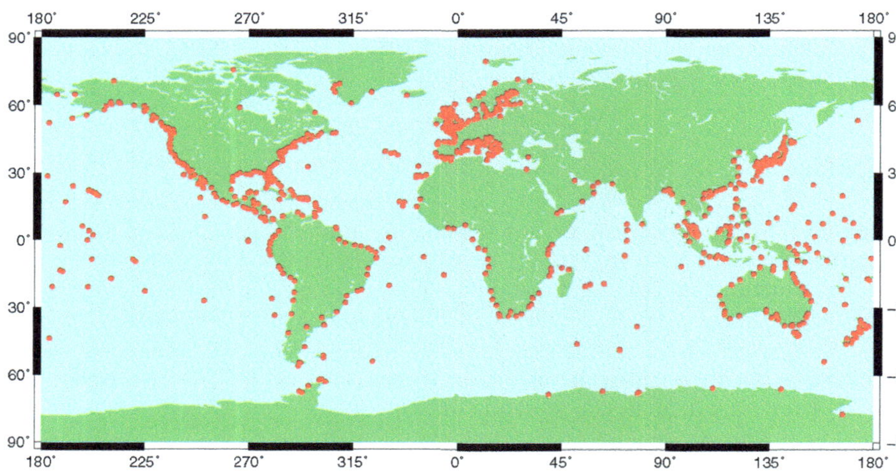

Fig. 1 Map of tide gauge stations with water surface elevations in the Global Extreme Sea Level Analysis (GESLA-2) dataset. Data from Woodworth et al. (2017)

complexity of coastal sea level is difficult to represent with only sparse tide gauges (Roemmich et al. 2017). Satellite altimetry would provide a unique and consistent data set from the open ocean up to the coasts. However, traditionally, data from standard products in the coastal zone (roughly 30 km from the coast) were not processed in this region and therefore flagged as bad and left unused. Therefore, traditional altimetry retrievals were unable to produce meaningful signals of sea level change in the coastal zone (Vignudelli et al. 2006).

This has motivated the development of coastal altimetry to improve the data quality closer to the coast with better spatial resolution, in order to extend the satellite-based sea level record toward the coast with quality comparable to that of the open ocean (Vignudelli et al. 2011a). Moreover, progress was made in technology, with new radar techniques, e.g., synthetic aperture radar (SAR) mode also called delay/Doppler altimeter (DDA) on CryoSat-2, Sentinel-3A and Sentinel-3B operating in Ku-band, and new experimental missions, e.g., the SARAL/AltiKa mission, operating in a conventional, or low-resolution model (LRM), but in Ka-band altimetry to become more capable close to the coast, opened new possibilities to better describe coastal ocean phenomena with high dynamics at fine spatial scales (Cipollini et al. 2017a, b). Therefore, coastal altimetry has the potential to deliver a unique and consistent sea level data set from the open ocean up to the coasts, which can be coupled with tide gauges and other observational techniques to improve the ability to understand coastal sea level changes (Marcos et al. 2019). Coastal altimetry can also measure changes in sea level in regions lacking in situ infrastructure.

The aim of this paper is to review the main issues when retrieving altimeter data (range and corrections) in the coastal zone and the associated techniques to get more and better data closer to the coastline. The paper also identifies the new observing capabilities of modern altimetry, new and improved data streams and products, with the ultimate aim of supporting coastal sea level research studies that are particularly important in the coastal zones subject to inundation, to understand actual conditions, determine rates of change and make reliable forecasting.

2 Satellite Altimetry and Issues in the Coastal Zone

Satellite altimetry has been originally designed for the open ocean, and the spatial and temporal resolution of sensors was supposed not to be high enough to get accurate sea levels in the coastal zone. Altimeter data require a complex sequence of processing steps to get usable information. The satellite altimetry system is based on a radar altimeter sending/receiving pulses/echoes toward/from the mean reflected surface. Over open ocean, the received echoes (called waveform) for classical altimetry follow a standard shape, with steeply rising leading edge followed by a trailing edge with gradually diminishing power. This standard shape is in agreement with the theoretical Brown model (Brown 1977) and hence can be modeled to estimate the signal round-trip time between the radar and the sea surface (Gómez-Enri et al. 2009). From this time value, a range (i.e., the distance between the satellite's center of mass and the mean reflected surface) can be determined. The recipe to transform the altimeter range into sea surface height (SSH) and sea level anomaly (SLA) also requires knowledge of auxiliary information [e.g., satellite altitude; atmospheric and sea surface corrections; mean sea surface (MSS)].

Radar altimetry waveforms can be distorted by any inhomogeneity in the properties of the surface observed (e.g., in altimeter footprints, Gómez-Enri et al. 2010). It is the case in land–ocean transition areas (e.g., Abileah et al. 2013). Ignoring these effects leads to severe errors in the range computation. In coastal areas, waveform retracking algorithms must be able to analyze these distorted waveforms. Moreover, algorithms for various corrections must be considered (Andersen and Scharroo 2011), together with accurate orbits. It is well known that standard altimetry corrections might have reduced the accuracy in the coastal zone for two principal reasons: direct influence of land on the measurement system; reduction in scale, temporal and spatial, of both oceanographic and atmospheric processes in the coastal zone.

The atmospheric-related effects induce a delay in the electromagnetic pulse travel time, which is taken into account through the ionospheric and the tropospheric (dry and wet) corrections (Fernandes et al. 2013). The water vapor correction (known as "wet tropospheric" correction, WTC) is one of the sources of error (Desportes et al. 2007). Strong near-coast gradients in water vapor produce changes in path delay equivalent to several centimeters that must be corrected, but the open-ocean correction based on microwave radiometers is unusable closer than 20–50 km as land enters the radiometer footprint (Vieira et al. 2018).

It has been shown that the dry tropospheric correction (DTC) has strong height dependence (Fernandes et al. 2014). The DTC has a mean variation of −2.5 cm per each 100 m (Cipollini et al. 2017a, b). The DTC for most of the satellite radar altimetry missions, except for, e.g., Sentinel-3A, is interpolated in time and space from values provided at the level of the smoothed representation of the terrain of the adopted model (Cipollini et al. 2017a, b).

The sea state and wind induce effects that must be corrected: radar signals are better reflected from troughs than crests (electromagnetic bias), the median sea level is not the mean sea level (skewness bias) and the range retrieval might be biased (tracker bias); all these are combined into the sea state bias (SSB) correction. The SSB is currently one of the range corrections with the largest uncertainty in the coastal zone (Pires et al. 2016, 2018).

We also need to remove oceanographic signals whose temporal periods are not resolved by altimetry in order to avoid important aliasing errors: tides and the high frequency response to wind and pressure changes. Large errors in tidal modeling still exist in the coastal zone (Ray and Egbert 2017); therefore, subtracting this signal remains a problem (Ray et al. 2011), as tidal range in coastal regions is larger than in open ocean and more complex due to various causes (e.g., bottom friction and resonance). Moreover, the signal has much higher frequency than the sampling of the satellite. Coastal tidal models are improving, but these also require detailed bathymetric data (Toublanc et al. 2018).

The dynamic atmospheric correction (known as DAC, i.e., combining the high-frequency barotropic sea level elevations and the low-frequency sea level elevations from the inverted barometer law) is also usually applied to the altimeter range (Carrère and Lyard 2003). The performances of global models used to estimate DAC in open ocean depend on forcing weather fields and bathymetry that are not at the required resolution and accuracy for the typical variability scales of the coastal zone (Carrère et al. 2016).

Other issues must also be addressed to optimize satellite altimetry in the coastal regions including the use of the MSS (Andersen and Scharroo 2011), which is computed as a spatial and temporal average of the along-track altimetric SSH measurements (Pujol et al. 2018). Typical approaches make use of interpolation and prediction techniques, as, for instance, least squares collocation (Hwang et al. 2002). Moreover, altimeter standard data are often missing in the coastal band from the coastline to 50 km offshore; therefore, the resolution of MSS products derived from altimetry data is degraded (Roblou et al. 2011).

From the studies mentioned above and others published in the literature, a reasonable consensus emerges on the fact that the ongoing data reprocessing efforts in the coastal zone are crucial for coastal sea level monitoring. This reprocessing relies on preprocessing (e.g., retracking, new/improved corrections) and on post-processing of higher rate data (e.g., editing). While the waveforms at high sampling rate (20/40/80 Hz corresponding to ~350/175/85 m depending on the altimeter mission) are all included within the products delivered, as well as range, significant wave height (SWH) and sigma-0 (Backscatter coefficient) that all are available at that resolution, the geophysical corrections are provided at 1 Hz (corresponding to ~7 km), and an interpolation step has to be performed to resample these fields to the native 20/40/80 Hz rate of the altimeter measurements.

3 Coastal Altimetry: A Set of Techniques

Coastal altimetry, i.e., the extension of satellite radar altimetry into the oceanic coastal zone, is an active field of research. Standard geophysical data records (GDRs) are almost useless for coastal applications, as most of the data in the coastal zone are flagged as "bad" because they are processed with the criteria used for open-ocean altimetry (Vignudelli et al. 2011b). This impediment to the use of altimetry for understanding coastal ocean processes can, however, in most cases, be overcome by removing or mitigating unwanted effects caused by the instrument, atmosphere, ocean and land. As stated previously, until recently, these effects were not sufficiently understood in the coastal zone, but the situation is rapidly evolving thanks to intense research in this field.

Coastal altimetry has made steady progress in recent years (Restano et al. 2018; Cipollini et al. 2017a, b; Vignudelli et al. 2011a) and has become a recognized mission objective for present and future satellite altimeters (Cipollini et al. 2014). Coastal altimetry can be considered as a set of techniques aiming at retrieving more and better data closer to the coast, where land contamination and inhomogeneity of radar backscattering degrade range, SSB and WTC corrections.

The traditional coastal reprocessing for conventional altimetry follows the approach based on de-flagging over-conservative flags, ad hoc filtering-out spikes in the data or in the corrections, re-interpolating missing corrections, and other processing recipes and screening applied to 1 Hz data to retain small-scale signals (e.g., Birol et al. 2006, 2017; Roblou et al. 2011).

A second generation of coastal altimetry reprocessing uses all the improvements of the first generation but also aims at getting closer to the coast, typically up to 1–5 km. As shown previously in this case there are additional problems: land which enters the footprint of the altimeter; quasi-specular reflections from stretches of calm water (for instance from a sheltered area); steepening of the waves; short-scale variability of the surface characteristics. All these factors cause a departure of the received radar waveforms from the open-ocean "Brown" model (Brown 1977) in pulse-limited altimeters used for the estimation of the parameters. Therefore, it becomes necessary to fit alternate models to the waveforms, in other words to "retrack" the waveforms (Gómez-Enri et al. 2009).

During recent years, significant improvements have been achieved thanks to more sophisticated reprocessing that now uses robust retracking algorithms for retrieving the range from altimeter's radar echoes. Some approaches are based on some form of classification of the waveforms depending on their shape and the use of a different functional form for the fitting of each class (e.g., Deng and Featherstone 2006; Berry et al. 2010; Yang et al. 2012). Other methods process a stack of successive waveforms to detect the signature of bright targets as proposed by Gómez-Enri et al. (2010), for the purpose of "cleaning" the stack prior to retracking (Quartly 2010). A more recent approach is based on the partitioning of the waveform in a sub-waveform containing the leading edge, thus excluding the tail section where most artifacts due to spurious bright targets from bordering land appear (e.g., Guo et al. 2010; Yang et al. 2011; Idris and Deng 2012; Passaro et al. 2014; Roscher et al. 2017; Peng and Deng 2018). The algorithms of the various authors differ in the estimator used and the method adopted to isolate the portion of the real waveform to fit with the Brown ocean model.

Advances in the observational capabilities through delay-Doppler technology and SAR/DDA processing have brought an improved observability of the small scales (Heslop et al. 2017; Raynal et al. 2018) and higher accuracy in sea level estimations (Boy et al. 2017). A growing number of publications show that the new SAR mode from CryoSat-2 and now globally from Sentinel-3A and Sentinel-3B has been particularly beneficial in the coastal zone, by virtue of the higher along-track resolution and lower noise than conventional altimetry, when the satellite ground track is perpendicular to the coastline (e.g., Gómez-Enri et al. 2018; Dinardo et al. 2018).

In situations where the satellite is orbiting parallel to the coast, the SRAL (Sentinel-3 Ku/C SAR Radar Altimeter) ground resolution cell has a greater proportion of land coverage (Boy et al. 2017). Conventional altimetry also has a greater proportion of land coverage when near the coast, as the ground resolution cell is a circle and then a ring. The difference is that it does not matter what orientation the track has. Some preliminary studies, however, limited to specific areas of investigation, seem to show some impact of land contamination (Birgiel et al. 2018), with reduced precision across track (Cotton et al. 2016). In these situations, two approaches exist to recover more data, one removing contamination using SARin mode (applicable to CryoSat-2 only) and constructing the waveform only from the remaining part (García et al. 2018), and a second one focusing on the waveform to a narrow beam (called fully focused), so that contamination can be excluded (Egido and Smith 2017). Both techniques are still in their infancy but show some promising results. The SAR mode can be processed simply unfocused up to 80 Hz, and a higher rate can be achieved with the fully focused approach.

Following the successful launch in February 2013 of the SARAL/AltiKa, the first Ka-band radar altimetry mission, new capabilities emerged in the coastal zone. SARAL/AltiKa takes advantage of a reduced footprint to about 100 km^2, compared with larger (~ 300 km^2) footprints of conventional altimetry (e.g., Jason series) as reported in Fig. 1.17 in Stammer and Cazenave (2017). Due to the smaller footprint, the altimeter can provide better results closer to the coasts. SARAL/AltiKa has also higher spatial resolution (up to 40 Hz) than the present conventional Ku-band (up to 20 Hz), thus enabling data retrieval much closer to the coast (Bonnefond et al. 2018; Verron et al. 2018). Progress has been made in reducing the altimeter footprints and noise going closer to the coast, but also in processing algorithms, corrections, and products for coastal applications (Valladeau et al. 2015). Moreover, the higher Ka-band frequency (35 GHz vs. 13 GHz for Ku-band) permits the use of a larger bandwidth than other altimeters, thus enhancing the resolution of the waveform gates to 0.3 m (Verron et al. 2018).

Reprocessed experimental products dedicated to the monitoring of coastal sea level are now available (e.g., COASTALT, ALES, XTRACK, PISTACH, SARvatore, TUDaBo). Compared to standard products, they include higher along-track resolution, new/improved retrackers, new/improved corrections, refined preprocessing, and/or post-processing. Cipollini et al. (2017a, b) summarized the main characteristics of the available products. The above products differ for their processing approach, applied geophysical corrections, coverage, satellite missions. An updated table is accessible at www.coastalt.eu/datasets, as algorithms and methodological approaches will continue to mature over the coming decades.

X-TRACK is a 1-Hz along-track product available in 23 regions with consistent and homogeneous coastal processing for some altimetric missions (TOPEX/Poseidon, Jason-1&2&3, Geosat Follow-on, Envisat, SARAL). However, a global 20-Hz product for all available missions is not yet available. The European Space Agency (ESA) Climate Change Initiative (CCI) project on "Sea Level" has reprocessed altimeter data from nine satellite missions over 1993–2015 to provide homogenous sea level for all altimetry missions (Legeais et al. 2018) over a grid of around 25 km, with the objective of improving estimations of climate-related sea level changes (Ablain et al. 2017) and consequently proposed a climate processing standard that has been replicated in other processing systems. The CCI+ new phase will address the last 50 km to the coast, with a coastal reprocessing for all missions and generation of a coastal altimetry product dedicated to long-term coastal sea level monitoring (Cazenave et al. 2018).

At the time of writing, there are height altimetry satellites currently in service (Jason-2, Jason-3, SARAL/AltiKa, HY2-A/B, CryoSat-2, Sentinel-3A and Sentinel-3B), plus the SWIM real-aperture Ku-band radar (Hauser et al. 2017) on board the China-France CFOSAT satellite, which also takes nadir-view altimetric measurements, and more than 25 years of data archived from previous satellite missions (Fig. 2). This multi-mission data set with coastal-oriented reprocessing applied represents an important asset to support sea level research in the coastal zone.

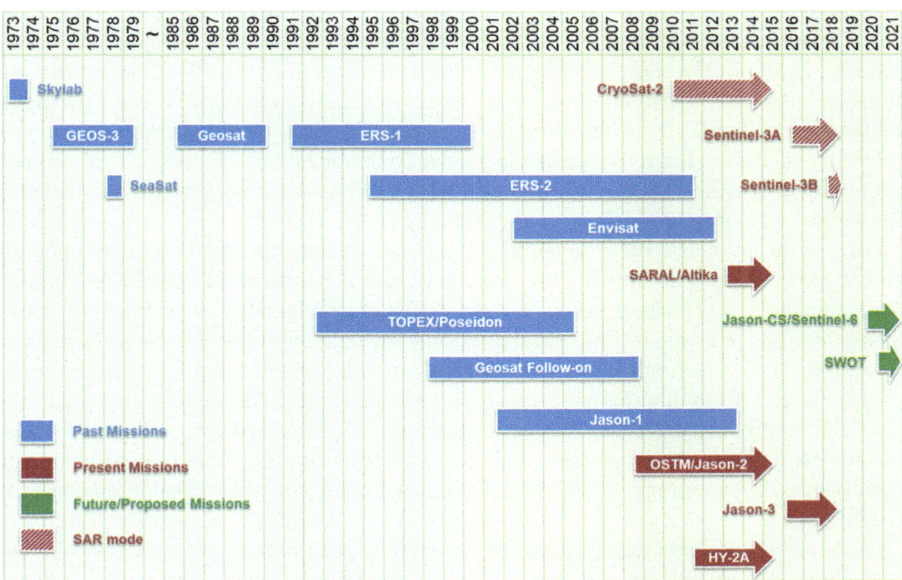

Fig. 2 Global satellite altimetry missions: past, now and then (Courtesy: JPL/PO.DAAC). Fill pattern with dots is used to identify satellite missions operating in SAR mode

4 Impact of Geophysical Corrections Near the Coast

As shown previously, some of the corrections applied to the altimeter range suffer from large uncertainties in the coastal zone and/or in shallow waters (Vignudelli et al. 2005; Andersen and Scharroo 2011; Ray et al. 2011) either because they have large spatiotemporal variability that is poorly reproduced by numerical models (e.g., ocean tide and DAC corrections), or because they are less precisely estimated by onboard sensors than over the open ocean (e.g., the radiometer-based WTC that suffers severe land contamination), or even because they are deduced from the altimeter measurements impacted by the proximity of land (e.g., the ionospheric correction and the SSB). As a consequence, near coastlines, the quality of the resulting SSH data degrades as the quality of the corrections applied diminishes. A complete review on this issue can be found in Vignudelli et al. (2011a).

At a global scale, the geophysical corrections that may induce the larger errors on radar altimetry coastal sea level data are: the wet tropospheric delay, the ocean tide correction, the DAC, and the SSB (Andersen and Scharroo 2011). The radiometer-based WTC degrades rapidly in a coastal band of 10–40 km, leading to errors of a few centimeters (depending on the radiometer onboard the satellite, see Fig. 6 of Cipollini et al. 2017a, b). In Jason-2/3 missions, new dedicated algorithms are implemented to largely reduce the effects of land contamination in the radiometer footprint (Brown 2010) and the improved correction is now available in classical GDR products This correction can also be derived from atmospheric models, but their resolution does not allow capturing the spatial and temporal short-scale changes in water vapor in the coastal zone. Other solutions consist in removing the contamination coming from the surrounding land from the radiometer measurements (Brown 2010; Obligis et al. 2011). The GNSS-derived Path Delay Plus (GPD+) correction, combining valid measurements from the onboard radiometer, from GNSS coastal and island stations and from scanning radiometers on board various remote sensing missions, is one of the most recent algorithms to retrieve improved WTC for most radar altimeter missions (Fernandes et al. 2015; Fernandes and Lázaro 2016). The operational computation of the GPD+ correction has been implemented for all altimeter missions at University of Porto (Joana Fernandes, personal communication). The use of this correction improves significantly the altimeter coastal sea level estimations and the estimation of regional sea level trends (Cipollini et al. 2017a, b).

For coastal altimetry, the availability of accurate ocean tide and DAC corrections in shallow water areas is a critical issue (Andersen and Scharroo 2011). These geophysical effects tend to be much larger, complex and associated with higher wavenumbers in coastal waters than in deep waters. Considerable efforts have already been dedicated to improve the numerical tidal solutions. Regular exercises of tidal model inter-comparisons [as in Stammer et al. (2014)] highlight that much progress has been achieved in global tidal solutions. But significant differences are still observed in some coastal areas: For the major constituents, the difference between ocean tide observations and global model solutions is larger than 5 cm on average [compared to less than 1 cm in the open ocean, Stammer et al. (2014)].

Modeling individual coastal regions offers significant progress for both the tidal and atmospherically forced high-frequency corrections (Roblou et al. 2011) and regional model corrections start to be available over some coastal areas (Maraldi et al. 2007; Pairaud et al. 2008; Le Bars et al. 2010). We expect to see further important progresses in coastal ocean tide and DAC corrections thanks to the efforts done on increasing the spatial model resolution and improving numerical schemes, data assimilation techniques, and better knowledge of the coastal bathymetry and the coastline (which still suffer from significant errors in many coastal areas, as reported in Stammer et al. 2014). Note also that for some coastal altimetry applications (storm surges or assimilation in numerical models that simulate ocean tides), the ocean tide and DAC corrections may not be a source of errors since they do not need to be removed from the sea level estimates.

The SSB is also a major source of uncertainty in coastal altimetry. Present-day methods for correcting this bias are based on wave and wind information derived from the altimeter, using empirical formulations. The latter are regularly refined (Labroue et al. 2006; Tran et al. 2010), but they are established for the open ocean. Near the coast, where wind and wave conditions change rapidly in both space and time, the development of a dedicated algorithm is needed. Another strong limitation is due to the fact that the SSB computation is based on parameters derived from the retracking of the radar waveforms (SWH and wind). Near coastlines (10–15 km from the coast), where the waveforms are much more complex, the quality of the SSB correction degrades with the performance of the waveform retracker (Andersen and Scharroo 2011). Different studies indicate that the SSB estimation may be improved by inclusion of wave model information (Tran et al. 2006), use of retrackers adapted to coastal waveforms (Gómez-Enri et al. 2016) or more simply computation of regional empirical models (Passaro et al. 2018).

Finally, every shoreline is affected by specific geophysical processes and the correction issue may be significantly different from one coastal region to another. This is illustrated in Fig. 3, which shows the standard deviation of the SLA and of the different geophysical corrections as a function of latitude for 8 years of Jason-2 data. We consider two tracks located in two regions characterized by different ocean dynamics. The SLA has been computed using all the corrections whose statistics are shown in Fig. 3. We assume that a sudden and brief increase in standard deviation values indicates errors in the correction. Comparing the standard deviation of the SLA and of the individual corrections allows us to investigate the relative impact of errors in each time-variable correction in the sea level estimation. Note first that the typical values of the variability of the different corrective terms are approximately the same in both regions, except for the ocean tides (0–250 cm for track 239 against 6–8 cm for track 85, located in a microtidal region, i.e., where the tidal range is less than 2 m).

The corrections that have the largest variability are the DAC and the ocean tides. This stresses the importance of having accurate estimates of these geophysical signals particularly along macro-tidal coasts such as over the NW European shelf seas. The corrections that have the lowest variability appear to be the ionospheric and the DTC. Concerning WTC, the GPD+ solution is used here. The values of the corresponding standard deviation appear very stable and do not indicate any degradation of the correction quality when approaching the coast. This result confirms that the GPD+ offers a significant improvement in coastal sea level estimations compared to the model and radiometer solutions. The standard deviation of the SSB (in the range 2–6 cm) appears more variable in space and suddenly increases in the last kilometers near the coast, where the standard deviation of the SLA exhibits unrealistic variations. This behavior is expected because waveforms are degraded by the land contamination in this coastal strip, thus impacting the estimation of epoch, SWH and wind amplitude that are used to compute SSB. These results indicate that in addition to the progress expected from future tidal and DAC model solutions, the computation of the SSB correction is clearly a field where effort is needed to gain accuracy in coastal altimetry data.

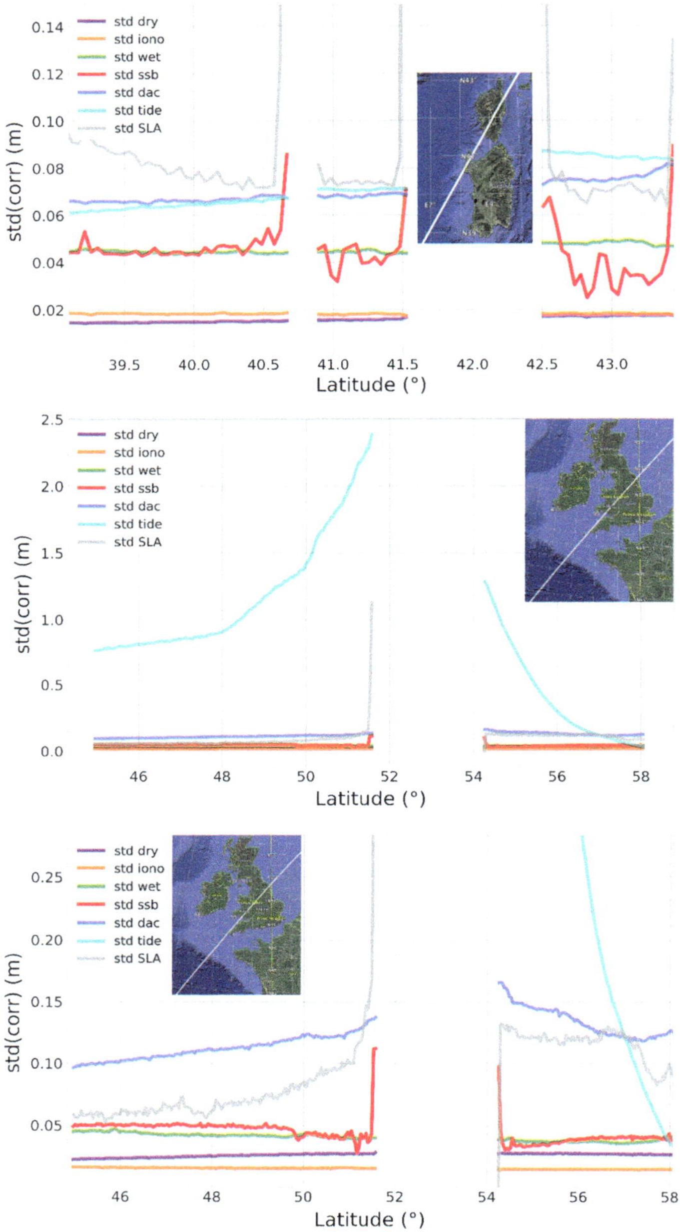

Fig. 3 Standard deviation (in meters) of the SLA and of the different geophysical corrections computed from cycles 1 to 296 of Jason-2 data along the track 85 in the Northwestern Mediterranean Sea (top) and along the track 239 in the North East Atlantic (middle and bottom). The figure at the bottom is an amplitude zoom of the figure at the middle. For each track, the region considered in indicated on the map superimposed on the figure. The corrections are derived from the RADS (Radar Altimeter Database System) database, except the wet tropospheric correction which is produced by University of Porto and distributed by the CTOH (Centre of Topography of the Oceans and the Hydrosphere)

5 Altimeter Performance Near the Coast

The onboard altimeters were initially designed to measure large-scale SSH variations in the open ocean. Their high accuracy and the large period sampled allowed improvements to our understanding of the large-scale oceanic circulation and its evolution. The extension of these observations to the coast is one of the greatest current challenges in particular for the observability of mesoscale and sub-mesoscale oceanic processes and to measure the impact of sea-level rise on our environment. However, for altimeter performances near the coasts, one of the most well-known sources of error is the footprint contamination by land surfaces. This error strongly depends on the altimeter characteristics.

Figure 4a illustrates the percentage of valid measurements computed for three different kinds of altimeter: Poseidon-3 (Jason-3), AltiKa (SARAL/AltiKa) and SRAL (Sentinel-3A), respectively, operating in LRM Ku-band, LRM Ka-band and SARM (SAR mode) Ku-band. In order to compare relevant metrics derived from the different satellites ground tracks, this statistic is computed for all ocean coastal areas over a period of 1 month. The validity criterion chosen is based on a threshold applied on SLA measurements. Indeed,

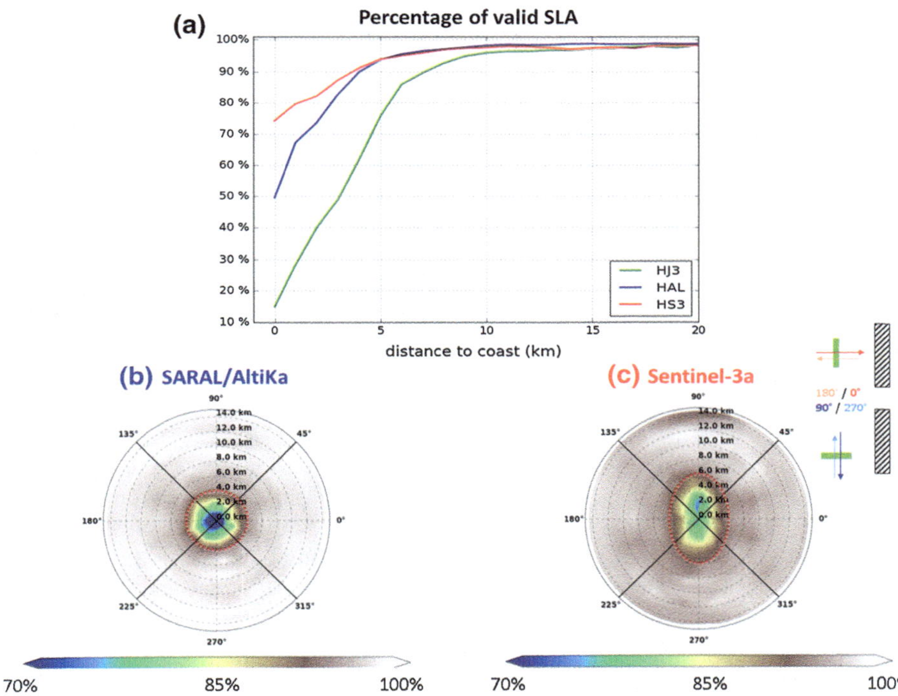

Fig. 4 Plot **a** shows the percentage of 20 Hz valid measurements computed for Sentinel-3A (red curve), SARAL/AltiKa (blue curve), and Jason-3 (green curve) datasets as a function of the distance to the coast. For this diagnosis, a measurement is considered as valid if the unbiased SLA does not exceed 1 m. Plots **b**, **c** show the percentage of valid measurements for SARAL/AltiKa and Sentinel-3A datasets (respectively, **b** and **c**). The radius of the circle corresponds to the distance of the measurement from the closest coast line. The perimeter of the circle corresponds to the angle formed between the ground track of the satellite and the closest coastline. 0° and 180° angles correspond to a perpendicular approach, whereas 90° and 270° angles correspond to parallel displacement

the usual 1 Hz editing provided in users handbooks is not relevant for high-rate measurements. Moreover, this choice of a 1-m threshold across the SLA mean value is a compromise for removing the strong outliers and keeping the measurements affected by the coast to illustrate the different kinds of altimeter performance (Figs. 4a, 6). The result shows a clear decrease in the number of valid measurements when the satellites approach the coast. However, the impact of the land contamination differs for the three altimeters:

- For Jason-3, the percentage of valid measurements starts to decrease around 10 km off the coast. From more than 98% in open ocean, it reaches only 15% at hundreds of meters to the coast. The value of 10 km roughly corresponds to the radius of the altimeter footprint.
- For SARAL/AltiKa, the decrease is smoother and starts around 6 km from the coast. This is explained by the smaller Ka footprint for which the radius equals 5.7 km on average. Moreover, the antenna gain pattern allows reducing the energy of the signals the farthest from the nadir (factor 2 for range gates at 4.5 km from nadir). Within 4.5 km to the coast, 50% of the measurements are still exploitable for estimating sea level.
- Finally, in the case of Sentinel-3A SARM mode dataset, the percentage of valid measurements decreases but more slightly than for other altimeters. This is explained by the specific geometry of the SARM footprint with its 300 m of resolution in the along-track direction.

The two polar plots show for SARAL/AltiKa (Fig. 4b) and Sentinel-3A (Fig. 4c) the percentage of valid SLA measurements as a function of the distance to the coast (radius of the circle) and as a function of the angle formed between the satellite ground track and the coastline (degrees of the circle). For AltiKa, as expected the direction of the satellite with respect to the coastline has no impact on the data quality (the footprint shape is circular). However, for Sentinel-3A SARM datasets an asymmetry is observed. When the satellite ground track is perpendicular to the coastline, the footprint contamination occurs much later (theoretically at 300 m from the coast). This result would mean that in these specific cases, the SARM range measurements are almost not impacted by the coast.

In addition to the altimeter signal and antenna characteristics, the tracker performances also play an important role in coastal areas. The tracker is responsible for the acquisition of the backscattered signal (Roca et al. 2009; Desjonquères et al. 2010). Two different tracking modes could be distinguished: the conventional close loop (CL) mode and (implemented for the first time on Jason-2 Poseidon-3 altimeter) the open loop (OL) mode. While in CL mode the tracker adjusts the position of the observation windows as a function of the level of energy of the backscattered signal; in OL mode an onboard predetermined digital elevation model is used. Figure 5 illustrates the altimeter tracking performances in terms of number of available measurements (with respect to the theoretical high-resolution ground track) derived from different satellites as a function of the distance to the coast. Once again, in order to compare results derived from the different satellites ground track, the diagnoses were performed over a period of 1 month including all the ocean coastal areas. Over this period, while SRAL and Poseidon-3 tracker operate in OL mode, the AltiKa tracker is in CL mode (SARAL/AltiKa geodetic phase). Despite its smaller footprint, the percentage of missing measurements for AltiKa starts to increase at 10 km from the coast, while it stays flat for Sentinel-3A. This result means that 3% (respectively, 8%) of the time, at 5 km (respectively, 0 km) from the coast, AltiKa tracker loses the signal and thus cannot provide sea surface measurements. The

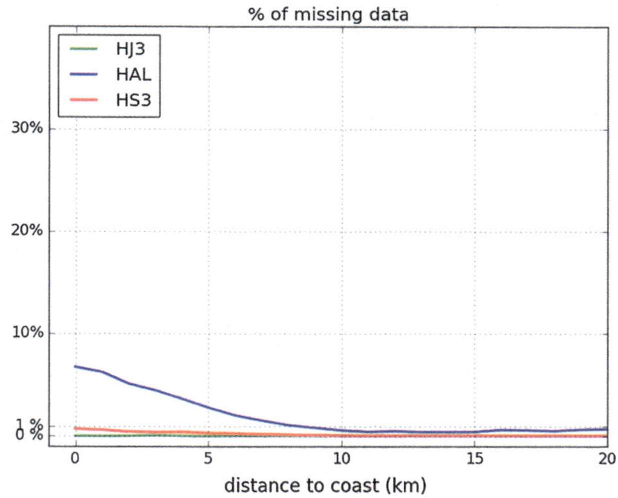

Fig. 5 Percentage of 20 Hz missing measurements computed for Sentinel-3A (red curve), SARAL/AltiKa (blue curve), and Jason-3 (green curve) datasets as a function of the distance to the coast. This percentage is computed with respect to their respective high-resolution theoretical ground track

slight difference observed between Jason-3 and Sentinel-3A (around 0.6%) could be explained by the fact that, for Sentinel-3A, all the ocean coastal areas are acquired in OL mode except the Indonesian sea area. Thus over this small region, more measurements are lost by the Sentinel-3A tracker operating in CL mode.

We have just seen that the data quality and the percentage of available measurements in coastal areas depend on the altimeter characteristics. Figure 6 aims at describing the impact on the final SSH. Global statistics of mean SLA were computed for Jason-3 (a), AltiKa (b) and Sentinel-3A SARM (c) datasets. First, this analysis shows, in the case of conventional altimetry (a and b plots), that when the satellites approach the coast, the trackers lose the return signal. For Jason-3, this loss appears at 6 km from the coast with an SLA decrease of 5 cm followed by a significant increase at 4 km. For AltiKa, the same thing is observed, respectively, at 4 and 2 km. For both satellites, the waveforms are disturbed by land backscattered signal. It occurs at different distances from the coast because of the different footprint sizes. The estimated geophysical parameters are impacted since the Brown model dedicated to oceanic waveforms (Brown 1977) is not suitable to retrack this kind of artifacts. Thanks to the smaller Sentinel-3A SARM footprint in the along-track direction, these SLA variations are not observed. The SLA signal appears flat until hundreds of meters from the coast. Examining in more detail the different angle configurations (Fig. 6d), it appears that:

- in the worst case (when Sentinel-3A ground track is parallel to the coast line) the SLA behaves similarly as for conventional altimetry (black curve). From 5 to 2 km to the coast, a decrease is observed followed by an increase in the SLA.
- in the best configuration (Sentinel-3A ground track perpendicular to the coastline), the SLA slightly increases continuously until the coastline.

Although this result (the gray curve) includes the errors related to the geophysical corrections (as mentioned in the previous section), it gives a first measure of the signal we expect to observe close to the coast when the altimeter footprint is not corrupted by land surfaces. The use of high-accuracy regional models combined with the exploitation

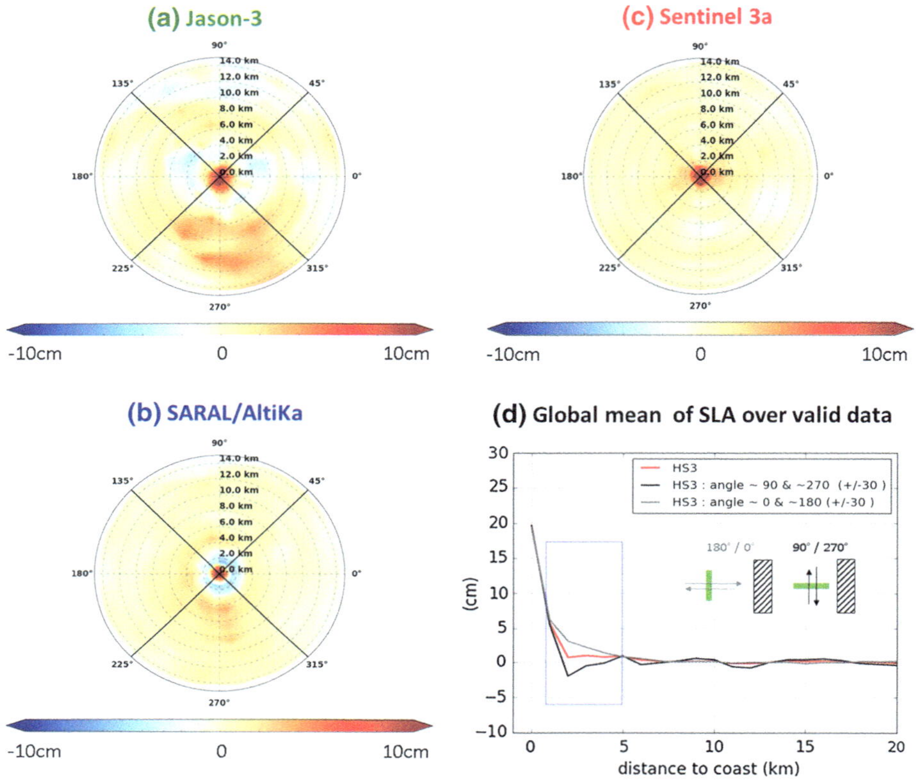

Fig. 6 Global average of the SLA derived from Jason-3, SARAL/AltiKa, and Sentinel-3A datasets (respectively, **a**–**c**). For the three first plots, the radius of the circle corresponds to the distance of the measurement from the closest coast line. The perimeter of the circle corresponds to the angle formed between the ground track of the satellite and the closest coastline. 0° and 180° angles correspond to a perpendicular approach, whereas 90° and 270° angles correspond to parallel displacement. Plot **d** is a one-dimensional representation of the Sentinel-3A SARM SLA average as a function of the distance to the coast in the global case (red curve) in the optimal case (gray curve) and in the worst case (black curve)

of optimal Sentinel-3A ground tracks (in perpendicular configuration with respect to the coastline) would allow us to compute relevant SSH measurements very close to the coast.

The diagnoses presented in this section mainly addressed the altimeter performances in the last 20 km band from the coast. Of course, the definition of coastal areas is not restricted to that narrow coastal strip; it also includes all the complex, regionally specific oceanic processes that could occur at hundreds of kilometers from the coast. We are confident in the altimeter capabilities to sample the large-scale and mesoscale signals in such areas. However, further work is needed to precisely describe their performances in order to exploit the shorter wavelengths.

6 A Selection of Coastal Altimetry Improvements

A number of studies in recent years have demonstrated the improvements in both quantity of valid measurements and quality as a function of distance from coast when waveforms are reprocessed and corrections optimized. Today, retracked pulse-limited altimetry, with optimized corrections, provides valid measurements to within 5 km from the coastline (Cipollini et al. 2017a, b).

The intrinsic capabilities of the innovative AltiKa Ka-band altimetry have confirmed expectations that, compared to conventional altimetry, the standard deviation of the range remains stable for AltiKa (lower than 10 cm) to less than 5 km from the coastline (Cipollini et al. 2017a, b). Much progress has been also achieved in assessing the quantity and quality of AltiKa sea level in coastal regions (Troupin et al. 2015).

The inherent improved capability of SAR mode in the coastal zone confirms that sea level is less noisy and more data are retained. The standard deviation of SLAs, which increases near coast, is the smallest for SAR data processed with SAMOSA+ (SAR Altimetry MOde Studies and Applications) and within the expected range until 2–3 km from the coast (Fenoglio-Marc et al. 2019). The accuracy of high-resolution along-track SLA from CryoSat-2 in SAR mode is in line with pulse-limited SARAL/AltiKa (Fenoglio-Marc et al. 2015; Gómez-Enri et al. 2018), and expected with Sentinel-3A and Sentinel-3B too.

Several studies have dealt with the comparison of various altimetric data sets with independent measurements (Xu et al. 2018; Vu et al. 2018) as well as the quality assessment of Sentinel-3A and CryoSat-2 (e.g., Bonnefond et al. 2018) and AltiKa data (Bonnefond et al. 2018). After 10 years of validation of coastal altimetry products in the Gulf of Cadiz and the Strait of Gibraltar (southwestern Iberian peninsula), the results clearly show that coastal-oriented retracking techniques (such as Adaptive Leading Edge Subwaveform (ALES)) and more accurate corrections provide around 20% of RMSE improvement for the high-resolution along-track SLA reprocessed using ALES retracker with respect to the operational GDR (Gómez-Enri et al. 2016). The comparison of sea level trends for tide gauges and the nearest along-track altimeter point shows some agreements but also some challenging discrepancies (Gharineiat and Deng 2018) when using along-track 1-Hz data supplied by the Radar Altimeter Database System (RADS) (Scharroo et al. 2013).

7 A Selection of Coastal Altimetry Applications

The availability of new experimental coastal altimetry products stimulated their usage for oceanographic studies (e.g., Birol et al. 2017). We will show a few examples to illustrate the contribution of coastal altimetry to sea level research studies in the coastal zone.

An improved coastal altimetry data set of sea level allowed the study of the flow variability through the Strait of Gibraltar (Gómez-Enri et al. 2019a). The study showed that global tidal models have in this region performances very close to a local model. However, in other regions global tidal models might not reproduce properly the tidal field. On the other hand, global MSS models in complex regions such as the Strait of Gibraltar show that residual errors may mask some of the sea level variability, making difficult its oceanographic interpretation. In the same area of investigation, Gómez-Enri et al. (2019b) show that sea level cross-strait differences are significantly correlated with zonal winds when a local along-track MSS based on ERS and Envisat retracked data is used instead of MSS models.

Regional studies of coastal sea level variability are other applications of coastal altimetry. For example, coastal altimetry datasets have revealed higher annual amplitudes in the presence of narrow coastal currents (Passaro et al. 2015, 2016), improved the knowledge of coastal tides (Piccioni et al. 2018) and permitted the extraction of coastal tidal mixing front signals (Dong et al. 2018).

Coastal altimetry plays also a critical role in storm surge forecasting studies. The value of improved altimeter data in capturing storm surges, if the satellite passes over the area at the right time, has been demonstrated by many authors. For example, Antony et al. (2014) analyzed altimeter data from the various missions in the Bay of Bengal during storm surge events. By coincidence, the Chinese HY2-A satellite passed at the right time to be above hurricane Sandy. The altimeter measured a storm surge of almost 1.5 m, with significant wave heights of nearly 8 m, making it the largest surge to date to be captured by satellite altimetry (Lillibridge et al. 2013). Coastal altimetry data have also been used for defining initial conditions in storm surge models to improve model performances in forecasting sea level peaks in the Venice region (Bajo et al. 2017) and in the Baltic Sea (Madsen et al. 2015).

Sea-level rise is seriously impacting coasts and coastal communities globally (Wright et al. 2018). For instance, in the Mediterranean Sea, the risk due to storm surges and coastal erosion under high sea level rise places vast portions of European coastline and United Nations Educational, Scientific and Cultural Organization (UNESCO) heritage sites at risk. It is thus important to have accurate sea-level observations in these sites in order to better assess the climate-related contribution. Tide gauge trends account for not only water volume changes but also land subsidence, which is observable using different techniques (e.g., GNSS, InSAR) in a limited number of sites. Coastal altimetry is aiming at extending the sea level climate record to the coastal zone with quality comparable to open ocean, thus contributing to answer the question if the sea level rate is similar or differs between open-ocean and the coastal zones. An example is the case of city of Venice, where the long-term implications of sea level rise have not been thoroughly investigated yet, and the contribution of the various processes to the coastal sea level change has not been noticeably quantified. A preliminary analysis of sea level changes around Venice (Vignudelli et al. 2019) shows that smaller trend has been found from altimetry (4.25 ± 1.25 mm/year) than those measured offshore (5.65 ± 1.25 mm/year) and in the lagoon (5.29 ± 1.27 mm/year), all local trends being much higher than that for the global mean sea level (GMSL) which is around 3.3 mm/year (Legeais et al. 2018). The differences might be explained in terms of VLM. However, the coastal zone needs specific processing, and the increased uncertainty in this area is not reflected in the trend error in the present version of the sea level CCI, which is based on open-ocean altimetry.

The new coastal altimetry datasets have many other uses as well. An example is the analysis of the surface signature due to a heavy Guadalquivir River discharge event (Gómez-Enri et al. 2018). The freshwater input will reduce the salinity levels in the surface layer during these episodes, resulting in a bump in the along-track CryoSat-2 sea level profile. Piecuch et al. (2018) highlighted the importance to get accurate satellite-based sea level measurements within a few kms of the coast and in estuaries (Durand et al. 2019). The analysis of river levels and tidal measurements from gauges installed throughout the eastern USA clearly illustrates that variations in river discharge can raise or lower coastal mean sea level by several centimeters.

Another study shows how the sparse coverage of tide gauges and their potential discontinuity in measuring sea level limit the accurate assessment of long-term changes in important coastal regions, such as the Pearl River delta (He et al. 2014) and that the

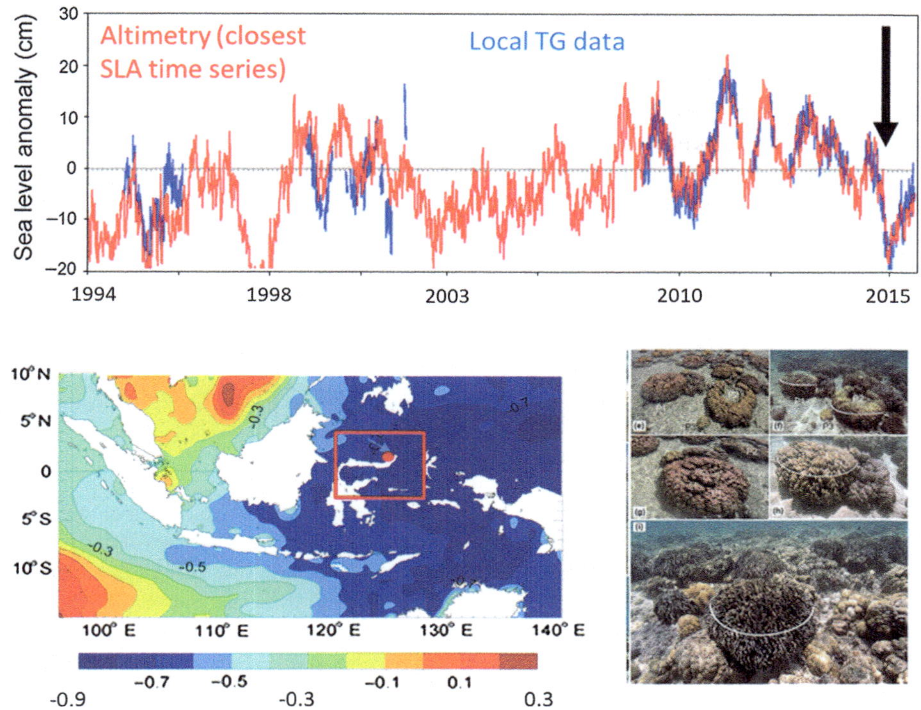

Fig. 7 Lower panel left: Bunaken location in the north of Sulawesi (Indonesia). Lower panel right: Bunaken reef flats and close-up of various coral colonies in **a**–**i**. Upper panel: SLAs measured by the Bitung tide gauge (TG) station (low-quality data), and overlaid on altimetry ADT anomaly data for the 1993–2016 period. To be noted the gaps in the tide gauge time series. Adapted from Ampou et al. (2017)

synergy with coastal altimetry data can contribute to reconstruct regionally consistent SLAs.

High-resolution coastal altimeter data are being used to monitor areas where recent mortality in coral communities was observed after an El Niño-induced sea level fall. For instance on Bunaken Island (Indonesia), radar altimetry and tide gauge data showed a rapid and significant sea level fall (Fig. 7), with a clear link to mortality (Ampou et al. 2017).

The new SARin mode operating on CryoSat-2 offers an additional possibility of discriminating land contamination signals from off-nadir land targets over coastal regions, thus helping to interpret sea level changes in complex morphologies. Idžanović et al. (2018) used SARin data to demonstrate the potential improvement of coastal sea level estimates around Norwegian coasts that are characterized by the presence of many islands, mountains, and deep, narrow fjords.

8 Perspectives from New Altimetry Missions

The space agencies are currently developing long-term scenarios aiming at filling gaps and satisfying emerging priority user needs. The coastal zone has two specific requirements in terms of spatial variability due to local effects and temporal evolution due to short events. The present constellation of eight altimeters provides an advantage for that type of monitoring. Coastal altimetry is a legitimate component of the coastal observing system (Benveniste et al. 2019) and now part of the new processing platforms, which allow researchers to rapidly process Earth observation data (Clerc et al. 2016). From a technological point of view, there will be a consolidation of the SAR mode in future radar altimeters and an important change of paradigm using SAR interferometry with radar altimetry becoming an imaging sensor.

8.1 SAR Altimetry

The recent developments in SAR mode toward higher resolution (up to 300 m along track) that contributed to the scientific advancement for coastal sea level studies will continue with forthcoming Sentinel-3C/D and Sentinel-6A/B. Those missions will be based on the heritage of previous Sentinel-3A and Sentinel-3B. An important innovation in Sentinel-6 will be the adoption of the continuous high-rate pulse mode (interleaved mode), compared to the closed burst mode used on Sentinel-3 and CryoSat-2 missions. Additionally, Sentinel-6A and Sentinel-6B will perform simultaneously LRM and SAR mode measurements, which will permit a very-high-accuracy link to the previous reference missions (TOPEX/Poseidon and Jason series). It is also important to mention the SKIM (Sea surface KInematics Multiscale monitoring), which is an ESA-EE9 candidate satellite mission that would carry on board a radar altimeter and adopt a processing of the nadir beam similar to Sentinel-3C/D and Sentinel-6A/B (Ardhuin et al. 2019).

The Envisat radar altimeter made available individual echoes (IE) in bursts of a maximum of 2000 complex echo samples (1.114 s) every 3 min. SARAL includes a similar capability. These individual echoes with higher spatial resolution (every 3.8 m along the ground track) opened new ways in processing and extracting the very detailed information encoded in them (Abileah et al. 2013), stimulating the development of further research (Abileah et al. 2017), and now applicable to CryoSat-2 (SAR and SARin modes) and Sentinel-3 where individual echoes come in short burst with 89 m ground spacing (Abileah et al. 2017).

A recommendation made by the radar altimetry community during the Ocean Surface Topography Science Team Meeting in Venice, Italy, in 2012, was to consider a second radiometer for future operational altimetry missions such as next-generation Sentinel missions to operate at high frequencies to resolve km-scale water vapor to improve coastal altimetry applications. A multi-frequency radiometer antenna and feed system that could provide such accurate atmospheric corrections will be included on the Sentinel-6 mission.

The so-called Copernicus Space Component (CSC) Expansion program has identified a Polar Ice and Snow Topographic Mission. This mission will provide enhanced retrieval of land ice sheet/glacier elevation, sea ice thickness and freeboard as well as ocean surface elevation, wave height and wind speed by higher spatial resolution measurements. The primary high-level objectives are to monitor critical climate signals: ice sheet, ice cap melting and sea level, as well as to monitor variability of Arctic and Southern Ocean sea ice and its snow-loading. Other objectives are to support applications related to coastal and inland waters and contribute to the observation of ocean topography.

A study concerning the Copernicus long-term scenario (jointly developed by ESA-EC-EUMETSAT) has just started to prepare the Copernicus next generation of satellite missions. The vision is to have the topographic measurement family supporting operational oceanography ensuring enhanced continuity of Sun-synchronous (Sentinel-3) and enhanced continuity of reference mission (Sentinel-6) as well as complementary polar orbiting mission for enhanced ice monitoring.

8.2 Interferometry on the Surface Water and Ocean Topography (SWOT) mission

8.2.1 Introduction

The present altimetric constellation includes conventional missions and missions with new SAR (along-track) and SAR-Interferometry (along-track and cross-track) technology that provide enhanced spatial resolution of the observations of SSH. Such capability has improved the spatial resolution near the coast over conventional altimetry. The benefit of SAR mode is already demonstrated, especially when the satellite approaches the coast at a perpendicular angle, maximizing the resolution by the SAR sampling and processing, while in the across-track direction the expected improvements are not observed, although at present the analyses are at early stage (as already explained in Sect. 3). The advantage of SAR-Interferometry along-track only recently started with some studies [e.g., Abulaitijiang et al. (2015) show that data from 0 to 7 km inland can be re-allocated to the coast using the off-nadir range correction]. Despite the current constellation in orbit, the major limitation of altimeter satellites is related to its nadir only sampling. There is clearly a need to

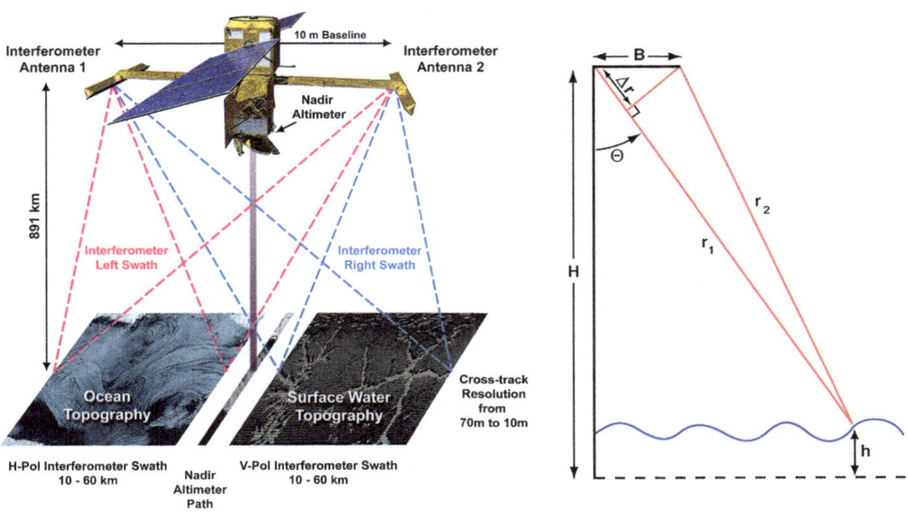

Fig. 8 The measurement system of SWOT is shown on the left. The two interferometer antennae, part of the Ka-Band Radar Interferometer (KaRIN), are separated by a 10-m mast. Each will transmit and receive radar signals. The signals received by the two antennae from the same target will allow the performance of interferometry as shown on the right. See text for explanations

improve the spatial and temporal sampling of those complex zones by providing 2D maps of the SSH.

In the future, two-dimensional wide-swath observations of the ocean surface topography will be made from the international Surface Water and Ocean Topography (SWOT) Mission (Fu and Ubelmann 2014), planned for launch in 2021. SWOT will make high-resolution observations using the SAR radar interferometry technique (Fig. 8). Two SAR antennae will be carried on board at the ends of a rigid mast 10 m long. The phase difference between the signals received by the two antennae allows the determination of the height of sea surface,

$$h = H - r_1 \cos(\theta) \tag{1}$$

The error of h can be expressed

$$\delta h = r_1 \lambda \tan(\theta) \frac{\delta \varphi}{2\pi B} \tag{2}$$

To minimize the height error, both the radar wavelength, λ, and look angle, ϑ, should be small. For SWOT, the wavelength as chosen to be Ka-band, ~1 cm, the look angle is near nadir, 0.4°–4° (compromise between ocean and inland water needs), forming a swath from 10 to 60 km from the nadir on each side of the nadir track for an altitude of 891 km of the spacecraft.

With measurements over a swath of 120 km (20 km nadir gap), SWOT will map the entire Earth within $\pm 77.6°$ latitudes with a repeat cycle of 21 days after a 3-month Cal/Val phase with a repeat cycle of 1 day. Over the ocean, these new measurements will extend the two-dimensional resolution of ocean surface topography estimated from conventional radar altimetry from 150 km wavelength to possibly 15 km (Fu and Ubelmann 2014), offering opportunities to observe the oceanic dynamic processes at these scales that act as one of the main gateways connecting the interior of the ocean to the upper layer. These processes provide both sinks and sources for the kinetic energy at larger scales, involving both low-frequency geostrophically balanced motions and high-frequency internal tides and gravity waves (Qiu et al. 2018). The active vertical exchanges linked to these scales are a key aspect of the role of the ocean in the climate system. These vertical exchanges have impacts on the local and global budgets of heat, carbon and nutrients for biogeochemical cycles (Klein and Lapeyre 2009).

8.2.2 Measurement Requirements

Figure 9 is the measurement performance requirement in the form of the wavenumber spectra of SSH signals and measurement errors (Rodríguez 2016). The spatial resolution is defined as the wavelength where the signal intersects with the error. Approximately over 68% of the ocean, the resolution is expected to be about 15 km under 2 m SWH. The measurement noise increases with SWH, making the SWOT resolution seasonally and geographically dependent (Wang et al. 2019).

Figure 10 is a plot of the height error over water bodies on land as function of the area over which the data are averaged to the area indicated (Desai 2018). It should be valid for estuaries and coastal waters not contaminated by land. The error increases with decreasing amount of averaging, reaching 0.5 m for an area of 100 m × 100 m. In coastal zones, the

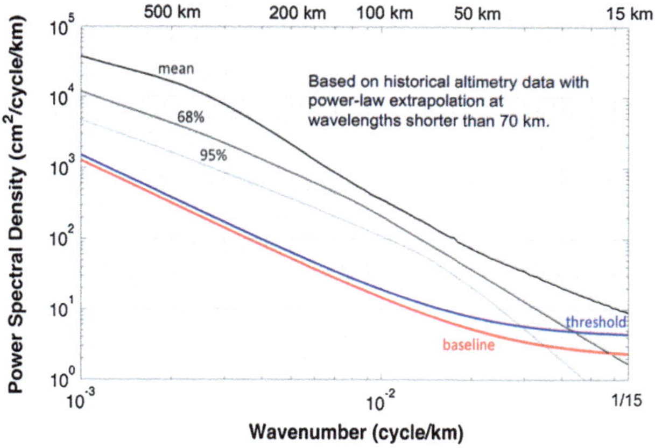

Fig. 9 SSH baseline requirement spectrum (red curve) as a function of wavenumber. Blue curve is the threshold requirement. Shown, for reference, is the global mean SSH spectrum estimated from the Jason-1 and Jason-2 observations (thick black line), the lower boundary of 68% of the spectral values (the upper gray dotted line), and the lower boundary of 95% of the spectral values (the lower gray dotted line). The intersections of the two dotted lines with the baseline spectrum at ~ 15 km (68%) and ~ 30 km (95%) determine the resolving capabilities of the SWOT measurement. The respective resolution for the threshold requirement is ~ 25 km (68%) and ~ 35 km (95%)

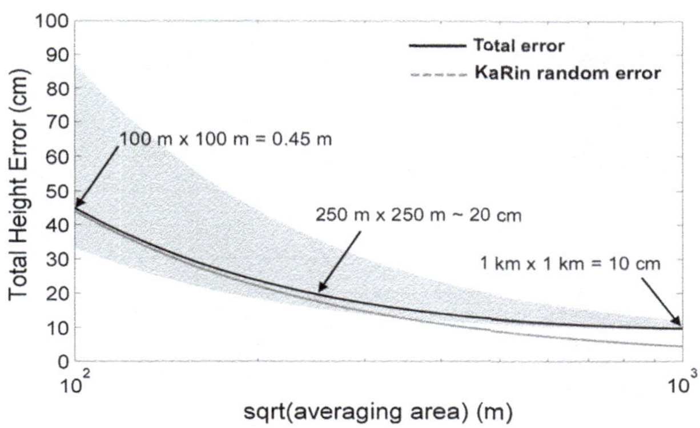

Fig. 10 Estimated non-vegetated water body total height accuracy for water-only pixels as a function of averaging area used to form the estimate (solid curve). Shown, for reference, is the KaRIN random error only contribution to the height accuracy (dashed curve). The total height accuracy is 10 cm for an equivalent water area of 1 km^2, 21 cm for (250 m)^2, and 50 cm for (100 m)^2. Due to changes in spatial resolution and signal-to-noise ratio, the performance will vary across the swath. The shaded area shows the expected variability in performance as a function of the averaging area

small size of the resolved pixels, on the order of 50 m, allows water detection without land contamination as in the case of conventional altimeters. The two-dimensional mapping of water bodies will enable the tackling of many coastal processes, such as inundation from storm surges, the interaction or river flow with the open ocean, etc.

8.2.3 A Fast-Sampling Phase for Calibration and Validation

To mitigate the challenge of the temporal sampling, the first 90 days of the mission after the commissioning phase for engineering checkout and adjustment will be flown in a 1-day repeat fast-sampling phase for calibration and validation.

This much-improved temporal sampling will allow enhanced understanding of the measurement at 15–150 km wavelengths in terms of signals and measurement errors. In particular, there will be two measurements a day at the crossover diamond-shaped regions, where the two-dimensional measurement at twice daily interval will provide the maximum amount of information on rapidly changing signals and errors. During the calibration and validation phases, in situ observations of the dynamic height of the ocean will be deployed to evaluate the relationship of the SSH measurement to the internal processes of the ocean. An airborne LiDAR system will also be flown to measure the SSH for comparison to the satellite observations.

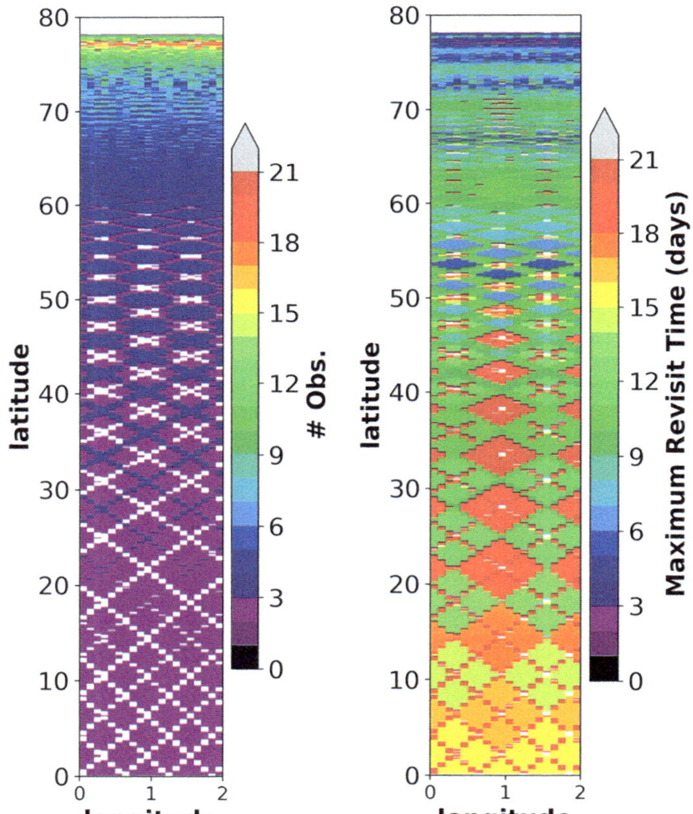

Fig. 11 Sampling pattern of the 21-day orbit for the Science Phase. The left panel shows the number of observations at a given location during the 21-day repeat period. The right panel shows the maximum gap in days between two successive observations

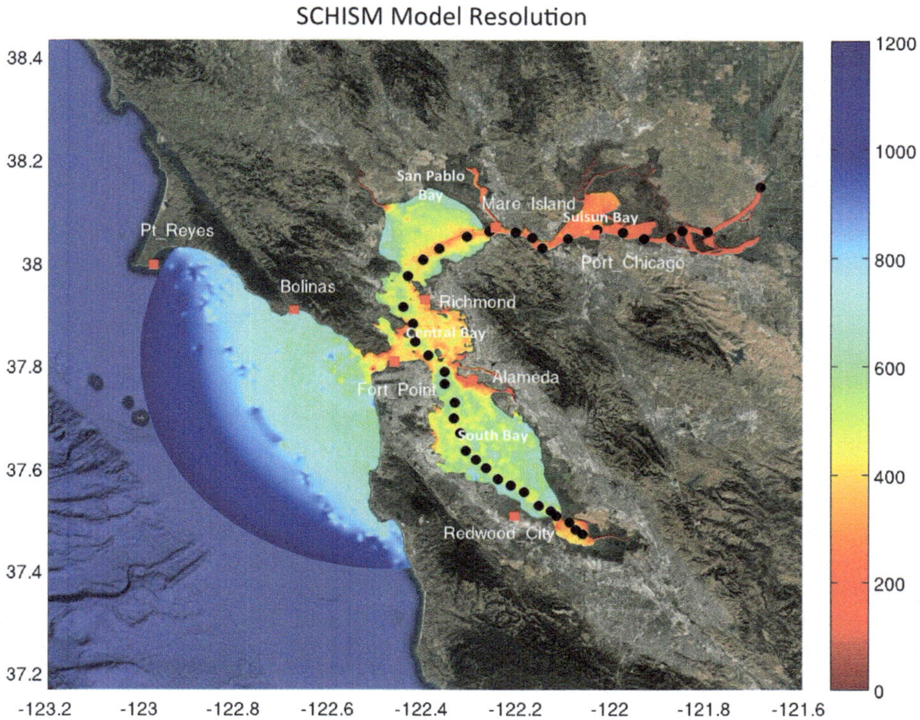

Fig. 12 The color shades of the map show the SCHISM model domain and spatial resolution (meters) of the San Francisco Bay configuration. The black dots show the locations of 37 USGS water quality monitoring stations; the red squares show the locations of tide gauge stations. Adapted from Chao et al. (2017)

8.2.4 Scientific Applications

The SWOT mission's topics of oceanographic investigations cover mesoscale and submesoscale processes; modeling and data assimilation; tides, waves, and high-frequency processes; calibration and validation; coastal and estuarine processes. Because of the challenges posed by the coarse temporal sampling (Fig. 11) and measurement errors, it is expected that the science investigation will heavily depend on modeling and assimilation for the construction of high-level gridded products. Efforts are being made to meet the challenges, by modeling the low-frequency balanced motions and high-frequency tides and internal gravity waves and by testing the assimilation of SWOT-like data into the models with the aim of constructing the ocean state in both space and time.

In the coastal zones, SWOT will largely improve data resolution, coverage and accuracy to address problems of the interaction of estuaries and coastal oceans. Shown in Fig. 12 is illustration of such applications in the context of a high-resolution ocean model called Semi-implicit Cross-scale Hydroscience Integrated System Model (SCHISM) (Chao et al. 2017). The color shades of the map show the SCHISM model domain and spatial resolution (meters) of the San Francisco Bay configuration. The black dots show the locations of 37 United States Geological Survey (USGS) water quality monitoring stations; the red squares show the locations of tide gauge stations. SWOT data will have resolutions progressing from scale of 1 km in the open ocean to ~ 100 m in the San Francisco Bay and upstream to the Sacramento River. The combination of data and modeling will allow studies of processes such as tidal mixing, storm surges and salt water intrusions.

9 Remaining Challenges and Concluding Remarks

A great progress has been made in coastal altimetry during the last decade to maintain as much as possible the open-ocean sea level accuracy while approaching the coast (Benveniste et al. 2019). Several approaches have been proposed to detect and take care of anomalous samples in waveforms collected from various pulse-limited altimetry missions, in particular in the strip of 10 km from the coast, bringing improvement in coastal sea level data. Recent technology advances in processing (SAR mode adopted in both CryoSat-2 and Sentinel-3 missions) already demonstrate that it is possible to enhance the quality and quantity of the sea level record close to the coast. Similarly, the better signal-to-noise ratio, smaller footprint, and high along-track sampling of SARAL/AltiKa acquire less-corrupted data, thus enhancing data availability in the 0–10 km coastal strip.

Beyond 10 km from the coast, users can benefit from recent coastal altimetry processing improvements (e.g., optimized geophysical corrections and high-resolution products). However, it is still a challenge to obtain accurate coastal sea levels in the 0–10 km band. Conventional altimetry still suffers from artifacts in the presence of complex coastal morphologies (e.g., steep relief, islands around, estuaries). SAR altimetry performances can be reliant on the angle the satellite approaches the coastline, with waveforms resulting contaminated and requiring dedicated retracking (Dinardo et al. 2018). Most of auxiliary information (orbit, ionosphere and tropospheric corrections, SSB) is still provided at standard rate (1 Hz). The need to have an SSB correction at 20 Hz and a specific SSB for each retracker has been highlighted (Pires et al. 2018). With retracked ranges and improved corrections, an enhanced MSS accuracy would be achieved because more and more accurate data would be available for the temporal averaging process. An inaccurate MSS might also mask some of the sea level variability making difficult the interpretation of oceanographic signals. The computation of some auxiliary information necessary to transform range in usable quantities (e.g., tidal and atmospheric corrections) requires models that, however, still use coarse bathymetry. There is a need to enhance bathymetry in order to increase the accuracy of those models in the coastal zone.

The continuous improvement in data processing and the recent progress in technology have allowed the development of various experimental coastal altimetry products suitable for coastal zone studies, which are now validated and being used for sea level research. The contribution of coastal altimetry is considered essential to within 0–10 km to link the sea level changes derived from the altimetry with those observed at tide gauges (Ponte et al. 2019). As the sampling of a single altimeter cannot be optimized to observe the complex variability of sea level at coastal scale, the merging of different missions that accounts for usage of 20 Hz high-resolution data, requires rethinking the typical grid approach used with 1 Hz data to downscale data at higher resolution from open ocean to coasts. Wide-swath altimetry that will be embarked for the first time on SWOT mission and envisaged for Sentinel-3 new generation will largely improve the temporal and spatial sampling of those complex zones.

Acknowledgements Thanks go to the European Space Agency that supported the development and exploitation of coastal altimetry with various scientific projects (COASTALT, Contract No. 21201/08/I-LG;

eSurge Venice, Contract No. 4000104485/11/I-LG; C-TEP, Contract No. C_TEP.1313.ACR-CNR.i1r0; CCI+ Bridging phase, Contract No. 4000109872/13/I-NB; SCOOP, Contract No. 4000115385/15/I-BG and that has organized and financially supported the gathering of the Coastal Altimetry Community with regular Coastal Altimetry Workshops in the past 10 years.

References

Abileah R, Gómez-Enri J, Scozzari A, Vignudelli S (2013) Coherent ranging with Envisat radar altimeter: a new perspective in analyzing altimeter data using Doppler processing. Remote Sens Environ 139:271–276. https://doi.org/10.1016/j.rse.2013.08.005

Abileah R, Scozzari A, Vignudelli S (2017) Envisat RA-2 individual echoes: a unique dataset for a better understanding of inland water altimetry potentialities. Remote Sens 9(6):605. https://doi.org/10.3390/rs9060605

Ablain M, Legeais JF, Prandi P, Marcos M, Fenoglio-Marc L, Dieng HB, Benveniste A, Cazenave A (2017) Satellite altimetry-based sea level at global and regional scales. In: Cazenave A, Champollion N, Paul F, Benveniste J (eds) Integrative study of the mean sea level and its components, vol 58. Space sciences series of ISSI. Springer, Cham, pp 9–33. https://doi.org/10.1007/978-3-319-56490-6_2

Abulaitijiang A, Andersen OB, Stenseng L (2015) Coastal sea level from inland CryoSat-2 interferometric SAR altimetry. Geophys Res Lett 42(6):1841–1847. https://doi.org/10.1002/2015GL063131

Ampou EE, Johan O, Menkes CE, Niño F, Birol F, Ouillon S, Andréfouët S (2017) Coral mortality induced by the 2015–2016 El-Niño in Indonesia: the effect of rapid sea level fall. Biogeosciences 14(4):817–826. https://doi.org/10.5194/bg-14-817-2017

Andersen OB, Scharroo R (2011) Range and geophysical corrections in coastal regions: and implications for mean sea surface determination. In: Vignudelli S, Kostianoy A, Cipollini P, Benveniste J (eds) Coastal altimetry. Springer, Berlin, pp 103–146. https://doi.org/10.1007/978-3-642-12796-0_5

Antony C, Testut L, Unnikrishnan AS (2014) Observing storm surges in the Bay of Bengal from satellite altimetry. Estuar Coast Shelf Sci 151:131–140. https://doi.org/10.1016/j.ecss.2014.09.012

Ardhuin F, Brandt P, Gaultier L, Donlon C, Battaglia A, Boy F, Casal T, Chapron B, Collard F, Cravatte S, Delouis JM (2019) SKIM, a candidate satellite mission exploring global ocean currents and waves. Front Mar Sci 6(209):1–8. https://doi.org/10.3389/fmars.2019.00209

Bajo M, De Biasio F, Umgiesser G, Vignudelli S, Zecchetto S (2017) Impact of using scatterometer and altimeter data on storm surge forecasting. Ocean Model 113:85–94. https://doi.org/10.1016/j.ocemod.2017.03.014)

Benveniste J, Cazenave A, Vignudelli S, Fenoglio-Marc L, Shah R, Almar R, Andersen O, Birol F, Bonnefond P, Bouffard J, Calafat F, Cardellach E, Cipollini P, Dufau C, Fernandes J, Garrison J, Frappart F, Gommenginger C, Han G, Høyer JL, Kourafalou V, Le Cozannet G, Leuliette E, Li Z, Loisel H, Madsen KS, Marcos M, Melet A, Meyssignac B, Passaro M, Pasqual A, Passaro M, Ribo S, Scharroo R, Song T, Speich S, Wilkin J, Woodworth P, Wöppelmann G (2019) Requirements for a coastal hazard observing system, OceanObs'19 community white paper. Front Mar Sci J Spec Sect Coast Ocean Process 6:348. https://doi.org/10.3389/fmars.2019.00348

Berry PAM, Freeman JA, Smith RG (2010) An enhanced ocean and coastal zone retracking technique for gravity field computation. In: Mertikas SP (ed) Gravity, geoid and Earth observation International Association of Geodesy Symposia, vol 135. Springer, Berlin, pp 213–220. https://doi.org/10.1007/978-3-642-10634-7_28

Birgiel E, Ellmann A, Delpeche-Ellmann N (2018) Examining the performance of the Sentinel-3 coastal altimetry in the Baltic Sea using a regional high-resolution geoid model. In: Proceedings of 2018 Baltic geodetic congress (BGC Geomatics), Olsztyn, Poland, 21–23 June 2018. https://doi.org/10.1109/bgc-geomatics.2018.00043

Birol F, Roblou L, Lyard F, Llovel W, Durand F, Renault L, Dewitte R, Morrow R, Ménard Y (2006) Towards using satellite altimetry for the observation of coastal dynamics. In: Danesy D (ed) Proceedings of 15 years of progress in radar altimetry joint ESA-CNES symposium, Venice, Italy, 13–18 March 2006, ESA SP-614. ISBN: 92-9092-925-1

Birol F, Fuller N, Lyard F, Cancet M, Nino F, Delebecque C, Fleury S, Toublanc F, Melet A, Saraceno M, Léger F (2017) Coastal applications from nadir altimetry: example of the X-TRACK regional products. Adv Space Res 59(4):936–953. https://doi.org/10.1016/j.asr.2016.11.005

Bonnefond P, Verron J, Aublanc J, Babu KN, Bergé-Nguyen M, Cancet M, Chaudhary A, Crétaux JF, Frappart F, Haines BJ, Laurain O, Ollivier A, Poisson JC, Prandi P, Sharma R, Thibaut P, Watson

C (2018) The benefits of the Ka-band as evidenced from the SARAL/Altika altimetric mission: quality assessment and unique characteristics of Altika data. Remote Sens 10(1):83. https://doi.org/10.3390/rs10010083

Boy F, Desjonquères J-D, Picot N, Moreau T, Raynal M (2017) CryoSat-2 SAR-mode over oceans: processing methods, global assessment, and benefits. IEEE Trans Geosci Remote Sens 55(1):148–158. https://doi.org/10.1109/TGRS.2016.2601958

Brown G (1977) The average impulse response of a rough surface and its applications. IEEE Trans Antennas Propag 25(1):67–74. https://doi.org/10.1109/TAP.1977.1141536

Brown S (2010) A novel near-land radiometer wet path-delay retrieval algorithm: application to the Jason-2/OSTM advanced microwave radiometer. IEEE Trans Geosci Remote Sens 48(4):1986–1992. https://doi.org/10.1109/TGRS.2009.2037220

Carrère L, Lyard F (2003) Modeling the barotropic response of the global ocean to atmospheric wind and pressure forcing-comparisons with observations. Geophys Res Lett. https://doi.org/10.1029/2002gl016473

Carrere L, Faugère Y, Ablain M (2016) Major improvement of altimetry sea level estimations using pressure-derived corrections based on ERA-Interim atmospheric reanalysis. Ocean Sci 12:825–842. https://doi.org/10.5194/os-12-825-2016

Cazenave A, Palanisamy H, Ablain M (2018) Contemporary sea level changes from satellite altimetry: what have we learned? What are the new challenges? Adv Space Res 62(7):1639–1653. https://doi.org/10.1016/j.asr.2018.07.017

Chao Y, Farrara JD, Zhang H, Zhang YJ, Atelijevich E, Chai F, Davis CO, Dugdale R, Wilkerson F (2017) Development, implementation, and validation of a modeling system for the San Francisco Bay and Estuary. Estuar Coast Shelf Sci 194:40–56. https://doi.org/10.1016/j.ecss.2017.06.005

Cipollini P, Vignudelli S, Benveniste J (2014) The coastal zone: a mission target for satellite altimeters. EOS Trans AGU 95(8):72. https://doi.org/10.1002/2014EO080006

Cipollini P, Calafat FM, Jevrejeva S, Melet A, Prandi P (2017a) Monitoring sea level in the coastal zone with satellite altimetry and tide gauges. Surv Geophys 38:33–57. https://doi.org/10.1007/s10712-016-9392-0

Cipollini P, Benveniste J, Birol F, Fernandes MJ, Obligis E, Passaro M, Strub PT, Valladeau G, Vignudelli S, Wilkin J (2017b) Satellite altimetry in coastal regions. In: Stammer D, Cazenave A (eds) Satellite altimetry over oceans and land surfaces. CRC Press, Boca Raton, FL, pp 343–380

Clerc S, O' Mahony C, Mangin A, Datcu M, Vignudelli S, Illuzzi D, Craciunescu V, Leone R, Campbell G (2016) New perspectives for the observation of coastal zones with the Coastal Thematic Exploitation Platform. In: Proceedings of European Space Agency living planet symposium, 9–13 May 2016, Prague, Czech Republic, ESA SP 740, August 2016

Cotton PD, Garcia PN, Cancet M, Andersen O, Stenseng L, Martin F, Cipollini P, Calafat FM, Passaro M, Ambrózio A, Benveniste J (2016) Improved oceanographic measurements with cryosat sar altimetry: application to the coastal zone and arctic. In: Proceedings of European Space Agency living planet symposium, 9–13 May 2016, Prague, Czech Republic, ESA SP 740, August 2016

Deng X, Featherstone WE (2006) A coastal retracking system for satellite radar altimeter waveforms: application to ERS-2 around Australia. J Geophys Res Oceans. https://doi.org/10.1029/2005jc003039

Desai S (2018) Surface water and ocean topography mission (SWOT) project. Science requirements doc., revision B. California Institute of Technology Jet Propulsion Laboratory Publ. JPL D-61923

Desjonquères J, Carayon G, Steunou N, Lambin J (2010) Poseidon-3 radar altimeter: new modes and in-flight performances. Mar Geod 33(Suppl.):57–79. https://doi.org/10.1080/01490419.2010.488970

Desportes C, Obligis E, Eymard L (2007) On the wet tropospheric correction for altimetry in coastal regions. IEEE Trans Geosci Remote Sens 45(7):2139–2149. https://doi.org/10.1109/TGRS.2006.888967

Dinardo S, Fenoglio-Marc L, Buchhaupt C, Becker M, Scharroo R, Fernandes MJ, Benveniste J (2018) Coastal SAR and PLRM altimetry in German Bight and West Baltic Sea. Adv Space Res 62(6):1371–1404. https://doi.org/10.1016/j.asr.2017.12.018

Dong C, Xu G, Han G, Chen N, He Y, Chen D (2018) Identification of tidal mixing fronts from high-resolution along-track altimetry data. Remote Sens Environ 209:489–496. https://doi.org/10.1016/j.rse.2018.02.047

Durand F, Piecuch CG, Becker M, Papa F, Raju SV, Khan JU, Ponte RM (2019) Impact of continental freshwater runoff on coastal sea level. Surv Geophys. https://doi.org/10.1007/s10712-019-09536-w

Egido A, Smith WH (2017) Fully focused SAR altimetry: theory and applications. IEEE Trans Geosci Remote Sens 55(1):392–406. https://doi.org/10.1109/TGRS.2016.2607122

Emery KO, Aubrey DG (eds) (1991) Sea levels, land levels, and tide gauges. Springer, Berlin. https://doi.org/10.1007/978-1-4613-9101-2

Fenoglio-Marc L, Dinardo S, Scharroo R, Roland A, Sikiric MD, Lucas B, Becker M, Benveniste J, Weiss R (2015) The German bight: a validation of CryoSat-2 altimeter data in SAR mode. Adv Space Res 55(11):2641–2656. https://doi.org/10.1016/j.asr.2015.02.014

Fenoglio-Marc L, Dinardo S, Buchhaupt C, Scharroo R, Becker M, Benveniste J (2019) Calibrating the SAR sea surface heights of CryoSat-2 and Sentinel-3 along the German coasts. In: Proceedings of international association of geodesy symposia. Springer, Berlin. https://doi.org/10.1007/1345_2019_73

Fernandes MJ, Lázaro C (2016) GPD+ wet tropospheric corrections for CryoSat-2 and GFO altimetry missions. Remote Sens 8(10):851. https://doi.org/10.3390/rs8100851

Fernandes MJ, Pires N, Lázaro C, Nunes AL (2013) Tropospheric delays from GNSS for application in coastal altimetry. Adv Space Res 51(8):1352–1368. https://doi.org/10.1016/j.asr.2012.04.025

Fernandes MJ, Lázaro C, Nunes AL, Scharroo R (2014) Atmospheric corrections for altimetry studies over inland water. Remote Sens 6(6):4952–4997. https://doi.org/10.3390/rs6064952

Fernandes MJ, Lázaro C, Ablain M, Pires N (2015) Improved wet path delays for all ESA and reference altimetric missions. Remote Sens Environ 169:50–74. https://doi.org/10.1016/j.rse.2015.07.023

Fu LL, Cazenave A (eds) (2001) Satellite altimetry and earth sciences: a handbook of techniques and applications. Academic Press, London

Fu L-L, Ubelmann C (2014) On the transition from profile altimeter to swath altimeter for observing global ocean surface topography. J Ocean Atmos Technol 31(2):560–568. https://doi.org/10.1175/JTECH-D-13-00109.1

García P, Martin-Puig C, Roca M (2018) SARin mode, and a window delay approach, for coastal altimetry. Adv Space Res 62(6):1358–1370. https://doi.org/10.1016/j.asr.2018.03.015

Gharineiat Z, Deng X (2018) Description and assessment of regional sea-level trends and variability from altimetry and tide gauges at the northern Australian coast. Adv Space Res 61(10):2540–2554. https://doi.org/10.1016/j.asr.2018.02.038

Gómez-Enri J, Vignudelli S, Quartly G, Gommenginger C, Benveniste J (2009) Bringing satellite radar altimetry closer to shore. In: SPIE (Society of Photo-Optical Instrumentation Engineers) Newsroom, pp 1–3. https://doi.org/10.1117/2.1200908.1797

Gómez-Enri J, Vignudelli S, Quartly GD, Gommenginger CP, Cipollini P, Challenor PG, Benveniste J (2010) Modeling ENVISAT RA-2 waveforms in the coastal zone: case study of calm water contamination. IEEE Geosci Remote Sens Lett 7(3):474–478. https://doi.org/10.1109/LGRS.2009.2039193

Gómez-Enri J, Cipollini P, Passaro M, Vignudelli S, Tejedor B, Coca J (2016) Coastal altimetry products in the strait of Gibraltar. IEEE Trans Geosci Remote Sens 54(9):5455–5466. https://doi.org/10.1109/tgrs.2016.2565472

Gómez-Enri J, Vignudelli S, Cipollini P, Coca J, González CJ (2018) Validation of CryoSat-2 SIRAL sea level data in the eastern continental shelf of the Gulf of Cadiz (Spain). Adv Space Res 62(6):1405–1420. https://doi.org/10.1016/j.asr.2017.10.042

Gómez-Enri J, González CJ, Passaro M, Vignudelli S, Álvarez O, Cipollini P, Mañanes R, Bruno M, Lopez-Carmona P, Izquierdo A (2019a) Wind-induced cross-strait sea level variability in the Strait of Gibraltar using coastal altimetry and in-situ measurements. Remote Sens Environ 221:596–608. https://doi.org/10.1016/j.rse.2018.11.042

Gómez-Enri J, Vignudelli S, Izquierdo A, Passaro M, González C J, Cipollini P, Bruno M, Álvarez O, Mañanes R (2019b) Sea level variability in the Strait of Gibraltar from along-track high spatial resolution altimeter products. In: Proceedings of international association of geodesy symposia—international review workshop on satellite altimetry Cal/Val activities and applications, 23–26 April 2018, Crete, Greece. Springer, Berlin, pp 1–10. https://doi.org/10.1007/1345_2019_54

Guo J, Gao Y, Hwang C, Sun J (2010) A multi-subwaveform parametric retracker of the radar satellite altimetric waveform and recovery of gravity anomalies over coastal oceans. Sci China Earth Sci 53(4):610–616. https://doi.org/10.1007/s11430-009-0171-3

Halpern BS, Frazier M, Potapenko J, Casey KS, Koenig K, Longo C et al (2015) Spatial and temporal changes in cumulative human impacts on the world's ocean. Nat Commun 6:7615. https://doi.org/10.1038/ncomms8615

Hauser D, Tison C, Amiot T, Delaye L, Corcoral N, Castillan P (2017) SWIM: the first spaceborne wave scatterometer. IEEE Trans Geosci Remote Sens 55(5):3000–3014. https://doi.org/10.1109/TGRS.2017.2658672

He L, Li G, Li K, Shu Y (2014) Estimation of regional sea level change in the Pearl River Delta from tide gauge and satellite altimetry data. Estuar Coast Shelf Sci 141:69–77. https://doi.org/10.1016/j.ecss.2014.02.005

Heslop EE, Sánchez-Román A, Pascual A, Rodríguez D, Reeve KA, Faugère Y, Raynal M (2017) Sentinel-3A views ocean variability more accurately at finer resolution. Geophys Res Lett. https://doi.org/10.1002/2017GL076244

Hwang C, Hsu HY, Jang RJ (2002) Global mean sea surface and marine gravity anomaly from multi-satellite altimetry: applications of deflection-geoid and inverse Vening Meinesz formulae. J Geod 76(8):407–418. https://doi.org/10.1007/s00190-002-0265-6

Idris NH, Deng X (2012) The retracking technique on multi-peak and quasi-specular waveforms for Jason-1 and Jason-2 missions near the coast. Mar Geod 35(sup1):217–237. https://doi.org/10.1080/01490419.2012.718679

Idžanović M, Ophaug V, Andersen OB (2018) Coastal sea level from CryoSat-2 SARIn altimetry in Norway. Adv Space Res 62(6):1344–1357. https://doi.org/10.1016/j.asr.2017.07.043

Klein P, Lapeyre G (2009) The oceanic vertical pump induced by mesoscale and submesoscale turbulence. Annu Rev Mar Sci 1:351–375. https://doi.org/10.1146/annurev.marine.010908.163704

Kummu M, De Moel H, Salvucci G, Viviroli D, Ward PJ, Varis O (2016) Over the hills and further away from coast: global geospatial patterns of human and environment over the 20th–21st centuries. Environ Res Lett 11(3):034010. https://doi.org/10.1088/1748-9326/11/3/034010

Labroue S, Gaspar P, Dorandeu J, Ogor F, Zanife OZ (2006) Overview of the improvements made on the empirical determination of the sea state bias correction. In: Proceedings of 15 years of progress in radar altimetry symposium, Venice, 13–18 March, 2006, ESA SP614

Le Bars Y, Lyard F, Jeandel C, Dardengo L (2010) The AMANDES tidal model for the Amazon estuary and shelf. Ocean Model 31(3):132–149. https://doi.org/10.1016/j.ocemod.2009.11.001

Legeais JF, Ablain M, Zawadzki L, Zuo H, Johannessen JA, Scharffenberg MG, Fenoglio-Marc L, Fernandes J, Andersen OB, Rudenko S, Cipollini P, Quartly GD, Passaro M, Cazenave A, Cipollini P (2018) An improved and homogeneous altimeter sea level record from the ESA climate change initiative. Earth Syst Sci Data 10:281–301. https://doi.org/10.5194/essd-10-281-2018

Lillibridge J, Lin M, Shum CK (2013) Hurricane Sandy storm surge measured by satellite altimetry. Oceanography 26(2):8–9. https://doi.org/10.5670/oceanog.2013.18

Madsen KS, Hoyer JL, Fu W, Donlon C (2015) Blending of satellite and tide gauge sea level observations and its assimilation in a storm surge model of the North Sea and Baltic Sea. J Geophys Res Oceans 120(9):6405–6418. https://doi.org/10.1002/2015JC011070

Maraldi C, Galton-Fenzi B, Lyard F, Testut L, Coleman R (2007) Barotropic tides of the southern Indian Ocean and the Amery Ice Shelf cavity. Geophys Res Lett. https://doi.org/10.1029/2007gl030900

Marcos M, Wöppelmann G, Matthews A, Ponte RM, Birol F, Ardhuin F, Coco G, Santamaría-Gómez A, Ballu V, Testut L, Chambers D, Stopa JE (2019) Coastal sea level and related fields from existing observing systems. Surv Geophys. https://doi.org/10.1007/s10712-019-09513-3

Neumann B, Vafeidis AT, Zimmermann J, Nicholls RJ (2015) Future coastal population growth and exposure to sea-level rise and coastal flooding: a global assessment. PLoS ONE 10:e0118571. https://doi.org/10.1371/journal.pone.0118571

Obligis E, Desportes C, Eymard L, Fernandes ML, Lázaro C, Nunes AL (2011) Tropospheric corrections for coastal altimetry. In: Vignudelli S, Kostianoy A, Cipollini P, Benveniste J (eds) Coastal altimetry. Springer, Berlin, pp 147–176. https://doi.org/10.1007/978-3-642-12796-0_6

Pairaud IL, Lyard F, Auclair F, Letellier T, Marsaleix P (2008) Dynamics of the semi-diurnal and quarter-diurnal internal tides in the Bay of Biscay. Part 1: barotropic tides. Cont Shelf Res 28(10):1294–1315. https://doi.org/10.1016/j.csr.2008.03.004

Passaro M, Cipollini P, Vignudelli S, Quartly GD, Snaith HM (2014) ALES: a multi-mission adaptive subwaveform retracker for coastal and open ocean altimetry. Remote Sens Environ 145:173–189. https://doi.org/10.1016/j.rse.2014.02.008

Passaro M, Cipollini P, Benveniste J (2015) Annual sea level variability of the coastal ocean: the Baltic Sea-North Sea transition zone. J Geophys Res Oceans 120(4):3061–3078. https://doi.org/10.1002/2014JC010510

Passaro M, Dinardo S, Quartly GD, Snaith HM, Benveniste J, Cipollini P, Lucas B (2016). Cross-calibrating ALES Envisat and CryoSat-2 Delay–Doppler: a coastal altimetry study in the Indonesian Seas. Adv Space Res 58(3):289–303

Passaro M, Nadzir ZA, Quartly GD (2018) Improving the precision of sea level data from satellite altimetry with high-frequency and regional sea state bias corrections. Remote Sens Environ 18:245–254. https://doi.org/10.1016/j.rse.2018.09.007

Peng F, Deng X (2018) Validation of improved significant wave heights from the Brown-Peaky (BP) retracker along the east coast of Australia. Remote Sens 10(7):1072. https://doi.org/10.3390/rs10071072

Piccioni G, Dettmering D, Passaro M, Schwatke C, Bosch W, Seitz F (2018) Coastal improvements for tide models: the impact of ALES retracker. Remote Sens 10(5):700

Piecuch CG, Bittermann K, Kemp AC, Ponte RM, Little CM, Engelhart SE, Lentz SJ (2018) River-discharge effects on United States Atlantic and Gulf coast sea-level changes. Proc Natl Acad Sci. https://doi.org/10.1073/pnas.1805428115

Pires N, Fernandes MJ, Gommenginger C, Scharroo R (2016) A conceptually simple modeling approach for Jason-1 sea state bias correction based on 3 parameters exclusively derived from altimetric information. Remote Sens 8(7):576. https://doi.org/10.3390/rs8070576

Pires N, Fernandes MJ, Gommenginger C, Scharroo R (2018) Improved sea state bias estimation for altimeter reference missions with altimeter-only three-parameter models. IEEE Trans Geosci Remote Sens 99:1–15. https://doi.org/10.1109/TGRS.2018.2866773

Ponte R, Carson M, Cirano M, Domingues C, Jevrejeva S, Marcos M, Mitchum G, Van de Wal RSW, Woodworth PL, Ablain M, Ardhuin F, Ballu V, Becker M, Benveniste J, Birol F, Bradshaw E, Cazenave A, Demey-Fremaux P, Durand F, Ezer T, Fu LL, Fukumori I, Gordon K, Gravelle M, Griffies SM, Han W, Hibbert A, Hughes CW, Idier D, Kourafalou VH, Little CM, Matthews A, Melet A, Merrifield M, Meyssignac B, Minobe S, Penduff T, Picot N, Piecuch C, Ray RD, Richards L, Santamaria- Gómez A, Stammer D, Staneva J, Testut L, Thompson K, Thompson P, Vignudelli S, Williams J, Williams SDP, Wöppelmann G, Zanna L, Zhang X (2019) Towards comprehensive observing and modeling systems for monitoring and predicting regional to coastal sea level, OceanObs'19 community white paper. Front Mar Sci J Spec Sect Coast Ocean Process. https://doi.org/10.3389/fmars.2019.00437

Pujol MI, Schaeffer P, Faugère Y, Raynal M, Dibarboure G, Picot N (2018) Gauging the improvement of recent mean sea surface models: a new approach for identifying and quantifying their errors. J Geophys Res Oceans 123(8):5889–5911. https://doi.org/10.1029/2017JC013503

Qiu B, Chen S, Klein P, Wang J, Fu L-L, Menemenlis D (2018) Seasonality in transition scale from balanced to unbalanced motions in the world ocean. J Phys Oceanogr 48:591–605. https://doi.org/10.1175/JPO-D-17-0169.1

Quartly GD (2010) Hyperbolic retracker: removing bright target artefacts from altimetric waveform data. In: Proceedings of living planet symposium 2010, Bergen, Norway, 28 June–2 July 2007, ESA SP-686, ESA Publication, SP-686

Ray RD, Egbert GD (2017) Tides and satellite altimetry. In situ observations needed to complement, validate, and interpret satellite altimetry. In: Stammer D, Cazenave A (eds) Satellite altimetry over oceans and land surfaces. CRC Press, Boca Raton, FL, pp 427–458

Ray RD, Egbert GD, Erofeeva SY (2011) Tide predictions in shelf and coastal waters: status and prospects. In: Vignudelli S, Kostianoy AG, Cipollini P, Benveniste J (eds) Coastal altimetry. Springer, Berlin, pp 191–216. https://doi.org/10.1007/978-3-642-12796-0_8

Raynal M, Labroue S, Moreau T, Boy F, Picot N (2018) From conventional to Delay Doppler altimetry: a demonstration of continuity and improvements with the Cryosat-2 mission. Adv Space Res 62(6):1564–1575. https://doi.org/10.1016/j.asr.2018.01.006

Restano M, Passaro M, Benveniste J (2018) New achievements in coastal altimetry. Eos. https://doi.org/10.1029/2018EO106087

Roblou L, Lamouroux J, Bouffard J, Lyard F, Le Hénaff M, Lombard A, Marsaleix P, De Mey P, Birol F (2011) Post-processing altimeter data towards coastal applications and integration into coastal models. In: Vignudelli S, Kostianoy A, Cipollini P, Benveniste J (eds) Coastal altimetry. Springer, Berlin, pp 217–246. https://doi.org/10.1007/978-3-642-12796-0_9

Roca M, Laxon S, Zeli C (2009) The EnviSat-RA2 instrument design and tracking performance. IEEE Trans Geosci Remote Sens 47:3489–3506. https://doi.org/10.1109/TGRS.2009.2020793

Rodríguez E (2016) Surface water and ocean topography mission project. Science requirements doc., revision A. California Institute of Technology Jet Propulsion Laboratory Publ. JPL D-61923

Roemmich D, Woodworth P, Jevrejeva S, Purkey S, Lankhorst M, Send U, Nikolai Maximenko N (2017) In situ observations needed to complement, validate, and interpret satellite altimetry. In: Stammer D, Cazenave A (eds) Satellite altimetry over oceans and land surfaces. CRC Press, Boca Raton, FL, pp 113–147

Roscher R, Uebbing B, Kusche J (2017) STAR: spatio-temporal altimeter waveform retracking using sparse representation and conditional random fields. Remote Sens Environ 201:148–164. https://doi.org/10.1016/j.rse.2017.07.024

Scharroo R, Leuliette EW, Lillibridge JL, Byrne D, Naeije MC, Mitchum GT (2013) RADS: consistent multi-mission products. In: Proceedings of 20 years of progress in radar altimetry symposium, Venice, Italy, 24–29 September 2012, ESA SP-710. https://doi.org/10.5270/esa.sp-710.altimetry2012

Stammer D, Cazenave A (2017) Satellite altimetry over oceans and land surfaces. CRC Press, Boca Raton, FL, p 670

Stammer D, Ray RD, Andersen OB, Arbic BK, Bosch W, Carrère L, Cheng Y, Chinn DS, Dushaw BD, Egbert GD, Erofeeva SY, Fok HS, Green JAM, Griffiths S, King MA, Lapin V, Lemoine FG, Luthcke SB, Lyard F, Morison J, Müller M, Padman L, Richman JG, Shriver JF, Shum CK, Taguchi E, Yi Y (2014) Accuracy assessment of global barotropic ocean tide models. Rev Geophys 52(3):243–282. https://doi.org/10.1002/2014RG000450

Toublanc F, Ayoub NK, Lyard F, Marsaleix P, Allain DJ (2018) Tidal downscaling from the open ocean to the coast: a new approach applied to the Bay of Biscay. Ocean Model 124:16–32. https://doi.org/10.1016/j.ocemod.2018.02.001

Tran N, Vandemark D, Chapron B, Labroue S, Feng H, Beckley B, Vincent P (2006) New models for satellite altimeter sea state bias correction developed using global wave model data. J Geophys Res 111:C09009. https://doi.org/10.1029/2005JC003406

Tran N, Labroue S, Philipps S, Bronner E, Picot N (2010) Overview and update of the sea state bias corrections for the Jason-2, Jason-1 and TOPEX missions. Mar Geod 33:348. https://doi.org/10.1080/01490419.2010.487788

Troupin C, Pascual A, Valladeau G, Pujol I, Lana A, Heslop E, Ruiz S, Torner M, Picot N, Tintoré J (2015) Illustration of the emerging capabilities of SARAL/AltiKa in the coastal zone using a multi-platform approach. Adv Space Res 55(1):51–59. https://doi.org/10.1016/j.asr.2014.09.011

Valladeau G, Thibaut P, Picard B, Poisson JC, Tran N, Picot N, Guillot A (2015) Using SARAL/AltiKa to improve Ka-band altimeter measurements for coastal zones, hydrology and ice: the PEACHI prototype. Mar Geod 38(sup1):124–142. https://doi.org/10.1080/01490419.2015.1020176

Verron J, Bonnefond P, Aouf L, Birol F, Bhowmick SA, Calmant S, Conchy T, Crétaux J-F, Dibarboure G, Dubey AK, Faugère Y, Guerreiro K, Gupta PK, Hamon M, Jebri F, Kumar R, Morrow R, Pascual A, Pujol M-I, Rémy E, Rémy F, Smith WHF, Tournadre J, Vergara O (2018) The benefits of the Ka-band as evidenced from the SARAL/AltiKa altimetric mission: scientific applications. Remote Sens 10:163. https://doi.org/10.3390/rs10020163

Vieira T, Fernandes MJ, Lázaro C (2018) Independent assessment of on-board microwave radiometer measurements in coastal zones using tropospheric delays from GNSS. IEEE Trans Geosci Remote Sens. https://doi.org/10.1109/TGRS.2018.2869258

Vignudelli S, Cipollini P, Roblou L, Lyard F, Gasparini GP, Manzella G, Astraldi M (2005) Improved satellite altimetry in coastal systems: case study of the Corsica Channel (Mediterranean Sea). Geophys Res Lett 32:L07608. https://doi.org/10.1029/2005GL022602

Vignudelli S, Snaith HM, Lyard F, Cipollini P, Birol F, Bouffard J, Roblou L (2006) Satellite radar altimetry from open ocean to coasts: challenges and perspectives. In: Proceedings of 5th Society of Photo-Optical Instrumentation Engineers (SPIE) Asia-Pacific remote sensing symposium, Panaji, Goa, India, 13–17 November 2006, 6406, 64060L, pp 1–12. https://doi.org/10.1117/12.694024

Vignudelli S, Vignudelli S, Kostianoy AG, Cipollini P, Benveniste J (eds) (2011a) Coastal altimetry. Springer, Berlin. https://doi.org/10.1007/978-3-642-12796-0

Vignudelli S, Cipollini P, Gommenginger C, Snaith H, Coelho H, Fernandes J, Lazaro C, Nunes A, Gómez-Enri J, Martin-Puig C, Woodworth P, Dinardo S, Benveniste J (2011b) Satellite altimetry: sailing closer to the coast. In: Gower J, Levy G, Heron M, Tang D, Katsaros K, Singh R (eds) Remote sensing of the changing oceans. Springer, Berlin, pp 217–238. https://doi.org/10.1007/978-3-642-16541-2_11

Vignudelli S, De Basio F, Scozzari A, Zecchetto S, Papa A (2019) Sea level trends and variability in the Adriatic Sea and around Venice. In: Proceedings of international association of geodesy symposia—international review workshop on satellite altimetry Cal/Val activities and applications, 23–26 April 2018, Crete, Greece, 1–10, Springer, Berlin. https://doi.org/10.1007/1345_2018_51

Vu PL, Frappart F, Darrozes J, Marieu V, Blarel F, Ramillien G, Bonnefond P, Birol F (2018) Multisatellite altimeter validation along the French Atlantic Coast in the Southern Bay of Biscay from ERS-2 to SARAL. Remote Sens 10(1):93. https://doi.org/10.3390/rs10010093

Wang J, Fu LL, Torres HG, Chen S, Qiu B, Menemenlis D (2019) On the spatial scale to be resolved by the surface water and ocean topography Ka-band fadar interferometer. J Atmos Ocean Technol 36(1):87–99. https://doi.org/10.1175/JTECH-D-18-0119.1

Woodworth PL, Hunter JR, Marcos M, Caldwell P, Menéndez M, Haigh I (2016) Towards a global higher-frequency sea level dataset. Geosci Data J 3(2):50–59. https://doi.org/10.5285/3b602f74-8374-1e90-e053-6c86abc08d39

Woodworth PL, Wöppelmann G, Marcos M, Gravelle M, Bingley RM (2017) Why we must tie satellite positioning to tide gauge data. Eos 98(4):13–15. https://doi.org/10.1029/2017EO064037

Wright LD, Nichols CR (2018) Tomorrow's coasts: complex and impermanent, vol 27. Coastal research library. Springer, Berlin. https://doi.org/10.1007/978-3-319-75453-6

Wright LD, Syvitski JPM, Nichols CR (2018) Sea level rise: recent trends and future projections. In: Wright LD, Nichols CR (eds) Tomorrow's coasts: complex and impermanent. Springer, Berlin. https://doi.org/10.1007/978-3-319-75453-6

Xu XY, Birol F, Cazenave A (2018) Evaluation of coastal sea level offshore Hong Kong from Jason-2 altimetry. Remote Sens 10(2):282. https://doi.org/10.3390/rs10020282

Yang Y, Hwang C, Hsu HJ, Dongchen E, Wang H (2011) A subwaveform threshold retracker for ERS-1 altimetry: a case study in the Antarctic Ocean. Comput Geosci 41:88–98. https://doi.org/10.1016/j.cageo.2011.08.017

Yang L, Lin M, Liu Q, Pan D (2012) A coastal altimetry retracking strategy based on waveform classification and sub-waveform extraction. Int J Remote Sens 33(24):7806–7819. https://doi.org/10.1080/01431161.2012.701350

Affiliations

Stefano Vignudelli[1] · Florence Birol[2] · Jérôme Benveniste[3] · Lee-Lueng Fu[4] · Nicolas Picot[5] · Matthias Raynal[6] · Hélène Roinard[6]

Florence Birol
florence.birol@legos.obs-mip.fr

Jérôme Benveniste
Jerome.Benveniste@esa.int

Lee-Lueng Fu
llf@jpl.nasa.gov

Nicolas Picot
nicolas.picot@cnes.fr

Matthias Raynal
mraynal@cls.fr

Hélène Roinard
hroinard@cls.fr

1 Consiglio Nazionale delle Ricerche (CNR-IBF), Via Moruzzi 1, 56127 Pisa, Italy

2 Laboratoire d'Etudes en Géophysique et Océanographie Spatiales (LEGOS), 18, av. Edouard Belin, 31401 cédex 9 Toulouse, France

3 European Space Agency (ESA-ESRIN), Largo Galileo Galilei, 1, 00044 Frascati, Rome, Italy

4 Jet Propulsion Laboratory (JPL), National Aeronautics and Space Administration (NASA), 4800 Oak Grove Dr, Pasadena, CA 91109, USA

5 Centre National d'Études Spatiales (CNES), 18 Avenue Edouard Belin, 31400 Toulouse, France

6 Collecte Localisation Satellites (CLS), 11 Rue Hermès 31520 Ramonville-Saint-Agne, France

Surveys in Geophysics (2019) 40:1351–1397
https://doi.org/10.1007/s10712-019-09531-1

Forcing Factors Affecting Sea Level Changes at the Coast

Philip L. Woodworth[1] · Angélique Melet[2] · Marta Marcos[3,4] · Richard D. Ray[5] · Guy Wöppelmann[6] · Yoshi N. Sasaki[7] · Mauro Cirano[8] · Angela Hibbert[1] · John M. Huthnance[1] · Sebastià Monserrat[4] · Mark A. Merrifield[9]

Received: 30 September 2018 / Accepted: 4 April 2019 / Published online: 8 May 2019

Abstract
We review the characteristics of sea level variability at the coast focussing on how it differs from the variability in the nearby deep ocean. Sea level variability occurs on all timescales, with processes at higher frequencies tending to have a larger magnitude at the coast due to resonance and other dynamics. In the case of some processes, such as the tides, the presence of the coast and the shallow waters of the shelves results in the processes being considerably more complex than offshore. However, 'coastal variability' should not always be considered as 'short spatial scale variability' but can be the result of signals transmitted along the coast from 1000s km away. Fortunately, thanks to tide gauges being necessarily located at the coast, many aspects of coastal sea level variability can be claimed to be better understood than those in the deep ocean. Nevertheless, certain aspects of coastal variability remain under-researched, including how changes in some processes (e.g., wave setup, river runoff) may have contributed to the historical mean sea level records obtained from tide gauges which are now used routinely in large-scale climate research.

Keywords Coastal sea level variability · Sea and land level observations · Meteorological and oceanographic forcings · Coastal climate change

✉ Philip L. Woodworth
plw@noc.ac.uk

1 National Oceanography Centre, 6 Brownlow Street, Liverpool L3 5DA, UK

2 Mercator-Ocean, 31520 Ramonville Saint-Agne, France

3 IMEDEA(UIB-CSIC), Miquel Marquès, 21, 07190 Esporles, Balearic Islands, Spain

4 Department of Physics, University of the Balearic Islands, Cra. Valldemossa, km 7.5, 07122 Palma, Spain

5 Code 698, NASA Goddard Space Flight Center, Greenbelt, MD 20771, USA

6 LIENSs, Université de La Rochelle-CNRS, La Rochelle, France

7 Science 8th Building, 8-3-20 Faculty of Science, Hokkaido University, N10, W8, Sapporo 060-0810, Japan

8 Department of Meteorology, Institute of Geosciences, Federal University of Rio de Janeiro, Rio de Janeiro 21941-901, Brazil

9 Scripps Institution of Oceanography, University of California, San Diego, La Jolla, CA 92093, USA

1 Introduction

Sea level variability at the coast can be similar to, or differ from, that in the neighbouring deep ocean, depending on location and timescale. For example, large spatial- and temporal-scale changes, such as a rise in mean sea level (MSL) due to climate change, might be expected to be similar, to first order at least, at the coast and in the ocean nearby.[1]

However, there are many processes which introduce sea level variability with shorter spatial scales, or which result in a coastal modification in the character of the larger-scale variability. These processes occur primarily due to coastal waters being shallow (by definition) and coastlines having complicated shapes and features such as estuaries and harbours. In addition, the coast provides one of the boundaries (the other being the continental shelf edge) which result in dynamical changes in the ocean circulation and thereby in the sea level variability observed over larger spatial scales. Runoff from rivers introduces another source of sea level variability from the landward side.

As one example, Fig. 1 (from Vinogradov and Ponte 2011) shows the correlation between monthly means of sea level measured at the coast by tide gauges and in the nearby ocean by satellite altimetry. The correlation is far from perfect and (leaving aside for the moment any questions of data imprecision) indicates that there are processes at work resulting in differences in sea level variability between coast and ocean, even on monthly timescales. This means that coastal processes need to be identified and understood as far as possible, partly so that they can be studied in their own right, and partly so that they can be clearly separated from the large-scale, climate-related signals.

In fact, there are many such coastal processes, operating at different timescales, for which in many cases the physics responsible is well understood. Many occur across the short spatial scales of the shelf (e.g., storm surges) or even shorter (e.g., harbour seiches), and timescales much shorter than the monthly and annual timescales of interest in climate studies. Others can occur on quite large spatial scales along the coast and on longer timescales. Examples include the trapped Kelvin waves along the Pacific coast associated with the El Niño–Southern Oscillation (ENSO) (Enfield and Allen 1980; Pugh and Woodworth 2014), or the long-distance correlations of sea level (or sub-surface pressure) along the shelf and slope (Hughes and Meredith 2006). Table 1 provides a list of such processes, while Fig. 2 demonstrates schematically the space and timescales of many of them.

The following sections of this paper discuss a number of forcing factors of coastal sea level variability. The first one refers to the tides, which are the dominant signal in sea level variability along all coastlines and which span a wide range of timescales. We then move to a discussion of a number of other processes, ordered approximately in terms of timescale instead of possible importance (magnitude), although sometimes processes again span different timescales, so the reader will have to be aware that such a division is not straightforward. We consider processes responsible for extreme sea levels, as well as MSL, extremes being of particular interest at the coast.

[1] Mean sea level (MSL) in altimetry usually refers to the average sea surface height at a point in the ocean over a period such as a month or year measured relative to a reference ellipsoid. MSL in tide gauge work is the average sea level measured by a tide gauge over a month or year relative to the height of a benchmark on the nearby land. The two types of MSL can be considered on the same basis when the height of the benchmark relative to the ellipsoid is measured using Global Navigation Satellite System (GNSS) equipment. Tide gauge MSL averaged over an extended period (traditionally 18.6 years) is often used as a national surveying datum. See Pugh and Woodworth (2014) and Gregory et al. (2019) for more detailed definitions of MSL.

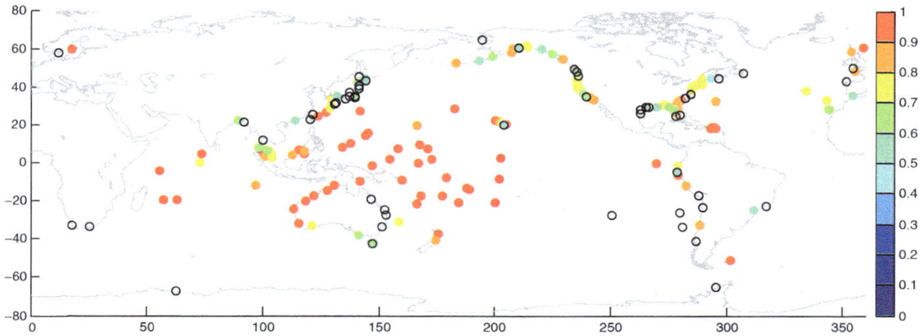

Fig. 1 Correlations between IB-corrected monthly mean sea levels measured at the coast by tide gauges and sea levels recorded by satellite altimetry in the nearby deep ocean over the period 1993–2008. Locations with correlations statistically indistinguishable from zero at 95% confidence level are shown as open circles. From Vinogradov and Ponte (2011)

However, it can be appreciated that, while there are many processes, there is only one ocean, so changes in depth introduced by one process necessarily introduce modifications to others. For example, there are interactions between tides and storm surges in coastal waters, due to both processes modifying the instantaneous depth. In addition, the generally deeper coastal waters arising from a rise in global MSL will result in an increase in tidal wavelengths and modification of patterns of tidal variability. Such interactions between processes are discussed in detail by Idier et al. (2019).

2 Tides

There is one topic that arises in a discussion of nearly every timescale: the tides (Pugh and Woodworth 2014). The dominant half-daily and daily periods of tidal variability are obvious, but tidal periods range from much shorter to very much longer than these. At shorter periods, compound tides such as M_4 (period 6.21 h) reach 25 cm at places like Dover, UK, and higher overtides such as M_{12} (2.07 h) or higher are often detectable and are sometimes even needed for precise predictions. At longer periods, the astronomical tides are all relatively small and sea level variability at these timescales is usually dominated by non-tidal processes, yet the impact of tides on long-term properties of extreme water levels can be pronounced; important tidal periodicities for extreme high water include fortnightly, 4.4 years and 18.6 years, and these will be referred to below. On even longer timescales, short period (semidiurnal and diurnal) tides are found to respond to long-term changes in the oceanic medium, seasonally in particular, but also at longer periods, even secular, leading to tentative connections between tides and climate.

Considerable progress has been made in recent years in modelling the tides of the deep ocean (Stammer et al. 2014), and Ray and Egbert (2017) have summarised major recent research progress in determining the energy budgets of the barotropic tides and in the transmission of internal tides across ocean basins (Zhao et al. 2016). Where internal tides break on a distant coast many days later, they can result in increased seiche activity on timescales typical of the shelf or harbour (e.g., Wijeratne et al. 2010).

Table 1 A highly schematic list of processes which contribute to sea level variability at the coast, in approximate order of timescale

	Process	Space scale	Magnitude	Comments	Example References
Waves and swell	Wind waves	1–10s km	10s cm to metres	Period 1–10 s	LeBlond and Mysak (1978)
	Ocean swell	10–100s km	Sometimes several metres	Period 10–20 s	LeBlond and Mysak (1978)
High frequency (min to hours)	Seiches	Harbour, Bay, Shelf-width, Basin	Typically decimetres, sometimes much larger (up to several metres) when externally forced by long waves (tsunamis or meteotsunamis)	Forced oscillations of variation in elevations and currents, usually forced by the wind, tide or breaking internal tide, or waves, or an impulse such as a tsunami or earthquake. Also generated importantly at the coast by the long waves of meteotsunamis	Monserrat et al. (2006). Rabinovich (2010). Wijeratne et al. (2010). Vilibić and Šepić (2017)
	Meteotsunamis	100s km in generation, harbour/bay scale in impact	Centimetric in the open ocean. 10s cm to potentially several metres after reaching the coast where associated harbour resonances are generated	Probably not appreciated as much as they should be as they need very high-frequency meteorological data to understand properly. Destructive when they amplify a seiche response by resonance	Monserrat et al. (2006). Rabinovich (2010)
High frequency to daily	Coastal trapped waves	100s to 1000s km along-shelf	Typically decimetres, sometimes metres as tidal Kelvin waves or storm surges	Coastal trapped waves underlie along-shelf propagation of responses to forcing. Scales (time, space, magnitude) depend on the forcing	Huthnance (2001). Hughes et al. (2019)
Daily	Tides	Basin scale in generation but more complex spatially in shallow water at the coast	Metres or 10s metres in shelf areas of resonance	Temporally and spatially complex tides in coastal waters	Ray et al. (2011). Ray and Egbert (2017). Pugh and Woodworth (2014)

Table 1 (continued)

	Process	Space scale	Magnitude	Comments	Example References
	Internal tides	Basin scale	Several cm	When break at the coast they can generate seiche activity	Ray and Egbert (2017)
	Inverse barometer	100s–1000s km synoptic weather scale	Decimetres and potentially ± 50 cm	1 cm change in sea level for 1 mbar change in air pressure (to within 0.5%). The ocean takes time to move so there is also a 'dynamic' air pressure change component on timescales of ~ 1 day	Wunsch and Stammer (1997). Discovery of IB effect described by Roden and Rossby (1999)
	Storm surges	100s km (shelf scale)	1–3 m or potentially ~ 10 m during extra-tropical and tropical cyclones, respectively	Generated by wind stress/water depth and air pressure according to the nonlinear shallow water (NLSW) equations	Gönnert et al. (2001). WMO (2011). Pugh and Woodworth (2014)
Examples of processes spanning timescales	Wave setup	Few 100 m for sloping beaches, harbour scales	Decimetres during a storm when high waves, potentially ~ 1 m in some harbours or lagoons	Contributes to MSL variability in the surf zone. Depends on offshore incident wave height, period, direction, still water level and on foreshore slope. Modulated over a range of timescales	Thompson and Hamon (1980). Stockdon et al. (2006). Dean and Walton (2009). Vetter et al. (2010). Aucun et al. (2012), Becker et al. (2014)

Table 1 (continued)

	Process	Space scale	Magnitude	Comments	Example References
	Swash and wave runup	As for setup	Zero contribution to mean sea level in that mean swash is zero and mean runup is equal to the setup	Oscillatory contribution. Depends on offshore incident wave height, period, direction, still water level and on foreshore slope. Large factor in coastal flooding and in shaping coastlines	Stockdon et al. (2006). Roelvink et al. (2009). Kennedy et al. (2016). Poate et al. (2016)
	River runoff	10–100 km (or even larger for the Amazon)	Several cm for most rivers. Major contribution to MSL seasonal cycle in large deltas.	Largely neglected (so far) contributor to sea level variability on timescales other than seasonal	Meade and Emery (1971). Laiz et al. (2014). Wijeratne et al. (2008). Piecuch et al. (2018)
Seasonal	Steric changes	Basin or shelf-scale	Decimetres	Due to seasonal expansion/contraction of the water column	Gill (1982)
	Met changes	Shelf scale	Decimetres	Due to seasonal cycles in air pressure, winds, runoff, etc.	Vinogradov and Ponte (2010)
	Upwelling/downwelling	100s km	Decimetres	Due to seasonal variations in local winds	Middleton and Cirano (1999). Middleton (2000)
	Tides	Shelf-scale	Centimetric	The main tidal harmonics have small seasonal sidebands in the tidal potential. However, on shelves they can vary annually by a much larger amount (typically 1%) due to shelf processes	Pugh and Vassie (1976, 1992). Müller (2012). Gräwe et al. (2014)

Table 1 (continued)

	Process	Space scale	Magnitude	Comments	Example References
	Extremes	Shelf-scale	Decimetres to potentially a metre	Obvious seasonal cycle in sea level extremes due to the weather	Menéndez and Woodworth (2010)
Interannual	ENSO, NAO, etc.	Largely basin scale although with some global teleconnections	Decimetres	In addition to contributing to MSL directly, an impact on mean offshore wave conditions (height, direction, period) and hence setup	Stopa and Cheung (2014). Han et al. (2017a,b, 2018a,b)
Decadal and internal variability	PDO, IOD, etc.	Basin scale	Decimetres	Primarily large scale rather than coastal scale, but there can be associated impacts on coastal processes	Han et al. (2014, 2017a, b, 2018a, b)
Ocean dynamics	Western Boundary Currents	100s km	Decimetres	The coast acts as a low-pass filter for sea level change in the nearby ocean	Bingham and Hughes (2009). Sallenger et al. (2012). Boon (2012). Yin and Goddard (2013). Higginson et al. (2015)
	Eastern coastal currents	1000s km along-shelf, 100 km cross-shelf	Sub-decimetric	Depends on along-shore coastal wind stress	Calafat et al. (2012)
	Coherent variability in SSP along continental shelf and slope	1000s km along continental shelf and slope	Mostly centimetric	Observed in altimeter data and confirmed by models	Hughes and Meredith (2006)
	Mesoscale (eddies, Rossby waves) at ocean islands	~ 100 km and ~ 10 day timescale	Decimetres	Observed in some island sea level records	Mitchum (1995). Williams and Hughes (2013)

Table 1 (continued)

	Process	Space scale	Magnitude	Comments	Example References
Long-term/climate change	Sea level rise	Global although regional variations. Associated changes in water depth (relative sea level) will depend on regional vertical land movements	Decimetres to metre or so by 2100	Changes in water depth modify tides, surges and waves (see Idier et al., 2019). Changes in winds in response to climate change induce changes in mean offshore wave conditions, including height, direction and period, which in turn induce changes in wave setup and runup	Church et al. (2013)
	Tides	Global/regional/local	Secular changes in tidal constituents of order 0.1% in amplitude have been observed that are not well understood	Changes in tides in the future will depend on changes in depth (MSL) from other processes, changes in thermal structure of the water column, etc.	Jay (2009), Ray (2009), Woodworth (2010), Müller et al. (2011), Haigh et al. (2019)
Vertical land movements	Change in the level of the crust (submergence or emergence) relative to the geocentre	Global scale for Global Isostatic Adjustment (GIA). Local scale for natural causes such as earthquakes and a number of anthropogenic factors	Decimetres to metres or so by 2100	GIA is only process that can be modelled on a global basis	Tamisiea and Mitrovica (2011). Peltier et al. (2015). Wöppelmann and Marcos (2016)
Anthropogenic factors					See text

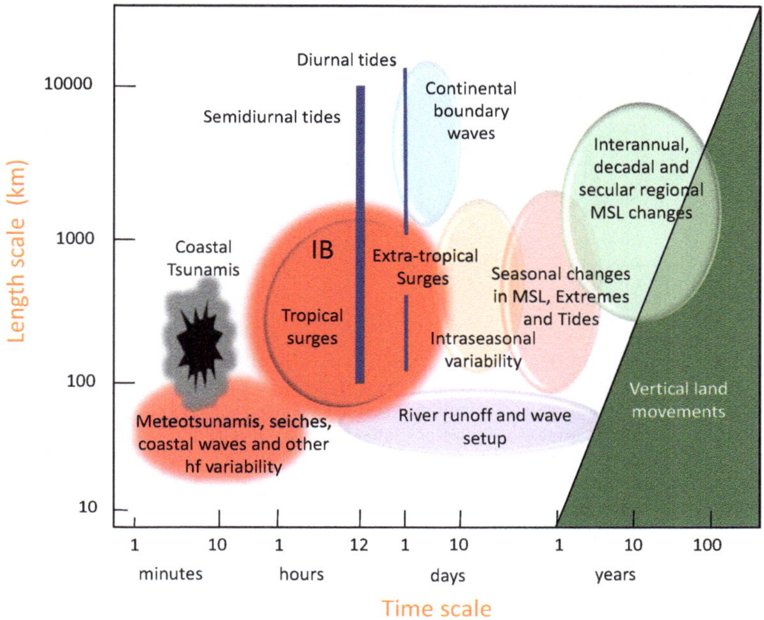

Fig. 2 A schematic overview of processes contributing to sea level variability at the coast indicating the space and timescales involved. Note that Table 1 contains a fuller list of processes than those shown here. Very high frequency processes with timescales less than 1 min (wind waves, swash, etc.) are not included. See Hughes et al. (2019) for a detailed review of different types of coastal trapped waves

The ocean tides are largely generated in the deep ocean. However, their transition to the shelves and to the coast results in their amplification, partly through resonance depending on the shape of the coast and depth of coastal waters, and the generation of higher harmonics of their main frequencies. As a result, many difficulties remain in parameterising the more complex tides which occur near the coast (Ray et al. 2011). Figure 3a provides a demonstration of the complexity of the tide at one coastal location (Eastport, Maine, NE USA). The main semidiurnal and diurnal lines to the left of the spectrum, and a number of others, are now represented well in global ocean tide models (e.g., FES2014 2018). However, it can be appreciated that a major challenge remains to parameterise spatially the many harmonics at frequencies higher than 2 cpd, and also the subtleties of variability and interaction hidden within the tidal cusps.

Figure 3b provides a contrasting spectrum obtained from a bottom pressure (BP) sensor on a Deep-ocean Assessment and Reporting of Tsunami (DART) buoy deployed at 2600 m depth just south of the New England shelf. Although the main semidiurnal and diurnal tides have similar amplitudes to those at Eastport, the higher tidal harmonics are either considerably weaker or absent, those at 5, 7 and 9 cpd in (b) being due to atmospheric tides in BP and not oceanic tides. One may also note the lower non-tidal background provided by a BP record compared to the sea level record of a conventional coastal tide gauge.

One subtlety to do with tidal variability concerns the apparent long-term changes in tidal amplitudes and phases along the coast; it is not yet known whether similar changes are occurring in the deep ocean. Of course, the tide changes over long timescales in response

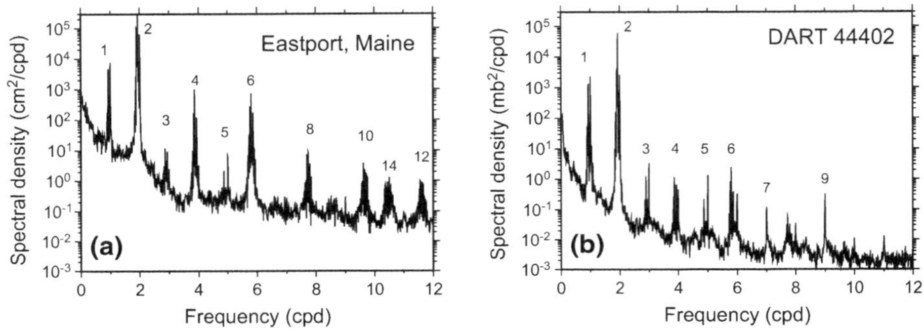

Fig. 3 **a** A sea level spectrum from Eastport, Maine, on the US NE Atlantic coast, highlighting the main tidal band. The dominant tidal constituent is the lunar semidiurnal M_2, but strong nonlinear compound tides appear at higher frequencies. Numerical labels denote tidal species, where each species *n* consists of multiple spectral lines clustering around *n* cycles per lunar day. The spectrum is obtained from four years of hourly spot readings from the Eastport tide gauge. The Nyquist frequency is therefore 12 cpd, so species 14 is aliased into lower frequencies. **b** The corresponding spectrum of bottom pressure (BP) obtained from a nearby deep-ocean buoy (2600 m depth, south of the New England shelf). The higher oceanic tide harmonics are much reduced, the peaks at 5, 7 and 9 cpd being due to atmospheric tides in the BP record

to changes in the orbit of the Moon (Green et al. 2017), and when coastlines and water depths change. However, the presently observed tidal changes (mostly during the past half-century) cannot be explained by simple arguments and constitute an important topic in tidal research (Hill 2016; Haigh et al. 2019).

3 High-Frequency to Daily Coastal Variability

Sub-daily oscillations of sea level near the coast are strongly controlled by bathymetry and local topography. Seiches provide examples of such oscillations. Seiches are a type of resonance in which the sea level oscillates at a natural period of an inlet, harbour, bay or continental shelf (Rabinovich 2010). They were observed first in lakes (Forel 1876) and have since been found to be present in almost all tide gauge records (e.g., Airy 1878). Even larger bodies of water such as the Adriatic Sea and Baltic experience seiches (Lisitzin 1974).

The physical characteristics of a seiche in a lake can be considered similar to that of a guitar string tied at both ends (i.e. a node at each end), while a seiche in a semi-enclosed basin such as a coastal inlet is analogous to a string tied (i.e. a node) at only one of its ends. Resonances can therefore occur with wavelengths twice the lake length in the former case, or four times the inlet length in the latter. Similarly, 'quarter-wavelength seiches' occur across continental shelves, with a node at the land end and an anti-node at the shelf edge. The frequency of a seiche is then given by its wavelength divided by $\sqrt{gh}$ where g is acceleration due to gravity and h is water depth. In the case of complicated coastal geometries, additional factors also play a role (Rabinovich 2010; Wiegel 1964; Wilson 1972).

Free oscillations of a natural system (their so-called natural resonant periods or 'eigenperiods') occur as a response to any external input of energy. In the case of coastal seiches, the forcing is normally in the form of long waves entering through the coastal basin mouth. These periods may be considered as a fundamental property of a particular location and are independent of the type of external forcing (see below). Natural basins generally oscillate with periods ranging between a few minutes and several hours, with amplitudes of centimetres to decimetres. However, at some locations and in some circumstances seiches can have amplitudes comparable to the tide. A maximum response will occur when an external forcing impinges on a basin mouth with a frequency corresponding to its eigen-frequencies. Seiche amplitudes may be then strongly amplified, and the currents associated with them and the resulting flooding inside the basin may cause serious damage to boats and harbour infrastructure. This is particularly the case when the amplification at resonance, characterised by the so-called quality factor Q, is particularly high. In basins with a high Q, generally those that are elongated and narrow, high levels of background seiche energy are also more likely to be present, even with a low level of external forcing (Rabinovich 2010).

There are several processes in nature which are able to generate oceanic long waves with periods matching the eigen-periods of basins and which are able to force them resonantly. Amongst them, tsunamis are probably the best-known phenomena. Tsunami wave properties are determined by the characteristics of the sea floor displacements (earthquakes) which generate them. They propagate as surface long waves with typical wavelengths of hundreds of kilometres and wave periods of up to an hour. The most energetic events affect the coast indiscriminately. However, less energetic tsunamis can also have a major impact where seiche frequencies match those of the tsunami itself, when a resonant coupling takes place and a seiche response is amplified at the local eigen-frequencies. As a consequence, there can be catastrophic consequences for harbours and bays with high Q-factors (Miller 1972; Rabinovich 1997; Rabinovich and Thomson 2007).

Seiches may also be forced by a number of other mechanisms, the most common processes being of atmospheric origin, either due to direct generation of long waves by pressure or wind forcing on the sea surface, or by transferring energy from low-frequency motions (storm surges) or high-frequency gravity waves (wind waves and swell) through nonlinear processes. The first mechanism is the most important because it is responsible for the generation of destructive seiche oscillations (meteotsunamis) all around the world (Defant 1961; Rabinovich and Monserrat 1996; Monserrat et al. 2006).

Destructive meteotsunamis are observed at certain locations in the world ocean where two mechanisms play a successive role: (1) the initial atmospheric energy is optimally transferred into the ocean through some specific resonant process, namely Proudman resonance (when atmospheric disturbance velocity equals the long wave phase speed of the ocean waves), Greenspan resonance (when atmospheric velocity matches that of edge wave modes, see below) or shelf resonance (when the atmospheric disturbance and associated generated ocean wave have periods and/or wavelengths equal to the resonant values for the shelf region); and (2) the generated long ocean waves approach the entrance of a bay or harbour and induce hazardous oscillations in the basin, exciting the basin seiche through harbour resonance (Monserrat et al. 2006).

Vilibić and Šepić (2017) demonstrated that many tide gauge records contain high-frequency variability on timescales from a few minutes to 2 h, which will include any energy due to seiches, although will not necessarily be exclusively due to seiches. They showed that such high-frequency variability, which is often not considered in studies of extreme sea levels based on hourly values from tide gauges, can contribute up to 50% of sea level extremes in some low-tidal areas.

Other high-frequency sea level oscillations can occur at the coast due to existence of the continental shelf, with the shelf characteristics (width and depth) playing a key role in determining their properties. For example, there are waves that travel along the coast or shelf and decay away from the coast: these include edge waves (periods of minutes to hours) and coastal trapped waves. The latter term usually applies to waves with periods longer than an inertial period and is at least partially dependent on the Earth's rotation and vorticity dynamics. A summary of their properties may be found in Huthnance (1978), Huthnance et al. (1986), Huthnance (2001) and references therein. Kelvin waves, with an elevation maximum at the coast and the greatest offshore extent (no offshore nodes of elevation), span the frequency range from edge waves (super-inertial) to coastal trapped waves (sub-inertial). (A 'mode-0' barotropic Kelvin wave in an idealised (straight shelf) context can propagate at super-inertial frequencies without losing energy, as can internal Kelvin waves against a wall. Stratification makes little difference to the mode-0 Kelvin wave. Edge waves are exclusively super-inertial.)

The temporal and spatial scales of these waves depend mainly on the forcing (tides, weather, adjacent oceanic features) and the width of the continental shelf or slope, and on stratification for baroclinic waves. Modes with scales best matching the forcing tend to be favoured. Thus, tides propagating as Kelvin waves may have an amplitude of metres (e.g., Pugh and Woodworth 2014), while amplitudes of coastal trapped wave components are more typically 0.1 m. For example, weather- and oceanic-forced coastal trapped waves have magnitudes of typically 0.1 m, but extreme storm surges may be $\pm$ 1 m or more (e.g., Gönnert et al. 2001; Merrifield et al. 2013).

Hughes et al. (2019) discuss further the physical mechanisms for generation, propagation and decay of coastal trapped waves and their role in determining differences in sea level between deep-ocean, shelf and coast and in transmitting dynamical signals rapidly around the ocean.

4 Daily Coastal Sea Level Variability

In this section, we refer to several types of processes with meteorological forcing which result in sea level variability on timescales of several hours to several days (which we denote as 'daily'). Some of these are well known and are described adequately in text books.

One of the most important meteorological forcings of sea level variability over the open ocean, as well near the coast, is variability in surface air pressure. The inverse barometer (IB) effect, whereby an increase of 1 mbar in air pressure results in approximately 1 cm decrease in sea level (to within approximately half a per cent), was discovered in Sweden by Nils Gissler (Roden and Rossby 1999). An historical example of the IB effect using data collected in 1842 is given in Fig. 4. Other historical examples from the early nineteenth century are discussed by Daussy (1831), Lubbock (1836) and Ross (1854). As the ocean takes some time to adjust to a new equilibrium (typically ~ 1 day), there is a transient 'dynamic air pressure effect' (e.g., Ponte et al. 1991). Within the spectrum of air pressure variability in some parts of the ocean, and consequently within that of sea level variability, are modes with particular periods. These include the Madden–Julian 5-day waves which are, in principle, global in scale but are most evident in the tropics where the overall magnitude of air pressure variability is less (Luther 1982; Woodworth et al. 1995). (These are not to be confused with the approximately 4-day equatorial-trapped waves discussed by Wunsch and Gill 1976.)

Wind stress is the shear force that the wind exerts on the ocean surface and is proportional to the square of the wind speed (Pugh and Woodworth 2014). Wind stress is a relatively more important forcing of sea level variability than air pressure in shallow-water areas, where increases in sea level gradients are proportional to wind stress divided by

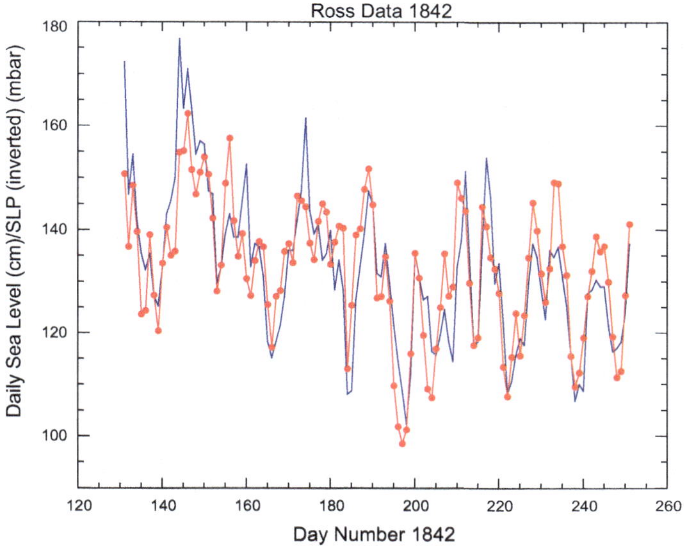

Fig. 4 Historical demonstration of the IB effect. Daily values of sea level (i.e. mean tide level, MTL) in 1842 at Port Louis, Falkland Islands (blue) together with daily values of sea level air pressure (SLP) (red), both measured by James Clark Ross. Air pressure values are shown inverted and their average adjusted to equal that in MTL. The MTL daily values are defined as the average of the average of high waters and average of low waters recorded each day. From Woodworth et al. (2010)

water depth. In addition, the coastal boundary acts to block wind-driven transport, leading to sea level elevation at the coast. As a result, coastal sea level variability on daily to monthly timescales departs significantly from an IB response to air pressure change (e.g., for the east coast of the UK, Thompson 1980; Woodworth 2018).

At times, the sea level changes resulting from a combination of air pressures and winds, called storm surges, can result in catastrophic flooding and loss of life. Depth-averaged (or barotropic) tides and storm surges can be modelled using the depth-averaged (2D) nonlinear shallow-water (NLSW) equations (Gönnert et al. 2001; WMO 2011; Pugh and Woodworth 2014; Piecuch et al. 2019). Such modelling schemes are used operationally in many countries (Flather 2000) and can be employed in delayed mode in research studies of coastal sea level variability (Carrère and Lyard 2003; Wakelin et al. 2003) and sea level extremes (Muis et al. 2016). Tides, winds and waves can also energise seiches (quasi-resonant modes of oscillation of sea level in inlets, bays, harbours and shelves, see Sect. 3) that can be superimposed on a storm surge and can consequently result in a higher measured extreme sea level.

An insight into waves is important for simulating accurately the daily variations in sea level in numerical models. Bottom friction coefficients used in barotropic modelling have been shown to depend on wave height (Madsen et al. 1988; Wolf 1999; Soulsby and Clarke 2005), although in practice such dependence is not usually taken into account. Nevertheless, this provides a further example of interaction between processes (tide-surge-wave) discussed by Idier et al. (2019).

The storm surges caused by tropical cyclones are different in character to those produced by higher latitude storms. Tropical storm surges tend to be of smaller spatial scale (~500 km rather than ~1000 km) and usually have a shorter duration (hours to days rather than several days), but are much larger in amplitude (sometimes 5–10 m rather than typically 2–3 m) (von Storch and Woth 2008). Extreme sea levels occur by the combination of surge and astronomical tide and clearly have their most extreme values when both tide and surge are large and coincide. Extreme sea levels are usually studied by techniques such as percentile analysis (Menéndez and Woodworth 2010). In strongly semi-diurnal tide regimes, the high percentiles have a perigean (~4.4 year) dependence, while in strongly diurnal tide regimes the high percentiles vary over the lunar nodal cycle (18.6 years) (Haigh et al. 2011).

Merrifield et al. (2013) made maps of mean annual maximum sea level (relative to annual mean MSL, thereby excluding consideration of interannual variability) at many locations round the world coastline, and also maps of the individual contributions to mean annual maximum sea level from either the tide, seasonal cycle in sea level or low and high-frequency variations. The low-frequency components were defined by timescales longer than approximately a month but less than seasonal, whereas high-frequency variations were identified using a running 1-month median filter. Mean annual maximum levels occur where tide and low-frequency components are both large, such as the coasts of the North East Pacific, North West European continental shelf and North West Australia, while high-frequency variability was shown to be relatively more important along the American Atlantic coast and in North West Europe and South Australia (see their Figs. 3, 4).

One concern arises from the fact that the largest extremes (and so the events with the most catastrophic flooding) might not be represented adequately in tide gauge data sets. This reservation applies particularly to extremes caused by tropical storms. By definition, these events are rare ones and, when they do occur, the highest sea level may not be located exactly at the gauge, but some distance away. Therefore, this type of event may not be sampled adequately, even in a record spanning many decades. Furthermore, some gauges may not be able to record very high sea levels, and during an energetic storm, a gauge might be destroyed and so the extreme may not be recorded. To some extent, this is a sampling issue that can be addressed by analysing the tide gauge data in combination with numerical ocean modelling (e.g., Haigh et al. 2014a, b).

Changes in MSL are a major driver of changes in extreme sea levels at interannual and longer timescales (Lowe et al. 2010; Menéndez and Woodworth 2010; Woodworth et al. 2011; Marcos and Woodworth 2017, 2018). For example, Fig. 5 shows that linear trends of annual 99th percentiles of total sea level since 1960 (these are a good approximation of annual extreme levels), and of skew surges over the same period, can be accounted for to a great extent by trends in MSL. However, MSL is not the only driver: analyses of high-frequency tide gauge records, once the effect of MSL has been removed, reveal variations in the storm surge contribution associated with changes in storminess on long timescales (Menéndez and Woodworth 2010; Marcos et al. 2015; Marcos and Woodworth 2017). The intensity and frequency of storm surge changes unrelated to MSL show regionally coherent patterns that have been linked to large-scale climate indices, such as the North Atlantic Oscillation (NAO) in the North Atlantic (Marcos et al. 2015; Wahl and Chambers 2015; Marcos and Woodworth 2017). Similar conclusions on MSL being a major, if not the only, driver of changes in extremes were obtained using a small number of very long tide gauge records starting in the mid-nineteenth century.

Semidiurnal and diurnal variations in meteorological forcings that can potentially lead to sea level variability are of particular interest in the tropics. For example, air pressure has a predominantly semidiurnal cycle throughout the tropics (Pugh and Woodworth 2014, Sect. 5.5), with an amplitude of more than 1 mbar, peaking at about 10:00 and 22:00 h local time. Small diurnal variations in wind speed occur in the synoptic trades (e.g., in

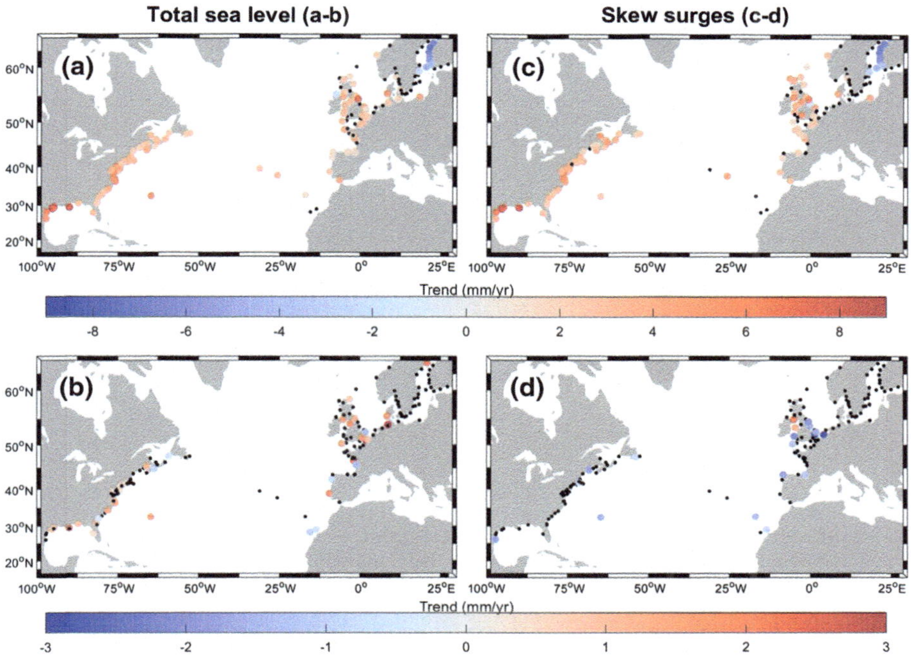

Fig. 5 **a** Linear trends of annual 99th percentiles of total sea level and **b** with median removed. **c** Linear trends of annual 99th percentiles of skew surges and **d** with median removed. Tide gauge data from 1960 to present are used. Black dots indicate where the trends are not significant. From Marcos and Woodworth (2018)

the Caribbean, Cook and Vizy 2010) and are best measured in situ by ocean buoys well away from land. However, much larger diurnal cycles in wind speed are found in data from some coastal land stations. These occur due to local sea and land breeze effects, which at locations in the tropics can extend 10s of km from the coast (Miller et al. 2003; Gille et al. 2005), and can affect many physical and biological processes including the local ocean circulation (e.g., Walter et al. 2017) and conceivably sea level to some extent. Inevitably, the sea and land breezes are not represented well in the large-scale meteorological products that are used for storm surge modelling.

5 Examples of Processes Spanning Timescales

As a demonstration of the difficulty of drawing simple diagrams such as Fig. 2, with some processes spanning a range of timescales, this section considers the importance to sea level studies of ocean waves. Waves manifest themselves at the high-energy end of the instantaneous sea level spectrum, and yet it will be seen that through long-term changes in wave climate waves can also contribute to long-term changes in MSL. This section also considers river runoff as a further example of processes spanning timescales that can contribute to MSL variability.

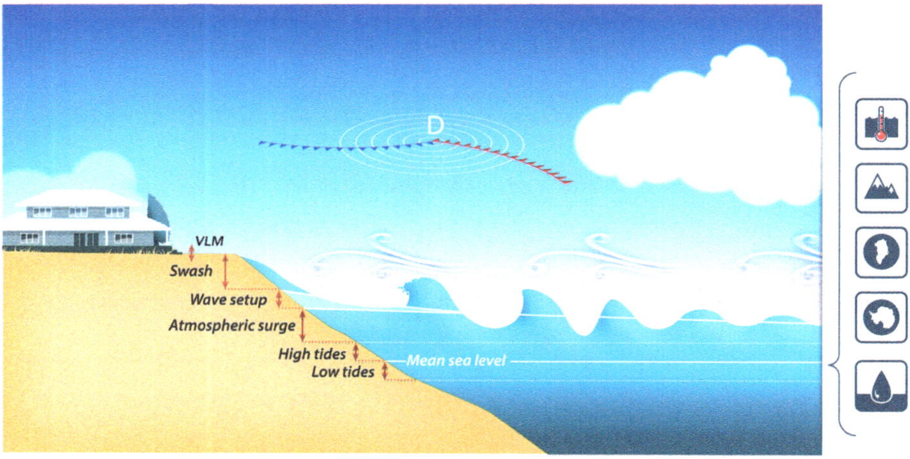

Fig. 6 Schematic of processes contributing to total water level changes at the coast. The mean sea level derived from radar altimetry data includes contributions from ocean thermal expansion and ocean circulation, transfer of water from land to ocean due to mass loss from glaciers and the Arctic and Antarctic ice sheets, as well as from land water storage changes (pictograms on the right, top to bottom). Sea level variability from tides and coastal processes including storm surges due to air pressure effects and wind setup, as well as wave setup and swash are superimposed on the larger-scale changes. Vertical land movements are denoted by VLM. The rotation of the depression (D) applies to the northern hemisphere. Adapted from Melet et al. (2018)

5.1 Wave Setup

Tides, surges and MSL together make up the 'still water level' superimposed upon which there are ocean wind waves. Wind waves span a range of period typically 1–25 s (LeBlond and Mysak 1978). The wave field impinging on a given location at the coast is usually composed of waves of different origins, ages and periods. Part of that field will consist of locally generated waves with shorter periods, while waves with longer periods will partly comprise ocean swell that could have travelled 1000s of km from distant storms (Ardhuin et al. 2009). Distantly generated swell has been found to result in major impacts on coastlines far from its generation (e.g., Harangozo 1993; Hoeke et al. 2013).

Wind waves are of great practical importance to coastal protection (e.g., Roelvink et al. 2009). Wave energy flux is a key driver of coastal erosion and contributes significantly to the evolution of shorelines, for example through modification of beach profiles due to sea level rise (Bruun 1962). Wind waves also play a role in flooding through overflowing, overtopping and breaching of natural barriers (e.g., dunes) or flood defences (e.g., dykes). Coastal flooding impacts are different in character in each case. Overflowing refers to when the water level (which includes wave setup) exceeds the height of the barrier. In the case of overtopping, when the crests of the waves exceed the barrier height, water with high momentum pours intermittently onto the coastal land. When breaching occurs, even greater flooding can take place, as the original barrier is no longer effective.

In spite of their importance, waves are often ignored in sea level studies, especially when those studies are not focused on extreme events. As waves propagate into shallow water, wave amplitudes increase until the waves become unstable and break (Dodet et al. 2019, in review). Breaking and wave dissipation raise water levels in the surf zone in a process known as wave setup (Fig. 6). The reduction in wave energy due to breaking leads to a radiation stress gradient, with momentum transferred from waves to the water column (Longuet-Higgins and Stewart 1962; Bowen et al. 1968; Holman and Sallenger 1985; Dean and Walton 2009; Pugh and Woodworth 2014). Assuming steady-state conditions, the radiation stress gradient is balanced by higher water levels at the shore. Wave setup is proportional to the offshore significant wave height and can contribute to elevated water levels that are an appreciable fraction (20–30%) of the incident deep water significant wave height. The magnitude of setup can be estimated if one has either measured or modelled wave data and has knowledge of coastal bathymetry (e.g., Stockdon et al. 2006; Dietrich et al. 2009; Melet et al. 2016; Marsooli and Lin 2018; Pedreros et al. 2018). Spatial gradients in wave setup, due, for example, to variations in breaker height, can cause local circulations such as rip currents. Characteristic periods of wave setup are tens of the dominant incident wind-wave periods (O(1 min)). However, it is modulated on longer timescales through its dependence on the height, period and direction of incident waves and on the still water level (Idier et al. 2019, in review).

Wave setup is a particular concern for island shorelines that are otherwise protected from wave energy by coral reefs (Vetter et al. 2010; Becker et al. 2014; Hoeke et al. 2015; Buckley et al. 2018). At these locations, wave setup can be the largest single non-tidal contributor to extreme water levels (Merrifield et al. 2014).[2]

Because tide gauges are usually located in large protected harbours, where wave breaking is limited, wave setup in most cases will be negligible in tide gauge records, although notable exceptions can occur (e.g., Thompson and Hamon 1980; Aucan et al. 2012). In these cases, it can be appreciated that, although wave events and wave setup occur on the 'daily' timescale, wave setup will inevitably contribute to MSL variability on seasonal and even interannual timescales. Consequently, there is a possibility in some cases of contamination of existing long-term MSL records by variations in wave setup in the past, and the character of that contamination might change again if wave climate changes in the future (Melet et al. 2018, discussed in Aucan et al. 2019 and Melet et al. 2019). For example, in the Arctic, wave climate will depend on future sea ice conditions (Stopa et al. 2016). A further technical issue is that tide gauge measurements, whatever the technique employed, can be affected to some extent by waves (e.g., see discussion of wave effects on radar tide gauge data in Intergovernmental Oceanographic Commission, IOC 2016).

Before leaving waves, we can refer to a further process called 'swash' (Fig. 6). Wave swash is the oscillation in shoreline position due to wave propagation onto upper parts of the beach. It plays an important role in shaping the coastline through sediment transport, and in flooding through overtopping and breaching. Wave runup is defined as the combination of wave setup and swash, with setup being the mean component of runup averaged over some time window, and swash therefore having zero contribution to sea level over that window. On wave-exposed, open-coast beaches, wave runup can reach several metres during extreme events (Kennedy et al. 2016; Poate et al. 2016) and at times wave energy can cause significant modifications to the coast (e.g., Cox et al. 2018). Like setup, the importance of swash is site dependent, being determined by the height, period and direction of the incident waves. Therefore, it is modulated at low frequencies in a similar way to wave

[2] A distinction is usually made between low-frequency modulation of waves on the timescale of wave groups, which is sometimes called surf beat, and longer-term averages of the wave field associated with a steady setup component. Dynamically, setup is generally computed assuming that steady state, over a timescale in which acceleration terms are small compared to other terms in the momentum balance (say longer than about 15 min).

setup. However, unlike setup, it does not contribute to variability in what we refer to usually as 'sea level'.

5.2 River Runoff

A process with a similar potential contribution to coastal sea level measurement across a wide range of timescales is freshwater runoff from rivers (Durand et al. 2019, in review). The process is known to contribute to signals of the order of centimetres in sea level variability on daily timescales for some rivers in Europe, with plumes extending ~10 km from the river mouth (e.g., Laiz et al. 2014). Gómez-Enri et al. (2017) have suggested that such discharges of small rivers can be detected as sea surface height anomalies in coastal altimeter data. Runoff will undoubtedly be a much larger factor in large river deltas. For example, Wijeratne et al. (2008) pointed to the large (~1 m) seasonal cycle in MSL in the Ganges Delta, although it is not clear whether this is due to only runoff per se, or also to an associated thermosteric contribution (Fabien Durand, private communication; Neetu et al. 2012). Meade and Emery (1971) suggested a link between runoff and interannual variability in MSL at US tide gauges, a link which has been confirmed by recent research (Piecuch et al. 2018). The most extreme contribution from runoff is probably that associated with the Amazon River (e.g., Korosov et al. 2015), where the spreading of the river plume can be traced for distances larger than a 1000 km from its mouth. A climate model simulation by Jahfer et al. (2015) has shown that Amazon runoff can impact climate and sea level in a much broader sense, by contributing to the strength of the Atlantic Meridional Overturning Circulation (AMOC).

6 Seasonal Variability in Coastal Sea Level

The seasonal cycle is one of the most important non-tidal components of sea level records, especially in the mid- to high latitudes.[3] Seasonal variability in sea level is forced by a variety of mechanisms, including atmospheric pressure and winds, precipitation, river runoff, ice melting, ocean circulation changes and variations in steric height. The latter, driven by expansion/contraction of the water column above the seasonal thermocline in response to heat flux exchanges with the atmosphere, is the dominant contributor in most oceanic regions (Gill and Niller 1973).

The mean seasonal sea level cycle at the coast was investigated by Tsimplis and Woodworth (1994) using a data set of 1043 tide gauges distributed globally around the world coastlines. They reported high spatial variability in the annual and the semi-annual signals with annual amplitudes reaching several decimetres along some parts of the coast. However, coastal seasonal oscillations may significantly differ from those in the open ocean (Vinogradov and Ponte 2010). While in the deep ocean the annual cycle is driven by steric changes and the large-scale wind field (Chen et al. 2000; Vinogradov et al. 2008), near the coast other factors, such as local wind patterns, rivers or seasonal upwelling/downwelling, become dominant (Middleton and Cirano 1999; Middleton 2000). In general, annual amplitudes are larger along the coasts and over continental shelves due to the impact of

[3] The seasonal cycle of MSL also contains small long-period astronomical tidal contributions with periods of 6 months and 1 year (Pugh and Woodworth 2014).

these coastal processes. Seasonal changes in the atmospheric forcing also induce variability at these timescales in higher-frequency processes such as storm surges, which result in larger extremes of sea level during the winter season (Menéndez and Woodworth 2010; Merrifield et al. 2013; Marcos and Woodworth 2017). The same applies for offshore wave conditions as a result of the seasonality in storminess and thereby in the propagation of swell waves (e.g., Semedo et al. 2011). Seasonal changes in wave height, period and direction are more pronounced in extratropical regions, and highest in the Northern Hemisphere (Young 1999). As a result, wave setup also contributes to seasonal water level changes at the coast (Melet et al. 2016).

The major constituents of the ocean tide also display seasonality. For example, Pugh and Vassie (1976, 1992) demonstrated that the amplitude of the predominant M_2 constituent along North Sea coasts varies through the year by several per cent and is a maximum in summer. This variation is due to a well-developed thermocline in summer and a well-mixed water column during winter (Müller 2012; Gräwe et al. 2014). Similar variations have been observed in other shelf areas (e.g., Yellow Sea, Kang et al. 1995, and the Canadian Pacific, Foreman et al. 1995). As far as we know, such studies have not been made on a global basis. However, inspection of the Admiralty Tide Tables (UK Hydrographic Office, UKHO 2017) and other tidal databases shows evidence for similar seasonality in other shelf areas. One suspects that it is not so apparent at deep-ocean islands where tidal amplitudes anyway tend to be smaller than in continental shelf areas.

Despite the seasonal sea level cycle often being considered as a steady signal, many studies have reported significant temporal changes in seasonality. Interannual to multidecadal variability has been related to changes in atmospheric pressure and wind fields (e.g., Plag and Tsimplis 1999, in the North and Baltic Seas; Marcos and Tsimplis 2007, in Southern Europe; Torres and Tsimplis 2012, in the Caribbean Sea) which, in turn, are linked to climate indices such as NAO. They have also been associated with variability in ocean currents, especially where these are strong (e.g., in the NW Pacific (Feng et al. 2015) or western Atlantic (Calafat et al. 2018)), or to changes in large-scale forcing patterns in steric height or sea surface temperature (SST) (Wahl et al. 2014). The study of Amiruddin et al. (2015) made use of both tide gauge and altimeter data from the South China Sea, finding significant differences between the coastal seasonal cycle and that of the nearby deeper ocean. Both types of data have also been applied to studies of the coastal seasonal cycle on a quasi-worldwide basis by Etcheverry et al. (2015), finding differences of ~ 2 cm between data types in the observed amplitudes of the annual cycle of MSL.

7 Interannual and Decadal Sea Level Variability

7.1 Importance of Climate Modes to Interannual Variability

Climate modes are large-scale patterns of coherent variability in meteorological or oceanographic parameters such as air pressure or SST, with the amplitude of the variability represented by a mode index. Since these parameters, and additional ones associated with them (e.g., winds), are known to be forcings of sea level variability (e.g., see Sect. 4 for discussion of wind forcing), it is unsurprising that large-scale patterns of variability in mean and extreme sea levels similar to the climate modes have also been observed (e.g., Menéndez and Woodworth 2010). Han et al. (2017a, b, 2018a, b) have already provided an overview of ocean modes, with a focus on the Pacific and Indian Oceans. We comment below on the importance of such modes from the primary perspective of coastal sea level.

The modes have large impacts on coastal oceans by means of forcing by local winds associated with them and by remote influence from the ocean interior. For example, surface winds associated with the El Niño–Southern Oscillation (ENSO) and Indian Ocean Dipole (IOD), discussed below, induce eastward-propagating equatorial Kelvin waves; upon arriving at the eastern boundary, the energy subsequently propagates poleward as coastal trapped waves, affecting sea level in a long distance along the coastlines of the eastern Pacific (e.g., Enfield and Allen 1980) and eastern Indian Ocean, respectively.

ENSO is the best-known climate mode, consisting of a coupled atmospheric and oceanic oscillatory mode that originates in the tropical Pacific and acts on typical timescales of 5–7 years. ENSO 'warm events' are characterised by both a lowering of sea level air pressure and a weakening of the easterly trade winds over the eastern tropical Pacific, allowing an area of anomalously high SST to spread eastwards, accompanied by a shift in the main area of convection from Indonesia to the central Pacific (Rasmussen and Carpenter 1982). This reduces upwelling, deepens the thermocline and increases sea levels at the eastern boundary. In contrast, 'cold events' or 'La Niña' episodes are associated with anomalously low SST in the central and eastern Pacific and warmer surface waters to the western Pacific, which strengthens the easterly trade winds, increasing upwelling at the eastern margins. In both warm and cold events, sea level anomalies are transmitted polewards along the Pacific coast of the Americas in the form of coastal trapped Kelvin waves (Enfield and Allen 1980; Pugh and Woodworth 2014). Recently, Merrifield and Thompson (2018) have pointed to differences in ENSO climatology between the pre-1970 period, when ENSO variability was relatively low, and post-1970 when it was greater. The effects of ENSO are widespread, and ENSO influences have been identified in MSL variability along both the Pacific and Atlantic coastlines of the USA (Hamlington et al. 2015), while Marcos and Woodworth (2017) noted an ENSO influence on wintertime extreme sea levels along the US Atlantic coast.

In polar regions, annular climate modes dominate atmospheric variability, reflecting the meridional pressure contrast between a mid-latitude ring of high pressure and a polar low, which determines the strength of the westerlies in each hemisphere. In the Southern Hemisphere, Hall and Visbeck (2002) proposed the existence of a large-scale oceanic response to the Southern Annular Mode (SAM) or Antarctic Oscillation (AAO), describing how a positive state SAM index (associated with stronger eastward wind stress) would increase equatorward Ekman transport, coastal divergence and upwelling along the Antarctic coast, generating a simultaneous lowering of coastal sea levels and increased outcropping of isopycnals at the sea surface, and resulting in both a barotropic and a baroclinic response in circumpolar transport. Observational studies using sub-surface pressure (sea level corrected for the IB effect) from Southern Ocean coastal tide gauge and bottom pressure recorders have substantiated this, identifying a virtually instantaneous large-scale coherent and inverse sea level response to subseasonal variability of the SAM at coastal locations (Aoki 2002; Hughes et al. 2003; Meredith et al. 2004, Woodworth et al. 2006, Hibbert et al. 2010), with covariability having been shown to hold for interannual timescales in some studies (Hughes et al. 2003; Meredith et al. 2004, Hibbert et al. 2010).

The Northern Hemisphere counterpart to the SAM, the Northern Annular Mode (NAM) or Arctic Oscillation (AO), is characterised by centres of low air pressure over the Arctic and higher pressure over the North Pacific and central North Atlantic oceans. There is a close correspondence between this pattern and that of the NAO which is focused on the Icelandic Low and the Azores High, and it is usually agreed that the

NAO is a regional expression of the NAM (Thompson and Wallace 1998; Cohen and Barlow 2005).

Modelling studies of the Arctic Ocean suggest that coastal sea levels respond to periodic reversals of the ocean circulation (i.e. cyclonic or anticyclonic) (Proshutinsky and Johnson 1997; Proshutinsky et al. 2002; Dukhovsky et al. 2004), depending on the phase of the NAM (Newton et al. 2006; Proshutinsky et al. 2007). However, Häkkinen and Geiger (2000) reported the existence of two separate modes of sea surface height variability: one related to the NAM and a second associated with the NAO. Hughes and Stepanov (2004) used a barotropic model referenced to tide gauge observations, finding evidence of a highly coherent (but not dominant) Arctic Ocean sea level mode at interannual timescales that was associated with both the NAO and NAM. They concluded that variability of these atmospheric patterns caused changes in the eastward wind stress of atmospheric flows from the Atlantic, altering onshore Ekman flow and sea levels along the Arctic coast. These results are largely supported by observational studies (Dvorkin et al. 2000; Pavlov 2001, Proshutinsky et al. 2004; Richter et al. 2012; Calafat et al. 2013). Correlations between sea level and NAO/NAM decrease travelling east from the Norwegian Sea (Dvorkin et al. 2000; Calafat et al. 2013).

At lower latitudes, on the Eastern US coast, associations between the NAO and coastal sea levels have also been established (e.g., Andres et al. 2013), though it is unclear whether this arises from the dynamic effects of NAO-related variability on regional wind stress and air pressure (Andres et al. 2013; Ezer et al. 2013; Kenigson et al. 2018), or whether ocean heat anomalies associated with the NAO modulate the strength of the Atlantic Meridional Overturning Circulation, AMOC (Häkkinen 2000; McCarthy et al. 2015), or alternatively from some combination of the two (Goddard et al. 2015). Here, sea levels have been shown to exhibit a negative poleward gradient, with elevated sea levels in the vicinity of the subtropical gyre to the south of Cape Hatteras, and lower sea levels to the north in the colder waters of the sub-polar gyre. Variability in this sea level gradient has been strongly associated with heat exchange between the two gyres forcing changes in the AMOC, such that positive heat anomalies advected to the sub-polar gyre inhibit the AMOC (Bingham and Hughes 2009; Yin et al. 2009).

On the eastern boundary of the North Atlantic, a large-scale coherent sea level signal has been noted, which is highly correlated with the NAO at decadal timescales and which has been attributed to the association of the NAO with regional wind changes and to a lesser extent with air pressure (Wakelin et al. 2003; Miller and Douglas 2007; Calafat et al. 2012). The latter study noted that the region of coherent variability was largely confined to the continental shelf, postulating that along-shore winds force sea level anomalies that propagate polewards as coastal trapped waves (see below).

The Quasi-Biennial Oscillation (QBO) (Angell and Korshover 1964) describes a periodic reversal in the predominant direction (easterly or westerly) of the equatorial stratospheric winds that occurs approximately every 14 months. The phase of this is determined by upward fluxes of westerly and easterly momentum supplied by equatorially trapped Kelvin waves and Rossby-gravity waves, respectively (Lindzen and Holton 1968; Holton and Lindzen 1972), generating alternate wind regimes that gradually propagate downwards, dissipating at the tropopause. Unlike the climate modes discussed so far, the QBO is a stratospheric phenomenon, and, intuitively, a connection to sea level would be unexpected. However, Andrew et al. (2006) noted a statistically significant relationship between QBO index and sea level from altimetry in the tropical South Atlantic, but was unable to establish a dynamical explanation. Hibbert et al. (2010) identified an extratropical sea level response to the QBO along the coast of Antarctica, which was ascribed to modulation of the westerlies by the poleward focusing of planetary wave activity during an easterly QBO phase.

There is also an important intraseasonal mode of tropical atmospheric variability called the Madden–Julian Oscillation (MJO) (Madden and Julian 1971). The MJO is characterised by the generation and eastward propagation of coupled atmospheric deep convection and precipitation anomalies on timescales of 30–100 days (Xie and Arkin 1997), but most commonly 40–50 days (Madden and Julian 1994). These eastward-propagating systems typically originate in the Indian Ocean and are discernible in observations of zonal wind and precipitation (Zhang 2005). Oliver and Thompson (2010) performed a global analysis of altimeter data, validated using tide gauge sea levels, and established three key regions of strong connection between sea level and the MJO, the most significant of which was found to be the equatorial region and eastern boundary of the Pacific. It was suggested that zonal winds induced sea level anomalies that propagate eastwards along the equator and then polewards in both hemispheres along the coast of the Americas in the form of coastal trapped waves. Along the coast of Sumatra, a similar mechanism was proposed, but in this case, the poleward-propagating waves were thought to be accompanied by westward-travelling Rossby waves. In contrast, sea level setup by MJO-related onshore winds was the underlying mechanism in the Gulf of Carpentaria. Matthews and Meredith (2004) identified a sea level response to the MJO on the Antarctic coast, which was attributed to the development of an extratropical atmospheric wave train.

Similar large-scale patterns to those of variability in coastal MSL associated with climate modes have also been observed in extreme sea levels (Menéndez and Woodworth 2010; Marcos et al. 2009; Talke et al. 2014; Marcos et al. 2015; Wahl and Chambers 2016). For example, a strong wintertime dependence of MSL and storm surge elevations on the NAO has been noted on the NW European shelf (Wakelin et al. 2003; Woodworth et al. 2007; Marcos and Woodworth 2017). Interannual changes in wind-wave height, period and direction are also influenced by climate modes (e.g., Semedo et al. 2011; Stopa and Cheung 2014 and references therein). Wave-driven processes in the coastal zone are therefore also directly dependent on large-scale teleconnection patterns such as ENSO, SAM and PDO (Pacific Decadal Oscillation), with remote responses of wave setup and runup through the propagation of swell across ocean basins (and, in turn, as noted above, wave setup can contribute to coastal sea level, Melet et al. 2018). Similarly, rates of coastal erosion will be affected by the variability in storm surges, MSL and wave direction and energy flux, and consequently will have a dependence on climate modes. Such an association between coastal erosion and ENSO has been observed on Pacific coasts (Barnard et al. 2015).

7.2 Decadal Sea Level Variability

Decadal variability can perhaps be claimed to be more important than interannual variability in some respects, owing to the longer periods being more comparable to the lengths of sea level records, and thereby being a determining factor in obtaining reliable secular sea level trends. Two of the main climate modes that exhibit energetic decadal timescale variability are the Pacific Decadal Oscillation (Mantua and Hare 2002) and the Indian Ocean Dipole (IOD) (Saji and Yamagata 2003). (In fact, the PDO also has an energetic interannual component. However, it has proportionally more decadal energy than ENSO modes.)

The PDO occurs in the same ocean areas as ENSO (primarily the Pacific), but on longer timescales, as reflected in Pacific SST north of 20°N. The IOD is a quasi-periodic oscillation of SST between the western and eastern tropical Indian Ocean, which impacts

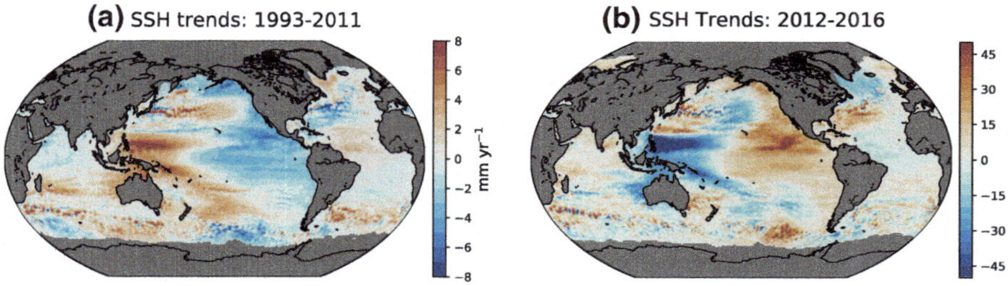

Fig. 7 Sea surface height (SSH) trends from **a** 1993 to 2011 and **b** from 2012 to 2016 based on Aviso gridded SSH data. These patterns in SSH trends are similar to those in sea surface temperatures, these two periods being times of decreasing and increasing PDO index, respectively. Adapted from Merrifield and Thompson (2018)

significantly on the regional monsoonal weather. Major IOD events occur less frequently than ENSO ones, but the two phenomena are clearly linked components of the climate system.

Although these two decadal indices are defined in terms of SST, they are also reflected in similar regional patterns of sea level change. For example, Merrifield and Thomson (2018) (see also Hamlington et al. 2016) pointed to a shift in PDO index and trade wind fields between 1993–2011 and 2012–2016 which manifests itself in patterns of sea level change of opposite sign in the two periods (Fig. 7). Reviews of Indian Ocean decadal variability, including discussion of the IOD and sea level, are given by Han et al. (2014, 2018a, b).

All of these decadal signals are regional, or even basin scale, in extent, rather than being particularly coastal. Nevertheless, the temperature and sea level variability associated with them can result in coastal impacts in, for example, coral bleaching or flooding of low-lying coral islands (e.g., Dunne et al. 2012).

Finally, one can mention that the nodal astronomical tide will contribute to variability in MSL. If this has a magnitude comparable to its equilibrium expectations, then it will be at the centimetre level or less at most locations (Woodworth 2012). Occasionally, larger nodal signals are reported in analyses of tide gauge data (e.g., Baart et al. 2012). However, these anomalous findings are mostly likely due to localised sea level variability (e.g., in river estuaries), or to genuine ocean variability with a similar period that is not adequately separable from the nodal tide in a short record.

8 Coastal Circulation Dynamics and Sea Level

The dynamics of the coastal ocean circulation are controlled by, amongst other things, bathymetry and the shape of the coastal boundaries. The dynamics introduces differences in sea level variability observed both along-shore and between the coast and deep ocean. These dynamics are discussed in detail by Hughes et al. (2019). However, for present purposes, we can point to three important aspects which are demonstrated in many studies: (1) the relative importance to sea level variability of atmospheric forcing, in particular wind stress, in shallow shelf seas, (2) the benefit of taking (1) into account when looking for longer-term trends in sea level variability, and (3) the sea level responses to forcing propagate along the shelf and slope, primarily cyclonically around an ocean basin (i.e. in the sense of Kelvin waves).

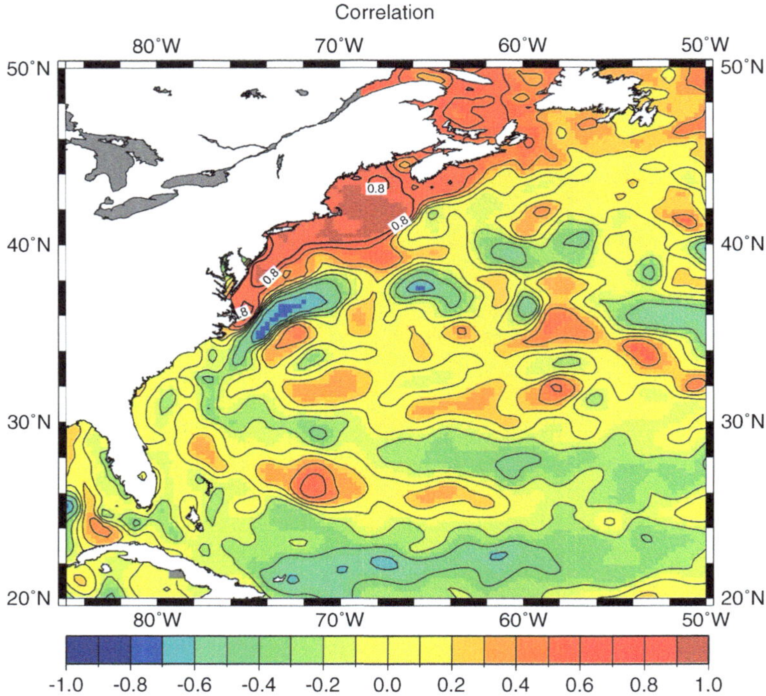

Fig. 8 Correlations of detrended annual mean values of sea level from altimeter data over 1993–2009 with those at a point on the shelf to the east of Cape Cod (42°N, 69°W). Sea level on the shelf can be seen to vary differently from that in the ocean. From Woodworth et al. (2014)

Dynamical processes along continental shelves have been investigated most intensively along the Atlantic coast of North America, where there is interesting dynamics related to the Gulf Stream, and high-quality tide gauge and meteorological data sets are available (e.g., Thompson and Mitchum 2014; Frederiske et al. 2017). The latter found a strong correlation between coastal sea level and decadal steric variability in the subpolar gyre which is probably caused by variability in the Labrador Sea that is propagated southward. They cite theory and modelling literature regarding coastal trapped waves as an explanation of the findings from their analysis of sea level measurements showing this propagation. The steric signal explains the majority of the observed decadal sea level variability. Much other research has focused on differences in variability north and south of Cape Hatteras and between shelf and deep ocean (Woodworth et al. 2014, 2017a; McCarthy et al. 2015), interannual variability north of the Cape being largely wind-driven over the shelf (Andres et al. 2013; Piecuch et al. 2016; Kenigson et al. 2018), while that to the south is controlled more by fluctuations in the Gulf Stream. As a result, coastal sea level variability, especially in the north, has little correspondence to that in the nearby deep ocean (Fig. 8). In addition, balances between the forces of bottom and lateral friction, which are larger where the flow is faster, and sea level gradient, result in along-shore tilts in sea level being smaller than in the deep ocean. In this situation, the sea level variations observed at the coast are said to be insulated from those in deeper ocean by the shelf (Fig. 9) (Higginson et al. 2015).

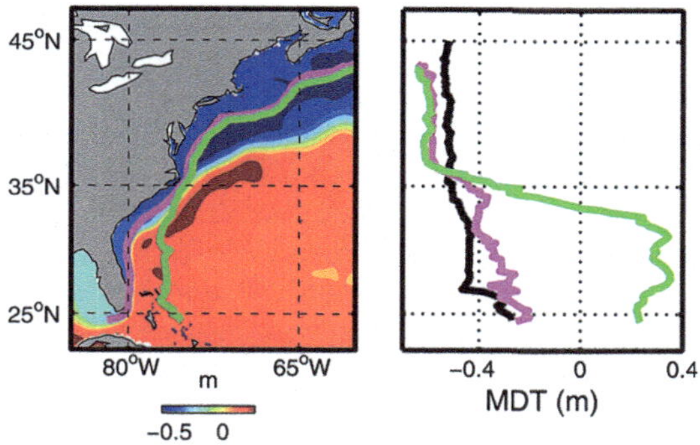

Fig. 9 (left) Mean dynamic topography (MDT) (in m) from the HYbrid Coordinate Ocean Model (HYCOM) data-assimilative ocean model. The magenta and green lines show the smoothed location of the 200 m and 2000 m isobaths, respectively. (right) MDT along the coastline (black) and along the 200 m (magenta) and 2000 m (green) isobaths, plotted against latitude. Note that the Gulf Stream signal in green is much attenuated on the shelf. From Higginson et al. (2015)

Links have been made between changes in the strength of the overturning circulation and sea level gradients on the US coast (Bingham and Hughes 2009; Yin et al. 2009; Yin and Goddard 2013). Consequently, the high rates of sea level rise ('accelerations') observed in recent years at stations in the Middle Atlantic Bight have been interpreted in terms of overturning changes (Sallenger et al. 2012; Boon 2012) with possible additional Greenland and Antarctic mass loss changes (Davis and Vinogradova 2017). Other links have been made between coastal sea level gradients, the strength of the Gulf Stream circulation and climate indices including the NAO (McCarthy et al. 2015) and the Atlantic Multidecadal Oscillation (AMO), an index defined by Atlantic sea surface temperatures (Kenigson and Han 2014). Most recently, Domingues et al. (2018) suggested two processes at work: warming of the Florida Current in the south, and air pressure changes in the north.

Sea level variability on the eastern boundary of the North Atlantic has been shown to be controlled largely by along-shore wind stress (Calafat et al. 2012). It is not known at present what the across-shelf spatial scale of such variability is, and so whether it can be considered 'coastal'. Nevertheless, one can suggest that it is due to a first-mode coastal trapped wave. Such a coastal trapped wave has the form of a Kelvin wave confined to the shelf, if the shelf width exceeds the barotropic radius of deformation at that location, and with the wind stress having a spatial scale exceeding the shelf width. There will be an along-shelf flow in the same sense across the whole shelf, with a node (zero) of elevation near the shelf break (Huthnance 1992). In the North Sea, Dangendorf et al. (2014) found that local atmospheric forcing mainly initiates MSL variability on timescales up to a few years; the IB effect being important in the northern North Sea, and wind stress in the shallower southern North Sea which is susceptible to storm surges. On decadal timescales, MSL variability was found to mainly reflect steric changes, which are largely forced remotely. They found evidence for a coherent signal extending between the Canary Islands and the Norwegian shelf, supporting the theory that along-shore wind forcing along the eastern boundary of the North Atlantic may cause coastal trapped waves that propagate thousands of kilometres along the continental slope. Similarly, Thompson et al. (2014) emphasised the need to account for atmospheric forcing and especially wind stress along North East Pacific coasts. They found that along-shore wind stress and local wind-stress curl are less important than (remote) equatorial forcing, the response to which propagates northwards.

Some general points can be made on the importance of along-shore winds based on the above literature. In the idealised context of uniform forcing and straight uniform shelf and slope, an along-shore wind tends to accelerate along-shore flow against bottom friction. The Coriolis force sets up cross-shelf transport which affects sea surface elevation at the coast relative to offshore (on the scale of the Rossby radius of deformation, or the shelf width if less). This sea surface slope balances the accelerating along-shore flow geostrophically, if bottom friction is relatively weak. Stronger friction tends to align the surface slope with the wind stress and limit the flow magnitude. Non-uniform or time-dependent forcing and non-uniform shelves result in propagating wave responses, so that the influence of the forcing extends over wave decay distances (greater for wide shelves and weak friction). Responses around very large islands may be considered in the same way. However, islands of much smaller scale than the forcing will experience an approximate averaging of the surrounding oceanic sea level.

Returning to the Pacific, the ENSO-related coastal sea levels along the American coast have already been referred to above. On the western side of the North Pacific, the Kuroshio Extension (KuE) provides the western boundary current of the subtropical gyre and is the Pacific counterpart of the Gulf Stream after separation at Cape Hatteras. As for the case of the Gulf Stream, interannual to decadal fluctuations of the KuE can have large impacts on coastal sea level variability.

Sasaki et al. (2014) have researched sea level variability along the coasts of Japan, primarily on decadal timescales. The first empirical orthogonal function (EOF) mode of sea level variability in the KuE region had previously been shown to describe well the meridional displacements of the KuE on decadal timescales (e.g., Taguchi et al. 2007). Sasaki et al. (2014) found that northward shifts of the KuE jet and the Kuroshio Current southeast of Japan are accompanied by higher sea levels at the coast. The decadal variability of the KuE latitude is mainly induced by westward-propagating, wind-forced Rossby waves from the eastern North Pacific (Qiu and Chen 2005; Yasuda and Sakurai 2006). These waves are concentrated along the KuE jet axis as jet-trapped Rossby waves. The resulting sea level changes along the Japan coast were found to be spatially variable, with large values along the south-eastern coast that are directly influenced by the jet-trapped Rossby waves, and also on the west coast, but small values north of the KuE jet. This is because any wind-induced Rossby waves will be trapped along the KuE axis (Sasaki et al. 2013). Hence, the area north of the KuE becomes a shadow zone which an incoming Rossby wave does not enter (Sasaki et al. 2014). Instead, a wind-forced coastal wave is one of the causes of interannual coastal sea level variability north of the KuE (e.g., Nakanowatari and Ohshima 2014). Kourafalou et al. (2015) described a case study, from the perspective of ocean forecasting, of an event in September 2011 that caused flooding in southern Japan. Sea level anomalies of ~30 cm were observed that resulted from the passage of coastal trapped waves induced by short-term fluctuations of the Kuroshio around 34°N, 140°E.

Sasaki et al. (2014) stress the importance of understanding the dynamical reasons for such variability in order to reliably predict future sea level changes. In a later modelling study of Japan sea level variability over 1906–2010, Sasaki et al. (2017) further pointed to the need to understand natural variability on decadal timescales for understanding future regional sea level change.

Another interesting feature is the bimodality of the Kuroshio path south of Japan. That changes between a straight path (along the south coast of Japan) and a large-meander path (away from the coast) on interannual to decadal timescales. This path variability induces sea level changes of about 10 cm along the south coast of Japan (Kawabe 1988; Usui et al. 2011). The Kuroshio transport, which is determined by the large-scale wind, is a key factor in determining the Kuroshio path (e.g., Tsujino et al. 2013). Its transport in the East China Sea has been found to be highly correlated with the PDO (Andres et al. 2009). The variability of the Kuroshio transport also causes coastal sea level change in the upstream region, such as along the coasts of Taiwan (Chang and Oey 2011) and Philippines (e.g., Zhuang et al. 2013).

Elsewhere in the Pacific and Indian Oceans, there has long been evidence for wind-driven coastal trapped waves along Australian coasts, mostly on monthly timescales. These include the coastal trapped waves on the south coast forced by strong westerly winds and the wide shelf, on the west coast that propagate southwards, and on the east coast propagating north (White et al. 2014 and references therein).

One interesting dynamical aspect of near-coastal sea level (or sub-surface pressure, SSP) variability concerns coherence of variability in SSP on intraseasonal timescales (timescales less than a year and not including the regular seasonal cycle) over great distances along the shelf and slope around continental boundaries (Hughes and Meredith 2006). The existence of such coherence, investigated first using altimeter data, has since been verified with ocean models (Roussenov et al. 2008; Hughes et al. 2018, 2019) and demonstrates that 'coastal' (or at least 'shelf slope') variability need not always be 'short spatial scale'.

With regard to sea levels on island coasts, we can mention the important role of eddies in the dynamics of the global ocean circulation. Open-ocean eddies have been found to be responsible for decimetric signals in some sea level records from ocean islands. For example, Mitchum (1995) relates 90-day oscillations at Wake Island (western Pacific) to Rossby waves propagating westwards (possibly from eddies generated by flow impinging on Hawaii). As Wake Island is very small and at latitude $< 20°$, it is expected to show the surface oscillations of the arriving Rossby waves. Modelled differences between coastal sea levels observed at islands and in the open ocean (Williams and Hughes 2013) show poor correlation for islands surrounded by ocean in which a large fraction of steric variability is at frequencies and wavelengths lacking baroclinic Rossby wave propagation. This is more likely at higher latitudes, so that coherence between island and open-ocean sea level decreases away from the Equator, until at yet higher latitudes the steric signal decreases and coherence increases once again.

Finally, on a similarly small spatial scale, one can refer to coastal bays and estuaries and their interaction with larger-scale dynamics that is sometimes reflected in sea level. For example, Feng and Li (2010) discussed the flushing of coastal bays in Louisiana due to the passage of cold fronts. This process takes place on timescales of less than 40 h and results in sea level changes of ~25 cm. On longer timescales, the strong winds and air pressure variations which are important to the coastal dynamics on shelves and the large-scale ocean circulation discussed above can result in particularly energetic (several decimetre) sub-tidal sea level variability in bays and estuaries. Examples for the American coast are discussed by Salas-Monreal and Valle-Levinson (2008) and Waterhouse and Valle-Levinson (2010).

9 Long-Term Changes in MSL

A major consequence of climate change is sea level rise resulting from changes in the density of sea water (steric effect) and from water mass transfer from land to the ocean from melting glaciers, ice sheets and groundwater storage changes (Church et al. 2013). Analysis of the first years of altimeter data suggested that MSL might be rising at a greater rate near to the coast than in the nearby deeper ocean (Holgate and Woodworth 2004) although such a difference was not considered significant by others (White et al. 2005; Prandi et al. 2009), and, as far as we are aware, there is at present no evidence for such differences.

As the depths of coastal waters increase, then many of the processes mentioned above will change:

- Tidal wavelengths will increase, and tidal patterns over the continental shelves will change. In fact, coastal tides are already known to be changing (e.g., Woodworth 2010; Haigh et al. 2019) for reasons that are not well understood. Sea level rise will result in further changes to the tides (e.g., Devlin et al. 2017; Idier et al. 2017; Pickering et al. 2017);
- Storm surge spatial gradients and magnitudes will reduce because of their dependence on 1/depth (Pugh and Woodworth 2014);
- Changes to tides and surges imply changes to extreme sea levels;
- Ocean waves break when entering water with depths ~2.6 times the wave amplitude (Dean and Walton 2009). As the MSL rises, waves with greater height and larger periods will impinge on coastal zones, with associated changes in wave setup and runup (Chini et al. 2010). This will cause amplified potential flooding impacts (Arns et al. 2017);
- Climate change may result in modifications to large-scale climate patterns (ENSO, NAO, etc.) and associated wind fields (and also heat content), resulting in regional changes in MSL and extreme sea level (Kirtman et al. 2013).

In addition to changes due to the depth of coastal waters, coastal sea level could also be affected by other changes in response to climate change including:

- Changes in regional patterns of atmospheric surface pressure and winds;
- Changes in ocean circulation (e.g., strengthening/weakening of coastal currents and of upwelling/downwelling);
- Changes in wind fields also imply further changes in wind waves and, therefore, in changes in wave setup, runup and overtopping.

Trends in surface winds have been observed over the last few decades, with notably a strengthening of the westerlies in the Southern Ocean and of the trade winds in the Pacific (e.g., Young et al. 2011; Swart and Fyfe 2012; Takahashi and Watanabe 2016). Climate change projections for the twenty-first century indicate significant changes in annual mean wave conditions over large ocean regions, notably with increased wave energy in the Southern Ocean that will impact remote regions through northward swell propagation (Hemer et al. 2013). Wave-driven contributions to water level at the coast could, therefore, exhibit trends in response to climate change over parts of the global ocean (Melet et al. 2018), which could lead to important coastal impacts. Long-term changes in wave direction may also induce changes in wave refraction and diffraction patterns, in along-shore current and associated sediment transport due to non-normal wave incidence. Together with changes in wave energy, they could result in altered patterns of beach erosion/accretion, and position and orientation of the shoreline.

All of these aspects of sea level variability are linked in various ways. In particular, trends observed in extreme sea levels in tide gauge records have been found to be related to trends in local MSL (see Sect. 4). Therefore, a gradual increase in MSL can thereby rapidly increase the frequency and severity of coastal flooding (Sweet and Park 2014). It has been estimated that 10 to 20 cm of sea level rise expected by 2050 will more than double the frequency of extreme events in the tropics (Vitousek et al. 2017). Extreme wave energy fluxes are projected to increase during this century implying potentially amplified impacts on the coast (Mentaschi et al. 2017). The many interactions between the various processes mentioned above are discussed in greater detail by Idier et al. (2019).

10 Vertical Land Movements at the Coast

Vertical land motion contributes to relative sea level change observed by tide gauges at the coast, which can therefore differ from a change in sea level in the open ocean observed by altimetry. In other words, the ocean volume could remain unchanged, and yet sea level changes and coastal impacts could be observed due to vertical land motion only. As a matter of fact, the vertical position of the land surface at the coast (measured relative to the centre of the Earth) could be changing as much as the position of the sea surface itself, sometimes by a factor of ten or more. For instance, coastal subsidence in excess of a centimetre per year has been observed at Manila, Philippines (Raucoules et al. 2013), due to sub-surface anthropogenic activities and at Grand Isle, Louisiana (Törnqvist et al. 2008; Kolker et al. 2011), due to a combination of natural and anthropogenic processes, whereas coastal uplift up to a centimetre per year has been observed in Fennoscandia (Kierulf et al. 2014) or at Hudson Bay (Sella et al. 2007) due to ice mass unloading from the last deglaciation and glacial isostatic adjustment (GIA). What is more, ignoring vertical land motion, especially in active tectonic regions, can result in mistakes in attributing the reasons for sea level change and thereby in adoption of strategies for protecting populations and assets against coastal flooding (Ballu et al. 2011). Therefore, vertical land motion deserves as much attention as climate change in coastal sea level studies.

In fact, there are many phenomena that can cause vertical land motion, operating at different time and spatial scales (Fig. 2 and Table 1), resulting both from natural processes (e.g., GIA, tectonics and sediment compaction) and from anthropogenic activities (e.g., groundwater depletion, dam building or settling of landfill in urban areas) over a broad range of space and timescales. GIA is the most widely known phenomenon, operating globally at decadal to millennia timescales for which geodynamic models are available on a global basis (e.g., Peltier et al. 2015). This geological process includes deformational, gravitational and rotational effects due to the waxing and waning of the great ice sheets. It is essential to know the rheology of the Earth's interior and the histories of the ice sheets in order to predict accurately the viscoelastic response of the solid Earth and the resulting rates of vertical land movement (crustal displacement). There are important differences in such geodynamic modelling if the melting of land ice relates to the late Pleistocene ice sheets or to the present-day ice sheets, although the calculations are based on the same physics. For instance, the rheological behaviour of the Earth's interior can be approximated to that of an elastic body for short (decade to century) contemporary timescales of melting (Tamisiea and Mitrovica 2011; Riva et al. 2017; Spada 2017).

Water mass redistributions on the Earth's surface, and the associated loading of the solid Earth, can also result in significant vertical land motion. These include natural processes such as non-tidal atmospheric, oceanic and continental water mass loading variations, operating at interannual to decadal timescales with vertical displacements of the order of a mm/year (Santamaría-Gómez and Mémin 2015). To a lesser extent (at the level of 0.5 mm/year over multidecadal timescales), anthropogenic activities associated with water impoundment behind dams (Fiedler and Conrad 2010) and groundwater depletion (Veit and Conrad 2016) can also be important.

Earthquakes are instantaneous co-seismic vertical displacements of the Earth's surface. However, the earthquakes themselves are only one aspect of a set of tectonic processes within the earthquake deformation cycle. That cycle consists of steady interseismic motion that can last for years, decades or longer, punctuated by the instantaneous displacements during the earthquakes themselves. Following the earthquakes, there will be a postseismic relaxation during which deformation will occur lasting months to years before reverting to steady interseismic motion. For example, Ballu et al. (2011) reported a steady interseismic subsidence of the order of a cm/year at Torres Islands, Vanuatu, in between the magnitude Mw 7.8 earthquakes of 1997 and 2009. Those two earthquakes resulted in sudden vertical displacements of several hundreds of millimetres (subsidence of 500–1000 mm in 1997 and uplift of about 200 mm in 2009). These vertical displacements in land level thereby translated into abrupt coastal sea level changes in the opposite direction (sea level rise in the case of land subsidence and sea level fall in the case of land uplift). One may note that in this case study the interseismic vertical land motion (~ 1 cm/year) was three times larger than the rise of global MSL observed during the satellite altimetry era. Hence, it can be seen that such geological processes can play major roles in magnifying coastal risks from sea level change at such locations.

Prediction of the epochs and magnitudes of co-seismic and postseismic displacements are still beyond the present-day means of geophysical modelling. However, some progress has recently been accomplished regarding the interseismic motion. Smith-Konter et al. (2014) used a 3-D elastic/viscoelastic earthquake cycle model of the San Andreas Fault System, and identified in the sea level records along the California coastline the tectonic signals associated with the flexure of the elastic plate caused by bending moments at the ends of the locked faults. Unfortunately, such estimates of tectonic vertical land motion are not yet readily available for regions outside California.

Magma flow and pressure in active volcanoes, whether associated with tectonic plate boundaries or hot spots, can cause large inflation/deflation ground deformation events over days to months, and sometimes even longer periods. For example, at Socorro Island, part of a shield volcano located 200 km west of the Pacific coast of Mexico, Cazenave et al. (1999) observed a large post-eruptive 30 cm subsidence of the island during the 3 years following a submarine volcanic eruption in 1993.

In delta regions, land subsidence occurs naturally through sediment compaction when water is lost from interstitial spaces caused by the weight of overlying sediment or through rearrangement of sediment particles (Törnqvist et al. 2008). Observed rates of deltaic subsidence over the last few decades range from 3 to 100 mm/year. For instance, average subsidence rates of 4–6 mm/year have been reported for the Ganges–Brahmaputra Delta (Brown and Nicholls 2015) with much larger rates up to 10–20 mm/year in densely populated areas. This includes an estimated long-term contribution from sediment loading and sea level rise during the Holocene amounting to 1.1–1.7 mm/year, depending on the values for lithospheric thickness and Earth mantle viscosity considered (Karpytchev et al. 2018). These are all significant rates of vertical land movement when compared to the 3 mm/year rate of global MSL rise observed by satellite altimetry over the same time span. In highly populated delta areas, the extraction of groundwater, oil and gas that fill pore spaces can significantly exacerbate, and sometimes dominate, the rate of compaction and resulting subsidence (Kolker et al. 2011).

Locally, all contributions to sea level changes are important, whether arising from oceanic or vertical land motion processes. The factors controlling relative sea level differ from one coastline to another, and oceanic effects may not be the largest. In some coastal regions of the world, vertical land motion clearly dominates. In other areas, they might

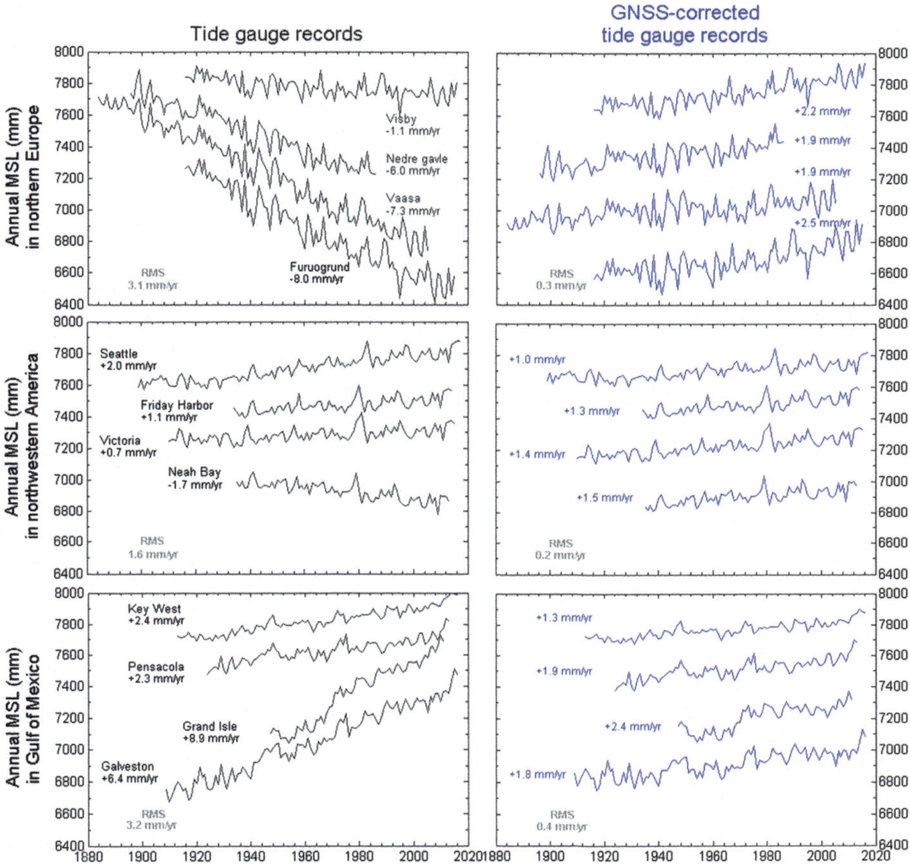

Fig. 10 Time series of annual MSL from (left) tide gauge records, and (right) GNSS-adjusted tide gauge records in (top) N Europe, (middle) NW America and (bottom) Gulf of Mexico. MSL data are from the Permanent Service for Mean Sea Level (PSMSL, https://psmsl.org), while GNSS information was acquired using the ULR6a solutions of the Système d'Observation du Niveau des Eaux Littorales (SONEL, http://www.sonel.org). The time series are displayed with arbitrary offsets for presentation purposes. Units mm. RMS indicates the root-mean-square of the trends shown in each panel

be of the same order of magnitude as oceanic (climate) factors (Wöppelmann and Marcos 2016). There is a clear need for measurements by modern geodetic techniques that provide accurate estimates of vertical land motion, which underlie the observed relative sea level changes, for application to sustainable management plans for the coast. This is why the new implementation plan of the international Global Sea Level Observing System (GLOSS) programme (see Marcos et al. 2019) calls for an important upgrade to its core network by requesting the installation of continuous Global Navigation Satellite System (GNSS) stations at tide gauges. GNSS will thereby measure the local vertical land movement of whatever origin. Figure 10 provides a demonstration of how trends of MSL measured by different tide gauges can be made more regionally consistent when GNSS information is employed to measure vertical land movements. The modern geodetic techniques are also required to place the tide gauge data into the same geocentric reference frame as for the altimeter data as required for altimeter calibration studies (Mitchum 2000; IOC 2016).

11 Human Influences on Coastal Sea Level Variability

A full discussion of modifications in coastal sea level variability, which occur due to human intervention in coastal processes via coastal engineering, is outside the scope of this paper. However, several examples may be mentioned in order to demonstrate that there can indeed be such man-made impacts.

It is well known that the amplitudes and phases of tides in harbours and lagoons can be altered by engineering to their inlets, thereby altering the tidal prism. Similarly, both natural and anthropogenic changes in the sedimentation of coastal lagoons affect the tide (Araújo et al. 2008). Dredging in river estuaries will tend to lower low waters but leave high waters relatively unchanged, with a consequent increase in tidal range (Siefert 1982). Coastal engineering can affect the tides (de Boer et al. 2011), and schemes such as beach nourishment, which modify near-shore gradients, will modify wave setup and overtopping (Dean 1991). Similarly, a rise in MSL (which in itself could be said to be man-made) will modify the vertical profiles of some coastlines (Bruun 1962). MSL records exist which demonstrate the effect of human-induced sedimentation in coastal embayments (e.g., Manila), or the consequences of submergence due to ground water pumping (e.g., Bangkok, Shanghai), leading to anomalous local rates of relative sea level rise (see examples in Pugh and Woodworth 2014).

These examples demonstrate that the history of any changes to the area around a tide gauge station can be reflected in its record, as can relocations of recording within a large harbour, or changes in tide gauge technology.

12 Conclusions

We have shown that there are many processes which result in coastal sea level variability, operating on timescales from seconds to centuries and on spatial scales from local to global. Many of the processes (summarised in Table 1) are understood well (in principle at least), such as tides and surges, although some remain relatively little researched and under-represented in sea level studies. In fact, there are others that have not been included here as they are not particularly coastal in character. Compendiums such as Pugh and Woodworth (2014) and Cazenave and Stammer (2017) provide more information on some of them, while several are discussed in greater detail in other papers in this volume. The scientific aim must be to be able to understand and model as many of these processes as possible.

We have also shown that each process will depend on the others to some extent due to the associated changes in water depth. It has also been shown that it is mistake to think that coastal sea level variability always has a 'local' forcing (although it often does), given that there are also for instance processes that result in signals trapped by and propagating along the continental shelves.

Some questions for consideration in future research are:

- How well can ocean models of various kinds reproduce the time series of sea level variability observed at the coast by tide gauges and offshore by altimetry (i.e. understanding the differences akin to those shown in Fig. 1)? Models will inevitably perform well for some regions and timescales, but less well for others (e.g., Chepurin et al. 2014; Becker et al. 2016; Meyssignac et al. 2017). In particular, models that are capable of reproducing coastal sea level variability observed to date will provide confidence in projecting future coastal sea level change (Ponte et al. 2019).
- Concerning our knowledge of tides at the coast, users of satellite altimetry in the deep ocean have grown accustomed to having reliable tide models that account for that dominant component of variability in their data. However, when altimetry is applied to the near-coastal zones, the existing models are less reliable and must be developed to greater complexity with many additional constituents. Deep-water versus shallow-water spectra (Fig. 3) readily convey the challenges of modelling coastal tides. In addition, a better determination and understanding is required of secular and other low-frequency changes in coastal tides that have been observed (this question relates to the need for 'data archaeology' mentioned below).
- With regard to waves, how much are historical MSL records contaminated by wave setup and can any contributions be modelled efficiently and so removed from the records? This question applies especially to composite records obtained from gauges at different locations within a bay or port. Should there be a comprehensive global coastal wave monitoring network to collect the data needed to assess the setup contribution to MSL? How will the wave setup contribution change in the future if wave climate changes?
- Similarly, how much have historical MSL records been contaminated by contributions from river runoff, and therefore misrepresent open-ocean conditions?
- There are several important questions in geodesy. How well can models of the solid Earth predict the motion (primarily vertical) of geodetic benchmarks at the coast over decadal to century timescales, specifically at tide gauges? Also, can the terrestrial reference frame be implemented in an accurate and stable manner in order to predict accurately the positions and motions of geodetic stations? Geophysical modelling and space geodesy observations have suggested that we should target vertical land motion predictability at the level of 0.1 mm/year over decadal to century timescales (Blewitt et al. 2010).
- In climate research, what mechanisms have been responsible for past changes in extreme levels (other than changes in MSL) and how might forcings and extremes change in the future? In particular, how will the extremely damaging storm surges associated with tropical cyclones change?
- In coastal modelling, because atmospheric forcing (and in particular wind stress) is relatively important in shallow shelf seas, there are challenges (1) to remove its shorter-term effects on coastal sea levels when estimating longer-term trends, and (2) to separate its longer-term effect from open-ocean sea level trends as drivers of coastal sea level change. Additionally, (3) as discussed in Sect. 8, because responses to forcing propagate along the shelf and slope, with forms and speed dependent on the shelf and slope topography, there is a need for models to be developed with sufficient resolution and 'upstream' extent over the distance in which the propagating signals decay. An additional challenge relates to modelling in greater detail the sea level variability around islands (including any surrounding shelves) located at different latitudes and with different sizes (larger and smaller than the baroclinic deformation radius) to understand where models and measurements differ.

Progress cannot be made with these and many other questions to do with sea level variability without access to the best, and most complete, observational and modelling data sets, as discussed further by Ponte et al. (2019). One may note:

- It is essential that the global network of tide gauges and other essential in situ data sets be completed and analysed in combination with satellite altimeter data sets (Roemmich et al. 2017). The global tide gauge network is currently challenged with maintaining many existing stations and installing new ones where required. Where appropriate, GNSS-reflection tide gauges may be more suitable than conventional techniques (Larson et al. 2017). In addition, there is a need for continuous monitoring of vertical land motion at tide gauges, requiring the installation of permanent GNSS stations at as many tide gauges as possible, and as near as possible to the tide gauges, and the undertaking of regular levelling campaigns between the tide gauge benchmarks and GNSS benchmarks (Woodworth et al. 2017b). See also discussion of this topic in Marcos et al. (2019) and Ponte et al. (2019).
- It is important also to extend the historical coastal sea level data set via a programme in 'data archaeology' (Bradshaw et al. 2015) and the use of 'proxy' (geological) data sets (e.g., Barlow et al. 2014).
- High-frequency (timescales ~ 1 h or less) sea level variability due to seiches, meteotsunamis and other high-frequency processes are frequently under-represented in sea level studies (Vilibić and Šepić 2017), and yet contribute to the extreme sea levels which are of great research interest and importance to coastal dwellers. In particular, an important objective should be to derive via barotropic modelling a global data set of seiche climatology.
- Similarly, it is highly desirable that barotropic tide-surge modelling, presently providing typically hourly values of modelled sea level on a global grid back to the mid-twentieth century, be extended back to the mid-nineteenth century using newly available reanalysis wind fields (Compo et al. 2011). Such model data sets would have many applications in understanding sea level variability.
- Access to new sets of coastal altimetry data, uncontaminated by reflections from the altimeter footprint over land and with improved geophysical corrections, should illuminate to a greater extent the reasons for differences between coastal and ocean sea level variability (Vignudelli et al. 2011; Cipollini et al. 2012, 2017; Birol et al. 2017). However, in our opinion, these data sets will never be a substitute for tide gauges in the coastal zone, given their temporal resolution and accuracy. The continuity of both in situ and space-based instrumentation is essential for a proper monitoring and understanding changes in sea level. The several techniques in combination will thereby enable us to understand as well as possible the evolution of coastal zones (Cazenave et al. 2017).

Acknowledgements We are grateful to Déborah Idier and Chris Piecuch for helpful comments. This work was supported partly by Natural Environment Research Council National Capability funding (for Woodworth, Hibbert and Huthnance) and by a research grant from CNPq (for Cirano). The paper arose from the Workshop on 'Understanding the Relationship between Coastal Sea Level and Large-Scale Ocean Circulation' held at the International Space Science Institute (ISSI), Bern, Switzerland, on 5–9 March 2018.

References

Airy GB (1878) On the tides at Malta. Philos Trans R Soc 169:123–138. https://doi.org/10.1098/rstl.1878.0006

Amiruddin AM, Haigh ID, Tsimplis MN, Calafat FM, Dangendorf S (2015) The seasonal cycle and variability of sea level in the South China Sea. J Geophys Res Oceans 120:5490–5513. https://doi.org/10.1002/2015JC010923

Andres M, Park J-H, Wimbush M, Zhu X, Nakamura Kim K, Chang K-I (2009) Manifestation of the Pacific decadal oscillation in the Kuroshio. Geophys Res Lett 36:L16602. https://doi.org/10.1029/2009GL039216

Andres M, Gawarkiewicz GG, Toole JM (2013) Interannual sea level variability in the western North Atlantic: regional forcing and remote response. Geophys Res Lett 40:5915–5919. https://doi.org/10.1002/2013GL058013

Andrew JAM, Leach HL, Woodworth PL (2006) The relationships between tropical Atlantic sea level variability and major climate indices. Ocean Dynam 56:452–463. https://doi.org/10.1007/s10236-006-0068-z

Angell JK, Korshover J (1964) Quasi-biennial variations in temperature, total ozone and tropopause height. J Atmos Sci 21:479–492. https://doi.org/10.1175/1520-0469(1964)021<0479:QBVITT>2.0.CO;2

Aoki S (2002) Coherent sea level response to the Antarctic Oscillation. Geophys Res Lett 29:11-1–11-4. https://doi.org/10.1029/2002gl015733

Araújo IB, Dias JM, Pugh DT (2008) Model simulations of tidal changes in a coastal lagoon, the Ria de Aveiro (Portugal). Cont Shelf Res 28:1010–1025. https://doi.org/10.1016/j.csr.2008.02.001

Ardhuin F, Chapron B, Collard F (2009) Observation of swell dissipation across oceans. Geophys Res Lett 36:L06607. https://doi.org/10.1029/2008GL037030

Arns A, Dangendorf S, Jensen J, Talke S, Bender J, Pattiaratchi C (2017) Sea level rise induced amplification of coastal protection design heights. Sci Rep 7:40171. https://doi.org/10.1038/srep40171

Aucan J, Hoeke R, Merrifield MA (2012) Wave-driven sea level anomalies at the Midway tide gauge as an index of North Pacific storminess over the past 60 years. Geophys Res Lett 39:L17603. https://doi.org/10.1029/2012GL052993

Aucan J, Hoeke RK, Storlazzi CD, Stopa J, Wandres M, Lowe R (2019) Waves do not contribute to global sea-level rise. Nat Clim Change 9:2. https://doi.org/10.1038/s41558-018-0377-5

Baart F, van Gelder PHAJM, de Ronde J, van Koningsveld M, Wouters B (2012) The effect of the 18.6-year lunar nodal cycle on regional sea-level rise estimates. J Coast Res 28:511–516. https://doi.org/10.2112/JCOASTRES-D-11-00169.1

Ballu V, Bouin MN, Siméoni P, Crawford WC, Calmant S, Boré JM, Kanas T, Pelletier B (2011) Comparing the role of absolute sea-level rise and vertical tectonic motions in coastal flooding, Torres Islands (Vanuatu). Proc Natl Acad Sci USA 108:13019–13022. https://doi.org/10.1073/pnas.1102842108

Barlow NLM, Long AJ, Saher MH, Gehrels WR, Garnett MH, Scaife RG (2014) Salt-marsh reconstructions of relative sea-level change in the North Atlantic during the last 2000 years. Quat Sci Rev 99:1–16. https://doi.org/10.1016/j.quascirev.2014.06.008

Barnard PL et al (2015) Coastal vulnerability across the Pacific dominated by El Niño/Southern Oscillation. Nat Geosci 8:801–808. https://doi.org/10.1038/ngeo2539

Becker JM, Merrifield MA, Ford M (2014) Water level effects on breaking wave setup for Pacific Island fringing reefs. J Geophys Res Oceans 119:914–932. https://doi.org/10.1002/2013JC009373

Becker M, Karpytchev M, Marcos M, Jevrejeva S, Lennartz-Sassinek S (2016) Do climate models reproduce complexity of observed sea level changes? Geophys Res Lett 43:5176–5184. https://doi.org/10.1002/2016GL068971

Bingham RJ, Hughes CW (2009) Signature of the Atlantic meridional overturning circulation in sea level along the east coast of North America. Geophys Res Lett 36:L02603. https://doi.org/10.1029/2008GL036215

Birol F, Fuller N, Lyard F, Cancet M, Niño F, Delebecque C, Fleury S, Toublanc F, Melet A, Saraceno M, Léger F (2017) Coastal applications from nadir altimetry: example of the X-TRACK regional products. Adv Space Res 59:936–953. https://doi.org/10.1016/j.asr.2016.11.005

Blewitt G, Altamimi Z, Davis J, Gross R, Kuo C-Y, Lemoine FG, Moore AW, Neilan RE, Plag H-P, Rothacher M, Shum CK, Sideris MG, Schöne T, Tregoning P, Zerbini S (2010) Geodetic observations and global reference frame contributions to understanding sea-level rise and variability. In: Church JA, Woodworth PL, Aarup T, Wilson WS (eds) Understanding sea-level rise and variability. Chapter 9. Wiley, London, pp 256–284

Boon JD (2012) Evidence of sea level acceleration at U.S. and Canadian tide stations, Atlantic coast, North America. J Coast Res 28:1437–1445. https://doi.org/10.2112/JCOASTRES-D-12-00102.1

Bowen AJ, Inman DL, Simmons VP (1968) Wave 'set-down' and set-up. J Geophys Res 73:2569–2577. https://doi.org/10.1029/JB073i008p02569

Bradshaw E, Rickards L, Aarup T (2015) Sea level data archaeology and the Global Sea Level Observing System (GLOSS). GeoResJ 6:9–16. https://doi.org/10.1016/j.grj.2015.02.005

Brown S, Nicholls RJ (2015) Subsidence and human influences in mega deltas: the case of the Ganges–Brahmaputra–Meghna. Sci Total Environ 527–528:362–374. https://doi.org/10.1016/j.scitotenv.2015.04.124

Bruun P (1962) Sea-level rise as a cause of shore erosion. J Waterways Harbors Div 88:117–130

Buckley ML, Lowe RJ, Hansen JE, van Dongeren AR, Storlazzi CD (2018) Mechanisms of wave-driven water level variability on reef-fringed coastlines. J Geophys Res Oceans 123:3811–3831. https://doi.org/10.1029/2018JC013933

Calafat FM, Chambers DP, Tsimplis MN (2012) Mechanisms of decadal sea level variability in the eastern North Atlantic and the Mediterranean Sea. J Geophys Res 117:C09022. https://doi.org/10.1029/2012JC008285

Calafat FM, Chambers DP, Tsimplis MN (2013) Inter-annual to decadal sea-level variability in the coastal zones of the Norwegian and Siberian Seas: the role of atmospheric forcing. J Geophys Res Oceans 118:1287–1301. https://doi.org/10.1002/jgrc.20106

Calafat FM, Wahl T, Lindsten F, Williams J, Frajka-Williams E (2018) Coherent modulation of the sea-level annual cycle in the United States by Atlantic Rossby waves. Nat Commun 9:2571. https://doi.org/10.1038/s41467-018-04898-y

Carrère L, Lyard F (2003) Modeling the barotropic response of the global ocean to atmospheric wind and pressure forcing—comparisons with observations. Geophys Res Lett 30:1275. https://doi.org/10.1029/2002GL016473

Cazenave A, Stammer D (eds) (2017) Satellite altimetry over oceans and land surfaces. CRC Taylor and Francis, Boca Raton, p 644

Cazenave A, Dominh F, Ponchaut F, Soudarin L, Cretaux JF, Le Provost C (1999) Sea level changes from Topex-Poseidon altimetry and tide gauges, and vertical crustal motions from DORIS. Geophys Res Lett 26:2077–2080. https://doi.org/10.1029/1999GL900472

Cazenave A, Le Cozannet G, Benveniste J, Woodworth P (2017) Monitoring the change of coastal zones from space. Eos, Transactions of the American Geophysical Union, 98. Published on 02 Nov 2017. https://eos.org/opinions/monitoring-coastal-zone-changes-from-space

Chang Y-L, Oey L (2011) Interannual and seasonal variations of Kuroshio transport east of Taiwan inferred from tide-gauge data. Geophys Res Lett 38:L08603. https://doi.org/10.1029/2011GL047062

Chen JL, Shum CK, Wilson CR, Chambers DP, Tapley BD (2000) Seasonal sea level change from TOPEX/Poseidon observation and thermal contribution. J Geodesy 73:638–647. https://doi.org/10.1007/s001900050

Chepurin GA, Carton JA, Leuliette E (2014) Sea level in ocean reanalyses and tide gauges. J Geophys Res Oceans 119:147–155. https://doi.org/10.1002/2013JC009365

Chini N, Stansby P, Leake J, Wolf J, Roberts-Jones J, Lowe J (2010) The impact of sea level rise and climate change on inshore wave climate: a case study for East Anglia (UK). Coast Eng 57:973–984. https://doi.org/10.1016/j.coastaleng.2010.05.009

Church JA, Clark PU, Cazenave A, Gregory JM, Jevrejeva S, Levermann A, Merrifield MA, Milne GA, Nerem RS, Nunn PD, Payne AJ, Pfeffer WT, Stammer D, Unnikrishnan AS (2013) Sea level change. In: Stocker TF, Qin D, Plattner G-K, Tignor M, Allen SK, Boschung J, Nauels A, Xia Y, Bex V, Midgley PM (eds) Climate change 2013: the physical science basis. Contribution of working group I to the fifth assessment report of the intergovernmental panel on climate change. Cambridge University Press, Cambridge

Cipollini P, Calafat FM, Jevrejeva S, Melet A, Prandi P (2017) Monitoring sea level in the coastal zone with satellite altimetry and tide gauges. Surv Geophys 38:33–57. https://doi.org/10.1007/s10712-016-9392-0

Cohen J, Barlow M (2005) The NAO, the AO and global warming: how closely related? J Clim 18:4498–4513. https://doi.org/10.1175/JCLI3530.1

Compo GP, Whitaker JS, Sardeshmukh PD, Matsui N, Allan RJ, Yin X, Gleason BE, Vose RS, Rutledge G, Bessemoulin P, Brönnimann S, Brunet M, Crouthamel RI, Grant AN, Groisman PY, Jones PD, Kruk M, Kruger AC, Marshall GJ, Maugeri M, Mok HY, Nordli Ø, Ross TF, Trigo RM, Wang XL, Woodruff SD, Worley SJ (2011) The twentieth century reanalysis project. Q J R Meteorol Soc 137:1–28. https://doi.org/10.1002/qj.776

Cook KH, Vizy EK (2010) Hydrodynamics of the Caribbean low-level jet and its relationship to precipitation. J Clim 23:1477–1494. https://doi.org/10.1175/2009JCLI3210.1

Cox R, Jahn KL, Watkins OG, Cox P (2018) Extraordinary boulder transport by storm waves (west of Ireland, winter 2013–2014), and criteria for analysing coastal boulder deposits. Earth Sci Rev 177:623–636. https://doi.org/10.1016/j.earscirev.2017.12.014
Dangendorf S, Calafat FM, Arns A, Wahl T, Haigh ID, Jensen J (2014) Mean sea level variability in the North Sea: processes and implications. J Geophys Res Oceans 119:6820–6841. https://doi.org/10.1002/2014JC009901
Daussy P (1831) Mémoire sur les Marées des côtes de France. Connaissance des Tems [...] pour l'année 1834. Bureau des Longitudes, Paris, pp 74–87
Davis JL, Vinogradova NT (2017) Causes of accelerating sea level on the East Coast of North America. Geophys Res Lett 44:5133–5141. https://doi.org/10.1002/2017GL072845
de Boer WP, Roos PC, Hulscher SJMH, Stolk A (2011) Impact of mega-scale sand extraction on tidal dynamics in semi-enclosed basins. An idealized model study with application to the Southern North Sea. Coast Eng 58:678–689. https://doi.org/10.1016/j.coastaleng.2011.03.005
Dean RG (1991) Equilibrium beach profiles: characteristics and applications. J Coast Res 7: 53–84. https://www.jstor.org/stable/4297805
Dean RG, Walton TL (2009) Wave setup. Chapter 1 in, Handbook of coastal and ocean engineering. World Scientific Publishing Co. Ltd. http://www.worldscibooks.com/engineering/6914.html
Defant A (1961) Physical oceanography. Pergamon Press, London
Devlin AT, Jay DA, Talke SA, Zaron ED, Pan J, Lin H (2017) Coupling of sea level and tidal range changes, with implications for future water levels. Sci Rep 7:17021. https://doi.org/10.1038/s41598-017-17056-z
Dietrich JC, Bunya S, Westerink JJ, Ebersole BA, Smith JM, Atkinson JH, Jensen R, Resio DT, Luettich RA, Dawson C, Cardone VJ, Cox AT, Powell MD, Westerink HJ, Roberts HJ (2009) A high-resolution coupled riverine flow, tide, wind, wind wave, and storm surge model for Southern Louisiana and Mississippi. Part II: synoptic description and analysis of Hurricanes Katrina and Rita. Mon Weather Rev 138:378–404. https://doi.org/10.1175/2009MWR2907.1
Dodet G, Melet A, Ardhuin F, Bertin X, Idier D, Almar R (2019) The contribution of wind generated waves to coastal sea level changes. Surv Geophys (in review)
Domingues R, Goni G, Baringer M, Volkov D (2018) What caused the accelerated sea level changes along the United States East Coast during 2010–2015? Geophys Res Lett 45:13367–13376. https://doi.org/10.1029/2018GL081183
Dukhovsky DS, Johnson MA, Proshutinsky A (2004) Arctic decadal variability: an auto-oscillatory system of heat and fresh water exchange. Geophys Res Lett 31:L03302. https://doi.org/10.1029/2003GL019023
Dunne RP, Barbosa SM, Woodworth PL (2012) Contemporary sea level in the Chagos Archipelago, central Indian Ocean. Glob Planet Change 82–83:25–37. https://doi.org/10.1016/j.gloplacha.2011.11.009
Durand F, Piecuch C, Cirano M, Becker M, Papa F (2019) Runoff impact on coastal sea level. Surv Geophys (in review)
Dvorkin EN, Kochanov SY, Smirnov NP (2000) The North Atlantic Oscillation and long-term changes in the level of the Arctic Ocean. Russ Meteorol Hydrol 3:59–64
Enfield DB, Allen JS (1980) On the structure and dynamics of monthly mean sea level anomalies along the Pacific coast of North and South America. J Phys Oceanogr 10:557–578. https://doi.org/10.1175/1520-0485(1980)010<0557:OTSADO>2.0.CO;2
Etcheverry LAR, Saraceno M, Piola AR, Valladeau G, Möller OO (2015) A comparison of the annual cycle of sea level in coastal areas from gridded satellite altimetry and tide gauges. Cont Shelf Res 92:87–97. https://doi.org/10.1016/j.csr.2014.10.006
Ezer T, Atkinson LP, Corlett WB, Blanco JL (2013) Gulf stream's induced sea level rise and variability along the U.S. mid-Atlantic coast. J Geophys Res Oceans 118(2):685–697. https://doi.org/10.1002/jgrc.20091
Feng Z, Li C (2010) Cold-front-induced flushing of the Louisiana Bays. J Mar Syst 82:252–264. https://doi.org/10.1016/j.jmarsys.2010.05.015
Feng X, Tsimplis MN, Marcos M, Calafat FM, Zheng J, Jorda G, Cipollini P (2015) Spatial and temporal variations of the seasonal sea level cycle in the northwest Pacific. J Geophys Res Oceans 120:7091–7112. https://doi.org/10.1002/2015JC011154
FES2014 (2018) Description of the FES2014 ocean tide model, obtained from https://www.aviso.altimetry.fr/en/data/products/auxiliary-products/global-tide-fes/description-fes2014.html. Downloaded Jan 2018
Fiedler JW, Conrad CP (2010) Spatial variability of sea level rise due to water impoundment behind dams. Geophys Res Lett 37:L12603. https://doi.org/10.1029/2010GL043462

Flather RA (2000) Existing operational oceanography. Coast Eng 41:13–40. https://doi.org/10.1016/S0378-3839(00)00025-9

Forel F-A (1876) Note sur un limnimètre enregistreur établi á Morges (Lac Léman) pour étudier les seiches. Annales de Chimie et de Physique (5th series) 9:90–92

Foreman MGG, Walters RA, Henry RF, Keller CP, Dolling AG (1995) A tidal model for eastern Juan de Fuca Strait and the southern Strait of Georgia. J Geophys Res 100:721–740. https://doi.org/10.1029/94JC02721

Frederikse T, Simon K, Katsman CA, Riva R (2017) The sea-level budget along the Northwest Atlantic coast: gIA, mass changes, and large-scale ocean dynamics. J Geophys Res Oceans 122:5486–5501. https://doi.org/10.1002/2017JC012699

Gill AE (1982) Atmosphere–ocean dynamics. Academic Press, New York, p 662

Gill AE, Niller PP (1973) The theory of the seasonal variability in the ocean. Deep Sea Res Oceanogr Abstr 20(2):141–177. https://doi.org/10.1016/0011-7471(73)90049-1

Gille ST, Llewellyn Smith SG, Statom NM (2005) Global observations of the land breeze. Geophys Res Lett 32:L05605. https://doi.org/10.1029/2004GL022139

Goddard PB, Yin J, Griffies SM, Zhang S (2015) An extreme event of sea-level rise along the Northeast coast of North America in 2009–2010. Nat Commun 6:6346. https://doi.org/10.1038/ncomms7346

Gómez-Enri J, Vignudelli S, Cipollini P, Coca J, González CJ (2017) Validation of CryoSat-2 SIRAL sea level data in the eastern continental shelf of the Gulf of Cadiz (Spain). Adv Space Res. https://doi.org/10.1016/j.asr.2017.10.042 (in press)

Gönnert G, Dube SK, Murty T, Siefert W (2001) Global storm surges: theory, observations and applications. Die Küste Volume 63. http://www.kfki.de

Gräwe U, Burchard H, Müller M, Schuttelaars HM (2014) Seasonal variability in M2 and M4 tidal constituents and its implications for the coastal residual sediment transport. Geophys Res Lett 41:5563–5570. https://doi.org/10.1002/2014GL060517

Green JAM, Huber M, Waltham D, Buzan J, Wells M (2017) Explicitly modelled deep-time tidal dissipation and its implication for Lunar history. Earth Planet Sci Lett 461:46–53. https://doi.org/10.1016/j.epsl.2016.12.038

Gregory J, Hughes C, Stammer D, Griffies S, Idier D, Fukumori I, Ponte R (2019) Concepts and terminology for sea level: mean, variability and change, both local and global. Surv Geophys. https://doi.org/10.1007/s10712-019-09525-z

Haigh ID, Eliot M, Pattiaratchi C (2011) Global influences of the 18.61 year nodal cycle and 8.85 year cycle of lunar perigee on high tidal levels. J Geophys Res 116:C06025. https://doi.org/10.1029/2010jc006645

Haigh ID, Wijeratne EMS, MacPherson LR, Pattiaratchi CB, Mason MS, Crompton RP, George S (2014a) Estimating present day extreme water level exceedance probabilities around the coastline of Australia: tides, extra-tropical storm surges and mean sea level. Clim Dynam 42:121–138. https://doi.org/10.1007/s00382-012-1652-1

Haigh ID, MacPherson LR, Mason MS, Wijeratne EMS, Pattiaratchi CB, Crompton RP, George S (2014b) Estimating present day extreme water level exceedance probabilities around the coastline of Australia: tropical cyclone-induced storm surges. Clim Dynam 42:139–157. https://doi.org/10.1007/s00382-012-1653-0

Haigh ID, Pickering MD, Green JAM, Arbic BK, Arns A, Dangendorf S, Hill D, Horsburgh K, Howard T, Idier D, Jay DA, Lee SB, Müller M, Schindelegger M, Talke SA, Wilmes S-B, Woodworth PL (2019) The tides they are a-changin'. Submitted to Reviews of Geophysics

Häkkinen S (2000) Decadal air-sea interaction in the North Atlantic based on observations and modelling results. J Clim 13:1195–1219. https://doi.org/10.1175/1520-0442(2000)013<1195:DASIIT>2.0.CO;2

Häkkinen S, Geiger CA (2000) Simulated low-frequency modes of circulation in the Arctic Ocean. J Geophys Res Oceans 105:6549–6564. https://doi.org/10.1029/2000JC900003

Hall A, Visbeck M (2002) Synchronous variability in the Southern Hemisphere atmosphere, sea ice, and ocean resulting from the Annular Mode. J Clim 15:3043–3057. https://doi.org/10.1175/1520-0442(2002)015<3043:SVITSH>2.0.CO;2

Hamlington BD, Leben RR, Kim K-Y, Nerem RS, Atkinson LP, Thompson PR (2015) The effect of the El Niño-Southern Oscillation on U.S. regional and coastal sea level. J Geophys Res Oceans 120:3970–3986. https://doi.org/10.1002/2014JC010602

Hamlington BD, Cheon SH, Thompson PR, Merrifield MA, Nerem RS, Leben RR, Kim K-Y (2016) An ongoing shift in Pacific Ocean sea level. J Geophys Res Oceans 121:5084–5097. https://doi.org/10.1002/2016JC011815

Han W, Vialard J, McPhaden MJ, Lee T, Masumoto Y, Feng M, de Ruijter WPM (2014) Indian Ocean decadal variability: a review. B Am Meteorol Soc 95:1679–1703. https://doi.org/10.1175/BAMS-D-13-00028.1

Han W, Meehl GA, Stammer D, Hu A, Hamlington B, Kenigson J, Palanisamy H, Thompson P (2017a) Spatial patterns of sea level variability associated with natural internal climate modes. Surv Geophys 38:217–250. https://doi.org/10.1007/s10712-016-9386-y

Han W, Meehl GA, Hu A, Zheng J, Kenigson J, Vialard J, Rajagopalan B, Yanto (2017b) Decadal variability of Indian and Pacific Walker Cells: do they co-vary on decadal timescales? J Clim 30:8447–8468. https://doi.org/10.1175/JCLI-D-16-0783.1

Han W, Stammer D, Meehl GA, Hu A, Sienz F, Zhang L (2018a) Multi-decadal trend and decadal variability of the regional sea level over the Indian Ocean since the 1960s: roles of climate modes and external forcing. Climate 6:51. https://doi.org/10.3390/cli6020051

Han W, Vialard J, McPhaden M, Roxy MK, Feng M, Shinoda T, Lee T (2018b) Regional sea-level variability and change. Chapter 14. In: Vialard J, Beal L (eds) Indian ocean observing system (IndOOS) decadal review. CLIVAR, Qingdao (in press)

Harangozo SA (1993) Flooding in the Maldives and its implications for the global sea level rise debate. In: Woodworth PL, Pugh DT, De Ronde JG, Warrick RG, Hannah J (eds) Sea level changes: determination and effects, vol 69. Geophysical monograph series. American Geophysical Union, Washington, pp 95–99. https://doi.org/10.1029/gm069

Hemer MA, Fan Y, Mori N, Semedo A, Wang XL (2013) Projected future changes in wind-wave climate in a multi-model ensemble. Nat Clim Change 3:471–476. https://doi.org/10.1038/nclimate1791

Hibbert A, Leach H, Woodworth P, Hughes CW, Roussenov V (2010) Quasi-biennial modulation of the Southern Ocean Coherent Mode. Q J R Meteor Soc 136:755–768. https://doi.org/10.1002/qj.581

Higginson S, Thompson KR, Woodworth PL, Hughes CW (2015) The tilt of mean sea level along the east coast of North America. Geophys Res Lett 42:1471–1479. https://doi.org/10.1002/2015GL063186

Hill DF (2016) Spatial and temporal variability in tidal range: evidence, causes, and effects. Curr Clim Change Rep 2:232–241. https://doi.org/10.1007/s40641-016-0044-8

Hoeke RK, McInnes KL, O'Grady J (2015) Wind and wave setup contributions to extreme sea levels at a tropical high island: a stochastic cyclone simulation study for Apia, Samoa. J Mar Sci Eng 3:1117–1135. https://doi.org/10.3390/jmse3031117

Hoeke RK, McInnes KL, Kruger JC, McNaught RJ, Hunter JR, Smithers SG (2013) Widespread inundation of Pacific islands triggered by distant-source wind-waves. Global Planet Change 108:128–138. https://doi.org/10.1016/j.gloplacha.2013.06.006

Holgate SJ, Woodworth PL (2004) Evidence for enhanced coastal sea level rise during the 1990s. Geophys Res Lett 31:L07305. https://doi.org/10.1029/2004GL019626

Holman RA, Sallenger AH Jr (1985) Setup and swash on a natural beach. J Geophys Res 90(C1):945–953. https://doi.org/10.1029/JC090iC01p00945

Holton JR, Lindzen RS (1972) An updated theory for quasi-biennial cycle of tropical stratosphere. J Atmos Sci 29:1076–1080. https://doi.org/10.1175/1520-0469(1972)029<1076:AUTFTQ>2.0.CO;2

Hughes CW, Meredith MP (2006) Coherent sea-level fluctuations along the global continental slope. Philos Trans R Soc A 364:885–901. https://doi.org/10.1098/rsta.2006.1744

Hughes CW, Stepanov VN (2004) Ocean dynamics associated with rapid J2 fluctuations: importance of circumpolar modes and identification of a coherent Arctic mode. J Geophys Res 109:C06002. https://doi.org/10.1029/2003JC002176

Hughes CW, Woodworth PL, Meredith MP, Stepanov V (2003) Coherence of Antarctic sea levels, Southern Hemisphere Annular Mode, and flow through Drake Passage. Geophys Res Lett 30:1464. https://doi.org/10.1029/2003GL017240

Hughes CW, Williams J, Blaker A, Coward A, Stepanov V (2018) A window on the deep ocean: the special value of ocean bottom pressure for monitoring the large-scale, deep-ocean circulation. Prog Oceanogr 161:19–46. https://doi.org/10.1016/j.pocean.2018.01.011

Hughes CW, Thompson K, Minobe S, Fukumori I, Griffies S, Huthnance J, Spence P (2019) Sea level and the role of coastal-trapped waves in mediating the interaction between the coast and open ocean. Surv Geophys. https://doi.org/10.1007/s10712-019-09535-x

Huthnance JM (1978) On coastal trapped waves: analysis and numerical calculation by inverse iteration. J Phys Oceanogr 8:74–92. https://doi.org/10.1175/1520-0485(1978)008<0074:OCTWAA>2.0.CO;2

Huthnance JM (1992) Extensive slope currents and the ocean-shelf boundary. Prog Oceanogr 29:161–196. https://doi.org/10.1016/0079-6611(92)90023-S

Huthnance JM (2001) Coastal trapped waves. In: Steele JH, Thorpe SA, Turekian KK (eds) Encyclopedia of ocean sciences, 1st edn. Academic Press, San Diego, pp 489–496

Huthnance JM, Mysak LA, Wang DP (1986) Coastal trapped waves. In: Mooers CNK (ed) Baroclinic processes on continental shelves, vol 3. Coastal and estuarine sciences. American Geophysical Union, Washington DC, pp 1–18. https://doi.org/10.1029/co003

Idier D, Paris F, Le Cozannet G, Boulahya F, Dumas F (2017) Sea-level rise impacts on the tides of the European Shelf. Cont Shelf Res 137:56–71. https://doi.org/10.1016/j.csr.2017.01.007

Idier D, Bertin X, Thompson P, Pickering MD (2019) Interactions between mean sea-level, tide, surge, waves and flooding: mechanisms and contributions to sea level variations at the coast. Surv Geophys (in review)

IOC (2016) Manual on sea-level measurements and interpretation, volume V: Radar Gauges. Paris, Intergovernmental Oceanographic Commission of UNESCO. 104 pp. (IOC Manuals and Guides No.14, vol. V; JCOMM Technical Report No. 89) (English). http://unesdoc.unesco.org/images/0024/002469/246981E.pdf which includes a Supplement: Practical Experiences. Accessed 1 Mar 2019

Jahfer S, Vinayachandran PN, Nanjundiah RS (2015) Long-term impact of Amazon river runoff on northern hemispheric climate. Nature 7:10989. https://doi.org/10.1038/s41598-017-10750-y

Jay DA (2009) Evolution of tidal amplitudes in the eastern Pacific Ocean. Geophys Res Lett 36:L04603. https://doi.org/10.1029/2008GL036185

Kang SK, Chung J, Lee S-R, Yum K-D (1995) Seasonal variability of the M2 tide in the seas adjacent to Korea. Cont Shelf Res 15:1087–1113. https://doi.org/10.1016/0278-4343(94)00066-V

Karpytchev M, Ballu V, Krien Y, Becker M, Goodbred S, Spada G, Calmant S, Shum CK, Khan Z (2018) Contribution of a strengthened early Holocene monsoon and sediment loading to present-day subsidence of the Ganges–Brahmaputra delta. Geophys Res Lett 45:1433–1442. https://doi.org/10.1002/2017GL076388

Kawabe M (1988) Variability of Kuroshio velocity assessed from the sea-level difference between Naze and Nishinoomote. J Oceanogr Soc Japan 44:293–304. https://doi.org/10.1007/BF02302572

Kenigson JS, Han W (2014) Detecting and understanding the accelerated sea level rise along the east coast of the United States during recent decades. J Geophys Res Oceans 119:8749–8766. https://doi.org/10.1002/2014JC010305

Kenigson JS, Han W, Rajagopalan B, Yanto Jasinski M (2018) Decadal shift of NAO-linked interannual sea level variability along the U.S. Northeast coast. J Clim 31:4981–4989. https://doi.org/10.1175/JCLI-D-17-0403.1

Kennedy AB, Mori N, Zhang Y, Yasuda T, Chen S-E, Tajima Y, Pecor W, Toride K (2016) Observations and modelling of coastal boulder transport and loading during Super Typhoon Haiyan. Coast Eng J 58:1640004-1–1640004-25. https://doi.org/10.1142/S0578563416400040

Kierulf HP, Steffen H, Simpson MJR, Lidberg M, Wu P, Wand H (2014) A GPS velocity field for Fennoscandia and a consistent comparison to glacial isostatic adjustment models. J Geophys Res Solid Earth 119:6613–6629. https://doi.org/10.1002/2013JB010889

Kirtman B, Power SB, Adedoyin JA, Boer GJ, Bojariu R, Camilloni I, Doblas-Reyes FJ, Fiore AM, Kimoto M, Meehl GA, Prather M, Sarr A, Schär C, Sutton R, van Oldenborgh GJ, Vecchi G, Wang HJ (2013) Near-term climate change: projections and predictability. In: Stocker TF, Qin D, Plattner G-K, Tignor M, Allen SK, Boschung J, Nauels A, Xia Y, Bex V, Midgley PM (eds) Climate change 2013: the physical science basis. Contribution of working group I to the fifth assessment report of the intergovernmental panel on climate change. Cambridge University Press, Cambridge, New York

Kolker AS, Allison MA, Hameed S (2011) An evaluation of subsidence rates and sea-level variability in the northern Gulf of Mexico. Geophys Res Lett 38:L21404. https://doi.org/10.1029/2011GL049458

Korosov A, Counillon F, Johannessen JA (2015) Monitoring the spreading of the Amazon freshwater plume by MODIS, SMOS, Aquarius, and TOPAZ. J Geophys Res-Oceans 120:268–283. https://doi.org/10.1002/2014JC010155

Kourafalou VH, De Mey P, Le Hénaff M, Charria G, Edwards CA, He R, Herzfeld M, Pascual A, Stanev EV, Tintoré J, Usui N, van der Westhuysen AJ, Wilkin J, Zhu X (2015) Coastal Ocean Forecasting: system integration and evaluation. J Oper Oceanogr 8(S1):s127–s146. https://doi.org/10.1080/1755876X.2015.1022336

Laiz I, Ferrer L, Plomaritis TA, Charria G (2014) Effect of river runoff on sea level from in situ measurements and numerical models in the Bay of Biscay. Deep Sea Res Pt II 106:49–67. https://doi.org/10.1016/j.dsr2.2013.12.013

Larson KM, Ray RD, Williams SDP (2017) A ten year comparison of water levels measured with a geodetic GPS receiver versus a conventional tide gauge. J Atmos Ocean Technol 34:295–307. https://doi.org/10.1175/JTECH-D-16-0101.1

LeBlond PH, Mysak LA (1978) Waves in the ocean. Elsevier Scientific Publishing, Amsterdam, p 602

Lindzen RS, Holton JR (1968) A theory of quasi-biennial oscillation. J Atmos Sci 25:1095–1107. https://doi.org/10.1175/1520-0469(1968)025<1095:ATOTQB>2.0.CO;2

Lisitzin E (1974) Sea-level changes. Elsevier, Amsterdam, p 286

Longuet-Higgins MS, Stewart RW (1962) Radiation stress and mass transport in gravity waves, with applications to "surf beats". J Fluid Mech 13:481–504. https://doi.org/10.1017/S0022112062000877

Lowe JA, Woodworth PL, Knutson T, McDonald RE, McInnes K, Woth K, Von Storch H, Wolf J, Swail V, Bernier N, Gulev S, Horsburgh K, Unnikrishnan AS, Hunter J, Weisse R (2010) Past and future changes in extreme sea levels and waves. Chapter 11. In: Church JA, Woodworth PL, Aarup T, Wilson WS (eds) Understanding sea-level rise and variability. Wiley-Blackwell, London

Lubbock JW (1836) On the tides at the port of London. Philos Trans R Soc London 126:217–266. https://doi.org/10.1098/rstl.1836.0017

Luther DS (1982) Evidence of a 4–6 day barotropic, planetary oscillation of the Pacific Ocean. J Phys Oceanogr 12:644–657. https://doi.org/10.1175/1520-0485(1982)012<0644:EOADBP>2.0.CO;2

Madden RA, Julian PR (1971) Detection of a 40–50 day oscillation in zonal wind in Tropical Pacific. J Atmos Sci 28:702–708. https://doi.org/10.1175/1520-0469(1971)028<0702:DOADOI>2.0.CO;2

Madden RA, Julian PR (1994) Observations of the 40–50-day tropical oscillation—a review. Mon Weather Rev 122:814–837. https://doi.org/10.1175/1520-0493(1994)122<0814:OOTDTO>2.0.CO;2

Madsen OS, Poon YK, Graber HC (1988) Spectral wave attenuation by bottom friction: theory. Coast Eng Proc 21:492–504. https://doi.org/10.9753/icce.v21.%25p

Mantua NJ, Hare SR (2002) The Pacific decadal oscillation. J Oceanogr 58:35–44. https://doi.org/10.1023/A:1015820616384

Marcos M, Tsimplis MN (2007) Variations of the seasonal sea level cycle in southern Europe. J Geophys Res 112:C12011. https://doi.org/10.1029/2006JC004049

Marcos M, Woodworth PL (2017) Spatio-temporal changes in extreme sea levels along the coasts of the North Atlantic and the Gulf of Mexico. J Geophys Res Oceans 122:7031–7048. https://doi.org/10.1002/2017JC013065

Marcos M, Woodworth PL (2018) Changes in extreme sea levels. CLIVAR Exch/US CLIVAR Var 16:20–24. https://doi.org/10.5065/D6445K82

Marcos M, Tsimplis MN, Shaw AGP (2009) Sea level extremes in southern Europe. J Geophys Res 114:C01007. https://doi.org/10.1029/2008JC004912

Marcos M, Calafat FM, Berihuete A, Dangendorf S (2015) Long-term variations in global sea level extremes. J Geophys Res Oceans 120:8115–8134. https://doi.org/10.1002/2015JC011173

Marcos M, Wöppelmann G, Matthews A, Ponte RM, Birol F, Ardhuin F, Coco G, Santamaría-Gómez A, Ballu V, Testut L, Chambers D, Stopa JE (2019) Coastal sea level and related fields from existing observing systems. Surv Geophys. https://doi.org/10.1007/s10712-019-09513-3

Marsooli R, Lin N (2018) Numerical modeling of historical storm tides and waves and their interactions along the U.S. east and Gulf Coasts. J Geophys Res Oceans 123:3844–3874. https://doi.org/10.1029/2017JC013434

Matthews AJ, Meredith MP (2004) Variability of Antarctic circumpolar transport and the Southern Annular Mode associated with the Madden-Julian Oscillation. Geophys Res Lett 31:L24312. https://doi.org/10.1029/2004GL021666

McCarthy GD, Smeed DA, Johns WE, Frajka-Williams E, Moat BI, Rayner D, Baringer MO, Meinen CS, Collins J, Bryden HL (2015) Measuring the Atlantic Meridional overturning circulation at 26°N. Prog Oceanogr 130:91–111. https://doi.org/10.1016/j.pocean.2014.10.006

Meade RH, Emery KO (1971) Sea level as affected by river runoff, Eastern United States. Science 173:425–428. https://doi.org/10.1126/science.173.3995.425

Melet A, Almar R, Meyssignac B (2016) What dominates sea level at the coast: a case study for the Gulf of Guinea. Ocean Dynam 66:623–636. https://doi.org/10.1007/s10236-016-0942-2

Melet A, Meyssignac B, Almar R, Le Cozannet G (2018) Under-estimated wave contribution to coastal sea-level rise. Nat Clim Change 8: 234–239. https://doi.org/10.1038/s41558-018-0088-y. Correction in Nat Clim Change 8: 840. https://doi.org/10.1038/s41558-018-0234-6

Melet A, Meyssignac B, Almar R, Le Cozannet G (2019) Reply to ''Waves do not contribute to global sea-level rise". Nat Clim Change 9:3. https://doi.org/10.1038/s41558-018-0378-4

Menéndez M, Woodworth PL (2010) Changes in extreme high water levels based on a quasi-global tide-gauge dataset. J Geophys Res 115:C10011. https://doi.org/10.1029/2009JC005997

Mentaschi L, Vousdoukas M, Voukouvalas E, Dosio A, Feyen L (2017) Global changes of extreme coastal wave energy fluxes triggered by intensified teleconnection patterns. Geophys Res Lett 44:2416–2426. https://doi.org/10.1002/2016GL072488

Meredith MP, Woodworth PL, Hughes CW, Stepanov V (2004) Changes in the ocean transport through Drake Passage during the 1980s and 1990s, forced by changes in the Southern Annular Mode. Geophys Res Lett 31:L21305. https://doi.org/10.1029/2004GL021169

Merrifield MA, Thompson PR (2018) Interdecadal sea level variations in the Pacific: distinctions between the tropics and extratropics. Geophys Res Lett 45:6604–6610. https://doi.org/10.1029/2018GL077666

Merrifield MA, Genz AS, Kontoes CP, Marra JJ (2013) Annual maximum water levels from tide gauges: contributing factors and geographic patterns. J Geophys Res 118:2535–2546. https://doi.org/10.1002/jgrc.2017

Merrifield MA, Becker JM, Ford M, Yao Y (2014) Observations and estimates of wave-driven water level extremes at the Marshall Islands. Geophys Res Lett 41:7245–7253. https://doi.org/10.1002/2014GL061005

Meyssignac B, Slangen ABA, Melet A, Church JA, Fettweis X, Marzeion B, Agosta C, Ligtenberg SRM, Spada G, Richter K, Palmer MD, Roberts CD, Champollion N (2017) Evaluating model simulations of twentieth-century sea-level rise. Part II: regional sea-level changes. J Climate 30:8565–8593. https://doi.org/10.1175/JCLI-D-17-0112.1

Middleton JF (2000) Wind-forced upwelling: the role of the surface mixed layer. J Phys Oceanogr 30:745–763. https://doi.org/10.1175/1520-0485(2000)030<0745:WFUTRO>2.0.CO;2

Middleton JF, Cirano M (1999) Wind-forced downwelling slope currents: a numerical study. J Phys Oceanogr 29:1723–1742. https://doi.org/10.1175/1520-0485(1999)029<1723:WFDSCA>2.0.CO;2

Miller GR (1972) Relative spectra of tsunamis. Hawaii Inst. Geophys Report, HIG-72-8. University of Hawaii, Hawaii

Miller L, Douglas BC (2007) Gyre-scale atmospheric pressure variations and their relation to 19th and 20th century sea level rise. Geophys Res Lett 34:L16602. https://doi.org/10.1029/2007GL030862

Miller STK, Keim BD, Talbot RW, Mao H (2003) Sea breeze: structure, forecasting, and impacts. Rev Geophys 41:1011. https://doi.org/10.1029/2003RG000124

Mitchum GT (1995) The source of 90-day oscillations at Wake Island. J Geophys Res 100(C2):2459–2475. https://doi.org/10.1029/94JC02923

Mitchum GT (2000) An improved calibration of satellite altimetric heights using tide gauge sea levels with adjustment for land motion. Mar Geod 23:145–166. https://doi.org/10.1080/01490410050128591

Monserrat S, Vilibić I, Rabinovich AB (2006) Meteotsunamis: atmospherically induced destructive ocean waves in the tsunami frequency band. Nat Hazards Earth Syst Sci 6:1035–1051. https://doi.org/10.5194/nhess-6-1035

Muis S, Verlaan M, Winsemius HC, Aerts JCJH, Ward PJ (2016) A global reanalysis of storm surge and extreme sea levels. Nat Commun 7:1–11. https://doi.org/10.1038/ncomms11969

Müller M (2012) The influence of changing stratification conditions on barotropic tidal transport and its implications for seasonal and secular changes of tides. Cont Shelf Res 47:107–115. https://doi.org/10.1016/j.csr.2012.07.003

Müller M, Arbic BK, Mitrovica JX (2011) Secular trends in ocean tides: observations and model results. J Geophys Res 116:C05013. https://doi.org/10.1029/2010JC006387

Nakanowatari T, Ohshima KI (2014) Coherent sea level variation in and around the Sea of Okhotsk. Prog Oceanogr 126:58–70. https://doi.org/10.1016/j.pocean.2014.05.009

Neetu S, Lengaigne M, Vincent EM, Vialard J, Madec G, Samson G, Ramesh Kumar MR, Durand F (2012) Influence of upper-ocean stratification on tropical cyclone-induced surface cooling in the Bay of Bengal. J Geophys Res 117:C12020. https://doi.org/10.1029/2012JC008433

Newton B, Tremblay LB, Cane MA, Schlosser P (2006) A simple model of the Arctic Ocean response to annular atmospheric modes. J Geophys Res Oceans 111:C09019. https://doi.org/10.1029/2004JC002622

Oliver ECJ, Thompson KR (2010) Madden-Julian Oscillation and sea level: local and remote forcing. J Geophys Res 115:C01003. https://doi.org/10.1029/2009JC005337

Pavlov VK (2001) Seasonal and long-term sea level variability in the marginal seas of the Arctic Ocean. Polar Res 20:153–160. https://doi.org/10.3402/polar.v20i2.6512

Pedreros R, Idier D, Muller H, Lecacheux S, Paris F, Yates-Michelin M, Dumas F, Pineau-Guillou L, Sénéchal N (2018) Relative contribution of wave setup to the storm surge: observations and modeling based analysis in open and protected environments (Truc Vert beach and Tubuai island). J Coast Res 85:1046–1050. https://doi.org/10.2112/SI85-210.1

Peltier WR, Argus DF, Drummond R (2015) Space geodesy constrains ice-age terminal deglaciation: the global ICE-6G_C (VM5a) model. J Geophys Res Solid Earth 120:450–487. https://doi.org/10.1002/2014JB011176

Pickering MD, Horsburgh KJ, Blundell JR, Hirschi JJ-M, Nicholls RJ, Verlaan M, Wells NC (2017) The impact of future sea-level rise on the global tides. Cont Shelf Res 142:50–68. https://doi.org/10.1016/j.csr.2017.02.004

Piecuch CG, Dangendorf S, Ponte RM, Marcos M (2016) Annual sea level changes on the North American northeast coast: influence of local winds and barotropic motions. J Clim 29:4801–4816. https://doi.org/10.1175/JCLI-D-16-0048.1

Piecuch CG, Bittermann K, Kemp AC, Ponte RM, Little CM, Engelhart SE, Lentz SJ (2018) River-discharge effects on United States Atlantic and Gulf coast sea-level changes. Proc Natl Acad Sci USA. https://doi.org/10.1073/pnas.1805428115 (in press)

Piecuch CG, Calafat FM, Dangendorf S, Jordà G (2019) The ability of barotropic models to simulate historical mean sea level changes from coastal tide gauge data. Surv Geophys. https://doi.org/10.1007/s10712-019-09537-9

Plag H-P, Tsimplis MN (1999) Temporal variability of the seasonal sea-level cycle in the North Sea and Baltic Sea in relation to climate variability. Global Planet Change 20:173–203. https://doi.org/10.1016/S0921-8181(98)00069-1

Poate TG, McCall RT, Masselink G (2016) A new parameterisation for runup on gravel beaches. Coast Eng 117:176–190. https://doi.org/10.1016/j.coastaleng.2016.08.003

Ponte RM et al. (2019) Towards comprehensive observing and modeling systems for monitoring and predicting regional to coastal sea level. Submitted to Front Sci

Ponte RM, Salstein DA, Rosen RD (1991) Sea level response to pressure forcing in a barotropic numerical model. J Phys Oceanogr 21:1043–1057. https://doi.org/10.1175/1520-0485(1991)021%3c1043:SLRTPF%3e2.0.CO;2

Prandi P, Cazenave A, Becker M (2009) Is coastal mean sea level rising faster than the global mean? A comparison between tide gauges and satellite altimetry over 1993–2007. Geophys Res Lett 36:L05602. https://doi.org/10.1029/2008GL036564

Proshutinsky AY, Johnson MA (1997) Two circulation regimes of the wind driven Arctic Ocean. J Geophys Res Oceans 102:12493–12514. https://doi.org/10.1029/97JC00738

Proshutinsky A, Bourke RH, McLaughlin FA (2002) The role of the Beaufort Gyre in Arctic climate variability: seasonal to decadal climate scales. Geophys Res Lett 29:L02100. https://doi.org/10.1029/2002GL015847

Proshutinsky A, Ashik IM, Dvorkin EN, Häkkinen S, Krishfield RA, Peltier WR (2004) Secular sea level change in the Russian sector of the Arctic Ocean. J Geophys Res 109:C03042. https://doi.org/10.1029/2003JC002007

Proshutinsky A, Ashik IM, Häkkinen S (2007) Sea level variability in the Arctic Ocean from AOMIP models. J Geophys Res 112:C04S08. https://doi.org/10.1029/2006jc003916

Pugh DT, Vassie JM (1976) Tide and surge propagation off-shore in the Dowsing region of the North Sea. Deutsche Hydrographische Zeitschrift 29:163–213

Pugh DT, Vassie JM (1992) Seasonal modulations of the principal semi diurnal lunar tide. In: Beven K, Chatwin P, Millbank J (eds) Mixing and transport in the environment. A memorial volume for Catherine M. Allen (1954–1991). Wiley, Chichester, pp 247–267

Pugh DT, Woodworth PL (2014) Sea-level science: Understanding tides, surges, tsunamis and mean sea-level changes. Cambridge University Press, Cambridge. ISBN 9781107028197

Qiu B, Chen S (2005) Variability of the Kuroshio Extension jet, recirculation gyre, and mesoscale eddies on decadal time scales. J Phys Oceanogr 35:2090–2103. https://doi.org/10.1175/JPO2807.1

Rabinovich AB (1997) Spectral analysis of tsunami waves: separation of source and topography effects. J Geophys Res Oceans 102:12663–12676. https://doi.org/10.1029/97JC00479

Rabinovich AB (2010) Seiches and harbor oscillations (Chapter 9). In: Kim YC (ed) Handbook of coastal engineering. World Scientific Publishing, Hackensack, pp 193–236

Rabinovich AB, Monserrat S (1996) Meteorological tsunamis near the Balearic and Kuril Islands: descriptive and Statistical analysis. Nat Hazards 13:55–90. https://doi.org/10.1007/BF00156506

Rabinovich AB, Thomson RE (2007) The 26 December 2004 Sumatra tsunami: analysis of tide gauge data from the World Ocean Part 1. Indian Ocean and South Africa. Pure appl Geophys 164:261–308. https://doi.org/10.1007/s00024-006-0164-5

Rasmussen EM, Carpenter TH (1982) Variations in tropical sea surface temperature and surface wind fields associated with the Southern Oscillation/El Niño. Mon Weather Rev 110:354–384. https://doi.org/10.1175/1520-0493(1982)110%3c0354:VITSST%3e2.0.CO;2

Raucoules D, Le Cozannet G, Wöppelmann G, de Michele M, Gravelle M, Daag A, Marcos M (2013) High nonlinear urban ground motion in Manila (Philippines) from 1993 to 2010 observed by DInSAR: implications for sea-level measurement. Remote Sens Environ 139:386–397. https://doi.org/10.1016/j.rse.2013.08.021

Ray RD (2009) Secular changes in the solar semidiurnal tide of the western North Atlantic Ocean. Geophys Res Lett 36:L19601. https://doi.org/10.1029/2009GL040217

Ray RD, Egbert GD (2017) Tides and satellite altimetry. In: Stammer D, Cazenave A (eds) Satellite altimetry over oceans and land surfaces. CRC Taylor and Francis, Boca Raton, pp 427–458

Ray RD, Egbert GD, Erofeeva SY (2011) Tide predictions in shelf and coastal waters: status and prospects. In: Vignudelli S et al (eds) Coastal altimetry. Springer, Berlin, pp 191–216. https://doi.org/10.1007/978-3-642-12796-0_8

Richter K, Nilsen JEØ, Drange H (2012) Contributions to sea level variability along the Norwegian coast for 1960–2010. J Geophys Res 117:C05038. https://doi.org/10.1029/2011JC007826

Riva REM, Frederikse T, King MA, Marzeion B, van den Broeke MR (2017) Brief communication: the global signature of post-1900 land ice wastage on vertical land motion. The Cryosphere 11:1327–1332. https://doi.org/10.5194/tc-11-1327-2017

Roden GI, Rossby HT (1999) Early Swedish contribution to oceanography: nils Gissler (1715–71) and the inverted barometer effect. B Am Meteorol Soc 80:675–682. https://doi.org/10.1175/1520-0477(1999)080%3c0675:ESCTON%3e2.0.CO;2

Roelvink D, Reniers A, van Dongeren A, van Thiel de Vries J, McCall R, Lescinski J (2009) Modelling storm impacts on beaches, dunes and barrier islands. Coast Eng 56:11–12. https://doi.org/10.1016/j.coastaleng.2009.08.006

Roemmich D, Woodworth P, Jevrejeva J, Purkey S, Lankhorst M, Send U, Maximenko N (2017) In situ observations needed to complement, validate, and interpret satellite altimetry (Chapter 3). In: Stammer D, Cazenave A (eds) Satellite altimetry over oceans and land surfaces. CRC Press, Boca Raton, pp 113–147

Ross JC (1854) On the effect of the pressure of the atmosphere on the mean level of the ocean. Philos Trans R Soc London 144:285–296. https://doi.org/10.1098/rstl.1854.0013

Roussenov VM, Williams RG, Hughes CW, Bingham RJ (2008) Boundary wave communication of bottom pressure and overturning changes for the North Atlantic. J Geophys Res 113:C08042. https://doi.org/10.1029/2007JC004501

Saji NH, Yamagata T (2003) Possible impacts of Indian Ocean Dipole Mode events on global climate. Clim Res 25:151–169

Salas-Monreal D, Valle-Levinson A (2008) Sea-level slopes and volume fluxes produced by atmospheric forcing in estuaries: chesapeake Bay case study. J Coast Res 24(Supplement 2B):208–217. https://doi.org/10.2112/06-0632.1

Sallenger AH Jr, Doran KS, Howd PA (2012) Hotspot of accelerated sea-level rise on the Atlantic coast of North America. Nat Clim Change 2:884–888. https://doi.org/10.1038/nclimate1597

Santamaría-Gómez A, Mémin A (2015) Geodetic secular velocity errors due to interanual Surface loading deformation. Geophys J Int 202:763–767. https://doi.org/10.1093/gjo/ggv190

Sasaki YN, Minobe S, Schneider N (2013) Decadal response of the Kuroshio Extension jet to Rossby waves: observation and thin-jet theory. J Phys Oceanogr 43:442–456. https://doi.org/10.1175/JPO-D-12-096.1

Sasaki YN, Minobe S, Miura Y (2014) Decadal sea-level variability along the coast of Japan in response to ocean circulation changes. J Geophys Res ceans 119:266–275. https://doi.org/10.1002/2013JC009327

Sasaki YN, Washizu R, Yasuda T, Minobe S (2017) Sea level variability around Japan during the twentieth century simulated by a regional ocean model. J Clim 30:5585–5595. https://doi.org/10.1175/JCLI-D-16-0497.1

Sella GF, Stein S, Dixon TH, Craymer M, James TS, Mazzotti S, Dokka RK (2007) Observation of glacial isostatic adjustment in "stable" North America with GPS. Geophys Res Lett 34:L02306. https://doi.org/10.1029/2006GL027081

Semedo A, Sušelj K, Rutgersson A, Sterl A (2011) A global view on the wind sea and swell climate and variability from ERA-40. J Clim 24:1461–1479. https://doi.org/10.1175/2010JCLI3718.1

Siefert W (1982) Bemerkenswerte Veränderungen der Wasserstände in den deutschen Tideflüssen. Die Küste 37: 1–36. http://www.kfki.de

Smith-Konter BR, Thornton GM, Sandwell DT (2014) Vertical crustal displacement due to interseismic deformation along the San Andreas fault: constraints from tide gauges. Geophys Res Lett 41:3793–3801. https://doi.org/10.1002/2014GL060091

Soulsby RL, Clarke S (2005) Bed shear-stresses under combined waves and currents on smooth and rough beds. HR Wallingford Report TR 137

Stammer D et al (2014) Accuracy assessment of global barotropic ocean tide models. Rev Geophys 52:243–282. https://doi.org/10.1002/2014RG000450

Stockdon HF, Holman RA, Howd PA, Sallenger AH Jr (2006) Empirical parameterization of setup, swash, and runup. Coast Eng 53:573–588. https://doi.org/10.1016/j.coastaleng.2005.12.005

Stopa JE, Cheung KF (2014) Periodicity and patterns of ocean wind and wave climate. J Geophys Res Oceans 119:5563–5584. https://doi.org/10.1002/2013JC009729

Stopa JE, Ardhuin F, Girard-Ardhuin F (2016) Wave climate in the Arctic 1992–2014: seasonality and trends. The Cryosphere 10:1605–1629. https://doi.org/10.5194/tc-10-1605-2016
Swart NC, Fyfe JC (2012) Observed and simulated changes in the Southern Hemisphere surface westerly wind-stress. Geophys Res Lett 39:L16711. https://doi.org/10.1029/2012GL052810
Sweet WV, Park J (2014) From the extreme to the mean: acceleration and tipping points of coastal inundation from sea level rise. Earth's Future 2:579–600. https://doi.org/10.1002/2014EF000272
Taguchi B, Shang-Ping X, Schneider N, Nonaka M, Sasaki H, Sasai Y (2007) Decadal variability of the Kuroshio Extension: observations and an eddy-resolving model hindcast. J Climate 20:2357–2377. https://doi.org/10.1175/JCLI4142.1
Takahashi C, Watanabe M (2016) Pacific trade winds accelerated by aerosol forcing over the past two decades. Nat Clim Change 6:768–772. https://doi.org/10.1038/nclimate2996
Talke SA, Orton P, Jay DA (2014) Increasing storm tides in New York Harbor, 1844–2013. Geophys Res Lett 41:3149–3155. https://doi.org/10.1002/2014GL059574
Tamisiea ME, Mitrovica JX (2011) The moving boundaries of sea level change: understanding the origins of geographic variability. Oceanography 24:24–39. https://doi.org/10.5670/oceanog.2011.25
Thompson KR (1980) An analysis of British monthly mean sea level. Geophys J R Astr Soc 63:57–73. https://doi.org/10.1111/j.1365-246X.1980.tb02610.x
Thompson R, Hamon BV (1980) Wave setup of harbor water levels. J Geophys Res 85:1151–1152. https://doi.org/10.1029/JC085iC02p01151
Thompson PR, Mitchum GT (2014) Coherent sea level variability on the North Atlantic western boundary. J Geophys Res Oceans 119:5676–5689. https://doi.org/10.1002/2014JC009999
Thompson DWJ, Wallace JM (1998) The Arctic Oscillation signature in the wintertime geopotential height and temperature fields. Geophys Res Lett 25:1297–1300. https://doi.org/10.1029/98GL00950
Thompson PR, Merrifield MA, Wells JR, Chang CM (2014) Wind-driven coastal sea level variability in the Northeast Pacific. J Climate 27:4733–4751. https://doi.org/10.1175/JCLI-D-13-00225.1
Törnqvist TE, Wallace DJ, Storms JEA, Wallinga J, van Dam RL, Blaauw M, Deksen MS, Klerks CJW, Meijneken C, Snijders EMA (2008) Mississippi Delta subsidence primarily caused by compaction of Holocene strata. Nat Geosci 1:173–176. https://doi.org/10.1038/ngeo129
Torres RR, Tsimplis MN (2012) Seasonal sea level cycle in the Caribbean Sea. J Geophys Res 117:C07011. https://doi.org/10.1029/2012JC008159
Tsimplis MN, Woodworth PL (1994) The global distribution of the seasonal sea level cycle calculated from coastal tide gauge data. J Geophys Res 99:16031–16039. https://doi.org/10.1029/94JC01115
UKHO (2017) Admiralty Tide Tables (including Tidal Stream Tables). NP204, Taunton, United Kingdom Hydrographic Office
Usui N, Tsujino H, Nakano H, Fujii Y, Kamachi M (2011) Decay mechanism of the 2004/05 Kuroshio large meander. J Geophys Res 116:C10010. https://doi.org/10.1029/2011JC007009
Veit E, Conrad CP (2016) The impact of groundwater depletion on spatial variations in sea level change during the past century. Geophys Res Lett 43:3351–3359. https://doi.org/10.1002/2016GL068118
Vetter O, Becker JM, Merrifield MA, Pequignet A-C, Aucan J, Boc SJ, Pollock CE (2010) Wave setup over a Pacific Island fringing reef. J Geophys Res 115:C12066. https://doi.org/10.1029/2010JC006455
Vignudelli S, Kostianoy A, Cipollini P, Benveniste J (eds) (2011) Coastal altimetry. Springer, Berlin
Vilibić I, Šepić J (2017) Global mapping of nonseismic sea level oscillations at tsunami timescales. Sci Rep 7:40818. https://doi.org/10.1038/srep40818
Vinogradov SV, Ponte RM (2010) Annual cycle in coastal sea level from tide gauges and altimetry. J Geophys Res 115:C04021. https://doi.org/10.1029/2009JC005767
Vinogradov SV, Ponte RM (2011) Low-frequency variability in coastal sea level from tide gauges and altimetry. J Geophys Res 116:C07006. https://doi.org/10.1029/2011JC007034
Vinogradov SV, Ponte RM, Heimbach P, Wunsch C (2008) The mean seasonal cycle in sea level estimated from a data-constrained general circulation model. J Geophys Res 113:C03032. https://doi.org/10.1029/2007JC004496
Vitousek S, Barnard PL, Fletcher CH, Frazer N, Erikson L, Storlazzi CD (2017) Doubling of coastal flooding frequency within decades due to sea-level rise. Sci Rep 7:1399. https://doi.org/10.1038/s41598-017-01362-7
von Storch H, Woth K (2008) Storm surges: perspectives and options. Sustain Sci 3:33–43. https://doi.org/10.1007/s11625-008-0044-2
Wahl T, Chambers DP (2015) Evidence for multidecadal variability in US extreme sea level records. J Geophys Res Oceans 120:1527–1544. https://doi.org/10.1002/2014JC010443
Wahl T, Chambers DP (2016) Climate controls multidecadal variability in U. S. extreme sea level records. J Geophys Res Oceans 121:1274–1290. https://doi.org/10.1002/2015JC011057

Wahl T, Calafat FM, Luther ME (2014) Rapid changes in the seasonal sea level cycle along the US Gulf coast from the late 20th century. Geophys Res Lett 41:491–498. https://doi.org/10.1002/2013GL058777

Wakelin SL, Woodworth PL, Flather RA, Williams JA (2003) Sea-level dependence on the NAO over the NW European Continental Shelf. Geophys Res Lett 30:1403. https://doi.org/10.1029/2003GL017041

Walter RK, Reid EC, Davis KA, Armenta KJ, Merhoff K, Nidzieko NJ (2017) Local diurnal wind-driven variability and upwelling in a small coastal embayment. J Geophys Res Oceans 122:955–972. https://doi.org/10.1002/2016JC012466

Waterhouse AF, Valle-Levinson A (2010) Transverse structure of subtidal flow in a weakly stratified subtropical tidal inlet. Cont Shelf Res 30:281–292. https://doi.org/10.1016/j.csr.2009.11.008

White NJ, Church JA, Gregory JM (2005) Coastal and global averaged sea level rise for 1950 to 2000. Geophys Res Lett 32:L01601. https://doi.org/10.1029/2004GL021391

White NJ, Haigh ID, Church JA, Koen T, Watson CS, Pritchard TR, Watson PJ, Burgette RJ, McInnes KL, You Z-J, Zhang X, Tregoning P (2014) Australian sea levels—trends, regional variability and influencing factors. Earth Sci Rev 136:155–174. https://doi.org/10.1016/j.earscirev.2014.05.011

Wiegel RL (1964) Tsunamis, storm surges, and harbor oscillations. Chapter 5 in Oceanographical engineering. Prentice-Hall, Englewood Cliffs, pp 95–127

Wijeratne EMS, Woodworth PL, Stepanov VN (2008) The seasonal cycle of sea level in Sri Lanka and Southern India. Western Indian Ocean J Mar Sci 7:29–43. https://doi.org/10.4314/wiojms.v7i1.48252

Wijeratne EMS, Woodworth PL, Pugh DT (2010) Meteorological and internal wave forcing of seiches along the Sri Lanka coast. J Geophys Res 115:C03014. https://doi.org/10.1029/2009JC005673

Williams J, Hughes CW (2013) The coherence of small island sea level with the wider ocean: a model study. Ocean Sci 9:111–119. https://doi.org/10.5194/os-9-111-2013

Wilson B (1972) Seiches. Adv Hydrosci 8:1–94. https://doi.org/10.1016/B978-0-12-021808-0.50006-1

Wolf J (1999) The estimation of shear stresses from near-bed turbulent velocities for combined wave–current flows. Coast Eng 37:529–543. https://doi.org/10.1016/S0378-3839(99)00042-3

Woodworth PL (2010) A survey of recent changes in the main components of the ocean tide. Cont Shelf Res 30:1680–1691. https://doi.org/10.1016/j.csr.2010.07.002

Woodworth PL (2012) A note on the nodal tide in sea level records. J Coast Res 28:316–323. https://doi.org/10.2112/JCOASTRES-D-11A-00023.1

Woodworth PL (2018) Sea level change in Great Britain between 1859 and the present. Geophys J Int 213:222–236. https://doi.org/10.1093/gji/ggx538

Woodworth PL, Windle SA, Vassie JM (1995) Departures from the local inverse barometer model at periods of 5 days in the central South Atlantic. J Geophys Res 100:18281–18290. https://doi.org/10.1029/95JC01741

Woodworth PL, Hughes CW, Blackman DL, Stepanov VN, Holgate SJ, Foden PR, Pugh JP, Mack S, Hargreaves GW, Meredith MP, Milinevsky G, Fierro Contreras JJ (2006) Antarctic peninsula sea levels: a real time system for monitoring Drake Passage transport. Antarct Sci 18:429–436. https://doi.org/10.1017/S0954102006

Woodworth PL, Flather RA, Williams JA, Wakelin SL, Jevrejeva S (2007) The dependence of UK extreme sea levels and storm surges on the North Atlantic Oscillation. Cont Shelf Res 27:935–946. https://doi.org/10.1016/j.csr.2006.12.007

Woodworth PL, Pugh DT, Bingley RM (2010) Long term and recent changes in sea level in the Falkland Islands. J Geophys Res 115:C09025. https://doi.org/10.1029/2010JC006113

Woodworth PL, Menéndez M, Gehrels WR (2011) Evidence for century-timescale acceleration in mean sea levels and for recent changes in extreme sea levels. Surv Geophys 32:603–618. https://doi.org/10.1007/s10712-011-9112-8 (erratum page 619)

Woodworth PL, Morales Maqueda MÁ, Roussenov VM, Williams RG, Hughes CW (2014) Mean sea-level variability along the northeast American Atlantic coast and the roles of the wind and the overturning circulation. J Geophys Res Oceans 119:8916–8935. https://doi.org/10.1002/2014JC010520

Woodworth PL, Morales Maqueda MÁ, Gehrels WR, Roussenov V, Williams RG, Hughes CW (2017a) Variations in the difference between mean sea level measured either side of Cape Hatteras and their relation to the North Atlantic Oscillation. Clim Dynam 49:2451–2469. https://doi.org/10.1007/s00382-016-3464-1

Woodworth PL, Wöppelmann G, Marcos M, Gravelle M, Bingley RM (2017b) Why we must tie satellite positioning to tide gauge data. Eos Trans Am Geophys Union 98(4): 13–15. https://doi.org/10.1029/2017eo064037, https://eos.org/opinions/why-we-must-tie-satellite-positioning-to-tide-gauge-data

Wöppelmann G, Marcos M (2016) Vertical land motion as a key to understanding sea level change and variability. Rev Geophys 54:64–92. https://doi.org/10.1002/2015RG000502

World Meteorological Organization (2011) Guide to Storm Surge Forecasting. WMO Report No. 1076. Geneva: World Meteorological Organization. https://library.wmo.int. Accessed 14 Apr 2019

Wunsch C, Gill AE (1976) Observations of equatorially trapped waves in Pacific sea level variations. Deep Sea Res Oceanogr Abstr 23:371–390. https://doi.org/10.1016/0011-7471(76)90835-4

Wunsch C, Stammer D (1997) Atmospheric loading and the oceanic "inverted barometer" effect. Rev Geophys 35:79–107. https://doi.org/10.1029/96RG03037

Xie PP, Arkin PA (1997) Global precipitation: a 17-year monthly analysis based on gauge observations, satellite estimates, and numerical model outputs. B Am Meteorol Soc 78:2539–2558. https://doi.org/10.1175/1520-0477(1997)078%3c2539:GPAYMA%3e2.0.CO;2

Yasuda T, Sakarai K (2006) Interdecadal variability of the sea surface height around Japan. Geophys Res Lett 33:L01605. https://doi.org/10.1029/2005GL024920

Yin J, Goddard PB (2013) Oceanic control of sea level rise patterns along the East Coast of the United States. Geophys Res Lett 40:5514–5520. https://doi.org/10.1002/2013GL057992

Yin JJ, Schlesinger ME, Stouffer RJ (2009) Model projections of rapid sea level rise on the northeast coast of the United States. Nat Geosci 2:262–266. https://doi.org/10.1038/ngeo462

Young IR (1999) Seasonal variability of the global ocean wind and wave climate. Int J Climatol 19:931–950. https://doi.org/10.1002/(SICI)1097-0088(199907)19:9%3c931:AID-JOC412%3e3.0.CO;2-O

Young IR, Zieger S, Babanin AV (2011) Global trends in wind speed and wave height. Science 332:451–455. https://doi.org/10.1126/science.1197219

Zhang C (2005) Madden-Julian oscillation. Rev Geophys 43:RG2003. https://doi.org/10.1029/2004RG000158

Zhao Z, Alford MH, Girton JB, Rainville L, Simmons HL (2016) Global observations of open-ocean mode-1 M2 internal tides. J Phys Oceanogr 46:1657–1684. https://doi.org/10.1175/JPO-D-15-0105.s1

Zhuang W, Qiu B, Du Y (2013) Low-frequency western Pacific Ocean sea level and circulation changes due to the connectivity of the Philippine Archipelago. J Geophys Res Oceans 118:6759–6773. https://doi.org/10.1002/2013JC009376

Surveys in Geophysics (2019) 40:1399–1435
https://doi.org/10.1007/s10712-019-09537-9

The Ability of Barotropic Models to Simulate Historical Mean Sea Level Changes from Coastal Tide Gauge Data

C. G. Piecuch[1] · F. M. Calafat[2] · S. Dangendorf[3] · G. Jordà[4]

Received: 27 September 2018 / Accepted: 24 April 2019 / Published online: 6 May 2019

Abstract

The nature of mean sea level variation over the global coastal ocean is considered based on 219 historical tide gauge records and three barotropic ocean circulation models forced by reanalysis surface air pressure and wind stress. The consistency of the models and their ability to reproduce the data are considered on nonseasonal timescales (seasonal cycles and linear trends removed) from bimonthly to multidecadal over 1900–2010. Models consistently simulate stronger sea level variability at higher latitude, higher frequency, between winters, and over broad shallow shelves and semi-enclosed marginal seas; standard deviations in modeled monthly sea level grow from 1–2 cm on average at low latitude (0°–30°) to 5–10 cm at high latitude (60°–90°), with larger values simulated over some shelf areas (e.g., North Sea). Models are more consistent over narrow shelf regions adjacent to deep basins and less consistent along the broad shallow continental shelf. On monthly timescales, discrepancies between models arise mostly from differences in model configuration (e.g., fine vs. coarse horizontal resolution), whereas model configuration and surface forcing (i.e., choice of atmospheric reanalysis) contribute comparably to model differences on annual timescales. Model solutions become more uncertain at earlier times (e.g., prior to 1950). The models show more skill explaining variance in tide gauge data at higher latitude, higher frequency, between winters, and over broad shallow shelves and within semi-enclosed marginal seas; at middle and high latitudes (poleward of 45°), model sea level solutions on average explain 30–50% of the monthly variance and 35–70% of the variance from one winter to the next in the tide gauge data records. Statistically significant relationships between the model solutions and observational data persist on long decadal periods. The relative skill of individual models is sensitive to region and timescale, such that no one model considered here consistently performs better than the others in all cases. Results suggest that barotropic models are useful for reducing noise in tide gauge records for studies of sea level rise and motivate additional model comparison studies in the context of sea level extremes.

Keywords Coastal sea level · Climate change and variability · Barotropic modeling · Wind forcing · Inverted barometer

✉ C. G. Piecuch
cpiecuch@whoi.edu

Extended author information available on the last page of the article

1 Introduction

Understanding coastal sea level variation and change as a function of space and time is an important and challenging problem in climate science. A rise in the coastal sea surface elevation relative to Earth's crust (i.e., relative sea level, as measured by a tide gauge) can have adverse impacts on the coastal zone, including saltwater intrusion, beach erosion, and habitat loss (e.g., Jordà et al. 2012a; Gonneea et al. 2013; Theuerkeuf et al. 2014; Field et al. 2017; Thorne et al. 2018). Depending on spatial and temporal scales, relative sea level can be controlled by any number of processes involving the ocean, atmosphere, cryosphere, land surface, solid Earth, and their coupling and interaction (e.g., Milne et al. 2009; Stammer et al. 2013; Kopp et al. 2015; Horton et al. 2018). See Woodworth et al. (2019) in this volume for a general overview of processes contributing to coastal sea level variation as a function of space and time.

Identifying the causes of historically observed coastal sea level anomalies is central to piecing together the past and predicting future sea level evolution over the global ocean, as well as anticipating the attendant coastal impacts. Depending on the application, the imprint of any particular process on the sea level record can represent unwanted noise, best removed from the data, or the desired signal (e.g., Ponte et al. 2018). Consider barometric pressure and wind stress acting over the ocean surface. Changes in these forcings can redistribute water volume throughout the ocean, hence affecting sea level regionally and locally. Yet, because they minimally alter the total volume of water contained within the ocean (cf. Gille 2004; Piecuch and Ponte 2014), these forcings have little influence on globally averaged sea level. Thus, in the case of accurately simulating the coastal ocean response to storm events (e.g., Calafat et al. 2014b; Dangendorf et al. 2014b; Marcos et al. 2015), this wind- and pressure-driven sea level variation is the quantity of interest. However, in the case of reconstructing global-mean sea level rise from tide gauge records (e.g., Hay et al. 2015; Thompson et al. 2016; Dangendorf et al. 2017), such wind and pressure effects largely contaminate the data and obscure the sought-after global-mean signal. Moreover, regional sea level variations resulting from natural modes of wind and pressure fluctuation can obscure underlying secular trends, hampering the detection of anthropogenic signals at individual locations (e.g., Calafat and Chambers 2013; Haigh et al. 2014; Dangendorf et al. 2015). In all cases, good model estimates of the sea level response to variable wind and pressure forcing are informative.

In recent years, long atmospheric retrospective analyses—or reanalyses—have become available, providing estimates of the time-varying atmospheric state over the last century or longer (e.g., Compo et al. 2011; Poli et al. 2013; Laloyaux et al. 2016). Using these reanalyses as boundary conditions, it is possible to produce ocean model estimates of the historical sea level response to past atmospheric variability (e.g., Chepurin et al. 2014). In this paper, we take advantage of these advances in atmospheric reanalysis, exploring the influence of the ocean's barotropic response to wind stress and isostatic adjustment to air pressure on historical coastal sea level changes on timescales from bimonthly to multidecadal. To this end, we compare monthly observations of coastal mean relative sea level from a quasi-global network of tide gauges to sea level simulated by a set of homogeneous ocean general circulation model solutions forced by reanalysis surface air pressure and wind stress fields over 1900–2010. We address the following questions:

1. How consistent are barotropic model estimates of sea level variation related to wind and pressure (e.g., forced by different atmospheric reanalyses)?

2. How much coastal sea level data variance is explained by barotropic model estimates of the sea level response to variable wind and pressure forcing?
3. How do answers to these questions depend on space and time?

This paper is an outcome of the International Space Science Institute (ISSI) Workshop on, "Understanding the Relationship between Coastal Sea Level and Large-Scale Ocean Circulation," held on 5–9 March 2018 in Bern, Switzerland. Our work addresses the Workshop's goals of identifying the processes driving coastal sea level changes, describing the space-time structure of sea level variation near the coast, and evaluating the ability of models to simulate coastal sea level changes in historical records. This effort furthers earlier studies by Ponte (1994) and Greatbatch et al. (1996) on the sea level response over an ocean basin from short simulations (1–2 year) of barotropic ocean general circulation models driven by surface wind and pressure forcing. This paper also complements past studies of air pressure effects on sea level changes over the global ocean (e.g., Ponte 1992, 1993, 2006; Wunsch and Stammer 1997; Stammer and Hüttemann 2008; Piecuch et al. 2016b), assessments of the skill of barotropic models in reproducing sea level data along particular coastlines and marginal seas (e.g., Tsimplis et al. 2005; Gomis et al. 2006, 2008; Marcos and Tsimplis 2007, 2008; Pascual et al. 2008; Jordà et al. 2012b; Calafat et al. 2014b; Piecuch and Ponte 2015b; Piecuch et al. 2016a), as well as focused investigations elucidating wind- or pressure-driven mechanisms underlying sea level changes at particular tide gauge stations (e.g., Woodworth et al. 2010; Sturges and Douglas 2011; Calafat et al. 2012, 2013; Richter et al. 2012; Andres et al. 2013; Woodworth et al. 2014; Thompson and Mitchum 2014; Piecuch and Ponte 2015a).

The remainder of this manuscript is structured as follows: in Sect. 2, we introduce the tide gauge data and barotropic model solutions to be analyzed; in Sect. 3, we present the main results, with a focus on the spatiotemporal structure of coastal sea level variation observed by tide gauges, the consistency of barotropic ocean model solutions, and the ability of the models to reproduce the observations; in Sect. 4, we summarize and discuss our results, and draw out broader implications.

2 Methods

2.1 Tide Gauge Records

To investigate coastal sea level variation, we use monthly revised local reference (RLR) tide gauge data provided by the Permanent Service for Mean Sea Level (PSMSL) database (Holgate et al. 2013; PSMSL 2018). These records, which represent sea level observations made relative to Earth's crust, were extracted from the PSMSL RLR database on 5 March 2018. To focus on variation on long periods, we use records spanning ≥ 50 years and returning ≥ 40 years of valid sea level data during 1900–2010, ignoring missing values and values flagged for quality concerns. This time period corresponds to the common duration of the barotropic model experiments described below. We do not consider tide gauges from a few marginal seas (e.g., Baltic Sea, Black Sea) that are not represented by the barotropic models (see below). After applying these criteria to the PSMSL RLR database, we are left with 219 tide gauge records constituting 14,722 gauge-years of data, corresponding to an average of ~ 67 years of data per tide gauge. These data are unevenly distributed in space and time: 78% of tide gauge measurements were taken after 1950, and 45% were made after 1975 (Fig. 1); 91% of the tide gauges are stationed in the Northern Hemisphere, and 55% are situated along the coast of North America or Europe (e.g., Fig. 2).

We apply minimal adjustments to the data. Time means, longterm trends, seasonal cycles, and extreme events are not considered. Rather, our focus is on nonseasonal fluctuations in mean sea level. So, we remove simultaneous least squares fits of time means, linear trends plus annual and semi-annual harmonics to the available monthly data from the tide gauge time series over their respective record lengths. Because sea level signals driven by air pressure variations are of interest, we do not make the standard inverted barometer correction (Wunsch and Stammer 1997; Ponte 2006).

2.2 Numerical Model Solutions

To interpret the data, we use monthly sea surface height from three barotropic ocean circulation models. These models solve discretized versions of the depth-averaged nonlinear shallow water equations for a constant-density global ocean forced by surface wind stress and air pressure. The solutions can differ in terms of model framework, horizontal resolution, or atmospheric reanalysis used for the surface wind and pressure forcing fields, among other details (see below).

Given their structure (single level, constant density, static bathymetry, etc.), the models simulate the barotropic (or external) mode of sea surface height variability related to wind

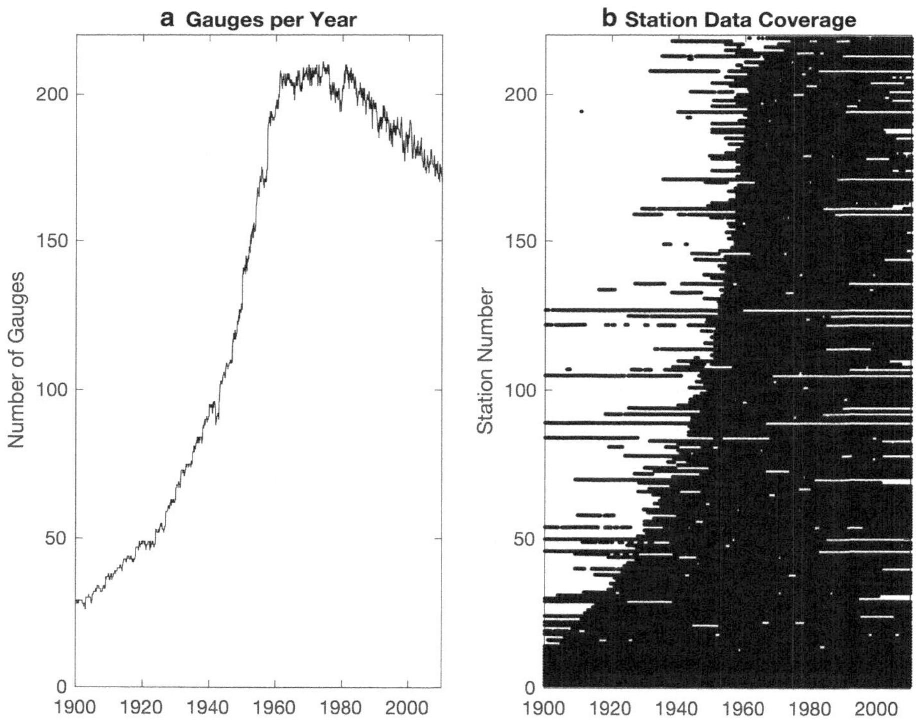

Fig. 1 **a** Histogram counting the number of tide gauges in the dataset used here returning monthly data values versus time. **b** Timeline of data availability. Dots indicate times during which any of the 219 tide gauge stations returned valid monthly data

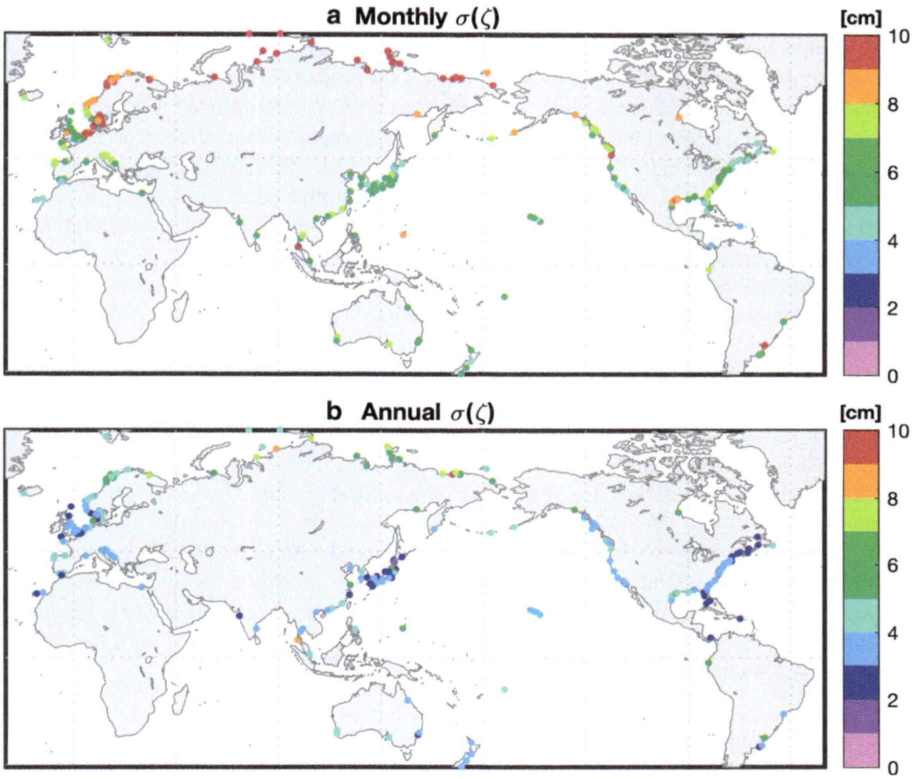

Fig. 2 **a** Standard deviation σ values computed from available monthly tide gauge ζ records (with seasonal cycles and linear trends removed) over 1900–2010. **b** As in **a** but values are based on annual ζ time series

and pressure over a finite areal extent. Differences between models and data can result from vertical land motion, stratification effects, unresolved local processes, the spatial separation between the tide gauge station and the model grid cell (see below), or other forcing mechanisms (e.g., surface heat or freshwater exchanges), which are not represented in the models but can impact the data, in addition to any model or data errors.

To match the model solutions to the data record for a given tide gauge, we choose the simulated sea level time series from the model grid cell whose centroid is closest to that particular tide gauge. As with the sea level data, we use least squares to remove time means, linear trends, and seasonal cycles from the model solutions. For comparisons between models and data described in Sect. 3.3, we impart gaps into the model sea level series as with the respective tide gauge data and remove time means, linear trends, and seasonal cycles estimated only using the remaining model "data" points.

2.2.1 Low-Resolution Solutions

The first two models are produced by nearly identical configurations of the Massachusetts Institute of Technology general circulation model (Marshall et al. 1997). The model is described in Piecuch et al. (2016a) and our description follows theirs. The model grid has a nominal horizontal resolution of 1° and is based on the "longitude latitude cap 90" (LLC90) topology and bathymetry from the version 4 ocean state estimate of the Estimating the Circulation and Climate of the Ocean (ECCO) project (Forget et al. 2015). A single vertical level is used, and partial cells (Adcroft et al. 1997) are employed to represent variable bathymetry. We select a linear free surface and represent bottom friction as a quadratic drag term. Along the bottom and sides, we implement no-slip boundary conditions. The vertical eddy viscosity is 1×10^{-3} m^2 s^{-1}, and the horizontal eddy viscosity is a variable function of grid cell area. We use time steps of 900 s and 3600 s for the momentum equations and free surface condition, respectively.

The difference between the two models is that distinct atmospheric reanalyses are used for the surface boundary conditions. The first solution is driven by monthly fields from the National Oceanic and Atmospheric Administration (NOAA) twentieth-century Reanalysis Version 2 (20CR; Compo et al. 2011), which is based on an ensemble Kalman filter and covers 1871–2012 with a 2° horizontal grid spacing. The second solution is forced by monthly wind stress and surface pressure from the European Centre for Medium-Range Weather Forecasts (ECMWF) Atmospheric Reanalysis of the twentieth century (ERA 20C; Poli et al. 2013), which makes use of 4DVAR data assimilation and covers 1900–2010 with a horizontal resolution of $\sim$ 125 km. These model runs are substantially longer than the solution studied by Piecuch et al. (2016a), which is forced with ECMWF ERA-Interim reanalysis fields that span from 1979 to present. Both models are started from rest. We choose a 5-year spin-up period, during which time the model is forced with mean years in surface pressure and wind stress. After spinning up, the model oceans are forced with the respective monthly reanalysis fields.

2.2.2 High-Resolution Solution

In addition to the two lower-resolution models described above, we also consider a higher-resolution barotropic model. This simulation is based on the numerical model T-UGOm, which represents ocean dynamics on a series of unstructured meshes. T-UGOm is an evolution of the well known MOG2D model (Carrère and Lyard 2003), which has been extensively used to model storm surges and tides at regional and global scale. Here, we use a very similar configuration to what is used to de-alias satellite altimetry data (e.g., Pascual et al. 2008). The model is run in a 2D configuration using a finite element triangular grid with 248,427 nodes. The spatial resolution ranges from $\sim$ 1 km in complex coastal areas to $\sim$ 100 km in open ocean regions, and the model uses a semi-implicit numerical scheme combined with a sub-step time process that makes it possible to maintain a larger time step for most calculations. Bottom friction is parameterized by a quadratic law and dissipation is introduced to take into account the barotropic-to-baroclinic energy transfer by means of internal wave generation over topography. The model is forced by 6-hourly wind stress and sea level pressure field from NOAA 20CR.

2.3 Some Clarifications, including on Terminology and Notation

For simplicity, we refer to the physical quantity measured by tide gauges and the state variable simulated by the numerical models both as "sea level." To be precise, the tide gauges measure sea level relative to a point on land, whereas the models simulate the height of the sea surface. As noted earlier, differences between the two are rendered by vertical land motion. Here, given the timescales of interest, we ignore crustal motions, and regard relative sea level and sea surface height as equivalent. While the influence of vertical land motion should be substantially reduced by the removal of linear trends, we acknowledge that nonlinear crustal motion effects will not always be negligible over the timescales of interest and could contribute to variability in the tide gauge records (e.g., Featherstone et al. 2015; Karegar et al. 2016; Frederikse et al. 2017).

Also, rather than repeatedly write precise but cumbersome phrases such as "sea level from the low-resolution barotropic model forced by NOAA reanalysis fields," we use mathematical symbols to indicate quantities of interest. We use ζ to denote sea level from a tide gauge. To distinguish model solutions from observational data, we use η to signify sea level from the barotropic model solutions. Subscripts differentiate the model solutions: η_E, η_N, and η_H, respectively, connote sea level from the low-resolution ERA-forced, low-resolution NOAA-forced, and high-resolution NOAA-forced barotropic model estimates. An overbar indicates the ensemble mean of model solutions,

$$\overline{\eta} \doteq \frac{1}{3} \sum_{A \in \{H,N,E\}} \eta_A . \tag{1}$$

Other commonly used symbols are also defined over the course of the paper. A complete listing is given in Table 1.

Finally, a clarification regarding interpretation of our results. At several points in the paper, for economy, we make summary statements, invoking percentages with reference to data locations, along the formulaic lines of, "*abc* is observed at *xyz*% of tide gauge stations." Given the spatially heterogeneous distribution of the data (e.g., Fig. 2), such statements are specific to the particular set of tide gauges considered here, and should not be conflated with truly representative spatial statistics. For example, the preceding toy sentence is not equivalent to the statement, "*abc* is observed at *xyz*% of coastal locations worldwide."

3 Results

3.1 Spatiotemporal Structure of ζ Variability

To establish basic patterns of ζ variability, Fig. 2a shows a global map of standard deviations (σ) computed from monthly tide gauge ζ records. Large-scale spatial structure is apparent, and magnitudes of ζ variability increase with latitude. For example, whereas 75% of monthly σ values between 0° and 30° latitude are $\lesssim 7$ cm, 75% of monthly σ values between 60° and 90° are $\gtrsim 9$ cm. This meridional dependence is clearly illustrated in Fig. 3a, which shows monthly σ versus latitude. Some of the lowest σ values (< 4 cm) are observed in the Caribbean Sea (e.g., Cristóbal, Isla Magueyes), while some of the highest (> 14 cm) are seen in the North Sea (e.g., Esbjerg, Delfzijl). Superimposed on this overarching meridional structure are more subtle regional and local details. On the US east coast, σ values are higher on the South Atlantic Bight (~ 7 cm) than on the Middle Atlantic Bight or Gulf of Maine (~ 5 cm), even though the latter regions are poleward of the former. These features could indicate that ζ in these different regions is controlled by distinct physical processes. Despite their tropical or subtropical locations, tide gauges at Koh Tapao Noi (Thailand) and Montevideo (Uruguay) register monthly σ values in excess of 10 cm, which is much larger than would be expected based solely on their latitude, perhaps indicative of more localized processes (e.g., related to a broad continental shelf).

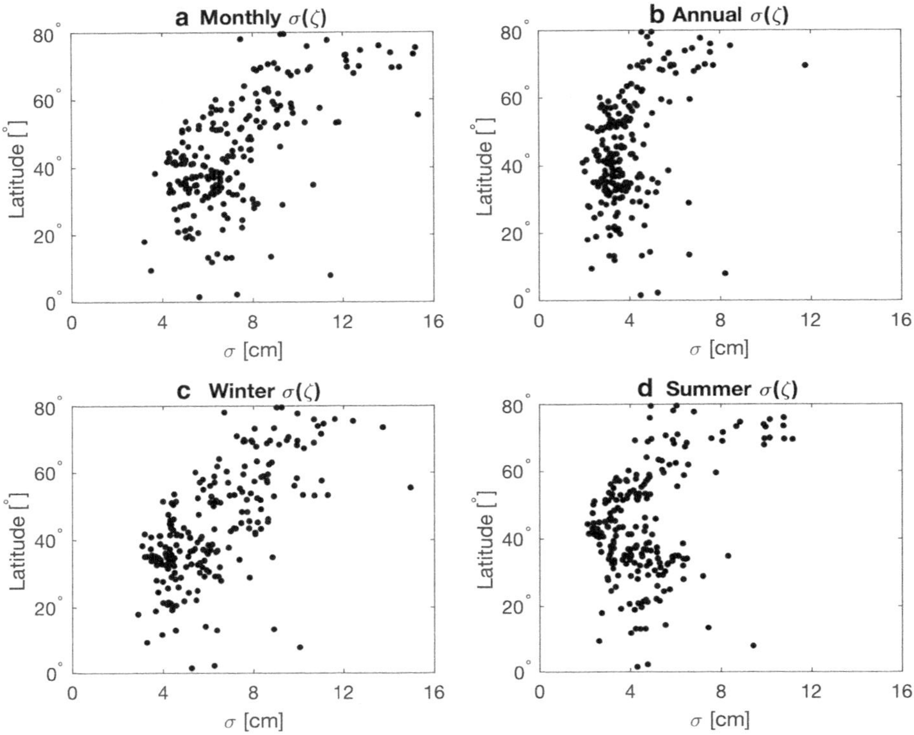

Fig. 3 Scatterplots of σ versus the absolute value of latitude of the corresponding tide gauge station, shown for **a** monthly, **b** annual, **c** wintertime, and **d** summertime ζ records

A rough sense of timescale dependence can be inferred by comparing monthly σ in Fig. 2a to σ computed from annually averaged ζ records in Fig. 2b (cf. Fig. 3a, b). In cases where most of the energy in the data is concentrated at intraseasonal periods, monthly σ values will be larger than the corresponding annual values, whereas monthly and annual σ will be more comparable in cases where ζ time series are dominated by interannual and decadal fluctuations or processes with longterm memory (e.g., Bos et al. 2014; Dangendorf et al. 2015; Royston et al. 2018). For about half (56%) of study locations, monthly σ values are 50–100% larger than the colocated annual σ values. Examples are found mainly on subtropical and midlatitude shorelines facing the open ocean, such as the east and west coasts of North America, the coast of Spain and northwest Africa, northern Norway, and the Japan coast. For roughly one-third (32%) of tide gauge stations, differences between monthly and annual σ values are starker, and monthly values are more than twice as large as corresponding annual values. Such instances are usually seen on broad shelves or in marginal seas, including the Italy and Croatia coasts on the Adriatic Sea, or the coasts of Denmark, UK, and the Netherlands on the North Sea. For the remaining approximately one-tenth (12%) of study sites, variations in monthly and annual time series are more similar, and monthly σ values are no more than 50% larger than annual values. Examples are mostly found at low latitudes or oceanic islands, including Hawaii, Guam, American Samoa, Ecuador, and the Philippines.

Partitioning the data by season sheds more light on the spacetime structure of ζ variability. Figure 4a shows a map of σ from boreal-wintertime (January, February, March) averages of the ζ records, whereas Fig. 4b shows σ based on boreal-summertime (July, August, September) averages (cf. Fig. 3c, d). Since most tide gauges are located in the Northern Hemisphere, we drop the understood prefix "boreal" with reference to winter and summer. Depending on latitude, there can be strong differences between amplitudes of winter-to-winter and summer-to-summer variability. At tropical and subtropical latitudes, winter-to-winter and summer-to-summer magnitudes are comparable to one another ($\sigma \sim 5$ cm on average). At midlatitudes, however, ζ fluctuations from one winter to the next are generally about twice as large as variations in ζ between summers. As such, latitude dependence of σ (increasing values from the equator to the poles) is more pronounced for winter-to-winter variability (Fig. 3c, d). Differences between winter-to-winter and summer-to-summer σ are strongest along the coasts of Europe and North America. The comparatively higher ζ variability observed at midlatitudes from one winter to the next could reflect fluctuations in extratropical wintertime storminess (e.g., Thompson et al. 2013; Dangendorf et al. 2014b).

To confer a more concrete sense of the nature of coastal ζ variability, and illustrate some of the basic data features discussed above, Fig. 5 shows monthly and annual ζ time series from four tide gauges at different latitudes: IJmuiden (52.5°N), New York City (40.7°N), Honolulu (21.3°N), and Cristóbal (9.35°N). These four data records are shown as particular

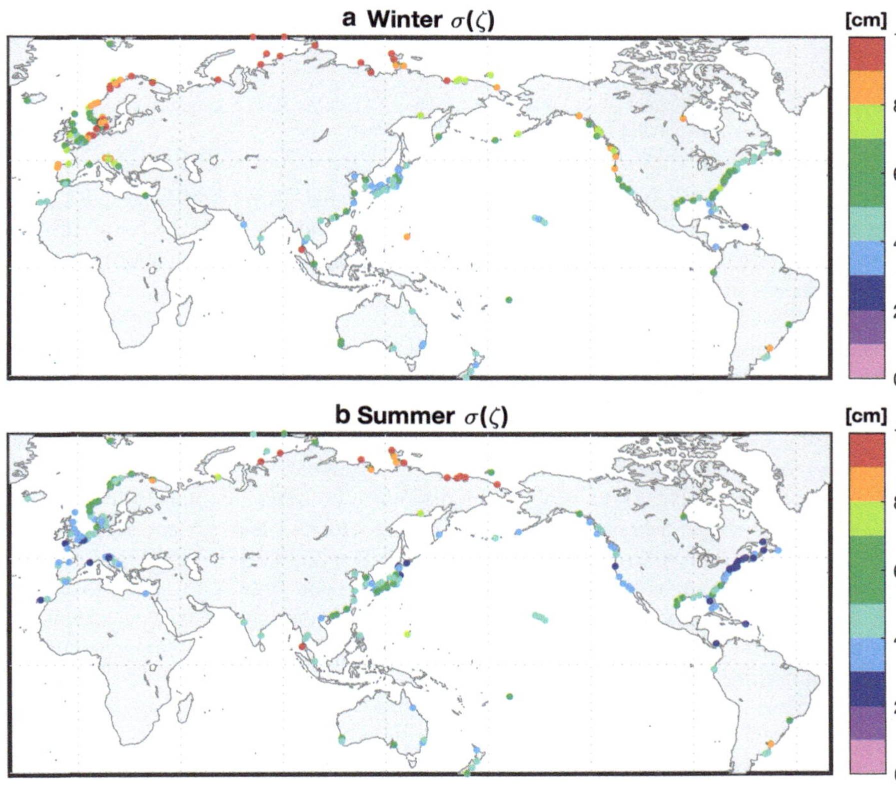

Fig. 4 Maps of σ as in Fig. 2 but based on **a** wintertime and **b** summertime averages of ζ records

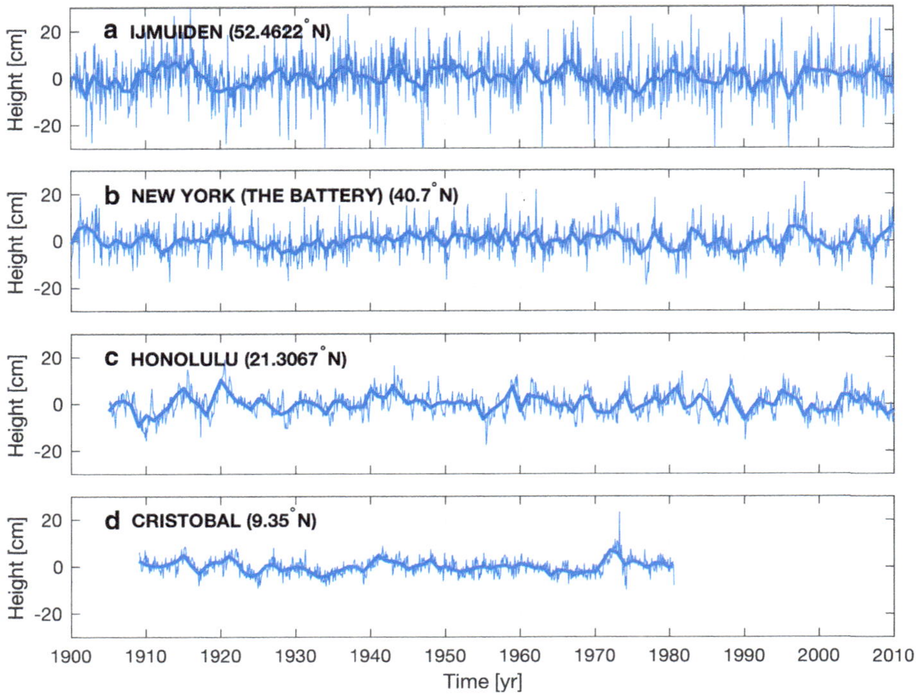

Fig. 5 Monthly (thin) and annual (thick) tide gauge sea level ζ records from **a** IJmuiden (Netherlands), **b** New York City (USA), **c** Honolulu (USA), and **d** Cristóbal (Panama)

instances that exemplify more general behavior at tide gauges from similar latitudes. Clear from visual inspection of the panels is the latitudinal dependence of ζ variability: the time series from lower latitudes (Honolulu, Cristóbal) have comparatively smaller σ, whereas the data records from higher latitudes (New York City, IJmuiden) show relatively larger σ values. This overall increase in σ with latitude is more apparent in the monthly data, and the annual ζ time series from these four locations exhibit variations that are more comparable to one another in magnitude (cf. Fig. 3a, b).

Considering the data from Cristóbal (Fig. 5d), we observe that monthly ζ fluctuations are superimposed on clear interannual and decadal undulations. Correspondingly, values of σ from monthly and annual averages from this tide gauge record are grossly similar (3.5 and 2.3 cm, respectively). There is not much difference between σ computed from wintertime- and summertime-averaged values from this record (3.3 and 2.6 cm, respectively). Analogous conclusions follow from inspection of the Honolulu tide gauge (Fig. 5c). These findings are consistent with our earlier reasoning based on Figs. 2, 3 and 4 that, for a typical tide gauge at low latitude or an oceanic island, σ computed from ζ records is less dependent on time averaging (monthly versus annual) or seasonal partitioning (wintertime versus summertime) of the data.

In contrast is the ζ record from IJmuiden (Fig. 5a). While lower-frequency decadal variations are present in this time series, similar to Cristóbal and Honolulu, they are masked by pronounced higher-frequency intraseasonal fluctuations. Consequently, monthly and annual averages of this time series yield very different σ values (9.1 and 3.6 cm, respectively). There are also sharp distinctions between σ from winter- and summer-averaged data (8.2 and 4.4 cm, respectively). Similar findings emerge from study of the tide gauge data in New York City (Fig. 5b). These results agree with more general conclusions drawn from the broad patterns in Figs. 2, 3 and 4 that, for a midlatitude tide gauge, σ values are relatively larger for monthly and wintertime records compared to annual and summertime ζ data.

In the sections that follow, we quantify to what extent these spacetime features in the tide gauge records can be understood in terms of a homogeneous ocean response to wind and pressure forcing.

3.2 Barotropic Ocean Model Consistency

Having established basic patterns of observed ζ variability, we now consider the model η solutions. Before comparing models to data, we evaluate the consistency between model η estimates. Recall that the models can have important differences, including horizontal resolution and forcing dataset. Let each model series $\eta_A(t)$, where $A \in \{H, N, E\}$, be represented as the sum of the common model signal $\overline{\eta}(t)$ plus a model-specific deviation $\eta'_A(t)$, *viz.*,

$$\eta_A(t) = \overline{\eta}(t) + \eta'_A(t). \tag{2}$$

Similarly to Ponte and Dorandeu (2003) and Piecuch et al. (2016b) we define

$$\begin{aligned} \mu &\doteq \sqrt{\frac{1}{3} \sum_{A\in\{H,N,E\}} \text{var}\left(\eta_A\right)}, \\ &\equiv \sqrt{\text{var}\left(\overline{\eta}\right) + \frac{1}{3} \sum_{A\in\{H,N,E\}} \text{var}\left(\eta'_A\right)}, \end{aligned} \tag{3}$$

and

$$\begin{aligned} \delta &\doteq \sqrt{\frac{1}{12} \sum_{A\in\{H,N,E\}} \sum_{B\neq A} \text{var}\left(\eta_A - \eta_B\right)}, \\ &\equiv \sqrt{\frac{1}{3} \sum_{A\in\{H,N,E\}} \text{var}\left(\eta'_A\right) - \frac{1}{6} \sum_{A\in\{H,N,E\}} \sum_{B\neq A} \text{cov}\left(\eta'_A, \eta'_B\right)}, \end{aligned} \tag{4}$$

where var and cov are variance and covariance, respectively. Given these definitions, μ is the root average variance of the model solutions, whereas δ is the root average variance of differences between model solutions. That is, μ is a measure of the average variability across models, whereas δ reflects the spread between models; while μ quantifies how much the models agree and generate similar variability, δ quantifies how much they disagree and generate dissimilar variability. To the extent that the common signal variance [the left term under the square root in Eq. (3)] is large relative to the mean deviation variance [right summand under the square root in (3)], μ will approximate to the standard deviation σ of the model average series $\overline{\eta}$. To the degree that covariance between model deviations [the right summand under the square root in Eq. (4)] is relatively small, δ will tend toward the root mean deviation variance.

To provide a rough sense of variability typical of the models, Fig. 6a shows a global map of μ based on monthly η at tide gauge stations. Similar to the monthly tide gauge ζ data (Fig. 2a), monthly model η solutions feature clear meridional structure, with average μ values growing from ~ 1 cm at low latitudes (0–30°) to ~ 7 cm at high latitudes (60–90°). Indeed, the spatial correlation coefficient between σ and μ values in Figs. 2a and 6a is ~ 0.8. Nearly identical μ patterns are found from consideration of annually averaged model output, albeit with reduced amplitudes compared to the monthly magnitudes (not shown). Stronger magnitudes of barotropic adjustment to atmospheric variation are generally expected at higher latitudes, given the overall increase in atmospheric variability from equator to poles (e.g., Ponte 1994, 2006). Particularly elevated monthly μ values (> 10 cm) are found over some broad mid- and high-latitude coastal seas (e.g., North, Laptev, and East Siberian Seas). In these regions, wind forcing is distributed over a relatively shallow water column, which leads to a more intense oceanic response, due to the inverse depth dependence of the wind forcing term in the shallow water momentum equations (e.g., Csanady 1982; Gill 1982).

Figure 6b shows a global map of δ computed from monthly η, providing a measure of uncertainty. There is a strong correspondence between μ and δ values in Fig. 6a, b (correlation coefficient between the two panels is ~ 1). That is, regions with stronger common

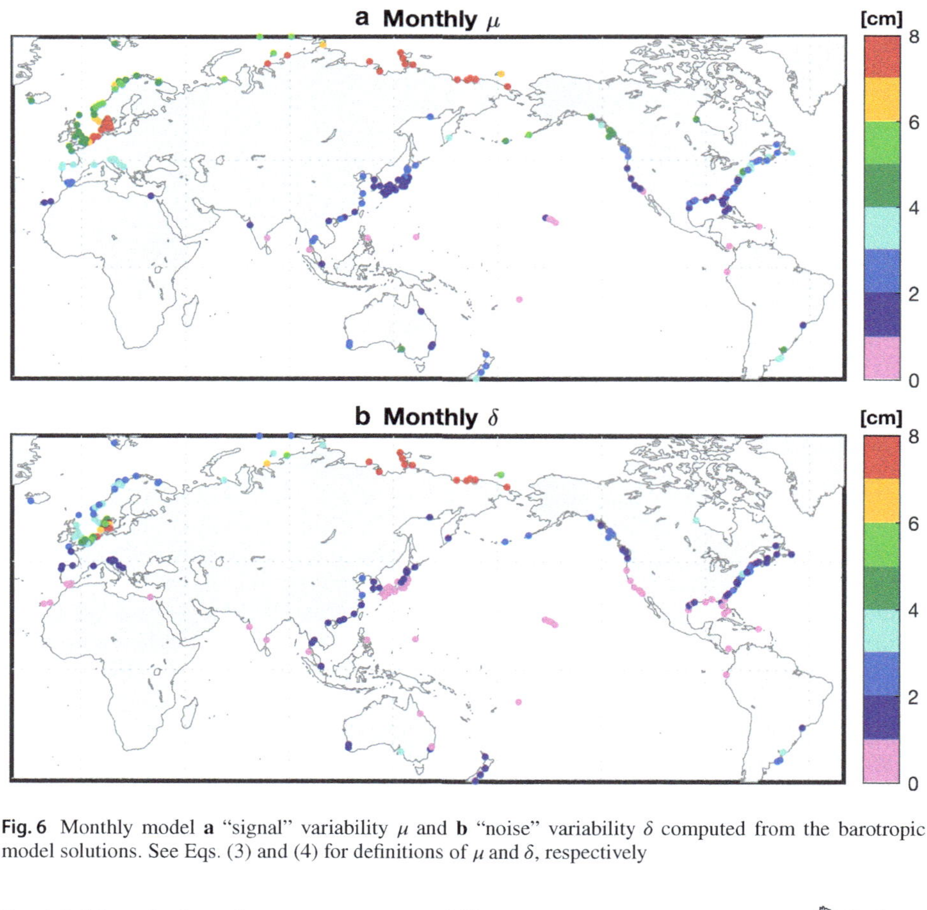

Fig. 6 Monthly model **a** "signal" variability μ and **b** "noise" variability δ computed from the barotropic model solutions. See Eqs. (3) and (4) for definitions of μ and δ, respectively

model variability also show elevated differences between models in absolute terms. For example, model differences grow larger with increasing latitude and are more pronounced over broad shallow shelf seas (Fig. 6b). Simple models of the barotropic coastal ocean response to wind forcing (e.g., through storm surge or wind setup mechanisms) represent η as proportional to the forcing but also as dependent on the details of bathymetry and representation of bottom friction (e.g., Sandstrom 1980). Thus, model differences in Fig. 6b could relate to distinctions in the surface forcing or the representation of the oceanic response to a given forcing.

To quantify the relative roles of different model representation (e.g., resolution) and surface forcing (i.e., reanalysis) choices in contributing to the uncertainties in Fig. 6b, Fig. 7a shows the ratio

$$\rho \doteq \frac{\sigma(\eta_N - \eta_H)}{\sigma(\eta_N - \eta_E)} \tag{5}$$

computed from monthly model output. Since η_H and η_N share common surface forcing fields (NOAA), but are produced by distinct models, the numerator represents differences related to model configuration. In what follows, our interpretations reflect the assumption

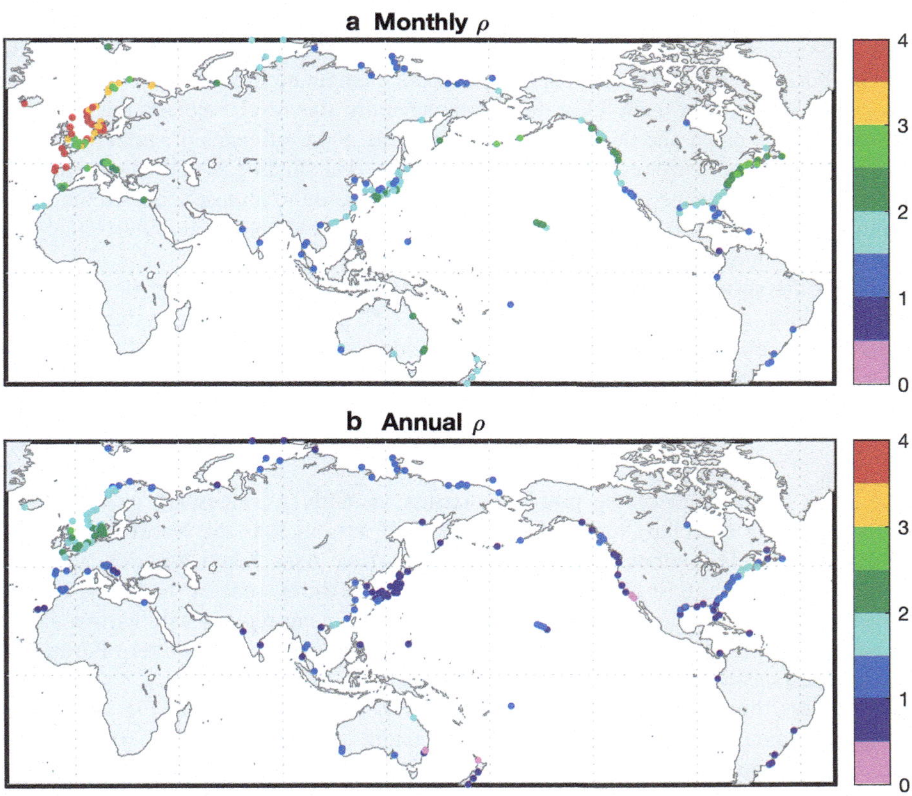

Fig. 7 **a** Monthly ratio ρ quantifying uncertainty due to model configuration relative to surface forcing. **b** As in **a** but for annual values. See Eq. (5) for definition of ρ

that the most important difference between model configurations is horizontal resolution, but we acknowledge that other details (e.g., parameterization of friction and dissipation, temporal resolution of surface forcing) could also be important. Because η_E and η_N are produced by the same barotropic model setup, but are generated using different reanalyses (NOAA versus ERA), the denominator corresponds to model differences related to discrepancies in surface boundary conditions. Thus, ρ values $\gg 1$ ($\ll 1$) indicate that differences between η solutions are dominated by model configuration (surface forcing) choices, whereas $\rho \sim 1$ signifies that model configuration and surface forcing contribute comparably to differences in η solutions.

Almost universally, monthly ρ values are > 1, indicating that differences in monthly η are controlled more by differences in model configuration than surface forcing. The highest ρ values ($\sim$ 3–4) occur on the coast of northwestern Europe, suggesting the sensitivity of model solutions to the prescribed details of bathymetry over broad shallow shelf regions. Elsewhere, notably at tropical latitudes and islands in the open ocean, monthly ρ values are ~ 1, meaning that model configuration and surface forcing choices contribute comparably to simulated η differences.

The relative roles of model configuration and surface forcing in contributing to differences in η estimates also depend on timescale. Figure 7b shows a map of ρ values based on annual η. While ρ spatial patterns shown in Fig. 7a, b are similar (correlation coefficient between panels is ~ 0.7), and the highest values are again seen over the northwest Europe shelf, ρ magnitudes in Fig. 7b are less than half as large as those in Fig. 7a on average. In fact, at 38% of tide gauges, annual ρ values are < 1, suggesting that the selection of surface forcing dataset can be more influential than model configuration choices in contributing to model η uncertainty at many locations. More generally, this result suggests that, for simulations of interannual and decadal variability, having good estimates of surface forcing is as important as properly representing ocean physics. This finding is consistent with basic theory: moving to longer time scales, the oceanic response to atmospheric forcing can be typified by larger spatial scales (e.g., Philander 1978; Willebrand et al. 1980), suggesting that fine resolution might be less crucial at low frequencies.

Given the strong correlation between global μ and δ patterns shown in Fig. 6, it is informative to consider their relative amplitudes. To determine where η simulations are more or less consistent, Fig. 8a shows a map based on monthly η solutions of the signal-to-noise ratio, which we define as

$$\Sigma \doteq \frac{\mu}{\delta}. \tag{6}$$

Interesting in the light of the preceding results, monthly Σ values are independent of latitude and not especially high over shallow shelf seas such as the North Sea and East Siberian Sea. Indeed, along with the southeast coasts of Asia, South America, and North America, the North, East Siberian, and Chukchi Seas exhibit some of the lowest monthly Σ values anywhere. In contrast, higher Σ values occur along regions with narrow shelves or adjacent to deep basins, such as western Canada, northern Norway, western Europe, and the Mediterranean Sea.

To assess timescale dependence, we consider Σ based on annual η (Fig. 8b). Spatial patterns of annual Σ are broadly similar to monthly values (cf. Fig. 8a, b). For example, higher annual Σ values are seen along western Canada, northern Norway, western Europe, and the Mediterranean, whereas lower annual Σ is observed along the North, East Siberian, and Chukchi Seas and southeastern Asia, South America, and North America

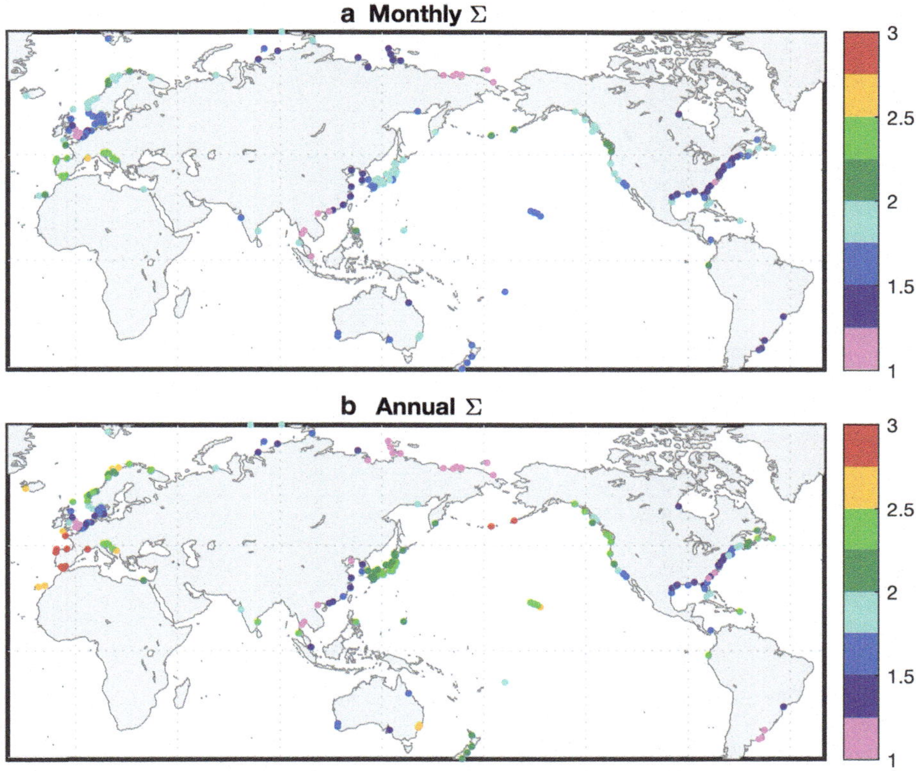

Fig. 8 Model signal-to-noise ratio Σ computed for **a** monthly and **b** annual values. See Eq. (6) in the text for the definition of Σ

(Fig. 8b). Interestingly, while their spatial structures are similar, annual Σ values are larger than monthly Σ at a majority (74%) of tide gauge locations, suggesting that year-to-year variations in the barotropic ocean response are more consistent than month-to-month fluctuations.

To allow a more detailed look at the consistency between models at a couple example locations, Fig. 9 shows η solutions and their differences at Ketchikan (55.3°N) and Auckland (36.8°S). Monthly time series are shown at the former location and annual time series at the latter to confer a sense of the dependence of the results on timescale.

At Ketchikan, monthly η time series consistently portray pronounced wintertime fluctuations on the order of ±10 cm (Fig. 9a). Correlation coefficients between estimates (0.6–0.9) are highly significant ($p < 0.01$). These results are reflected in a relatively high Σ value (1.8) at this site. Despite the similarities, there are discrepancies between solutions that are illustrated by the difference time series $\eta_N - \eta_H$ and $\eta_N - \eta_E$ in Fig. 9b. Fluctuations in $\eta_N - \eta_H$ are roughly twice as large as $\eta_N - \eta_E$ variations, meaning that monthly model simulations at Ketchikan are more sensitive to model configuration choices (e.g., horizontal resolution) than alternative choices of surface forcing. This exemplifies our general conclusion that monthly model η uncertainty is controlled more by the details of model configuration than selection of surface forcing dataset.

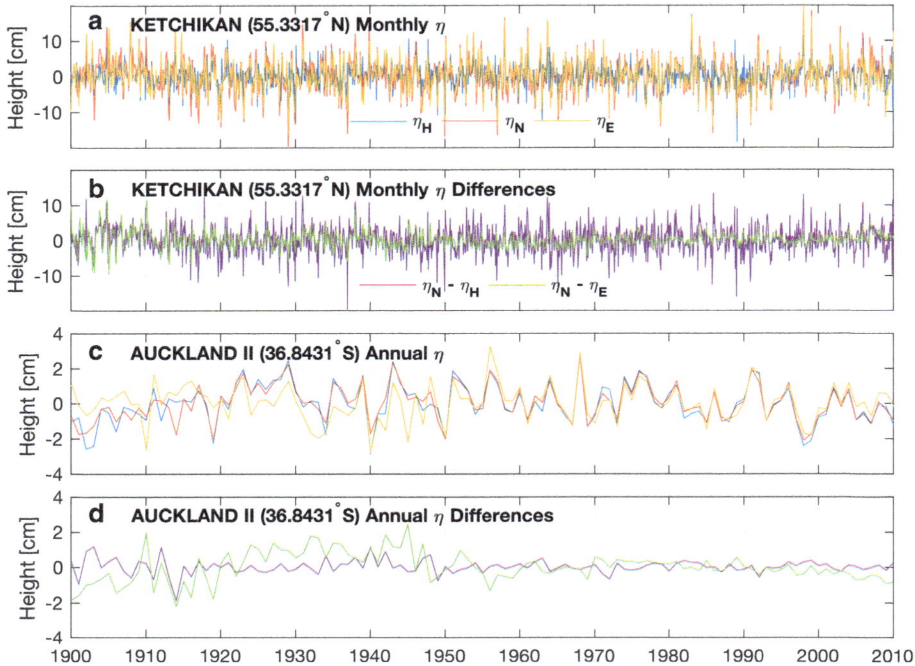

Fig. 9 **a** Monthly time series of barotropic model estimates η_H (blue), η_N (orange), and η_E (yellow) from Ketchikan (USA). **b** Monthly time series of differences $\eta_N - \eta_H$ (purple) and $\eta_N - \eta_E$ (green) at Ketchikan. **c** Annual time series of barotropic model estimates η_H, η_N, and η_E from Auckland (Australia). **d** Annual time series of differences $\eta_N - \eta_H$ and $\eta_N - \eta_E$ at Auckland

Annual model η solutions at Auckland also show strong similarities (Fig. 9c). The η time series depict similarly strong interannual variations, with amplitudes at times exceeding ± 2 cm. The annual signal-to-noise ratio Σ is comparatively high (2.1), reflecting the statistically significant correlation coefficients between η estimates (0.7–0.9; $p < 0.01$). Also apparent upon inspection of Fig. 9c are disagreements between model simulations, which are made clearer by the time series of differences between solutions shown in Fig. 9d. Differences between annual η_N and η_E are about twice as big as between η_N and η_H (Fig. 9d), revealing that different surface forcing choices contribute more than model configuration choices to uncertainties in annual η at this location. This result for Auckland accords with our more general argument made earlier that, for annual η, having good estimates of surface forcing fields and properly representing model physics are equally important.

An interesting feature of the models at Ketchikan and Auckland is that the $\eta_N - \eta_E$ time series are heteroscedastic, and $\eta_N - \eta_E$ fluctuations become larger going back in time; elevated variability is evident at Ketchikan for years before $\sim$ 1920 and at Auckland prior to $\sim$ 1950 (Fig. 9). This could suggest that reanalyses are more uncertain for earlier times. To investigate this systematically, Fig. 10a, b shows monthly Σ computed for times before and after 1950, respectively. Values computed for the two periods are similar (correlation coefficient between Fig. 10a, b is $\sim$ 0.9). While drastic differences between values computed before and after midcentury are not obvious, Σ computed for 1951–2010 is consistently greater (at 78% of tide gauges) than Σ calculated for 1900–1950 (median difference of

Table 1 Description of symbols used in the text

Symbol	Description
ζ	Tide gauge sea level
η	Barotropic model sea level
η_{ib}	Isostatic (inverted barometer) sea level response to barometric pressure [cf. Eq. (9)]
η_E	Sea level from coarse-resolution barotropic model forced by ERA 20C reanalysis
η_N	Sea level from coarse-resolution barotropic model forced by NOAA 20CR reanalysis
η_H	Sea level from high-resolution barotropic model forced by NOAA 20CR reanalysis
$\overline{\eta}$	Ensemble average of barotropic model sea level solutions [cf. Eq. (1)]
$'$	Model deviation from ensemble average [cf. Eq. (2)]
σ	Standard deviation
μ	Model signal variance [cf. Eq. (3)]
δ	Model noise variance [cf. Eq. (4)]
ρ	Model standard deviation ratio $\doteq \sigma(\eta_N - \eta_H)/\sigma(\eta_N - \eta_E)$ [cf. Eq. (5)]
Σ	Model signal-to-noise ratio $\doteq \mu/\delta$ [cf. Eq. (6)]
$\mathcal{V}$	Percentage variance explained [cf. Eq. (7)]
G_{xy}	One-sided cross-spectral density between x and y
H_{xy}	Admittance (transfer function) between x and y
var	Variance
cov	Covariance

~ 0.1). This demonstrates that model solutions are more uncertain at earlier times, consistent with there being fewer historical observations available to constrain atmospheric reanalyses earlier in time (Krueger et al. 2013).

3.3 Comparison Between Data and Models

Having quantified the consistency between models as a function of space and time, we now compare models to data, determining to what extent observed ζ variation can be understood in terms of simulated η behavior. Figure 11a shows a global map of the percent variance $\mathcal{V}$ in monthly ζ explained by the ensemble mean solution $\overline{\eta}$, where following Fukumori et al. (2015) we define

$$\mathcal{V} \doteq 100\% \times \left[1 - \frac{\text{var}(\zeta - \overline{\eta})}{\text{var}(\zeta)}\right]. \tag{7}$$

As defined in Eq. (7), $\mathcal{V}$ is a measure of agreement between ζ and $\overline{\eta}$ that depends on amplitude and phase. Values $\mathcal{V} \sim 1$ occur when the two time series agree in both amplitude and phase, whereas values $\mathcal{V} < 0$ occur if ζ and $\overline{\eta}$ are out of phase or if the magnitude of the latter is much greater than the former. Unless otherwise indicated, all model-data comparisons in this section are performed using the ensemble average of model solutions $\overline{\eta}$. Note that $\mathcal{V}$ is not synonymous with the coefficient of determination from simple linear regression. For more details on $\mathcal{V}$ and its properties, the interested reader is referred to Appendix A of Fukumori et al. (2015).

Model $\overline{\eta}$ explains more monthly ζ variance at higher latitudes (Figs. 11a, 12a). For example, for 95% of tide gauge stations equatorward of 30° latitude, $\overline{\eta}$ explains $\lesssim 20\%$ of

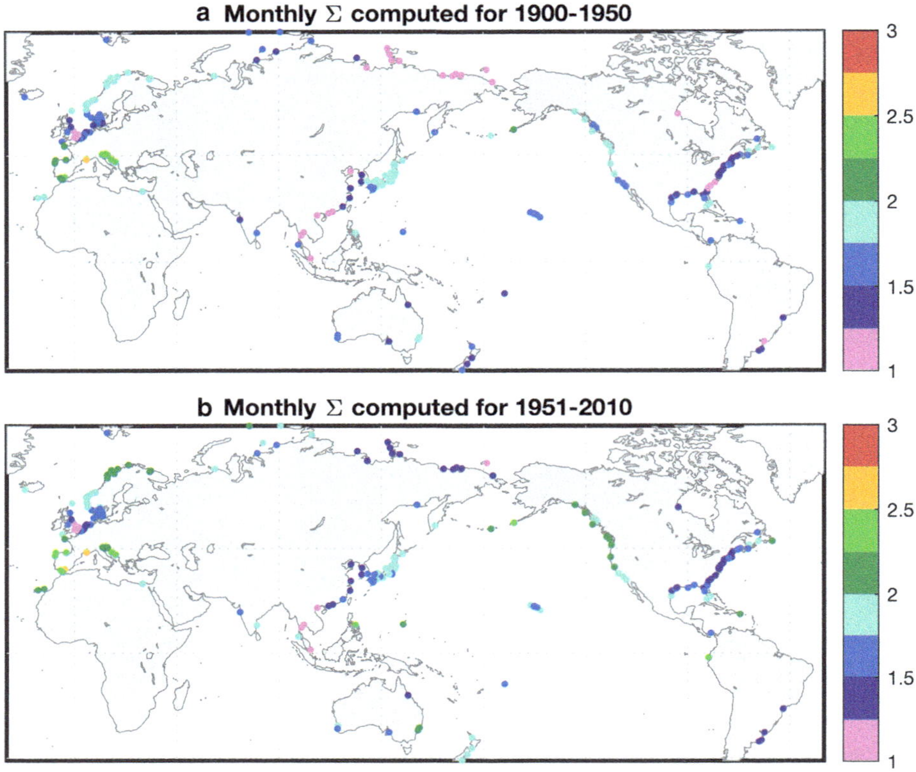

Fig. 10 Model signal-to-noise ratio Σ computed for monthly values **a** before 1950 and **b** after 1950. See Eq. (6) in the text for the definition of Σ

the observed monthly ζ variance, whereas $\overline{\eta}$ explains $\gtrsim 30\%$ of monthly ζ data variance at 75% of locations poleward of 40° (Fig. 12a). This gross result is consistent with basic physical expectations. Because transient adjustment timescales grow with latitude, owing in part to the latitudinal dependencies of the Coriolis parameter and its meridional derivative, the baroclinic response can be more locally trapped and barotropic effects are comparatively more important at higher latitudes compared to lower latitudes (e.g., Gill 1982; Frankignoul et al. 1997). More generally, see the Appendix for a dedicated scaling analysis, which establishes that barotropic processes grow relatively more important compared to baroclinic effects at higher latitude, higher frequency, larger scale, weaker stratification, and shallower depth. Regional "hotspots" are also apparent, such that model $\overline{\eta}$ explains upward of $\sim 50\%$ of monthly ζ variance. Such regions include the Kara, North, and Adriatic Seas, along with the Gulf of Lion, Norway shelf, western Canada, and along the Aleutians. These regions tend to be characterized by strong forcing, shallow depth, weak stratification, or are at high latitude, thus favoring the barotropic response.

Considering annual model and data records, we find similar spatial patterns of ζ variance explained by $\overline{\eta}$ (Figs. 11b, 12b). We observe analogous regional hotspots of enhanced annual $\mathcal{V}$ (e.g., Kara, North, and Adriatic Seas), and a tendency for annual $\mathcal{V}$ to increase with latitude, from a median value of $\sim 5\%$ for locations equatorward of 30° latitude to a

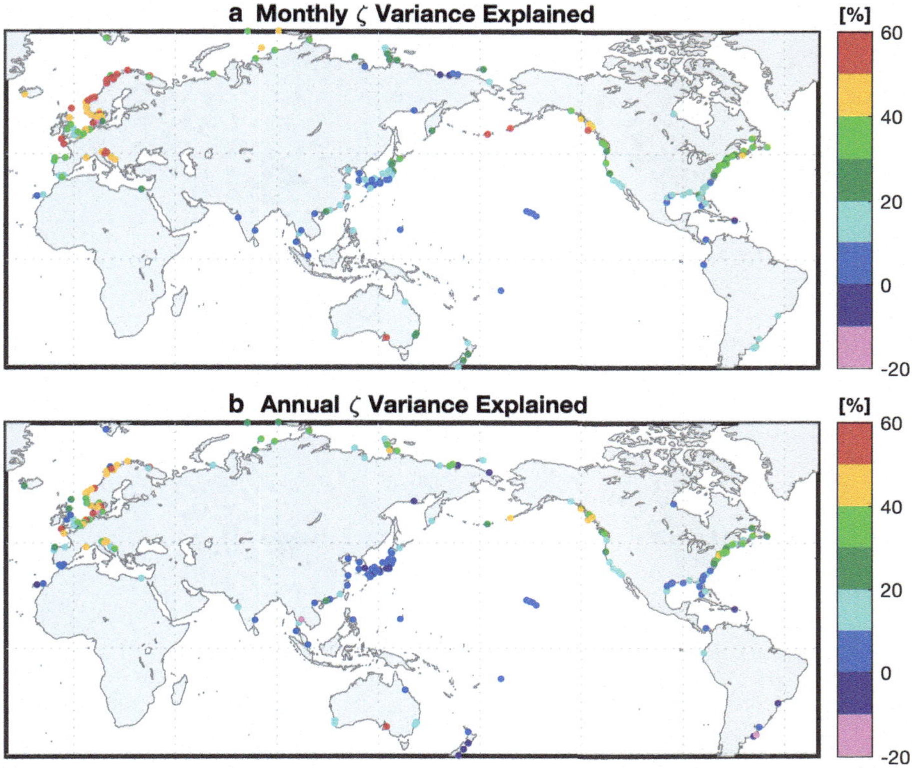

Fig. 11 **a** Percent variance explained $\mathcal{V}$ in monthly tide gauge sea level ζ records by the ensemble average barotropic model solution $\overline{\eta}$. **b** As in **a** but for annual values. See Eq. (7) in the text for the definition of $\mathcal{V}$

median of ∼ 30% for sites poleward of 40° (Fig. 12b). However, magnitudes of ζ variance explained by $\overline{\eta}$ are somewhat smaller based on annual relative to monthly time series. This result is expected given the frequency dependence of the oceanic response to atmospheric forcing—at lower frequencies, there becomes increasingly sufficient time for the ocean to adjust baroclinicly, so the relative importance of barotropic adjustment becomes less important at longer timescales (see the Appendix).

Global maps of winter-to-winter and summer-to-summer data variance explained by the models are shown in Fig. 13a, b, respectively (cf. Fig. 12c, d). In these cases, as with monthly and annual records (cf. Fig. 11), more ζ variance is explained by $\overline{\eta}$ at higher latitudes, and familiar regions are revealed as hotspots of high $\mathcal{V}$ values. However, there is seasonal dependence in terms of overall magnitudes. At most (79%) sites, more winter-to-winter ζ variance is explained by $\overline{\eta}$ compared to summer-to-summer variance. Averaging over all locations, the median winter-to-winter ζ variance explained by $\overline{\eta}$ is 27%, whereas it is only 13% for summer-to-summer values. Broadly over the coastal ocean (42% of study sites), $\overline{\eta}$ explains > 40% of the ζ variance between winters. Such regions include swaths of the Canada coast, Mediterranean and North Seas, Norway shelf, and Barents and Kara Seas. In contrast, only at 12% of tide gauge stations (mainly scattered along coastal Norway or the East Siberian and Chukchi Seas) does $\overline{\eta}$ explain > 40% of the summer-to-summer ζ

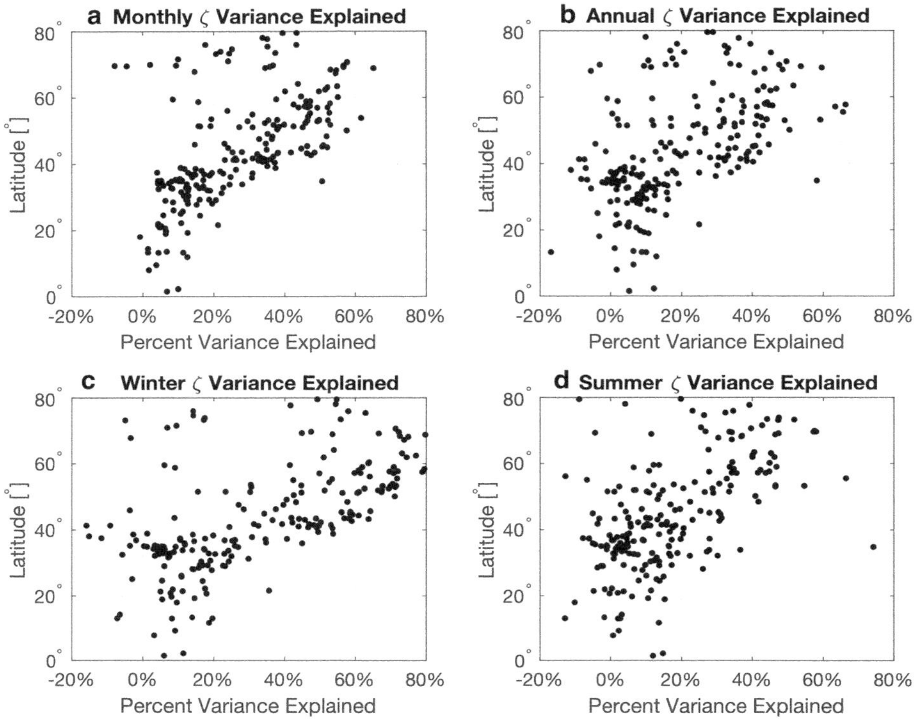

Fig. 12 Scatterplots of $\mathcal{V}$ versus the absolute value of latitude of the corresponding tide gauge station, shown for **a** monthly, **b** annual, **c** wintertime, and **d** summertime ζ and $\overline{\eta}$ time series

variance. That the barotropic models tend to explain more winter-to-winter variance compared to between summers is consistent with physical intuition. Summertime conditions are characterized by warmer surface temperatures and stronger density stratification and are more susceptible to baroclinic adjustment processes, which are not represented in the barotropic models (see also the Appendix). In fall, the stratification breaks down (e.g., due to surface cooling and wind-driven mixing associated with storms; Forsyth et al. 2018). These more unstratified wintertime conditions favor a barotropic response.

In some regions (21% of locations), $\overline{\eta}$ explains more summer-to-summer ζ variance than it does between winters. Such tends to be the case at low latitude, where little ζ variance is explained by $\overline{\eta}$ regardless of season. However, an interesting instance is apparent at high latitude along the Laptev, East Siberian, and Chukchi Seas (cf. Fig. 13). Here, $\overline{\eta}$ estimates explain 44% of the summer-to-summer variance in the ζ records on average, whereas the models show little if any skill explaining the regional observations from one winter to the next. This result could reflect the absence of sea ice in the models. These regions are covered in ice during winter, muting the oceanic response to atmospheric forcing. Since this buffering effect is absent in the models, the simulated oceanic response to atmospheric variability from one winter to the next is too strong relative to observations (not shown). During summer, sea ice has mostly retreated, leaving the ocean more directly exposed to the atmosphere. Thus, the observed variation between summers is more faithfully simulated by the models. A barotropic ocean model coupled to a model of sea ice would be more useful in this setting (e.g., Proshutinsky and

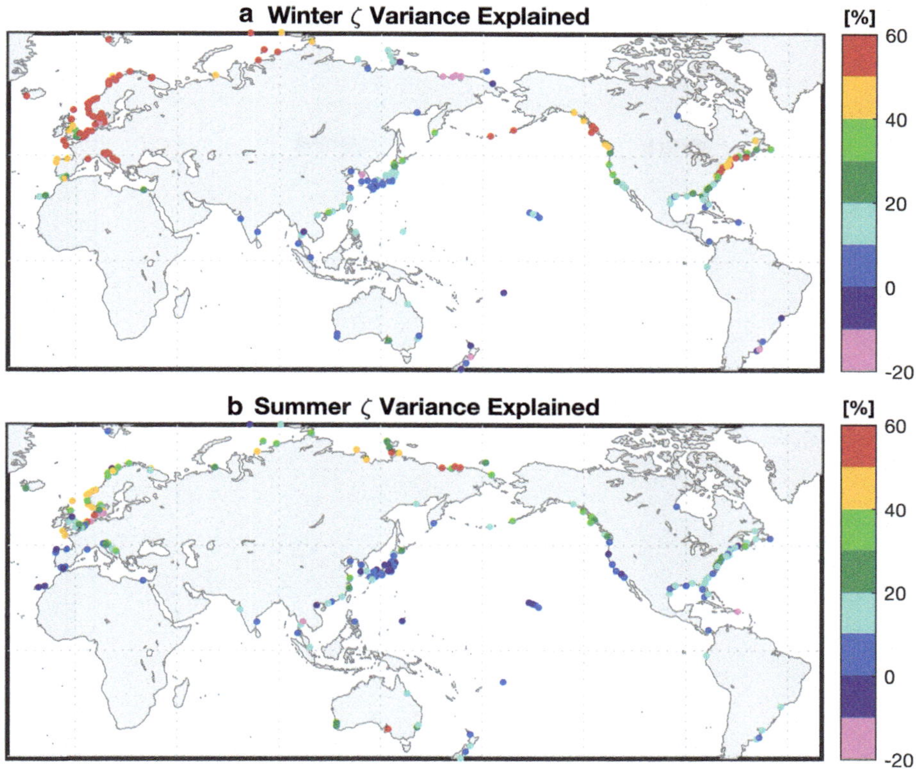

Fig. 13 Maps of $\mathcal{V}$ as in Fig. 11 but based on **a** wintertime and **b** summertime averages of ζ and $\overline{\eta}$ time series

Johnson 1997). Also worth noting, observed winter-to-winter ζ variability is accurately captured by the $\overline{\eta}$ solutions just to the west over the Barents and Kara seas, which are less prone to wintertime ice cover.

The spatial structure of ζ variance explained by $\overline{\eta}$ (Figs. 11, 12, 13) is consistent with results from past studies that focused solely on air pressure contributions to tide gauge records (e.g., Ponte 2006; Piecuch et al. 2016b). For example, Ponte (2006) finds that, while having no explanatory power near the equator, the isostatic ocean response to barometric pressure can explain 40% or more of the variance in monthly and annual tide gauge ζ records at midlatitudes. The question thus arises as to how much our results reflect the effects of wind or pressure forcing. To infer the relative roles of wind versus pressure, Figs. 14 and 15 show global maps of the *difference* in variance explained

$$\Delta\mathcal{V} \doteq 100\% \times \left[\frac{\mathrm{var}(\zeta - \overline{\eta}_{ib}) - \mathrm{var}(\zeta - \overline{\eta})}{\mathrm{var}(\zeta)}\right], \tag{8}$$

for different choices of time averaging, with $\overline{\eta}_{ib}$ being the local inverted barometer response to air pressure forcing,

$$\overline{\eta}_{ib} \doteq -\frac{\overline{P}_a}{\rho_0 g}, \tag{9}$$

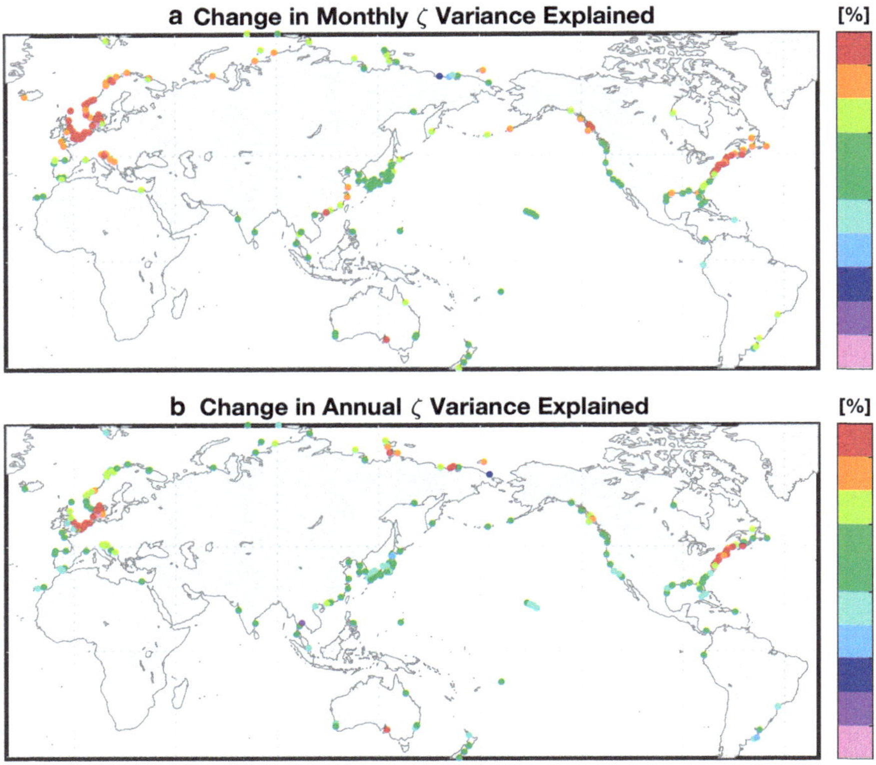

Fig. 14 **a** Additional percentage variance explained $\Delta\mathcal{V}$ in monthly tide gauge ζ data by the barotropic model solution $\overline{\eta}$ compared to a local inverted barometer response $\overline{\eta}_{ib}$. **b** As in **a** but for annual values. See Eq. (8) in the text for the definition of $\Delta\mathcal{V}$

where $\overline{P}_a$ is the barometric pressure used to force the models, ρ_0 is a reference density (1029 kg m^{-3}), and g is gravitational acceleration (9.81 m s^{-2}). Overbar again denotes ensemble mean over all models. Positive $\Delta\mathcal{V}$ values indicate that more ζ variance is explained when wind forcing is included in the models. Note that separate low-resolution model runs, where surface forcing is only by air pressure (not shown), confirm the basic expectation that the oceanic response to barometric pressure is isostatic on monthly and longer time scales, and almost perfectly described by an inverted barometer.

Including wind forcing in the models is advantageous in terms of explaining monthly ζ variance (Fig. 14a). At 97% of locations, $\overline{\eta}$ explains more monthly ζ variance than $\overline{\eta}_{ib}$ (i.e., $\Delta\mathcal{V} > 0$). The monthly impact of wind forcing can be fairly modest along tropical and subtropical coastlines and around oceanic islands ($\Delta\mathcal{V} \sim$ 0–10%), including California, Hawaii, Japan, India, and the Maritime Continent. Monthly wind effects can be more substantial ($\Delta\mathcal{V} \sim$ 10–20%) in the Mediterranean Sea and along the coasts of China, Alaska, and the Russian Arctic. Along the northeast US coast (Middle Atlantic Bight and Gulf of Maine) and over the North Sea (UK, Netherlands, Denmark, Norway coasts), the influence of wind forcing on monthly ζ records is particularly pronounced ($\Delta\mathcal{V} > 20\%$).

Similar $\Delta\mathcal{V}$ patterns emerge from analysis of annual time series (Fig. 14b). This suggests that barotropic ocean response to wind stress forcing is important for understanding

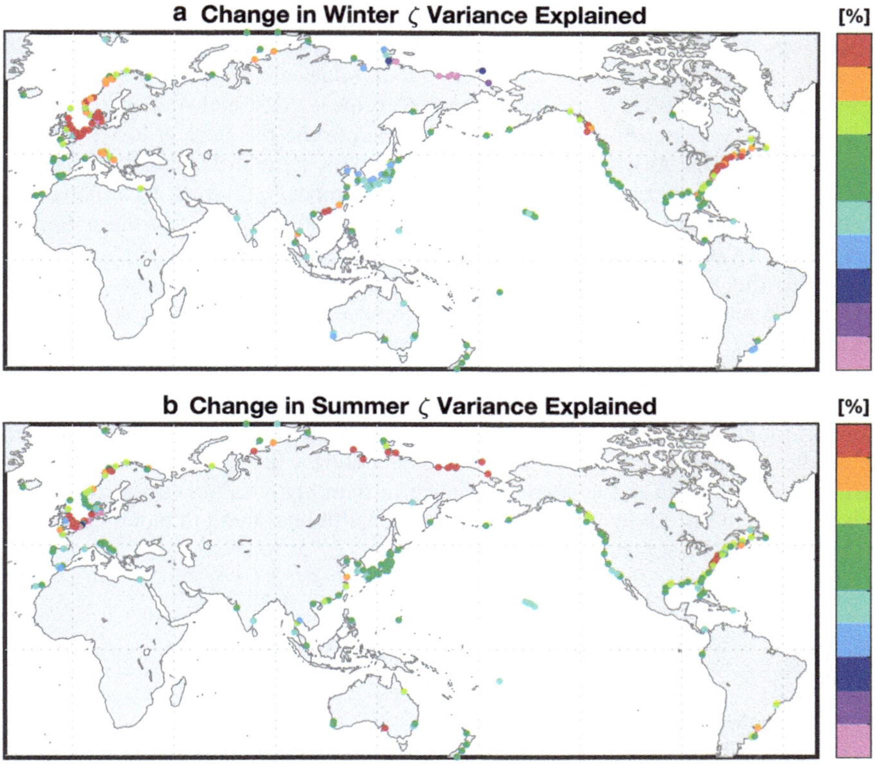

Fig. 15 Maps of $\Delta\mathcal{V}$ as in Fig. 14 but based on **a** wintertime and **b** summertime averages of ζ and $\overline{\eta}$ time series

ζ variations in tide gauge records even over longer timescales. However, the advantage of including barotropic wind effects (in the sense of explaining more ζ variance) is somewhat smaller in quantitative terms for annual compared to monthly time series: while the mean monthly $\Delta\mathcal{V}$ value over all tide gauges is 14%, the annual mean $\Delta\mathcal{V}$ is only 9% (cf. Fig. 14a, b).

Studying differences between winter-to-winter ζ variance explained by $\overline{\eta}$ and $\overline{\eta}_{ib}$, we observe analogous spatial structure in $\Delta\mathcal{V}$ (Fig. 15a). For example, the wind-driven response of a barotropic ocean is central to the character of ζ variations from one winter to the next over the northeast US coast and the North Sea, as it is from month to month and year to year (cf. Fig. 14). Note that including wind forcing in the models actually reduces the winter-to-winter ζ variance explained in the East Siberian and Chukchi Seas relative to considering only pressure forcing, possibly related to the absence of sea ice effects in the models alluded to earlier. Interesting in this context, including wind forcing substantially increases the summer-to-summer ζ variance explained in the East Siberian and Chukchi Seas (Fig. 15b).

To provide a more granular view of the relationship between ζ and $\overline{\eta}$ as a function of space and time, Fig. 16 shows time series of the data records and model estimates averaged over four coastlines: northern Europe (50.1–60.2°N, 5.5°W–12.5°E), northeastern USA (36.8–44.9°N, 67.0–76.5°W), California coast (32.7–41.7°N, 117.2–124.4°W), and southern Australia (32.1–34.8°S, 115.7–151.8°E). Consistent with Figs. 6 and 11, both barotropic variability and data variance explained by the models increase with latitude (cf. the Appendix), such that relatively higher values are apparent along northern Europe and northeastern USA compared to the California coast and southern Australia. Also evident is the decreasing importance of the barotropic response at lower frequencies in California and Australia, where the data exhibit clear interannual and decadal variability that is mostly unapparent in the barotropic models. Overall, $\overline{\eta}$ explains 53%, 35%, 19%, and 28% of the variance in regionally averaged ζ over northern Europe, northeastern USA, California, and southern Australia, respectively.

To garner the impact of adjusting the observations using the models, we show monthly and annual time series of residual differences $\zeta - \overline{\eta}$ over these same coastal regions in Fig. 17. Removing $\overline{\eta}$ from ζ has an important influence on the spatiotemporal structure, such that the residual variability shows less of a tendency to increase with latitude. For example, σ values from the four monthly $\zeta - \overline{\eta}$ time series shown in Fig. 17 are similar, ranging from 3.9 to 4.9 cm. This compares to the larger σ range of 4.3–7.1 cm from the "unadjusted" monthly regional ζ data shown in Fig. 16. More generally, removing $\overline{\eta}$ from ζ reduces the spatial variance in monthly σ values across tide gauge locations shown in Fig. 2a by 25%, and reduces the latitudinal trend in monthly σ apparent in Fig. 3a by 42% (not shown).

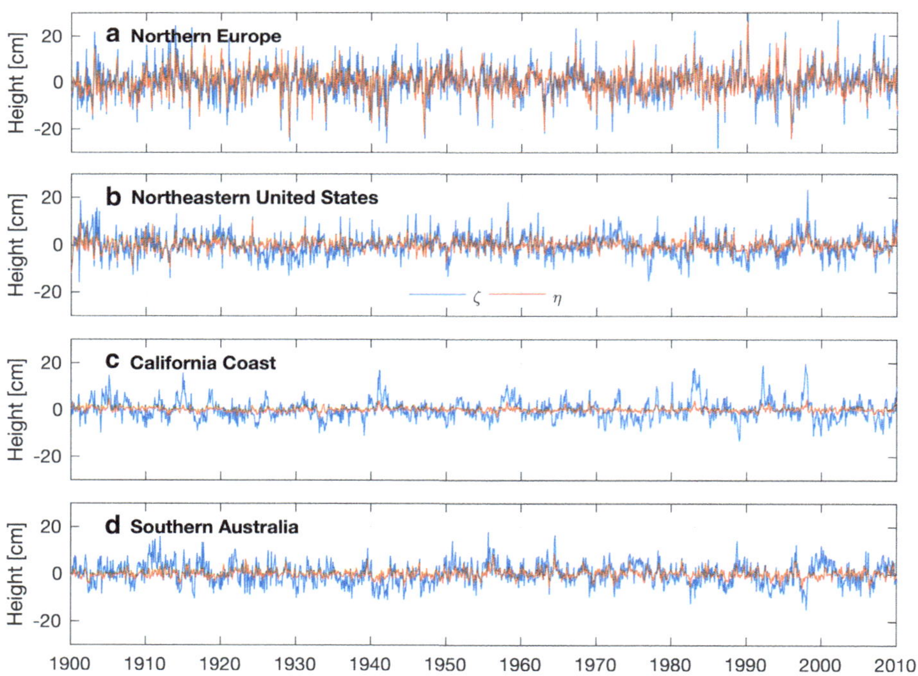

Fig. 16 Monthly time series of ζ from tide gauges (blue) and $\overline{\eta}$ from barotropic models (orange) averaged over **a** northern Europe (50.1–60.2°N, 5.5°W–12.5°E), **b** northeastern USA (36.8–44.9°N, 67.0–76.5°W), **c** California coast (32.7–41.7°N, 117.2–124.4°W), and **d** southern Australia (32.1–34.8°S, 115.7–151.8°E)

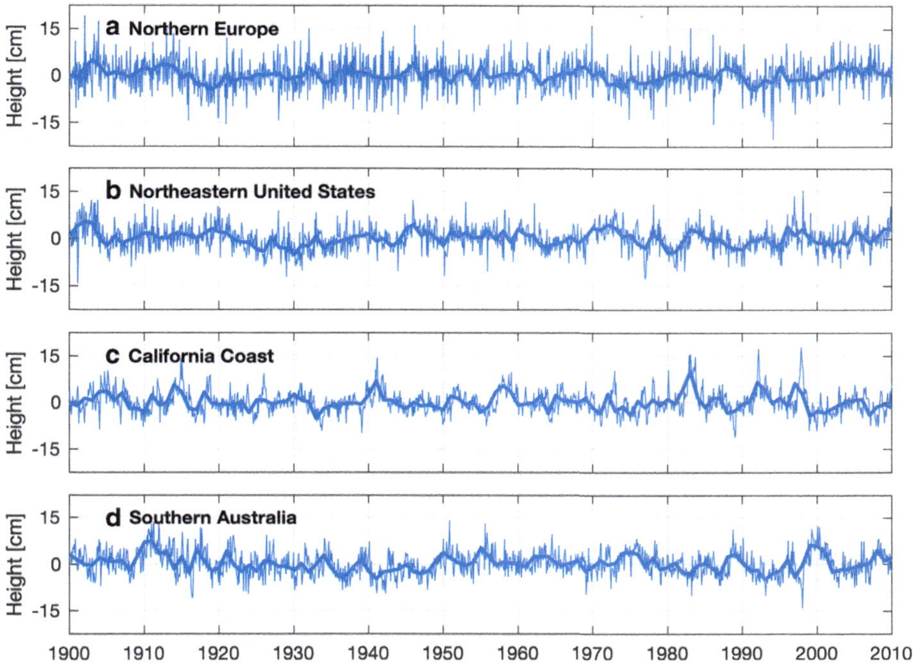

Fig. 17 Monthly (thin) and annual (thick) time series of data-model residual differences $\zeta - \overline{\eta}$ averaged over **a** northern Europe (50.1–60.2°N, 5.5°W–12.5°E), **b** northeastern USA (36.8–44.9°N, 67.0–76.5°W), **c** California coast (32.7–41.7°N, 117.2–124.4°W), and **d** southern Australia (32.1–34.8°S, 115.7–151.8°E)

More insight onto timescale dependence and the relative roles of air pressure versus wind forcing is facilitated by an admittance analysis. Given an input x and output y, the admittance (or transfer function) is given by

$$H_{xy}(f) \doteq \frac{G_{xy}(f)}{G_{xx}(f)}, \tag{10}$$

where f is frequency and G is the respective one-sided spectral density or cross-spectral density. The admittance in the frequency domain is analogous to the more familiar regression coefficient in the time domain. Figure 18 shows amplitudes of the admittance between ζ and $\overline{\eta}$ and between ζ and $\overline{\eta}_{ib}$ based on the regionally averaged time series from Fig. 16, using the data as input and models as the output. Admittance amplitudes ~ 1 indicate that the model faithfully reproduces the data, whereas amplitudes ~ 0 occur when the model solutions substantially underestimate the observed variability.

In all regions, statistically significant ($p < 0.05$) admittance is apparent between ζ and $\overline{\eta}$ across frequency bands from intraseasonal to decadal, underscoring the importance of the barotropic ocean response to wind stress and pressure forcing even on long timescales. Depending on region, admittance amplitudes between ζ and $\overline{\eta}$ can vary substantially. Larger amplitudes ($\sim$ 0.5–1.0) are found between ζ and $\overline{\eta}$ along northern Europe and the northeastern USA over intra- to interannual frequencies (Fig. 18a, b), whereas lower values ($\sim$ 0.2–0.4) are seen along the California and southern Australia coasts (Fig. 18c, d). These results agree with our earlier inspection of spatially

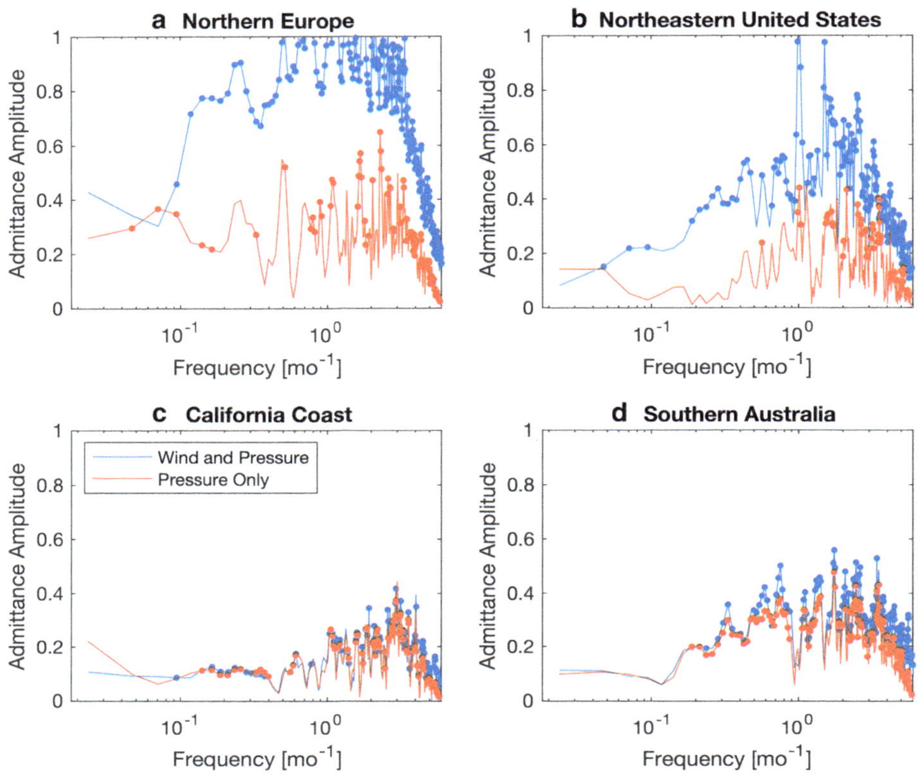

Fig. 18 Admittance amplitudes between ζ and either $\overline{\eta}$ (blue) or $\overline{\eta}_{ib}$ (orange) for **a** northern Europe (50.1–60.2°N, 5.5°W–12.5°E), **b** northeastern USA (36.8–44.9°N, 67.0–76.5°W), **c** California coast (32.7–41.7°N, 117.2–124.4°W), and **d** southern Australia (32.1–34.8°S, 115.7–151.8°E). Solid dots indicate values that are significant at the $p < 0.05$ level, where significance is evaluated using repeated simulations of synthetic time series

averaged ζ and $\overline{\eta}$ time series suggesting a strong relationship between the two in the former regions and a weak correspondence in the latter regions. More generally, these results are also consistent with Figs. 11, 12 and 13, which show that more ζ variance is explained by $\overline{\eta}$ at higher latitudes and over broad shelf regions.

These regions are also distinguished by the relative influences of wind and pressure effects. In northern Europe and along the northeastern USA, barotropic response to wind stress contributes importantly to the observed variability across timescales, evidenced by admittance amplitudes between ζ and $\overline{\eta}$ that are considerably higher than between ζ and $\overline{\eta}_{ib}$ (Fig. 18a, b). Along the California and southern Australia coasts, barotropic adjustment to wind stress is less important, and admittances between ζ and $\overline{\eta}$ are nearly identical to those computed between ζ and $\overline{\eta}_{ib}$ (Fig. 18c, d), reflecting the dominant control of pressure forcing on the model solutions in these regions. Consistently over all four regions, admittances between ζ and $\overline{\eta}_{ib}$ are largely significant, even at decadal frequencies, but have low or modest amplitudes (~ 0.2). This is consistent with arguments made by Piecuch et al. (2016b) that the inverted barometer response is a significant but minor overall contributor to ζ changes over long periods—while ζ and $\overline{\eta}_{ib}$ are correlated at low frequencies, the latter explains only a small fraction of the latter's variance.

The preceding comparisons between models and data (Figs. 11, 12, 13, 14, 15, 16, 17, 18) are based on the average model estimate $\overline{\eta}$. Given the differences between solutions (Figs. 6, 7, 8, 9, 10), it is informative to compare the individual models in terms of ζ variance explained. Figures 19 and 20 show maps indicating which of the three barotropic model η solutions explains the most variance in the tide gauge ζ records for different time averaging of the data (monthly, annual, wintertime, and summertime). Generally speaking, the maps show nonrandom spatial structure, meaning that particular models can perform better than others consistently over broad stretches of coastline.

The high-resolution solution η_H explains more monthly ζ variance than either of the low-resolution model estimates η_N and η_E for a majority (58%) of tide gauge stations, including those along the coasts of western Canada, Alaska and the Aleutian Islands, New Zealand, Japan, the Mediterranean Sea, western Europe, and northern Norway (Fig. 19a). Some of these regions have narrow shelves and abut deep basins, so this result could suggest that having good representation of topography is important for simulating monthly variability in these regions. Elsewhere, the low-resolution models perform comparatively better, including over broader shelf regions such as the North,

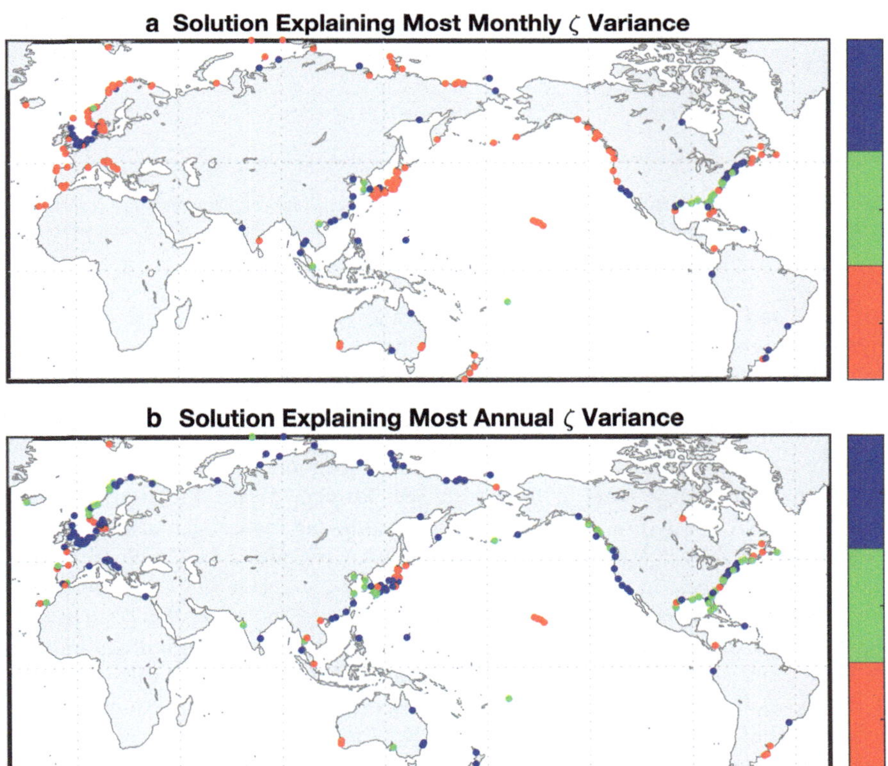

Fig. 19 **a** Colored dots indicate which of the three barotropic ocean model solutions (η_H red; η_N green; η_E blue) explains the most monthly ζ variance at a particular tide gauge station. **b** As in **a** but for annual values

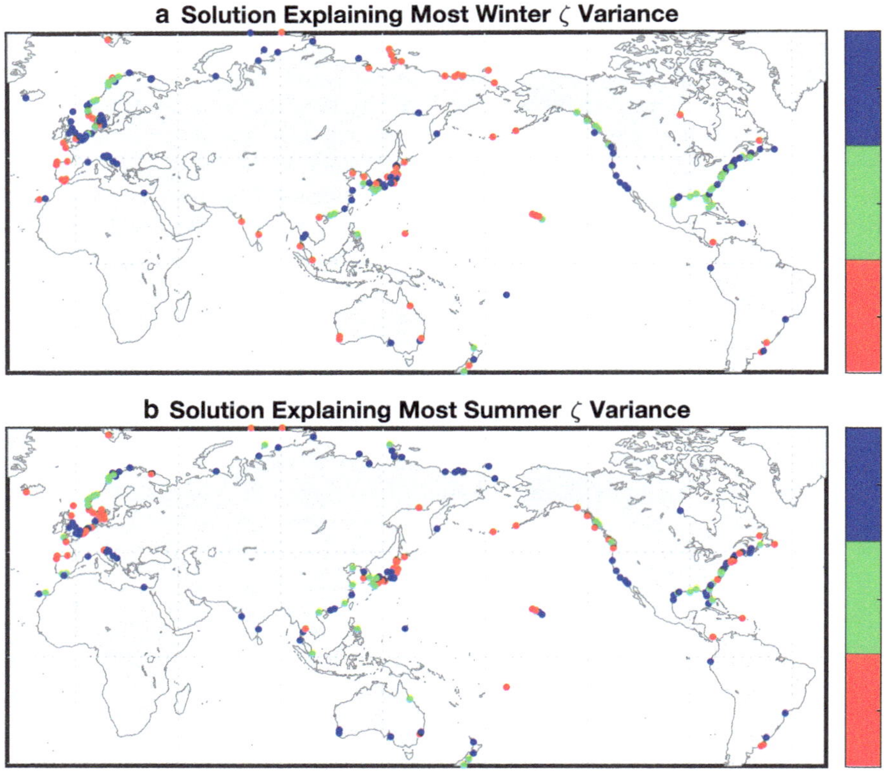

Fig. 20 Maps indicating which barotropic model (η_H red; η_N green; η_E blue) explains the most ζ variance at a tide gauge as in Fig. 19 but based on **a** wintertime and **b** summertime averages of ζ and $\overline{\eta}$ time series

East China, and South China Seas, and the Middle Atlantic Bight, where having fine bathymetry might be less crucial for simulating monthly behavior.

In contrast, considering annually averaged time series, we find that η_H explains more ζ variance than η_N and η_E only at a fraction (19%) of sites. Rather, for annual records, the low-resolution solution forced with ERA fields η_E performs better than either of the models forced with the NOAA reanalysis η_N and η_H for more than half (56%) of study locations, including large parts of the North Sea, Russian Arctic, Mediterranean Sea, and western USA coast (Fig. 19b), possibly related to the higher spatial resolution of the ERA product ($\sim$ 125 km) compared to the NOAA reanalysis ($\sim$ 2°). Some regions where η_E performs best in terms of explaining *annual* ζ variance (e.g., Mediterranean, western USA) are the same regions where η_H explains the most *monthly* ζ variance of all models. This demonstrates that model performance in a given region can be time-scale dependent. Comparing winter-to-winter and summer-to-summer values, we also find that the skill of models to reproduce the observed variability can exhibit seasonal dependence (Fig. 20). For example, whereas ζ variance between winters over the East Siberian and Chukchi Seas is best explained by the high-resolution model solution η_H, low-resolution solutions η_N and η_E show more skill over this region in terms of reproducing summer-to-summer ζ variance.

While some models perform quantitatively better than others over certain stretches of coastline (Figs. 19, 20), the models simulations are qualitatively similar in general. For example, the mean monthly ζ variance explained by the models is 9–21%, while the mean annual ζ variance explained is 9–19%, depending on model. That is, on the whole, the models simulate robust spatiotemporal structures, and show broadly similar correspondence to the data.

4 Summary and Discussion

We used a network of 219 coastal tide gauge records and three barotropic ocean circulation models to consider the nature of historical mean sea level variation. We examined the consistency of the barotropic model simulations and their ability to reproduce the sea level observations as functions of space and time. The models were forced at the surface by air pressure and wind stress from atmospheric reanalysis. Focus was on nonseasonal behavior over timescales from bimonthly to multidecadal during 1900–2010.

The barotropic models show stronger variability at higher latitudes, shorter timescales, between winters, and along broad shallow shelves and semi-enclosed marginal seas (Figs. 6, 9). Consistency between models is higher along regions with narrow shelves adjacent to deep basins and lower over broad shallow shelf regions (Fig. 8). For simulated monthly variability, model differences are controlled more by details of model configuration (e.g., fine versus coarse horizontal resolution) than by the nature of the surface forcing (e.g., choice of atmospheric reanalysis), whereas model configuration and surface forcing contribute comparably to model differences in terms of simulated annual variability (Fig. 7). Model solutions become more uncertain for earlier periods (Figs. 9, 10), due to increasing errors in the forcing datasets as one goes back in time.

Consistent with basic expectations given the vertical structure of the ocean's response to atmospheric forcing, barotropic models show more skill and explain more variance in the tide gauge data at higher latitudes and higher frequencies, over broad shallow shelves and within semi-enclosed marginal seas, and regions without seasonal ice cover (Fig. 11). The models show considerable skill in accounting for data variance from one winter to the next (Fig. 13). Barotropic ocean response to wind stress forcing is particularly relevant for understanding the observed variability at midlatitudes and from winter to winter (Figs. 14, 15, 16). Significant relationships between the data and the models are observed even on long decadal timescales (Fig. 18). The relative performance of individual models in terms of explaining data variance is a sensitive function of space and time (Figs. 19, 20), and no one model considered here consistently performs better than the others in all cases.

This work builds on previous efforts, and corroborates past studies of wind and pressure effects on mean sea level changes from coastal tide gauge data (e.g., Tsimplis et al. 2005; Gomis et al. 2006, 2008; Ponte 2006; Marcos and Tsimplis 2007, 2008; Pascual et al. 2008; Woodworth et al. 2010, 2014; Sturges and Douglas 2011; Sündermann and Pohlmann 2011; Jordà et al. 2012b; Calafat et al. 2012, 2013, 2014b; Richter et al. 2012; Andres et al. 2013; Dangendorf et al. 2013, 2014a, b; Thompson and Mitchum 2014; Piecuch and Ponte 2015a, b; Piecuch et al. 2016a, b). Spatial patterns of data variance explained by the models in Figs. 11, 12 and 13 are consistent with past regional works suggesting that barotropic ocean response to atmospheric forcing is central to the nature of intraseasonal-to-decadal sea level variation in the Mediterranean Sea (e.g., Tsimplis et al. 2005; Marcos and Tsimplis 2007, 2008; Gomis et al. 2008; Calafat et al. 2012), North Sea (e.g., Dangendorf et al.

2013, 2014a), coastal Norway and Russian Arctic (e.g., Proshutinsky et al. 2001, 2004; Proshutinksy et al. 2007; Richter et al. 2012; Calafat et al. 2013), and the northeastern USA (e.g., Andres et al. 2013; Woodworth et al. 2014; Piecuch and Ponte 2015a; Piecuch et al. 2016a, b; Kenigson et al. 2018), but less crucial for understanding data records on these time scales along the USA West Coast (e.g., Thompson et al. 2014; Merrifield and Thompson 2018), the coast of Japan (e.g., Sasaki et al. 2014, 2017), and the tropical Indo-Pacific (e.g., Clarke and Liu 1994; Feng et al. 2004; Qiu and Chen 2006, 2010, 2012), where baroclinic processes have been shown to be more influential. Having considered in combination more ocean models, a larger spatial domain, and a longer temporal duration than previous investigations, our efforts advance the state of the science regarding the processes driving coastal sea level changes, the spacetime structure of sea level variation near the coast, and the ability of models to simulate coastal sea level changes in historical records.

We have shown that wind and pressure effects from barotropic models can explain an important percentage of the spatiotemporal variance in coastal tide gauge records. This result has implications for efforts to reconstruct global-mean sea level rise since the Industrial Revolution (e.g., Hay et al. 2015; Thompson et al. 2016; Dangendorf et al. 2017) as well as attempts to detect an anthropogenic influence or significant acceleration in sea level rise at coastal tide gauge stations (e.g., Calafat and Chambers 2013; Haigh et al. 2014; Dangendorf et al. 2015). To reduce noise in tide gauge data, authors in such sea level studies typically remove the estimated effects of particular processes (e.g., related to air pressure, postglacial rebound) that are not relevant to the problem at hand (e.g., Calafat et al. 2014a). Consistent with previous regional results (e.g., Marcos and Tsimplis 2008; Dangendorf et al. 2014b), our global findings suggest that the noise in tide gauge records can be further reduced by removing barotropic model estimates of wind and pressure effects. For example, removing ensemble mean model estimates of wind and pressure effects from the monthly (annual) tide gauge records reduces the data variance by 26% (20%) on average, whereas making the standard inverted barometer adjustment only reduces the monthly (annual) variance in the data by 12% (11%) on average. Since relative model skill shows spatial and temporal dependencies (Figs. 19, 20), and no model performs better than others in all cases, we recommend—as a general strategy in global sea level studies—to adjust tide gauge data using an ensemble average of multiple barotropic model solutions whenever possible, since the ensemble average tends to perform better on balance than the individual models. For example, whereas the ensemble mean of barotropic models explains 26% (20%) of the monthly (annual) tide gauge data variance on average over all data sites, individual models explain 9–21% (9–19%) of the monthly (annual) tide gauge data variance on average. However, for sea level studies focused more locally, we note that specially tailored regional model products might be more useful (e.g., Tsimplis et al. 2005; Marcos and Tsimplis 2008; Calafat et al. 2014b).

Motivated by the recent ISSI Workshop on, "Understanding the Relationship between Coastal Sea Level and Large-Scale Ocean Circulation," our focus has been on monthly and longer timescales relevant to ocean circulation and climate studies. However, it would be informative to address these same topics—consistency of models and ability to capture observations—in the context of sea level extremes, which are relevant to studies of coastal exposure and impacts. Some steps have been taken in this direction, for example, by (among others) Calafat et al. (2014b), who consider the ability of a particular model to simulate observed sea level extremes within a specific marginal sea, and by Stammer et al. (2014), who compare global barotropic ocean models in the context of the astronomical tides. Given the recent proliferation of extreme sea level databases (Woodworth et al. 2017), we recommend future studies to undertake investigations involving different global barotropic ocean models, evaluating their consistency and comparing to observed sea level extremes over the global ocean.

Acknowledgements This work was supported by National Science Foundation awards OCE-1558966 and OCE-1834739 as well as the J. Lamar Worzel Assistant Scientist Fund and the Penzance Endowed Fund in Support of Assistant Scientists at the Woods Hole Oceanographic Institution. This paper is an outcome of the ISSI Workshop on, "Understanding the Relationship between Coastal Sea Level and Large-Scale Ocean Circulation," held on 5–9 March 2018 in Bern, Switzerland. Helpful comments from Magdalena Andres and an anonymous reviewer are acknowledged.

Appendix: Scaling of the Relative Influences of Barotropic and Baroclinic Effects on ζ Variability

Following past works (Gill and Niiler 1973; Willebrand et al. 1980; Frankignoul et al. 1997), we perform a scaling analysis to establish the basic controls on the relative contributions of barotropic and baroclinic processes on ζ variability. The words "barotropic" and "baroclinic" have various usages and meanings in physical oceanography and geophysical fluid dynamics (Holton 1992; Pedlosky 1987). Here, we use these words in a similar sense to the separation of variables and normal vertical modes in a continuously stratified fluid (Gill 1982; Kundu and Cohen 2004). We define the barotropic component of a depth-dependent variable as the depth-averaged value, and the baroclinic component at a given depth as the deviation from the depth average. In the case of ζ, which has no explicit depth dependence, we define the barotropic component as the scaled depth-averaged hydrostatic pressure p (cf. Gill 1982),

$$\langle\zeta\rangle \doteq \frac{1}{\rho_0 g}\frac{1}{\zeta + H}\int_{-H}^{\zeta} p(z)\,\mathrm{d}z, \tag{11}$$

where H is ocean depth, ρ_0 a constant reference density, and g gravitational acceleration. The baroclinic ζ component is defined as the difference between total and barotropic components,

$$\zeta'' \doteq \zeta - \langle\zeta\rangle. \tag{12}$$

Usage of angled brackets and double primes to denote the barotropic and baroclinic components follows Peixoto and Oort (1992). It can be shown that, by applying the hydrostatic equation,

$$\frac{\mathrm{d}p}{\mathrm{d}z} = -\rho g, \tag{13}$$

ζ'' can be rewritten in terms of a double integral of ocean density ρ,

$$\zeta'' = -\frac{1}{\rho_0}\frac{1}{\zeta + H}\int_{-H}^{\zeta}\int_{z}^{0} \rho(z')\,\mathrm{d}z'\,\mathrm{d}z. \tag{14}$$

See Piecuch et al. (2015) for more details on how (14) can be derived from (13) and (12).

To compare the magnitudes of $\langle\zeta\rangle$ and ζ'' variations, we consider basic ocean dynamics. Given the timescales of interest to this study (monthly to decadal), we generally expect an equilibrium (time-independent) barotropic response to surface atmospheric forcing, while we anticipate a transient (time-dependent) baroclinic adjustment. For simplicity, we suppose that the only surface forcing is by a variable wind stress $\boldsymbol{\tau}$. (Indeed, the above expressions for $\langle\zeta\rangle$

and ζ'' neglect any surface loading by barometric pressure.) Thus, to scale the p integrand in Eq. (11), we assume that the equilibrium barotropic adjustment takes the form of a Sverdrup balance,

$$\mathbf{J}\left(p, \frac{H}{f}\right) = -\nabla \times \left(\frac{\boldsymbol{\tau}}{f}\right), \tag{15}$$

where $\mathbf{J}$ is the Jacobian operator, $\nabla\times$ is the vertical component of the curl operator, and f is the Coriolis parameter. Eq. (15) represents a balance between vertical stretching of the water column by the curl of $\boldsymbol{\tau}$ and advection of the water column across contours of ambient potential vorticity by geostrophic flows (Pedlosky 1987). Combining Eqs. (11) and (15), we find that $\langle\zeta\rangle$ is of order,

$$\mathcal{O}(\langle\zeta\rangle) \sim \frac{\tau f}{\rho_0 g H \beta}, \tag{16}$$

where β is the meridional derivative of f.

To scale the ρ integrand in Eq. (14), we assume the transient baroclinic response is such that density changes arise solely due to heaving of the mean stratification by an anomalous velocity w,

$$\frac{\partial \rho}{\partial t} = \rho_0 \frac{N^2}{g} w, \tag{17}$$

where N^2 is the square of the buoyancy frequency. For simplicity, we assume a vertical structure for w such that it is equal to the Ekman pumping velocity,

$$w_{\text{ek}} = \nabla \times \left(\frac{\boldsymbol{\tau}}{\rho_0 f}\right), \tag{18}$$

within some shallow upper layer of vertical thickness δ, and zero everywhere below that depth. Combining Eqs. (14), (17), and (18), we find that ζ'' scales as

$$\mathcal{O}(\zeta'') \sim \frac{N^2 \delta \boldsymbol{\tau}}{\rho_0 \omega g L f}, \tag{19}$$

where ω is the angular frequency of the density variation and L is a representative length scale of the surface forcing. Thus, the ratio of the barotropic to the baroclinic ζ term is on the order of

$$\frac{\mathcal{O}(\langle\zeta\rangle)}{\mathcal{O}(\zeta'')} \sim \frac{\omega f^2 L}{N^2 \delta H \beta}. \tag{20}$$

That is, barotropic response becomes increasingly important relative to baroclinic adjustment for progressively higher latitude (f^2/β increases in magnitude with latitude), higher frequency, larger spatial scale, weaker stratification, and shallower water column thickness. These simple arguments are borne out and corroborated by more realistic ocean general circulation model experiments (Vinogradova et al. 2007; Bingham and Hughes 2008).

References

Adcroft A, Hill C, Marshall J (1997) Representation of topography by shaved cells in a height coordinate ocean model. Mon Weather Rev 125:2293–2315

Andres M, Gawarkiewicz GG, Toole JM (2013) Interannual sea level variability in the western North Atlantic: regional forcing and remote response. Geophys Res Lett 40:5915–5919. https://doi.org/10.1002/2013GL058013

Bingham RJ, Hughes CW (2008) The relationship between sea-level and bottom pressure variability in an eddy permitting ocean model. Geophys Res Lett 35:L03602

Bos MS, Williams SDP, Araújo IB, Bastos L (2014) The effect of temporal correlated noise on the sea level rate and acceleration uncertainty. Geophys J Int 196:1423–1430. https://doi.org/10.1093/gji/ggt481

Calafat FM, Chambers DP (2013) Quantifying recent acceleration in sea level unrelated to internal climate variability. Geophys Res Lett 40:3661–3666. https://doi.org/10.1002/grl.50731

Calafat FM, Chambers DP, Tsimplis MN (2012) Mechanisms of decadal sea level variability in the eastern North Atlantic and the Mediterranean Sea. J Geophys Res 117:C09022. https://doi.org/10.1029/2012JC008285

Calafat FM, Chambers DP, Tsimplis MN (2013) Inter-annual to decadal sea-level variability in the coastal zones of the Norwegian and Siberian Seas: the role of atmospheric forcing. J Geophys Res Oceans 117:1287–1301. https://doi.org/10.1002/jgrc.20106

Calafat FM, Chambers DP, Tsimplis MN (2014a) On the ability of global sea level reconstructions to determine trends and variability. J Geophys Res Oceans 119:1572–1592. https://doi.org/10.1002/2013JC009298

Calafat FM, Avgoustoglou E, Jordà G, Flocas H, Zodiatis G, Tsimplis MN, Kouroutzoglou J (2014b) The ability of a barotropic model to simulate sea level extremes of meteorological origin in the Mediterranean Sea, including those caused by explosive cyclones. J Geophys Res Oceans 119:7840–7853

Carrère L, Lyard F (2003) Modeling the barotropic response of the global ocean to atmospheric wind and pressure forcing: comparisons with observations. Geophys Res Lett 30(6):1275. https://doi.org/10.1029/2002GL016473

Chepurin GA, Carton JA, Leuliette E (2014) Sea level in ocean reanalyses and tide gauges. J Geophys Res Oceans 119:147–155. https://doi.org/10.1002/2013JC009365

Clarke AJ, Liu X (1994) Interannual sea level in the northern and eastern Indian Ocean. J Phys Oceanogr 24:1224–1235

Compo GP, Whitaker JS, Sardeshmukh PD, Matsui N, Allan RJ, Yin X, Gleason BE, Vose RS, Rutledge G, Bessemoulin P, Brönnimann S, Brunet M, Crouthamel RI, Grant AN, Groisman PY, Jones PD, Kruk MC, Kruger AC, Marshall GJ, Maugeri M, Mok HY, Nordli Ø, Ross TF, Trigo RM, Wang XL, Woodruff SD, Worley SJ (2011) The twentieth century reanalysis project. Q J R Meteorol Soc 137:1–28. https://doi.org/10.1002/qj.776

Csanady GT (1982) Circulation in the coastal ocean. D. Reidel Publishing Compeny, Dordrecht, p 279

Dangendorf S, Mudersbach C, Wahl T, Jensen J (2013) Characteristics of intra-, inter-annual and decadal sea-level variability and the role of meteorological forcing: the long record of Cuxhaven. Ocean Dyn 63:209–224. https://doi.org/10.1007/s10236-013-0598-0

Dangendorf S, Rybski D, Mudersbach C, Müller A, Kaufmann E, Zorita E, Jensen J (2014a) Evidence for long-term memory in sea level. Geophys Res Lett 41:5530–5537. https://doi.org/10.1002/2014GL060538

Dangendorf S, Müller-Navarra S, Jensen J, Schenk F, Wahl T, Weisse R (2014b) North Sea storminess from a novel storm surge record since AD 1843. J Climate 27:3582–3595

Dangendorf S, Marcos M, Müller M, Zorita E, Riva R, Berk K, Jense J (2015) Detecting anthropogenic footprints in sea level rise. Nat Commun 6:7849. https://doi.org/10.1038/ncomms8849

Dangendorf S, Marcos M, Wöppelmann G, Conrad CP, Frederikse T, Riva R (2017) Reassessment of 20th century global mean sea level rise. Proc Natl Acad Sci USA 114(23):5946–5951. https://doi.org/10.1073/pnas.1616007114

Featherstone WE, Penna NT, Filmer MS, Williams SDP (2015) Nonlinear subsidence at Fremantle, a long-recording tide gauge in the Southern Hemisphere. Geophys Res Lett 120:7004–7014. https://doi.org/10.1002/2015JC011295

Feng M, Li Y, Meyers G (2004) Multidecadal variations of Fremantle sea level: footprint of climate variability in the tropical Pacific. Geophys Res Lett 31:L16302. https://doi.org/10.1029/2004GL019947

Field CR, Bayard TS, Gjerdrum C, Hill JM, Meiman S, Elphick CS (2017) High-resolution tide projections reveal extinction threshold in response to sea-level rise. Glob Change Biol 23:2058–2070. https://doi.org/10.1111/gcb.13519

Forget G, Campin J-M, Heimbach P, Hill CN, Ponte RM, Wunsch C (2015) ECCO version 4: an integrated framework for non-linear inverse modeling and global ocean state estimation. Geosci Model Dev 8:3071–3104. https://doi.org/10.5194/gmd-8-3071-2015
Forsyth J, Gawarkiewicz G, Andres M, Chen K (2018) The interannual variability of the breakdown of fall stratification on the New Jersey shelf. J Geophys Res Oceans. https://doi.org/10.1029/2018JC014049
Frankignoul C, Müller P, Zorita E (1997) A simple model of the decadal response of the ocean to stochastic wind forcing. J Phys Oceanogr 27:1533–1546
Frederikse T, Simon K, Katsman CA, Riva R (2017) The sea-level budget along the Northwest Atlantic coast: GIA, mass changes, and large-scale ocean dynamics. J Geophys Res Oceans 122:5486–5501. https://doi.org/10.1002/2017JC012699
Fukumori I, Wang O, Llovel W, Fenty I, Forget G (2015) A near-uniform fluctuation of ocean bottom pressure and sea level across the deep ocean basins of the Arctic Ocean and the Nordic Seas. Prog Oceanogr 134:152–172
Gill AE (1982) Atmosphere-ocean dynamics. Academic Press, New York, p 662
Gill AE, Niiler PP (1973) The theory of the seasonal variability in the ocean. Deep See Res 20:141–177
Gille ST (2004) How nonlinearities in the equation of state of seawater can confound estimates of steric sea level change. J Geophys Res 109:C03005. https://doi.org/10.1029/2003JC002012
Gomis D, Tsimplis MN, Martín-Míguez B, Ratsimandresy AW, García-Lafuente J, Josey SA (2006) Mediterranean Sea level and barotropic flow through the Strait of Gibraltar for the period 1958–2001 and reconstructed since 1659. J Geophys Res 111:C11005. https://doi.org/10.1029/2005JC003186
Gomis D, Ruiz S, Sotillo MG, Álvarez-Fanjul E, Terradas J (2008) Low frequency Mediterranean sea level variability: the contribution of atmospheric pressure and wind. Glob Planet Change 63:215–229
Gonneea ME, Mulligan AE, Charette MA (2013) Climate-driven sea level anomalies modulate coastal groundwater dynamics and discharge. Geophys Res Lett 40:2701–2706. https://doi.org/10.1002/grl.50192
Greatbatch RJ, Lu Y, de Young B (1996) Application of a barotropic model to North Atlantic synoptic sea level variability. J Mar Res 54:451–469
Haigh ID, Wahl T, Rohling EJ, Price RM, Pattiaratchi CB, Calafat FM, Dangendorf S (2014) Timescales for detecting a significant acceleration in sea level rise. Nat Commun 5:3635. https://doi.org/10.1038/ncomms4635
Hay CC, Morrow E, Kopp RE, Mitrovica JX (2015) Probabilistic reanalysis of twentieth-century sea-level rise. Nature 517:481–484
Holgate SJ, Matthews A, Woodworth PL, Rickards LJ, Tamisiea ME, Bradshaw E, Foden PR, Gordon KM, Jevrejeva S, Pugh J (2013) New data systems and products at the permanent service for mean sea level. J Coast Res 29(3):493–504
Holton JR (1992) An introduction to dynamic meteorology. Academic Press, San Diego, p 507
Horton BP, Kopp RE, Garner AJ, Hay CC, Khan NS, Roy K, Shaw TA (2018) Mapping sea-level change in time, space, and probability. Annu Rev Environ Resour. https://doi.org/10.1146/annurev-environ-102017-025826
Jordà G, Marbà N, Duarte CM (2012a) Mediterranean seagrass vulnerable to regional climate warming. Nat Clim Change 2:821–824
Jordà G, Gomis D, Álvarez-Fanjul E, Somot S (2012b) Atmospheric contribution to Mediterranean and nearby Atlantic sea level variability under different climate change scenarios. Glob Planet Change 80–81:198–214
Karegar MA, Dixon TH, Engelhart SE (2016) Subsidence along the Atlantic Coast of North America: insights from GPS and late Holocene relative sea level data. Geophys Res Lett 43:3126–3133. https://doi.org/10.1002/2016GL068015
Kenigson JS, Han W, Rajagopalan B, Yanto Jasinski M (2018) Decadal shift of NAO-linked interannual sea level variability along the U.S. Northeast Coast J Clim 31:4981–4989
Kundu PK, Cohen IM (2004) Fluid mechanics, 3rd edn. Elsevier Academic Press, Amsterdam, p 759
Kopp RE, Hay CC, Little CM, Mitrovica JX (2015) Geographic variability of sea-level change. Curr Clim Change Rep 1(3):192–204
Krueger O, Schenk F, Feser F, Weisse R (2013) Inconsistencies between long-term trends in storminess derived from the 20CR reanalysis and observations. J Clim 26:868–874
Laloyaux P, Balmaseda M, Dee D, Mogensen K, Janssen P (2016) A coupled data assimilation system for climate reanalysis. Q J R Meteorol Soc 142:65–78. https://doi.org/10.1002/qj.2629
Marcos M, Tsimplis MN (2007) Forcing of coastal sea level rise patterns in the North Atlantic and the Mediterranean Sea. Geophys Res Lett 34:L18604. https://doi.org/10.1029/2007GL030641
Marcos M, Tsimplis MN (2008) Coastal sea level trends in Southern Europe. Geophys J Int 175:70–82. https://doi.org/10.1111/j.1365-246X.2008.03892.x

Marcos M, Calafat FM, Berihuete Á, Dangendorf S (2015) Long-term variations in global sea level extremes. J Geophys Res Oceans 120:8115–8134. https://doi.org/10.1002/2015JC011173
Marshall J, Adcroft A, Hill C, Perelman L, Heisey C (1997) A finite-volume, incompressible Navier Stokes model for studies of the ocean on parallel computers. J Geophys Res 102(C3):5753–5766. https://doi.org/10.1029/96JC02775
Merrifield MA, Thompson PR (2018) Interdecadal sea level variations in the Pacific: distinctions between the tropics and extratropics. Geophys Res Lett. https://doi.org/10.1029/2018GL077666
Milne GA, Gehrels WR, Hughes CW, Tamisiea MA (2009) Identifying the causes of sea-level change. Nat Geosci 2:471–478
Pascual A, Marcos M, Gomis D (2008) Comparing the sea level response to pressure and wind forcing of two barotropic models: validation with tide gauge and altimetry data. J Geophys Res 113:C07011. https://doi.org/10.1029/2007JC004459
Pedlosky J (1987) Geophysical fluid dynamics, 2nd edn. Springer, New York, p 710
Peixoto JP, Oort AH (1992) Physics of Climate. American Institute of Physics, New York, p 520
Philander SGH (1978) Forced oceanic waves. Rev Geophys 16(1):15–46
Piecuch CG, Ponte RM (2014) Mechanisms of global-mean steric sea level change. J Clim 27:824–834
Piecuch CG, Ponte RM (2015a) Inverted barometer contributions to recent sea level changes along the northeast coast of North America. Geophys Res Lett 42:5918–5925. https://doi.org/10.1002/2015GL064580
Piecuch CG, Ponte RM (2015b) A wind-driven nonseasonal barotropic fluctuation of the Canadian inland seas. Ocean Sci 11:175–185. https://doi.org/10.5194/os-11-175-2015
Piecuch CG, Fukumori I, Ponte RM, Wang O (2015) Vertical structure of ocean pressure variations with application to satellite-gravimetric observations. J Atmos Ocean Technol 32:603–613
Piecuch CG, Dangendorf S, Ponte RM, Marcos M (2016a) Annual sea level changes on the North American Northeast Coast: influence of local winds and barotropic motions. J Clim 29:4801–4816
Piecuch CG, Thompson PR, Donohue KA (2016b) Air pressure effects on sea level changes during the twentieth century. J Geophys Res Oceans 121:7917–7930. https://doi.org/10.1002/2016JC012131
Poli P, Hersbach H, Tan D, Dee D, Thépaut J-N, Simmons A, Peubey C, Laloyaux P, Komori T, Berrisford P, Dragani R, Trémolet Y, Hólm E, Bonavita M, Isaksen L, Fisher M (2013) The data assimilation system and initial performance evaluation of the ECMWF pilot reanalysis of the 20th-century assimilating surface observations only (ERA-20C). ERA report series 14
Ponte RM (1992) The sea level response of a stratified ocean to barometric pressure forcing. J Phys Oceanogr 22:109–113
Ponte RM (1993) Variability in a homogeneous global ocean forced by barometric pressure. Dyn Atmos Oceans 18:209–234
Ponte RM (1994) Understanding the relation between wind- and pressure-driven sea level variability. J Geophys Res 99(C4):8033–8039
Ponte RM (2006) Low-frequency sea level variability and the inverted barometer effect. J Atmos Ocean Technol 23:619–629
Ponte RM, Dorandeu J (2003) Uncertainties in ECMWF surface pressure fields over the ocean in relation to sea level analysis and modeling. J Atmos Ocean Technol 20:301–307
Ponte RM, Quinn KJ, Piecuch CG (2018) Accounting for gravitational attraction and loading effects from land ice on absolute sea level. J Atmos Ocean Technol 35:405–410
Proshutinsky AY, Johnson MA (1997) Two circulation regimes of the wind-driven Arctic Ocean. J Geophys Res 102(C6):12493–12514
Proshutinsky A, Pavlov V, Bourke RH (2001) Sea level rise in the Arctic Ocean. Geophys Res Lett 28(11):2237–2240
Proshutinsky A, Ashik IM, Dvorkin EN, Häkkinen S, Krishfield RA, Peltier WR (2004) Secular sea level change in the Russian sector of the Arctic Ocean. J Geophys Res 109:C03042. https://doi.org/10.1029/2003JC002007
Proshutinksy A, Ashik I, Häkkinen S, Hunke E, Krishfield R, Maltrud M, Maslowski W, Zhang J (2007) Sea level variability in the Arctic Ocean from AOMIP models. J Geophys Res 112:C04S08. https://doi.org/10.1029/2006JC003916
Permanent Service for Mean Sea Level (PSMSL) (2018) Tide gauge data. http://www.psmsl.org/data/obtaining/. Retrieved 5 Mar 2018
Qiu B, Chen S (2006) Decadal variability in the large-scale sea surface height field of the South Pacific Ocean: observations and causes. J Phys Oceanogr 36:1751–1762
Qiu B, Chen S (2010) Interannual-to-decadal variability in the bifurcation of the North Equatorial Current off the Philippines. J Phys Oceanogr 40:2525–2538

Qiu B, Chen S (2012) Multidecadal sea level and gyre circulation variability in the northwestern tropical Pacific Ocean. J Phys Oceanogr 42:193–206
Richter K, Nilson JEØ, Drange H (2012) Contributions to sea level variability along the Norwegian coast for 1960–2010. J Geophys Res 117:C05038. https://doi.org/10.1029/2011JC007826
Royston S, Watson CS, Legrésy B, King MA, Church JA, Bos MS (2018) Sea-level trend uncertainty with Pacific climatic variability and temporally-correlated noise. J Geophys Res Oceans 123:1978–1993. https://doi.org/10.1002/2017JC013655
Sandstrom H (1980) On the wind-induced sea level changes on the Scotian shelf. J Geophys Res 85(C1):461–468
Sasaki YN, Minobe S, Miura Y (2014) Decadal sea-level variability along the coast of Japan in response to ocean circulation changes. J Geophys Res 119:266–275. https://doi.org/10.1002/2013JC009327
Sasaki YN, Washizu R, Yasuda T, Minobe S (2017) Sea level variability around Japan during the twentieth century simulated by a regional ocean model. J Clim 30:5585–5595
Stammer D, Hüttemann S (2008) Response of regional sea level to atmospheric pressure loading in a climate change scenario. J Clim 21:2093–2101
Stammer D, Cazenave A, Ponte RM, Tamisiea ME (2013) Causes for contemporary regional sea level changes. Annu Rev Mar Sci 5:21–46
Stammer D, Ray RD, Andersen OB, Arbic BK, Bosch W, Carrère L, Cheng Y, Chinn DS, Dushaw BD, Egbert GD, Erofeeva SY, Fok HS, Green JAM, Griffiths S, King MA, Lapin V, Lemoine FG, Luthcke SB, Lyard F, Morison J, Müller M, Padman L, Richman JG, Shriver JF, Shum CK, Taguchi E, Yi Y (2014) Accuracy assessment of global barotropic ocean tide models. Rev Geophys 52:243–282. https://doi.org/10.1002/2014RG000450
Sturges W, Douglas BC (2011) Wind effects on estimates of sea level rise. J Geophys Res 116:C06008. https://doi.org/10.1029/2010JC006492
Sündermann J, Pohlmann T (2011) A brief analysis of North Sea physics. Oceanologia 53(3):663–689
Theuerkeuf EJ, Rodriguez AB, Fegley SR, Luettich RA (2014) Sea level anomalies exacerbate beach erosion. Geophys Res Lett 41:5139–5147. https://doi.org/10.1002/2014GL060544
Thompson PR, Mitchum GT (2014) Coherent sea level variability on the North Atlantic western boundary. J Geophys Res 119:5676–5689. https://doi.org/10.1002/2014JC009999
Thompson PR, Mitchum GT, Vonesch C, Li J (2013) Variability of winter storminess in the eastern United States during the twentieth century from tide gauges. J Clim 26:9713–9726
Thompson PR, Merrifield MA, Wells JR, Chang CM (2014) Wind-driven coastal sea level variability in the northeast Pacific. J Clim 27:4733–4751
Thompson PR, Hamlington BD, Landerer FW, Adhikari S (2016) Are long tide gauge records in the wrong place to measure global mean sea level rise? Geophys Res Lett 43:10403–10411. https://doi.org/10.1002/2016GL070552
Thorne K, MacDonald G, Guntenspergen G, Ambrose R, Buffington K, Dugger B, Freeman C, Janousek C, Brown L, Rosencranz J, Holmquist J, Smol J, Hargan K, Takekawa J (2018) U.S. Pacific coastal wetland resilience and vulnerability to sea-level rise. Sci Adv 4:eaao3270
Tsimplis MN, Álvarez-Fanjul E, Gomis D, Fenoglio-Marc L, Pérez B (2005) Mediterranean Sea level trends: atmospheric pressure and wind contribution. Geophys Res Lett 32:L20602. https://doi.org/10.1029/2005GL023867
Vinogradova NT, Ponte RM, Stammer D (2007) Relation between sea level and bottom pressure and the vertical dependence of oceanic variability. Geophys Res Lett 34:L03608
Willebrand J, Philander SGH, Pacanowski RC (1980) The oceanic response to large-scale atmospheric disturbances. J Phys Oceanogr 10:411–429
Woodworth PL, Pouvreau N, Wöppelmann G (2010) The gyre-scale circulation of the North Atlantic and sea level at Brest. Ocean Sci 6:185–190
Woodworth PL, Morales Maqueda MÁ, Roussenov VM, Williams RG, Hughes CW (2014) Mean sea-level variability along the northeast American Atlantic coast and the roles of the wind and the overturning circulation. J Geophys Res Oceans 119:8916–8935. https://doi.org/10.1002/2014JC010520
Woodworth PL, Morales Maqueda MÁ, Gehrels WR, Roussenov VM, Williams RG, Hughes CW (2017) Variations in the difference between mean sea level measured either side of Cape Hatteras and their relation to the North Atlantic Oscillation. Clim Dyn 49(7–8):2451–2469
Woodworth PL, Melet A, Marcos M, Ray RD, Wöppelmann G, Sasaki YN, Cirano M, Hibbert A, Huthnance JM, Montserrat S, Merrifield MA (2019) Forcing factors affecting sea level changes at the coast. Surv Geophys. https://doi.org/10.1007/s10712-019-09531-1
Wunsch CW, Stammer D (1997) Atmospheric loading and the oceanic "inverted barometer" effect. Rev Geophys 35(1):79–107

Affiliations

C. G. Piecuch[1] · F. M. Calafat[2] · S. Dangendorf[3] · G. Jordà[4]

[1] Woods Hole Oceanographic Institution, 266 Woods Hole Road, Woods Hole, MA 02543, USA

[2] National Oceanography Centre, Joseph Proudman Building, 6 Brownlow Street, Liverpool L3 5DA, UK

[3] Forschungsinstitut Wasser und Umwelt, Universität Siegen, 57076 Siegen, Germany

[4] Instituto Español de Oceanografía (IEO), Centre Oceanogràfic de Balears, c./ Moll de Ponent s/n, 07015 Palma de Mallorca, Spain

Surveys in Geophysics (2019) 40:1437–1466
https://doi.org/10.1007/s10712-019-09536-w

Impact of Continental Freshwater Runoff on Coastal Sea Level

Fabien Durand[1] · Christopher G. Piecuch[2] · Mélanie Becker[3] · Fabrice Papa[1] · Sherin V. Raju[4] · Jamal U. Khan[1,5] · Rui M. Ponte[6]

Received: 13 December 2018 / Accepted: 23 April 2019 / Published online: 11 May 2019

Abstract

Freshwater discharge to the coastal ocean is a fundamental component of the global water cycle. It can impact coastal sea level over a broad range of spatial and temporal scales. Here we review the status of the current knowledge based on observational and modeling approaches. The main limitation in studies of the influence of rivers on coastal sea level has been the lack of consolidated discharge databases. We first provide an inventory of the main data sources currently available. We then review the existing knowledge about the runoff forcing of coastal sea level, differentiating between the mass and steric height contributions. Both mechanisms are important for coastal sea level budget, although they act on different scales. The mass contribution is related to a global ocean response that is established on relatively short timescales through barotropic processes while the steric contribution is associated with more of a regional adjustment that takes place on longer timescales by means of baroclinic dynamics. While numerical models required to simulate the runoff impact on coastal sea level variability have been improving over the past decades, a similar evolution is awaited for observational techniques, both for in situ observation and for remote sensing.

Keywords Sea level · Runoff · Discharge · River plumes · Salinity

✉ Fabien Durand
fabien.durand@ird.fr

1 LEGOS, Université de Toulouse, CNES, CNRS, IRD, UPS, 14 Avenue Edouard Belin, 31400 Toulouse, France

2 Woods Hole Oceanographic Institution, MS#21, Woods Hole, MA 02543-1050, USA

3 LIENSs, Université de La Rochelle, CNRS, 2 rue Olympe de Gouges, 17000 La Rochelle, France

4 Indo-French Cell for Water Sciences, Indian Institute of Science, Bangalore 560 012, India

5 Institute of Water and Flood Management, Bangladesh University of Engineering and Technology, Dhaka, Bangladesh

6 Atmospheric and Environmental Research, Inc., 131 Hartwell Avenue, Lexington, MA 02421-3126, USA

1 Introduction

1.1 Geographical and temporal scope

Continental freshwater runoff or discharge is a major constituent of the climatic system. Indeed, it represents a key component of the global water cycle (Trenberth et al. 2007). River discharge returns back to the ocean water that partly comes from evaporation over the oceans and was precipitated over continents, thereby maintaining a long-term balance of freshwater in the oceans. Rivers also play an important role in global biogeochemical cycles, discharging large amounts of sediment and nutrients to the oceans (Dai et al. 2009). In the present study, we review the current knowledge about the influence of river discharge on coastal sea level, focusing on large river deltas and large estuaries with strong outflows, and specifically on the best documented systems with some of the world's largest discharges (e.g., Amazon, Ganges–Brahmaputra–Meghna, Yangtze). Several other river outflows, although weaker in terms of overall discharge but extensively studied in recent years, will also be presented. We restrict our review to the regions dynamically connected to the ocean, which means that the upstream parts of the estuaries and deltas, under the primary influence of riverine hydraulics in terms of water level, are left out of our review. We focus our review on long timescales, typically seasonal scales and longer.

1.2 Why Should We Care About Runoff?

The coastal zone is a dynamic interface, where the rivers, land, and ocean interact. Throughout history, these regions have been attractive for humans due to their extremely rich resources (subsistence, ecologic, economic, logistic, recreative). In the year 2000, more than 10% of the world's population (625 million) lived in low-lying coastal areas located at less than 10 metres above sea level (Neumann et al. 2015). In these regions, very large numbers of people are particularly vulnerable to sea level rise, storm surge, natural and/or anthropogenic land subsidence, and variability of the sediment transports. This vulnerability is aggravated for low-lying deltaic regions, with large rivers and population densities among the highest of the world, such as the delta systems of Ganges–Brahmaputra, Mekong, Yangtze and Niger, to name a few (Fig. 1; Becker et al. 2019). Moreover, many of the world's megacities are located in the coastal zone and many of these are situated in large deltas. In this regard, Asia stands out as a prominent zone of vulnerability (Dhaka, Kolkata, Shanghai, Ho Chi Minh City, Bangkok; Fig. 2).

In deltaic and estuarine areas, a large river runoff can induce sea level fluctuations at the river mouths on a variety of timescales, acting in concert with other environmental factors, and making their interpretation more complex (Meade and Emery 1971). Although this issue is important for a better understanding of coastal zone vulnerability, the contribution of river runoff to sea level fluctuations has received little attention (e.g., Meade and Emery 1971; Aubrey et al. 1988; Tsimplis and Woodworth 1994; Piecuch et al. 2018). The typical magnitude of regional sea level variability induced by river runoff can be of the order of 1–10 cm for the largest discharges (Piecuch et al. 2018). This implies that runoff has a significant contribution to the overall sea level budget, in the regions under the influence of continental discharge, at our timescales of interest. Quantifying those impacts is of great interest to oceanographic and climate studies. Therefore, there is now a widespread need

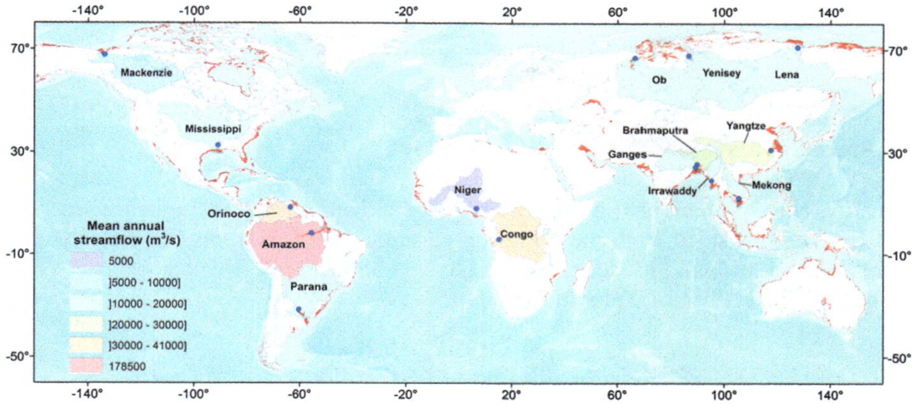

Fig. 1 Major river basins of the world (listed in Table 1). The global digital elevation model GTOPO30 (lta.cr.usgs.gov/GTOPO30) is used to map elevation less than 10 meters (in red). The blue dots locate the Global Runoff Data Center (GRDC, 2014, 2018) gauge stations listed in Table 1. The color of the basins represents their mean annual streamflow (m^3/s)

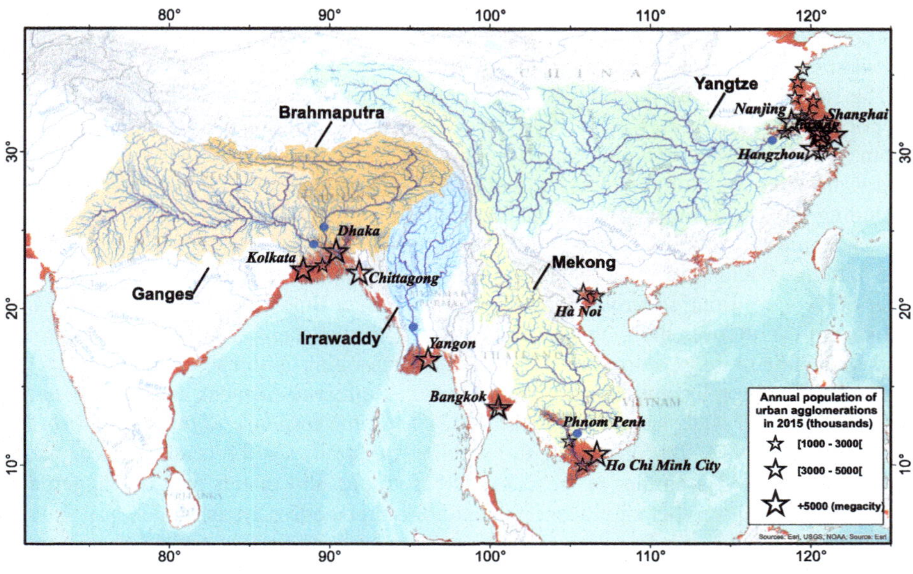

Fig. 2 Major Asian deltas. The global digital elevation model GTOPO30 (lta.cr.usgs.gov/GTOPO30) is used to map elevation less than 10 meters (in red). The stream network is provided by Hydrological data and maps based on SHuttle Elevation Derivatives at multiple Scales (HydroSHEDS, hydrosheds.cr.usgs.gov/hydro.php). The blue dots locate the Global Runoff Data Center (GRDC, 2014, 2018) gauge stations listed in Table 1. The stars correspond to large urban agglomerations with 1 million inhabitants or more in 2015 (from United Nations world urbanization prospects: The 2014 Revision, esa.un.org/unpd/wup/cd-Rom/)

for access to comprehensive continental discharge estimates globally. An up-to-date inventory of the available estimates will be presented in Sect. 2.

1.3 Processes and associated space/timescales

Primarily, one can think of two different means for riverine water to influence sea level. This can be understood from the following equation, which presents the breakdown of hydrostatic sea level into its steric, bottom pressure and atmospheric components (see for instance Gill and Niller 1973) for full details):

$$\eta = \frac{P'_b}{g\rho_0} - \frac{1}{\rho_0}\int_{-H}^{0} \rho' dz + \frac{P_{atm}}{g\rho_0} \tag{1}$$

where η represents the deviation of sea level around its mean, g is the acceleration of gravity, P'_b is the deviation of ocean bottom pressure, ρ_0 is a representative (constant) seawater density, H is the ocean depth, ρ' is the deviation of seawater density around its mean, P_{atm} is the deviation of atmospheric pressure. In the present study we do not consider the effects of atmospheric pressure on sea level variability (cf. Piecuch et al. 2019). Henceforth, we will consider only the first two terms, reflecting the two effects known as the ocean mass contribution and the steric effect, respectively.

The first effect is the ocean mass contribution (termed as "manometric sea level" by Gregory et al., this issue), which has received relatively little attention (Dobslaw and Thomas 2007). All else being equal, freshwater discharged into the sea increases the total water mass and volume of the global ocean, hence raising the global-mean sea level. Excluding any other forcing, basic physical intuition suggests that the oceanic adjustment to surface mass loading occurs rapidly, similar to what happens under atmospheric pressure loading (Ponte 1993). Facilitated by barotropic waves, equilibrium is reached on the order of days, resulting in an isostatic response on longer timescales; mass is redistributed and spread evenly over the global ocean surface such that there are negligible horizontal pressure gradients (e.g., Ponte 2006). This basic reasoning ignores complicating factors like coasts, topography, and stratification, which can effect resonances and other nonequilibrium responses (Dobslaw and Thomas 2007), as in the response to other ocean surface loading (Ponte 1993, 2006). One of the pending questions for the scientific community regards the detailed dynamics of the transient barotropic adjustments that are triggered by river outflows and whether significant nonequilibrium responses are possible.

Given the global ocean's relatively large surface area, one might anticipate that freshwater discharged into the ocean by rivers has a negligible influence on globally averaged sea level. However, this is not necessarily the case. Figure 3 shows the freshwater volume discharged by the Amazon River observed at Óbidos (Brazil) during 1993–2010, converted to units of equivalent global-mean sea level. That is, the river discharge time series has been integrated in time and divided by the global ocean's surface area. For comparison, the contemporaneous global-mean sea level time series from satellite altimetry is also shown. To emphasize low-frequency (interannual) variation, linear trends and seasonal cycles were removed from both time series, and a 13-month low-pass filter was applied. The standard deviation computed from the Amazon River time series is 0.4 mm, which is not small compared to the standard deviation of 1.0 mm calculated

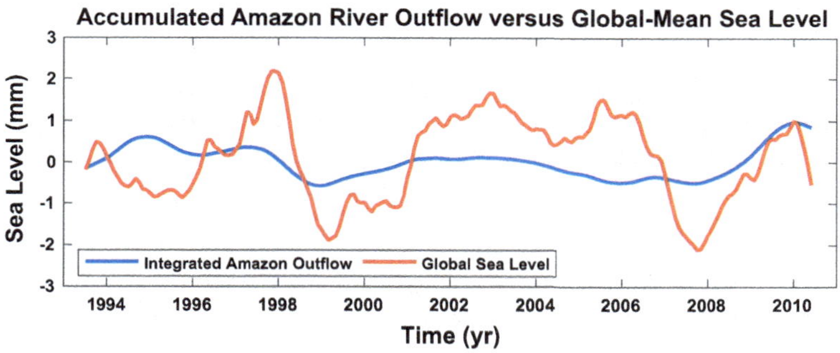

Fig. 3 Comparison of accumulated Amazon River outflow and global-mean sea level. Blue curve is the time integral of monthly discharge from the Amazon River observed at Óbidos (Brazil) from the database of Dai (2016) and normalized by global ocean surface area. Red curve is global-mean sea level observed by satellite altimetry. Both time series have had a linear trend and seasonal cycle removed, and have been smoothed with a 13-month low-pass filter to emphasize low-frequency variations

from the satellite altimetry time series. This simple exercise suggests that the impact of freshwater discharged by rivers on sea level is potentially important, not only at regional scales, but also at global scales.

The second way a river discharge can influence the sea level is through the steric effect, and more precisely the halosteric effect. Commonly, an outflow of riverine water is less dense than the surrounding salty water. This strong density contrast is only partly eroded by mixing and entrainment of ambient coastal ocean water into the buoyant coastal freshwater plume. Thus, a riverine discharge results in a lens of fresher, lighter water that retains its identity while "floating" over the saltier, denser ocean water. Such density anomalies involve sea level signals, baroclinic pressure gradients, and associated currents. As this regional dynamic response is believed to be locally more important than the ocean mass contribution effect (which is more broadly spread over the global ocean) around most of river outlets, it has received considerably more attention in the past decades. It is associated with longer response timescales, and has a regional impact, hence its relevance for coastal sea level variability.

A key question for understanding the associated variability of coastal sea level can be stated as follows: what is the dynamics of the spreading of the fresh anomaly induced by a river plume along the neighboring coastlines, away for the river mouth? "Spreading" here is to be understood generally both in the sense of mixing of the riverine waters with the ambient ocean water, and of transport of the riverine waters away from the river mouth. Strictly speaking, there is also a related thermal effect, due to the fact that a river outflow does not necessarily have the same temperature as the ambient ocean water. However, sea level and density anomalies resulting from this difference of temperature are not considered in this review. This omission is justified based on simple scaling arguments. Assuming a typical haline contraction coefficient of 8×10^{-4} PSU^{-1} and thermal expansion coefficient of 2×10^{-4} degC^{-1}, and given a 1 practical salinity unit, 1 PSU (10 PSU) salinity contrast between the river water and ocean water, a corresponding temperature difference of several degC (several tens of degC) is needed for temperature effects on density to be comparable to salinity effects.

The two above-cited processes, mass contribution and halosteric effect, will be discussed in Sect. 3, in theoretical and realistic frameworks.

2 State-of-the-Art Runoff and Freshwater Flux Products

Direct observational river runoff estimates across the global ocean are largely scattered, incomplete and inhomogeneous, even for the major rivers. This has considerably hampered the scientific progress on our topic. This section aims at improving matters and providing a comprehensive inventory of state-of-the-art databases.

The primary estimation of river flow and discharge is based on in situ observations (Fekete et al. 2000, 2015). In situ gauging networks have been installed for several decades in many river basins, distributed non-uniformly throughout the world, usually managed at local or country level, and primarily motivated by socioeconomic applications (e.g., water resources allocation, navigation and infrastructures, hydroelectric energy, flood hazard). However, the achievement of a comprehensive data collection of continental discharge to the oceans with in situ observations faces many challenges (Trenberth et al. 2007). One of the major obstacles in estimating continental discharge to the ocean is the sparse and incomplete gauging records or unmonitored streamflow. In many regions, especially in the tropics and in high-latitude environments, the collection of data is made difficult by the complexity of the physics of water flow across vast remote and inaccessible regions. For other countries, the cost of data collection can be limited due to economic reasons. As a result, a vast portion of the freshwater discharge to the ocean is ungauged, not adequately measured or has experienced loss of gauges in the past decades (Shiklomanov et al. 2002). Finally, when such collection of data exists, their dissemination is in general restricted, being considered sensitive national information, thus limiting their public access and use for environmental and climate studies (Papa et al. 2012a).

In recent decades, the systematic and global monitoring of rivers became a fundamental objective of the international community, including United Nations organisations, governments, and other public or private institutions. The primary archive for global in situ river discharge data is now the Global Runoff Data Center (GRDC, 2018) that operates under the auspices of the World Meteorological Organisation (WMO).

The GRDC provides a unique collection of river discharge data collected at daily or monthly intervals from more than 8000 stations located in 157 countries, available for non-commercial use upon request (www.bafg.de/GRDC/EN/Home/ homepage_node.html) Table 1 summarizes, as of November 2018, the data available (daily or monthly discharge observations) from GRDC for a selection of 15 of the world's largest rivers at the farthest downstream station before reaching the ocean. As seen in Table 1, while GRDC offers long-term, recent and up-to-date times series (latest observations within the last 5 years for Mississippi, Rio Parana, Ob, Yenisei, Mackenzie), other large river systems show very limited records in time (Mekong, Ganges) and/or not up-to-date (Amazon, Congo, Lena, Yangtze, Orinoco, Brahmaputra, Irrawaddy). Some stations offering long-term monitoring (several decades) also suffer from large amounts of missing data on daily or monthly records (Mississippi, Yenisei, Lena, Niger, Yangtze, Brahmaputra).

For specific studies, in order to improve the record length and obtain more recent measurements, users can complement the large database of GRDC by using additional sources providing streamflow data. Those sources can come from in situ or satellite-derived observations, and are provided by institutional websites and databases or through personal contacts. Our objectives here are to provide the community with the current and most relevant sources, with a balance between the length of the records,

Table 1 River discharge data at the farthest downstream stations for 15 of the world's largest ocean-reaching rivers from GRDC (2018): characteristics and availability as of November 2018

River name	Station name, country, GRDC number	Lat (deg)	Lon (deg)	Catchment size ($10^6 \times km^2$); Distance of the station to the river mouths (km)	Period of daily data availability	Length of daily time series in years (% of missing data)	Period of monthly data availability	Length of monthly time in years (% of missing data)	Mean annual stream flow (m^3/s)	Mean annual volume (km^3)
Amazon	Óbidos, Brazil, 3629001	1.92S	55.51W	4.680; 700	1968–2008	41 (6.15)	1968–2008	41 (n.a)	178,500	5600
Congo	Brazzaville, Congo, 1447150	4.27S	15.32E	3.475; 550	n.a	n.a	1971–1983	13 (0.0)	41,000	1300
Mississippi	Vicksburg, MS, USA, 4127800	32.32N	90.91W	2.965; 350	1931–2018	88(1.35)	1928–1983	56 (63.23)	17,500	550
Rio Parana	Chapeton, Argentina, 3265600	31.57S	60.33W	n.a; 450	1975–2014	40 (0.48)	1975–2014	40 (0.43)	17,800	560
Ob	Shalekard, Russia 2912600	66.57N	66.53E	2.950; 287	1954–2010	57 (1.76)	1930–2015	86 (12.79)	12,900	410
Yenisei	Igarka, Russia, 2909150	67.48N	86.5E	2.440; 697	1955–2011	57 (13.05)	1936–2015	80 (15.0)	19,250	610
Lena	Kusur, Russia, 2903420	70.7N	127.65E	2.430; 211	1935–2011	77 (0.16)	1934–2000	67 (0.0)	17,100	540
Niger	Lokoja, Nigeria 1834101	7.80N	6.77E	n.a,; 500	1970–2006	37 (12.03)	2007–2012	6 (44.4)	5000	160

Table 1 (continued)

River name	Station name, country, GRDC number	Lat (deg)	Lon (deg)	Catchment size ($10^6 \times km^2$); Distance of the station to the river mouths (km)	Period of daily data availability	Length of daily time series in years (% of missing data)	Period of monthly data availability	Length of monthly time in years (% of missing data)	Mean annual stream flow (m^3/s)	Mean annual volume (km^3)
Yangtze	Datong, China, 2181900	30.77N	117.62E	1.706; 510	2004–2004	1 (0.0)	1922–1988	67 (25.44)	25,000	790
Mackenzie	Arctic Red River, Canada, 4208025	67.54N	133.75W	1.660; 292	1972–2016	45 (1.76)	1972–1996	25 (0)	9200	290
Mekong	Kompong Cham, Cambodia, 2569003	11.99N	105.47E	0.660; 420	1964–1974	11 (2.40)	n.a	n.a	13,500	425
Orinoco	Puente Angostura, Venezuela, 3206720	8.15N	63.60W	0.836; 380	1923–1989	67 (1.33)	1923–1989	67 (1.25)	31,200	985
Irrawaddy	Pyay, Myanmar, 2260600	18.80N	95.22E	0.346; 400	1996–2010	15 (0.0)	1996–2010	15 (0)	11,800	372
Ganges	Hardinge bridge, Bangladesh, 2646200	24.08N	89.03E	0.846; 250	1985–1992	8 (1.21)	1985–1992	8 (1.19)	10,900	345
Brahmaputra	Bahadurabad, Bangladesh, 2651100	25.18N	89.67E	0.636; 350	1985–1992	8 (0.0)	1969–1992	24 (44.80)	23,800	750

Table 2 Proposed sources for river discharge data and time series for 15 of the world's largest ocean-reaching rivers: characteristics and availability as of November 2018

River name	Data sources	Station name, country,	Lat (deg); Lon (deg)	Period of data availability and temporal sampling	Data acquisition procedure	Web address or contact
Amazon	In situ, Hybam and ANA (Brazilian National Water Agency)	Óbidos, Brazil	1.94722S; 55.5111W	23/02/1968–31/10/2017 (daily) 02/1968–10/2017 (monthly)	Website database/download (login)	http://www.ore-hybam.org http://www.snirh.gov.br/hidroweb
Congo	In situ, Hybam	Beach Brazzaville, Congo,	4,2823S; 15,3008E	01/01/1990–10/06/2018 (daily) 01/1990–06/2018 (monthly)	Website database/download (login)	http://www.ore-hybam.org
Mississippi	In situ, GRDC	Vicksburg, MS, USA,	32.32N; 90.91W	1931–2018 (daily)	Website database/upon request	www.bafg.de/GRDC
Rio Parana	In situ, GRDC	Chapeton, Argentina,	31.57S; 60.33W	1975–2014 (daily)	Website database/upon request	www.bafg.de/GRDC
Ob	In situ, GRDC	Shalekard, Russia	66.57N; 66.53E	1954–2010 (daily) 1930–2015 (monthly)	Website database/upon request	www.bafg.de/GRDC
Yenisei	In situ, GRDC	Igarka, Russia,	67.48N 86.50E	1955–2011	Website database/upon request	www.bafg.de/GRDC
Lena	In situ, GRDC	Kusur, Russia,	70.7N; 127.65E	1935–2010 (monthly)	Website database/direct download	www.bafg.de/GRDC
Niger	Satellite/In situ	Lokoja, Nigeria	7.80N; 6.77E	2006–2014 (daily)	Upon request	www.hydrology.irpi.cnr.it/people/angelica-tarpanelli/
Yangtze	In situ, GRDC	Datong, China,	30.77N; 117.62E	2004–2004	Website database/upon request	www.bafg.de/GRDC
Mackenzie	In situ, GRDC	Arctic Red River, Canada,	67.54N; 133.75W	1972–2016 (daily)	Website database/upon request	www.bafg.de/GRDC
Mekong	Satellite/in situ (Biancamaria et al., 2017)	Chroy Chang Var, Cambodia	11.98N; 104.98E	1993–2018	Upon request	http://www.legos.obs-mip.fr/members/biancamaria

Table 2 (continued)

River name	Data sources	Station name, country,	Lat (deg); Lon (deg)	Period of data availability and temporal sampling	Data acquisition procedure	Web address or contact
Orinoco	In situ, Hybam	Ciudad Bolivar, Venezuela	8,1432N; 63,6074W	01/01/2003–13/06/2017 (daily) 01/2003–06/2017 (monthly)	Website database/download (login)	http://www.ore-hybam.org
Irrawaddy	In situ, GRDC	Pyay, Myanmar	18.80N 95.22E	1996–2010 (daily)	Website database/upon request	www.bafg.de/GRDC
Irrawaddy	Satellite/in situ	Pyay, Myanmar	18.80N 95.22E	01/1993–12/2016 (monthly)	Upon request	http://www.legos.obs-mip.fr/members/papa
Ganges	Satellite/in situ (Papa et al. 2012a)	Hardinge bridge, Bangladesh	24.08N 89.03E	01/1993–12/2016 (monthly) 06/2008–12/2016 (10-day)	Upon request	http://www.legos.obs-mip.fr/members/papa
Brahmaputra	Satellite/in situ (Papa et al. 2012a)	Bahadurabad, Bangladesh	25.18N 89.67E	01/1993-12/2016 (monthly) 06/2008-12/2016 (10-day)	Upon request	http://www.legos.obs-mip.fr/members/papa

their temporal sampling interval and the availability of up-to-date observations. Table 2 summarizes the proposed collections, their sources, the main characteristics of the time series and how to get access to those data.

For 6 out of the 15 largest rivers we considered, the GRDC database turns out to be the most adequate source for providing river discharge time series. For Mississippi, Mackenzie, Rio Parana, GRDC provides long-term records with recent/up-to-date observations, similar for instance to what is available on the U.S. Geological Survey website (http://nwis.waterdata.usgs.gov/nwis/). For the large Siberian rivers (Ob, Yenisei, Lena), the project R-ArcticNet (A Regional, Electronic, Hydrographic Data Network For the Arctic Region, www.r-arcticnet.sr.unh.edu, Lammers et al. 2001) offers time series similar to GRDC.

For large tropical rivers, alternatives to GRDC limited records range from data archives from international observatories, river basins and water management institutes, to collections that can be obtained only through personal contacts. For the Amazon, Orinoco and Congo rivers, the Observation Service (SO) HyBAm (HYBAM, 2018), "Geodynamical, hydrological and biogeochemical control of erosion/alteration and material transport in the Amazon, Orinoco and Congo basins", provides the research community with long-term and up-to-date time series of river discharge at daily and monthly timescales. As of November 2018, time series of in situ river discharge over the Amazon River (1968–2017 at Óbidos), the Congo River (1990–2018 at Brazzaville) and the Orinoco River (2003–2017 at Ciudad Bolivar) are available on the website http://www.ore-hybam.org. Note that for the Amazon River, the Brazilian National Water Agency (ANA) also provides up-to-date river discharge time series (http://hidroweb.ana.gov.br/)

For the Yangtze River, to our knowledge, no alternative to the short 1-year time series of GRDC is available, despite the fact that longer (since 1950) and more recent (at least 2001–2006) time series from the Changjiang Water Resources Commission exist, as reported in Xu and Milliman (2009).

For large rivers of the Indian subcontinent, public access to long-term and recent river discharge observations is generally restricted. Recent efforts have been undergone to provide to the public such measurements for Indian non-transboundary rivers, including large basins such as Mahanadi, Godavari, Krishna, and Cauvery flowing into the Bay of Bengal. Those data are available on the "Generation of Database and Implementation of Web Enabled Water Resources Information System in the Country" short named as India-WRIS WebGIS (Water Resources Information System of India, www.india-wris.nrsc.gov.in/). However, observations of large Indian transboundary rivers (mainly the Ganges–Brahmaputra-Meghna system and Indus River) are still not freely available. Historically, hydrological observations in the Ganges–Brahmaputra Rivers across Bangladesh have also been carried out by the Bangladesh Water Development Board since the early 1920s (www.bwdb.gov.bd/). However, long-term and recent data records are difficult to obtain in the region and public access is often limited (Jian et al. 2009; Durand et al. 2011) especially for long-term daily Ganges and Brahmaputra discharge time series.

Given the importance of Ganges - Brahmaputra freshwater flux to the Bay of Bengal and its impacts on the regional climate (Neetu et al. 2012; Sengupta et al. 2016), Papa et al. (2012a) developed a methodology using satellite altimetry observations (TOPEX-Poseidon, ERS-2, ENVISAT, Jason2/3 missions) to locally estimate river discharge from the systematic monitoring of water levels of these two rivers. Altimetry-derived river water heights are correlated with in situ observed river discharge or height to construct empirical regression curves (called rating curves) so as to provide altimetry-based discharge estimates for times when in situ discharge observations are missing, or even to extend river discharge series forward or backward in time (for more details, refer to Papa et al. (2012a)).

This technique, despite several limitations (Alsdorf et al. 2007; Papa et al. 2012b), has been shown to be extremely valuable as a complement to ground-based observations where traditional gauge data can be irregular and difficult to obtain. It has been proven advantageous to provide important information for oceanography studies (Akhil et al. 2014; Chaitanya et al. 2015). Over the Ganges and Brahmaputra rivers, altimetry-derived discharge time series are available for each river (Table 2) and as a Ganges–Brahmaputra combined freshwater flux to the Bay of Bengal at the river mouth for 1993–2016 (monthly basis) and for 2008–2016 (10-day basis). Uncertainties are around 10%, well within the range of errors acceptable for large rivers (a 15–20% accuracy is generally considered as acceptable (Fekete et al. 2000)). A similar approach has been used for the Irrawaddy River (Frappart et al. 2015), and an altimetry-derived discharge time series for 1993–2016 on a monthly timescale is also available to the community (Table 2) and provides additional valuable information to the traditional gauge data available on the GRDC collection (1996–2010, daily).

For the Mekong River, several institutional sources, such as the Mekong Central Water Commission (MCWC, www.portal.mrcmekong.org) or the Vietnam Southern Regional Hydrometeorological Center (VSRHC, http://www.kttv-nb.org.vn/) also provide in situ water level and discharge information on their data portal. For instance, Tan Chau (10.48°N, 105.13°E) and Chau Doc (10.42°N, 105.06°E) stations on the Mekong would offer precious information on continental freshwater flux, but timeseries can be irregular, incomplete, not up-to-date or difficult to obtain. As a complement, and similarly to what is proposed on the Ganges–Brahmaputra or the Irrawaddy rivers, an alternative based on long-term and continuous radar altimetry observations is available and a time series of Mekong river discharge for 1993–2018 can be now accessed for environmental studies (Biancamaria et al. 2017).

Finally, for the Niger River in Africa, very recent satellite-based products inferring river discharge at Lokoja are also available upon request (see Table 2; Tarpanelli et al. 2017, 2018). These estimates are based on a combination on multi-satellite sensors (Moderate-Resolution Imaging Spectroradiometer MODIS and radar altimetry observations) with a neural network approach, and were found to be a very reliable tool to infer Niger River discharge (2006–2014, daily) with a relative root-mean-square error of 0.12%.

As a complement to in situ archives and satellite-derived river discharge products, efforts have been also made by the community to characterize long-term variations and recent changes of continental discharge to the global ocean using modeling approaches (GRDC 2014; Peel et al. 2006, Fekete et al. 2000). As several methods and results are available, we will not discuss them here in detail. For the oceanographic community, widely used datasets are the ones from Dai and Trenberth (2002) and Dai et al. (2009), where in their latest versions, they combined observations from in situ gauges and simulations from a land surface model to create a dataset of historical monthly streamflow for the world's 925 largest ocean-reaching rivers for 1948–2004. This compilation has been recently updated to include earlier data (going back to the year 1900 in some cases) and more recent records (extending through the year 2010), and is described in Dai (2016). While this dataset represents unprecedented and valuable information on continental discharge into the global ocean, for individual river systems where in situ discharge observations are not available, estimates from Dai et al. (2009) have difficulty in reproducing the interannual variability characterized by large anomalous events. This is the case for instance after 1996 for the Ganges–Brahmaputra, which might have strong impacts on the coastal ocean at various timescales (Durand et al. 2011). Similarly, several recent studies based on observations, models or model-data combinations (Clark et al. 2015; Chandanpurkar et al. 2017;

Do et al. 2018; Gudmundsson et al. 2018; Suzuki et al. 2018) also provide new global and long-term datasets of continental discharge estimates and freshwater flux to the oceans.

In the near future, the Surface Water and Ocean Topography mission (SWOT, Prigent et al. 2016), now planned for September 2021, is set to measure surface water bodies and to infer river discharge with a repeat cycle of 21 days. Unlike previous altimeters used for hydrological applications (Papa et al. 2012a) that only measure along-track 1-D heights, SWOT will carry a Ka-band radar interferometer across a 120 km swath capable of deriving 2-D images of surface water height (along with river height, width and slope) with a vertical accuracy of about 1 cm per 1 km^2. The calculation of river discharge will still rely on algorithms that account for the unknown channel depths and flow velocities; however SWOT is expected to provide unprecedented global and continuous discharge measurements from space with spatial and temporal resolutions adequate to oceanographic studies.

3 Theory, Observation, and Modeling of Continental Freshwater Runoff Impacts on Regional Sea Level

Here we review current understanding of the influence of continental freshwater runoff from rivers on coastal sea level, including the roles of mass and steric changes, considering theoretical and idealized frameworks as well as more realistic data and model settings.

3.1 Qualitative Relationships Between Tide Gauge Records and River Runoff

Previous studies consider the influence of forcing by river runoff on sea level from tide gauge data. Many of these studies are qualitative, based on intuitive reasoning or statistical methods, such as correlation or regression analysis. While it is difficult to generalize, these studies find that river runoff can have more or less influence on coastal sea level, depending on space and timescales, region and time period. Here we summarize the main findings from some example studies, with an emphasis on the relevant timescales, time periods, and geographic regions.

Roden (1960) observes that between 15 and 50% of the anomalous sea level variation at Astoria, Oregon (US West Coast) is due to anomalous Columbia River discharge, depending on timescale (cf. Chelton and Davis 1982; Chelton and Enfield 1986). Meade and Emery (1971) argue that river runoff accounts for between 20 and 31% of detrended interannual sea level variance during 1930–1970 along the US East and Gulf Coasts. Royer (1979) discusses the influence of runoff on annual changes in coastal steric sea level along the Gulf of Alaska. Blaha (1984) shows that freshwater runoff from the Savannah River and Chesapeake Bay does not explain variance in nonseasonal monthly tide gauge sea level records at Fernandina, Charleston, and Norfolk (US Southeast Coast) during 1955–1975. In a study of tide gauges on the east coast of South America, Aubrey et al. (1988) note large monthly sea level variations in tide gauge data from locations near or within major rivers—such as Isla Martin Garcia (Argentina), Colonia (Uruguay), and Montevideo (Uruguay)—situated in the Río de la Plata. Tsimplis and Woodworth (1994) study the sea level seasonal cycle from globally distributed tide gauges and interpret large amplitudes observed in tide gauge data along the Ganges and Irrawaddy Deltas, Mahi River, Yellow River, St. Lawrence River, and Río Uruguay as the consequence of river outflows. Based on correlation analyses, Gough and Robinson (2000) suggest that discharge from the Churchill River explains 43% of the monthly sea level variance in the Churchill tide gauge records in Hudson Bay (Canada) from 1974 to 1994. Hong et al. (2000) describe their effort to find a statistically significant relationship between observed decadal variability in US East Coast sea level and river runoff as "fruitless". Judging from simulations with a reduced-gravity ocean model, Han and Webster (2002) find that the influence of river discharge on interannual sea level variability in the Bay of Bengal is negligible. Using monthly river runoff data along with sea level from tide gauges and satellite altimetry, Han (2002) reasons that runoff from the St. Lawrence River (Canada) did not cause an interannual decline in sea level on the eastern Scotian Shelf during 1997–1999.

Based on study of tide gauge data and a barotropic model, Proshutinsky et al. (2004) find that seasonal increases in Arctic sea level at locations near river mouths during June and July result from increased river discharge associated with melting snow, but note that long-term (1948–2002) coastal sea level trends in the Arctic due to river runoff are small and negligible. Vinogradov and Ponte (2011) suggest that strong river runoff could be responsible for discrepancies observed between interannual sea level changes from tide gauge records and satellite altimeter data around the Ganges River delta from 1993 to 2008; similar suggestions are made more recently by Ruiz Etcheverry et al. (2015) for the annual cycle in that region. Torres and Tsimplis (2012) suggest that outflow from the Magdalena and Atrato Rivers contributes to the sea level seasonal cycle in the southeastern Colombian Basin (Caribbean Sea). Studying the seasonal cycle in coastal sea level from monthly tide gauge data in the Gulf of Cadiz (Portugal and Spain), Laiz et al. (2013) argue that runoff from the Guadalquivir River explains 18% of the barometrically corrected sea level variance at nearby Bonanza, mostly due to strong discharge events in winter and autumn, but they find that runoff from the Tinto-Odiel River System has no impact on sea level as observed at the close-by Huelva tide gauge. Saramul and Ezer (2014) determine that river discharge has only a small impact on seasonal changes in sea level in the Gulf of Thailand. Becker et al. (2014) explain that tide gauge data in the St. Lawrence River and Gulf of St. Lawrence are affected by strong discharge from upstream runoff. Svendsen et al. (2016) note that, given their location in the Gulf of Ob, sea level observations from the Antipayuta tide gauge (Russian Arctic) are largely indicative of river runoff. Calafat et al. (2018) compare the sea level annual cycle from tide gauges on the US Southeast Coast to river discharge from major rivers flowing into the Atlantic Ocean and do not find good agreement. Piecuch et al. (2018) corroborate earlier findings from Meade and Emery (1971) using updated datasets over longer and more recent time periods along the US East and Gulf Coasts.

Together, these studies reveal that river runoff can be an important driver of coastal sea level variation on monthly and longer timescales, but seldom is it the dominant forcing mechanism. Moreover, these works clarify that something like a "first law of geography" does not hold for the relationship between variable river runoff and coastal sea level—it is not necessarily true that sea level at some location geographically closer to a river mouth is more strongly affected by river discharge than in another location farther away. For example, the fact that Laiz et al. (2013) find no relation between discharge from the Tinto-Odiel River System and sea level at nearby Huelva could in part be because that tide gauge is situated slightly southeast of the river mouth, whereas—under the influence of Earth's rotation—seasonal river discharge would have the tendency to "turn away" and flow northwest along the coast in the sense of a coastal Kelvin wave (Piecuch et al. 2018). This underscores the need to better understand physical processes mediating relationships between river runoff and sea level at the coast.

3.2 Ocean mass Contribution of Runoff

One way of investigating the ocean mass contribution of river outflows is through "hosing experiments" performed with ocean numerical models. These experiments simulate the sea level response to local inputs of water mass into the ocean. As such, they can help understand what would result from anomalous runoff in river outlets or coastal ice bodies. Based on idealized ice-melting experiments, Lorbacher et al. (2012) observed that the sea level response to mass input is mediated by barotropic waves, which propagate very quickly across the global ocean. They also determined that the global ocean gets roughly uniformly adjusted within a few days. As emphasized by Stammer (2010), this implies that the sea level response to the ocean mass contribution of localized runoff is essentially global, not regional, whatever the location of the source point. However, further studies are needed based on idealized experiments or theoretical analyses, in particular focusing on specific geometries such as shallow shelves and narrow semi-enclosed basins (e.g., Ponte 2006; Dobslaw and Thomas 2007).

As an example of rivers discharging to the open ocean, the ocean mass contribution of runoff was assessed by Laiz et al. (2014) for the case of the Gironde (west coast of France, northeastern Atlantic). In their regional circulation model, even when focusing only on flood periods, the ocean mass contribution of the sea level response to discharge is sub-centimetric, including in the immediate vicinity of the river mouth. This modest signature may be related to the weak discharge of the river considered (1100 m^3/s mean outflow). Still, one cannot exclude significant regional impact on coastal sea level driven by more powerful rivers, in particular those outflowing in marginal seas. For instance, Fig. 4 presents the amplitude of the annual cycle of sea level simulated in a barotropic model of the Bay of Bengal. The combined discharge of the rivers outflowing in the Northern Bay of Bengal (Ganges–Brahmaputra–Meghna and Hooghly rivers) is large (see Sect. 2), with

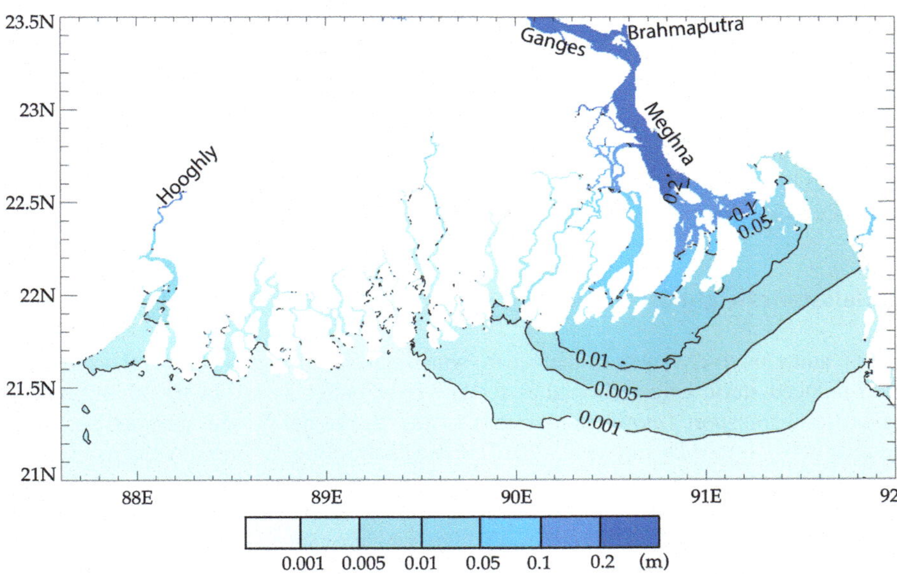

Fig. 4 Amplitude of the annual harmonic of sea level in a barotropic model of the Bay of Bengal forced by seasonally varying rivers discharges

summer season discharge roughly equivalent to the Amazon yearly average discharge. The model setup is similar to Krien et al. (2016). The tidal forcing comprises only high-frequency constituents (diurnal, semi diurnal, semi-monthly and monthly periods), and the model is forced by time-varying discharge at its upstream boundaries. Hence, any low-frequency (seasonal-to-annual) variability of the simulated water level can only result from the mass contribution of these rivers. Figure 4 can thus be seen as a measure of the ocean mass contribution of these rivers to the regional annual sea level variability. The amplitude of the annual sea surface height variability decays sharply when moving away from the mouth of Meghna along the coasts of the Bengal delta, from values of about 20 cm right at the mouth, to about 1 cm some 70 km away. Beyond 150 km from the outlet, the amplitude is less than 1 mm.

In the same vein, Dobslaw and Thomas (2007) as well as Peralta-Ferriz and Morison (2010) investigated the seasonal changes in Arctic Ocean bottom pressure (primarily equivalent to ocean mass, and thus contributing to sea surface height). They suggested that the observed changes, reaching 2 cm in amplitude, can be reasonably well explained by a partial trapping of the discharged water within the Arctic basin. This trapping appears to result from a barotropic geostrophic circulation (involving the whole water column) around the Arctic Ocean, accompanied by an outflow to the adjacent ocean basins through narrow frictional straits. A similar dynamics may be expected in other semi-enclosed basins subject to intense runoff, such as the Baltic Sea or the Black Sea. Volkov et al. (2016) considered the specific case of the Black Sea, a marginal basin connected to the Mediterranean Sea through a series of narrow and shallow choke points. They suggested the possibility of significant mass accumulation driven by freshwater input, at seasonal and longer timescales. Given that more than half of the freshwater received by the Black Sea comes from rivers (Danube, Dnepr and Don in particular), their study calls for a careful examination of the specific role of hydrologic variability of this large drainage basin, among others, on the seasonal-to-decadal sea level variability.

In summary, the contribution of mass effects to coastal sea level anomalies associated with runoff is expected to be relatively weak in most cases because of the rapid isostatic adjustment through barotropic dynamics. However, stronger dynamic mass effects are possible, for example, in the case of discharge into a semi-enclosed marginal sea connected to the global ocean through a narrow strait, where frictional processes can locally trap the mass input on certain timescales (e.g., Peralta-Ferriz and Morison 2010; Volkov et al. 2016). Careful evaluation on a case by case basis is warranted, apart from consideration of mass effects on estuarine sea level, which will likely be important in most cases.

3.3 Halosteric Height Contribution of Runoff

The spreading of river waters in the ocean, which governs the spatiotemporal structure of runoff-induced steric height anomalies for any river outlet, is driven by mixing (mostly vertical) and transport (mostly horizontal) of the freshwater in the surrounding ocean. The review by Horner-Devine et al. (2015) distinguishes three adjacent domains in a river plume: the near-field, close to the source, where the plume is marked, thick (typically occupying the whole water column), hence where the halosteric sea level effect is expected to be strong; the mid-field, located further offshore, where rotation effects are prominent; and the far-field, where the memory of the initial momentum of the discharge is lost, but where the water mass still shows distinct characteristics (in particular lower salinity) compared to ambient waters. The latter domain can extend hundreds of kilometers or more from the river mouth in some cases, as we shall see in the next section. Garvine (2001) and Wu et al. (2014) identified three dominant types of river plumes. The first type turns right (in the northern hemisphere) upon entering the ocean, and hugs the coast in the direction of propagation of coastally trapped waves. This pattern is commonly observed in numerical simulations with idealized geometry (e.g., McCreary et al. 1997), where the size of the outlet is large compared to the Rossby radius of deformation (typically in broad deltas). The second type also includes spreading to the left of the river mouth, in the northern hemisphere, under some special conditions for discharge rates, flow structure, bathymetry and mixing at the mouth (e.g., Garvine 1999, 2001; Yankovsky 2000); it is commonly seen in idealized numerical experiments but rarely found in nature. The third type of plume turns right (in the northern hemisphere) but gets trapped in an anticylonic bulge, that never reaches a steady state despite export by a geostrophic coastal current (Pichevin and Nof 1997; Nof and Pichevin 2001; Garvine 2001; Fong and Geyer, 2002; Nof 2005). A growing sea level anomaly can occur in the absence of background circulation, significant mixing or external forcing.

Simpson (1997) and Horner-Devine et al. (2015) reviewed the various processes that can alter the idealized picture of plume spreading presented in the previous paragraph. Four different kinds of processes govern the spreading of a freshwater plume: (1.) transport by the low-frequency, large-scale to mesoscale coastal circulation (typically geostrophic flow, including the buoyancy-driven anticyclonic flow generated along the outer edge of a river plume); (2.) transport by the wind-driven ageostrophic circulation (typically Ekman drift); (3.) mixing (on the horizontal and on the vertical) of the plume waters with surrounding ocean waters; and (4.) transport by the tidal flow. We hereafter illustrate each of these processes through a few representative, realistic cases reported in the literature.

3.3.1 Transport of River Discharge by Large-Scale to Mesoscale Coastal Circulation

Probably on account of the nature of western boundary currents as swift and turbulent, the influence of regional circulation on river plumes transport has been mostly studied in western boundary regimes. Muller-Karger et al. (1988) suggested that the Amazon plume propagates northwestward, hugging the northern coast of South America, only during the winter-spring season, whereas it is carried offshore by the seasonal North Brazil Countercurrent, all the way to Africa, during summer–fall. Similarly, Guo and Valle-Levinson (2007) evidenced the role of the boundary current of the northwestern Atlantic in the export pathway of the Chesapeake Bay plume. The southward-flowing coastal current appears responsible for the southward export of the fresh plume. Along the same shoreline, but considered at a larger scale (all along the US East Coast), Piecuch et al. (2018) investigated the variability of the buoyancy-driven along-shore flow (and its associated change in coastal sea level) induced by the interannual to interdecadal variability of continental discharge. They concluded that river discharge and the associated alongshore flow make a significant contribution to variability in coastal sea level. In the tropics, Benshila et al. (2014) modeled the transport of Ganges–Brahmaputra freshwater along the western boundary of the Bay of Bengal, resulting in a so-called "river in the sea" (Chaitanya et al. 2014) that extends more than 2000 km from the river mouth when the southward-flowing western boundary current is fully developed. This basin, like several others, is subject to intense monsoonal winds, which induce an annual reversal of the boundary currents. This study illustrated that the seasonal export of riverine freshwater far from the source results both from the basin-scale boundary

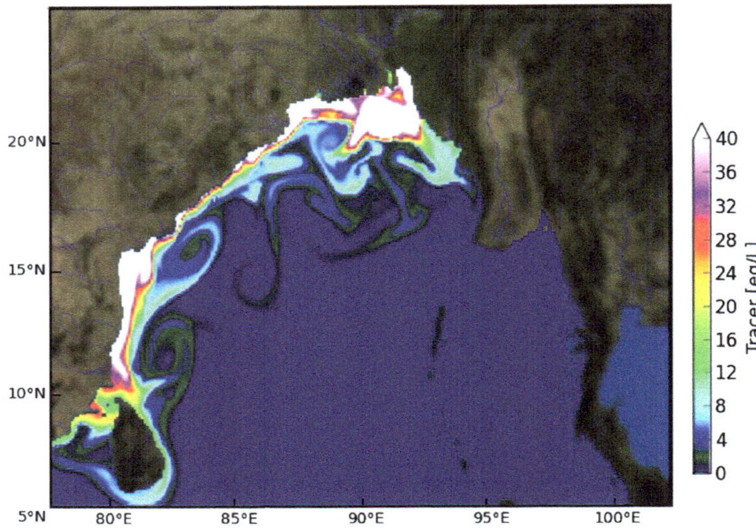

Fig. 5 Passive tracer concentration in a numerical model simulation of the Ganges–Brahmaputra outflow in a regional circulation model of the Bay of Bengal on 22/11/2003. The colour scale (in arbitrary units) represents the concentration of the water of riverine origin. After Benshila et al. (2014)

current, that conveys the plume up to the southern limit of the Bay of Bengal, and from mesoscale instabilities of the boundary current, inducing recirculation and offshore export of the fresh plume (Fig. 5). It was found that a similar transport by the basin-scale coastal circulation is largely reponsible for the export of Ganges–Brahmaputra plume waters at interannual timescales (Durand et al. 2011; Chaitanya et al. 2015). In the western tropical Atlantic, Coles et al. (2013) and Fournier et al. (2017a) similarly put forward the role of mesoscale eddies in the transient offshore export of the Amazon plume waters.

In the specific case of monsoonal outflows, caution is needed when trying to interpret the observed freshwater plumes pathways and the associated impact on coastal sea level. Indeed, the monsoonal variability of the atmosphere does not only induce vigorous seasonal changes of precipitation and discharge, but also—and primarily—seasonally reversing winds. Over the tropical oceans, such reversing winds have the potential to trigger marked changes in the vertical density profile in the water column, through baroclinic adjustments. These baroclinic perturbations are associated with significant thermosteric sea level changes (e.g., Shankar et al. 2002, 2010) that can interfere constructively or destructively with the halosteric anomalies associated with the river plumes, depending on the relative timing of the monsoonal winds compared to the seasonal timing of precipitation and runoff. For the specific case of the coastline of the Bay of Bengal for instance, the relative timings of the two factors are such that the wind-driven thermosteric sea level variability is largely in phase with the riverine halosteric contribution, with comparable contributions of the two processes near the mouth of Ganges–Brahmaputra during the summer monsoon sea level rise (April–June) (Fig. 6). Similar interfering effects may exist in the other monsoonal outflows, with phasing of thermosteric and halosteric sea level changes being probably highly site-dependent.

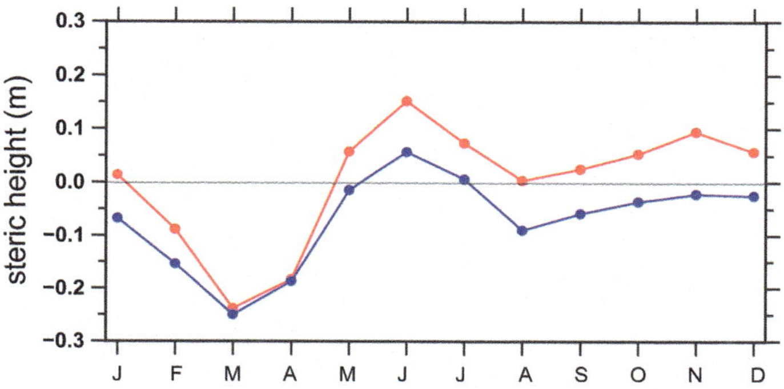

Fig. 6 Seasonal cycle of steric height anomaly observed off the mouths of Ganges–Brahmaputra in the northern Bay of Bengal (88.53°E, 20.5°N), from the in situ dataset of Sherin et al. (2018). The red curve represents the total steric height, whereas the blue curve represents the thermosteric component only (computed by assuming a constant salinity, hereby canceling the halosteric height anomaly)

3.3.2 Transport of River Discharge by Local Wind-Driven Circulation

The strong stratification existing at the base of a surface-advected plume tends to prevent the downward transfer of momentum injected by the wind, favouring swift surface-trapped Ekman drift, that in turn can significantly influence the plume pathway and its imprint on coastal sea level. Fong et al. (1997) observed very contrasted patterns of the coastal plume of the Gulf of Maine (northwestern Atlantic), under contrasted wind regimes. The offshore plume extent was typically 4 times larger during upwelling-favorable wind events, compared to downwelling-favorable periods. They concluded that this was explained by reversing cross-shore currents, well consistent with Ekman drift. Similarly, Sree Lekha et al. (2018) analyzed the offshore export of Ganges–Brahmaputra freshwater in the northern Bay of Bengal. They concluded that the overall export is largely driven by Ekman drift, under the favorable conditions of along-shore winds. The thin freshwater lens overlays a sharp pycnocline that concentrates wind-driven momentum in this shallow layer. It results in a swift offshore Ekman flow that drains the coastal plume away from the shore, with salinity advective rates-of-change several times larger than whatever has been reported in oceanic regimes located far from any river outflow.

3.3.3 Mixing and Small-Scale Processes Influencing Discharged Waters

The extreme magnitude of the seawater density gradients associated with river plumes at fine scale, both on the horizontal at their outer edge, as well as on the vertical at their bottom, puts stringent constraints on the skill of the numerical models used to simulate their spatiotemporal evolution and the associated impact on coastal sea level. However, an appropriate modeling of the density gradients is an obvious pre-requisite in any numerical study targeting a proper representation of the coastal sea level in plume regimes. Beyond the issue of model grid resolution, the sub-grid-scale parameterizations are instrumental for the realism of state-of-the-art models in such regimes. Vertical mixing in particular appears as a key ingredient of the evolution of plumes simulated by the numerical models. Li et al. (2005) analyzed the sensitivity of the fresh plume of Chesapeake Bay to various mixing schemes in a high-resolution regional model. They came to the conclusion that none of the vertical mixing schemes they tested allows to curb the excess vertical diffusion seen in their model through the bottom of the river plume; however the turbulent closure schemes they tested are commonly used among the community, even today.

In line with these results, Kärnä et al. (2015) investigated the sensitivity of freshwater plume characteristics to their model numerical setup for Columbia River, by varying the spatial grid size and time step. They restricted their analysis to super-fine grids, with resolution better than 100 m, which stands at the forefront of the modeling setups currently used in regional simulations of large river deltas and large estuaries outflows. In the plume region, in the near-shore domain, they evidenced a high sensitivity of the model skill to the size of both the spatial grid and the time step, even within this context of well-resolved grids. This suggests that a major issue for the near future regards the computational cost of the numerical models targeting a proper representation of river plumes and associated coastal sea level variability at regional scales. These authors all agree that model skill is more limited in conditions of peak flood plumes than in conditions of moderate discharge.

3.3.4 Effect of the Tides on River Discharge

For coastal plumes being restricted to shallow regions, the tidal flow naturally appears as a possible prominent driver of the freshwater plume pathways and associated imprints on the regional sea level. Essentially two aspects of the tidal influence can be identified in the plume regions. The first one is the direct transport of the freshwater by the tidal flow, which can consist of the advection by tidal residual current (i.e., nonzero long-term mean of the tidal flow) or Stokes drift (i.e., nonlinear interaction between tidal elevation and tidal flow, resulting in a net transport of freshwater in the direction of tide propagation). Wu et al. (2014) quantified these contributions for the Yangtze plume outflow in the East China Sea. They concluded that the Stokes drift is largely responsible for the northward along-shore propagation of the plume upon entering the ocean. For this particular case of the Yangtze plume, Wu et al. (2011) evidenced that the overall contribution of the various tidal effects dominate the freshwater dispersal in the neighborhood of the mouth, including under windy conditions, while the wind forcing and the transport by shelf currents become prominent further away (typically off the shelf edge).

The second way for the tide to impact river plume pathways and coastal halosteric sea level anomalies is by indirectly modifying the background (non-tidal) coastal flow. A river plume is inherently associated with a very strong density stratification at its base, driven by the vertical salinity gradient. This stratification has the potential to modulate the shear instability, and thus the production of turbulence, in the frictional bottom boundary layer (e.g., Simpson 1997). When the tidal flow is strong enough (typically in macrotidal regimes and/or during spring tides), the flow can become unstable and the horizontal momentum becomes vertically mixed. In such a case, the salinity also becomes vertically mixed, resulting in a so-called bottom-advected plume, as opposed to a surface-advected plume (Guo and Valle-Levinson 2007). The enhanced vertical mixing generally leads to reduced surface velocity, hereby impacting the offshore export of the plume waters far from the river mouth, which in turn influences the coastal sea level anomaly. This mechanism was identified as responsible for the contrasting pattern of the freshwater front at the mouth of the Amazon during spring and neap tides (Geyer 1995; Geyer and Kineke 1995). Guo and Valle-Levinson (2007) also observed that the same process of tidally driven vertical mixing was needed to ensure a proper simulation of the Chesapeake

Bay plume in their model. Similarly, Palma and Matano (2012) concluded that this process largely shapes up the Magellan plume along the southeastern coast of South America. Hordoir et al. (2006) reviewed possible strategies to parameterize the tidal mixing in order to realistically simulate the fate of river plumes in coarse and/or non-tide-resolving ocean general circulation models.

4 Observational Challenges

At this stage, it is clear that most of our background knowledge is based on numerical modeling studies. This can be explained by the fact that many observing systems are designed for the deep ocean, and turn out to be of limited use for the monitoring of coastal sea level in plume regions. Here we review these limitations, for both in situ and satellite observational techniques.

4.1 Spaceborne Altimetry

Originally conceived for accurate monitoring of the sea surface height in the offshore ocean, spaceborne altimetry performs relatively poorly in the near-shore regions due to errors in the altimetric observations themselves as well as uncertainties in the corrections that need to be applied (Cippolini et al. 2010; Vignudelli et al. 2011; Vignudelli et al., this issue). In order to obtain acceptable error budget of altimetry products in the coastal domain, one has to operate dedicated re-processing of existing datasets (e.g., Passaro et al. 2015; Gómeze-Enri et al. 2016; Birol et al. 2017). Still, the resulting errors are typically in the range of several dozens of centimeters in coastal plumes. River runoff and associated signals (sea level, alongshore currents, etc.) can be strongly trapped to the coast (Horner-Devine et al. 2015). The offshore scale of the trapping is on the order of the baroclinic Rossby radius, which can be expressed as a nonlinear function of river outflow (e.g., Piecuch et al. 2018). For a river with strong outflow at mid-latitudes (e.g., Mississippi River), the Rossby radius is <10 km. This offshore length scale is important, because the quality of data from satellite altimetry, even today, is degraded within $\sim$10–20 km of the coast.

These simple scalings suggest that satellite altimeters might not register coastal sea level signals driven by river runoff (Vinogradov and Ponte 2011). However, the above considerations are somewhat idealized and omit other relevant complicating factors, such as sloping bathymetry, alongshore winds, and mean flows. For example, discharge from the Mississippi River hit a 63-year high during the summer of 1993; this exceptional runoff was driven far offshore on the shallow shelf due to persistent westerly and southwesterly winds during July and August of that year and interactions with the Loop Current (e.g., Walker et al. 1994). As the performance of coastal altimetry is gradually improving (Vignudelli et al., this issue), it will be timely to re-visit the signature of river plumes (in particular the largest ones) on near-shore sea level based on the latest re-processed altimetric datasets. The limitations of the classical radar altimetry missions also put considerable expectation in the upcoming synthetic aperture radar (SAR) missions, and in particular in the swath SAR altimetry such as foreseen from the SWOT mission (NASA/CNES), which will yield effective sea level measurements within a few hundreds of meters off the shoreline (Dufau et al. 2016; Biancamaria et al. 2016).

4.2 Spaceborne Salinity

The last decade has seen a series of satellite missions dedicated to the observation of sea surface salinity, based on microwave radiometry. The first two missions, Soil Moisture Ocean Salinity (SMOS by ESA) and Aquarius (NASA and the Space Agency of Argentina) were initially found not to perform well in coastal regions, including in plume regions (e.g., Reul et al. 2014; Akhil et al. 2016). Basically these early missions were not usable in the first 100 km coastal belt. Lately, the situation has significantly improved, through dedicated re-processing of early datasets (e.g., Boutin et al. 2018). The latest Soil Moisture Active Passive (SMAP) satellite mission (NASA) also allowed the scientific community to move forward in the monitoring of coastal salinity, with measurements typically usable as close as 40 km from the shore in large plume regimes (Fournier et al. 2017a, b; da Silva and Castelao 2018). However, one has to keep in mind that these spaceborne radiometers provide estimates of surface salinity only, which can not be directly related to halosteric sea level anomalies as the vertical extent of the plumes is not observed.

4.3 Tide Gauges

Tide gauges are the main tool for monitoring the coastal sea level changes since the mid-19th century. Compared to satellite altimeters, tide gauges have a relative advantage in terms of observing the impact of river runoff on sea level. Located along the coast within harbors or inside estuaries, tide gauges can in principle detect the narrow coastally trapped sea level signals typically associated with river runoff, which are not always faithfully captured by satellite altimetry. However, tide gauges are not without their own issues, and there are particular difficulties associated with the analysis of these data. Tide gauge records represent measurements made at a point in space. Given a single tide gauge time series, all wavenumbers are aliased, and it is impossible to infer the spatial scales associated with the sea level signals being observed.

Another challenge relates to the nature of the measurement itself; since tide gauges are affixed to land, the measure is relative in nature, as it reflects not only changes in sea surface height, but also any motions of the Earth's crust. Such vertical land motion can be due to glacial isostatic adjustment, tectonic activity (Ballu et al. 2011), groundwater withdrawal (Emery and Aubrey 1991), sediment loading (Karpytchev et al. 2018), among other effects. These effects can be substantial in large estuaries and deltas, as well as in regions uplifting or subsiding in ongoing response to the last deglaciation. For example, during the last half century, sea level has risen much faster than the global mean due to groundwater extraction in Bangkok (Thailand) (Emery and Aubrey 1991; Phien-wej et al. 2006) and in Manila (Philippines) (Rodolfo and Siringan 2006), whereas sea level has been falling for centuries in Stockholm (Sweden) due to postglacial rebound in response to the melting of the former Fennoscandian Ice Sheet (Ekman 1996). For this reason, it is important to have data of vertical land motion (e.g., from continuous Global Positioning System devices) colocated with or nearby to tide gauges to distinguish sea surface height from vertical crustal motion (e.g., Santamaria-Gomez et al. 2017; Marcos et al. 2019).

4.4 In Situ Moorings, Ship-Borne Surveys

The estuarine and riverine neighborhoods are shallow, and in general subject to swift tidal currents, where fishing and navigation activities can be intense. As a result, many in situ surveys conducted in the past consisted of dedicated ship-borne cruises, operated on large vessels. One example is the AMASSEDS (A Multidisciplinary Amazon Shelf SEDiment Study) project (Nittrouer et al. 1991) dedicated to the observation of the Amazon outflow. This ambitious program turned out to be very successful in regards to the general understanding of the physics of the Amazon fresh plume (e.g., Geyer 1995; Lentz and Limeburner 1995), but the constraints of in situ operations in such environments prevent tackling timescales longer than about one season in the surveys. This limits the scientific scope of the subsequent process studies, precluding in particular the assessment of the longer timescales. Long-term deployments of in situ moorings, for instance, are often not tractable in strong river plumes. The deltas and estuaries being obviously located in exclusive economic zones, territorial issues also arise when it comes to designing long-term international in situ observing networks. This has led, in several cases, to confinement of in situ surveys of river plumes to international waters (beyond the 200 nautical miles limit), which precludes a detailed investigation of the plume dynamics at its source, and of its imprint on coastal sea level. One such example (among others) is the recent OMM-ASIRI (Ocean Mixing and Monsoons—Air-Sea Interactions in the Northern Indian Ocean) international program (Wijesekera et al. 2016), that could survey the narrow band of international waters of the central Bay of Bengal.

4.5 Toward the Future

Gliders and profiling floats, which require typically at least 50 m depth of water to operate safely, do not currently appear as relevant means of observing the near-shore plumes. However, lightweight surface vehicles, either towed or autonomous, fitted with GNSS receivers, offer promising performances (Marcos et al. 2019) and can already be used in plume regions. Figure 7 displays an example of a towed GNSS blanket experiment carried out across the plume of Ganges–Brahmaputra along the coast of Bangladesh, during the post-monsoon season of 2015. At this time of the monsoonal cycle, the cumulated discharge of Ganges–Brahmaputra to the Northern Bay of Bengal reached 900 km^3. Figure 7 shows that such a device can monitor the sea surface slope associated with the plume front, separating

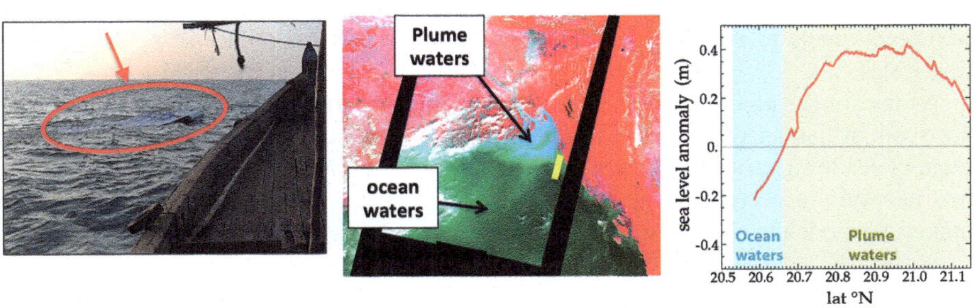

Fig. 7 Towed GNSS blanket experiment carried out in the Ganges–Brahmaputra plume region in November 2014. (left) Experimental setup with the GNSS blanket highlighted in red. (centre) Trajectory of the ship (in yellow), across the front separating the plume waters (blueish) from the ocean waters (green); the background is the quasi-true-color imagery obtained from PROBA-V satellite. (right) Sea level anomaly retrieved along the transect, after removing the tide signature and other high-frequency features. The domains of plume waters and ocean waters, as seen from the satellite imagery, are highlighted in brown and blue, respectively. Adapted from Durand et al. (2017)

the fresh plume waters (with high steric height) from the saltier ocean waters (with lower steric height).

5 Conclusions

Given the stakes of the coastal sea level variability with regard to the vulnerability of the shorelines of the major riverine and estuarine regions, in an era when the large ship-borne observational programs become less feasible in many countries, there is a need by the scientific community to invent the next generation of in situ observing networks. These networks will undoubtedly heavily rely on the development of cost-effective, research-quality, autonomous platforms. In order to discern between the various effects that can induce coastal sea level variability, including runoff, a comprehensive observing system, integrating not only runoff but also the other important variables, needs to be put in place in the coastal ocean.

The successful modeling of coastal sea level variability driven by river outflows remains challenging. This is due to the variety of processes involved (background regional circulation, tides, fine scale processes), that are all instrumental in the realistic representation of river plumes by numerical models, and that cover very broad spatial and temporal spectra. The numerical models need to be cross-scale enabled, encompass the continent - ocean continuum as a whole, and be numerically robust. Fortunately, the new generation of circulation models, in particular the tri-dimensional models implemented on varying-resolution grids, now allow an explicit resolution of the above processes, even over large regions. Just now, these tools are becoming mature enough, across several modeling teams around the world (e.g., Ye et al. 2016, Stanev et al. 2017, 2018, for the Chesapeake Bay, Black Sea, and Baltic Sea, respectively). Still the specific nature of river plumes, in particular the strong density gradients they induce, both horizontally and vertically, call for dedicated research to work out novel turbulent closure models, that can be adopted by the next generation of circulation models. From Sect. 4, it appears that the long timescales (interannual to interdecadal, including long-term changes) remain largely unaddressed in the literature. At a time when major river systems are suggesting significant long-term trends in the discharge in the past decades (Syed et al. 2010), and when the latest climate projections suggest significant changes in the global water cycle for the next century (Tao et al. 2014), it appears timely to address the variability of coastal sea level induced by runoff at these timescales.

As part of the global shoreline, the surroundings of large river mouths are particularly hot spots of human vulnerability to global change. It is now the right time to re-visit the topic of sea level variability driven by river discharge, building on the strong (though limited in several aspects) existing literature, taking advantage of the latest developments in numerical modeling and emerging observation technologies.

Acknowledgements We are thankful to Valérie Ballu and Stéphane Calmant for sharing the GNSS blanket dataset. Rachid Benshila carried out the Bay of Bengal passive tracer modeling experiment. We thank GRDC for providing discharge data on request. FD and JK were hosted by LIENSs—Université de La Rochelle, France during this work. CGP was supported by the Independent Research & Development Program at Woods Hole Oceanographic Institution. JK was supported by Centre National d'Etudes Spatiales (CNES), FRANCE, and by the Embassy of France in Bangladesh. FP and FD were supported by the CNES-TOSCA program via the BANDINO and AltiKest projects. MB was supported by the French research agency (Agence Nationale de la Recherche; ANR) under the DELTA project (ANR-17-CE03-0001). RMP was supported by NASA contract NNH16CT01C to AER. The in situ data presented in Fig. 6 were collected in the northern Bay of Bengal with support from the Ministry of Earth Sciences (MoES), Government of India. The authors thank all the project staff for their efforts in collecting these data.

References

Akhil VP, Durand F, Lengaigne M, VialardJ Keerthi MG, Gopalakrishna VV, Deltel C, Papa F, de Boyer Montegut C (2014) A modeling study of the processes of surface salinity seasonal cycle in the Bay of Bengal. J Geophys Res Oceans 119:3926–3947. https://doi.org/10.1002/2013jc009632

Akhil VP, Lengaigne M, Durand F, Vialard J, Chaitanya AVS, Keerthi MG, Gopalakrishna VV, Boutin J, de Boyer Montégut C (2016) Assessment of seasonal and year-to-year surface salinity signals retrieved from SMOS and Aquarius missions in the Bay of Bengal. Int J Remote Sens 37(5):1089–1114. https://doi.org/10.1080/01431161.2016.1145362

Alsdorf DE, Rodriguez E, Lettenmaier DP (2007) Measuring surface water from space. Rev Geophys 45:1–24. https://doi.org/10.1029/2006rg000197

Aubrey DG, Emery KO, Uchipi E (1988) Changing coastal sea levels of South America and the Caribbean region from tide gauge records. Tectonophysics 154:269–284

Ballu V, Bouin MN, Siméoni P, Crawford WC, Calmant S, Boré JM et al (2011) Comparing the role of absolute sea-level rise and vertical tectonic motions in coastal flooding, Torres Islands (Vanuatu). Proc Natl Acad Sci USA 108(32):13019–13022

Becker M, Karpytchev M, Lennartz-Sassink S (2014) Long-term sea level trends: natural or anthropogenic? Geophys Res Lett 41:5571–5580

Becker M, Karpytchev M, Papa F (2019) Hotspots of relative sea level rise in the tropics, chapter 7. In: Vuruputur V, Sukhatme J, Murtugudde R, Roca R (eds) Tropical extremes: natural variability and trends: observations, modeling, and theoretical expectations. Elsevier, Amsterdam

Benshila R, Durand F, Masson S, Bourdallé-Badie R, de Boyer Montégut C, Papa F, Madec G (2014) The upper Bay of Bengal salinity structure in a high-resolution model. Ocean Model 74:36–52

Biancamaria S, Lettenmaier DP, Pavelsky TM (2016) The SWOT mission and its capabilities for land hydrology. Surv Geophys 37(2):307–337

Biancamaria S, Frappart F, Normandin C, Blarel F, Bourrel L, Aumont M, Azémar P, Vu P-L, Lubac B, Darrozes J (2017) Tonle Sap lake water storage change over 24 years from satellite observation and its link with Mekong River discharge and climate events. AGU fall meeting, 11–15 December 2017, New Orleans, LA, USA

Birol F, Fuller N, Lyard F, Cancet M, Niño F, Belebecque Fleury S, Toublanc F, Melet A, Saraceno M, Leger F (2017) Coastal applications from nadir altimetry: example of the X-TRACK regional products. Adv Space Res 59:936–953

Blaha JP (1984) Fluctuations of monthly sea level as related to the intensity of the gulf stream from key west to Norfolk. J Geophys Res 89(C5):8033–8042

Boutin J, Vergely JL, Marchand S, D'Amico F, Hasson A, Kolodziejczyk N, Reul N, Reverdin G, Vialard J (2018) New SMOS sea surface salinity with reduced systematic errors and improved variability. Remote Sens Environ 214:115–134. https://doi.org/10.1016/j.rse.2018.05.022

Calafat FM, Wahl T, Lindsten F, Williams J, Frajka-Williams E (2018) Coherent modulation of the sea-level annual cycle in the United States by Atlantic Rossby wave. Nat Commun 9:2571

Chaitanya AVS, Lengaigne M, Vialard J, Gopalakrishna VV, Durand F, Kranthikumar C, Amritash S, Suneel V, Papa F, Ravichandran M (2014) Fishermen-operated salinity measurements reveal a "river in the sea" flowing along the east coast of India. BAMS 95:1897–1908. https://doi.org/10.1175/BAMS-D-12-00243.1

Chaitanya AVS, Durand F, Mathew S, Gopalakrishna VV, Papa F, Lengaigne M, Vialard J, Kranthikumar C, Venkatesan R (2015) Observed year-to-year sea surface salinity variability in the Bay of Bengal during the period 2009–2014. Ocean Dyn 65:173–186. https://doi.org/10.1007/s10236-014-0802-x

Chandanpurkar HA, Reager JT, Famiglietti JS, Syed TH (2017) Satellite- and reanalysis-based mass balance estimates of global continental discharge (1993–2015). J Clim 30:8481–8495. https://doi.org/10.1175/JCLI-D-16-0708.1

Chelton DB, Davis RE (1982) Monthly mean sea-level variability along the west coast of North America. J Phys Oceanogr 12:757–784

Chelton DB, Enfield DB (1986) Ocean signals in tide gauge records. J Geophys Res 91(B9):9081–9098

Cipollini P, et al (2010) The role of altimetry in coastal observing systems. In: Hall J, Harrison DE, Stammer D(eds) Proceedings of OceanObS09: sustained ocean observations and information for society (vol 2), Venice, Italy, 21–25 September 2009. ESA Publication WPP-306

Clark EA, Sheffield J, Van Vliet MTH, Nijssen B, Lettenmaier DP (2015) Continental runoff into the Oceans (1950–2008). J Hydrometeorol 16:1502–1520. https://doi.org/10.1175/jhm-d-14-0183.1
Coles VJ, Brooks MT, Hopkins J, Stukel MR, Yager PL, Hood RR (2013) The pathways and properties of the Amazon River Plume in the tropical North Atlantic Ocean. J Geophys Res Oceans 118:6894–6913. https://doi.org/10.1002/2013jc008981
da Silva CE, Castelao RM (2018) Mississippi River plume variability in the Gulf of Mexico from SMAP and MODIS-Aqua observations. J Geophys Res Oceans 123:6620–6638. https://doi.org/10.1029/2018JC014159
Dai A (2016) Historical and future changes in streamflow and continental runoff: a review. In: Tang Q, Oki T (eds) Terrestrial water cycle and climate change: natural and human-induced impacts. Geophysical monograph 221. AGU, Wiley, Hoboken, pp 17–37. https://doi.org/10.1002/9781118971772
Dai A, Trenberth KE (2002) Estimates of freshwater discharge from continents: latitudinal and seasonal variations. J Hydrometeorol 3(6):660–687
Dai A, Qian T, Trenberth KE (2009) Changes in continental freshwater discharge from 1948 to 2004. J Clim 22(10):2773–2792. https://doi.org/10.1175/2008jcli2592.1
Do HX, Gudmundsson L, Leonard M, Westra S (2018) The global streamflow indices and metadata archive (GSIM)—Part 1 : The production of a daily streamflow archive and metadata. Earth Syst Sci Data 10:765–785. https://doi.org/10.5194/essd-10-765-2018
Dobslaw H, Thomas M (2007) Impact of river run-off on global ocean mass redistribution. Geophys J Int 168:527–532
Dufau C, Orsztynowicz M, Dibarboure G, Morrow R, Le Traon P-Y (2016) Mesoscale resolution capability of altimetry: present and future. J Geophys Res Oceans 121:4910–4927
Durand F, Papa F, Rahman A, Bala SK (2011) Impact of Ganges–Brahmaputra interannual discharge variations on Bay of Bengal salinity and temperature during the 1992–99 period. J Earth Syst Sc. 120(5):859–872
Durand F, Calmant S, Calzas M, Ballu V, Testut L, Valty P, Krien Y, Bonnefond P, Papa F (2017) Geodetic survey of the freshwater front of the Ganges–Brahmaputra freshwater plume in the northern Bay of Bengal from CalNaGeo GNSS device. OSTST2017, Miami, USA, Oct 2017
Ekman M (1996) A consistent map of the postglacial uplift of Fennoscandia. Terra Nova 8:158–165. https://doi.org/10.1111/j.1365-3121.1996.tb00739.x
Emery KO, Aubrey DG (1991) Sea levels, land levels, and tide gauges. Springer, New York, p 237
Fekete B, Vörösmarty CJ, Grabs W (2000) Report no. 22: global composite runoff fields based on observed discharge and simulated water balances. Global Runoff Data Centre/Federal Institute of Hydrology (BfG) Rep., 108 pp
Fekete B, Robarts RD, Kumagai M, Nachtnebel HP, Odada E, Zhulidov AV (2015) Time for in situ renaissance. Science 349(6249):685–686. https://doi.org/10.1126/science.aac7358
Fong D, Geyer WR (2002) The alongshore transport of freshwater in a surface trapped river plume. J Phys Oceanogr 32:957–972
Fong D, Geyer WR, Signell R (1997) The wind-forced response on a buoyant coastal current: observations of the western Gulf of Maine. J Mar Syst 12:69–81
Fournier S, Vandemark D, Gaultier L, Lee T, Jonsson B, Gierach MM (2017a) Interannual variation in offshore advection of Amazon–Orinoco plume waters: observations, forcing mechanisms, and impacts. J Geophys Res : Oceans 122:8966–8982. https://doi.org/10.1002/2017JC013103
Fournier S, Vialard J, Lengaigne M, Lee T, Gierach MM, Chaitanya AVS (2017b) Modulation of the Ganges–Brahmaputra river plume by the Indian Ocean dipole and eddies inferred from satellite observations. J Geophys Res: Oceans 122:9591–9604. https://doi.org/10.1002/2017JC013333
Frappart F, Papa F, Marieu V, Malbeteau Y, Jordy F, Calmant S, Durand F, Bala S (2015) Preliminary assessment of SARAL/ALTIKA observations over the Ganges–Brahmaputra and Irrawaddy rivers. Mar Geodesy 38:568–580. https://doi.org/10.1080/01490419.2014.990591
Garvine RW (1999) Penetration of buoyant coastal discharge onto the continental shelf: a numerical model experiment. J Phys Oceanogr 29:1892–1909
Garvine RW (2001) The impact of model configuration in studies of buoyant coastal discharge. J Mar Res 59:193–225
Geyer WR (1995) Tide-induced mixing in the Amazon frontal zone. J Geophys Res 100(C2):2341–2353. https://doi.org/10.1029/94jc02543
Geyer WR, Kineke GC (1995) Observations of currents and water properties in the Amazon frontal zone. J Geophys Res 100(C2):2321–2339. https://doi.org/10.1029/94jc02657
Gill AE, Niller PP (1973) The theory of the seasonal variability in the ocean. Deep Sea Res 20(2):141–177. https://doi.org/10.1016/0011-7471(73)90049-1

Gómeze-Enri J, Cipollini P, Passaro M, Vignudelli S, Tejedor B, Coca J (2016) Coastal altimetry products in the strait of Gibralar. IEEE T Geosci Remote 54(9):5455–5466

Gough WA, Robinson CA (2000) Sea-level variation in Hudson Bay, Canada, from Tide–Gauge data. Arct Antarct Alp Res 32(3):331–335

GRDC (2014) Global freshwater fluxes into the world oceans/online provided by global runoff data centre, 2014 edn. Federal Institute of Hydrology (BfG), Koblenz

GRDC (2018) Long-Term statistics and annual characteristics of GRDC timeseries data/online provided by the global runoff data centre of WMO. Federal Institute of Hydrology (BfG), Koblenz. Accessed 29 Nov 2018

Gudmundsson L, Do HX, Leonard M, Westra S (2018) The global streamflow indices and metadata archive (GSIM)—Part 2: quality control, time-series indices and homogeneity assessment. Earth Syst Sci Data 10:787–804. https://doi.org/10.5194/essd-10-787-2018

Guo X, Valle-Levinson A (2007) Tidal effects on estuarine circulation and outflow plume in the Chesapeake Bay. Cont Shelf Res 27(1):20–42. https://doi.org/10.1016/j.csr.2006.08.009

Han G (2002) Interannual sea-level variations in the Scotia-Maine region in the 1990s. Can J Remote Sens 28(4):581–587

Han W, Webster PJ (2002) Forcing mechanisms of sea level interannual variability in the Bay of Bengal. J Phys Oceanogr 32:216–239

Hong BG, Sturges W, Clarke AJ (2000) Sea level on the U.S. east coast: decadal variability caused by open ocean wind-curl forcing. J Phys Oceanogr 29:2088–2098. https://doi.org/10.1175/1520-0485(2000)030

Hordoir R, Nguyen KD, Polcher J (2006) Simulating tropical river plumes, a set of parametrizations based on macroscale data: a test case in the Mekong Delta region. J Geophys Res 111:C09036. https://doi.org/10.1029/2005jc003392

Horner-Devine AR, Hetland RD, MacDonal DG (2015) Mixing and transport in coastal river plumes. Annu Rev Fluid Mech 47:569–594

HYBAM (2018) Contrôles géodynamique, hydrologique et biogéochimique de l'érosion/altération et des transferts de matière dans les bassins de l'Amazone, de l'Orénoque et du Congo. http://www.ore-hybam.org. Accessed 29 Nov 2018

Jian J, Webster PJ, Hoyos CD (2009) Large-scale controls on Ganges and Brahmaputra river discharge on intraseasonal and seasonal time scales. Q J R Meteorol Soc 135:353–370. https://doi.org/10.1002/qj.384

Kärnä T, Baptista AM, Lopez JE, Turner PJ, McNeil C, Sanford TB (2015) Numerical modeling of circulation in high-energy estuaries: a Columbia River estuary benchmark. Ocean Model 88:54–71. https://doi.org/10.1016/j.ocemod.2015.01.001

Karpytchev M, Ballu V, Krien Y, Becker M, Goodbred S, Spada G, Calmant S, Shum CK, Khan Z (2018) Contributions of a strengthened early holocene monsoon and sediment loading to present-day subsidence of the Ganges-Brahmaputra delta. Geophys Res Lett 45(3):1433–1442. https://doi.org/10.1002/2017GL076388

Krien Y, Mayet C, Testut L, Durand F, Tazkia AR, Islam AKMS, Gopalakrishna VV, Becker M, Calmant S, Papa F, Ballu V, Shum CK, Khan ZH (2016) Improved bathymetric dataset and tidal model for the head Bay of Bengal. Marine Geodesy 39:422–438. https://doi.org/10.1080/01490419.2016.1227405

Laiz I, Gómez-Enri J, Tejedor B, Aboitiz A, Villares P (2013) Seasonal sea level variations in the gulf of Cadiz continental shelf from in situ measurements and satellite altimetry. Cont Shelf Res 53:77–88. https://doi.org/10.1016/j.csr.2012.12.008

Laiz I, Ferrer L, Plomaritis TA, Charria G (2014) Effect of river runoff on sea level from in situ measurements and numerical models in the Bay of Biscay. Deep-Sea Res II 106:49–67. https://doi.org/10.1016/j.dsr2.2013.12.013i

Lammers RB, Shiklomanov AI, Vörosmarty CJ, Fekete BM, Peterson BJ (2001) Assessment of contemporary Arctic river runoff based on observational discharge records. J Geophys Res 106:3321–3334. https://doi.org/10.1029/2000jd900444

Lentz SJ, Limeburner R (1995) The Amazon River Plume during AMASSEDS: spatial characteristics and salinity variability. J of Geophys Res 100(C2):2355. https://doi.org/10.1029/94jc01411

Li M, Zhong L, Boicourt WC (2005) Simulations of Chesapeake Bay estuary: sensitivity to turbulence mixing parameterizations and comparison with observations. J Geophys Res 110(C12004)

Lorbacher KS, Marsland J, Church JA, Griffies SM, Stammer D (2012) Rapid barotropic sea level ris from ice sheet melting. J Geophys Res. https://doi.org/10.1029/2011jc007733

Marcos M, Wöppelmann G, Matthews A et al (2019) Coastal sea level and related fields from existing observing systems. Surv Geophys 10:15–20. https://doi.org/10.1007/s10712-019-09513-3

McCreary JP, Zhang S, Shetye SR (1997) Coastal circulation driven by river outflow in a variable-density 11/2-layer model. J Geophys Res 102:15535–15554
Meade RH, Emery KO (1971) Sea level as affected by river runoff, eastern United States. Science 173:425–428
Muller-Karger FE, McClain CR, Richardson PL (1988) The dispersal of the Amazon's water. Nature 333(6168):56–59. https://doi.org/10.1038/333056a0
Neetu S, Lengaigne M, Vincent EM, Vialard J, Madec G, Samson G, Ramesh Kumar MR, Durand F (2012) Influence of upper-ocean stratification on tropical cyclones-induced surface cooling in the Bay of Bengal. J Geophys Res 117:C12020
Neumann B, Vafeidis AT, Zimmermann J, Nicholls RJ (2015) Future coastal population growth and exposure to sea-level rise and coastal flooding—a global assessment. PLoS ONE 10(3):e0118571. https://doi.org/10.1371/journal.pone.0118571
Nittrouer CA, DeMaster DJ, Figueiredo AG, Rine JM (1991) AmasSeds: an interdisciplinary investigation of a complex coastal environment. Oceanography 4(1):3–7. https://doi.org/10.5670/oceanog.1991.14
Nof D (2005) The momentum imbalance paradox revisited. J Phys Oceanogr 35:1928–1939
Nof D, Pichevin T (2001) The ballooning of outflows. J Phys Oceanogr 31:3045–3058
Palma ED, Matano RP (2012) A numerical study of the Magellan Plume. J Geophys Res 117:C05041. https://doi.org/10.1029/2011jc007750
Papa F, Bala SK, Kumar Pandey R, Durand F, Gopalakrishna VV, Rahman A, Rossow WB (2012a) Ganga-Brahmaputra river discharge from Jason-2 radar altimetry: an update to the long-term satellite-derived estimates of continental freshwater forcing flux into the Bay of Bengal. J Geophys Res 117:C11021. https://doi.org/10.1029/2012jc008158
Papa F, Biancamaria S, Lion C, Rossow WB (2012b) Uncertainties in mean river discharge estimates associated with satellite altimeters temporal sampling intervals: a case study for the annual peak flow in the context of the future SWOT hydrology mission. IEEE Geosci Remote Sens Lett 9(4):569–573. https://doi.org/10.1109/lgrs.2011.2174958
Passaro M, Cipollini P, Benveniste J (2015) Annual sea level variability of the coastal ocean: the Baltic Sea-North Sea transition zone. J Geophys Res Oceans 120:3061–3078
Peralta-Ferriz C, Morison J (2010) Understanding the annual cycle of the Arctic Ocean bottom pressure. Geophys Res Lett 37:L10603. https://doi.org/10.1029/2010gl042827
Phien-wej N, Giao PH, Nutalaya P (2006) Land subsidence in Bangkok. Thailand. Eng Geol 82(4):187–201. https://doi.org/10.1016/j.enggeo.2005
Pichevin T, Nof D (1997) The momentum imbalance paradox. Tellus 49:298–319
Piecuch CG, Bittermann K, Kemp AC, Ponte RM, Little CM, Engelhart SE, Lentz SJ (2018) River-discharge effects on United States Atlantic and Gulf coast sea-level changes. Proc Natl Acad Sci 115(30):7729–7734. https://doi.org/10.1073/pnas.1805428115
Piecuch CG, Calafat FM, Dangendorf S, Jordà G (2019) The ability of barotropic models to simulate historical mean sea level changes from coastal tide gauge data. https://doi.org/10.1007/s10712-019-09537-9
Ponte RM (1993) Variability in a homogeneous global ocean forced by barometric pressure. Dyn Atmos Oceans 18:209–234
Ponte RM (2006) Oceanic response to surface loading effects neglected in volume-conserving models. J Phys Oceanogr 36:426–434
Prigent C, Lettenmaier DP, Aires F, Papa F (2016) Towards a high resolution monitoring of continental surface water extent and dynamics, at global scale: from GIEMS (global inundation extent from multi-satellites) to SWOT (surface water ocean topography). Surv Geophys 37(2):339–355. https://doi.org/10.1007/s10712-015-9339-x
Proshutinsky A, Ashik IM, Dvorkin EN, Hakkinen S, Krishfield RA, Peltier WR (2004) Secular sea level change in the Russian sector of the Arctic Ocean. J Geophys Res 109:C03042
Reul N, Quilfen Y, Chapron B, Fournier S, Kudryavtsev V, Sabia R (2014) Multisensor observations of the Amazon-Orinoco river plume interactions with hurricanes. J Geophys Res Oceans 119:8271–8295. https://doi.org/10.1002/2014jc010107
Roden GI (1960) On the nonseasonal variations in sea level along the west coast of North America. J Geophys Res 65(9):2809–2826
Rodolfo KS, Siringan FP (2006) Global sea-level rise is recognised, but flooding from anthropogenic land subsidence is ignored around northern Manila Bay, Philippines. Disasters 30(1):118–139
Royer TC (1979) On the effect of precipitation and runoff on coastal circulation in the Gulf of Alaska. J Phys Oceanogr 9:555–563
Ruiz Etcheverry LA, Saraceno M, Piola AR, Valladeau G, Moeller OO (2015) A comparison of the annual cycle of sea level in coastal areas from gridded satellite altimetry and tide gauges. Cont Shelf Res 92:87–97

Santamaria-Gomez A, Gravelle M, Dangendorf S, Marcos M, Spada G, Woppelmann G (2017) Uncertainty of the 20th century sea-level rise due to vertical land motion errors. Earth Planet Sci Lett 473:24–32

Saramul S, Ezer T (2014) Spatial variations of sea level along the coast of Thailand: impacts of extreme land subsidence, earthquakes and the seasonal monsoon. Global Planet Change 122:70–81

Sengupta D, Bharath Raj GN, Ravichandran M, Sree Lekha J, Papa F (2016) Near-surface salinity and stratification in the north Bay of Bengal from moored observations. Geophys Res Lett 43:4448–4456. https://doi.org/10.1002/2016GL068339

Shankar D, Vinayachandran P, Unnikrishnan AS (2002) The monsoon currents in the north Indian Ocean. Prog Oceanogr 52:63–120

Shankar D, Gandhi Aparna Saieesh, McCreary JP, Suresh I, Neetu S, Durand F, Shenoi SSC, Al Saafani MA (2010) Minima of interannual sea-level variability in the Indian Ocean. Progress in Oceanography 83:225–241. https://doi.org/10.1016/j.pocean.2009.10.002

Sherin VR, Durand F, Gopalakrishna VV, Anuvinda S, Chaitanya AVS, Bourdalle-Badie R, Papa F (2018) Signature of Indian Ocean dipole on the western boundary current of the Bay of Bengal revealed from 27 years of repeated in situ observations. DSR-I 136:91–106. https://doi.org/10.1016/j.dsr.2018.04.002

Shiklomanov AI, Lammers RB, Vorosmarty CJ (2002) Widespread decline in hydrological monitoring threatens Pan-Arctic Research. EOS Trans Am Geophys Union 83:13. https://doi.org/10.1029/2002eo000007

Simpson JH (1997) Physical processes in the ROFI regime. J Mar Syst 12(1–4):3–15. https://doi.org/10.1016/s0924-7963(96)00085-1

Sree Lekha J, Buckley JM, Tandon A, Sengupta D (2018) Subseasonal dispersal of freshwater in the northern Bay of Bengal in the 2013 summer monsoon season. J. Geophys Res Oceans 123:6330–6348. https://doi.org/10.1029/2018jc014181

Stammer D (2010) Reply to comment by J. F. R. Gower on "Response of the global ocean to Greenland and Antarctic ice melting. J Geophys Res 115:C10010. https://doi.org/10.1029/2010jc006457

Stanev EV, Grashorn S, Zhang Y (2017) Cascading ocean basins: numerical simulations of the circulation and interbasin exchange in the Azov-Black-Marmara-Mediterranean Seas system. Ocean Dyn 67:1003–1025. https://doi.org/10.1007/s10236-017-1071-2

Stanev EV, Pein J, Grashorn S, Zhang Y, Schrum C (2018) Dynamics of the Baltic Sea straits via numerical simulation of exchange flows. Ocean Model 131:40–58

Suzuki T, Yamazaki D, Tsujino H, Komuro Y, Nakano H, Urakawa S (2018) A dataset of continental river discharge based on JRA–55 for use in a global ocean circulation model. J Oceanogr 74:421–429. https://doi.org/10.1007/s10872-017-0458-5

Svendsen PL, Andersen OB, Nielsen AA (2016) Stable reconstruction of Arctic sea level for the 1950-2010 period. J Geophys Res Oceans 121:5697–5710

Syed TH, Famiglietti JS, Chambers DP, Willis JK, Hilburn K (2010) Satellite-based global-ocean mass balance estimates of interannual variability and emerging trends in continental freshwater discharge. PNAS 107(42):7916–17921. https://doi.org/10.1073/pnas.1003292107

Tao B, Tian H, Ren W, Yang J, Yang Q, He R, Cai W, Lohrenz S (2014) Increasing Mississippi river discharge throughout the 21st century influenced by changes in climate, land use, and atmospheric CO2. Geophys Res Lett 41:4978–4986. https://doi.org/10.1002/2014gl060361

Tarpanelli A, Amarnath G, Brocca L, Massari C, Moramarco T (2017) Discharge estimation and forecasting by MODIS and altimetry data in Niger-Benue River. Remot Sens Env 195:96–106. https://doi.org/10.1016/j.rse.2017.04.015

Tarpanelli A, Santi E, Tourian MJ, Filippucci P, Amarnath G, Brocca L (2018) Daily river discharge estimates by merging satellite optical sensors and radar altimetry through artificial neural network. IEEE Trans Geosci Remote Sens 10:15–20. https://doi.org/10.1109/tgrs.2018.2854625

Torres RR, Tsimplis MN (2012) Seasonal sea level cycle in the Caribbean Sea. J Geophys Res 117:C07011

Trenberth KE, Smith L, Qian T, Dai A, Fasullo J (2007) Estimates of the global water budget and its annual cycle using observational and model data. J Hydrometeorol 8:758–769. https://doi.org/10.1175/JHM600.1

Tsimplis MN, Woodworth PL (1994) The global distribution of the seasonal sea level cycle calculated from coastal tide gauge data. J Geophys Res 99(C8):16031–16039

Vignudelli S, Kostianoy A, Cipollini P, Benveniste J (2011) Coastal altimetry. Springer, Berlin, p 565

Vinogradov SV, Ponte RM (2011) Low-frequency variability in coastal sea level from tide gauges and altimetry. J Geophys Res 116:C07006

Volkov DL, Johns WE, Belonenko TV (2016) Dynamic response of the Black Sea elevation to intraseasonal fluctuations of the Mediterranean sea level. Geophys Res Lett 43:283–290. https://doi.org/10.1002/2015gl066876

Walker ND, Gargion GF, Rouse LJ, Biggs DC (1994) The great flood of summer 1993: Mississippi river discharge studied. EOS Trans Am Geophys Union 75:36

Wijesekera HW et al (2016) ASIRI: an ocean-atmosphere initiative for Bay of Bengal. Bull Am Meteor Soc 97(10):1859–1884. https://doi.org/10.1175/BAMS-D-14-00197.1

Wu H, Zhu J, Shen J, Wang H (2011) Tidal modulation on the Changjiang River plume in summer. J Geophys Res 116:08017. https://doi.org/10.1029/2011JC007209

Wu H, Shen J, Zhu J, Zhang J, Li L (2014) Characteristics of the Changjiang plume and its extension along the Jiangsu Coast. Cont Shelf Res 76:108–123. https://doi.org/10.1016/j.csr.2014.01.007

Xu K, Milliman JD (2009) Seasonal variations of sediment discharge from the Yangtze River before and after impoundment of the Three Gorges Dam. Geomorphology 104:276–283. https://doi.org/10.1016/j.geomorph.2008.09.004

Yankovsky AE (2000) The cyclonic turning and propagation of buoyant coastal discharge along the shelf. J Mar Res 58:585–607

Ye F, Zhang YJ, Friedrichs MAM, Wang HV, Irby ID, Shen J, Wang Z (2016) A 3D, cross-scale, baroclinic model with implicit vertical transport for the Upper Chesapeake Bay and its tributaries. Ocean Model 107:82–96. https://doi.org/10.1016/j.ocemod.2016.10.004

Surveys in Geophysics (2019) 40:1467–1492
https://doi.org/10.1007/s10712-019-09535-x

Sea Level and the Role of Coastal Trapped Waves in Mediating the Influence of the Open Ocean on the Coast

Chris W. Hughes[1,2] · Ichiro Fukumori[3] · Stephen M. Griffies[4] · John M. Huthnance[2] · Shoshiro Minobe[5] · Paul Spence[6] · Keith R. Thompson[7] · Anthony Wise[1,2]

Received: 14 October 2018 / Accepted: 19 April 2019 / Published online: 2 May 2019

Abstract
The fact that ocean currents must flow parallel to the coast leads to the dynamics of coastal sea level being quite different from the dynamics in the open ocean. The coastal influence of open-ocean dynamics (dynamics associated with forcing which occurs in deep water, beyond the continental slope) therefore involves a hand-over between the predominantly geostrophic dynamics of the interior ocean and the ageostrophic dynamics which must occur at the coast. An understanding of how this hand-over occurs can be obtained by considering the combined role of coastal trapped waves and bottom friction. We here review understanding of coastal trapped waves, which propagate cyclonically around ocean basins along the continental shelf and slope, at speeds which are fast compared to those of baroclinic planetary waves and currents in the open ocean (excluding the large-scale barotropic mode). We show that this results in coastal sea-level signals on western boundaries which, compared to the nearby open-ocean signals, are spatially smoothed, reduced in amplitude, and displaced along the coast in the direction of propagation of coastal trapped waves. The open-ocean influence on eastern boundaries is limited to signals propagating polewards from the equatorial waveguide (although a large-scale diffusive influence may also play a role). This body of work is based on linearised equations, but we also discuss the nonlinear case. We suggest that a proper consideration of nonlinear terms may be very important on western boundaries, as the competition between advection by western boundary currents and a counter-propagating influence of coastal trapped waves has the potential to lead to sharp gradients in coastal sea level where the two effects come into balance.

Keywords Sea level · Coastal trapped waves · Continental shelf waves · Ocean dynamics

1 Introduction

In the open ocean, sea-level gradients [strictly, dynamic sea-level gradients as defined in Gregory et al. (this volume)] are, to first order, in geostrophic balance with currents near the surface, with wind stress adding an additional flow in the surface Ekman layer. This

✉ Chris W. Hughes
cwh@liv.ac.uk

Extended author information available on the last page of the article

implies a geostrophic flow perpendicular to the sea-level gradient. The mean ocean currents sustain sea-level differences of around 3 m between the North Pacific subtropical gyre and the Weddell Sea near Antarctica (Rio et al. 2014).

If sea level slopes along the coast, the implied geostrophic flow is towards or away from the coast, inconsistent with the coastal boundary condition of no normal flow. Thus, as the coast is approached, a different dynamical balance must come into play. This change in dynamical balance has, in many cases, the effect of reducing the size of the signal, so that sea-level changes at the coast can be smaller than nearby open-ocean changes.

When a change of forcing occurs on the ocean, the oceanic response to that change can be felt at distant locations after some time. This information transfer happens in part because of advection by ocean currents, but usually the fastest response is mediated by waves. Thus waves, and in particular those in the coastal waveguide, known as coastal trapped waves (CTWs), play an important role in setting up the coastal sea-level response to open-ocean changes. In this paper, we focus on the way in which an understanding of CTWs informs the interpretation of this coastal response. We will find that, for continental boundaries, the strong mesoscale variability in the ocean interior is strongly damped at the coast, meaning the basin-scale signals are the main consideration. We start here by summarising elements of wave phenomenology, identifying salient features to be described in more detail later in this paper.

1.1 Waves in a Flat-Bottom Ocean

In idealised models of the ocean with a flat bottom and vertical sidewalls, linear ocean waves can be sorted into orthogonal vertical modes with different vertical structures. These modes are enumerated by the number of vertical nodes (i.e., depths at which the amplitude is zero). For each mode of subinertial frequency (wave frequency σ less than f or periods longer than the inertial period of $2\pi/f$, where f is the Coriolis parameter), the waves can be classified as Rossby waves in the interior (arising from meridional gradients in the Coriolis parameter), and Kelvin waves at the boundary. Rossby waves have westward phase speeds, yet only long Rossby waves (whose wavelength is longer than 2π times the Rossby deformation radius) have westward group velocity whereas shorter Rossby waves have eastward group velocity. Superinertial waves (waves with frequencies greater than f and periods less than $2\pi/f$) are characterised differently. For this review, we focus on the subinertial regime for which coastal trapping is possible.

Kelvin waves are a form of CTW, with the Rossby deformation radius acting as an exponential decay scale away from the vertical side boundary. Kelvin waves propagate cyclonically around an ocean basin with the boundary on the right (facing in the direction of propagation) in the northern hemisphere and on the left in the southern hemisphere. They also generally move much faster than Rossby waves of the corresponding mode. In particular, Rossby waves travel fastest at the equator, at one third of the equatorial Kelvin wave speed, and they slow dramatically with increasing latitude whereas Kelvin waves do not. This contrast is illustrated for the first baroclinic mode (mode-1) in Fig. 1.

Mode-0 waves (the barotropic mode) adjust rapidly, with the Kelvin wave speed being of order 200 m s^{-1} and the Rossby radius of order 2000 km. Consequently, Mode-0 Kelvin waves transfer forcing change information globally in just a few days (Lorbacher et al. 2012). For higher wave modes, the adjustment time scale can be much longer. The Mode-1 (first baroclinic) equatorial Kelvin wave speed is typically 2.5 m s^{-1}. Furthermore, the corresponding Mode-1 Rossby-wave speed drops below 10 cm s^{-1} poleward of about 20°,

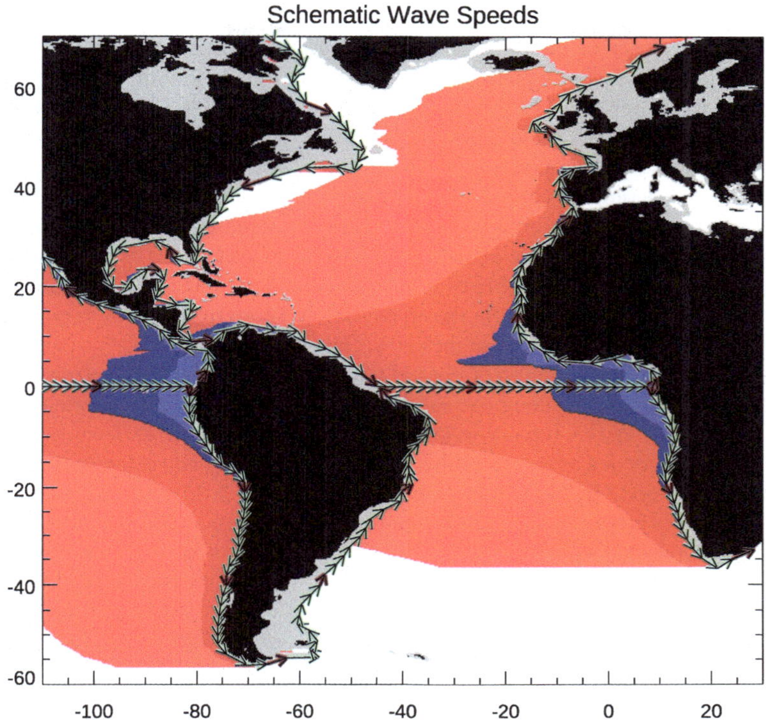

Fig. 1 Illustration of subinertial wave speeds in a flat-bottomed ocean, showing the fastest (long wavelength) mode-1 waves, and assuming a spatially uniform typical Kelvin wave speed of 2.5 m s^{-1}. Arrows show the distance covered per day by Kelvin waves, with every tenth day highlighted. Colours show the westward distance covered by Rossby waves from the eastern boundary in ten days (pale blue), one month (dark blue), one year (red) and ten years (light red). For each, the boundary of the ocean is taken as the 500 m isobath (shallower regions are grey). In a more realistic ocean with variable stratification and bathymetry, the Rossby-wave speeds would be reduced, and the boundary wave speeds increased, at high latitudes

with theoretical speeds below 1 cm s^{-1} poleward of about 60° (Chelton and Schlax 1996). The ocean, of course, does not have a flat bottom. Away from the continental slopes, even the relatively weakly sloping seafloor has an influence on the structure of Rossby waves, strongly reducing the amplitude of the Mode-1 Rossby wave at the seafloor and slightly altering its dispersion relation, but otherwise the general results from flat-bottom theory remain valuable (LaCasce 2017).

1.2 The Disparity Between Coastal and Open-Ocean Wave Speeds

There is a great disparity in wave speeds and length scales between coastal signals and open-ocean signals. The open-ocean adjustment process is dominated by basin-scale Rossby waves, whereas boundary waves are trapped to the continental slope over a length scale that is the larger of the Rossby radius (in the case of a Kelvin wave) and the width of the slope itself (as we will see for other kinds of coastal trapped waves). This length scale is typically tens of kilometres outside the tropics, and a maximum of about 250 km near the equator (excluding the rapidly adjusting mode-0, which is basin scale). Within a few equatorial Rossby radii of the equator, equatorial Kelvin waves and Yanai waves (mixed Rossby-gravity waves) carry signals rapidly to the east, thus removing the coastal trapping found away from the equator. The above dynamics is standard and is described in oceanography textbooks such as that of Gill (1982).

The disparity in wave properties means that the coast is a special place, with communication of signals along the coastal boundary moving rapidly compared to the ocean interior. There is hence the possibility of a decoupling between coastal and open-ocean sea-level signals. Such a decoupling is seen in observations and ocean models, which show quite different spectra of sea level between the coast and the open ocean in many regions, though most dramatically away from the equatorial and eastern boundary regions (Hughes and Williams 2010; Bingham and Hughes 2012; Hughes et al. 2018).

The effect of rapid propagation of coastal trapped waves is seen in the coastal sea-level response to El Niño events along the eastern boundary of the Pacific (Enfield and Allen 1980; Kurapov et al. 2017). It has also been noted indirectly via the uniformity of sea-level signals around Antarctica as discussed by Hughes et al. (2014) and references therein, and by an analogous mode in the Arctic (see Fukumori et al. 2015 and references therein). These polar modes are manifestations of the response to near-coastal winds being trapped and rapidly propagated along the coast, a phenomenon also seen in the eastern North Atlantic (Calafat et al. 2012, 2013), and discussed in more detail elsewhere in this volume. Further indirect evidence of the influence of CTWs is seen in the coherence of sea-level signals above long stretches of the global continental slope (Hughes and Meredith 2006). Recent model-based analysis suggests that much of the shelf coherence results from the strong suppression of mesoscale variability over the continental slope, thus permitting the large-scale barotropic mode to be seen in the resulting quiet regions (Hughes et al. 2018), representing an indirect manifestation of CTW effects.

1.3 Importance of the Continental Slope

The influence of the continental slope on the results described above highlights an important aspect of the real ocean, namely it does not have vertical sidewalls. Instead, as illustrated in Fig. 2, typical offshore bathymetry at the coast consists of a gently sloping shelf

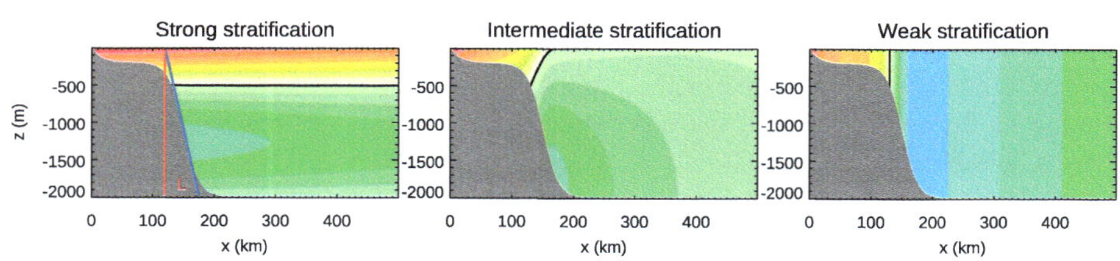

Fig. 2 Schematic showing the typical configuration of topography, coordinate system, and mode-1 CTW characteristics for various strengths of stratification as defined by the Burger number (see text). The y direction is into the page and would be to the north if the boundary is on the west of the ocean. Grey shading represents topography, with a typical gently sloping shelf region, followed by a steeply sloping continental slope. The topographic length scale L corresponding to a particular position (where the blue line is tangent to the slope) is illustrated in the first panel. Shading represents the perturbation pressure associated with the mode, with the node (zero value) marked with a black contour. In the northern hemisphere, the wave would be propagating out of the page (the opposite in the southern hemisphere). The offshore decay in the strong stratification case is exaggerated, to make it more visible

region, followed by a steeply sloping continental slope down to the abyssal plain of the open ocean. In the presence of a sloping sidewall, CTWs are no longer pure Kelvin waves. Given that the rapid propagation of CTWs appears to be responsible for the above-mentioned decoupling between the coast and open ocean, we assume that physical characteristics of CTWs play an important role in mediating the influence of the open ocean on the coastal region. The purpose of this paper is to review the extent to which this assumption offers a valuable framework for understanding how the open-ocean communicates with the coast. We begin by considering properties of CTWs when sloping topography is present. The complementary question of how CTWs act to trap and propagate sea-level signals that are themselves generated close to the coast, rather than in the open ocean, is considered elsewhere in this volume.

At subinertial frequencies, and assuming f to be constant (the f-plane approximation is almost ubiquitous in the theory of CTWs; this is a significant issue which we will pick up later on), it remains the case even with nontrivial topography that plane waves cannot propagate away from the shore. There are still waves that travel along-shelf with an off-shelf decay. Hence, the concept of CTWs remains valid. However, the presence of topography breaks the decomposition into vertical modes. Typically, these CTWs form a sequence with an increasing number of nodes in bottom pressure, spaced down the slope, as we see in baroclinic Kevin waves for the vertical sidewall case. What is different is that the nodes reach the sea floor at different distances from the shore, because of the finite slope, and their extension away from the sea floor is no longer horizontal as it is in baroclinic Kelvin waves, but at some angle, becoming vertical in the barotropic limit (Huthnance 1978), as seen in Fig. 2.

For a given along-shelf wavelength, higher modes (with more offshore nodes) have lower frequency and propagate more slowly. Mode-0, which depends on the surface of the ocean being free to move (i.e., not rigid) is termed a (barotropic) Kelvin wave. Even in the presence of topography, the mode-0 Kelvin wave usually has maximum elevation at the coast and offshore decay with no change of sign and is much like the barotropic Kelvin wave in the flat-bottom case. Typically mode-1 also has maximum elevation at the coast and a node near the shelf break. As the forms with simplest and largest-scale spatial structure (shelf-width scale for mode-1) modes 0 and 1 are most naturally generated by large-scale forcing (from atmosphere, deep ocean or tides) with resulting maximal effects of elevation at the coast. Along-shelf phase propagation remains cyclonic around an ocean basin with typical speeds of hundreds of metres per second for a mode-0 Kelvin wave and several metres per second for mode-1. The speeds other than mode-0 tend to be similar to, or faster than, the corresponding pure (i.e., vertical sidewall) baroclinic Kelvin wave speeds.

2 Properties of *f*-plane Coastal Trapped Waves

CTWs are subinertial waves (wave frequency σ less than the magnitude of the inertial frequency $|f|$), with along-shelf propagation and off-shelf decay. We here present a summary of their properties on the f-plane. Far more details, including mathematical derivations, can be found in the review papers by Huthnance (1978), Mysak (1980a), Mysak (1980b), Huthnance et al. (1986), Huthnance (2001) and references therein. We follow the usual convention whereby the waves are described using a coordinate system with $\hat{\mathbf{x}}$ (the unit vector along the x-axis) pointing in the off-shelf direction into the ocean interior (as in Fig. 2) and the y-axis direction, $\hat{\mathbf{y}}$, directed along the coast (pointing into the page in Fig. 2). Hence, northern hemisphere waves propagate in the $-\hat{\mathbf{y}}$ direction for a right-handed coordinate system in which $\hat{\mathbf{z}}$ points upwards (note that $\hat{\mathbf{y}}$ points approximately to the north on western ocean boundaries, and to the south on eastern boundaries).

We are concerned with the following restoring mechanisms leading to ocean wave propagation: gravity (tending to level the sea surface and interior isopycnals; the Kelvin wave mechanism) and potential vorticity conservation (tending to constrain any bottom-reaching flow to be along depth contours in the f-plane limit). The latter is analogous to the Rossby-wave mechanism that gives westward phase propagation in the open ocean due to the meridional gradient of the Coriolis parameter. We thus refer to "topographic Rossby waves" when the potential vorticity gradient is predominantly due to gradients in water depth (i.e., topographic β), rather than gradients in the Coriolis parameter (planetary β). In this manner, cyclonic around an ocean basin corresponds to the westward phase propagation of Rossby waves. Another common term for CTWs, especially in the unstratified case, is "continental shelf waves".

The two relevant length scales are the cross-shelf scale of the topography, L, and the first baroclinic Rossby deformation radius, L_{d}. The cross-shelf length scale is given by $L = h/|s|$, where $z = -h(x, y)$ is the vertical position of the ocean bottom topography and $s = \partial h/\partial x$ is its offshore slope. The deformation radius L_{d} scales approximately as $NH/|f|$ where H is the vertical scale and N is the buoyancy frequency measuring the strength of stratification: $N^2 \equiv -(g/\rho_0)\mathrm{d}\rho/\mathrm{d}z$ where z is the vertical coordinate (positive upward), g is acceleration due to gravity, $\rho(z)$ is the background vertical structure of potential density at rest and ρ_0 is a reference background density. When stratification is strong, i.e., the Rossby radius of deformation exceeds the cross-shelf topographic scale, the continental slope and shelf may be "seen" by the wave as a near-vertical sidewall. Waveforms in this limit are modes of vertical structure with off-shelf decay on the scale of the Rossby radius of deformation, i.e., they act like "Kelvin waves". Strong stratification corresponds to a narrow shelf slope compared to the Rossby radius: $(L_{\mathrm{d}}/L)^2 \gg 1$. Here, $(L_{\mathrm{d}}/L)^2$ is approximately equivalent to the Burger number

$$S \equiv N^2H^2/f^2L^2 \approx (L_{\mathrm{d}}/L)^2. \tag{1}$$

The spatial structure of a wave mode changes as stratification, topography and/or latitude changes. Nodal lines of perturbation pressure typically tilt upward towards the surface, from horizontal (strong stratification/steep topography/low latitude, $S \gg 1$) in the Kelvin wave limit to vertical (weak stratification/broad topography/high latitude, $S \ll 1$) in the barotropic topographic Rossby-wave limit. Figure 2 schematically illustrates the progression from strong-to-weak stratification for mode-1, with the nodal lines marked in black. In the Kelvin wave limit, the modes have the same offshore structure as the corresponding open-ocean vertical modes. As stratification weakens, the slope becomes less steep, or $|f|$ increases, the CTW modes evolve more complex structures which no longer match the interior modes, and are not separable in the vertical coordinate, until they become simply barotropic in the low S limit. A clear example of this transformation of modal structure from equator to high latitude is given by Allen and Romea (1980), who also explain how (in the absence of scattering by small-scale topography) energy is retained within a particular mode even as its structure changes with latitude.

2.1 Characteristic Properties in Various Limits

For mode-1 in the relatively weak stratification limit (i.e., a topographic Rossby wave or "continental shelf wave"), the cross-shelf scale tends to match the shelf width L. At low frequencies, the waves become nondispersive with a propagation speed of order Lf, which is $\mathcal{O}(10\ \mathrm{m\ s^{-1}})$ for $f = 10^{-4}\ \mathrm{s^{-1}}$, $L = 100$ km. Hence, long period implies long wavelength. Mode-1 tends to have a maximum (subinertial) frequency at which the along-shelf scale is comparable with the shelf width. Shorter waves then have lower frequency so that energy propagation at the group velocity is reversed (phase propagation remains cyclonic around the deep ocean). This behaviour is again analogous to Rossby waves: the frequency maximum for Rossby waves is at a length scale (wavelength divided by 2π) which is comparable to the smaller of the Rossby radius and the meridional length scale, whereas for CTWs the frequency maximum is at a length scale comparable to the shelf width. As the stratification increases, the waves transition towards (internal) Kelvin waves with a propagation speed of order NH, which is $\mathcal{O}(1\ \mathrm{m\ s^{-1}})$ for a bottom-top density difference $0.001\rho_0$ in depth 100 m. Correspondingly, for stratification-dominated waves (the Kelvin wave limit) the dispersion relation for frequency σ as a function of along-slope wavenumber k can approach and even pass smoothly through the inertial frequency as k increases (Dale et al. 2001).

For short along-slope wavelengths (large k), the general coastal trapped wave form is bottom trapped. Bottom-trapped waves (Rhines 1970) are a limiting case in simple geometry, with uniform stratification N^2 and motion everywhere parallel to a plane sloping seafloor; they decay away from the seafloor. They can propagate up or down the slope, but always with a component along the slope cyclonically around the deeper water. In more general geometries, CTWs in the large k limit become bottom-trapped waves confined near the seafloor where Ns is maximum, with frequency given by $\sigma = Ns$ (Huthnance 1978).

With increasing distance from the equator, the inertial frequency f increases from zero in proportion to the sine of latitude. Oceanic stratification also generally decreases. For any given offshore profile of coastal bathymetry, these changes imply a poleward trend from more to less stratification (decreasing Rossby radius of deformation or decreasing Burger number). This transition of the Burger number thus leads to a transition from (internal) Kelvin waves towards topographic Rossby waves. An implicit assumption is that changes in f, the stratification, and the continental shelf form are small over one wavelength, so that local wave forms are roughly as for a uniform shelf. Then also individual wave modes conserve along-shelf energy flux. However, in realistic cases the shelf-depth profile can vary relatively rapidly, thus causing scattering between wave modes.

The shelf width may be the most important factor in determining whether stratification is "strong", i.e., if the Rossby radius of deformation exceeds the cross-shelf scale L so that the Burger number is larger than unity. With a bottom-top density difference of $0.001\rho_0$, $f = 10^{-4}\mathrm{s^{-1}}$ and $L = 100$ km, the Burger number is $S = 10^{-4}H$ where H is the water depth measured in metres. For this case with a fairly wide shelf, stratification is weak, especially over the shelf where H is small. For a narrower shelf of $L = 10$ km, then $S = 10^{-2}H$ (again, with H in metres). In this case, stratification is strong especially over the adjacent slope. At a latitude of about 12.5° the factor f^{-2} in S becomes ten times larger than the typical midlatitude value of f assumed above, thus making stratification ten times more effective than in the above scalings.

2.2 The Long-Wave Limit

The long-wave limit is (as we will show below) the most relevant to open-ocean interaction with the coast at periods longer than a few days. At very low frequencies and negligible bottom friction, with correspondingly small along-shelf wavenumber, and with shelf-width scales much smaller than the barotropic Rossby radius ($gH/f^2L^2 \gg 1$), we use the linear, inviscid boundary equations:

$$\rho_0 f v' = \frac{\partial p'}{\partial x}, \tag{2}$$

$$\rho_0 \frac{\partial v'}{\partial t} + \rho_0 f u' = -\frac{\partial p'}{\partial y}, \tag{3}$$

$$\rho_0 \frac{\partial \rho'}{\partial t} + \rho_0 \frac{N^2}{g} w' = 0, \tag{4}$$

where primes represent perturbations about a stably stratified state of rest. Assuming a wave-like form travelling along the boundary, with $(u', v', w', \rho', p') = (u, v, w, \rho, p)e^{i(ky-\sigma t)}$, and substituting into the momentum equations, we find that velocity components are related to pressure p by

$$\rho_0 f^2(u, v) = \left(-ik\left[-c\frac{\partial p}{\partial x} + fp\right], f\frac{\partial p}{\partial x}\right). \tag{5}$$

Here we are assuming a wave propagating in the y direction (along-slope). This means that the wave phase speed is $c = \sigma/k$ (we will find that c takes the opposite sign to f), and imaginary quantities are 90° out of phase with real quantities. Thus along-shelf flow v is in phase with the pressure field, but cross-shelf flow u lags it by 90°. Within Eq. (5), the pressure p obeys

$$\frac{\partial^2 p}{\partial x^2} + \frac{f^2}{N^2}\frac{\partial^2 p}{\partial z^2} = 0. \tag{6}$$

The boundary condition of no normal flow through the seafloor $w = -u\mathrm{d}h/\mathrm{d}x$ at $z = -h(x)$ means that at the bottom we have

$$\frac{\partial h}{\partial x}\left(\frac{\partial p}{\partial z} - \frac{fp}{c}\right) + \frac{f^2}{N^2}\frac{\partial p}{\partial z} = 0. \tag{7}$$

Assuming a rigid lid boundary condition, which is usually a good approximation for modes 1 and higher, but not the mode-0 Kelvin wave, the equivalent boundary condition at the top is

$$\frac{\partial p}{\partial z} = 0. \tag{8}$$

Since only c appears in Eq. (7), rather than σ and k separately, the eigenmodes that satisfy Eq. (6) and its boundary condition all have the same speed c for all wavelengths in this long wavelength limit. This means that long waves are nondispersive and characterised by a single propagation speed for each mode.

Given speeds measured in metres per second (hundreds of kilometres per day), these long waves are clearly the appropriate limit for considering the coastal influence of open-ocean currents with natural time scales of more than a few days. However, as time scales become longer, it becomes important to consider the role of friction.

Friction causes cross-shelf phase shifts, altered amplitude distributions, and significant damping of CTWs (e.g., Brink 1982, 1991). Qualitatively, this effect can be understood by thinking in terms of how the ocean responds to an externally imposed along-shelf wind stress τ rather than the along-shelf pressure gradient which is a part of the wave itself. For idealised uniform conditions (no along-shelf pressure gradient and no on-offshore transport), the depth-integrated alongshore momentum balance is

$$\partial v/\partial t + rv/h = \tau/\rho_0 h. \tag{9}$$

In this equation, v is the along-shelf component of flow and r is a bottom friction coefficient with units of speed. This friction coefficient expresses a linear drag law proportional to bottom velocity, based on an assumed quadratic drag linearised around a background, usually tidal velocity u_0. The momentum equation (9) means that the along-shelf flow is in phase with the forcing wind stress τ if the frequency of oscillation of the stress is much smaller than r/h (in which case the time tendency term can be dropped). In contrast, the flow lags more as the frequency increases to approach r/h. Since drag becomes important more rapidly (i.e., at higher frequency) in shallower water, its effect is to bias v to greater amplitude in deeper water, which in turn mitigates the damping effect (Huthnance 2001). For example, nearshore currents lag the wind less than currents in deeper water offshore. Within damped CTWs, it is found that v shifts from being in a geostrophic balance $v \propto \partial p/\partial x$ offshore (where h is large) to a frictional balance in which flow is down the slope of sea level $v \propto \partial p/\partial y$ in shallow water.

Damping rates may be estimated as $r/h = \mathcal{O}(0.003\, u_0\, h^{-1})$, where the value 0.003 is a standard non-dimensional quadratic drag coefficient. This leads to a decay time less than 4 days for a typical current with $u_0 = 0.1$ m s^{-1} and depth $h = 100$ m. This decay time converts to a decay distance $c_g h/r$ for a wave with energy propagation speed c_g. Such decay distances are largest (hundreds to a thousand kilometres or more) for long waves with 'forward' energy propagation; much less for (short) waves with slow 'backward' energy propagation.

Thus, although CTWs are an important factor in regulating the link between the ocean and coast, for time scales of days and longer it is important to include the role of friction. In order to understand this effect in more detail, we reintroduce bottom drag and consider the low frequency limit for which the coastal adjustment to open-ocean changes may be considered to be complete, and a steady state has been reached.

2.3 The Low Frequency Limit

We now examine how variability on the middle and outer shelf can influence coastal sea level as $\sigma \to 0$, remaining on an f-plane, showing that the effect of the continental slope is to smooth the open-ocean sea-level signal, and shift it in the direction of CTWs before it reaches the coast.

To simplify the discussion, we follow Csanady (1982) and references therein, and assume a straight coast at $x = 0$ and a "wedge" depth profile of the form $h = sx$ defined over a coastal strip of width l. The flow is assumed to be steady, linear and barotropic and the wind stress is zero. A further simplification (which results from the along-shelf currents being much larger than the cross-shelf currents) is the neglect of bottom stress in the cross-shelf direction leaving a geostrophically balanced alongshore flow.

Under the above assumptions, the sea-level distribution over the coastal strip ($0 < x < l$) satisfies

$$\frac{\partial \eta}{\partial y} = -\frac{r}{fs}\frac{\partial^2 \eta}{\partial x^2}. \tag{10}$$

As noted by Csanady (1978), this is a diffusion equation with alongshore distance in the direction of CTW propagation playing the role of time. The coastal boundary condition of no normal flow, combined with the alongshore momentum balance as depth tends to zero, leads to a boundary condition $\partial\eta/\partial x = 0$ under the present assumptions. The offshore boundary condition specifies $\eta(l, y)$.

This highly idealised model illustrates two important consequences of the coastal boundary condition. First, spatial variations of mean sea level "diffuse" along the coastal strip in the same direction as CTW propagation, i.e., cyclonically. This feature explains the use of "Arrested Topographic Wave" to describe Csanady's model. Second, this diffusive effect leads to coastal sea level being smoother than the variability offshore. More specifically, if the sea level at the offshore boundary of the coastal strip is taken to be $\eta(l, y) = \cos(ky)$ then sea level at the coast is given by $A(k)\cos(ky + \phi)$ where the gain $A(k) \rightarrow 1$ from below as $k \rightarrow 0$; only infinite wavelengths diffuse completely to the coast (Fig. 3).

A more complete analysis includes the effect of stratification (Huthnance 2004). Consistent with the above discussion it is concluded that coastal tide gauges can only monitor large-scale oceanic motion with scales of thousands of kilometres. Lin et al. (2015) provide observational evidence for the smoothness of mean sea level along extended coastlines exposed to the open ocean. Based on an analysis of mean sea level observed by 31 tide gauges along west coast of North America, and a realistic model of the geoid, they showed that changes of coastal mean sea level have a range of about 0.3 m between 30 and 60°N. They then used the Arrested Topographic Wave model to show that the primary driver of this alongshore variability was wind forcing over the shelf rather than the open ocean, consistent with simulations by realistic ocean models.

On other coastlines, however, different dynamics apply. Tide gauge data, satellite altimetry, and ocean model simulations agree on the general features of the global coastal mean dynamic topography (Woodworth et al. 2012; Andersen et al. 2018), which shows smooth variations on eastern boundaries (except at the Strait of Gibraltar where the Mediterranean inflow allows for a step, Hughes et al. 2015), but larger and sharper steps in places along western boundaries, with different models in particular showing significant differences in the latter case. The sharp steps appear to be associated with western boundary currents, the Gulf Stream in particular being a clear example (Higginson et al. 2015), but the steps are smaller than those across the western boundary currents and occur equatorward of the main open-ocean step as if displaced in the direction of CTW propagation.

In summary, the coastal boundary condition of no normal flow has a profound influence on the way signals originating in the open ocean are transmitted across the shelf to the coast: spatially smoothing the ocean signal and diffusing it along the shelf in the same direction as CTW propagation. It is important to note, however, that the Arrested Topographic Wave model is only relevant on the inner shelf and describes how sea-level variability on the middle to outer shelf is transmitted to the coast. It is not meant to model the transmission of signals across the slope to the open ocean. We return to this more complicated problem in Sect. 3.

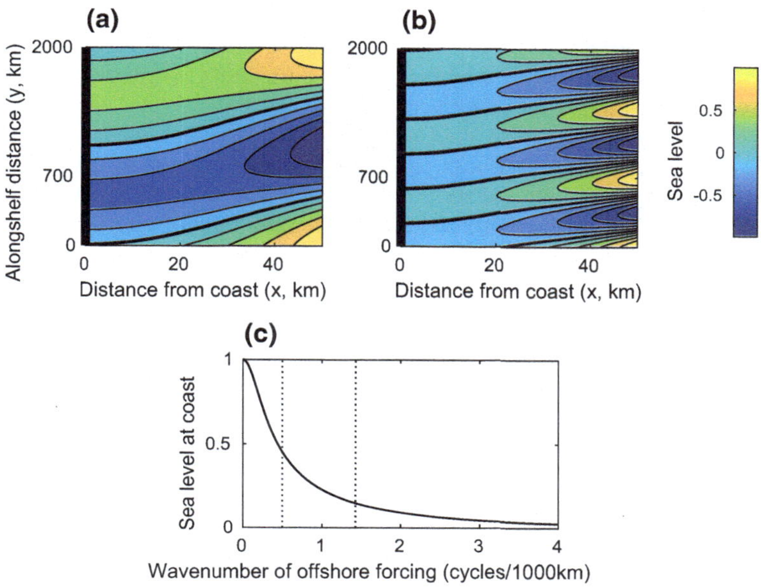

Fig. 3 Response of coastal sea level to steady sinusoidal forcing specified at the offshore boundary of a narrow coastal strip, calculated using Csanady's Arrested Topographic Wave model (see text for details). **a**, **b** Sea level as a function of cross (x) and along (y) shore distance. The coast is at $x = 0$ and marked by the thick black vertical line. The offshore boundary is at $x = 50$ km where sea level is assumed to be sinusoidal with unit amplitude and alongshore wavelength of **a** 2000 km and **b** 700 km. Zero contours are shown by the thicker black lines. **c** The amplitude of coastal sea level as a function of the wavenumber of the offshore forcing. The wavenumbers used in **a** and **b** are indicated by the dotted lines. The linear friction coefficient is 5×10^{-4} m s^{-1}, the Coriolis parameter is 10^{-4} s^{-1} and the slope of the wedge-shaped bathymetry is 3×10^{-3} (implying a depth of 150 m at the offshore boundary)

Given the apparent importance of bottom friction in allowing the ocean sea-level signal to "diffuse" towards the coast, we now consider the possibility of dynamical effects that may reduce the role of bottom friction.

2.4 Slippery Bottom Boundaries

It has been pointed out (MacCready and Rhines 1993 and references therein) that the presence of stratification can have an important effect on the operation of bottom friction. Friction induced by a bottom current along isobaths will result in an Ekman flux perpendicular to those isobaths, advecting buoyancy up or down the slope. The resulting upwelling or downwelling leads to horizontal density gradients near the bottom which in turn produce a change in the bottom geostrophic flow, as a result of the associated change in thermal wind balance. The result is always a tendency to reduce the near-bottom geostrophic flow, and hence reduce the friction, thus making the bottom effectively more "slippery" than might initially be thought (although the flow near the bottom has been reduced, this Ekman flux-induced adjustment means the frictional interaction of the flow with the bottom is subsequently reduced). In fact, a similar process applies over a flat bottom, as a result of the convergence or divergence of the Ekman flux, but the presence of a slope can accelerate the process as it does not require the Ekman flux to be divergent.

The logical extreme of this idea is that, after some time, the bottom geostrophic flow tends to zero and bottom friction ceases to act at all. It is important to put this interpretation into a broader context to see why it cannot be correct in general, though there are circumstances in which it may be a useful concept.

First, in the context set out by MacCready and Rhines (1993), the bottom geostrophic flow does not decay to zero, but to a particular value determined by a balance between vertical diffusion and upslope Ekman flux of density. It could only approach zero in the absence of diffusivity. Furthermore, diffusion is the only form of forcing in this scenario, as the problem considered involves no wind stress and no influence from the open ocean (which we will discuss below in terms of the addition of varying Coriolis parameter) other than the establishment of a background stratification.

Second, if we consider the steady, linear, along-slope, depth-integrated momentum budget, as there is no variation in depth in the along-slope direction, bottom form stress does not appear and the budget can be written as

$$fU = -\frac{\partial P}{\partial y} + \tau_{\mathrm{s}} - \tau_{\mathrm{b}}, \tag{11}$$

where U is the depth-integrated offshore mass transport, P is the depth-integrated pressure, τ_{s} is the alongshore surface wind stress, and τ_{b} is the alongshore stress on the bottom. The terms on the right-hand side represent the offshore geostrophic, wind-driven Ekman, and bottom Ekman flows, respectively. As the depth approaches zero at the coast, both U and P must approach zero, being depth integrals of finite quantities, so the balance becomes one between wind stress and bottom stress, meaning that bottom friction cannot reduce to zero. This is consistent with the steady-state form of Eq. (10) in Sect. 2.3 describing the Arrested Topographic Wave: in the absence of wind stress, the bottom stress must decay to zero at the coast, but balance the depth-integrated pressure gradient offshore.

Third, if we take the curl of the steady, depth-integrated linear momentum equations (e.g., substitute constant f, $H = h(x)$, $Q = 0$ and $\partial/\partial t = 0$ into equation 20 of Hughes 2008), then we obtain

$$\frac{\partial p_{\mathrm{b}}}{\partial y}\frac{\mathrm{d}h}{\mathrm{d}x} = \hat{\boldsymbol{k}} \cdot \nabla \times \boldsymbol{\tau}, \tag{12}$$

where p_{b} is the bottom pressure and $\boldsymbol{\tau}$ is the vector surface minus bottom stress. In this equation, we have ignored nonlinear terms in the momentum equation and the very small effect of stress due to atmospheric pressure acting on the free surface slope of the ocean, but otherwise the equation is general and applies in either stratified or unstratified oceans. Integrating along characteristics (contours of h in this case) shows that, in the absence of any bottom stress, bottom pressure must vary along the contours in a manner determined by wind stress. The resulting bottom pressure field will in general imply the presence of geostrophic flows at the bottom, which is inconsistent with the slippery boundary assumption. This aspect of the analysis leads us to consider the connection to distant forcing, and hence to open-ocean dynamics, for which we must abandon the assumption of constant f. This scenario will be considered further in the next section.

Finally, the assumption that the bottom flow can be shut down relies on there being sufficient stratification. Advection of denser water up or down the slope will tend to reduce the alongshore bottom velocity, but by an amount which depends on the density contrast. For strong currents in weak stratification, it may be impossible to generate sufficient density contrast to shut down the bottom flow. This is the likely to be the case on the inner shelf.

In summary, while the bottom Ekman layer produces an adjustment which tends to reduce the bottom geostrophic flow, there are fundamental reasons why this bottom flow cannot generally shut down. It is required in order to balance the (wind or buoyancy) forcing.

3 The Influence of Ocean Dynamics at the Coast

We have seen above that CTWs propagate rapidly compared to the typical speeds associated with baroclinic open-ocean dynamics. Mode-0 is sufficiently fast that a large-scale adjustment can occur globally in a matter of a few days. Furthermore, low modes also typically propagate at speeds measured in metres per second, and are trapped to the coast with a length scale which is (outside the equatorial waveguide) small compared to ocean basin scales. This disparity in length scales and propagation speeds requires special consideration in both theoretical and numerical models of ocean circulation. A common approach is to use a framework in which the shelf response is assumed to be in a steady equilibrium with the instantaneous ocean interior, effectively assigning an infinite speed to the CTWs.

An example is the quasigeostrophic (QG) approximation, in which sidewalls must be vertical and the CTWs become an infinitely fast series of Kelvin waves. This introduces some subtleties into the boundary conditions, which are resolved by considering volume conservation in each of the ocean's density layers. Once the correct boundary conditions are applied, a boundary-trapped mode is added to the equations enabling the evolution of the ocean circulation to mimic the case with explicitly resolved Kelvin waves (Milliff and McWilliams 1994). This is an unusual case in which the boundary signal has been explicitly considered. It is more usual in idealised ocean circulation studies (such as Stommel 1948; Munk 1950 and their descendants) to solve for the interior circulation plus a western boundary current in a manner which eliminates pressure from the equations, and not to explicitly consider the boundary pressure or sea-level values. Although this is simply a choice of solution method, it does have the effect of obscuring the physics associated with sea level and boundary pressures.

Something similar occurs in the linear shallow water equation approximation used by Johnson and Marshall (2002) to describe the overturning circulation. Again, vertical sidewalls are assumed, with boundary (and equatorial) Kelvin waves travelling fast compared to other time scales. And again, a volume integral constraint is needed to determine the boundary pressure values. By allowing the waves to travel rapidly, causality is obscured, and the entire boundary appears to "know" about the interior ocean simultaneously.

Another system which exhibits similar behaviour is the linear planetary geostrophic equations with topography. Here, wherever the topography is steep enough to produce closed contours of f/h (or, equivalently, of gh/f which we will later show to be a more useful quantity in the sea-level context), it is found that baroclinic signals impinging on the topography can effectively "jump" zonally across the topography, disappearing from one side and appearing more rapidly than expected on the other side, a phenomenon termed a "Rossby wormhole" (Marshall 2011). When the disturbance originates outside the topography, it jumps across from east to west. When it originates inside the topography, as in a basin configuration, the jump is back from west to east, enabling resonant basin modes to occur (as Kelvin waves would do in a vertical sidewall basin). The hidden mechanism involved here is the implicit (infinitely fast) propagation of barotropic topographic Rossby waves around the closed gh/f contours, thus setting up a bottom pressure signal which absorbs the baroclinic disturbance at one side and re-radiates it on the other side of the topography. Here, the implied boundary waves are barotropic (a limitation of the planetary geostrophic approximation which cannot support Kelvin waves, in which relative vorticity is significant), complementing the baroclinic Kelvin waves of the vertical sidewall case to represent the opposite extreme of the family of CTWs: topographic Rossby waves. Between the quasigeostrophic and planetary geostrophic approximations, we have two illustrations of how CTWs can have a profound effect on ocean adjustment processes, in the baroclinic Kelvin wave limit and the barotropic continental shelf wave limit, respectively.

3.1 Implications of Rapidly Propagating Waves: Smoothing

The implication of these idealised systems is that the continental slope should act as a smoother, taking signals which impinge on it and propagating them rapidly around the boundary. A similar conclusion can be drawn from a scaling argument based on vorticity balance (Hughes et al. 2018). Essentially, if a mesoscale eddy interacts with the sloping seafloor, the lack of flow through the boundary means that horizontal velocities induce vertical velocities at the bottom. However, using the same mesoscale eddy velocity in the vorticity balance results in a much smaller scaling for vertical velocity at the bottom; the vorticity constraint means that the large vertical velocity required by the bottom boundary condition cannot, in fact, be supplied.

As a result, the bottom velocities must be much smaller than typical mesoscale velocities, and the mesoscale is not strongly represented in bottom pressure on the continental slope. In effect, the eddies are "fended off" by the continental slope, although some fluid exchange occurs at scales smaller than the mesoscale; see e.g., Cherian and Brink (2016) for an illustration of this process. Bottom pressures on the slope should therefore be coherent over large distances, in contrast to sea level in the ocean interior which decorrelates rapidly over the mesoscale. The scaling involved here is a reflection of the rapid propagation of CTWs compared to Rossby waves. A related argument can be made in the case of vertical sidewalls as described by Kanzow et al. (2009).

The latest ocean models can now be run with sufficient resolution that it is no longer necessary to artificially smooth the topography to avoid a vertical sidewall, although even at 1/12° resolution, which is still considered high resolution for a global ocean model, the slope remains only marginally resolved in some regions of very steep topography, and details on the slope are certainly not resolved. As a result, it is becoming possible to test these theoretical ideas. It is found that, in a model with realistic mesoscale energy and spectra, the bottom pressure on continental slopes does indeed display coherence over distances measured in tens of thousands of kilometres (Hughes et al. 2018). Using this coherence, it is possible to identify the circuit times for mode-1 and mode-2 CTWs in the (model) North Atlantic as 115 and 205 days, respectively. This defines a time scale with respect to which the system evolution must be "slow" to justify the assumption that CTWs are in equilibrium with the interior (the mode-0 adjustment time is too fast to clearly resolve). The mode-1 time is equivalent to an average CTW speed of around 4–5 m s^{-1}, significantly faster than the corresponding Kelvin wave speed anywhere in the North Atlantic (Chelton et al. 1998). The fact that the speed is faster than a Kelvin wave speed shows that the finite inclination of the continental slope is an important factor in this boundary adjustment process, so the planetary geostrophic limit (implied barotropic topographic Rossby waves) may be more applicable than the QG limit (implied baroclinic Kelvin waves) over much of the domain.

The model results also confirm the strong suppression of bottom pressure variability amplitude on the continental slope, compared to the mesoscale, and show that the mesoscale spectrum does not penetrate strongly into coastal regions (with the exception of a resonant basin mode in the Caribbean Sea, where the coastal signal has a strong 120-day period excited by mesoscale variability, Hughes et al. 2016). This lack of penetration to the coast is consistent with what is seen in satellite altimetry: sea-level spectra near western boundaries differ strongly between the coast and open ocean, the two regions being typically separated by a minimum of variability near the top of the continental slope (Hughes and Williams 2010; Zhai et al. 2010).

It is worth remarking in this context that small islands are a rather special case. The continental slope smoothing effect is rather ineffective because the slope is closed over relatively small distances, so the mesoscale is only averaged over distances smaller than the mesoscale length scale. For this reason, model diagnostics show little difference between the open-ocean sea level and island coastal sea level, unless the length scales in the open ocean are smaller than the island scale (Williams and Hughes 2013). Thus, the special dynamics at boundaries do not upset the traditional interpretation of island gauges as good sites for monitoring ocean sea-level variations (Woodworth 1991), which is why they have proved so useful for satellite altimeter validation, e.g., Mitchum (1994).

3.2 Oceans with Vertical Sidewalls

Having established that most of the mesoscale variability is filtered out by the continental slope, we are left with the question of the basin-scale variability and how that affects coastal sea level. For many idealised studies, the pressure field (and hence sea level) is implicit in the solution, but is not explicitly shown.

It is helpful first to consider a simple case, for which an explicit solution can easily be found: the linear Munk (1950) or Stommel (1948) two-gyre ocean with vertical sidewalls and constant layer thickness H. Here, we would typically have an eastward wind stress which is maximum at some middle latitude and decays to zero to the north and south. The wind stress curl then excites a cyclonic subpolar gyre on the poleward side (here, sea level falls from east to west, before rising rapidly again across the western boundary current), and an anticyclonic subtropical gyre on the equatorward side (where sea level rises from east to west, before falling across the boundary current). We can sidestep all the vorticity balance arguments, retaining only the information that friction acts dominantly in the western boundary (it is western boundary current friction that balances the alongshore sea-level slope in these models, so this assumption locates that slope on the western rather than eastern boundary), and calculate the coastal sea level simply from the wind stress. Since, when integrating over longitude and depth, there is no net northward transport across any closed section, the effect of the Coriolis force integrates out and the steady, linear, zonal momentum balance (or, strictly, angular momentum about the Earth's axis) becomes a balance between the wind stress and the pressure difference between eastern and western sidewalls:

$$\int_{\mathrm{W}}^{E} \tau_{\mathrm{s}}^{(x)} = \int_{-H}^{0} \left(p_{\mathrm{E}} - p_{\mathrm{W}}\right) \mathrm{d}z, \tag{13}$$

where subscripts E and W refer to the eastern and western boundary, and $\tau_{\mathrm{s}}^{(x)}$ is the eastward wind stress (we have neglected sea level in comparison with total open-ocean depth H in the pressure integral). Using the fact that the boundary current is on the west, so pressure on the east is independent of latitude (Hughes and de Cuevas 2001; Hughes et al.

2018), we can subtract off a function of depth only which represents the eastern pressure at any latitude, giving

$$\int_{\mathrm{W}}^{E} \tau_{\mathrm{s}}^{(x)}\,\mathrm{d}x = -Hp'_{\mathrm{W}}, \tag{14}$$

where p'_{W} is the western boundary pressure minus the reference value at the east. Finally, we can use hydrostatic balance to write $p'_{\mathrm{W}} = \rho_0 g \eta_{\mathrm{W}}$, giving

$$\eta_{\mathrm{W}} = -\frac{1}{\rho_0 g H}\int_{\mathrm{W}}^{E} \tau_{\mathrm{s}}^{(x)}\,\mathrm{d}x, \tag{15}$$

for sea level at the western boundary relative to an assumed constant eastern boundary sea level. The western boundary sea level is therefore lowest between the gyres, at the latitude where the zonally integrated wind stress is strongest.

This pattern can alternatively be understood as the effect of friction in the western boundary currents, which must be flowing down the pressure gradient as they converge towards the intergyre boundary. However, the angular momentum argument is insensitive to details of friction and can even be extended to include nonlinear terms which only become important where there is curvature of the boundary current (Hughes and de Cuevas 2001). In terms of sea level, the final pattern in this simple Munk or Stommel model looks as if the low sea levels of the subpolar gyre are being "advected" towards the equator by CTWs and leaking through the coast in a diluted form somewhat further south (see the middle panels of Fig. 4). This is in fact a good analogy, as we will see.

A simple thermohaline circulation can also be added to this model by assuming that the dynamics discussed above refer to an active layer above a deep, passive abyssal layer. The thermohaline flow is then represented by adding a net northward flow into the active layer, and imagining it to be returned to the south in the abyssal layer. The constant poleward mass transport then does induce a (negative) western sea-level signal via the Coriolis force, and this signal is proportional to f, so it grows in size at higher latitudes.

While the angular momentum argument is pedagogically useful, the real ocean is not in perfect Sverdrup balance and the ocean circulation near to the western boundary can produce more complex patterns than the simple two-gyre solution. However, it has been shown (Minobe et al. 2017) that the linkage between western boundary sea level and sea level at the western end of ocean interior or eastern end of western boundary layer can be understood in the linear limit, by mass conservation, to be given by

$$\eta[x_{\mathrm{W}}(y), y, t] = \frac{f(y)}{f(y_{\mathrm{p}})}\eta[x_{\mathrm{W}}(y_{\mathrm{p}}), y_{\mathrm{p}}, t] + f(y)\int_{y}^{y_{\mathrm{p}}} \frac{\beta}{f^2}\eta[x_{\mathrm{I}}(y'), y', t]\mathrm{d}y', \tag{16}$$

where x_{W} and x_{I} are the zonal positions of the western boundary and western end of the ocean interior, respectively, y_{p} is a reference meridional position that is located poleward of the position y, and $\beta = \mathrm{d}f/\mathrm{d}y$. This equation indicates that the western boundary sea level at a particular latitudinal position y is determined by the coastal sea level at a reference position y_{p} poleward of y, and cumulative effects of ocean interior sea level between y and y_{p}. The physical mechanism is that the mass flux to the western boundary layer due to incident Rossby waves from the ocean interior must be carried by CTWs equatorward. The corresponding meridional transport is well approximated by a current in geostrophic balance, accompanied by a sea-level difference between the western boundary and the ocean interior. The first term on the right-hand side reduces in amplitude in proportion to f on

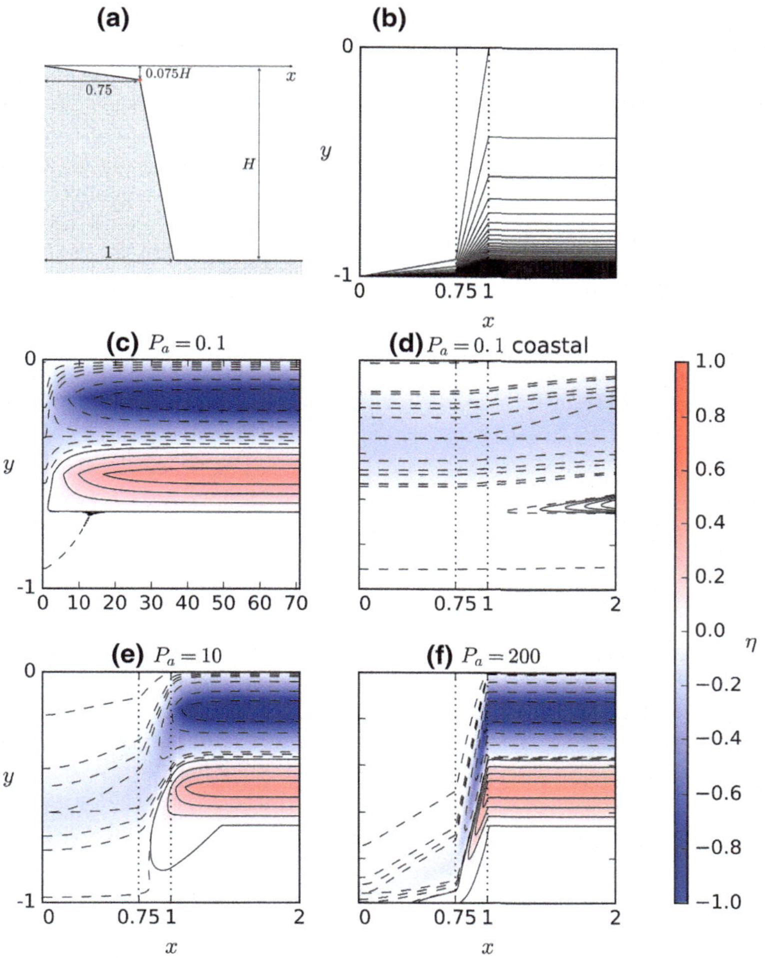

Fig. 4 Western ocean sea level in a barotropic model with topography, adapted from Figs. 3, 4 and 5 of Wise et al. (2018). **a** Geometry of the western boundary topography, with x measured in units such that the foot of the continental slope is at $x = 1$. **b** Corresponding contours of the string function gh/f, with equal spacing (values increase to the south). The y-axis represents a range of 6000 km from the equator at $y = -1$ to the northern boundary at $y = 0$, on this constant-beta geometry. **c** High friction solution, similar to the vertical sidewall case, resolving the full width of the Stommel boundary layer (P_a is the width of the topography measured in units of Stommel boundary layer width). **d** Blow-up of **c**, focusing on the region with topography. **e**, **f** similar to **d**, but with lower friction (narrower Stommel boundary layers)

approaching the equator, reflecting the smaller sea-level signal needed for the same transport to occur at lower latitudes.

The relation (16) is derived for a single-layer linear model, but based on a decomposition into vertical modes, and given the absence of ocean depth in (16), it is suggested that the relation can be used for sea level itself without knowing the detailed vertical mode structures. An important feature of (16) is that the relative importance between the first and second terms are strongly dependent on latitude, because of the aforementioned latitudinal dependency of the Rossby-wave speed. In lower latitudes, where Rossby waves are fast, interior sea level contributes more strongly than in higher latitudes, and vice versa. That is, the insulation of coastal sea level from the ocean interior sea level is stronger in higher latitudes than in lower latitudes. Hence, in mid-latitudes and high latitudes, the contributions of western boundary sea level at a higher latitude propagating equatorward due to CTWs are generally important. Consistently with this, it is suggested that the projected future sea-level rise seen in coupled climate models between the end of the twentieth century and the end of the twenty-first century in northeast North America, known as a sea-level rise hot spot, is strongly related to the sea-level rise in the Labrador Sea (Minobe et al. 2017).

The results of Minobe et al. (2017) as summarised by Eq. (16) are entirely compatible with the angular momentum argument expressed in Eq. (15). The same western boundary sea level can be derived directly from some assumed wind stress, and the interior sea level can also be so calculated if it is considered to be determined by Sverdrup balance from the same wind stress. These interior and boundary sea levels are then found to be consistent with Eq. (16) (Wise et al. 2018).

3.3 Oceans with Topography

The above results for the vertical sidewall ocean are a rather special case, as can be seen from the dependence of Eq. (15) on the constant depth H. The angular momentum balance relies on knowing the vertical extent of the pressure perturbation on the "sidewalls" of the ocean. When there is a continental slope, currents can flow in different directions over different ocean depths leading to a distribution of "sidewall pressure" which can no longer be calculated based on independent vertical modes, and thus complicating the relationship between the open-ocean circulation and the coastal sea level. At the simplest level, the more surface-intensified the circulation becomes, the smaller the effective H, and hence the larger the associated coastal sea-level signal. However, reversals in the flow can complicate the relationship further, making it questionable whether a meaningful value of H can be determined.

3.4 A Linear, Barotropic Case

An investigation of the simplest (linear, single layer) version of the problem with topography (Wise et al. 2018) has proved revealing. The problem can be reduced to an analogous "advection-diffusion" problem in which a source of water (either a literal source, or the convergence of the Ekman flux due to wind stress) causes a rise in sea level which then behaves as if it is "advected" along characteristics (we use quotation marks to denote words used to describe the analogous problem, it is not a literal advection), while being "diffused" (blurred) by the action of bottom friction. The characteristics in this case are contours of gh/f as shown in Fig. 4b for the bathymetry illustrated in Fig. 4a. These contours can be thought of as the streamfunction responsible for the "advection", so the speed of "advection" is given by the size of the gradient of gh/f, and directed perpendicular to that gradient (along the contours at a speed inversely proportional to their spacing). This "advection" speed was first described by Tyler and Käse (2000) who coined the term "string function" for gh/f to avoid confusion with a true stream function associated with currents. In the constant-slope, f-plane case this "advection" becomes simply a constant speed along the coast, leading to the Arrested Topographic Wave interpretation in which diffusion to the coast happens over "time", but "time" is actually distance along the coast in the direction of CTW propagation. A similar analogy, expressed in terms of streamfunction rather than bottom pressure or sea level, was exploited by Welander (1968) and Becker and Salmon (1997) giving similar results, although it is much harder to extract information about coastal sea level from this formulation.

In this interpretation, sea level is "advected" westwards in the flat-bottomed ocean interior (at the long Rossby-wave speed) until it encounters the continental slope, whereupon the "advection" turns equatorward and accelerates, due to the convergence of characteristics (string function contours), carrying the sea-level pattern with it. This is a natural extension of the Arrested Topographic Wave concept which allows for a dynamical connection between the open ocean and the coast to be made. Note that, although we are here considering a steady state, this only implies that variation in time is slow compared to the relatively short time taken to establish the coastal response by propagation of CTWs.

In the small friction limit, this "advection-diffusion" balance results in all the diffusion occurring close to the equator, where all gh/f contours converge at the western coast, and no sea-level signal penetrates to the coast. Figure 4f shows a case approaching this limit. This is an unrealistic limit: not only does it assume unrealistically small friction, it also assumes the flow can remain barotropic and coastally trapped right to the equator, which is far from the case with realistic stratification. However, as friction increases (other panels in Fig. 4), penetration of the interior signal to the coast increases and occurs further from the equator. The largest and most rapid penetration (meaning with least southward deflection) occurs in the limit of high friction or narrow continental shelf and slope (these are equivalent limits) and coincides with the vertical sidewall result of Minobe et al. (2017).

The physics of these solutions can be usefully considered in terms of the balance (11). Far offshore, the bottom stress term can be neglected (we ignore local wind stress in this boundary problem), and the alongshore pressure gradient is balanced by a depth-integrated onshore (say) geostrophic flow. Close to the coast, the depth-integrated flow becomes negligible and the balance is between the pressure gradient and the bottom stress. This is the same switch from geostrophic to frictional balance that occurs in damped CTWs. Between these two limits, either the bottom stress must build up to provide an offshore Ekman flux which balances the onshore geostrophic flow, or the pressure gradient must reduce as the geostrophic flow is deflected along the slope. In the former case, there is "diffusion" of the sea-level signal across gh/f contours, and a coastal response appears. In the latter case, there is no "diffusion", and no coastal response. This interpretation explains an apparent contradiction with Csanady (1978), who found that all the open-ocean signal would eventually make it to the coast for long enough wavelengths. In that study (with constant f), the depth-integrated onshore flow was always taken to be zero (consistent with the design of the Arrested Topographic Wave to model circulation over the inner shelf), meaning that the geostrophic onshore flow was always balanced by an offshore flow in the bottom Ekman layer, and a connection with the open ocean (where the pressure gradient is not balanced by bottom stress) was not truly made.

Thus, the size and position of the coastal signal depend on both friction and the shape of the boundary topography. This conclusion is consistent with Higginson et al. (2015), who found that the northward drop in U.S. Atlantic coastal sea level was much smaller and further south than the interior ocean signal, as the above discussion would suggest. They also found that different ocean models disagreed as to the extent of this southward deflection, with some showing much more of a step near Cape Hatteras than would be suggested by the observations, which show almost all the step in south Florida. This is suggestive of the kind of sensitivity to details of topography and friction that the linear barotropic model indicates should be expected.

Further analytical work on the linear barotropic model (Wise et al. 2019) has shown that certain features are robust. The western boundary coastal signal can always be computed as a weighted integral of the open-ocean signal from poleward of the point in question just as in the vertical sidewall case as expressed in Eq. (16), but the weightings of the interior and poleward sea-level signals become different from those in (16). The weighted integral can also still be interpreted as a series of damped boundary modes which propagate information towards the equator. The idea that the interior signal is carried equatorward by CTWs while being leaked across the slope by bottom friction (Huthnance 1987, 2004) is therefore a useful interpretation of the dynamics.

It should be noted, however, that the coastal modes in this interpretation can become somewhat more complicated than conventional *f*-plane CTWs. If *f* is allowed to vary, a new time scale is introduced, which is the shortest period at which Rossby waves can exist. This period is given by $4\pi/\beta L_{\mathrm{d}}$. Using $L_{\mathrm{d}} = c/|f|$ where c is the gravity wave speed for the same vertical mode, and approximating c as about 2.5 m s^{-1} for the first baroclinic mode (Chelton et al. 1998), this can be approximated as $T \approx |\tan\phi|$ where T is measured in years and ϕ is latitude (although near the poles, the separation of variables used to derive the standard Rossby-wave dispersion relation no longer applies). For a truly barotropic mode, taking $c \approx 200$ m s^{-1}, the critical period T is 80 times shorter. The few early studies of CTWs which allowed for variations in *f*, e.g., Allen and Romea (1980), Grimshaw (1977), limited the frequency range to exclude Rossby waves. When Rossby waves are possible, energy can leak away from the boundaries as short Rossby waves from the west, or long Rossby waves from the east. As shown in the vertical sidewall case by Marshall and Johnson (2013), this results in the boundary signals transitioning from Kelvin to Rossby waves, or to Munk (1950) or Stommel (1948) boundary layers as friction becomes important. More work is needed to understand the implications of this, but initial work (Wise et al. 2019) suggests that the general conclusions carry over to the case with topography, suggesting that great care needs to be exercised in the interpretation of measurement of signals propagating along boundaries, as phase speeds can be quite different from those seen in *f*-plane or higher frequency CTWs.

Nonetheless, the linear barotropic model does show that signals generated in the interior are "advected" to the west at the long Rossby-wave speed, and then along *gh*/*f* countours along the boundary at a speed which can be considered to be the relevant CTW speed, while being "diffused" by bottom friction.

3.5 Considerations of Nonlinearity

The model considered above remains highly simplified, being linear and with only rudimentary stratification (although barotropic, the open-ocean part of this model can also be thought of as a model with a single active layer above a passive abyss) There are hints that nonlinear effects may produce a richer array of behaviours on western boundaries, including the formation of fronts in boundary pressure, and hence in sea level. The essential mechanism is the overwhelming of CTW propagation by the flow itself, leading to a reversal of the characteristic velocity along part of the boundary (such reversals of characteristic velocity also lie at the heart of longstanding questions of the extent to which western boundary currents can be considered to be passive in ocean thermocline theory). The flow must oppose the wave propagation to achieve this reversal, implying that the reversal is in the subtropical gyre region (the Gulf Stream in the North Atlantic). In a vertical sidewall case, the relevant waves are Kelvin waves which, at least for high enough modes, can certainly be halted by realistic boundary currents. Loss of balance (generation of small-scale gravity waves which remove energy from the "balanced" part of the flow which can be determined from the potential vorticity equation) is found to occur at the point of convergence of opposing characteristic velocities at the boundary, leading to formation of fronts there (Dewar and Hogg 2010; Deremble et al. 2017). This mechanism was sketched out (in a case with sloping topography modelled on the Gulf Stream geometry) by Stern (1998) and has gained qualitative support from model sensitivity studies (Schoonover et al. 2017), in which CTW speeds are compared with current speeds to suggest the plausibility of this mechanism as an explanation of Gulf Stream separation.

Nonlinear behaviour may, in fact, arise even without the nonlinear terms in the momentum equations. It has proved possible to solve a variety of special cases of the planetary geostrophic equations with sloping boundaries, and these also show a rich variety of behaviours with the formation of fronts, and recirculations either side of the boundary current extension (Salmon 1994; Ford 2000). Again, these solutions can be considered in terms of characteristic "velocities", "advecting" the dynamical quantities, coupled with a form of "diffusion". These "velocities" are compounded of a westward component associated with the baroclinic Rossby-wave speed, a component along the topography in the direction of CTW propagation, a genuine advection by the flow, and a modification of the Rossby-wave speed due to finite deformation of the stratification (particularly strong in the subpolar gyre). In several cases, the characteristic "velocity" at the western boundary is found to be polewards in the equatorward part of the subtropical gyre, converging with an equatorward velocity from the subpolar gyre, and forming a front at the convergence [a little further offshore the front is found much further polwards, see figures 5–7 of Salmon (1994)]. This suggests the possibility of sharp steps in coastal sea level mediated by this competition between advection by the flow and "advection" by CTWs, although the "advected" quantity in these more complex solutions is no longer as simple as the bottom pressure. This is an area ripe for further exploration, with potentially important consequences for understanding and predicting coastal sea level.

3.6 Eastern Boundaries

The above has focused on western boundaries, where the dynamics are rather complicated. At eastern boundaries things are more straightforward. The open-ocean characteristic "velocities" near to eastern boundaries are dominated by the westward Rossby-wave speed except at the equator where the influence of the eastward-propagating equatorial Kelvin and Yanai waves is felt. Along the boundary, the CTWs propagate away from the equator, so all coastal signals should either propagate from the equator, or be generated by local forcing close to the coast. The vertical sidewall analytical models suggest that the signal propagating from the equator would, on time scales longer than the basin circuit time, be determined by the layerwise mass balance constraint.

Model diagnostics are consistent with this interpretation (Hughes et al. 2018). They show that, below about 200 m, the bottom pressure variations propagate away from the equator at speeds typical of CTWs, becoming at interannual time scales almost uniform along the entire eastern boundary, and very small (less than 1 cm of water). Variations in sea level along the eastern boundary (and they do occur) must therefore be generated either from equatorial sources or by shelf sea dynamics, with some of the effects radiating out into the open ocean. Illustrating this, it is found that regional model simulations of the US Pacific coast perform better when using "clamped" boundary conditions to the south, directly importing the observed properties at that boundary via a data assimilating global model, as opposed to the "radiation plus nudging" conditions applied at other boundaries (Durski et al. 2015). Both boundary wave propagation and local winds play important roles in the coastal sea level in this region (Kurapov et al. 2017). The radiation of Rossby waves has been suggested as a mechanism for the formation of poleward-flowing undercurrents below the equatorward winds on certain boundaries (Samelson 2017), an example of the coastal variability influencing the open ocean rather than vice versa.

4 Conclusions

The interaction between open ocean and the coast is a subtle issue, especially at western boundaries. We have found that it is possible to think of CTWs as effectively advecting sea level (or bottom pressure) signals rapidly along the continental slope, in the direction of CTW propagation, with bottom friction acting to diffuse the signal slowly across the slope. Thus the coastal sea-level signal emerges from the balance between these two processes and can become very small when bottom friction is small. The sea-level signals reach the continental slope as a result of a similar Rossby-wave "advection" from east to west in much of the ocean, or a Kelvin wave "advection" to the east at the equator. Thus eastern boundary coastal sea-level signals are only influenced by the equatorial open ocean, as well as near-coastal direct forcing. The western boundary coastal sea level, on the other hand, is influenced by the open ocean from all latitudes.

The conventional vertical sidewall case appears to produce the largest western boundary coastal signals, which are still significantly smaller than the associated open-ocean signals, and displaced towards the equator. More realistic topography and lower bottom friction act to reduce the size of these signals further, and push them further towards the equator. Thus, it is expected that western boundary coastal signals should be smaller than interior ocean signals and should smooth those interior signals over long distances (greatly reducing the influence of mesoscale variability). In the linear limit, western boundary coastal sea level should only be affected by ocean signals poleward of the latitude being considered.

Nonlinear effects, however, may be very important, permitting an advective influence of open-ocean sea level from equatorward of the coastal point, associated with poleward-flowing western boundary currents. Sharp steps along western boundaries may be a manifestation of the convergence of this propagation of influence from poleward (by CTWs) and equatorward (by western boundary currents). More work is needed to clarify these issues.

The smoothing and the equatorward "advection" of open-ocean sea-level signals, both of which act to reduce the magnitude of the signal, only apply when the continental slope is long and spans a wide latitude range. In the case of small islands, the smoothing is limited to the length of the depth contours which close around the island, and the equatorward displacement is similarly limited. This means that the open-ocean influence is felt much more strongly at small islands, increasing the risks from sea-level change, but also meaning that measurements from tide gauges on small islands are representative of the surrounding ocean, in contrast to the case for, especially extratropical, continental tide gauges.

For all cases, it should be stressed that we have here considered only the dynamical component of sea-level change, which results in the sea surface not being level. On top of this component, any increase in the volume of water in the ocean will transmit freely to the coast, with a distribution depending purely on the response of the solid Earth and its gravity field to the redistribution of mass, as considered elsewhere in this volume. In addition, we have ignored the inverse barometer response to atmospheric pressure changes, which would also be felt at the coast just as strongly as in the open ocean.

Acknowledgements This work was partly supported by the Natural Environment Research Council: (Anthony Wise NE/L002469/1) and (Chris W. Hughes NE/K012789/1). SM is supported by the Japan Society for the Promotion of Science (JSPS) KAKENHI Grant Nos. 18H04129 and 18H04911.

References

Andersen OB, Nielsen K, Knudsen P, Hughes CW, Bingham R, Fenoglio-Marc L, Gravelle M, Kern M, Padilla Polo S (2018) Improving the coastal mean dynamic topography by geodetic combination of tide gauge and satellite altimetry. Mar Geod 41(6):517–545. https://doi.org/10.1080/01490419.2018.1530320

Allen JS, Romea RD (1980) On coastal trapped waves at low latitudes in a stratified ocean. J Fluid Mech 98:555–585

Becker JM, Salmon R (1997) Eddy formation on a continental slope. J Mar Res 55:181–200

Bingham RJ, Hughes CW (2012) Local diagnostics to estimate density-induced sea level variations over topography and along coastlines. J Geophys Res 117(C1):C01013. https://doi.org/10.1029/2011JC007276

Brink KH (1982) The effect of bottom friction on low-frequency coastal trapped waves. J Phys Oceanogr 12:127–133

Brink KH (1991) Coastal trapped waves and wind-driven currents over the continental shelf. Annu Rev Fluid Mech 23(1991):389–412

Calafat FM, Chambers DP, Tsimplis MN (2012) Mechanisms of decadal sea level variability in the eastern North Atlantic and the Mediterranean Sea. J Geophys Res Oceans 117:C09022. https://doi.org/10.1029/2012JC008285

Calafat FM, Chambers DP, Tsimplis MN (2013) Inter-annual to decadal sea-level variability in the coastal zones of the Norwegian and Siberian Seas: the role of atmospheric forcing. J Geophys Res Oceans 118:1287–1301. https://doi.org/10.1002/jgrc.20106

Chelton DB, Schlax MA (1996) Global observations of oceanic Rossby waves. Science 272:234–238

Chelton DB, de Szoeke RA, Schlax MA, El Naggar K, Siwertz N (1998) Geographical variability of the first baroclinic Rossby radius of deformation. J Phys Oceanogr 28:433–460

Cherian DA, Brink KH (2016) Offshore transport of shelf water by deep-ocean eddies. J Phys Oceanogr 46:3599–3621. https://doi.org/10.1175/JPO-D-16-0085.1

Csanady GT (1978) The arrested topographic wave. J Phys Oceanogr 8:47–62

Csanady GT (1982) Circulation in the coastal ocean, vol 2. Springer, Dordrecht, p 279

Deremble B, Johnson ER, Dewar WK (2017) A coupled model of interior balanced and boundary flow. Ocean Model 119:1–12. https://doi.org/10.1016/j.ocemod.2017.09.003

Dewar WK, Hogg A (2010) Topographic inviscid dissipation of balanced flow. Ocean Model 32:1–13. https://doi.org/10.1016/j.ocemod.2009.03.007

Dale A, Huthnance JM, Sherwin TJ (2001) Coastal trapped internal waves and tides at near-inertial frequencies. J Phys Oceanogr 31(10):2958–2970

Durski SM, Kurapov AL, Allen JS, Kosro PM, Egbert GD, Shearman RK, Barth JA (2015) Coastal Ocean variability in the US Pacific Northwest region: seasonal patterns, winter circulation, and the influence of the 2009–2010 El Niño. Ocean Dyn 65(12):1643–1663. https://doi.org/10.1007/s10236-015-0891-1

Enfield DB, Allen JS (1980) On the structure and dynamics of monthly mean sea level anomalies along the Pacific coast of North and South America. J Phys Oceanogr 10:557–578. https://doi.org/10.1175/1520-0485(1980) 010<0557:OTSADO>2.0.CO;2

Ford R (2000) A baroclinic western boundary current over a continental slope. J Mar Res 58(3):327–373

Fukumori I, Wang O, Llovel W, Fenty I, Forget G (2015) A near-uniform fluctuation of ocean bottom pressure and sea level across the deep ocean basins of the Arctic Ocean and the Nordic Seas. Prog Oceanogr 134:152–172. https://doi.org/10.1016/j.pocean.2015.01.013

Gill AE (1982) Atmosphere-ocean dynamics, International geophysics series, 30. Academic Press, Cambridge

Gregory JM, Griffies SM, Hughes CW, Lowe JA, Church JA, Fukumori I, Gomez N, Kopp RE, Landerer F, Ponte RM, Stammer D, Tamisiea ME, van de Wal RS Concepts and terminology for sea level—mean, variability and change, both local and global. Surv Geophys (this volume)

Grimshaw R (1977) The effects of a variable Coriolis parameter, coastline curvature and variable bottom topography on continental-shelf waves. J Phys Oceanogr 7:547–554

Higginson S, Thompson KR, Woodworth PL, Hughes CW (2015) The tilt of mean sea level along the east coast of North America. Geophys Res Lett 42(5):1471–1479. https://doi.org/10.1002/2015GL063186

Hughes CW (2008) A form of potential vorticity equation for depth-integrated flow with a free surface. J Phys Oceanogr 38:1131–1136

Hughes CW, de Cuevas BA (2001) Why western boundary currents in realistic oceans are inviscid: a link between form stress and bottom pressure torques. J Phys Oceanogr 31(10):2871–2885. https://doi.org/10.1175/1520-0485(2001)031%3C2871:WWBCIR%3E2.0.CO;2

Hughes CW, Meredith MP (2006) Coherent sea-level fluctuations along the global continental slope. Philos Trans R Soc Lond A 364(1841):885–901. https://doi.org/10.1098/rsta.2006.1744

Hughes CW, Williams SDP (2010) The color of sea level: importance of spatial variations in spectral shape for assessing the significance of trends. J Geophys Res 115(C10):C10048. https://doi.org/10.1029/2010JC006102

Hughes CW, Williams Joanne, Coward AC, de Cuevas BA (2014) Antarctic circumpolar transport and the southern mode: a model investigation of interannual to decadal time scales. Ocean Sci 10:215–225. https://doi.org/10.5194/os-10-215-2014

Hughes CW, Bingham RJ, Roussenov V, Williams Joanne, Woodworth PL (2015) The effect of Mediterranean exchange flow on European time mean sea level. Geophys Res Lett 42(2):466–474. https://doi.org/10.1002/2014GL062654

Hughes CW, Williams Joanne, Hibbert A, Boening C, Oram J (2016) A Rossby whistle: a resonant basin mode observed in the Caribbean Sea. Geophys Res Lett 43:7036–7043. https://doi.org/10.1002/2016GL069573

Hughes CW, Williams Joanne, Blaker A, Coward A, Stepanov V (2018) A window on the deep ocean: the special value of ocean bottom pressure for monitoring the large-scale, deep-ocean circulation. Prog Oceanogr 161:19–46. https://doi.org/10.1016/j.pocean.2018.01.011

Huthnance JM (1978) On coastal trapped waves: analysis and numerical calculation by inverse iteration. J Phys Oceanogr 8:74–92

Huthnance JM (1987) Effects of longshore shelf variations on barotropic continental shelf waves. Prog Oceanogr 19:177–220

Huthnance JM (2001) Coastal trapped waves. In: Steele JH, Thorpe SA, Turekian KK (eds) Encyclopedia of ocean sciences. Academic Press, San Diego, pp 489–496

Huthnance JM (2004) Ocean-to-shelf signal transmission: a parameter study. J Geophys Res 109:C12029. https://doi.org/10.1029/2004JC002358

Huthnance JM, Mysak LA, Wang DP (1986) Coastal trapped waves. In: Mooers CNK (ed) Coastal and Estuarine sciences 3: Baroclinic processes on continental shelves. American Geophysical Union, Washington, pp 1–18

Johnson HL, Marshall DP (2002) A theory for the surface Atlantic response to thermahaline variability. J Phys Oceanogr 32:1121–1132

Kanzow T, Johnson HL, Marshall DP, Cunningham SA, Hirschi JJM, Mujahid A, Bryden HL, Johns WE (2009) Basinwide integrated volume transports in an eddy-filled ocean. J Phys Oceanogr 39:3091–3109. https://doi.org/10.1175/2009JPO4185.1

Kurapov AL, Erofeeva SY, Myers E (2017) Coastal sea level variability in the US West Coast Ocean Forecast System (WCOFS). Ocean Dyn 67:23–36. https://doi.org/10.1007/s10236-016-1013-4

LaCasce JH (2017) The prevalence of oceanic surface modes. Geophys Res Lett 44:11097–11105. https://doi.org/10.1002/2017GL075430

Lin H, Thompson KR, Huang J, Veronneau M (2015) Tilt of mean sea level along the Pacific coasts of North America and Japan. J Geophys Res Oceans 120:6815–6828. https://doi.org/10.1002/2015JC010920

Lorbacher K, Marsland SJ, Church JA, Griffies SM, Stammer D (2012) Rapid barotropic sea level rise from simulated ice-sheet melting scenarios. J Geophys Res 117:C06003. https://doi.org/10.1029/2011JC007733

MacCready P, Rhines PB (1993) Slippery bottom boundary layers on a slope. J Phys Oceanogr 23:5–22

Marshall DP (2011) Rossby wormholes. J Mar Res 69:309–330

Marshall DP, Johnson HL (2013) Propagation of meridional circulation anomalies along western and eastern boundaries. J Phys Oceanogr 43:2699–2717
Milliff RF, McWilliams JC (1994) The evolution of boundary pressure in ocean basins. J Phys Oceanogr 24:1317–1338
Minobe S, Terada M, Qiu B, Schneider N (2017) Western boundary sea level: a theory, rule of thumb, and application to climate models. J Phys Oceanogr 47(5):957–977
Mitchum G (1994) Comparison of TOPEX sea surface heights and tide gauge sea levels. J Geophys Res 99(C12):24541–24553
Munk WH (1950) On the wind-driven ocean circulation. J Meteorol 7:79–93
Mysak LA (1980) Topographically trapped waves. Annu Rev Fluid Mech 12:45–76
Mysak LA (1980) Recent advances in shelf wave dynamics. Rev Geophys Space Phys 18:211–241
Rhines PB (1970) Edge, bottom and Rossby waves. Geophys Fluid Dyn 1:273–302
Rio M-H, Mulet S, Picot N (2014) Beyond GOCE for the ocean circulation estimate: synergetic use of altimetry, gravimetry, and in situ data provides new insight into geostrophic and Ekman currents. Geophys Res Lett 41:8918–8925. https://doi.org/10.1002/2014GL061773
Salmon R (1994) Generalized two-layer models of ocean circulation. J Mar Res 52:865–9082
Samelson RM (2017) Time-dependent linear theory for the generation of poleward undercurrents on eastern boundaries. J Phys Oceanogr 47:3037–3059. https://doi.org/10.1175/JPO-D-17-0077.1
Schoonover J, Dewar WK, Wienders N, Deremble B (2017) Local sensitivities of the Gulf Stream separation. J Phys Oceanogr 47:353–373. https://doi.org/10.1175/JPO-D-16-0195.1
Stern M (1998) Separation of a density current from the bottom of a continental shelf. J Phys Oceanogr 28:2040–2049. https://doi.org/10.1175/1520-0485(1998)028%3C2040:SOADCF%3E2.0.CO;2
Stommel H (1948) The westward intensification of wind-driven ocean currents. Trans Am Geophys Union 29:202–206
Tyler RH, Käse R (2000) A "string function" for describing the propagation of large-scale energy anomalies in a rotating fluid. Geophys Astrophys Fluid Dyn 92:31–64
Welander P (1968) Wind-driven circulation in one- and two-layer oceans of variable depth. Tellus 20:1–15
Williams Joanne, Hughes CW (2013) The coherence of small island sea level with the wider ocean: a model study. Ocean Sci 9:111–119. https://doi.org/10.5194/os-9-111-2013
Wise A, Hughes CW, Polton J (2018) Bathymetric influence on the coastal sea level response to ocean gyres at western boundaries. J Phys Oceanogr 48:2949–2964. https://doi.org/10.1175/JPO-D-18-0007.1
Wise A, Hughes CW, Polton J, Huthnance JM (2019) Leaky slope waves: unusual consequences of the beta-effect along western boundaries with bottom topography and dissipation. J Phys Oceanogr (submitted)
Woodworth PL (1991) The permanent service for mean sea level and the global sea level observing system. J Coast Res 7(3):699–710
Woodworth PL, Hughes CW, Bingham RJ, Gruber T (2012) Towards worldwide height system unification using ocean information. J Geod Sci 2(4):302–318. https://doi.org/10.2478/v10156-012-0004-8
Zhai X, Johnson HL, Marshall DP (2010) Significant sink of ocean-eddy energy near western boundaries. Nat Geosci 3:609–612

Affiliations

Chris W. Hughes[1,2] · Ichiro Fukumori[3] · Stephen M. Griffies[4] · John M. Huthnance[2] · Shoshiro Minobe[5] · Paul Spence[6] · Keith R. Thompson[7] · Anthony Wise[1,2]

[1] Department of Earth, Ocean and Ecological Sciences, University of Liverpool, Jane Herdman Building, 4 Brownlow Street, Liverpool L69 3GP, UK

[2] National Oceanography Centre, 6 Brownlow Street, Liverpool L3 5DA, UK

[3] Jet Propulsion Laboratory, California Institute of Technology, 4800 Oak Grove Dr, Pasadena, CA 91109, USA

[4] NOAA Geophysical Fluid Dynamics Laboratory, Princeton University Program in Atmospheric and Oceanic Sciences, Princeton University Forrestal Campus, 201 Forrestal Road, Princeton, NJ 08540-6649, USA

[5] Department of Earth and Planetary Sciences, Faculty of Science, Hokkaido University, N10, W8, Kita-ku, Sapporo 060-0810, Japan

[6] Climate Change Research Centre, University of New South Wales, Level 4, Mathews Building, Sydney, NSW 2052, Australia

[7] Department of Oceanography, Dalhousie University, LSC, Room 3631, 1355 Oxford Street, PO BOX 15000, Halifax, NS B3H 4R2, Canada

Surveys in Geophysics (2019) 40:1493–1541
https://doi.org/10.1007/s10712-019-09562-8

Impacts of Basin-Scale Climate Modes on Coastal Sea Level: a Review

Weiqing Han[1] · Detlef Stammer[2] · Philip Thompson[3] · Tal Ezer[4] · Hindu Palanisamy[5] · Xuebin Zhang[6] · Catia M. Domingues[7,8,9] · Lei Zhang[1] · Dongliang Yuan[10,11]

Received: 23 February 2019 / Accepted: 1 August 2019 / Published online: 19 August 2019

Abstract
Global sea level rise (SLR) associated with a warming climate exerts significant stress on coastal societies and low-lying island regions. The rates of coastal SLR observed in the past few decades, however, have large spatial and temporal differences from the global mean, which to a large part have been attributed to basin-scale climate modes. In this paper, we review our current state of knowledge about climate modes' impacts on coastal sea level variability from interannual-to-multidecadal timescales. Relevant climate modes, their impacts and associated driving mechanisms through both remote and local processes are elaborated separately for the Pacific, Indian and Atlantic Oceans. This paper also identifies major issues and challenges for future research on climate modes' impacts on coastal sea level. Understanding the effects of climate modes is essential for skillful near-term predictions and reliable uncertainty quantifications for future projections of coastal SLR.

Keywords Coastal sea level change · Sea level variability · Climate variability · Climate modes

✉ Weiqing Han
whan@colorado.edu

1 Department of Atmospheric and Oceanic Sciences, University of Colorado, Boulder, CO 80309, USA

2 Center für Erdsystem Wissenschaften und Nachhaltigkeit, Universität Hamburg, 20146 Hamburg, Germany

3 Department of Oceanography, SOEST, University of Hawai'i at Mānoa, Honolulu, HI 96822, USA

4 Center for Coastal Physical Oceanography, Old Dominion University, Norfolk, VA 23508, USA

5 LEGOS – OMP – CNES, UMR 5566, 31400 Toulouse, France

6 Centre for Southern Hemisphere Oceans Research (CSHOR), CSIRO Oceans and Atmosphere, Hobart, TAS 7000, Australia

7 Institute for Marine and Antarctic Studies, University of Tasmania, Hobart, TAS 7004, Australia

8 ARC Centre of Excellence for Climate Extremes, University of Tasmania, Hobart, TAS 7001, Australia

9 Antarctic Climate and Ecosystem Cooperative Research Centre, Hobart, TAS 7001, Australia

10 Key Laboratory of Ocean Circulation and Waves, and Center for Ocean Mega-Science, Institute of Oceanology, Chinese Academy of Sciences, and Qingdao National Laboratory for Marine Science and Technology, Qingdao, China

11 University of Chinese Academy of Sciences, 266071 Beijing, China

1 Introduction

1.1 Background

Sea level rise (SLR) and extreme events associated with a warming climate are direct threats to human society in low-lying coastal areas and island nations (Wong et al. 2014; Wahl et al. 2018). For adaptation purposes, planners and decision makers require skillful decadal predictions and longer-term projections of SLR along coastlines (e.g., Milne et al. 2009; Church and White 2011; Church et al. 2014; National Research Council (NRC) Report 2012). Producing reliable predictions and future projections of coastal sea level, however, remains challenging due to the complex causes for coastal sea level variations, which differ significantly from the global mean and vary along shore. In addition to non-climate-related local human interferences (e.g., groundwater extraction that causes land subsidence) and geodetic factors, coastal sea level responds to local and remote changes in atmospheric and oceanic circulations. These circulation changes may result from natural internal climate variability, natural external forcing (e.g., solar and volcano) and anthropogenic forcing (e.g., Church et al. 2014; Kopp et al. 2015a, b; Carson et al. 2016).

It is virtually certain ($P = 0.99$) that at least 45% of the global mean SLR over the past century is of anthropogenic origin (Bindoff et al. 2013; Church et al. 2014; Dangendorf et al. 2015; Kopp et al. 2016; Slangen et al. 2016). In contrast, the spatially uneven regional and coastal sea level variability at interannual-to-multidecadal timescales observed since the 1950s has been attributed primarily to internal climate variability, with a large fraction being associated with basin-scale climate modes such as the El Niño and Southern Oscillation (ENSO; e.g., Stammer et al. 2013; Bilbao et al. 2015; Han et al. 2017a). Progress has been made in understanding the impacts of climate modes on basin-wide patterns of sea level variability (Han et al. 2017a). Yet, our understanding of coastal sea level variability caused by climate modes and associated mechanisms is far from complete. In particular, it is unclear to what extent and how remote sea level signals from the open ocean can affect the coasts, as the continental slope can act as a barrier for the communication between the shelf areas and the open ocean (e.g., Brink 1998; Bingham and Hughes 2012; Hughes et al. 2019).

1.2 Purpose of This Review

Given the importance of climate modes in causing open-ocean sea level variability on interannual-to-multidecadal timescales, a thorough understanding of their impacts on coastal sea level is instrumental for improving reliability of decadal predictions and uncertainty quantifications of future SLR projections at coasts. In this paper, we first review the dynamics of communication between coastal and open ocean (Sect. 2); then we summarize the observational evidence for, and our current understanding of, coastal sea level variability from interannual-to-multidecadal timescales induced by climate variability, particularly basin-scale climate modes, in the Pacific, the Indian and the Atlantic Oceans (Sects. 3–5). In Sect. 6, we provide a summary and discuss science issues and future outlook. In this review, unless specified otherwise "decadal-to-multidecadal variability (including multi-decadal trend)" is collectively referred to as "decadal" variability (periods ≥ 10 years), and "interannual" refers to periods < 10 years.

2 Communication Between the Open Ocean and Coasts: Dynamics

The idea that open-ocean variability can impact coastal sea level has been suggested early on (e.g., Montgomery 1938). Sea level signals in the open ocean and over the shelf communicate through different processes for the eastern and western ocean boundaries. Along the eastern ocean boundaries, sea level anomalies (SLAs) can be significantly affected by signals originated from the equatorial basin through eastward-propagating equatorial Kelvin waves (e.g., Wyrtki 1975) and subsequently poleward-propagating coastally trapped waves after the equatorial Kelvin waves impinge on the coast. If the ocean bottom is flat and coasts are vertical walls, sea level signals along the eastern boundary radiate westward as Rossby waves in regions equatorward of Rossby waves' critical latitudes, and poleward as coastal Kelvin waves poleward of the critical latitudes. Bottom topography and bottom friction associated with continental shelf and slope, however, can trap part of the incoming equatorial Kelvin waves' energy to the coast, producing poleward-propagating sea level signals even in regions below the critical latitudes (e.g., Clarke and Vangorder 1994). Compared to meridional coastlines, slanted eastern ocean boundaries affect critical latitudes and somewhat increase the poleward propagation speed, but they do not alter the fundamental nature of coastally trapped sea level signals (e.g., Clarke and Vangorder 1994; Han et al. 2011).

Along the western ocean boundaries, it has been shown that SLAs at particular latitude can be expressed by the sum of contributions from interior SLAs propagating onto the boundary via Rossby waves at and above that latitude, and the western boundary SLAs at higher latitudes via coastally trapped waves (Minobe et al. 2017). This result is based on a linear ocean model that excludes bottom topography and western boundary current. In real coastal oceans, however, continental shelf and slope exist. Under geostrophic approximation and neglecting planetary beta, circulations over the shelf have distinct separations from the large-scale circulations in the open ocean: Currents flow along the isobaths of the continental slope (Brink 1998), setting a "barrier" for cross-isobath flows and thus constraining the remote influence from the open ocean on the coast. The generation of cross-isobath currents must be through ageostrophic processes (e.g., external forcing, nonlinear eddy transport, friction). The long continental slopes in high latitudes also strongly suppresses the effects of open-ocean mesoscale eddies on coasts (e.g., Hughes and Williams 2010; Bingham and Hughes 2012; Hughes et al. 2018, 2019).

By including planetary beta and considering time-dependent large-scale circulations (i.e., greater than Rossby radius), some Rossby waves' energy is able to cross the "barrier" and arrive at the western boundary, particularly at lower latitude where the topographic effect is weaker due to its dependence on Coriolis parameter (Yang et al. 2013). The degree of the open-ocean impact on coastal sea level depends on bottom friction and on the shapes of the shelf and slope (e.g., width and depth), based on the experiments using a linear model that extends the Minobe et al. (2017) solution by including idealized shelf and slope (Wise et al. 2018). Observational analyses support these theoretical results, showing that offshore sea level is likely to be representative of the coastal signal in areas where the shelf is narrow (e.g., the Florida Straits in the Atlantic), but not likely over the broad shelf of the mid-Atlantic Bight (e.g., Higginson et al. 2015).

At the latitudes of subtropical and subpolar gyres, western boundary currents prevail and they can affect the incoming Rossby waves through advection, and the advection effect is less on the first baroclinic mode Rossby wave compared to higher baroclinic modes (Liu 1999). Observational analyses find that variations of the western boundary currents (e.g., the Gulf Stream and Kuroshio) are significantly correlated with the variability of coastal sea level (e.g., Blaha 1984; Haigh et al. 2011; Ezer et al. 2013; Sasaki et al. 2014). Baroclinic Rossby waves driven by open-ocean wind stress curl propagate westward, affecting the transport of the western boundary currents and therefore the cross-current sea level gradients (i.e., alongshore geostrophy). Given that the cross-shore sea level gradients are weak over the shelf compared to the sea level gradients across the boundary current, SLAs at the inshore side of the boundary current were used to represent coastal SLAs (Hong et al. 2000).

3 The Pacific Ocean

In this section, we first provide observational evidence for coastal sea level variability using tide gauge and satellite observations (Sect. 3.1). Since the dynamics of sea level variability along the eastern and western boundaries are different, we review our understanding of the causes for SLAs first along the eastern boundary (Sect. 3.2) and then along the western boundary (Sect. 3.3). For each boundary, we first focus on remote and local processes that induce the observed SLAs and then assess the effects of climate modes. The reviews for the Indian and Atlantic Oceans follow a similar structure.

It is worth noting that satellite altimeters do not observe sea level within 10–20 km of the coast (partly due to land contamination), but they provide a near-global coverage albeit with a relatively short span (~26 years since October 1992). In the immediate vicinity of the coast, information about sea level variability relies on tide gauge observations, which provide long records but only at particular locations. Consequently, reconstructed and reanalysis products, which provide near global sea level with relatively long time span (e.g., since 1950s when more in situ data are available), are often used in sea level studies. However, neither the satellite altimetry data over the shelf nor reconstruction or reanalysis products are able to capture the full magnitude of interannual sea level events observed by tide gauges in most coastal areas (e.g., Hamlington et al. 2015).

3.1 Observations

Satellite altimetry data show unambiguous regional differences in sea level trends since the early 1990s (Church et al. 2014; Fig. 1). Near the eastern boundary of the Pacific, satellite data show no or weak rising trends from 1993 to 2018, and similar situations are also shown in tide gauge data at San Francisco of the North Pacific and Antofagasta of the South Pacific for the same time period (Fig. 1). The multidecadal trend of 1950–2018 at San Francisco tide gauge, however, shows SLR, suggesting that sea level along the Pacific east coast exhibits large-amplitude decadal variability. Indeed, strong interannual and decadal variability has been detected in a number of long, high-quality tide gauge records along the US west coast, and San Francisco holds the longest record since 1854 (e.g., Enfield and Allen 1980; Chelton and Davis 1982; Clarke 1992; Ramp et al. 1997; Meyers et al. 1998; Strub and James 2002; Ponte 2006; Papadopoulos and Tsimplis 2006; Chambers et al. 2012; Breaker and Ruzmaikin 2013; Hamlington et al. 2015). South of the equator, tide gauge records are generally shorter; however, interannual and decadal variability is clearly observed (Fig. 1; Pizarro et al. 2001).

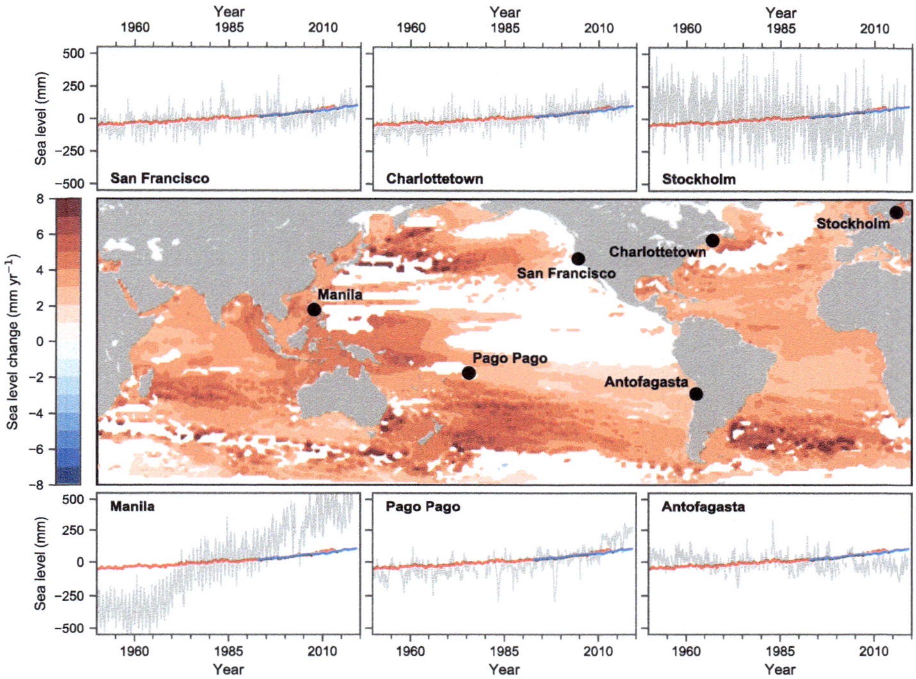

Fig. 1 Map of rates of change (trends) in sea surface height (SSH; geocentric sea level) for the period 1993–2018 from satellite altimetry; trend values exceeding 90% significance are shown in color and those below 90% significance are shown in white. Also shown are relative sea level changes (gray lines) from selected tide gauge stations for the period 1950–2018. For comparison, estimates of global mean sea level change from tide gauges (red lines) and satellite altimetry (blue lines) are shown with each tide gauge time series. The relatively large, short-term oscillations in local sea level (gray lines) are due to the natural climate variability, such as the large deviations at Pago Pago of the western Pacific and San Francisco of the eastern Pacific are associated with the El Niño-Southern Oscillation. This is an updated figure of Church et al. (2014)

Near the western boundary of the Pacific, satellite data observed marked SLR from 1993 to 2018, with maximum rise occurring in the tropics (Fig. 1). Compared to the eastern Pacific, the western Pacific has complex basin geometry and topography, hosting various marginal seas, broad and narrow shelves and slopes, multitude islands and straits that connect with the Indian Ocean (i.e., the Indonesian Throughflow (ITF); see Sect. 4). These can complicate our understanding of the western boundary sea level variability. The satellite-observed sea level trends in the marginal seas (e.g., the South China Sea, East China Sea and Sea of Japan) and near the ITF straits show the same sign as that of the western Pacific Ocean, indicating that open-ocean signals may exert significant influence on coastal ocean. Consistent with satellite observations, tide gauge data at Manila of the Philippines and Pago Pago in the tropical south Pacific also show SLR from 1993 to 2018, albeit with larger rates. Overlying the multidecadal trends of 1950–2018, sea level at both tide gauges exhibit strong interannual and decadal variations (Fig. 1). Indeed, tide gauges detected coherent multi-scale variability in various subregions along the western boundary of the North and South Pacific (e.g., Senjyu et al. 1999; Church et al. 2006; Sect. 3.3.1).

3.2 Eastern Boundary of the Pacific

3.2.1 Remote Versus Local Processes

On interannual timescales, sea level variability along the Pacific eastern boundary is dominated by wind forcing, and the relative contributions of remote versus local wind vary geographically. From the equator to Southern California, interannual SLAs primarily reflect remotely forced, coastally trapped signals of tropical origin (Enfield and Allen 1980; Chelton and Davis 1982). Trade wind anomalies in the equatorial Pacific force eastward-propagating equatorial Kelvin waves; after they impinge upon the eastern boundary, a portion of the energy is reflected back into the ocean interior as Rossby waves, and a portion propagates poleward as coastally trapped waves due to bottom friction and topography, as illustrated by the analytic solutions to a linear ocean model (Clarke and Vangorder 1994) and discussed in Sect. 2. Coherent signatures of these propagating SLAs have been observed as far north as Alaska (Clarke 1992; Ramp et al. 1997; Meyers et al. 1998; Strub and James 2002).

North of San Francisco, however, the impacts of local longshore wind and atmospheric pressure increase with latitude (Enfield and Allen 1980; Chelton and Davis 1982; Hermann et al. 2009). Atmospheric sea level pressure affects sea level via loading, often referred to as inverted barometer (IB) effect (Close 1918; Wunsch and Stammer 1997), which can account for substantial fractions (20–60%) of monthly sea level variance at locations in the Pacific Northwest and Gulf of Alaska regions (Ponte 2006). Longshore winds can produce onshore/offshore Ekman transport, which generates a poleward (equatorward) longshore sea level gradient for southerly (northerly) wind anomalies. The longshore wind and sea level pressure anomalies are, in large part, related to the strength and position of the Aleutian Low (Emery and Hamilton 1985), which is the dominant feature of atmospheric circulation over the Northeast Pacific. Increased strength or eastward displacement of the Aleutian Low raises coastal sea level along the west coast of North America by lowering sea level pressure and increasing the southerly component of wind stress. Along the Canada/Alaska coast, interannual SLAs result from the signals propagating from lower latitudes and those forced by local longshore winds (Qiu 2002).

At decadal time scales, remote tropical forcing—rather than local forcing—is the dominant mechanism. Decadal variations in thermocline depth and sea level of the eastern Pacific as far north as southern California are remotely driven by variability in trade winds of the tropical Pacific (Clarke and Lebedev 1999; Thompson et al. 2014; Merrifield and Thompson 2018). Further north, recent decadal sea level trends at the coast are more closely related to remote equatorial wind forcing with a substantially smaller contribution from local longshore winds (Thompson et al. 2014), even though local forcing is important for interannual SLAs in the higher latitude region; local wind stress curl may also be an important driver (Bromirski et al. 2011), but it is ineffective in accounting for coastal sea level variance in statistical regressions (Chelton and Davis 1982; Thompson et al. 2014). Certainly, wind stress curl is an important driver of open-ocean SLAs (Lagerloef et al. 1995; Fu and Qiu 2002), which propagate westward away from the eastern ocean boundary, leaving the relationship between open-ocean wind stress curl and eastern boundary sea level unclear.

South of the equator, the dynamics of remotely forced SLAs along the eastern boundary largely mirror that of the North Pacific (Enfield and Allen 1980; Pizarro et al. 2001) with interannual SLAs of tropical origin being detected at the southern tip of South America in satellite altimetry (Strub and James 2002; Colas et al. 2008). In contrast to the North Pacific, however, the role of local atmospheric forcing is smaller at higher latitudes, which is reflected by the overall poleward decrease in coastal sea level variance measured by tide gauges (Pizarro et al. 2001). This is at least partially due to the smaller IB effect (<20%) on monthly mean sea level variance along the South American west coast (Ponte 2006). The role of longshore winds is smaller than in the North Pacific as well, but the effect is not negligible as longshore winds modulate the remotely forced SLAs and account for the seasonal asymmetry between hemispheres in the coastal sea level response to interannual tropical forcing (Strub and James 2002).

3.2.2 Effects of Climate Modes

The major modes of climate variability over the Pacific are ENSO (Bjerknes 1969), the Pacific Decadal Oscillation (PDO; Mantua et al. 1997; Zhang et al. 1997), Interdecadal Pacific Oscillation (IPO; Power et al. 1999; Folland et al. 2002) and North Pacific Gyre Oscillation (NPGO; Di Lorenzo et al. 2008). While the PDO is defined as the first empirical orthogonal function (EOF) of monthly sea surface temperature (SST) anomalies in the North Pacific (north of 20°N; with time series of global mean SST removed), the IPO is often regarded as the Pacific-wide manifestation of the PDO (Folland et al. 2002; Trenberth and Jones 2007). On decadal timescales, the indices of PDO, IPO and decadal variability of ENSO are all highly correlated, with correlation coefficients for PDO-IPO and IPO-NINO3.4 (8 year low-passed indices) being both 0.88 during 1900–2008 (Zhang and Church 2012; Han et al. 2014a; Newman et al. 2016). The NPGO is defined as the second EOF of sea surface height anomalies over (180°–110°W, 25°–62°N) of the Northeast Pacific (Di Lorenzo et al. 2008). Since the Southern Annual Mode (SAM) has very weak influence on Indo-Pacific coastal and open-ocean sea level (e.g., Haigh et al. 2011; White et al. 2014; Frankcombe et al. 2015), its effect will not be further discussed in this review.

Climate modes manifest themselves in basin-wide patterns of sea level variability (Han et al. 2017a). The relative importance of these modes in the basin interior, however, differs from the coastal region along the eastern boundary. Eastern boundary sea level is more closely related to remote and local wind forcing along the equatorial and coastal waveguides, whereas SLAs due to open-ocean forcing propagate westward away from the eastern boundary. Thus, coastal SLAs in the East Pacific are expected to correlate with climate modes that have a strong expression in the tropics and/or atmospheric centers of action that affect longshore winds and sea level pressure. Existing studies demonstrate that interannual SLAs along the East Pacific coasts are highly correlated with ENSO, with El Niño (La Niña) causing large-amplitude coastal sea level rise (fall) (Fig. 2a; e.g., Enfield and Allen 1980; Chelton and Davis 1982; Emery and Hamilton 1985; Clarke and Vangorder 1994; Meyers et al. 1998; Strub and James 2002; Papadopoulos and Tsimplis 2006; Hermann et al. 2009; Thompson et al. 2014; Hamlington et al. 2015). Indeed, large sea level increases during major El Niño events are clearly seen in San Francisco tide gauge data since 1880 (Fig. 3) and are identifiable in Antofagasta tide gauge at the South American west coast since 1950 (Fig. 1).

Below, we use the monthly mean sea level from the long and highest-quality tide gauge records to explore the relative importance of climate modes on coastal sea level

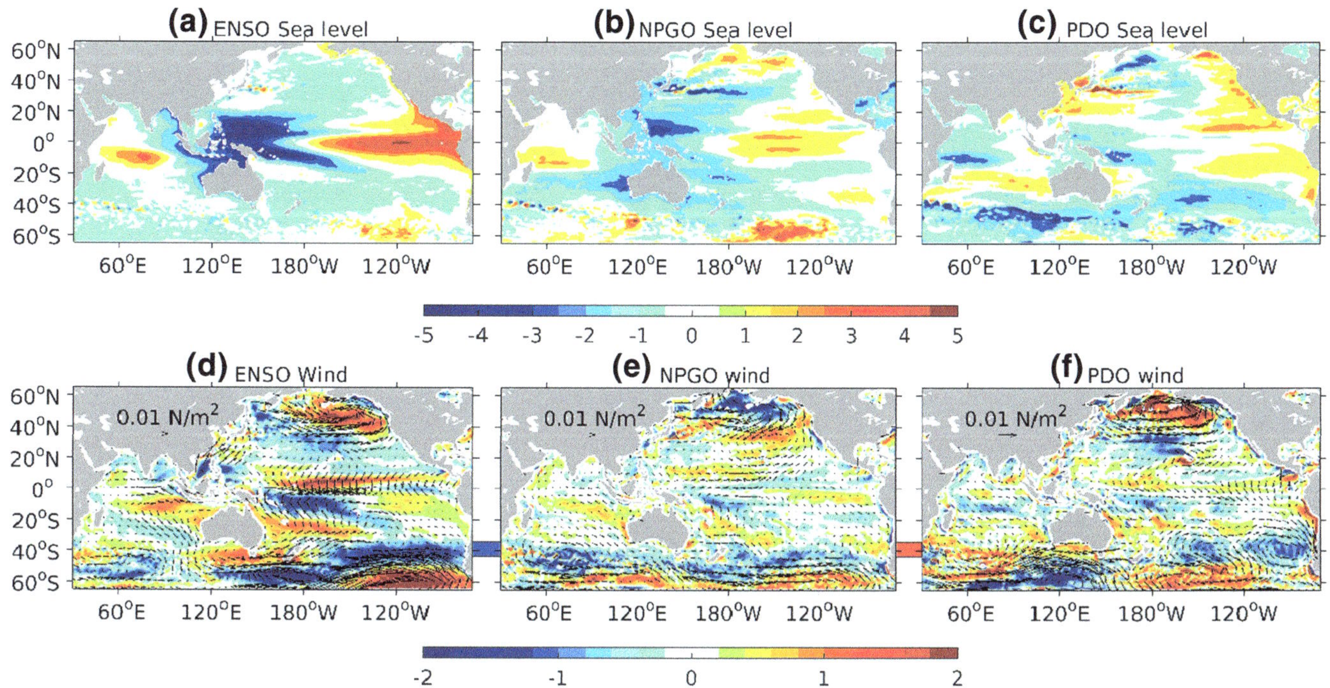

Fig. 2 **a** Regression coefficients of sea level (unit: cm) over the Indo-Pacific basin with respect to **a** ENSO, **b** -NPGO and **c** PDO indices based on multiple linear regression analysis of the ECMWF ORAS5 for 1958–2017. **d**–**f**, same as **a**–**c**, but for regression coefficient of wind stress curl (shading; unit: 10–8 N m^{-3}) and wind stress (vector). The multiple linear regression is modified from Zhang and Church (2012) by adding the NPGO index, in which sea level anomalies (SLAs) are regressed to temporarily high-passed MEI, low-passed NPGO and PDO indices simultaneously. Note for ease of comparison, the regression coefficients with NPGO index are plotted in panels (**b**) and (**e**). The low-pass filter used here is successive application of a 25- and 37-month running mean to the climate indices, which half power point at a period of 6.2 years. Therefore, the low-pass filtered data contain mainly variability at decadal and longer time scales, while the corresponding high-pass filtered data are derived by removing the low-pass-filtered data from the original data, and contain variability mainly at interannual and shorter time scales (Vimont 2005; Zhang and Church 2012). Regression to the IPO index is similar to that of PDO (Frankcombe et al. 2015)

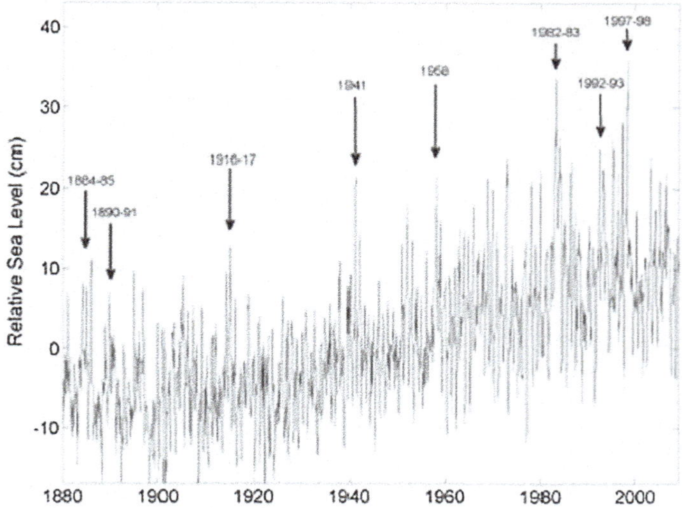

Fig. 3 San Francisco tide gauge record showing relative sea level increases during major El Niño events. Tide gage data from the Permanent Service for Mean Sea Level. Figure from NRC report (2012)

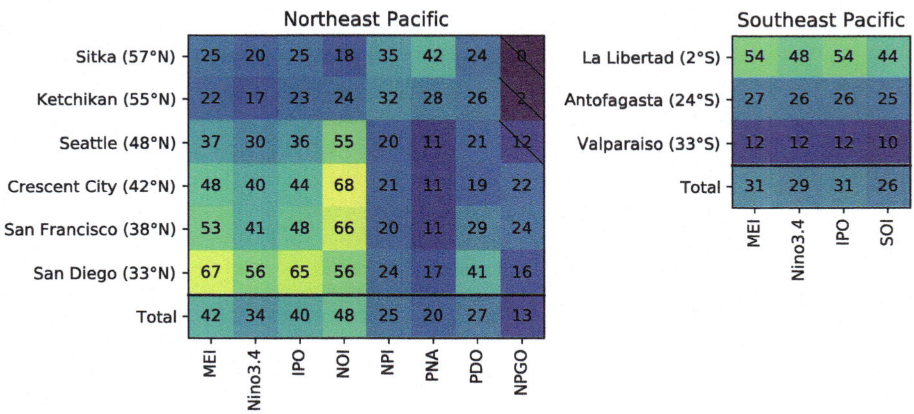

Fig. 4 Percentage of interannual and longer variance accounted for by Pacific climate indices in detrended sea level observations from long, high-quality tide gauges in the East Pacific from 1950 to 2017. Colors map to values; large (small) percentages of variance are highlighted in yellow (purple). Values not significant at the 95% level are marked with a diagonal line. "Total" is the ratio between the sum of (variance accounted for by climate mode at each tide gauge record) and sum of (total sea level variance at each record). A low-pass convolution filter was applied to monthly tide gauge data and climate indices to isolate variability with periods longer than 18 months. The analysis was restricted to the period 1950–2017, which is the period spanned by all climate indices considered here and satisfies the requirement of at least 50 years for separating the influence of climate modes from trends in Pacific sea level (Frankcombe et al. 2015). Tide gauge data are from Permanent Service for Mean Sea Level (Holgate et al. 2013), and detrending is performed using the fitted trend from the regression with the index. See Sect. 3.1.3 of the text for the definitions of climate indices

along the eastern boundary of the North Pacific. In addition, we have also examined the effects of other climate indices (Fig. 4). For each tide gauge and index pair, we perform a least-squares, multiple linear regression of the tide gauge data onto a linear trend and the climate index in question; then the trend is removed before calculating the variance for Fig. 4. We do not perform regressions onto multiple indices simultaneously, because in some cases the indices are highly correlated. Thus, our results reflect the maximum amount of variance that might be attributed to any particular mode or index.

Of particular interest is that the PDO and NPGO are among the least effective climate modes in capturing interannual and decadal sea level variance along the eastern boundary (Fig. 4). To be clear, these modes are dominant drivers of basin-wide patterns of open-ocean sea level variability in the North Pacific (e.g., Han et al. 2017a), but this does not necessarily make them optimal predictors of coastal sea level. The multivariate ENSO index (MEI; Wolter and Timlin 2011) and IPO index (defined here as a SST tri-pole as in Henley et al. 2015) are far more effective as predictors of eastern boundary SLAs at low- to mid-latitudes, presumably because they capture tropical processes that induce the remotely forced, propagating SLAs observed in tide gauge records. In agreement with Frankcombe et al. (2015), the fraction of variance accounted for by the tropical indices decreases with latitude as the influence of local atmospheric forcing becomes more important.

Between San Francisco and Seattle, although ENSO and IPO still explain large fractions of variance, coastal SLAs are most effectively captured by the Northern Oscillation Index (NOI; Schwing et al. 2002), which is defined as the atmospheric sea level pressure difference between Darwin, Australia and the North Pacific High. The NOI is highly correlated with both the MEI and IPO ($r = -0.83$ in both cases), but the NOI is particularly effective as a predictor of sea level along the US west coast (Fig. 4) due to the inclusion of the North Pacific High as a center of action, which better captures variability in the longshore wind stress there. Such a mechanism has been proposed as an explanation for a large (≈ 80 cm peak to trough) multidecadal fluctuation in San Francisco sea level spanning the late nineteenth and early twentieth centuries prior to the establishment of other gauges in the region (Miller and Douglas 2007). Note that lengthening the filter from 18 months to 7 years to isolate decadal variations results in a substantial increase in the fraction of coastal sea level variance accounted for by the NPGO (not shown), though statistical significance drops below 95% for the three northern most gauges due to the reduction in degrees of freedom caused by the heavier filter. The increase in variance captured by the NPGO is likely due to the fact that at longer time scales it becomes difficult to statistically distinguish between the various modes and indices. Using the seven-year filter, the correlation between the NPGO and NOI increases from 0.44 to 0.58 (both significant at the 99% level), while anticorrelation between the NPGO and IPO increases from -0.37 to -0.67 (both at 99% significance).

For high latitudes in the Gulf of Alaska, the most effective predictors of coastal SLAs are the North Pacific Index (NPI; Trenberth and Hurrell 1994) and the Pacific/North American pattern (PNA; Wallace and Gutzler 1981). Both of which are closely related to variability in the Aleutian low with NPI being a direct measure of the Aleutian low intensity and the latter incorporating the Aleutian low as a primary center of action. The NOI, NPI and PNA are significantly correlated with ENSO, IPO, PDO and NPGO, but they are more effective predictors of coastal SLAs, due to the dynamic link between Aleutian low variability and SLAs via the effects on local sea level pressure and longshore winds. This is related to the fact that PDO is an empirical mode and can be caused by both extratropical and tropical processes. This issue is further discussed in Sect. 6.

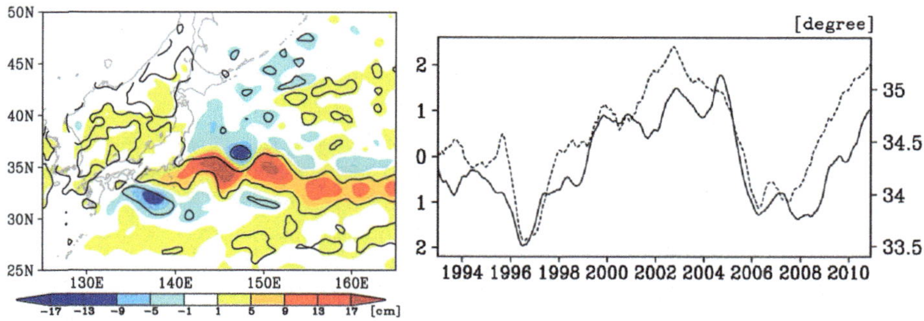

Fig. 5 (Left) Regression coefficient map of satellite SLAs onto the normalized time series of the 1st SVD mode (between satellite and tide gauge) from satellite data during 1993–2010, which is the solid curve on the right panel; the line contour indicates the regions where the corresponding correlations are significant at 95% confidence level. (Right) Normalized time series of the 1st SVD mode of satellite SLA (solid line; left axis) and the latitude (dashed line; right axis) of the Kuroshio Extension jet averaged for 140°E–165°E. From Sasaki et al. (2014)

In the South Pacific, ENSO indices—i.e., MEI, Niño3.4 index and southern oscillation index (SOI)—and IPO, the climate modes that are centered in the tropics, do not capture large fractions of coastal sea level variance outside the tropics (Fig. 4, right panel; Frankcombe et al. 2015). This is partially due to the regional tectonic and seismic activities that cannot be removed from tide gauge data due to the short GPS record as well as the inability of ENSO and IPO indices to capture a greater fraction of the variance. For example, the MEI accounts for less than 30% of the interannual and longer variance at Valparaiso prior to 1977 and more than 50% of the variance during 1993–present. The relationship during the latter period is dominated by the 1997–98 El Niño event, which suggests that the largest tropical events do affect coastal sea level at mid- to high latitudes along the South Pacific eastern boundary and supports previous findings suggesting this connection (e.g., Strub and James 2002).

More recently, sea level in the East Pacific has undergone a shift from near-zero trends during most of the first two decades of satellite altimetry (Bromirski et al. 2011; Thompson et al. 2014) to large positive trends since around 2012 (Hamlington et al. 2016). It is difficult to distinguish the effects of individual climate modes on sea level over the altimetry period alone (e.g., Zhang and Church 2012), as the Pacific indices can be highly correlated over short periods. For example, after applying the 18-month low-pass filter described above, the PDO index is correlated at magnitude 0.65 or greater (and exceeding the 99% significance level) with all of the following indices during 1993–present: MEI, IPO, NOI, SOI, NPI and NPGO. This underscores the importance of process-oriented studies of the relationships between climate indices and coastal sea level, as not all of these indices represent processes with a clear physical link to sea level along the eastern boundary of the basin. Nevertheless, the inflection in decadal sea level trends can be statistically decoupled from canonical ENSO sea level fluctuations during recent decades (Hamlington et al. 2016), which suggests that recent trends may reflect a phase change in basin-scale Pacific climate.

3.3 Western Boundary of the Pacific

3.3.1 Remote Versus Local Processes

In the subpolar western North Pacific, interannual SLAs along the east coast of Kuril islands are determined by the wind-driven, westward-propagating baroclinic Rossby waves (Qiu 2002). In the Sea of Japan, ocean general circulation model (OGCM) experiments suggest that the tide-gauge observed bidecadal variability of sea level around Japanese coastlines results from the westward propagation of Rossby waves forced by winds in the central and eastern North Pacific basin (Yasuda and Sakurai 2006). Prominent decadal variability of sea level was found along the Kuroshio Extension jet, due to the westward-propagating Rossby waves from the east Pacific (Fig. 5) causing north–south shifts of the jet and thus inducing SLAs around the Japanese coasts, as observed by both tide gauge and satellite data from 1993 to 2010 (Sasaki et al. 2014). The SLAs are large along the southeast coast of Japan due to the direct influence of the jet-trapped Rossby waves, and along the west coast of Japan likely due to coastally trapped waves excited by the incoming Rossby waves.

Along the China east coast, sea level variations are strongly influenced by coastally trapped waves (Hsueh and Pang 1989; Hsueh and Yuan 1997). Over the continental shelf of the East China Sea, local wind stress curl is suggested to be the cause for decadal SLAs (Moon and Song 2017). In the South China Sea, Rossby waves from the western tropical Pacific impinge on the east coast of the Philippines, where their associated SLAs propagate clockwise as coastally trapped waves, causing interannual-to-decadal SLAs around the Philippine coasts (e.g., Liu et al. 2011; Zhuang et al. 2013; Cheng et al. 2016). The effect of local longshore wind is important for SLAs along the west coasts of Borneo and Palawan islands (Cheng et al. 2016).

In the western tropical Pacific, interannual and decadal SLAs around the multitude of islands and ITF straits are primarily attributed to the variability of the easterly trade winds. On interannual timescales, variations in zonal wind in the equatorial Pacific cause SLAs along the Arafura/Australia shelf break via equatorial Rossby waves, which excite coastally trapped waves off the western tip of New Guinea, with portion of the energy entering the Indian Ocean through the Indonesian Archipelago (e.g., Clarke 1991; Wijffels and Meyers 2004; also see Sect. 4). Theoretical studies suggest that SLA signals in the western equatorial Pacific and on the western boundaries of the major landmasses should be in phase and have similar amplitudes based on the island rule (Clarke 1991; Godfrey 1996). Recent observations suggest that nonlinear interactions between the Rossby waves and the Mindanao Current result in significant elevation of sea level in the northern Indonesian seas, which forces significant ITF transport into the Indian Ocean (Yuan et al. 2018).

On decadal timescales, rapid SLR in the western tropical Pacific during recent decades, which opposes the sea level fall in the eastern tropical Pacific basin, has been detected by satellite, tide gauge, reconstructed and reanalysis data (Fig. 1; e.g., Church et al. 2006; Merrifield 2011; Zhang and Church 2012). Both observational analyses and ocean modeling experiments show that the steady intensification of the trade wind is the primary cause for the rapid SLR since the early 1990s (Merrifield 2011; McGregor et al. 2012; Merrifield and Maltrud 2011; Qiu and Chen 2012; Meyssignac et al. 2012; Nidheesh et al. 2013; Han et al. 2014a; Hamlington et al. 2014; Palanisamy et al. 2015). Furthermore, intensified amplitudes of SLAs at 8–20 year periods since the late 1980s were observed and attributed to the intensified decadal variability of easterly trade and its associated off-equatorial wind stress curl (Han et al. 2014a). Interannual and decadal fluctuations of the easterly trade, which are linked to climate modes and inter-basin interactions (see Sect. 3.3.2), cause the west–east seesaw of decadal SLAs (e.g., Carton et al. 2005; Bindoff and Willebrand 2007; Kohl et al. 2007; Lombard et al. 2009; Timmermann et al. 2010; McGregor et al. 2012; England et al. 2014; Han et al. 2014a; Merrifield and Thompson 2018). Local land subsidence, however, may also be an important factor in the amplification of relative SLR (e.g., Ballu et al. 2011; Becker et al. 2012).

In the western South Pacific, the leading EOF pattern from 16 tide gauge records around the Australian coasts explains 69% of the total sea level variance, with larger amplitudes occurring at the northern and western Australian coasts of the Indian Ocean, from where SLAs propagate counterclockwise around the coasts as coastally trapped waves with magnitude decreasing with distance (White et al. 2014). Direct influence from the western equatorial Pacific on SLAs along the Australian east coast is weak, because there is no direct oceanic pathway. Instead, westward-propagating Rossby waves from the subtropical Pacific interior directly impact coastal sea level and the East Australian Current (EAC; Holbrook et al. 2011), with the Indian Ocean (via coastally trapped waves) and Southern Ocean having much weaker influence (White et al. 2014). Interannual-to-decadal variations of EAC transport and SLA measured at the Fort Denison tide gauge in Sydney Harbor are significantly correlated; Rossby waves generated by winds in the Tasman Sea explain the large variances of EAC transport and coastal sea level, and remotely forced Rossby waves from the South Pacific interior account for the multidecadal sea level trend along the New South Wales coast (Holbrook et al. 2011). Observational analysis and OGCM experiments showed that decadal variations of wind stress curl in the South Pacific interior excite baroclinic Rossby waves, causing decadal SLAs along the east coast of New Zealand; subsequently, Rossby waves emanated from New Zealand propagate into the Tasman Sea, causing decadal SLA along Australian southeast coast and the coasts of Tasmania (Sasaki et al. 2008).

3.3.2 Effects of Climate Modes

The trade wind anomalies that cause the sea level east–west seesaw and interannual variability in the western tropical Pacific result primarily from ENSO (Fig. 2; e.g., Nerem et al. 1999; Landerer et al. 2008; Zhang and Church 2012; Wu et al. 2017). Sea level is low (high) in the western tropical Pacific during El Niño (La Niña), and its variability exhibits pronounced seasonality and north–south asymmetry. During El Niño, low sea level appears north of the equator (e.g., Guam and Marshall islands) from July to December and south of the equator (e.g., American Samoa islands) from January to June, due to the seasonal evolution of westerly wind anomalies in the western and central equatorial basin (Chowdhury et al. 2007). On decadal timescales, the IPO phase transitions are linked to SLAs in the western tropical Pacific, such as the rapid SLR since the early 1990s (e.g., Merrifield et al. 2012; Meyssignac et al. 2012; Zhang and Church 2012; Hamlington et al. 2013, 2014; Moon et al. 2013; Han et al. 2014a; Palanisamy et al. 2015; Lyu et al. 2017). The intensified wind and SLAs during recent decades, however, cannot be fully explained by the IPO (Han et al. 2014a); decadal variability of SST over the tropical Indian and Atlantic Oceans also had significant contributions (Luo et al. 2012; Han et al. 2014a; McGregor et al. 2014).

In the western North Pacific, ENSO influence on coastal SLAs weakens with latitude, as shown by the analysis of 27 tide gauges along the China Coastline from 1968 to 2016 and satellite altimetry (Wang et al. 2018). From 1993 to 2015, ENSO-SLA correlations are the largest in the South China Sea (> 0.6 in most areas; also see Cheng et al. 2015), weaker in the East China Sea (> 0.4 in most areas) and weakest in the Bohai and Yellow Seas (< 0.4), with all correlation coefficients being statistically significant at the 95% confidence level. Significant correlations between PDO index and interannual SLAs (up to 10 cm) have also been found in the northwest Pacific including the East China Sea (Papadopoulos and Tsimplis 2006; Han and Huang 2008). On decadal timescales, SLAs are significantly correlated with the PDO in the East China Sea (Han and Huang 2008) and South China Sea in recent decades, due to Rossby waves forced by PDO-associated wind stress curl propagating to the South China Sea through the Philippine Archipelago (Cheng et al. 2016). Moon and Song (2017), however, found that decadal SLAs in the East China Sea in the past 50 years were highly correlated with the NPGO rather than PDO (also see Merrifield 2011), although the PDO can explain the multidecadal trend reversal since the mid-1980s. Indeed, either NPGO or PDO can dominate coastal SLAs, depending on locations and periods (Fig. 2).

In the western South Pacific, variations of the wind stress curl that drive interannual-to-decadal Rossby waves and coastal SLAs along the east coasts of Australia and New Zealand and around the coasts of Tasman Sea are associated with ENSO (e.g., Sasaki et al. 2008; Haigh et al. 2011; Holbrook et al. 2011; White et al. 2014). As discussed above, due to the lack of direct oceanic pathway the impacts of ENSO and IPO on sea level along the Australian east coast are not as strong as those along the north and west coasts (Fig. 2; e.g., Zhang and Church 2012; Frankcombe et al. 2015; Wu et al. 2017).

Wu et al. (2017) examined the interannual and decadal (6-year low-passed) SLAs as well as trend associated with ENSO and PDO over 1993–2011 and found that the SLAs and trend were well explained by the steric component in the open ocean, with a major contribution from the thermosteric component while the halosteric component only played a minor role in the western equatorial Pacific region. Over the shallow shelves of the western Pacific boundary, however, mass component plays a significant role (their Fig. 4).

4 The Indian Ocean

4.1 Observations

Tide gauge observations show evident multidecadal trends and interannual-to-interdecadal sea level variability around the coastal and island regions of the Indian Ocean (e.g., Shankar and Shetye 1999; Unnikrishnan and Shankar 2007; Han et al. 2010; Frankcombe et al. 2015; Unnikrishnan et al. 2015; Parekh et al. 2017; black lines of Fig. 6). Centennial trends of SLR are also detected at Mumbai, the west coast of India (Shankar and Shetye 1999) and Fremantle, the west coast of Australia (Feng et al. 2004), the only two tide gauges within the Indian Ocean with record lengths longer than 100 years (Bradshaw et al. 2015). The rates of SLR and amplitudes of sea level variability, however, differ considerably from region to region. In particular, a falling trend was detected in a ~20-year tide gauge record in recent decades at Zanzibar, the east coast of Tanzania and the western boundary of the Indian Ocean, while rising trends were observed at all other tide gauges since the 1960s/1970s.

Overlying the multidecadal trend, coastal sea level exhibits strong interannual and decadal variations (Fig. 6), with apparently larger amplitudes along the coasts of the east basin (stations 3–8 around the Bay of Bengal and Australian coasts) compared to that of the west

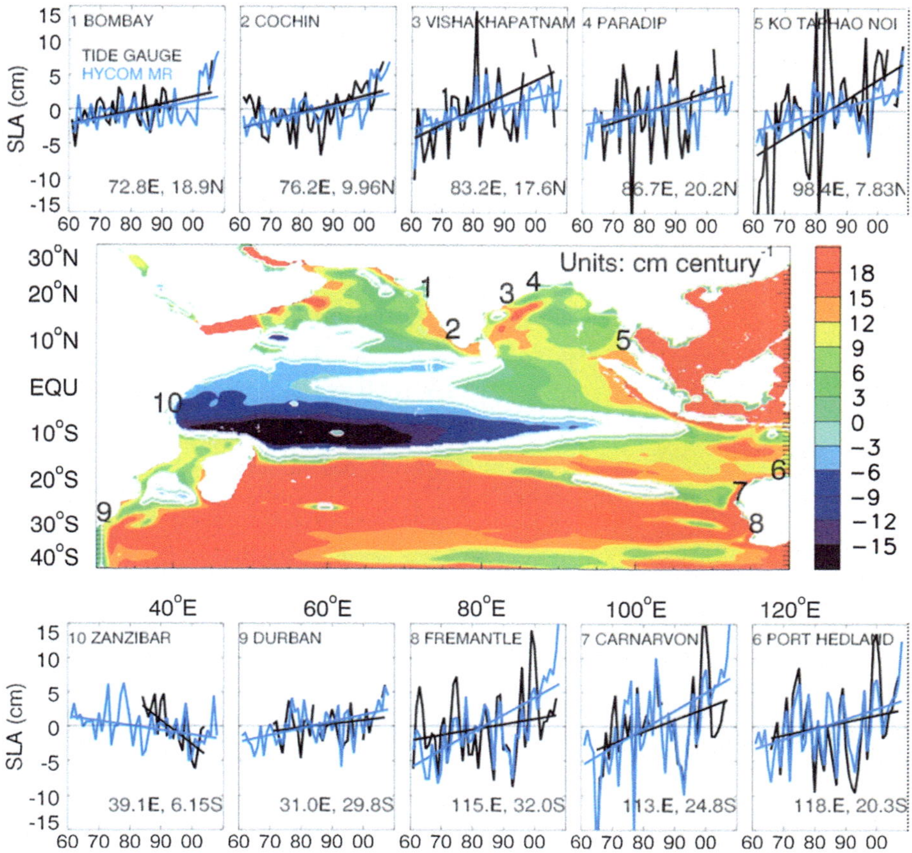

Fig. 6 Tide gauge observed and HYCOM simulated annual mean sea level anomalies (SLA) and their Kendall Theil trends during 1961–2008. The 10 tide gauge stations with records longer than 30 years (20 years for Zanzibar) are shown. All trends exceed 95% significance except for stations 6 and 9 tide gauge data. Middle color panel shows Kendall Theil trend of HYCOM simulated SLA for 1961–2008. Light blue/green regions are below and the rest above 95% significance. Tide gauge locations are marked by 1–10. Customized from Han et al. (2010)

basin (stations 1–2 of the Indian west coast and 9–10 of the South African coast). These results agree with the variance map of Shankar et al. (2010), showing the SLA minima in the central equatorial basin and eastern Arabian Sea, but large variance along the boundaries of the East Indian Ocean. Indeed, tide gauge observations detected coherent interannual SLAs along the 8000 km coastline from Java to Mumbai (Clarke and Liu 1994).

Satellite altimetry since the early 1990s (Fig. 7c) and various reanalysis and reconstructed sea level products since the 1960s show strong interannual-to-decadal SLAs over the Seychelles islands and Chagos Archipelago regions of the tropical South Indian Ocean where the thermocline is shallow (McCreary et al. 1993; Murtugudde et al. 1999), referred to as the Seychelles–Chagos thermocline ridge (SCTR; e.g., Hermes and Reason 2008; Yokoi et al. 2008). Large spread, however, exists among different reanalysis and reconstructed products, suggesting large uncertainties in detecting sea level variability using these datasets (Nidheesh et al. 2017). Decadal variations are evident, although the

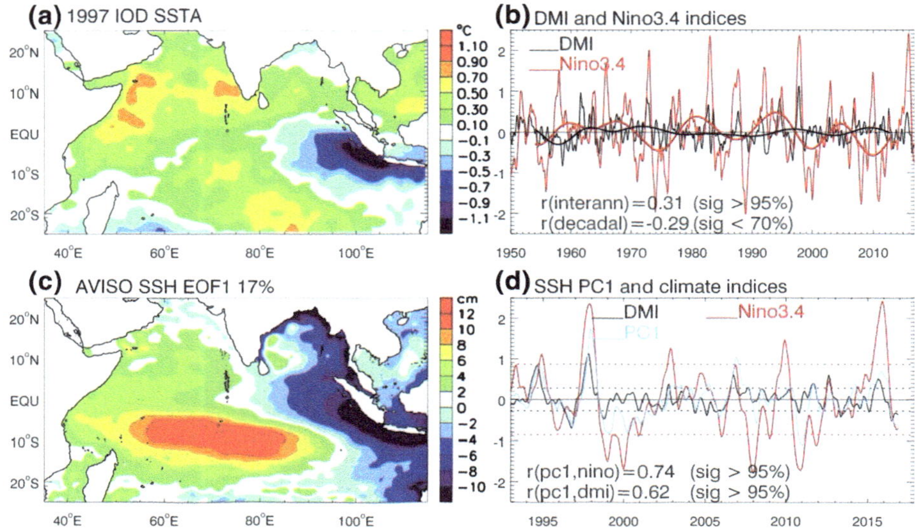

Fig. 7 **a** September, October and November (SON) mean SSTA for the 1997 positive IOD-El Nino co-occurrence, based on detrended and demeaned HadISST data from 1950 to 2012; **b** 5-month running mean Dipole Mode Index (DMI; thin black curve) based on monthly SSTA, defined as SSTA difference between western pole (50°E–70°E, 10°S–10°N average) and eastern pole (90°E–110°E, 10°S–0°N average); thin red curve shows 5-month running mean Nino3.4 index; corresponding thick curves are their 8-year low-passed indices; **c** EOF1 of monthly AVISO SSHA (linear trend and monthly climatology removed); **d** SSHA PC1 (blue), DMI and Nino3.4 indices. Horizontal dashed lines show the ± 1STD of DMI (black) and Nino3.4 (red) index

magnitudes are weaker than that of interannual (e.g., Shankar and Shetye 1999; Feng et al. 2004, 2010, 2011; Holgate and Woodworth 2004: Nidheesh et al. 2013; Figs. 6 and 7d). Indeed, decadal reversals of basin-wide sea level trend patterns have been observed in satellite data (e.g., Lee and McPhaden 2008; Thompson et al. 2016; Srinivasu et al. 2017). The leading EOF of satellite SLAs for 1993–2016 agrees with the tide gauge results, showing larger amplitudes around the boundaries of the east basin and over SCTR, compared to the weaker magnitude in the central equatorial basin and east Arabian Sea (Fig. 7c, d).

4.2 Eastern and Northern Indian Ocean Boundaries and the Seychelles-Chagos Thermocline Ridge (SCTR) Region

Unique to the Indian Ocean, its northern boundary is located in the tropics and its eastern boundary is separated by the ITF, which connects the Indian and Pacific Oceans, the only low-latitude connection between ocean basins in the world. As a result, sea level signals generated in the equatorial basin can propagate southward to Sumatra and Java coasts (e.g., Wijffels and Meyers 2004) and northward into the Bay of Bengal until the west coast of India along equatorial and coastal waveguides (Clarke and Liu 1994), and those signals generated in the equatorial Pacific can exert strong influence on the west coast of Australia (i.e., southeast coast of the Indian Ocean).

4.2.1 Remote Versus Local Processes

The multidecadal sea level trends observed by tide gauges around the coasts are associated with a basin-wide spatial pattern, with sea level fall in the tropical southwest basin (including Zanzibar) accompanying SLR elsewhere (including all other tide gauge stations; map of Fig. 6). Similar patterns have been shown in various reconstructed and reanalysis sea level products (e.g., Church et al. 2004; Hamlington et al. 2011; Dunne et al. 2012; Han et al. 2018) and in ocean model simulations (e.g., Timmermann et al. 2010; see Han et al. 2014b and 2017a for reviews). The changing surface winds over the Indian Ocean are the major driver for this distinct pattern (Han et al. 2010; Timmermann et al. 2010; Schwarzkopf and Böning 2011), although the ITF has a significant contribution to the SCTR sea level fall in an OGCM experiment (Schwarzkopf and Böning 2011; Han et al. 2014b). Natural internal variability dominates external forcing in causing the spatially uneven distribution of sea level trends (Fig. 2 of Han et al. 2018). Over the SCTR region, the falling rate of sea level obtains its maximum, and internal variability (external forcing) contributes ~ 81% (19% ± 2.4%) after global mean SLR removed, based on the reanalysis data and large ensemble climate model simulations.

On interannual timescales, the observed interannual SLAs (up to 10–25 cm) in the Bay of Bengal result mainly from surface wind forcing, with influence from buoyancy flux being weak (Han and Webster 2002). Equatorial wind is the main driver of SLAs along the eastern and northern Bay boundaries, by exciting equatorial Kelvin waves and subsequently coastally trapped waves. In the western Bay (i.e., east coasts of India and Sri Lanka), wind within the Bay has a comparable effect as equatorial wind especially during the summer monsoon season, because longshore winds around the Bay generate coastally trapped waves and wind stress curl in the Bay interior cause westward-propagating Rossby waves. Near the Australian west coast, remote forcing by wind from the equatorial Pacific is much more important than local forcing for determining interannual SLAs (e.g., Feng et al. 2003; Wijffels and Meyers 2004; Trenary and Han 2012; White et al. 2014; Deepa et al. 2018), even though composite analyses showed that during some seasons (e.g., May), forcing over the Indian Ocean has a larger effect (Fig. 11 of Trenary and Han 2012). Recent theoretical and modeling studies showed that the sloping ocean bottom plays a crucial role in trapping the Leeuwin current to the coast, even though some energy radiates offshore via Rossby waves (Furue et al. 2013; Benthuysen et al. 2014).

In the central equatorial basin (e.g., the Maldives) and east Arabian Sea (e.g., Indian west coast), interannual SLAs attain their minima (Figs. 7c, 8 and 9), due to the destructive interference between the direct wind-forced signals and reflected Rossby waves from the eastern ocean boundary (Shankar et al. 2010). Over the interior South Indian Ocean, interannual SLAs obtain the maximum in the SCTR region, and they are primarily driven by westward-propagating Rossby waves forced by wind stress curl east of the SCTR (e.g., Tozuka et al. 2010; Trenary and Han 2012), with local wind forcing also playing a non-negligible role (Tozuka et al. 2010).

On decadal timescales, surface wind over the Indian Ocean is suggested to be the dominant forcing for SLAs in most regions (Nidheesh et al. 2013; Trenary and Han 2013; Li and Han 2015), and equatorial wind variability is crucial for driving decadal SLAs in the Bay of Bengal (Nidheesh et al. 2013). Along the west coast of Australia, decadal SLAs are strongly influenced by remote forcing from the trade wind anomalies in the equatorial Pacific (e.g., Feng et al. 2004, 2010; Deepa et al. 2019), although local forcing also has comparable contributions (Trenary and Han 2013). While surface wind is an important

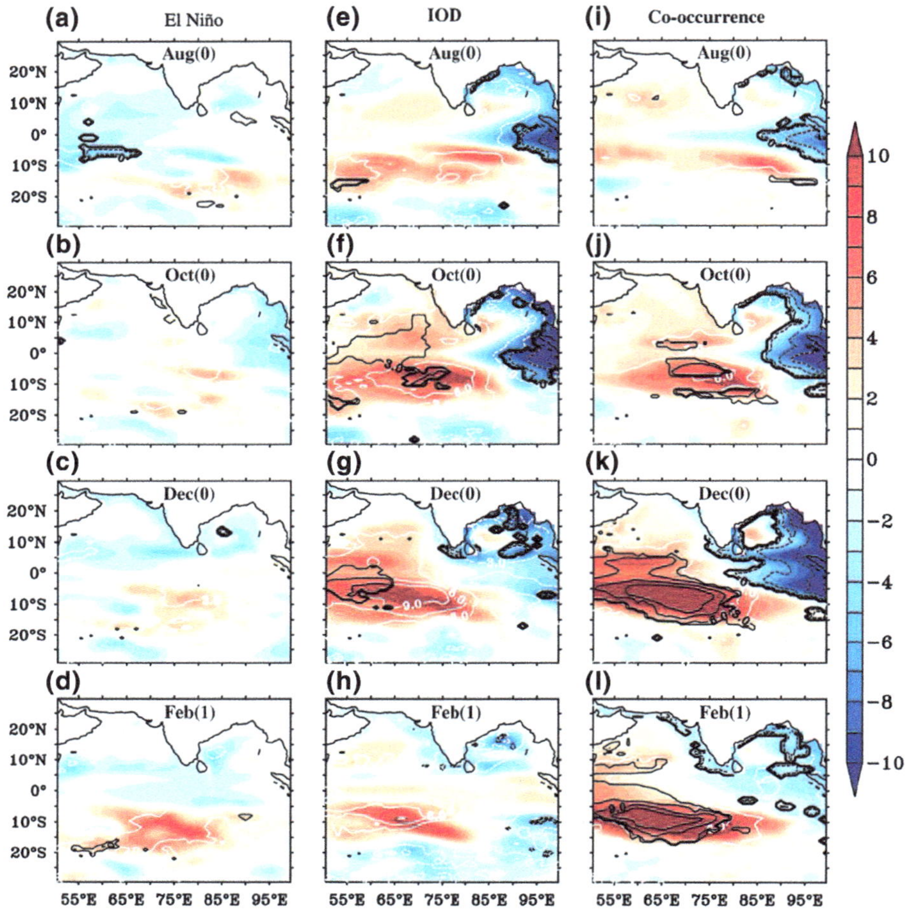

Fig. 8 Spatial SLA composite (cm) during El Niño years of 1965, 1976, 1986, 1987 and 2002 (**a**–**d**); pure positive IOD years of 1961, 1967, 1977 and 1994 (e–h); and co-occurrence years of 1963, 1972, 1982, 1997 and 2006 (**i**–**l**) for the months August, October, December and February based on ORAS4 reanalysis (color shaded) and OGCM experiment (white contours) from 1959 to 2008. Black contours are OGCM results significant at 90% confidence level. Figure from Deepa et al. (2018)

driver, changes in salinity due to regional precipitation may also play a role in some regions. For instance, the century-long-tide gauge at Mumbai observed interdecadal sea level variations, which mimic the variability of monsoon rainfall over the Indian subcontinent, suggesting the influence of halosteric effects on coastal sea level (Shankar and Shetye 1999). While thermosteric sea level dominates the observed SLAs in most regions, halosteric sea level also has apparent contributions in some areas, such as the north and west coasts of Australia and the coasts of Bay of Bengal and India (e.g., Fukumori and Wang 2013; Nidheesh et al. 2013; Llovel and Lee 2015; Wu et al. 2017).

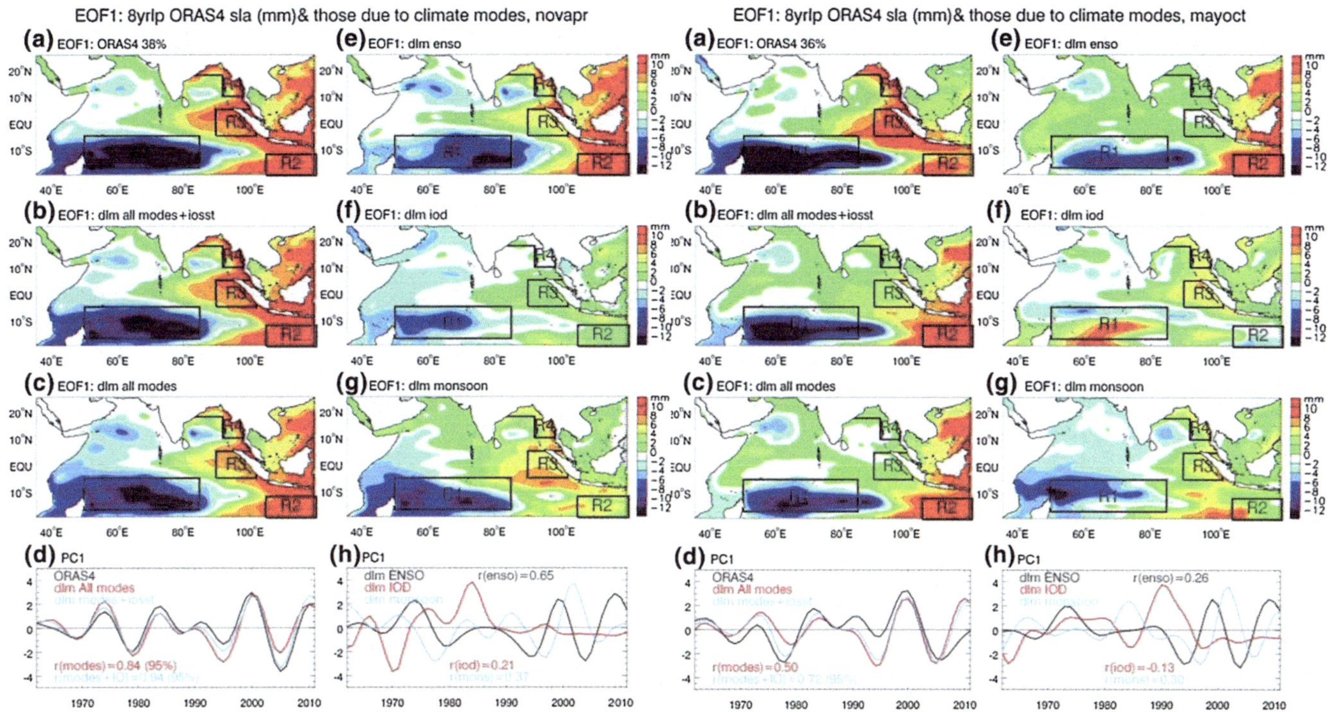

Fig. 9 A (left two columns): The leading Empirical Orthogonal Function (EOF1) of the 8-year low-passed northern winter (November–April) mean SLA over the tropical Indian Ocean for the period of 1962–2011 from (**a**) ORAS4 data; (**b**) Bayesian DLM simulation from the sum of all modes and IOSST (ENSO + IOD + monsoon + IOSST); and (**c**) DLM simulation from all modes (ENSO + IOD + monsoon); (**d**) the principal component of EOF1 (PC1) for ORAS4 (black), all modes + IOSST (blue), and all modes (red); (**e**)–(**g**) are the same as (**c**) except for the DLM simulation from ENSO, IOD and monsoon, respectively; (**h**) Same as (d) except for the PC1 of ENSO (black), IOD (red) and monsoon (blue). The correlation coefficients shown in (**d**) and (**h**) are with the observed ORAS4 PC1 (the black curve of panel (d)). Boxes mark the large-amplitude SLA areas. Figure 9B (right two columns): Same as Fig. 9A but for northern summer season of May–October. From Han et al. (2018)

4.2.2 Effects of Climate Modes

Over the tropical Indian Ocean, the most influential climate modes are ENSO and the Indian Ocean Dipole (IOD). The IOD is a coupled ocean–atmosphere mode operating at interannual timescale (e.g., Saji et al. 1999; Webster et al. 1999) but with significant decadal modulation (Song et al. 2007; Tozuka et al. 2007). Its positive phase is associated with cold SST anomaly (SSTA) in the tropical southeast Indian Ocean and warm SSTA in the tropical western basin, reaching peak amplitudes during September–November (Fig. 7a, b). Its temporal variability is measured by the Dipole Mode Index (DMI), which exhibits large interannual variability with decadal modulation (Fig. 7b). While some IOD events co-occur with ENSO, others are ENSO-independent (e.g., Meyers et al. 2007; Sun et al. 2015; Yang et al. 2015). Additionally, variations of monsoon winds, which are often correlated with ENSO and IOD but sometimes act independently, also induce variability in sea level over the Indian Ocean (Han et al. 2017b; Swapna et al. 2017). In the south Indian Ocean, the subtropical Indian Ocean dipole (SIOD) was identified as a coupled ocean–atmosphere mode (Behera and Yamagata 2001; Suzuki et al. 2004). Its temporal variability is measured by Subtropical Dipole Mode Index (SDMI), which peaks in January–March and is the weakest during July–September (Fig. 10b). Like the IOD, while some SIOD events are associated with ENSO, others act independently (Zhang et al. 2019).

For the multidecadal sea level trends, it is unknown to what extent the dominant effect of natural internal variability discussed above can be attributed to climate modes. For interannual variability, existing studies demonstrate the importance of ENSO and IOD in causing the observed SLAs in different coastal and island regions. Over the north Indian Ocean, the IOD-related basin-scale wind is an important cause for interannual SLAs along the coasts of Java, Sumatra and Bay of Bengal (e.g., Han and Webster 2002; Chen et al. 2016), but ENSO can also play a significant role (Sreenivas et al. 2012). Along the Indian west coast, interannual variability of boreal fall (September–November mean) sea level is correlated with the IOD (Parvathi et al. 2017), even though the magnitude is overall small there (Shankar et al. 2010; Fig. 7c, d). Over the South Indian Ocean, ENSO-related trade wind variations induce SLAs in the western tropical Pacific (Sect. 3.3), which propagate to the west coast of Australia via the ITF (e.g., Pariwono et al. 1986; Pearce and Phillips 1988; Clarke and Liu 1994; Godfrey 1996; Meyers 1996; Feng et al. 2003, 2013; Wijffels and Meyers 2004; Holgate and Woodworth 2004). Using Geosat sea level data from 1985 to 1989, Perigaud and Delecluse (1993) showed large interannual SLAs in 10°S–20°S of the Indian Ocean, with the strongest variability occurring in the El Niño year of 1986–1987.

Correlation, regression and composite analyses suggest that the IOD (ENSO) dominates interannual SLAs north (south) of ~ 10°S (e.g., Rao and Behera 2005; Yu et al. 2005; Gnanaseelan and Vaid 2010). Similar results are shown in the SLA composites for pure El Niño and pure positive IOD years from 1959 to 2008, and the ENSO-IOD co-occurrence significantly enhances the SLA magnitudes (Fig. 8; Deepa et al. 2018; also see Webster et al. 1999; Rao et al. 2002; McPhaden and Nagura 2014). Along the Indian west coast, the weak SLAs are indeed affected by IOD but also ENSO (Fig. 8). The leading EOF of SLAs over the Indian Ocean is significantly correlated with ENSO ($r = 0.74$) and IOD (0.62) during 1993–2016 (Fig. 7c, d). The somewhat higher correlation with ENSO is likely due to the inclusion of the entire tropical South Indian Ocean where ENSO's influence is strong. The effect of monsoon wind variability that is independent of ENSO and IOD on interannual coastal SLAs requires systematic investigation.

On decadal time scales, the impacts of climate modes have strong seasonality and spatial variability (Han et al. 2018). During boreal winter, climate modes account for most observed decadal SLAs from 1962 to 2011, with the total effects of IPO, IOD and monsoon accounting for 86%, 84%, 80% and 78% of the observed SLA standard deviation (STD) near the Australian coast, SCTR region, coasts of Sumatra and coasts of the eastern-northern Bay of Bengal, respectively. During summer, they explain 95% of observed STD near the Australian coast but only 67%, 58% and 63%, respectively, over the SCTR, Sumatra and Bay of Bengal coasts. In the equatorial and North Indian Ocean, wind associated with IPO is the major cause for coastal SLAs along the coasts of Java, Sumatra and Bay of Bengal during winter. However, during summer, winds associated with decadal IOD and to a lesser degree monsoon control the coastal SLAs, through both remote forcing from the equator and local forcing adjacent to the coasts (Han et al. 2018). In the South Indian Ocean, IPO dominates SLAs near the Australian coast and, to a lesser extent, the SCTR region (Frankcombe et al. 2015; Deepa et al. 2019) during both winter and summer (Han et al. 2018), with a sea level fall in the SCTR islands region corresponding to a SLR along the boundaries of the East Indian Ocean (Fig. 9A, B). The trade wind anomalies in the tropical Pacific associated with the IPO are the major cause for decadal SLAs along the Australian west coast via the ITF (Feng et al. 2004, 2010; Behera and Yamagata 2010), with local winds, which are partly associated with the IPO (Han et al. 2018) playing a comparable role (Trenary and Han 2013). Over the SCTR region, IPO drives the SLAs through affecting the surface wind over the Indian Ocean, with the influence of ITF being negligible (Deepa et al. 2019; Han et al. 2018). Decadal variations of winter and summer monsoon winds also have significant contributions, and the effect of IOD is non-negligible during winter (Fig. 9A).

The impact of SIOD on interannual SLAs shows a dipole structure over the southwest basin and its influence is negligible along the eastern and northern Indian Ocean boundaries (Fig. 10). A positive SIOD corresponds to negative SLA over the Chagos Archipelago of the SCTR and positive SLA over the Mascarene islands (e.g., Réunion, Mauritius and Rodrigues) southeast of Madagascar. Therefore, the SIOD primarily affects sea level of the island nations of the southwest Indian Ocean. The basin-scale wind stress curls associated with the SIOD excite Rossby waves propagating from the east; combined with forcing by the local wind stress curl, they produce the interannual SLA dipole, which also exhibits significant decadal variations (Zhang et al. 2019).

4.3 Western Indian Ocean Boundary

4.3.1 Remote Versus Local Processes

Compared to the eastern and northern boundaries, studies on sea level variability along the western boundary (African coastline) are lacking, likely due to the relatively weaker SLA amplitude and shorter tide gauge records there. Along the east coasts of South and North Africa, multidecadal trend and interannual-to-decadal SLAs seem to be connected to the open-ocean SLAs with substantially reduced magnitudes (Figs. 6, 7c and 9), indicating that part of the open-ocean Rossby waves' energy may pass the slope barrier (Sect. 2) to arrive at the western boundary. Near Zanzibar (Fig. 6), the continental slope is steep and the shelf is narrow; therefore, signals from the open ocean could have a significant impact on the observed SLA, including the observed falling trend there (see Sect. 2).

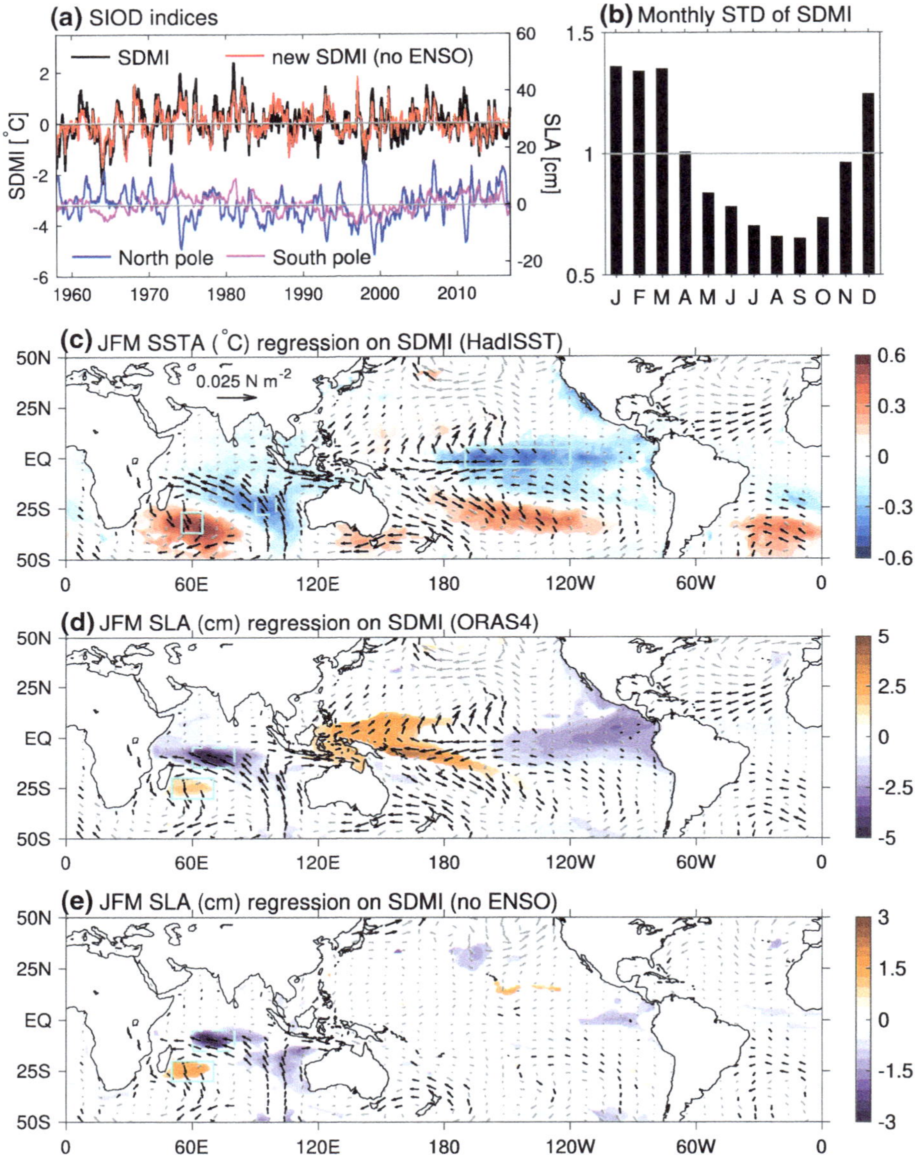

Fig. 10 **a** Time evolution of the subtropical dipole mode index (SDMI; °C; black line), defined as the difference of SSTA from HadISST data averaged over (55°E–65°E, 37°S–27°S) and (90°E–100°E, 28°S–18°S), boxed regions in (**c**). Red line shows the SDMI independent of ENSO; blue and purple lines denote monthly SLA (cm) time series averaged in the SLA dipole areas of SCTR region in the north and Mascarene islands region in the south, respectively. Data are detrended with monthly climatology removed. **b** Monthly standard deviation of the normalized SDMI. **c** Regression of January–March (JFM) mean SSTA onto normalized JFM SDMI (°C), and vectors denote regression of the JFM surface wind stress from ECMWF twentieth-century reanalysis (N m^{-2}). Box in the tropical Pacific denotes the Niño-3.4 region. **d** Same as (**c**) but for regression of JFM SLA (cm). SLA data are from ORAS4 reanalysis. Boxes in the Indian Ocean denote the SLA dipole region (60°E–80°E, 15°S–5°S and 50°E–70°E, 30°S–20°S). **e** Same as (**d**) but for regressions of SLA and wind stress residuals (with ENSO signals removed by removing linear regression on the November–January mean Niño-3.4 index) onto SDMI. Shading and black vectors in **c**–**e** denote results that are statistically significant at 90% confidence level

4.3.2 Effects of Climate Modes

While both ENSO and IOD are associated with interannual and decadal SLAs in some areas of the western boundary including the coast of Madagascar (Figs. 7, 8, 9), and the SIOD is associated with weak SLAs along the Somali coast (Fig. 10), variations of monsoon appear to have an overall larger effect on decadal SLAs for both winter and summer (Figs. 9A, B). How the Rossby waves generated in the basin interior affect the Somali current, East African coastal current and western boundary SLAs remains unknown. How the climate modes affect sea level in the Persian Gulf and Red Sea remains unclear.

5 The Atlantic Ocean

Different from the Pacific and Indian Oceans whose coastal sea level variability is dominated by the wind-driven ocean circulation, sea level along the Atlantic coasts—particularly the east coast of North America—may also be influenced by the Atlantic Meridional Overturning Circulation (AMOC) driven by buoyancy flux, as suggested by OGCM and coupled climate model studies. Observational evidence, however, has not yet firmly established the relationship between AMOC and coastal sea level variability.

5.1 Observations

The spatial distribution of sea level variability in the Atlantic as seen in altimeter data from 1993 to 2017 (Fig. 11) identifies several regions of large-amplitude SLAs, most notably the Gulf Stream in the western North Atlantic, the Brazil Current in the western South Atlantic, the South African coast in the eastern South Atlantic where the Agulhas rings shed from the Indian Ocean, and the North Sea as well as other European shelf regions of the eastern North Atlantic. Tide gauge records also show large-amplitude interannual and decadal SLAs along the European coast, and to a lesser extent the east coast of North America (Figs. 1 and 12). Spectral peaks at interannual, 12–14 year, bidecadal 20–30 year and 50–70 year periods were detected in most of the tide gauges along the US northeast coast (e.g., Figure 1 of Kenigson and Han 2014; Sects. 5.2 and 5.3), and the near 60-year cycle was also observed along European coasts and other ocean basins (Chambers et al. 2012).

Using long-tide gauge records, several recent studies detected a region of rapid SLR acceleration along the US northeast coast from Cape Hatteras to Cape Cod during recent decades particularly in the ~ 1990–2010 period (e.g., Boon 2012; Ezer and Corlett 2012; Sallenger et al. 2012). Sallenger et al. (2012) dubbed the region of SLR rate much faster than the global mean, from Cape Hatteras to Cape Cod, the "hotspot." From 2010 to 2015, however, the area of the highest SLR rate shifts to south of Cape Hatteras, suggesting interannual and decadal variability of the rapidest SLR region (Valle-Levinson et al. 2017; Domingues et al. 2018; Ezer 2019).

Long-tide gauge records with lengths ≥ 75 years and no major gaps (blue dots of Fig. 11) are available primarily along the west and east coasts of the North Atlantic, with only a few available along the coasts of the South Atlantic. Nevertheless, coherent interannual SLAs were also detected by tide gauges along the South Atlantic west and east coasts, respectively (Brundrit et al. 1984, 1987; Douglas 2001; Papadopoulos and Tsimplis 2006). Based on the data availability and dynamical distinctions, in our discussion below we divide the Atlantic into three regions: the western North Atlantic, the eastern North Atlantic and the

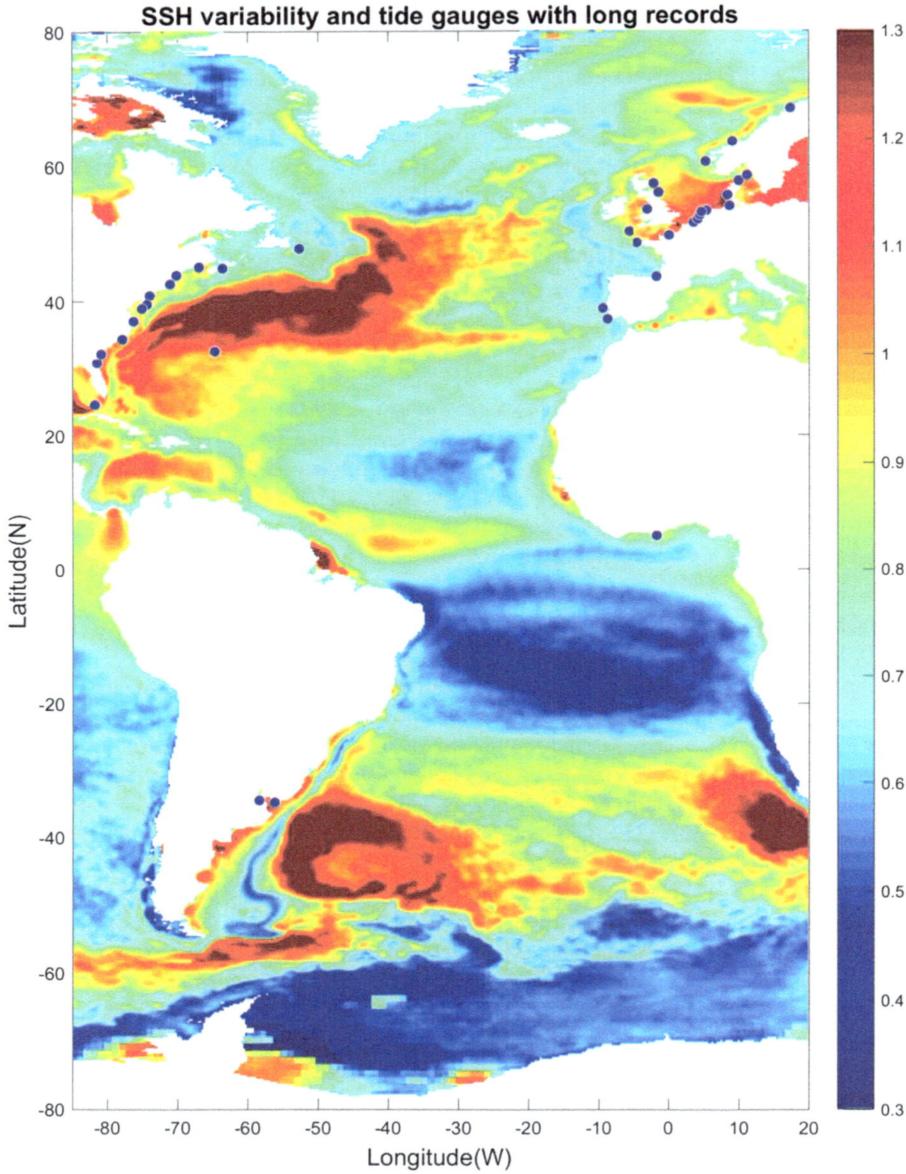

Fig. 11 Sea surface height anomaly (SSHA) (units are log of root mean square in cm) from satellite altimeter data (1993–2017) and location of tide gauge stations (blue dots) with records of 75 years and longer and no major gaps. Altimeter data are from the Permanent Service for Mean Sea Level (PSMSL) organization (https://las.aviso.oceanobs.com/) and tide gauge data are from the Permanent Service for Mean Sea Level (PSMSL) organization (http://www.psmsl.org/)

South Atlantic. Each region is not only unique in the dynamics involved, but also in the amount of data available (Fig. 11), leading to substantial differences in our understanding of the relevant processes and time scales of variability.

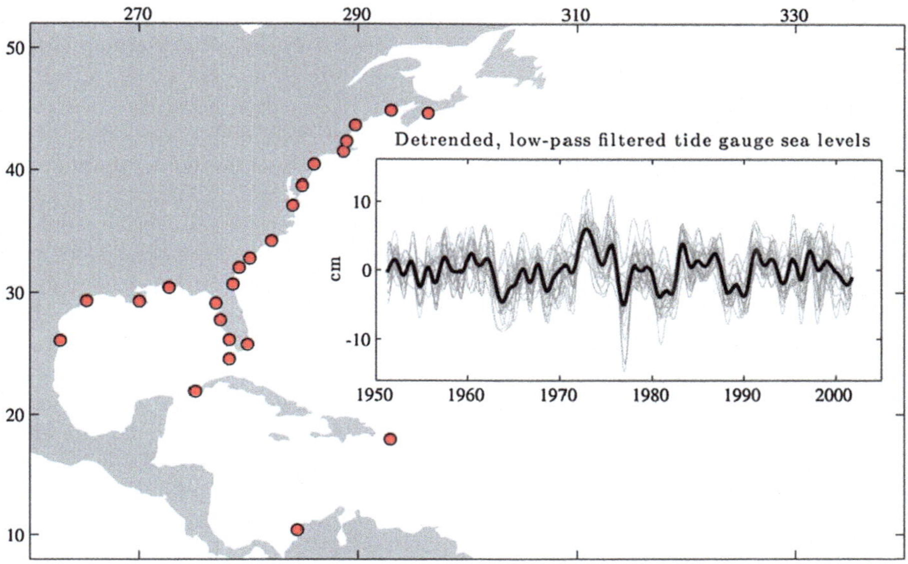

Fig. 12 Tide gauge locations (red circles) and the detrended, 18-month low-pass filtered sea level anomaly time series (gray lines) with monthly climatology removed at each tide gauge, based on the PSMSL monthly tide gauge observations from 1950 to 2010. The thick black line is the average of the individual time series and accounts for greater than 50% of the variance in the low-passed data set. The filter passed more than 90% of the amplitudes at periods longer than 1.9 years, and thus the SLA represents interannual-to-decadal variability. From Thompson and Mitchum (2014)

5.2 Western Boundary of the North Atlantic

5.2.1 Remote Versus Local Processes and Buoyancy Versus Wind-Driven

Sea level along the US east coast has received renewed attention in recent years, due to the detection of the accelerated SLR in the mid-Atlantic Bight (Sallenger et al. 2012; Ezer 2013; Ezer et al. 2013; Yin and Goddard 2013; Goddard et al. 2015; Ezer 2015). While the IB effect was suggested to contribute 10–30% of the acceleration (Piecuch and Ponte 2015), a slowdown of the AMOC was suggested to be an important cause (Sallenger et al. 2012), based on a qualitative comparison between the observed coastal SLR pattern with that of climate model experiments driven by buoyancy flux of Yin et al. (2009). Extensive modeling studies showed that surface warming and freshwater flux into the subpolar North Atlantic increased steric sea level, weakened the AMOC, reduced the sharp sea level gradients across the Gulf Stream and North Atlantic Current, and resulted in rapid dynamical SLR along the northeast coast of North America (e.g., Hakkinen 2001; Hakkinen and Rhines 2004; Levermann et al. 2005; Hewitt et al. 2006; Landerer et al. 2007; Kleinen et al. 2009; Yin et al. 2009; Lorbacher et al. 2010; Hu et al. 2011; den Toom et al. 2014; Brunnabend et al. 2015; Yu et al. 2016; Hu and Bates 2018). Because the mean sea level is low on the inshore side but 1–1.5 m higher on the open-ocean side of the Gulf Stream, a weakened cross-stream gradient corresponds to a rising sea level inshore and falling sea level offshore of the Gulf Stream; these signals are clear in climate model solutions (e.g., Yin et al. 2009).

On interannual timescales, OGCM experiments showed an anticorrelation between the US northeast coast SLAs and variability of the Atlantic meridional overturning circulation (AMOC) strength, with a 2 cm drop in sea level corresponding to a 1 Sverdrup (Sv) increase in the AMOC (Bingham and Hughes 2009). It is unclear, however, whether this anticorrelation represents the effect of buoyancy-driven geostrophic component of the AMOC or reflects large-scale wind-driven ocean circulation. Note that the northward transport of AMOC's upper branch consists of three components: the Gulf Stream (or at higher latitudes, the North Atlantic Current), meridional Ekman transport driven by wind and upper-mid-ocean transport driven by wind and buoyancy flux in the open ocean (McCarthy et al. 2015; Ezer 2015; Piecuch et al. 2019).

Using the RAPID monitoring array at 26°N and tide gauge data along the New England coasts during 2004–2017, Piecuch et al. (2019) found that the anticorrelation between intraseasonal/interannual coastal SLAs and AMOC transport was forced by large-scale wind patterns. While the local longshore winds drive negative coastal SLAs, open-ocean winds along 26°N force positive (northward) Ekman transport, resulting in an anticorrelation between SLAs and the AMOC. The geostrophic component of AMOC (Gulf Stream plus upper-mid-ocean transport), however, is uncorrelated with coastal SLAs. In fact, correlations of 0.70–0.95 are shown between the Ekman component of AMOC transport and three interannual modes from empirical mode decomposition (EMD) of the SLA difference between Atlantic City and Bermuda, using the RAPID data and tide gauge observations during 2004–2012; the correlations are low between the geostrophic AMOC and SLA difference except for the ~ 6-year EMD mode, which shows a correlation of 0.89 but it only has one cycle during the 2004–2012 period (Fig. 8 of Ezer 2015; also see Ezer et al. 2013). Wind stress curl in the Labrador Sea shows significant correlation with interannual SLAs along the US northeast coast (Andres et al. 2013; Kenigson et al. 2018), and IB effect accounts for ~ 25% in the region (Piecuch and Ponte 2015). These results agree with Piecuch et al. (2019), suggesting that the anticorrelation between AMOC and US northeast coast SLAs on interannual timescales during the RAPID period are primarily wind-driven. Further studies are needed to explore the relationship between geostrophic AMOC and US east coast interannual SLAs using observations.

Modeling solutions support the above observational results. The local longshore winds (Woodworth et al. 2014) are shown to be important for interannual SLAs all the way from Cape Hatteras to Nova Scotia (Andres et al. 2013; Kenigson et al. 2018). Using a global barotropic model, Piecuch et al. (2016) showed that local wind stress over the continental shelf and slope is the major forcing for interannual SLAs along the coast north of Cape Hatteras from 1980 to 2015, explaining 50% of tide gauge variance.

On decadal timescales, modeling studies showed that variations of both surface buoyancy flux and wind stress over the North Atlantic can induce AMOC variability (e.g., Marshall et al. 2001; Schloesser et al. 2012, 2014; Yeager and Danabasoglu 2014; Danabasoglu et al. 2016; Elipot et al. 2017). OGCM experiments, however, suggested that changes of downward heat flux were the major cause for the spin down/up in the Subpolar Gyre and AMOC, causing the 12–14 year SLAs along the US northeast coast (Hakkinen 2000, 2001; Hakkinen and Rhines 2004), with 1 Sv weakening of AMOC corresponds to 1.5 cm SLR along the US northeast coast (Woodworth et al. 2014). Local longshore winds may also affect the decadal SLAs (Woodworth et al. 2014). Due to the short data record of the RAPID array, observational relationship between geostrophic AMOC and US east coast SLAs on decadal timescales has not yet been established.

South of Cape Hatteras, interior wind stress curl is the dominant forcing for coastal SLAs at interannual-to-decadal time scales (e.g., Sturges and Hong 1995; Ezer 1999; Hong et al. 2000; Woodworth et al. 2014). Baroclinic Rossby waves generated by open-ocean wind stress curl propagate westward, affecting the Gulf Stream transport, cross-stream sea level gradient and thus coastal sea level (Hong et al. 2000; Sect. 2). Both wind stress curl and surface heat flux in the basin interior could cause interannual-to-decadal variability of the Gulf Stream (e.g., Curry and McCartney 2001; Di Nezio et al. 2009; Meinen et al. 2010; Chaudhuri et al. 2011), but these studies did not explicitly examine coastal sea level. Indeed, data analyses and modeling experiments showed significant anticorrelations between the Gulf Stream transport and US east coast SLAs on a wide range of time scales, from a few days to decades (Hong et al. 2000; Ezer 2001; Sturges and Hong 2001; Papadopoulos and Tsimplis 2006; Ezer 2013; Ezer et al. 2013; Kopp 2013; Ezer and Atkinson 2014, 2017; Park and Sweet 2015).

It has also been argued that variations in the Gulf Stream position are related to variations in the southward-flowing Slope Current in the mid-Atlantic-Bight (Rossby et al. 2010), which connects the recirculation gyre between the coast and the Gulf Stream. When the Gulf Stream moves offshore, the northern recirculation gyre between the Gulf Stream and the coast can expand and the Slope Current along the coast can increase its flow, resulting in increased coastal sea level (Ezer et al. 2013; Ezer 2015, 2019). Conversely, other studies suggest that intrusion of the Labrador Sea Water into the Slope Sea affects coastal sea level gradients and therefore the latitudinal position and separation point of the Gulf Stream (e.g., Rossby 1999; Hameed and Piontkovski 2004; Andres et al. 2013).

Despite the dynamical differences between coastal regions north and south of Cape Hatteras, there are multidecadal periods when coherent SLAs were observed from the Caribbean to Nova Scotia (e.g., Maul and Hanson 1991; Hakkinen 2000; Douglas 2005; Thompson and Mitchum 2014; Calafat et al. 2018; Fig. 12). This coherence is surprising given the substantial longshore distances and the distinct dynamical regimes partitioned by the Gulf Stream separation and the Straits of Florida. Analyses of ocean hindcasts find that the spatial coherence is largely the result of changes in upper ocean heat content spanning the coastal and open-ocean areas of the western boundary region rather than changes in slope across the boundary current (Hakkinen 2000, Thompson and Mitchum 2014). During a large part of the second half of the twentieth century, the spatial coherent coastal SLAs are largely driven by changes in basin-wide wind stress curl that force basin-scale, zonal redistributions of volume into and out of the western boundary region (Thompson and Mitchum 2014). It has also been shown that Rossby waves have coherent modulation on the amplitudes of sea level annual cycle along US east coast (Calafat et al. 2018).

5.2.2 Effects of Climate Modes on US East Coast Sea Level

Two climate modes dominate the variability of the North Atlantic Ocean: the North Atlantic Oscillation (NAO)—representing variations in the amplitude of a dipole pattern in sea level pressure over the Atlantic (e.g., Barnston and Livezey 1987; Hurrell 1995)—and the Atlantic Multidecadal Oscillation (AMO)—representing the average SST over the North Atlantic (e.g., Schlesinger and Ramankutty 1994; Delworth and Mann 2000; Kerr 2000; Enfield et al. 2001a, b). Both have imprints in surface wind stress and buoyancy flux and thus are closely connected with variations in gyre strength and AMOC (e.g., Curry and McCartney 2001; Schloesser et al. 2014). The NAO and AMO have different time scales, with more interannual-to-decadal variability in NAO compared to ~ 60–80-year time scales of the AMO (Delworth and Mann 2000). It has been hypothesized that at multidecadal timescales the SST variability of the AMO reflects the temporal integration of the ocean

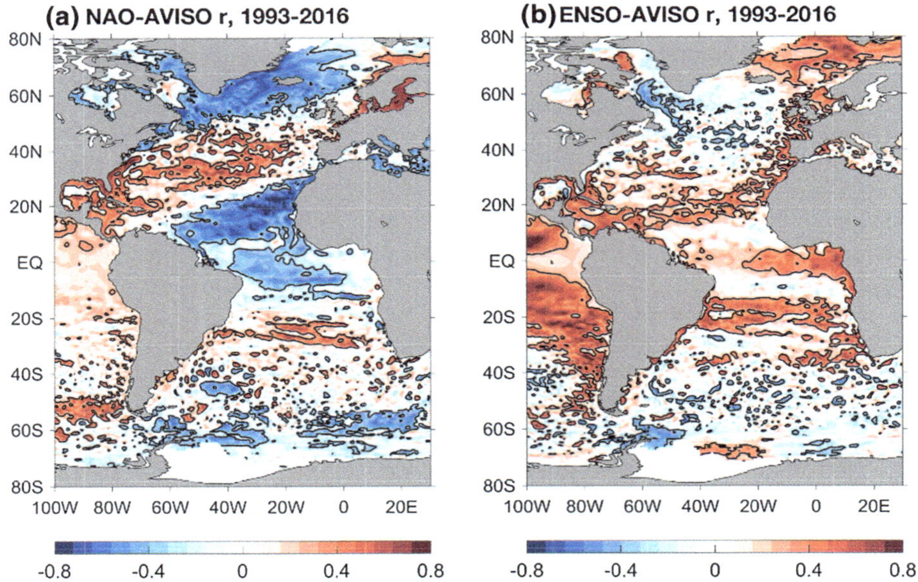

Fig. 13 **a** Correlation map between winter (DJFM mean) NAO index and annual mean AVISO satellite SSHA over the Atlantic Ocean for the 1993–2016 period; correlation coefficients of ± 0.3 are shown by the black line contours; **b** Same as **a** but for the correlation between ENSO and satellite SSHA. (The NAO index is downloaded from: www.climatedataguide.ucar.edu/climate-data/hurrell-north-atlantic-oscillation-nao-index-station-based.)

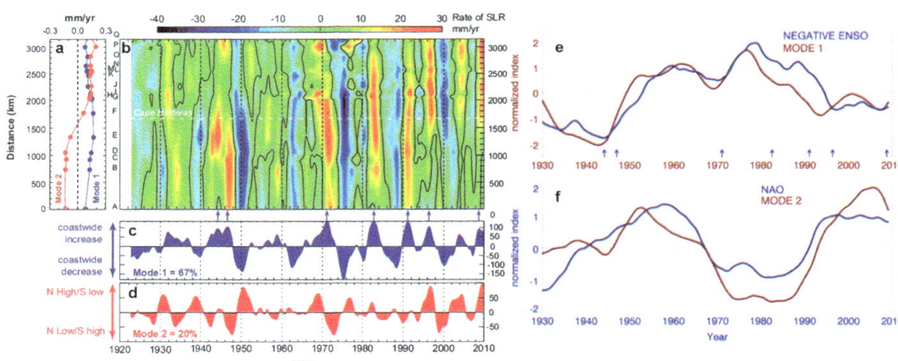

Fig. 14 The 5-year rates of sea level change (in mm/yr) calculated from the detrended, 1-year filtered data for the long time series of tide gauge along the US east coast from 1920 to 2010. **a** Spatial structures of the first two EOF modes; **b** Hovmöller diagram of the sea level change rate along US east coast from tide gauge A (southern tip of Florida) to Q (Maine); the white-dashed horizontal line shows the location of Cape Hatteras; **c**, **d** time series of the principle components (or temporal variability) of EOF modes 1 and 2 shown in **a**. The blue arrows above **c** show that the highest peaks in Mode 1 correspond to the timing of the SLR hot spots in **b**. Cumulative and 7-year filtered versions of **e** EOF Mode 1 and negative ENSO index and **f** EOF2 and NAO index. The blue arrows are like those between panels (**b**) and (**c**). Customized from Valle-Levinson et al. (2017)

circulation (and associated heat transport) variability forced by wind stress associated with the NAO (McCarthy et al. 2015; Woodworth et al. 2016); therefore, NAO and AMO may not be fully independent of each other. It has also been argued that variations of the AMO SST index in the past few decades resulted partly from external forcing (natural and anthropogenic; e.g., Booth et al. 2012; Knudsen et al. 2014; Mann et al. 2014) and partly from natural variability (Ting et al. 2009; Zhang et al. 2013). In addition, a recent study suggested the influence of ENSO on multidecadal variability of US east coast sea level (Valle-Levinson et al. 2017).

The surface wind and heat flux, which drive interannual and decadal SLAs along the west coast of North Atlantic through both remote and local processes (Sect. 5.2.1) are in part associated with the NAO. Satellite observations from 1993 to 2016 show that the NAO is associated with distinct spatial patterns of coastal SLA (Fig. 13), showing opposite SLA signs between north and south of Cape Hatteras with lower (higher) sea level in the north (south) during a positive NAO. Tide gauge records from 1920 to 2010 confirm this north–south contrast pattern, which appears in the 2nd EOF mode of coastal SLAs (Fig. 14a, red line). This EOF2 mode however is not significantly correlated with the NAO index using 1 year filtered data (Valle-Levinson et al. 2017), which is inconsistent with the correlation shown in Fig. 13; but the 7 year filtered cumulative EOF2 and NAO index agree well (Fig. 14f), showing coherent 50–70 year cycle. This result indicates that cumulative ocean response to NAO forcing can produce ~ 60 year cycle in coastal SLA.

The inconsistency of correlations between coastal SLA and NAO using satellite data of 1993–2016 and tide gauge data of 1920–2010 indicates that NAO impact may exhibit significant decadal variability. Empirical analyses showed that the NAO impact on interannual SLAs is strong during some decades but weak during others (e.g., Woolf 2003; Andres et al. 2013; Woodworth et al. 2017), due to changes of local longshore wind associated with changes in NAO-related wind patterns near the coast (Kenigson et al. 2018). A strong negative NAO superimposed on a 30% AMOC reduction likely caused the 2009–2010 extreme SLR along the US Northeast coast (Goddard et al. 2015; Ezer 2015), with up to 50% of the sea level increase resulted from the IB effect (Piecuch and Ponte 2015).

Tide gauge data showed that the ~ 60-year cycle in US northeast coast sea level coincided with the positive transition of the AMO index, with SST warming since ~ 1970 corresponding to rapid SLR in the mid-Atlantic Bight (Kopp 2013; Ezer 2013; Ezer et al. 2013; Scafetta 2014). Kenigson and Han (2014) demonstrated that the ~ 60-year cycle has contributed a large portion to the SLR acceleration along the US northeast coast since ~ 1970; without the ~ 60-year cycle, the acceleration dramatically reduces. Empirical analyses indicated that the US northeast coast SLR acceleration is also linked to the sea level pressure and winds associated with the NAO (e.g., Ezer 2015). Tide gauge data during the past 95 years showed that the locations of accelerated SLR exhibit significant intra-decadal variability, and they were not correlated with the AMO (Valle-Levinson et al. 2017). While the multidecadal variation of the spatially coherent SLAs along the entire US east coast (EOF1 of Fig. 14a, black line) agrees well with the 7-year filtered cumulative ENSO index (Fig. 14e), the EOF2 mode, which shows opposite signs north and south of Cape Hatteras, corresponds to cumulative NAO index. They suggested that the cumulative ocean response to the combined ENSO and NAO forcing determines the timing and location of the accelerated SLR, even though direct correlations for EOF1-ENSO (also see Fig. 13b) and EOF2-NAO were not found. Near the coasts of Caribbean and Gulf of Mexico, ENSO has higher correlations with coastal SLAs (Fig. 13b).

5.3 The Eastern Boundary of the North Atlantic Ocean

5.3.1 Remote Versus Local Processes

Along the east coast of the North Atlantic, while some studies suggested the likely link between coastal SLAs and changes of gyre-scale ocean circulation (Miller and Douglas 2007; Woodworth et al. 2010), others show the dominance of remote and local coastal processes, rather than remote forcing from the basin interior, are the primary causes for coastal SLAs (e.g., Sturges and Douglas 2011; Calafat et al. 2012; Wahl et al. 2013; Dangendorf et al. 2014; Chafik et al. 2019). Interannual and decadal SLAs at Cascais tide gauge, Portugal (39°N, 9°W), was primarily forced by longshore wind integrated from the equator to Cascais, suggesting the dominant role played by northward propagation of coastally trapped waves driven by longshore wind (Sturges and Douglas 2011). Along the European west coast and in the Mediterranean Sea (27°N–55°N), decadal SLAs up to 15 cm in tide-gauge data are highly correlated with the cumulative longshore wind stress, which further demonstrates the deterministic role of coastally trapped waves forced by longshore wind (e.g., Calafat et al. 2012; Chafik et al. 2019); the IB effect contributes 14–27% sea level variance and forcing by local wind and heat flux is weak (Calafat et al. 2012). These coastal SLA signals can propagate into the Norwegian coast, Barents Sea and Kara Sea, affecting coastal sea level there (Richter et al. 2012; Calafat et al. 2013). In the Mediterranean Sea, coastal sea level variability results from the IB effect, surface wind forcing and mass exchange with the Atlantic Ocean, and mass exchange dominates other factors during some years such as 2010 (e.g., Fukumori et al. 2007; Menemenlis et al. 2007; Gomis et al. 2008; Calafat et al. 2012; Landerer and Volkov 2013; Tsimplis et al. 2013; Volkov 2019). South of 27°N, decadal SLAs along the African west coast of the North Atlantic are associated with heat advection by Ekman transport (Calafat et al. 2012).

In the North Sea, various processes account for interannual SLAs detected by tide gauge data around the coasts (Dangendorf et al. 2014). While the IB effect dominates the SLAs along the UK and Norwegian coasts, wind controls the SLAs in the south from Belgium up to Denmark. On decadal time scales, SLAs mainly reflect steric changes and result largely from remote longshore wind forcing. Spatial correlation analyses of altimetry observations and steric heights suggest coherent SLAs extending from the Norwegian shelf in the north down to the Canary islands of Spain in the South, further supporting the importance of longshore wind-forced coastally trapped waves.

5.3.2 Effects of Climate Modes

Since the NAO index is based on sea level pressure pattern west of the European coast, a strong influence from NAO on sea level via changes in wind stress and sea level pressure (IB effect) is expected. Numerous studies find that IB effect and large-scale wind patterns that drive the coastal SLAs along the eastern boundary of the North Atlantic spanning

Fig. 15 (Top) Location of tide gauge stations near European coast; (Bottom) low-frequency modes of SLA ▶ (colored, thin lines) obtained from Ensemble Empirical Mode Decomposition (EEMD) method and indices of NAO (solid, heavy, black line) and AMO (dashed, heavy, black line) for 1865–2012 at six of the eight tide gauge stations shown in the top panel; the amplitude is normalized by the standard deviation (SD), which is listed for each record (NAO and AMO have no units; sea level is in mm). Adapted from Ezer et al. (2016)

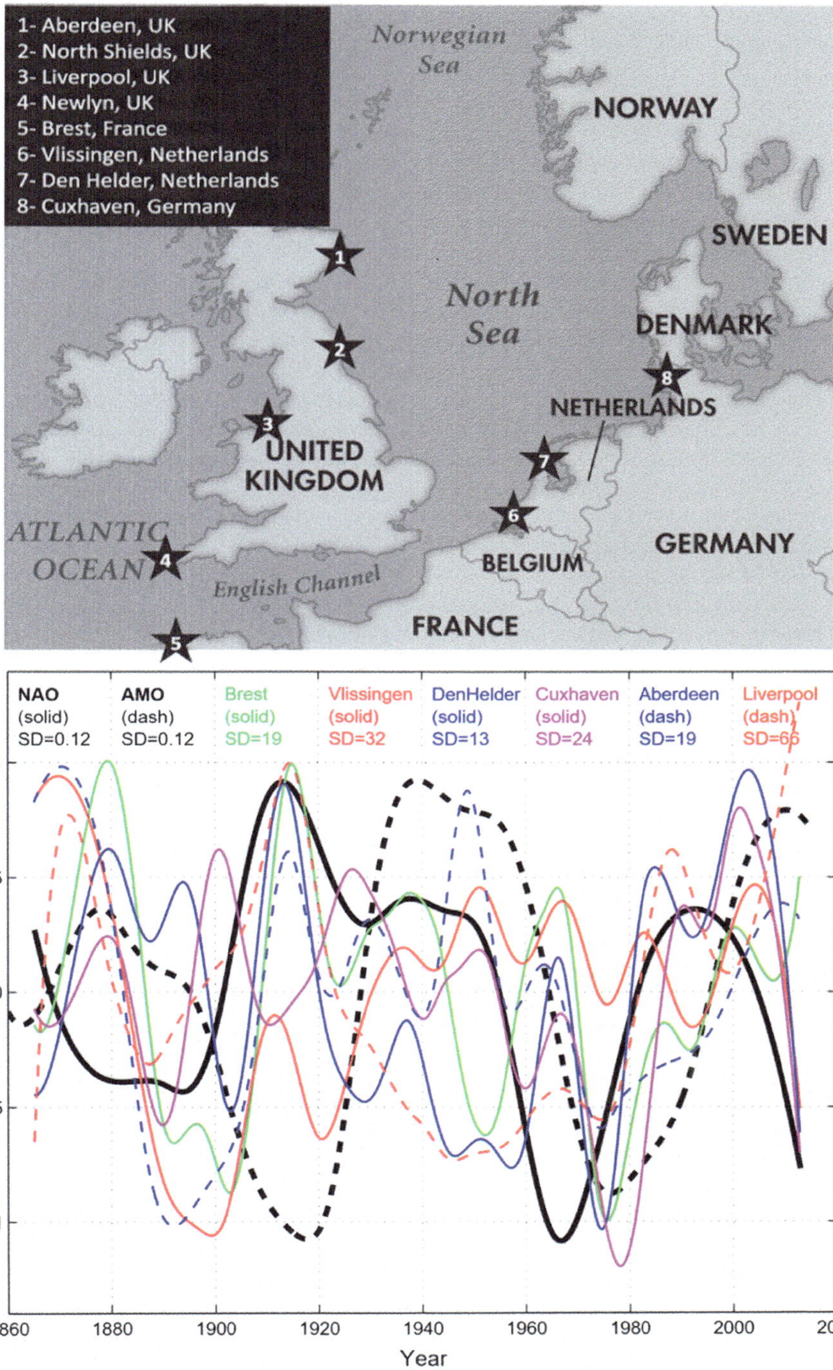
1- Aberdeen, UK
2- North Shields, UK
3- Liverpool, UK
4- Newlyn, UK
5- Brest, France
6- Vlissingen, Netherlands
7- Den Helder, Netherlands
8- Cuxhaven, Germany
Norwegian Sea
NORWAY
SWEDEN
North Sea
DENMARK
NETHERLANDS
UNITED KINGDOM
ATLANTIC OCEAN
English Channel
BELGIUM
GERMANY
FRANCE
NAO (solid) SD=0.12
AMO (dash) SD=0.12
Brest (solid) SD=19
Vlissingen (solid) SD=32
DenHelder (solid) SD=13
Cuxhaven (solid) SD=24
Aberdeen (dash) SD=19
Liverpool (dash) SD=66
Norm. Amp.
Year
1860
1880
1900
1920
1940
1960
1980
2000
202
1
0.5
0
−0.5
−1

the coasts of Morocco, Europe and Mediterranean Sea, largely result from the NAO (e.g., Wakelin et al. 2003; Woolf et al. 2003; Yan et al. 2004; Hughes and Meredith 2006; Tsimplis et al. 2006; Miller and Douglas 2007; Gomis et al. 2008; Tsimplis and Shaw 2008; Calafat et al. 2012; Tsimplis et al. 2013; Dangendorf et al. 2014; Ezer et al. 2016). The NAO impacts, however, are spatially and temporally variable, with stronger NAO influence observed during the second half of the twentieth century relative to the first half. Spatial variations of the NAO influences are evident, with positive coastal SLA-NAO correlations appearing in the North Sea and northern coasts of Europe, but negative correlations in the south as revealed by satellite altimetry data from 1993 to 2016 (Fig. 13a). Changes in the center of action of the Icelandic low and Azores high associated with the NAO, which affect surface wind, sea level pressure and SST patterns, play a crucial role in affecting decadal sea level variability and multidecadal trend along both the east and west coasts of the North Atlantic Ocean (Kolker and Hameed 2007).

The decadal variations of coastal sea level along the coasts of the North Sea and the UK can be either dominated by low-frequency variations of the NAO or AMO, depending on the temporal periods (Ezer et al. 2016). The ~ 60-year cycle of AMO is evident in Fig. 15 with negative AMO phases in ~ 1910–1920 and ~ 1970–1980 and positive AMO phases in ~ 1930–1950 and ~ 2000–2012; however, the very low-frequency variations of the NAO are in different phases. Around 1915–1920 when NAO is positive and AMO is negative, five of the six stations show positive SLA maxima indicating that NAO may dominate the sea level variability (i.e., the positive correlation in Fig. 13a), while around 1980 when AMO is negative and NAO is near zero, all 6 stations show peak negative SLAs indicating that AMO is likely dominating the SLAs. The bidecadal variations of tide-gauge observed SLAs along the east and west coasts of the North Atlantic were also shown to be associated with the AMO (Frankcombe and Dijkstra 2009). In addition, ENSO also seems to be correlated with SLAs near the eastern boundary of the North Atlantic (Fig. 13b).

5.4 The Western and Eastern Boundaries of the South Atlantic Ocean

5.4.1 Remote Versus Local Processes

Due to the very limited long-term tide gauge records in the South Atlantic Ocean, studies of remote influence on coastal sea level are rare and often involve numerical model simulations rather than observations. The few analyses of tide gauge data, such as studies of sea level trends at the southernmost tip of South America (e.g., Dragani et al. 2014), show significant interannual variations, but the lack of long-term records prevents researchers from fully understanding the sources of this variability. In the western South Atlantic, circulations near the coast of South America are largely influenced by local winds and tides (e.g., Tonini and Palma 2011). Modeling studies suggest that the upwelling dynamics of the shallow coastal area near the Brazilian coast are largely influenced by a combination of local winds and the interaction of the Brazil Current with the coastal topography (Palma and Matano 2009). While this study focused on seasonal upwelling, one may expect that longer-term variations in the wind and the Brazil Current would also impact the coastal sea level. Observations by Olson et al. (1988) found that the Brazil Current as well as the Malvinas (Falkland) Current (a cold current flowing northward along the tip of South America opposing the Brazil Current) have significant interannual variations in their separation point from the coast, which can thus cause interannual variations in coastal sea level. No studies are available that examine the forcing mechanisms of coastal sea level variability.

Piecuch and Ponte (2013) used models to study interannual SLAs in the tropical South Atlantic Ocean. They showed that Rossby waves forced by surface wind and buoyancy fluxes communicated across the basin in a similar fashion to processes found in other tropical and subtropical regions. By analyzing ocean reanalysis data, Vianna and Menezes (2013) showed that the leading Complex EOF mode of the bidecadal sea level signals over the entire Atlantic basin is characterized by in phase variations of Subtropical Gyres in the North and South Atlantic with an opposite sign in the tropical and subpolar regions, and it is associated with the AMOC variability. For the second CEOF mode, the North and South Subtropical Gyres are not in phase, and it is associated with westward propagation of temperature anomalies via Rossby waves (also see Sevellec and Fedorov 2013). The impacts of AMOC and Rossby waves on coastal sea level along the South American coasts, however, remain unclear. Their interactions with the western boundary current, the southward-flowing Brazil Current (maximum variability around ~ 50°W, 40°S; Fig. 11) and thus coastal SLAs are not known. One of the few observations of AMOC in the South Atlantic is the 35°S section from Africa to South America (Dong et al. 2009), which shows seasonal and interannual variations that impact variations in the northward heat transport. These observations also indicate large interannual variability in the eastern and western boundary currents, but the influence of these variations on coastal sea level has not been evaluated.

Along the eastern boundary of South Atlantic (i.e., west coast of Africa), remote influence from the equatorial Atlantic by events similar to the Pacific El Niño can cause coherent interannual sea level variability of up to 10–20 cm along the entire coast (Brundrit et al. 1984, 1987). Years of 1963, 1974 and 1984 are the years similar to Pacific El Niño, causing SLR along the west African coast. Although the modeling work of Piecuch and Ponte (2013) focused on the open ocean, their results suggest the importance of wind forcing versus effects of buoyancy, ocean internal variability and nonlinear ocean response in causing interannual SLAs near the west coast of Africa (their Fig. 2). The effects longshore winds versus equatorial forcing, local versus remote longshore wind and buoyancy versus wind, however, have not been examined. The influence of northward flowing Benguela Current along the western coast of Africa is not known. In the southeast Atlantic basin, energetic rings shed from the Agulhas Current over the southern tip of Africa (e.g., Olson and Evans 1986) propagate northwestward and contribute to considerable sea level variability there (~ 10°E, 40°S; Fig. 11). These rings are generally larger than Gulf Stream eddies, and they are shed in an irregular frequency with a signature clearly seen in satellite altimetry data (e.g., Schouten et al. 2000; review of Beal et al. 2011). The impact of the rings on coastal sea level has not been studied, however.

5.4.2 Effects of Climate Modes

Existing studies found that the AMOC in the South Atlantic is correlated with SST, which leads to a reconstruction of South Atlantic AMOC (Lopez et al. 2017); this study shows a strong connection between the South Atlantic AMOC, SST and the IPO. Therefore, decadal variations in the South Atlantic Ocean are expected to be quite different from those in the North Atlantic Ocean, which are largely influenced by the NAO. ENSO has significant impacts on coastal SLAs along the southwest Atlantic coast ($r = 0.5$ for SLA and SOI index from 1958 to 1997) and the correlation increased after 1980, likely through the Pacific–South American teleconnection mechanism by affecting surface wind, sea level pressure and precipitation (Papadopoulos and Tsimplis 2006; also see Douglas 2001). While ENSO is significantly correlated with SLAs at tide gauge Buenos Aires, east coast of Argentina within the estuary, from the late 1910 to early 1980s, the SLAs at tide gauge Quequen, which is somewhat south of Buenos Aires near the open ocean, are not correlated with ENSO (Douglas 2001). This result further suggests the complication of coastal processes relative to open-ocean sea level.

Correlation analyses using satellite altimetry data from 1993 to 2016 show weak influence of NAO on south Atlantic coastal sea level except for some areas along the southeast coast of South America (Fig. 13a), but ENSO appears to have significant effects near the coasts of Caribbean Sea, and the north as well as some regions of the southeast coast of South America (Fig. 13b). Comprehensive studies using both observations analysis and modeling experiments are needed to understand the climate modes impact on coastal sea level at various time scales in the South Atlantic Ocean.

6 Summary, Issues and Future Outlook

6.1 Summary

While reviewing coastal sea level variability and underlying mechanisms, one has to emphasize on the significant impacts of climate modes on coastal oceans via both local and remote processes, such as sea level signals from the open ocean. Tide gauge data detected large interannual and decadal sea level variability around the coasts of the Pacific, Indian and Atlantic Oceans. The variability amplitudes show strong regional differences, consistent with satellite observations (Figs. 1, 3, 6, 7, 11, 12, 14 and 15). While at least more than 45% of the global mean SLR over the past century has been attributed to anthropogenic climate change, interannual and decadal variability of coastal sea level mainly reflects internal climate variability, with a large fraction being associated with climate modes.

Over the Pacific Ocean, ENSO, PDO/IPO and NPGO are the dominant climate variability modes, which exert significant influence on coastal sea level (Sect. 3). Variations of trade wind in the equatorial Pacific related to ENSO (IPO) drive eastward-propagating equatorial Kelvin waves and westward-propagating Rossby waves, causing an east–west SLA seesaw that dominates coastal SLAs at interannual (decadal) timescales along the eastern and western boundaries of the tropical basin. Upon impinging on the eastern boundary, part of the equatorial Kelvin waves' energy propagates poleward as coastally trapped waves, resulting in coherent SLAs all the way through Alaska in the North and southern tip of South America in the South (Figs. 2 and 3; Sect. 3.2). North of San Francisco, the effects of longshore wind and sea level pressure (atmospheric loading or IB effect), with a large part being associated with the PDO, increase with latitudes on interannual timescales, but remote forcing from the tropics remains the dominant factor for decadal SLAs. The PDO and NPGO indices, however, are least effective in capturing sea level variance along the coasts of Northeast Pacific, whereas the NOI, NPI and PNA, which are significantly correlated with the PDO and IPO, are much more effective predictors there (Fig. 4). This is likely because NOI, NPI and PNA can better capture the local longshore wind and air pressure than the PDO and NPGO indices. In extratropical western North and South Pacific, westward-propagating Rossby waves driven by interior wind stress curl related to ENSO, PDO/IPO and NPGO are the dominant force for interannual and decadal SLAs around the coasts and marginal seas. Rossby waves can excite coastally trapped waves upon impinging on the coasts and affect the location and transport of the western boundary currents and thus coastal SLAs (Sect. 2; Fig. 5). Local longshore wind and wind stress curl within the marginal seas can also be important in some coastal regions (Sect. 3.3).

Over the Indian Ocean, the most influential climate modes are ENSO, IOD and SIOD plus monsoon variability. Large-amplitude interannual and decadal SLAs occur along the eastern boundary and over the Seychelles–Chagos islands (SCTR) region (Sect. 4.1; Figs. 7c, 8 and 9). Along the Australian west coast, remote forcing by trade wind in the equatorial Pacific related to ENSO (IPO) via the ITF is the dominant cause for interannual (decadal) SLAs for all seasons, while IPO-associated wind over the Indian Ocean also plays a comparable role for decadal SLAs. From Java to the northern Bay of Bengal, coastal SLAs are primarily forced by equatorial winds at both interannual and decadal timescales, and IOD likely dominates ENSO for interannual SLAs; but quantitative assessment on their relative importance remains to be done. Along the east coast of India and Sri Lanka, longshore wind and wind stress curl in the Bay of Bengal interior are equally important as equatorial wind forcing in driving interannual SLAs during boreal summer. On decadal timescales, IPO dominates coastal SLAs during northern winter, but IOD and monsoon dominate during summer (Fig. 9). Over the SCTR region, Indian Ocean winds associated with ENSO (IPO) are the major cause for interannual (decadal) SLAs, with IOD and monsoon also having significant contributions. The SIOD has its largest influence on SLAs over the SCTR and Mascarene island regions, with negligible effect on the eastern and north boundaries of the Indian Ocean. Along the western boundary, monsoon variability appears to have larger impact on decadal SLAs compared to decadal ENSO (or IPO) and IOD (Fig. 9), and SIOD is associated with weak SLAs along the Somali coast (Fig. 10). Although Rossby waves associated with ENSO and IOD have been discussed, their impacts on coastal SLAs have not been explicitly examined. Even though the multi-decadal trend of Indian Ocean sea level (with global SLR removed) since the 1960s was attributed largely to internal variability, contributions by climate modes remain unclear.

In the Atlantic Ocean, the dominant climate modes are NAO and AMO. Along the east coast of the South Atlantic, coherent interannual SLAs were observed and attributed to remote forcing from the equator. Along the east coast of the North Atlantic, Ekman heat transport associated with variations of subtropical gyre is the major cause for SLAs south of ~27°N. North of ~27°N particularly along the European coast, local and remote longshore wind (integrated from the equator), which drive coastally trapped waves, together with air pressure associated with the NAO are the major causes for interannual SLAs (Sect. 5.2). On decadal timescales, the effects of NAO may dominate coastal SLAs during some decades and AMO dominate during other decades (Figs. 13a and 15). Along the west coast of the North Atlantic, instraseasonal and interannual SLAs along the US northeast coast north of Hatteras results mainly from longshore wind forcing and IB effect; the influence of NAO is strong during some decades but weak during others, depending on its influence on longshore wind. No correlation was found between intraseasonal and interannual SLAs along New England coast and AMOC geostrophic transport, based on tide gauge and RAPID observations from 2004 to 2017. On decadal timescales, modeling experiments suggest that SLAs along US northeast coast are linked to AMOC changes, which are largely driven by basin-wide buoyancy flux associated with the NAO over the North Atlantic, with ~1.5 cm SLR corresponding to ~1 Sv AMOC weakening. Observational evidence, however, has not been established due to the short data records. South of Cape Hatteras and in subpolar region, westward-propagating Rossby waves and subsequently coastally trapped waves are the major causes for interannual and decadal SLAs. Rossby waves can affect the location and transport of the Gulf Stream and thus coastal

SLAs (Sect. 5.3). Along the west coast of South Atlantic, ENSO-associated wind, sea level pressure and precipitation near the coast were suggested to be the major cause for coastal SLAs. The impacts of Rossby waves and AMOC on coastal SLAs remain elusive.

6.2 Science Issues and Future Outlook

(a) Coastal and open-ocean connections. Currently, our understanding of the open-ocean impact on coastal sea level is based primarily on linear ocean models using idealized continental shelf and slope geometry. In the real ocean, however, shelf, slope and bottom shape vary largely from region to region. To what extent the remote equatorial SLA signals are trapped to the eastern boundary of each ocean basin as coastally trapped waves, and to what extent the open-ocean SLAs can pass through the slope barrier to arrive at the western boundary in different regions of each ocean are not well understood. From observational perspective, continued and new tide gauge records, together with satellite observations such as the Surface Water and Ocean Topography (SWOT) mission, which aims to detect sea level within 10 km from the coasts, will significantly improve our understanding of coastal and open-ocean connections. From modeling perspective, high-resolution models that can adequately resolve continental shelf, slope and western boundary currents are needed, to understand the crosstalk between coastal and the open ocean and to quantify the relative effects of coastal versus open-ocean processes on coastal sea level.

(b) Representation of climate modes. Climate modes are represented by their indices, which are either the principle component (PC) of an EOF mode or time series of SSTA over specific regions. Regression analyses onto these indices are used to extract their associated winds and sea level pressure that force coastal sea level variability. These methods, however, may not well represent the climate modes' effects on sea level, because climate modes, such as ENSO dynamics, are best represented by a few eigenmodes with different periods and decay rates but nonorthogonal spatial patterns (e.g., Penland and Sardeshmukh 1995; Alexander et al. 2008; Compo and Sardeshmukh 2010; Solomon and Newman 2012). Using a fixed EOF pattern to represent climate mode (e.g., PDO) may not depict the temporal changes of their spatial patterns. Improved representations of climate modes need to be sought, in order to achieve more accurate depictions of their impacts on coastal sea level. Since local longshore wind and IB effect are important for driving coastal SLAs in extratropical oceans, it is important to make the distinction between extratropical climate indices (e.g., PDO) and tropical-centered indices (e.g., IPO), even though they are highly correlated. For instance, the PDO index can capture the PDO phase transitions in the North Pacific, whereas the IPO index cannot always capture them (Thompson et al. 2014; Merrifield and Thompson 2018). This is because the PDO is an empirical mode and not a physical mode, which reflects a superposition of multiple processes including teleconnection to the tropics, variability of Aleutian Low due to stochastic weather noise, and oceanic processes in the North Pacific (Schneider and Cornuelle 2005; Newman et al. 2016). Therefore, PDO phase transitions caused by extratropical processes may not correspond to phase changes of IPO or ENSO in the tropics.

Climate mode indices can be significantly correlated especially on decadal time scales (Sect. 3.2.2), either because of the relatively short data record that cannot make statistically significant distinctions or because they are physically connected. Robust relationships between coastal SLAs and decadal climate modes require long data records. While changes of AMOC and Gulf Stream were thought to be important for causing decadal SLAs along the US east coast, studying their long-term relationship using observations is challenging, because continuous observations of the Florida Current transport started only in 1982 and the RAPID observations of AMOC in 2004. Therefore, the impacts of AMOC on coastal SLAs are based exclusively on modeling studies. Long observational records are needed to confirm the modeling results. Furthermore, variations in SST indices of decadal climate modes (e.g., PDO and AMO) can be partly caused by external forcing (e.g., Booth et al. 2012; Dong et al. 2014). Due to these complications, extracting the effect of internal climate modes on coastal sea level from that of external forcing using observational analysis remains a challenge. To this end, the recently available large ensemble experiments of climate models with long integrations using anthropogenic, natural, and all forcing, respectively, will be helpful; however, climate models suffer from significant biases in simulating climate modes (e.g., Lyu et al. 2016).

(c) Relation with global SLR. Due to the global SLR, US east coast communities see acceleration in flooding incidents and severity; even small temporal elevated sea level due to internal variability, which were undetected in the past, can now pass a threshold and cause unpredictable flooding (Ezer and Atkinson 2014; Sweet and Park 2014; Park and Sweet 2015). When sea level increases induced by climate modes are added to global SLR and land subsidence, which is especially large in the mid-Atlantic Bight region (Boon 2012; Karegar et al. 2017), they can cause unexpected year-to-year variations in coastal sea level and flooding. For instance, El Niño years are found to be more prone for flooding; the extremely strong negative NAO was associated with higher coastal sea level along US east coast in 2009–2010, and flooding increased in many locations (2009 was one of the most flooded years in Norfolk; Ezer 2015; Goddard et al. 2015). Further research is needed to understand climate modes impacts on coastal floods in a changing climate.

Acknowledgements WH and LZ are supported by National Science Foundation (NSF) AGS 1446480, NSF OCE 1658132, NASA Ocean Surface Topography Science Team NNX17AI63G and NASA Physical Oceanography Program NNX17AH25G. DS is funded in part through the DFG SPP 1889 on Sea Level Change and Society. CMD is funded the Australian Research Council (FT130101532 and DP160103130). XZ was supported by Centre for Southern Hemisphere Oceans Research (CSHOR), a joint international research centre between QNLM (China) and CSIRO (Australia). DY was supported by grants 41421005, 41720104008, 91858204. The paper is an outcome of the International Space Science Institute (ISSI) Workshop on "Understanding the relationship between coastal sea level and large-scale ocean circulation" held during March 5–9, 2018, in Bern, Switzerland.

References

Alexander MA, Matrosova L, Penland C, Scott JD, Chang P (2008) Forecasting Pacific SSTs: linear inverse model predictions of the PDO. J Clim 21(2):385–402

Andres M, Gawarkiewicz GG, Toole JM (2013) Interannual sea level variability in the western North Atlantic: regional forcing and remote response. Geophys Res Lett 40(22):5915–5919

Ballu V, Bouin MN, Simeoni P, Crawford WC, Calmant S, Bore JM, Kanas T, Pelletier B (2011) Comparing the role of absolute sea-level rise and vertical tectonic motions in coastal flooding, Torres Islands (Vanuatu). Proc Natl Acad Sci USA 108(32):13019–13022

Barnston AG, Livezey RE (1987) Classification, seasonality and persistence of low-frequency atmospheric circulation patterns. Mon Weather Rev 115(6):1083–1126

Beal LM, De Ruijter WP, Biastoch A, Zahn R, Cronin M, Hermes J, Bornman T (2011) On the role of the Agulhas system in ocean circulation and climate. Nature 472(7344):429–436
Becker M, Meyssignac B, Letetrel C, Llovel W, Cazenave A, Delcroix T (2012) Sea level variations at tropical Pacific islands since 1950. Glob Planet Change 80–81:85–98
Behera SK, Yamagata T (2001) Subtropical SST dipole events in the southern Indian ocean. Geophys Res Lett 28(2):327–330
Behera S, Yamagata T (2010) Imprint of the El Niño Modoki on decadal sea level changes. Geophys Res Lett. https://doi.org/10.1029/2010gl045936
Benthuysen J, Furue R, McCreary JP, Bindoff NL, Phillips HE (2014) Dynamics of the Leeuwin Current: part 2. Impacts of mixing, friction, and advection on a buoyancy-driven eastern boundary current over a shelf. Dyn Atmos Oceans 65:39–63
Bilbao RAF, Gregory JM, Bouttes N (2015) Analysis of the regional pattern of sea level change due to ocean dynamics and density change for 1993–2099 in observations and CMIP5 AOGCMs. Clim Dyn 45(9–10):2647–2666
Bindoff NL, Willebrand J (2007) Observations: oceanic climate change and sea level. Climate Change 2007: The Physical Science Basis, pp 385–432
Bindoff NL, Stott PA, AchutaRao KM, Allen MR, Gillett N, Gutzler D, Hansingo K, Hegerl G, et al (2013) Chapter 10—Detection and attribution of climate change: from global to regional. In: Climate Change 2013: the physical science basis. IPCC working group I contribution to AR5. Cambridge University Press, Cambridge
Bingham RJ, Hughes CW (2009) Signature of the Atlantic meridional overturning circulation in sea level along the east coast of North America. Geophys Res Lett 36:L02603. https://doi.org/10.1029/2008GL036215
Bingham RJ, Hughes CW (2012) Local diagnostics to estimate density-induced sea level variations over topography and along coastlines. J Geophys Res Oceans 117(C1):C01013. https://doi.org/10.1029/2011JC007276
Bingham F, Foltz G, McPhaden M (2012) Characteristics of the seasonal cycle of surface layer salinity in the global ocean. Ocean Sci 8:915–929
Bjerknes J (1969) Atmospheric teleconnections from equatorial pacific. Mon Weather Rev 97(3):163
Blaha JP (1984) Fluctuations of monthly sea-level as related to the intensity of the Gulf-Stream from Key West to Norfolk. J Geophys Res Oceans 89(Nc5):8033–8042
Boon JD (2012) Evidence of sea level acceleration at U.S. and Canadian tide stations, Atlantic Coast, North America. J Coast Res 28(6):1437–1445
Booth BBB, Dunstone NJ, Halloran PR, Andrews T, Bellouin N (2012) Aerosols implicated as a prime driver of twentieth-century North Atlantic climate variability. Nature 484(7393):228-U110
Bradshaw E, Richards L, Aarup T (2015) Sea level data archaeology and the Global Sea Level Observing System (GLOSS). GeoResJ 6(3):9–16
Breaker LC, Ruzmaikin A (2013) Estimating rates of acceleration based on the 157-year record of sea level from San Francisco, California, USA. J Coast Res 29(1):43–51
Brink KH (1998) Deep-sea forcing and exchange processes. In: Brink KH, Robinson AR (eds) The sea, vol 10. The global coastal ocean: processes and methods. Wiley, New York
Bromirski PD, Miller AJ, Flick RE, Auad G (2011) Dynamical suppression of sea level rise along the Pacific coast of North America: indications for imminent acceleration. J Geophys Res 116:C07005
Brundrit GB, Decuevas B, Shipley AM (1984) Significant sea-level variations along the west-coast of Southern-Africa 1979–83. S Afr J Sci 80(2):80–82
Brundrit GB, Decuevas BA, Shipley AM (1987) Long-term sea-level variability in the eastern South-Atlantic and a comparison with that in the Eastern Pacific. S Afr J Mar Sci 5:73–78
Brunnabend SE, Schroter J, Rietbroek R, Kusche J (2015) Regional sea level change in response to ice mass loss in Greenland, the West Antarctic and Alaska. J Geophys Res Oceans 120(11):7316–7328
Calafat FM, Chambers DP, Tsimplis MN (2012) Mechanisms of decadal sea level variability in the eastern North Atlantic and the Mediterranean Sea. J Geophys Res Oceans 117:C09022. https://doi.org/10.1029/2012JC008285
Calafat FM, Chambers DP, Tsimplis MN (2013) Inter-annual to decadal sea-level variability in the coastal zones of the Norwegian and Siberian Seas: the role of atmospheric forcing. J Geophys Res Oceans 118(3):1287–1301
Calafat FM, Wahl T, Lindsten F, Williams J, Frajka-Williams E (2018) Coherent modulation of the sea-level annual cycle in the United States by Atlantic Rossby waves. Nat Commun 9:1
Carson M, Kohl A, Stammer D, Slangen ABA, Katsman CA, van de Wal RSW, Church J, White N (2016) Coastal sea level changes, observed and projected during the 20th and 21st century. Clim Change 134(1–2):269–281

Carton JA, Giese BS, Grodsky SA (2005) Sea level rise and the warming of the oceans in the Simple Ocean Data Assimilation (SODA) ocean reanalysis. J Geophys Res Oceans 110(C9), C09006. https://doi.org/10.1029/2004JC002817

Chafik L, Nilsen JEO, Dangendorf S, Reverdin G, Frederikse T (2019) North Atlantic ocean circulation and decadal sea level change during the altimetry era. Sci Rep UK 9:1041

Chambers DP, Merrifield MA, Nerem RS (2012) Is there a 60-year oscillation in global mean sea level? Geophys Res Lett 39

Chaudhuri AH, Gangopadhyay A, Bisagni JJ (2011) Response of the Gulf Stream transport to characteristic high and low phases of the North Atlantic Oscillation. Ocean Model 39(3–4):220–223

Chelton DB, Davis RE (1982) Monthly mean sea-level variability along the west-coast of North-America. J Phys Oceanogr 12(8):757–784

Chen G, Han W, Li Y, Wang D (2016) Interannual variability of equatorial Eastern Indian ocean upwelling: local versus remote forcing. J Phys Oceanogr 46:789–807

Cheng YC, Plag HP, Hamlington BD, Xu Q, He YJ (2015) Regional sea level variability in the Bohai Sea, Yellow Sea, and East China Sea. Cont Shelf Res 111:95–107

Cheng XH, Xie SP, Du Y, Wang J, Chen X, Wang J (2016) Interannual-to-decadal variability and trends of sea level in the South China Sea. Clim Dyn 46(9–10):3113–3126

Chowdhury MR, Chu PS, Schroeder T (2007) ENSO and seasonal sea-level variability—a diagnostic discussion for the US-Affiliated Pacific Islands. Theor Appl Climatol 88(3–4):213–224

Church JA, White NJ (2011) Sea-level rise from the late 19th to the early 21st century. Surv Geophys 32(4–5):585–602

Church JA, White NJ, Coleman R, Lambeck K, Mitrovica JX (2004) Estimates of the regional distribution of sea level rise over the 1950–2000 period. J Clim 17(13):2609–2625

Church JA, White NJ, Hunter JR (2006) Sea-level rise at tropical Pacific and Indian Ocean islands. Global Planet Change 53(3):155–168

Church JA, Clark PU, Cazenave A, Gregory JM, Jevrejeva S, Levermann A, Merrifield MA, Milne GA, Nerem RS, Nunn PD, Payne AJ, Pfeffer WT, Stammer D, Unnikrishnan AS, Bahr D, Box JE, Bromwich DH, Carson M, Collins W, Fettweis X, Forster P, Gardner A, Gehrels WR, Giesen R, Gleckler PJ, Good P, Graversen RG, Greve R, Griffies S, Hanna E, Hemer M, Hock R, Holgate SJ, Hunter J, Huybrechts P, Johnson G, Joughin I, Kaser G, Katsman C, Konikow L, Krinner G, Le Brocq A, Lenaerts J, Ligtenberg S, Little CM, Marzeion B, McInnes KL, Mernild SH, Monselesan D, Mottram R, Murray T, Myhre G, Nicholas JP, Nick F, Perrette M, Pollard D, Radic V, Rae J, Rummukainen M, Schoof C, Slangen A, van Angelen JH, van de Berg WJ, van den Broeke M, Vizcano M, Wada Y, White NJ, Winkelmann R, Yin JJ, Yoshimori M, Zickfeld K (2014) Sea level change. Climate change 2013: The physical science basis, pp 1137–1216

Clarke AJ (1991) On the reflection and transmission of low-frequency energy at the irregular Western Pacific-Ocean boundary. J Geophys Res Oceans 96:3289–3305

Clarke AJ (1992) Low-frequency reflection from a nonmeridional eastern ocean boundary and the use of coastal sea-level to monitor eastern pacific equatorial Kelvin waves. J Phys Oceanogr 22(2):163–183

Clarke AJ, Lebedev A (1999) Remotely driven decadal and longer changes in the coastal Pacific waters of the Americas. J Phys Oceanogr 29(4):828–835

Clarke AJ, Liu X (1994) Interannual sea-level in the Northern and Eastern Indian-Ocean. J Phys Oceanogr 24(6):1224–1235

Clarke AJ, Vangorder S (1994) On Enso coastal currents and sea levels. J Phys Oceanogr 24(3):661–680

Close C (1918) The fluctuations of mean sea-level with special reference to those caused by variations in barometric pressure. Geogr J 52(1):51–58

Colas F, Capet X, McWilliams JC, Shchepetkin A (2008) 1997-1998 El Nino off Peru: a numerical study. Prog Oceanogr 79(2–4):138–155

Compo GP, Sardeshmukh PD (2010) Removing ENSO-related variations from the climate record (vol 23, pg 1957, 2010). J Clim 23(22):6124–6127

Curry RG, McCartney MS (2001) Ocean gyre circulation changes associated with the North Atlantic Oscillation. J Phys Oceanogr 31(12):3374–3400

Danabasoglu G, Yeager SG, Kim WM, Behrens E, Bentsen M, Bi DH, Biastoch A, Bleck R, Boning C, Bozec A, Canuto VM, Cassou C, Chassignet E, Coward AC, Danilov S, Diansky N, Drange H, Farneti R, Fernandez E, Fogli PG, Forget G, Fujii Y, Griffies SM, Gusev A, Heimbach P, Howard A, Ilicak M, Jung T, Karspeck AR, Kelley M, Large WG, Leboissetier A, Lu JH, Madec G, Marsland SJ, Masina S, Navarra A, Nurser AJG, Pirani A, Romanou A, Melia DSY, Samuels BL, Scheinert M, Sidorenko D, Sun S, Treguier AM, Tsujino H, Uotila P, Valcke S, Voldoire A, Wang Q, Yashayaev I (2016) North Atlantic simulations in Coordinated Ocean-ice reference experiments phase II (CORE-II). Part II: inter-annual to decadal variability. Ocean Model 97:65–90

Dangendorf S, Calafat FM, Arns A, Wahl T, Haigh ID, Jensen J (2014) Mean sea level variability in the North Sea: processes and implications. J Geophys Res Oceans 119(10):6820–6841
Dangendorf S, Marcos M, Müller A, Zorita E, Riva R, Berk K, Jensen J (2015) Detecting anthropogenic footprints in sea level rise. Nat Commun 6:7849
Deepa JS, Gnanaseelan C, Kakatkar R, Parekh A, Chowdary JS (2018) The interannual sea level variability in the Indian Ocean as simulated by an Ocean General Circulation Model. Int J Climatol 38(3):1132–1144
Deepa JS, Gnanaseelan C, Sandeep Mohapatra JS, Chowdary AK, Kakatkar R, Parekh A (2019) The tropical Indian Ocean decadal sea level response to the Pacific Decadal Oscillation forcing. Clim Dyn 52:5045. https://doi.org/10.1007/s00382-018-4431-9
Delworth TL, Mann ME (2000) Observed and simulated multidecadal variability in the Northern Hemisphere. Clim Dyn 16(9):661–676
den Toom M, Dijkstra HA, Weijer W, Hecht MW, Maltrud ME, van Sebille E (2014) Response of a strongly eddying Global Ocean to North Atlantic freshwater perturbations. J Phys Oceanogr 44(2):464–481
Di Lorenzo E, Schneider N, Cobb K, Franks P, Chhak K, Miller A, Mcwilliams J, Bograd S, Arango H, Curchitser E (2008) North Pacific Gyre Oscillation links ocean climate and ecosystem change. Geophys Res Lett 35:L08607. https://doi.org/10.1029/2007GL032838
Di Nezio PN, Gramer LJ, Johns WE, Meinen CS, Baringer MO (2009) Observed interannual variability of the Florida Current: wind forcing and the North Atlantic oscillation. J Phys Oceanogr 39(3):721–736
Domingues R, Goni G, Baringer M, Volkov D (2018) What caused the accelerated sea level changes along the U.S. East Coast during 2010–2015? Geophys Res Lett 45:13367–13376. https://doi.org/10.1029/2018GL081183
Dong SF, Garzoli S, Baringer M, Meinen C, Goni G (2009) Interannual variations in the Atlantic meridional overturning circulation and its relationship with the net northward heat transport in the South Atlantic. Geophys Res Lett 36:L20606. https://doi.org/10.1029/2009GL039356
Dong L, Zhou TJ, Chen XL (2014) Changes of Pacific decadal variability in the twentieth century driven by internal variability, greenhouse gases, and aerosols. Geophys Res Lett 41(23):8570–8577
Douglas BC (2001) Chapter 3 Sea level change in the era of the recording tide gauge. Int Geophys 75:37–64. https://doi.org/10.1016/S0074-6142(01)80006-1
Douglas BC (2005) Gulf of Mexico and Atlantic coast sea level change. In: Sturges W, Lugo-Fernández A (eds) Circulation in the Gulf of Mexico: observations and models. Geophysical monograph series. AGU, Washington, pp 111–121
Dragani WC, D'Onofrio E, Alonso G, Fiore M, Oreiro F (2014) Sea-level trend at the southernmost region of South America. J Coast Res 30(1):210–213
Dunne RP, Barbosa SM, Woodworth PL (2012) Contemporary sea level in the Chagos Archipelago, central Indian Ocean. Global Planet Change 82–83:25–37
Elipot S, Frajka-Williams E, Hughes CW, Olhede S, Lankhorst M (2017) Observed basin-scale response of the North Atlantic meridional overturning circulation to wind stress forcing. J Clim 30(6):2029–2054
Emery WJ, Hamilton K (1985) Atmospheric forcing of interannual variability in the Northeast Pacific-Ocean—connections with El-Nino. J Geophys Res Oceans 90(Nc1):857–868
Enfield DB, Allen JS (1980) On the structure and dynamics of monthly mean sea-level anomalies along the Pacific Coast of North and South-America. J Phys Oceanogr 10(4):557–578
Enfield DB, Mestas-Nunez AM, Trimble PJ (2001a) The Atlantic multidecadal oscillation and its relation to rainfall and river flows in the continental US. Geophys Res Lett 28(10):2077–2080
Enfield DB, Mestas-Nunez AM, Trimble PJ (2001b) The Atlantic multidecadal oscillation and its relation to rainfall and river flows in the continental US. Geophys Res Lett 28(10):2077–2080
England MH, McGregor S, Spence P, Meehl GA, Timmermann A, Cai WJ, Sen Gupta A, McPhaden MJ, Purich A, Santoso A (2014) Recent intensification of wind-driven circulation in the Pacific and the ongoing warming hiatus. Nat Clim Change 4(3):222–227
Ezer T (1999) Decadal variabilities of the upper layers of the subtropical North Atlantic: an ocean model study. J Phys Oceanogr 29(12):3111–3124
Ezer T (2001) Can long-term variability in the Gulf Stream transport be inferred from sea level? Geophys Res Lett 28(6):1031–1034
Ezer T (2013) Sea level rise, spatially uneven and temporally unsteady: why the US East Coast, the global tide gauge record, and the global altimeter data show different trends. Geophys Res Lett 40(20):5439–5444
Ezer T (2015) Detecting changes in the transport of the Gulf Stream and the Atlantic overturning circulation from coastal sea level data: the extreme decline in 2009-2010 and estimated variations for 1935–2012. Global Planet Change 129:23–36

Ezer T (2019) Regional differences in sea level rise between the Mid-Atlantic Bight and the South Atlantic Bight: is the Gulf Stream to blame? Earth's Future. https://doi.org/10.1029/2019ef001174
Ezer T, Atkinson LP (2014) Accelerated flooding along the US East Coast: on the impact of sea-level rise, tides, storms, the Gulf Stream, and the North Atlantic Oscillations. Earths Future 2(8):362–382
Ezer T, Atkinson LP (2017) On the predictability of high water level along the US East Coast: can the Florida Current measurement be an indicator for flooding caused by remote forcing? Ocean Dyn 67(6):751–766
Ezer T, Corlett WB (2012) Is sea level rise accelerating in the Chesapeake Bay? A demonstration of a novel new approach for analyzing sea level data. Geophys Res Lett 39:19605. https://doi.org/10.1029/2012GL053435
Ezer T, Atkinson LP, Corlett WB, Blanco JL (2013) Gulf Stream's induced sea level rise and variability along the U.S. mid-Atlantic coast. J Geophys Res Oceans 118(2):685–697
Ezer T, Haigh ID, Woodworth PL (2016) Nonlinear sea-level trends and long-term variability on Western European coasts. J Coast Res 32(4):744–755
Feng M, Meyers G, Pearce A, Wijffels S (2003) Annual and interannual variations of the Leeuwin Current at 32 S. J Geophys Res 108(C11):3355. https://doi.org/10.1029/2002jc001763
Feng M, Li Y, Meyers G (2004) Multidecadal variations of Fremantle sea level: Footprint of climate variability in the tropical Pacific. Geophys Res Lett 31(16):16302. https://doi.org/10.1029/2004GL019947
Feng M, McPhaden MJ, Lee T (2010) Decadal variability of the Pacific subtropical cells and their influence on the southeast Indian Ocean. Geophys Res Lett 37:L09606. https://doi.org/10.1029/2010GL042796
Feng M, Böning C, Biastoch A, Behrens E, Weller E, Masumoto Y (2011) The reversal of the multi-decadal trends of the equatorial Pacific easterly winds, and the Indonesian Throughflow and Leeuwin Current transports. Geophys Res Lett 38(11):L11604
Feng M, McPhaden MJ, Xie SP, Hafner J (2013) La Nina forces unprecedented Leeuwin Current warming in 2011. Sci Rep UK 3:1277
Folland C, Renwick J, Salinger M, Mullan A (2002) Relative influences of the interdecadal Pacific oscillation and ENSO on the South Pacific convergence zone. Geophys Res Lett 29(13):21-1
Frankcombe LM, Dijkstra HA (2009) Coherent multidecadal variability in North Atlantic sea level. Geophys Res Lett 36:L15604. https://doi.org/10.1029/2009GL039455
Frankcombe LM, McGregor S, England MH (2015) Robustness of the modes of Indo-Pacific sea level variability. Clim Dyn 45(5–6):1281–1298
Fu LL, Qiu B (2002) Low-frequency variability of the North Pacific Ocean: the roles of boundary- and wind-driven baroclinic Rossby waves. J Geophys Res Oceans 107(C12):13-1
Fukumori I, Wang O (2013) Origins of heat and freshwater anomalies underlying regional decadal sea level trends. Geophys Res Lett 40(3):563–567
Fukumori I, Menemenlis D, Lee T (2007) A near-uniform basin-wide sea level fluctuation of the Mediterranean Sea. J Phys Oceanogr 37:338–358. https://doi.org/10.1175/Jpo3016.1
Furue R, McCreary JP, Benthuysen J, Phillips HE, Bindoff NL (2013) Dynamics of the Leeuwin Current: part 1. Coastal flows in an inviscid, variable-density, layer model. Dyn Atmos Oceans 63:24–59
Gnanaseelan C, Vaid BH (2010) Interannual variability in the Biannual Rossby waves in the tropical Indian Ocean and its relation to Indian Ocean Dipole and El Nino forcing. Ocean Dyn 60(1):27–40
Goddard PB, Yin JJ, Griffies SM, Zhang SQ (2015) An extreme event of sea-level rise along the Northeast coast of North America in 2009–2010. Nat Commun 6:6346
Godfrey JS (1996) The effect of the Indonesian throughflow on ocean circulation and heat exchange with the atmosphere: a review. J Geophys Res Oceans 101(C5):12217–12237
Gomis D, Ruiz S, Sotillo MG, Alvarez-Fanjul E, Terradas J (2008) Low frequency Mediterranean sea level variability: the contribution of atmospheric pressure and wind. Glob Planet Change 63(2–3):215–229
Haigh ID, Eliot M, Pattiaratchi C, Wahl T (2011) Regional changes in mean sea level around Western Australia between 1897 and 2008. In: Proceedings of the 20th Australasian coastal and ocean engineering conference, Perth, 28–30 September
Hakkinen S (2000) Decadal air-sea interaction in the North Atlantic based on observations and modeling results. J Clim 13(6):1195–1219
Hakkinen S (2001) Variability in sea surface height: a qualitative measure for the meridional overturning in the North Atlantic. J Geophys Res Oceans 106(C7):13837–13848
Hakkinen S, Rhines PB (2004) Decline of subpolar North Atlantic circulation during the 1990s. Science 304:555–559
Hameed S, Piontkovski S (2004) The dominant influence of the Icelandic Low on the position of the Gulf Stream northwall. Geophys Res Lett 31:L09303. https://doi.org/10.1029/2004GL019561

Hamlington BD, Leben RR, Nerem RS, Han W, Kim KY (2011) Reconstructing sea level using cyclostationary empirical orthogonal functions. J Geophys Res Oceans 116:C12015. https://doi.org/10.1029/2011JC007529
Hamlington BD, Leben RR, Strassburg MW, Nerem RS, Kim KY (2013) Contribution of the Pacific decadal oscillation to global mean sea level trends. Geophys Res Lett 40:5171–5175
Hamlington BD, Strassburg MW, Leben RR, Han W, Nerem RS, Kim KY (2014) Uncovering an anthropogenic sea-level rise signal in the Pacific Ocean. Nat Clim Change 4(9):782–785
Hamlington BD, Leben RR, Kim KY, Nerem RS, Atkinson LP, Thompson PR (2015) The effect of the El Nino-Southern Oscillation on US regional and coastal sea level. J Geophys Res Oceans 120(6):3970–3986
Hamlington BD, Cheon SH, Thompson PR, Merrifield MA, Nerem RS, Leben RR, Kim KY (2016) An ongoing shift in Pacific Ocean sea level. J Geophys Res Oceans 121(7):5084–5097
Han GQ, Huang WG (2008) Pacific decadal oscillation and sea level variability in the Bohai, Yellow, and East China seas. J Phys Oceanogr 38(12):2772–2783
Han W, Webster PJ (2002) Forcing mechanisms of sea level interannual variability in the Bay of Bengal. J Phys Oceanogr 32(1):216–239
Han W, Meehl GA, Rajagopalan B, Fasullo JT, Hu A, Lin J, Large WG, Wang J, Quan XW, Trenary LL (2010) Patterns of Indian Ocean sea-level change in a warming climate. Nat Geosci 3(8):546–550
Han WQ, McCreary JP, Masumoto Y, Vialard J, Duncan B (2011) Basin resonances in the equatorial Indian Ocean. J Phys Oceanogr 41(6):1252–1270
Han W, Meehl G, Hu A, Alexander M, Yamagata T, Yuan D, Ishii M, Pegion P, Zheng J, Hamlington B, Quan X-W, Leben R (2014a) Intensification of decadal and multi-decadal sea level variability in the western tropical Pacific during recent decades. Clim Dyn 43(5–6):1357–1379
Han WQ, Vialard J, McPhaden MJ, Lee T, Masumoto Y, Feng M, De Ruijter WPM (2014b) Indian Ocean decadal variability a review. Bull Am Meteor Soc 95(11):1679–1703
Han WQ, Meehl GA, Stammer D, Hu AX, Hamlington B, Kenigson J, Palanisamy H, Thompson P (2017a) Spatial patterns of sea level variability associated with natural internal climate modes. Surv Geophys 38(1):217–250
Han WQ, Meehl GA, Hu AX, Zheng J, Kenigson J, Vialard J, Rajagopalan B (2017b) Yanto, decadal variability of the Indian and Pacific walker cells since the 1960s: do they covary on decadal time scales? J Clim 30(21):8447–8468
Han WQ, Stammer D, Meehl GA, Hu AX, Sienz F, Zhang L (2018) Multi-decadal trend and decadal variability of the regional sea level over the Indian Ocean since the 1960s: roles of climate modes and external forcing. Climate 6(2):51
Henley B, Gergis J, Karoly D, Power S, Kennedy J, Folland C (2015) A tripole index for the interdecadal Pacific oscillation. Clim Dyn 45(11–12):3077–3090
Hermann AJ, Curchitser EN, Haidvogel DB, Dobbins EL (2009) A comparison of remote vs. local influence of El Nino on the coastal circulation of the northeast Pacific. Deep Sea Res Part II 56(24):2427–2443
Hermes J, Reason C (2008) Annual cycle of the South Indian Ocean (Seychelles-Chagos) thermocline ridge in a regional ocean model. J Geophys Res 113:C04035. https://doi.org/10.1029/2007JC004363
Hewitt CD, Broccoli AJ, Crucifix M, Gregory JM, Mitchell JFB, Stouffer RJ (2006) The effect of a large freshwater perturbation on the glacial north Atlantic Ocean using a coupled general circulation model. J Clim 19(17):4436–4447
Higginson S, Thompson KR, Woodworth PL, Hughes CW (2015) The tilt of mean sea level along the east coast of North America. Geophys Res Lett 42(5):1471–1479
Holbrook NJ, Goodwin ID, McGregor S, Molina E, Power SB (2011) ENSO to multi-decadal time scale changes in East Australian Current transports and Fort Denison sea level: oceanic Rossby waves as the connecting mechanism. Deep Sea Res Part II 58(5):547–558
Holgate SJ, Woodworth PL (2004) Evidence for enhanced coastal sea level rise during the 1990s. Geophys Res Lett 31:L07305. https://doi.org/10.1029/2004GL019626
Holgate SJ, Matthews A, Woodworth PL, Rickards LJ, Tamisiea ME, Bradshaw E, Foden PR, Gordon KM, Jevrejeva S, Pugh J (2013) New Data Systems and Products at the Permanent Service for Mean Sea Level. J Coast Res 29(3):493–504. https://doi.org/10.2112/JCOASTRES-D-12-00175.1
Hong BG, Sturges W, Clarke AJ (2000) Sea level on the US East Coast: decadal variability caused by open ocean wind-curl forcing. J Phys Oceanogr 30(8):2088–2098
Hsueh Y, Pang IC (1989) Coastally trapped long waves in the Yellow sea. J Phys Oceanogr 19(5):612–625
Hsueh Y, Yuan DL (1997) A numerical study of currents, heat advection, and sea-level fluctuations in the Yellow Sea in Winter 1986. J Phys Oceanogr 27(11):2313–2326

Hu A, Bates SC (2018) Internal climate variability and projected future regional steric and dynamic sea level rise. Nat Commun 9:1068
Hu A, Meehl G, Han W, Yin J (2011) Effect of the potential melting of the Greenland Ice Sheet on the meridional overturning circulation and global climate in the future. Deep Sea Res II 58:1914–1926
Hughes CW, Meredith CP (2006) Coherent sea-level fluctuations along the global continental slope. Philos Trans R Soc A 364(1841):885–901
Hughes CW, Williams SDP (2010) The color of sea level: importance of spatial variations in spectral shape for assessing the significance of trends. J Geophys Res Oceans 115:C10048. https://doi.org/10.1029/2010JC006102
Hughes CW, Williams J, Blaker A, Coward A, Stepanov V (2018) A window on the deep ocean: the special value of ocean bottom pressure for monitoring the large-scale, deep-ocean circulation. Prog Oceanogr 161:19–46
Hughes CW, Fukumori I, Griffies SM, Huthnance JM, Minobe S, Spence JP, Thompson KR, Wise A (2019) Sea level and the role of coastal trapped waves in mediating the interaction between the coast and open ocean. Surv Geophys. https://doi.org/10.1007/s10712-019-09535-x
Hurrell JW (1995) Decadal trends in the North-Atlantic oscillation—regional temperatures and precipitation. Science 269(5224):676–679
Karegar MA, Dixon TH, Malservisi R, Kusche J, Engelhart SE (2017) Nuisance flooding and relative sea-level rise: the importance of present-day land motion. Sci Rep UK 7:11197
Kenigson JS, Han W (2014) Detecting and understanding the accelerated sea level rise along the east coast of the United States during recent decades. J Geophys Res Oceans 119(12):8749–8766
Kenigson JS, Han WQ, Rajagopalan B, Yanto, Jasinski M (2018) Decadal shift of NAO-linked interannual sea level variability along the US northeast coast. J Clim 31(13):4981–4989
Kerr RA (2000) A North Atlantic climate pacemaker for the centuries. Science 288(5473):1984–1986
Kleinen T, Osborn TJ, Briffa KR (2009) Sensitivity of climate response to variations in freshwater hosing location. Ocean Dyn 59(3):509–521
Knudsen MF, Jacobsen BH, Seidenkrantz MS, Olsen J (2014) Evidence for external forcing of the Atlantic Multidecadal Oscillation since termination of the Little Ice Age. Nat Commun 5:3323
Kohl A, Stammer D, Cornuelle B (2007) Interannual to decadal changes in the ECCO global synthesis. J Phys Oceanogr 37(2):313–337
Kolker AS, Hameed S (2007) Meteorologically driven trends in sea level rise. Geophys Res Lett 34:L23616. https://doi.org/10.1029/2007GL031814
Kopp RE (2013) Does the mid-Atlantic United States sea level acceleration hot spot reflect ocean dynamic variability? Geophys Res Lett 40(15):3981–3985
Kopp RE, Horton BP, Kemp AC, Tebaldi C (2015a) Past and future sea-level rise along the coast of North Carolina, USA. Clim Change 132(4):693–707
Kopp RE, Kemp AC, Bittermann K, Horton BP, Donnelly JP, Gehrels WR, Hay CC, Mitrovica JX, Morrow ED, Rahmstorf S (2015b) Temperature-driven global sea-level variability in the common era. Proc Natl Acad Sci USA 113:E1434–E1441. https://doi.org/10.1073/pnas.1517056113
Kopp RE, Kemp AC, Bittermann K, Horton BP, Donnelly JP, Roland GW, Hay CC, Mitrovica JX, Morrow ED, Rahmstorf S (2016) Temperature-driven global sea-level variability in the Common Era. Proc Natl Acad Sci 113(11):E1434–E1441
Lagerloef GS, Swift CT, Le Vine DM (1995) Sea surface salinity: the next remote sensing challenge. Oceanography 8(2):44–50
Landerer FW, Volkov DL (2013) The anatomy of recent large sea level fluctuations in the Mediterranean Sea. Geophys Res Lett 40:553–557
Landerer FW, Jungclaus JH, Marotzke J (2007) Regional dynamic and steric sea level change in response to the IPCC-A1B scenario. J Phys Oceanogr 37(2):296–312
Landerer FW, Jungclaus JH, Marotzke J (2008) El Nino-Southern Oscillation signals in sea level, surface mass redistribution, and degree-two geoid coefficients. J Geophys Res Oceans 113:C08014. https://doi.org/10.1029/2008JC004767
Lee T, McPhaden MJ (2008) Decadal phase change in large-scale sea level and winds in the Indo-Pacific region at the end of the 20th century. Geophys Res Lett 35:L01605. https://doi.org/10.1029/2007GL032419
Levermann A, Griesel A, Hofmann M, Montoya M, Rahmstorf S (2005) Dynamic sea level changes following changes in the thermohaline circulation. Clim Dyn 24:347–354
Li Y, Han W (2015) Decadal sea level variations in the Indian Ocean investigated with HYCOM: roles of climate modes, ocean internal variability, and stochastic wind forcing. J Clim 28(23):9143–9165
Liu ZY (1999) Planetary wave modes in the thermocline: non-Doppler-shift mode, advective mode and Green mode. Q J R Meteorol Soc 125(556):1315–1339

Liu QY, Feng M, Wang DX (2011) ENSO-induced interannual variability in the southeastern South China Sea. J Oceanogr 67(1):127–133
Llovel W, Lee T (2015) Importance and origin of halosteric contribution to sea level change in the southeast Indian Ocean during 2005–2013. Geophys Res Lett 42(4):1148–1157
Lombard A, Garric G, Penduff T (2009) Regional patterns of observed sea level change: insights from a 1/4A degrees global ocean/sea-ice hindcast. Ocean Dyn 59(3):433–449
Lopez H, Goni G, Dong SF (2017) A reconstructed South Atlantic Meridional Overturning Circulation time series since 1870. Geophys Res Lett 44(7):3309–3318
Lorbacher K, Dengg J, Boning CW, Biastoch A (2010) Regional patterns of sea level change related to interannual variability and multidecadal trends in the Atlantic meridional overturning circulation. J Clim 23(15):4243–4254
Luo J-J, Sasaki W, Masumoto Y (2012) Indian Ocean warming modulates Pacific climate change. Proc Natl Acad Sci USA 109(46):18701–18706
Lyu KW, Zhang XB, Church JA, Hu JY (2016) Evaluation of the interdecadal variability of sea surface temperature and sea level in the Pacific in CMIP3 and CMIP5 models. Int J Climatol 36:3723–3740. https://doi.org/10.1002/joc.4587
Lyu KW, Zhang XB, Church JA, Hu JY, Yu JY (2017) Distinguishing the quasi-decadal and multidecadal sea level and climate variations in the Pacific: implications for the ENSO-like low-frequency variability. J Clim 30(13):5097–5117
Mann ME, Steinman BA, Miller SK (2014) On forced temperature changes, internal variability, and the AMO. Geophys Res Lett 41(9):3211–3219
Mantua NJ, Hare SR, Zhang Y, Wallace JM, Francis RC (1997) A Pacific interdecadal climate oscillation with impacts on salmon production. Bull Am Meteorol Soc 78(6):1069–1079
Marshall J, Johnson H, Goodman J (2001) A study of the interaction of the North Atlantic oscillation with ocean circulation. J Clim 14(7):1399–1421
Maul GA, Hanson K (1991) Interannual coherence between North-Atlantic atmospheric surface pressure and composite Southern USA sea-level. Geophys Res Lett 18(4):653–656
McCarthy GD, Haigh ID, Hirschi JJM, Grist JP, Smeed DA (2015) Ocean impact on decadal Atlantic climate variability revealed by sea-level observations. Nature 521(7553):508-U172
McCreary JP, Kundu PK, Molinari RL (1993) A numerical investigation of dynamics, thermodynamics and mixed-layer processes in the Indian Ocean. Prog Oceanogr 31(3):181–244
McGregor S, Sen Gupta A, England MH (2012) Constraining wind stress products with sea surface height Observations and implications for Pacific Ocean sea level trend attribution. J Clim 25(23):8164–8176
McGregor S, Timmermann A, Stuecker MF, England MH, Merrifield M, Jin FF, Chikamoto Y (2014) Recent Walker circulation strengthening and Pacific cooling amplified by Atlantic warming. Nat Clim Change 4(10):888–892
McPhaden MJ, Nagura M (2014) Indian Ocean dipole interpreted in terms of recharge oscillator theory. Clim Dyn 42(5–6):1569–1586
Meinen CS, Baringer MO, Garcia RF (2010) Florida Current transport variability: an analysis of annual and longer-period signals. Deep Sea Res Part I 57(7):835–846
Menemenlis M, Fukumori I, Lee T (2007) Atlantic to Mediterranean sea level difference driven by winds near Gibraltar Strait. J Phys Oceanogr 37:359–376. https://doi.org/10.1175/Jpo3015.1
Merrifield MA (2011) A shift in western tropical Pacific sea level trends during the 1990s. J Clim 24(15):4126–4138
Merrifield MA, Maltrud ME (2011) Regional sea level trends due to a Pacific trade wind intensification. Geophys Res Lett 38:L21605. https://doi.org/10.1029/2011GL049576
Merrifield MA, Thompson PR (2018) Interdecadal sea level variations in the Pacific: distinctions between the tropics and extratropics. Geophys Res Lett 45(13):6604–6610
Merrifield MA, Thompson PR, Lander M (2012) Multidecadal sea level anomalies and trends in the western tropical Pacific. Geophys Res Lett 39:L13602
Meyers G (1996) Variation of Indonesian throughflow and the El Nino Southern oscillation. J Geophys Res Oceans 101(C5):12255–12263
Meyers SD, Melsom A, Mitchum GT, O'Brien JJ (1998) Detection of the fast Kelvin wave teleconnection due to El Nino Southern oscillation. J Geophys Res Oceans 103(C12):27655–27663
Meyers G, McIntosh P, Pigot L, Pook M (2007) The years of El Nino, La Nina, and interactions with the tropical Indian ocean. J Clim 20(13):2872–2880
Meyssignac B, Melia DSY, Becker M, Llovel W, Cazenave A (2012) Tropical Pacific spatial trend patterns in observed sea level: internal variability and/or anthropogenic signature? Clim Past 8(2):787–802
Miller L, Douglas BC (2007) Gyre-scale atmospheric pressure variations and their relation to 19th and 20th century sea level rise. Geophys Res Lett 34:L16602. https://doi.org/10.1029/2007GL030862

Milne GA, Gehrels WR, Hughes CW, Tamisiea ME (2009) Identifying the causes of sea-level change. Nat Geosci 2(7):471–478

Minobe S, Terada M, Qiu B, Schneider N (2017) Western boundary sea level: a theory, rule of thumb, and application to climate models. J Phys Oceanogr 47(5):957–977

Montgomery RB (1938) Fluctuations in monthly sea level on eastern US coast as related to dynamics of western North Atlantic ocean. J Mar Res 1(2):165–185

Moon JH, Song YT (2017) Decadal sea level variability in the East China Sea linked to the North Pacific Gyre Oscillation. Cont Shelf Res 143:278–285

Moon JH, Song YT, Bromirski PD, Miller AJ (2013) Multidecadal regional sea level shifts in the Pacific over 1958–2008. J Geophys Res Oceans 118(12):7024–7035

Murtugudde RG, Signorini SR, Christian JR, Busalacchi AJ, McClain CR, Picaut J (1999) Ocean color variability of the tropical Indo-Pacific basin observed by SeaWiFS during 1997–1998. J Geophys Res Oceans 104(C8):18351–18366

National Research Council (2012) Sea-level rise for the coasts of California, Oregon, and Washington: past, present, and future. The National Academies Press, Washington, DC. http://www.nap.edu/catalog.php?record_id=13389

Nerem RS, Chambers DP, Leuliette EW, Mitchum GT, Giese BS (1999) Variations in global mean sea level associated with the 1997–1998 ENSO event: implications for measuring long term sea level change. Geophys Res Lett 26(19):3005–3008

Newman M, Alexander MA, Ault TR, Cobb KM, Deser C, Di Lorenzo E, Mantua NJ, Miller AJ, Minobe S, Nakamura H, Schneider N, Vimont DJ, Phillips AS, Scott JD, Smith CA (2016) The Pacific decadal oscillation, revisited. J Clim 29(12):4399–4427

Nidheesh AG, Lengaigne M, Vialard J, Unnikrishnan AS, Dayan H (2013) Decadal and long-term sea level variability in the tropical Indo-Pacific Ocean. Clim Dyn 41(2):381–402

Nidheesh AG, Lengaigne M, Vialard J, Izumo T, Unnikrishnan AS, Meyssignac B, Hamlington B, Montegut CD (2017) Robustness of observation-based decadal sea level variability in the Indo-Pacific Ocean. Geophys Res Lett 44(14):7391–7400

Olson DB, Evans RH (1986) Rings of the Agulhas current. Deep Sea Res 33(1):27–42

Olson DB, Podesta GP, Evans RH, Brown OB (1988) Temporal variations in the separation of Brazil and Malvinas currents. Deep Sea Res 35(12):1971–1990

Palanisamy H, Meyssignac B, Cazenave A, Delcroix T (2015) Is anthropogenic sea level fingerprint already detectable in the Pacific Ocean? Environ Res Lett 10(8):084024

Palma ED, Matano RP (2009) Disentangling the upwelling mechanisms of the South Brazil Bight. Cont Shelf Res 29(11–12):1525–1534

Papadopoulos A, Tsimplis MN (2006) Coherent coastal sea-level variability at interdecadal and interannual scales from tide gauges. J Coast Res 22(3):625–639

Parekh A, Gnanaseelan C, Deepa JS, Karmakar A, Chowdary JS (2017) Sea level variability and trends in the North Indian Ocean. In: Observed climate variability and change over the Indian region. Springer, Singapore, pp 181–192. https://doi.org/10.1007/978-981-10-2531-0

Pariwono JI, Bye JAT, Lennon GW (1986) Long-period variations of sea-level in Australasia. Geophys J Int 87(1):43–54

Park J, Sweet W (2015) Accelerated sea level rise and Florida Current transport. Ocean Sci 11(4):607–615

Parvathi V, Suresh I, Lengaigne M, Ethé C, Vialard J, Lévy M, Neetu S, Aumont O, Resplandy L, Naik H, Naqvi SWA (2017) Positive Indian Ocean Dipole events prevent anoxia along the west coast of India. Biogeosciences 14:1541–1559

Pearce AF, Phillips BF (1988) Enso events, the Leeuwin Current, and larval recruitment of the western rock lobster. J Conseil 45(1):13–21

Penland C, Sardeshmukh PD (1995) The optimal-growth of tropical sea-surface temperature anomalies. J Clim 8(8):1999–2024

Perigaud C, Delecluse P (1993) Interannual sea-level variations in the tropical Indian-Ocean from geosat and shallow-water simulations. J Phys Oceanogr 23(9):1916–1934

Piecuch CG, Ponte RM (2013) Buoyancy-driven interannual sea level changes in the tropical South Atlantic. J Phys Oceanogr 43(3):533–547

Piecuch CG, Ponte RM (2015) Inverted barometer contributions to recent sea level changes along the northeast coast of North America. Geophys Res Lett 42(14):5918–5925

Piecuch CG, Dangendorf S, Ponte RM, Marcos M (2016) Annual sea level changes on the North American northeast coast: influence of local winds and barotropic motions. J Clim 29(13):4801–4816

Piecuch CG, Dangendorf S, Gawarkiewicz GG, Little CM, Ponte RM, Yang J (2019) How is New England coastal sea level related to the Atlantic meridional overturning circulation at 26°N? Geophys Res Lett. https://doi.org/10.1029/2019gl083073

Pizarro O, Clarke AJ, Van Gorder S (2001) El Nino sea level and currents along the South American coast: comparison of observations with theory. J Phys Oceanogr 31(7):1891–1903
Ponte RM (2006) Low-frequency sea level variability and the inverted barometer effect. J Atmos Ocean Technol 23(4):619–629
Power S, Casey T, Folland C, Colman A, Mehta V (1999) Inter-decadal modulation of the impact of ENSO on Australia. Clim Dyn 15(5):319–324
Qiu B (2002) Large-scale variability in the midlatitude subtropical and subpolar North Pacific Ocean: observations and causes. J Phys Oceanogr 32(1):353–375
Qiu B, Chen S (2012) Multidecadal sea level and gyre circulation variability in the northwestern tropical Pacific Ocean. J Phys Oceanogr 42:193–206
Ramp SR, McClean JL, Collins CA, Semtner AJ, Hays KAS (1997) Observations and modeling of the 1991–1992 El Nino signal off central California. J Geophys Res Oceans 102(C3):5553–5582
Rao SA, Behera SK (2005) Subsurface influence on SST in the tropical Indian Ocean: structure and interannual variability. Dyn Atmos Oceans 39(1):103–135
Rao SA, Behera SK, Masumoto Y, Yamagata T (2002) Interannual subsurface variability in the tropical Indian Ocean with a special emphasis on the Indian Ocean Dipole. Deep Sea Res Part II 49(7–8):1549–1572
Richter K, Nilsen JEO, Drange H (2012) Contributions to sea level variability along the Norwegian coast for 1960–2010. J Geophys Res Oceans 117:C05038. https://doi.org/10.1029/2011JC007826
Rossby T (1999) On gyre interactions. Deep Sea Res Part II 46(1–2):139–164
Rossby T, Flagg C, Donohue K (2010) On the variability of Gulf Stream transport from seasonal to decadal timescales. J Mar Res 68(3–4):503–522
Saji N, Goswami B, Vinayachandran P, Yamagata T (1999) A dipole mode in the tropical Indian Ocean. Nature 401(6751):360–363
Sallenger AH, Doran KS, Howd PA (2012) Hotspot of accelerated sea-level rise on the Atlantic coast of North America. Nat Clim Change 2(12):884–888
Sasaki YN, Minobe S, Schneider N, Kagimoto T, Nonaka M, Sasaki H (2008) Decadal sea level variability in the South Pacific in a global eddy-resolving ocean model hindcast. J Phys Oceanogr 38(8):1731–1747
Sasaki YN, Minobe S, Miura Y (2014) Decadal sea-level variability along the coast of Japan in response to ocean circulation changes. J Geophys Res Oceans 119(1):266–275
Scafetta N (2014) Multi-scale dynamical analysis (MSDA) of sea level records versus PDO, AMO, and NAO indexes. Clim Dyn 43(1–2):175–192
Schlesinger ME, Ramankutty N (1994) An oscillation in the global climate system of period 65–70 years. Nature 367(6465):723–726
Schloesser F, Furue R, McCreary JP, Timmermann A (2012) Dynamics of the Atlantic meridional overturning circulation. Part 1: buoyancy-forced response. Prog Oceanogr 101(1):33–62
Schloesser F, Furue R, McCreary JP, Timmermann A (2014) Dynamics of the Atlantic meridional overturning circulation. Part 2: forcing by winds and buoyancy. Prog Oceanogr 120:154–176
Schneider N, Cornuelle BD (2005) The forcing of the Pacific decadal oscillation. J Clim 18(21):4355–4373
Schouten MW, de Ruijter WPM, van Leeuwen PJ, Lutjeharms JRE (2000) Translation, decay and splitting of Agulhas rings in the southeastern Atlantic Ocean. J Geophys Res Oceans 105(C9):21913–21925
Schwarzkopf FU, Böning CW (2011) Contribution of Pacific wind stress to multi-decadal variations in upper-ocean heat content and sea level in the tropical south Indian Ocean. Geophys Res Lett 38:L12602. https://doi.org/10.1029/2011GL047651
Schwing FB, Murphree T, Green PM (2002) The Northern Oscillation Index (NOI): a new climate index for the northeast Pacific. Prog Oceanogr 53(2–4):115–139
Senjyu T, Matsuyama M, Matsubara N (1999) Interannual and decadal sea-level variations along the Japanese coast. J Oceanogr 55:619–633
Sevellec F, Fedorov AV (2013) The leading, interdecadal eigenmode of the Atlantic meridional overturning circulation in a realistic ocean model. J Clim 26(7):2160–2183
Shankar D, Shetye SR (1999) Are interdecadal sea level changes along the Indian coast influenced by variability of monsoon rainfall? J Geophys Res Oceans 104(C11):26031–26042
Shankar D, Aparna S, Mccreary JP, Suresh I, Neetu S, Durand F, Shenoi S, Al Saafani M (2010) Minima of interannual sea-level variability in the Indian Ocean. Prog Oceanogr 84(3):225–241
Slangen ABA, Church JA, Agosta C, Fettweis X, Marzeion B, Richter K (2016) Anthropogenic forcing dominates global mean sea-level rise since 1970. Nat Clim Change 6(7):701
Solomon A, Newman M (2012) Reconciling disparate twentieth-century Indo-Pacific ocean temperature trends in the instrumental record. Nat Clim Change 2(9):691–699

Song Q, Vecchi GA, Rosati AJ (2007) Indian Ocean variability in the GFDL coupled climate model. J Clim 20(13):2895–2916

Sreenivas P, Gnanaseelan C, Prasad KVSR (2012) Influence of El Nino and Indian Ocean Dipole on sea level variability in the Bay of Bengal. Glob Planet Change 80–81:215–225

Srinivasu U, Ravichandran M, Han WQ, Sivareddy S, Rahman H, Li YL, Nayak S (2017) Causes for the reversal of North Indian Ocean decadal sea level trend in recent two decades. Clim Dyn 49(11–12):3887–3904

Stammer D, Cazenave A, Ponte RM, Tamisiea ME (2013) Causes for contemporary regional sea level changes. Annu Rev Mar Sci 5:21–46

Strub PT, James C (2002) The 1997–1998 oceanic El Nino signal along the southeast and northeast Pacific boundaries—an altimetric view. Prog Oceanogr 54(1–4):439–458

Sturges W, Douglas BC (2011) Wind effects on estimates of sea level rise. J Geophys Res Oceans 116:C06008. https://doi.org/10.1029/2010JC006492

Sturges W, Hong BG (1995) Wind forcing of the Atlantic thermocline along 32-degrees-N at low-frequencies. J Phys Oceanogr 25(7):1706–1715

Sturges W, Hong BG (2001) Gulf Stream transport variability at periods of decades. J Phys Oceanogr 31(5):1304–1312

Sun SW, Lan J, Fang Y, Tana, Gao XQ (2015) A triggering mechanism for the Indian Ocean dipoles independent of ENSO. J Clim 28(13):5063–5076

Suzuki R, Behera SK, Iizuka S, Yamagata T (2004) Indian Ocean subtropical dipole simulated using a coupled general circulation model. J Geophys Res Oceans 109:C09001. https://doi.org/10.1029/2003JC001974

Swapna P, Jyoti J, Krishnan R, Setti S, Griffies SM (2017) Multi-decadal weakening of Indian Ocean summer monsoon circulation induces an increasing northern Indian Ocean sea level. Geophys Res Lett. https://doi.org/10.1002/2017gl074706

Sweet WV, Park J (2014) From the extreme to the mean: acceleration and tipping points of coastal inundation from sea level rise. Earths Future 2(12):579–600

Thompson PR, Mitchum GT (2014) Coherent sea level variability on the North Atlantic western boundary. J Geophys Res Oceans 119(9):5676–5689

Thompson PR, Merrifield MA, Wells JR, Chang CM (2014) Wind-driven coastal sea level variability in the Northeast Pacific. J Clim 27(12):4733–4751

Thompson PR, Piecuch CG, Merrifield MA, McCreary JP, Firing E (2016) Forcing of recent decadal variability in the Equatorial and North Indian Ocean. J Geophys Res Oceans 121(9):6762–6778

Timmermann A, McGregor S, Jin FF (2010) wind effects on past and future regional sea level trends in the Southern Indo-Pacific. J Clim 23(16):4429–4437

Ting MF, Kushnir Y, Seager R, Li CH (2009) Forced and internal twentieth-century SST trends in the North Atlantic. J Clim 22(6):1469–1481

Tonini MH, Palma ED (2011) Barotropic response of north Patagonian gulfs in Argentina to tidal and wind forcing. Lat Am J Aquat Res 39(3):481–498

Tozuka T, Luo JJ, Masson S, Yamagata T (2007) Decadal modulations of the Indian Ocean dipole in the SINTEX-F1 coupled GCM. J Clim 20(13):2881–2894

Tozuka T, Yokoi T, Yamagata T (2010) A modeling study of interannual variations of the Seychelles Dome. J Geophys Res 115:C04005. https://doi.org/10.1029/2009JC005547

Trenary L, Han W (2012) Intraseasonal-to-interannual variability of South Indian Ocean sea level and thermocline: remote versus local forcing. J Phys Oceanogr 42:602–927

Trenary LL, Han W (2013) Local and remote forcing of decadal sea level and thermocline depth variability in the South Indian Ocean. J Geophys Res Oceans 118:381–398. https://doi.org/10.1029/2012JC008317

Trenberth KE, Hurrell JW (1994) Decadal atmosphere-ocean variations in the Pacific. Clim Dyn 9(6):303–319

Trenberth KE, Jones PD (2007) Observations: surface and atmospheric climate change. Climate change 2007: the physical science basis, pp 235–336

Tsimplis MN, Shaw AGP (2008) The forcing of mean sea level variability around Europe. Glob Planet Change 63(2–3):196–202

Tsimplis MN, Shaw AGP, Flather RA, Woolf DK (2006) The influence of the North Atlantic Oscillation on the sea-level around the northern European coasts reconsidered: the thermosteric effects. Philos Trans R Soc A 364(1841):845–856

Tsimplis MN, Calafat FM, Marcos M, Jorda G, Gomis D, Fenoglio-Marc L, Struglia MV, Josey SA, Chambers DP (2013) The effect of the NAO on sea level and on mass changes in the Mediterranean Sea. J Geophys Res Oceans 118(2):944–952

Unnikrishnan A, Shankar D (2007) Are sea-level-rise trends along the coasts of the north Indian Ocean consistent with global estimates? Glob Planet Change 57(3):301–307
Unnikrishnan AS, Nidheesh AG, Lengaigne M (2015) Sea-level-rise trends off the Indian coasts during the last two decades. Curr Sci India 108(5):966–971
Valle-Levinson A, Dutton A, Martin JB (2017) Spatial and temporal variability of sea level rise hot spots over the eastern United States. Geophys Res Lett 44(15):7876–7882
Vianna ML, Menezes VV (2013) Bidecadal sea level modes in the North and South Atlantic Oceans. Geophys Res Lett 40(22):5926–5931
Vimont DJ (2005) The contribution of the interannual ENSO cycle to the spatial pattern of decadal ENSO-like variability*. J Clim 18(12):2080–2092
Volkov DL (2019) Teleconnection between the Atlantic Meridional Overturning Circulation and Sea Level in the Mediterranean Sea. J Clim 32:935–955
Wahl T, Haigh ID, Woodworth PL, Albrecht F, Dillingh D, Jensen J, Nicholls RJ, Weisse R, Woppelmann G (2013) Observed mean sea level changes around the North Sea coastline from 1800 to present. Earth Sci Rev 124:51–67
Wahl T, Nilsen JEØ, Haigh I, Brown S (eds) (2018) Coastal sea levels, impacts and adaptation. Pages: VI, 334, 2018, ISBN 978-3-03842-847-3 (Pbk); ISBN 978-3-03842-848-0 (PDF); https://doi.org/10.3390/books978-3-03842-848-0 © 2018 by the authors; CC BY-NC-ND license
Wakelin SL, Woodworth PL, Flather RA, Williams JA (2003) Sea-level dependence on the NAO over the NW European Continental Shelf. Geophys Res Lett 30(7):1403. https://doi.org/10.1029/2003GL017041
Wallace JM, Gutzler DS (1981) Teleconnections in the Geopotential Height Field during the Northern Hemisphere Winter. Mon Weather Rev 109(4):784–812
Wang H, Liu KX, Wang AM, Feng JL, Fan WJ, Liu QL, Xu Y, Zhang ZJ (2018) Regional characteristics of the effects of the El Nio-Southern Oscillation on the sea level in the China Sea. Ocean Dyn 68(4–5):485–495
Webster PJ, Moore AM, Loschnigg JP, Leben RR (1999) Coupled ocean–atmosphere dynamics in the Indian Ocean during 1997–98. Nature 401(6751):356–360
White NJ, Haigh ID, Church JA, Koen T, Watson CS, Pritchard TR, Watson PJ, Burgette RJ, McInnes KL, You ZJ, Zhang XB, Tregoning P (2014) Australian sea levels-trends, regional variability and influencing factors. Earth Sci Rev 136:155–174
Wijffels S, Meyers G (2004) An intersection of oceanic waveguides: variability in the Indonesian throughflow region. J Phys Oceanogr 34(5):1232–1253
Wise A, Hughes CW, Polton JA (2018) Bathymetric influence on the coastal sea level response to ocean gyres at western boundaries. J Phys Oceanogr 48(12):2949–2964
Wolter K, Timlin MS (2011) El Niño/Southern Oscillation behaviour since 1871 as diagnosed in an extended multivariate ENSO index (MEI. ext). Int J Climatol 31(7):1074–1087
Wong PP, Losada IJ, Gattuso J-P, Hinkel J, Khattabi A, McInnes KL, Saito Y, Sallenger A (2014) Coastal systems and low-lying areas. In: Field CB, Barros VR, Dokken DJ, Mach KJ, Mastrandrea MD, Bilir TE, Chatterjee M, Ebi KL, Estrada YO, Genova RC, Girma B, Kissel ES, Levy AN, MacCracken S, Mastrandrea PR, White LL (eds) Climate change 2014: impacts, adaptation, and vulnerability. Part A: global and sectoral aspects. Contribution of working group II to the fifth assessment report of the intergovernmental panel on climate change. Cambridge University Press, Cambridge, pp 361–409
Woodworth PL, Pouvreau N, Woppelmann G (2010) The gyre-scale circulation of the North Atlantic and sea level at Brest. Ocean Sci 6(1):185–190
Woodworth PL, Maqueda MAM, Roussenov VM, Williams RG, Hughes CW (2014) Mean sea-level variability along the northeast American Atlantic coast and the roles of the wind and the overturning circulation. J Geophys Res Oceans 119(12):8916–8935
Woodworth PL, Hunter JR, Marcos M, Caldwell P, Menendez M, Haigh I (2016) Towards a global higher-frequency sea level dataset. Geosci Data J 3(2):50–59
Woodworth PL, Maqueda MAM, Gehrels WR, Roussenov VM, Williams RG, Hughes CW (2017) Variations in the difference between mean sea level measured either side of Cape Hatteras and their relation to the North Atlantic Oscillation. Clim Dyn 49(7–8):2451–2469
Woolf DK, Shaw AGP, Tsimplis MN (2003) The influence of the North Atlantic Oscillation on sea-level variability in the North Atlantic region. J Atmos Ocean Sci 9:145–167. https://doi.org/10.1080/10236730310001633803
Wu QR, Zhang XB, Church JA, Hu JY (2017) Variability and change of sea level and its components in the Indo-Pacific region during the altimetry era. J Geophys Res Oceans 122(3):1862–1881

Wunsch C, Stammer D (1997) Atmospheric loading and the oceanic "inverted barometer" effect. Rev Geophys 35(1):79–107
Wyrtki K (1975) Fluctuations of the dynamic topography in the Pacific Ocean. J Phys Oceanogr 5(3):450–459
Yan ZW, Tsimplis MN, Woolf D (2004) Analysis of the relationship between the North Atlantic oscillation and sea-level changes in northwest Europe. Int J Climatol 24(6):743–758
Yang J, Lin X, Wu D (2013) Wind-driven exchanges between two basins: some topographic and latitudinal effects. J Geophys Res Oceans 118:4585–4599
Yang Y, Xie SP, Wu LX, Kosaka Y, Lau NC, Vecchi GA (2015) Seasonality and predictability of the Indian Ocean DIPOLE MODE: ENSO forcing and internal variability. J Clim 28(20):8021–8036
Yasuda T, Sakurai K (2006) Interdecadal variability of the sea surface height around Japan. Geophys Res Lett 33:L01605. https://doi.org/10.1029/2005GL024920
Yeager S, Danabasoglu G (2014) The origins of late-twentieth-century variations in the large-scale North Atlantic circulation. J Clim 27(9):3222–3247
Yin JJ, Goddard PB (2013) Oceanic control of sea level rise patterns along the East Coast of the United States. Geophys Res Lett 40(20):5514–5520
Yin J, Schlesinger ME, Stouffer RJ (2009) Model projections of rapid sea-level rise on the northeast coast of the United States. Nat Geosci 2(4):262–266
Yokoi T, Tozuka T, Yamagata T (2008) Seasonal variation of the Seychelles Dome. J Clim 21(15):3740–3754
Yu W, Xiang B, Liu L, Liu N (2005) Understanding the origins of interannual thermocline variations in the tropical Indian Ocean. Geophys Res Lett 32:L24706. https://doi.org/10.1029/2005GL024327
Yu L, Gao YQ, Ottera OH (2016) The sensitivity of the Atlantic meridional overturning circulation to enhanced freshwater discharge along the entire, eastern and western coast of Greenland. Clim Dyn 46(5–6):1351–1369
Yuan DL, Li X, Wang Z, Li Y, Wang J, Yang Y, Hu XY, Tan SW, Zhou H, Wardana AK, Surinati D, Purwandana A, Ismail MFA, Avianto P, Dirhamsyah D, Arifin Z, von Storch JS (2018) Observed transport variations in the Maluku channel of the Indonesian seas associated with western boundary current changes. J Phys Oceanogr 48(8):1803–1813
Zhang XB, Church JA (2012) Sea level trends, interannual and decadal variability in the Pacific Ocean. Geophys Res Lett 39:L21701. https://doi.org/10.1029/2012GL053240
Zhang Y, Wallace JM, Battisti DS (1997) ENSO-like interdecadal variability: 1900–93. J Clim 10(5):1004–1020
Zhang R, Delworth TL, Sutton R, Hodson DLR, Dixon KW, Held IM, Kushnir Y, Marshall J, Ming Y, Msadek R, Robson J, Rosati AJ, Ting MF, Vecchi GA (2013) Have aerosols caused the observed atlantic multidecadal variability? J Atmos Sci 70(4):1135–1144
Zhang L, Han W, Li Y, Lovenduski N (2019) Variability of Sea Level and Upper-Ocean Heat Content in the Indian Ocean: Effects of Subtropical Indian Ocean Dipole and ENSO. J. Clim. https://doi.org/10.1175/JCLI-D-19-0167.1
Zhuang W, Qiu B, Du Y (2013) Low-frequency western Pacific Ocean sea level and circulation changes due to the connectivity of the Philippine Archipelago. J Geophys Res Oceans 118(12):6759–6773

Surveys in Geophysics (2019) 40:1543–1562
https://doi.org/10.1007/s10712-019-09571-7

Trends of Coastal Sea Level Between 1993 and 2015: Imprints of Atmospheric Forcing and Oceanic Chaos

Thierry Penduff[1] · **William Llovel**[2] · **Sally Close**[1] · **Ixetl Garcia-Gomez**[1] · **Stéphanie Leroux**[3]

Received: 13 December 2018 / Accepted: 10 September 2019 / Published online: 11 October 2019

Abstract
The observation and simulation of the variability of coastal sea level are impacted by various uncertainties, such as measurement errors and sampling biases, unresolved processes, and model and forcing biases. Ocean model simulations suggest that another uncertainty should be taken into account for the attribution of sea-level changes. Global ocean simulations indeed show that resolving mesoscale turbulence (even partly) promotes the emergence of low-frequency (LF) chaotic intrinsic variability (CIV) which causes substantial random fluctuations of sea level up to multiple decades in eddy-active regions of the world ocean. This random LFCIV is superimposed on the atmospherically forced (or simply "forced") fluctuations, which are directly controlled by the atmospheric variability. We show from a large ensemble of global oceanic hindcasts that this multi-decadal LFCIV leaves a substantial imprint on the long-term trends (1993–2015) of coastal sea level: over 17–20% of the global ocean coastal area, in particular along the coastlines of the northwestern Pacific and Indian Oceans, and around the Gulf of Mexico, random sea-level trends may blur their atmospherically forced counterpart, such that simulated (and potentially observed) coastal sea-level trends cannot be unambiguously attributed to atmospheric or anthropic causes. The steric and manometric sea-level change contributions of these uncertainties are discussed, suggesting that they mostly come from the manometric sea-level trends near the coasts.

Keywords Sea-level trend · Coastal ocean · Ensemble modeling · Intrinsic variability · Detection and attribution

✉ Thierry Penduff
Thierry.Penduff@cnrs.fr

[1] CNRS, IRD, Grenoble-INP, Institut des Géosciences de l'Environnement (IGE-MEOM), Université Grenoble Alpes, CS 40 700, Grenoble, France

[2] Laboratoire d'Études en Géophysique et Océanographie Spatiales (LEGOS)/CNRS/IRD/CNES/UPS, OMP, 14 Avenue Edouard Belin, 31400 Toulouse, France

[3] Ocean Next, 90 Chemin du Moulin, 38660 La Terrasse, Grenoble, France

1 Introduction and Context

1.1 Open Ocean and Coastal Sea-Level Evolution

The remote observation of sea level has reached an unprecedented level of accuracy and spatio-temporal coverage with the launch of the Topex/Poseidon altimeter satellite in 1992, followed by several successors up to the present day. Data from these successive missions have been inter-calibrated and merged into gridded fields, providing a continuous quasi-global monitoring of sea level at a spatio-temporal resolution ranging from the scale of mesoscale eddies to the global ocean, and from weekly timescales to more than two decades (Ablain et al. 2017; WCRP Global Sea Level Budget Group 2018). These data have yielded tremendous progress in physical oceanography for the description, understanding, modeling, and forecasting of the evolution of sea level (as well as related variables, including below the surface) over a wide range of scales.

Anthropogenic global warming is mostly being transferred to the ocean (Church et al. 2011; Rhein et al. 2013) and has a particularly clear imprint on global mean sea level, with a linear rise of 3 ± 0.4 mm year^{-1} since 1993 (Nerem et al. 2018). This globally averaged increase is mostly due to the thermal expansion of sea water (known as thermosteric sea-level contribution), and to the melting of ice sheets from Greenland and Antarctica and mountain glaciers. The continental freshwater input has a global imprint on global mean sea-level rise and is known as barystatic sea-level rise (Gregory et al. 2019). At regional scale, other physical processes are at play such as salinity changes that can compensate or enhance temperature changes (Llovel and Lee 2015), ocean dynamics and circulation (affecting seawater properties), atmospheric heat fluxes, precipitation, and evaporation (Church et al. 2013). The observed trends of sea level in fact have a complex and slowly varying spatial structure controlled by many oceanic and atmospheric processes, the geometry of ocean basins and coasts, the vertical displacements of the latter, etc. This means that in certain coastal regions, the observed sea-level trend can be substantially smaller or larger than its global average, raising in the latter case serious environmental concerns within highly populated coastal areas around the globe.

The monitoring, understanding, and mitigation of sea-level changes require accurate and stable measurements of open ocean and coastal sea level over long periods (see Marcos et al. 2019), together with numerical and process-oriented studies of the ocean dynamics. Another important issue also requires attention: it concerns the estimation of uncertainties associated with the measurements and processes of long-term sea-level variations, which are particularly large in coastal regions.

1.2 Low-Frequency Chaotic Intrinsic Variability (LFCIV) in the Ocean

One specific uncertainty about the low-frequency oceanic variations of regional sea level has been somewhat overlooked until recently and is now being recognized as substantial in the open ocean. Global ocean/sea-ice simulations, and especially those performed in the eddying regime (with grid spacings of 1/4° and finer) show that nonlinear ocean dynamics spontaneously produce a *Low-Frequency Chaotic Intrinsic Variability (LFCIV),* even without any low-frequency atmospheric forcing. Penduff et al. (2011) and Sérazin et al. (2015) have shown from long global ocean/sea-ice high-resolution simulations, repeatedly forced by the same annual cycle, that the LFCIV leaves a large imprint on sea level in many regions of the open ocean, and may explain in certain midlatitudes eddy-active regions up to 100% of the *full* interannual-to-decadal sea-level variability simulated in a *hindcast*.[1] This LFCIV questions the attribution to atmospheric or anthropic drivers of regional sea-level variability or long-term changes: the LFCIV in the turbulent ocean consists of a persistent low-frequency spatially-structured "noise" (with a random phase and an intermittent character) that may blur or even dominate the "signal" (i.e., the atmospherically *forced* variations) that is directly driven by the evolution of the external forcing. It is important to note that LFCIV is much weaker in non-turbulent ocean models[2] (Penduff et al. 2011), suggesting that the coarse-resolution ocean components of coupled climate models used for climate projections largely underestimate this source of uncertainty.

Sérazin et al. (2018) demonstrated that nonlinear interactions between mesoscale (turbulent, chaotic) eddies at subannual timescales spontaneously and persistently feed sea-level variability at longer timescales (i.e., decadal in the Southern Ocean).[3] This temporal inverse cascade is at work in 1/4° and 1/12° global ocean simulations; this process is basically equally strong under seasonal atmospheric forcing and under full reanalyzed forcing, and may thus be an important source of LFCIV in oceanic hindcasts.

1.3 Disentangling the LFCIV and the Atmospherically Forced Ocean Variability

The model studies mentioned above took advantage of pairs of simulations: a climatological run that isolates the LFCIV under repeated seasonal forcing, and a hindcast (driven by an atmospheric reanalysis including interannual variability) that simulates the "full" low-frequency ocean variability. These results suggested that the full ocean variability in this eddying regime might be a blend of LFCIV and atmospherically forced variability (Penduff et al. 2011). Pairs of simulations, however, are not sufficient to properly disentangle both components.

In order to separate both components, the OCCIPUT project produced a large ensemble (50 members) of 1/4°-resolution global ocean/sea-ice NEMO-based simulations (Penduff et al. 2014, Bessières et al. 2017). As explained in the next section, the integration strategy was designed to separate, quantify, and characterize the *forced* variability that is directly driven by the atmospheric variability, and the chaotic intrinsic variability (abbreviated as LFCIV for low frequencies) whose phase differs in each member, and which is independent of the atmospheric evolution.

Studies based on 1/4° and 1/12° climatological simulations have shown that the LFCIV not only has a strong imprint on sea level, but also on the Atlantic Meridional Overturning simulation (AMOC; see Hirschi et al. 2003; Grégorio et al. 2015). Analyses of the OCCIPUT ensemble have further demonstrated that the LFCIV, now diagnosed from ensemble statistics, remains comparable in amplitude to its counterpart in climatological runs (Leroux et al. 2018), and impacts other important climate-relevant oceanic variables: the interannual-to-decadal variability of ocean heat content (OHC) was, for example, shown to be dominantly chaotic in several regions of the global ocean (Sérazin et al. 2017).

[1] That is, a simulation driven by an atmospheric reanalysis, i.e., including the full range of timescales.

[2] Certain 1°-resolution simulations produce LFCIV, albeit with much weaker intensity (e.g., O'Kane et al. 2013).

[3] Although other processes such as large-scale baroclinic instability may also produce LFCIV (Huck et al. 2015).

While the globally integrated OHC interannual-to-decadal variability is almost totally forced by the atmosphere in the OCCIPUT ensemble, the LFCIV impact on certain large-scale climate-relevant oceanic indices can remain substantial at very large spatial scales. Zanna et al. (2018) thus showed that between 40 and 48°S, the LFCIV accounts for about 30% of the monthly to multi-decadal variability of the Meridional Heat Transport integrated over the whole range of longitudes.

1.4 Impacts of the Forcing and of the LFCIV on Long-Term Oceanic Trends

The chaotic component of the eddying ocean variability can exert a significant influence even at timescales of multiple decades and thus has an imprint on long-term trends. Sérazin et al. (2016) showed from a long climatological 1/4° NEMO simulation that multi-decadal LFCIV in strongly eddying regions may manifest itself as *random sea-level trends* over several decades. Sérazin et al. (2017) further showed that in such regions the 30-year trends of OHC fields, computed between 1980 and 2010 from the OCCIPUT ensemble, may also be mostly due to the oceanic chaos and not to the atmospheric (or anthropogenic) forcing. Llovel et al. (2018) showed that similar results hold for regional sea-level trends in many regions of the open ocean over the altimetric period (1993–2015).

These results strongly suggest that attributing low-frequency ocean variability, and certain long-term trends, to external (atmospheric, or anthropogenic) drivers is not straightforward in the eddying ocean. The ocean-driven multi-decadal LFCIV may manifest itself in certain finite-length time series as significant random trends. This raises important issues regarding the detection and attribution of oceanic changes in numerical simulations, and presumably in observations.

The aforementioned studies were, however, focused on the impacts of the LFCIV and atmospheric variability in the open ocean and gave no particular consideration to coastal regions. In this study, the OCCIPUT ensemble simulation is analyzed to disentangle the respective imprints of the atmospheric forcing and the low-frequency oceanic chaos on regional sea-level trends over the altimetric period (1993–2015), in particular in coastal regions. This paper addresses the following questions:

- How are the forced and random sea-level trends distributed in the coastal ocean?
- Where is the signal-to-noise ratio (ratio between the forced and random trends) largest and smallest in the coastal ocean?
- What are the contributions of steric and manometric (i.e., non-steric or bottom pressure changes, Gregory et al. 2019) effects in the forced and random sea-level trends in the coastal ocean?
- What are the implications of the above issues for the monitoring, analysis and forecast of sea-level trends?

Section 2 presents the OCCIPUT ensemble simulation, and the post-processing applied to the model outputs. Section 3 presents the respective imprints of forced and random sea-level trends, with a specific focus on coastal and shallow regions. Conclusions are given and discussed in the last section.

2 Post-processing of Model and Observed Data

The partners of the OCCIPUT project (OceaniC Chaos—ImPacts, strUcture, predicTability, Penduff et al. 2014) performed two kinds of 1/4° ocean/sea-ice simulations drawing on a common global model configuration based on NEMO3.5 (Bessières et al. 2017): the ensemble run presented above consists in 50 hindcasts with perturbed initial conditions, driven over 1960–2015 by the DFS5.2 forcing fields (based on ERA-Interim, see Dussin and Barnier 2013); a companion climatological simulation was repeatedly forced during 330 years by a climatological atmospheric annual cycle derived from DFS5.2. (This forcing is devoid of any low-frequency and trend.) The integration strategy is detailed in Leroux et al. (2018) and is summarized below.

2.1 Ensemble Simulation Strategy

All members of the ensemble simulation were initialized using the final state of a common 21-year spin-up. We then introduced slight stochastic perturbations within each ensemble member during 1960 (see Brankart 2013 and Bessières et al. 2017), switched off these perturbations at the end of 1960, and resumed the integration of the 50 members until 2015 using the same fully varying DFS5.2 forcing. Nonlinear ocean dynamics yield an initial growth of incipient perturbations, i.e., of chaotic mesoscale anomalies; the subsequent ensemble spread then approximately saturates in amplitude within a few months or years depending on the region (see Zanna et al. 2018). Nonlinear processes (e.g., eddy–eddy interactions, subsequent spatial and temporal inverse cascades) then contribute to extend the range of chaotic fluctuations toward lower wavenumbers and frequencies, hence feeding the LFCIV and larger structures which emerge around the ensemble mean within each member with a random phase. As shown in Sérazin et al. (2016) under seasonal forcing, and in Sérazin et al. (2017) and in Llovel et al. (2018) in the OCCIPUT ensemble, the LFCIV exerts an influence on decadal and longer periods as the OCCIPUT simulation proceeds, and leaves regional imprints on long-term trends in the form of random trends within each member. The present paper will assess whether (coastal) sea-level trends are also impacted by this random signal.

2.2 Computing Regional Sea-Level Trends

The full details of the post-processing are presented in Llovel et al. (2018) and summarized below. The diagnostics performed in this study started in 1993, i.e., after $21+34=55$ years of dynamical adjustment within each member. At every grid point of each ensemble member, we first compute the linear trend of sea level over the 23-year period 1993–2015. The imprint of the model numerical drift on sea-level trends is then estimated from the climatological run in a similar way: the drift-related linear sea-level trend is computed at every grid point from the climatological run after 55 years of adjustment, i.e., between years 56 and 78. This field is removed from the trends of the 50 ensemble members to retain the geophysical sea-level trend signals. Finally, we subtract the global average from these 50 sea-level trend fields (this being necessary in Boussinesq ocean models, see Greatbatch 1994), yielding 50 estimates of regional sea-level trends over 1993–2015, corrected for the model drift and relative to their global average. These processing steps yield a remarkably small root-mean-square difference between observed and ensemble mean sea-level trends (1.57 mm/year over the period 1993–2015, see Llovel et al. 2018).

Consistently with the above, steric sea-level fields are calculated from the monthly 3-dimensional temperature and salinity fields archived from the 50 ensemble members (between 1993 and 2015) at every grid point. We estimate the spurious drift of 3-D temperature and salinity from the climatological run (between years 56 and 78), remove this drift from the 3-D temperature and salinity fields from the 50 members, compute the full-depth steric sea-level trend fields, and finally remove their respective global averages. This yields 50 regional steric sea-level trend fields, corrected for the model drift and relative to their global average. Manometric sea-level trends are computed from each ensemble member as the difference between sea-level trends and full-depth steric sea-level trends. Note that manometric sea-level trends refer to the ocean bottom pressure term in regional sea-level changes (see Gregory et al. 2019 for more details).

The observed regional sea-level trend field is calculated over the same 1993–2015 period from the Climate Change Initiative (CCI, Legeais et al. 2018) dataset derived from several altimeter missions. The observed regional sea-level trend field is finally obtained by removing the global average from the latter field and used to assess the realism of the ensemble simulation.

2.3 Ensemble Statistics: Forced and Random Trends

The ensemble standard deviation (ESTD) of any oceanic field simulated with this initial perturbation ensemble modeling strategy quantifies the imprint of the chaotic variability on this field (i.e., the width of the ensemble spread). The ensemble mean (EMEAN) of any field provides an estimate of the atmospherically forced signal, since all members were driven by the same atmospheric forcing. For the purpose of this study, we estimated the forced sea-level trend (due to external influences, i.e., atmospheric variability and trend, anthropogenic influences, etc.) by the ensemble mean of the 50 sea-level trend maps, and the imprint of low-frequency chaotic variability by the ensemble standard deviation of these maps (which will quantify the amplitude of random trends in the following). These forced and random signals are estimated for the total, steric, and manometric regional sea-level trends. Using the Lilliefors test, we verified that local ensemble distributions of total and steric sea-level trend fields are Gaussian at the 95% significance level over 93% of the global ocean area. The use of EMEANs and ESTDs to estimate the forced and random trends is therefore adequate for our analysis.

3 Results from the 1/4° OCCIPUT Ensemble Simulation

Section 3.1 describes and compares the forced and random sea-level trends in the open ocean and summarizes the more detailed analysis presented by Llovel et al. (2018). The focus is put on coastal regions in the following sections.

3.1 Forced and Random Regional Sea-Level Trends in the Open Ocean

Figure 1a, b shows the regional trends of sea level over the period 1993–2015 from altimeter observations and from a randomly picked OCCIPUT member (member #1), respectively. While some discrepancies are visible in certain regions (in particular in the North Atlantic western Subpolar Gyre), the distribution and magnitude of regional sea-level trends are quite well reproduced by the model: Llovel et al. (2018) show that the

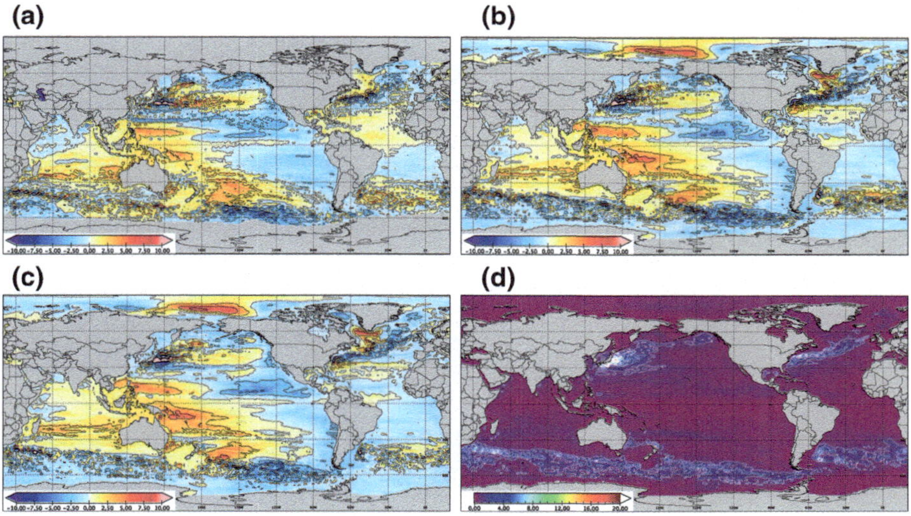

Fig. 1 1993–2015 regional sea-level trends from the CCI observational product (**a**) and from the OCCIPUT ensemble simulation: ensemble member #1 (**b**), forced trends (**c**, ensemble mean), and random trends (**d**, ensemble standard deviation)

root-mean-square difference between OCCIPUT and observed trends is smaller than any simulation considered in Griffies et al. (2014). Large-scale patterns of regional sea-level trends range between roughly -3 and $+3$ mm/year, and are found at similar locations in the model and the real ocean: large positive trends throughout most of the western Pacific and within the subtropical gyres of the South Indian, South Atlantic, and North Atlantic oceans; large negative trends over most of the eastern and southern Pacific, and along the Gulf Stream path.

We now take advantage of the information from the 50 members and split the simulated sea-level trends into their forced (EMEAN, Fig. 1c) and random (ESTD, Fig. 1d) components. The main large-scale patterns of regional sea-level trends simulated in member #1 happen to belong to the forced component over many regions (compare panels b and c); there indeed, random trends (panel d) remain smaller than about 1 mm/year, i.e., smaller than forced trends. The relative contributions of forced and random trends should, however, be compared more quantitatively to identify regions where the "signal," associated with the atmospheric fluctuations and climate change, can be considered as significantly larger than the "noise," associated with LFCIV.

We define at every grid point a signal-to-noise ratio (SNR) as the ratio of the absolute value of the forced sea-level trend to the random sea-level trend, respectively, given by the EMEAN and ESTD of local trends. The larger the SNR, the more confidently one can attribute the regional sea-level trend found in one particular realization (i.e., one ensemble member picked randomly) to the external forcing, whether it be natural atmospheric variability or anthropogenic influences. Conversely, the smaller the SNR the more the low-frequency chaotic variability impacts the sea-level trends in a given realization, with a smaller impact of external sources. As Sérazin et al. (2017, their section 4), we consider that one may attribute the regional trend found in a given realization to the external forcing where $SNR > 2$, while one cannot unambiguously do so

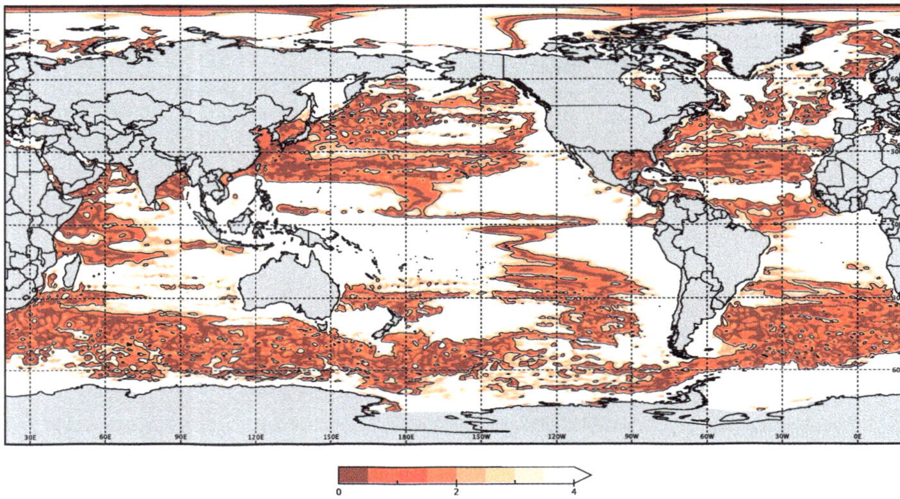

Fig. 2 Ratio between the forced and random 1993–2015 regional sea-level trends (i.e., ensemble mean divided by the ensemble standard deviation, or signal-to-noise ratio) deduced from the OCCIPUT ensemble simulation. Sea-level trends found in a single member cannot be unambiguously attributed to the atmospheric forcing (95% confidence interval) in regions enclosed by the SNR = 2 isocontour (black)

where SNR < 2 (at the 95% confidence level). In other words, regional sea-level trends in regions where SNR < 2 may just be random since they emerge from the LFCIV.

Figure 2 shows the global distribution of the sea-level trend SNR, and the black contour encircles regions where SNR < 2. Large forced trends are generally associated with large SNRs in vast areas of the intertropical Pacific, within most of the Eastern Pacific and Arctic oceans. This is no longer the case in many other parts of the global ocean: SNR < 2 over most of the South Atlantic (25–55°S), central and tropical parts of the North Atlantic (15–45°N, 0–10°N), western North Pacific (18–50°N, west of 180°W), western Indian ocean (west of 60°E, from 15°S to the northern boundary), and almost everywhere in the Antarctic Circumpolar Current (except in the South Pacific sector). There, our results suggest that regional sea-level trends are not certainly driven by external (atmospheric or anthropogenic) causes, but may be random since they are influenced by the intrinsic oceanic "noise" (LFCIV). In other words, sea-level trends in such regions are affected by a sizeable uncertainty due to chaotic ocean dynamics.

3.2 Forced and Random Regional Sea-Level Trends in Coastal Regions

Figure 2 shows that the SNR increases and passes the SNR = 2 threshold when approaching the coast in several regions, such as around Alaska, Antarctica, Australia and all islands located north of it, around all islands from Cuba to the lesser Antilles, or along the west coasts of America, Europe, and North Africa. Figure 3d shows that the coasts surrounding the southern tip of Africa (SA region) seem to be shielded from the very small SNR values found offshore within the strongly chaotic Agulhas Retroflexion. Along other coastlines, however, the opposite holds: the other panels of Fig. 3 show that over large coastal parts of the northwestern Pacific (NWP), western Indian

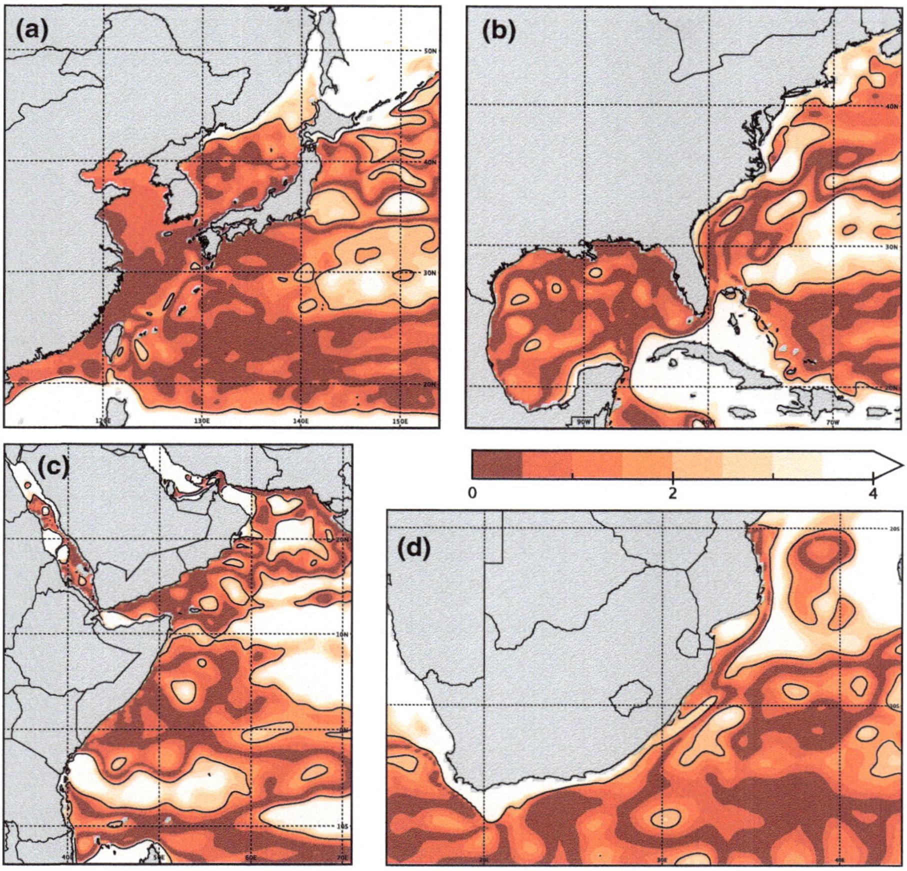

Fig. 3 Zooms of Fig. 2 in the Northwest Pacific (**a**), the Northwest Atlantic (**b**), the Northwest Indian (**c**), and around the south of Africa

(WI), Gulf of Mexico, and US east coast (MEX), the SNR remains smaller than 2 and may even fall below 0.5 locally. In the latter coastal regions, the modeled sea-level trends may thus be random and cannot be unambiguously attributed to the atmospheric (and anthropogenic) forcing.

We now try to identify generic differences between the open ocean and coastal regions in terms of forced and random sea-level trends (and/or their ratio, SNR). We will focus on five specific domains: the global ocean, and the four domains shown in Fig. 3. We will show the distributions of forced trends, random trends, and SNR considering all grid points of each specific domain, then considering two subregions within each specific domain: the coastal domain (CD) will include all grid points located less than 25 km away from the coastline, whether they be deep or shallow. In a complementary way, the shallow domain (SD) will include all grid points where depth is shallower than 25 m, whether they be close to or far away from the coasts.

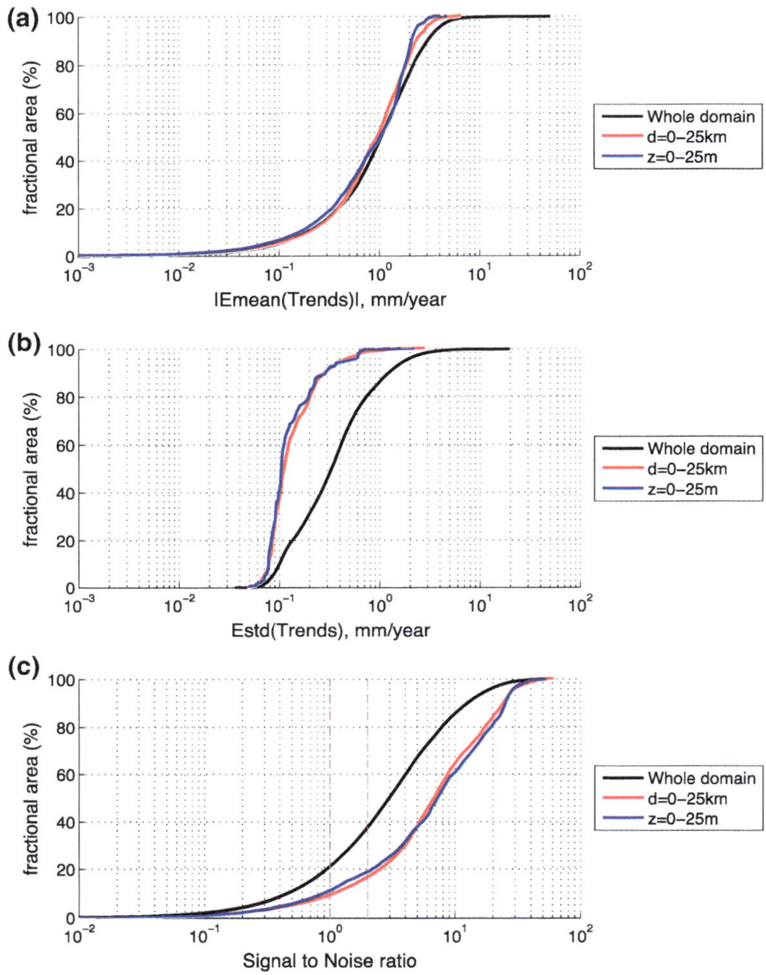

Fig. 4 Cumulative fractional area of the global ocean as a function of: **a** absolute value of the forced sea-level trends; **b** random sea-level trends; **c** local signal-to-noise ratio shown in Fig. 2. Black lines show the results for all model points, red lines for model points located within 0–25 km from the coasts, blue lines for model points located in regions shallower than 25 m

3.2.1 Scale of the global ocean

Let us first consider the global ocean domain. We sort in increasing order the signals (i.e., the absolute value of the forced sea-level trends) simulated at each grid point of the domain; we accumulate the areas of the corresponding grid points and express the result as a fraction (in %) of the total area of the domain. This result is shown in black in Fig. 4a (the fractional area is not shown for very small values of the signal): this line indicates for instance that the absolute value of forced sea-level trends is smaller than 0.4 mm/year over 20% of the global ocean area, smaller than 1 mm/year (the median) over half of it, larger than 3 mm/year over 10% of it, and does not exceed 50 mm/year anywhere. The same computation is done in the CD and SD subregions of the global ocean, and the results are shown in red and blue in the same figure. The differences between these 3 lines are generally small (median values are around 1 mm/year in the 3 regions), except for the largest signals: the signal exceeds 3 mm/year within only 5% of the area of CD, and barely anywhere in SD. We thus conclude that at global scale, the distribution of forced sea-level trends in shallow and coastal regions is comparable to their counterparts in the open ocean, except for extreme (and rare) signals which are much smaller near the coast.

The same three computations are repeated in the global ocean, substituting the signal with the noise (i.e., random trends or ensemble standard deviation). Figure 4b shows that noise values range between about 0.035 and 20 mm/year at global scale, with a median of 0.3–0.4 mm/year, that is 30–40% of the median of the signal. Unlike the signal however, the noise substantially decreases (by a factor of about 3 for the median, 10 for the maximum) when focusing on shallow (SD) and coastal (CD) domains. This reduction might be explained by one or several of the following hypotheses: the mesoscale processes that emerge and may locally feed LFCIV may be marginally resolved by the model since internal deformation radii are smaller in shallow regions (see, e.g., Hallberg 2013); the time-scales of the LFCIV generated in these regions may not reach multiple decades and have less imprint on long-term trends; the multi-decadal LFCIV present in the neighboring open ocean may be high-pass filtered when approaching the coasts and shallow waters. Other hypotheses might exist, and further work is required to explain these features, which nevertheless are quite robust according to Fig. 4b.

Figure 4c does not show the ratio of the lines in the previous two panels, but presents the result of the binning described above applied to local SNR values within the global ocean, and its CD and SD subdomains. The black line shows that sea-level trends can be considered to be dominantly driven by the atmosphere over more than half (62%) of the global open ocean area (where SNR > 2). Colored lines show that regional sea-level trends in coastal and shallow parts of the global ocean are characterized by larger SNR values than in the open ocean: the SNR remains larger than 2 in about 80–83% of their area; the coastal areas are also those where the largest values of the SNR may be found at global scale.

These model results conversely show that within 17–20% of the coastal and shallow areas of the global ocean, the 1993–2015 sea-level trends are likely to be random because of LFCIV and are not certainly forced by external drivers. This proportion decreases from 38 to 17–20% from the open ocean to the shallow and coastal domains because the imprint of LFCIV on sea-level trends significantly decreases there. In other words, the model suggests that the attribution of observed sea-level trends (from altimetry or from tide gauges) to non-oceanic sources is questionable over 38% of the global ocean area, and over about one-fifth of the coastal and shallow water area. The implications of these results are further discussed in the last section of this paper.

3.2.2 Zoom on Four Specific Regions

We now describe in more detail the respective imprints of the external forcing and of the oceanic chaos on sea-level trends in the four regional domains shown in Fig. 3, and in their coastal (CD) and shallow (SD) parts.

We saw that coastal SNR values tend to remain small in the region surrounding the Southern tip of Africa (SA, Fig. 3d). Figure 5d shows that the SNR changes from the whole SA domain to its shallow and coastal parts are comparable to those described at

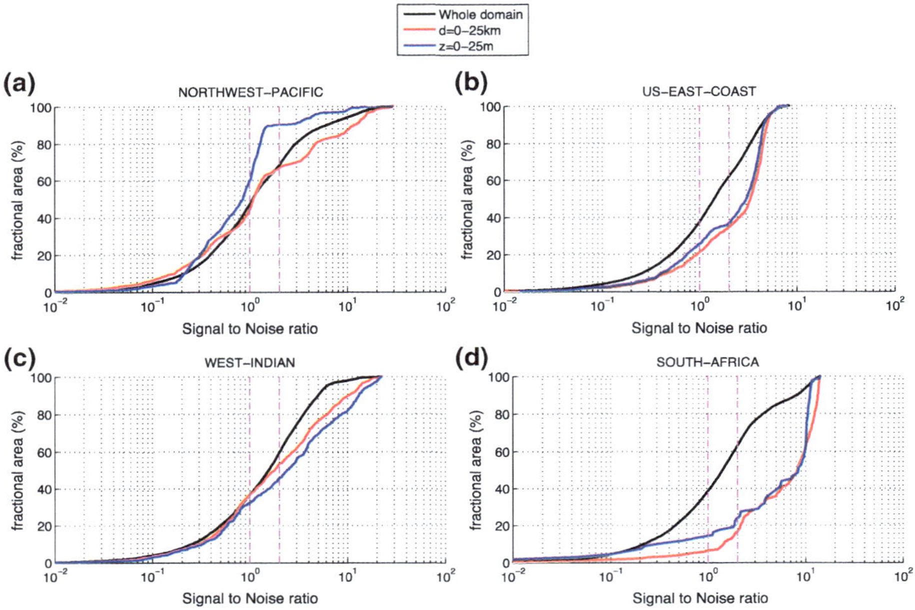

Fig. 5 Same as Fig. 4c for the four domains shown in Fig. 3 (with identically laid out panels)

global scale (Fig. 4c): while SNR values are smaller than 2 over most (62%) of the SA full domain, this proportion sharply decreases (17–23%) near the coasts and in shallow areas, except along the northeastern coasts of South Africa and the southeastern coast of Mozambique where the SNR remains smaller than 2 (and even less locally, see Fig. 3d). As in the global ocean, the decrease of SNR values in the coastal and shallow areas of the SA domain is essentially due to a sixfold decrease of the median (and more than a tenfold decrease of the maximum) of the LFCIV-induced noise, while the median of the signal remains very close to 1 mm/year (not shown). These resemblances suggest that in several parts of the global ocean, approaching the coastal and shallow oceans has comparable impacts on the forced and random parts of sea-level trends as in the SA region.

Figure 5b resembles Fig. 5d: within the whole region shown in Fig. 3b, SNR values are smaller than 2 over 62% of model grid points, and over substantially less (36–38%) grid points in its coastal and shallow parts, with a strong spatial inhomogeneity: coastal sea-level trends can be attributed to the forcing along most of US Atlantic coast (SNR > 2 from around Titusville, FL, to Nova Scotia at least) and along the coasts of the Caribbean islands. In contrast, our results suggest that coastal sea-level trends may be random over most of the Gulf of Mexico coastline (from southwest Florida to the southernmost point of the Gulf), with SNR values remaining even smaller than 0.5 everywhere between Pensacola, FL, to Caillou Bay, LO.

The structure of the forced and random trends is much more homogeneous along the coasts of the northwestern Pacific (NWP) domain, host of the strongly turbulent Kuroshio. Here as well, the SNR remains below 2 within most (about 68%) of its total area. In contrast with the other regions considered, however, this fractional area remains as large when only coastal regions are considered, and even increases (90%) in the shallow parts of the NWP domain. Figure 3a further shows that the sea-level trend SNR

Table 1 Main statistics (last 3 lines) of total, steric, and manometric sea-level trends (last three columns) over the global ocean: whole domain (black), grid points within 25 km of the coasts (red), grid points with depth shallower than 25 m (blue)

Global Ocean: Whole / Coastal / Shallow	Total sea level trends			Steric sea level trends			Manometric sea level trends		
	Whole	Coastal	Shallow	Whole	Coastal	Shallow	Whole	Coastal	Shallow
Median of the Signal Absolute value (Forced sea level trends, mm/yr)	1.0	1.0	1.0	1.0	0.9	0.9	0.1	0.4	1.0
Median of the Noise (Random sea level trends, mm/yr)	0.3	0.1	0.1	0.3	0.045	0.025	0.05	0.09	0.1
Fractional area where S/R < 2	38%	17%	20%	37%	5%	1%	56%	30%	14%

remains smaller than 2 (and becomes locally much smaller) almost everywhere along the continental and island coastlines located within the East China Sea, Yellow Sea, and Japan Sea, all the way between the cities of Haikou (South China) and Vladivostok, including most Japanese coastlines (except southern and northeastern Hokkaido). Further analysis in the NWP region (not shown) shows that the median forced sea-level trends now decrease by a factor 4–6 near the coasts and in shallow waters compared to the open ocean, while the imprint of LFCIV on these trends only decreases by a factor of 3, yielding these small SNR values over most of the coasts in this area. The NWP domain is therefore the region of the global ocean where attributing coastal sea-level trends to external drivers is the most questionable.

3.3 Steric and Manometric Contributions to the Coastal Sea-Level Trend Components

The total regional sea-level trends discussed above may be split in two components: steric trends result from the thermal expansion and haline contraction of seawater, and manometric (i.e., non-steric) sea-level trends come from local changes in the mass of seawater at each location. Note that the trends in the melting rate of glaciers and ice sheets are not taken into account in these simulations.

In this section, we investigate the respective imprints of steric and manometric components on the forced and random trends over the global ocean area, and in its shallow (SD), and coastal (CD) parts. Table 1 summarizes for each of these three domains the forced part, the random part, and the SNR of the total, steric and manometric regional sea-level trends. The last three lines in Table 1 are derived from the counterparts of Fig. 4 drawn for the steric and manometric sea-level trends (not shown); colors correspond to the whole global ocean, its coastal and shallow parts.

3.3.1 Steric and Manometric Coastal Sea-Level Trends: Forced Part

The second line in Table 1 concerns the median of the absolute value of the signal (i.e., of the forced trends). In Fig. 4a, this median corresponds to the abscissae where each line reaches the 50% fractional area. As explained in the previous section, the median absolute values of the forced total sea-level trends are basically the same over the open ocean, the coastal and shallow domains (close to 1 mm/year, see line 2, column 2). The next two columns of line 2 further indicate that forced steric trends are also typically close to 1 mm/year in absolute value over these 3 domains, but that forced manometric trends (last column) are 4 and 10 times stronger in the coastal and shallow domains, respectively.

This strong increase of forced manometric trends toward the coast is consistent with several studies using forced ocean circulation models (Griffies and Greatbatch 2012) and coupled climate models (Landerer et al. 2007a, b; Yin et al. 2009, 2010) at coarse resolution. Sea-level projections in the late twenty-first century show an increase of bottom pressure loading along shelves and marginal seas related to the expansion of open ocean water due to the increased concentration of greenhouse gases in the atmosphere. Such a forced increase of ocean heat content in the open ocean may create a steric sea-level gradient next to the continental shelf and push water masses toward the coast at the shelf break. As the deep open ocean can absorb more heat than shallower coastal regions, steric sea-level trends can be greater away from the coastal zone. Therefore, the steric sea-level change yields a dynamic topography gradient near the continental shelf areas, with lower dynamic topography on the shelves than in the open oceans. Dynamic topography gradients may then locally modify ocean currents through dynamical adjustments. Therefore, open ocean water is expected to progressively penetrate on the shelves, increase mass and therefore ocean bottom pressure in the coastal areas, yielding this enhanced forced manometric sea-level trend near the coasts.

3.3.2 Steric and Manometric Coastal Sea-Level Trends: Random Part

The third line in Table 1 concerns the median of the noise (random trends). In Fig. 4b, this median corresponds to the abscissae where each line reaches 50% fractional area. As mentioned in Sect. 3.2.1, the median amplitude of random total sea-level trends is close to 0.3 mm/year over the whole global ocean area, i.e., about 30% of the typical forced signal. Unlike the forced (total and steric) sea-level trends which were similar in the whole, coastal and shallow regions, typical values of their random counterparts drop by 70–99% when only coastal and shallow domains are considered (columns 2 and 3, line 3).

As was noted for its forced counterpart, the manometric random sea-level trend median increases (roughly doubles) from the open ocean to its coastal and shallow parts, and gets similar as the total random trend median (about 0.1 mm/year). This amplification toward the coasts of manometric trends thus concerns both the forced and random components, unlike the steric trends whose medians remain unchanged (forced component) or sharply drop (random component). The dynamical hypotheses presented in Sect. 3.3.1 to explain the coastal amplification of forced manometric trends are likely to hold for their random counterparts.

3.3.3 Steric and Manometric Coastal Sea-Level Trends: Signal-to-Noise Ratio

The reader might have noted that adding the medians of steric and manometric sea-level trends (columns 3 and 4 in lines 2 or 3) does not yield the median of total sea-level trends (column 2). Indeed, the fractional areas corresponding to steric and manometric components are computed independently after sorting their values by increasing order. In other words, the values given in rows 2 and 3 of Table 1 do not take into account the possibility of local compensations between steric and manometric signals. These possible compensations are now taken into account: the last line of the table gives the fraction of the area of the global ocean (full, coastal, and shallow domains) where the *local* signal-to-noise ratios (SNR) of total, steric, and manometric sea-level trends are smaller than 2. This is the percentage of the area where regional trends cannot be unambiguously attributed to external causes (95% confidence), but may be due to the LFCIV.

As mentioned earlier, attributing total sea-level trends to the atmospheric forcing is questionable over 38% of the global ocean area; this fraction decreases to 17–20% in its coastal and shallow parts (line 4, column 2). The changes of the forced and random parts of the steric and manometric signals when approaching the coast (described above separately) combine together when considering them locally, and yield a simpler picture in terms of SNR: the fractional area over which the oceanic LFCIV may affect the (steric, manometric, and total) sea-level trends consistently decrease when switching from the global ocean to its coastal and shallow parts. In the coastal regions located within 25 km of the coasts, the external forcing cannot be certainly held as the main driver of total sea-level trends over 17% of the oceanic area. This area proportion is slightly larger (30%) for manometric sea-level trends, and clearly smaller for steric sea-level trends (5%).

In summary, our results show that sea-level trends in coastal regions are somewhat shielded from the LFCIV, whose relative contribution compared to the forced signal is smaller than in the open ocean. The attribution of coastal sea-level trends to external forcing (atmospheric fluctuations, anthropogenic forcing) is thus valid over most of the globe, but requires care in regions where the SNR approaches 2, and may be invalid where SNR values drop below this level (i.e., within 17–20% of the global ocean coastal area). The model suggests that sea-level trends in such regions may be random since they are substantially impacted by the ocean-driven low-frequency chaotic variability.

4 Conclusions and Discussion

Sea-level trends have a complex distribution along the coasts, where the ongoing global mean sea-level rise can be either enhanced or reduced. The accurate monitoring and understanding of these coastal trends requires detailed analyses of their causes, and of the associated uncertainties. In this paper, we investigated the contributions of two drivers of coastal sea-level trends over the altimetric period (1993–2015): the trends driven by the atmospheric evolution (of natural or anthropic origin), and the trends driven by the oceanic Low-Frequency Chaotic Intrinsic Variability (LFCIV). The latter driver is substantial when mesoscale eddies are (even partly) resolved, and should be considered as a source of uncertainty for attributing coastal sea-level trends to external drivers: the LFCIV indeed induces random fluctuations on sea-level trends and other oceanic fields.

Using the outputs of a large ensemble of 1/4° global oceanic hindcasts, we showed that, in certain coastal areas, this "noise" may blur the detection of regional sea-level trends.

Our results do not concern (and do not question the anthropic origin of) the globally averaged 1993–2015 sea-level trend, which was removed from our datasets: they concern the regional contrasts of sea-level trends near the coasts, specifically their external or internal origin. Our main results may be summarized as follows:

- Coastal sea-level trends are not significantly impacted by the ocean-driven multi-decadal LFCIV over most (80–83%) of the global ocean area located less than 25 km away from the coasts. They may be attributed to non-oceanic (atmospheric or anthropic) causes with 95% confidence level.
- However, coastal sea-level trends cannot be unambiguously attributed to atmospheric drivers over the remaining 17–20% of the global ocean coastal area. There, the ocean-driven multi-decadal LFCIV is smaller than in the open ocean, but still induces random sea-level trends that represent more than half of the externally driven counterpart, and may blur the detection of the latter.
- These latter regions are inhomogeneously distributed around the globe and sit near strong eddy-active regions (Fig. 3). They include in particular all island and continental coastlines between 142°E and the Asian coast between 20 and 42°N, most of the Gulf of Mexico coastline, and several parts of the northwestern Indian Ocean coastlines.
- Steric sea-level trends are impacted by LFCIV over only 5% of the global ocean coastal area; manometric sea-level trends are impacted by LFCIV over a larger fraction (30%) of it.

These results suggest that the presently available 23-year altimeter record is not long enough to rigorously assess the externally forced character of sea-level trends along 17–20% of the coastlines. It is nevertheless likely that a longer altimetric record will progressively increase the percentage of coastal areas where the LFCIV does not perturb the attribution of sea-level changes. In this context, an interesting perspective of this study would be to assess the contribution of atmospherically forced and internally generated sea-level trends in coastal regions where (longer) tide gauge records are available.

The members of this ensemble simulation represent the observed distribution of regional sea-level trends with a very good degree of accuracy in the open ocean (as quantified in Llovel et al. 2018), except in a few areas such as the western Subpolar Gyre of the North Atlantic. As for any model-based study however, our results should be considered with caution. The fidelity of 1/4° simulations may decrease from the open ocean toward the coasts: certain coastal processes are either absent from our model (e.g., tides, surface gravity waves, etc.), or may be marginally resolved (mesoscale turbulence, edge waves, coastal wind drop-off, certain upwellings, etc.) since depth, hence the internal Rossby radii and the model effective resolution, generally decrease when approaching the coasts. Future investigations of forced and random coastal sea-level trends could utilize for instance higher resolution ensembles of regional coastal simulations (with adequate lateral forcing), and ideally ensembles gathering different types of models. The present study may in any case be seen as a proof of concept: it illustrates at least the potential of ensemble-based modeling strategies for disentangling internal and external sources of oceanic fluctuations over a wide range of scales.

As noted in Sect. 1.2, the ocean-driven LFCIV, and therefore random sea-level trends, are largely underestimated in laminar ocean simulations forced by the atmosphere, and presumably also in ocean–atmosphere coupled simulations where the oceanic mesoscale is absent. In other words, the LFCIV is an oceanic driver of coastal sea-level changes in the turbulent regime, which may compete with the external drivers examined in Woodworth et al. (2019) and with the ocean–atmosphere coupled modes presented by Han et al. (2019). More importantly, the random character of LFCIV suggests that it actually constitutes a source of uncertainty for the detection and attribution of coastal sea-level trends, in addition to those simulated by climate models (Carson et al. 2019), and that these uncertainties should also be taken into account for coastal sea-level projections (see Jevrejeva et al. 2019).

Fasullo and Nerem (2018) and Hamlington et al. (2019) used ocean–atmosphere coupled ensemble simulations (with a non-eddying ocean component) to extract the "internal" and "forced" sea-level trends. In their context however, (1) "internal" refers to the variability (e.g., ENSO, PDO, etc.) and trends that emerge from the air-sea coupling and in the turbulent atmosphere, whose phase are essentially random and differ among ensemble members; (2) and "forced" refers to the response of the coupled system to the sole anthropogenic forcing (greenhouse gases concentration increase in particular).

In our study, we have used an ocean-only ensemble simulation (with an eddying ocean model) driven by a prescribed atmospheric variability. As explained in Sérazin et al. (2017, their introduction) and in Penduff et al. (2018), this prescription of the atmospheric variability is mandatory to split the oceanic variability into its atmospherically forced component, and its intrinsic/chaotic variability that spontaneously arises in the turbulent ocean. In other words, what we called the "forced" ocean variability and trends are those driven by the atmospheric forcing (including the anthropogenic trends it contains), and what we called the LFCIV and the random trends emerge in the ocean from nonlinear processes without coupling to the atmosphere. It is important to recall, as mentioned in Sect. 1.2, that this oceanic LFCIV is very small in non-eddying ocean models (Penduff et al. 2011; Grégorio et al. 2015): Fasullo and Nerem (2018) and Hamlington et al. (2019)'s coupled simulations performed with a non-eddying ocean are thus certainly underestimating this chaotic variability that our eddying ocean model generates. In other words, the processes and signals that we have disentangled are distinct from those considered in the latter two studies.

Characterizing the imprints of LFCIV on, e.g., sea-level trends in a global eddying 50-member ensemble simulation coupled to the atmosphere would not only require huge computational resources; it would also require simulation and analysis strategies allowing to separate intrinsic and forced signals within two fluids in complex interaction, and such strategies are not clear yet. An intermediate step could consist of forcing atmospheric model ensembles with sea-surface temperature (or upper ocean heat content) fields simulated in several OCCIPUT members. This would help to answer important but open questions about the atmospheric response to random trends of the upper ocean heat content (Sérazin et al. 2017), which contribute to the steric sea-level trends discussed here. These ambitious modeling and physical objectives are left for the future.

Acknowledgements This work is a contribution to the OCCIPUT and PIRATE projects. PIRATE (https://sealevel.jpl.nasa.gov/science/ostscienceteam/scientistlinks/scientificinvestigations2017/penduff/) is funded by CNES through the Ocean Surface Topography Science Team (OST-ST). OCCIPUT (https://meom-group.github.io/projects/occiput/) was funded by ANR through contract ANR-13-BS06-0007-01. This work was also supported by the French national program LEFE/INSU and has received funding from the European Union Horizon 2020 research and innovation program under grant agreement No 633211. It is also part of the Copernicus Marine Environment Monitoring Service (CMEMS) GLO-HR project; CMEMS is implemented by Mercator Ocean International in the framework of a delegation agreement with the European Union. We acknowledge that the results of this research have been achieved using the PRACE Research Infrastructure resource CURIE based in France at TGCC. William Llovel was supported by C3S program, "Louis Gentil–Jacques Bourcart" fellowship from the French Académie des Sciences and by the OVALIE project from ESA Living Planet Fellowship fundings. The CCI product is freely available at http://www.esa-sealevel-cci.org/. The model dataset used for this study is freely available on http://zenodo.org (http://doi.org/10.5281/zenodo.1487983). We would like to thank two anonymous reviewers for their constructive comments and helpful suggestions.

References

Ablain M, Legeais JF, Prandi P, Marcos M, Fenoglio-Marc L, Dieng HB, Benveniste J, Cazenave A (2017) Satellite altimetry-based sea level at global and regional scales. Surv Geophys 38:7–31. https://doi.org/10.1007/s10712-016-9389-8

Bessières L, Leroux S, Brankart J-M, Molines J-M, Moine M-P, Bouttier P-A, Penduff T, Terray L, Barnier B, Sérazin G (2017) Development of a probabilistic ocean modelling system based on NEMO 3.5: application at eddying resolution. Geosci Model Dev 10:1091–1106. https://doi.org/10.5194/gmd-10-1091-2017

Brankart J-M (2013) Impact of uncertainties in the horizontal density gradient upon low resolution global ocean modelling. Ocean Model 66:64–76

Carson M, Lyu K, Richter K, Becker M, Domingues CM, Han W, Zanna L (2019) Climate model uncertainty and trend detection in regional sea level projections: a review. Surv Geophys. https://doi.org/10.1007/s10712-019-09559-3

Church JA, White NJ, Konikow LF, Domingues CM, Cogley JG, Rignot E, Gregory JM, van den Broeke MR, Monaghan AJ, Velicogna I (2011) Revisiting the Earth's sea-level and energy budgets from 1961 to 2008. Geophys Res Lett 38:L18601. https://doi.org/10.1029/2011GL048794

Church JA, Clark PU, Cazenave A, Gregory JM, Jevrejeva S, Levermann A, Merrifield MA, Milne GA, Nerem RS, Nunn PD, Payne AJ, Pfeffer WT, Stammer D Unnikrishnan AS (2013) Sea level change. In: Stocker TF, Qin D, Plattner G-K, Tignor M, Allen SK, Boschung J, Nauels A, Xia Y, Bex V, Midgley PM (eds) Climate change 2013: the physical science basis. Contribution of working group I to the fifth assessment report of the intergovernmental panel on climate change. Cambridge University Press, Cambridge and New York

Dussin R, Barnier B (2013) The making of DFS5.1. Drakkar project report, Grenoble, France

Fasullo JT, Nerem RS (2018) Altimeter-era emergence of the patterns of forced sea-level rise in climate models and implications for the future. Proc Nat Acad Sci 115(51):12944–12949. https://doi.org/10.1073/pnas.1813233115

Greatbatch RJ (1994) A note on the representation of steric sea level in models that conserve volume rather than mass. J Geophys Res 99(C6):12767–12771

Grégorio S, Penduff T, Sérazin G, Molines J-M, Barnier B, Hirschi J (2015) Intrinsic variability of the Atlantic meridional overturning circulation at interannual-to-multidecadal time scales. J Phys Oceanogr 45(7):1929–1946. https://doi.org/10.1175/JPO-D-14-0163.1

Gregory JM, Griffies SM, Hughes CW et al (2019) Concepts and terminology for sea level: mean, variability and change, both local and global. Surv Geophys. https://doi.org/10.1007/s10712-019-09525-z

Griffies SM, Greatbatch RJ (2012) Physical processes that impact the evolution of global mean sea level in ocean climate models. Ocean Model 51:37–72. https://doi.org/10.1016/j.ocemod.2012.04.003

Griffies SM, Yin J, Durack PJ, Goddard P, Bates SC, Behrens E, Bentsen M, Bi D, Biastoch A, Böning C, Bozec A, Chassignet E, Danabasoglu G, Danilov S, Domingues CM, Drange H, Farneti R, Fernandez E, Greatebatch RJ, Holland DM, Ilicak M, Large WG, Lorbacher K, Lu J, Marsland SJ, Mishra A, Nurser AJG, Salas-Mélia D, Palter JB, Samuels BL, Schröter J, Schwarzkopf FU, Sidorenko D, Treguier A-M, Tseng YH, Tsujino H, Uotila P, Valcke S, Voldoire A, Wang Q, Winton M, Zhang X (2014) An assessment of global and regional sea level for years 1993–2007 in a suite of interannual CORE-II simulations. Ocean Model 78:35–89. https://doi.org/10.1016/j.ocemod.2014.03.004

Hallberg R (2013) Using a resolution function to regulate parameterizations of oceanic mesoscale eddy effects. Ocean Model 72:92–103. https://doi.org/10.1016/j.ocemod.2013.08.007

Hamlington BD, Fasullo JT, Nerem RS, Kim KY, Landerer FW (2019) Uncovering the pattern of forced sea level rise in the satellite altimeter record. Geophys Res Lett 46(9):4844–4853. https://doi.org/10.1029/2018GL081386

Han W, Stammer D, Thompson P, Ezer T, Palanisamy H, Zhang X, Domingues CM, Zhang L, Yuan D (2019) Impacts of basin-scale climate modes on coastal sea level: a review. Surv Geophys. https://doi.org/10.1007/s10712-019-09562-8

Hirschi J, Baehr J, Marotzke J, Stark J, Cunningham S, Beismann J-O (2003) A monitoring design for the Atlantic meridional overturning circulation. Geophys Res Lett 30:1413. https://doi.org/10.1029/2002GL016776

Huck T, Arzel O, Sévellec F (2015) Multidecadal variability of the overturning circulation in presence of eddy turbulence. J Phys Oceanogr 45(1):157–173. https://doi.org/10.1175/jpo-d-14-0114.1

Jevrejeva S, Frederikse T, Kopp RE, Le Cozannet G, Jackson LP, van de Wal RSW (2019) Probabilistic sea level projections at the coast by 2100. Surv Geophys. https://doi.org/10.1007/s10712-019-09550-y

Landerer F, Jungclaus J, Marotzke J (2007a) Ocean bottom pressure changes lead to a decreasing length-of-day in a warming climate. Geophys Res Lett 34:L06307. https://doi.org/10.1029/2006GL029106

Landerer F, Jungclaus J, Marotzke J (2007b) Regional dynamic and steric sea level change in response to the IPCC-A1B scenario. J Phys Oceanogr 37:296–312

Legeais J-F, Ablain M, Zawadzki L, Zuo H, Johannessen JA, Scharffenberg MG, Fenoglio-Marc L, Fernandes MJ, Andersen OB, Rudenko S, Cipollini P, Quartly GD, Passaro M, Cazenave A, Benveniste J (2018) An improved and homogeneous altimeter sea level record from the ESA Climate Change Initiative. Earth Syst Sci Data 10:281–301. https://doi.org/10.5194/essd-10-281-2018

Leroux S, Penduff T, Bessières L, Molines J, Brankart J, Sérazin G, Barnier B, Terray L (2018) Intrinsic and atmospherically forced variability of the AMOC: insights from a large-ensemble ocean hindcast. J Clim 31:1183–1203. https://doi.org/10.1175/JCLI-D-17-0168.1

Llovel W, Lee T (2015) Importance and origin of halosteric contribution to sea level change in the southeast Indian Ocean during 2005–2013. Geophys Res Lett 42:1148–1157

Llovel W, Penduff T, Meyssignac B, Molines J-M, Terray L, Bessières L, Barnier B (2018) Contributions of atmospheric forcing and chaotic ocean variability to regional sea level trends over 1993–2015. Geophys Res Lett. https://doi.org/10.1029/2018GL080838

Marcos M, Wöppelmann G, Matthews A, Ponte RM, Birol F, Ardhuin F, Coco G, Santamaria-Gomez A, Ballu V, Testut L, Chambers D, Stop JE (2019) Coastal sea level and related fields from existing observing systems. Surv Geophys. https://doi.org/10.1007/s10712-019-09513-3

Nerem RS, Beckley BD, Fasullo JT, Hamlington BD, Masters D, Mitchum GT (2018) Climate-change-driven accelerated sea-level rise detected in the altimeter era. Proc Natl Acad Sci USA 115(9):2022–2025. https://doi.org/10.1073/pnas.1717312115

O'Kane TJ, Matear RJ, Chamberlain MA, Risbey JS, Sloyan BM, Horenko I (2013) Decadal variability in an OGCM Southern Ocean: intrinsic modes, forced modes and metastable states. Ocean Model 69:1–21. https://doi.org/10.1016/j.ocemod.2013.04.009

Penduff T, Juza M, Barnier B, Zika J, Dewar WK, Treguier A-M, Molines J-M, Audiffren N (2011) Sea-level expression of intrinsic and forced ocean variabilities at interannual time scales. J Clim 24:5652–5670. https://doi.org/10.1175/JCLI-D-11-00077.1

Penduff T, Barnier B, Terray L, Bessières L, Sérazin G, Grégorio S, Brankart J-M, Moine M-P, Molines J-M, Brasseur P (2014) Ensembles of eddying ocean simulations for climate. CLIVAR Exchanges, Special Issue on High Resolution Ocean Climate Modelling, 65, vol 19, no 2, July 2014

Penduff T, Sérazin G, Leroux S, Close S, Molines JM, Barnier B, Bessières L, Terray L, Maze G (2018) Chaotic variability of ocean: heat content climate-relevant features and observational implications. Oceanography 31(2):63–71. https://doi.org/10.5670/oceanog.2018.210

Rhein M, Rintoul SR, Aoki S, Campos E, Chambers D, Feely RA, Gulev S, Johnson GC, Josey SA, Kostianoy A et al (2013) Observations: ocean. Chapter 3 in climate change 2013: the physical science basis. In: Stocker TF, Qin D, Plattner G-K, Tignor M, Allen SK, Boschung J, Nauels A, Xia Y, Bex V, Midgley PM (eds) Contribution of working group I to the fifth assessment report of the intergovernmental panel on climate change. Cambridge University Press, Cambridge

Sérazin G, Penduff T, Grégorio S, Barnier B, Molines J-M, Terray L (2015) Intrinsic variability of sea-level from global 1/12° ocean simulations: spatio-temporal scales. J Clim 28:4279–4292. https://doi.org/10.1175/JCLI-D-14-00554

Sérazin G, Meyssignac B, Penduff T, Terray L, Barnier B, Molines J-M (2016) Quantifying uncertainties on regional sea-level rise induced by multi-decadal oceanic intrinsic variability. Geophys Res Lett. https://doi.org/10.1002/2016GL069273

Sérazin G, Jaymond A, Leroux S, Penduff T, Bessières L, Llovel W, Barnier B, Molines J-M, Terray L (2017) A global probabilistic study of the ocean heat content low-frequency variability: atmospheric forcing versus oceanic chaos. Geophys Res Lett 44:5580–5589. https://doi.org/10.1002/2017GL073026

Sérazin G, Penduff T, Barnier B, Molines J, Arbic BK, Müller M, Terray L (2018) Inverse cascades of kinetic energy as a source of intrinsic variability: a global OGCM study. J Phys Oceanogr 48:1385–1408. https://doi.org/10.1175/JPO-D-17-0136.1

WCRP Global Sea Level Budget Group (2018) Global sea-level budget 1993–present. Earth Syst Sci Data 10:1551–1590. https://doi.org/10.5194/essd-10-1551-2018

Woodworth PL, Melet A, Marcos M, Ray RD, Wöppelmann G, Sasaki YN, Cirano M, Hibbert A, Huthnance JM, Monserrat S, Merrifeld MA (2019) Forcing factors affecting sea level changes at the coast. Surv Geophys. https://doi.org/10.1007/s10712-019-09531-1

Yin J, Schlesinger M, Stouffer R (2009) Model projections of rapid sea-level rise on the northeast coast of the United States. Nat Geosci 2:262–266

Yin J, Griffies SM, Stouffer R (2010) Spatial variability of sea-level rise in 21st century projections. J Clim 23:4585–4607

Zanna L, Brankart JM, Huber M, Leroux S, Penduff T, Williams PD (2018) Uncertainty and scale interactions in ocean ensembles: from seasonal forecasts to multi-decadal climate predictions. Q J R Meteorol Soc. https://doi.org/10.1002/qj.3397

Surveys in Geophysics (2019) 40:1563–1601
https://doi.org/10.1007/s10712-019-09557-5

The Contribution of Wind-Generated Waves to Coastal Sea-Level Changes

Guillaume Dodet[1] · Angélique Melet[2] · Fabrice Ardhuin[1] · Xavier Bertin[3] · Déborah Idier[4] · Rafael Almar[5]

Received: 31 October 2018 / Accepted: 10 July 2019 / Published online: 29 July 2019

Abstract
Surface gravity waves generated by winds are ubiquitous on our oceans and play a primordial role in the dynamics of the ocean–land–atmosphere interfaces. In particular, wind-generated waves cause fluctuations of the sea level at the coast over timescales from a few seconds (individual wave runup) to a few hours (wave-induced setup). These wave-induced processes are of major importance for coastal management as they add up to tides and atmospheric surges during storm events and enhance coastal flooding and erosion. Changes in the atmospheric circulation associated with natural climate cycles or caused by increasing greenhouse gas emissions affect the wave conditions worldwide, which may drive significant changes in the wave-induced coastal hydrodynamics. Since sea-level rise represents a major challenge for sustainable coastal management, particularly in low-lying coastal areas and/or along densely urbanized coastlines, understanding the contribution of wind-generated waves to the long-term budget of coastal sea-level changes is therefore of major importance. In this review, we describe the physical processes by which sea states may affect coastal sea level at several timescales, we present the methods currently used to estimate the wave contribution to coastal sea-level changes, we describe past and future wave climate variability, we discuss the contribution of wave to coastal sea-level changes, and we discuss the limitations and perspectives of this research field.

Keywords Wind waves · Sea level · Coastal zone · Climate change

✉ Guillaume Dodet
guillaume.dodet@ifremer.fr

[1] UMR 6253 LOPS, CNRS-Ifremer-IRD-Univiversity of Brest Brest, ZI Pointe du Diable, CS10070, 29280 Plouzané, France

[2] Mercator Ocean, 8-10 rue Hermès, 31520 Ramonville Saint Agne, France

[3] UMR 7266 LIENSs, CNRS - La Rochelle University, 2 rue Olympe de Gouges, 17000 La Rochelle, France

[4] BRGM, 3 avenue Guillemin, 45060 Orléans Cédex, France

[5] UMR 5566 LEGOS, 18 avenue Edouard Belin, 31401 Toulouse Cédex 9, France

1 Introduction

Waves often play a significant role in high sea levels and inundations at the coast, whether associated with a local wind storm or with swells from a remote storm (Hoeke et al. 2013; Ford et al. 2018). This wave activity has a strong regional and interannual variability (Bromirski et al. 2005), and long-term trends in offshore significant wave height (H_s) exhibit strong regional variations, with possible trends of a few centimeters per year for the 90th percentile of offshore H_s (Wang and Swail 2001). The wave-driven contribution to the total water level generally varies with shoreline morphology and sea-state properties and can be a fraction of the offshore H_s that ranges from 10 to 200% (e.g., Stockdon et al. 2006; Poate et al. 2016). As a result, wave-driven contributions to the water level can contribute substantially to trends in coastal sea level (Melet et al. 2018).

The contribution of wave to coastal sea level adds to *ocean dynamic sea-level rise* (Gregory et al. 2019) and, where wave height or wave periods increase, enhances the threat to coastal zones (Cazenave and Cozannet 2014), or mitigates the threat where heights or periods decrease. First, because a higher sea level increases the frequency and amplitude of coastal hazards, such as flooding and erosion, but also because the social and economic stakes of the coasts have never been so valuable and fragile at the same time. Indeed, the increase in population density in coastal regions during the industrial period has fostered the urbanization of many coastlines of the world, enhancing their socioeconomic importance but also weakening their resilient capacity (Neumann et al. 2015). Therefore, densely populated and/or highly urbanized coastlines now require a detailed understanding of coastal sea-level changes, with possible costly adaptation strategy and accurate early warning systems in order to maintain economic activities and population safety.

Since the early 1990s, satellite altimetry has provided a comprehensive view of the global distribution of sea-level changes (Cazenave et al. 2018). However, these results concern the open ocean and, presently, cannot be easily extrapolated to the coastal regions. Indeed, coasts represent an important source of noise in radar altimetry, which prevents an accurate estimation of sea level closer than about 20 km from the coast (Cipollini et al. 2017). In addition, the coastal shelf and more particularly the narrow wave-breaking zone (with width of the order 10^1–10^4 m, Wright and Short 1984) is a very dynamic region that exhibits rapid changes in sea level and currents, as a result of the complex interactions between the waves and the sea floor (Munk and Traylor 1947). Indeed, wind-generated waves accumulate and transport momentum across ocean basins and release it to the water column when they break in the shallow surf zone. The rapid decrease in momentum flux is compensated by a tilting of the water surface between the breakpoint and the waterline (Longuet-Higgins and Stewart 1964), which can raise the time-averaged sea level at the waterline by up to 1 m (Pedreros et al. 2018; Guérin et al. 2018; Dodet et al. 2018). This effect, called the wave setup, is modulated by long waves with periods of the order of 1 min that travel at the speed of the wave groups and rapidly grow (from centimeters to decimeters) in the surf zone. These waves are called infragravity (IG) waves. Finally, the wave runup, which is the highest waterline elevation reached by individual waves, integrates both the setup and infragravity waves plus a short-wave component, and represents an important contributor of the total water level. Since the wave runup is directly responsible for wave overtopping, it is crucial to take it into account for the design of coastal defences. The wave setup, wave runup and infragravity waves are all directly controlled by incident wave conditions and nearshore bathymetry.

Similarly to the atmospheric circulation, the average wave fields present coherent patterns at the basin scale that can be described with statistical parameters. The wave climate integrates the effect of both distant and local wind conditions, which makes the interpretation of observed variabilities particularly challenging. Thanks to long-term wave buoy records, spectral wave models and satellite-based wave observations, the different modes of variability of the wave climate have been well investigated. The strong interannual variability of H_s at high latitudes and its link with climate modes such as the North Atlantic Oscillation (NAO), the Pacific Decadal Oscillation (PDO) or the Southern Annular Mode (SAM) has been evidenced in several studies (e.g., Dodet et al. 2010; Hemer et al. 2018; Bromirski et al. 2013). Similar findings were obtained for extreme wave heights based on wave buoy and satellite observations (Menéndez et al. 2008; Izaguirre et al. 2011). Analysis of satellite-based wave observations over the period 1985–2008 highlighted the existence of significant trends in H_s in several regions of the world, more pronounced for the 90th and 99th percentiles of H_s (Young et al. 2011). However, given the relatively short time coverage of this data set, it is likely that the observed trend values are mostly influenced by decadal climate oscillations. Bertin et al. (2013) analyzed the outputs of a 109-year numerical wave hindcasts for the North Atlantic and found significant trends in H_s in the North-East Atlantic, in the absence of any trends in NAO over the same period. While these long-term trends could be the result of external climate variability, the time consistency of the wind field reanalysis that feed wave hindcasts remains a major issue to be solved for gaining confidence in such results (e.g., Stopa et al. 2019). Nevertheless, given the significant contribution of wave-induced processes to coastal sea level, changes in the wave conditions over decadal or longer timescales will likely contribute to coastal sea-level changes and need to be further investigated.

The objective of this review paper is to discuss the current state of knowledge on wind-generated wave contributions to coastal sea-level changes, how these contributions are observed and modelled, and to identify future research needs in that regard. In the following section (Sect. 2), we describe the main physical processes through which wind-generated waves can affect coastal sea level. In Sect. 3, we introduce the methods used to characterize offshore significant wave conditions and we present our current understanding on past and future wave conditions, coastal sea level and wave conditions. In Sect. 4, we present the method used to estimate nearshore parameters required to investigate coastal sea level and we discuss the impact of waves on coastal sea level. Finally, in Sect. 5, we present the current limitations of our understanding of the wave impact on coastal sea level and we mention several perspectives that could improve our understanding in the near future.

2 Physical Processes

Wave-induced processes control the nearshore hydrodynamics of exposed coastline and cause fluctuations of the coastal sea level over a wide range of timescales. Three main processes are identified and correspond to distinct, yet overlapping, spatial and temporal scales. These processes and their associated scales are depicted in Fig. 1. First, infragravity waves (Fig. 1a, d), which travel out of phase with the wave groups they are bound to, have typical periods of ~ 1 min and wavelength of ~ 10 km. Second, the wave

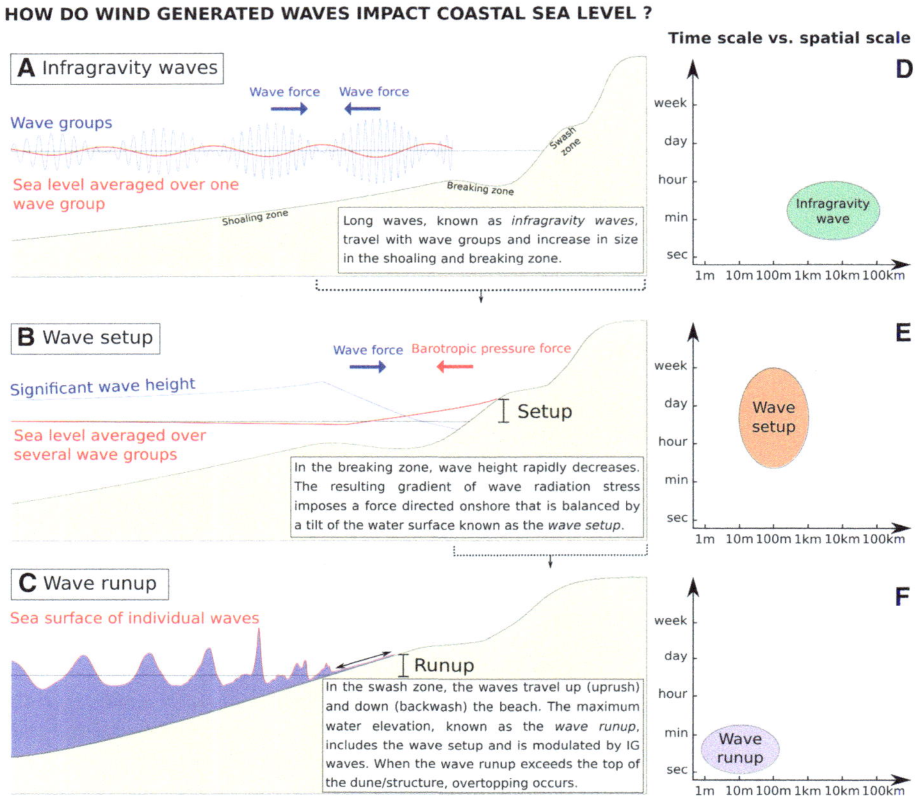

Fig. 1 Schematic description of wave-induced processes impacting coastal sea level and their associated temporal and spatial scales for **a–d** infragravity waves; **b–e** wave setup; and **c–f** wave runup. The horizontal dotted black line represents the still water level, which includes the mean sea level, the astronomical tide and the atmospheric surge components

setup (Fig. 1b, e), which develops in the surf zone, may extend from a dozen of meters in steep environments to several kilometers in low-sloping environments during stormy conditions. Since the magnitude of the wave setup is mostly controlled by the offshore significant wave height, period and spectrum shape (Guza and Feddersen 2012), its magnitude varies with local wind sea and swell conditions, from a few hours to several days. Third, the wave runup (Fig. 1c, f), which corresponds to the fluctuations of the highest instantaneous water level across the swash zone, extends from a few meters in reflective environments to a hundred meters in dissipative environments. Its timescale is controlled by the relative contribution of incident (periods of ~ 10 s) and infragravity (periods of ~ 1 min) wave energy that reach the shoreline after the incident waves have broken. These three processes all contribute to the total coastal sea level, which is here defined as the sum of the mean sea level (e.g., averaged over 1 year), the astronomical tide, the atmospheric surge (inverse barometer effect and wind-induced surge) and the wave runup. The wave runup is composed of a steady component, the wave setup, and a fluctuating component, the swash, itself composed of a high-frequency (incident waves) component and a low-frequency (infragravity waves) component. The following paragraphs present these processes in more detail.

2.1 Wave Setup

Wave setup corresponds to the increase in mean water level along the shoreline associated with the dissipation of wind-generated waves in the nearshore and was first reported by Saville (1961). It is usually measured relative to the still water level, defined here as the mean sea level outside the surf zone, including the astronomical tide and the atmospheric surge. Wave setup was investigated based on field observations for several decades (e.g., Guza and Thornton 1981; Holman and Sallenger 1985; Raubenheimer et al. 2001; Apotsos et al. 2007; Nicolae-Lerma et al. 2017; Guérin et al. 2018). Wave setup can exceed 1 m under storm waves (Pedreros et al. 2018; Guérin et al. 2018; Dodet et al. 2018) and can therefore have a relevant contribution in storm surges. As a rough guideline, wave setup along the shoreline of sandy beaches represents about 10 to 20% of the significant wave height at the breaking point. Along the coasts bordered by narrow continental shelves or at volcanic islands, wave setup can even represent the largest contribution of storms surges (e.g., Kennedy et al. 2012; Bertin et al. 2017; Pedreros et al. 2018). Several studies also showed that the setup driven by wave breaking over the ebb deltas of shallow inlets (Malhadas et al. 2009; Dodet et al. 2013) and large estuaries (Bertin et al. 2015; Fortunato et al. 2017; Bertin et al. 2017) could propagate outside surf zones and raise the water level at the scale of the whole lagoon/estuary. The tilting of the free surface elevation resulting from wave setup induces a barotropic pressure gradient, which partly drives a bed return flow or undertow (Garcez-Faria et al. 2000), which is one of the main processes responsible for coastal erosion.

The first theoretical explanation for the development of wave setup is due to Longuet-Higgins and Stewart (1964), who introduced the concept of radiation stresses, which correspond to the wind-generated wave momentum flux. In the near shore, the depth-limited dissipation of short waves causes a strong gradient of radiation stress, which acts as a horizontal pressure force toward the shore and tilts the water level until a balance is reached with the subsequent barotropic pressure gradient. As a result, the mean water level near the breaking point lowers (set-down) and the mean water level at the shoreline rises (setup). This wave-induced deformation of the water level was successfully reproduced in a wave channel by Bowen et al. (1968), as shown in Fig. 2.

2.2 Infragravity Waves

Infragravity (hereafter IG) waves are surface gravity waves with frequencies typically ranging from 0.004 to 0.04 Hz and related to the presence of groups in incident short waves (see Bertin et al. 2018 for a recent review). While IG waves are only a few millimeters to a few centimeters high in the deep ocean (e.g., Rawat et al. 2014; Crawford et al. 2015; Smit et al. 2018), they grow in the nearshore and their height can exceed 1 m at the shoreline (see Ruessink 2010; Sheremet et al. 2014; Fiedler et al. 2015; Inch et al. 2017). As a consequence, IG waves have a relevant contribution to the nearshore hydrodynamics, particularly under storm waves (e.g., Guza and Thornton 1982; Elgar et al. 1992; Ruessink et al. 1998).

Two main mechanisms typically explain the development of IG waves in the nearshore. First, the divergence of the momentum flux associated with the short waves at the scale of

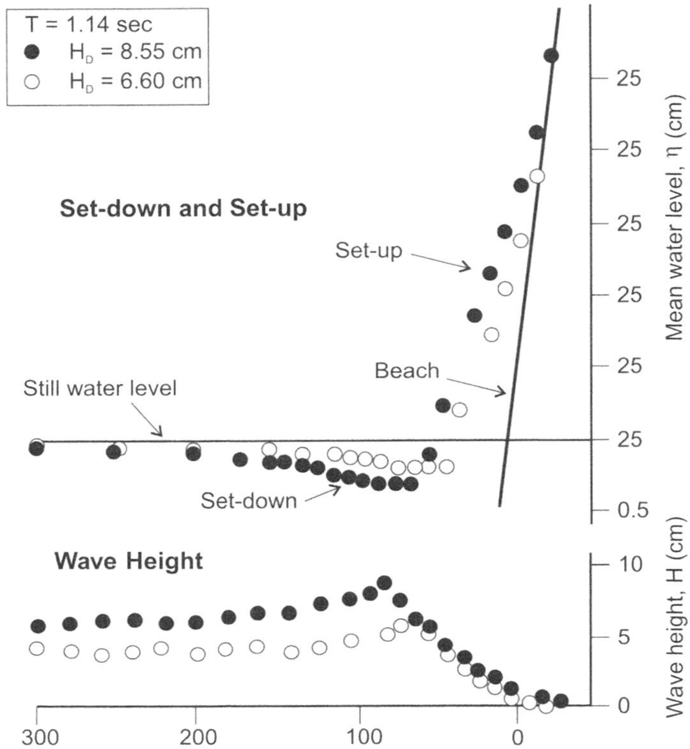

Fig. 2 Profile of the mean water level and the envelope of the wave height for two experiments of Bowen et al. (1968) with wave period = 1.14 s, $H_s = 6.60$ cm and $H_s = 8.55$ cm. Reprinted from Bowen (1969), as authorized by Wiley Online Library

wave groups drives the development of a long bound wave, out of phase with the energy envelope of the short waves (Biesel 1952; Longuet-Higgins and Stewart 1962). Hasselmann (1962) proposed an analytical solution to compute the bound wave for 2D random waves, which implies that the bound wave increases with the energy of the short wave, particularly when this energy is distributed over narrow-banded spectra. Second, due to the presence of wave groups, the cross-shore position of the breaking point varies in time and the equilibrium in the surf zone between the gradient of wave radiation stress and the subsequent barotropic pressure gradient becomes dynamic (see previous section and Fig. 1b). This process generates IG waves radiating from the breaking point seaward and shoreward (Symonds et al. 1982). Battjes et al. (2004) showed that the former mechanism is dominant at gently sloping beaches, while the latter is dominant in steep surf zones, such as in coral reefs (e.g., Pomeroy et al. 2012). However, a recent study of Moura and Baldock (2017) questioned these well-admitted findings and suggested that the breakpoint mechanism could also be dominant for wide surf zones under spilling breakers. Cheriton et al. (2016) and Gawehn et al. (2016) further showed that IG waves can trigger resonant processes in coral reefs, which result in the development of very-low-frequency motions.

In the surf zone, the dissipation of short waves through depth-limited breaking reduces their groupiness, so that IG waves are no longer bound and can propagate as free waves

(Battjes et al. 2004). In the inner surf zone, IG waves transfer the energy to higher frequencies, which results in their steepening and can lead to their dissipation by breaking, particularly at gently sloping beaches (Battjes et al. 2004; De Bakker et al. 2014). As beaches usually display a steeper profile in their upper part—called the berm—IG wave dissipation at high tide is reduced and IG waves can dominate the runup (Ruggiero et al. 2004; Fiedler et al. 2015). The IG wave energy that is not dissipated can be reflected offshore, where it can be trapped by refraction and promote the development of edge waves (Bowen and Guza 1978) or be leaked and propagate through the ocean with little dissipation (Rawat et al. 2014).

2.3 Wave Runup

When wind-generated waves reach the shores, they travel up (uprush) and down (backwash) the beach before being reflected seawards. This water displacement is called the swash, and the beach extent over which it occurs is the swash zone. The maximum vertical excursion of the waterline—called the wave runup—is usually measured with respect to the still water level, as for the wave setup. Therefore, the wave runup includes the contribution of both the swash and the wave setup. The swash energy is usually decomposed into a high-frequency band (incident band ~ 0.04 Hz–0.4 Hz) and a low-frequency band (infragravity band ~ 0.004 Hz–0.04 Hz). During extreme wave conditions, the wave runup can exceed 10 m (see Fig. 3; Poate et al. 2016). It is thus a key parameter for the design of coastal structures and the prediction of overtopping volumes

Fig. 3 Example of coastal defence overtopping at Chesil Beach, UK, caused by extreme swash events exceeding 10 m (see Poate et al. 2016) during Petra storm on February 5, 2014 (credits: Tim Poate)

during storm events. Given the strongly nonlinear nature of the wave-breaking process, the transition from undular bore to wave runup and the collision between uprush and backwash, analytical solutions have been derived for simplified cases only (e.g., Carrier and Greenspan 1958) and the cost of numerical simulations capable of representing such processes is often prohibitive for large-scale studies. Significant advances for the prediction of wave runup in natural environments stem from empirical approaches conducted either in the laboratory (Hunt 1959; Van der Meer and Stam 1992) or in the field (see Stockdon et al. 2006 for a description of major runup field experiments conducted between 1982 and 1997). These studies have shown that the wave runup mostly depends on the wave height (H), the wavelength (L) and the foreshore slope (β) (see Sect. 4.1.3 and Table 1 for a list of wave runup formulation). Since the wavelength scales with the square of the wave period in deep water, the wave period has actually a larger influence than the wave height on the runup. However, the range of wave period at a given site is usually lower than the range of wave heights, and this latter often display stronger correlations with the wave runup (Poate et al. 2016; Dodet et al. 2018). Several studies investigated more closely the spectral distribution of the wave energy in the swash zone and revealed that the energy in the incident band could be saturated in dissipative environments, such as high-energy low-sloping beaches, so that infragravity wave energy was dominant (Ruessink et al. 1998). In order to investigate the impact of the foreshore slope on the wave runup, some authors took advantage of the strong alongshore variability of sandy beaches (Ruggiero et al. 2004) or the large tidal range that modifies the foreshore morphology felt by the waves (Suanez et al. 2015), or carried out interfield comparisons (Stockdon et al. 2006). These studies show a significant impact of the foreshore slope on the runup for reflective conditions and a lesser or nonexistent impact for high-energy dissipative environments.

In this section, we have seen that wave-induced coastal processes have a significant impact on coastal sea level. All these processes are largely controlled by offshore wave conditions. Therefore, given the strong variability of the offshore wave climate at various timescales (seasonal, interannual, decadal) and its potential long-term evolution

Table 1 Wave setup (η) empirical formulations (non-exhaustive list)

References	Empirical equation	Applicability range
Guza and Thornton (1981)	$\eta = 0.17H_s$	
Holman and Sallenger (1985)	$\eta = 0.46 \tan\beta\sqrt{H_s L_0}$	$0.026 < \beta < 0.14$
Holman (1986)	$\eta = 0.2H_s$	$0.07 < \beta < 0.2$
Hanslow and Nielsen (1992)	$\eta = 0.048\sqrt{\frac{H_s}{\sqrt{2}} L_{0,s}}$	$0.03 < \beta < 0.16$
Komar (1998)	$\eta = 0.45 \tan\beta\sqrt{H_0 L_0}$	$0.026 < \beta < 0.14$
Hedges and Mase (2004)	$\eta = 0.34H_s$	$\xi_s < 3$
Stockdon et al. (2006)	$\eta = 0.35\beta\sqrt{H_0 L_0}$	$\xi_0 > 0.3$
Stockdon et al. (2006)	$\eta = 0.016\sqrt{H_0 L_0}$	$\xi_0 < 0.3$
Atkinson et al. (2017)	$\eta = 0.16H_s$	Model of models
Ji et al. (2018)	$\eta = 0.220H_s^{0.629} L_0^{0.371} (\tan\beta)^{0.538}$	$0.005 < \beta < 0.10$

β is the foreshore beach slope, H_s is the deep-water significant wave height, H_0 is the deep-water wave height, L_0 is the deep-water wavelength $L_{0,s}$ the deep-water wavelength computed using the significant period in the context of climate change, it is particularly important to better understand past and future changes in wave conditions and how these changes will translate in terms of coastal sea level.

3 Characterization and Variability of Offshore Wave Conditions

Since the first evidence of long-term changes in significant wave height measured by the Sevenstones Lightship wave recorder 25 km off Cornwall Land's End (UK) (Carter and Draper 1988), significant progress has been achieved on our comprehension of past and future evolution of the wave climate. Part of this progress can be attributed to the deployment and maintenance of large-scale buoy networks, the development of numerical models and the advent of satellite Earth Observation programs. In this section, we first describe the different methods that are used to characterize offshore wave conditions. Then, we present the current state of the art regarding past and future evolution of the wave climate at global scale, based on the IPCC 5th Assessment Report (AR5; chapter 3, Rhein et al. 2013 and chapter 13, Church et al. 2013) and the Special Report on Managing the Risks of Extreme Events and Disasters to Advance Climate Change Adaptation (SREX; chapter 3, Seneviratne et al. 2012) as well as more recent findings published since AR5.

3.1 In situ and Remote Sensing Observations of Offshore Wave Conditions

Wave measurements started with visual observations from the coast using a wind sea and swell separation method and estimations of wave heights and periods (Gain 1923; Munk and Traylor 1947). Such visual observation programs continue for offshore ship-based observations (e.g., Gulev et al. 2003), providing the longer time series of wave measurements (Gulev and Grigorieva 2004). Offshore of the surf zone and in regions where currents are under 1 m/s, the most common source of wave measurements is moored surface following buoys based on accelerometers (Longuet-Higgins et al. 1963; Allender et al. 1989) or GPS velocity measurements (Herbers et al. 2012). Although not coordinated under a single international program, the collection of wave buoy data has been facilitated by the Oceansites program (Send et al. 2010), as well as various efforts associated with the Global Ocean Observing System (GOOS) and the Copernicus Marine Environment Monitoring System (CMEMS). The actual response of the buoy to the water motion depends on the hull shape and sensor mounting (Jensen et al. 2015; Guimaraes et al. 2018). Where currents are strong. Acoustic Doppler current profilers (ADCPs) are interesting alternatives to measure both currents and waves (Herbers and Lentz 2010), and drifting surface buoys can also provide interesting information either with dedicated buoys (Thomson et al. 2012), or with motion packages added on drifters from the Global Surface Velocity Program (Lumpkin et al. 2016). In that context, in situ wave measurements are today provided by hundreds of wave buoy moored in both deep or coastal waters (typically in 15–100 m depth), with most time series extending over 20 to 40 years (e.g., US National Data Buoy Center, https://www.ndbc.noaa.gov/). These measurements cannot give the detailed wave information needed to estimate coastal sea levels, in particular over complex shorelines due to wave evolution outside of the surf zone, mostly due to refraction (Munk and Traylor 1947; Magne et al. 2007) and bottom friction (e.g., Ardhuin et al. 2003; Roland and Ardhuin 2014). Also, buoys do not measure the full directional spectrum, but moments of its

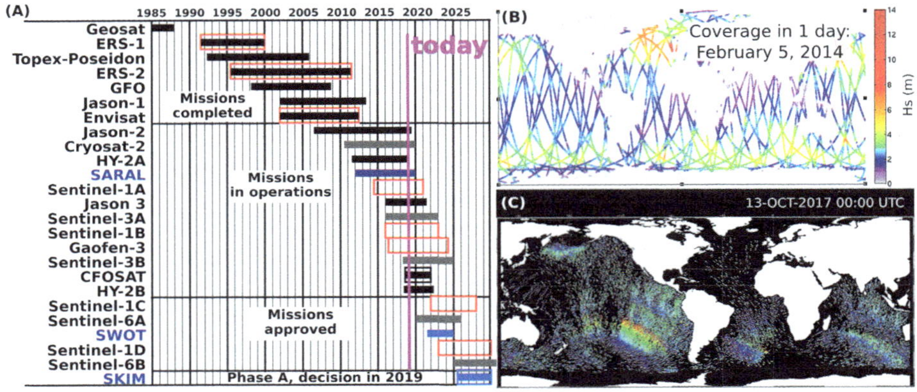

Fig. 4 **a** Time coverage of satellite missions from 1985 to 2030, including nadir and near-nadir altimeters (solid bars) missions monitoring ocean wave spectra (open box) using C-band Synthetic Aperture Radars (red), and real aperture radars in Ku-band (black) or Ka-band (blue). The light gray bars correspond to altimeters using delay Doppler processing. **b** Example of 1-day coverage for H_s measurements with four satellite altimeters, **c** snapshot of "fireworks," showing peak periods, and heights of swell partitions derived from Sentinel-1A and Sentinel-1B wave mode data. Reprinted from Ardhuin et al. (2019), as authorized by Frontiers copiright statements

distribution, that lead to important uncertainties when waves are propagated to the coast (e.g., Crosby et al. 2017).

A more complete spatial coverage of ocean waves is provided by satellite remote sensing, as illustrated in Fig. 4. Nowadays, satellites provide most of the background data for wave climatologies and detection of trends. Satellite altimeters, particularly, give an uninterrupted record of significant wave height since the launch of ERS-1 in 1991. Additional information on the sea state, in particular wave periods that are critical for estimating wave-induced water levels at the coast, can be obtained with other satellite remote sensing techniques. In particular, ERS-1, ERS-2, Envisat and the Sentinel 1 constellation carry synthetic aperture radars (SARs) that are operated in "wave mode" over most of the oceans (Hasselmann et al. 2012). SAR provides radar images from which the height, period and direction of swells can be estimated, provided that their wavelength is long enough, typically more than 200 m depending on their direction and on the wind speed (Kerbaol et al. 1998). Both altimeter H_s and SAR-derived swell partitions are assimilated into the CMEMS/Meteo-France operational global model (Aouf et al. 2006), which today provides the most accurate forecasts of wave heights (Bidlot 2017), with the swell assimilation impact strongest in the Pacific ocean.

3.2 Regional Modeling of Offshore Wave Conditions

Given the difficulty of monitoring waves over large spatial and temporal scales, numerical models are important tools, often combined with in situ measurements and remote sensing. A wide range of numerical techniques exist, each adapted to particular scales and physical processes to be accounted for (see Ardhuin and Orfila 2018 for a recent review). As long as time resolution shorter than the wave group scale (a few minutes) is not needed, the flow, water level and wave motion can be separated, and the waves are efficiently solved

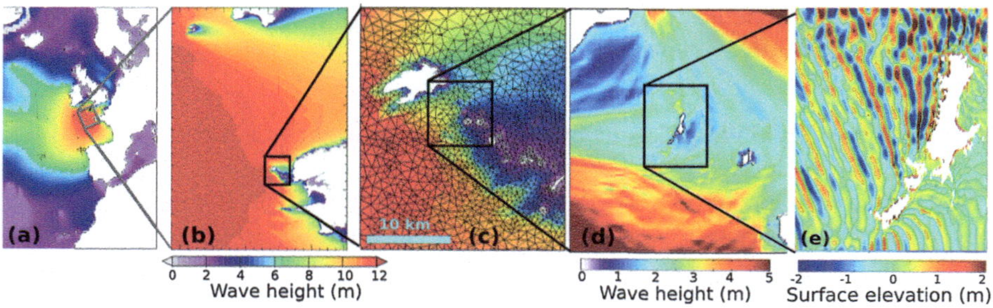

Fig. 5 Example of multiple scales wave modelling. **a–c** Phase-averaged wave model (WAVEWATCH III, the WAVEWATCH III Development Group 2016), **d** wave-group-resolving model (XBeach, Roelvink et al. 2018), and **e** phase-resolving wave model (SWASH, Zijlema et al. 2011), here applied at Banneg Island, France

with spectral wave models that are generally phase-averaged (e.g., the WAVEWATCH III Development Group 2016) and that may also include a bispectrum evolution for taking into account non-local nonlinear effects (Herbers and Burton 1997; Janssen et al. 2006). Spectral phase-averaged models can be applied at all spatial scales (Fig. 5).

Numerical models can provide good wave prediction, but are computationally time-consuming. Meta-models (also called "response surface", "surrogate model", "model emulators", "proxy models") provide an alternative approach to tackle the computation time issue. They are based on the definition of a statistical relationship between the inputs (X, called the "predictor") and the output (Y, called the "predictand"). Such fast-running model allows, for instance, performing sensitivity analysis, exploring the effect of uncertainties in X on the Y results, or performing ensemble simulations. From the literature review, wave meta-models can be divided into two categories (statistical downscaling (SD) and hybrid (H) models), the first one being the one used when investigating waves at a regional scale. Local waves resulting from the regional meteorology over a few days scale (Camus et al. 2014a), the SD models relate a large-scale predictor (most of the time the sea-level pressure fields or its squared gradient) with a local predictand (multivariate wave conditions, e.g., wave height, period and direction). They require atmospheric and sea-state databases. One of the key points in statistical downscaling is to reduce the dimension of the inputs, i.e. here the mean sea-level pressure (or its gradient), which has very high dimension (number of grid points times the number of time steps). This reduction is often based on principal component (PC) analysis. Then, two types of approaches have been pursued. In the first one, the SD model is defined as a linear combination of the most important PCs of the predictor defined specifically for the analyzed target location (see e.g., Camus et al. 2014a). In the second one, the SD model estimates the predictand based on the occurrence of weather types (see, e.g., Camus et al. 2014b, Laugel et al. 2014; Perez et al. 2015; Rueda et al. 2016). These weather types are obtained by clustering methods (e.g., K-means), initialized by a maximum dissimilarity algorithm. In many studies, a typical number of 100 weather types are used. Then, a regression model is built between these weather types and the wave conditions. At the end, a statistical model is built allowing emulation of the wave conditions with a negligible computation time. However, although revealing the dominant modes of wave climate variability and trends, the statistical downscaling methods still faces issues to predict extremes at high frequency (e.g., hour scale). It should be noted that statistical downscaling models aiming at predicting cyclone-induced wave conditions rely on the cyclone characteristics rather than on spatiotemporal meteorological fields (see, e.g., Jia and Taflanidis 2013; Rohmer et al. 2016).

3.3 Past Changes in Wave Conditions During the Twentieth Century

Buoy data and Voluntary Observing Ship (VOS) reports indicate statistically significant positive H_s trends during the second half of the twentieth century over the North Atlantic, north of 45°N, and over the central to eastern mid-latitude North Pacific with typical trends of up to 2 cm per year, as shown in Fig. 6a (Gulev and Grigorieva 2006; Ruggiero et al. 2010). However, these measurements suffer from limited spatial coverage, particularly in the Southern Ocean. In addition, some of the trends computed from the North Pacific buoy data were introduced by modifications of the measurement techniques (Gemmrich et al.

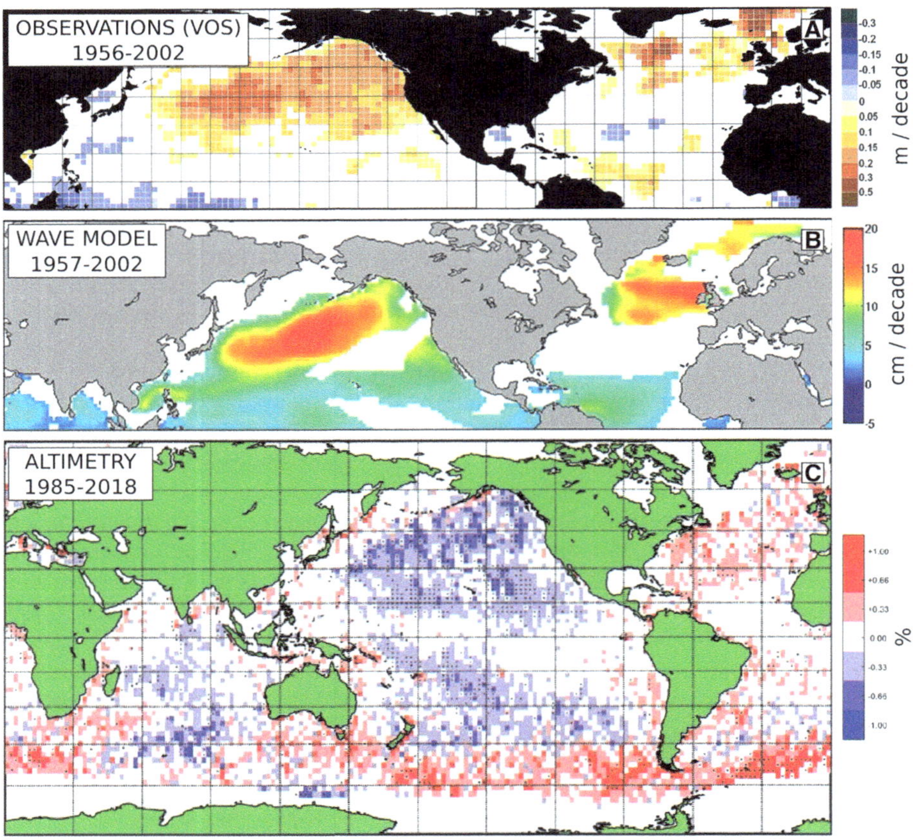

Fig. 6 Trends in significant wave height estimated from **a** visual observing ship observations over the period 1956–2002. Reprinted from Gulev and Grigorieva (2006), © American Meteorological Society. Used with permission; **b** numerical wave model hindcast over the period 1957–2002. Reprinted from Semedo et al. (2010), © American Meteorological Society. Used with permission; **c** satellite altimetry over the period 1985–2018. Reprinted from Young and Ribal (2019), with permission of AAAS. In each of these studies, values which are not statistically significant are either not shown (**a** and **b**) or not marked with black dots (**c**). Adapted from Gulev and Grigorieva (2004), Semedo et al. (2010) and Young and Ribal (2019)

2011). For these reasons, satellite altimeter observations available since the mid-1980s provide extremely valuable data source for investigating wave height variability at global scale. Using an extensive altimetry database, Young and Ribal (2019) found positive trends (up to 0.5 cm per year) for the mean annual H_s in some part of the Southern Ocean and negative trends in the central part of the North Pacific, with a global low level of statistical significance (Fig. 6c). They also obtained stronger positive trends (up to 1 cm per year) for the 99th H_s percentile in the Southern Ocean, North Atlantic and North West Pacific. Given the short time period covered by the data (1985–2018) and the strong link between variations in waves and internal climate variability, it is yet difficult to determine whether these results reflect long-term H_s trends or are a part of the decadal oscillation. The differences observed between the trends computed over the period 1985–2018 from satellite altimetry and the ones computed over the period 1957–2002 from observations and model results (compare Fig. 6a–c) also illustrate how the internal atmospheric variability may impact the H_s trends computed over a few decades.

Numerical wave hindcasts forced by general circulation models (GCMs) or regional climate model (RCM) reanalysis offer an additional alternative to study wave climate variability over a longer time period with a high resolution and global coverage, even though temporal inhomogeneity in the reanalysis data limits the confidence in the model results for long-term trend analysis (e.g., Stopa et al. 2019). A 45-year (1957–2002) hindcast forced by the ERA-40 reanalysis from the European Centre for Medium-Range Weather Forecasts (ECMWF) revealed positive H_s trends in the North Atlantic and North Pacific similar to the one obtained from in situ measurements (Semedo et al. 2010, Fig. 6b). Hemer et al. (2010) obtained positive trends across most of the Southern Hemisphere using a corrected ERA-40 reanalysis and showed that winter H_s was strongly correlated with the SAM. They also found an anticlockwise rotation of wave direction with the southward intensification of the Southern Ocean storm belt associated with the southern annular mode (SAM). In the North Atlantic, Dodet et al. (2010) found positive H_s trends (up to 15 cm/decade) north of 40°N and clockwise trends (up to 1°/decade) in mean wave direction south of 45°N during the period 1953–2009. They related these changes to a strengthening and northward shift of mid-latitude storms associated with changes in the North Atlantic Oscillation (NAO) that shifted from a negative phase in the 1960s to a positive phase in the 1990s. These results are consistent with the 1958–2002 wave hindcast of Charles et al. (2012). Bertin et al. (2013) performed a 109-year numerical wave hindcasts for the North Atlantic and found significant upward trends in yearly-mean H_s in the North-East Atlantic, reaching 10 cm/decade around 60°N, despite any trends in NAO over the same period. This upward trend was explained by an upward trend in 10-m winds, observed both in atmospheric hindcast and in observations from VOS (Gulev et al. 2003). More recently, Castelle et al. (2018) performed a wavelet analysis in a 69-year (1949–2017) wave hindcast in the North-East Atlantic and found an increase in H_s variability starting in the 1990s, that is also observed in the pressure-based index. In the Arctic Ocean, reduction in summer sea ice extent resulted in enhanced wave activity due to increased fetch area and longer duration of the open water season (Overeem et al. 2011; Stopa et al. 2016).

3.4 Projected Changes for the End of the Twenty-First Century

Given the usually coarse resolution (typically 250 km) of the atmospheric component of global coupled atmosphere–ocean general circulation model (GCM), global wave climate projections usually require dynamical (Wang and Swail 2006) or statistical (Camus

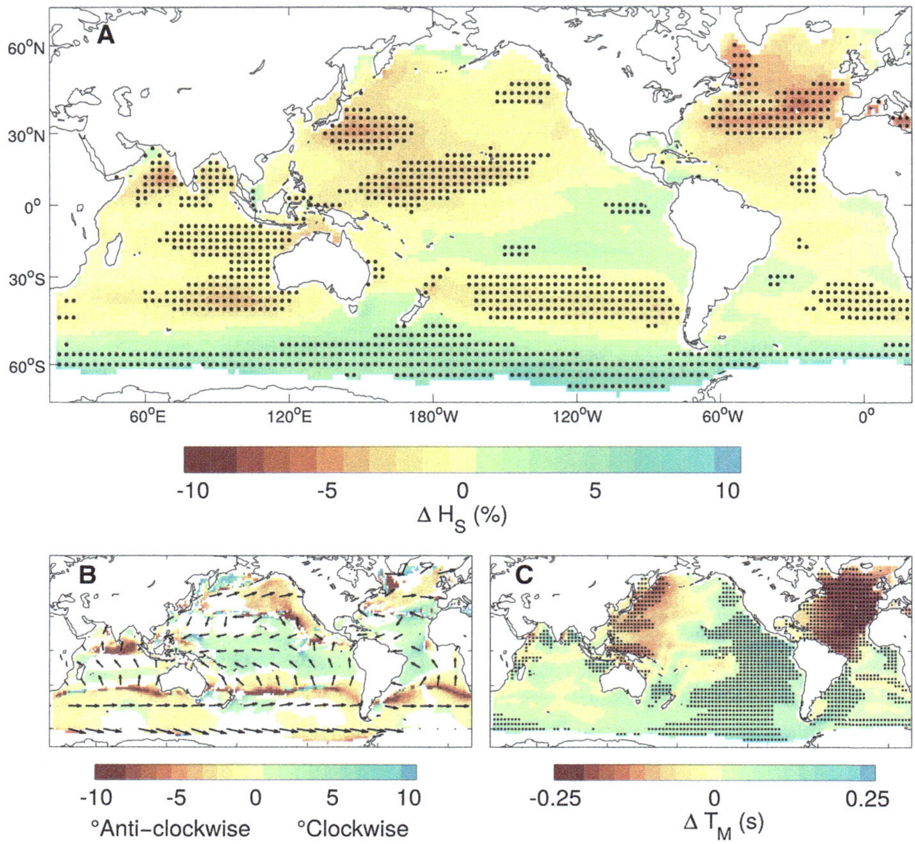

Fig. 7 Projected changes in wind-wave conditions (~ 2075–2100 compared with ~ 1980–2009) derived from the Coordinated Ocean Wave Climate Projection (COWCLIP) Project (Hemer et al. 2013a). **a** Percentage difference in annual mean H_s. **b** As for **a**, but displaying absolute changes in mean wave direction, with positive values representing projected clockwise rotation relative to displayed vectors, and colours shown only where ensemble members agree on the sign of change. **c** As for **a**, but displaying absolute changes in mean wave period. The symbol ~ is used to indicate that the reference periods differ slightly for the various model studies considered. Adapted from Church et al. (2013)

et al. 2017) downscaling approaches to increase the resolution of the forcing wind fields. Hemer et al. (2013a) analyzed the results of an ensemble of four dynamical and one statistical wave models developed as part of the Coordinated Ocean Wave Climate Project (COWCLIP) and compared the averaged multimodel wave parameters for the time-slice 2070–2100 with the ones for the time-slice 1979–2009 (Fig. 7). They found a statistically significant decrease in the annual H_s for 25.8% of the global ocean area and a statistically significant increase for 7.1% of the global ocean, predominantly in the Southern Ocean. These trends were more pronounced when focusing on the winter mean. The increase in wave activity in the Southern Ocean was shown to affect the wave period and wave direction in the other ocean basins, with a clockwise rotation of the wave direction in the tropics and larger wave periods in the eastern Pacific, as a result of enhanced wave generation in the Southern Ocean and northward swell propagation. In the North

Atlantic and North Pacific, a significant decrease in H_s and wave period is associated with weaker wind forcing projected in these regions. Wang et al. (2014) used a statistical model to derive project changes in H_s from changes in the sea-level pressure fields of 20 CMIP5 simulations. They obtained trend patterns similar to previous analysis, but also noted some differences with the results of studies based on CMIP3 GCM (Hemer et al. 2013a). For instance, they found a much more extensive H_s increase in the tropical South Pacific and an opposite H_s trend (increasing instead of decreasing) in the tropical South Atlantic, compared to Hemer et al. (2013a). Mentaschi et al. (2017) computed the projected changes in wave energy fluxes (integrating both H_s and the wave period) from the results of a wave model forced by an ensemble of five CMIP5 GCM models. They found a significant increase up to 30% in the 100-year return level for the majority of the coastal areas of the southern temperate zone and significant negative trend in large areas of the northern hemisphere. They explained these trends in extreme wave energy fluxes (WEFs) by the intensification of teleconnection patterns such as the Arctic Oscillation (AO), the El-Nino Southern Oscillation (ENSO) and the NAO. Casas-Prat et al. (2018) investigated the future wave projections in the Arctic using an unstructured spherical grid wave model forced with the wind fields and ice concentration of five CMIP5 GCM models. They found that by the end of the twenty-first century the wave climate in the Arctic region will be significantly different compared to the current climate due to ice retreat yielding new open water areas for wave generation. In particular, their ensemble projected mean H_s changes to reach 1.75 m by the end of the twenty-first century in newly open water. In the historical open water areas, the ensemble average projected some significant increases (up to 15%) in the Barents Sea, which can be related to the local increase in surface wind.

In summary, offshore wave conditions show strong spatial and temporal variability, which can be related to large-scale patterns in the atmospheric circulation. Although most available wave data are too short or overly inhomogeneous to clearly depict past long-term trends, most studies agree on significant positive H_s trends of the order of ~ 1 cm/year in the North Atlantic and Southern Ocean. In contrast, model projections for the end of the century tend to agree on a significant decrease in H_s in the North Atlantic and a significant increase in the Southern Hemisphere, but show contrasting results in other ocean basins such as the South Atlantic, the Indian Ocean or the North Pacific (Morim et al. 2018). In the following section, we will see how such changes may impact coastal sea level and add to ocean dynamic sea-level rise.

4 Wave Impacts on Coastal Sea Level

Measuring ocean properties in the nearshore environment is a challenging task. Contrary to deep-water environments, the nearshore bottom topography plays a fundamental role in the ocean dynamics, through refraction, diffraction, frictional, shoaling, breaking and resonant processes. Hence, the observed variability of most physical ocean parameters (wave height, sea level, currents) cannot be investigated without knowledge on the bottom topography, which is hardly available and may evolve rapidly. Also, the strong gradients in the bottom topography, currents and wave properties, which characterize the nearshore zone, often preclude the application of large-scale remote sensing techniques and coarse-resolution modelling strategy. Finally, the strong wave energy dissipation that occurs when wave break in the nearshore (see Sect. 2) makes the surf zone a very dynamic area with strong currents and rapid topographic changes, where long-term deployment of in situ measurements is very complicated. For these reasons, our knowledge on coastal sea level mostly relies on a few tide gauge time-series partly sheltered from the effect of wave and is therefore very limited compared to our knowledge on offshore sea-level changes. In this section, we present the current techniques used to measure and model nearshore topography, wave and sea level. Then, we discuss the impact of waves on coastal sea level based on recently published studies.

4.1 Topography, Waves and Sea Level in the Nearshore

4.1.1 Observation Techniques

Important nearshore observation programs have been developed in Australia, Europe or in the USA, with long-term monitoring of beach topography, nearshore wave conditions and water level that now extend over 30 years, but only at a few dedicated locations. The US Army Corps of Engineers Field Research Facility, located in Duck, North Carolina, is one of these sites with a continuous detailed monitoring of offshore and nearshore directional wave spectra, beach profiles and daytime video monitoring of the nearshore and intensive process studies (Birkemeier 1997; Holman and Stanley 2007). The Petten dike in the Netherlands (Wenneker et al. 2016), Narrabeen beach in Australia (Turner et al. 2016) or Truc Vert beach in France (Castelle et al. 2014) are other examples of coastal locations dedicated to long-term monitoring survey. At these sites, observations of sea level right at the shoreline have been combined with measurements of waves and nearshore topography to produce empirical parameterizations (see Sect. 4.1.3), suggesting that observing surf zone topography and waves outside of the surf zone could be a first step to extrapolate regional-scale storm surge levels all the way to sea levels right at the coast.

Close to the shoreline and across the surf zone, pressure-based systems have been developed (Barber et al. 1946; Munk et al. 1963) and are still widely used to measure the wave spectrum, giving the distribution of the surface elevation variance as a function of frequency, with recent improvements to correct for nonlinearities in the transformation from bottom pressure to surface elevation (Bonneton et al. 2017). Pressure is often combined with velocity measurements to provide a measurement of wave propagation direction as well as currents (e.g., Thornton and Guza 1983). Other instruments used routinely from structures include runup gauges (Wenneker et al. 2016) and shore-based video systems (Holman and Haller 2013). With the progress made on estimating variables from video imagery, such as wave height, sea level and runup, and morphology, this technique offers now access to an unequaled high frequency (hourly) and long-term description of the nearshore dynamics (Pianca et al. 2015; Almar et al. 2017; Brodie et al. 2018) including bathymetry (Holman et al. 2013; Bergsma and Almar 2018) and sea level (Abessolo Ondoa et al. 2019). The installation of shore-based video stations to monitor the nearshore is increasingly used due to their possibilities and low cost. Combining these video techniques with the use of unmanned aerial vehicle (UAV) has also greatly enlarged the scope of application of these methods (e.g., Turner et al. 2016; Matsuba and Sato 2018). Although video is limited to daytime monitoring, the development of LIDAR technology is expanding the possibilities of shore-based remote sensing (Blenkinsopp et al. 2010; Almeida et al. 2015; Brodie et al. 2015) and now offers an

Fig. 8 **a** Video camera system overlooking Biscarrosse beach, France (Marchesiello et al. 2015); **b** LIDAR scanner array fixed along a pier at Saltburn beach, UK (Martins et al. 2017); **c** array of ultrasonic sensors measuring swash and bed elevations at Truc Vert beach, France (Masselink et al. 2009, credits: Tim Scott); **d** wave buoy spotter; **e** pressure sensors installed on the rocky cliffs of Banneg Island, France (Dodet et al. 2018); **f** PUV system (pressure and current meter) partially immersed on the ebb shoal of the Obidos lagoon, Portugal (Bruneau et al. 2011)

attractive alternative to monitor high-frequency topography and runup or more recently, the detailed geometric properties of waves in the surf zone (Martins et al. 2018). First long-term deployments are being conducted (e.g., at Narrabeen, Australia) and should provide soon new insights in the quantification of multiscale runup dynamics and flooding events (Almeida et al. 2018). Combining measurements from shore-based lidars and

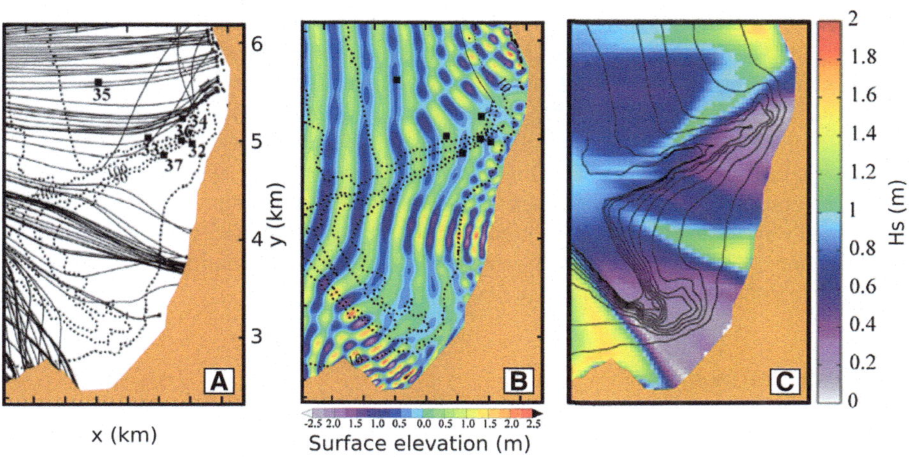

Fig. 9 Different representations of wave propagation over the Scripps-La Jolla submarine canyons. **a** Wave rays for 15 s with a constant offshore direction from the West and an offshore spacing of 20 m. **b** Solution of the mild slope equation for 1 m amplitude 15 s monochromatic swells, with a phase-resolving model. **c** Significant wave height computed for 15 s swells from the West with a phase-average spectral model. Reprinted from WISE Group (2007), as authorized by Elsevier

from tide gauges might allow to separate observed wave setup and runup from offshore sea-level variability. However, all these measurements are very localized and give a very partial view of the complex spatial patterns in waves and associated water levels. Figure 8 shows several instruments used to measure nearshore parameters.

4.1.2 Numerical Models

Spectral phase-averaged models are typically only limited by their poor representation of diffraction effects (e.g., Holthuijsen et al. 2003), which are typically negligible on natural topographies (e.g., Fig. 9 and Magne et al. 2007). In small areas, the effect of local winds may be neglected and backward ray tracing can be a very efficient linear model (O'Reilly and Guza 1993; Crosby et al. 2017). Phase-resolving models can also be used to better represent steep topographies and associated diffraction, as well as nonlinear shoaling effects; however, in their time-stepping version they can be prohibitively expensive in computation time for regions larger than about 10 km and timescales beyond a few hours. However, a great advantage of such models is that they solve the full flow, including water-level variations and currents, allowing the representation of rapid couplings, for example, in the swash zone, including inundation (e.g., Chen et al. 2002; Zijlema et al. 2011; Torres-Freyermuth et al. 2013).

Ocean circulation models (either based on the shallow water or the primitive equations) can be forced by phase-averaged forces to represent the wave effect on the mean sea level and the setup. This approach is generally successful except in very shallow water (Apotsos et al. 2007). Numerous coupled wave-current models have been developed in the last decade with some applications to coastal water levels (e.g., Walstra et al. 2000; Ozer et al. 2000; Kumar et al. 2012; Bennis et al. 2014; Stockdon et al. 2014; Cohn and Ruggiero 2016; Guérin et al. 2018). For depth-integrated motions, waves contribute to a horizontal force, that is usually represented by the divergence of a horizontal radiation stress tensor (Longuet-Higgins and Stewart 1964; Smith 2006). When vertical profiles of the current are considered, it is most convenient to write the equations for the flow momentum only (McWilliams et al. 2004; Ardhuin et al. 2008a, b, c; Suzuki and Fox-Kemper 2016).

The effect of infragravity waves has for long remained unaccounted for in wave-current models. However, the devastating impact of several hurricanes on the sandy coasts of Florida in 2004 has triggered the development of a new modeling approach to simulate water-level changes during storms including the effect of IG waves. The XBeach modelling system (Roelvink et al. 2009) uses this so-called surfbeat approach and couples a depth-integrated flow model with a spectral wave model, which represents the short-wave groups. IG waves can also be represented using phase-resolving models (e.g., Zijlema et al. 2011; Bonneton et al. 2011), although the large associated computational time limits such approach to domains a few km-large at maximum.

4.1.3 Empirical Models

Wave setup and runup cannot yet be modelled at large spatial scales (regional to global) with numerical hydrodynamic models or over the long periods needed to study, for instance, their contribution to water-level extremes (statistically) and their evolution under climate change, as they would need high-resolution mesh, knowledge of the full incident wave spectra and of nearshore morphology. To overcome these difficulties, empirical

Table 2 Wave runup empirical formulations (non-exhaustive list)

References	Empirical equation	Applicability range
Wassing (1957)	$R_{2\%} = 8\tan\beta H_{st}$	$0.05 < H/L < 0.07$
Hunt (1959)	$R_{2\%} = \tan\beta\sqrt{H_0 L_0}$	
Holman and Sallenger (1985)	$R_{2\%} = 0.92\tan\beta\sqrt{H_s L_0}$	$0.026 < \beta < 0.14$
Holman (1986)	$R_{2\%} = 0.2H_s + 0.83\tan\beta\sqrt{H_s L_p}$	$0.07 < \beta < 0.2$
Mase (1989)	$R_{2\%} = 1.86H_0\xi_s^{0.71}$	$0.03 < \beta < 0.20.007L_0 < H_0$
Powell (1990)	$R_{2\%} = H_s\left[2.86 - 62.69\left(\frac{H_s}{L_0}\right) + 443.29\left(\frac{H_s}{L_0}\right)^2\right]\left(\frac{-\ln 0.02}{4.2}\right)^{0.455}$	Gravel beaches, $H_s < 5$ m
Nielsen and Hanslow (1991)	$R_{2\%} = \mathrm{SWL} + 1.98 * 0.042\sqrt{H_s L_{0,s}}$ $R_{2\%} = \mathrm{SWL} + 1.85 * 0.052\tan\beta\sqrt{H_s L_{0,s}}$	$\beta < 0.10$ $\beta < 0.10$
Van der Meer and Stam (1992)	$R_{2\%} = 1.5\tan\beta\sqrt{H_{st} L_p}$	$0.5 < \xi_p < 2$
Ruggiero et al. (2001)	$R_{2\%} = 0.27\sqrt{\beta H_s L_p}$	$0.005 < \beta < 0.025$
Hedges and Mase (2004)	$R_{2\%} = 0.34H_s + 1.49\tan\beta H_s L_0$	$\xi_s < 3$
Stockdon et al. (2006)	$R_{2\%} = 1.1\left[0.35\beta\sqrt{H_s L_p} + 0.5\left(H_s L_p\sqrt{0.563\beta^2 + 0.004}\right)\right]$	$\xi_0 > 0.3$
Stockdon et al. (2006)	$R_{2\%} = 0.043\sqrt{H_s L_p}$	$\xi_0 < 0.3$
Pullen et al. (2007)	$R_{2\%} = 1.65\tan\sqrt{H_{m0} L_0}$	Dikes (of outer slope α)
Roberts et al. (2010)	$R_{2\%} = 1.00H_b$	$\xi_0 > 0.3$
Vousdoukas et al. (2012)	$R_{2\%} = 0.53\beta\sqrt{H_s L_p} + 0.58\tan\beta H_s + 0.45$	Reflective beaches
Poate et al. (2016)	$R_{2\%} = 0.21D_{50}^{-0.15}\sqrt{\tan\beta H_s T_{m-1m0} H_s}$ simplified to: $R_{2\%} = 0.49\sqrt{\tan\beta T_0 H_s}$	Gravel beaches $0.05 < tan\beta < 0.20$
Atkinson et al. (2017)	$R_{2\%} = 0.92\tan\beta\sqrt{H_s L_p} + 0.16H_s$	Model of models

β is the foreshore beach slope. Ω is the Dean parameter (Dean 1977), SWL is the still water level (see Nielsen and Hanslow 1991). ξ_s is calculated with respect to the deep-water significant wave height (H_s) and significant period (T_s). ξ_P corresponds to the Iribarren number calculated using the peak period and significant wave height. H_{st} is the significant wave height and H_{m0} is the wave height at the toe of the slope (for structures such as dikes), L_p is the peak period deep-water wavelength, L_0 the deep-water wavelength $L_{0,s}$ the deep-water wavelength computed using the significant period. H_0 is the deep-water wave height. D_{50} is the median sediment size parameterizations have been developed based on observations collected during field or laboratory experiments to estimate wave setup and runup for natural beaches and artificial structures.

Most studies have shown that the wave setup and the wave runup mostly depend on the offshore wave height (H_0), the offshore wavelength (L_0) and the foreshore slope (tan$\beta \sim \beta$), and can be expressed as a function of the Iribarren number = tan$(H_0/L_0)^{-0.5}$ (Iribarren and Nogales 1949), also known as the surf-similarity parameter (Battjes 1974). The most common scaling for runup is that of Hunt (1959), where runup is proportional to $\xi_0 H_0$, which is equal to tan$\beta(H_0 L_0)^{0.5}$. A non-exhaustive list of the most commonly used empirical formulations of setup and runup can be found in Tables 1 and 2, respectively, and in the references therein. A list of empirical swash formulations can be found in Passarella et al. 2018. Note that the definition of the beach slope is not straightforward for complex profiles (e.g., concave profiles, presence of sandbars, rocky cliffs time-evolving bathymetry), but on natural beaches, the value of β is often taken as the foreshore slope, in the region covered by the swash (Stockdon et al. 2006). The foreshore beach slope can substantially vary in time and alongshore and has been poorly measured so far. As the dependence of runup to the coastal morphology is stronger for non-dissipative beaches, several empirical formulations for runup were also derived without a dependence to the beach slope, to be applicable to dissipative beaches only (e.g., Mase 1989; Holman and Sallenger 1985; Powell 1990; Nielsen and Hanslow 1991; Stockdon et al. 2006; Roberts et al. 2010; Table 2).

Existing wave setup, swash or runup formulations were extensively tested (e.g., Atkinson et al. 2017; Di Luccio et al. 2018; Senechal et al. 2011; Vousdoukas et al. 2012; Cohn and Ruggiero 2016; Díaz-Sánchez et al. 2014; Stockdon et al. 2014; Passarella et al. 2018; Ji et al. 2018; Pullen et al. 2007; Power et al. 2019). Although most of these formulae have significant skills, the scatter between predicted and observed setup or runup can be substantial. This could be due to second-order processes (e.g., edge waves, variability of the beach slope, nearshore morphological control on runup that is not captured when only accounting for the beach slope) that are not represented by the formulations' predictors (e.g., Díaz-Sánchez et al. 2014). In addition, empirical setup and runup formulations have been calibrated and/or validated with short observational time series, and Power et al. 2019 showed that they are prone to significant errors when applied outside the range of conditions over which they have been calibrated. Finally, empirical setup and runup formulations have mostly been developed for natural sandy beaches, which are among the most vulnerable environments to sea-level changes (Wong et al. 2014) and cover a large fraction of the world's coast (Luijendijk et al. 2018). However, wave setup can exist in other coastal environments such as semi-enclosed bays, harbors (Thompson and Hamon 1980), rocky cliffs (Dodet et al. 2018) or steep-shelf small islands with fringing reefs (see, e.g., Merrifield et al. 2014). Some processes that may be negligible for sandy beaches may dominate in such environments. Recent experiments conducted on gravel beaches (Poate et al. 2016) and rocky cliffs (Dodet et al. 2018) have revealed the significant role of beach grain size, bottom roughness and water infiltration within fractured bedrock on the wave runup propagation. Therefore, research efforts are still actively ongoing to improve existing formulations for setup, swash and runup (e.g., Atkinson et al. 2017; Power et al. 2019; Ji et al. 2018; Passarella et al. 2018) and to cover other coastal environments including structures (e.g., van der Meer 1992; Pullen et al. 2007) and gravel beaches (e.g., Poate et al. 2016).

4.1.4 Hybrid Models

In comparison with the statistical downscaling models presented in Sect. 3.2, the hybrid models are more focused on a local scale as they propagate hydrodynamic conditions. They combine statistical techniques and numerical models. They have been used to predict nearshore wave conditions, wave runup or water level at the coast, based on offshore hydrodynamic conditions (see, e.g., Camus et al. 2011; Gouldby et al. 2014; Rohmer and Idier 2012; Gainza et al. 2018; Passarella et al. 2018). These hybrid models rely on the interpolation of process-based simulations or observations. In the former case, the first step is to define the process-based simulations to run (using, for instance, maximum dissimilarity algorithm as in Gainza et al. (2018); or adaptive sampling as in Rohmer and Idier (2012). For the interpolation, it can be done, for instance, by using radial basis functions (e.g., Camus et al. 2011; Gouldby et al. 2014), kriging (Rohmer and Idier 2012), or genetic programming (Passarella et al. 2018). It should be noted that the quality of meta-models based on process-based simulations cannot be better than the used numerical model and thus introduce additional errors. Passarella et al. (2018) used a genetic programming approach to predict the total and infragravity swash excursion from observed data sets extensively used in swash prediction studies. One of the originalities of this work is that the final solutions are selected based on a minimization of the error while ensuring the formula could be interpreted physically and avoiding overfitting. While their approach reduces the prediction errors compared to well-established parameterization, as the one of Stockdon et al. (2006), it still depends on the learning dataset and the choice of the variables taken into account. The comparison (visual inspection) of the runup prediction of that study (Fig. 5 in Passarella et al. 2018) and the modelling results of Nicolae-Lerma et al. (2016, Fig. 4a therein) on the Truc Vert dataset show similar prediction quality. However, as highlighted by Passarella et al. (2018), even if the parameters they took into account (H_0, T_p, L_0, β) are easily accessible, they oversimplify the processes that affect swash. In addition, it is unknown how the predictors will perform in settings beyond those of their work, contrary to the kriging method which provides an error estimate.

4.2 Wave Contribution to Coastal Sea-Level Changes

In Sect. 2, we have shown how wave-induced processes could impact the sea level at the coast. These local processes are mostly controlled by offshore wave conditions, particularly the significant wave height and the wave period, which have been shown (Sect. 3) to vary significantly over decadal time scales, due to internal climate oscillations. Given the projected changes in atmospheric circulation induced by external forcing, it is likely that the wave climate will respond to these changes and adapt to the future wind regimes. The ensemble modeling of projected change in wave conditions realized during the COWCLIP project provides a global picture of the potential wave conditions for the end of the twenty-first century (see Fig. 7 and Sect. 3.4). Such changes will likely impact future coastal sea level. In addition, other interactions between waves and sea level need to be taken into account in order to understand the contribution of waves to coastal sea level. For instance, changes in water depth due to sea-level rise will relax the depth limitation of waves and could lead to higher and longer-period waves reaching the coast. These aspects are presented in this section.

Global-scale studies of coastal sea-level changes or flood-related risk assessments are often based on tide gauge records, which are mostly located in wave-sheltered areas. Yet, regional- to global-scale studies accounting for wave contributions to past (e.g., Vousdoukas et al. 2016; Serafin et al. 2017; Rueda et al. 2017; Melet et al. 2018) and projected extreme sea levels (ESLs) at the coast are emerging (e.g., Vousdoukas et al. 2017, 2018a, b, Vitousek et al. 2017; Arns et al. 2017), although often assuming stationarity in the wave climate from past to future climate. These studies pinpoint the sizeable effects of wave contributions and the need to include them for coastal planning.

Vitousek et al. (2017) reported that when accounting for wave setup, wave runup, tides and storm surges, a sea-level rise of only 5–10 cm (expected to occur between 2030 and 2050) doubles the flooding frequency in many regions, particularly in the Tropics. Arns et al. (2017) reported that when accounting for wave contributions in future ESL, coastal protection design heights need to be increased by roughly 50% in the German Bight region relative to design heights inferred solely on sea-level rise. Focusing on future ESL along European coasts, Vousdoukas et al. (2017) showed that projected changes in storm surges and waves can substantially either enhance the effects of relative sea-level rise (along the majority of northern European coasts, locally with contributions up to 40%), or reduce it (along the Portuguese coast and the Gulf of Cadiz where reductions in surge and wave extremes offset relative sea-level rise by 20–30%). Global projections of ESL at the coast were recently provided by Vousdoukas et al. (2018a), accounting for wave setup. They reported a very likely increase in the globally averaged 100-year ESL of 34–76 cm under a moderate-emission-mitigation-policy scenario and of 58–172 cm under a business-as-usual scenario with wave setup being a non-dominant contributor to changes in extreme events. The important influence of changing wave contributions to coastal flooding due to increased water depth with sea-level rise was also reported in other studies (e.g., Hoeke et al. 2015; Wandres et al. 2017).

Wave setup and runup amplitude are modulated at longer timescales, notably through their dependence on offshore wave conditions. Wave height, period and direction vary

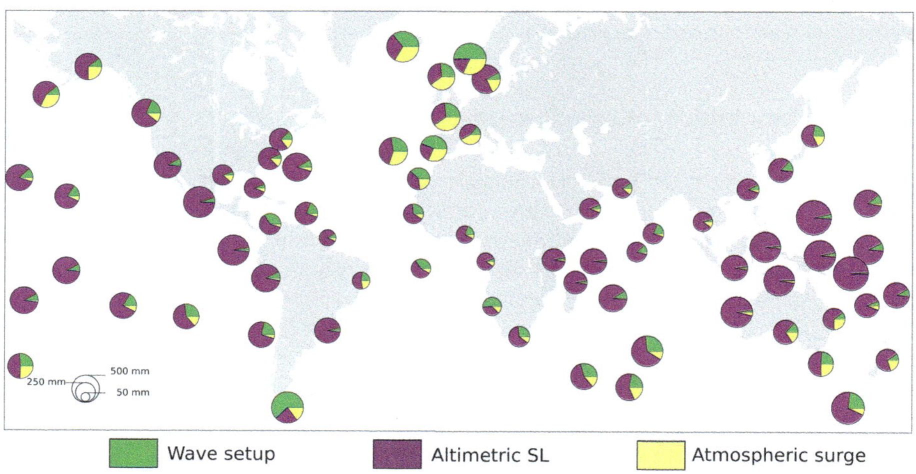

Fig. 10 Pie charts of the relative contribution of wave setup (green), altimetry-derived sea level (violet) and atmospheric surges (yellow) to total water-level detrended interannual-to-multidecadal variations over 1993–2015. The size of the pie charts indicates the standard deviation of detrended interannual-to-multidecadal sea-level variations, with scalings on the lower left corner. Wave setup was estimated from the Stockdon et al. (2006) generic formulation with a spatially uniform shoreface slope of 0.05 and ERA-interim deep-water wave height and period. Adapted from Melet et al. (2018)

over a broad range of timescales, from seasonal to interannual and multidecadal scales in response to both internal climate variability (e.g., seasonality in storminess, climate modes of variability such as ENSO) and climate change (Sect. 3, see also Woodworth et al. 2019). Long-term changes in offshore wave conditions can therefore modulate wave energy fluxes and extreme water levels at the coast (e.g., Barnard et al. 2015; Mentaschi et al. 2017), and affect wave setup and swash at long timescales. Melet et al. (2016) reported a large contribution from wave runup to past changes in total coastal water level in the Gulf of Guinea at seasonal timescales. A first-order, quasi-global estimate of wave setup and swash contribution to interannual-to-decadal coastal water-level changes was recently provided by Melet et al. (2018), considering wave setup and runup changes induced only by changes in offshore wave height and period. Interannual-to-decadal wave setup changes were found to be significant in over large parts of the world coastline over the last two decades compared to other contributors to coastal sea-level changes (see Melet et al. 2018; and Fig. 10 herein). As reported by Serafin et al. (2017), who investigated the relative contribution of tides, waves and non-tidal residuals to extreme total water levels at the shoreline of US West Coast sandy beaches, regional differences in the magnitude of extreme total water levels can be attributed, in part, to changes in incident wave conditions through their contribution to the wave setup and wave runup. Therefore, the offshore regional wave climate variability presented in Sect. 3 may explain the regional differences in coastal sea-level changes reported by several authors (e.g., Melet et al. 2018; Vousdoukas et al. 2018a, b). For some regions, changes in the wave setup can substantially either enhance or attenuate the effect of thermal expansion and ice mass transfer from land-over periods of several decades. Melet et al. (2018) found that changes in the wave runup over the past two decades were mostly caused by internal climate variability.

It is important to stress that most of the aforementioned studies on the contribution of wave-induced processes to ESL and sea-level changes at global scale use empirical parameterizations with approximated inputs, which can hardly provide accurate estimates and sharp conclusions on the potential role of waves on global coastal water levels (see the comments from Aucan et al. 2019 and the associated response from Melet et al. Aucan et al. 2019; Melet et al. 2019). The most important limitations of these approaches are therefore discussed in a dedicated Sect. 5.4. However, all these studies converge to show that given the actual projections of future wave climate, it is likely that wave-induced processes will significantly impact future trends in coastal sea level, which need to be taken into account in future studies on regional sea-level change projections.

4.3 Interactions with Other MSL-Related Processes

Several interactions between waves and lower-frequency sea-level components can be identified, among which are: (1) the effect of water depth modulation and currents on waves and (2) the effect of waves on atmospheric storm surge. Here, we introduce studies providing quantifications of these effects, mainly based on Idier et al. (2019), who also detail the related mechanisms.

In the nearshore, tides can significantly modify short waves. First, tide-induced water-level variations shift the cross-shore position of the surf zone, so that wave heights are modulated along a tidal cycle (e.g., Dodet et al. 2013). In addition, strong tidal currents (as in straits, estuaries or tidal inlets) can affect the waves (Rusu et al. 2011). As a consequence, wave setup along the shoreline or inside estuary can exhibit tidal modulations with a wave setup being smaller at high tide than at low tide (see, e.g., Kim et al. 2008), or the opposite (Dodet et al. 2018), depending on the curvature of the foreshore slope. At a given location, modulations of several centimeters to tens centimeters have been estimated in many studies, both in estuaries (see, e.g., Fortunato et al. 2017; Tagus estuary, Portugal) or on wave-dominated beaches (see, e.g., Pedreros et al. 2018; Truc Vert Beach, France). As an additional mechanism, we should note that, in estuaries, the wave setup can be also amplified through a resonant process (Fortunato et al. 2017).

Several studies investigated the effect of SLR on waves, taking into account tide changes or tide and atmospheric storm surges changes (see, e.g., Chini et al. 2010; Arns et al. 2017). In the German Bight, at the exposed westward-oriented coast, the modeling results of Arns et al. (2017) show that the significant wave height of the most damaging combination (still water level, wave height) of probability 0.01/year would exceed the present conditions by up to 0.25 m (0.78 m), for SLR = 0.54 m (1.74 m). They also show that with the sea-level rise, at a given location, the tide-induced modulation of waves decreases (see, e.g., Arns et al. 2017). However, the absolute results of these studies should be used with caution as the bathymetry is generally assumed unchanged (which is a strong assumption considering that sea-level rise should have significant effect).

Waves and wave setup are modified by water depth and currents, but they also have an effect on atmospheric storm surges, as the surface stress also depends on the sea state, through the sea-surface roughness (see, e.g., Stewart et al. 2013). These modifications of sea-surface roughness by waves can lead to atmospheric surge amplification up to tens of centimeters. For instance, Bertin et al. (2012) investigated the wave-induced processes explaining the large storm surge in the Bay of Biscay associated with the Xynthia storm in February 2010. They compared the atmospheric surges obtained with quadratic formulation to the ones obtained with wave-dependent parameterization to compute wind stress and they found that both approaches performed similarly except during the storm peak, where the surge with the wave-dependent parameterization was several tens of centimeters larger. Similar order of magnitudes is obtained, for instance, in the North Sea (Mastenbroek et al. 1993) or the Taiwan Strait (Zhang et al. 2010).

In coastal zones, the near-bottom orbital velocities associated with the propagation of short waves can become large and enhance bottom stress (Grant and Madsen 1986), including the formation of ripples (Ardhuin et al. 2002a, b). This enhancement should reduce the storm surges. However, this effect remains to be validated with field measurements in shallow water.

5 Limitation and Perspectives

5.1 Measurements of Waves

With seven altimeters in operations as of September 2018 (Fig. 4a), offshore wave heights are better monitored than ever, and higher along-track resolution is now available thanks to improved retracking and filtering. Because wave-induced sea level at the coast is a function of the wave periods (e.g., Stockdon et al. 2006; Poate et al. 2016; Dodet et al. 2018) and directional wave properties (Guza and Feddersen 2012), the availability of spectral wave information is critical. For large ocean basins, and in particular in the Pacific, SAR-derived swell measurements, such as from Sentinel-1, is a very rich source of data. Extending such measurements to shorter wave periods will allow the monitoring of wave periods

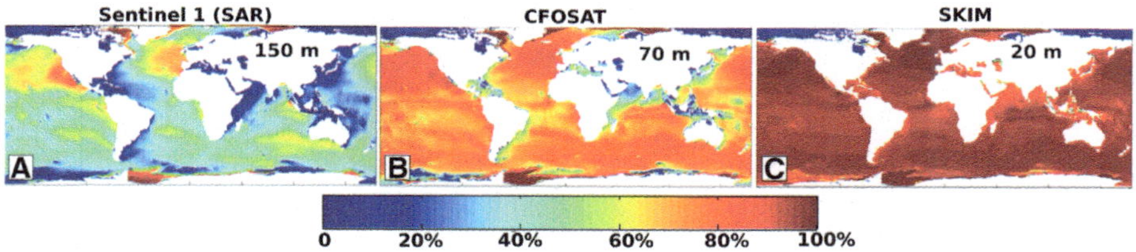

Fig. 11 Average fraction of simulated wave energy in January 2014 resolved when using a cutoff wavelength of 150 m (**a**), 70 m (**b**) and 20 m (**c**). Note that low values in the Arctic and other ice-covered regions are an artifact of the model that does not properly represent wave–ice interactions. January 2014 was very stormy in the North Atlantic

and directions in and near storms and in smaller basins. Indeed, the main limitation of SARs is due to the blurring associated with orbital velocities (Alpers and Rufenach 1979), which limits the effective resolution of waves that propagate in the satellite flight direction. This blurring is proportional to the altitude of the satellite. As a result, conditions are generally not satisfactory for measuring waves with SARs in enclosed basins or off eastern coasts (Fig. 11a). This is the main motivation for the development of specific "wave spectrometers," based on a conically scanning real aperture radars (RARs, see Jackson et al. 1985; Hauser et al. 2017; Nouguier et al. 2018). The first satellite to carry such a Ku-band RAR instrument is CFOSAT, successfully launched on October 29, 2018. This instrument is expected to resolve waves as short as 70 m, with a 180° ambiguity on the wave propagation direction (Fig. 11b). The next generation of such an instrument is ESA's Sea surface KInematics Multiscale (SKIM) monitoring mission, resolving much shorter wavelengths without direction ambiguity thanks to a Doppler measurement, and this could be launched in 2025 (Ardhuin et al. 2018). Such a resolution would allow the measurement of dominant waves in all seas, with a typical revisit time of 4 days (Fig. 11c).

All these wave measurements fail very close to the shore (50 km for altimeters, a few meters for SARs with a strong perturbation by the surf zone) and are typically used for validating the offshore part of numerical wave models that simulate waves up to the coast. However, recent developments in processing (e.g., Passaro et al. 2015; Ardhuin et al. 2017) or filtering techniques (Quilfen et al. 2018) enable data to be used at much higher resolution, possibly down to 20 km, whereas standard wave heights from altimeters (e.g., Sepulveda et al. 2015) are typically dominated by noise for scales shorter than 50 km.

Concerning our understanding of the complex wave deformation in the surf zone, new insights have been obtained with LiDAR scanners deployed along a pier at Saltburn beach, UK (Martins et al. 2017). This technique provides measurements of the sea-surface elevation from the break point to the runup limit at spatial (centimeters) and temporal (25 Hz) resolutions rarely achieved in field conditions. Such innovative measurements will undoubtedly foster our understanding of depth-limited wave-breaking mechanism and swash zone hydrodynamics and improve the accuracy of parametric formula used to infer nearshore parameters from deep-water wave measurements.

The modelling of waves right up to the coast requires a good knowledge of nearshore depths and currents that is missing in many regions. With some progress coming from the exceptional coverage of new optical sensors mounted on board of satellites such as Sentinel 2, both radiance-based methods (e.g., Purkis 2018) and new methods based on dispersion (e.g., Kudryavtsev et al. 2017; Romeiser and Graber 2018) will certainly lead to rapid progress on this topic. In addition, altimeter data can be efficiently used to apply directional correction to modeled wind sea and swell wave height, as demonstrated by Albuquerque et al. (2018).

Finally, the satellite remote sensing of a sea level that include wave effects, right at the coast, has not yet been demonstrated. Today's nadir altimeters only provide offshore sea levels, and it is unclear how much the noise in future measurements of SWOT's across-track SAR interferometer (Durand et al. 2010) may corrupt data across the surf zone, with additional velocity bunching and azimuthal cutoff effects.

5.2 Coastal Bathymetry

Recent studies have shown that extreme winter wave conditions can have a dramatic impact on beach morphologies at regional scale and over pluri-annual time periods (Masselink et al. 2016; Dodet et al. 2019). Therefore, it seems over-simplistic to consider that coastal vulnerability (shoreline retreat and flooding) can be represented as a simple response to sea-level change, assuming passive coastal bathymetry. Although constant efforts by the research community have been made toward either simple or complex paradigms of coastal evolution (e.g., static retreat by Bruun 1962), the coastal response to perpetually changing ocean-forcing conditions is still unclear (Cooper and Pilkey 2004; Ranasinghe 2016). Recently, several methods using satellite imagery have been proven reliable (Poupardin et al. 2016; Bergsma et al. 2019; Almar et al. 2019; Raucoules et al. 2019) in estimating large-sale coastal bathymetry at unprecedented resolution. One prominent approach is the use of multispectral imagery in estimating shallow bathymetry, until 20 m depth approximately in the case of clear waters. However, many coastal waters are very turbid, and this method requires ground-based calibration, which limits this technique to accessible areas. Other techniques to estimate bathymetry from optical or radar imagery make use of the wavelengths change during the shoaling of ocean waves. This allows resolving depths up to 40–50 m in regions where long swells are present. Among these methods, some use external data (measurements or offshore modeling), while others directly extract the wavelength and wave celerity information from the satellite images. Despite their high potential, these methods were only applied to a limited spatial domain (Danilo and Melgani 2016; Poupardin et al. 2016) using basic wave physics (none uses the information contained in the full spectrum in an optimal way) and can still be improved. Having access to high-resolution coastal bathymetry is one major prerequisite in order to reduce uncertainty in the estimation of wave contribution to coastal sea-level changes (e.g., Melet et al. 2018), and the aforementioned studies appear as promising avenue to tackle this challenge.

5.3 Stochastic Character of Wind-Generated Waves

Our ability to predict wave overtopping is crucial for coastal management. It should be reminded that an infinite number of time series could occur for a same-wave spectrum (Tuah and Hudspeth 1982). Pearson et al. (2001) raised the issue of the relationship between the length of the time series and the accuracy of the overtopping estimate. Pullen et al. (2007) recommend simulating a sequence of 1000 waves for each sea state tested. Pearson et al. (2001) and Romano et al. (2015) noticed that the overtopping discharge from tests using series of 500 waves is very close to that from tests with 1000 waves, while Williams et al. (2014) show that using more than 1000 waves does not affect the overtopping estimate. This suggests that the effect of stochastic character of waves on overtopping discharge depends on the time span during which the parameters influencing the waves are almost constant. Considering a wave period of 12 s, the time span should be larger than 1h40 min. In micro-tidal environment, such conditions could be met. However, in macro-tidal environments, as highlighted in Sect. 4.3, nearshore waves are modulated by tides, and water level can exhibit changes up to a few meters in a single hour. This implies that the stochastic character of waves should have a significant effect on flood occurrence or overtopping discharge, especially in macro-tidal environment. This subject should deserve more attention in the future.

5.4 Empirical Formulations for Wave Setup and Runup

While wave setup and runup derived from empirical formulations can compare well to observations when local characteristics of the coast are available (e.g., Vousdoukas et al. 2009; Stockdon et al. 2006), this approach can lead to uncertain results at global scales for several reasons: First, generic formulations of wave setup and runup involve the foreshore slope, which vary significantly in space and time (e.g., Hoeke et al. 2015; Karunarathna et al. 2016; Díez et al. 2017), and are usually within the 1–20% range (e.g., Komar 1998; Defeo and McLachlan 2013). Yet, as foreshore beach slopes are unknown over most of the world coastlines, regional- to global-scale studies have used constant values of the foreshore beach slope (e.g., Melet et al. 2018; Serafin et al. 2017), constant values of sediment grain size to infer beach slopes (Rueda et al. 2017), or formulations specific to dissipative beaches that do not depend on the beach slope (e.g., Vitousek et al. 2017). Wave setup estimates are very sensitive to the beach slope value and to the chosen empirical formulation, so that reported wave setup contributions are therefore to be modulated by the local beach slope compared to estimates using a uniform spatial value. It should also be noted that accounting for the variability of the beach slope should modulate the spatial heterogeneity of wave setup changes. Second, the widely used empirical formulation of Stockdon et al. (2006) for wave setup and runup has been derived from field observations on sandy beaches and does not encompass the variety of coastal environments that can be found worldwide (gravel beaches, cliffs, armored coasts, etc). It is therefore important to test and derive new empirical formula for other types of environment. In addition, deep-water wave characteristics derived from global numerical models to estimate wave setup and runup from empirical formulations also come with limitations. In particular for extreme events, storm winds tend to be underestimated in global simulations (especially for tropical cyclones). Finally, global-scale studies of coastal sea-level changes including the contribution from wave setup or runup do not account for interactions between the different contributors to sea-level changes (e.g., tides, waves, surges, ocean circulation, SLR) as global-scale numerical modeling studies including all the aforementioned processes are not available yet.

5.5 Projections from General Circulation Models

Predicting how wave-induced processes will contribute to future coastal sea-level changes requires accurate information on future wave conditions. For this purpose, general circulation models integrate the major physical processes of the atmosphere, ocean, cryosphere and land surface in order to simulate the response of the global climate system to increasing greenhouse gas concentrations. Although GCMs are extremely valuable tools to estimate the magnitude and trends of essential climate variables in the near future, their results are flawed by cumulative uncertainties inherent to each layer that constitutes these complex modeling systems (e.g., expected accumulation of greenhouse gases and aerosols in the atmosphere, response of the atmospheric circulation, interactions with the hydrosphere, cryosphere, lithosphere and biosphere, global-to-regional downscaling). Concerning ocean waves, the main driver is the atmospheric circulation and more particularly the 10-m wind fields that are usually used to force numerical wave models. As stated in the 5th Annual Report of the IPCC (chapter 13, Church et al. 2013), there is *low confidence* in global wave model projections because of uncertainties regarding future wind states, particularly storm geography, the limited number of model simulations used in the ensemble averages, and the different methodologies used to downscale climate model results to regional scales (Hemer et al. 2013b). In a recent paper, Morim et al. (2018) analyze 91 published global and regional wave climate projection studies and found a lack of consensus for projections of H_s over the eastern North Pacific and southern Indian and Atlantic Oceans, and everywhere, except for the Southern Ocean and the North Atlantic, for extreme H_s. They also note a distinct lack of research regarding projected changes in wave direction, which is of critical importance for the impact of waves on coastal sea level. Finally, they recommend a shift toward a systematic, community-based framework (as proposed by the Coordinated Ocean Wave Climate Project—COWCLIP, Hemer et al. 2018) to foster concerted efforts and to better inform the wide range of relevant decisions across ocean and coastal adaptation and mitigation assessments.

6 Conclusion

We have seen that the coastal sea level, as observed at the shores of exposed coastlines, is strongly influenced by wave-induced processes. Despite its central importance for risk mitigation and sustainable management of the coastal zone, the coastal sea level has for long been assimilated to the sea level estimated from tidal gauges located in sheltered areas, where the effect of the waves is limited. In addition, the rich information on global sea-level variability recorded by satellite altimeters over the last 30 years cannot be extrapolated to the coast where the presence of lands degrades altimeter echoes. As a consequence, our understanding of the regional and long-term variability of coastal sea level, and particularly its wave-related components, is still very limited. We claim in this paper that this topic deserves much attention. The three major wave-related processes that affect coastal sea level are (1) the wave setup: a tilt of the water surface in the surf zone caused by the rapid dissipation of wave energy at the breaking point; (2) the wave runup: the vertical excursion of the waterline when the waves enter the swash zone; (3) the infragravity waves: low-frequency (~ 0.01 Hz) oscillations of the water surface bound to and travelling with the wave groups that increase in size in the shoaling and breaking zone and significantly contribute to the swash motions. All these processes are controlled by offshore wave parameters, such as the significant wave height, the wave period and the wave direction. Given the strong variabilities (seasonal, interannual, decadal) of incident offshore wave conditions, the contribution of wave-related components is known to impact coastal sea level over a wide range of scales. Moreover, a number of studies on past and future trends in wave conditions indicate that significant changes in the height, direction and periods of wind-generated waves are imprinted by internal and external climate variabilities. These long-term changes in wave conditions will likely affect coastal sea level, and preliminary assessments of the wave-related contribution to coastal sea level have already confirmed this idea. However, severe limitations still restrain a clear understanding about the role of waves on coastal sea-level variability. These limitations concern: the lack of satellite information at the coast and on the wave period and direction, the difficulty to obtain accurate bathymetric information in the nearshore, where bottom features are constantly evolving, the high computational cost of high-resolution model needed to resolve the complex wave transformation from deep water to the shore, the overly simplistic form of empirical models used to derive wave setup and runup from offshore wave parameters, and the large uncertainties associated with future projections of wind and wave conditions at regional scales. Fortunately, great advances are currently shaping the fields of remote sensing observations, geophysical data analysis, and high-level computer science, which will pave the way for a deeper understanding of the contribution of wind-generated waves to coastal sea level.

Acknowledgements This paper arose from the international workshop on "Understanding the Relationship between Coastal Sea Level and Large-Scale Ocean Circulation" held at the International Space Science Institute (ISSI), Bern, Switzerland, on March 5–9, 2018. The authors are grateful to Anny Cazenave for taking charge of the implementation of this special issue. GD is supported by the ESA Sea State Climate Change Initiative. FA is supported by Labex Mer via Grant ANR-10-LABX-19-01, and the ESA Sea State Climate Change Initiative. XB is supported by the Regional Chair Project EVEX. DI is supported by BRGM and ANR projects (PSO COTIER and RISCOPE) and is thankful to Jérémy Rohmer for constructive discussions on the meta-models.

References

Abessolo Ondoa G, Almar R, Castelle B, Testut L, Leger F, Bonou F, Bergsma E, Meyssignac B, and Larson M (2019) On the use of shore-based video camera to monitor sea level at the coast: A case study in grand popo, benin (Gulf of Guinea, West Africa). J Atmos Ocean Technol (in review)

Albuquerque J, Antolínez JAA, Rueda A, Méndez FJ, Coco G (2018) Directional correction of modeled sea and swell wave heights using satellite altimeter data. Ocean Model 131:103–114. https://doi.org/10.1016/j.ocemod.2018.09.001

Allender J, Audunson T, Barstow SF, Bjerken S, Krogstad HE, Steinbakke P, Vardtal L, Borgman LE, Graham C (1989) The WADIC project: a comprehensive field evaluation of directional wave instrumentation. Ocean Eng 16:505–536

Almar R, Blenkinsopp C, Almeida LP, Cienfuegos R, Catalan P (2017) Wave runup video motion detection using the Radon Transform. Coast Eng 130:46–51

Almar R, Bergsma EWJ, Maisongrande P, Melo de Almeida LP (2019) Wave-derived coastal bathymetry from satellite video imagery: a showcase with Pleiades persistent mode. Remote Sens Environ. https://doi.org/10.1016/j.rse.2019.111263

Almeida LP, Masselink G, Russell PE, Davidson MA (2015) Observations of gravel beach dynamics during high energy wave conditions using a laser scanner. Geomorphology 228:15–27. https://doi.org/10.1016/j.geomorph.2014.08.019

Almeida LP, Almar R, Meyssignac B, Viet NT (2018) Contributions to coastal flooding events in southeast of Vietnam and their link with global mean sea level rise. Geosciences 8:437

Alpers W, Rufenach C (1979) The effect of orbital motions on synthetic aperture radar imagery of ocean waves. IEEE Trans Antennas Propag 27:685–690. https://doi.org/10.1109/TAP1979.1142163

Aouf L, Lefèvre JM, Hauser D, Chapron B (2006) On the combined assimilation of RA-2 altimeter and ASAR wave data for the improvement of wave forecasting. In: Proceedings of 15 years of radar altimetry symposium, Venice, March 13–18, 2006

Apotsos A, Raubenheimer B, Elgar S, Guza R, Smith JA (2007) Effects of wave rollers and bottom stress on wave setup. J Geophys Res Oceans 112(C2):C02003

Ardhuin F, Orfila A (2018) Wind waves. New Front Oper Oceanog 14:393–422. https://doi.org/10.17125/gov2018.ch14

Ardhuin F, Drake TG, Herbers THC (2002a) Observations of wave-generated vortex ripples on the North Carolina continental shelf. J Geophys Res Oceans 107:7-1–7-14. https://doi.org/10.1029/2001JC000986

Ardhuin F, Drake TG, Herbers THC (2002b) Observations of wave-generated vortex ripples on the North Carolina continental shelf. J Geophys Res 107:C10. https://doi.org/10.1029/2001JC000986

Ardhuin F, Herbers THC, Jessen PF, O'Reilly WC (2003) Swell transformation across the continental shelf. Part II: validation of a spectral energy balance equation. J Phys Oceanogr 33:1940–1953

Ardhuin F, Rascle N, Belibassakis KA (2008a) Explicit wave-averaged primitive equations using a generalized Lagrangian mean. Ocean Model 20(1):35–60

Ardhuin F, Jenkins AD, Belibassakis KA (2008b) Comments on the three-dimensional current and surface wave equations. J Phys Oceanogr 38(6):1340–1350

Ardhuin F, Rascle N, Belibassakis KA (2008c) Explicit wave-averaged primitive equations using a generalized Lagrangian mean. Ocean Model 20:35–60. https://doi.org/10.1016/j.ocemod.2007.07.001

Ardhuin F, Rascle N, Chapron B, Gula J, Molemaker J, Gille ST, Menemenlis D, Rocha C (2017) Small scale currents have large effects on wind wave heights. J Geophys Res 122(C6):4500–4517. https://doi.org/10.1002/2016JC012413

Ardhuin F, Aksenov Y, Benetazzo A, Bertino L, Brandt P, Caubet E, Chapron B, Collard F, Cravatte S et al (2018) Measuring currents, ice drift, and waves from space: the Sea surface KInematics Multiscale monitoring (SKIM) concept. Ocean Sci 14:337–354. https://doi.org/10.5194/os-2017-65

Ardhuin F, Stopa JE, Chapron B, Collard F, Husson R, Jensen RE, Johannessen J, Mouche A, Passaro M,Quartly GD, Swail V, Young I (2019) Observing sea states. Front Mar Sci. https://doi.org/10.3389/fmars.2019.00124

Arns A, Wahl T, Dangendorf S, Jensen J, Pattiaratchi C (2017) Sea-level rise induced amplification of coastal protection design heights. Nat Sci Rep. https://doi.org/10.1038/srep40171

Atkinson AL, Power HE, Moura T, Hammond T, Callaghan DP, Baldock TE (2017) Assessment of runup predictions by empirical models on non-truncated beaches on the south-east Australian coast. Coast Eng 119:15–31

Aucan J, Hoeke RK, Storlazzi CD, Stopa J, Wandres M, Lowe R (2019) Waves do not contribute to global sea-level rise. Nat Clim Change 9:2. https://doi.org/10.1038/s41558-018-0377-5

Barber NF, Ursell F, Darbyshire J, Tucker MJ (1946) A frequency analyser used in the study of ocean waves. Nature 158:329–335

Barnard PL, Short AD, Harley MD, Splinter KD, Vitousek S, Turner IL, Allan J, Banno M, Bryan KR, Doria A, Hansen JE, Kato S, Kuriyama Y, Randall-Goodwin E, Ruggiero P, Walker IJ, Heathfield DK (2015) Coastal vulnerability across the Pacific dominated by El Niño/Southern Oscillation. Nat Geosci 8:801–807. https://doi.org/10.1038/ngeo2539

Battjes JA (1974) Surf similarity. In: Proceedings of the 14th conference of Coast Eng. ASCE, 466–48

Battjes JA, Bakkenes HJ, Janssen TT, van Dongeren AR (2004) Shoaling of subharmonic gravity waves. J Geophys Res 109:c02009. https://doi.org/10.1029/2003JC001863

Bennis AC, Dumas F, Ardhuin F, Blanke B (2014) Mixing parameterization: impacts on rip currents and wave set-up. Ocean Eng 84:213–227

Bergsma EWJ, Almar R (2018) Video-based depth inversion techniques, a method comparison with synthetic cases. Coast Eng 138:199–209

Bergsma EWJ, Almar R and Maisongrande P (2019) Radon-augmented SentinelII satellite imagery to derive wave-patterns and regional bathymetry. IEEE Trans Geosci Remote Sens (in review)

Bertin X, Bruneau N, Breilh JF, Fortunato AB, Karpytchev M (2012) Importance of wave age and resonance in storm surges: the case Xynthia, Bay of Biscay. Ocean Model 42:16–30. https://doi.org/10.1016/j.ocemod.2011.11.001

Bertin X, Prouteau E, Letetrel C (2013) A significant increase in wave height in the North Atlantic Ocean over the 20th century. Glob Planet Change. https://doi.org/10.1016/j.gloplacha.2013.03.009

Bertin X, Li K, Roland A, Bidlot JR (2015) The contribution of short-waves in storm surges: two case studies in the Bay of Biscay. Cont Shelf Res 96:1–15

Bertin X, Olabarrieta M, MacCall R (2017) Hydrodynamics under storm conditions. In: Coastal storms: processes and impacts. Wiley, London

Bertin X, de Bakker A, van Dongeren A, Coco G, André G, Ardhuin F, Bonneton P, Bouchette F, Castelle B, Crawford WC, Davidson M, Deen M, Dodet G, Guérin T, Inch K, Leckler F, McCall R, Muller H, Olabarrieta M, Roelvink D, Ruessink G, Sous D, Stutzmann E, Tissier M (2018) Infragravity waves: from driving mechanisms to impacts. Earth Sci Rev 177:774–799. https://doi.org/10.1016/j.earscirev.2018.01.002

Bidlot JR (2017) Intercomparison of operational wave forecasting systems against buoys: data from ECMWF, MetOffice, FNMOC, ECCC, NCEP, MeteoFrance, DWD, BoM, SHOM, JMA, KMA, Puerto del Estado, DMI, NZM, METNO, SHN-SM, September 2017 to November 2017, tech. rep, Joint WMO-IOC Technical Commission for Oceanography and Marine Meteorology, 2017

Biesel F (1952) Équations générales au second ordre de la houle irrégulière. La Houille Blanche 7(3):372–376. https://doi.org/10.1051/lhb/1952033
Birkemeier WA (1997) The sandyduck '97 nearshore field experiment. Defense Technical Information Center, Fort Belvoir. https://doi.org/10.21236/ADA629329
Blenkinsopp CE, Mole MA, Turner IL, Peirson WL (2010) Measurements of the time-varying free-surface profile across the swash zone obtained using an industrial LIDAR. Coast Eng 57:1059–1065. https://doi.org/10.1016/j.coastaleng.2010.07.001
Bonneton P, Barthelemy E, Chazel F, Cienfuegos R, Lannes D, Marche F, Tissier M (2011) Recent advances in Serre-Green Naghdi modelling for wave transformation, breaking and runup processes. Eur J Mech B Fluids 30:589–597
Bonneton A, Lannes D, Martins K, Michallet H (2017) Nonlinear weakly dispersive method for recovering the elevation of irrotational surface waves from pressure measurements. Coast Eng. https://doi.org/10.1016/j.coastaleng.2018.04.005
Bowen AJ (1969) Rip currents. Theoretical investigations. J Geophys Res 74:5467–5478
Bowen AJ, Guza R (1978) Edge waves and surf beat. J Geophys Res 83:1913–1920
Bowen AJ, Inman DL, Simmons VP (1968) Wave 'set-down' and set-Up. J Geophys Res 73:2569–2577. https://doi.org/10.1029/JB073i008p02569
Brodie KL, Raubenheimer B, Elgar S, Slocum RK, McNinch JE (2015) Lidar and pressure measurements of inner-surfzone waves and setup. J Atmos Ocean Technol 32:1945–1959. https://doi.org/10.1175/JTECH-D-14-00222.1
Brodie KL, Palmsten ML, Hesser TJ, Dickhudt PJ, Raubenheimer B, Ladner H, Elgar S (2018) Evaluation of video-based linear depth inversion performance and applications using altimeters and hydrographic surveys in a wide range of environmental conditions. Coast Eng 136:147–160
Bromirski PD, Cayan DR, Flick RE (2005) Wave spectral energy variability in the northeast Pacific. J Geophys Res 110:C03005. https://doi.org/10.1029/2004JC002398
Bromirski PD, Cayan DR, Helly J, Wittmann P (2013) Wave power variability and trends across the North Pacific. J Geophys Res Oceans 118:6329–6348. https://doi.org/10.1002/2013JC009189
Bruneau N, Fortunato AB, Dodet G, Freire P, Oliveira A, Bertin X (2011) Future evolution of a tidal inlet due to changes in wave climate, Sea level and lagoon morphology (Óbidos lagoon, Portugal). Cont Shelf Res 31:1915–1930. https://doi.org/10.1016/j.csr.2011.09.001
Bruun P (1962) Sea-level rise as a cause of shore erosion. J Waterw Har Div 88:117–132
Camus P, Mendez FJ, Medina R (2011) A hybrid efficient method to downscale wave climate to coastal areas. Coast Eng 58:851–862. https://doi.org/10.1016/j.coastaleng.2011.05.007
Camus P, Mendez FJ, Losada I, Menendez M, Espejo A, Pérez J, Rueda A, Guanche Y (2014a) A method for finding the optimal predictor indices for local wave climate conditions. Ocean Dyn 64:1025–1038. https://doi.org/10.1007/s10236-014-0737-2
Camus P, Menendez M, Mendez FJ, Izaguirre C, Espejo A, Canovas V, Perez J, Rueda A, Losada IJ, Medina R (2014b) A weather-type statistical downscaling framework for ocean wave climate. J Geophys Res Oceans 119:7389–7405. https://doi.org/10.1002/2014jc010141
Camus P, Losada IJ, Izaguirre C, Espejo A, Menéndez M, Pérez J (2017) Statistical wave climate projections for coastal impact assessments. Earth's Future 5:918–933. https://doi.org/10.1002/2017EF000609
Carrier GF, Greenspan HP (1958) Water waves of finite amplitude on a sloping beach. J Fluid Mech 4:97–109. https://doi.org/10.1017/S0022112058000331
Carter DJT, Draper L (1988) Has the north-east Atlantic become rougher? Nature 332:494–494. https://doi.org/10.1038/332494a0
Casas-Prat M, Wang XL, Swart N (2018) CMIP5-based global wave climate projections including the entire Arctic Ocean. Ocean Model 123:66–85. https://doi.org/10.1016/j.ocemod.2017.12.003
Castelle B, Marieu V, Bujan S, Ferreira S, Parisot J.-P, Capo S, Sénéchal N, Chouzenoux T (2014) Equilibrium shoreline modelling of a highenergy meso-macrotidal multiple-barred beach. Mar Geol 347:85–94. https://doi.org/10.1016/j.margeo.2013.11.003
Castelle B, Dodet G, Masselink G, Scott T (2018) Increased winter-mean wave height, variability, and periodicity in the Northeast Atlantic over 1949–2017. Geophys Res Lett 45:3586–3596. https://doi.org/10.1002/2017GL076884
Cazenave A, Cozannet GL (2014) Sea level rise and its coastal impacts. Earth's Future 2:15–34. https://doi.org/10.1002/2013EF000188
Cazenave et al (WCRP Global Sea Level Budget Group) (2018) Global sea-level budget 1993–present. Earth Syst Sci Data 10:1551–1590. https://doi.org/10.5194/essd-10-1551-2018
Charles E, Idier D, Thiébot J, Le Cozannet G, Pedreros R, Ardhuin A, Planton S (2012) Present wave climate in the Bay of Biscay: spatiotemporal variability and trends from 1958 to 2001. J Climate 25:2020–2039. https://doi.org/10.1175/JCLI-D-11-00086.1

Chen Q, Kirby JT, Dalrymple RA, Shi F, Thornton EB (2002) Boussinesq modeling of longshore currents. J Geophys Res 108(C11):3362. https://doi.org/10.1029/2002jc001308
Cheriton OM, Storlazzi CD, Rosenberger KJ (2016) Observations of wave transformation over a fringing coral reef and the importance of low-frequency waves and offshore water levels to runup, overwash, and coastal flooding. J Geophys Res Oceans 121(5):3121–3140
Chini N, Stansby P, Leake J, Wolf J, Roberts-Jones J, Lowe J (2010) The impact of sea level rise and climate change on inshore wave climate: a case study for East Anglia (UK). Coast Eng 57(11–12):973–984. https://doi.org/10.1016/j.coastaleng.2010.05.009
Church JA, Clark PU, Cazenave A, Gregory JM, Jevrejeva S, Levermann A, Merrifield MA, Milne GA, Nerem RS, Nunn PD, Payne AJ, Pfeffer WT, Stammer D, Unnikrishnan AS (2013) Sea level change. In: Stocker TF, Qin D, Plattner G.-K, Tignor M, Allen SK, Boschung J, Nauels A, Xia Y, Bex V, Midgley PM (eds) Climate change 2013: the physical science basis. Contribution of working group I to the fifth assessment report of the intergovernmental panel on climate change. Cambridge University Press, Cambridge, pp 1137–1216. https://doi.org/10.1017/CBO9781107415324.026
Cipollini P, Benveniste J, Birol F, Joana Fernandes M, Obligis E, Passaro M, Ted Strub P, Valladeau G, Vignudelli S, Wilkin J (2017) Satellite altimetry in coastal regions. In: Satellite altimetry over oceans and land surfaces, pp 343–380. https://doi.org/10.1201/9781315151779
Cohn N, Ruggiero P (2016) The influence of seasonal to interannual nearshore profile variability on extreme water levels: modeling wave runup on dissipative beaches. Coast Eng 115:79–92
Cooper JAG, Pilkey OH (2004) Sea-level rise and shoreline retreat: time to abandon the Bruun Rule. Glob Planet Change 43:157–171. https://doi.org/10.1016/j.gloplacha.2004.07.001
Crawford W, Ballu V, Bertin X, Karpytchev M (2015) The sources of deep ocean infragravity waves observed in the North Atlantic Ocean. J Geophys Res 120:5120–5133. https://doi.org/10.1002/2014JC010657
Crosby SC, Cornuelle BD, O'Reilly WC, Guza RT (2017) Assimilating global wave model predictions and deep-water wave observations in nearshore swell predictions. J Atmos. Ocean Technol 34:1823–1836. https://doi.org/10.1175/JTECH-D-17-0003.1
Danilo C, Melgani F (2016) Wave period and coastal bathymetry using wave propagation on optical images. IEEE Trans Geosci Remote Sens 54:6307–6319. https://doi.org/10.1109/TGRS2016.2579266
De Bakker ATM, Tissier MFS, Ruessink BG (2014) Shoreline dissipation of infragravity waves. Cont Shelf Res 72:73–82. https://doi.org/10.1016/j.csr.2013.11.013
Dean RG (1977) Equilibrium beach profiles: U.S. atlantic and gulf coasts. Department of Civil Engineering and College of Marine Studies, University of Delaware
Di Luccio D, Benassai G, Budillon G, Mucerino L, Montella R, Pugliese Carratelli E (2018) Wave run-up prediction and observation in a micro-tidal beach. Nat Hazards Earth Syst Sci 18:2841–2857
Díaz-Sánchez R, López-Gutiérrez JS, Lechuga A, Negro V (2014) Runup variability due to time dependence and stochasticity in the beach profiles: two extreme cases of the Spanish coast. J Coast Res 70:1–6. https://doi.org/10.2112/SI70-001.1
Díez J, Uriarte A, Cánovas V, Medina R (2017) A parametric model for dry beach equilibrium profiles. Coast Eng 127:134–144
Dodet G, Bertin X, Taborda R (2010) Wave climate variability in the North-East Atlantic Ocean over the last six decades. Ocean Model 31:120–131. https://doi.org/10.1016/j.ocemod.2009.10.010
Dodet G, Bertin X, Bruneau N, Fortunato A, Nahon A, Roland A (2013) Wave-current interactions in a wave-dominated tidal inlet. J Geophys Res Ocean 118:1587–1905. https://doi.org/10.1002/jgrc.20146
Dodet G, Leckler F, Sous D, Ardhuin F, Filipot JF, Suanez S (2018) Wave runup over steep rocky cliffs. J Geophys Res Oceans 123:7185–7205. https://doi.org/10.1029/2018JC013967
Dodet G, Castelle B, Masselink G, Scott T, Davidson M, Floc'h F, Jackson D, Suanez S (2019) Beach recovery from extreme storm activity during the 2013/14 winter along the Atlantic coast of Europe. Earth Surf Process Landf. https://doi.org/10.1002/esp.4500
Durand M, Fu L, Lettenmaier DP, Alsdorf DE, Rodriguez E, Esteban-Fernandez D (2010) The surface water and ocean topography mission: Observing terrestrial surface water and oceanic submesoscale eddies. Proc IEEE 98:766–779. https://doi.org/10.1109/JPROC.2010.2043031
Elgar S, Herbers THC, Okihiro M, Oltman-Shay J, Guza RT (1992) Observations of infragravity waves. J Geophys Res Oceans 97:15573–15577. https://doi.org/10.1029/92JC01316
Fiedler JW, Brodie KL, McNinch JE, Guza RT (2015) Observations of runup and energy flux on a low-slope beach with high-energy, long-period ocean swell. Geophys Res Lett. https://doi.org/10.1002/2015gl066,124
Ford M, Merrifield MA, Becker JM (2018) Inundation of a low-lying urban atoll island: Majuro, Marshall Islands. Nat Hazards 91(3):1273–1297. https://doi.org/10.1007/s11069-018-3183-5

Fortunato AB, Freire P, Bertin X, Rodrigues M, Liberato MLR, Ferreira J (2017) A numerical study of the February 15, 1941 storm in the Tagus estuary. Cont Shelf Res 144:50–64. https://doi.org/10.1016/j.csr.2017.06.023

Gain L (1923) La prédiction des houles au Maroc. Revue Scientifique 61(19):605–615

Gainza J, Rueda A, Camus P, Tomas A, Méndez FJ, Sano M, and Tomlinson R (2018) A meta-modelling approach for estimating long-term wave run-up and total water level on beaches. J Coast Res 34(2):475–489. Coconut Creek (Florida), ISSN 0749-0208

Garcez-Faria A, Thornton E, Lippmann T, Stanton T (2000) Undertow over a barred beach. J Geophys Res Oceans 105(C7):16999–17010

Gawehn M, van Dongeren A, van Rooijen A, Storlazzi CD, Cheriton OM, Reniers A (2016) Identification and classification of very low frequency waves on a coral reef flat. J Geophys Res Oceans 121(10):7560–7574

Gemmrich J, Thomas B, Bouchard R (2011) Observational changes and trends in northeast Pacific wave records. Geophys Res Lett. https://doi.org/10.1029/2011GL049518

Gouldby B, Méndez FJ, Guanche Y, Rueda A, Mínguez R (2014) A methodology for deriving extreme nearshore sea conditions for structural design and flood risk analysis. Coast Eng 88:15–26. https://doi.org/10.1016/j.coastaleng.2014.01.012

Grant WD, Madsen OS (1986) The continental shelf bottom boundary layer. Annu Rev Fluid Mech 18:265–305

Gregory JM, Griffies SM, Hughes CW, Lowe JA, Church JA, Fukimori I, Gomez N, Kopp RE, Landerer F, Cozannet GL, Ponte RM, Stammer D, Tamisiea ME, van de Wal RSW (2019) Concepts and terminology for sea level: mean, variability and change, both local and global. Surv Geophys. https://doi.org/10.1007/s10712-019-09525-z

Guérin T, Bertin X, Coulombier T, de Bakker A (2018) Impacts of wave-induced circulation in the surf zone on wave setup. Ocean Model 123:86–97. https://doi.org/10.1016/j.ocemod.2018.01.006

Guimaraes PV, Ardhuin F, Sutherland P, Accensi M, Hamon M, Pérignon Y, Thomson J, Benetazzo A, Ferrant P (2018) A Surface KInematics Buoy (SKIB) for wave-current interactions studies. Ocean Sci Discuss. https://doi.org/10.5194/os-2018-45

Gulev SK, Grigorieva V (2004) Last century changes in ocean wind wave height from global visual wave data. Geophys Res Lett. https://doi.org/10.1029/2004GL021040

Gulev SK, Grigorieva V (2006) Variability of the winter wind waves and swell in the North Atlantic and North Pacific as revealed by the voluntary observing ship data. J Clim 19:5667–5685. https://doi.org/10.1175/JCLI3936.1

Gulev SK, Grigorieva V, Sterl A, Woolf D (2003) Assessment of the reliability of wave observations from voluntary observing ships: insights from the validation of a global wind wave climatology based on voluntary observing ship data. J Geophys Res 108(C7):3236

Guza RT, Feddersen F (2012) Effect of wave frequency and directional spread on shoreline runup. Geophys Res Lett 39:L11607

Guza RT, Thornton EB (1981) Wave set-up on a natural beach. J Geophys Res 86(C5):4133–4137

Guza RT, Thornton EB (1982) Swash oscillations on a natural beach. J Geophys Res 87:483–491. https://doi.org/10.1029/JC087iC01p00483

Hanslow DJ, Nielsen P (1992) Wave setup on beaches and in river entrances. In: Proceedings of 23rd international conference on coastal Engineering, pp 240–252

Hasselmann K (1962) On the non-linear energy transfer in a gravity-wave spectrum part 1. General theory. J Fluid Mech 12(04):481–500. https://doi.org/10.1017/S0022112062000373

Hasselmann K, Chapron B, Aouf L, Ardhuin F, Collard F, Engen G, Hasselmann S, Heimbach P, Janssen P, Johnsen H, Krogstad H, Lehner S, Li J-G, Li X-M, Rosenthal W, Schulz-Stellenfleth J (2012) The ERS SAR wave mode: a breakthrough in global ocean wave observations. ERS Missions: 20 Years of Observing Earth. European Space Agency, Noordwijk, pp 165–198

Hauser D, Tison C, Amiot T, Delaye L, Corcoral N, Castillan P (2017) SWIM: the first spaceborne wave scatterometer. IEEE Trans Geosci Remote Sens 55:3000–3014. https://doi.org/10.1109/TGRS2017.2658672

Hedges T, Mase H (2004) Modified Hunt's equation incorporating wave setup. J Waterw Port Coast Ocean Eng 130:109–113

Hemer MA, Church JA, Hunter JR (2010) Variability and trends in the directional wave climate of the Southern Hemisphere. Int J Climatol 30:475–491. https://doi.org/10.1002/joc.1900

Hemer MA, Fan Y, Mori N, Semedo A, Wang XL (2013a) Projected changes in wave climate from a multi-model ensemble. Nat Clim Change 3:471–476. https://doi.org/10.1038/nclimate1791

Hemer MA, Katzfey J, Trenham CE (2013b) Global dynamical projections of surface ocean wave climate for a future high greenhouse gas emission scenario. Ocean Modell Ocean Surf Waves 70:221–245. https://doi.org/10.1016/j.ocemod.2012.09.008

Hemer MA, Wang XL, Webb A, COWCLIP contributors (2018) Report of the 2018 meeting for the WCRP-JCOMM coordinated ocean wave climate project, Paris, 21–23 May, 2018. JCOMM technical report 92. https://www.jcomm.info/index.php?option=com_oe&task=viewDocumentRecord&docID=22378
Herbers THC, Burton MC (1997) Nonlinear shoaling of directionally spread waves on a beach. J Geophys Res 102(C9):21101–21114
Herbers THC, Lentz SJ (2010) Observing directional properties of ocean swell with an acoustic doppler current profiler (ADCP). J Atmos Ocean Technol 27:210–225
Herbers THC, Janssen TT, Colbert DB, MacMahan JH (2012) Observing ocean surface waves with gps-tracked buoys. J Atmos Ocean Technol 29:944–959
Hoeke RK, McInnes KL, Kruger JC, McNaught RJ, Hunter JR, Smithers SG (2013) Widespread inundation of Pacific islands triggered by distant-source wind-waves. Glob Planet Change 108:128–138. https://doi.org/10.1016/j.gloplacha.2013.06.006
Hoeke RK, McInnes KL, O'Grady JG (2015) Wind and wave setup contributions to extreme sea levels at a tropical high island: a stochastic cyclone simulation study for Apia. Samoa J Mar Sci Eng 3:1117–1135
Holman RA (1986) Extreme value statistics for wave run-up on a natural beach. Coast Eng 9:527–544
Holman R, Haller MC (2013) Remote sensing of the nearshore. Ann Rev Mar Sci 5:95–113. https://doi.org/10.1146/annurev-marine-121211-172408
Holman RA, Sallenger AH Jr (1985) Setup and Swash on a natural beach. J Geophys Res 90(C1):945–953
Holman RA, Stanley J (2007) The history and technical capabilities of Argus. Coast Eng 54:477–491. https://doi.org/10.1016/j.coastaleng.2007.01.003
Holman R, Plant NG, Holland KT (2013) cBathy: a robust algorithm for estimating nearshore bathymetry. J Geophys Res C Oceans 118:2595–2609. https://doi.org/10.1002/jgrc.20199
Holthuijsen LH, Herman A, Booij N (2003) Phase-decoupled refraction-diffraction for spectral wave models. Coast Eng 49:91–305
Hunt IA (1959) Design of seawalls and breakwaters. J Waterw Harbors Div 85:123–152
Idier D, Bertin X, Thompson P, Pickering MD (2019) Interactions between mean sea level, tide, surge, waves and flooding: mechanisms and contributions to sea level variations at the coast. Surv Geophys. https://doi.org/10.1007/s10712-019-09549-5
Inch K, Davidson M, Masselink G, Russell P (2017) Observations of nearshore infragravity wave dynamics under high energy swell and wind-wave conditions. Cont Shelf Res 138:19–31. https://doi.org/10.1016/j.csr.2017.02.010
Iribarren CR, Nogales C (1949) Protection des ports. In: XVIIth international navigation congress. Lisbon, Portugal, pp 31–80
Izaguirre C, Méndez FJ, Menéndez M, Losada IJ (2011) Global extreme wave height variability based on satellite data. Geophys Res Lett. https://doi.org/10.1029/2011GL047302
Jackson FC, Walton WT, Baker PL (1985) Aircraft and satellite measurement of ocean wave directional spectra using scanning-beam microwave radars. J Geophys Res 90:987–1004
Janssen TT, Herbers THC, Battjes JA (2006) Generalized evolution equation for nonlinear surface gravity waves over two-dimensional topography. J Fluid Mech 552:393–418
Jensen RE, Swail VR, Bouchard RH, Riley RE, Hesser TJ, Blaseckie M, MacIsaac C (2015) Field laboratory for ocean sea state investigation and experimentation: FLOSSIE intra-measurement evaluation of 6 N wave buoy systems. In: Proceedings of the 114th international workshop on wave hindcasting and forecasting & 5th coastal hazard symposium
Ji C, Zhang Q, Wu Y (2018) An empirical formula for maximum wave setup based on a coupled wave-current model. Ocean Eng 147:215–226
Jia G, Taflanidis AA (2013) Kriging metamodeling for approximation of high-dimensional wave and surge responses in real-time storm/hurricane risk assessment. Comput Methods Appl Mech Eng 261:24–38
Karunarathna H, Caraballo JH, Kuriyama Y, Mase H, Ranasinghe R, Reeve DE (2016) Linkages between sediment composition, wave climate and beach profile variability at multiple timescales. Mar Geol 381:194–208
Kennedy A, Westerink J, Smith J, Hope M, Hartman M, Taflanidis A, Tanaka S, Westerink H, Cheung K, Smith T, Hamann M, Minamide M, Ota A, Dawson C (2012) Tropical cyclone inundation potential on the hawaiian islands of Oahu and Kauai. Ocean Model 52–53:54–68
Kerbaol V, Chapron B, Vachon P (1998) Analysis of ERS-1/2 synthetic aperture radar wave mode imagettes. J Geophys Res 103(C4):7833–7846
Kim SY, Yasuda T, Mase H (2008) Numerical analysis of effects of tidal variations on storm surges and waves. App Ocean Res 30(4):311–322. https://doi.org/10.1016/j.apor.2009.02.003
Komar P (1998) Beach processes and sedimentation, 2nd edn. Prentice Hall, New Jersey

Kudryavtsev V, Yurovskaya M, Chapron B, Collard F, Donlon C (2017) Sun glitter imagery of surface waves. Part 2: waves transformation on ocean currents. J Geophys Res. https://doi.org/10.1002/2016jc012426
Kumar N, Voulgaris G, Warner JC, Olabarrieta M (2012) Implementation of the vortex force formalism in the coupled ocean-atmosphere-wavesediment transport (COAWST) modeling system for inner shelf and surf zone applications. Ocean Model 47:65–95. https://doi.org/10.1016/j.ocemod.2012.01.003
Laugel A, Menendez M, Benoit M, Mattarolo G, Méndez F (2014) Wave climate projections along the French coastline: dynamical versus statistical downscaling methods. Ocean Model 84:35–50. https://doi.org/10.1016/j.ocemod.2014.09.002
Longuet-Higgins M, Stewart R (1962) Radiation stress and mass transport in gravity waves, with application to surf beats. J Fluid Mech 13(4):481–504
Longuet-Higgins MS, Stewart R (1964) Radiation stresses in water waves; a physical discussion, with applications. Deep Sea Res Oceanogr Abstracts 11:529–562
Longuet-Higgins MS, Cartwright DE, Smith ND (1963) Observations of the directional spectrum of sea waves using the motions of a floating buoy. In: Ocean wave spectra, proceedings of a conference, Easton, Maryland, pp 111–136, National Academy of Sciences, Prentice-Hall
Luijendijk A, Hagenaars G, Ranasinghe R, Baart F, Donchyts G, Aarninkhof S (2018) The state of the world's beaches. Sci Rep 8:6641
Lumpkin T, Ozgokmen T, Centurioni L (2016) Advances in the application of surface drifters. Ann Rev Mar Sci. https://doi.org/10.1146/annurev-marine-010816-060641
Magne R, Belibassakis K, Herbers THC, Ardhuin F, O'Reilly WC, Rey V (2007) Evolution of surface gravity waves over a submarine canyon. J Geophys Res 112:C01002. https://doi.org/10.1029/2005JC003035
Malhadas MS, Leitão PC, Silva A, Neves R (2009) Effect of coastal waves on sea-level in Óbidos Lagoon, Portugal. Cont Shelf Res 29(9):1240–1250
Marchesiello P, Benshila R, Almar R, Uchiyama Y, McWilliams JC, Shchepetkin A (2015) On tridimensional rip current modeling. Ocean Model 96:36–48. https://doi.org/10.1016/j.ocemod.2015.07.003
Martins K, Blenkinsopp CE, Power HE, Bruder B, Puleo JA, Bergsma EWJ (2017) High-resolution monitoring of wave transformation in the surf zone using a LiDAR scanner array. Coast Eng 128:37–43. https://doi.org/10.1016/j.coastaleng.2017.07.007
Martins K, Blenkinsopp CE, Deigaard R, Power HE (2018) Energy dissipation in the inner surf zone: new insights from LiDAR-based roller geometry measurements. J Geophys Res Oceans (in press)
Mase H (1989) Random wave runup height on gentle slope. J Waterw Port Coast Ocean Eng 115:649–661
Masselink G, Russell P, Turner I, Blenkinsopp C (2009) Net sediment transport and morphological change in the swash zone of a high-energy sandy beach from swash event to tidal cycle time scales. Mar Geol 267:18–35. https://doi.org/10.1016/j.margeo.2009.09.003
Masselink G, Castelle B, Scott T, Dodet G, Suanez S, Jackson D, Floc'h F (2016) Extreme wave activity during 2013/2014 winter and morphological impacts along the Atlantic coast of Europe. Geophys Res Lett 43:2135–2143. https://doi.org/10.1002/2015GL067492
Mastenbroek C, Burgers G, Janssen PAEM (1993) The dynamical coupling of a wave model and a storm surge model through the atmospheric boundary layer. J Phys Oceanogr 23:1856–1866
Matsuba Y, Sato S (2018) Nearshore bathymetry estimation using UAV. Coast Eng J 60:51–59. https://doi.org/10.1080/21664250.2018.1436239
McWilliams JC, Restrepo JM, Lane EM (2004) An asymptotic theory for the interaction of waves and currents in coastal waters. J Fluid Mech 511:135–178
Melet A, Almar R, Meyssignac B (2016) What dominates sea level at the coast: a case study for the Gulf of Guinea. Ocean Dyn 66:623–636
Melet A, Meyssignac B, Almar R, Le Cozannet G (2018) Under-estimated wave contribution to sea-level rise. Nat Clim Change 8:234–239
Melet A, Meyssignac B, Almar R, Le Cozannet G (2019) Reply to ''Waves do not contribute to global sea-level rise''. Nat Clim Change 9:3. https://doi.org/10.1038/s41558-018-0378-4
Menéndez M, Méndez FJ, Losada IJ, Graham NE (2008) Variability of extreme wave heights in the northeast Pacific Ocean based on buoy measurements. Geophys Res Lett. https://doi.org/10.1029/2008GL035394
Mentaschi L, Vousdoukas MI, Voukouvalas E, Dosio A, Feyen L (2017) Global changes of extreme coastal wave energy fluxes triggered by intensified teleconnection patterns. Geophys Res Lett 44:2416–2426. https://doi.org/10.1002/2016GL072488
Merrifield MA, Becker JM, Ford M, Yao Y (2014) Observations and estimates of wave-driven water level extremes at the Marshall Islands. Geophys Res Lett 41:7245–7253. https://doi.org/10.1002/2014GL061005

Morim J, Hemer M, Cartwright N, Strauss D, Andutta F (2018) On the concordance of 21st century wind-wave climate projections. Glob Planet Change 167:160–171. https://doi.org/10.1016/j.gloplacha.2018.05.005

Moura T, Baldock TE (2017) Remote sensing of the correlation between breakpoint oscillations and infragravity waves in the surf and swash zone. J Geophys Res Oceans 122(4):3106–3122

Munk WH, Traylor MA (1947) Refraction of ocean waves: a process linking underwater topography to beach erosion. J Geol LV:1–26

Munk WH, Miller GR, Snodgrass FE, Barber NF (1963) Directional recording of swell from distant storms. Phil Trans R Soc Lond Ser A Math Phys Eng Sci 255:505–584. https://doi.org/10.1098/rsta.1963.0011

Neumann B, Vafeidis AT, Zimmermann J, Nicholls RJ (2015) Future coastal population growth and exposure to sea-level rise and coastal flooding—a global assessment. PLoS ONE. https://doi.org/10.1371/journal.pone.0118571

Nicolae-Lerma A, Pedreros R, Senechal N (2016) Wave set-up and run-up variability on a complex barred beach during highly dissipative storm conditions. J Coast Res 75:882–886. https://doi.org/10.2112/SI75-177.1

Nicolae-Lerma A, Pedreros R, Robinet A, Sénéchal N (2017) Simulating wave setup and runup during storm conditions on a complex barred beach. Coast Eng 123:29–41

Nielsen P, DJ Hanslow (1991) Wave runup distributions on natural beaches. J Coast Res 1139–1152

Nouguier F, Chapron B, Collard F, Mouche A, Rascle N, Ardhuin F, Wu X (2018) Sea surface kinematics from near-nadir radar measurements. IEEE Trans Geosci Remote Sens. https://doi.org/10.1109/tgrs2018.2833200

O'Reilly WC, Guza RT (1993) A comparison of two spectral wave models in the Southern California Bight. Coast Eng 19:263–282

Overeem I, Anderson RS, Wobus CW, Clow GD, Urban FE, Matell N (2011) Sea ice loss enhances wave action at the Arctic coast. Geophys Res Lett. https://doi.org/10.1029/2011GL048681

Ozer J, Padilla-Hernandez R, Monbaliub J, Fanjul EA, Albiach JCC, Osuna P, Yu JC, Wolf J (2000) A coupling module for tides, surges and waves. Coast Eng 41(1–3):95–124

Passarella M, Goldstein EB, De Muro S, Coco G (2018) The use of genetic programming to develop a predictor of swash excursion on sandy beaches. Nat Hazards Earth Syst Sci 18:599–611. https://doi.org/10.5194/nhess-18-599-2018

Passaro M, Fenoglio-Marc L, Cipollini P (2015) Validation of significant wave height from improved satellite altimetry in the German Bight. IEEE Trans Geosci Remote Sens 53:2146–2156

Pearson J, Bruce T, Allsop N (2001) Prediction of wave overtopping at steep seawalls—variabilities and uncertainties. Proc Waves 1:1797–1808

Pedreros R, Idier D, Muller H, Lecacheux S, Paris F, Yates-Michelin M, Dumas F, Pineau-Guillou L, Sénéchal N (2018) Relative contribution of wave setup to the storm surge: observations and modeling based analysis in open and protected environments (Truc Vert beach and Tubuai island). In: Shim J-S, Chun I, Lim HS (eds) Proceedings from the international coastal symposium (ICS) 2018 (Busan, Republic of Korea). J Coast Res 85:1046–1050. Coconut Creek (Florida), ISSN 0749-0208

Perez J, Menendez M, Camus P, Mendez FJ, Losada IJ (2015) Statistical multi-model climate projections of surface ocean waves in Europe. Ocean Model 96:161–170. https://doi.org/10.1016/j.ocemod.2015.06.001

Pianca C, Holman R, Siegle E (2015) Shoreline variability from days to decades: results of long-term video imaging. J Geophys Res Oceans 120(3):2159–2178

Poate TG, McCall RT, Masselink G (2016) A new parameterisation for runup on gravel beaches. Coast Eng 117:176–190. https://doi.org/10.1016/j.coastaleng.2016.08.003

Pomeroy A, Lowe R, Symonds G, Van Dongeren A, Moore C (2012) The dynamics of infragravity wave transformation over a fringing reef. J Geophys Res. https://doi.org/10.1029/2012jc008310

Poupardin A, Idier D, de Michele M, Raucoules D (2016) Water depth inversion from a single SPOT-5 dataset. IEEE Trans Geosci Remote Sens 54:2329–2342. https://doi.org/10.1109/TGRS2015.2499379

Powell KA (1990) Predicting short term profile response for shingle beaches. Hydraulics Research Limited, Wallingford, Oxfordshire. Report SR2 19

Power HE, Gharabaghi B, Bonakdari H, Robertson B, Atkinson AL, Baldock TE (2019) Prediction of wave runup on beaches using Gene-Expression Programming and empirical relationships. Coast Eng 144:47–61

Pullen T, Allsop N, Bruce T, Kortenhaus A, Schüttrumpf H, Van der Meer J (2007) EurOtop wave overtopping of sea defences and related structures: assessment manual. Environ Agency, UK

Purkis SJ (2018) Remote sensing tropical coral reefs: the view from above. Ann Rev Mar Sci 10(1):149–168. https://doi.org/10.1146/annurev-marine-121916-063249

Quilfen Y, Yurovskaya M, Chapron B, Ardhuin F (2018) Storm waves sharpening in the Agulhas current: satellite observations and modeling. Remote Sens Environ 216:561–571. https://doi.org/10.1016/j.rse.2018.07.020

Ranasinghe R (2016) Assessing climate change impacts on open sandy coasts: a review. Earth-Sci Rev 160:320–332. https://doi.org/10.1016/j.earscirev.2016.07.011

Raubenheimer B, Guza R, Elgar S (2001) Field observations of wave-driven setdown and setup. J Geophys Res Oceans 106(C3):4629–4638

Raucoules D, de Michele M, Idier D, Smai F, Foumelis M, Boulahya F, Volden E, Drakopoulou V, Przemysław M (2019) BATHYSENT—a method to retrieve coastal bathymetry from sentinel-2). In: IEEE international geoscience and remote sensing symposium (IGARSS)

Rawat A, Ardhuin F, Ballu V, Crawford W, Corela C, Aucan J (2014) Infragravity waves across the oceans. Geophys Res Lett 41(22):7957–7963. https://doi.org/10.1002/2014GL061604

Rhein M et al (2013) Observations: ocean. In: Stocker TF, Qin D, Plattner G-K, Tignor M, Allen SK, Boschung J, Nauels A, Xia Y, Bex V, Midgley PM (eds) Climate change 2013: the physical science basis. contribution of working group I to the fifth assessment report of the intergovernmental panel on climate change. Cambridge University Press, Cambridge, pp 255–316. https://doi.org/10.1017/cbo9781107415324.010

Roberts TM, Wang P, Kraus NC (2010) Limits of wave runup and corresponding beach-profile change from large-scale laboratory data. J Coast Res 26:184–198

Roelvink D, Reniers A, van Dongeren A, van Thiel de Vries J, McCall R, Lescinski J (2009) Modelling storm impacts on beaches, dunes and barrier islands. Coast Eng 56:1133–1152. https://doi.org/10.1016/j.coastaleng.2009.08.006

Roelvink D, McCall R, Mehvar S, Nederhoff K, Dastgheib A (2018) Improving predictions of swash dynamics in XBeach: the role of groupiness and incident-band runup. Coast Eng 134:103–123. https://doi.org/10.1016/j.coastaleng.2017.07.004

Rohmer J, Idier D (2012) A meta-modelling strategy to identify the critical offshore conditions for coastal flooding. Nat Hazards Earth Syst Sci 12:2943–2955. https://doi.org/10.5194/nhess-12-2943-2012

Rohmer J, Lecacheux S, Pedreros R et al (2016) Dynamic parameter sensitivity in numerical modelling of cyclone-induced waves: a multi-look approach using advanced meta-modelling techniques. Nat Hazards 84:1765. https://doi.org/10.1007/s11069-016-2513-8

Roland A, Ardhuin F (2014) On the developments of spectral wave models: numerics and parameterizations for the coastal ocean. Ocean Dyn 64(6):833–846. https://doi.org/10.1007/s10236-014-0711-z

Romano A, Bellotti G, Briganti R, Franco L (2015) Uncertainties in the physical modelling of the wave overtopping over a rubble mound breakwater: the role of the seeding number and of the test duration. Coast Eng 103:15–21. https://doi.org/10.1016/j.coastaleng.2015.05.005

Romeiser R, Graber HC (2018) Advanced ocean wave retrieval from time series of spotlight SAR subaperture images, EUSAR 2018. In: 12th European conference on synthetic aperture radar

Rueda A, Gouldby B, Méndez F, Tomás A, Losada I, Lara J, Díaz-Simal P (2016) Coastal flood risk assessment. J Flood Risk Manag 9:390–401. https://doi.org/10.1111/jfr3.12204

Rueda A, Vitousek S, Camus P, Tomas A, Epejo A, Losada IJ, Barnard P, Erikson L, Ruggiero P, Reguero BG, Mendez FJ (2017) A global classification of coastal flood hazard climates associated with large-scale oceanographic forcing. Sci Rep 7:5038

Ruessink BG (2010) Observations of turbulence within a natural surf zone. J Phys Oceanogr 40:2696–2712. https://doi.org/10.1175/2010JPO4466.1

Ruessink BG, Kleinhans MG, van den Beukel PGL (1998) Observations of swash under highly dissipative conditions. J Geophys Res 103:3111–3118. https://doi.org/10.1029/97JC02791

Ruggiero P, Komar PD, Marra JJ, McDougal WG, Beach RA (2001) Wave runup, extreme water levels and the erosion of properties backing beaches. J Coastal Res 17:407–419

Ruggiero P, Holman R, Beach R (2004) Wave run-up on a high-energy dissipative beach. J Geophys Res C Oceans 109(6):C06025, 1–12. https://doi.org/10.1029/2003jc002160

Ruggiero P, Komar PD, Allan JC (2010) Increasing wave heights and extreme value projections: the wave climate of the U.S. Pacific Northwest. Coast Eng 57:539–552. https://doi.org/10.1016/j.coastaleng.2009.12.005

Rusu L, Bernardino M, Guedes Soares C (2011) Modelling the influence of currents on wave propagation at the entrance of the Tagus estuary. Ocean Eng 38(10):1174–1183. https://doi.org/10.1016/j.oceaneng.2011.05.016

Saville T (1961) Experimental determination of wave set-up. In: Proceedings of the second technical conference on hurricanes, US Dept. of Commerce, National Hurricane Res. Proj, 1961, pp 242–252

Semedo A, Sušelj K, Rutgersson A, Sterl A (2010) A global view on the wind sea and swell climate and variability from ERA-40. J Clim 24:1461–1479. https://doi.org/10.1175/2010JCLI3718.1
Send U, Weller RA, Wallace D, Chavez F, Lampitt R, Dickey T, Honda M, Nittis K, Lukas R, McPhaden M, Feely R (2010) OceanSITES. In: Hall J, Harrison DE, Stammer D (eds) Proceedings of OceanObs'09: sustained ocean observations and information for society, Vol. 2. European Space Agency, pp 913–922
Senechal N, Coco G, Bryan KR, Holman RA (2011) Wave runup during extreme storm conditions. J Geophys Res 116:C07032. https://doi.org/10.1029/2010JC006819
Seneviratne SI et al (2012) Changes in climate extremes and their impacts on the natural physical environment. In: Field CB, Barros V, Stocker TF, Dahe Q (eds) Managing the risks of extreme events and disasters to advance climate change adaptation. Cambridge University Press, Cambridge, pp 109–230. https://doi.org/10.1017/cbo9781139177245.006
Sepulveda HH, Queffeulou P, Ardhuin F (2015) Assessment of SARAL AltiKa wave height measurements relative to buoy, Jason-2 and Cryosat-2 data. Mar Geodesy 38(S1):449–465. https://doi.org/10.1080/01490419.2014.1000470
Serafin KA, Ruggiero P, Stockdon HF (2017) The relative contribution of waves, tides, and nontidal residuals to extreme total water levels on US West Coast sandy beaches. Geophys Res Lett 44:1839–1847
Sheremet A, Staples T, Ardhuin F, Suanez S, Fichaut B (2014) Observations of large infragravity-wave run-up at Banneg island, France. Geophys Res Lett. https://doi.org/10.1002/2013gl058880
Smit PB, Janssen TT, Herbers THC, Taira T, Romanowicz BA (2018) Infragravity wave radiation across the shelf break. J Geophys Res Oceans 123:4483–4490. https://doi.org/10.1029/2018JC013986
Smith JA (2006) Wave-current interactions in finite-depth. J Phys Oceanogr 36:1403–1419
Stewart AL, Ferrari R, Thompson AF (2013) On the importance of surface forcing in conceptual models of the deep ocean. J Phys Oceanogr 44:891–899. https://doi.org/10.1175/JPO-D-13-0206.1
Stockdon HF, Holman RA, Howd PA, Sallenger AH Jr (2006) Empirical parameterization of setup, swash, and runup. Coast Eng 53:573–588. https://doi.org/10.1016/j.coastaleng.2005.12.005
Stockdon HF, Thompson DM, Plant NG, Long JW (2014) Evaluation of wave runup predictions from numerical and parametric models. Coast Eng 92:1–11
Stopa JE, Ardhuin F, Girard-Ardhuin F (2016) Wave climate in the Arctic 1992-2014: seasonality and trends. Cryosphere 10:1605–1629. https://doi.org/10.5194/tc-10-1605-2016
Stopa JE, Ardhuin F, Stutzmann E, Lecocq T (2019) Sea state trends and variability: consistency between models, altimeters, buoys, and seismic data (1979–2016). J Geophys Res Oceans. https://doi.org/10.1029/2018JC014607
Suanez S, Cancouët R, Floc'h F, Blaise E, Ardhuin F, Filipot J.-F, Cariolet J.-M, Delacourt C (2015) Observations and predictions of wave runup, extreme water levels, and medium-term dune erosion during storm conditions. J Mar Sci Eng 3:674–698. https://doi.org/10.3390/jmse3030674
Suzuki N, Fox-Kemper B (2016) Understanding Stokes forces in the wave-averaged equations. J Geophys Res Oceans 121:3579–3596. https://doi.org/10.1002/2015JC011566
Symonds G, Huntley DA, Bowen AJ (1982) Two-dimensional surf beat: long wave generation by a time-varying breakpoint. J Geophys Res Oceans 87:492–498. https://doi.org/10.1029/JC087iC01p00492
The WAVEWATCH III R Development Group (2016) User manual and system documentation of WAVEWATCH III R version 5.16," Tech. Note 329, NOAA/NWS/NCEP/MMAB, College Park, MD, USA, 2016. 326 pp. + Appendices
Thomson J (2012) Wave breaking dissipation observed with "swift" drifters. J Atmos Ocean Technol 29:1866–1882. https://doi.org/10.1175/JTECH-D-12-00018.1
Thompson RORY, Hamon BV (1980) Wave setup of harbor water levels. J Geophys Res Oceans 85:1151–1152. https://doi.org/10.1029/JC085iC02p01151
Thornton EB, Guza RT (1983) Transformation of wave height distribution. J Geophys Res Oceans 88:5925–5938. https://doi.org/10.1029/JC088iC10p05925
Torres-Freyermuth A, Puleo JA, Pokrajac D (2013) Modeling swash-zone hydrodynamics and shear stresses on planar slopes using reynolds-averaged navierstokes equations. J Geophys Res 118:1019–1033. https://doi.org/10.1002/jgrc.20074
Tuah H, Hudspeth RT (1982) Comparisons of numerical random sea simulations. J Waterw Port Coast Ocean Div ASCE 108(4):569–584
Turner IL, Harley MD, Drummond CD (2016) UAVs for coastal surveying. Coast Eng 114:19–24. https://doi.org/10.1016/j.coastaleng.2016.03.011
Van der Meer JW, Stam C-JM (1992) Wave runup on smooth and rock slopes of coastal structures. J Waterw Port Coast Ocean Eng 118:534–550. https://doi.org/10.1061/(ASCE)0733-950X(1992)118:5(534)

Vitousek S, Barnard PL, Fletcher CH, Frazer N, Erikson L, Storlazzi CD (2017) Doubling of coastal flooding frequency within decades due to sea-level rise. Nature 7:1399

Vousdoukas MI, Velegrakis AF, Dimou K, Zervakis V, Conley DC (2009) Wave run-up observations in microtidal, sediment-starved pocket beaches of the Eastern Mediterranean. J Mar Syst 78:S37–S47

Vousdoukas MI, Wziatek D, Almeida LP (2012) Coastal vulnerability assessment based on video wave run-up observations at a mesotidal, steep-sloped beach. Ocean Dyn 62(1):123–137

Vousdoukas MI et al (2016) Developments in large-scale coastal flood hazard mapping. Nat Hazards Earth Syst Sci 16:1841–1853

Vousdoukas MI, Mentaschi L, Voukouvalas E, Verlaan M, Feyen L (2017) Extreme sea levels on the rise along Europe's coasts. Earth's Future 5:304–323

Vousdoukas MI, Mentaschi L, Voukouvalas E, Verlaan M, Jevrejeva S, Jackson LP, Feyen L (2018a) Global probabilistic projections of extreme sea levels show intensification of coastal flood hazard. Nat Commun 9:2360

Vousdoukas MI, Mentaschi L, Voukouvalas E, Bianchi A, Dottori F, Feyen L (2018b) Climatic and socio-economic controls of future coastal flood risk in Europe. Nat Clim Change 8:776–780

Walstra DJR, Roelvink J, Groeneweg J (2000) Calculation of wave-driven currents in a 3D mean flow model. In: Proceedings of the 27th international conference on coastal engineering, Sydney, vol 2, pp 1050–1063, ASCE, 2000

Wandres M, Pattiaratchi C, Hemer MA (2017) Projected changes of the southwest Australian wave climate under two atmospheric greenhouse gas concentration pathways. Ocean Model 117:70–87

Wang XL, Swail VR (2001) Changes in extreme wave heights in Northern Hemisphere oceans and related atmospheric circulation regimes. J Clim 14:2204–2221. https://doi.org/10.1175/1520-0442(2001)014,2204:COEWHI2.0.CO;2

Wang XL, Swail VR (2006) Climate change signal and uncertainty in projections of ocean wave heights. Clim Dyn 26:109–126. https://doi.org/10.1007/s00382-005-0080-x

Wang XL, Feng Y, Swail VR (2014) Changes in global ocean wave heights as projected using multimodel CMIP5 simulations. Geophys Res Lett 41:1026–1034. https://doi.org/10.1002/2013GL058650

Wassing F (1957) Model investigation on wave run-up carried out in the Netherlands during the past twenty years. In: Proccedings of the 6th international coastal engineering conference, American Society of Civil Engineers, pp 700–714

Wenneker I, Spelt B, Peters H, de Ronde J (2016) Overview of 20 years of field measurements in the coastal zone and at the Petten sea dike in the Netherlands. Coast Eng 109:96–113. https://doi.org/10.1016/j.coastaleng.2015.12.009

Williams HE, Briganti R, Pullen T (2014) The role of offshore boundary conditions in the uncertainty of numerical prediction of wave overtopping using non-linear shallow water equations. Coas En 89:30–44. https://doi.org/10.1016/j.coastaleng.2014.03.003

WISE Group (2007) Wave modelling—the state of the art. Prog Oceanogr 75:603–674. https://doi.org/10.1016/j.pocean.2007.05.005

Woodworth PL, Melet A, Marcos M, Ray RD, Wöppelmann G, Sasaki YN, Cirano M, Hibbert A, Huthnance JM, Monserrat S, Merrifield MA (2019) Forcing factors affecting sea level changes at the coast. Surv Geophys. https://doi.org/10.1007/s10712-019-09531-1

Wong PP et al. In: Climate change 2014: impacts, adaptation, and vulnerability. Field CB et al (eds). IPCC, Cambridge Univ. Press, pp 361–409

Wright LD, Short AD (1984) Morphodynamic variability of surf zones and beaches: a synthesis. Mar Geol 56:93–118

Young IR, Ribal A (2019) Multiplatform evaluation of global trends in wind speed and wave height. Science 364:548. https://doi.org/10.1126/science.aav9527

Young IR, Zieger S, Babanin AV (2011) Global trends in wind speed and wave height. Science 332:451–455. https://doi.org/10.1126/science.1197219

Zhang WZ, Shi F, Hong HS, Shang SP, Kirby JT (2010) Tide-surge Interaction Intensified by the Taiwan Strait. J Geophys Res 115:C06012. https://doi.org/10.1029/2009JC005762

Zijlema M, Stelling G, Smit P (2011) Swash: an operational public domain code for simulating wave fields and rapidly varied flows in coastal waters. Coast Eng 58:992–1012. https://doi.org/10.1016/j.coastaleng.2011.05.015

Surveys in Geophysics (2019) 40:1603–1630
https://doi.org/10.1007/s10712-019-09549-5

Interactions Between Mean Sea Level, Tide, Surge, Waves and Flooding: Mechanisms and Contributions to Sea Level Variations at the Coast

Déborah Idier[1] · Xavier Bertin[2] · Philip Thompson[3] · Mark D. Pickering[4]

Received: 19 November 2018 / Accepted: 8 June 2019 / Published online: 26 June 2019

Abstract
Coastal areas epitomize the notion of 'at-risk' territory in the context of climate change and sea level rise (SLR). Knowledge of the water level changes at the coast resulting from the mean sea level variability, tide, atmospheric surge and wave setup is critical for coastal flooding assessment. This study investigates how coastal water level can be altered by interactions between SLR, tides, storm surges, waves and flooding. The main mechanisms of interaction are identified, mainly by analyzing the shallow water equations. Based on a literature review, the orders of magnitude of these interactions are estimated in different environments. The investigated interactions exhibit a strong spatiotemporal variability. Depending on the type of environments (e.g., morphology, hydrometeorological context), they can reach several tens of centimeters (positive or negative). As a consequence, probabilistic projections of future coastal water levels and flooding should identify whether interaction processes are of leading order, and, where appropriate, projections should account for these interactions through modeling or statistical methods.

Keywords Water level · Hydrodynamics · Interaction processes · Implications · Flood · Quantification · Modeling

✉ Déborah Idier
d.idier@brgm.fr

Xavier Bertin
xbertin@univ-lr.fr

Philip Thompson
philiprt@hawaii.edu

Mark D. Pickering
mdp053@gmail.com

1 BRGM, 3 av. C. Guillemin, 45060 Orléans Cédex, France

2 UMR 7266 LIENSs, CNRS - La Rochelle University, 2 rue Olympe de Gouges, 17000 La Rochelle, France

3 Department of Oceanography, University of Hawai'i at Manoa, 1000 Pope Road, Honolulu, HI 96822, USA

4 University of Southampton, University Road, Southampton SO17 1BJ, UK

1 Introduction

Coastal areas are considered ‘at-risk’ territories in the context of climate change and sea level rise (SLR). Knowledge of water level variability at the coast, especially the still water level and storm tide, is critical for coastal flooding assessment, both for present and for future climate. Still water level includes mean sea level, tide and atmospheric surge (Fig. 1a). Several definitions can be found for storm tides; here, we consider that they include mean sea level, tide, atmospheric storm surge and wave setup.

According to the IPCC 5th Assessment Report, the likely range of future global mean sea level (GMSL) for the high emissions scenarios is + 0.5 to + 1 m by 2100 (Church et al. 2013b), which does not preclude more extreme scenarios (Church et al. 2013a). Importantly, sea level will continue to rise beyond 2100 (Church et al. 2013b) and is likely to reach several meters by 2200 (Kopp et al. 2014). Such changes in mean sea level will produce significant societal impact.

A widely used approach to account for mean sea level changes in flood hazard assessment is to linearly add the sea level rise to selected still water level scenarios to estimate the flood hazard. Such an approach relies on the underlying assumption that there is no significant nonlinear interaction between contributions to water level variability, such as SLR, tide and surge. However, some studies show evidence that these interactions can represent a significant part of water level changes. For instance, using a numerical modeling approach, focusing on the German Bight area (SE of North Sea) and assuming a sea level rise of 0.54 m, Arns et al. (2015) show that taking into account the interactions between mean sea level, tide and atmospheric surge leads to a 50-year return still water level 12 cm larger than when these interactions are neglected, corresponding to a doubling of the frequency of 50-year return still water level obtained neglecting the interactions.

The present review focuses on water level resulting from mean sea level, tide and surge (atmospheric surge and wave setup) and investigates how this water level can be altered by interaction processes occurring between SLR, tides, storm surges, waves and flooding. Indeed, many mechanisms can affect the still water level (e.g., changes in seabed morphology, oceanographic circulations, tide–surge interactions, etc.). Figure 1b schematizes some

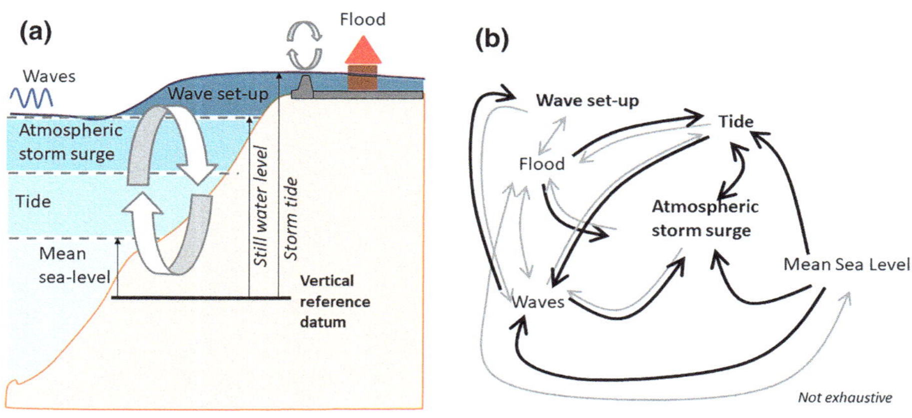

Fig. 1 **a** Components of storm tide, terminology and sketch of interactions. **b** Main interactions between mean sea level, waves, atmospheric storm surges, tide, wave setup and flooding. In bold and black: the focus of the present paper

of these interactions. The main interactions to be investigated in this review are: (1) the SLR effect on tides, atmospheric surges and waves, (2) the tide effect on atmospheric storm surges, waves and wave setup, (3) the flooding effect on tide and still water level (including human adaptation on tides), (4) the effect of short waves on atmospheric surges.

The present paper aims at highlighting these interaction mechanisms and at providing the orders of magnitude of the interactions contributions to the water level at the coast. One of the difficulties is to isolate the influence of each interaction. Observations (e.g., from tide gauges) can provide insights into changes in mean sea level, tides, surge, or even sometimes the wave setup, but, as highlighted by Woodworth (2010) and Haigh et al. (2018), many processes can affect tide changes (SLR, harbor infrastructures, long-term changes in the tidal potential, changes in internal tide, morphological changes, etc.), such that it is difficult to properly isolate the influence of each parameter based on these observations. Thus, the present review is mainly based on modeling studies.

The paper is organized as follows. First, the main mechanisms leading to changes in mean sea level, tidal amplitude, atmospheric surge and wave setup are reviewed together with their orders of magnitude (Sect. 2). Then, each of the interaction mechanisms is described and orders of magnitude are provided in different environments (Sect. 3). Section 4 provides a synthesis and examples of combined interactions, before discussing the limits of the review and the implications for projections of water level at the coast and flood hazard estimation. Remaining questions are also highlighted. Section 5 draws the main conclusions.

2 Mean Sea Level, Tide, Atmospheric Surge and Wave Setup: Mechanisms and Orders of Magnitude

What follows is a summary of the main mechanisms or factors leading to changes in mean sea level and leading to tide, atmospheric storm surge and wave setup. Here, mean sea level can be considered as a zeroth-order component (low frequency), while tide, atmospheric surge and wave setup (higher frequency) are considered as first-order components.

As highlighted by Woodworth et al. (2019), mean sea level can be affected by many factors. In addition to long-term trends related to climate change, mean sea level is subject to seasonal variability due to changes in thermal expansion and salinity variations (steric effect), air pressure and winds, land and sea ice melt, oceanographic circulation, river runoff, etc. Some inter-annual and decadal variability can also be observed as a result of the effect of climate modes like El Niño Southern Oscillation (ENSO), North Atlantic Oscillation (NAO) or Pacific Decadal Oscillation (POD) resulting in large-scale sea level change. Fifteen thousand years ago, GMSL was more than 100 m below present (Clark et al. 2016). According to Church et al. (2013a), GMSL will increase by several tens of centimeters and could exceed 1 m in 2100.

Tides are generated by gravitational forces acting over the whole water column in the deep ocean, with a gravitational feedback in tidal dynamics known as self-attraction and loading [SAL, Hendershott (1972)]. In deep water, tides have wavelengths of several hundreds of kilometers, i.e., much longer than the water depth. They propagate as shallow water waves, influenced by the Earth's rotation (Coriolis force), and are dissipated by bottom friction in shallow water on continental shelves and by energy loss to internal tides (Ray 2001). Local or basin-scale enhancements can occur due to resonance producing very large tides (Godin 1993). At the global scale, depending on the location, spring tidal ranges vary from a few tens of centimeters to several meters and can locally exceed 10 meters as in the Bay of Fundy (Pugh 1987). The atmospheric storm surges can also be regarded as long waves. They are generated by changes in atmospheric pressure and wind stress acting on the sea surface. Similar to tides, storm surges propagate to the coast as shallow water waves and are subject to seabed friction, Earth's rotation (Coriolis force), and local enhancements due to resonance producing large surges. Atmospheric surge of tens of centimeters and up to 1 m is frequently observed on the Northwest European shelf (e.g., Brown et al. 2010; Idier et al. 2012; Breilh et al. 2014; Pedreros et al. 2018) and can exceed 2–3 m under specific stormy conditions, such as in the North Sea in 1953 (Wolf and Flather 2005). It should be noted that these values correspond to the so-called practical storm surge, i.e., the difference between the still water level and the tide. In cyclonic environments, pure atmospheric surge (i.e., without accounting for tide–surge interaction) can reach almost 10 m (e.g., Nott et al. 2014).

In a first approximation, tides and surge can be modeled by the shallow water equations, which can be written as follows, omitting the horizontal viscosity term ($A\nabla^2 u$) for the sake of clarity:

$$\frac{\partial \xi}{\partial t} + \nabla \cdot (D \cdot \mathbf{u}) = 0 \tag{1}$$

$$\frac{\partial \mathbf{u}}{\partial t} + \mathbf{u} \cdot \nabla \mathbf{u} - f\mathbf{k} \cdot \mathbf{u} = -g\nabla\xi + \frac{1}{\rho}\nabla p_{\mathrm{a}} + \frac{\tau_{\mathrm{s}}}{\rho D} - \frac{\tau_{\mathrm{b}}}{\rho D} + \mathbf{F} + \mathbf{\Pi} \tag{2}$$

with $\mathbf{u}$ the depth-integrated current velocity, ξ the free surface, D the total water depth (equal to the sum of undisturbed water depth H and the free surface elevation ξ), ρ the density of sea water, g the gravitational acceleration, p_{a} the sea level atmospheric pressure, f the Coriolis parameter ($2\omega \sin \phi$, with ω the angular speed of Earth rotation and ϕ the latitude) and $\mathbf{k}$ a unit vector in the vertical. τ_{b} and τ_{s} are, respectively, the bed and wind shear stress, which can be written as follow (assuming a quadratic law):

$$\tau_{\mathbf{s}} = \rho_{\mathrm{a}} C_{D_{\mathrm{s}}} \mathbf{U}_{10} |\mathbf{U}_{10}| \tag{3}$$

$$\tau_{\mathbf{b}} = C_{D_{\mathrm{b}}} \mathbf{u} |\mathbf{u}| \tag{4}$$

where $C_{D_{\mathrm{s}}}$ and $C_{D_{\mathrm{b}}}$ are the free surface and bottom drag coefficients, respectively, ρ_{a} is the air density and $\mathbf{U}_{10}$ is the wind velocity at $z = 10$ m. Finally, $\mathbf{F}$ includes other forces such as the wave-induced forces leading to wave setup, and $\mathbf{\Pi}$ includes tide-related forcing terms (e.g., self attracting load, tidal potential forces). In the case of pure tides, the second, third and fifth terms of the right-hand side of Eq. (2) are equal to zero. In the case of pure atmospheric storm surge, the last term is equal to zero. From the equations, it can be readily seen that the effect of wind depends on water depth and increases as the depth decreases, whereas the atmospheric pressure effect is depth independent. In deep water, surge elevations are therefore approximately hydrostatic, while surge production by the wind stress can be large on shallow continental shelves.

In the nearshore, the dissipation of shortwaves through depth-limited breaking (with a small contribution from bottom friction) results in a force that drives currents and wave setup along the coast, which can substantially contribute to storm surges. Under energetic wave conditions, wave setup can even dominate storm surges along coasts bordered by narrow to moderately wide shelves or at volcanic islands (Kennedy et al. 2012; Pedreros et al. 2018). Several studies combining field observations with numerical modeling also demonstrated that wave breaking over the ebb shoals of shallow inlets (Malhadas et al. 2009; Dodet et al. 2013) as well as large estuaries (Bertin et al. 2015; Fortunato et al. 2017) results in a setup that can propagate at the scale of the whole backbarrier lagoon or estuary. Local wave setup of several tens of centimeters up to about 1 m have been observed (Pedreros et al. 2018; Guérin et al. 2018), while regional wave setup can reach values of tens of centimeters (Bertin et al. 2015). This does not imply that larger values could not exist. The first theoretical explanation for the development of wave setup is due to Longuet-Higgins and Stewart (1964), who proposed that the divergence of the shortwave momentum flux associated with wave breaking acts as a horizontal pressure force that tilts the water level until an equilibrium is reached with the subsequent barotropic pressure gradient. However, several studies reported that this model could result in a severe underestimation of wave setup along the coast (Raubenheimer et al. 2001; Apotsos et al. 2007), suggesting that other processes may be involved. Apotsos et al. (2007) and Bennis et al. (2012) proposed that bed shear stress associated with the undertow (bed return flow that develops in surf zones) could contribute to wave setup. Recently, Guérin et al. (2018) showed that the depth-varying currents that take place in the surf zone (horizontal and vertical advection and shear of the currents) could contribute to wave setup substantially, particularly when the bottom is steep.

A broader overview of all forcing factors causing sea level changes at the coast and of their orders of magnitude, from sub-daily (seiche, infra-gravity waves) to long-term scales (centuries), is provided by Woodworth et al. (2019), while Dodet et al. (2019) provide a review on wind-generated waves (processes, methods) and their contributions to coastal sea level changes.

3 Interaction Mechanisms and Orders of Magnitude

3.1 Sea Level Rise Effect on Tide and Atmospheric Surge

3.1.1 Mechanisms

Tides behave as shallow water waves and thus are strongly affected by water depth. There are several mechanisms by which mean sea level changes can alter tidal dynamics (Wilmes 2016; Haigh et al. 2018). Here, we focus on the direct effect of SLR on tides. First, large tidal amplitudes and dissipation occur when the tidal forcing frequency lies close to the natural period of an ocean basin or sea (Hendershott 1973). Therefore, increases in water depth due to MSL rise could push a shelf sea or embayment closer to resonance, increasing tidal range (e.g., in the Tagus estuary after the study of Guerreiro et al. (2015)), or away from resonance, reducing tidal range [e.g., in the Western English Channel according to Idier et al. (2017)]. The sensitivity to such water depth change increases as the basin approaches resonance. Second, the greater water depth implies a reduction in the energy dissipation at the bottom (see Eqs. 2, 4) and thus contributes to an increase in tidal range (see, e.g., the study of Green (2010) for numerical experiments in real cases). Third, increase in water depth alters the propagation speed of the tidal wave (and thus causes a spatial reorganization of the amphidrome). For instance, in a semi-enclosed basin and neglecting the dissipation terms, sea level rise causes the amphidromic point to shift toward the open boundary after the analytical solution of Taylor (1922).

In case of SLR, as for the tides, storm surges are affected by the bottom friction reduction which tends to increase storm surges. However, as illustrated by Arns et al. (2017) in the North Sea, the decreased bottom friction appears to be counteracted by the lessened effectiveness of surface wind stress. Indeed, the same wind forcing (surface stress) is less effective at dragging water and produces a smaller surge when water depth is larger (see the wind forcing term in Eq. 2). Finally, as a counterbalancing effect, SLR will also result, in some locations, in new flooded areas, which will act as additional dissipative areas for tide and surge. In the present section, for the sake of clarity, we do not consider the effect of these additional wet areas. The effect of flooding on tides and on still water level is discussed in Sects. 3.3 and 4.2, respectively.

3.1.2 Orders of Magnitude

The SLR effect on tides has been investigated at different scales (global, regional, local) and in different environments. The locations of the main studies presented below are indicated in Fig. 2 (in black). The values given in the next paragraphs correspond to changes in the tidal component alone (i.e., relative to the mean sea level) and not to the absolute tide level (which includes the mean sea level and thus SLR itself). In addition, the orders of magnitude provided below are extracted from model results obtained assuming a fixed shoreline (i.e., impermeable walls along the present-day shoreline).

First, at the global scale, tide response (*M*2 amplitude or mean high water level for instance) to SLR is widespread globally with spatially coherent non-uniform amplitude changes of both signs in many shelf seas, even considering uniform SLR (Green 2010;

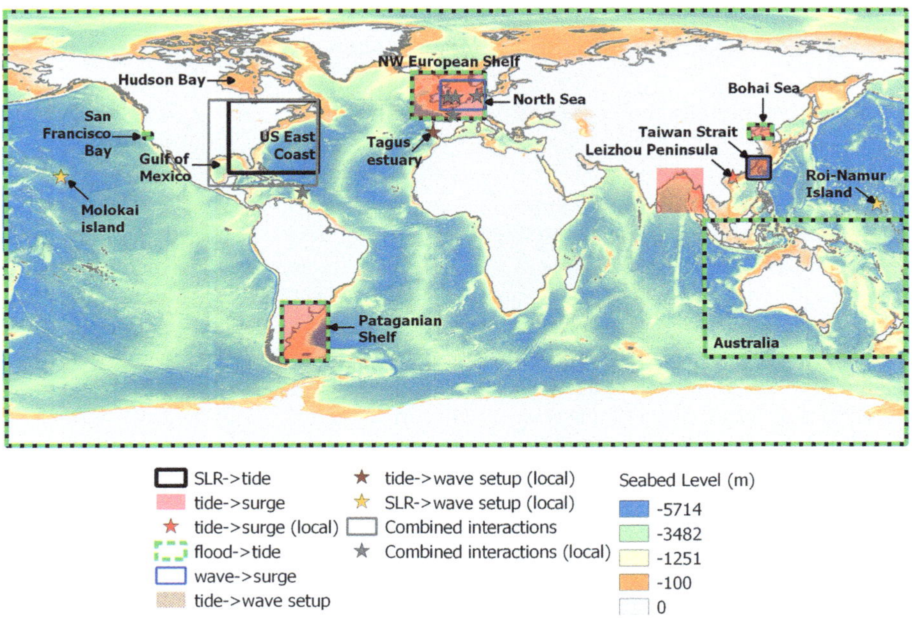

Fig. 2 Global bathymetry [seabed level (m), from The General Bathymetric Chart of the Oceans, GEBCO] and areas investigated in the papers selected to provide orders of magnitude of each of the interactions described in the present review. Stars correspond to very local studies

Pickering et al. 2017; Schindelegger et al. 2018). Response in the open ocean, where the relative depth change with SLR is small, is generally of a smaller magnitude but with a much greater horizontal length scale. Pickering et al. (2017), focusing on 136 cities of population larger than 1 million (in 2005), assuming fixed shorelines and a uniform SLR of 2 m, found changes in the mean high waters (MHW) varying from − 0.25 (Surabaya, Indonesia) to + 0.33 m (Rangoon, Myanmar) (Fig. 3b). The comparison of bathymetry (here The General Bathymetric Chart of the Oceans, GEBCO, Fig. 2) with the SLR-induced tide changes map of Pickering et al. (2017) (Fig. 2a therein, or Fig. 3b in the present paper) illustrates that along open coasts with narrow continental shelf, the SLR effect on tide appears negligible. In that study, they also investigated the effect of a spatially varying SLR, focusing on fingerprints of the initial elastic response to ice mass loss. These SLR perturbations weakly alter the tidal response with the largest differences being found at high latitudes (see the cumulative distribution of MHW changes for the 136 cities and for the assumption of a fixed shoreline, Fig. 3a).

Focusing on the NW European Shelf (spring tidal range varying from a few centimeters to more than 10 m, mainly in the Bay of Mont Saint Michel), Idier et al. (2017), Pickering et al. (2012) and Pelling et al. (2013a) show that for SLR = +2 m and under a 'no flood' assumption (also called fixed shoreline), the $M2$ amplitude changes up to ± 10–15% of SLR. In terms of high tide changes, Idier et al. (2017) show

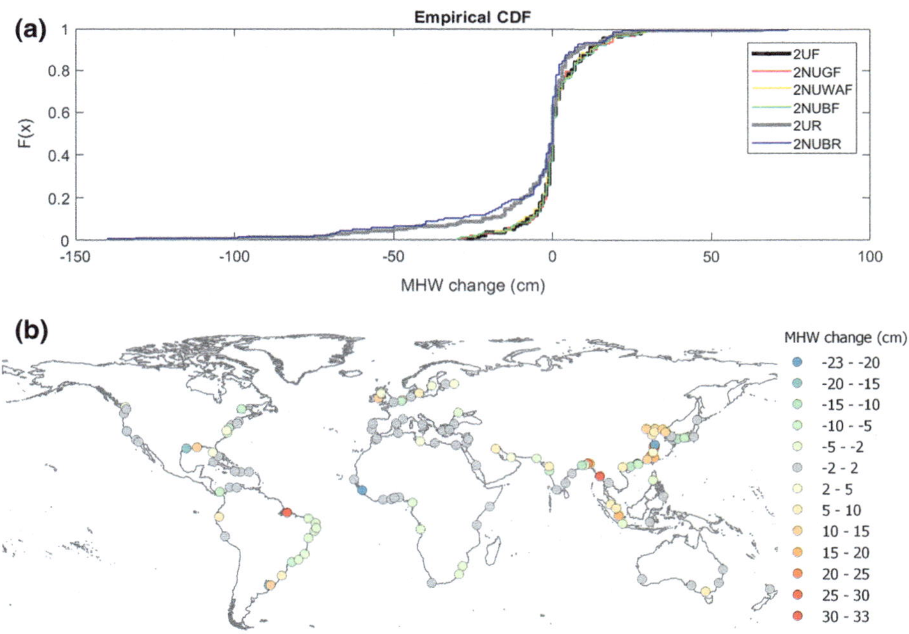

Fig. 3 Mean high water changes in the 136 cities of population larger than 1 million (in 2005) investigated by Pickering et al. (2017). **a** Empirical cumulative distribution for various SLR scenarios characterized by a global mean SLR of + 2 m: case of a fixed shoreline ('no flood') with a uniform SLR (2UF) or non-uniform SLR corresponding to the initial elastic response of ice sheet melt in Greenland (2NUGF), Western Antarctica (2NUWAF), or both (2NUBF); case with recession ('flood') with a uniform SLR (2UR) or non-uniform SLR corresponding to the initial elastic response of ice sheet melt in Greenland and Western Antarctica (2NUBR). **b** MHW change for the SLR scenario 2UF. Figures produced here based on the data provided in the supplementary material (Pickering et al. 2017)

that, depending on the location, changes in the highest tide of the year (in that study: 2009) range from − 15 to + 15% of SLR, i.e., several centimeters to about 15 cm for SLR = 1 m. They also show that, when it is assumed that land areas are protected from flooding, the tide components and the maximum tidal water levels vary proportionally to SLR over most of the domain, up to at least SLR = +2 m. Some areas show non-proportional behavior (e.g., the Celtic Sea and the German Bight). Consistently with the studies of Pelling et al. (2013a) and Pickering et al. (2017), the high tide level decreases in the western English Channel and increases in the Irish Sea, the southern part of the North Sea and the German Bight. The overall agreement between the different modeling experiments is fairly remarkable. Even using different tidal boundary conditions, different spatial resolutions, different models (even if all based on the shallow water equations), Idier et al. (2017), Pickering et al. (2012) and Pelling et al. (2013a) provide similar results in terms of $M2$ changes (see Figs. 3, 4, 6d in these studies, respectively). These studies agree on a decrease in the western English Channel and in the SW North Sea, and an increase in the eastern English Channel, the central part of the North Sea, the German Bight and the Irish Sea. The main discrepancy is the positive trend along the Danish coast given in Pickering et al. (2012), probably due to the closed model boundary to the Baltic Sea in that study. As an additional comparison, we can also refer to the study of Palmer et al. (2018), which shows strikingly similar spatial patterns of increase and decrease to the one of Pickering et al. (2012), except for the region that spreads out from the Bristol Channel. For a more detailed comparison on the modeling studies of the SLR effect on tides over the European shelf, see Idier et al. (2017).

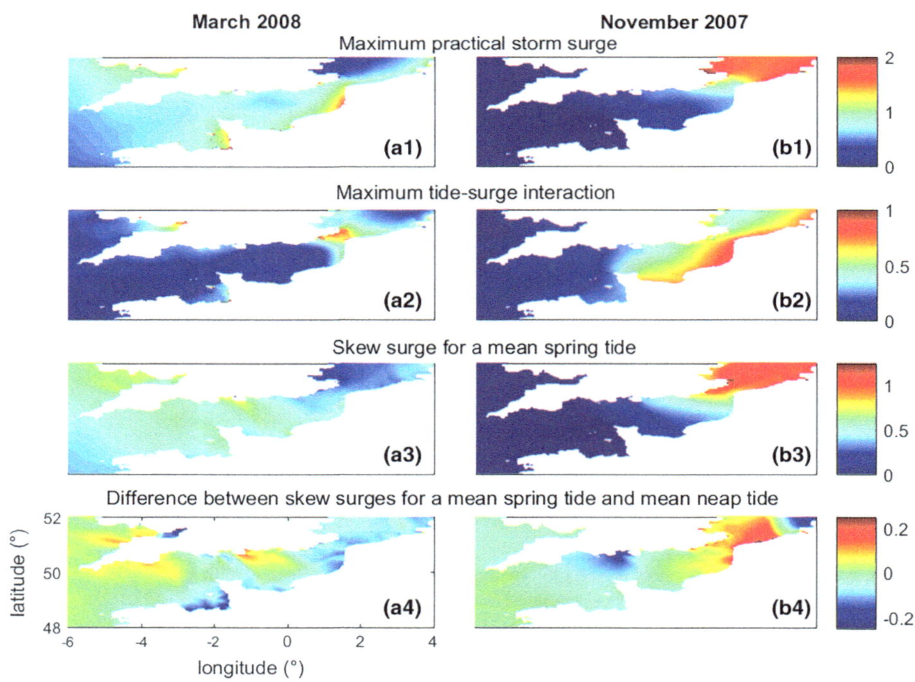

Fig. 4 Tide–surge interactions (in m) for the storms of the March 10–11, 2008, and November 9–10, 2007, in the English Channel, after the study of Idier et al. (2012)

Other regions have been investigated, such as the Taiwan Strait, which is a long (> 300 km) and wide (~ 140 km) shelf channel characterized by a mean tidal range varying from less than 1 m in the southeast end to more than 4 m in its northwest end. After Kuang et al. (2017), a SLR of 2 m induces an increase of 1–4 cm for *M*2 tidal component amplitude and 1 cm for K1 amplitude. For this area, the global study of Pickering et al. (2017) indicates even larger changes, with an increase of 17 cm of *M*2 amplitude at Xiamen (city located on the Chinese coast) and an increase in the maximal tidal range of 36 cm (for the same SLR of 2 m, assuming fixed present-day coastline).

The SLR effect on tides has also been investigated in the Bohai Sea (China, north of the Taiwan Strait, Fig. 2). For a 'no flood' case and SLR = 2 m, Pelling et al. (2013b) estimated *M*2 amplitude changes ranging from about − 0.1 to + 0.1 m. In addition, the effect of the sea level rise on *M*2 amplitude in this area is not proportional to the SLR amount.

In the Southern Hemisphere, along the coast of Australia, Harker et al. (2019) found *M*2 amplitude changes ranging from − 0.1 to + 0.1 m for a SLR of 1 m with amplitude changes that are not proportional to the SLR in this area, even if the patterns appear similar (in terms of areas of increase or decrease in *M*2 amplitude).

The effect of SLR on tides in the San Francisco Bay has also been investigated. This bay is characterized by an inlet (width of about 2.5 km) and two main bays (one to South, one to the North) of tens of kilometers length and widths varying from few kilometers up to almost 20 km. The mean tidal range varies from 1.8 to about 2.7 m, after the tide data provided by NOAA. With scenarios of hardened shoreline and a SLR of 1 m, the high tide exhibits an increase of 6 cm and 5 cm in the southern and northern bay, respectively, i.e., more than 10% of the natural tide amplification in these bays (Holleman and Stacey 2014).

Regarding the US East coast, the *M*2 amplitudes range from about 0.4–1.5 m (values extracted from the FES2014[1] tidal components database; Carrere et al. 2015). Ross et al. (2017) show that for SLR = 1 m, more than half of the Delaware Bay is projected to experience an *M*2 amplitude increase of at least 15 cm, while the Chesapeake Bay exhibits a small decrease at the mouth (− 2 cm), and an increase over most of the bay up to 10 cm at the head. It is also highlighted that changes are proportional to the SLR (especially for SLR = [− 1; + 1]m).

Along the Patagonian Shelf (spring tidal range between 0 and 3 m), Carless et al. (2016) show that for SLR = 1 m, *M*2 amplitude changes range between − 0.1 and + 0.1 m ('no flood' scenario).

All these studies converge to highlight that the effect of metric SLR can lead to tide changes (*M*2 component or spring high tide) up to ± 10–15% of SLR. We could not identify any studies focusing on the sole effect of SLR on atmospheric surge. However, several studies investigated the effect of SLR on still water level or practical storm surge. These studies implicitly take into account not only the effect of SLR on atmospheric surge but also on tides and the tide–surge interactions. The changes induced by these combined interactions are discussed in Sect. 4.2.

3.2 Tide Effect on Surge

The present subsection focuses on the effect of tide on surge. However, it should be kept in mind that this is a matter of point of view, and that strictly speaking the mechanisms

[1] Finite Element Solution 2014

can be referred to as tide–surge interactions. In addition, we focus on the practical storm surge (also called residual), which is the difference between the still water level and the tide level, such that it includes both the pure atmospheric storm surge and the effect of the tide on the surge.

3.2.1 Mechanisms

From Eqs. 1–4, it can be readily seen that there are several nonlinear terms of tide–surge interaction which can be classified in three nonlinear effects:

- the advective effect arising from the advective terms of the momentum Eq. (2).
- the shallow water effect, which arises from nonlinearity related to $D = (H + \xi)$ in Eqs. (1)–(3) in the following terms: advective term of the continuity equation, division by the depth D for the bed friction and wind forcing.
- the nonlinear effect of the bottom friction term with the quadratic parametrization in Eq. (4).

Thus, tidal current and tidal water level interact directly with the hydrodynamics induced by wind and pressure through the advection term, the shallow water effect and the nonlinear friction term related to velocity interactions (Flather 2001; Zhang et al. 2010). The advective term implies that, everything else being equal, the tide–surge interaction is larger for larger tidal currents, such that areas of strong tidal currents are potential areas of strong tide–surge interactions. Regarding the shallow water effect, it contributes to the modulated surge production. Indeed, under some assumptions (mainly 1-D flow and constant wind field) Pugh (1987) shows that the sea surface slope ($\partial\xi/\partial x$) is in equilibrium with $C_{D_s} U_{10}^2/(gD)$, such that the wind stress produces more surge in shallow water, leading to more surge at low tide than at high tide with other factors being equal. As explained by Horsburgh and Wilson (2007), such phenomena can lead to an increase in the phase lag of the practical storm surge compared to the tide, such that the storm surge can precede high water by more than 4 h. Regarding the nonlinear friction term, it appears to be the dominant term in tide–surge interaction in shallow water areas of strong tidal currents (Zhang et al. 2010; Idier et al. 2012). Wolf (1978) investigated the contribution of this nonlinear friction term to the tide–surge interaction. In that study, the definition was slightly different with the quadratic friction term including the water depth variations, i.e., one part of the shallow water effect. They solved analytically the motion equation of two plane progressive waves traveling together in a semi-infinite uniform channel and show that the increase in the interaction on rising tide is due to shallow water and advection effect, whereas the quadratic friction effect tends to reduce it at high tide. Besides, from Eq. (2), the increased force of bed stress due to the alignment of tidal and storm-induced current is offset by the pressure gradient force (surface slope) and then the surge residual, such that tide–surge interaction is intensified in cases of strong alignment of tide and storm surges. From the tide perspective, it should be noted that a positive storm surge (leading to a larger water depth) induces a faster propagating tide (see, e.g., Flather 2001).

3.2.2 Orders of Magnitude

The locations of the main studies presented below are indicated in Fig. 2 (in red). At the scale of the NW European shelf, Horsburgh and Wilson (2007) show that, for the storm of

January 29–30, 2000, tide modified the instantaneous surge of several tens of centimeters (exceeding 50 cm of changes at high tide for instance in the German Bight). Their analysis of results from selected locations along the East coast of the UK shows changes in the surge peak of tens of centimeters. Focusing on the English Channel, Idier et al. (2012) made surge computations with and without tide using a shallow water model (Fig. 4). For the two selected events (the November 2007 North Sea and March 2008 Atlantic storms), the instantaneous tide–surge interaction is seen to be non-negligible in the eastern half of the English Channel, reaching values of 74 cm (i.e., 50% of the same event's maximal storm surge) in the Dover Strait. Using the same hydrodynamic model, simple computations are performed with the same meteorological forcing while varying the tidal amplitude. Skew surges (defined as the difference between the maximum still water level and the maximum predicted tidal level regardless of their timing during the tidal cycle) appear to be tide-dependent, with negligible values (< 0.05 m) over a large portion of the English Channel, but reaching several tens of centimeters in some locations (e.g., the Isle of Wight and Dover Strait).

The Bay of Bengal is another region where tide–surge interactions are known to be very relevant (Johns et al. 1985). Krien et al. (2017b) performed numerical experiments during cyclone Sidr (2007), focusing on the head of the bay. They investigated the interaction between the tide and the total storm surge (including wave setup). As the computed wave setup ranged from 0.2 to 0.3 m and varies little over a tidal cycle, the tide–surge interactions analyzed by these authors mostly correspond to the effect of the tide on atmospheric surge and vice versa. They showed that tide–surge interactions in the range ± 0.6 m develop in shallow areas of this large deltaic zone. In addition, such interactions occurred at a maximum of 1–2 h after low tide due to the combination of a stronger wind contribution during periods of shallow depth and a faster propagating tide compared to a situation without surge. These findings corroborate those of Johns et al. (1985), Antony and Unnikrishnan (2013) and Hussain and Tajima (2017).

The Taiwan Strait is one example where the pattern of strong tidal currents and storm-induced currents along the channel direction enhances tide–surge interaction via nonlinear bottom friction (Zhang et al. 2010). This strait is subject to large storm surges frequently occurring during the typhoon season; from 1949 to 1990 there were 69 typhoons inducing storm surges over 1 m along at the western bank of the Taiwan Strait (Fujian coast), including four with storm surge larger than 2 m. Oscillations of about 0.4 m have been observed at tide gauges along the northern Fujian coast, the west bank of the Taiwan Strait, during Typhoon Dan (1999) (for this event, surge ranged from 0.6 m to more than 1 m at the tide gauges). The numerical experiments of Zhang et al. (2010) show that these oscillations are due to tide–surge interaction.

At the East of the Taiwan strait, tide–surge interactions have been investigated along the coast of the Leizhou Peninsula (LP) by Zhang et al. (2017) (Fig. 2). This area is characterized by extensive mudflats, large tidal ranges and a complex coastline. The largest amplitudes of tide–surge interaction are found in the shallow water region of the Leizhou Bay, with values up to 1 m during typhoon events. Numerical experiments reveal that nonlinear bottom friction is the main contributor to tide–surge interaction in this area.

Further east, the effect of tide on surge has been investigated in the Bohai Sea and the East China Sea. Xu et al. (2016) selected one typhoon, assumed that this typhoon arrives at 12 different times (the other conditions remaining constant) and analyzed the results in four tidal stations. The modeled storm surge elevations exhibit wide variations across the twelve cases, reaching differences up to 58 cm (at Yingkou tidal station).

Tide–surge interactions have also been investigated on the Patagonian Shelf. Etala (2009) found differences of tens of centimeters at the head of the bay and mouth of Rio de la Plata (Brazil).

The above studies converge to highlight that tide–surge interactions can produce tens of centimeters of water level at the coast with up to 1 m contributions in some cases.

3.3 Flooding Effect on Tide

3.3.1 Mechanisms

In Sects. 3.1 and 3.2, we considered that the shoreline was fixed. In other words, we assume that the coastal defenses (natural or man-made) are high enough to protect the lands from the flood. Removing this assumption can lead locally to more space for water, especially adding very shallow areas, i.e., areas of additional energy dissipation. Such effect can balance for instance the pure effect of SLR on tides. At the global scale, Pickering et al. (2017) investigated the impact of flood defenses and SLR on the tidal regime: SLR scenarios allowing for coastal recession (i.e., allowing for flood) tend increasingly to result in a reduction in tidal range. At this global scale, according to Pickering et al. (2017), the fact that the fixed and recession shoreline scenarios result mainly in changes of opposing sign is explained by the effect of the perturbations on the natural period of oscillation in the basin. At a regional scale, the effect of allowing dry land to flood is more complex. For instance, Pelling et al. (2013a) show that the North Sea is dominated by the flooding of the Dutch coast which shifts the areas of tidal energy dissipation from the present coastline to the new cells and thus moves the amphidromic points toward the coast.

3.3.2 Orders of Magnitude

The locations of the main studies presented below are indicated in green in Fig. 2. As in Sect. 3.1, the values given in the next paragraphs correspond to changes in the sole tidal component (i.e., relative to the mean sea level).

At the global scale, according to Pickering et al. (2017), assuming a receding shoreline except around Antarctica and a SLR of 2 m tends to result in a reduction in the tidal range, with more cities exhibiting mean high water reduction. For instance, Rotterdam (the Netherlands) experiences a change of − 0.69 m in MHW compared to the present-day MHW of 1.31 m. Changes occur at the coast but also in the open ocean, highlighting that the flood effect is not only local. In that study, tide changes appear more sensitive to the shoreline evolution (recession or fixed), than to the non-uniformity of SLR (Fig. 3a). Comparing the $M2$ amplitude changes of Schindelegger et al. (2018) with the ones of Pickering et al. (2017), $M2$ appears less sensitive to flooding in the former study. However, it should be kept in mind that these global modeling studies are run at a scale of $1/12°$ and $1/8°$, respectively.

On the NW European shelf, comparing 'flood' and 'no flood' scenarios, Pelling et al. (2013a) found $M2$ amplitude changes up to more than 10 cm (for SLR = 2 m), especially along the German and Danish coasts. From a quantitative point of view, the numerical experiment of Idier et al. (2017) shows that the sign of high-tide level changes obtained for the 'flood' and 'no flood' scenarios is the same across most of the NW European shelf area (57% of the computational domain). Significant local changes are observed especially along the German and Danish coasts (see, e.g., point C of Fig. 5). As highlighted by

Fig. 5 Changes in maximum annual high tide (2009) versus SLR for points A (Mont Saint Michel Bay) and C (German Bight), for the 'no flood' and 'flood' scenarios, after the study of Idier et al. (2017)

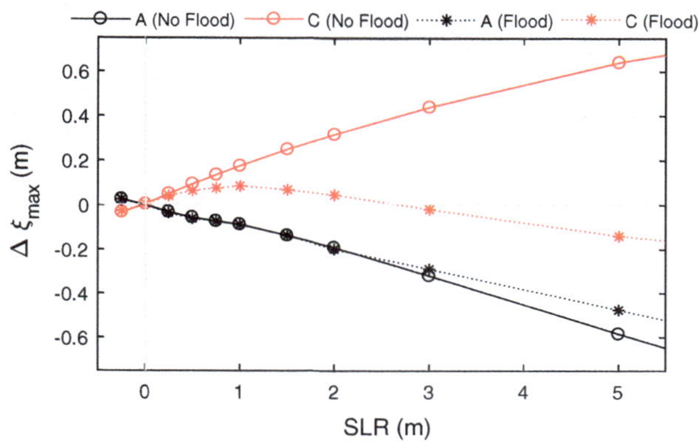

Pelling et al. (2013a), local flooding can have an effect at the basin scale: the flooding of the low-lying Dutch coast is the main forcing for the response of the *M*2 amplitude to SLR seen in the North Sea. It should be noted that there is a strong consistency between these modeling studies. Idier et al. (2017) and Pelling and Green (2014) provide very similar *M*2 amplitude changes in terms of order of magnitude and patterns. The main discrepancy is in the Bristol Channel, which may be due to the differences in spatial resolution and quality of the topographic data used in each case.

In San Francisco Bay, Holleman and Stacey (2014) and Wang et al. (2017) also investigated the effect of coastal defense scenarios. We discussed in Sect. 3.1 that a SLR of 1 m induces an increase of 6 and 5 cm in the southern and northern bay in the case of hardened shoreline scenario based on the study of Holleman and Stacey (2014). These authors made the same experiment with present coastal defenses and topography, finding a decrease in the high tide level (relative to the mean sea level) ranging from a few centimeters to 13 cm, i.e., an opposite change compared to results obtained with the hardened shoreline scenarios. Wang et al. (2017) also investigated the effect of coastal defenses on tides, considering two scenarios: existing topography and full-bay containment that follows the existing land boundary with an impermeable wall. Comparing the model results obtained for both scenarios, they found that the semidiurnal mode exhibits local changes at the shoreline up to 2 mm, changes in the diurnal mode extend into the bay (reaching values of about 1 mm), and overtide changes exhibit a significant spatial variability (with changes exceeding locally 2 mm). But the most important impact of the full-bay containment appears to be in the long-term process, with the changes in the long-term tidal mode being almost uniform in space, and exceeding 5 mm.

Along the coast of Australia, Harker et al. (2019) found that the effect of coastal defense on *M*2 and K1 amplitude is very small for a SLR of 1 m, with changes smaller than 1 cm. As stated by the authors, this is likely due to the fact that allowing land to flood only increases the wetted area by few cells for this SLR scenario. For a larger SLR (7 m), the effect of allowing dry land to flood is much larger with changes ranging between − 20 cm and + 20 cm.

On the Patagonian Shelf, Carless et al. (2016) show that allowing model cells to flood leads to *M*2 amplitude changes larger than in the case of a fixed shoreline, with more negative changes in the 'flood' scenario, but also that the sign of changes can be locally reversed. The absolute difference of *M*2 amplitude changes between the 'flood' and 'no flood' scenarios can locally exceed 15 cm for SLR = 1 m (Fig. 5).

The above studies show that, when previously dry land is allowed to flood, it can decrease the amplitude of high tide by a few or even tens of centimeters relative to the case where flooding is prevented. A key point is that initially flood defense schemes have localized benefits (they defend the coast line they protect). However, as shown for instance by Pelling and Green (2014), the process of flooding or not can have an impact on tides at the entire basin scale (e.g., North Sea).

3.4 Wave Effect on Atmospheric Storm Surges

3.4.1 Shear Stress at the Sea Surface

For a long time, the drag coefficient C_{D_s} used to compute the surface stress due to wind (see Eq. 3) was assumed to increase linearly with wind speed. Although such a simple approach appears attractive for implementation in storm surge models, it has several major shortcomings. First, several studies relying on field and laboratory measurements suggested that under extreme winds the sea surface roughness—and therefore the drag coefficient—could plateau after 30 m/s and even decrease for higher winds (e.g., Powell et al. 2003). This behavior was attributed to the development of wave-induced streaks of foam and sprays, which tend to smooth the sea surface. Second, for a given wind speed, significant scatter exists and C_{D_s} could vary by 30% or more. This scatter was partly explained by the fact that the sea surface roughness does not only depend on the wind speed but also depend on the sea state. Following the pioneering work of Van Dorn (1953) and Charnock (1955), Stewart (1974) proposed that, for a given wind speed, the sea surface roughness should also depend on the wave age, which is defined as the ratio between the shortwave velocity and the friction velocity. Using a coupled wave and storm surge model, Mastenbroek et al. (1993) showed that using a wave-dependent surface stress could increase the surface stress by 20% while better matching the observations. Performing a numerical hindcast of the February 1989 storm in the North Sea, they showed that using a wave-dependent drag parameterization rather than the ones of Smith and Banke (1975) (quadratic wind shear stress with $C_{D_s} = f(U_{10})$) leads to an increase of 20 cm for the modeled highest water level reached during the storm. In the Taiwan Strait, Zhang and Li (1996) show that the wave effect on atmospheric storm surges is significant, reaching about 20 cm for the typhoon Ellen (September 1983, 297 km/h gusts) and for an observed surge peak of almost 1 m. The dependence of the surface stress to the sea state was then corroborated in many studies (Moon et al. 2004, 2009; Bertin et al. 2012, 2015). In particular, Bertin et al. (2015) performed a high-resolution hindcast of the storm surge associated with the Xynthia (2010) storm in the Bay of Biscay and showed that the young sea state associated with this storm increased the surface stress by a factor of two. More precisely, they compared the surges obtained with quadratic formulation to the ones obtained with wave-dependent parameterization to compute wind stress. They found that both approaches perform similarly except during the storm peak, where the surge with the wave-dependent parameterization for wind stress is 30% larger, i.e., several tens of centimeters larger, bringing the model results closer to the observations. All these studies show that the wave effect on the sea surface roughness can lead to increases in storm surge of a few centimeters up to tens of centimeters.

3.4.2 Shear Stress at the Seabed

In coastal zones, the near-bottom orbital velocities associated with the propagation of short waves become large and enhance bottom stress (Grant and Madsen 1979). Several studies investigated the impact of wave-enhanced bottom stress on storm surges (Xie et al. 2003; Nicolle et al. 2009) although it is not really clear whether accounting for this process improves storm surge predictions or not (Jones and Davies 1998). Bertin et al. (2015) argued that, most of the time, the tide gauges used to validate storm surge models are located in harbors connected to deep navigation channels, where bottom friction is rather a second-order process and affect storm surges by less than 0.1 m. Further research is needed, including field measurements in shallow water.

3.5 Tide Effect on Waves and Wave Setup

3.5.1 Mechanisms

In the nearshore, tides can have a significant effect on short waves. First, tide-induced water level variations shift the cross-shore position of the surf zone, so that wave heights are modulated along a tidal cycle (Brown et al. 2013; Dodet et al. 2013; Guérin et al. 2018). Second, in coastal zones subjected to strong tidal currents such as estuaries and tidal inlets, tidal currents can substantially affect the wave field (Ardhuin et al. 2012; Rusu et al. 2011; Dodet et al. 2013). Neglecting dissipation, the conservation of the shortwave energy flux implies that, during the flood phase, waves following currents decrease while, during the ebb phase, waves propagating against currents increase (Dodet et al. 2013; Bertin and Olabarrieta 2016). However, during this ebb phase, as and when currents increase, the increase in wave height together with the decrease in wavelength increases the wave steepness. This increase in steepness can induce dissipation by whitecapping, although this process affects mostly higher frequencies (Chawla and Kirby 2002; Dodet et al. 2013; Bertin and Olabarrieta 2016; Zippel and Thomson 2015). In very shallow inlets and estuaries, tidal currents can also reach the group speed of the short waves so that full blocking can eventually occur (Dodet et al. 2013; Bertin and Olabarrieta 2016). As a consequence of wave setup being controlled mainly by the spatial rate of dissipation of short waves, wave setup along the shoreline or inside estuaries can exhibit large tidal modulations. Such modulation is illustrated by Dodet et al. (2013) and Fortunato et al. (2017) for the case of inlets; they show that wave breaking is more intense on ebb shoals at low tide so that the associated setup in the lagoon/estuary is higher at low tide.

3.5.2 Orders of Magnitude

In the Taiwan Strait, the numerical experiment of Yu et al. (2017) for Typhoon Morakot (2009) shows that an increase in significant wave height (H_s) of about 0.5 m occurred at Sansha (China coast) during high water levels induced by tidal change and atmospheric storm surge. The H_s difference at other estuary regions is also significant with a range of − 0.4 m at low water levels and 0.4 m at high water levels. In locations with larger currents or depths, H_s appear less correlated with water level variations. From the results of the numerical experiments, a weak modulation of the wave setup is observed (up to about 2 cm, based on Fig. 8 therein) for H_s of about 2–3 m.

Along the French Atlantic Coast (Truc Vert beach) during storm Johanna (March 10), Pedreros et al. (2018) estimated wave setup modulations of tens of centimeters, sometimes exceeding 40 cm. These modulations were found at a given nearshore location, i.e., a fixed point located in the surf zone. At the waterline, the modulation is found to be much weaker (few centimeters).

Fortunato et al. (2017) performed a high-resolution hindcast of the storm surge associated with the 1941 storm in the Tagus Estuary (Portugal, Fig. 2), which corresponds to the most damaging event to strike this region over the last century. Their numerical results suggest that the significant wave height of incident waves exceeded 10 m and dissipation of the waves on the ebb shoal resulted in the development of a wave setup reaching up to 0.35 m at the scale of the whole estuary. This setup was tidally modulated and ranged from 0.10 to 0.15 m at high tide (when dissipation was lowest) and 0.30–0.37 m at low tide. In addition, Fortunato et al. (2017) revealed a more subtle mechanism, where wave setup is also amplified along the estuary up to 25% through a resonant process.

3.6 Sea Level Rise Effect on Waves and Wave Setup

The impact of SLR on waves and wave setup is difficult to evaluate at sandy beaches. On the one hand, assuming an unchanged bathymetry (i.e., no morphological adaptation to SLR) and considering that the bottom slope increases along the beach profile (i.e., Dean 1991), SLR would imply that waves would break over a steeper bottom, which would result in an increase in wave setup. On the other hand, it is more likely that the beach profile will translate onshore due to SLR (Bruun 1962), so that wave setup would be globally unchanged. Due to large uncertainties concerning the response of sandy coastlines to SLR, we focus the review on studies investigating the effect of SLR on reef environment, assuming that the reef will weakly change for metric SLR.

Quataert et al. (2015) investigated this effect on Roi-Namur Island (Marshall Islands, Fig. 2), showing that an offshore water level increase (e.g., SLR) leads to a decrease in wave setup on the reef. According to their computations, a SLR of 1 m leads to a wave setup decrease in tens up to 50 cm (for $H_s = 3.9$ m and $T_p = 14$s). They also show that these changes are increased by narrow reef and steep fore reef slope. On the Molokai coral reefs (Hawaii), Storlazzi et al. (2011) show that the SLR effect on wave height and wave setup leads to changes in total water level (relative to SLR) of a few centimeters for SLR = 1 m. From these studies, assuming unchanged bathymetry in these coral reef environments, SLR has the potential to induce wave setup decreases of a few centimeters up to tens of centimeters or more.

4 Discussion

4.1 Synthesis

The literature review shows that site-specific knowledge of the importance of each interaction mechanism is very heterogeneous (Fig. 2) with some sites or regions receiving little attention (see, e.g., the West Africa coast) and others subject to many studies (e.g., NW European shelf). In the literature, there are few environments or sites where all the

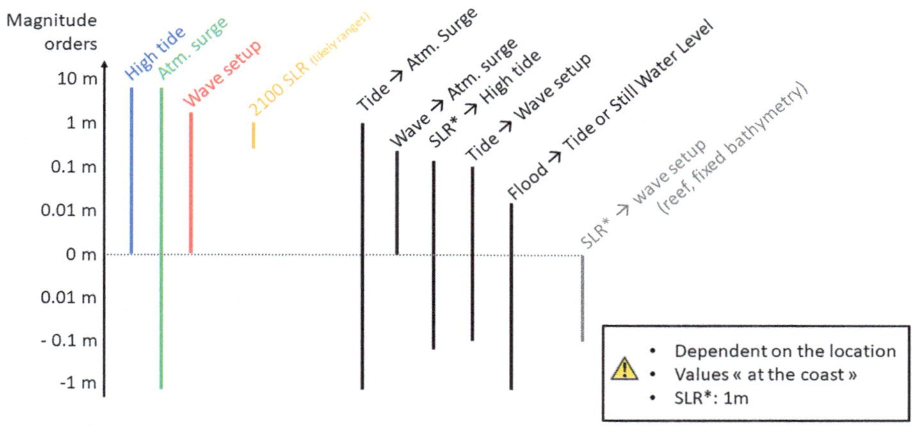

Fig. 6 Orders of magnitude of main water level components (in color) and some of the interactions (in black) investigated in the present paper. The orders of magnitude are based on the publications reviewed in the present paper and on Woodworth et al. (2019). It should be noted that these orders of magnitude are provided 'at the coast' (i.e., at the waterline). This does not exclude larger effect in the nearshore (for instance for tide modulation of wave setup in the surf zone)

interactions investigated here have been quantified separately. However, we can still extract some ranges (in order of magnitude) for some of the interactions (Fig. 6), to compare with the orders of magnitude of the main water level components, keeping in mind that the importance of interactions strongly depends on the location, the amount of SLR and the considered meteorological event.

High tide amplitudes (relative to mean sea level) range from decimetric to metric magnitudes (locally exceeding 8 m in the Bay of Fundy), but sea level rise can cause significant modifications. Changes in $M2$ amplitude or MHW changes of several centimeters to more than 10 cm for SLR scenarios of ~ 1 to 2 m have been obtained from modeling studies. Flooding of previously dry land can also induce tide changes of several centimeters to more than 10 cm nearshore with potential effects at the basin scale (as in the North Sea for instance). The flood effect is mainly negative (i.e., it reduces the high tide level).

Wave setup ranges between a few to tens of centimeters and up to about 1 m. We cannot, however, exclude that larger wave setup could occur. Tides can modulate wave setup from several centimeters on open beaches to tens of centimeters at inlet or estuary mouths (shoals). Nearshore areas (e.g., open sandy coasts and inlets) are known to have dynamic morphologies on event, seasonal or pluriannual timescales. On longer timescales, under the effect of SLR, the morphology is expected to change significantly such that providing specific estimates of the SLR effect on wave setup is perhaps too ambitious. However, assuming an unchanged bathymetry such as in reef environments, wave setup (at the lagoon scale) is expected to decrease $O(10\text{ cm})$, while on fixed open beaches, setup is expected to increase.

Atmospheric surges range from a few centimeters to tens of centimeters, reaching a few meters in exceptional cases and up to 10 m in cyclonic areas. Again, we cannot exclude larger atmospheric storm surges. Tide–surge interactions can lead to surge changes of a few to tens of centimeters and up to almost 1 m. In addition, the wave effect on the sea surface roughness can increase atmospheric surges up to a few tens of centimeters, especially under young sea states.

In summary, there exist locations where each interaction discussed in the present review can reach values of a few tens of centimeters while some interaction processes can contribute almost 1 m to coastal water level. These contributions to total water level are far from negligible and must be considered in planning and mitigation efforts. As highlighted above, site-specific knowledge of the importance of each interaction mechanism is heterogeneous. However, the sites discussed here give some indication where the significant interactions are likely to occur. According to the available literature, along the US East coast, the Patagonian coast, the NW European coasts, and in San Francisco Bay and Taiwan Strait, there exists a significant effect of SLR on tide and tide–surge interaction. All these sites are characterized by substantial shallow water areas. This suggests that there should be other shallow areas subject to non-negligible SLR–tide–surge interactions, such as Indonesia, for instance. Along open coasts with narrow continental shelves, the SLR effect on tide, surge and tide–surge interaction is expected to be negligible. Similarly, based on the shallow water equations and the literature review, significant effects from waves on atmospheric storm surges are expected only in shallow water areas. Regarding the effect on tides of letting previously dry areas flood or not, it is not straightforward to identify the potential areas where this will be a significant effect. However, we can still expect significant changes in shallow water areas characterized by low-lying coasts, especially in estuaries or tidal inlets. As a result, the following areas (not exhaustive) appear sensitive to at least one of the interactions investigated in the present paper: Hudson Bay, European continental shelf, straits with significant tidal currents (e.g., Taiwan), the northern coast of Australia, the Patagonian shelf, Gulf of Mexico and San Francisco Bay.

4.2 Combined Interactions

The present review focused on a few of the possible interactions and on studies providing results concerning each individual interactions. However, multiple studies address the combined effect of multiple interactions, such as taking into account coincident interactions between tides, atmospheric surges, waves and wave setup (e.g., Brown et al. 2013), mainly at local scales.

At the scale of the US East and Gulf coasts Marsooli and Lin (2018) investigated historical storm tides resulting from tide, atmospheric surge and wave setup and the interactions between these components using a numerical modeling approach, focusing on past tropical cyclones (1988–2015). Model results show that the maximum water level rise due to nonlinear tide–surge interaction in most regions along the US East and Gulf Coasts (especially in Long Island Sound, Delaware Bay, Long Bay and along the western coast of Florida) was relatively large but did not occur at the timing of the peak storm tide. Model results at the location of selected tide gauges showed that the contribution of tide–surge interaction to the peak storm tide was between − 25 and + 20% (from − 0.35 to 0.31 m). During the most extreme storm events (i.e., tropical cyclones that caused a storm tide larger than 2 m), the tide–surge interaction contribution ranged between − 12 and 5%. Brown et al. (2013) found a similar behavior on the Liverpool Bay, showing that the maximum wave setup occurs at low water, stressing the effect of the banks (or shoals) at the mouth of the estuary.

Several studies quantified the effect of large coastal flooding on the still water level (i.e., on tide and surge, implicitly including the tide effect on surge), mainly at regional or local scales. For instance, Townend and Pethick (2002) showed that the removal of coastal defenses along several English estuaries allowed the flooding of extensive areas and result in a water level reduction locally exceeding 1 m. Bertin et al. (2014) and Huguet et al. (2018) showed that the massive flooding associated with Xynthia (February 2010, central part of the Bay of Biscay) induced a still water level decrease ranging from 0.1 m at the entrance of the estuaries to more than 1.0 m inside estuaries compared to a situation where the flooding would have been prevented. Note that these two studies revealed that the impact of freshwater discharges was negligible in the case of Xynthia, mostly because freshwater discharges were close to yearly mean values. Different conclusions might be drawn for tropical hurricanes, which are usually associated with heavy rainfall. These findings and the corresponding orders of magnitude have been corroborated in other French estuarine environments (Chaumillon et al. 2017; Waeles et al. 2016).

While there are few studies focusing on the sole effect of SLR on pure atmospheric surges, there are several studies investigating the effect on the still water level or practical storm surge. For instance Arns et al. (2017) show that SLR scenarios of 54 cm, 71 cm, and 174 cm lead to decreases of the practical atmospheric storm surge (still water level minus tide) of 1.8%, 2.3% and 5.1%, on average in the German Bight area. They show that, with SLR and a fixed bathymetry, the modulation of waves by the storm tide should decrease. The observed correlation between waves and storm tides decreases with SLR, such that waves and storm tides become more independent with SLR.

As a last example of studies providing quantitative values on combined interactions, Krien et al. (2017a) investigated the effect of SLR on 100-year surge levels (including atmospheric surge and wave setup) along the coasts of Martinique (Caribbean islands). They show that a 1 m SLR leads to changes in the 100-year surge levels ranging between − 0.3 and + 0.5 m in areas of coral reef and shelf. Most of the domain (especially between the eastern shoreline and coral reefs) is subject to a decrease (larger water depths induce a decrease in wave setup and wind induced storm surge), while increase is observed in very local low-lying regions where the inundation extent is strongly enhanced by the sea level rise.

4.3 Implications for Water Level and Flood Projections

Interactions between the contributions to coastal water level have significant implications for projected changes in the frequency and amplitude of future extreme events, yet most projections neglect the interactions discussed in this paper and consider only linear additions of the relevant processes (Muis et al. 2016; Vitousek et al. 2017; Melet et al. 2018; Vousdoukas et al. 2018). Often, projected SLR is added to current tidal datums with the assumption that a given increment of SLR corresponds to an equivalent increment in the average high tide (i.e., MHW) or some other relevant datum. As discussed above and demonstrated for instance by Pickering et al. (2017), this assumption is not valid in many shelf seas across the global ocean. The obvious implication of the nonlinear relationship between SLR and tidal amplitude is an enhancement or reduction in future water level at high tide. From a planning perspective, however, it is also important to consider how the nonlinear response of tidal amplitude to SLR affects the timing of impacts. Rates of SLR will be on the order of 10 cm per decade under the plausible scenario that GMSL rises by 1 m during the twenty-first century. The nonlinear response of tidal amplitude to 1 m of SLR is also on the order of ± 10 cm in some locations (Pickering et al. 2017). Thus, the effect of tidal amplification on the MHW datum can be roughly equivalent to the effect of ± 1 decade of SLR. Depending on the sign and magnitude of the tidal amplification at a given location, optimal planning horizons may need to be adjusted earlier or later to account for the non-linear response of tidal amplitude and its effect on the frequency of high-tide flooding.

In addition, changes in mean sea level will cascade through the different interaction mechanisms with the net effect potentially resulting in several tens of centimeters of additional (or reduced) water level at the coast during extreme events (e.g., Arns et al. 2017). SLR will directly affect water levels associated with tides, atmospheric storm surges and wave setup with additional indirect effects on surges through tide–surge interactions. Even excluding the interaction between these processes, a 10 cm increase in mean sea level corresponds to a doubling of the frequency of former 50-year return total water levels over much of the global ocean, with approximately 25 cm required for the doubling in areas most affected by storm surge (Vitousek et al. 2017). These mean sea level changes are of the same order of magnitude as the interaction effects (Fig. 6), suggesting that the frequency of the most extreme water level events could increase much more rapidly than currently projected in locations where constructive interactions between processes are strongest.

Explicitly accounting for the interactions between processes in projections of future total water level is not trivial. In practice, a detailed accounting of the interactions requires high-resolution tide, wave, and surge models (including wave setup) with high-quality bathymetry and reasonable estimates of local bottom friction. Indeed, even if in many cases a resolution of few hundred meters is sufficient to capture tide, atmospheric surge and their interaction (see, e.g., Idier et al. 2012; Muller et al. 2014, in which 2 km resolution models are used), it is not sufficient to capture regional and local wave setups, which, depending on the environment, require resolutions of tens and few meters, respectively, but also high-quality bathymetry (see, e.g., Bertin et al. 2015; Pedreros et al. 2018). The quality of the topography (especially on the coastal defenses) is also crucial to account for the flooding effect on coastal water level. As highlighted here and in Sect. 4.4 (penultimate paragraph), there are downscaling challenges, but there are also upscaling issues (indeed, local processes as for instance dissipation by floods or on intertidal areas or tidal bedforms may also affect the regional dynamic). In addition, to account for the uncertainties in the future climate projections, many simulations should be done. Thus, global modeling assessments currently exceed what is computationally feasible, while accurate bathymetric and bottom friction information is not available in many locations.

Given these challenges, a statistical approach should be employed when possible to include process interactions in projections of flood frequency and return periods of extreme events. Probabilistic projections of extreme water levels (e.g., Vousdoukas et al. 2018) offer an opportunity to include statistical representations of process interactions, but this approach has yet to be implemented. Fortunato et al. (2016) proposed a solution to account for tide–surge interactions in extreme value statistics for the coasts of the Iberic Peninsula, although the interactions are not the strongest in this region. To include process interactions in probabilistic projections of extreme water level events, statistical covariance relationships must be established between the processes contributing to total water level. For example, one can envisage a spatially variable covariance relationship between mean sea level and tidal amplitude derived from scenario-based tide modeling studies such as Pickering et al. (2017) or Schindelegger et al. (2018). General covariance relationships between other processes could be estimated by leveraging regional and local modeling frameworks designed for specific local case studies. Exploring physically reasonable parameter spaces in a small number of locations that span general classes of coastal environments (e.g., reef-lined islands, shelf seas, etc.) could provide reasonable estimates of covariance relationships that could be applied more generally to coastal environment classes in a global probabilistic framework. Regardless of approach, a high priority must be placed on developing covariance relationships between contributions to total water level in order to provide accurate projections of water level extremes.

4.4 Limits, Gaps and Remaining Questions

The values and orders of magnitude provided in the present review should be used with some caution. Indeed, this study is based on a literature review, keeping in mind that some areas or environments have been subject to fewer investigations than others, and that the values are dependent on the considered scenarios (e.g., SLR values) and/or meteorological events. In addition, the review relies on modeling studies (as this is the only way to distinguish every component and contribution), such that even if most of the modeling experiments have been validated with observations, there are still some epistemic uncertainties related either to the water level measurements or the modeling (errors in input data, e.g., bathymetry, atmospheric forcing, etc.; representation or omission of the underlying dominant process). For instance, Apotsos et al. (2007) showed that wave setup estimates based on the depth-integrated approach of Longuet-Higgins and Stewart (1964) can be biased low by a factor of two along the shoreline. While most storm surge modeling systems rely on a similar approach, one can expect that wave setup is not always well represented in 2D models. Also, field measurements in surf zones under storm waves are limited to a very few studies (Guérin et al. 2018; Pedreros et al. 2018). These difficulties highlight an urgent need for detailed field observations of wave setup under storm wave conditions.

Regarding validation of modeled tide changes, Schindelegger et al. (2018) investigated the SLR effect on tides and made a thorough comparison of model results with 45 tide gauge records. Their model reproduces the sign of observed amplitude trends in 80% of the cases and captures considerable fractions of the absolute $M2$ variability, specifically for stations in the Gulf of Mexico and the Chesapeake–Delaware Bay system. This result gives strong support to the fact that, in many locations, a significant part of observed tide changes could be attributed to the effect of SLR. Still, discrepancies in models/data remain in several key locations, such as the European Shelf. Indeed, as highlighted by Haigh et al. (2018), many processes can cause changes in tides (sea ice coverage, seabed roughness, ocean stratification, internal tides, etc.), and it remains difficult to associate observed changes in tide over the instrumental period with particular forcing factors. Furthermore, it remains unclear how some of these forcing factors would change with SLR and more 'generally' with the future climate. Finally, while the agreement in local- to regional-scale tidal changes from differing models (e.g., on the NW European Shelf) provides some confidence, it would be of value to conduct further investigations of macro-tidal regions (such as the Bristol Channel) with consideration of interim 'partial recession' or 'flood' scenarios depending on coastal management priorities and sensitivities to the resulting change.

In the present review, we focus on SLR, tide, atmospheric surge, wave and wave setup interactions. However, in estuaries and inlets, when not negligible, the interaction between water level and river discharge should also be considered. Water depth changes are dependent on river discharge (Q_r) in estuarine locations. An increase in Q_r will increase mean sea level locally, but the increased friction of the incoming tide interacting with the outgoing river discharge will lead to a decrease in tidal amplitude (Devlin et al. 2017). Krien et al. (2017b) performed a high-resolution hindcast of the storm surge and flooding associated with cyclone Sidr (2007) in the head of the Bay of Bengal. They showed that, while tide–surge interactions can impact the storm surge by − 0.5 to + 0.5 m, accounting for river discharge can also impact storm-induced flooding substantially.

The interactions investigated in the present review exhibit different spatial scales; the wave setup changes induced by tidal water level and currents or SLR occur mainly at a local scale, while tide–surge interactions and SLR effects have local, regional and global scales. Indeed, tide and atmospheric surge dynamics result from global-, regional- and local-scale mechanisms. A few studies have provided maps of the SLR effect on tide at the global scale. First, as much as possible, at least in regions exhibiting a significant effect of SLR on tides, it is recommended to take into account the global-scale changes in the open boundary conditions of regional or local modeling studies (as in Harker et al. 2019, for instance). Second, to the authors' knowledge there is no study at a global scale investigating tide–surge interaction or SLR effect on atmospheric surge (except tide gauge based studies, which provide local information, non-uniformly spread around the world; see, e.g., Arns et al. 2019). Such studies would be very helpful for hindcasts and projections of still water level or for coastal flood hazard assessment by allowing areas sensitive to SLR, tide and atmospheric surge interactions to be identified.

As mentioned above, one of the main issues when focusing on nearshore water level is the temporal evolution of the seabed topography/morphology. Indeed, such changes, especially for sandy beaches exposed to waves, can have a significant effect on the wave setup (at different timescales: event, seasonal, inter-annual to longer term). For instance, Thiébot et al. (2012) and Brivois et al. (2012) show how, depending on the wave and water level characteristics, different morphologies can emerge on doubled sandbar systems, and thus can alter water level at the coast, especially the wave setup. Morphological changes can also alter the tidal dynamics and related water levels. Ferrarin et al. (2015) investigated the effect of morphology changes and MSL on tides in the Venice lagoon over the last 70 years. While tidal amplitudes in the North Adriatic Sea did not change significantly (even if they exhibit some fluctuations), morphological changes that occurred in the lagoon in the last century produced an increase in the amplitude of major tidal constituents (e.g., $M2$ increase up to about 20% with respect to the imposed tidal wave). This raises the question of how the sole effect of a changing seabed morphology (related to SLR, wave climate change, or human intervention) compares with the interactions investigated in this review.

5 Conclusions and Perspectives

The present paper focused on water level at the coast resulting from the interaction between SLR, tides, atmospheric surge and wave setup. While the discussed mechanisms of interaction were previously known, we provide an overview of quantifications of the interactions based on modeling studies. The largest identified interaction is the tide–surge interaction which can lead to changes in the practical atmospheric surge up to 1 m or more. SLR with a metric value can induce high tide changes (positive or negative) exceeding 10 cm, while waves can increase the atmospheric storm surge a few centimeters up to tens of centimeters. The flood effect on tide and still water level can induce changes (mainly negative) ranging from a few centimeters up to more than 1 m in estuaries. The modulation of wave setup by the tide can represent a few centimeters at the shoreline, but can reach tens of centimeters on ebb shoals. The effect of SLR on wave setup is more debatable, but could be positive or negative depending on the nearshore bathymetry and beach slope.

The review also suggests that these interactions have smaller magnitudes in deeper areas and can thus be considered as negligible in some locations. On the contrary, many studies show significant interactions in shallow water. The sensitive areas we identified include Hudson Bay, European continental shelves, straits with significant tidal currents (e.g., Taiwan), the northern coast of Australia, the Patagonian shelf and the Gulf of Mexico. However, the spatial distribution of studies focusing on these interactions is heterogeneous.

In areas where non-negligible interactions are expected, we suggest these interactions to be taken into account (either by numerical modeling or by statistical methods) in assessments of nearshore water levels and induced coastal flooding. Including interaction mechanisms is especially important when projecting future coastal flooding including SLR.

The present review focused on a subset of the possible interactions, but within the estimation of future water levels, additional complexity arises. Regarding future tide changes, further investigations are needed to better identify if and which phenomena other than the sea level rise could have a significant effect on tides. Finally, the nearshore area is a key zone for tide and surge dissipation, but also wave setup. However, especially under a rising sea level, significant morphological changes are expected in these nearshore areas. The effect of changes in nearshore bathymetry deserves more attention, at least considering scenarios to better characterize the sensitivity of water level to these changes in comparison with changes induced by the interactions discussed in the present paper.

Acknowledgements The authors are grateful to Philip Woodworth and Martin Verlaan for fruitful discussions. This paper arose from the workshop on 'Understanding the Relationship between Coastal Sea Level and Large-Scale Ocean Circulation,' held at the International Space Science Institute (ISSI), Bern, Switzerland on March 5–9, 2018. The authors wish also to thank Anny Cazenave for the initiative of the workshop and associated Special Issue. Contributions to this work from Déborah Idier were funded by BRGM and the ECLISEA project (which is part of ERA4CS, an ERA-NET initiated by JPI Climate with co-funding by the European Union, Grant 690462). Contributions from Xavier Bertin were funded through the Regional Chair Program 'EVEX.' Contributions from Philip Thompson were funded by the NOAA Research Global Ocean Monitoring and Observing Program in support of the University of Hawaii Sea Level Center (NA16NMF4320058).

References

Antony C, Unnikrishnan AS (2013) Observed characteristics of tide–surge interaction along the east coast of India and the head of Bay of Bengal. Estuar Coast Shelf Sci 131:6–11. https://doi.org/10.1016/j.ecss.2013.08.004

Apotsos A, Raubenheimer B, Elgar S, Guza RT, Smith J (2007) Effects of wave rollers and bottom stress on wave setup. J Geophys Res Oceans 112:C02003. https://doi.org/10.1029/2006JC003549

Ardhuin F, Roland A, Dumas F, Bennis A-C, Sentchev A, Forget P, Wolf J, Girard F, Osuna P, Benoit M (2012) Numerical wave modeling in conditions with strong currents: dissipation, refraction, and relative wind. J Phys Oceanogr 42(12):2101–2120. https://doi.org/10.1175/JPO-D-11-0220.1

Arns A, Wahl T, Dangendorf S, Jensen J (2015) The impact of sea level rise on storm surge water levels in the northern part of the German Bight. Coast Eng 96:118–131. https://doi.org/10.1016/j.coastaleng.2014.12.002

Arns A, Wahl T, Dangendorf S, Jensen J, Pattiaratchi C (2017) Sea-level rise induced amplification of coastal protection design heights. Sci Rep 7:40171. https://doi.org/10.1038/srep40171

Arns A, Wahl T, Wolff C, Vafeidis A, Jensen J (2019) Global estimates of tide surge interaction and its benefits for coastal protection. EGU General Assembly 2019, Geophysical Research Abstracts 21, EGU2019-7307-1

Bennis A-C, Dumas F, Ardhuin F, Blanke B (2012) Mixing parameterization: impacts on rip currents and wave set-up. Ocean Eng 84:213–227. https://doi.org/10.1016/j.oceaneng.2014.04.021

Bertin X, Olabarrieta M (2016) Relevance of infragravity waves in a wave-dominated inlet. J Geophys Res Oceans 121:1–15. https://doi.org/10.1002/2015JC011444

Bertin X, Bruneau N, Breilh J-F, Fortunato AB, Karpytchev M (2012) Importance of wave age and resonance in storm surges: the case Xynthia, Bay of Biscay. Ocean Model 42:16–30. https://doi.org/10.1016/j.ocemod.2011.11.001

Bertin X, Li K, Roland A, Zhang YJ, Breilh JF, Chaumillon E (2014) A modeling-based analysis of the flooding associated with Xynthia, central Bay of Biscay. Coast Eng. https://doi.org/10.1016/j.coastaleng.2014.08.013

Bertin X, Li K, Roland A, Bidlot J-R (2015) The contribution of short-waves in storm surges: two case studies in the Bay of Biscay. Cont Shelf Res 96:1–15. https://doi.org/10.1016/j.csr.2015.01.005

Breilh J-F, Bertin X, Chaumillon E, Giloy N, Sauzeau T (2014) How frequent is storm-induced flooding in the central part of the Bay of Biscay? Glob Planet Change 122:161–175. https://doi.org/10.1016/j.gloplacha.2014.08.013

Brivois O, Idier D, Thiébot J, Castelle B, Le Cozannet G, Calvete D (2012) On the use of linear stability model to characterize the morphological behaviour of a double bar system. Application to Truc Vert beach (France). CR Geosci 344:277–287. https://doi.org/10.1016/j.crte.2012.02.004

Brown JM, Souza AJ, Wolf J (2010) An investigation of recent decadal-scale storm events in the eastern Irish Sea. J Geophys Res 115:C05018. https://doi.org/10.1029/2009JC005662

Brown JM, Bolaños R, Wolf J (2013) The depth-varying response of coastal circulation and water levels to 2D radiation stress when applied in a coupled wave-tide–surge modelling system during an extreme storm. Coast Eng 82:102–113. https://doi.org/10.1016/j.coastaleng.2013.08.009

Bruun P (1962) Sea level rise as a cause of shore erosion. J Waterw Harb Div 88:117–130

Carless SJ, Green JAM, Pelling HE, Wilmes S-B (2016) Effects of future sea-level rise on tidal processes on the Patagonian Shelf. J Mar Syst 163:113–124. https://doi.org/10.1016/j.jmarsys.2016.07.007

Carrere L, Lyard F, Cancet M, Guillot A, Picot N (2015) FES 2014, a new tidal model—validation results and perspectives for improvements. Geophys Res Abstracts 17:EGU2015-5481-1, EGU General Assembly 2015

Charnock H (1955) Wind stress on a water surface. Q J R Meteor Soc 81:639–640

Chaumillon E, Bertin X, Fortunato AB, Bajo M, Schneider J-L, Dezileau L, Walsh JP, Michelot A, Chauveau E, Créach A, Hénaff A, Sauzeau T, Waeles B, Gervais B, Jan G, Baumann J, Breilh J-F, Pedreros R (2017) Storm-induced marine flooding: lessons from a multidisciplinary approach. Earth Sci Rev 165:151–184. https://doi.org/10.1016/j.earscirev.2016.12.005

Chawla A, Kirby JT (2002) Monochromatic and random wave breaking at blocking points. J Geophys Res Oceans 107:1–19. https://doi.org/10.1029/2001JC001042

Church JA, Clark PU, Cazenave A, Gregory JM, Jevrejeva S, Levermann A, Merrifield MA, Milne GA, Nerem RS, Nunn PD, Payne A, Pfeffer W, Stammer D, Unnikrishnan AS (2013a) Sea-level rise by 2100. Science 342(6165):1445–1445. https://doi.org/10.1126/science.342.6165.1445-a

Church J, Clark P, Cazenave A, Gregory J, Jevrejeva S, Merrifield M, Milne G, Nerem R, Nunn P, Payne A, Pfeffer W, Stammer D, Unnikrishnan AS (2013b) Sea level change, pages 1137–1216. Climate change 2013: the physical science basis. Contribution of working group I to the fifth assessment report of the intergovernmental panel on climate change. Cambridge University Press, Cambridge

Clark PU, Shakun JD, Marcott SA, Mix AC, Eby M, Kulp S, Levermann A, Milne GA, Pfister PL, Santer BD, Schrag DP, Solomon S, Stocker TF, Strauss BH, Weaver AJ, Winkelmann R, Archer D, Bard E, Goldner A, Lambeck K, Pierrehumbert RT, Plattner G-K (2016) Consequences of twenty first-century policy for multi-millennial climate and sea-level change. Nat Clim Change 6:360–369. https://doi.org/10.1038/nclimate2923

Dean RG (1991) Equilibrium beach profiles: characteristics and applications. J Coast Res 7:53–84

Devlin AT, Jay DA, Talke SA, Zaron ED, Pan J, Lin H (2017) Coupling of sea level and tidal range changes, with implications for future water levels. Sci Rep 7:17021. https://doi.org/10.1038/s41598-017-17056-z

Dodet G, Bertin X, Bruneau N, Fortunato A, Nahon A, Roland A (2013) Wave–current interactions in a wave-dominated tidal inlet. J Geophys Res Oceans 118:1587–1905. https://doi.org/10.1002/jgrc.20146

Dodet G, Melet A, Ardhuin F, Bertin X, Idier D, Almar R (2019) The contribution of wind generated waves to coastal sea level changes. Surv Geophys (in review)

Etala P (2009) Dynamic issues in the SE South America storm surge modeling. Nat Hazards 51:79–95. https://doi.org/10.1007/s11069-009-9390-3

Ferrarin C, Tomasin A, Bajo M, Petrizzo A, Umgiesser G (2015) Tidal changes in a heavily modified coastal wetland. Cont Shelf Res 101:22–33. https://doi.org/10.1016/j.csr.2015.04.002

Flather RA (2001) Storm surges. In: Steele JH, Thorpe SA, Turekian KK (eds) Encyclopedia of Ocean Sciences. Academic, San Diego, pp 2882–2892

Fortunato A, Li K, Bertin X, Rodrigues M, Miguez BM (2016) Determination of extreme sea levels along the Iberian Atlantic coast. Ocean Eng 111:471–482. https://doi.org/10.1016/j.oceaneng.2015.11.031

Fortunato AB, Freire P, Bertin X, Rodrigues M, Liberato MLR, Ferreira J (2017) A numerical study of the February 15, 1941 storm in the Tagus estuary. Cont Shelf Res 144:50–64. https://doi.org/10.1016/j.csr.2017.06.023

Godin G (1993) On tidal resonance. Cont Shelf Res 13(1):89–107. https://doi.org/10.1016/0278-4343(93)90037-X

Grant WD, Madsen OS (1979) Combined wave and current interaction with a rough bottom. J Geophys Res Oceans 84:1797–1808

Green JAM (2010) Ocean tides and resonance. Ocean Dyn 60:1243–1253. https://doi.org/10.1007/s10236-010-0331-1

Guérin T, Bertin X, Coulombier T, de Bakker A (2018) Impacts of wave-induced circulation in the surf zone on wave setup. Ocean Model 123:86–97. https://doi.org/10.1016/j.ocemod.2018.01.006

Guerreiro M, Fortunato AB, Freire P, Rilo A, Taborda R, Freitas MC, Andrade C, Silva T, Rodrigues M, Bertin X, Azevedo A (2015) Evolution of the hydrodynamics of the Tagus estuary (Portugal) in the 21st century. J Integr Coast Zone Manag 15(1):65–80. https://doi.org/10.5894/rgci515

Haigh ID, Green M, Pickering MD, Arbic B, Arns A, Dangendorf S, Hill D, Horsburgh K, Howard T, Idier D, Jay D, Lee S, Müller M, Schindelegger M, Talke S, Wilmes S-B, Woodworth P (2018) The tides they are a-Changin'. Rev Geophys. (Submitted)

Harker A, Green JAM, Schindelegger M (2019) The impact of sea-level rise on tidal characteristics around Australia. Ocean Sci Discuss. https://doi.org/10.5194/os-15-147-2019

Hendershott MC (1972) The effects of solid earth deformation on global ocean tides. Geophys J R Astron Soc 29:389–402

Hendershott MC (1973) Ocean tides. Eos Trans AGU 54(2):76–86. https://doi.org/10.1029/EO054i002p00076-02

Holleman RC, Stacey MT (2014) Coupling of sea level rise, tidal amplification, and inundation. J Phys Oceanogr. https://doi.org/10.1175/JPO-D-13-0214.1

Horsburgh KJ, Wilson C (2007) Tide–surge interaction and its role in the distribution of surge residuals in the North Sea. J Geophys Res Oceans 112:C08003. https://doi.org/10.1029/2006JC004033

Huguet J-R, Bertin X, Arnaud G (2018) Managed realignment to mitigate storm-induced flooding: a case study in La Faute-sur-mer, France. Coast Eng 134:168–176. https://doi.org/10.1016/j.coastaleng.2017.08.010

Hussain MA, Tajima Y (2017) Numerical investigation of surge–tide interactions in the Bay of Bengal along the Bangladesh coast. Nat Hazards 86(2):669–694. https://doi.org/10.1007/s11069-016-2711-4

Idier D, Dumas F, Muller H (2012) Tide–surge interaction in the English channel. Nat Hazard Earth Sys 12:3709–3718. https://doi.org/10.5194/nhess-12-3709-2012

Idier D, Paris F, Le Cozannet G, Boulahya F, Dumas F (2017) Sea-level rise impacts on the tides of the European Shelf. Cont Shelf Res 137:56–71. https://doi.org/10.1016/j.csr.2017.01.007

Johns B, Rao AD, Dube SK, Sinha PC (1985) Numerical modelling of tide–surge interaction in the Bay of Bengal. Phil Trans R Soc Lond A 313:507–535

Jones JE, Davies AM (1998) Storm surge computations for the Irish Sea using a three-dimensional numerical model including wave–current interaction. Cont Shelf Res 18:201–251

Kennedy AB, Westerink JJ, Smith JM, Hope ME, Hartman M, Taflanidis AA, Tanaka S, Westerink H, Cheung KF, Smith T, Hamann M, Minamide M, Ota A, Dawson C (2012) Tropical cyclone inundation potential on the Hawaiian Islands of Oahu and Kauai. Ocean Model 52–53:54–68. https://doi.org/10.1016/j.ocemod.2012.04.009

Kopp RE, Horton RM, Little CM, Mitrovica JX, Oppenheimer M, Rasmussen DJ, Strauss BH, Tebaldi C (2014) Probabilistic 21st and 22nd century sea-level projections at a global network of tide-gauge sites. Earth Fut 2:383–406. https://doi.org/10.1002/2014EF000239

Krien Y, Dudon B, Roger J, Arnaud G, Zahibo N (2017a) Assessing storm surge hazard and impact of sea level rise in the Lesser Antilles case study of Martinique. Nat Hazard Earth Sys 17:1559–1571. https://doi.org/10.5194/nhess-17-1559-2017

Krien Y, Testut L, Islam AKMS, Bertin X, Durand F, Mayet C, Tazkia AR, Becker M, Calmant S, Papa F, Ballu V, Shum CK, Khan ZH (2017b) Towards improved storm surge models in the northern Bay of Bengal. Cont Shelf Res 135:58–73. https://doi.org/10.1016/j.csr.2017.01.014
Kuang C, Liang H, Mao X, Karney B, Gu J, Huang H, Chen W, Song H (2017) Influence of potential future sea-level rise on tides in the China Sea. J Coast Res 33(1):105–117. https://doi.org/10.2112/JCOASTRES-D-16-00057.1
Longuet-Higgins MS, Stewart RW (1964) Radiation stresses in water waves: a physical discussion, with applications. Deep Sea Res Oceanogr Abstr 11:529–562
Malhadas MS, Leitao PC, Silva A, Neves R (2009) Effect of coastal waves on sea level in Obidos Lagoon, Portugal. Cont Shelf Res 1999:1240–1250. https://doi.org/10.1016/j.csr.2009.02.007
Marsooli R, Lin N (2018) Numerical modeling of historical storm tides and waves and their interactions along the US east and Gulf Coasts. J Geophys Res Oceans 123:3844–3874. https://doi.org/10.1029/2017JC013434
Mastenbroek C, Burgers G, Janssen PAEM (1993) The dynamical coupling of a wave model and a storm surge model through the atmospheric boundary layer. J Phys Oceanogr 23:1856–1866
Melet A, Meyssignac B, Almar R, Le Cozannet G (2018) Under-estimated wave contribution to coastal sea-level rise. Nat Clim change 8(3):234–239. https://doi.org/10.1038/s41558-018-0088-y
Moon I-J, Ginis I, Hara T (2004) Effect of surface waves on Charnock coefficient under tropical cyclones. Geophys Res Lett. https://doi.org/10.1029/2004GL020988
Moon I-J, Kwon JI, Lee J-C, Shim J-S, Kang SK, Oh IS, Kwon SJ (2009) Effect of the surface wind stress parameterization on the storm surge modeling. Ocean Model 29(2):115–127. https://doi.org/10.1016/j.ocemod.2009.03.006
Muis S, Verlaan M, Winsemius HC, Aerts JCJH, Ward PJ (2016) A global reanalysis of storm surges and extreme sea levels. Nat Commun 7(11):969. https://doi.org/10.1038/ncomms11969
Muller H, Pineau-Guillou L, Idier D (2014) Ardhuin F (2014) Atmospheric storm surge modeling methodology along the French (Atlantic and English Channel) coast. Ocean Dyn 64:1671–1692. https://doi.org/10.1007/s10236-014-0771-0
Nicolle A, Karpytchev M, Benoit M (2009) Amplification of the storm surges in shallow waters of the Pertuis Charentais (Bay of Biscay, France). Ocean Dyn 59:921. https://doi.org/10.1007/s10236-009-0219-0
Nott J, Green C, Townsend I, Callaghan J (2014) The world record storm surge and the most intense southern hemisphere tropical cyclone: new evidence and modeling. Bull Am Meteor Soc 95:757–765. https://doi.org/10.1175/BAMS-D-12-00233.1
Palmer M, Howard T, Tinker J, Lowe J, Bricheno L, Calvert D, Edwards T, Gregory J, Harris G, Krijnen J, Pickering M, Roberts C, Wolf J (2018) Maine projections. UKCP18 marine report (Met Office)
Pedreros R, Idier D, Muller H, Lecacheux S, Paris F, Yates-Michelin M, Dumas F, Pineau-Guillou L, Sénéchal N (2018) Relative contribution of wave setup to the storm surge: observations and modeling based analysis in open and protected environments (Truc Vert beach and Tubuai island). In: Shim J-S, Chun I, Lim HS (eds) Proceedings from the international coastal symposium (ICS) 2018 (Busan, Republic of Korea). J Coast Res SI85:1046-1050. Coconut Creek (Florida). ISSN 0749-0208. https://doi.org/10.2112/SI85-210.1
Pelling HE, Green JAM (2014) Impact of flood defences and sea-level rise on the European Shelf tidal regime. Cont Shelf Res 85:96–105. https://doi.org/10.1016/j.csr.2014.04.011
Pelling HE, Green JAM, Ward SL (2013a) Modelling tides and sea-level rise: to flood or not to flood. Ocean Model 63:21–29. https://doi.org/10.1016/j.ocemod.2012.12.004
Pelling HE, Uehara K, Green JAM (2013b) The impact of rapid coastline changes and sea level rise on the tides in the Bohai Sea, China. J Geophys Res Oceans 118:3462–3472. https://doi.org/10.1002/jgrc.20258
Pickering MD, Wells NC, Horsburgh KJ, Green JAM (2012) The impact of future sea-level rise on the European Shelf tides. Cont Shelf Res 35:1–15. https://doi.org/10.1016/j.csr.2011.11.011
Pickering MD, Horsburgh KJ, Blundell JR, Hirschi JJ-M, Nicholls RJ, Verlaan M, Wells NC (2017) The impact of future sea-level rise on the global tides. Cont Shelf Res 142:50–68. https://doi.org/10.1016/j.csr.2017.02.004
Powell MD, Vickery PJ, Reinhold TA (2003) Reduced drag coefficient for high wind speeds in tropical cyclones. Nature 422:279–283. https://doi.org/10.1038/nature01481
Pugh DT (1987) Tides, surges and mean sea-level: a handbook for engineers and scientists. Wiley, Hoboken, pp 472
Quataert E, Storlazzi C, van Rooijen A, Cheriton O, van Dongeren A (2015) The influence of coral reefs and climate change on wave-driven flooding of tropical coastlines. Geophys Res Lett 42:6407–6415. https://doi.org/10.1002/2015GL064861

Raubenheimer B, Guza RT, Elgar S (2001) Field observations of wave-driven setdown and setup. J Geophys Res Oceans 106:4629–4638. https://doi.org/10.1029/2000JC000572
Ray RD (2001) Internal tides. In: Steele JH (ed) Encyclopedia of ocean sciences. Academic, Berlin, pp 258–265. https://doi.org/10.1016/B978-012374473-9.00125-9
Ross AC, Najjar RG, Li M, Lee SB, Zhang F, Liu W (2017) Fingerprints of sea level rise on changing tides in the Chesapeake and Delaware Bays. J Geophys Res Oceans 122:8102–8125. https://doi.org/10.1002/2017JC012887
Rusu L, Bernardino M, Guedes Soares C (2011) Modelling the influence of currents on wave propagation at the entrance of the Tagus estuary. Ocean Eng 38(10):1174–1183. https://doi.org/10.1016/j.oceaneng.2011.05.016
Schindelegger M, Green JAM, Wilmes S-B, Haigh ID (2018) Can we model the effect of observed sea level rise on tides? J Geophys Res Oceans. https://doi.org/10.1029/2018JC013959
Smith SD, Banke EG (1975) Variation of the sea surface drag coefficient with windspeed. Q J R Meteorol Soc 101:665–673
Stewart RW (1974) The air-sea momentum exchange. Boundary Layer Meteorol 6:151–167
Storlazzi CD, Elias E, Field ME, Presto MK (2011) Numerical modeling of the impact of sea-level rise on fringing coral reef hydrodynamics and sediment transport. Coral Reefs 30:83–96. https://doi.org/10.1007/s00338-011-0723-9
Taylor GI (1922) Tidal oscillations in gulfs and rectangular basins. Proc Lond Math Soc 20:148–181
Thiébot J, Idier D, Garnier R, Falquès A, Ruessink G (2012) The influence of wave direction on the morphological response of a double sandbar system. Cont Shelf Res 32:71–85. https://doi.org/10.1016/j.csr.2011.10.014
Townend I, Pethick J (2002) Estuarine flooding and managed retreat. Proceedings of "Flood risk in a changing climate". Philos Trans R Soc A 360:1477–1495
Van Dorn WG (1953) Wind stress on a artificial pond. J Mar Res 12:249–276
Vitousek S, Barnard PL, Fletcher CH, Frazer N, Erikson L, Storlazzi CD (2017) Doubling of coastal flooding frequency within decades due to sea-level rise. Sci Rep 7(1):1399. https://doi.org/10.1038/s41598-017-01362-7
Vousdoukas MI, Mentaschi L, Voukouvalas E, Verlaan M, Jevrejeva S, Jackson LP, Feyen L (2018) Global probabilistic projections of extreme sea levels show intensification of coastal flood hazard. Nat Commun 9(1):2360. https://doi.org/10.1038/s41467-018-04692-w
Waeles B, Bertin X, Chevaillier D, Breilh J-F, Li K, Le Mauff B (2016) Limitation of high water levels in bays and estuaries during storm flood events. In: Gourbesville P, Cunge JA, Caignaert G (eds) Advances in hydroinformatics, SIMHYDRO, pp 439–449
Wang RQ, Herdman LM, Erikson L, Barnard P, Hummel M, Stacey MT (2017) Interactions of estuarine shoreline infrastructure with multiscale sea level variability. J Geophys Res Oceans 122:9962–9979. https://doi.org/10.1002/2017JC012730
Wilmes S-B (2016) The impact of large-scale sea-level changes on tides in the past, present and future. PhD thesis, Prifysgol Bangor University
Wolf J (1978) Interaction of tide and surge in a semi-infinite uniform channel, with application to surge propagation down the east coast of Britain. Appl Math Model 2:245–253
Wolf J, Flather RA (2005) Modelling waves and surges during the 1953 storm. Phil Trans R Soc A 363:1359–1375. https://doi.org/10.1098/rsta.2005.1572
Woodworth PL, Melet A, Marcos M, Ray R, Woppelmann G, Sasaki N, Cirano M, Hibbert A, Huthnance JM, Montserrat S (2019) Forcing factors causing sea level changes at the coast. Surv Geophys. https://doi.org/10.1007/s10712-019-09531-1
Woodworth PL (2010) A survey of recent changes in the main components of the ocean tide. Cont Shelf Res 30:1680–1691. https://doi.org/10.1016/j.csr.2010.07.002
Xie L, Pietrafesa LJ, Wu K (2003) A numerical study of wave–current interaction through surface and bottom stresses: coastal ocean response to hurricane Fran of 1996. J Geophys Res Oceans 108:3049–3066. https://doi.org/10.1029/2001JC001078
Xu JL, Zhang YH, Cao AZ, Liu Q, Lv XQ (2016) Effects of tide–surge interactions on storm surges along the coast of the Bohai Sea, Yellow Sea, and East China Sea. Sci China Earth Sci 59:1308–1316. https://doi.org/10.1007/s11430-015-5251-y
Yu X, Pan W, Zheng X, Zhou S, Tao X (2017) Effects of wave–current interaction on storm surge in the Taiwan Strait: insights from Typhoon Morakot. Cont Shelf Res 146:47–57. https://doi.org/10.1016/j.csr.2017.08.009
Zhang MY, Li YS (1996) The synchronous coupling of a third-generation wave model and a two-dimensional storm surge model. Ocean Eng 23(6):533–543. https://doi.org/10.1016/0029-8018(95)00067-4

Zhang W-Z, Shi F, Hong H-S, Shang S-P, Kirby JT (2010) Tide–surge interaction intensified by the Taiwan Strait. J Geophys Res 115:C06012. https://doi.org/10.1029/2009JC005762

Zhang H, Cheng W, Qiu X, Feng X, Gong W (2017) Tide–surge interaction along the east coast of the Leizhou Peninsula, South China Sea. Cont Shelf Res 146:47–57. https://doi.org/10.1016/j.csr.2017.08.009

Zippel S, Thomson J (2015) Surface wave breaking over sheared currents: observations from the Mouth of the Columbia River. J Geophys Res Oceans 222:3311–3328. https://doi.org/10.1002/2016JC012498

Surveys in Geophysics (2019) 40:1631–1653
https://doi.org/10.1007/s10712-019-09559-3

Climate Model Uncertainty and Trend Detection in Regional Sea Level Projections: A Review

Mark Carson[1] · Kewei Lyu[2] · Kristin Richter[3] · Mélanie Becker[4] · Catia M. Domingues[5] · Weiqing Han[6] · Laure Zanna[7]

Received: 6 November 2018 / Accepted: 18 July 2019 / Published online: 10 August 2019

Abstract
Projections of future sterodynamic sea level change from global climate models are associated with different sources of uncertainty. From a scientific, societal and policy-making perspective, it is relevant to both understand and reduce uncertainty in projections of climate change. Here, we review recent findings which describe, and shed light on, climate model uncertainty focusing particularly on two types of model uncertainty that contribute to the currently large spread in dynamical sea level patterns (i.e., regional sea level relative to the global mean). These uncertainties are: (1) intermodel uncertainty due to differences in models' responses in a warming climate and (2) internal model variability due to an individual model's own climate variability. On timescales longer than about 50 years from now, anthropogenic sterodynamic (dynamic plus global mean) sea level trends from middle- and high-end forcing scenarios will be larger than internal model variability. By 2100, these anthropogenic trends will also be larger than intermodel uncertainty when global mean thermosteric sea level rise and/or melting contributions from land ice are considered along with dynamic sea level changes. Furthermore, we discuss projections of future coastal sea level from the perspective of global climate models as well as from downscaled efforts based on regional climate models. Much knowledge and understanding has been achieved in the last decade from intermodel experiments and studies of sea level process-based model; here, the prospects for improving coastal sea level and reducing sea level uncertainty are discussed.

Keywords Sea level · Climate projections · Regional sea level · Uncertainty · Trends · Trend detection · Time of emergence · Climate model

1 Introduction

Global mean sea level (GMSL) will continue to rise over the next centuries as a consequence of increases in global mean temperature caused by anthropogenic climate forcing. About 70% of global coastlines are projected to experience a relative sea level

✉ Mark Carson
mark.carson@uni-hamburg.de

Extended author information available on the last page of the article

change within 20% of global mean sea level rise by the end of this century (Church et al. 2013). Proper appraisal of uncertainty in projections of global and dynamic sea level is essential for risk assessment in policy responses and results in more effective risk management as part of adaptation and mitigation efforts (IPCC 2014: Summary for Policymakers).

Sea level projections are typically made using coupled climate models (e.g., Yin 2012; Church et al. 2013), statistical (e.g., Perrette et al. 2013) and semiempirical methods (e.g., Moore et al. 2013). While statistical and semiempirical methods can both provide an estimate of sea level change along with some measure of uncertainty, ensembles of coupled climate models directly provide both an estimate of intermodel uncertainty—which is the sensitivity of dynamical sea level projections to model structure, parameterizations and numerics—and an estimate of the uncertainty due to natural variability over different timescales. In these multi-model projections, uncertainty arises from different sources, with their relative significance varying as a function of lead time and spatiotemporal averaging scales (Hawkins and Sutton 2009; Northrop and Chandler 2014). Models under discussion in this review are largely models contributing to phase 5 of CMIP (Coupled Model Intercomparison Project, hereafter CMIP5; Taylor et al. 2009).

Climate models also provide valuable process-based information, such as low-frequency climate variability and anthropogenically forced trends on timescales up to centuries, which can be used for detecting the emergence of anthropogenic sterodynamic (often referred to as "regional" or "local") sea level trends. These trends are detected when their signal emerges above the "background noise", that is, above the range of variability which is externally forced by natural processes (e.g., solar and volcanic) and variability internal (unforced) to the climate system (e.g., known climate modes of variability). Such detection efforts can be used to assess how quickly sea level changes outside the range of natural variability will impact a specific coastal region. Thus, detection of anthropogenic sea level trends is crucial not only to better understand physical processes by climate scientists but also to the public sector and local governments to inform urban planning and elaboration of effective climate change adaptation and mitigation strategies. However, it is important that climate models can accurately estimate both internal variability and regional responses to anthropogenic forcings in order for such detection methods to yield results with confidence.

This review focuses on recent advances into understanding the spread in model projections of local, sterodynamic sea level change related to ocean processes, i.e., ocean heat uptake, mass, heat and freshwater redistribution. The ways in which this has been achieved, as well as the problems and answers which have been found so far, inform on how well we can directly estimate or infer future sea level changes at the coast and regionally in the open ocean and how much confidence we are able to place on them. Though sea level rise due to mass loss from the Greenland and Antarctic ice sheets is expected to increase (e.g., Church et al. 2013), the respective sea level fingerprints are still obscured by the decadal to multidecadal sea level variability observed in satellite altimetry. Richter et al. (2017b) showed that the internal decadal to multidecadal (modeled) contribution of glaciers mass change to sea level variability is small compared to ocean variability. Little is known, however, about the internal variability of the Greenland and Antarctic ice sheets.

As we employ various specific terms regarding sea level, variability and uncertainty, a terminology list is found in the following subsection. These terms will be linked to those found in Gregory et al. 2019, where possible. In Sect. 2, we cover relevant literature on the sources of climate model uncertainty for projected local, sterodynamic sea level trends and on model representation of internal climate variability of sea level in comparison with satellite altimetry and tide gauge observations. Some focus is specific to understanding model internal climate variability, a partially irreducible source of uncertainty in trend detection given that it is a natural feature of the climate system.

Research into trend detection for anthropogenic sterodynamic sea level change is presented in Sect. 3. As an application of the uncertainties explored in Sect. 2, here we summarize model studies that assess the effect of internal variability and intermodel spread on the detection of future sterodynamic sea level trends. These studies provide a timeframe proxy for anthropogenic sea level trends that are expected to emerge from natural variability in the observational record. A subset of these results that are applied specifically at the coasts is also presented.

In Sect. 4, we examine research which covers the coastal aspect of sea level projections, including recent downscaling efforts based on regional models of considerably higher spatial grid resolution than global climate models, and what still needs to be accomplished or improved in coastal sea level projections. Sources of uncertainty that are specific to modeled coastal sea level projections are explored. Finally, Sect. 5 contains some brief concluding remarks.

1.1 Terminology

- *Dynamic sea level*—the spatially and time-dependent sea level referenced to the geoid and provides geostrophic surface currents, chosen such that its global mean is zero; dynamic sea level here does not contain any other sea level signal (e.g., no global mean thermosteric sea level, no land ice melt, no land motion, no inverse barometer effects). This is term N13 ocean dynamic sea level change in Gregory et al. 2019, minus the inverse barometer (IB) correction, and is the same as the "zos" variable reported for CMIP5 models.
- *Global mean thermosteric sea level*—the increase in global mean sea level through thermal expansion of warming water (e.g., Domingues et al. 2008), where the global mean is being derived from ocean model density via a common calculation (Greatbatch 1994) in which a mean, time-independent salinity is used. In CMIP5 model output alone, this is normally synonymous with global mean sea level. This is term N17 in Gregory et al. (2019).
- *Sterodynamic sea level*—in modeling studies often called "regional or local sea level," it is the dynamic sea level plus global mean thermosteric sea level; the sterodynamic sea level (associated with changes in ocean density and circulation, see Gregory et al. 2019) can be derived directly from coupled climate models and does not include any other sea level components which are not commonly calculated in CMIP5 models. This is term N20 in Gregory et al. (2019).
- *Total sea level*—the sterodynamic sea level, plus all other known components to sea level that contribute a substantial amount to the sterodynamic sea level changes relative to the adjacent coast, or the ocean floor, as presented in the AR5 report (Church et al. 2013; i.e., land ice melt, vertical land motion from glacial isostatic adjustment, land water storage and inverse barometer (IB) effects). It is the IB-corrected relative sea level change (see term N15, Gregory et al. 2019), the sea level measured relative to the sea floor, and therefore includes the contribution from vertical land motion, but includes also changes in the geoid and the change in total mass (volume) of the ocean. This is the only quantity in this paper that relies on data external to the typical CMIP5 coupled climate models' ocean component model.

- *Internal variability*—dynamic sea level variability occurring within the pre-industrial control runs of individual models.
- *Intermodel uncertainty*—differences between models in dynamic sea level changes over a fixed time frame.
- *Uncertainty*—a general term used for the property of statistical uncertainty or error associated with changes (usually mean differences or trends) in dynamic, sterodynamic or total sea level over a specified time interval, but also used as a term for the range of values obtained when applying a set of different forcings in model experiments that may not span the range of possible forcing values due to unknown or unknowable factors. An example of the latter is scenario uncertainty (Yip et al. 2011; see Sect. 2).
- *Time of emergence (ToE)/trend detection*—the length of time over which a trend from linear least squares fitted to sterodynamic sea level will be statistically significant against the local, unforced, sea level variability (i.e., the internal variability) is the time of (signal) emergence; the process is also called trend detection. In order to identify the ToE for anthropogenic sterodynamic sea level change, one must estimate sterodynamic sea level variability from internal climate processes on a wide range of timescales (e.g., Becker et al. 2014; Carson et al. 2015; Little et al. 2015; Han et al. 2018; see Sect. 3 for uncertainty arising from internal variability).
- *Regional*—this adjective is used to draw specific attention to the fact that a spatially local property is being examined, as opposed to a global or global mean property.

2 Climate Model Uncertainty in Future Sea Level Projections

Future projections of sterodynamic sea level are generally developed based on multi-model ensembles all using the same forcing protocol design (e.g., Eyring et al. 2016). These global climate model simulations are averaged together to provide a mean estimate, called the ensemble mean, as this averages out random noise and transient dynamic features. The multi-model ensemble also provides an uncertainty estimate found from the spread of the ensemble members (Fig. 1). Note that the averaging, however, does not remove systematic errors that might be common to the ensemble of models.

The major sources of uncertainty related to changes in global mean thermosteric and dynamic process-based sea level projections include:

1. internal variability due to differences in the timing, spatial patterns and magnitudes of multidecadal climate variability (e.g., the interdecadal Pacific Oscillation, Di Lorenzo et al. 2008) within and among individual models (e.g., Hu and Deser 2013; Bordbar et al. 2015; Carson et al. 2015; Hu et al. 2017, Hu and Bates 2018); due to these differences, the ensemble average of different model results may not be able to fully remove the internal climate variability and its associated sea level variability (although it can be greatly reduced, see below);
2. intermodel uncertainty due to differences in responses among projections of different climate models under the same forcing scenario (e.g., Church et al. 2013; Melet and Meyssignac 2015; Gregory et al. 2016);
3. scenario uncertainty due to the future path of anthropogenic forcing (Moss et al. 2010; Yip et al. 2011); and
4. model–scenario uncertainty "due to the variation of model deviations from the ensemble mean across different scenarios" (Yip et al. 2011).

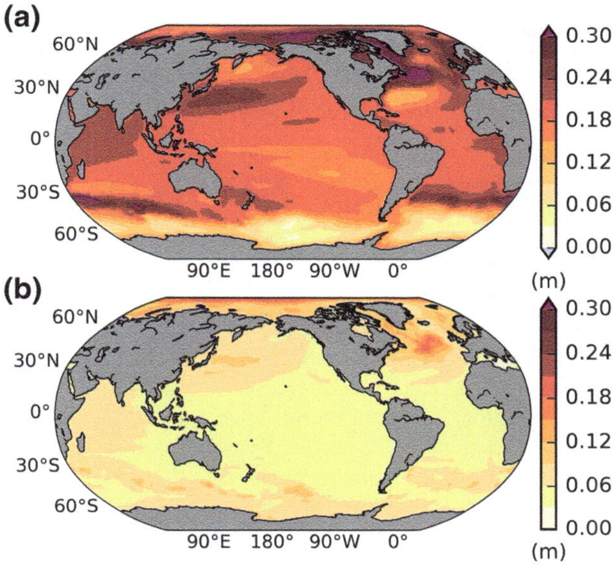

Fig. 1 From AR5, Chapter 13, Fig. 13.16. Projections of future sterodynamic (dynamic plus global mean thermosteric) sea level change resulting from the RCP4.5 scenario forcings, as a difference of the 2081–2100 mean minus the 1986–2005 mean sea level. The RCP4.5 scenario is a prescribed "middle" scenario for climate projection model experiments that includes some anthropogenic climate forcing mitigation through 2100 (Moss et al. 2010). **a** The ensemble mean sea level change from 21 ensemble members, in meters (m). **b**) The spread in sea level among ensemble members, calculated as the RMS (root mean square) deviation around the ensemble mean [in (**a**)], in m. Note that, because we only show results from RCP4.5, the ensemble spread does not contain any deviations due to differing forcing scenarios

These types of uncertainty apply to projections of both global mean thermosteric sea level change (e.g., Melet and Meyssignac 2015) and regional anomalies from the global mean, dynamic sea level (e.g., Yin 2012; Gregory et al. 2016). The model spread of global mean thermosteric sea level change is generally smaller than the model spread in dynamic sea level change by 2100 in most regions outside the tropics (Yin 2012; Church et al. 2013), by more than a factor of two in parts of the North Atlantic and Arctic regions. In the tropics, the ensemble spread of global mean thermosteric sea level change is of similar magnitude to the total spread in sterodynamic (global mean thermosteric + dynamic) sea level.

To allow for the partitioning of the relative contribution of the four types of uncertainty listed above, with respect to the total uncertainty in the projections, Yip et al. (2011) proposed the use of a statistical procedure known as analysis of variance (ANOVA, e.g., Von Storch and Zwiers 2001).

Using this approach and the same subset of CMIP5 models as in the IPCC AR5 (Church et al. 2013), Little et al. 2015 found that the total uncertainty in RCP4.5 projections of sterodynamic sea level rise by 2090 was composed of 40–70% due to intermodel uncertainty; 30–40% due to scenario uncertainty; and a smaller fraction (< 5%) due to internal variability and model–scenario uncertainty. All of these relative contributions vary locally due to the magnitude of both forced (anthropogenic or natural) and unforced (control-run) variability. At regional scales and on the relatively shorter timescales of 10–50 years, the largest uncertainties in future projections of sterodynamic sea level arise from intermodel differences and internal variability (Lyu et al. 2014, 2015; Richter and Marzeion 2014; Carson et al. 2015; Little et al. 2015; Han et al. 2018). Therefore, we will focus on the sources and causes of these two model-derived uncertainties for the rest of this section.

2.1 Sources of Intermodel Uncertainty

Several techniques have been employed in order to assess the causes of uncertainty in ocean-only sea level projections from global climate models, i.e., sterodynamic sea level. Bouttes and Gregory (2014) applied surface flux changes from different models to a single coupled climate model and found that heat flux and wind changes dominate both the patterns of sterodynamic sea level change and their intermodel spread. The CMIP6-endorsed FAFMIP project (Flux-Anomaly-Forced Model Intercomparison Project) is being carried out to quantify the drivers of dynamic sea level variability in models and the key ocean processes responsible for the large spread in projections (Gregory et al. 2016). Initial results based on a small number of CMIP5 model simulations show that heat flux perturbations are largely responsible for the modeled sterodynamic sea level changes over most of the ocean, except in the Southern Ocean, where wind forcing has a comparable contribution in driving the strong sea level gradient across the Antarctic Circumpolar Current (Gregory et al. 2016).

Based on an eddy-permitting ocean model, Saenko et al. (2015) also found that surface heat forcing is a dominant process in driving dynamic sea level changes under the RCP4.5 scenario. In this eddy-permitting experiment, both wind and heat surface forcing contributed to the large belt of sea level changes along the Southern Ocean, as in FAFMIP, but wind forcing drove larger sea level changes in the North Pacific and Atlantic compared to FAFMIP. Using a different approach from FAFMIP, Huber and Zanna (2017) tested the magnitudes of uncertainties from air–sea fluxes versus ocean model parameterizations and found that the uncertainties from air–sea fluxes were larger than those from ocean parameterizations, especially for the Atlantic Meridional Overturning Circulation (AMOC) and Atlantic Ocean heat content. In a similar vein to FAFMIP, Garuba and Klinger (2018) and Zanna et al. (2018) explored individual surface flux perturbations on ocean-only models, finding that heat, freshwater and wind flux perturbations all have various, and large, regional responses in ocean heat uptake, and therefore sterodynamic sea level. In addition, Melet and Meyssignac (2015) find that the majority of the model spread in global mean thermosteric sea level in coupled simulations is due to differences in ocean heat uptake efficiency, and the overall effective climate feedback parameter of models. Combining results from ocean-only simulations together with coupled models can shed light on processes responsible for intermodel spread in ocean heat uptake and associated sterodynamic sea level change (Kuhlbrodt and Gregory 2012; Marshall and Zanna 2014; Saenko et al. 2018).

To quantify uncertainty introduced by internal variability, most studies used multimodel ensembles (Yin et al. 2010; Little et al. 2015) or sea level projections from a single model, where each realization was forced by the identical scenario, but run with perturbed initial conditions. By taking this approach, Bordbar et al. (2015) demonstrated that the sterodynamic sea level projections by 2100 were strongly dependent on ocean initial conditions. In the same way, Hu et al. (2017), who analyzed a large ensemble from a single model, found that perturbations on initial ocean conditions led to larger changes in sterodynamic sea level rise than initial atmospheric perturbations. To improve our understanding and estimation of the internal variability uncertainty on sea level projections, studies analyzing both atmospheric and oceanic initial conditions effects are required.

Although the text above does not summarize all possible mechanisms responsible for uncertainty in ocean-only sea level changes from process-based models, it lists the major sources of uncertainty causing spread in dynamic sea level projections.

2.2 Quantifying Internal Climate Variability

The internal variability of dynamic sea level is the main source of interannual and decadal variability of sterodynamic sea level, which could overwhelm any early anthropogenic signals of sterodynamic sea level change (Meyssignac et al. 2012; Zhang and Church 2012). It is also possible, but not clearly detected, that land ice volume low-frequency (multidecadal) variability might also be able to drive some sterodynamic sea level variability (Chylek et al. 2004; Bjørk et al. 2012). Therefore, climate model simulations have been evaluated against historical observations with the goal of evaluating model performance in simulating internal sea level variability.

To what extent the climate models can simulate realistic internal sea level variability is an open question (e.g., Bordbar et al. 2015; Hu et al. 2017). Even when a model reproduces dynamic sea level of similar magnitude to the real ocean, the internal variability in model simulations is not in phase and future projections differ in spatial patterns for regional variability on the timescales of 10–40 years and in spatial patterns of regional trends over 80–100 years (Richter and Marzeion 2014; Carson et al. 2015; Little et al. 2015). Internal variability, combined with model errors and cross-model differences, therefore yields a complex picture of uncertainties that apply to projected sea level changes.

Comparisons of modeled and observed sea level variability over multidecadal periods are possible using tide gauge data (e.g., Becker et al. 2016; Meyssignac et al. 2017). The extraction of the dynamic sea level signal from tide gauges is complicated by the fact that they constitute point measurements that can be contaminated by land motion (Emery and Aubrey 1991; Santamaría-Gómez et al. 2014), and tide gauges also measure all other sources of local, relative sea level, such as land ice melt, groundwater retention and vertical land motion. Tide gauge variability on decadal timescales—i.e., not secular trends—is usually associated with dynamic sea level variability (e.g., in the North Atlantic: Calafat et al. 2012; Richter et al. 2012; Ezer et al. 2013; Dangendorf et al. 2014a), or in certain cases with global mean thermosteric sea level (e.g., large volcanic eruptions, Church et al. 2011) or large transient water mass changes (Fasullo et al. 2013).

Meyssignac et al. (2017) compared 27 historical tide gauge records (> 70 years) with an ensemble mean of 12 CMIP5 models. They showed that the simulated sea level in CMIP5 models is generally in close agreement with multidecadal variability from the tide gauge record during 1900–2015. They pointed out, however, that the interannual variability in models may overestimate or underestimate tide gauge variability, depending on the region. These differences are due to a variety of effects that models do not represent well, including river runoff, extreme ENSO events and ocean variability in shallow seas (Meyssignac et al. 2017). Becker et al. (2016) also found mismatches in variability between climate model ocean and tide gauges. Their analysis employed the methods developed by Lennartz and Bunde (2009) and was based on the property of sea level fluctuations to exhibit long-term correlations modeled as outcomes of stochastic power-law processes (Agnew 1992; Beretta et al. 2005; Barbosa et al. 2006, 2008; Hughes and Williams 2010; Bos et al. 2013; Becker et al. 2014; Dangendorf et al. 2014b). By comparing scaling properties in sea level changes simulated in 36 CMIP5 models to those in 23 historical tide gauge records (> 100 years), Becker et al. (2016) found that the majority of models overestimates the scaling of sea level fluctuations, particularly in the North Atlantic. Consequently, the models may underestimate a portion of sea level rise due to external forcing, in particular the anthropogenic footprint in the twentieth-century projections. This is likely, in part, due to not including volcanic forcing in the control runs of some models, which lead to lower estimates of ocean heat content uptake for these models (Gregory et al. 2013).

There are also studies comparing internal sea level variability in climate model simulations to historical datasets using satellite altimeter observations and other sea level products, including ocean reanalyses and sea level reconstructions that are available for longer time periods than altimetry data. Climate models generally reproduce large-scale features of the interannual and decadal sea level variability patterns, despite considerable intermodel spread. Monselesan et al. (2015) showed that the climate models can also simulate the spatially coherent features that interannual sea level variability is predominantly in the tropics, and on longer timescales, the sea level variance moves to higher latitudes. However, compared to available observations, most climate models underestimate the magnitude of internal sea level variability in the Pacific on both interannual and decadal timescales (Landerer et al. 2014; Lyu et al. 2016; Peyser and Yin 2017).

3 Sterodynamic Trend Signal Detection

3.1 Trend Detection in Future Model Projections

The time of emergence (or ToE, in trend detection) is the length of time needed to be able to detect significant secular trends in sterodynamic sea level against the background climate variability. If reliable model estimates of sea level variability can be made, then the statistical significance and ToE of sterodynamic sea level trends can also be estimated. The significance estimate provides confidence both in the estimated sea level trends and in the estimated ToE, thereby delivering a possible time frame of detectable sea level changes for the purposes of, e.g., civil engineering project planning, among other sociopolitical uses. In this section, we review the current state of estimating the time frame for projected sterodynamic sea level trend detection (time of signal emergence). Note that all statistical significance tests are for trends over a specified time period that emerge from the background internal climate variability of the model.

A common method of estimating an individual model's internal climate variability, which examines the model's control runs and calculates the variability of arising from control simulation data on a variety of timescales, is used in many of the studies discussed here. This yields an important question: Is sterodynamic sea level variability expected to remain of the same magnitude or substantially change when under additional, changing, climate forcing conditions? The IPCC AR5 report found changes in the ensemble interannual variability of detrended data between the intervals 1951–2005 and 2081–2100 to be mostly below 10% for the RCP4.5 scenario, outside of the high-latitude Arctic region (Church et al. 2013). This includes both positive and negative changes in the intensity of interannual variability, though there are large positive changes in Arctic variability (Fig. 13.15, Church et al. 2013). Hu and Bates (2018) report that decadal variability changes, as compared to future changes in interannual variability in the AR5, are more consistently positive in sign, and larger in magnitude, over more of the ocean, and more so for RCP8.5 than for RCP4.5.

In contrast to the AR5 report, Hu and Bates (2018) use a single model with a larger ensemble of projections. Further modeling studies to explore the commonality of these variability changes between different models, forcings and resolutions will prove useful.

Hu and Deser (2013) used a large ensemble of projected sea level runs from a single model, under the same forcing but with different initial conditions, and estimated that the 95% uncertainty on sea level trends (2000–2060) was greater than the magnitude of sterodynamic trends in the Southern Ocean and Arctic and nearly equal to the trend magnitude in parts of the equatorial Pacific and high latitudes in the Pacific and Atlantic. Thus, trends in these regions were not statistically significant. However, for the rest of the ocean, sterodynamic sea level trends were statistically significant over this time frame.

Using multi-model ensembles from the CMIP5 project, three studies explored regional trend signal detection using differing methodologies and different sets of the models (Lyu et al. 2014; Richter and Marzeion 2014; Carson et al. 2015). A common aspect of their methodologies is that the test of trends (of varying time frames) against the internal climate variability, from control runs, is performed on a per-model basis, with a central estimate for the ensemble presented. Lyu et al. (2014) and Richter and Marzeion (2014) consider the spread in control-run-based trends between models in some way (see the details in each study below), although Carson et al. (2015) only show results for the central estimate of the ensemble's control-run internal variability. Also, sea level variability due to volcanic forcing is not considered, as internal variability is estimated from control runs. All results generally converge on a range of values between ~ 40 and 60 years for the length of a future sea level record needed to resolve a trend in sterodynamic (dynamic plus global mean thermosteric) sea level larger than the underlying internal variability for ocean processes alone.

Lyu et al. (2014) also compared a more complete sea level projection signal containing land ice, water impoundment and glacial isostatic adjustment (GIA) to model control-run estimated internal variability. They estimated internal variability threshold to be two times the standard deviation of 200-year, annual detrended control-run time series in each grid box. For the sterodynamic sea level projection that includes both regional dynamic and global mean thermosteric sea level rise, sea level rise is detected from the noise of internal variability over half of the ocean by the 2040s; by 2080, most of the ocean outside of the Southern Ocean shows a significant trend (Fig. 3). When including all other known components contributing to future sterodynamic sea level change, i.e., "total sea level" as defined above, this time frame is much shorter, with significant trends found over half of the ocean by 2020, relative to the reference period 1986–2005. Only regions where at least 84% of the models in the ensemble exhibit signal emergence by 2080 are shown, as a measure of ensemble uncertainty (Fig. 3, right panels).

Richter and Marzeion (2014) estimated internal variability by computing overlapping trends from control-run data (per grid box) on a sequence of window lengths, from 10- to 100-year windows. Then, the sequence of trends from the RCP4.5 scenario, including both dynamic and global mean thermosteric sea level, was computed, and the time point at which the 95% anthropogenically forced trend uncertainty no longer intersects with the 95% uncertainty of the internal variability trends (and afterward for all future time points) is found to be the time of emergence at that location. They find that most of the ocean (again, outside of the Southern Ocean, and some high-latitude regions) shows significant sea level trends by 2040 or 2050, depending on the time frame over which the forced trend is estimated (cf. their Fig. 4). In a follow-up study, Richter et al. (2017b) showed that the addition of the glacier contribution increases the signal-to-noise ratio of sterodynamic sea level changes, thus leading to an earlier emergence by 10–20 years away from the sources of ice mass loss.

Carson et al. (2015) uses a very similar approach to Richter and Marzeion (2014) for estimating internal model variability: overlapping trends calculated for specific time frames. While the paper's focus is not on time of emergence, it was found that sea level trends are larger than two times the internal variability estimate over most regions of the ocean, for RCP4.5's dynamic plus global mean thermosteric sea level (their Fig. 3). This is in good agreement with the results from the other studies discussed above, though here looking at the ensemble mean trend and not individual trends from a single run.

When considering the same data as in these previous studies but restricting the analysis to coastal-only grid boxes, most coastal regions should expect statistically significant sea level trends by the mid-twenty-first century (Table 1). This statistical significance is higher in the lower and mid-latitudes, due to the presence of higher multidecadal variability at high latitudes in models. Although using somewhat different methodologies, with differing models and aims, these four papers (Hu and Deser 2013; Lyu et al. 2014; Richter and Marzeion 2014; Carson et al. 2015) generally agree that dynamic plus global mean thermosteric sea level trends over large portions of the ocean will have emerged from the background climate variability present in the models by the mid-twenty-first century.

Common to the studies that only examine sterodynamic sea level in climate models is that the trend and its emergence from the noise are certainly underestimated, as land ice melt is expected to contribute an ever increasing amount to sea level over the next few centuries. Glacial isostatic adjustment (GIA) and land water storage change are also expected to lower sea level trends in some locales, but increase them in others (Church et al. 2013, Slangen et al. 2014a). Studies that include additional components of sea level change, such as land ice, groundwater storage changes and vertical land motion contributions (Lyu et al. 2014; Richter et al. 2017b), give an earlier emergence time. Accelerations in sea level changes (changes in the local or global rate of change of sea level) would also be a sign of a change in the climate likely due to anthropogenic forcing, much like trend detection. Haigh et al. (2014), in a study that artificially extended tide gauges using the scaling from an ensemble of model projections and added random noise to represent variability, found that accelerations in local sea level should be detectable within the next two decades. The results from Haigh et al. (2014) mirror the finding in Lyu et al. (2014) when including the additional non-ocean model sea level components (total sea level) and are also reflected in Dieng et al. (2017), who find that an already detectable acceleration in GMSL (as opposed to local) is driven largely by Greenland mass loss. Nevertheless, several questions remain unanswered: How much real variability exists, and will exist, in these additional non-ocean sea level components and thus how much would such variability modify the noise part of the signal-to-noise ratio and the emergence of anthropogenic trends.

The estimated ToE is less certain in some areas compared to others, with the regions of low overall ensemble spread having a better estimate than regions of higher ensemble spread. Better ToE estimates are likely in much of the tropical Atlantic, the eastern side of large ocean basins, and possibly in the tropical ocean regions in general, since decadal variability is generally lower in these regions in climate models than mid- and high-latitude regions (see Fig. 1b and also Carson et al. 2015, their Figs. 3b and 4b). Moreover, the coarse resolution of models does not allow capturing of the oceanic mesoscale turbulence, a manifestation of intrinsic ocean fluctuation, i.e., it emerges without any atmospheric interaction (Sérazin et al. 2016; Zanna et al. 2018; Llovel et al. 2018; Llovel et al. 2018). At similar interdecadal timescales, the trend detection results cited here for regions of high intrinsic variability also may not provide accurate estimates of time of emergence. These regions happen to also coincide with the regions of larger ensemble spread, so the same regions listed above probably have better ToE estimates relative to this unmeasured internal variability as well, compared to the mid- and high-latitude and western boundary current regions.

3.2 Trends in Historical Data and Model Simulations

As outlined in the previous section, detection of an anthropogenically forced local trend can only be expected by the mid-twenty-first century due to the low signal-to-noise ratio on regional scales. In order to compare the ability of model simulations to accurately capture trends, and to explore the issues surrounding trend estimation in observed data, we discuss the results of different studies on the trend estimates over historical periods from observed data and model simulations. Richter et al. (2017b) showed that extensive spatial smoothing is necessary to detect a forced signal in steric and dynamic sea level change on regional scales within historical observations, depending on the time period. On global scales, various studies found an anthropogenically forced signal in mean thermosteric sea level change (Marcos and Amores 2014; Slangen et al. 2014b), in the glacier mass balance contribution (Marzeion et al. 2014) and in global sea level rise (Dangendorf et al. 2015; Slangen et al. 2016). These studies distinguish between internal and forced signals by comparing unforced control simulations to simulations with selected forcings (Marcos and Amores 2014; Slangen et al. 2014b, 2016; Marzeion et al. 2014), or by using statistical methods (Becker et al. 2014; Dangendorf et al. 2015) to compare the results of either approach with observations to detect an externally forced signal.

There are some difficulties attached to comparing model simulations of historical sea level changes to the available historical observations. Satellite altimetry covers much of the ocean for the time after 1993, but this is still a short time frame for low-frequency sea level variability on some regional scales (e.g., Bilbao et al. 2015). Tide gauges can have much longer time series, and while there are sometimes issues of gaps and instrument changes, the largest source of errors comes from unmeasured vertical land motion (Douglas 1991; Wöppelmann and Marcos 2016). The papers in this section generally attempt to account for vertical land motion by making corrections to the tide gauge data; this information can be found in the individual citations. Other sources of sea level rise not normally accounted for in climate models, such as land ice mass loss, are measured by tide gauges and altimetry, and studies cited below draw some conclusions regarding how well model data compare with observations when including or not including offline estimates of land ice contributions.

Comparisons between satellite altimetry and model simulations for the altimetry era have been examined to explore the quality of model hindcasts and projections in producing realistic trends (Gregory et al. 2001; Meyssignac et al. 2012, 2017; Landerer et al. 2014; Bilbao et al. 2015; Monselesan et al. 2015; Richter et al. 2017a; Watson 2018). These studies have shown that CMIP5 models tend to simulate well recent global mean sea level rise, i.e., trends, particularly during the satellite altimetry era. However, before the satellite era, the discrepancies are larger, due to not including other components of local sea level change such as changes in land ice and water impoundment (Meyssignac et al. 2017). While Meyssignac et al. (2017) found that model trends over the same 20-year period generally have weaker trends than in satellite altimetry data, they note that other contributing factors to sterodynamic sea level, such as land ice, are not present in CMIP5 coupled climate models. When taking the land ice contribution into account (Meyssignac et al. 2017; Richter et al. 2017a), observed trends in the northern North Atlantic over 1993–2012 are reproduced to varying degrees, depending on the climate model.

Marcos and Amores (2014) provided an analysis based on empirical orthogonal function (EOF; Preisendorfer 1988) that maximizes the signal-to-noise ratio, estimated the forced sea level response in historical CMIP5 simulations and found that natural variability enhanced the basin-mean anthropogenic thermosteric sea level rise in the North Atlantic over the period 1970–2005 while the opposite was true in the Western Pacific Ocean (Marcos and Amores 2014, their Fig. 2). A more widely used approach for detecting an anthropogenically forced trend in sterodynamic sea level is through calculation of a multi-model

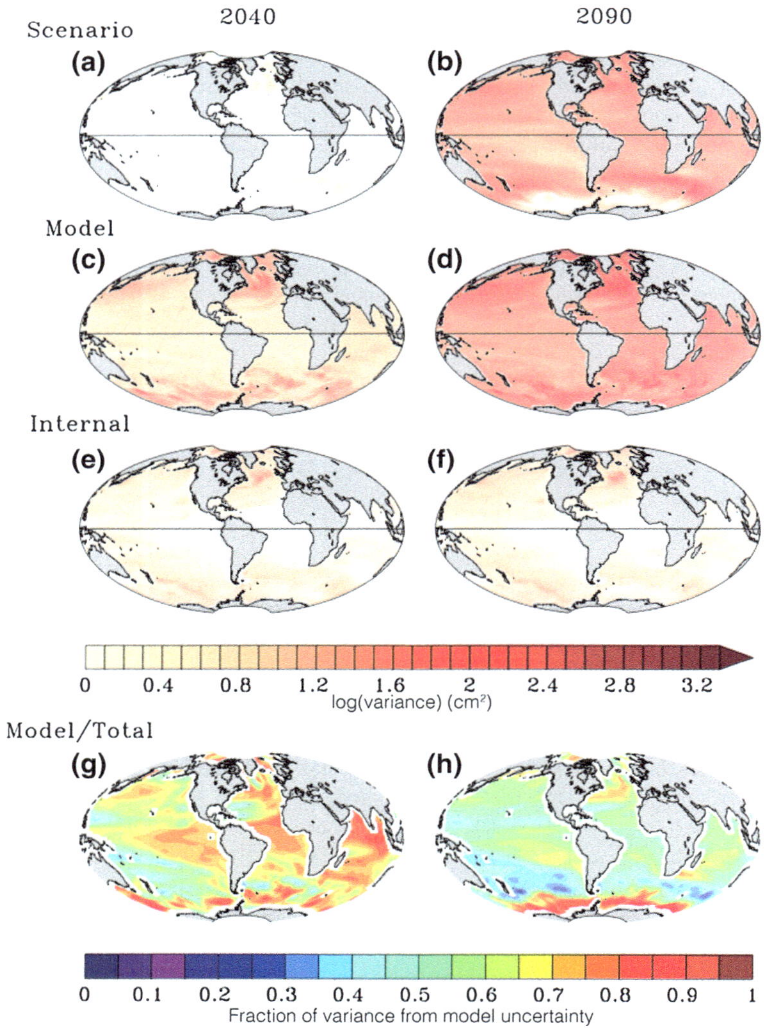

Fig. 2 From Little et al. (2015), Fig. 4. Sterodynamic sea level change variance in cm^2 by 2040 (left column) and by 2090 (right column) for the following uncertainty components: **a**, **b** scenario uncertainty (RCPs 2.6, 4.5, 6.0, 8.5); **c**, **d** intermodel uncertainty (16 models, with various numbers of realizations); **e**, **f** internal climate variability uncertainty; and **g**, **h** fractional variance of the intermodel uncertainty (from **c**, **d**) divided by the total uncertainty

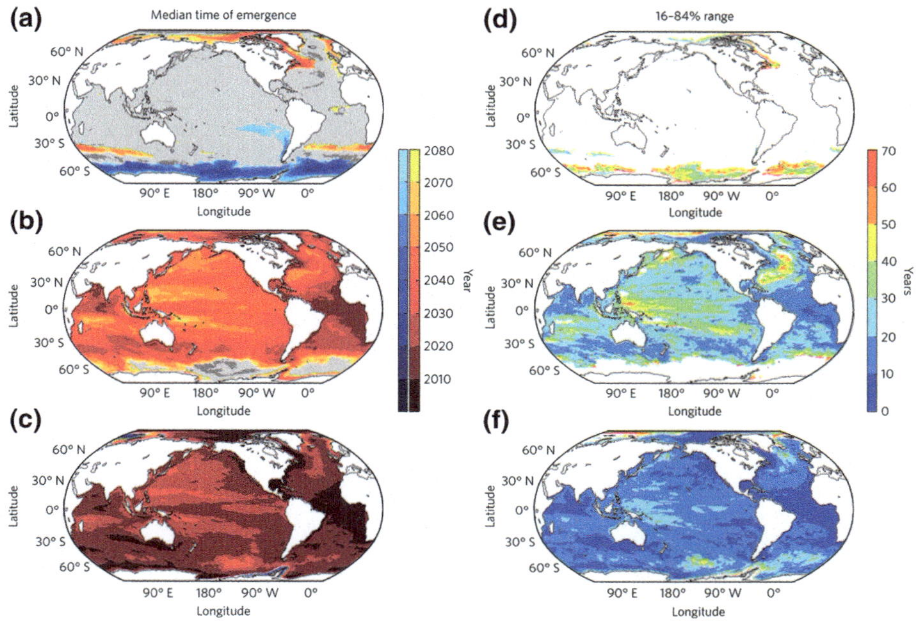

Fig. 3 From Lyu et al. (2014), Fig. 2. Time of emergence (multi-model ensemble median) of regional sea level change signal under RCP8.5 relative to 1986–2005, by year, for: **a** dynamic sea level, **b** dynamic plus global mean thermosteric sea level and **c** all contributing components to regional sea level (total sea level). Gray color means that no signal has yet emerged by 2080 or no agreement among models. The 16–84% uncertainty ranges for the same sea level change projection estimates are shown in the right panels. The ranges are only shown where at least 84% of the models in the ensemble exhibit signal emergence before 2080

ensemble mean over the period of interest. Given a model ensemble large enough (e.g., 16 models in Little et al. (2015), see Sect. 2), this approach assumes that internal variability is strongly reduced by averaging when computing an ensemble mean, which then largely displays the anthropogenic response, in addition to other external natural forcings, like volcanic aerosol and solar forcings. This pattern, together with modeled internal variability (from control simulations), is compared to the observed pattern of sterodynamic sea level change. Using this approach, Richter et al. (2017a) concluded that the observed dynamic sea level rise over the period 1993–2012 in the North Atlantic subpolar gyre is consistent with internal variability and therefore not anthropogenically forced. Similarly, Meyssignac et al. (2012) found the unusual sea level rise pattern in the tropical Pacific over the period 1993–2009 to be not anthropogenically forced. However, these conclusions strongly depend on the model's ability to reproduce and simulate the geographical pattern and strength of naturally forced variability realistically. For the tropical Pacific Ocean, this has been challenged. While the modeled spatiotemporal patterns are consistent with observations, their magnitudes may be underestimated (Bilbao et al. 2015).

In the Indian Ocean, Han et al. (2018) analyzed sea level trends using a set of reanalysis products for winds and sea level, as well as large ensembles from climate models. From 1958 to 2005, sea level rose in the eastern Indian Ocean (after removing the global mean sea level, and including coastal regions) but fell in the western basin, with the largest drop

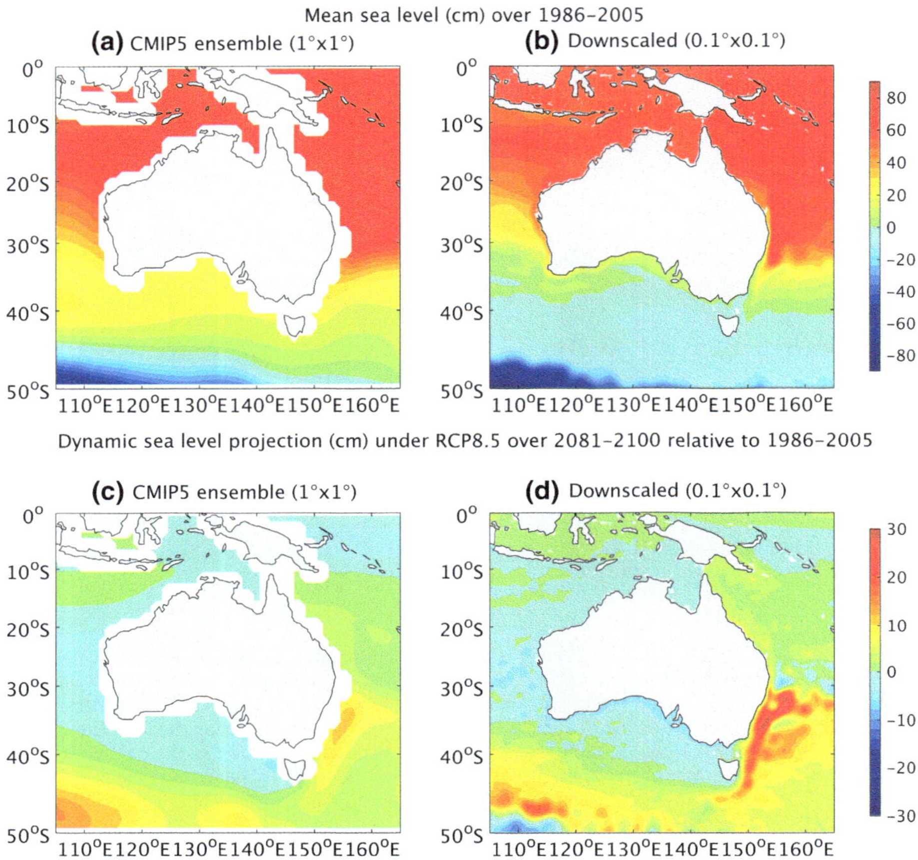

Fig. 4 Mean fields (cm; average over 1986–2005) and future change projections under RCP8.5 (cm; difference between averages of 1986–2005 and 2080–2099) for dynamic sea level around Australia, based on CMIP5 multi-model mean (left panels) and 1/10° ocean model dynamical downscaling (right panels). Redrawn from Zhang et al. (2016, 2017)

Table 1 Sea level rise by 2050 in the RCP4.5 scenario

References	% of total coastline	% of coastline between ± 58°
Lyu et al. (2014)	80.3	82.6
Richter and Marzeion (2014)	91.4	99.2
Carson et al. (2015)	97.2	100

Percentage of the coastline where sea level trends statistically emerge from the background natural sea level variability by 2050, based on estimates from multi-model CMIP5 climate model control runs (only constant climate forcings are applied). The first column is for the whole global coastline, as a percentage of coastline length, the second column is for the coastline between 58°S and 58°N, to mask out Antarctica and high-latitude Northern Hemisphere regions of lower population density. These regions contain more model uncertainty and natural, low-frequency variability. Data are provided by the authors as used in the listed references occurring over the Seychelles. Using the twentieth-century simulations from the 100-member ensemble of the Max-Planck Institute of Meteorology model and 40-member ensemble of the National Center for Atmospheric Research (NCAR) Community Earth System Model version 1 (CESM1), Han et al. (2018) found that the observed maximum sea level fall over the Seychelles results largely from natural internal variability, with anthropogenic forcing contributing 19% ± 2.4%. For decadal sea level anomalies, the uncertainties of external forcing are comparable to the signals, with a standard deviation ratio of externally forced/observed decadal sea level anomalies being 18% ± 17% over Seychelles and 17% ± 11% near the Indonesian Throughflow regions. Even for the ensemble means of large-ensemble members, externally forced sea level trend patterns in that region differ largely (even being opposite in sign in some areas) between the two models, which suggests a strong model dependence of external forcing effects on sterodynamic sea level trends.

It should also be noted that trend detection in historical data using models suffers the same kind of intermodel uncertainty that could plague trend detection in future projections (discussed at the end of the previous section). Thus, while regions of large interdecadal variability like the North Pacific or the high-latitude North Atlantic (Zanna et al. 2019) would be additionally difficult regions for trend detection (due to larger internal variability and intermodel spread there), "quieter" regions like southern parts of the Atlantic and Pacific basins might yield a detectable sea level signal sooner. Marcos et al. (2017) also provide a review regarding the estimation and separation of internal variability and anthropogenically forced signals in sea level.

4 Connecting Open-Ocean Projections to Coastal Regions

The state-of-the-art global climate models provide important information about how the large-scale ocean circulation and sterodynamic sea level could change in the future. Since the local relative sea level change at the coast is what the coastal communities essentially care about, it is important to link large-scale ocean changes to coastal sea level and identify the contributing to similarities or differences between coastal and open-ocean changes, and how drivers of this relationship might change in the future. In some specific regions, there have been well-established dynamical connections between changes in coastal sea level and large-scale ocean circulation. In other many regions, decoupling between shallow and deep water sea level variations, observed by satellite altimetry, is evident on timescales shorter than several months (Hughes and Williams 2010). Rates of sea level change at the coast can differ significantly from the open ocean nearby for several reasons, particularly through (1) coastal topography acting as barriers to the propagation of open-ocean signals, (2) open-ocean changes just being local and (3) local processes such as the coastal winds, currents, atmospheric pressures and river runoff playing important roles (White et al. 2005; Deng et al. 2011; Vinogradov and Ponte 2011; Bingham and Hughes 2012; Williams and Hughes 2013; see also Durand et al. 2019 in this volume).

The connections between large-scale ocean circulation and coastal sea level in the western boundary regions have been explored in a number of studies. Particularly along the eastern coast of North America, coastal sea level variations and changes across a range of timescales are significantly modulated by ocean dynamics (Ezer et al. 2013; Yin and Goddard 2013; Fraser et al. 2019). For example, a robust feature from climate model projections is a rapid dynamical sea level rising near the northeastern coast of North America associated with a weakening of meridional overturning circulation in the Atlantic (Yin et al. 2009). McCarthy et al. (2015) proposed that an index defined as coastal sea level differences between north and south of Cape Hatteras is a good indicator for ocean circulation changes, which drive phase changes in the Atlantic decadal climate variability through ocean heat transport. Calafat et al. (2018) showed that changes in the amplitude of sea level annual cycle along the Gulf of Mexico and the United States Southeast coasts are primarily induced by incident Rossby waves from the open ocean that generate boundary waves.

The open-ocean signals usually do not exert impacts on the coastal sea level in a direct and uniform way. Sasaki et al. (2014) identified that westward propagating Rossby waves along the Kuroshio Extension have different impacts on coastal sea level around Japan. While the resulting sea level changes are largest along the southeastern coast due to meridional shifts of the Kuroshio Path, the excited coastal waves propagate southwestward and also induce a large signal in the western coast of Japan but leave the northeastern coast as the shadow zone. Recently Minobe et al. (2017) proposed a theory based on Johnson and Marshall (2002) to explain western boundary sea level changes by considering both incoming Rossby waves from ocean interior, which bring mass input to the western boundary layer and mass redistribution along the western boundary in the form of equatorward wave propagation. Their theoretical framework can explain the main features of western boundary dynamical sea level future changes from climate model projections, e.g., the lower sea level near the coast of Japan and Argentina relative to the nearby open ocean, and coastal sea level rise of similar magnitude to the open ocean along the US East Coast (see Fig. 1a). Including a continental slope yields a similar situation, but the magnitude of the impact of open-ocean sea level rise on the coasts is sensitive to model resolution and friction (Wise et al. 2018), indicating the importance of topography on coastal sea level anomalies. Long continental slopes at high latitudes such as along the Mid-Atlantic Bight also strongly suppress the influence of open-ocean mesoscale eddies (Hughes et al. 2018).

In light of the close relations of coastal sea level to large-scale ocean circulation and nearby boundary currents, the uncertainties for coastal sea level projection arise from not only the poor representation of coastal processes in current coarse-resolution climate models (generally ~ 1° for the ocean model component) but also from model deficiencies and biases in simulating ocean dynamics in the ocean interior and surrounding regions. To reduce these uncertainties and to provide sea level information closer to the coastline than climate models can, there have been some efforts using high-resolution ocean models to downscale ocean changes from climate model projections, either regionally or globally. For example, Liu et al. (2016) used a regional ocean model with an eddy-permitting horizontal resolution of 0.25° to downscale future projections from three CMIP5 models in the western North Pacific region. Recently, a near-global eddy-resolving (0.1°) ocean model was used to downscale both historical changes and future projections of the ocean state throughout 1979–2101, driven by atmospheric forcing fields from reanalysis and the ensemble average of 17 CMIP5 models (Zhang et al. 2016, 2017). It has been shown that ocean models with refined spatial resolution better represent the strong western boundary currents and associated large sea level gradient (Fig. 4a, b). Penduff et al. (2010) have also shown that increasing the ocean model horizontal resolution would improve the sea level simulations in terms of mean sea level and also the magnitudes and spatial patterns of interannual sea level anomalies. For the future projections, dynamical downscaling models show a narrow band of large sea level changes off the coast as a result of future changes in western boundary currents, e.g., up to 30 cm around the East Australian Current (Zhang et al. 2017), which are rather smoother, weaker (~ 10 cm) and further offshore located in CMIP5 models (Fig. 4c, d). Differences between high-resolution and low-resolution projections are relatively smaller along the coastline than offshore. Zhang et al. (2017) reported that the downscaled dynamic sea level changes around the Australian coastline are generally larger by 1–3 cm than for the CMIP5 ensemble. Given the substantial computational resources required, these dynamical downscaling products represent valuable resources to assess the uncertainties of coastal sea level projection from coarse-resolution models. Also, further downscaling toward the coast with a nested coastal model would be useful to better resolve fine-scale details in local topography and land–sea interfaces as well as to consider the interaction with tides, waves, storm surges and other dynamical processes near the coast.

Vertical land motions, either geological or due to human-induced activities, add additional uncertainties for coastal sea level projections that can be comparable or even larger than climate-induced sea level change over the same period (e.g., Wöppelmann and Marcos 2016). For example, Ballu et al. (2011) estimated that from 1997 to 2009 the relative sea level rise rate (total sea level rise) around the Torres Islands in the Southwest Pacific was 12 mm/year, of which 9.4 mm/year was due to island subsidence. Raucoules et al. (2013) reported that the difference between altimetry data and tide gauge record near Manila city implies a land subsidence of ~ 10 mm/year over the altimetry era (since 1993) mainly due to intensive groundwater pumping. In addition to these smaller-scale uncertainties, there are also large-scale uncertainties in sterodynamic sea level rise due to uncertainty in projections of land ice melt and glacial isostatic adjustment (e.g., Church et al. 2013; Slangen et al. 2014a). All these sources of uncertainties added together affect our capability to deliver reliable sea level projections near the coast, which would be essential for coastal community adaptation and mitigation planning.

5 Concluding Remarks

Intermodel uncertainty is the dominant climate model uncertainty in ensemble projections of multidecadal to centennial sterodynamic sea level change, for the ocean-only components of dynamic sea level plus global mean thermosteric sea level (Little et al. 2015). Scenario uncertainty is large, but it is due to a range of forcings applied to models, and not a function of the models themselves. Other contributions to sea level projections are calculated "offline," i.e., not within the models themselves (Church et al. 2013). Intermodel comparison studies (e.g., Gregory et al. 2016) and model data comparisons (with tide gauges and altimetry products) provide a better understanding of the origins of climate model differences and inform improvements for the next generation of climate models. Such improvement will yield more confidence in sterodynamic sea level projections. But, with changes in model resolution (in addition to other possible changes to climate models) in the upcoming Coupled Model Intercomparison Project, phase 6 (CMIP6) models, there may be new difficulties to overcome, such as uncertainty due to intrinsic ocean variability (Sérazin et al. 2016), and interaction with better resolved coastal shelves (Durand et al. 2019).

The time of emergence for anthropogenic signals in sea level can be estimated by applying internal model variability to trend estimates of sea level projections. Detection of sea level trends on a global scale is easier than at regional scales due to its higher signal-to-noise ratio. There have been mixed and disputed results in detecting regional forced sea level trends (secular and not part of the background variability), although detection of the global trend is virtually certain, along with a likely acceleration (e.g., Church et al. 2013;

Cazenave et al. 2018). At local scales, only some long-term individual tide gauges are available, but they are affected by, among others, decadal variability and vertical land motion contaminating the signal, making them trickier to use. In addition, continuous worldwide coverage of sterodynamic sea level has only been possible since the advent of continuous satellite altimetry in late 1992. Even though this altimetry record is now 26 years long, there are still not enough data to corroborate some of the longer multidecadal sea level signals suspected in certain regions, nor to unambiguously resolve the anthropogenic signal-to-internal variability noise ratio completely, although progress continues to be made (Fasullo and Nerem 2018; Hamlington et al. 2019). Maintaining the tide gauge network and calibrating the costal altimetry product would be also essential to provide high-quality coastal sea level observations (Cipollini et al. 2017).

On the modeling side, reliable detection of trends moving forward depends on how well models produce natural (i.e., non-anthropogenic) variability that matches real-world sea level variability, on long timescales. For the previous generation of models, as presented in the AR5 report (Church et al. 2013), the results converge to the vast majority of ocean coastlines experiencing statistically significant anthropogenic sea level rise by mid-twenty-first century, not including contributions from land ice and water impoundment (Lyu et al. 2014; Richter and Marzeion 2014; Carson et al. 2015). These trends are expected to be detectable sooner and be significantly larger when these components are included (Lyu et al. 2014). It is also useful to note that the intermodel uncertainty from climate model ensembles is not generally the largest local uncertainty for coastal sea level projections, when compared to sea level components not included in climate models, such as land ice mass loss, GIA, and groundwater storage changes (Carson et al. 2016). In addition, these uncertainties have interdependencies, and Le Bars (2018) uses models to explore the correlations and dependencies between sea level components in projections.

The dynamics of how large-scale changes in ocean dynamics in a warming scenario will impact coastal regions are still being studied, with substantial progress having been made over the last 10 years. However, further work to understand links between open-ocean sea level rise and coastal risks is required. Improved theoretical frameworks along with sustained observations from the coast to the open-ocean and higher-resolution modeling will help to improve our understanding of regional and coastal sea level changes, to better characterize and reduce sources of uncertainty and, ultimately, to better inform policy and decision making.

Acknowledgements Thanks to the ISSI for hosting the Workshop on Coastal Sea Level from which this paper was conceived and to Xuebin Zhang for his help in producing Fig. 4. And thanks to Chris Little for his comments on an early version of the manuscript. MC was supported in part through the DFG funded CliSAP Excellence Cluster of the University of Hamburg, through the BMBF (Federal Ministry of Education and Science) Project RACE and through a DFG-funded special research effort on regional sea level (SPP1889). KR is funded by the Austrian Science Fund (FP302560). KL is funded by CSHOR, a joint research Centre for Southern Hemisphere Oceans Research between QNLM and CSIRO. CMD is supported by Australian Research Council FT130101532 and DP160103130. LZ is funded by the Natural Environment Research Council (NE/R000727/1 and NE/P019218/1) and thanks to Princeton AOS and GFDL visiting faculty program for additional support. MB is supported by the French National Centre for Space Studies (CNES) TOSCA program.

References

Agnew DC (1992) The time-domain behavior of power-law noises. Geophys Res Lett 19(4):333–336. https://doi.org/10.1029/91GL02832

Ballu V, Bouin MN, Siméoni P, Crawford WC, Calmant S, Boré JM, Kanas T, Pelletier B (2011) Comparing the role of absolute sea-level rise and vertical tectonic motions in coastal flooding, Torres Islands (Vanuatu). Proc Natl Acad Sci 108:13019–13022. https://doi.org/10.1073/pnas.1102842108

Barbosa SM, Fernandes MJ, Silva ME (2006) Long-range dependence in North Atlantic sea level. Phys A 371:725–731. https://doi.org/10.1016/j.physa.2006.03.046

Barbosa SM, Silva ME, Fernandes MJ (2008) Time series analysis of sea-level records: characterising long-term variability. In: Donner RV, Barbosa SM (ed) Nonlinear time series analysis in the geosciences. Springer, Berlin, pp 157–173. https://doi.org/10.1007/978-3-540-78938-3_8

Becker M, Karpytchev M, Lennartz-Sassinek S (2014) Long-term sea level trends: natural or anthropogenic? Geophys Res Lett 41:5571. https://doi.org/10.1002/2014gl061027

Becker M, Karpytchev M, Marcos M, Jevrejeva S, Lennartz-Sassinek S (2016) Do climate models reproduce complexity of observed sea level changes? Geophys Res Lett 43:5176. https://doi.org/10.1002/2016gl068971

Beretta A, Roman HE, Raicich F, Crisciani F (2005) Long-time correlations of sea-level and local atmospheric pressure fluctuations at Trieste. Phys A 347:695–703

Bilbao RA, Gregory JM, Bouttes N (2015) Analysis of the regional pattern of sea level change due to ocean dynamics and density change for 1993–2099 in observations and CMIP5 AOGCMs. Clim Dyn 45:2647

Bingham RJ, Hughes CW (2012) Local diagnostics to estimate density-induced sea level variations over topography and along coastlines. J Geophys Res 117(C1):C01013. https://doi.org/10.1029/2011JC007276

Bjørk AA et al (2012) An aerial view of 80 years of climate-related glacier fluctuations in southeast Greenland. Nat Geosci 5:427. https://doi.org/10.1038/ngeo148110.1038/ngeo1481

Bordbar MH, Martin T, Latif M, Park W (2015) Effects of long-term variability on projections of twenty-first century dynamic sea level. Nat Clim Change 5:343–347. https://doi.org/10.1038/nclimate2569

Bos MS, Williams SDP, Araújo IB, Bastos L (2013) The effect of temporal correlated noise on the sea level rate and acceleration uncertainty. Geophys J Int 196:1423–1430. https://doi.org/10.1093/gji/ggt481

Bouttes N, Gregory JM (2014) Attribution of the spatial pattern of CO_2-forced sea level change to ocean surface flux changes. Environ Res Lett 9:034004. https://doi.org/10.1088/1748-9326/9/3/034004

Calafat FM, Chambers DP, Tsimplis MN (2012) Mechanisms of decadal sea level variability in the eastern North Atlantic and the Mediterranean Sea. J Geophys Res Oceans 117:C9

Calafat FM, Wahl T, Lindsten F, Williams J, Frajka-Williams E (2018) Coherent modulation of the sea-level annual cycle in the United States by Atlantic Rossby waves. Nat Commun 9(1):2571

Carson M, Köhl A, Stammer D (2015) The impact of regional multidecadal and century-scale internal climate variability on sea level trends in CMIP5 models. J Clim 28:853–861. https://doi.org/10.1175/JCLI-D-14-00359.1

Carson M, Köhl A, Stammer D, Slangen ABA, Katsman CA, van de Wal RSW, Church J, White N (2016) Coastal sea level changes, observed and projected during the 20th and 21st century. Clim Change 134:269–281. https://doi.org/10.1007/s10584-015-1520-1

Cazenave A et al (2018) Global sea-level budget 1993–present. Earth Syst Sci Data 10:1551–1590. https://doi.org/10.5194/essd-10-1551-2018

Church JA, White NJ, Konikow LF, Domingues CM, Cogley JG, Rignot E, Gregory JM, van den Broeke MR, Monaghan AJ, Velicogna I (2011) Revisiting the Earth's sea-level and energy budgets from 1961 to 2008. Geophys Res Lett 38:L18601. https://doi.org/10.1029/2011GL048794

Church JA, Clark PU, Cazenave A, Gregory JM, Jevrejeva S, Levermann A, Merrifield MA, Milne GA, Nerem RS, Nunn PD, Payne AJ, Pfeffer WT, Stammer D, Unnikrishnan AS (2013) Sea level change. In: Stocker TF, Qin D, Plattner G-K, Tignor M, Allen SK, Boschung J, Nauels A, Xia Y, Bex V, Midgley PM (eds) Climate change 2013: the physical science basis. Contribution of working group I to the fifth assessment report of the intergovernmental panel on climate change. Cambridge University Press, Cambridge

Chylek P, Box JE, Lesins G (2004) Global warming and the Greenland ice sheet. Clim Change 63:201–221. https://doi.org/10.1023/B:CLIM.0000018509.74228.03

Cipollini P, Calafat FM, Jevrejeva S, Melet A, Prandi P (2017) Monitoring sea level in the coastal zone with satellite altimetry and tide gauges. Surv Geophys 38:33–57

Dangendorf S, Calafat FM, Arns A, Wahl T, Haigh ID, Jensen J (2014a) Mean sea level variability in the North Sea: processes and implications. J Geophys Res Oceans 119(10):50

Dangendorf S, Rybski D, Mudersbach C, Müller A, Kaufmann E, Zorita E, Jensen J (2014b) Evidence for long-term memory in sea level. Geophys Res Lett 41:5530–5537. https://doi.org/10.1002/2014GL060538/

Dangendorf S, Marcos M, Müller A, Zorita E, Riva R, Berk K, Jensen J (2015) Detecting anthropogenic footprints in sea level rise. Nat Commun 6:7849. https://doi.org/10.1038/ncomms8849
Deng X, Griffin DA, Ridgway K, Church JA, Featherstone WE, White NJ, Cahill M (2011) Satellite altimetry for geodetic, oceanographic, and climate studies in the Australian region. In: Vignudelli S, Kostianoy AG, Cipollini P, Benveniste J (eds) Coastal altimetry. Springer, Berlin, pp 473–508
Di Lorenzo E et al (2008) North Pacific Gyre oscillation links ocean climate and ecosystem change. Geophys Res Lett 35:L08607. https://doi.org/10.1029/2007GL032838
Dieng HB, Cazenave A, Meyssignac B, Ablain M (2017) New estimate of the current rate of sea level rise from a sea level budget approach. Geophys Res Lett 44:3744–3751. https://doi.org/10.1002/2017GL073308
Domingues CM, Church JA, White NJ, Gleckler PJ, Wijffels SE, Barker PM, Dunn JR (2008) Improved estimates of upper-ocean warming and multi-decadal sea-level rise. Nature 453:1090–1093. https://doi.org/10.1038/nature07080
Douglas BC (1991) Global sea level rise. J Geophys Res 96(C4):6981–6992. https://doi.org/10.1029/91JC00064
Durand F, Piecuch CG, Becker M, Papa F, Raju SV, Khan JU, Ponte RM (2019) Impact of continental freshwater runoff on coastal sea level. Surv Geophys 1:1
Emery KO, Aubrey DG (1991) Sea levels, land levels, and tide gauges. Springer, New York
Eyring V, Bony S, Meehl GA, Senior CA, Stevens B, Stouffer RJ, Taylor KE (2016) Overview of the coupled model intercomparison project phase 6 (CMIP6) experimental design and organization. Geosci Model Dev 9:1937–1958. https://doi.org/10.5194/gmd-9-1937-2016
Ezer T, Atkinson LP, Corlett WB, Blanco JL (2013) Gulf Stream's induced sea level rise and variability along the US mid-Atlantic coast. J Geophys Res Oceans 118(2):685–697
Fasullo JT, Nerem RS (2018) Altimeter-era emergence of the patterns of forced sea-level rise in climate models and implications for the future. Proc Natl Acad Sci 115(51):12944–12949. https://doi.org/10.1073/pnas.1813233115
Fasullo JT, Boening C, Landerer FW, Nerem RS (2013) Australia's unique influence on global sea level in 2010–2011. Geophys Res Lett 40:4368–4373. https://doi.org/10.1002/grl.50834
Fraser R, Palmer M, Roberts C, Wilson C, Copsey D, Zanna L (2019) Investigating the predictability of North Atlantic sea surface height. Clim Dyn 53:2175. https://doi.org/10.1007/s00382-019-04814-0
Garuba OA, Klinger BA (2018) The role of individual surface flux components in the passive and active ocean heat uptake. J Clim 31:6157–6173. https://doi.org/10.1175/JCLI-D-17-0452.1
Greatbatch RJ (1994) A note on the representation of steric sea level in models that conserve volume rather than mass. J Geophys Res 99(C6):12767–12771. https://doi.org/10.1029/94JC00847
Gregory JM, Church JA, Boer GJ, Dixon KW, Flato GM, Jackett DR, Lowe JA, O'Farrell SP, Roeckner E, Russell GL, Stouffer RJ, Winton M (2001) Comparison of results from several AOGCMs for global and regional sea-level change 1900–2100. Clim Dyn 18:225–240. https://doi.org/10.1007/s003820100180
Gregory JM, White NJ, Church JA, Bierkens MF, Box JE, van den Broeke MR, Cogley JG, Fettweis X, Hanna E, Huybrechts P, Konikow LF, Leclercq PW, Marzeion B, Oerlemans J, Tamisiea ME, Wada Y, Wake LM, van de Wal RS (2013) Twentieth-century global-mean sea level rise: is the whole greater than the sum of the parts? J Clim 26:4476–4499. https://doi.org/10.1175/JCLI-D-12-00319.1
Gregory JM et al (2016) The flux-anomaly-forced model intercomparison project (FAFMIP) contribution to CMIP6: investigation of sea-level and ocean climate change in response to CO_2 forcing. Geosci Model Dev 9:3993–4017. https://doi.org/10.5194/gmd-9-3993-2016
Gregory JM et al (2019) Concepts and terminology for sea level: mean, variability and change, both local and global. Surv Geophys. https://doi.org/10.1007/s10712-019-09525-z
Haigh ID, Wahl T, Rohling EJ, Price RM, Pattiaratchi CB, Calafat FM, Dangendorf S (2014) Timescales for detecting a significant acceleration in sea level rise. Nat Commun 5:3635. https://doi.org/10.1038/ncomms4635
Hamlington BD, Fasullo JT, Nerem RS, Kim K-Y, Landerer FW (2019) Uncovering the pattern of forced sea level rise in the satellite altimeter record. Geophys Res Lett. https://doi.org/10.1029/2018gl081386
Han W, Stammer D, Meehl GA, Hu A, Sienz F, Zhang L (2018) Multi-decadal trend and decadal variability of the regional sea level over the Indian Ocean since the 1960s: roles of climate modes and external forcing. Climate 6:51. https://doi.org/10.3390/cli6020051
Hawkins E, Sutton R (2009) The potential to narrow uncertainty in regional climate predictions. Bull Am Meteorol Soc 90:1095–1108. https://doi.org/10.1175/2009BAMS2607.1
Hu A, Bates SC (2018) Internal climate variability and projected future regional steric and dynamic sea level rise. Nat Commun 9:1068. https://doi.org/10.1038/s41467-018-03474-8
Hu A, Deser C (2013) Uncertainty in future regional sea level rise due to internal climate variability. Geophys Res Lett 40:2768–2772. https://doi.org/10.1002/grl.50531

Hu A, Meehl GA, Stammer D, Han W, Strand WG (2017) Role of perturbing ocean initial condition in simulated regional sea level change. Water 9(6):401. https://doi.org/10.3390/w9060401
Huber MB, Zanna L (2017) Drivers of uncertainty in simulated ocean circulation and heat uptake. Geophys Res Lett 44:1402–1413. https://doi.org/10.1002/2016GL071587
Hughes CW, Williams SDP (2010) The color of sea level: importance of spatial variations in spectral shape for assessing the significance of trends. J Geophys Res 115:C10048. https://doi.org/10.1029/2010JC006102
Hughes CW, Williams J, Blaker A, Coward A, Stepanov V (2018) A window on the deep ocean: the special value of ocean bottom pressure for monitoring the large-scale, deep-ocean circulation. Prog Oceanogr 161:19–46. https://doi.org/10.1016/j.pocean.2018.01.011
IPCC (2014) Summary for policymakers. In: Edenhofer O, Pichs-Madruga R, Sokona Y, Farahani E, Kadner S, Seyboth K, Adler A, Baum I, Brunner S, Eickemeier P, Kriemann B, Savolainen J, Schlömer S, von Stechow C, Zwickel T, Minx JC (eds) Climate change 2014: mitigation of climate change. Contribution of working group III to the fifth assessment report of the intergovernmental panel on climate change. Cambridge University Press, Cambridge
Johnson HL, Marshall DP (2002) A theory for the surface Atlantic response to thermohaline variability. J Phys Oceanogr 32:1121–1132. https://doi.org/10.1175/1520-0485(2002)032%3c1121:ATFTSA%3e2.0.CO;2
Kuhlbrodt T, Gregory J (2012) Ocean heat uptake and its consequences for the magnitude of sea level rise and climate change. Geophys Res Lett 39(18):L18608. https://doi.org/10.1029/2012GL052952
Landerer FW, Gleckler PJ, Lee T (2014) Evaluation of CMIP5 dynamic sea surface height multi-model simulations against satellite observations. Clim Dyn 43:1271–1283. https://doi.org/10.1007/s00382-013-1939-x
Le Bars D (2018) Uncertainty in sea level rise projections due to the dependence between contributors. Earth's Future 6:1275. https://doi.org/10.1029/2018ef000849
Lennartz S, Bunde A (2009) Trend evaluation in records with long-term memory: application to global warming. Geophys Res Lett 36:L16706. https://doi.org/10.1029/2009GL039516
Little CM, Horton RM, Kopp RR, Oppenheimer M, Yip S (2015) Uncertainty in twenty-first-century CMIP5 sea level projections. J Clim 28:838–852. https://doi.org/10.1175/JCLI-D-14-00453.1
Liu Z-J, Minobe S, Sasaki YN, Terada M (2016) Dynamical downscaling of future sea-level change in the western North Pacific using ROMS. J Oceanogr 72:905–922. https://doi.org/10.1007/s10872-016-0390-0
Llovel W, Penduff T, Meyssignac B, Molines J-M, Terray L, Bessières L, Barnier B (2018) Contributions of atmospheric forcing and chaotic ocean variability to regional sea level trends over 1993–2015. Geophys Res Lett 45:13405–13413. https://doi.org/10.1029/2018GL080838
Lyu K, Zhang X, Church JA, Slangen ABA, Hu J (2014) Time of emergence for regional sea-level change. Nat Clim Change 4:1006–1010. https://doi.org/10.1038/nclimate2397
Lyu K, Zhang X, Church JA, Hu J (2015) Quantifying internally generated and externally forced climate signals at regional scales in CMIP5 models. Geophys Res Lett 42:9394–9403. https://doi.org/10.1002/2015GL065508
Lyu K, Zhang X, Church JA, Hu J (2016) Evaluation of the interdecadal variability of sea surface temperature and sea level in the Pacific in CMIP3 and CMIP5 models. Int J Climatol 36(11):3723–3740
Marcos M, Amores A (2014) Quantifying anthropogenic and natural contributions to thermosteric sea level rise. Geophys Res Lett 41:2502–2507. https://doi.org/10.1002/2014GL059766
Marcos M, Marzeion B, Dangendorf S, Slangen ABA, Palanisamy H, Fenoglio-Marc L (2017) Internal variability versus anthropogenic forcing on sea level and its components. Surv Geophys 38:329–348
Marshall DP, Zanna L (2014) A conceptual model of ocean heat uptake under climate change. J Clim 27(22):8444–8465
Marzeion B, Cogley JG, Richter K, Parkes D (2014) Attribution of global glacier mass loss to anthropogenic and natural causes. Science 345:919–921. https://doi.org/10.1126/science.1254702
McCarthy GD, Haigh ID, Hirschi JJM, Grist JP, Smeed DA (2015) Ocean impact on decadal Atlantic climate variability revealed by sea-level observations. Nature 521(7553):508
Melet A, Meyssignac B (2015) Explaining the spread in global mean thermosteric sea level rise in CMIP5 climate models. J. Climate 28:9918–9940. https://doi.org/10.1175/JCLI-D-15-0200.1
Meyssignac B, Salasy Melia D, Becker M, Llovel W, Cazenave A (2012) Tropical Pacific spatial trend patterns in observed sea level: internal variability and/or anthropogenic signature? Clim Past 8:787–802. https://doi.org/10.5194/cp-8-787-2012
Meyssignac B, Slangen ABA, Melet A, Church JA, Fettweis X, Marzeion B, Agosta C, Ligtenberg SRM, Spada G, Richter K, Palmer MD, Roberts CD, Champollion N (2017) Evaluating model simulations

of twentieth-century sea-level rise. Part II: regional sea-level changes. J. Clim 30:8565–8593. https://doi.org/10.1175/jcli-d-17-0112.1

Minobe S, Terada M, Qiu B, Schneider N (2017) Western boundary sea level: a theory, rule of thumb, and application to climate models. J Phys Oceanogr 47:957–977. https://doi.org/10.1175/JPO-D-16-0144.1

Monselesan DP, O'Kane TJ, Risbey JS, Church JA (2015) Internal climate memory in observations and models. Geophys Res Lett 42:1232–1242. https://doi.org/10.1002/2014GL062765

Moore JC, Grinsted A, Zwinger T, Jevrejeva S (2013) Semiempirical and process-based global sea level projections. Rev Geophys 51(3):484–522. https://doi.org/10.1002/rog.20015

Moss RH, Edmonds JA, Hibbard KA, Manning MR, Rose SK, van Vuuren DP, Carter TR, Emori S, Kainuma M, Kram T, Meehl GA, Mitchell JFB, Nakicenovic N, Riahi K, Smith SJ, Stouffer RJ, Thomson AM, Weyant JP, Wilbanks TJ (2010) The next generation of scenarios for climate change research and assessment. Nature 463:747–756. https://doi.org/10.1038/nature08823

Northrop PJ, Chandler RE (2014) Quantifying sources of uncertainty in projections of future climate. J Clim 27:8793–8808. https://doi.org/10.1175/JCLI-D-14-00265.1

Penduff T, Juza M, Brodeau L, Smith GC, Barnier B, Molines J-M, Tréguier A-M, Madec G (2010) Impact of global ocean model resolution on sea-level variability with emphasis on interannual time scales. Ocean Sci. 6:269–284. https://doi.org/10.5194/os-6-269-2010

Perrette M, Landerer F, Riva R, Frieler K, Meinshausen M (2013) A scaling approach to project regional sea level rise and its uncertainties. Earth Syst Dyn 4:11–29. https://doi.org/10.5194/esd-4-11-2013

Peyser C, Yin J (2017) Interannual and decadal variability in tropical Pacific Sea Level. Water 9(6):402

Preisendorfer RW (1988) Principal component analysis in meteorology and oceanography. Elsevier, Amsterdam, p 425

Raucoules D, Le Cozannet G, Wöppelmann G, De Michele M, Gravelle M, Daag A, Marcos M (2013) High nonlinear urban ground motion in Manila (Philippines) from 1993 to 2010 observed by DInSAR: implications for sea-level measurement. Remote Sens Environ 139:386–397

Richter K, Marzeion B (2014) Earliest local emergence of forced dynamic and steric sea-level trends in climate models. Environ Res Lett 9:114009. https://doi.org/10.1088/1748-9326/9/11/114009

Richter K, Nilsen JE, Drange H (2012) Contributions to sea level variability along the Norwegian coast for 1960–2010. J Geophys Res Oceans 117(C5):1

Richter K, Øie Nilsen JE, Raj RP, Bethke I, Johannessen JA, Slangen AB, Marzeion B (2017a) Northern North Atlantic sea level in CMIP5 climate models: evaluation of mean state, variability, and trends against altimetric observations. J Clim 30(23):9383–9398

Richter K, Marzeion B, Riva R (2017b) The effect of spatial averaging and glacier melt on detecting a forced signal in regional sea level. Environ Res Lett 12(3):034004

Saenko OA, Yang D, Gregory JM, Spence P, Myers PG (2015) Separating the influence of projected changes in air temperature and wind on patterns of sea level change and ocean heat content. J Geophys Res Oceans 120:5749–5765. https://doi.org/10.1002/2015JC010928

Saenko OA, Yang D, Gregory JM (2018) Impact of mesoscale eddy transfer on heat uptake in an eddy-parameterizing ocean model. J Clim 31:8589–8606. https://doi.org/10.1175/JCLI-D-18-0186.1

Santamaría-Gómez A, Gravelle M, Wöppemann G (2014) Long-term vertical land motion from double-differenced tide gauge and satellite altimetry data. J Geodyn 88:207–222. https://doi.org/10.1007/s00190-013-0677-5

Sasaki YN, Minobe S, Miura Y (2014) Decadal sea-level variability along the coast of Japan in response to ocean circulation changes. J Geophys Res Oceans 119(1):266–275

Sérazin G, Meyssignac B, Penduff T, Terray L, Barnier B, Molines JM (2016) Quantifying uncertainties on regional sea level change induced by multidecadal intrinsic oceanic variability. Geophys Res Lett 43:8151–8159

Slangen ABA, Carson M, Katsman C, van de Wal R, Koehl A, Vermeersen L, Stammer D (2014a) Projecting twenty-first century regional sea-level changes. Clim Change 124:317–332. https://doi.org/10.1007/s10584-014-1080-9

Slangen ABA, Church JA, Zhang X, Monselesan D (2014b) Detection and attribution of global mean thermosteric sea-level change. Geophys Res Lett 41:5951–5959. https://doi.org/10.1002/2014GL061356

Slangen ABA, Church JA, Agosta C, Fettweis X, Marzeion B, Richter K (2016) Anthropogenic forcing dominates global mean sea-level rise since 1970. Nat Clim Change 6:701–705. https://doi.org/10.1038/NCLIMATE2991

Taylor KE, Stouffer RJ, Meehl GA (2009) A summary of the CMIP5 experiment design. PCMDI Technical Report, 33 pp. Available online at http://cmip-pcmdi.llnl.gov/cmip5/docs/Taylor_CMIP5_design.pdf

Vinogradov SV, Ponte RM (2011) Low-frequency variability in coastal sea level from tide gauges and altimetry. J Geophys Res Oceans 116(C7):1

Von Storch H, Zwiers FW (2001) Statistical analysis in climate research. Cambridge University Press, Cambridge, p 496

Watson PJ (2018) How well do AR5 sea surface-height model projections match observational rates of sea-level rise at the regional scale? J Mar Sci Eng 6:11. https://doi.org/10.3390/jmse6010011

White NJ, Church JA, Gregory JM (2005) Coastal and global averaged sea level rise for 1950 to 2000. Geophys Res Lett 32:L01601. https://doi.org/10.1029/2004GL021391

Williams J, Hughes CW (2013) The coherence of small island sea level with the wider ocean: a model study. Ocean Sci 9:111–119

Wise A, Hughes CW, Polton J (2018) Bathymetric influence on the coastal sea level response to ocean gyres at western boundaries. J Phys Oceanogr 48:2949

Wöppelmann G, Marcos M (2016) Vertical land motion as a key to understanding sea level change and variability. Rev Geophys 54:64–92. https://doi.org/10.1002/2015RG000502

Yin J (2012) Century to multi-century sea level rise projections from CMIP5 models. Geophys Res Lett 39:L17709. https://doi.org/10.1029/2012GL052947

Yin J, Goddard PB (2013) Oceanic control of sea level rise patterns along the East Coast of the United States. Geophys Res Lett 40:5514–5520. https://doi.org/10.1002/2013GL057992

Yin J, Schlesinger ME, Stouffer RJ (2009) Model projections of rapid sea-level rise on the northeast coast of the United States. Nat Geosci 2(4):262

Yin J, Griffies SM, Stouffer RJ (2010) Spatial variability of sea-level rise in twenty-first century projections. J Clim 23:4585–4607. https://doi.org/10.1175/2010JCLI3533.1

Yip S, Ferro CAT, Stephenson DB, Hawkins E (2011) A simple, coherent framework for partitioning uncertainty in climate predictions. J Clim 24:4634–4643. https://doi.org/10.1175/2011JCLI4085.1

Zanna L, Brankart JM, Huber M, Leroux S, Penduff T, Williams PD (2018) Uncertainty and scale interactions in Ocean Ensembles: from seasonal forecasts to multi-decadal climate predictions. QJRMS. https://doi.org/10.1002/qj.3397

Zanna L, Khatiwala S, Gregory J, Ison J, Heimbach P (2019) Global reconstruction of historical ocean heat storage and transport. Proc Natl Acad Sci 116(4):1126–1131. https://doi.org/10.1073/pnas.1808838115

Zhang X, Church JA (2012) Sea level trends, interannual and decadal variability in the Pacific Ocean. Geophys Res Lett 39:L21701. https://doi.org/10.1029/2012GL053240

Zhang X, Oke P, Feng M, Chamberlain MA, Church JA, Monselesan D, Sun C, Matear RJ, Fiedler R (2016) A near-global eddy-resolving OGCM for climate studies. Geosci Model Dev Discuss 2016:1–52. https://doi.org/10.5194/gmd-2016-17

Zhang X, Church JA, Monselesan D, McInnes KL (2017) Sea level projections for the Australian region in the 21st century. Geophys Res Lett 44:8481–8491. https://doi.org/10.1002/2017GL074176

Affiliations

Mark Carson[1] · Kewei Lyu[2] · Kristin Richter[3] · Mélanie Becker[4] · Catia M. Domingues[5] · Weiqing Han[6] · Laure Zanna[7]

[1] Centrum für Erdsystemforschung und Nachhaltigkeit, Universität Hamburg, Hamburg, Germany

[2] Centre for Southern Hemisphere Oceans Research (CSHOR), CSIRO Oceans and Atmosphere, Hobart, TAS, Australia

[3] Institute for Atmospheric and Cryospheric Sciences, University of Innsbruck, Innrain 52f, 6020 Innsbruck, Austria

[4] Littoral, Environment and Societies (LIENSs) - UMR 7266, CNRS, La Rochelle, France

[5] IMAS - ACE CRC - CLEX, University of Tasmania, Tasmania, Australia

[6] Department of Atmospheric and Oceanic Sciences, University of Colorado, Boulder, CO, USA

[7] Department of Physics, Atmospheric Ocean and Planetary Physics, University of Oxford, Oxford, England, UK

Surveys in Geophysics (2019) 40:1655–1671
https://doi.org/10.1007/s10712-019-09575-3

Uncertainties in Long-Term Twenty-First Century Process-Based Coastal Sea-Level Projections

R. S. W. van de Wal[1,2] · X. Zhang[3] · S. Minobe[4,5] · S. Jevrejeva[6,7] · R. E. M. Riva[8] · C. Little[9] · K. Richter[10] · M. D. Palmer[11]

Received: 12 October 2018 / Accepted: 9 October 2019 / Published online: 21 October 2019

Abstract
Many processes affect sea level near the coast. In this paper, we discuss the major uncertainties in coastal sea-level projections from a process-based perspective, at different spatial and temporal scales, and provide an outlook on how these uncertainties may be reduced. Uncertainty in centennial global sea-level rise is dominated by the ice sheet contributions. Geographical variations in projected sea-level change arise mainly from dynamical patterns in the ocean response and other geophysical processes. Finally, the uncertainties in the short-duration extreme sea-level events are controlled by near coastal processes, storms and tides.

Keywords Uncertainties · Coastal sea level

✉ R. S. W. van de Wal
R.S.W.vandeWal@uu.nl

1 Institute for Marine and Atmospheric Research Utrecht, Utrecht University, Princetonplein 5, 3584, CC, Utrecht, The Netherlands

2 Department of Physical Geography, Utrecht University, Utrecht, The Netherlands

3 Centre for Southern Hemisphere Oceans Research (CSHOR), CSIRO Oceans and Atmosphere, Hobart, TAS, Australia

4 Graduate School of Science, Hokkaido University, Sapporo, Japan

5 Faculty of Science, Hokkaido University, Sapporo, Japan

6 National Oceanography Centre, Liverpool, UK

7 Centre for Climate Research Singapore, Singapore, Singapore

8 Department of Geoscience and Remote Sensing and TUDelft Climate Institute, Delft University of Technology, Delft, The Netherlands

9 Atmospheric and Environmental Research, Inc., Lexington, MA, USA

10 Institute of Atmospheric and Cryospheric Sciences, Universität Innsbruck, Innsbruck, Austria

11 Met Office Hadley Centre, Exeter, UK

1 Introduction

Sea-level projections have a long tradition in climate research, and it has long been known that both the observed and projected rates of sea-level change vary regionally. As one moves from global to regional scales, additional processes have the potential to affect sea level, often increasing the uncertainty in future projections. In this paper, we consider global scale projections as our starting point, and then highlight additional uncertainty associated with processes influencing coastal and regional sea level. We define regional sea-level projections as those at a scale of approximately 100-km resolution—the same ocean horizontal scales as represented in the Coupled Model Intercomparison Project Phase 5 (CMIP5) experiments. CMIP5 data are also used to provide lateral boundary conditions for dynamical downscaling experiments that can provide sea-level projections at local coastal scales less than 10 km. Uncertainties in projections usually increase in time, as for most climate variables. In this paper, we are mainly concerned with a typical time scale of 100 years. The uncertainties with sea-level changes on geological time scales are not discussed. It is important to note that the uncertainty of the "open ocean" sea-level projections represented in CMIP5 climate models increases as we approach the coast as more processes need to be considered (Carson et al. 2019). While climate models explicitly represent sea-level rise associated with global thermal expansion and local changes in ocean circulation and density, the ice-related and land water storage components are calculated offline. This implies that the sea-level rise information is restricted to the climate model resolution and physical processes associated with climate models. Consequently, they are unable to represent important coastal processes, like erosion, sedimentation changes associated with changes in waves and tides, etc.

Figure 1 shows the key contributions to sea-level changes at the different operational scales used in this paper. The contribution of glaciers, ice sheets and land water storage changes are calculated using offline models forced with boundary conditions derived from climate model projections (mainly temperature and precipitation), implying that feedbacks between freshwater flux and ocean circulation are not captured. This furthermore implies that the uncertainty caused by the covariance of the different components is often not fully captured both at global and regional scales, hindering a proper uncertainty estimate (Le Bars 2018). One of the main reasons for this approach is the limited resolution of climate

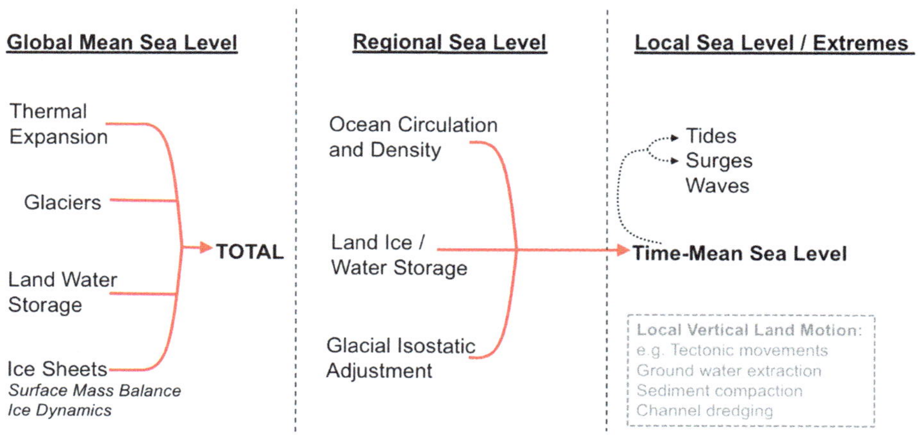

Fig. 1 Components of global mean sea level (GMSL), regional sea level (RSL) and local sea level (LSL)

models, which itself is a result of finite computing resources. For the calculation of changes in glacier volume and area, one would ideally use climate information at 1-km scale, which cannot be provided on 100-year time scales by global climate models (GCMs); hence, downscaling techniques are required. Similarly, high resolution (~ 10 km) is required to accurately calculate changes for the Greenland and Antarctic ice sheets in order to simulate the surface mass balance and ice dynamical processes. Further complications arise in Earth System Models for the inclusion of coupled ice sheet models, due to their long response time to environmental changes and our limited physical understanding of ice sheet dynamics (e.g., Schoof 2007; Pattyn 2018). Finally, land water storage changes are not resolved in climate models as they require non-RCP-driven[1] information on human behaviour and geological information to make projections of terrestrial water changes.

Figure 1 shows that, for regional sea-level changes, additional processes need to be considered. This includes ocean circulation and density changes that can be derived directly from the GCMs, as well as the regional imprint of land water storage and land ice changes. These two latter terms lead to a redistribution of mass between land and ocean and, consequently, the sea-level equation (Farrell and Clark 1976) needs to be resolved to calculate the pattern of the sea-level change (e.g., Mitrovica et al. 2001; Slangen et al. 2012, 2014; Perrette et al. 2013) to account for gravitational and rotational effects related to the mass redistribution. At local scales, one also needs to consider the contribution from vertical land motion induced by changes in loading of the crust due to ice mass changes. Together, these effects are referred to as "GRD" (gravitation, rotation, deformation) (Gregory et al. 2019).

IPCC AR5 (Church et al. 2013) presented projections for regional sea-level changes for the next century based on CMIP5 model simulations. For a given RCP scenario, these represent the change in the mean sea level over time due to climate change. However, it is important to note that local non-climatic processes, such as subsidence, can be much larger than the climate-driven component of relative sea-level change. In addition to the "*likely* range" projections presented in IPCC AR5, probabilistic approaches covering regional sea-level have been developed that aim to more fully represent the distribution of projected changes [e.g., Kopp et al. 2014; Jackson and Jevrejeva 2016; De Winter et al. (2017)]. Those results can be used by stakeholders who need more information than the *likely* range provides.

Figure 1 also indicates what is needed to resolve not only the sea-level trend, but also in addition the coastal high water levels associated with short-duration extreme events (e.g., surges and waves) on time scales ranging from hours to decades. For this reason, we discuss the uncertainties in global and regional projections as well as the uncertainties associated with shorter time scales particularly near the coast. We will focus on the extreme water-level variability rather than the morphodynamical processes that also play a role in the coastal zone and are particularly important in delta regions. Finally, we will briefly discuss the challenges of using sea-level rise projections in an adaptation framework (Stammer et al. 2019; Hinkel et al. 2019).

2 Sources of Uncertainties in Global Projections

Global mean sea-level (GMSL) rise occurs due to global thermal expansion (associated with ocean warming), and gain of ocean mass from glaciers, ice sheets and changes in the terrestrial water storage. Figure 2 shows a compilation of our understanding of the

[1] RCP is Representative Concentration Pathway, i.e. the greenhouse gas concentration trajectory adopted by the IPCC for its fifth Assessment Report (AR5).

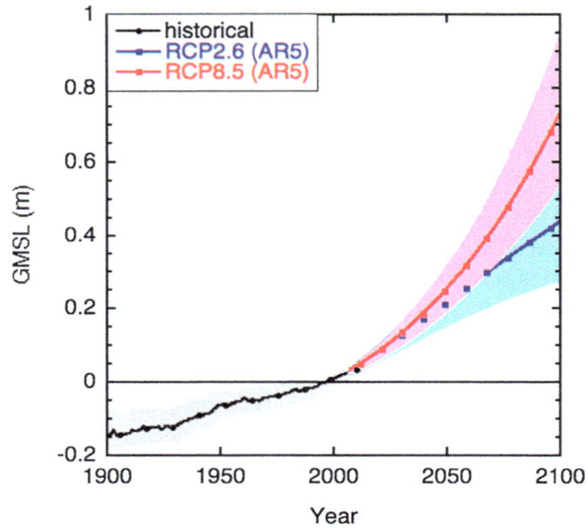

Fig. 2 A compilation of uncertainties in GMSL over the period 1900–2100 based on historical sea-level reconstructions, see text and projections presented by Church et al. (2013). The shading indicates the likely range around the mean reconstruction or projection

uncertainties of global sea-level reconstructions over the last century and projections over the twenty-first century. The reconstruction over the last century is based on equally weighting the reconstructions by Ray and Douglas (2011), Church and White (2011), Jevrejeva et al. (2014), Hay et al. (2015) and Dangendorf et al. (2017). The uncertainties for the projections are based on the assessed "*likely* range" (17–83‰) presented in IPCC AR5 (Church et al. 2013). Uncertainties decrease from the past to present and increase again further ahead in time, related to the chosen reference period in the present (e.g., 1986–2005). Typically, uncertainties in projections for the second half of the twenty-first century are larger than the uncertainty over the historical period. The uncertainty in global mean sea-level projections strongly depends on the emission scenario as shown in Fig. 2. The uncertainty does not include the potential collapse of the marine-based sectors of the Antarctic ice sheet (Church et al. 2013). Hence, uncertainties are possibly larger than shown.

The components that explain the sea-level change over the last century (Gregory et al. 2012), which was dominated by global thermal expansion and glacier mass loss, will continue to contribute to the sea-level change for the next century, but not in the same ratios. This is already emerging from the observations of current rates of sea-level change which shows an acceleration of sea-level rise (Cazenave et al. 2018), that, for a large part, can be attributed to an increase in the mass loss of the ice sheets (Shepherd et al. 2018; Mouginot et al. 2019; Rignot et al. 2019). The projections presented by Church et al. (2013) provide an indication of the contribution of each GMSL term to the total variance in projected sea-level change over the twenty-first century (Fig. 3).

As shown in Fig. 2, the projections do not account for the potential collapse of the marine-based sectors of Antarctica (Church et al. 2013). Twenty-first century sea-level rise substantially larger than 1 m is only thought to be possible with a significant contribution from the major ice sheets of Greenland and Antarctica. As such, there is a wide consensus that for centennial projections of sea-level change, the major source of uncertainty is related to ice sheet processes, since the largest uncertainty in any other component is only at the 10 cm level. The large uncertainty in estimates of mass loss in Antarctica is due to our limited physical understanding of the dynamic response of the ice sheet (Pattyn 2018).

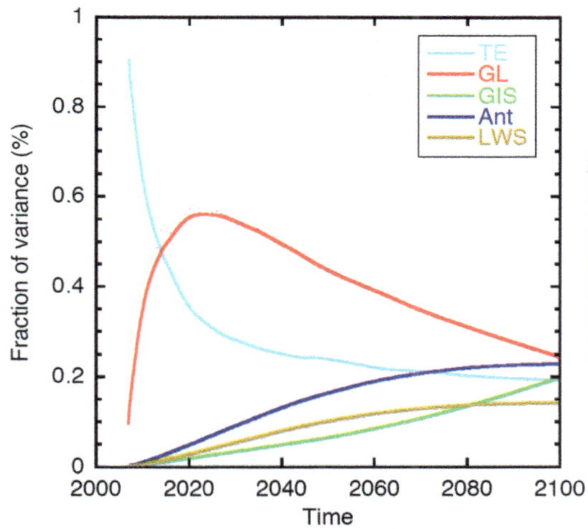

Fig. 3 Evolution of the relative contribution of thermal expansion (TE), glaciers (GL), the Greenland ice sheet (GIS), Antarctica (Ant) and land water storage changes (LWS) as presented by Church et al. (2013) to the total variance. The dotted blue line indicates qualitatively the increase in the dynamic contribution of the Antarctic ice sheet if marine-based sectors of Antarctica collapse

For Greenland, sea-level projections are driven largely by surface mass balance changes, which have a smaller uncertainty. The uncertainty in the ice dynamical component is related to the limited observational evidence and our ability to understand and simulate key ice dynamic processes (Edwards et al. 2019). Improved and prolonged satellite-based techniques are rapidly changing the field (e.g., Shepherd et al. 2018).

Different mechanisms can lead to mass changes of the Antarctic ice sheet. Traditionally, emphasis has been on the possibility of changes in accumulation, whereby, in a warmer climate, accumulation rates increase because warmer air can contain more moisture, promoting a gain of ice sheet mass and a decrease in the sea-level contribution. Currently, emphasis is more on interplay of the dynamical processes and the environmental changes whereby the environmental changes are no longer restricted to atmospheric processes but apply also to the ocean changes surrounding the ice sheet. Currently, the ice sheet is losing mass (Joughin et al. 2014; Rignot et al. 2014) in restricted areas in west Antarctica, and the general understanding is that these changes are driven by changes in the ocean water temperature which controls the basal melt rates below the ice shelves. Whether these changed water temperatures are due to ocean variability or are driven by climate change remains to be seen (Jenkins et al. 2018). As a result, it is at present difficult to assess, which term in the mass balance is driving future changes of the ice sheet.

Though accumulation changes are likely to be too small to explain the observed mass loss, the dynamic implications of changes in Antarctic surface mass balance may be important. Increased ablation rates at the surrounding shelves of Antarctica have locally increased such that the firn layer of the snow is saturated and the remaining water penetrates the deeper parts of the ice shelf and destabilizes the shelves. This process of hydrofracturing was a contributor to the rapid break up of Larsen-B (Rott et al. 1996). Disappearance of the ice shelves does not lead directly to a sea-level contribution, but the shelves are crucial for the stability of the grounded ice. In the study by DeConto and Pollard (2016), the hydrofracturing mechanism combined with marine ice cliff instability plays an important role in the rapid deglaciation of Antarctica. However, results from a carefully calibrated regional climate model (Kuipers Munneke et al. 2014; Trusel et al. 2015) do suggest that the amounts of melt are too small on most ice shelves until the end of the century to cause large-scale hydrofracturing on the major ice shelves.

The point at which increased basal melt will trigger destabilization of ice shelves is largely unknown because of limitations in our knowledge of the topography of the ice cavities below the ice shelves and our understanding of future changes in ocean circulation on the continental shelves surrounding the ice shelves. Basal melt models including the local circulations in ice cavities are now emerging (Lazeroms et al. 2018; Reese et al. 2017). While they capture the changes in basal melt rates under changed geometrical conditions, the feedback from increased fresh water production on the ocean circulation itself is not explicitly included in ocean models. In addition, models describing the physics of calving of floating ice shelves at the open ocean side are only starting to be developed (e.g., Borstad et al. 2012), and the first direct measurements of basal melt rates are just emerging (Sutherland et al. 2019).

On top of the uncertainties in the forcing of the ice shelves, we have to consider the uncertainty in the dynamical response to the changes in the forcing. What matters for the ice sheet from a dynamical point of view is the loss of buttressing. The lower the buttressing, the faster the ice sheet will lose mass, and hence sea-level rise will occur. Traditionally, it was thought that, in particular, on retrograde slopes, an initial retreat of the grounding line could lead to an irreversible retreat (Marine Ice Sheet Instability, MISI). Recently, it has been suggested that even for prograding slopes, the ice sheet may experience a rapid retreat via marine ice cliff instability (MICI) (Bassis and Walker 2012). Currently, MISI is captured by state-of-the-art ice sheet models if the resolution is sufficiently detailed and the subglacial topography known, but MICI is only treated in a highly parameterized way (DeConto and Pollard 2016). In particular, the wastage term determines how much ice is lost to the ocean by ice cliff instability. A possible precursor to both instability mechanisms of ice mass loss is a destabilization of the ice shelves. Retreat or weakening of ice shelves can therefore act as a tipping point for ice sheet mass loss. Quantification is challenging as it depends both on the projections of increased atmospheric warming driving hydrofracturing as well as changes in ocean water circulation and temperature changes on the continental shelves driving the basal melting of the shelves.

3 Sources of Uncertainties in Regional Sea-Level Projections

3.1 Ocean Processes

Sea-level changes due to changes in ocean density and circulation with inverse barometer correction of sea-level pressure are here referred to as sterodynamic sea-level changes (Gregory et al. 2019), while sterodynamic sea-level change minus global mean thermosteric sea-level change is referred to as dynamic sea-level change (e.g., Yin 2012). Over the twenty-first century, regional dynamic sea-level changes can be as large as the global mean thermosteric sea-level change (Yin 2012), thereby doubling the respective regional ocean-driven sea-level change in some areas. Unlike the contributions from land ice and land water, sterodynamic and dynamic sea-level changes are directly simulated by GCMs, and uncertainties are commonly assessed as the spread over the available ensemble.

By the end of the twenty-first century, uncertainties associated with ocean processes are the largest in regions of high ensemble mean sterodynamic sea-level change such as the Arctic Ocean and the northern North Atlantic (Slangen et al. 2014; Little et al. 2015), particularly along the densely populated north-eastern North American coast (Carson et al. 2016), as shown in Fig. 4.

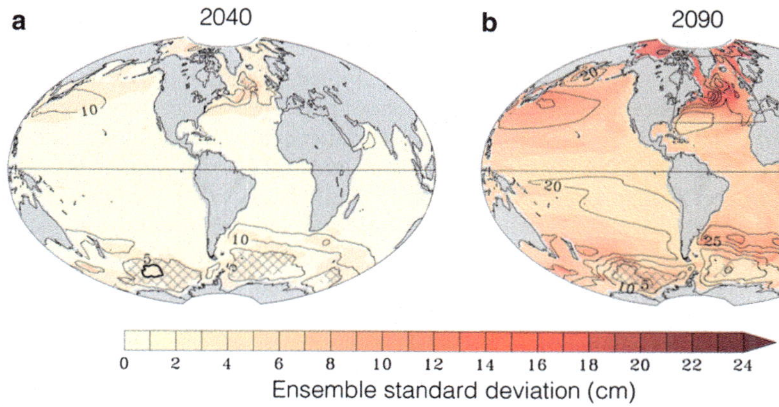

Fig. 4 CMIP5 sterodynamic component of sea-level change for (left) 2040 and (right) 2090 as multimodel, multiscenario, multirealization decadal mean (contours, in cm) and the ensemble standard deviation (colours). Cross-hatching indicates regions in which the ensemble mean divided by the ensemble standard deviation is less than one, figure from Little et al. (2015)

In the Arctic Ocean, this is caused by the sea ice—ocean interaction, whereas for the North American coast, deviations are driven by changes in the Atlantic Meridional Overturning Circulation (AMOC). The AMOC is projected to decline over the twenty-first century (Collins et al. 2013), resulting in a dynamic sea-level rise along the north-eastern American coast. Widely varying representation of the AMOC across models leads to a large uncertainty in this region (e.g., Yin et al. 2009; Little et al. 2019). This model or structural uncertainty was found to be the largest contributor to regional sea-level uncertainty by ocean processes throughout the twenty-first century, to varying degrees in different regions. Uncertainty due to internal variability and scenario uncertainty contributed significantly in the beginning and, towards the end of the century, respectively (Little et al. 2015).

Heat fluxes across the atmosphere–ocean interface cause changes in global and regional sterodynamic sea level. The simulated global mean thermosteric sea-level rise, and therefore also regional sterodynamic sea-level changes, depend on the climate feedback parameter and the ocean heat uptake efficiency, both of which vary across models due to different parameterizations and representations of oceanic and atmospheric processes (Melet and Meyssignac 2015 and references therein). They form an important source of variability in regional sea-level projections at present and will continue to do so in the future (Yin et al. 2010; Yin 2012; Church et al. 2013; Slangen et al. 2014; Gregory et al. 2016).

Where and to what depth the excess heat enters the ocean directly affects thermosteric sea-level change, one major component of sterodynamic sea-level change, as the thermal expansion coefficient depends on pressure, temperature and salinity. This effect contributes to locally high rates of thermosteric sea-level rise in regions where the ocean heat uptake is relatively large in the current climate, such as those associated with mode water formation (Suzuki and Ishii 2011; Terada and Minobe 2018). At the same time, local halosteric effects depend on the salinity versus freshwater input which is particularly important at high latitudes in the North Atlantic Ocean (Yin et al. 2010). Additionally, the projected warming that takes place in the deep ocean below the depth of shallow continental shelves drives an ocean mass redistribution that contributes strongly to sea-level rise in coastal areas (Landerer et al. 2007; Yin et al. 2010; Richter et al. 2013). However, the consistency of the climate models with respect to shelf mass loading has not yet been evaluated, and is likely hindered by the limited resolution of GCMs.

The sea-level changes originating in the deep ocean affect coastal sea-level via westward propagating Rossby waves that subsequently travel equatorward along the western boundaries as coastally trapped waves (Minobe et al. 2017). However, interaction with currents and topography may affect this mechanism (Little et al. 2019). Additionally, as a consequence of the limited resolution (typically 100 km in CMIP5 climate models), the current generation of GCMs fails to capture and simulate future changes in strong and narrow western boundary currents such as the Gulf Stream and the Kuroshio, both of which are important for local sea-level changes. This can be addressed by dynamical downscaling using high-resolution ocean models (Liu et al. 2016; Zhang et al. 2017). For example, Liu et al. (2016) reported that over the twenty-first century, the sea-level rise difference is less than 10 cm along the coast of the main islands of Japan but can reach nearly 50 cm in the deep ocean east of Japan.

In contrast to atmosphere–ocean heat fluxes, momentum fluxes do not induce changes in global sea level. However, changes in the magnitude and location of major wind systems greatly affect regional sea level via the wind-driven ocean circulation. In particular, the poleward shift of mid-latitude westerly winds causes poleward expansion of the subtropical oceanic gyres, particularly in the Southern hemisphere (Saenko et al. 2005; Bouttes et al. 2012; Zhang et al. 2017). This poleward gyre-boundary migration is accompanied by sea-level rise around the gyre boundary as subtropical gyres lead to higher sea level than subpolar gyres. This mechanism partly contributes to the sea-level rise in the Kuroshio Extension region with a large inter-model spread (Zhang et al. 2014; Terada and Minobe 2018).

Climate models are not yet routinely coupled to glacier and ice sheet models; thus, the impact of freshwater fluxes from melting land ice on the ocean circulation is not simulated and represents an additional uncertainty, particularly in the northern North Atlantic and Arctic Ocean. This region is particularly sensitive to the input of meltwater from the surrounding ice-covered land masses in north-eastern Canada and Greenland that is associated with the strength of the AMOC (e.g., Stammer 2008; Yin et al. 2009). A study by Slangen and Lenaerts (2016) with a fully coupled version of the Community Earth System Model (CESM) shows that freshwater forcing from the ice sheets leads to an ocean-driven change of locally over 0.1 m over the twenty-first century in the Southern Ocean, the Arctic Ocean and the northern North Atlantic including the east coast of North America. Similarly, Bronselaer et al. (2018) used a CMIP5 model to study effects of meltwater from the ice sheets and ice shelves of Antarctica, and they found that meltwater can induce subsurface ocean warming, leading to a positive feedback in further ice mass loss. Golledge et al. (2019) argue that meltwater from Antarctica will be trapped near the sea surface and increases ice mass loss.

On shorter (decadal and interannual) time scales, sea-level changes are largely associated with natural variability and climate modes such as Pacific decadal oscillation (PDO)/interdecadal Pacific oscillation (IPO), Atlantic multidecadal oscillation and El Nino and Southern oscillation. How these and other climate phenomena influenced sea-level are documented by Woodworth et al. (2019) and Han et al. (2018, 2019). In particular, the rapid sea-level rise observed in the western tropical Pacific during the satellite era is related to the PDO/IPO variability (Zhang and Church 2012; Hamlington et al. 2013). These modes are not predictable on time scales longer than a few years (Kim et al. 2012; Chikamoto et al. 2015; Meehl et al. 2016), and are therefore ignored in projections.

To account for natural variability in sea-level projections, it is important that climate models (1) represent the observed variability adequately and (2) capture potential future changes in frequency and magnitude of natural climate modes. Regarding (1), it has been suggested that the decadal variability in ocean models is too low in the tropical Pacific Ocean (Bilbao et al. 2015) over the altimetric record. Peyser and Yin (2017) showed that CMIP5 models underestimate sea-level variability associated with El Nino and the PDO. With respect to (2), some features of climate modes are expected to change in future (Hu and Bates 2018). Cai et al. (2014) reported that the frequency of extreme El Nino will increase, implying that extreme sea-level anomalies associated with El Nino may occur more frequently (Widlansky et al. 2015).

On somewhat longer time scales, Hu and Deser (2013) found that the decadal variability in sea level did not change between 2041–2060 and 1980–1999 based on analyses of 40 ensemble members of a single climate model, and Little et al. (2015) reported that decadal sea-level variability around New York City is expected to be roughly constant throughout the twenty-first century.

3.2 Other Geophysical Processes

Regional sea-level changes as experienced in coastal zones are not only the result of ocean processes, but also of changes in the solid earth topography and gravity field (Tamisiea and Mitrovica 2011), which are the subject of this section.

As the solid earth is not rigid, the height of the surface determining the relative sea level is a result of a balance between Earth dynamic processes, such as mantle convection and plate tectonics and buoyancy forces (Conrad 2013). When mass accumulates at a specific location, the additional weight depresses the surface and raises the geoid, causing sea level to rise in its proximity and to fall in the far field. This solid earth–water interaction is described by the sea-level equation (Farrell and Clark 1976; Kendall et al. 2005) and is mainly instantaneous. The major uncertainty in the pattern is the uncertainty in the loading changes by the ice.

The main geophysical process that contributes to regional sea-level change on century time scales is Glacial Isostatic Adjustment (GIA), which is the ongoing response of the solid earth to the loading–unloading effect of the last glacial cycle (Tamisiea 2011). Uncertainties from forward GIA models are usually not available, since they are mainly due to uncertainties in earth structure and glacial history that are very difficult to assess. The only systematic study of GIA uncertainties has been recently published by Melini and Spada (2019), where they have shown that both input uncertainties (ice history and Earth mechanical properties) and structural uncertainties (differences in GIA models and in observational constraints) are equally important contributors to the total error budget. At many locations, the solid Earth response is small, and signals at the cm/year level are only expected close to the former ice sheets (e.g., Hudson Bay Baltic Sea). Other regions where the GIA signals are important are those in the peripheral areas of the former ice sheets, like the US East coast, where vertical land motion rates are about 1–2 mm/year. As the solid Earth processes are slow, we can assume the GIA signal to be linear at the centennial scale; hence, if we assume an uncertainty of about 0.5 mm/year (Frederikse et al. 2017), it will contribute no more than 5 cm to the uncertainty near the end of the twenty-first century.

A second process affecting the uncertainty in regional and coastal sea-level changes is the accumulation of sediments at the estuaries of major rivers, which induces both bathymetry changes and gravitational effects. The accumulation of large amounts of sediments loads the crust, which causes subsidence, and attracts ocean waters; both processes result in regional sea-level rise. A few studies have considered the Mississippi (Ivins et al. 2007) and the Indus (Ferrier et al. 2015) basins, where relative sea-level rates can locally amount to a few mm/year due to sediment accumulation.

Changes in the amount of freshwater stored on land will also affect relative sea level in both a direct way (water exchange between continents and oceans), as well as through induced changes in the solid earth. Examples are the effects of natural processes such as droughts (Borsa et al. 2014), intensified periods of rainfall on land (Boening et al. 2012), but also anthropogenic changes like dam building (Fiedler and Conrad 2010) and groundwater extraction (Veit and Conrad 2016). With respect to sea-level changes at centennial scales, the main uncertainty will likely arise from groundwater extraction, which depends strongly on socio-economic factors. Regional sea-level changes could amount to several millimetres per year, especially in California, Pakistan and NW India. In addition, local groundwater extraction is causing some megacities to subside by several centimetres per year (e.g., Abidin et al. 2015); whether this trend will continue in the future is dependent on political and socio-economic factors (Nicholls 2011).

Finally, the occurrence of earthquakes can affect local sea level due to both instantaneous elastic deformation of the crust, mostly affecting sea level very close to the earthquake location, and the subsequent viscoelastic adjustment in the earth curst and upper mantle, which might affect regional changes (Broerse et al. 2014), with rates largely dependent on the earthquake size (Melini et al. 2004). However, it is almost impossible to make projections of the effect of earthquakes, since recurrence times of large events are usually several centuries. Of all the processes listed above, only GIA and the effect of freshwater changes on land are usually incorporated into regional sea-level projections.

4 Sources of Uncertainties in Extreme Sea Level

Extreme sea level (ESL) is defined here as an event of extremely high sea level along the coast occurring over a relatively short period of one to a few days (sometimes also called "extreme water level"), triggered by storm surges, waves, tides or a combination of these processes. ESL events take place on top of the long-term trends in sea level and play an important role in flood risk. Flood risks may increase due to the long-term trend in mean sea level, but also by a change in the frequency or magnitude of extreme events (often expressed in terms of return periods). Changes in historical flood risk have been dominated by long-term sea-level rise, but whether that also holds for changes in future ESLs is uncertain.

Beside changes in climate modes as discussed in Sect. 3, ESL characteristics might also be affected by changes in frequency or magnitude of cyclones, waves and tides. Most AOGCM models show that the frequency of cyclones will either decrease or remain unchanged, but the intensity is expected to increase (Christensen et al. 2013). How this affects the extreme sea-level characteristics for those coastlines vulnerable to cyclone activity remains to be seen.

Close to the coast, many processes may influence ESL characteristics. Arns et al. (2017) showed that an increase in mean sea level reduces the depth limitation of waves in shallow seas yielding larger waves and higher run-up of the waves. Melet et al. (2018) demonstrate, by analysing coastal sea-level observations, that decadal changes in wave climate have an important role in dampening or enhancing local rates of the sea-level change. Coupled climate and hydrodynamical models are needed to resolve the importance of these local-scale processes for local sea-level changes, as pioneered by Vousdoukas et al. (2018).

In addition to waves, tidal characteristics may change over time. Historically, ocean tides have been considered stationary because of their close relationship to astronomical motions (Cartwright and Tayler 1971) including a small nodal cycle with a length of 18.6 years. Nevertheless, long-term tidal evolution has been reported for some locations (Cartwright 1972; Amin 1983; Bowen 1972; Familkhalili and Talke 2016), mainly associated with harbour modifications and changes in water depth. In addition, recent studies, however, provide evidence that ocean tides are changing in some ocean basins at diverse rates without any relationship to astronomical forcing (Mawdsley et al. 2015; Muller 2011). Changes in tides have been observed in the Gulf of Maine, (Ray 2006) in the North Atlantic (Muller 2011) and in China (Feng et al. 2015). Analysis for the Pacific Ocean (Devlin et al. 2017) suggests that sea-level variability is correlated with interannual tidal variability at most of the tide gauges in the Pacific. These tidal anomalies, while influenced by basin-scale climate processes and sea-level changes, appear to be locally forced and not coherent over amphidromic points (i.e. tidal nodes) or basin-scale. A further possibility for tides to change is related to increased water depths associated with sea-level rise (Pickering et al. 2017; Howard et al. 2019) leading to shifts of the amphidromic points and local tidal characteristics. Detailed hydrodynamical models may capture these uncertainties in near future simulations.

Seasonal changes to stratification and thermocline depth caused by variations in water temperature and wind produce a steric sea-level signal and alter the surface manifestation of internal tides, creating a detectable change in tide gauge records (Colosi and Munk 2006). Seasonal changes in wave speed in shallow coastal areas also modify propagation and dissipation of tides (Arbic and Garrett 2010). Furthermore, river flows and changes in run off directly influence bottom friction and modify stratification, leading to changes in tidal dynamics (Guo et al. 2015).

A recent study by Vousdoukas et al. (2018) demonstrates that future changes in tides are driven by sea-level trends, and projected changes in tides are higher for the RCP8.5 scenario compared to the RCP4.5. Increase in tidal range of several cm is projected along parts of north Australia, east Patagonia and the Sea of Okhotsk. However, for most of the world regional changes in tides are insignificant in comparison with the other components of sea-level rise at centennial time scales.

5 Discussion and Conclusions

As sea-level is expected to rise for over the twenty-first century and beyond (Oppenheimer et al. 2019), and likely at an accelerated pace, there is a need for more detailed information near the coasts. CMIP5 generation climate models (GCMs) are unable to represent important processes relating to extreme sea level (ESL) events and coastal processes. This poses challenges from an adaptation point of view, as sometimes a full probability density function is needed including high-end scenarios, whereas climate models as used in IPCC context (Church et al. 2013) only offer, for good reasons, a likely range. Risk adverse users of this information may wish to take a more conservative approach that explicitly considers information on the "tail risks" (Stammer et al. 2019; Hinkel et al. 2019; Jevrejeva et al. 2019). A key limitation is our understanding of the future response of the ice sheets, particularly from ice dynamic processes, and the potential for accelerated sea-level rise. As a result, conditional probability distributions are provided in the literature which assume a certain Antarctic contribution based on expert judgement or on a single ice dynamical study (e.g., Bamber and Aspinall 2013; Kopp et al. 2014; Jackson and Jevrejeva 2016; Slangen and Lenaerts 2016; Bamber et al. 2019).

However, in order to get to the local scale where adaptation measures are to be taken, many other issues must also be resolved. Variations in ESL are among the factors to be considered; for this reason, adaptation measures are very local and need to evolve over time and are therefore sometimes framed as adaptation pathways (Haasnoot et al. 2011). One possibility to inform adaptation strategies is to include more detailed climate models near the coast, which help to resolve the shallowing of the bathymetry near the coast and its effect on local water level. Such models may also be combined with hydrodynamical models to better represent small-scale coastal processes. Around the Antarctic ice sheet, higher resolution in climate models may help to resolve processes associated with coastal water masses and/or circulation on the continental shelf and result in improved simulations of future ice sheet response. Nevertheless, improved resolution is not a panacea for the problems arising from a lack of small-scale physical processes in climate models. Particular challenges are the representation of the AMOC in models for patterns of sea-level change in the North Atlantic region and more generally the ocean mass distribution near the continental shelves, which is critical for coastal sea-level change.

Inclusion of small-scale processes like ice shelf hydrofracturing will likely need to be parameterized for the foreseeable future, and GCMs are yet to include the effects of tides and wave set-up on simulated sea level. Hence, to answer questions with respect to local coastal sea level, we have to improve the physics of climate models and combine them with hydrodynamical and/or regional ocean models which capture changes in local bathymetry, the interaction between surges, waves and tides, such that we can provide more information than only the RSL at 100-km resolution and move towards projections of high water levels at 10-km resolution. A more detailed outline for model improvements is provided by Ponte et al. (2019), but combining hydrodynamical and regional ocean models is already feasible and data for validation are available. Combining this with new data assimilation techniques will promote more realistic coastal information which is better suited for coastal decision making.

Acknowledgements Benoit Meyssignac is thanked for providing the data compilation of the historical sea-level reconstruction used in Fig. 2. ISSI is acknowledged for organizing a Workshop on coastal sea level in spring 2018 where the idea of this paper shaped. REMR acknowledges funding from the Netherlands Organization for Scientific Research through VID Grant No. 864.12.012. KR is funded by the Austrian Science Fund (FP302560). RvdW acknowledges funding from NWO/NPP. XZ acknowledges funding from the Centre for Southern Hemisphere Oceans Research Centre (CSHOR), jointly funded by QNLM and CSIRO. MDP was supported by the Met Office Hadley Centre Climate Programme funded by BEIS and Defra. SJ was supported by the Natural Environmental Research Council under Grant Agreement No. NE/P01517/1 and by the EPSRC NEWTON Fund Sustainable Deltas Programme, Grant Number EP/R024537/1. CL's contribution was supported by NASA Contract NNH16CT01C.

References

Abidin HZ, Andreas H, Gumilar I, Brinkman JJ (2015) Study on the risk and impacts of land subsidence in Jakarta. Proc IAHS 372:115–120. https://doi.org/10.5194/piahs-372-115-2015

Amin M (1983) On perturbations of harmonic constants in the Thames Estuary. Geophys J Int 73(3):587–603

Arbic BK, Garrett C (2010) A coupled oscillator model of shelf and ocean tides. Cont Shelf Res 30(6):564–574. https://doi.org/10.1016/j.csr.2009.07.008

Arns A et al (2017) Sea-level rise induced amplification of coastal protection design heights. Sci Rep 7:40171

Bamber J, Aspinall W (2013) An expert judgement assessment of future sea level rise from the ice sheets. Nat Clim Change 3(4):424–427

Bamber JL et al (2019) Ice sheet contributions to future sea-level rise from structured expert judgment. Proc Natl Acad Sci 116:11195–11200

Bassis JN, Walker CC (2012) Upper and lower limits on the stability of calving glaciers from the yield strength envelope of ice. Proc R Soc A 468:913–931

Bilbao RA, Gregory JM, Bouttes N (2015) Analysis of the regional pattern of sea-level change due to ocean dynamics and density change for 1993–2099 in observations and CMIP5 AOGCMs. Clim Dyn 45(9–10):2647–2666

Boening C et al (2012) The 2011 La Niña: so strong, the oceans fell. Geophys Res Lett. https://doi.org/10.1029/2012GL053055

Borsa AA, Agnew DC, Cayan DR (2014) Ongoing drought-induced uplift in the western United States. Science 345(6204):1587–1590

Borstad CP, Khazendar A, Larour E, Morlighem M, Rignot E, Schodlok MP, Seroussi H (2012) A damage mechanics assessment of the Larsen B ice shelf prior to collapse: toward a physically-based calving law. Geophys Res Lett 39:L18502. https://doi.org/10.1029/2012GL053317

Bouttes N, Gregory JM, Kuhlbrodt T, Suzuki T (2012) The effect of wind stress change on future sea-level change in the Southern Ocean. Geophys Res Lett. https://doi.org/10.1029/2012GL054207

Bowen AJ (1972) The tidal regime of the River Thames; long-term trends and their possible causes. Philos Trans R Soc Lond A Math Phys Eng Sci 272(1221):187–199

Broerse T, Riva R, Vermeersen B (2014) Ocean contribution to seismic gravity changes: the sea level equation for seismic perturbations revisited. Geophys J Int 199(2):1094–1109

Bronselaer B, Winton M, Griffies SM, Hurlin WJ, Rodgers KB, Sergienko OV, Stouffer RJ, Russell JL (2018) Change in future climate due to Antarctic meltwater. Nature 564(7734):53

Cai W et al (2014) Increasing frequency of extreme El Nino events due to greenhouse warming. Nat Clim Change 4:111–116. https://doi.org/10.1038/NCLIMATE2100

Carson M, Köhl A, Stammer D, Slangen ABA, Katsman CA, van de Wal RSW, Church J, White N (2016) Coastal sea level changes, observed and projected during the 20th and 21st century. Clim Change 134:269–281. https://doi.org/10.1007/s10584-015-1520-1

Carson M, Lyu K, Richter K, Becker M, Domingues CM, Han W, Zanna L (2019) Climate model uncertainty and trend detection in regional sea level projections: a review. Surv Geophys. https://doi.org/10.1007/s10712-019-09559-3

Cartwright DE (1972) Secular changes in the oceanic tides at Brest, 1711–1936. Geophys J Int 30(4):433–449

Cartwright DE, Tayler RJ (1971) New computations of the tide-generating potential. Geophys J R Astron Soc 23:45–74. https://doi.org/10.1111/j.1365-246X.1971.tb01803.x

Cazenave MA, Bamber J, Barletta V, Beckley B, Benveniste J, Berthier E, Blazquez A, Boyer T, Caceres D, Chambers D, Champollion N, Chao B, Chen J, Cheng L, Church JA, Cogley JG, Dangendorf S, Desbruyères D, Döll P, Domingues C, Falk U, Famiglietti J, Fenoglio-Marc L, Forsberg R, Galassi G, Gardner A, Groh A, Hogg A, Horwath M, Humphrey V, Husson L, Ishii M, Jaeggi A, Jevrejeva S, Johnson G, Kolodziejczyk N, Kusche J, Lambeck K, Landerer F, Leclercq P, Legresy B, Leuliette E, Llovel W, Longuevergne L, Loomis BD, Luthcke SB, Marcos M, Marzeion B, Merchant C, Merrifield M, Meyssignac B, Milne G, Mitchum G, Mohajerani Y, Monier M, Nerem S, Palanisamy H, Paul F, Perez B, Piecuch CG, Ponte RM, Purkey SG, Reager JT, Rietbroek R, Rignot E, Riva R, Roemmich DH, Sandberg Sørensen L, Sasgen I, Schrama EJO, Seneviratne SI, Shum CK, Spada G, Stammer D, van de Wal RSW, Velicogna I, von Schuckmann K, Wada Y, Wang Y, Watson C, Wiese D, Wijffels S, Westaway R, Woppelmann G, Wouters B (2018) Global sea-level budget 1993-present. Earth Syst Sci Data 10:1551–1590

Chikamoto Y et al (2015) Skilful multi-year predictions of tropical trans-basin climate variability. Nat Commun 6:6869

Christensen JH et al (2013) Climate phenomena and their relevance for future regional climate change. In: Stocker TF, Qin D, Plattner G-K, Tignor M, Allen SK, Boschung J, Nauels A, Xia Y, Bex V, Midgley PM (eds) Climate change 2013: the physical science basis. Contribution of working group I to the fifth assessment report of the intergovernmental panel on climate change, Cambridge University Press, Cambridge, United Kingdom and New York, NY, USA
Church JA, White NJ (2011) Sea-level rise from the late 19th to the early 21st century. Surv Geophys 32(4–5):585–602
Church JA, Clark PU, Cazenave A, Gregory JM, Jevrejeva S, Levermann A, Merrifield MA, Milne GA, Nerem RS, Nunn PD, Payne AJ, Pfeffer WT, Stammer D, Unnikrishnan AS (2013) Sea-level change. in: climate change 2013: the physical science basis. In: Stocker TF, Qin D, Plattner GK, Tignor M, Allen SK, Boschung J, Nauels A, Xia Y, Bex V, Midgley PM (eds) Contribution of working group I to the fifth assessment report of the intergovernmental panel on climate change. Cambridge University Press, Cambridge, pp 1137–1216. https://doi.org/10.1017/cbo9781107415324.026
Collins M, Knutti R, Arblaster J, Dufresne J-L, Fichefet T, Friedlingstein P, Gao X, Gutowski WJ, Johns T, Krinner G, Shongwe M, Tebaldi C, Weaver AJ, Wehner M (2013) Long-term climate change: projections, commitments and irreversibility. In: Stocker TF, Qin D, Plattner G-K, Tignor M, Allen SK, Boschung J, Nauels A, Xia Y, Bex V, Midgley PM (eds) Climate change 2013: the physical science basis. Contribution of working group I to the fifth assessment report of the intergovernmental panel on climate change. Cambridge University Press, pp 1029–1136. https://doi.org/10.1017/cbo9781107415324.024
Colosi JA, Munk W (2006) Tales of the venerable Honolulu tide gauge. J Phys Oceanogr 36:967–996. https://doi.org/10.1175/jpo2876.1
Conrad CP (2013) The solid Earth's influence on sea level. Geol Soc Am Bull 125(7–8):1027–1052
Dangendorf S et al (2017) Reassessment of 20th century global mean sea-level rise. Proc Natl Acad Sci 114:5946–5951
De Winter R et al (2017) Impact of asymmetric uncertainties in ice sheet dynamics on regional sea level projections. Nat Hazards Earth Syst Sci 17:2125–2141
DeConto RM, Pollard D (2016) Contribution of Antarctica to past and future sea-level rise. Nature 531(7596):591–597. https://doi.org/10.1038/nature17145
Devlin AT, Jay DA, Zaron ED, Talke SA, Pan J, Lin H (2017) Tidal variability related to sea-level variability in the Pacific Ocean. J Geophys Res Oceans 122:8445–8463. https://doi.org/10.1002/2017JC013165
Edwards TL, Brandon MA, Durand G, Edwards NR, Golledge NR, Holden PB et al (2019) Revisiting Antarctic ice loss due to marine ice-cliff instability. Nature 566(7742):58–64. https://doi.org/10.1038/s41586-019-0901-4
Familkhalili R, Talke SA (2016) The effect of channel deepening on storm surge: case study of Wilmington, NC. Geophys Res Lett 43:9138–9147. https://doi.org/10.1002/2016GL069494
Farrell WE, Clark JA (1976) On postglacial sea level. Geophys J R Astron Soc 46(3):647–667
Feng X, Tsimplis MN, Woodworth PL (2015) Nodal variations and long-term changes in the main tides on the coasts of China. J Geophys Res Oceans 120:1215–1232. https://doi.org/10.1002/2014JC010312
Ferrier KL, Mitrovica JX, Giosan L, Clift PD (2015) Sea-level responses to erosion and deposition of sediment in the Indus River basin and the Arabian Sea. Earth Planet Sci Lett 416:12–20
Fiedler JW, Conrad CP (2010) Spatial variability of sea-level rise due to water impoundment behind dams. Geophys Res Lett 37(12):1–3. https://doi.org/10.1029/2010GL043462
Frederikse T, Simon K, Katsman CA, Riva R (2017) The sea-level budget along the Northwest Atlantic coast: GIA, mass changes, and large-scale ocean dynamics. J Geophys Res Oceans 122(7):5486–5501
Golledge NR et al (2019) Global environmental consequences of twenty-first-century ice-sheet melt. Nature 566(7742):65–72. https://doi.org/10.1038/s41586-019-0889-9
Gregory JM, White NJ, Church JA, Bierkens MFP, Box JE, van den Broeke MR, Cogley JG, Fettweis X, Hanna E, Huybrechts P, Konikow LF, Leclercq PW, Marzeion B, Oerlemans J, Tamisiea ME, Wada Y, Wake LM, van de Wal RSW (2012) Twentieth-century global-mean sea-level rise: is the whole greater than the sum of the parts? J Clim. https://doi.org/10.1175/JCLI-D-12-00319.1
Gregory JM et al (2016) The flux-anomaly-forced model intercomparison project (FAFMIP) contribution to CMIP6: investigation of sea-level and ocean climate change in response to CO_2 forcing. Geosci Model Dev 9(11):3993–4017
Gregory JM, Griffies SM, Hughes CW, Lowe JA, Church JA, Fukimori I, Gomez N, Kopp R, Landerer F, Ponte R, Stammer D, Tamisiea M, van de Wal RSW (2019) Concepts and terminology for sea

level-mean, variability and change, both local and global. Surv Geophys. https://doi.org/10.1007/s10712-019-09525-z
Guo L, van der Wegen M, Jay DA, Matte P, Wang ZB, Roelvink D, He Q (2015) River-tide dynamics: Exploration of nonstationary and nonlinear tidal behavior in the Yangtze River estuary. J Geophys Res Oceans 120:3499–3521. https://doi.org/10.1002/2014JC010491
Haasnoot M, Middelkoop H, van Beek E, van Deursen WPA (2011) A method to develop sustainable water management strategies for an uncertain future. Sustain Dev 19:369–381. https://doi.org/10.1002/sd.438
Hamlington BD, Leben R, Strassburg MW, Nerem RS, Kim KY (2013) Contribution of the Pacific decadal oscillation to global mean sea-level trends. Geophys Res Lett 40:5171–5175. https://doi.org/10.1002/grl.50950
Han W, Meehl GA, Stammer D, Hu A, Hamilington B, Kenigson J, Palanisamy H, Thompson P (2018) Spatial patterns of sea level variability associated with natural internal climate modes. Surv Geophys 38:217–250. https://doi.org/10.1007/s10712-016-9386-y
Han W, Stammer D, Thompson P, Ezer T, Palanisamy H, Zhang X, Domingues C, Zhang L, Yuan D (2019) Impacts of basin-scale climate modes on coastal sea level: a review. Surv Geophys. https://doi.org/10.1007/s10712-019-09562-8
Hay CC, Morrow E, Kopp RE, Mitrovica JX (2015) Probabilistic reanalysis of twentieth-century sea-level rise. Nature 517(7535):481–484
Hinkel J, Le Cozannet G, Lowe J, Gregory J, Lambert E, McInnes K, Nicholls R, Church J, van de Pol T, van de Wal RSW (2019) Meeting user needs for sea-level rise information: a decision analysis perspective. Earths Future. https://doi.org/10.1029/2018EF001071
Howard T, Palmer MD, Bricheno LM (2019) Contributions to 21st century projections of extreme sea-level changearound the UK, Environ. Res. Commun. https://doi.org/10.1088/2515-7620/ab42d7
Hu A, Bates SC (2018) Internal climate variability and projected future regional steric and dynamic sea-level rise. Nat Commun 9(1):1068. https://doi.org/10.1038/s41467-018-03474-8
Hu A, Deser C (2013) Uncertainty in future regional sea-level rise due to internal climate variability. Geophys Res Lett 40:2768–2772. https://doi.org/10.1002/grl.50531
Ivins ER, Dokka RK, Blom RG (2007) Post-glacial sediment load and subsidence in coastal Louisiana. Geophys Res Lett 34(16):1-3. https://doi.org/10.1029/2007GL030003
Jackson LP, Jevrejeva S (2016) A probabilistic approach to 21st century regional sea-level projections using RCP and high-end scenarios. Glob Planet Change 146:179–189
Jenkins A et al (2018) West Antarctic Ice Sheet retreat in the Amundsen Sea driven by decadal oceanic variability. Nat Geosci. https://doi.org/10.1038/s41561-018-0207-4
Jevrejeva S, Grinsted A, Moore JC (2014) Upper limit for sea-level projections by 2100. Environ Res Lett 9(10):104008
Jevrejeva SA, Carson M, Le Cozannet G, Frederikse T, Kopp R, Jackson L, van de Wal RSW (2019) Probabilistic sea level projections at the coast by 2100. Surv Geophys. https://doi.org/10.1007/s10712-019-09550-y
Joughin I, Smith BE, Medley B (2014) Marine ice sheet collapse potentially under way for the thwaites glacier basin. West Antarctica. Science 344(6185):735–738. https://doi.org/10.1126/science.1249055
Kendall RA, Mitrovica JX, Milne GA (2005) On post-glacial sea level—II. Numerical formulation and comparative results on spherically symmetric models. Geophys J Int 161:679–706
Kim H-M, Webster PJ, Curry JA (2012) Evaluation of short-term climate change prediction in multi-model CMIP5 decadal hindcasts. Geophys Res Lett 39:L10701. https://doi.org/10.1029/2012GL051644
Kopp RE et al (2014) Probabilistic 21st and 22nd century sea-level projections at a global network of tide-gauge sites. Earth's Future 2(8):383–406
Kuipers Munneke P, Ligtenberg SRM, Van Den Broeke MR, Vaughan DG (2014) Firn air depletion as a precursor of Antarctic ice-shelf collapse. J Glaciol 60(220):205–214. https://doi.org/10.3189/2014JoG13J183
Landerer FW, Jungclaus JH, Marotzke J (2007) Ocean bottom pressure changes lead to a decreasing length-of-day in a warming climate. Geophys Res Lett. https://doi.org/10.1029/2006GL029106
Lazeroms WM, Jenkins A, Gudmundsson GH, van de Wal RS (2018) Modelling present-day basal melt rates for Antarctic ice shelves using a parametrization of buoyant meltwater plumes. Cryosphere 12(1):49
Le Bars D (2018) Uncertainty in sea Level rise projections due to the dependence between contributors. Earth Future. https://doi.org/10.1029/2018EF000849
Little CM, Horton RM, Kopp RE, Oppenheimer M, Yip S (2015) Uncertainty in twenty-first-century CMIP5 sea-level projections. J Clim 28(2):838–852. https://doi.org/10.1175/JCLI-D-14-00453.1

Little CM, Hu A, Hughes CW, McCarthy GD, Piecuch CG, Ponte RM, Thomas MD (2019) The Relationship between United States East Coast Sea Level and the Atlantic Meridional Overturning Circulation: a review. J Geophys Res Oceans. https://doi.org/10.1029/2019JC015152

Liu Z-J, Minobe S, Sasaki YN, Terada M (2016) Dynamical downscaling of future sea-level change in the western North Pacific using ROMS. J Oceanogr 72:905–922. https://doi.org/10.1007/s10872-016-0390-0

Mawdsley RJ, Haigh ID, Wells NC (2015) Global changes in tidal high water, low water and range. Earth's Future 3(2):66–81

Meehl GA, Hu A, Teng H (2016) Initialized decadal prediction for transition to positive phase of the Interdecadal Pacific Oscillation. Nat Commun 7:11718

Melet A, Meyssignac B (2015) Explaining the spread in global mean thermosteric sea-level rise in CMIP5 climate models. J Clim 28(24):9918–9940

Melet A, Meyssignac B, Almar R, Le Cozannet G (2018) Under-estimated wave contribution to coastal sea-level rise. Nat Clim Change 8:234

Melini D, Spada G (2019) Some remarks on glacial isostatic adjustment modelling uncertainties. Geophys J Int 218:401–413

Melini D, Piersanti A, Spada G, Soldati G, Casarotti E, Boschi E (2004) Earthquakes and relative sea-level changes. Geophys Res Lett. https://doi.org/10.1029/2003GL019347

Minobe S, Terada M, Qiu B, Schneder N (2017) Western boundary sea level: a theory, rule of thumb, and application to climate models. J Phys Oceanogr 47:957–977. https://doi.org/10.1175/JPO-D-16-0144.1

Mitrovica JX, Tamisiea ME, Davis JL, Milne GA (2001) Recent mass balance of polar ice sheets inferred from patterns of global sea-level change. Nature 409:1026–1029

Mouginot J, Rignot E, Bjørk AA, van den Broeke MR, Millan R, Morlighem M, Noël B, Scheuchl B, Wood M (2019) Forty-six years of Greenland Ice Sheet mass balance from 1972 to 2018. PNAS. https://doi.org/10.1073/pnas.1904242116

Muller M (2011) Rapid change in semi-diurnal tides in the North Atlantic since 1980. Geophys Res Lett 38:L11602. https://doi.org/10.1029/2011GL047312

Nicholls RJ (2011) Planning for the impacts of sea-level rise. Oceanography 24(2):144–157

Oppenheimer M, Glavovic B, Hinkel J, Van de Wal RSW, Magnan AK, Abd-Elgawad A, Cai R, Cifuentes-Jara M, DeConto RM, Ghosh T, Hay J, Isla F, Marzeion B, Meyssignac B, Sebesvari Z (2019) Sea level rise and implications for low lying Islands, coasts and communities. In: Pörtner H-O, Roberts DC, Masson-Delmotte V, Zhai P, Tignor M, Poloczanska E, Mintenbeck K, Nicolai M, Okem A, Petzold J, Rama B, Weyer N (eds) IPCC special report on the ocean and cryosphere in a changing climate

Pattyn F (2018) The paradigm shift in Antarctic ice sheet modelling. Nat Commun. https://doi.org/10.1038/s41467-018-05003-z

Perrette M et al (2013) A scaling approach to project regional sea-level rise and its uncertainties. Earth Syst Dyn 4(1):11–29. https://doi.org/10.5194/esd-4-11-2013

Peyser CE, Yin J (2017) Interannual and decadal variability in tropical Pacific Sea level. Water 9(6):402. https://doi.org/10.3390/w9060402

Pickering MD, Horsburgh KJ, Blundell JR, Hirschi JJ-M, Nicholls RJ, Verlaan M, Wells NC (2017) The impact of future sea-level rise on the global tides. Cont Shelf Res 142:50–68

Ponte RM, Carson M, Cirano M, Domingues C, Jevrejeva S, Marcos M, Mitchum G, van de Wal RSW, Woodworth PL, Ablain M, Ardhuin F, Ballu V, Becker M, Benveniste J, Birol F, Bradshaw E, Cazenave A, De Mey-Frémaux P, Durand F, Ezer T, Fu L-L, Fukumori I, Gordon K, Gravelle M, Griffies SM, Han W, Hibbert A, Hughes CW, Idier D, Kourafalou VH, Little CM, Matthews A, Melet A, Merrifield M, Meyssignac B, Minobe S, Penduff T, Picot N, Piecuch C, Ray RD, Rickards L, Santamaría-Gómez A, Stammer D, Staneva J, Testut L, Thompson K, Thompson P, Vignudelli S, Williams J, Williams SDP, Wöppelmann G, Zanna L, Zhang X (2019) Towards comprehensive observing and modeling systems for monitoring and predicting regional to coastal sea level. Front Mar Sci. https://doi.org/10.3389/fmars.2019.00437

Ray R (2006) Secular changes of the M2 tide in the Gulf of Maine. Cont Shelf Res 26:422–427

Ray RD, Douglas BC (2011) Experiments in reconstructing twentieth-century sea levels. Prog Oceanogr 91(4):496–515

Reese R et al (2017) Antarctic sub-shelf melt rates via PICO. Cryosphere 2:1969–1985. https://doi.org/10.5194/tc-12-1969-2018

Richter K, Riva REM, Drange H (2013) Impact of self-attraction and loading effects induced by shelf mass loading on projected regional sea-level rise. Geophys Res Lett 40(6):1144–1148. https://doi.org/10.1002/grl.50265

Rignot E et al (2014) Widespread, rapid grounding line retreat of Pine Island, Thwaites, Smith, and Kohler glaciers, West Antarctica, from 1992 to 2011. Geophys Res Lett 41(10):3502–3509. https://doi.org/10.1002/2014GL060140

Rignot E et al (2019) Four decades of Antarctic Ice Sheet mass balance from 1979–2017. Proc Natl Acad Sci 116(4):1095–1103. https://doi.org/10.1073/pnas.1812883116
Rott H, Skvarca P, Nagler T (1996) Rapid collapse of northern Larsen Ice Shelf. Antarct Sci 271:788–792
Saenko OA, Fyfe JC, England MH (2005) On the response of the oceanic wind-driven circulation to atmospheric CO2 increase. Clim Dyn 25(4):415–426
Schoof C (2007) Marine ice-sheet dynamics, Part 1, The case of rapid sliding. J Fluid Mech 573:27–55. https://doi.org/10.1017/S0022112006003570
Shepherd A et al (2018) Mass balance of the Antarctic Ice Sheet from 1992 to 2017. Nature 558:219–222
Slangen ABA, Lenaerts JTM (2016) The sea-level response to ice sheet freshwater forcing in the Community Earth System Model. Environ Res Lett 11:104002
Slangen ABA, Katsman C, van de Wal RSW, Vermeersen LLA, Riva REM (2012) Towards regional projections of the twenty-first century sea-level change based on IPCC SRES scenario. Clim Dyn. https://doi.org/10.1007/s00382-011-1057-6
Slangen ABA, Carson M, Katsman CA, Van de Wal RSW, Köhl A, Vermeersen LLA, Stammer D (2014) Projecting twenty-first century regional sea-level changes. Clim Change 124(1–2):317–332. https://doi.org/10.1007/s10584-014-1080-9
Stammer D (2008) Response of the global ocean to Greenland and Antarctic ice melting. J Geophys Res Oceans. https://doi.org/10.1029/2006JC004079
Stammer D, van de Wal RSW, Nicholls RJ, Church J, Le Cozannet G, Lowe JA, Horton B, White K, Behar D, Hinkel J (2019) Framework for high-end estimates of sea-level rise for stakeholder applications. Earth Fut. https://doi.org/10.1029/2019EF001163
Sutherland DA et al (2019) Melt and subsurface geometry at a tidewater glacier. Sci Adv 365:369–373
Suzuki T, Ishii M (2011) Regional distribution of sea-level changes resulting from enhanced greenhouse warming in the model for interdisciplinary research on climate version 3.2. Geophys Res Lett 38:L02601. https://doi.org/10.1029/2010gl045693
Tamisiea ME (2011) Ongoing glacial isostatic contributions to observations of sea-level change. Geophys J Int 186(3):1036–1044
Tamisiea ME, Mitrovica JX (2011) The moving boundaries of sea-level change: understanding the origins of geographic variability. Oceanography 24(2):24–39
Terada M, Minobe S (2018) Projected sea-level rise, gyre circulation and water mass formation in the western North Pacific: CMIP5 inter-model analysis. Clim Dyn 50:4767–4782. https://doi.org/10.1007/s00382-017-3902-8
Trusel LD et al (2015) Divergent trajectories of Antarctic surface melt under two twenty-first-century climate scenarios. Nat Geosci 8:927. https://doi.org/10.1038/ngeo2563
Veit E, Conrad CP (2016) The impact of groundwater depletion on spatial variations in sea-level change during the past century. Geophys Res Lett 43(7):3351–3359
Vousdoukas MI, Mentaschi L, Voukouvalas E, Verlaan M, Jevrejeva S, Jackson LP, Feyen L (2018) Global probabilistic projections of extreme sea levels show intensification of coastal flood hazard. Nat Commun. https://doi.org/10.1038/s41467-018-04692-w
Widlansky MJ, Timmermann A, Cai W (2015) Future extreme sea level seesaws in the tropical Pacific. Sci Adv 1(8):e1500560. https://doi.org/10.1126/sciadv.1500560
Woodworth PL, Melet A, Marcos M et al (2019) Forcing factors affecting sea level changes at the coast Surv Geophys. https://doi.org/10.1007/s10712-019-09531-1
Yin J (2012) Century to multi-century sea-level rise projections from CMIP5 models. Geophys Res Lett. https://doi.org/10.1029/2012GL052947
Yin J, Schlesinger ME, Stouffer RJ (2009) Model projections of rapid sea-level rise on the northeast coast of the United States. Nat Geosci 2(4):262. https://doi.org/10.1038/NGEO462
Yin J, Griffies SM, Stouffer RJ (2010) Spatial variability of sea-level rise in twenty-first century projections. J Clim 23(17):4585–4607. https://doi.org/10.1175/2010JCLI3533.1
Zhang X, Church JA (2012) Sea level trends, interannual and decadal variability in the Pacific Ocean. Geophys Res Lett 39:L21701. https://doi.org/10.1029/2012GL053240
Zhang X, Church JA, Platten SM, Monselesan D (2014) Projection of subtropical gyre circulation and associated sea-level changes in the Pacific based on CMIP3 climate models. Clim Dyn 43:131–144
Zhang XJA, Monselesan CD, McInnes K (2017) Regional sea level projections for Australian Coasts in the 21st century. Geophys Res Lett 44:8481–8491. https://doi.org/10.1002/2017GL074176

Surveys in Geophysics (2019) 40:1673–1696
https://doi.org/10.1007/s10712-019-09550-y

Probabilistic Sea Level Projections at the Coast by 2100

S. Jevrejeva[1] · T. Frederikse[2] · R. E. Kopp[3] · G. Le Cozannet[4] · L. P. Jackson[5] · R. S. W. van de Wal[6,7]

Received: 13 November 2018 / Accepted: 12 June 2019 / Published online: 14 August 2019

Abstract
As sea level is rising along many low-lying and densely populated coastal areas, affected communities are investing resources to assess and manage future socio-economic and ecological risks created by current and future sea level rise. Despite significant progress in the scientific understanding of the physical mechanisms contributing to sea level change, projections beyond 2050 remain highly uncertain. Here, we present recent developments in the probabilistic projections of coastal mean sea level rise by 2100, which provides a summary assessment of the relevant uncertainties. Probabilistic projections can be used directly in some of the decision frameworks adopted by coastal engineers for infrastructure design and land use planning. However, relying on a single probability distribution or a set of distributions based upon a common set of assumptions can understate true uncertainty and potentially misinform users. Here, we put the probabilistic projections published over the last 5 years into context.

Keywords Sea level rise · Probabilistic sea level projections · Coastal impact · Climate change

1 Introduction

For the more than 600 million people living in low-elevation coastal areas less than 10 metres above sea level, sea level rise is one of the primary damaging aspects of climate change (IPCC 2014). The global coastline is characterized by high population

✉ S. Jevrejeva
sveta@noc.ac.uk

1 National Oceanography Centre, Liverpool L3 5DA, UK

2 Jet Propulsion Laboratory, California Institute of Technology, Pasadena, CA 91109, USA

3 Department of Earth and Planetary Sciences and Institute of Earth, Ocean, and Atmospheric Sciences, Rutgers University, New Brunswick, NJ 08901, USA

4 BRGM, French Geological Survey, 45060 Orléans, France

5 Nuffield College, Oxford University, Oxford OX1 1NF, UK

6 Institute for Marine and Atmospheric Research Utrecht, Utrecht University, 3584, CC, Utrecht, The Netherlands

7 Department of Physical Geography, Utrecht University, 3584, CB, Utrecht, The Netherlands

density, a substantial fraction of global economic activity and the presence of critical infrastructure (IPCC 2014, Hallegatte et al. 2013; Hinkel et al. 2014). Changes in mean sea level affect the height and frequency of extreme water levels (Woodworth et al. 2011), thus altering flood and inundation risks for low-lying areas (Nicholls and Cazenave 2010). Impact and risk assessment, adaptation policies and long-term decision-making in coastal areas are crucially informed by projections of coastal mean sea level and extreme water level events. (IPCC 2014; Nicholls et al. 2014; Hinkel et al. 2014, 2015; Kopp et al. 2014, 2017; Jevrejeva et al. 2016, 2018; Le Cozannet et al. 2017a). There is thus considerable societal demand for projections of future mean sea level and extreme water level changes with well communicated uncertainties.

Since the Intergovernmental Panel on Climate Change's Fifth Assessment Report (IPCC AR5), there has been considerable progress in observing mean sea level changes and the different components contributing to it (Cazenave and WCRP Global Sea Level Budget Group 2018). Advances in climate and ice sheet models (Griffies et al. 2016; Nowicki et al. 2016; Nowicki and Seroussi, 2018) have also led to improved understanding of the oceanic and cryospheric response to radiative forcing and better characterization of their associated uncertainties. Despite recent progress in climate change and sea level science, projections of long-term future sea level changes under different emissions scenarios remain highly uncertain, mainly due to the large uncertainty in estimates of future mass loss from the Greenland and Antarctic ice sheets. Recent publications reveal an increase in observed Antarctic sheet mass loss (e.g., Shepherd et al. 2018; Cazenave and WCRP Global Sea Level Budget Group 2018; Rignot et al. 2019), while model projections range widely (e.g., Ritz et al. 2015; Golledge et al. 2015; DeConto and Pollard, 2016; Edwards et al. 2019). These have fuelled a discussion about the increasing possibility of considerably higher future sea level rise than suggested in IPCC AR5 (Church et al. 2013a; Kopp et al. 2017; Horton et al. 2018; Garner et al. 2018). As a consequence, there has been an increase in the number of publications constructing regional and local mean sea level projections (e.g., Kopp et al. 2014, 2017; Grinsted et al. 2015; Slangen et al. 2016; Carson et al. 2016). This reflects the need for mean sea level rise projections suitable for risk assessment and decision-making by policymakers, planners, coastal engineers and general public in coastal areas (Hinkel et al. 2015, 2019).

Recent coastal and local sea level rise projections (e.g., Kopp et al. 2014, 2017; Grinsted et al. 2015; Jackson and Jevrejeva, 2016; Le Cozannet et al. 2017b) have moved away from IPCC AR5's focus on median and central range projections (Church et al. 2013a; Slangen et al. 2014). IPCC AR5 focused particularly on the "likely range" of projections. Under the IPCC's calibrated uncertainty language (Mastrandrea et al. 2010), *likely* refers to a probability of at least 66%. An exegesis by the authors of AR5′s sea level rise chapter (Church et al. 2013a) indicates that, in the context of sea level rise projections, IPCC AR5 ascribed a probability of about two-thirds to the likely range (Church et al. 2013b). However, for impact assessment, risk management and adaptation strategy in coastal areas there is a need for the low-probability, high-impact upper range of future sea level rise, which is not provided by AR5 IPCC "likely range" sea level projections.

Probabilistic sea level projections provide probability density functions (PDFs) that are conditional upon emissions pathways, which self-consistently project both likely values of mean sea level rise and the likelihood of high-risk, low-probability conditions such as those associated with rapid ice mass loss of Antarctica or Greenland which are physically poorly understood. Those projections explicitly labelled "probabilistic" include not only central or "likely" ranges, but also the tails of these distributions; Garner et al. (2018) empirically distinguish them as studies reporting more than three quartiles of a projected distribution. Probabilistic projections also provide a summary assessment of the relevant uncertainties, which are consistent with some of the decision frameworks used by coastal engineers for infrastructure design and land use planning (e.g., Hunter et al. 2013; Buchanan et al. 2016). In this paper, we also discuss that for many stakeholders, probabilistic projections require simplification into a range-spanning set of sea level scenarios (Nicholls et al. 2014; Hinkel et al. 2019). Unlike probabilistic projections, which are explicitly conditional upon emissions scenarios, sea level scenarios may or may not be tied to emissions scenarios (e.g., Representative Concentration Pathways) or other climate change scenarios (e.g., 1.5 °C above pre-industrial global mean surface temperature).

In this paper, we present an overview of recent work on probabilistic projections of changes in mean sea level and extreme sea levels by 2100. We discuss the user needs for multiple probabilistic sea level projections at the coast and the main challenges for coastal sea level projections including future changes in extreme sea levels.

2 Probabilistic Approach to Sea Level Changes

In many ways, the IPCC has become authoritative in assessing climate change; thus, unsurprisingly, its assessment, including the statements on uncertainties, influenced decision makers (Nicholls et al. 2014). A number of regional- and national-level assessments build upon the IPCC framework (e.g., Tran et al. 2016) or have developed their own along similar lines of reasoning, but often from a more national perspective (e.g., Katsman et al. 2011; NYPCC15; Hall et al. 2016). Notwithstanding the difficulties in producing them, probabilistic projections have been recognized as potentially useful information to support adaptation and mitigation since the 1990s (Titus and Narayanan 1995). This utility is due in part to the desire amongst the decision/planning community to gain insight into possible futures in which a low-probability, high-impact sea level rise occurs—discussed further in Sect. 4: Challenges for coastal sea level projections.

Several modelling frameworks exist to produce sea level projections. For example, process-based projections estimate the contribution of each process causing sea level rise (e.g., Katsman et al. 2011; Church et al. 2013a), while semi-empirical projections are simulated by reduced-form models calibrated to historical observations (e.g., Rahmstorf 2007, Jevrejeva et al. 2012; Kopp et al. 2016; Mengel et al. 2016). In a process-based approach, such as that used by Church et al. (2013a), various sources of information, including numerical simulations, are combined to model the evolution of different sea level components. Global mean sea level (GMSL) changes over time (t) are represented as the sum of projected sea level components, including thermostatic expansion (T), ice mass loss from different glaciers (GIC_i), ice mass loss from the Greenland Ice Sheet (GrIS), ice mass loss from the Antarctic Ice Sheet (AIS), often separated into East and West (EAIS and WAIS), and the contribution from land water storage (LWS_j) changes:

$$GMSL(t) = T(t) + \sum_i GIC_i(t) + GrIS(t) + WAIS(t) + EAIS(t) + \sum_j LWS_j(t). \quad (1)$$

In some studies, the individual PDFs of each term are considered independent. This assumption could result in underestimation of the upper tail of the projections (see Le Bars et al. 2018 for a review of dependence and correlation schemes used so far in the area of probabilistic sea level rise projections). In Church et al. (2013a), the sum of these components, with their uncertainties, provided an estimate of the median and 90% range (5th–95th percentiles) of sea level change under each representative concentration pathway

(RCP) scenario (Moss et al. 2010). This range was then assessed as a *likely range* (~2/3 probability) within the IPCC framework. Different research groups have taken alternative approaches to tackling this interpretation to "fill in" the remaining approximately one-third of the distribution (e.g., Kopp et al. 2014, 2017; Jevrejeva et al. 2014; Grinsted et al. 2015; Jackson and Jevrejeva, 2016; Le Cozannet et al. 2017b).

Regional sea level (RSL) rise displays complex spatial patterns due to atmosphere/ocean dynamics and the gravitational, rotational and crustal deformation effects of the redistribution of ocean mass, associated with ice loss from mountain glaciers, ice mass changes in the Greenland and Antarctic ice sheets and changes to land–water storage by artificial reservoirs and groundwater extraction.

RSL projections at locations x can be represented as:

$$\begin{aligned}\mathrm{RSL}(\mathrm{x}, t) = {} & T(t) + DSL(x, t) + \sum_i F_i(x)GIC_i(t) \\ & + \mathrm{F}_{GrIS}(\mathrm{x})GrIS(t) + \mathrm{F}_{WAIS}(\mathrm{x})WAIS(t) + \mathrm{F}_{EAIS}(\mathrm{x})EAIS(t) \\ & + \sum_{\mathrm{j}} F_{LWS_j}(x)LWS_j(t) + Bkgd(x, t),\end{aligned} \tag{2}$$

where RSL(x,t) is relative sea level, $DSL(x,t)$ is the dynamic sea level contribution and F_{GIC_i}, F_{GrIS}, F_{WAIS}, F_{EAIS} and F_{LWS_j} are the normalized gravitational, rotational and deformational fingerprints associated, respectively, with different glacial regions, GrIS, WAIS, EAIS and different land water storage regions. *Bkgd* references to background processes, unassociated with contemporary climate change that contribute to local sea level changes; in some projections, this includes only glacial isostatic adjustment (GIA), whereas in others it includes localized processes such as sediment compaction.

In general, the process-based modelling approach for regional sea level projections sums the contribution of sea level components. The mass contribution (e.g., glaciers, ice sheets, land water) is scaled by spatial "fingerprints" associated with gravitational, deformation and rotational effects (e.g., Mitrovica et al. 2001). In studies prior 2013 (e.g., Katsman et al. 2011), contributions from Greenland and Antarctica ice sheets are represented by "low" and "high" ("modest" and "severe" in Katsman et al. 2011) scenarios, mainly due to lack of ice sheet model simulations of ice mass loss from ice sheets with emission or climate scenarios. The RSL changes associated with dynamic sea level effects are determined from an ensemble of global climate models, with the spread between individual model ensemble members often used as an estimate of the uncertainty. This approach was taken by Katsman et al. (2011) and Slangen et al. (2014).

Kopp et al. (2014), Grinsted et al. (2015) and Jackson and Jevrejeva (2016) further developed this approach by embedding it into a probabilistic framework, such that the global mass and volume contributions were represented as PDFs (Fig. 1). The PDFs were then sampled using a Monte Carlo approach (e.g., Kopp et al.. 2014; Grinsted et al. 2015) or a semi-analytical method (De Winter et al. 2017), and draws across components to yield total sea level at either a global scale (Fig. 1) or individual locations (Fig. 2). These summed draws define a new PDF for a given point in time and space, thus providing the probabilistic regional sea level projections.

Kopp et al. (2014), Grinsted et al. (2015) and Jackson and Jevrejeva (2016) utilized the expert elicitation by Bamber and Aspinall (2013) to introduce non-Gaussian uncertainty into the tails of Greenland and Antarctic ice sheet contributions. Kopp et al. (2014) used information about tail shape, while retaining the central range of AR5; Grinsted et al. (2015) and

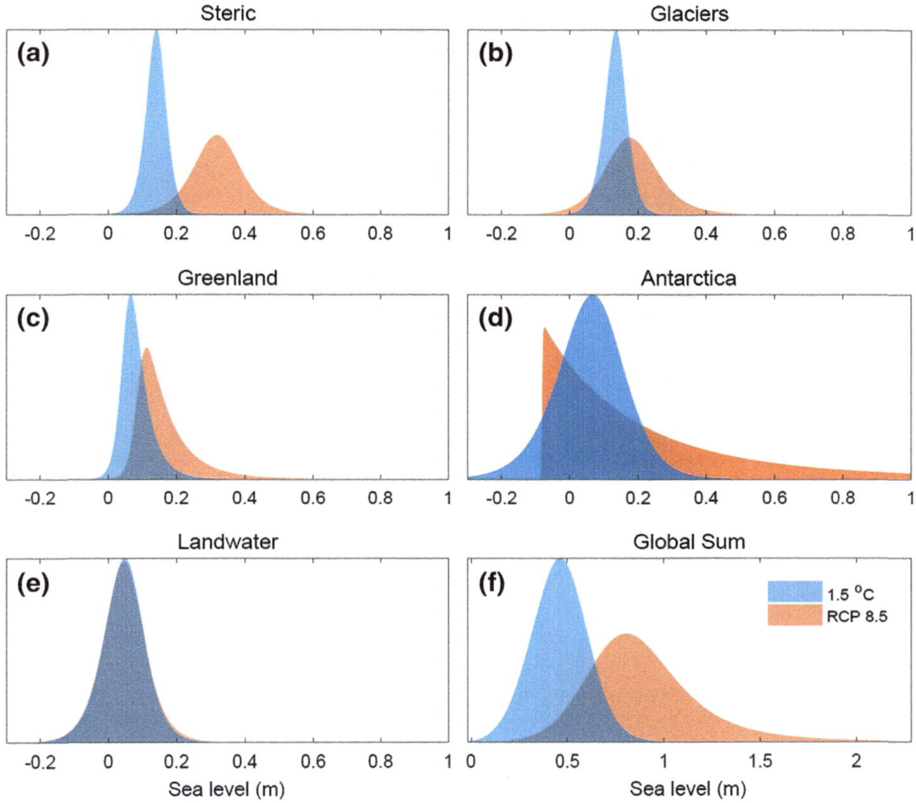

Fig. 1 Probability density functions for global sea level and its components in 2100 for two scenarios: warming of 1.5 °C and RCP8.5 (after Jevrejeva et al. 2018). Note that the land-based water component is scenario independent

Jackson and Jevrejeva (2016) used the full distribution of Bamber and Aspinall (2013). Both cases yielded a heavy-tailed distribution for the Antarctic ice sheet and hence total sea level. Additional interpretation of Bamber and Aspinall (2013) was made by De Vries and Van de Wal (2015; see also response by Bamber et al. 2016) and was consequently used by de Winter et al. (2017). Several other probabilistic projections have been made based on a recent Antarctic ice sheet modelling studying by DeConto and Pollard (2016) (e.g., Kopp et al. 2017).

In a scaling approach (Perrette et al. 2013), authors sample distributions for the global contributions and use a Monte Carlo to combine these with the spatial fingerprints. The spread mostly comes from the sampled global distributions (Model for assessment of greenhouse gas induced climate change (MAGICC) probabilistic projections), whereas the global circulation model (GCM) spread only imprints in the scaling relationships (ocean heat uptake to steric expansion, global mean temperature to local ocean dynamic). In fact, this study describes a regional SLR emulator, to make flexible, probabilistic projections, in the same spirit as Nauels et al. (2017). Probabilistic projections have also been constructed using semi-empirical sea level models (e.g., Rahmstorf 2007, Jevrejeva et al. 2012; Kopp et al. 2016; Mengel et al. 2016), simple climate models (e.g., Goodwin et al. 2017) and statistical emulators (e.g., Nauels et al. 2017). Because these approaches are not directly

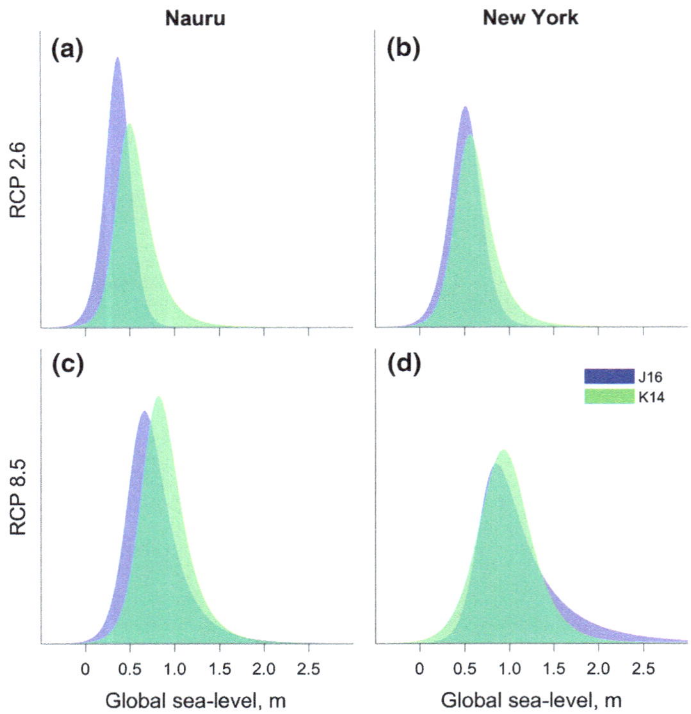

Fig. 2 Probability density functions for sea level in Nauru (Pacific island) and New York in 2100 for RCP2.6 and RCP8.5. Green colour corresponds to the results from Kopp et al. (2014), named as K14, and blue to the results from Jackson and Jevrejeva (2016), J16

dependent upon the RCP-driven projections of global climate models, they are more flexible with respect to scenarios considered (e.g., Kopp et al. 2016; Jevrejeva et al. 2018; Nauels et al. 2017). One limitation of most semi-empirical approaches is that they simulate only global sea level. The advantage of all these methods is their computational efficiency and their ability to explore numerous future pathways with policy intervention (e.g., Rasmussen et al. 2018; Mengel et al. 2018). In all cases, these methods, when embedded into a Monte Carlo or Bayesian framework, allow projection of a distribution under the assumptions of the model formulation.

3 Sea Level Projections and Scenarios: A User Perspective

3.1 Current Uses of Sea Level Projections and Scenarios

Coastal adaptation practitioners have had access to sea level information for decades (Hoffman et al. 1983). While the first probabilistic projections were produced nearly 25 years ago (Titus and Narayan, 1995), current adaptation planning largely relies on discrete scenarios, often informed by IPCC projections, defining possible future trajectories of sea level rise (Nicholls et al. 2014; Le Cozannet et al. 2017b). In some countries, sea level rise scenarios are defined at a national level and used across government agencies, as in the Netherlands (Van den Hurk et al. 2014). In other countries, such as the USA, sea level rise scenarios may differ amongst entities. For example, in the USA, the US Department of Defense (Hall et al. 2016), the US National Climate Assessment process (Sweet et al. 2017) and different states may employ different projections (see Hall et al. 2019, for a review). Furthermore, sea level rise scenarios can eventually be included in the regulation or design guidance, as in California, New York City or France (Rosenzweig et al. 2011; Le Cozannet et al. 2017b).

The overall process producing these sea level projections is driven by a demand of coastal users on the one hand and by efforts of the scientific community to produce these projections and transfer them to the practice of coastal adaptation on the other hand. In fact, the coastal engineering community has long used probabilistic approaches to estimate extreme water levels at the coast and design infrastructures with appropriate safety levels (e.g., extreme value analysis).

Probabilistic sea level projections are useful for analysing, understanding and communicating the cascade of uncertainties that propagate from sea level rise and other forcing factors throughout coastal impact models applicable at global to local scales. In this area, sensitivity analyses are especially useful to help identify input parameters or modelling assumptions that drive the variability of model outcomes such as the magnitude of shoreline retreat or the frequency and intensity of coastal flooding (e.g., Hallegatte et al. 2013; Hinkel et al. 2014). Typical sensitivity analyses are based on variance, which is relatively

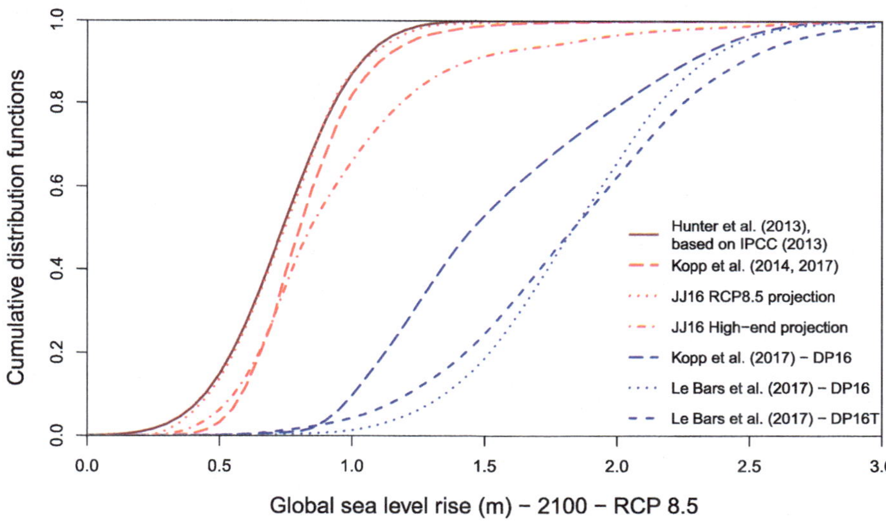

Fig. 3 Projections of globally mean sea level rise (GMSL, in m) by 2100 under RCP8.5 represented in a cumulative distribution diagram. (Church et al. 2013a; Kopp et al. 2014; Jackson and Jevrejeva, 2016; Kopp et al. 2017; Le Bars et al. 2017). Here, the curve labelled as "Hunter et al. (2013), based on IPCC (Church et al. 2013a)", is a modification of the median and likely range provided by Church et al. (2013a), following the interpretation of Hunter et al. (2013), which assumes a symmetric Gaussian extrapolation of the IPCC likely range and median values. DP16 is reference to the estimate of contribution from Antarctica ice sheet by DeConto and Pollard (2016), which is used in studies by Kopp et al. (2017) and Le Bars, et al. (2017); JJ16 is reference to Jackson and Jevrejeva, 2016 (including RCP8.5 scenarios, labelled as JJ16 RCP8.5 projection, and the high-end scenario, labelled as JJ16 High-end projection)

insensitive to the tail of the distribution. For that reason, as long as sea level projections considering Marine Ice Cliff Instability (DeConto and Pollard, 2016) are excluded (Fig. 3), the results of these variance-based sensitivity analyses remain relatively insensitive to different assumptions in probabilistic sea level projections, because projections mainly differ in their upper tail (Le Cozannet et al. 2015).

3.2 Dealing with Multiple Probabilistic Sea Level Projections: A User Perspective

Today, the processes that will cause sea level rise during the twenty-first century remain imperfectly understood. In particular, the dynamic response of the Antarctic ice sheet is a critical unknown, as its contribution to global sea level rise by 2100 could be either limited to a few tens of centimetres (Ritz et al. 2015), or reach one metre or more if ice shelf hydrofracturing and marine ice cliff instability lead to a dramatic increase in melt (DeConto and Pollard, 2016). Producers of probabilistic sea level projections need to choose which processes are included in their projections. Furthermore, they need to make assumptions about the dependencies between the different contributions of sea level rise. These choices can have a strong impact on the final probabilistic sea level projections produced for time periods after 2050 (Church et al. 2013a, Kopp et al. 2017; Le Bars, 2018), as well as on the coastal impacts to be expected.

Hence, several probabilistic sea level projections are available for users concerned with adaptation. Figure 3 displays a few probabilistic global sea level projections for RCP 8.5 in 2100 published recently. This figure is only for illustration, because coastal adaptation practitioners need sea level projections applicable locally and not global sums. However, this figure shows clearly that two very different subsets of probabilistic sea level projections coexist today:

- Those assuming that Antarctic dynamics will be mostly driven by marine ice sheets instability (red curves in Fig. 3)
- Those involving marine ice cliffs instability and ice shelf hydrofracturing (blue curves in Fig. 3).

At the level of the median, the difference between the two subsets of sea level projections is close to one metre. Importantly, coastal adaptation practitioners usually do not have the expertise to estimate the likelihood of the assumptions underpinning each sea level projections.

Instead of trying to identify a single probabilistic sea level projection corresponding to a “best estimate”, coastal adaptation practitioners may choose to consider all existing probabilistic sea level projections or a set of projections that span the range of probability distributions, for example, in order to test the robustness of their adaptation options against a suite of probabilistic projections (Horton et al. 2018). It follows that for coastal adaptation practitioners, the challenge is to identify the particular probabilistic projection that is best aligned with their level of risk aversion (Buchanan et al. 2016; Hinkel et al. 2019). For example, managers of critical infrastructures with long lifetimes (e.g., nuclear power stations) may consider the most pessimistic probabilistic projection in order to test their resilience to the full range of future possible sea level changes. These different probabilistic projections could be used within flexible adaptation pathways approaches (e.g., Haasnoot et al. 2013), employing probability distributions for the time period of good agreement (through about 2050) and developing structured contingency plans to follow as the fate of future sea level becomes clearer.

3.3 Strengths and Weaknesses of Probabilistic Projections in Operational Contexts

Today, many potential users of probabilistic projections have questions regarding the maturity and the transferability of probabilistic projections to operational practices and still remain reluctant to move from scenarios to probabilistic projections. For example, suggestions to consider probabilistic projections or scenarios besides the regulatory 60-cm sea level rise scenario defined by regulation for 2100 in France have not surpassed the level of technical reports so far (BRGM 2018). This example, amongst others, shows that scenarios are used in the practice of adaptation (Le Cozannet et al. 2017a).

Building on the review of current coastal climate services conducted within the framework of the World Climate Research Programme (WCRP) Grand Challenge on sea level rise, it appears, however, that probabilistic projections could be directly useful for several applications (Table 1), with the caveat that relying on a single probabilistic projection may not be sufficient (see Fig. 3). The first line in this table highlights that using existing probabilistic projections in combination with global coastal impact models to assess the benefits of mitigation in coastal area is a straightforward research avenue. Probabilistic projections can also be used to quantify and rank sources of uncertainties and identify which research is needed to reduce uncertainties in coastal impacts and adaptation assessments. Other needs listed in Table 1 relate to global or local adaptation. In this area, there is a need for probabilistic prediction (i.e. probabilistic description of sea level rise unconditional to greenhouse gas emissions) in order to address adaptation needs and optimize investments to prevent chronic flooding occurring during the highest tides, as this is increasingly occurring in low-lying sheltered areas (Table 1, line 4; Sweet and Park, 2014). The needs in this area may be that further efforts involving users with sea level information providers to co-design appropriate projections will be essential in this area.

4 Challenges for Coastal Sea Level Projections

The primary sources for a sea level rise beyond one metre this century are the polar ice sheets though a key aspect of the uncertainty is how they will respond to further warming. This is reflected in a significant spread amongst the research community's opinion (e.g., Bamber and Aspinall, 2013), a wide range of estimates for potential ice mass loss simulations (e.g., DeConto and Pollard, 2016; Edwards et al. 2019; Golledge et al. 2015; Ritz et al. 2015; Church et al. 2013) and the latest estimates of ice mass loss from observations (e.g., Shepherd et al. 2018; Cazenave and WCRP Global Sea Level Budget Group 2018; Bevis et al. 2019; Rignot et al. 2019). The current state of ice sheet modelling and reasons for the large uncertainty is presented by van de Wal et al. (2019) and discussed in several recent publications (Horton et al. 2018; Kopp et al. 2017; Jackson et al. 2018).

While the future of the ice sheets remains a prominent uncertainty, other challenges for coastal sea level projections remain. Current climate and Earth system models (e.g., Coupled Model Intercomparison Project Phase 5 (CMIP5, Taylor et al. 2012)), used for sea level projections, lack both the horizontal and vertical resolution to resolve small-scale

Table 1 Potential of probabilistic sea level projections to respond to current needs (after Le Cozannet et al. 2017a)

Need	Key challenge	Timescales of sea level projections required	Example of methods potentially using probabilistic projections
To identify benefits of mitigation	To discriminate impacts amongst different scenarios	From 2050 onward	Probabilistic propagation of uncertainties across climate and coastal impact models and sensitivity analysis (e.g., extending Hinkel et al. 2014[a])
To identify research needs	To identify the prominent sources of uncertainties in modelling outcomes	All	Sensitivity analysis assessing the sources of uncertainties in modelling outcomes (e.g., Kopp et al. 2014; Horton et al. 2018)
To quantify global coastal adaption needs	To discriminate SLR impacts from those due to other processes	All	Probabilistic propagation of uncertainties across climate and coastal impact models and sensitivity analysis (e.g., extending Hinkel et al. 2014)
To prepare for changing flooding hazards	Detailed coastal flood analysis (accuracy requirement in the order of 10 to 20 cm)	Up to 2050	Probabilistic propagation of uncertainties to support cost–benefit analysis (e.g., extending Hallegatte et al. 2013) or robust decision-making (Lempert and Schlesinger 2000)
To quantify local adaptation needs	To reduce uncertainties in SLR projections; to include environmental and societal changes in coastal change projections; to identify timescales of changes	All	Propagation of uncertainties across climate and coastal impact models (Le Cozannet et al. 2015; Lin and Shullman, 2017); extreme value analysis
To evaluate local adaptation strategies (e.g., Hallegatte, 2009)	To differentiate local to regional impacts of SLR according to different adaptation options	All	Probabilistic propagation of uncertainties to support cost–benefit analysis, or robust decision-making, the coastal tipping points approach (Kwadijk et al. 2010; Hall et al. 2012), or dynamic adaptive policy pathways or robustness approach (Haasnoot et al. 2013)

[a]In Hinkel et al. 2014, the contribution from land-ice components is represented as the scenarios (low, medium, high); however, these scenarios are based on probabilistic projections from the land-ice contributions

processes, which may be important for sea level rise. One such a challenge relates to the ability of ocean models to simulate realistic sea surface height (changes) in coastal areas. Part of the reason for this issue is the coarse resolution (the average across CMIP5 models is ~ 1°) compared to the length scale desirable for coastal analysis. Most of the models in CMIP5 are not eddy permitting and require parameterizations for eddy-induced transport of mass, heat and freshwater (Landerer et al. 2014; Griffies et al. 2016). This issue is compounded by coarse bathymetry on the continental shelf and the lack of physical mechanisms modelled in large-scale climate simulation driving coastal sea level variability on time scales of seasons to years.

In addition, mean sea level rise projections are often focused on long-term averages over extended periods. In most coastal locations (Carson et al. 2016, Church et al. 2013a), observations reveal the presence of strong seasonal, interannual and decadal variability. Carson et al. (2016) show that internal variability is also present in individual simulations of the models, but the variance in the models is underestimated (Hay et al. 2013) (Fig. 4).

Ocean dynamics can be misallocated or appear as diffuse features whose signal is smeared coastward. For example, Landerer et al. (2014) showed the meridional maximum sea surface height gradient of the Antarctic circumpolar current was shifted equatorward by ~ 4 degrees in CMIP5 models, which was correlated with a positioning bias in the zonal wind stress maxima. Many of these dynamic issues are likely to be resolved by using high resolution ocean models (e.g., Roberts et al. 2016) that resolve long-standing biases in the mean ocean state, which is critical for reliable climate projections.

One key issue is related to the combining of regional sea level projections with local land motion to project local relative sea level change (e.g., Kopp et al. 2014). A crucial shortcoming is that at present there is no global, coastal field of continuous subsidence or uplift. While simulations of the global field of global field of glacial isostatic adjustment (GIA) are available from a number of research groups, it forms only one component of uplift (Fig. 5) and is frequently presented without uncertainties in the context of probabilistic projections. At local scales, the uncertainty in GIA may be up to 6 mm yr^{-1}, which is a substantial fraction of the total rates of regional sea level at those locations even for high scenarios at the end of the century. For the global mean, it is a small source of uncertainty.

Besides GIA, natural and anthropogenic processes such as tectonics, volcanism, groundwater extraction and mining activity can cause vertical land motion. The land motion resulting from these processes is difficult to model quantitatively; thus, coastal adaptation often relies on geodetic observations such as permanent Global Navigation Satellite System (GNSS) stations, levelling surveys or synthetic aperture radar interferometry (InSAR)

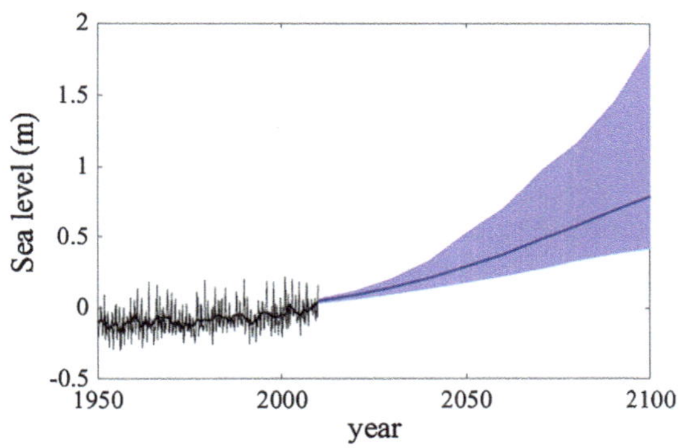

Fig. 4 Observed (black, based on monthly mean tide gauge data) and projected (thick blue line represents the median and blue shows 5–95th percentile) sea level changes with RCP8.5 at Newlyn (UK). Note that projections are usually presented as mean annual values excluding the temporal variability at higher frequencies

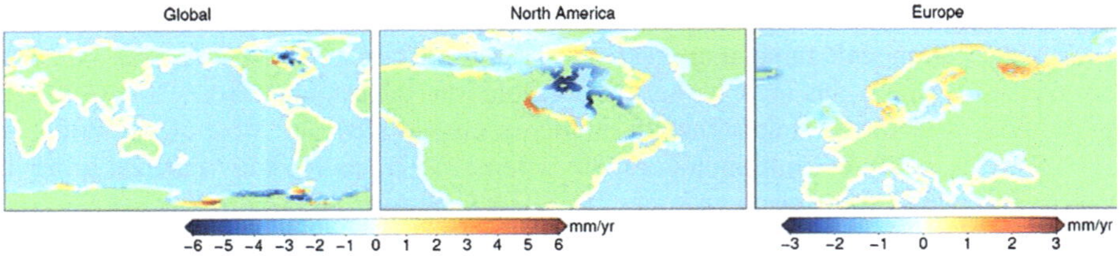

Fig. 5 Difference between the GIA from ICE6G-VM5a (Peltier et al. 2015) and ICE5G-VM2 (Peltier 2004) at coastal locations. Choice of GIA model is critical for the locations in North America and Europe, where the difference could be up to 6 mm·yr^{-1} (North American coast) and up to 3 mm·yr^{-1} (European coast). The largest differences occur at places where sea level will drop substantially due to GIA which are rather sparsely populated (Hudson Bay and Barents Sea), while for most locations of interest with a substantial GIA signal (US East Coast, Western Europe, etc.), the uncertainty is often only on the order of 1 mm·yr^{-1} or less

to estimate the future contribution of uplift/subsidence to sea level rise (Wöppelmann and Marcos, 2016). These data sets are complementary: for example, the pointwise measurements in a geocentric framework obtained from GNSS records can be complemented with levelling or InSAR deformation maps, which are relative to a local terrestrial framework. Ultimately, the combination of these techniques allows one to obtain up to sub-millimetre estimates of coastal vertical land motions (e.g., Dixon et al. 2006; Erban et al. 2014; Wöppelmann et al. 2013).

Coastal vertical land motion remains a major unknown when it comes to producing sea level projections applicable to individual locations because (e.g., Raucoules et al. 2013): (1) maps of vertical land motion are often lacking; (2) nonlinear vertical land motion remains difficult to predict. All projections that include non-GIA vertical land motion implicitly assume that rates occurring over the observational record will continue in the future (e.g., Kopp et al. 2014), though in some cases rates of vertical land movement are closely tied to human activities (e.g., groundwater extraction) and exhibit significant variability over the historical period. In areas where vertical land motion is fairly steady but the observational record is short, geological data can in some cases provide a useful additional constraint (e.g., Horton et al. 2018). In the coming years, the SAR Sentinel 1 data, which are characterized by a more frequent revisit time and larger swaths, are expected to produce nation-wide ground deformation maps, at least in Europe.

5 Probabilistic Projections for Coastal Extremes

For coastal communities, knowledge about the expected changes in the height and frequency of extreme sea level (ESL) events is of importance to decide on sufficient and cost-effective adaptation strategies in coastal communities (Hinkel et al. 2014). The height and return frequency of ESL events are mostly driven by tides, storm surges, waves and river discharge (Wahl et al. 2015; Ward et al. 2018; Williams et al. 2016; Melet et al. 2018). Since for most locations mean sea level is expected to change relative to the present-day level, the height and frequency of ESL events relative to present-day mean sea level at a specific location are expected to change as well. Furthermore, the characteristics of tides, surges, waves and river discharge can be affected by changes in the climate system. All aforementioned processes are subject to uncertainty, and probabilistic projections of the height and frequency of future extreme water level events are needed to incorporate these uncertainties.

Changes in ESL events are often expressed as changes to the return curves. A return curve shows height above present-day mean sea level (or another reference level) as a function of the return period (inverse of the expected frequency) of ESL events that exceed that height. Figure 6 shows estimated return curves for three coastal locations. These return curves can be derived from tide gauge observations or from hydrodynamic models. Changes in ESL events due to climate change will result in a changing return curve, relative to present-day mean sea level. These changes can be caused by changes in mean sea level or by changes in the characteristics of tides and surges. The green lines in Fig. 6 show the effect of a 30-cm rise of MSL on the return curves: they shift vertically, which results in higher exceedance frequencies for a given height above present-day mean sea level.

Two quantities are widely used to characterize these changing return curves. The first one is the frequency amplification factor (AF) (Tebaldi et al. 2012; Buchanan et al. 2016). The AF describes how many times more or less often a specific event is expected to occur in a future scenario compared to present-day conditions. This factor is a metric of the increase in flood risk when assets and defence structures are not adapted to sea level changes. The purple arrows in Fig. 6 show these changes in return frequencies, from which the amplification factor can be directly inferred. The second quantity is the sea level allowance, which describes the height change (unit metres) for which the projected exceedance frequency stays constant under sea level changes (Hunter 2012; Hunter et al. 2013; Buchanan et al. 2016; Slangen et al. 2017). The red arrow in Fig. 6 depicts the allowances. Projections of future ESL events have been traditionally modelled using statistical frameworks based on high-frequency tide gauge observations. Another approach consists in using hydrodynamical models to provide estimate of extreme water levels and flooding heights and velocities where no tide gauge records are available. Here, we discuss both modelling and statistical approaches.

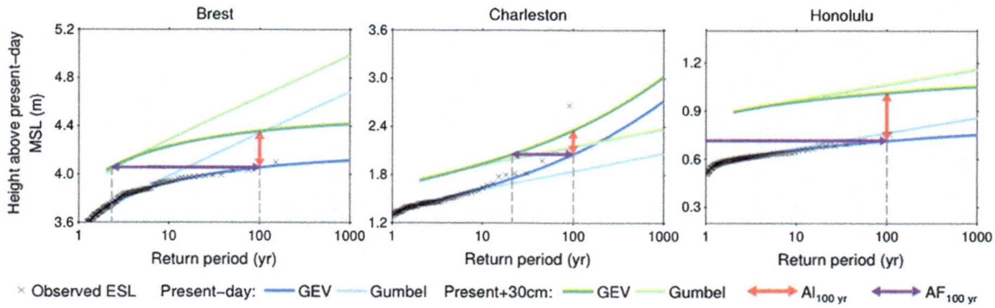

Fig. 6 Example of the statistical method to project future ESL events for three stations. The black crosses show the height and return frequency of observed ESL events from tide gauge records (Woodworth et al. 2016). The blue lines show the return curve for the Gumbel (light) and generalized extreme value (GEV, dark) distribution fitted to the annual maximum water levels under present-day conditions. The green lines show the return curve for a sea level rise of 30 cm. These lines have been computed following the procedure in Wahl et al. (2017). The red arrow shows the 100-year allowance, and the purple arrow denotes the 100-year amplification factor

5.1 The Statistical Approach

The statistical approach is grounded on the assumption that the distribution of water level extremes relative to the mean sea level do not change significantly. It is thus assumed that the tidal, wave and storm surge regime does not change significantly in a future climate. Observations over the last century provide support for this assumption, since variations in the occurrence of ESL events have been dominated by changes in mean sea level (Menendez and Woodworth 2010), although the changes in the climate system over the last century were significantly smaller than those foreseen in the twenty first century.

Critical in the approach is the fitting of the characteristics of ESL events with an extreme value distribution (EVD) to the tail of high-frequency sea level observations, generally obtained from high-frequency tide gauge records. Since tide gauges are often mounted in stilling wells or use similar low-pass filtering techniques, and the sampling frequency is typically a few minutes or more, the effects of waves are commonly not included in this type of analysis. Commonly used distributions are the Gumbel, generalized extreme value and generalized Pareto distributions (Wahl et al. 2017). These distributions are fitted to a number of extreme events, which are determined using a threshold approach or the annual or monthly highest values. These distributions all have a location parameter, which relate the height of a typical ESL event to mean sea level. To simulate ESL events under a future scenario, the location parameter is changed by the projected mean sea level change.

The curves in Fig. 6 have been computed using the GEV and Gumbel distributions. The shape of the return curve has a profound effect on the resulting amplification factors (AFs): for locations where the ESL events have an upper limit, such as in Honolulu, small changes in mean sea level lead to large amplification factors. In this example, the distribution parameters and mean sea level change are considered deterministic. Various methods have been derived to compute probabilistic estimates of the allowances and amplification factors. Hunter et al. (2013) computed allowances for a global set of tide gauge locations with the uncertainty in mean sea level projections taken into account. As a consequence, the allowance is always larger than the projected median mean sea level change. This method can also be applied to mean sea level projections with non-Gaussian confidence intervals (Slangen et al. 2017). A further extension of the concept has been introduced by Buchanan et al. (2016) and Rasmussen et al. (2018) who also combine uncertainty in the projected MSL changes with uncertainties in the fitted EVD parameters into account when computing allowances and AFs.

The advantages of the statistical methods are the low computational costs, the ease of implementation and inherent consistency with the observational record. When using observed ESL events, no direct care has to be taken of the possible joint probability of the individual processes, such as compound river-discharge–surge–waves–tide events. A limitation is that the available tide gauge records only sparsely cover the global coastline, with large parts of the global coasts ungauged, especially along the African coast (Woodworth et al. 2016). In addition, the length of the tide gauge records is generally only about a few decades, and the EVD is thus fitted through a limited number of ESL events. One way to use the short observational records more effectively is to separate the observations into a tide and surge component, which could uncover surges that occurred during low tides (Tawn et al. 1989; Tawn 1992; Batstone et al. 2013; Mazas et al. 2014). Since tides and surges can be dependent, the distributions of tides and surges cannot be added directly. The skew surge, which is the difference between the highest observed sea level and the predicted tidal high water, instead of the surge height, can be used as a good estimate of the tide-independent surge level (Williams et al. 2017).

Furthermore, the treatment of the data and the choice of a specific EVD and which water level extremes are used to fit the EVD have a considerable impact on the estimated return frequencies (Arns et al. 2013; Wahl et al. 2017), especially for events with small return frequencies. The two distributions shown in Fig. 6 show this divergence at low frequencies, which strongly affects the estimated return levels at those frequencies. Another challenge for the statistical method is the modelling of ESL behaviour in locations that are prone to tropical cyclones and hurricanes. These events are very rare, but can generate very high surge levels. The highest observed surge in Charleston in Fig. 6 was caused by Hurricane Hugo in 1989. The EVD does not adequately model these events, and for locations prone to similar events, the statistical method likely underestimates the flood frequencies. Also in regions not affected by these events, the inclusion of single surge events could have a significant impact on the projected EVD behaviour (Dangendorf et al. 2016).

5.2 Towards Global Hydrodynamical Modelling of Extreme Sea Level Events

To obtain estimates of ESL changes along ungauged coastlines, and to avoid the assumption that the ESL characteristics are invariant under future changes in the climate system, the use of hydrodynamic models to project future changes has gained popularity over the last few years (Wahl, 2017). Multiple studies show that the assumption of invariant ESL behaviour is generally not valid: from regional to local scales, mean sea level changes cause changes in tidal regimes (Pickering et al. 2017; Du et al. 2018), surges (Arns et al. 2017) and waves (Vitousek et al. 2017; Melet et al. 2018) so detailed coastal modelling is required for accurate coastal impact assessments (e.g., Barnard et al. 2019). Additionally, various environmental models indicate future changes in tropical cyclones, wind patterns and river discharge, which will modulate surge and wave conditions in the regions affected by these changes (Nohara et al. 2006; Wang et al. 2014; Piecuch et al. 2018).

By replacing the observed present-day ESL curves and using model results rather than a shift in the location parameter to project future ESL characteristics, the aforementioned limitations due to sparse tide gauge records can be resolved. The improved resolution of atmospheric reanalysis data sets and hydrodynamical models have been used to reconstruct present-day tide and surge levels during extreme events (Muis et al. 2016, 2017). Regional ESL projections have been developed for the German and European coastlines: Arns et al. (2017) forced a hydrodynamic model of the German Bight with updated mean sea level projections and found that due to the nonlinear response of tides, waves and surges to mean sea level changes in most locations, the changes in required coastal design heights exceeded the mean sea level change with an average of about 50 per cent. For RCP scenarios Vousdoukas et al. (2016) used wind fields from CMIP5 model simulations and global mean sea level projections to estimate ESL changes, finding that changes in wind patterns result in higher ESL projections along a majority of the European coastlines.

Recently, two studies investigated the global changes in ESL characteristics based on hydrodynamic models. In the first study by Vitousek et al. (2017), a combination of tide, surge and wave models were used to estimate present-day ESL return curves on a global grid. They subsequently combined these return curves with regional mean sea level projections to derive a grid of expected amplification factors to obtain a global estimate of ESL change projections. Vousdoukas et al. (2018) built on this approach by explicitly modelling the changes in surge, tide and wave characteristics that result in changes in mean sea level and wind forcing under various climate scenarios. Changes in ESL characteristics and the accompanying confidence intervals were derived using a Monte Carlo approach. They found that under both RCP4.5 and RCP8.5 scenarios, AFs above 100 are expected along most of the world's coastlines. On average, the largest changes in ESL are driven by regional mean sea level changes. They also found that the mean sea level changes form the largest source of uncertainty for determining future ESL changes.

The use of models to project future changes in ESL behaviour at broad scale is a recent area of research, and not all relevant processes, such as river discharge, are included in the models. Since ESL events are often a combination of multiple contributing processes, the probability of these events is based on the joint probability of the individual processes, which are often not independent (Wahl et al. 2015; Little et al. 2015), and some processes, such as local subsidence and changes in river discharge, are not present in the current generation of hydrodynamic models. Similar to challenges faced by the statistical model, tropical regions still pose questions for hydrodynamic models, which is partially caused by the atmospheric reanalysis products whose resolution generally falls short to simulate the large gradients in winds during tropical hurricanes and cyclones. A solution to this problem is to combine the hydrodynamic model with synthetic cyclone forcing. Using this approach, Haigh et al. (2014a, 2014b) were able to compute an exceedance curve for the Australian coastline which is subject to both tropical and extratropical storms and in agreement with tide gauges in the region. Synthetic tropical cyclones have also been used in studies of the New York City area (e.g., Garner et al. 2017) and La Réunion island (Lecacheux et al. 2012).

6 Ways Forward

6.1 Probabilistic Sea Level Projections at the Coast

In this review, we have demonstrated that probabilistic sea level projections in coastal areas are a valuable solution and a step forward for the risk assessment and decision-making of stakeholders, providing a probability density function, conditional upon emissions, that self-consistently projects likely outcomes and also the likelihood of high-risk, low-probability states of the world. However, there are several challenges for probabilistic sea level projections in coastal areas. In addition to the uncertainties in global sea level projections, e.g., ice mass loss from ice sheets in Greenland and Antarctica (Church et al. 2013a; Jevrejeva et al. 2014) and the large uncertainties in regional sea level projections (e.g., due to ocean circulation), which have been widely discussed (Kopp et al. 2014; Grinsted et al. 2015; Jackson and Jevrejeva, 2016), there are a wide range of specific uncertainties for coastal and local projections.

Currently, interactions between some of the sea level components (e.g., the interaction between fresh water fluxes due to ice mass loss from ice sheets and ocean dynamics) are not represented in standard climate model experiments. The understanding and modelling of ocean dynamic processes and incorporation of fresh water forcing as a result of ice sheet mass loss in climate models is a goal of CMIP6 experiments (Eyring et al. 2016). In addition, CMIP5 models lack both the horizontal and vertical resolution and representation of the main physical mechanisms driving the variability in sea level in shallow areas of continental shelf and along the coast. This leads to difficulties providing probabilistic projections for marginal seas, such as the Baltic Sea (Grinsted et al. 2015) and the Mediterranean Sea (Slangen et al. 2016). Interactions between fundamental physical mechanisms in coastal areas such as river run-off, tide, waves, storm surges and their link to the changes in mean sea level are still poorly understood and currently not included in coastal sea level projections and the projections of extreme water levels (Zhang et al. 2017).

The lack of local vertical land movement measurements in the areas vulnerable to sea level rise, e.g., river deltas, low-lying island and coastal cities, and inability to project the future change in local vertical land movement introduces additional uncertainties to sea level projections for individual locations. In some areas, especially those affected by significant groundwater extraction activity (e.g., Jakarta, Manila and Bangkok) the rate of local subsidence is larger than any projected rate of sea level rise by 2100 (Chaussard et al. 2013; Raucoules et al. 2013; Phien-wej et al. 2006; Jevrejeva et al. 2016).

Moreover, there are currently considerable challenges modelling high-end ice sheet contributions to sea level rise. Alternative physical characterizations in the period since AR5 have led to Antarctic ice sheet projections for 2100 that span 30 cm (Ritz et al. 2015) to more than a metre (DeConto and Pollard, 2016). In particular, DeConto and Pollard (2016) introduced new physical mechanisms that had not previously been represented in continental-scale ice sheet models, leading to model projections that included potential metre-scale contributions to sea level by the end of the twenty-first century. The wide spread of the Antarctic projections reflects the deep uncertainty surrounding these processes, and while subsequent papers and conference presentations suggest increasing convergence amongst continental-scale projections (Edwards et al. 2019), it would be premature to assume that this will be the last episode in which new physical insights lead to substantial changes in projected ice sheet behaviours. This deep uncertainty highlights both the need for an improved physical understanding of the problem as well as the value of structured expert judgement studies focused on characterizing tail risk of deeply uncertain sea level components (e.g., Bamber and Aspinall, 2013), and the use of extra probabilistic methods, discussed below.

6.2 Needs for Sea Level Information Beyond Probabilistic Projections

The previous sections have shown that the various probabilistic projections available today can display large differences. Globally, this is due primarily to differences in the treatment of ice mass loss contributions from ice sheets. Regionally, ocean dynamics and local vertical land movement are key drivers of both uncertainty within projections and differences amongst projections. As mentioned in Sect. 3, this poses a particular difficulty for coastal adaptation practitioners, who do not necessarily have the expertise to select a particular sea level projection amongst those available. To overcome this issue, coastal adaptation has adopted for at least 30 years a pragmatic approach consisting of considering a few sea level rise scenarios, including some corresponding to the most unfavourable cases considered by sea level science (Nicholls et al. 2014; Hinkel et al. 2015; Sweet et al. 2017). Here, it can be noticed that probabilistic projections may not meet the need for information of the most risk-averse users, because their highest quartile remains poorly constrained (Hinkel et al. 2015; Le Cozannet et al. 2017b). For example, estimating the value of sea level rise corresponding to an exceedance of 1% by 2100 would require a large confidence in the tail of the distributions. Here, we suggest that defining actionable sea level scenarios requires identifying interlinkages between sea level and coastal impact science and the operational workflows of users (Le Cozannet et al. 2017b), for example, by crossing sea level scenarios with the desired security margins and decision time horizon (Hallegatte, 2009). Flexible adaptation pathways, which in advance identify triggers (e.g., when sea level exceeds a given height) for key decisions (e.g., when to replace a storm barrier) and chart out possible options, provide another key tool for coping with this deep uncertainty (Haasnoot et al. 2013).

Extraprobabilistic approaches can be seen as an attempt to reconcile probabilistic sea level projections and sea level rise scenarios into a single mathematical object (see Ben Abdallah et al. 2014 for a first application in the area of sea level rise). Recognizing that the probability of sea level rise cannot be precisely estimated, extra probabilistic approaches assign an uncertainty to this probability and provide the analytical tools to work with families of probabilistic projections. Such approaches can be used when conflicting expert opinions (whether probabilistic or not) need to be considered and represented (Ben Abdallah et al. 2013; Le Cozannet et al. 2017b). Extra probabilistic projections can be visualized in the form of probability boxes, which bound all probability functions considered possible at a given date. In Fig. 7, the extra probabilistic projection is presented in the form of a probability box (p-box), which bounds all possible probability functions compliant with a set of assumptions. In this case, these assumptions are the IPCC AR5 likely range as defined by the guidance of the IPCC AR5 (Mastrandrea et al. 2010), as well as more recent studies attempting to provide maximum and minimum values for sea level rise by 2100 for RCP8.5. As these boundaries are uncertain, different weights are associated with maximum values as given in Table 3 of Le Cozannet et al. (2017a). Importantly, Fig. 7 shows that probabilistic projections relying on DeConto and Pollard (2016) are not included in the probability box and therefore disagree with the IPCC likely range. To summarize, instead of attempting to provide minimum and maximum values for future sea level rise the extra probabilistic approach attempts to provide constraints to probability functions in particular considering the needs of the most risk-averse users (Hinkel et al. 2019), and they allow for performing propagation of uncertainties and sensitivity analysis even when different probability functions coexist, which is hardly achievable within a scenario approach with complex coastal impact models (Rohmer et al. 2019). This example shows that approaches in the area of mathematical theories of uncertainties can

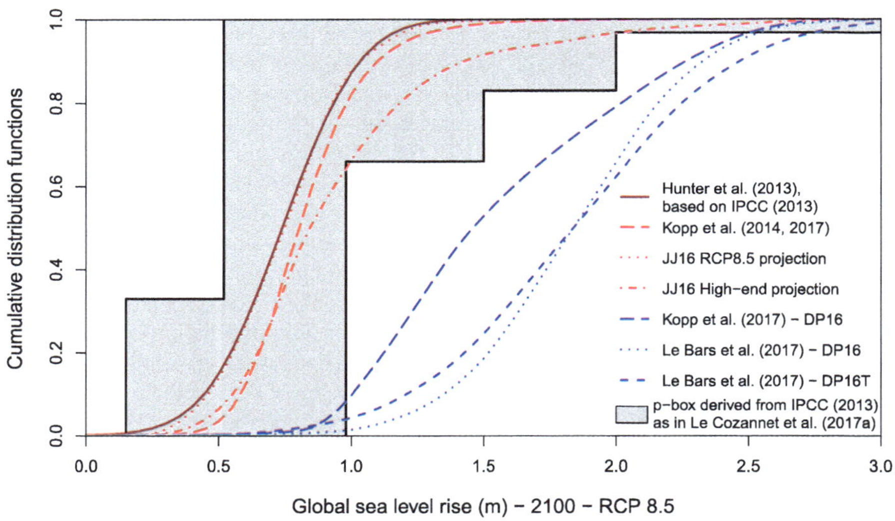

Fig. 7 Probability box (p-box; grey area bounded by dark lines) displaying the uncertainty of global sea level rise projections in 2100, conditional to the RCP 8.5 scenario, with respect to 1986–2005. These p-boxes are compared with probability functions shown in Fig. 3

be beneficial to support coastal adaptation to sea level rise, in particular if large differences remain between probabilistic projections of sea level rise over the coming years to decades.

7 Conclusions

This paper has reviewed the current status of probabilistic sea level projections. Initially, probabilistic projections were demanded by some users who required a more complete description of uncertainties than existing products, especially the IPCC projections that were limited to a "likely range". However, probabilistic projections are themselves uncertain, and the differences are very large as their mean can differ by up to one metre or so (see Figs. 3, 7). So far, the large differences of probabilistic assessments have often prevented users from replacing their standard sea level scenarios with state-of-the-art probabilistic sea level projections. This means that research is still needed to tailor probabilistic projections to the needs of adaptation practitioners.

We identify four research challenges potentially beneficial for coastal adaptation:

- include coastal processes in probabilistic SLR projections, e.g., changing meso-scale ocean processes acting at the scale of the continental shelf and semi-enclosed seas in regional probabilistic projections or vertical land motions at regional to local scales;
- provide information regarding future changes in extreme water levels;
- beside 2050 and 2100, address other timescales relevant to adaptation according to each user requirement;
- conduct research at the interface between decision-making and sea level science to provide uncertainty assessments relevant to user needs and ultimately support operational adaptation.

Acknowledgements This paper arose from the workshop on "Understanding the Relationship between Coastal Sea Level and Large-Scale Ocean Circulation" held at the International Space Science Institute (ISSI), Bern, Switzerland on 5–9 March 2018. Parts of this research (TF) were carried out at the Jet Propulsion Laboratory, California Institute of Technology, under a contract with the National Aeronautics and Space Administration and a NWO-NPP grant. REK was supported by National Aeronautics and Space Administration (NASA) Grant 80NSSC17K0698 and National Science Foundation grant ICER-1663807. GLC and RvdW were supported by the ERA4CS ECLISEA and INSeaPTION projects (Grant 690462). SJ was supported by the Natural Environmental Research Council under Grant Agreement No. NE/P01517/1 and by the EPSRC NEWTON Fund Sustainable Deltas Programme, grant number EP/R024537/1. LPJ is funded by the Robertson Foundation through the Climate Econometrics project (Grant Numbers: 9908921 and 9907422). RvdW received funding from NWO, grant 866.13.001.

References

Arns A, Wahl T, Haigh ID, Jensen J, Pattiaratchi C (2013) Estimating extreme water level probabilities: a comparison of the direct methods and recommendations for best practise. Coast Eng 81:51–66. https://doi.org/10.1016/j.coastaleng.2013.07.003

Arns A et al (2017) Sea-level rise induced amplification of coastal protection design heights. Sci Rep. https://doi.org/10.1038/srep40171

Bamber JL, Aspinall WP (2013) An expert judgement assessment of future sea level rise from the ice sheets. Nat Clim Change 3(4):424

Bamber JL, Aspinall WP, Cooke RM (2016) A commentary on "how to interpret expert judgment assessments of twenty-first century sea-level rise" by Hylke de Vries and Roderik SW van de Wal. Clim Change 137(3–4):321–328

Barnard PL et al (2019) Dynamic flood modeling essential to assess the coastal impacts of climate change. Sci Rep. https://doi.org/10.1038/s41598-019-40742-z

Batstone C et al (2013) A UK best-practice approach for extreme sea-level analysis along complex topographic coastlines. Ocean Eng 71:28–39. https://doi.org/10.1016/j.oceaneng.2013.02.003

Ben Abdallah N et al (2014) Combining statistical and expert evidence using belief functions: application to centennial sea level estimation taking into account climate change. Int J Approx Reason 55:341–354

Bevis M (2019) Accelerating changes in ice mass within Greenland, and the ice sheet's sensitivity to atmospheric forcing. Proceedings of the national academy of sciences of the united states of america, vol 116, pp 1934–1939. https://doi.org/10.1073/pnas.1806562116

BRGM (2018) Annula report, BRGM, the French geological survey. http://www.brgm.eu/news-media/2017-annual-report

Buchanan MK et al (2016) Allowances for evolving coastal flood risk under uncertain local sea-level rise. Clim Change 137(3–4):347–362. https://doi.org/10.1007/s10584-016-1664-7

Carson M et al (2016) Coastal sea level changes, observed and projected during the 20th and 21st century. Clim Change 134(1–2):269–281

Cazenave A and WCRP Global Sea Level Budget Group (2018) Global sea-level budget 1993–present. Earth Syst Sci Data 10:1551–1590. https://doi.org/10.5194/essd-10-1551-2018

Chaussard E et al (2013) Sinking cities in Indonesia: aLOS PALSAR detects rapid subsidence due to groundwater and gas extraction. Remote Sens Environ 128:150–161. https://doi.org/10.1016/j.rse.2012.10.015

Church FN et al (2013a) Sea level change. In: Stocker TF, Qin D, Plattner G-K, Tignor M, Allen SK, Boschung J, Nauels A, Xia Y, Bex V, Midgley PM (eds) Climate change. The physical science basis. Contribution of working group I to the fifth assessment report of the intergovernmental panel on climate change. Cambridge University Press, Cambridge

Church JA et al (2013b) Sea-level rise by 2100. Science 342(6165):1445–1445. https://doi.org/10.1126/science.342.6165.1445-a

Cozannet Le et al (2015) Evaluating uncertainties of future marine flooding occurrence as sea-level rises. Environ Model Softw 73:44–56. https://doi.org/10.1016/j.envsoft.2015.07.021

Cozannet Le et al (2017a) Sea level change and coastal climate services: the way forward. J Mar Sci Eng 5(4):49

Cozannet Le et al (2017b) Bounding probabilistic sea-level projections within the framework of the possibility theory. Environ Res Lett 12(1):014012

Dangendorf S et al (2016) The exceptional influence of storm 'Xaver' on design water levels in the german bight. Environ Res Lett 11:054001. https://doi.org/10.1088/1748-9326/11/5/054001

De Vries H, van de Wal RS (2015) How to interpret expert judgment assessments of 21st century sea-level rise. Clim Change 130(2):87–100

DeConto RM, Pollard D (2016) Contribution of Antarctica to past and future sea-level rise. Nature 531(7596):591

Dixon TH et al (2006) Space geodesy: subsidence and flooding in New Orleans. Nature 441(7093):587

Du J et al (2018) Tidal response to sea-level rise in different types of estuaries: the importance of length, bathymetry, and geometry: tidal response to sea-level rise. Geophys Res Lett 45:227–235. https://doi.org/10.1002/2017GL075963

Edwards TL et al (2019) Revisiting Antarctic ice loss due to marine ice cliff instability. Nature. https://doi.org/10.1038/s41586-019-0901-4

Erban LE, Gorelick SM, Zebker HA (2014) Groundwater extraction, land subsidence, and sea-level rise in the Mekong Delta, Vietnam. Environ Res Lett 9(8):084010

Eyring V et al (2016) Overview of the Coupled Model Intercomparison Project Phase 6 (CMIP6) experimental design and organization. Geosci Model Dev 9:1937–1958. https://doi.org/10.5194/gmd-9-1937-2016
Garner AJ et al (2017) Impact of climate change on New York City's coastal flood hazard: increasing flood heights from the preindustrial to 2300 CE. Proc Natl Acad Sci. https://doi.org/10.1073/pnas.1703568114
Garner AJ et al (2018) Evolution of 21st century sea-level rise projections. Earth's Future 1:1. https://doi.org/10.1029/2018EF000991
Golledge NR et al (2015) The multimillenial Antarctic commitment to future sea-level rise. Nature 526:421–425. https://doi.org/10.1038/nature15706
Goodwin P, Haigh ID, Rohling EJ, Slangen A (2017) A new approach to projecting 21st century sea-level changes and extremes. Earth's Future 5(2):240–253
Griffies SM et al (2016) OMIP contribution to CMIP6: experimental and diagnostic protocol for the physical component of the Ocean Model Intercomparison Project. Geosci Model Dev 9:3231–3296. https://doi.org/10.5194/gmd-9-3231-2016
Grinsted A et al (2015) Sea level rise projections for Northern Europe under RCP8.5. Clim Res 64:15–23. https://doi.org/10.3354/cr01309
Haasnoot M et al (2013) Dynamic adaptive policy pathways: a method for crafting robust decisions for a deeply uncertain world. Glob Environ Change 23(2):485–498. https://doi.org/10.1016/j.gloenvcha.2012.12.006
Haigh ID et al (2014a) Estimating present day extreme water level exceedance probabilities around the coastline of Australia: tropical cyclone-induced storm surges. Clim Dyn 42:139–157. https://doi.org/10.1007/s00382-012-1653-0
Haigh ID et al (2014b) Estimating present day extreme water level exceedance probabilities around the coastline of australia: tides, extra-tropical storm surges and mean sea level. Clim Dyn 42:121–138. https://doi.org/10.1007/s00382-012-1652-1
Hall JW et al (2012) Robust climate policies under uncertainty: a comparison of robust decision making and info-gap methods. Risk Anal 32:1657–1672
Hall JA et al (2016) Regional sea level scenarios for coastal risk management: managing the uncertainty of future sea level change and extreme water levels for Department of Defense coastal sites worldwide. Department of Defense, Strategic Environmental Research and Development Program, Alexandria
Hall JA et al (2019) Rising sea levels: helping decision-makers confront the inevitable. Coast Manag. https://doi.org/10.1080/08920753.2019.1551012
Hallegatte S (2009) Strategies to adapt to an uncertain climate change. Glob Environ Change 19(2):240–247
Hallegatte S et al (2013) Future flood losses in major coastal cities. Nat Clim Change 3:802–806. https://doi.org/10.1038/nclimate1979
Hay CC, Morrow E, Kopp RE, Mitrovica JX (2013) Estimating the sources of global sea level rise with data assimilation techniques. Proc Natl Acad Sci 110(Supplement 1):3692–3699
Hinkel J et al (2014) Coastal flood damage and adaptation costs under 21st century sea-level rise. Proc Natl Acad Sci 111:3292–3297. https://doi.org/10.1073/pnas.1222469111
Hinkel J et al (2015) Sea-level rise scenarios and coastal risk management. Nat Clim Change 5:188–190
Hinkel J et al (2019) Meeting user needs for sea-level rise information: a decision analysis perspective. Earth's Future 1:1. https://doi.org/10.1029/2018EF001071
Hoffman JS, Keyes D, Titus JG (1983) Projecting future sea level rise; methodology, estimates to the year 2100, and Research needs. Environmental Protection Agency, Washington, pp 115–121
Horton BP et al (2018) Mapping sea-level change in time, space and probability. Ann Rev Environ Resour. https://doi.org/10.1146/annurev-environ-102017-025826
Hunter J (2012) A simple technique for estimating an allowance for uncertain sea-level rise. Clim Change 113(2):239–252. https://doi.org/10.1007/s10584-011-0332-1
Hunter JR et al (2013) Towards a global regionally varying allowance for sea-level rise. Ocean Eng 71:17–27
IPCC (2014) Summary for policymakers. In: Field CB, Barros VR, Dokken DJ, Mach KJ, Mastrandrea MD, Bilir TE, Chatterjee M, Ebi KL, Estrada YO, Genova RC, Girma B, Kissel ES, Levy AN, MacCracken S, Mastrandrea PR, White LL (eds) Climate change 2014: impacts, adaptation, and vulnerability. Part A: global and sectoral aspects. contribution of working group II to the fifth assessment report of the intergovernmental panel on climate change. Cambridge University Press, Cambridge, pp 1–32
Jackson LP, Jevrejeva S (2016) A probabilistic approach to 21st century regional sea-level projections using RCP and High-end scenarios. Global Planet Change 146:179–189

Jackson LP et al (2018) 21st century sea-level rise in line with the Paris accord. Earth's Future 6:213–229. https://doi.org/10.1002/2017EF000688
Jevrejeva S, Moore JC, Grinsted A (2012) Sea level projections to AD2500 with a new generation of climate change scenarios. Global Planet Change 80:14–20
Jevrejeva S, Grinsted A, Moore J (2014) Upper limit for sea level projections by 2100. Environ Res Lett 9:104008
Jevrejeva S et al (2016) Coastal sea-level rise with warming above 2 degree. Proc Natl Acad Sci. https://doi.org/10.1073/pnas.1605312113
Jevrejeva S, Jackson LP, Grinsted A, Lincke D, Marzeion B (2018) Flood damage costs under the sea level rise with warming of 1.5° C and 2° C. Environ Res Lett 13(7):074014
Katsman CA et al (2011) Exploring high-end scenarios for local sea level rise to develop flood protection strategies for a low-lying delta—the Netherlands as an example. Clim Change 109:617–645
Kopp RE et al (2014) Probabilistic 21st and 22nd century sea-level projections at a global network of tide-gauge sites. Earth's Future 2(8):383–406
Kopp RE et al (2016) Temperature-driven global sea-level variability in the Common Era. Proc Natl Acad Sci 13:E1434–E1441
Kopp RE et al (2017) Evolving understanding of Antarctic ice-sheet physics and ambiguity in probabilistic sea-level projections. Earth's Future 5(12):1217–1233
Landerer FW, Gleckler PJ, Lee T (2014) Evaluation of CMIP5 dynamic sea surface height multi-model simulations against satellite observations. Clim Dyn 43(5–6):1271–1283
Le Bars D (2018) Uncertainty in sea level rise projections due to the dependence between contributors. Earth's Future. https://doi.org/10.1029/2018ef000849
Le Bars D, Drijfhout S, de Vries H (2017) A high-end sea level rise probabilistic projection including rapid Antarctic ice sheet mass loss. Environl Res Lett 12(4):044013
Lecacheux S et al (2012) A method to characterize the different extreme waves for islands exposed to various wave regimes: a case study devoted to Reunion Island. Nat Hazards Earth Syst Sci 12(7):2425–2437
Lempert R, Schlesinger ME (2000) Robust strategies for abating climate change. Clim Change 45:387–401
Lin N, Shullman E (2017) Dealing with hurricane surge flooding in a changing environment: part I. Risk assessment considering storm climatology change, sea level rise, and coastal development. Stoch Env Res Risk Assess. https://doi.org/10.1007/s00477-016-1377-5
Little CM et al (2015) Joint projections of US East Coast sea level and storm surge. Nat Clim Change 5(12):1114–1120. https://doi.org/10.1038/nclimate2801
Mastrandrea MD et al (2010) Guidance note for lead authors of the IPCC 5th assessment report on consistent treatment of uncertainties. Intergovernmental Panel on Climate Change. Available at https://archive.ipcc.ch/pdf/supporting-material/uncertainty-guidance-note.pdf
Mazas F et al (2014) Applying POT methods to the Revised Joint Probability Method for determining extreme sea levels. Coast Eng 91:140–150. https://doi.org/10.1016/j.coastaleng.2014.05.006
Melet A et al (2018) Under-estimated wave contribution to coastal sea-level rise. Nat Clim Change 8(3):234–239. https://doi.org/10.1038/s41558-018-0088-y
Menéndez M, Woodworth PL (2010) Changes in extreme high water levels based on a quasi-global tide-gauge data set. J Geophys Res. https://doi.org/10.1029/2009JC005997
Mengel M et al (2016) Future sea level rise constrained by observations and long-term commitment. Proc Natl Acad Sci 113:2597–2602
Mengel M, Nauels A, Rogelj J, Schleussner CF (2018) Committed sea-level rise under the Paris Agreement and the legacy of delayed mitigation action. Nat Commun 9(1):601
Mitrovica JX, Tamisiea ME, Davis JL, Milne GA (2001) Recent mass balance of polar ice sheets inferred from patterns of global sea-level change. Nature 409(6823):1026
Moss RH et al (2010) The next generation of scenarios for climate change research and assessment. Nature 463(7282):747
Muis S et al (2016) A global reanalysis of storm surges and extreme sea levels. Nat Commun 7:11969. https://doi.org/10.1038/ncomms11969
Muis S et al (2017) A comparison of two global datasets of extreme sea levels and resulting flood exposure. Earth's Future 5(4):379–392. https://doi.org/10.1002/2016EF000430
Nauels A et al (2017) Linking sea level rise and socioeconomic indicators under the Shared Socioeconomic Pathways. Environ Res Lett 12(11):114002
Nicholls RJ, Cazenave A (2010) Sea-level rise and its impact on coastal zones. Science 328(5985):1517–1520
Nicholls RJ et al (2014) Sea-level scenarios for evaluating coastal impacts. Rev Clim Change 5:129–150
Nohara D et al (2006) Impact of climate change on river discharge projected by multimodel ensemble. J Hydrometeorol 7(5):1076–1089. https://doi.org/10.1175/JHM531.1

Nowicki S, Seroussi H (2018) Projections of future sea level contributions from the Greenland and Antarctic Ice Sheets: challenges beyond dynamical ice sheet modeling. Oceanography 31:2. https://doi.org/10.5670/oceanog.2018.216

Nowicki SMJ et al (2016) Ice sheet model intercomparison project (ISMIP6) contribution to CMIP6. Geosci Model Dev 9:4521–4545. https://doi.org/10.5194/gmd-9-4521-2016

Peltier WR (2004) Global glacial isostasy and the surface of the ice-age Earth: the ICE-5G (VM2) model and GRACE. Annu Rev Earth Planet Sci 32(1):111–149. https://doi.org/10.1146/annurev.earth.32.082503.144359

Peltier WR, Argus DF, Drummond R (2015) Space geodesy constrains ice age terminal deglaciation: the global ICE-6G_C (VM5a) model: global glacial isostatic adjustment. J Geophys Res Solid Earth 120(1):450–487. https://doi.org/10.1002/2014JB011176

Perrette M et al (2013) A scaling approach to project regional sea level rise and its uncertainties. Earth Syst Dyn 4(1):11–29

Phien-wej N, Giao PH, Nutalaya P (2006) Land subsidence in Bangkok, Thailand. Eng Geol 82:187–201

Pickering MD et al (2017) The Impact of future sea-level rise on the global tides. Cont Shelf Res 142:50–68. https://doi.org/10.1016/j.csr.2017.02.004

Piecuch CG et al (2018) River-discharge effects on united states atlantic and gulf coast sea-level changes. Proc Natl Acad Sci. https://doi.org/10.1073/pnas.1805428115

Rahmstorf S (2007) A semi-empirical approach to projecting future sea-level rise. Science 315(5810):368–370

Rasmussen DJ et al (2018) Extreme sea level implications of 1.5° C, 2.0° C, and 2.5° C temperature stabilization targets in the 21st and 22nd centuries. Environ Res Lett 13(3):034040

Raucoules D et al (2013) High nonlinear urban ground motion in Manila (Philippines) from 1993 to 2010 observed by DInSAR: implications for sea-level measurement. Remote Sens Environ 139:386–397

Ritz C et al (2015) Potential sea-level rise from Antarctic ice-sheet instability constrained by observations. Nature 528(7580):115

Rignot E et al (2019) Four decades of Antarctic Ice Sheet mass balance from 1979–2017. PNA. https://doi.org/10.1073/pnas.1812883116

Roberts MJ et al (2016) Impact of ocean resolution on coupled air-sea fluxes and large-scale climate. Geophys Res Lett 43(19):10–430

Rohmer J et al (2019) Addressing ambiguity in probabilistic assessments of future coastal flooding using possibility distributions. Clim Change. https://doi.org/10.1007/s10584-019-02443-4

Rosenzweig C, Solecki WD, Blake R, Bowman M, Faris C, Gornitz V, Horton R, Jacob K, LeBlanc A, Leichenko R, Linkin M (2011) Developing coastal adaptation to climate change in the New York City infrastructure-shed: process, approach, tools, and strategies. Clim Change 106(1):93–127. https://doi.org/10.1007/s10584-010-0002-8

Shepherd A et al (2018) Mass balance of the Antarctic Ice Sheet from 1992 to 2017. Nature 556:219–222

Slangen ABA et al (2014) Projecting twenty-first century regional sea-level changes. Clim Change 124(1–2):317–332

Slangen ABA et al (2016) A review of recent updates of sea-level projections at global and regional scales. Surv Geophys 38:385

Slangen A et al (2017) The impact of uncertainties in ice sheet dynamics on sea-level allowances at tide gauge locations. J Mar Sci Eng 5(2):21. https://doi.org/10.3390/jmse5020021

Sweet WV, Park J (2014) From the extreme to the mean: acceleration and tipping points of coastal inundation from sea level rise. Earth's Future 2:579–600

Sweet et al (2017) Global and Regional Sea Level Rise Scenarios for the United States. NOAA technical report nos CO-OPS 083. https://tidesandcurrents.noaa.gov/publications/techrpt83_Global_and_Regional_SLR_Scenarios_for_the_US_final.pdf Cited 6 January 2018

Tawn JA (1992) Estimating probabilities of extreme sea-levels. Appl Stat 41(1):77. https://doi.org/10.2307/2347619

Tawn JA, Vassie JM, Gumbel EJ (1989) Extreme sea levels: the joint probabilities method revisited and revised. Proc Inst Civ Eng 87(3):429–442. https://doi.org/10.1680/iicep.1989.2975

Taylor K, Stouffer RJ, Meehl GA (2012) An overview of CMIP5 and the experiment design. Bull Am Meteorol Soc 93(4):485–498. https://doi.org/10.1175/BAMS-D-11-00094.1

Tebaldi C et al (2012) Modelling sea level rise impacts on storm surges along US Coasts. Environ Res Lett 7(1):014032. https://doi.org/10.1088/1748-9326/7/1/014032

Titus JG, Narayanan VK (1995) The probability of sea level rise; US Environmental Protection Agency: Washington, DC, USA; Office of Policy, Planning, and Evaluation: Bethesda, MD, USA; Climate Change Division, Adaptation Branch: Washington, DC, USA, 1995; vol 95

Tran T et al (2016) Climate change and sea level rise scenarios for Viet Nam. Viet Nam Institute of meteorology, hydrology and climate, http://www.imh.ac.vn/files/doc/2017/CCS%20final.compressed.pdf

van den Hurk B et al (2014) Climate change scenarios for the 21st century—a Netherlands perspective Scientific Report WR2014-01 KNMI, De Bilt, the Netherlands. www.climatescenarios.nl

van de Wal RSW, Zhang X, Minobe S, Jevrejeva S, Riva, REM, Little C, Richter K, Palmer M (2019) Uncertainties in long-term process-based coastal sea-level projections, Surv Geophys 40 (**in review**)

Vitousek S et al (2017) Doubling of coastal flooding frequency within decades due to sea-level rise. Sci Rep. https://doi.org/10.1038/s41598-017-01362-7

Vousdoukas MI et al (2016) Extreme sea levels on the rise along Europe's coasts. Earth's Future 5(3):304–323. https://doi.org/10.1002/2016EF000505

Vousdoukas M et al (2018) Global probabilistic projections of extreme sea levels show intensification of coastal flood hazard. Nat Commun. https://doi.org/10.1038/s41467-018-04692-w

Wahl T (2017) Sea-level rise and storm surges, relationship status: complicated! Environ Res Lett 12(11):111001. https://doi.org/10.1088/1748-9326/aa8eba

Wahl T et al (2015) Increasing risk of compound flooding from storm surge and rainfall for major US cities. Nat Clim Change 5(12):1093–1097. https://doi.org/10.1038/nclimate2736

Wahl T et al (2017) Understanding extreme sea levels for broad-scale coastal impact and adaptation analysis. Nat Commun 8:16075. https://doi.org/10.1038/ncomms16075

Wang XL et al (2014) Changes in global ocean wave heights as projected using multimodel CMIP5 simulations. Geophys Res Lett 41(3):1026–1034. https://doi.org/10.1002/2013GL058650

Ward PJ et al (2018) Dependence between high sea-level and high river discharge increases flood hazard in global deltas and estuaries. Environ Res Lett 13(8):084012. https://doi.org/10.1088/1748-9326/aad400

Williams J et al (2016) Tide and skew surge independence: new insights for flood risk. Geophys Res Lett 43(12):6410–6417. https://doi.org/10.1002/2016GL069522

Winter De et al (2017) Impact of asymmetric uncertainties in ice sheet dynamics on regional sea level projections. Nat Hazards Earth Syst Sci 17(2125–2141):2017. https://doi.org/10.5194/nhess-17-2125-2017

Woodworth PL, Menéndez M, Gehrels WR (2011) Evidence for century-timescale acceleration in mean sea levels and for recent changes in extreme sea levels. Surv Geophys 32(4–5):603–618

Woodworth PL et al (2016) Towards a global higher-frequency sea level dataset. Geosci Data J 3(2):50–59. https://doi.org/10.1002/gdj3.42

Wöppelmann G, Marcos M (2016) Vertical land motion as a key to understanding sea level change and variability. Rev Geophys 54(1):64–92

Wöppelmann G et al (2013) Is land subsidence increasing the exposure to sea level rise in Alexandria, Egypt? Geophys Res Lett 40(12):2953–2957

Zhang X et al (2017) Sea level projections for the Australian region in the 21st century. Geophys Res Lett. https://doi.org/10.1002/2017gl074176

Printed by Printforce, the Netherlands